# THE OXFORD

## Essential
## Geographical
## Dictionary

AMERICAN EDITION

*Also Available*

THE OXFORD DESK DICTIONARY AND THESAURUS
THE OXFORD ESSENTIAL BIOGRAPHICAL DICTIONARY
THE OXFORD ESSENTIAL DICTIONARY
THE OXFORD ESSENTIAL DICTIONARY OF FOREIGN TERMS IN ENGLISH
THE OXFORD ESSENTIAL SPELLING DICTIONARY
THE OXFORD ESSENTIAL THESAURUS
THE OXFORD FRENCH DICTIONARY
THE OXFORD GERMAN DICTIONARY
THE OXFORD ITALIAN DICTIONARY
THE OXFORD PORTUGUESE DICTIONARY
THE OXFORD RUSSIAN DICTIONARY
THE OXFORD NEW SPANISH DICTIONARY

# THE OXFORD

## Essential
## Geographical
## Dictionary

AMERICAN EDITION

BERKLEY BOOKS, NEW YORK

THE OXFORD ESSENTIAL GEOGRAPHICAL DICTIONARY

A Berkley Book / published in mass market paperback by arrangement with Oxford University Press, Inc.

PRINTING HISTORY
Berkley edition / August 1999

The Penguin Putnam Inc. World Wide Web site address is
http://www.penguinputnam.com

ISBN: 0-425-16994-4

BERKLEY®
Berkley Books are published by
The Berkley Publishing Group, a division of Penguin Putnam Inc.,
375 Hudson Street, New York, New York 10014.
BERKLEY and the "B" design are trademarks
belonging to Penguin Putnam Inc.

PRINTED IN THE UNITED STATES OF AMERICA

10  9  8  7  6  5  4  3  2  1

# Contents

# Staff

# Introduction

The *Oxford Essential Geographical Dictionary* provides concise geographical information for more than 10,000 places around the world. Each place may be thought of as either physical, political, or cultural. The *physical* places included are continents, oceans, mountain ranges, rivers, lakes, and other natural features. *Political* entries include nations, provinces or states, territories, capitals, cities and towns, and other creations of human government. A *cultural* entry, broadly speaking, covers any place that may have no definite physical or political definition but that has significance for any of a wide variety of reasons—because its name is associated with a certain concept (*Madison Avenue*), or it was the site of an important historical event or development (*Waterloo* or *Broadway*), or it is commonly talked about (*Hollywood*), even though it does not exist as an "official" political entity.

For each entry in this dictionary, the user will find the following information: the name of the place, an indication of correct word division (if applicable), the pronunciation (unless accurate pronunciation could not be determined); any alternate spellings of the name, or alternate names of the place; and a concise definition of the place, which gives location and some indication of significance.

Depending on the place, an entry may also include any of the following: area (of a physical feature) or population (of a political jurisdiction or settlement); identification of components such as a national or regional capital, largest city, etc.; additional historical, physical, or cultural data; or cross reference to places related in some special way. In appropriate cases derivative forms, like the adjective *Spanish* from *Spain*, are included.

About one-third of the entries in the *Oxford Essential Geographical Dictionary* cover places in North America. This focus on material of particular interest to American readers is also reflected in the handling of all 50 U.S. states in special feature boxes, which give an expanded range of information, including such items as state flowers and nicknames, and in the inclusion of more information on Canadian provinces and territories and on Mexican states than on analogous political entities elsewhere in the world.

# How to Use This Book

The "entry map" below explains the different parts of a typical entry in this book:

> **Ka·li·nin·grad** |kə'lēnen,grəd| **1** port on the Baltic Sea.... Pop. 406,000....
>
> **Kan·dy** |'kændē| city in Sri Lanka.... □ **Kandyan** *adj. & n.*
>
> **Ka·tah·din, Mount** |kə'tädn| (also **Ktaadn**) peak in .... At 5,267 ft./1,606 m....

1. **Boldface:** Main entries, alternate names, and derivative forms appear in **boldface.**

**Word division:** Dots within the main entries mark places where a name can be divided correctly, as at the end of a line of text. Many names will not have dots at each syllable, because the dots are intended to show optimum word division points. Thus, one-letter syllables at the beginning or end of a name are not marked with dots (**Aus·tria**, not **Aus·tri·a**; **Avon**, not **A·von**). No divisions are marked in hyphenated names, because they are best divided at the hyphen. Standard generic terms that are used in many place names, such as *river* and *mountain*, are not marked for word division.

2. **Cross-references** appear in small capitals.

> **Ka·tan·ga** |kə'tæNGgə| former name (until 1972) for SHABA, Congo (formerly Zaire).

3. **Sense numbers** are used to group closely related places under a single main entry where the places occur within a single country

> **Oa·xa·ca** |wä'häkə| **1** state of S Mexico. Area: 36,289 sq. mi./93,952 sq. km. Pop. 3,022,000. **2** its capital city, an historic cultural and commercial center. Pop. 213,000. Full name **Oaxaca de Juárez**.

But where a single place name occurs in more than one country—as in the case of **Perth**, Scotland, and **Perth**, Australia—each place is treated as a separate entry and appears in alphabetical order by the country name, or by the name of the most commonly known next higher political division. In the case of such "homographs" (two or more names spelled exactly the same, although the two are separate places, and the names may have no relation to each other), entry order is indicated by a superscript number given with each entry.

4. The name under which a place is listed is, in some cases (for example, *Venice, Rome,* and *Italy*) not the official "native" form or spelling, but is the form in which Americans are likely to use the name. In some other cases, the form under which a name is entered is better known than the official form or spelling; for example, San Buenaventura, California, is not as well known by that (official) name as by the entry form given, **Ventura**.

5. The characterization of the **status** of a place, it should be noted, is also subject to language and national differences. For entries in the United States and Canada, terms like *city, town,* and *village* used in this dictionary reflect official usage, which is a matter of municipal organization, not population or land area; for example, the town of Hempstead, N.Y.; the village of Skokie, Illinois; and the city of Sitka, Alaska. In other parts of the world, governmental form and municipal designation take many forms (and are sometimes difficult to determine with certainty). For places outside the United States and Canada, this book adopts general usage, and the term *city,* for example, usually denotes an urban place larger than a town or village. There are, of course, many different designations for populated places, some more familiar than others, such as *commune, borough,* and *parish*; some of these are used here, following the most reliable source information that could be obtained.

6. **Population figures:** For populated places in the United States and Canada, the latest official census figures are used. For populated places in the rest of the world, sources vary, but recently released figures are used, rounded off, in almost all cases, to the nearest thousand.

7. **Measurements** are given in standard units first, followed by a conversion into metric measurement. This conforms to prevalent usage in the United States. Thus miles (mi.) are also given in kilometers (km.); feet (ft.) in meters (m.); and square miles (sq. mi.) in square kilometers.

## Appendixes

At the back of the *Oxford Essential Geographical Dictionary* are several appendixes that present, in handy tabular format, factual geographical information on oceans and seas, continents, mountains and volcanoes, lakes and rivers, and the largest metropolitan areas.

# Pronunciation Key

Main entries are normally followed by a pronunciation. The pronunciation appears within upright vertical lines immediately after the main entry, for example:

**Ker·ou·ac** |ˈkerəwæk|

The pronunciations use a simple respelling system to represent English and some non-English sounds, as shown below. Pronunciations generally are an "Americanized" rendering that is acceptable in almost all contexts. In certain cases, especially with unusual names (sometimes of non-English origin) whose pronunciations are less familiar, the pronunciations are approximations of the way the name is pronounced in the particular foreign language of origin. Where information on the pronunciations preferred by a certain individual or family could be determined, that preferred pronunciation is given. In a small percentage of entries, when reliable data could not be obtained, no pronunciation is given.

## VOWELS:

| Symbol: | as in: | Example: |
|---|---|---|
| æ | cat | **Nash** \|næSH\| |
| ā | mate | **Ma·jor** \|ˈmājər\| |
|   | father | **Scott** \|skt\| |
| e | let | **Penn** \|pen\| |
| ē | feet | **Reeves** \|rēvz\| |
| i | it | **Mil·ler** \|ˈmilər\| |
| ī | tide | **Price** \|prīs\| |
| aw | fall | **Al·bright** \|ˈawlbrīt\| |
| ō | cove | **Stone** \|stōn\| |
| ŏŏ | hook | **Bush** \|booSH\| |
| ŏŏ | loose | **Shu·la** \|ˈSHōōlə\| |
| ə | but, banana | **But·ler** \|ˈbətlər\| |

## DIPHTHONGS:

| oi | foil | **Con·roy** \|ˈknˌroi\| |
|---|---|---|
| ow | couch | **Ei·sen·how·er** \|ˈīzənˌhowər\| |

## CONSONANTS:

| | | |
|---|---|---|
| b | boot | **Ba·bel** \|'bābəl; 'bæbəl\| |
| CH | church | **Chad** \|CHæd\| |
| d | dog | **Do·ver**[1] \|'dōvər\| |
| f | fate | **Flag·staff** \|'flæg,stæf\| |
| g | go; bigger | **Get·tys·burg** \|'getēz,bərg\| |
| h | hot; behave | **Han·ni·bal** \|'hænəbəl\| |
| j | jack; magic | **Ja·pan** \|jə'pæn\| |
| k | kettle; cut | **Keene** \|kēn\|; **Can·a·da** \|'kænədə\| |
| l | lap; cellar; cradle | **Lang·ley** \|'læNGlē\| |
| m | main | **Mem·phis**[2] \|'mem(p)fəs\| |
| n | honor; maiden | **Na·pa** \|'næpə\|; **Jor·dan** \|'jawrdn\| |
| NG | singer | **Fin·ger Lakes** \|'fiNGgər\| |
| p | put | **Pam·plo·na** \|pæm'plōnə\| |
| r | root; carry | **Roch·es·ter**[1] \|'räCHəstər\| |
| s | sit | **Sar·a·so·ta** \|,særə'sōtə\| |
| SH | shape; wish | **Shaw·nee**[1] \|SHaw'nē; SHänē\| |
| t | top; butter | **Tam·pa** \|'tæmpə\|; **Cal·cut·ta** \|kæl'kətə\| |
| TH | thing; path | **Thebes**[1] \|'THēbz\| |
| <u>TH</u> | this; mother | **Neth·er·lands** \|'neTHərlən(d)z\| |
| v | never | **Ven·ice**[1] \|'venəs\| |
| w | wait; quick | **Wales** \|wālz\| |
| y | yes; beyond | **York**[1] \|yawrk\| |
| z | lazy; fuse | **Zu·rich** \|'tsYriKH; 'zʊʊrik\| |
| ZH | beige; leisure | **Bei·jing** \|ba'jiNG; 'ba'zHiNG\| |

## FOREIGN SOUNDS:

| | | |
|---|---|---|
| KH | Bach | **Rei·chen·bach** \|'rīKHən,bäk\| |
| N | vin | **Ly·ons** \|lyawN\| |
| Œ | Goethe | **Köln** \|'kœln\| |
| Y | über | **Brux·elles** \|brY(k)'sel\| |

## STRESS

Each stressed syllable is preceded by a small upright stroke, showing that the following syllable that has a stressed vowel sound. Primary stress is shown by an upright stroke above the line, while secondary stress is shown by an upright stroke below the line:

**Col·os·se·um** \|,kälə'sēəm\|

# Aa

**Aa·ben·raa** |'awbən,raw| (also **Åbenrå**) port and resort town in SE Jutland, Denmark. Pop. 21,000.

**Aa·chen** |'äкнən| (French name **Aix-La-Chapelle**) industrial city and spa in western Germany, in North Rhine–Westphalia; Charlemagne's capital and favorite residence. Pop. 244,440.

**Aal·borg** |'awl,bawrg| (also **Ålborg**) industrial city and port in N Jutland, Denmark. Pop. 155,000.

**Aa·len** |'älən| industrial city in S Germany, on the Kocher River, E of Stuttgart. Pop. 65,000. The city is noted for its old half-timbered houses. It gives its name to the Aalen period in geological history.

**Aale·sund** |'awlə,sōōn| commercial seaport and fishing town in W Norway, on three islands. Pop. 36,000. It is linked by tunnel to several offshore islands.

**Aals·meer** |'äls,mer| town in W central Netherlands, SW of Amsterdam. Pop. 22,000. It is famous for its huge flower market.

**Aalst** |'älst| industrial city in W central Belgium. Pop. 77,000.

**Aa·re River** |'ärə| river (184 mi./295 km. long) in Switzerland. Rising in the Bernese Alps, it flows NW to the Rhine opposite the German town of Waldshut and is the longest river entirely in Switzerland.

**Aar·gau** |'är,gow| canton in N Switzerland, in a fertile agricultural region. Area: 543 sq. mi./1,405 sq. km. Pop. 490,000. Capital: Aarau.

**Aar·hus** |'awr,hōōs| (also **Århus**) city on the coast of E Jutland, Denmark. Pop. 261,440.

**A·ba** |ə'bä| industrial city in S Nigeria, NE of Port Harcourt. Pop. 264,000.

**Aba·co Islands** |'æbə,kō| forested island group in the N Bahamas.

**Aba·dan** |,äbə'dän| major port and oil-refining center on an island of the same name on the Shatt al-Arab waterway in W Iran. Pop. 308,000.

**Aba·kan** |,äbə'kän|, ,əbə'kän| (until 1931 **Ustabakanskoe**) industrial city in S central Russia, capital of the republic of Khakassia. Pop. 154,000.

**Abbe·ville**[1] |äbə'vēl| industrial and commercial town in N France. Pop. 25,000. It gives its name to early Paleolithic pickaxe industries (*c.* 500,000 B.C.), remains of which were found here. □ **Abbevillian** *adj. & n.*

**Ab·be·ville**[2] |'æbē,vil| historic city in NW South Carolina. Pop. 5,778.

**Ab·bey Road** |'æbē| road in NW London, England, W of Regents Park, site of recording studios associated with the Beatles and other pop music figures.

**Ab·bey Theatre** |'æbē| theater in Abbey Street, Dublin, Ireland, opened in 1904 and associated with Yeats and other writers and with Irish culture in general.

**Ab·bots·ford** |'æbətsfərd| district municipality in SW British Columbia, near the Washington border. Pop. 18,864.

**Ab·bot·ta·bad** |'æbətə,bäd| resort city in N Pakistan, in the foothills of the Himalayas. Pop. 66,000.

**ABC Islands** |'ā'bē'sē| acronym for the Dutch Caribbean islands of Aruba, Bonaire, and Curaçao.

**Ab·de·ra** |æb'dirə| city in ancient Greece, on the Aegean Sea, E of the mouth of the Mesta River. It was home to several prominent Greek philosophers, among them Protagoras and Democritus.

**Abé·ché** |,äbā'shä| (also **Abeshr**) historic commercial city in E Chad. Pop. 188,000. Once capital of the Ouaddaï Empire, it is a trade center for the Sahel.

**Abe·o·ku·ta** |ä'baōkōō,tä| city in SW Nigeria, capital of the state of Ogun. Pop. 308,800.

**Aber·deen**[1] |'æbər,dēn| town in NE Maryland, on Chesapeake Bay. Pop. 13,087. A major military test range is nearby.

**Aber·deen**[2] |'æbər,dēn| city and seaport in NE Scotland, the administrative capital of Grampian region. It is a center of the offshore North Sea oil industry. Pop. 201,100.

**Aber·deen**[3] |,æbər'dēn| city in NE South Dakota, a dairy center. Pop. 24,927.

**Aber·deen·shire** |,æbər'dēnsнər, ,æbər-'dēn,sнir| former county of NE Scotland. It became a part of Grampian region in 1975.

**Aber·fan** |,æbər'væn| village in S Wales where, in 1966, a slag heap collapsed, overwhelming houses and a school and killing 28 adults and 116 children.

**Aber·foyle** |,æbər'foil| resort village in SW Scotland, in the Trossachs, N of Glasgow. It is associated with the writings of Sir Walter Scott.

**Abe·ryst·wyth** |,æbə'rist,wiTH| resort and

cultural town on Cardigan Bay, W Wales. Pop. 10,000.

**Ab·ha** |ˈäb,hä| (also **Ebha; Ibha**) city in SW Saudi Arabia, in the highland area of Asir province. Pop. 112,000.

**Abi·djan** |ˌæbəˈjän| chief port of Côte d'Ivoire, the capital 1935–83. Pop. 1,850,000.

**Abi·lene**¹ |ˈæbəˌlēn| commercial city in E central Kansas, famed as the first terminus of the Chisholm Trail. Pop. 6,242.

**Abi·lene**² |ˈæbəˌlēn| city in N central Texas, an agricultural and oil industry center. Pop. 106,654.

**Abi·quiu** |ˌæbəˈkēōō| ranching community in N New Mexico, noted as the longtime home of artist Georgia O'Keeffe.

**Ab·kha·zia** |äbˈkʜäzēə| autonomous territory in the NW republic of Georgia, S of the Caucasus Mts. on the Black Sea. Pop. 537,500. Capital: Sokhumi. In 1992 Abkhazia unilaterally declared itself independent, sparking armed conflict with Georgia, and the following year drove Georgian forces from its territory. □ **Abkhazian** adj. & n. **Abkhazi** adj. & n.

**Abo·mey** |ˌæbəˈmä; əˈbōmē| town in S Benin, capital of the former kingdom of Dahomey. Pop. 54,400.

**Abra·ham, Plains of** |ˈäbrə,hæm| see PLAINS OF ABRAHAM.

**Abruz·zi** |əˈbrōōtsē| mountainous region of E central Italy. Capital: Aquila.

**Ab·sa·ro·ka Range** |æbˈsawrkē| range of the Rocky Mts. in Montana and Wyoming.

**A·bu Dha·bi** |ˌäbōō ˈdäbē| **1** the largest of the seven member states of the United Arab Emirates, lying between Oman and the Persian Gulf coast. Pop. 670,125. The former sheikhdom joined the federation of the United Arab Emirates in 1971. **2** the capital of this state. Pop. 242,975. It is also the federal capital of the United Arab Emirates.

**Abu·ja** |əˈbōōjə| newly built city in central Nigeria, designated in 1982 to replace Lagos as the national capital. Pop. 378,670.

**Abu·kir** |ˌäbōōˈkir| see ABU QIR,.

**Abu Mu·sa** |ˌäbōō ˈmōōsə| small island in the Persian Gulf. Formerly held by the emirate of Sharjah, it has been occupied by Iran since 1971.

**Abu Qir** |ä'bōō 'kir| (also **Abukir** or **Aboukir**) village in N Egypt, NE of Alexandria, on Abu Qir Bay. The British won the Battle of the Nile (1798) in the bay. Ancient Canopus was in this locality.

**Abu Sim·bel** |ˌäbōō 'simbəl| (also **Ipsambul**) former village in S Egypt. Rock temples here were removed to high ground in the 1960s, after building of the Aswan Dam on the Nile River.

**Aby·dos**¹ |əˈbides| town of ancient Egypt, on the Nile River N of Thebes, the site of burial of many early pharaohs.

**Aby·dos**² |əˈbides| town of ancient Asia Minor, in present-day NW Turkey, on the S side of the Dardanelles. It is across from Sestos and NE of modern Canakkale, and is associated with the legend of Hero and Leander.

**Abys·si·nia** |ˌæbəˈsinēə| former name for ETHIOPIA. □ **Abyssinian** adj. & n.

**Aca·dia** |əˈkādēə| former French colony established in 1604 in the territory that later formed Nova Scotia. It was contested by France and Britain until it was ceded to Britain in 1763. Acadians were deported to other parts of North America; some migrated to Louisiana (where they became known as Cajuns). □ **Acadian** adj. & n.

**Aca·jut·la** |ˌäkəˈhōōtlə| seaport town in W El Salvador, the leading Pacific port in the country. Pop. 17,000.

**Aca·pul·co** |ˌäkəˈpōōlkō| port and resort in S Mexico, on the Pacific coast. Pop. 592,290. Full name **Acapulco de Juárez**.

**Ac·cra** |əˈkrä| capital of Ghana, a port on the Gulf of Guinea. Pop. 867,000.

**Aceh** |ˈä,cʜä| (also **Atjeh; Achin**) province and special region of Indonesia, on N Sumatra. Area: 21,395 sq. mi./55,392 sq. km. Pop. 2,611,000. Capital: Banda Aceh.

**Achaea** |əˈkēə| region of ancient Greece on the North coast of the Peloponnese. □ **Achaean** adj. & n.

**Ache·lous River** |ˌækəˈlōəs| second-longest river in Greece (137 mi./219 km). It rises in the Pindus Mts. and flows into the Ionian Sea near the Gulf of Patras.

**Ache·ron River** |ˈækə,rän| in Greek mythology, a river that flowed through Hades. The name is also given to several rivers in Greece that pass through underground caverns and caves.

**Achill Island** |ˈækəl| island in County Mayo, NW Ireland, a noted fishing center.

**Áco·ma** |ˈäkə,maw; ˈækə,maw| Indian community atop a mesa in NW New Mexico, one of the oldest known human settlements in North America.

**Acon·ca·gua** |ˌækənˈkägwə| extinct volcano in the Andes, on the border between Chile and Argentina, rising to 22,834 ft./6,960 m. It is the highest mountain in the W hemisphere.

**Açores** |əˈsawris| Portuguese spelling for AZORES Islands.

**Acre**[1] |'äkrə| state of western Brazil, on the border with Peru. Capital: Rio Branco.

**Acre**[2] |'akər; 'äkər| industrial seaport of NW Israel. Pop. 39,100. Also called **Akko**.

**Ac·ro·po·lis, the** |ə'kräpələs| hill (260 ft./80 m. high) in Athens, Greece, atop which is the Parthenon, a temple to Athena, and other ancient sites, some built as early as the 5th century B.C. The Acropolis was destroyed by the Persians in 480 B.C.

**Ac·te** |'äktē| peninsula in NE Greece, one of three fingers at the end of Chalcidice, extending into the Aegean Sea between the Strymonic Gulf and Singitic Gulf. Mount Athos is at its tip.

**Adak** |'a‚dæk| island in the Aleutian Islands of SW Alaska, site of a U.S. naval base.

**Ada·ma·wa** |‚ädə'mä-wə| plateau region of W Africa, in N central Cameroon and E Nigeria. It is also the name of a Nigerian state and a province of Cameroon.

**Adam's Bridge** |'ædəmz| line of shoals lying between NW Sri Lanka and the SE coast of Tamil Nadu in India, separating the Palk Strait from the Gulf of Mannar.

**Adam's Peak** |'ædəmz| mountain in S central Sri Lanka, rising to 2,243 m./7,360 ft. It is regarded as sacred by Buddhists, Hindus, and Muslims.

**Ada·na** |‚ädə'nä| a town in S Turkey, capital of a province of the same name. Pop. 916,150.

**Ada·pa·za·ri** |‚ädə‚päzə'rə| commercial and industrial city in NW Turkey, in Sakarya province. Pop. 171,000.

**Ad Dam·mam** |‚äd dä'mäm| port town in Saudi Arabia, on the Persian Gulf coast. Pop. 1,224,000.

**Ad·dis Aba·ba** |‚ædəs 'æbəbə| capital and largest city of Ethiopia, in the central plateau. Pop. 2,113,000. It is the commercial and cultural center of Ethiopia, and has light industries.

**Ad·di·son** |'ædəsən| village in NE Illinois, a suburb NW of Chicago. Pop. 32,058.

**Ade·laide** |'ædl‚äd| industrial port city, the capital of South Australia state, Australia. Pop. 1,050,000.

**Adé·lie Land** |ə'dälē| (also **Adélie Coast**) section of the Antarctic continent S of the 60th parallel, between Wilkes Land and King George V Land.

**Aden, Gulf of** |'ädn; 'ædn| part of the E Arabian Sea lying between the S coast of Yemen and the Horn of Africa.

**Aden** |'adən| port in Yemen at the mouth of the Red Sea. Pop. 417,370. Aden was formerly under British rule, first as part of British India (from 1839), then from 1935 as a Crown Colony. It was capital of the former South Yemen from 1967 until 1990.

**Adi·ge River** |'ädə‚ja| river (255 mi./408 km.) in NE Italy, rising in the Rhaetian Alps and flowing into the Adriatic Sea between Venice and the mouth of the Po River.

**Adi·ron·dack Mountains** |‚ædə'rän‚dæk| (also **the Adirondacks**) range of mountains in New York, source of the Hudson and Mohawk rivers. It is part of the Canadian Shield.

**Adi·ron·dack Park** |‚ædə'rän‚dæk| state preserve in N central New York, the largest park in the contiguous U.S.

**Adis A·be·ba** |‚ædəs 'æbəbə| variant spelling of ADDIS ABABA.

**Adi·ya·man** |‚ädēə'män| city in SE Turkey, capital of Adiyaman province. Pop. 100,000.

**Ad·mi·ral·ty Islands** |'ædm(ə)rəltē| group of about forty islands in the W Pacific, part of Papua New Guinea.

**Ado-Ekiti** |‚ädō‚a'kētē| city in SW Nigeria, in the Yoruba Hills. Pop. 317,000.

**Adrar des Ifo·ras** |ä'drär dō‚zēfaw'rä| massif region in the central Sahara, on the border between Mali and Algeria.

**Adri·an** |'ädrēən| city in SE Michigan. Pop. 22,097

**Adri·at·ic Sea** |‚ädrē'ætik| arm of the Mediterranean Sea between the Balkans and the Italian peninsula.

**Ad·wa** |'ädwə| (also **Adua**) historic commercial town in N Ethiopia, in Tigré province, site of an 1896 defeat of the Italians by Menelik II. Pop. 25,000.

**Ady·gea** |‚ädə'gəə| autonomous republic in the NW Caucasus in SW Russia, with a largely Muslim population. Pop. 432,000. Capital: Maikop. Full name **Adygei Autonomous Republic.**

**Ad·zha·ria** |ə'järēə| (also **Adjaria** or **Adzharistan**) autonomous republic in the Republic of Georgia, on the Black Sea. Its capital is Batumi. Pop. 382,000.

**Ae·ge·an Islands** |i'jēən| group of islands in the Aegean Sea, forming a region of Greece. The principal islands of the group are Chios, Samos, Lesbos, the Cyclades, and the Dodecanese.

**Ae·ge·an Sea** |i'jēən| part of the Mediterranean Sea lying between Greece and Turkey, bounded to the S by Crete and Rhodes and linked to the Black Sea by the Dardanelles, the Sea of Marmara, and the Bosporus.

**Ae·gi·na** |i'jinə| resort and seaport in E Greece, on the Saronic Gulf, SW of Athens. Pop. 11,000.

**Ae·go·spo·ta·mi** |ˌēgəˈspätə,mī| small river of ancient Thrace flowing into the Hellespont (now the Dardanelles). Near its mouth the Athenian fleet was defeated by Lysander in 405 B.C., ending the Peloponnesian War.

**Ae·o·lian Islands** |ēˈōlyən| ancient name for LIPARI ISLANDS.

**Ae·o·lis** |ˈēələs| ancient Greek colony in NW Asia Minor (present-day Turkey).

**Ae·to·lia** |iˈtōlyə| region of ancient Greece, now part of the modern department of Aetolia and Acarnania, in central Greece. Pop. 231,000. The capital is Mesolóngion.

**Afar** |əˈfär| desert region of NE Ethiopia, on the borders of Eritrea and Djibouti.

**Af·ghan·i·stan** |æfˈgænə,stæn| mountainous landlocked republic in central Asia. Area: 250,173 sq. mi./647,697 sq. km. Pop. 16,600,000. Languages, Pashto and Dari (Persian). Capital and largest city: Kabul. Long dominated by British and Russian interests, Afghanistan has been in turmoil since Soviet withdrawal in 1989. Most of the country is in the Hindu Kush; agriculture, textiles, and natural gas are important to the economy. □ **Afghan** *adj. & n.*

**Afghanistan**

**Af·ri·ca** |ˈæfrikə| the second largest (11.62 million sq. mi./30.1 million sq. km.) continent, a S projection of the Old World land mass divided roughly in two by the equator and surrounded by sea except where the Isthmus of Suez joins it to Asia. Largest country: Sudan. Largest city: Cairo, Egypt. In the N Africa is dominated by the Sahara Desert, S of which is the transitional Sahel, with a central plateau and surrounding tropical lowlands farther S. In the far S, much of South Africa is temperate. □ **African** *adj. & n.*

**Af·ton** |ˈæftən| (also **Afton Water** stream in SW Scotland, in the Strathclyde region, immortalized by the poet Robert Burns.

**Af·yon** |äfˈyōn| (also **Afyonkarahisar**) city in W Turkey, capital of Afyon province.

Pop. 96,000. The area is noted for its opium production.

**Aga·dir** |ˌägəˈdir| seaport and resort on the Atlantic coast of Morocco. Pop. 110,500.

**Aga·na** |əˈgänyə| the capital of Guam, on the Philippine Sea. Pop. 1,139.

**Agar·ta·la** |ˌəgərtˈlä| city in the far NE of India, capital of the state of Tripura, near the border with Bangladesh. Pop. 157,640.

**Agas·siz, Lake** prehistoric glacial lake of the Pleistocene epoch, covering parts of present-day Minnesota, North Dakota, Manitoba, and Ontario.

**Age·nais** |äzHəˈnä| ancient region of SW France. The major town is Agen. The region corresponds roughly to the present department of Lot-et-Garonne.

**Aghi·os Ni·ko·la·os** |ˈāyē,aws niˈkōlä,aws| fishing port and resort on the N coast of Crete, E of Heraklion. Pop. 8,100. Greek name **Áyios Nikólaos.**

**Agin·court** |ˈæjən,kawrt; ˈäzHən,kŏŏr| village in the Pas-de-Calais, N France. In 1415, during the Hundred Years War, King Henry V of England defeated a much larger French force here. Modern French name, **Azincourt.**

**Agou·ra Hills** |əˈgawrə| city in SW California, a suburb NW of Los Angeles. Pop. 20,390.

**Ag·ra** |ˈägrə| city on the Jumna River in Uttar Pradesh state, N India. Pop. 899,000. Founded in 1566, Agra was the capital of the Mogul empire until 1658. It is the site of the TAJ MAHAL.

**Ag·ri** |ˈärē; äˈrə| capital of Agri province in extreme E Turkey, near the Armenian and Iranian borders. Pop. 58,000.

**Ag·ri·gen·to** |ˌägriˈjen,tō| market and tourist center in Sicily, in S Italy, capital of Agrigento province. Pop. 57,000. On a hill overlooking the Mediterranean Sea, the town has many ancient monuments.

**Agua Pri·e·ta** |ˈägwəprēˈätə| city in Sonora, NW Mexico, near the Arizona border. Pop. 38,000.

**Aguas·ca·lien·tes** |ˌägwəskälˈyen,täs| **1** state of central Mexico. Area: 2,217 sq. mi./5,471 sq. km. Pop. 720,000. **2** its capital, a health resort noted for its hot springs. Pop. 506,000.

**Agul·has, Cape** |əˈgələs| the most southerly (34° 52′ S) point of the continent of Africa, in the province of Western Cape, South Africa.

**Agul·has Current** |əˈgələs| ocean current flowing S along the E coast of Africa.

**Ah·len** |ˈälən| industrial city in NW Germany, S of Münster. Pop. 53,000.

**Ah·ma·da·bad** |'ämədə,bäd| (also **Ahmedabad**) industrial city in the state of Gujarat in W India. Pop. 2,873,000.

**Ah·mad·na·gar** |,äməd'nəgər| (also **Ahmednagar**) commercial and industrial city in W central India, in Maharashtra state. Pop. 222,000.

**Ahua·cha·pán** |,äwəchə'pän| commercial city in SW El Salvador, capital of Ahuachapán department. Pop. 25,000. It is in an area noted for its coffee and its geothermal power production.

**Ah·vaz** |ä'wäz| (also **Ahwaz**) historic commercial and industrial city in W Iran, in an oil-producing area. Pop. 725,000.

**Ah·ve·nan·maa** |'ävänən,mä| Finnish name for **Åland Islands**.

**Ai·ken** |'aken| resort city in W central South Carolina. Pop. 19,872.

**Ain·tab** |in'tæb| former name (until 1921) for **Gaziantep**, Turkey.

**Ain·tree** |'äntrē| suburb of Liverpool, England, site of a racecourse over which the Grand National steeplechase is run.

**Aire River** |ær;er| river in W Yorkshire, England. Leeds lies on it, and its upper valley, **Airedale**, gave its name to the dog breed.

**Aisne River** |en; än| river (150 mi./240 km.) that rises in the Argonne area in NE France and flows NW to meet the Oise River at Compiègne.

**Aix-en-Pro·vence** |eks än prō'väNs| historic spa and cultural city in Provence in S France. Pop. 126,850.

**Aix-la-Cha·pelle** |,eks lä sHä'pel| French name for **Aachen**.

**Ai·zawl** |i'zowl| city in the far NE of India, capital of the state of Mizoram. Pop. 154,000.

**Ajac·cio** |ä'yäcHō; äzHäks'yō| port on the W coast of Corsica. Pop. 59,320. It is the capital of the department of Corse-du-Sud.

**Ajan·ta Caves** |ə'jəntə| series of caves in the state of Maharashtra, S central India, containing Buddhist frescos and sculptures dating from the 1st century B.C. to the 7th century A.D.

**Ajax** |'a,jæks| industrial town in S Ontario. Pop. 57,350.

**Aj·man** |æj'män; äj'mæn| **1** smallest of the seven emirates of the United Arab Emirates. Pop. 64,320. **2** its capital city.

**Aj·mer** |əj'mir; əj'mer| commercial city in NW India, in Rajasthan. Pop. 402,000.

**Ajo·dhya** |ə'yōdyə| see **Ayodhya**, India.

**Akar·naí** |ä,kärnä'e| (also **Akharnai, Acharnae**) town in S Greece, N of Athens. Aristophanes set his play *The Acharnians* here. Pop. 40,000.

**Aka·shi** |'äkə,sHē; ə'käsHē| industrial port city in W central Japan, on SW Honshu. Pop. 271,000. Standard time for Japan is set here.

**Ak·he·ta·ten** |,äkə'tätn| ancient Egyptian capital built by Akhenaten in *c.*1375 B.C. when he established the new worship of the sun disc Aten, but abandoned after his death. See also **Amarna, Tell el-**.

**Aki·ta** |ä'kētə| industrial port city in NE Japan, on N Honshu. Pop. 302,000.

**Ak·kad** |'æk,æd; 'äk,äd| ancient city on the Euphrates River in central Mesopotamia, its exact location unknown. It gave its name to the Akkadian Empire and language. □ **Akkadian** *adj. & n.*

**Ak-Mechet** |,äk mə'cHet| former name for **Simferopol**, Ukraine.

**Ak·mo·la** |äk'mawlə| alternate spelling for **Aqmola**, Kazakhstan.

**Ako·la** |ə'kōlə| commercial and industrial city in W central India, in Maharashtra state. Pop. 328,000.

**Ak·ron** |'ækrən| city in NE Ohio. Pop. 223,000. Through much of the 20th century it was the center of the tire and rubber industry in the U.S.

**Ak·sai Chin** |'äk'si 'cHin| region of the Himalayas between Tibet and Xinjiang, occupied by China since 1950. It is claimed by India as part of Kashmir.

**Ak·su** |'äk'soo| city in Xinjiang, W China, on the Aksu River in the foothills of the Tian Shan range. Pop. 341,000. It was the Mongol capital in the 14th century.

**Ak·sum** |'äk,soom| (also **Axum**) a town in the province of Tigray in N Ethiopia. It was a religious center and the capital of a powerful kingdom between the 1st and 6th centuries A.D. □ **Aksumite** *adj. & n.*

**Ak·tyu·binsk** |äk'tyoobinsk| **1** subdivision of W central Kazakhstan. Pop. 753,000.

**Aku·mal** |,äkoo'mäl| village in SE Mexico, in Quintana Roo state, on the Gulf of Mexico, noted as a diving and beach resort.

**Ala·bama** |,ælə'bæmə| see box, p. 6. □ **Alabaman** *adj. & n.*

**Ala·bama River** |,ælə'bæmə| river in S Alabama, flowing 315 mi./507 km. into the Mobile River.

**Ala·goas** |,älə'gōəs| state in E Brazil, on the Atlantic coast. Pop. 2,513,000. Capital: Maceió.

**Alai Range** |'ä,li| mountain range in SW Kyrgyzstan. The highest peak reaches 19,554 ft./5,960 m.

**Ala·me·da** |,ælə'mēdə| port city in N central California, just SW of Oakland on San Francisco Bay. Pop. 76,459.

## Alabama

**Capital:** Montgomery
**Largest city:** Birmingham
**Other cities:** Athens, Decatur, Dothan, Gadsden, Huntsville, Mobile, Tuscaloosa
**Population:** 4,040,587 (1990); 4,351,999 (1998); 4,631,000 (2005 proj.)
**Population rank (1990):** 22
**Rank in land area:** 30
**Abbreviation:** AL; Ala.
**Nicknames:** The Heart of Dixie; Yellowhammer State
**Motto:** *Audemus jura nostra defendere* (Latin: 'We Dare Defend Our Rights')
**Bird:** flicker; yellowhammer
**Fish:** tarpon
**Flower:** camellia
**Tree:** Southern longleaf pine
**Song:** "Alabama"
**Noted physical features:** Appalachian Mountains
**Tourist attractions:** Azalea Trail Festival; Civil Rights Memorial/Museum, Alabama Shakespeare Festival; Carver Museum; W.C. Handy Home & Museum; Alabama Space and Rocket Center; Moundville State Monument; Pike Pioneer Museum; USS *Alabama* Memorial Park; Russell Cave National Monument; Vulcan Statue.
**Admission date:** December 14, 1819
**Order of admission:** 22
**Name origin:** For the Alabama River, which was possibly named for Choctaw Indians who lived along it.

**Ala·me·da²** |ˌäləˈmädə| public park in the center of Mexico City, Mexico, named for its cottonwood trees.

**Ala·mo, the** |ˈæləˌmō| historic site in San Antonio, Texas. In 1836 Mexican forces overwhelmed American defenders here.

**Ala·mo·gor·do** |ˌæləməˈgawrdō| city in S New Mexico. Pop. 27,596. White Sands and other military and aerospace facilities are nearby.

**Åland Islands** |ˈawˌlän| (Finnish name **Ahvenanmaa**) group of islands in the Gulf of Bothnia, forming an autonomous region of Finland. Capital: Mariehamn (known in Finnish as Maarianhamina).

**Ala·nia** |əˈlänyä| (formerly **Caucasian Republic of North Ossetia**), republic in S Russia, on the N slopes of the central Caucasus Mts. Pop. 695,000. The capital is Vladikavkaz.

**Alap·pu·zha** |ˌələˈpōozə| see ALLEPEY, India.

**Alas·ka** |əˈlæskə| see box. □ **Alaskan** *adj.* & *n.*

**Alas·ka, Gulf of** |əˈlæskə| part of the NE Pacific, bounded by the Alaska Peninsula and the Alexander Archipelago.

**Alas·ka Highway** |əˈlæskə| see ALCAN HIGHWAY.

**Alas·ka Peninsula** |əˈlæskə| peninsula on the S coast of Alaska. It extends SW into the NE Pacific between the Bering Sea and the Gulf of Alaska, and is continued in the Aleutian Islands.

**Alas·ka Range** |əˈlæskə| mountain chain lying across S Alaska. Mt. McKinley (20,320 ft./6,194 m.) is its high point.

**Ála·va** |ˈäləvə| largest of the three Basque provinces in N Spain. Pop. 272,000. Capital: Vitoria.

## Alaska

**Capital:** Juneau
**Largest city:** Anchorage
**Other cities:** Barrow, Fairbanks, Ketchikan, Kodiak, Nome, Sitka
**Population:** 550,043 (1990); 614,010 (1998); 700,000 (2005 proj.)
**Population rank (1990):** 49
**Rank in land area:** 1
**Abbreviation:** AK; Alas.
**Nicknames:** Great Land; Sourdough State; Last Frontier; Land of the Midnight Sun
**Motto:** 'North to the Future'
**Bird:** willow ptarmigan
**Fish:** chinook (king salmon)
**Flower:** forget-me-not
**Tree:** Sitka spruce
**Song:** "Alaska's Flag"
**Noted physical features:** Glacier Bay, Prudhoe Bay; Prince William Sound; Gulf of Alaska; Gastineau Channel; Malaspina Glacier; Mount McKinley (Alaska Range); Chilkoot Pass; Kenai, Alaska, Seward peninsulas; Alexander Archipelago; Whitehorse Rapids; Beaufort Sea; Bering Strait
**Tourist attractions:** Mount McKinley; Portage Glacier, Mendenhall Glacier; Ketchikan Totems; Glacier Bay National Park and Preserve; Denali National Park; Mt. Roberts Tramway; Pribilof Islands; St. Michael's Russian Orthodox Cathedral; Katmai National Park & Preserve.
**Admission date:** January 3, 1959
**Order of admission:** 49
**Name origin:** From the Aleutian word *alakshak*, meaning 'peninsula,' 'great land,' or 'mainland.'

**Al·ba·ce·te** |ˌälbə'sā͟ˌtā| commercial city, in an agricultural province of the same name in SE Spain. Pop. 134,600.

**Al·ba Iu·lia** |ˌälbə 'yo͞olyə| city in W central Romania, to the N of the Transylvanian Alps. Pop. 72,330. Founded by the Romans in the 2nd century A.D., it was the capital of Transylvania.

**Al·ba Lon·ga** |ˌälbə 'lawNGgə| ancient city in the Alban Hills in central Italy, according to legend the birthplace of Romulus and Remus, founders of Rome.

**Al·ba·nia** |æl'bānēə; awl'bānēschwa.| republic in SE Europe, in the Balkan Peninsula, on the Adriatic Sea. Area: 11,104 sq. mi./28,748 sq. km. Pop. 3,300,000. Language, Albanian. Capital and largest city: Tirana. Part of the Byzantine, later the Ottoman, empires, Albania became independent in 1912. After World War II until 1992 it was an isolationist communist state. Agriculture has given way to industry in many areas, but the economy remains underdeveloped. □ **Albanian** adj. & n.

**Albania**

**Al·ba·ny**[1] |ˌawl'benē; æ'bānē| commercial city in SW Georgia. Pop. 78,122.

**Al·ba·ny**[2] |'awlbənē| state capital of New York, an industrial port and commercial and educational center on the Hudson River. Pop. 101,080.

**Al·ba·ny**[3] |'awlbənē| city in NW Oregon. Pop. 29,462.

**Al·be·marle Sound** |'ælbə͟märl| inlet of the Atlantic in NE North Carolina, inside the Outer Banks.

**Al·bert, Lake** |'ælbərt| lake in the Rift Valley of E central Africa, on the border between the Democratic Republic of the Congo (formerly Zaire) and Uganda. It is linked to Lake Edwards by the Semliki River and to the White Nile by the Albert Nile. Also called **Lake Mobutu Sese Seko**.

**Al·ber·ta** |æl'bərtə| prairie province in W Canada, bounded on the S by the U.S. and on the W by the Rocky Mts. Area: 255,287

sq. mi./661,190 sq. km. Pop. 2,545,553. Capital: Edmonton. Largest city: Calgary. Oil and gas, wheat and other crops, and tourism are important to the economy of Alberta, which also has various industries in its urban centers. □ **Albertan** adj. & n.

**Al·bert Canal** |'ælbərt| canal in NE Belgium, 80 mi./128 km. long, that links the Meuse and Scheldt rivers, connecting the cities of Liège and Antwerp.

**Al·bert Nile** |äber'vēl| upper part of the White Nile, flowing through NW Uganda between Lake Albert and the Ugandan–Sudanese border.

**Al·bert·ville** |ælbərtˌvil| winter resort in SE France, in the Rhône-Alps region, near the Italian border. Pop. 18,000. The 1992 Winter Olympics were held here.

**Al·bi** |ˌäl'bē| town in S France. Pop. 48,700. The Albigensian heretical movement of the 12th and 13th centuries took its name from **Albiga**, the ancient name of the town, a center of the movement.

**Al·bi·on** |'ælbēən| ancient and literary name for the island of Great Britain.

**Al·bu·quer·que** |'ælbəˌkərkē| city in N central New Mexico, on the Rio Grande. Pop. 384,736. A commercial and research center, it is the largest city in New Mexico.

**Al·bu·ry** |'awlbərē| commercial town in SE Australia, on the N side of the Murray River in New South Wales. Pop. 40,000.

**Al·ca·lá de He·na·res** |ˌälkə'lä də ə'nä͟ˌräs| city in central Spain, on the Henares River NE of Madrid. Pop. 162,780.

**Al·can Highway** |'ælˌkæn| (also **Alaska Highway**) military road, built during World War II to link Dawson Creek, in the Yukon Territory, with Fairbanks, Alaska, as part of a supply route to the Soviet Union and the Pacific.

**Al·ca·traz** |'ælkəˌtræz| rocky island in San Francisco Bay, California. It was, between 1934 and 1963, the site of a maximum security Federal prison, nicknamed "The Rock."

**Al·cá·zar, the** |ˌælkə'zär; æl'kæzər| 12th-century Moorish palace in Seville, SW Spain, later used by Spanish kings. The term is also applied to palaces in Toledo and other Spanish cities.

**Al·cor·cón** |ˌälkawr'kōn| SW suburb of Madrid, in central Spain. Pop. 140,000.

**Al·da·bra** |æl'dæbrə| coral island group in the Indian Ocean, NW of Madagascar. Formerly part of the British Indian Ocean Territory, it became an outlying dependency of the Seychelles in 1976.

**Al·dan River** |əl'dän| river (1,400 mi./

2,240 km.) in E Siberia, Russia. It rises in the Stanovoy Khrebet Mts. and flows into the Lena River E of Yakutsk.

**Al·de·burgh** |'äldəbərə| town on the coast of Suffolk, E England. Pop. 3,000. It is the site of an annual music festival established (1948) by Benjamin Britten.

**Al·der·ney** |'awldərnē| island in the English Channel, to the NE of Guernsey. Pop. 2,130. It is the third largest of the Channel Islands. French name **Aurigny**.

**Al·der·shot** |'awldər,SHät| town in S England, in Hampshire, site of a major military training center. Pop. 54,358.

**Alek·san·drovsk** |,ælik'ændrəfsk| former name (until 1921) for ZAPORIZHZHYA, Ukraine.

**Alen·çon** |äläN'sawN| capital of the department of Orne, NW France. Pop. 35,000. The town is known for its fine lace.

**Alen·te·jo** |ə,leN'tezHŌŌ| region and former province of E central Portugal.

**Alep·po** |ə'lepō| city in N Syria. Pop. 1,355,000. This ancient city was formerly an important commercial center on the trade route between the Mediterranean and the countries of the East. Arabic name **Halab**.

**Ales·san·dria** |,älə'sändrēə| agricultural market and industrial center in NW Italy, capital of Alessandria province. Pop. 93,000.

**Aletsch·horn** |'älicH,hawrn| mountain in Switzerland, in the Bernese Alps, rising to 13,763 ft./4,195 m. Its glaciers are among the largest in Europe.

**Aleu·tian Islands** |ə'lōōSHən| (also **the Aleutians**) chain of volcanic islands in Alaska, extending W and S from the Alaska Peninsula.

**Aleu·tian Range** |ə'lōōSHən| extension of the Coast Ranges in SW Alaska. It contains many volcanoes.

**Alex·an·der Archipelago** |,ælg'zændər| group of about 1,100 islands off the coast of SE Alaska, the remnants of a submerged mountain system.

**Alex·an·dret·ta** |,ælig,zæn'dretə| former name for ISKENDERUN, Turkey.

**Alex·an·dria**[1] |,ælig'zændrēə| the chief port of Egypt. Pop. 2,893,000. Alexandria was a major center of Hellenistic culture, renowned in ancient times for its library and for the Pharos lighthouse. □ **Alexandrian** adj. & n.

**Alex·an·dria**[2] |,ælig'zændrēə| industrial city in central Louisiana, on the Red River. Pop. 49,188.

**Alex·an·dria**[3] |,ælig'zændrēə| city in N Virginia, on the Potomac River opposite Washington, D.C. Pop. 111,183.

**Al·föld** |'awl,foeld| great central plain of Hungary, extending into Serbia and W Romania. On the main invasion route to W Europe, it has often been a battleground. It is now an agricultural and cattle-raising area. The Little Alföld, W Hungary, extends into Austria and S Slovakia.

**Al·gar·ve, the** |äl'gärvə| the southernmost province of Portugal, on the Atlantic coast, noted as a resort area. Capital: Faro.

**Al·ge·ci·ras** |,æljə'sirəs| ferry port and resort in S Spain. Pop. 101,365.

**Al·ge·ria** |æl'jirēə| republic on the Mediterranean coast of N Africa. Area: 919,595 sq. mi./2.32 million sq. km. Pop. 25,800,000. Language, Arabic. Capital and largest city: Algiers. The second-largest African nation, Algeria is dominated in the S by the Sahara Desert. France held it as a colony from the 19th century until 1962. Oil and gas are now central to the economy, and there is some agriculture in the N. □ **Algerian** adj. & n.

Algeria

**Al·giers** |æl'jirz| the capital and largest city of Algeria, one of the leading Mediterranean ports of N Africa. Pop. 1,722,000.

**Al·goa Bay** |æl'gōə| inlet of the Indian Ocean in SE South Africa, in the Cape province. Port Elizabeth is here.

**Al·gon·quin Pro·vin·cial Park** |æl'gäNGkwin| park in S central Ontario, noted for its lakes and scenery.

**Al·ham·bra, the** |æl'hæmbrə; æl'hämbrə| Moorish palace and citadel in Granada, Spain. Built 1248–1354, it is an important example of Moorish architecture.

**Al·ham·bra** |æl'hæmbrə; æl'hämbrə| city in SW California, a suburb NE of Los Angeles. Pop. 82,106.

**Al Hil·lah** |æl 'hilə| commercial port city in central Iraq, on an irrigation canal branching off from the Euphrates River. Pop. 220,000.

**Al·i·can·te** |ˌälə'käntä; ˌælə'kæntē| seaport on the Mediterranean coast of SE Spain, the capital of a province of the same name. Pop. 270,950.

**Alice** |'æləs| city in S Texas. Pop. 19,788.

**Alice Springs** |'æləs| town, a railway terminus and supply center serving the outback of Northern Territory, Australia. Pop. 20,450.

**Al·i·garh** |ˌälē'gär; ˌälē'gər| city in N India, in Uttar Pradesh. Pop. 480,000. The city comprises the ancient fort of Aligarh and the former city of Koil.

**Al Ji·zah** |æl 'jēzə| variant form of GIZA, Egypt.

**Al·ju·bar·ro·ta** |ˌälzHŏŏbə'rōtə| village in W central Portugal. The most important battle in Portuguese history took place here in 1385 when John I defeated invaders from Castile.

**Al Ka·rak** |äl'kärək; ˌælkə'rɔek| (also **Karak**; ancient name **Kir Moab**) historic commercial city in W Jordan, near the S end of the Dead Sea. Pop. 50,000. It was a Moabite city in biblical times.

**Alk·maar** |'älk‚mär| city in the NW Netherlands. Pop. 91,000. It has a famous Edam cheese market.

**Al·la·gash River** |'ælə‚gæsH| river in N Maine, noted as a canoeing route.

**Al·la·ha·bad** |ˌäləhə'bäd| city in the state of Uttar Pradesh, N central India. Pop. 806,000. Situated at the confluence of the sacred Juma and Ganges rivers, it is a place of Hindu pilgrimage.

**All-American Canal** |ˌawl ə'merəkən| water conduit from the Colorado River across S California, supplying the Imperial Valley and nearby farm areas.

**Al·le·ghe·ny Mountains** |ˌælə'gānē| (also the **Alleghenies**) a relatively low (2,000–4,000 ft./610–1,460 m.) mountain range of the Appalachian system in the U.S. extending through Pennsylvania, Maryland, Virginia, West Virginia. Its E slopes are called the Allegheny Front.

**Al·le·ghe·ny River** |ˌælə'gānē| river that flows 325 mi./523 km. through New York and Pennsylvania, joining the Monongahela River at Pittsburgh, Pennsylvania to form the Ohio River.

**Al·len, Bog of** |'ælən| series of peat bogs in central Ireland, between Dublin and the Shannon River. It covers 375 sq. mi./970 sq. km.

**Al·len·town** |'ælən‚town| commercial and industrial city in E Pennsylvania, on the Lehigh River. Pop. 105,090.

**Al·lep·pey** |ə'lepē| (also called **Alappuzha**) commercial port city in S India, on the Malabar Coast of Kerala state. Pop. 265,000. .

**All·gau Alps** |'awl‚goi| (in German, **Allgäuer Alpen**) a range of the Alps that separates Bavaria from the Austrian Tyrol. Madelegabel is the highest peak: 8,678 ft./2,645 m.

**Al·li·ance** |ə'līəns| city in NE Ohio. Pop. 23,393.

**Al·lier** |äl'yā| river of central France that rises in the Cévennes and flows 258 mi./410 km. NW to meet the Loire.

**Al·lo·way** |'ælə‚wā| village in Strathclyde, SW Scotland, the birthplace (1759) of the poet Robert Burns.

**Al·ma** |'ælmə| city in S central Quebec, on the Saguenay River. Pop. 25,910.

**Alma-Ata** |ˌælmə'ɔtä| older name for AL-MATY, Kazakhstan.

**Al·ma·dén** |ˌälmə'dän| town in S central Spain, in the Sierra Morena Mts. Pop. 15,000. Mercury mines are located nearby.

**Al·ma·di·es, Cape** |ˌælmə'dēəs| westernmost point of Africa, a promontory NW of Dakar, Senegal, at 17° 33' W.

**Al Ma·di·nah** |ˌæl mə'dēnə| Arabic name for MEDINA.

**Al·ma·ty** |əl'mätē| (also **Alma-Ata**) largest city and former capital (until 1998) of Kazakhstan, an industrial, research, and educational center. Pop. 1,515,300. Former name (until 1921) **Verny**.

**Al·me·ría** |ˌälmə'rēə| industrial port city, capital of Almería province, Andalusia, S Spain. Pop. 157,760.

**Al·mi·ran·te Brown** |ˌälmə'rän‚tä 'brown| city in E Argentina, forming part of the Buenos Aires metropolitan area. Pop. 449,100.

**Alo·ha** |ə'lō‚hä| community in NW Oregon, a suburb W of Portland. Pop. 34,284.

**Alo·ha State** |ələ‚hä| informal name for HAWAII.

**Alor Se·tar** |'äl‚awr sē'tär| the capital of the state of Kedah in Malaysia, near the W coast of the central Malay Peninsula. Pop. 71,682.

**Al·phe·us River** |æl'fēəs| river in S Greece, rising in Arcadia and flowing NW into the Ionian Sea near Pyrgos. In Greek mythology it ran underground to the fountain of Arethusa, in Syracuse, Sicily. Also **Alphios**.

**Alps** |ælps| mountain system in Europe consisting of several ranges extending in a curve from the coast of SE France through

NW Italy, Switzerland, Liechtenstein, and S Germany into Austria. The highest peak of the Alps, Mont Blanc, rises to 15,771 ft./4,807 m. □ **Alpine** *adj.*

**Al Qa·hi·ra** |ăl 'kähe,raw| Arabic name for CAIRO, Egypt.

**Al·sace** |ăl'säs; ăl'săs| region of NE France, on the borders with Germany and Switzerland. Alsace was annexed by Prussia, along with part of Lorraine (forming *Alsace-Lorraine*), after the Franco-Prussian War of 1870–1, and restored to France after World War I. Alsace is noted for its industry, agriculture, and historic sites. □ **Alsatian** *adj. & n.*

**Al·ta·de·na** |,ăltə'dēnə| residential suburb in SW California, just N of Pasadena. Pop. 42,658.

**Al·tai** |'ăl,tī| (also **Altay**) a krai (administrative territory) of Russia in SW Siberia, on the border with Kazakhstan. Capital: Barnaul.

**Al·tai Mountains** |'ăl,tī| mountain system of central Asia extending about 1,000 mi./1,600 km. E from Kazakhstan into W Mongolia and NChina.

**Al·ta·mi·ra**[1] |,ăltə'mirə| city in N central Brazil, on the Xingu River in Pará state, a commercial center in the Amazon basin. Pop. 79,000.

**Al·ta·mi·ra**[2] |,ăltə'mirə| cave in NE Spain, site of noted prehistoric rock paintings. Discovered in 1879, the art depicts bison, deer, and other animals.

**Al·ta·mont** |'ăltə,mänt| site in N central California, NE of Livermore, scene of a famous 1969 rock concert.

**Alt·dorf** |'ält,dawrf| town in central Switzerland, near Lucerne, the capital of Uri canton. Pop. 8,000. Altdorf was the home of the legendary William Tell.

**Al·ten·burg** |'ältən,bərg| industrial city in eastern Germany, on the Pleisse River. Pop. 53,000.

**Al·ti·pla·no** |,awltə'plänō| high plains region in the Andes Mts. in W Bolivia and S Peru. Lake Titicaca and the city of La Paz are in this region, where agriculture and mining are important and where most Bolivians live.

**Al·to A·di·ge** |,ältō 'ädə,ja| autonomous German-speaking region in NE Italy. Pop. 891,000. It includes the N part of the former Trentino–Alto Adige region.

**Al·ton** |'awltn| industrial city in SW Illinois, on the Mississippi River N of St. Louis, Missouri. Pop. 32,905.

**Al·to·na** |äl'tōnə; ăl'tōnə| former city, incorporated into Hamburg, N Germany,

in 1937. The city is a port on the Elbe River.

**Al·too·na** |ăl'tōōnə| city in S central Pennsylvania, in the Allegheny Mts. Pop. 51,881. A famed railroad center, it is near Horseshoe Curve, where rails first crossed the Alleghenies.

**Al·tus** |'ăltəs| city in SW Oklahoma. Pop. 21,910.

**Al Uq·sur** |äl'ooksoor| Arabic name for LUXOR, Egypt.

**Al·vin** |'ălvən| city in SE Texas. Pop. 19,220.

**Al·war** |'əlwər| industrial and commercial city in N central India, in Rajasthan state. Pop. 211,000.

**Ama·ga·sa·ki** |ə,mägə'säkē| industrial port city in W central Japan, on S Honshu. Pop. 499,000.

**Amal·fi** |ə'mälfē| port and resort on the W coast of Italy, on the Gulf of Salerno. Pop. 5,900.

**Ama·na Colonies** |ə'mænə| group of seven villages in E central Iowa. Settled by a German religious group, they are famous for manufacturing appliances.

**Ama·pá** |,ämə'pä| state of N Brazil, on the Atlantic coast, lying between the Amazon delta and the border with French Guiana. Capital: Macapá. It is a region of dense rainforest. Pop. 289,000.

**Ama·ril·lo** |,æmə'rilō| industrial and commercial city in NW Texas, in the Panhandle. Pop. 157,615.

**Amar·na, Tell el-** |'tel ,el ə'märnə| the site of the ruins of the ancient Egyptian capital Akhetaten, on the E bank of the Nile.

**Amas·ya** |,äməs'yä| (ancient name **Amasia**) historic commercial city in N Turkey, the capital of Amasya province. Pop. 163,000. It was a Cappadocian capital.

**Ama·zon River** |'æmə,zän| river in South America, flowing over 4,150 mi./6,683 km. through Peru, Colombia, and Brazil into the Atlantic. It drains two-fifths of the continent, and in terms of water flow it is the largest river in the world. □ **Amazonian** *adj. & n.*

**Ama·zo·nas** |,æmə'zōnəs| largest (604,266 sq. mi./1,564,445 sq. km.) state of NW Brazil. Capital: Manaus. It is traversed by the Amazon and its numerous tributaries. Pop. 2,103,000.

**Ama·zo·nia** |,æmə'zōnēə| **1** region surrounding the Amazon River, principally in Brazil but also extending into Peru, Colombia, and Bolivia. It contains about one third of the world's remaining tropical rainforest. **2** national park protecting 3,850 sq.

mi./10,000 sq. km. of rainforest in the state of Pará, N Brazil.

**Am·ba·to** |äm'bätō| market town in the Andes of central Ecuador. Pop. 229,190.

**Am·ber Coast** |'æmbər| name for the N coast of the Dominican Republic, on the Atlantic around Puerto Plata. Nearby mountains are the leading world source of amber.

**Am·berg** |'ämberk| city in S central Germany, on the Vils River, E of Nuremberg. Pop. 43,000.

**Am·boise** |ˌäN'bwäz| town in N central France, in the Loire valley. It is known chiefly for its Gothic and Renaissance chateau, of which only parts remain. Leonardo da Vinci died at Amboise and is buried in its chapel.

**Am·bon** |äm'bawn; 'æm,bän| (also **Amboina**) **1** mountainous island in E Indonesia, one of the Moluccas Islands. **2** port on this island, the capital of the Moluccas. Pop. 80,000.

**Am·brym** |'ämbrim| (also **Ambrim**) island in NE Vanuatu, noted for its folk arts and black volcanic ash.

**Am·chit·ka** |æm'CHitkə| island in the Aleutian Islands of SW Alaska. It has been used as a military base and for nuclear testing.

**Amer·i·ca** |ə'merəkə| **1** (also **the Americas**) land mass of the W hemisphere consisting of the continents of North and South America joined by the Isthmus of Panama. The continent was originally inhabited by American Indians and Inuit peoples. The NE coastline of North America was visited by Norse seamen in the 8th or 9th century, but European colonization followed the explorations of Columbus, who reached the West Indies in 1492 and the South American mainland in 1498. **2** widely used informal name for the United States. The name **America** dates from the early 16th century and is believed to derive from the Latin form (*Americus*) of the given name of Amerigo Vespucci, who explored the E coast of South America in at least two voyages between 1499 and 1502. Vespucci's explorations convinced Europeans that these lands were not part of Asia (as Columbus thought) but rather a "New World." The name first appeared on maps by German cartographer Martin Weldseemüller in 1507. □ **American** *adj. & n.*

**Amer·i·can River** |ə'merəkən| river in N central California, joining the Sacramento River at Sacramento. Gold was discovered here in 1848, setting off the California gold rush.

**Amer·i·can Sa·moa** |ə'merəkən sə'mōə| unincorporated overseas territory of the U.S. comprising a group of islands in the S Pacific, to the E of the state of SAMOA and S of the Kiribati group. Pop. 46,770. Capital: Fagatogo. In 1899 the U.S. took control of the islands by agreement with Germany and Britain.

**American Samoa**

**Amer·i·cus** |ə'merəkəs| city in SW Georgia. Pop. 16,512.

**Amers·foort** |'ämərs,fawrt| transportation and manufacturing center in the central Netherlands. Pop. 102,000.

**Ames** |āmz| city in central Iowa, home to Iowa State University. Pop. 47,198.

**Am·ha·ra** |äm'härə| region and former kingdom of NW Ethiopia, which gave its name to the Amharic language. Gondar is the principal city in the area.

**Am·herst¹** |'æm(h)ərst| town in W central Massachusetts, home to several colleges. Pop. 35,228.

**Am·herst²** |'æm(h)ərst| town in W New York, a suburb NE of Buffalo. Pop. 111,711.

**Ami·ens** |äm'yeN| commercial and industrial city in N France. Pop. 136,230. An historic textile center, it attracts tourism.

**Amin·di·vi Islands** |ˌəmən'dēvē| the northernmost group of islands in the Indian territory of Lakshadweep in the Indian Ocean.

**Ami·ran·te Islands** |'æmə,rænt| group of coral islands in the Indian Ocean, forming part of the Seychelles.

**Amish Country** |'ämisH| name for areas, chiefly in SE Pennsylvania and NE Ohio, inhabited by the Amish, an agricultural religious sect.

**Am·man** |ə'män| the capital, largest city, and industrial and commercial center of Jordan. Pop. 1,160,000.

**Amol** |'aw,mōl| (also **Amul**) commercial city in N Iran, in the foothills of the Elburz Mts. Pop. 140,000.

**Amoy** |ä'moi| another name for XIAMEN, China.

**Am·ra·va·ti** |əm'rävətē; äm'rävətē| industrial and commercial city in W central India, in Maharashtra state. Pop. 434,000. It has the largest cotton market in India.

**Am·rit·sar** |əm'ritsər; äm'ritsər| city in the state of Punjab in NW India. Pop. 709,000. The center of the Sikh faith and the site of its holiest temple, the Golden Temple.

**Am·ro·ha** |əm'rōhə| town in N India, in Uttar Pradesh state. Pop. 137,000. It is a Muslim center of pilgrimage.

**Am·stel·veen** |'ämstəl,vän| industrial suburb of Amsterdam, the Netherlands. Pop. 70,000. Schiphol International Airport is located here.

**Am·ster·dam**[1] |'æmpstər,dæm| the capital and largest city of the Netherlands. Pop. 702,440. Although Amsterdam is the capital, the country's seat of government and administrative center is at The Hague. Amsterdam, a European commercial and cultural center, is crossed by canals, which have made it known as the Venice of the N.

**Am·ster·dam**[2] |'ämstər,dæm; 'æmstər,dæm| city in E central New York, on the Mohawk River and the Erie Canal. Pop. 20,714.

**Amu Dar·ya** |,ämoo 'däryə| river of central Asia, rising in the Pamirs and flowing 1,500 mi./2,400 km. into the Aral Sea. In classical times it was known as the Oxus.

**Amund·sen Gulf** |'ämənsən| arm of the Beaufort Sea N of the mainland Northwest Territories and Nunavut and S of Banks Island, in the Canadian arctic.

**Amund·sen Sea** |'ämənsən| arm of the South Pacific Ocean on the coast of Antarctica, off Marie Byrd Land.

**Amur River** |ə'moor| (Chinese name **Heilong Jiang**) river of NE Asia, flowing 1,786 mi./2,874 km. along the Russia-China border then NE through Russia to the Tatar Strait.

**Ana·con·da** |,ænə'kändə| mining city in SW Montana. Pop. 10,278.

**Ana·cos·tia** |,ænə'kawstēə; ,ænə'kästēə| residential section of SE Washington, D.C., across the Anacostia River from the rest of the District of Columbia.

**Ana·dyr River** |,änə'dir| river (694 mi./1,117 km.) in NE Siberian Russia. It rises in the mountains S of Chukotshoye Nagor'ye and flows into the Gulf of Anadyr.

**Ana·heim** |'ænə,hīm| city in California, on the SE side of metropolitan Los Angeles. Pop. 266,400. It is the site of the amusement park Disneyland.

**Aná·huac** |ə'nä,wäk| name for the central plateau of Mexico, including the Mexico City area (the Valley of Mexico).

**Aná·po·lis** |ä'näpoo,lēs| commercial city in central Brazil, in Goiás state. Pop. 265,000. It is a rail center shipping coffee and other agricultural and mine products.

**Ana·to·lia** |,ænə'tōlēə| the W peninsula of Asia, bounded by the Black Sea, the Aegean, and the Mediterranean, that forms the greater part of Turkey. □ **Anatolian** *adj. & n.*

**An·chor·age** |'æNGk(ə)rij| the largest city in Alaska, a seaport on Cook Inlet, off the Pacific. Pop. 226,340.

**An·co·na** |äNG'kōnə; æNG'kōnə| port on the Adriatic coast of central Italy, capital of Marche region. Pop. 103,270.

**An·cy·ra** |æn'sīrə| ancient Roman name for ANKARA, Turkey.

**An·da** |'ändä| city in Heilongjiang province, NE China, between Daqing and Harbin. Pop. 423,000.

**An·da·lu·sia** |ändə'loosēə| the southernmost region of Spain, bordering on the Atlantic and the Mediterranean. Capital: Seville. The region was under Moorish rule from 711 to 1492. Spanish name **Andalucía**. □ **Andalusian** *adj. & n.*

**An·da·man and Ni·co·bar Islands** |'ændəmən ən 'nikə,bär| two groups of islands in the Bay of Bengal, constituting a Union Territory of India. Pop. 279,110. Capital: Port Blair.

**An·der·lecht** |'ändər,leKHt| industrial suburb of Brussels, Belgium. Pop. 88,000. It was the home of the scholar Erasmus in the 16th century.

**An·der·son**[1] |'ændərsən| industrial city in E central Indiana. Pop. 59,459.

**An·der·son**[2] |'ændərsən| city in NW South Carolina. Pop. 26,184.

**An·der·son·ville** |'ændərsən,vil| village in SW Georgia, near Americus, site of a major Confederate prison camp during the Civil War.

**An·des** |'ændēz| major mountain system running the length of the Pacific coast of South America. It extends over some 5,000 mi./8,000 km., with a continuous height of more than 10,000 ft./3,000 m. Its highest peak is Aconcagua, which rises to a height of 22,834 ft./6,960 m. □ **Andean** *adj.*

**Andh·ra Pra·desh** |'ändrə prə'deSH| state in SE India, on the Bay of Bengal. Pop. 66,305,000. Capital: Hyderabad.

**An·di·zhan** |,ändi'zän| (also **Andijon**) **1** administrative subdivision in E Uzbekistan. Area: 1,660 sq. mi./4,299 sq. km. Pop.

1,795,000. **2** its capital, an industrial city. Pop. 298,000.

**An·dor·ra** |æn'dawrə| small (181 sq. mi./468 sq. km.) autonomous principality in the S Pyrenees, between France and Spain. Pop. 55,000. Languages: Catalan, Spanish, and French. Capital: Andorra la Vella. Its independence dates from the late 8th century, when Charlemagne is said to have granted the Andorrans self-government for their help in defeating the Moors. It has a pastoral and resort economy, with international offices. □ **Andorran** adj. & n.

Andorra

**An·do·ver** |'æn,dōvər; 'ændəvər| town in NE Massachusetts, home to Phillips Academy, a famous prep school. Pop. 29,151.

**An·dre·an·of Islands** |,ændrē'æn,awf; ,ændrē'ænəf| island group in SW Alaska, part of the Aleutian Islands.

**An·dros¹** |'ændrəs| largest (2,300 sq. mi./5,955 sq. km.) island of the Bahamas, in the W part.

**An·dros²** |'ændrəs; 'æn,draws| island in Greece, northernmost island of the Cyclades, in the Aegean Sea. Pop. 9,000. Its capital is Andros.

**An·dro·scog·gin River** |,ændrə'skägən| river that flows 175 mi./280 km. from N New Hampshire through SW Maine to the Atlantic.

**Ané·ho** |ä'nähō| commercial port town in S Togo, E of Lomé. Pop. 14,000. It was formerly a colonial capital and slave-trade center.

**Ane·to, Pi·co de** |'pēkō ,dā ə'netō| mountain peak in the Maladeta range in NE Spain, just S of the French border. It is the tallest peak in the Pyrénées (11,168 ft./3,404 m.).

**An·ga·ra River** |,ängə'rä| river (1.039 mi./1,779 km.) in SE Siberia, Russia. It flows from Lake Baikal NW and W, meeting the Yenisei River S of Yeniseysk.

**An·garsk** |ən'gärsk| industrial city in E Siberia, Russia, NW of Irkutsk. Pop. 267,000.

**An·gel Falls** |'änjəl| waterfall in the Guiana Highlands of SE Venezuela. It is the highest waterfall in the world, with an uninterrupted descent of 3,210 ft./978 m. The falls were discovered in 1935 by the American aviator and prospector James Angel.

**An·gel Island** |'änjəl| island in San Francisco Bay, N central California, that was the chief immigration station on the U.S. W coast. It is now a state park.

**An·geln** |'äNGəln| region in NW Schleswig-Holstein, Germany, noted as a cattle-raising area and as the traditional home of the Angles, who invaded Britain in the 5th century.

**An·gers** |äN'ZHā| industrial and commercial city in W France, capital of the former province of Anjou. Pop. 146,160.

**Ang·kor** |'æNGkawr; 'äNG,kawr| the capital of the ancient kingdom of the Khmer in NW Cambodia; long abandoned, the site was rediscovered in 1860, and is noted for its temples, especially the Angkor Wat (mid 12th century).

**An·gle·sey** |'æNGgəl,sē| island of NW Wales, separated from the mainland by the Menai Strait. The ferry port at Holyhead is on Holy Island, just NW.

**An·glia** |'æNGglēə| Latin name for England, the land of the Angles (Latin *Angli*), a Germanic people who settled here in the 5th century. *England* has the same meaning.

**An·go·la** |æNG'gōlə; æn'gōlə| republic on the W coast of southern Africa. Area: 481,186 sq. mi./1.25 million sq. km. Pop. 10,301,000. Capital and largest city: Luanda. Languages: Portuguese (official), Bantu languages. Held by the Portuguese for almost 400 years before 1975, Angola has a central plateau with headwaters of the Congo and Zambezi rivers. Timber, coffee, tobacco, and diamonds are important to the economy. Oil is central especially to the

Angola

coastal exclave of Cabinda. □ **Angolan** adj. & n.

**An·go·ra** |æNG'gawrə; æn'gawrə| old name for ANKARA, Turkey, source of the name of a type of wool.

**An·go·stu·ra** |ˌæNgə'st(y)ŏŏrə| old name for CIUDAD BOLÍVAR, Venezuela.

**An·gou·lême** |ˌäNGgŏŏ'lem| industrial and transportation center in W France, on the Charente River. Pop. 46,000.

**An·guil·la** |æNG'gwilə; æn'gwilə| the most northerly of the Leeward Islands in the West Indies. Pop. 7,020. Languages, English (official), English Creole. Capital: The Valley. Formerly a British colony, and briefly united with St. Kitts and Nevis (1967), the island is now a self-governing dependency of the UK. □ **Anguillan** adj. & n.

**An·gus** |'æNGgəs| former county of NE Scotland, known from the 16th century until 1928 as Forfarshire. It became an administrative district of Tayside region in 1975.

**An·hui** |'än'hwä| (also **Anhwei**) province in E China. Pop. 59,380,000. Capital: Hefei.

**An·jou¹** |'æn,jŏŏ; äN'ZHŏŏ| former province of W France, on the Loire. It was an English possession from 1154 to 1204. Angers was the chief town. □ **Angevin** adj. & n.

**An·jou²** |äNZHŏŏ| residential city in S Quebec, immediately NE of Montreal. Pop. 37,210.

**An·ka·ra** |'æNGkərə; 'äNGkərə| the capital of Turkey since 1923. Pop. 2,559,470. Prominent in Roman times as Ancyra, it later declined in importance until chosen by Kemal Atatürk in 1923 as his seat of government. Former name (until 1930) **Angora**.

**Ann, Cape** |æn| peninsula in NE Massachusetts, noted for its resorts and scenery.

**An·na·ba** |'æn'äbə| port of NE Algeria. Pop. 348,000. The modern town is adjacent to the site of Hippo Regius, a prominent city in Roman Africa and the home and bishopric of St. Augustine of Hippo from 396 to 430. Former name **Bône**.

**An Na·jaf** |ˌän nə'yäf| (also called **Mashad Ali**) city in S central Iraq, on a lake W of the Euphrates River. Pop. 243,000. The tomb of Ali, son-in-law of the Prophet Muhammad, is here.

**An·nam** |ə'næm; ə'näm| former independent kingdom (c.10th to 19th centuries) in SE Asia, in territory that is now a region in central Vietnam. □ **Annamese** adj. & n.

**An·nan·dale** |'ænən,däl| residential sub-

urb in N Virginia, SW of Washington, D.C. Pop. 50,975.

**An·na·po·lis** |ə'næp(ə)liəs| city, the capital of Maryland, on Chesapeake Bay. Pop. 33,190. It is the home of the U.S. Naval Academy.

**An·na·po·lis Roy·al** |ə'næp(ə)ləs 'roiəl| historic town in SW Nova Scotia, on the Annapolis River. Pop. 633.

**An·na·pur·na** |ˌænə'pŏŏrnə| ridge of the Himalayas, in N central Nepal. Its highest peak rises to 26,503 ft./8,078 m.

**Ann Ar·bor** |æn 'ärbər| city in SE Michigan, home to the University of Michigan. Pop. 109,592.

**Anne·cy** |än'sē| capital of the department of Haute-Savoie, in SE France. Pop. 51,000. It is an industrial center and resort.

**An Nhon** |'än'nŏn| (formerly **Binh Dinh**) city in SE Vietnam, SSE of Da Nang, near Quy Nhon. It was once the capital of Annam.

**An·nis·ton** |'ænə,stən| industrial and military city in NE Alabama. Pop. 26,623.

**An·no·bón** |ˌänŏ'bawn| island of Equatorial Guinea, in the Gulf of Guinea. Also called **Pagalu**.

**An·qing** |'än'CHiNG| city in Anhui province, E China, at the mouth of the Yangtze River. Pop. 441,000.

**An·shan** |'än'SHän| city in Liaoning, China. Pop. 1,370,000. Anshan is situated close to major iron-ore deposits and China's largest iron-and-steel complex is nearby.

**An·shun** |'än'SHŏŏn| city in Guizhou province, S China, noted for green tea and sugar production. Pop. 174,000.

**An·tak·ya** |ˌäntä'kyä| Turkish name for ANTIOCH.

**An·tal·ya** |ˌäntl'yä| port in S Turkey. Pop. 378,200.

**An·ta·na·na·ri·vo** |ˌäntə,nänə'rēvŏ| capital, largest city, and commercial center of Madagascar, situated in the central plateau. Pop. 802,390. Former name (until 1975) **Tananarive**.

**Ant·arc·ti·ca** |ænt'är(k)tikə| continent surrounding the South Pole, situated mainly within the Antarctic Circle and almost entirely covered by ice sheets. Area: 5.4 million sq. mi./13.9 million sq. km.

**Ant·arc·tic Circle** |ænt'är(k)tik| the parallel of latitude 66° 33′ S of the equator. It marks the southernmost point at which the sun is visible on the S winter solstice and the northernmost point at which the midnight sun can be seen on the S summer solstice.

**Antarctica**

**Antigua & Barbuda**

**Ant·arc·tic Convergence** |ˌænˈ(t)ärˈ(k)tik kənˈvərjəns; æntˈärˈ(k)tik| the zone of the Antarctic Ocean where cold, nutrient-laden Antarctic surface water sinks beneath the warmer waters to the N.

**Ant·arc·tic Ocean** |æntˈärˈ(k)tik| the sea surrounding Antarctica, consisting of parts of the S Atlantic, the S Pacific, and the S Indian Ocean. Also called **Southern Ocean**.

**Ant·arc·tic Peninsula** |æntˈärˈ(k)tik| mountainous peninsula of Antarctica between the Bellingshausen sea and the Weddell Sea, extending N toward Cape Horn and the Falkland Islands.

**An·thra·cite Belt** |ˈænTHrəˌsīt| area of NE Pennsylvania, around Scranton and Wilkes-Barre, where hard coal has been central to economic development.

**An·tibes** |änˈtēb| fishing port and resort in SE France, on the Riviera. Pop. 70,690. Just S is the well-known Cap d'Antibes.

**An·ti·cos·ti Island** |ˌæntəˈkawstē| largely uninhabited island in E Quebec, in the mouth of the Saint Lawrence River.

**An·tie·tam** |ænˈtētəm| historic site on Antietam Creek, in NW Maryland, SE of Sharpsburg, scene of a major Civil War battle in September 1862.

**An·ti·go·nish** |ˌæntəgiˈnisH| town in N central Nova Scotia. Pop. 4,924.

**An·ti·gua** |ænˈtēgwə| (also **Antigua Guatemala**) historic town in the central highlands of Guatemala. Pop. 26,630.

**An·ti·gua and Bar·bu·da** |ænˈtigwə ənd ˌbärˈbo͞odə; änˈtēgwə ənd ˌbärˈbo͞odə; ænˈtēg(w)ənd bärˈbo͞odə| republic consisting of two islands in the Leeward Islands in the West Indies. Area: 171 sq. mi./442 sq. km. Pop 80,000. Languages: English (official), Creole. Capital: St. John's (on Antigua). Discovered in 1493 by Columbus and settled by the English in 1632, Antigua became a British colony with Barbuda as its dependency; the islands gained independence within the Commonwealth in 1981. Tourism and sugar have been mainstays of the economy. □ **Antiguan** *adj. & n.*

**Anti-Lebanon Mountains** |ˌæntiˈlebənən| range of mountains running N to S along the border between Lebanon and Syria, E of the Lebanon range.

**An·til·les** |ænˈtilēz| group of islands, forming the greater part of the West Indies. The *Greater Antilles*, extending roughly E to W, comprise Cuba, Jamaica, Hispaniola (Haiti and the Dominican Republic), and Puerto Rico; the *Lesser Antilles*, to the SE, include the Virgin Islands, Leeward Islands, Windward Islands, and various small islands to the N of Venezuela. See also NETHERLANDS ANTILLES.

**An·ti·och**[1] |ˈæntēˌäk| city in N central California. Pop. 62,195.

**An·ti·och**[2] |ˈæntēˌäk| city in S Turkey, near the Syrian border. Pop. 123,871. Antioch was the ancient capital of Syria under the Seleucid kings, who founded it. Turkish name **Antakya**.

**An·tip·o·des, the** |ænˈtipədˌēz| from the term for any two points opposite each other on the earth's surface, an old (chiefly British) popular name for Australia and New Zealand.

**An·to·fa·gas·ta** |ˌäntōfəˈgästə| industrial port city in N Chile, the capital of Antofagasta region. Pop. 227,000. Mining and tourism are central to its economy.

**An·trim** |ˈæntrəm| **1** one of the Six Counties of Northern Ireland. **2** town in this county, on the NE shore of Lough Neagh. Pop. 21,000.

**Ant·si·ra·be** |ˌäntsirˈäbə| spa town in central Madagascar, in the Ankaratra Mts. Pop. 120,000.

**An·tung** |ˈänˈdo͞oNG| former name for DANDONG, China.

**Ant·werp** |ˈænˌtwərp| port in N Belgium, on the Scheldt. Pop. 467,520. By the 16th century it became a leading European commercial and financial center. French name **Anvers**, Flemish name **Antwerpen**.

**Anu·ra·dha·pu·ra** |ˌənəˌrädəˈpo͝orə| city in N central Sri Lanka, capital of a district of the same name. Pop. 36,000.The ancient capital of Sri Lanka, it is a center of Buddhist pilgrimage.

**An·vers** |änˈver(s)| French name of ANTWERP, Belgium.

**An·yang** |ˈänˈyäNG| industrial city in Henan province, central China. Pop. 480,000. It was the last capital (1330–1066 B.C.) of the Shang dynasty.

**An·za Bor·re·go** |ˈænzə bəˈrägö| desert region, much of it a state park, in S California.

**An·zio** |ˈäntsēˌō; ˈænzēō| seaport, W Italy, S of Rome. Pop. 36,000. It was a popular resort for citizens of ancient Rome. Allied troops landed here in January 1944; amid fierce fighting, to begin their drive on Rome.

**Ao·mo·ri** |ˌäōˈmawrē| industrial port city in N Japan, on N Honshu. Pop. 288,000.

**Ao·ran·gi** |owˈräNGē| Maori name for MOUNT COOK, New Zealand.

**Aos·ta** |äˈawstə| city in NW Italy, capital of Valle d'Aosta region. Pop. 36,095.

**Ao·te·a·roa** |ˌow͟ˌtäəˈrōə| Maori name for NEW ZEALAND.

**Aou·zou Strip** |owˈzōō| narrow corridor of disputed desert land in N Chad, stretching the full length of the border between Chad and Libya.

**Apa·che Junction** |əˈpæCHē| city in S central Arizona, a suburb SE of Phoenix. Pop. 18,100.

**Apa·la·chi·co·la River** |ˌæpəˌlæCHiˈkōlə| see CHATTAHOOCHEE RIVER.

**Apel·doorn** |äpəlˌdawrn| town in the E central Netherlands. Pop. 148,200.The site of the summer residence of the Dutch royal family.

**Apen·nines** |ˈæpəˌnīnz| mountain range running 880 mi./1,400 km. down the length of Italy, from the NW to the S tip of the peninsula. □ **Apennine** *adj.*

**Aphro·di·si·as** |ˌæfrəˈdizēəs| ancient city of W Asia Minor, site of a temple dedicated to Aphrodite. Now in ruins, it is situated 50 mi./80 km. W of Aydin, Turkey.

**Apia** |äˈpēə| port city, the capital and economic and cultural center of the state of Samoa (Western Samoa). Pop. 32,200.

**Apos·tle Islands** |əˈpäsəl| island group in N Wisconsin, in Lake Superior.

**Ap·pa·la·chia** |ˌæpəˈläsHə; ˌæpəˈlæCHə| term for areas in the Appalachian Mts. of the E U.S. that exhibit longterm poverty and distinctive folkways. □ **Appalachian** *adj.*

**Ap·pa·la·chian Mountains** |ˌæpəˈläsHən; ˌæpəˈlæCHən| (also **the Appalachians**) a mountain system of E North America, stretching from Quebec and Maine in the N to Georgia and Alabama in the S. Its highest peak is Mount Mitchell in North Carolina, which rises to 6,684 ft./2,037 m. Other ranges in the Appalachian system include the White Mts. of New Hampshire, the Green Mts. of Vermont, the Catskills of New York, and the Allegheny, Blue Ridge, and Cumberland mountains. □ **Appalachian** *adj.*

**Ap·pa·la·chian Trail** |ˌæpəˈläsHən; ˌæpəˈlæCHən| 2,000-mi./3,200-km. footpath through the Appalachian Mts., from Mount Katahdin in Maine to Springer Mt. in Georgia.

**Ap·pian Way** |ˈæpēən| the principal road S from Rome in classical times, named after Appius Claudius Caecus, who in 312 B.C. built the section to Capua; it was later extended to Brindisi. Latin name **Via Appia**.

**Ap·ple Isle** |ˈæpəl| (also **Apple Island**) an informal Australian name for Tasmania.

**Ap·ple·ton** |ˈæpəltən| industrial and academic city in E central Wisconsin. Pop. 65,695.

**Ap·ple Valley**[1] |ˈæpəl| town in SW California, a suburb NE of Los Angeles. Pop. 46,079.

**Ap·ple Valley**[2] |ˈæpəl| city in SE Minnesota, a suburb S of Minneapolis. Pop. 34,598.

**Ap·po·mat·tox** |ˌæpəˈmætəks| historic site in central Virginia, at the head of the Appomattox River, where Robert E. Lee surrendered his Confederate forces in April 1865, ending the Civil War.

**Ap·ra Harbor** |ˈäprə| military and commercial port on Guam. Pop. 7,956.

**Apu·lia** |əˈp(y)o͞olyə| region of SE Italy, extending into the "heel" of the peninsula. Capital: Bari. Italian name **Puglia**.

**Apu·re River** |äˈpo͝orə| river that flows 500 mi./800 km. from the Andes in Colombia across W central Venezuela, into the Orinoco River.

**Apu·ri·mac River** |ˌäpəˈrē͟ˌmäk| river that flows 430 mi./690 km. through central Peru, to join the Urubamba River in forming the Ucayali River, an important headwater of the Amazon.

**Aqa·ba** |äkəkəbə; ˈækəbə| Jordan's only port, at the head of the Gulf of Aqaba. Pop. 40,000.

**Aqa·ba, Gulf of** |äkˈmawlətow.; ˈækəbə|

part of the Red Sea extending N between the Sinai and Arabian peninsulas.

**Aq·mo·la** |äk'mawlə| (also **Akmola**) former name of ASTANA.

**Aq·taū** |'äk,tow| (formerly **Shevchenko**) town in SW Kazakhstan, on the E coast of the Caspian Sea. Pop. 169,000.

**Aq·tö·be** |äk'tœbe| (formerly known as **Aktyubinsk**) industrial city in Kazakhstan, in the S foothills of the Ural Mts. Pop. 261,000.

**Aquid·neck** former name of the largest island in Narragansett Bay, now called Rhode Island; part of the state of Rhode Island.

**Aqui·la** |'äkwilə| city in E central Italy, capital of Abruzzi region. Pop. 67,820. Italian name **L'Aquila**.

**Aqui·taine** |'ækwə,tān| region and former province of SW France, on the Bay of Biscay, centered on Bordeaux. It was an English possession 1259–1453. Latin name **Aquitania**.

**Ara·bia** |ə'rābēə| (also **Arabian Peninsula**) a peninsula of SW Asia, largely desert, lying between the Red Sea and the Persian Gulf and bounded on the N by Jordan and Iraq. The original homeland of the Arabs and the historic center of Islam, it comprises the states of Saudi Arabia, Yemen, Oman, Bahrain, Kuwait, Qatar, and the United Arab Emirates. □ **Arabian** adj. & n.

**Ara·bian Desert** |ə'rābēən| desert in E Egypt, between the Nile and the Red Sea. Also called the **Eastern Desert**.

**Ara·bian Gulf** another name for the PERSIAN GULF.

**Ara·bian Peninsula** |ə'rābēən| another name for ARABIA.

**Ara·bian Sea** |ə'rābēən| the NW part of the Indian Ocean, between Arabia and India.

**Ara·by** |'ærəbē| archaic term for ARABIA.

**Ara·ca·jú** |,ärəkə'ZHōō| port in E Brazil, on the Atlantic coast, capital of the state of Sergipe. Pop. 404,828.

**Arad** |ä'räd| commercial and industrial city in W Romania, capital of Arad county, on the Mures River. Pop. 191,000.

**Ara·fu·ra Sea** |,ærə'fŏŏrə| sea lying between N Australia, the islands of E Indonesia, and New Guinea.

**Ara·gon** |'ærə,gän| (Spanish name **Aragón**) autonomous region of NE Spain, bounded on the N by the Pyrenees and on the E by Catalonia and Valencia. Capital: Saragossa. Formerly an independent kingdom, it was united with Catalonia in 1137

and with Castile in 1479. □ **Aragonese** adj. & n.

**Ara·guaía River** |,ærə'gwīyə| river that flows 1,300 mi./2,100 km. from Mato Grosso state, S central Brazil, N to the Tocantins River. Bananal Island, which lies in its course, is over 200 mi./320 km. long.

**Arak** |ə'räk| commercial city in W central Iran, in the Zagros Mts. SW of Tehran. Pop. 331,000. It is famous for its carpets.

**Araks River** |ə'räks| (ancient name **Araxes;** Turkish name **Aras**) river that flows 566 mi./900 km. E from Armenia to the Caspian Sea, at times forming the Turkey-Iran and Armenia-Azerbaijan borders. Its valley has been claimed to be the legendary Garden of Eden.

**Aral Sea** |'ærəl| inland sea in central Asia, on the border between Kazakhstan and Uzbekistan. Its area was reduced to two-thirds of its original size between 1960 and 1990, after water was diverted for irrigation, with serious consequences for the environment.

**Aram** |'ærəm| ancient country of SW Asia, roughly the equivalent of present-day Syria. Its language, Aramaic, was a lingua franca in the region, and came to be spoken by many Jews.

**Aran Islands** |'ærən| group of three islands, Inishmore, Inishmaan, and Inisheer, off the W coast of the Republic of Ireland.

**Aran·juez** |ärän'hwäтн| agricultural market town and former royal summer residence in central Spain, near Madrid. Pop. 36,000.

**Ara·rat, Mount** |'ærə,ræt| pair of volcanic peaks in E Turkey, near the borders with Armenia and Iran. The higher peak, which rises to 16,946 ft./5,165 m., is the traditional site of the resting place of Noah's ark after the Flood (Gen. 8:4).

**Arau·ca·nia** |,är,owkä'nēə| region of S Chile, S of the Bío-Bío River. Temuco is its capital. The Araucanian Indians lived in the area before Europeans arrived, and resisted settlement until the 1880s. □ **Araucanian** adj.

**Ara·val·li Range** |ə'rävələ| mountain range in NW India, running from N Gujarat state to central Rajasthan state.

**Ar·bil** |'är,bēl| (also **Erbil; Irbil**) historic city in N Iraq, capital of the Kurdish province of Arbil. Pop. 334,000.

**Ar·broath** |är'brōтн| port town in Tayside, E Scotland. Pop. 24,000. The independence of Scotland from England was proclaimed here in 1320.

**Ar·buck·le Mountains** |'är,bəkəl| low

**Ar·ca·dia**[1] |är'kadēə| city in SW California, a suburb NE of Los Angeles. Pop. 48,290. The Santa Anita racetrack is here.

**Ar·ca·dia**[2] |är'kadēə| (also **Arcady**; Greek name **Arkhadia**) mountainous district in the Peloponnese of S Greece. In poetic fantasy it represents a pastoral paradise and in Greek mythology it is the home of Pan. □ **Arcadian** adj.

**Ar·ca·ta** |,är'kätə| city in NW California, on Humboldt Bay off the Pacific. Pop. 15,197.

**Arch·an·gel** |'är,kānjəl| industrial port of NW Russia, on the White Sea. Pop. 419,000. It is named after the monastery of the Archangel Michael situated here. Russian name **Arkhangelsk**.

**Ar·chi·pié·la·go de Co·lón** |,ärCH'pyälä-,gō ,dä kə'lōn| official Ecuadorian name for GALAPAGOS ISLANDS.

**Arc·tic, the** |'är(k)tik| regions on or N of the Arctic Circle.

**Arc·tic Archipelago** |'är(k)tik| name for all the islands lying N of mainland Canada and the Arctic Circle. Sparsely populated, they have varied mineral resources and wildlife. Baffin Island is the largest in the group.

**Arc·tic Circle** |'är(k)tik| the parallel of latitude 66° 33′ N of the equator. It marks the northernmost point at which the sun is visible on the N winter solstice and the southernmost point at which the midnight sun can be seen on the N summer solstice.

**Arc·tic National Wildlife Refuge** |'är(k)tik| preserve on the North Slope of NE Alaska, scene of controversies over oil exploration and drilling.

**Arc·tic Ocean** |'är(k)tik| ocean that surrounds the North Pole, lying within the Arctic Circle. Much of it is covered with pack ice throughout the year.

**Ar·da·bil** |,ärdə'bēl| (also **Ardebil**) historic city in NW Iran. Pop. 311,000. It is famous for its carpets and rugs.

**Ar·dèche** |är'deSH| department in E France, in the Rhône-Alpes region. Area: 2,136 sq. mi./5,529 sq. km. Pop. 278,000. The capital is Privas.

**Ar·den, Forest of** |'ärdən| forest in Warwickshire, central England, remnant of a much greater wilderness and associated with *As You Like It* by Shakespeare. The name has come to connote idyllic pastoral life.

**Ar·dennes** |är'den| forested upland region extending over parts of SE Belgium, NE France, and Luxembourg. It was the scene of fierce fighting in both world wars.

**Ard·more** |'ärd,mawr| city in S Oklahoma, in an oil-producing and agricultural area. Pop. 23,079.

**Ard·na·mur·chan** |,ärdnə'mərKHən| peninsula on the coast of Highland Region in W Scotland.

**Are·ci·bo** |,ärə'sēbō| community in NW Puerto Rico, W of San Juan. Pop. 49,545. It is an academic center noted for its huge radio telescope facility.

**Are·op·a·gus** |,ærē'äpəgəs| rocky hill in Athens, Greece, W of the Acropolis. Once the meeting place of the prime council (the Areopagus) of Greece, it was the site of Saint Paul's address to the Athenians.

**Are·qui·pa** |,ärə'kēpə| commercial city in the Andes of S Peru. Pop. 634,500.

**Are·thu·sa** |,ærə'THŌŌzə; ,ærə'THŌŌsə| see ALPHEUS river, Greece.

**Arez·zo** |ə'retsō| agricultural trade center in central Italy, capital of Arezzo province. Pop. 92,000.

**Ar·gen·teuil** |ärzHən'twœi| industrial NW suburb of Paris, on the Seine River. Pop. 94,000. Many painters have worked in Argenteuil, including Monet.

**Ar·gen·tia** |är'jenCHə| locality in SE Newfoundland, on Placentia Bay, former site of naval facilities important in World War II.

**Ar·gen·ti·na** |,ärjən'tēnə| republic occupying much of the S part of South America. It is the second largest country in the continent. Area: 1,073,809 sq. mi./ 2,780,092 sq. km. Pop. 32,646,000; official language, Spanish. Capital and largest city: Buenos Aires. Also called **the Argentine Republic.** With the Andes in the W, the pampa in the center, and the Atlantic coast in the E, Argentina is a major producer of grains and cattle. Oil, gas, and minerals are also important, and there is much industry. □ **Argentine** n. **Argentinian** adj. & n.

**Argentina**

**Ar·geş River** |'är,jeSH| river in S Romania that rises in the Transylvanian Alps and flows S to the Danube River SE of Bucharest; it is linked to the city by canals.

**Ar·go·lis** |'ärgələs| ancient region of the Peloponnese, SE Greece, dominated by Argos and home to the Argives. A modern prefecture retains the name.

**Ar·gonne** |är'gawn; är'gän| wooded plateau in NE France, near the Belgian border. The region is thinly populated. A major Allied offensive was staged here during World War I; during World War II the region was occupied by Germany in 1940–44.

**Ar·gos** |'är,gəs| city in the NE Peloponnese of Greece. Pop. 20,702. One of the oldest cities of ancient Greece, it dominated the Peloponnese and the W Aegean in the 7th century B.C. □ **Argive** adj. & n.

**Ar·gyll·shire** |är'gīl,SHir; är'gilSHər| former county on the W coast of Scotland. It was divided between Strathclyde and Highland regions in 1975.

**Ar·i·a·na** |,ærē'änə; ,ärē'änə| name for E provinces of the ancient Persian Empire lying to the S of the Oxus (present-day Amu Darya) River.

**Ar·i·ca** |ä'rēkä| port city in extreme N Chile, near the Peruvian border. Pop. 195,000. It provides foreign trade facilities for landlocked Bolivia, to the E.

**Ar·i·ma·thea** |,ærəmə'THēə| (also **Arimathaea**) unidentified biblical town, the home of Joseph who placed Jesus in his tomb and who is identified with the AVALON legend.

**Ar·i·zo·na** |,ærə'zōnə| see box. □ **Arizonan** adj. & n.

**Ar·kan·sas** |'ärkən,saw| see box. □ **Arkansan** adj. & n.

**Ar·kan·sas River** |'ärkən,saw; är'kænzəs| river in the SW U.S., flowing 1,450 mi./2,320 km. from the Rockies in Colorado to join the Mississippi River in Arkansas. It has been made navigable by oceangoing vessels as far W as Tulsa, Oklahoma.

**Ar·khan·gelsk** |,ər'KHängilsk; är'kæn,gelsk| Russian name for ARCHANGEL.

**Arl·berg** |'ärl,berk; 'ärlbərg| mountain valley and pass in the Tyrolean Alps, W Austria. A tunnel (6.3 mi./10.1 km.) through the pass, completed in 1884, links Bludenz, Landeck, and Innsbruck.

**Arles** |ärl| historic city in SE France. Pop. 52,590. It was the capital of the medieval kingdom of Arles, formed in the 10th century by the union of the kingdoms of Provence and Burgundy.

**Ar·ling·ton** |'ärliNGtən| town in E Massa-

---

## Arizona

**Capital/largest city:** Phoenix
**Other cities:** Flagstaff, Glendale, Mesa, Phoenix, Scottsdale, Tempe, Tucson
**Population:** 3,665,228 (1990); 4,668,631 (1998); 5,230,000 (2005 proj.)
**Population rank (1990):** 24
**Rank in land area:** 6
**Abbreviation:** AZ; Ariz.
**Nickname:** Grand Canyon State
**Motto:** *Ditat Deus* (Latin: 'God Enriches')
**Bird:** cactus wren
**Flower:** blossom of the saguaro cactus
**Tree:** paloverde
**Songs:** "Arizona March Song"; "Arizona"
**Noted physical features:** Grand Canyon; Sonora Desert, Painted Desert; Petrified Forest; Canyon de Chelly; Meteor Crater; London Bridge; Biosphere 2; Navajo National Monument.
**Tourist attractions:** Grand Canyon; Painted Desert; Petrified Forest; Hoover Dam
**Admission date:** February 14, 1912
**Order of admission:** 48
**Name origin:** From the Pima or Papago Indian word *arizonac*, which may mean 'place of small springs.'

---

## Arkansas

**Capital/largest city:** Little Rock
**Other cities:** Fayetteville, Fort Smith, Hot Springs, North Little Rock, Pine Bluff
**Population:** 2,350,725 (1990); 2,538,303 (1998); 2,750,000 (2005 proj.)
**Population rank (1990):** 33
**Rank in land area:** 29
**Abbreviation:** AR; Ark.
**Nickname:** Land of Opportunity
**Motto:** *Regnat populus* (Latin: 'The People Rule')
**Bird:** mockingbird
**Flower:** apple blossom
**Tree:** pine
**Songs:** "Arkansas"; "The Arkansas Traveler"
**Noted physical features:** Magazine Mountain
**Tourist attractions:** Hot Springs National Park; Eureka Springs; Ozark Folk Center; Crater of Diamonds; Toltec Mounds Archaeological State Park.
**Admission date:** June 15, 1836
**Order of admission:** 25
**Name origin:** From the French name for the Quapaw tribe of the Sioux, whose name is translated 'downstream people.'

chusetts, a suburb NW of Boston. Pop. 44,630.

**Ar·ling·ton²** |'ärliNGtən| industrial city in N Texas, between Dallas and Fort Worth. Pop. 261,720.

**Ar·ling·ton³** |'ärliNGtən| county in N Virginia, forming a suburb of Washington, D.C. Pop. 170,936. It is the site of the Pentagon and the Arlington National Cemetery.

**Ar·ling·ton Heights** |'ärliNGtən 'hīts| village in NE Illinois, a suburb NW of Chicago. Pop. 75,460.

**Ar·lon** |är'lawN| town in SE Belgium, capital of the province of Luxembourg. Pop. 23,420.

**Ar·ma·ged·don** |,ärmə'gedn| biblical hill of **Megiddo**, an archaeological site on the plain of Esdraelon, S of present-day Haifa, Israel. In the book of Revelation, Armageddon is the site of the last battle between good and evil.

**Ar·magh** |är'mä; 'är,mä| **1** one of the Six Counties of Northern Ireland, formerly an administrative area. **2** the chief town of this county. Pop. 12,700. It has been the religious capital of Ireland since the 5th century.

**Ar·ma·gnac** |,ärmən,yäk; ,ärmən'yæk| region in SW France, in Aquitaine, constituting most of the department of Gers. It is best known for its medieval fortified villages (*bastides*) and its brandy.

**Ar·ma·vir** |ər,mə'vir| industrial city and transportation center in S central Russia, in the foothills of the Caucasus Mts. Pop.162,000.

**Ar·me·nia¹** |är'mänyə| city in W central Colombia, in a coffee growing district. Pop. 212,000.

**Ar·me·nia²** |är'mēnēə| landlocked republic in the Caucasus of SE Europe. Area: 11,510 sq. mi./29,800 sq. km. Pop. 3,360,000. Languages, Armenian and Russian. Capital and largest city: Yerevan. The remnant of a much larger historical

country, Armenia has been dominated by Turkey and by Russia, and became independent in 1992 after the Soviet Union dissolved. Cotton, rice, fruit, tobacco, and small manufactures are important. Christian Armenia has had uneasy relations with its Muslim neighbors. □ **Armenian** *adj. & n.*

**Ar·men·tières** |,ärmäN'tyer| industrial town in extreme N France. Pop. 26,000. It became known through the World War I song "Mademoiselle from Armentières."

**Ar·mor·i·ca** |är'mawrikə| ancient region of NW France between the Seine and the Loire. It is usually identified with all or the N part of Brittany. □ **Armorican** *adj. & n.*

**Arn·hem** |'ärn,hem; 'ärnəm| town in the E Netherlands, on the Rhine River, capital of the province of Gelderland. Pop. 131,700. During World War II, in September 1944, British airborne troops made a landing nearby but were overwhelmed by German forces.

**Arn·hem Land** |'ärnəm ,lænd| peninsula in Northern Territory, Australia whose chief town is Nhulunbuy. In 1976 Arnhem Land was declared an Aboriginal reservation.

**Ar·no River** |'ärnō| river that rises in the Apennines of N Italy and flows W 150 mi. (240 km.) through Florence and Pisa to the Ligurian Sea.

**Arns·berg** |'ärns,berk| industrial city in western Germany, on the Ruhr River. Pop. 76,000.

**Aroos·took County** |ə'roostək; ə'roostək| northernmost and largest county in Maine, noted for its potato production.

**Ar·rah** |'ərə| (also **Ara**) industrial city in NE India, in Bihar state. Pop. 157,000.

**Ar Ra·ma·di** |,är rə'mädē| (also **Ramadie; Rumadiya**) town in central Iraq, on the Euphrates River. Pop. 137,000.

**Ar·ran** |'ærən| island in the Firth of Clyde, in the W of Scotland.

**Ar·ras** |ä'räs| town in NE France, in the Pas-de-Calais. Pop. 42,700. In medieval times, it was the capital of Artois, and a center for the manufacture of tapestries.

**Ar·row·head Region** |'ærə,hed| highland region of NE Minnesota, largely on the Canadian Shield, noted for its mines and wilderness recreation.

**Ar·thur's Seat** |'ärTHərz 'sēt| volcanic hill in and overlooking Edinburgh, Scotland, from which King Arthur is supposed to have watched his army defeat the forces of the Picts.

**Ar·tois** |är'twä| region and former province

Armenia

of NW France. Known in Roman times as Artesium, the area gave its name to a type of well, which was first sunk in the 12th century.

**Aru·ba** |əˈrōōbə| island in the Caribbean Sea, close to the Venezuelan coast. Pop. 60,000. Capital: Oranjestad. Formerly part of the Netherlands Antilles, it separated from that group in 1986 to become a self-governing territory of the Netherlands. It is a popular resort destination.

Aruba

**Aru·na·chal Pra·desh** |ˌärəˈnāCHəl prəˈdeSH| mountainous state in the far NE of India, lying on the borders of Tibet to the N and Burma (Myanmar) to the E. Capital: Itanagar.

**Aru·sha** |əˈrōōSHə| industrial city in N Tanzania, the capital of the Arusha region. Pop. 140,000. It is a safari base in a coffee-growing area. Mount Kilimanjaro is nearby.

**Ar·va·da** |ärˈvædə; ärˈvädə| city in N central Colorado, a suburb NW of Denver. Pop. 89,235.

**Ar·za·mas** |ˌärˌzəˈmäs| town and rail junction in W Russia, S of Nizhni Novgorod. Pop. 111,000.

**Asa·hi·ka·wa** |ˌäˌsähēˈkäwə; ˌäsäˈhēkäwə| commercial and industrial city in N Japan, on central Hokkaido. Pop. 359,000.

**Asan·sol** |ˌəsənˈsōl| industrial city in NE India, in West Bengal, NW of Calcutta. Pop. 262,000.

**As·bes·tos** |ˌābesˈtōs; æzˈbestəs| city in S Quebec, E of Montreal, a center of asbestos mining. Pop. 6,487.

**As·bury Park** |ˈæz,berē ˈpärk; ˈæzb(ə)rē ˈpärk| city in E central New Jersey, on the Atlantic shore, long a noted resort. Pop. 16,799.

**As·ca·lon** |ˈäskə,lawn; ˈæskə,län| ancient Greek name for ASHQELON, Israel.

**Ascen·sion Island** |əˈsenCHən| small island in the South Atlantic, incorporated with St. Helena, with which it is a dependency and strategic asset of the U.K. Pop. 1,007.

**Aschaf·fen·burg** |äˈsHäfən,bŏŏrk| river port in S Germany, on the Main River, ESE of Frankfurt am Main. Pop. 64,000.

**As·co·li** |ˈäskəlē| (also **Ascoli Piceno**) tourist resort and market town in the Marche region of E central Italy and capital of Ascoli Piceno province. Pop. 53,000.

**As·cot** |ˈæs,kät| town in Berkshire, England, SW of Windsor. Its racetrack on Ascot Heath is the site of the annual Royal Ascot races.

**ASEAN** |ˈäsē,än| acronym for the Association of South East Asian Nations, founded in 1967 by Indonesia, Malaysia, the Philippines, Singapore, and Thailand. Brunei joined in 1984. ASEAN has economic, security, and diplomatic purposes.

**Ashan·ti** |əˈsHäntē| (also **Asante**) region of central and S Ghana. From the 17th century it was the center of the Ashanti Empire, with its capital at Kumasi, whose king occupied the Golden Stool. With a complex, matrilinal, village-centered social organization, the Ashanti people dominated the region, which is noted for its agriculture, especially cacao production, gold mining and goldwork, and colorful Kente cloth. Conflict with British colonial incursions marked much of the 19th century and finally the Ashanti region was annexed by Britain in 1902, becoming part of the former British colony of the Gold Coast.

**Ash·dod** |ˈæsH,däd; äsHˈdōd| seaport on the Mediterranean coast of Israel, situated to the S of Tel Aviv. Pop. 62,000.

**Ashe·ville** |ˈæsHvəl; ˈæsH,vil| city in W North Carolina, a resort in the Blue Ridge Mts. Pop. 61,607. The famed Biltmore estate is here.

**Ash·ford** |ˈæsHfərd| industrial town in Kent, SE England. Pop. 91,000. One terminus of the Channel Tunnel from France is here.

**Ash·ga·bat** |ˈæsHgə,bät| (also **Ashkhabad**) the capital of the central Asian republic of Turkmenistan. Pop. 407,200. Former name (1919–27) **Poltoratsk**.

**Ashi·ka·ga** |ˌäsHəˈkägə| commercial city in N central Japan, on central Honshu. Pop. 168,000. It gave its name to a Japanese dynasty.

**Ash·kha·bad** |ˈäsHkə,bäd| variant spelling of ASHGABAT, Turkmenistan.

**Ash·land** |ˈæsHlənd| city, a coal industry center, in NE Kentucky, on the Ohio River. Pop. 23,622.

**Ash·land**[2] |'æSHlənd| city in N central Ohio. Pop. 20,079.

**Ash·more and Car·tier Islands** |'æSHmôr ən 'kärtyā| external territory of Australia in the Indian Ocean, comprising the uninhabited Ashmore Reef and Cartier Islands.

**Ash·qe·lon** |'äSHkə,lōn; 'æSHkə,län| (also **Ashkelon**) ancient Mediterranean city, situated to the S of modern Tel Aviv, in Israel. Greek name **Ascalon**.

**Ash Sha·ri·qah** |äSH'shärēkə| variant form of SHARJAH, United Arab Emirates.

**Ash·ta·bu·la** |,æSHtə'byoolə| port city in NE Ohio, on Lake Erie. Pop. 21,633.

**Ash·ta·roth** |'æSHtə,räTH; 'æSHtə,rōTH| ancient city in SW Syria, E of the Sea of Galilee, a center of worship of the Phoenician goddess Astarte.

**Asia** |'āZHə| largest (17 million sq. mi./44 million sq. km.) of the world's continents, constituting nearly one-third of the land mass, lying N of the equator except for some SE Asian islands. It is connected to Africa by the Isthmus of Suez, and borders Europe (part of the same land mass) along the Ural Mts., the Caspian Sea, the Caucasus Mts., and the Black Sea. Largest country: Russia. Largest cities: Seoul, South Korea; Calcutta and Bombay, India; Tokyo, Japan. □ **Asian** adj. & n. **Asiatic** adj.

**Asia Minor** |'āZHə 'mīnər| the W peninsula of Asia, which now constitutes the bulk of Turkey (Anatolia). For over 2,500 years before the 6th century A.D., it was a center of Asian and European cultures.

**Asir Mountains** |ä'sir| range of mountains in SW Saudi Arabia, running parallel to the Red Sea.

**As·ma·ra** |æs'märə| industrial and commercial center, the capital and largest city of Eritrea. Pop. 358,000.

**Asnières-sur-Seine** |än'yer soor 'sen| industrial NW suburb of Paris, France, on the Seine River. Pop. 72,000.

**Aso Mountain** |'äsō| (Japanese name **Asosan**) volcano with five peaks in S Japan, on Kyushu. Its crater is one of the world's largest: 75 mi./121 km. in circumference.

**As·pen** |'æspən| resort city in S central Colorado. Pop. 6,850. Formerly a silvermining town, it is now a thriving recreational center, noted particularly for its skiing facilities.

**As·sam** |ä'sæm| state in NE India. Capital: Dispur. Most of the state lies in the valley of the Brahmaputra River; it is noted for the production of tea. □ **Assamese** adj. & n.

**As·sa·teague Island** |'æsə,tēg| barrier island in SE Maryland and NE Virginia, on the Atlantic, noted for its wild ponies.

**As·si·ni·boine River** |ə'sinə,boin| river that flows 590 mi. from E Saskatchewan into Manitoba, joining the Red River at Winnipeg.

**As·si·si** |ə'sēsē; ə'sēzē| town in the province of Umbria in central Italy. Pop. 24,790. It is famous as the birthplace of St. Francis, whose tomb is here.

**As Su·lay·ma·ni·yah** |äs ,sooli,mä'nēyə| variant form of SULAYMANIYAH, Iraq.

**As·sur** |ä'soor; 'äsoor| (also **Asur** or **Ashur**) an ancient city-state of Mesopotamia, situated on the present-day Tigris River to the south of modern Mosul, Iraq. The Assyrian empires were centered on the city.

**As·syr·ia** |ə'sirēə| ancient country in what is now N Iraq. From the early part of the 2nd millennium B.C. Assyria was the center of a succession of empires; it was at its peak in the 8th and late 7th centuries B.C., when its rule stretched from the Persian Gulf to Egypt. It fell in 612 B.C. to a coalition of Medes and Chaldeans. □ **Assyrian** adj. & n.

**Asta·na** |äs'tänə| capital of Kazakhstan (since 1998). Pop. 287,000. Formerly called **Aqmola** and, earlier, **Tselinograd**.

**As·ti** |'ästē| city in NW Italy and capital of Asti province. Pop.77,000. It is at the center of a wine-producing region.

**As·to·ria**[1] |ə'stawrēə| section of NW Queens, New York City, noted for its large Greek-American population.

**As·to·ria**[2] |ə'stawrēə| city in NW Oregon, near the mouth of the Columbia River on the Pacific coast. Pop. 10,069. In the 19th century it was a famous fur-trading center.

**As·tra·khan** |'æstrə,kæn| city in S Russia, on the delta of the Volga River. Pop. 509,000. Astrakhan fleeces were given their name because traders from the city brought them into Russia from central Asia.

**As·tu·ri·as** |ä'stooryəs| autonomous region and former principality of NW Spain. Capital: Oviedo. □ **Asturian** adj. & n.

**Asun·ci·ón** |ä,soonse'ōn| the capital, largest city, industrial center, and chief port of Paraguay, on the Paraguay River. Pop. 729,300.

**As·wan** |äs'wän| city on the Nile in S Egypt, 10 mi./16 km. N of Lake Nasser. Pop. 195,700. Two dams across the Nile have been built nearby. The controlled release of water from Lake Nasser behind the High

Dam produces the greater part of Egypt's electricity.

**As•yut** |ˌäsˈyōōt| industrial and commercial city in E central Egypt, on the Nile River. Pop. 313,000. It was the ancient Lycopolis.

**Ata•ca•ma Desert** |ˌätəˈkämə| arid region of W Chile, extending roughly 600 mi./965 km. S from the Peruvian border.

**Atas•ca•de•ro** |əˌtæskəˈderō| city in SW California. Pop. 23,138.

**Atchaf•a•laya River** |(ə)ˌCHæfəˈlīə| river in S central Louisiana that flows 170 mi./275 km. S to the Gulf of Mexico. It is used to control flooding on the Red and Mississippi rivers.

**Atch•i•son** |ˈæCHisən| city in NE Kansas, the birthplace of the Santa Fe (Atchison, Topeka & Santa Fe) Railroad. Pop. 10,656.

**Ath•a•bas•ca River** |ˌæTHəˈbæskə| river that flows 765 mi./1,230 km. NE from the Rocky Mts. across Alberta to Lake Athabasca, the fourth-largest lake within Canada. The river valley has large oil tar deposits.

**Ath•ens**[1] |ˈæTHənz| city in NE Georgia, seat of the University of Georgia. Pop. 45,734.

**Ath•ens**[2] |ˈæTHənz| the capital of Greece. Pop. 3,096,775. A flourishing city-state of ancient Greece, Athens was an important cultural center from the 5th century B.C. It came under Roman rule in 146 B.C. and fell to the Goths in A.D. 267. After its capture by the Turks in 1456 Athens declined in status until chosen as the capital of a newly independent Greece in 1834. Greek name transliterated **Athínai**. □ **Athenian** adj. & n.

**Ath•ens**[3] |ˈæTHənz| city in SE Ohio, seat of Ohio University. Pop. 21,265.

**Ath•er•ton Tableland** |ˈæTHərtən| plateau in the Great Dividing Range in NE Queensland, Australia.

**Athí•nai** |əˈTHēˌnä| transliteration for the Greek name **Athens**.

**Ath•os, Mount** |ˈæˌTHäs; ˈäˌTHäs| narrow, mountainous peninsula in NE Greece, projecting into the Aegean Sea. It is inhabited by monks of the Orthodox Church, who forbid women and even female animals to set foot on the peninsula. □ **Athonite** adj. & n.

**Atit•lán** |ˌätētˈlän| dormant volcano in central Guatemala, SW of Guatemala City; 11,633 ft./3,546 m. **Lake Atitlán**, in a crater on the N, is famed for its scenery.

**At•lan•ta** |ətˈlæntə| the state capital of Georgia and its largest city. Pop. 394,000. Founded at the end of a railway line in 1837, the city was originally called Terminus; in 1843 it was incorporated as Marthasville, and in 1845 its name was finally changed to Atlanta. During the Civil War it was an important Confederate supply depot, but much of the city was burned after its capture in 1864 by Sherman. In recent decades the Atlanta metropolitan area has grown tremendously, and is a major center of industry and commerce. □ **Atlantan** adj. & n.

**At•lan•tic City** |ətˈlæntik| resort city in SE New Jersey, on the Atlantic. Pop. 37,986. It is famed for its gambling casinos.

**Atlantic Intracoastal Waterway** |ətˈlæntik ˈintərˌkōstəl| route that allows sheltered boat passage for 1,900 mi./3,100km. along the Atlantic coast between Boston, Massachusetts and Key West, Florida.

**At•lan•tic Ocean** |ətˈlæntik| the ocean lying between Europe and Africa to the E and N and South America to the W. It is divided by the equator into the N Atlantic and the S Atlantic oceans.

**At•lan•tic Provinces** |ətˈlæntik| name for the MARITIME PROVINCES of Canada together with NEWFOUNDLAND AND LABRADOR.

**At•lan•tis** |ətˈlæntəs| legendary island that sank in a volcanic explosion in ancient times, destroying a great civilization. Some place it in the Atlantic, W of Gibraltar. Others identify it with the Greek island of THERA.

**At•las Mountains** |ˈætləs| range of mountains in N Africa extending from Morocco to Tunisia in a series of chains.

**At•ti•ca**[1] |ˈætikə| triangular promontory of E mainland Greece. With the islands in the Saronic Gulf it forms a department of Greece, of which Athens is the capital. □ **Attic** adj. & n.

**At•ti•ca**[2] |ˈætikə| town in W New York, scene of a bloody 1971 prison uprising. Pop. 7,383.

**At•tle•boro** |ˈætlbərə| industrial city in SE Massachusetts, NE of Providence, Rhode Island. Pop. 38,383.

**At•tu** |ˈæˌtōō| westernmost of the Aleutian Islands in SW Alaska. During World War II it was occupied by Japanese forces.

**At•wa•ter** |ˈæt,wawtər; ˈæt,wätər| city in central California. Pop. 22,282.

**Aube** |ōb| department in NE France. Area: 2,319 sq. mi./6,004 sq. km. Pop. 289,000. The capital is Troyes. The area is part of the region that produces champagne.

**Au•ber•vil•liers** |ˌōber,vēlˈya| industrial town NE of Paris, in N central France. Pop.

68,000. It was a medieval pilgrimage destination.

**Au·burn**[1] |'awbərn| academic city in E Alabama, home to Auburn University. Pop. 33,830.

**Au·burn**[2] |'awbərn| industrial city in SW Maine, on the Androscoggin River opposite Lewiston. Pop. 24,309.

**Au·burn**[3] |'awbərn| industrial and commercial city in W central New York, on Owasco Lake. Pop. 31,258.

**Au·burn**[4] |'awbərn| industrial city in W central Washington. Pop. 33,102.

**Au·burn Hills** |'awbərn| city in SE Michigan, a residential and commercial suburb E of Pontiac and NE of Detroit. Pop. 17,076.

**Au·bus·son** |ˌōbyˈsawN| town in central France, on the Creuse River. It is famous for its tapestry and carpet works, which date to the 15th century. There is also some light industry.

**Auck·land** |'awklənd| the largest city and chief seaport of New Zealand, on North Island. Pop. 309,400. It was the site of the first Parliament of New Zealand in 1854, remaining the capital until 1865.

**Aude** |ōd| department in SW France. Area: 2,371 sq. mi./6,139 sq. km. Pop. 299,000. The capital is Carcassonne.

**Augh·rim** |'awgrəm| village in E Galway, W Ireland, scene of a conclusive victory by the Protestant William of Orange over Catholic forces on July, 12, 1691 (Orangemen's Day in Northern Ireland).

**Au·gra·bies Falls** |aw'gräbēz| series of waterfalls on the Orange River in the province of Northern Cape, South Africa.

**Augs·burg** |'owks,bŏŏrk; 'awgz,bərg| historic commercial and industrial city in S Germany, in Bavaria. Pop. 259,880.

**Au·gus·ta**[1] |ə'gəstə| commercial and resort city in E Georgia. Pop. 44,640. The Augusta National golf course is here.

**Au·gus·ta**[2] |ə'gəstə| state capital of Maine, on the Kennebec River. Pop. 21,320.

**Au·lis** |'awləs; 'owləs| small port in ancient Greece, from which, in Homeric legend, the Greeks sailed against Troy at the start of the Trojan War.

**Au·rang·a·bad** |ow'rəNG(g)ə,bäd| commercial and industrial city in W India, in Maharashtra state. Pop. 572,000. The magnificent mausoleum of the wife of the Mogul emperor Aurangzeb is here.

**Au·ri·gnac** |awrēn'yäk| village, S France, in the foothills of the Pyrenees, SW of Toulouse. Significant remains from the Paleolithic era were found in a cave here in

1860; the Aurignacian period takes its name from the village.

**Au·ro·ra**[1] |ə'rawrə| city in N central Colorado, a largely residential suburb E of Denver. Pop. 222,103.

**Au·ro·ra**[2] |ə'rawrə| industrial city in NE Illinois. Pop. 99,581.

**Au·ro·ra**[3] |ə'rawrə| town in S Ontario, a suburb N of Toronto. Pop. 29,454.

**Ausch·witz** |'owSH,vits; 'owSH,wits| (Polish name **Oświęcim**) town in S Poland, near Cracow. Site of one of the largest and most infamous of the Nazi concentration camps during World War II.

**Aus·ter·litz** |'owstər,lits; 'awstə,lits| agricultural town in the SE Czech Republic. On December 2, 1805, in the "battle of the three emperors" here, Napoleon defeated Austrian troops under Emperor Francis II and Russian troops led by Czar Alexander I.

**Aus·tin**[1] |'awstən| city in SE Minnesota, noted for its meatpacking industry. Pop. 21,907.

**Aus·tin**[2] |'awstən| capital of Texas, on the Colorado River in the S central part. Pop. 465,622. A research and industrial center, it is also known as the seat of the University of Texas.

**Aus·tral·asia** |ˌawstrə'lāZHə| the region consisting of Australia, New Zealand, New Guinea, and the neighboring islands of the Pacific. □ **Australasian** adj. & n.

**Aus·tra·lia** |aw'strālyə| island country and continent of the S hemisphere, in the SW Pacific. Area: 2.97 million sq. mi./7.68 million sq. km. Pop. 17,500,000. Language, English. Capital: Canberra. Largest city: Sydney. Noted for its unique fauna, Australia was inhabited by Aboriginal peoples of mixed stock before British colonization began in the late 18th century. Largely flat plains, the country has strong agricultural and livestock-raising sectors, along with extensive mining and varied industry. □ **Australian** adj. & n.

**Australia**

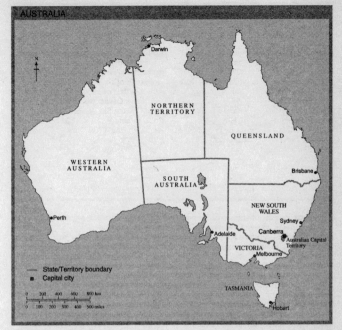

**Aus·tra·lian Alps** |aw'strālyən 'ælps| the SE section of the E highlands of Australia, in the states of Victoria and New South Wales.

**Aus·tra·lian Ant·arc·tic Territory** |aw-'strālyən ænt'är(k)tik| area of Antarctica administered by Australia, lying between longitudes 142° E and 136° E.

**Aus·tra·lian Cap·i·tal Territory** |,aw'strālyən| federal territory in New South Wales, Australia, consisting of one enclave ceded by New South Wales in 1911 to contain Canberra. Formerly included Jervis Bay 1915–88.

**Aus·tra·sia** |aw'strāzHə| kingdom of the Merovingian Franks in the 6th–8th centuries, incorporating N European lands from E France to Bohemia.

**Aus·tria** |'awstrēə| mountainous landlocked republic in central Europe. Area: 32,389 sq. mi./83,854 sq. km. Pop. 7,700,000. Language, German. Capital and largest city: Vienna. German name **Österreich**. Long the center of the Habsburg and Austro-Hungarian empires, the republic was dominated by Nazi Germany in 1938–45. Its economy is based on agriculture and forest industries, mining, tourism, and manufacturing. Vienna is a great cultural center. □ **Austrian** adj. & n.

**Austria-Hungary** |'awstrēə'hənGgərē| (also **Austro-Hungarian Empire** or **Dual Monarchy**) kingdom that existed from 1867 until the outbreak of World War I. Austria and Hungary were sovereign states, and parts of present-day Croatia, Slovakia, Romania, Slovenia, Italy, Poland, Bosnia, and the Czech Republic were subject to the crown.

**Aus·tro·ne·sia** |,awstrə'nēzHə| name sometimes used to designate the islands of the Pacific, where Austronesian, or Malayo-Polynesian, languages are spoken. These languages, however, extend as far W as Madagascar. □ **Austronesian** adj. & n.

**Au·teuil** |ō'tœ| district in Paris, France. Formerly a town, between the Seine River and the SE entrance to the Bois de Boulogne, it was absorbed into Paris 1860.

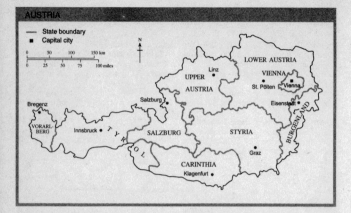

**Au·vergne** |ō'vern(yə)| region of S central France and a province of the Roman Empire. The region is mountainous and contains the extinct volcanic cones known as the Puys.

**Au·xerre** |ō'ser| commercial town and capital of Yonne district in N central France. Pop. 40,000. It is the center of the Chablis wine trade.

**Au·yu·it·tuq National Park** |‚ow'yōͬōətək| preserve on Baffin Island in Nunavut, the first Canadian park within the Arctic Circle.

**Ava·lon** |'ævə‚län| in Arthurian legend, the land of the dead, long identified with Glastonbury, in Somerset, SW England, where an ancient abbey was said to have been founded by Joseph of Arimathea.

**Ava·lon Peninsula** |'ævə‚län| historic region in SE Newfoundland, home to most residents of the province since early European settlement.

**Ave·bury** |'avb(ə)rē| village in Wiltshire, SW England, site of one of Britain's major henge monuments of the late Neolithic period. The monument consists of a bank and ditch containing the largest known stone circle, with two smaller circles within it.

**Avei·ro** |ə'vārōͬō; ə'verōͬō| seaport town on the Aveiro lagoon in SW Portugal, capital of Aveiro district. Pop. 35,000.

**Avel·la·ne·da** |‚äväzHä'nä'uädä| city in E Argentina, a major industrial suburb of Buenos Aires. Pop. 347,000.

**Avel·li·no** |‚ävel'lēnō| market and manufacturing center in S Italy, E of Naples. Pop. 56,000. The town has suffered significant earthquake damage, but many medieval buildings survive.

**Aver·nus** |ə'vərnəs| lake near Naples in Italy, which fills the crater of an extinct volcano. It was described by Virgil and other Latin writers as the entrance to the underworld.

**Avey·ron** |‚ävä'rōN| department in S France, at the S edge of the Massif Central. Area: 3,374 sq. mi./8,735 sq. km. Pop. 270,000. The capital is Rodez.

**Avi·gnon** |‚vēn'yawN| city on the Rhône in SE France. Pop. 89,440. From 1309 until 1377 it was the residence of the popes during their exile from Rome, and was papal property until the French Revolution.

**Avi·la** |ə'vēlə| (also **Avila de los Caballeros**) ancient city in N central Spain, the capital of Avila province. Pop. 50,000. Its medieval buildings attract tourists.

**Avi·lés** |‚ävē'läs| port and industrial center in N Spain, on the Bay of Biscay. Pop. 84,000.

**Avo·ca** |ə'vōkə| short river and its valley (the **Vale of Avoca**) in Wicklow, E Ireland, S of Dublin, famed for its beauty.

**Avon**[1] |'avən| river of central England that rises near the Leicestershire-Northamptonshire border and flows 96 mi./154 km. SW through Stratford to the Severn River.

**Avon**[2] |'avən| river of SW England that rises near the Gloucestershire-Wiltshire border and flows 75 miles (121 km) through Bath and Bristol to the River Severn.

**Avon**[3] |'avən| county of SW England, formed in 1974 from parts of N Somerset and Gloucestershire; county seat, Bristol.

**Axis, the** |'æksəs| term for Germany, Italy, and Japan, along with countries allied to them, during World War II.

**Ax·min·ster** |'æk,sminstər| town in Devon, SW England. Pop. 5,000. It was formerly famous for its carpets.

**Ax·um** |'äk,sōōm| variant spelling of Aksum, Ethiopia.

**Aya·cu·cho** |,ïə'kōōCHō| historic commercial city in the Andes of S central Peru. Pop. 101,600.

**Ay·din** |ï'din| (ancient name **Tralles**) historic commercial city in SW Turkey, on the Menderes River. Pop. 107,000. It is the capital of Aydin province, a mining region.

**Ayers Rock** |ærz| red rock mass in Northern Territory, Australia, SW of Alice Springs. One of the largest monoliths in the world, it is 1,143 ft./348 m. high and about 6 mi./9 km. in circumference. It is named after Sir Henry Ayers, premier of South Australia 1872–73. Aboriginal name **Uluru.**

**Ayles·bury** |'älzb(ə)rē| town in S central England, the county seat of Buckinghamshire. Pop. 50,000.

**Ayl·mer** |'älmər| city in SW Quebec, a suburb just W of Hull and NW of Ottawa, Ontario. Pop. 32,244.

**Ayodh·ya** |ə'yōdyə| (also **Ajodhya**) village in N central India, part of the city of Faizabad, in Uttar Pradesh state. It is one of Hinduism's seven sacred sites.

**Ayr·shire** |'ær,sHir; 'ær,sHər| former county of SW Scotland, on the Firth of Clyde. It became a part of Strathclyde region in 1975.

**Ayut·la** |ä'yōōtlə| (official name **Ayutla de los Libres**) historic town in Guerrero state, S Mexico, noted for the 1854 Plan of Ayutla, a protest and statement of principles for a new government.

**Ayut·tha·ya** |,äyōō'tïyə| historic city in S central Thailand, N of Bangkok. Pop. 61,000.

**Azad Kash·mir** |ä'zäd käsH'mēr| autonomous state in NE Pakistan, formerly part of Kashmir; administrative center, Muzaffarabad. It was established in 1949 after Kashmir was split as a result of the partition of India.

**Aza·nia** |ə'zänēə| alternative name for South Africa, proposed in the time of apartheid by some supporters of majority rule for the country.

**Azer·bai·jan** |,æzər,bï'zHän| republic in the Caucasus of SE Europe, on the W shore of the Caspian Sea. Area: 33,450 sq. mi./86,600 sq. km. Pop. 7,219,000. Languages, Azerbaijani, Russian. Capital and largest city: Baku. Dominated for centuries by Persia and then Russia, Azerbaijan became independent in 1991, on the breakup of the Soviet Union. The mountainous country has an economy based on agriculture and oil. □ **Azerbaijani** *adj. & n.*

Azerbaijan

**Azores** |'ä,zawrz| group of volcanic islands in the Atlantic, W of Portugal, in Portuguese possession but partially autonomous. Pop. 241,590. Capital: Ponta Delgada. Portuguese name **Açores.**

**Azov, Sea of** |ə'zawf; 'æ,zawf| inland sea of S Russia and Ukraine, separated from the Black Sea by the Crimea and linked to it by a narrow strait.

**Azu·sa** |ə'zōōsə| city in SW California, an industrial and residential suburb NE of Los Angeles. Pop. 41,333.

**Az Zar·qa** |ä'zärkə| variant form of Zarqa, Jordan.

# Bb

**Baal·bek** |'bäl,bek| town in E Lebanon, site of the ancient city of Heliopolis.

**Ba·ba·ho·yo** |,bäbə'hōyō| commercial town in W Ecuador, in tropical lowlands along the Babahoyo River. Pop. 50,000.

**Ba·bar Islands** |'bä,bär| island group in E Indonesia, in the Banda Sea between Timor and the Taninbar Islands.

**Ba·bel** |'bäbəl; 'bæbəl| biblical site of a tower built in the plain of Shinar, Mesopotamia, in an attempt to reach heaven.

**Bab el Man·deb** |'bæb el 'män,deb| strait, 17 mi./27 km. wide, between E Africa and the Arabian Peninsula, linking the Red Sea with the Gulf of Aden, part of the Indian Ocean.

**Ba·bine Lake** |bæ'bēn| lake in central British Columbia, noted for its fishing and salmon spawning grounds. The Babine Mts. run along its W side.

**Ba·bi Yar** |,bäbē 'yär| ravine near Kiev, Ukraine, where in two days in 1943 Nazis slaughtered 33,000 Jews. In all, the Nazis are believed to have killed 100,000 persons, primarily Jews, Gypsies, and Russian prisoners of war, over a period of months here.

**Ba·bol** |bä'bōl; bäbōol| (also **Babul**) commercial city in N Iran, just S of the Caspian Sea. Pop. 137,000.

**Ba·bo·qui·vi·ri Mountains** |,bäbōkə-'väre| range in S Arizona, rising to 7,734 ft./2,357 m. at Baboquivri Peak.

**Bab·ru·isk** |bə'brŏŏisk| (also **Babruysk**, **Bobruisk**, or **Bobruysk**) a river port in central Belarus, on the Berezina River SE of Minsk. Pop. 222,900.

**Ba·bu·yan Islands** |,bäbŏŏ'yän| group of twenty-four volcanic islands lying to the N of the island of Luzon in the N Philippines.

**Bab·y·lon**[1] |'bæbələn; 'bæbə,län| ancient city in Mesopotamia, the capital of Babylonia in the 2nd millennium B.C. The city (of which only ruins now remain) lay on the Euphrates River and was noted for its luxury, its fortifications, and particularly for the Hanging Gardens of Babylon. □ **Babylonian** *adj. & n.*

**Bab·y·lon**[2] |'bæbələn; 'bæbə,län| town on the South Shore of Long Island, New York, including Babylon, Amityville, and other villages. Pop. 202,889.

**Bab·y·lo·nia** |,bæbə'lōnēə| ancient region of Mesopotamia, formed when the kingdoms of Akkad in the N and Sumer in the S combined the first half of the 2nd millennium B.C. Babylonia was dominated by Assyria, formerly its dependency, from the 14th to the 7th century B.C. The throne was held by the Chaldeans from 625 to 539 B.C., and Babylonia was conquered by Cyrus the Great of Persia in 539 B.C. □ **Babylonian** *adj. & n.*

**Ba·ca·bal** |,bəkə'bäl| commercial city in NE Brazil, on the Rio Mearim. Pop. 99,000.

**Ba·cău** |bə'kow| industrial town in NE Romania, in the foothills of the Carpathian Mts., on the Bistriţa. River. Pop.193,000.

**Bac·ca·rat** |,bäkə'rä| town in NE France, on the W edge of the Vosges Mts. The town is famous for its crystal works, established in 1764.

**Back Bay** |bæk| historic residential and commercial district of W Boston, Massachusetts, on land along the Charles River that was reclaimed in the 19th century.

**Ba·co·lod** |bə'kō,lōd| city on the NW coast of the island of Negros in the central Philippines. Pop. 364,180. It is the chief city of the island and a major port.

**Bac·tria** |'bæktrēə| ancient country in central Asia, corresponding to the N part of modern Afghanistan. Traditionally the home of Zoroaster, it was the seat of a powerful Indo-Greek kingdom in the 3rd and 2nd centuries B.C. □ **Bactrian** *adj. & n.*

**Ba·da·csóny** |'bädə,CHŌnē| district in Hungary, NW of Lake Balaton, noted for its white wines.

**Ba·da·joz** |,bädə'hōs| market center and industrial city in W Spain, capital of Badajoz province. Pop. 130,000.

**Ba·da·lo·na** |,bädə'lōnə| seaport in NE Spain, NE of Barcelona, on the Mediterranean Sea. Pop. 206,000.

**Ba·den** |'bädn| spa town in Austria, S of Vienna. Pop. 24,000. It was a royal summer retreat and fashionable resort in the 19th century.

**Baden-Baden** |'bädn'bädn| spa town in the Black Forest, SW Germany. Pop. 48,700. It was a fashionable resort in the 19th century.

**Baden-Württemberg** |,bädn'vʏrtəm-,berg| state of western Germany. Capital: Stuttgart.

**Bad·ger State** |'bæjər| nickname for WISCONSIN.

**Bad Hom·burg** |,bät 'awm,bŏŏrg| (also called **Homburg** or **Bad Homburg vor der**

**Höhe**) spa and resort in the Taunus Mts., in central Germany. Homburg hats originated here.

**Bad Kreuz·nach** |ˌbät ˈkroit‚snäk| historic spa and industrial city in western Germany, in Rhineland-Palatinate. Pop. 43,000.

**Bad·lands, the** |ˈbæd‚lændz| highland region chiefly in SW South Dakota, S of the Black Hills, noted for its harsh terrain.

**Bad·min·ton** |ˈbædmintn| name of two villages in SW England. Badminton House, a local estate, gave its name to the game first played here.

**Baf·fin Bay** |ˈbæfən| extension of the N Atlantic between Baffin Island and Greenland, linked to the Arctic Ocean by three passages. It is largely icebound in winter.

**Baf·fin Island** |ˈbæfən| large island in the Canadian Arctic, situated at the mouth of Hudson Bay. It is separated from Greenland by Baffin Bay.

**Ba·fous·sam** |bäˈfoosəm| commercial city in W Cameroon, in a coffee-producing region. Pop. 113,000.

**Bagh·dad** |ˈbæg‚dæd; bægˈdæd| capital of Iraq, on the Tigris River. Pop. 4,648,600. A thriving city under the Abbasid caliphs in the 8th and 9th centuries, it was taken by the Ottoman sultan Suleiman in 1534 and remained under Ottoman rule until World War I. In 1920 it became the capital of the newly created state of Iraq. Today it is the administrative, commercial, and cultural center of the country.

**Ba·guio** |ˈbägēō| summer capital of the Philippines, a mountain resort on NW Luzon. Pop. 183,000. Noted for its woodcarvings, it is also the center of a major gold-producing area.

**Ba·ha·mas** |bəˈhäməz| (official name **Commonwealth of the Bahamas**) republic consisting of an archipelago off the SE coast of Florida. Area: 5,380 sq. mi./13,939 sq. km. Pop. 225,050. Languages, English, Creole. Capital and largest city: Nassau. It was on one of these West Indian islands that Columbus made his first landfall in the New World. The islands were a British colony from the 18th century until they gained independence in 1973. Tourism, finance, fishing, and some industry are important to the economy. □ **Bahamian** adj. & n.

**Ba·ha·ram·pur** |ˈbähərəm‚poor| town in NE India, in West Bengal state, near the border with Bangladesh. Pop. 126,000.

**Ba·ha·wal·pur** |bəˈhäwəl‚poor| city of central Pakistan, in Punjab province. Pop. 250,000. It was formerly the capital of a princely state established by the nawabs of Bahawalpur.

**Ba·hia** |bäˈēə| **1** State of E Brazil, on the Atlantic coast. Pop. 11,855,000. Capital: Salvador. **2** an earlier name for SALVADOR.

**Ba·hía Blanca** |bäˈēə ˈbläNGkə| port in Argentina serving the S part of the country. Pop. 271,500.

**Bah·raich** |bəˈrik| commercial town in N India, in Uttar Pradesh state, NE of Lucknow. Pop. 135,000. It is a place of pilgrimage for Hindus and Muslims.

**Bah·rain** |bäˈrān| sheikhdom consisting of a group of islands in the Persian Gulf. Area: 255 sq. mi./691 sq. km. Pop. 518,000. Language, Arabic. Capital and largest city: Manama. Formerly under Portuguese, Persian, and British domination, Bahrain became independent in 1971. Pearls were once central to the economy; today oil refining and exporting are. □ **Bahraini** adj. & n.

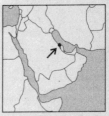

Bahrain

**Bahr al-Ghazal** |ˌbär æl gəˈzäl| river in S Sudan, a tributary to the White Nile. The name was also formerly that of a province of S Sudan.

**Ba·ia Ma·re** |ˈbīə ˈmärä| industrial city in NW Romania, capital of Maramureş county. Pop. 150,000.

**Bai·cheng** |ˈbīˈCHəNG| city in Jilin province, NE China. Pop. 218,000.

Bahamas

**Bai·kal, Lake** |bī'kawl; bī'kæl| (also **Baykal**) large lake in S Siberia, the largest freshwater lake in Eurasia and, with a depth of 5,714 ft./1,743 m., the deepest lake in the world.

**Baie-Comeau** |ba 'kōmō; ˌbakō'mō| industrial port city in SE Quebec, at the mouth of the Manicouagan River on the St. Lawrence River, NE of Quebec City. Pop. 26,012.

**Bai·ko·nur** |ˌbīkə'nŏŏr| (also **Baykonur**) mining town in central Kazakhstan. The world's first satellite (1957) and the first manned space flight (1961) were launched from the former Soviet space center nearby.

**Bain·bridge Island** |'bānbrij| island in W Washington, in Puget Sound, a largely-residential suburb W of Seattle.

**Bai·ri·ki** |'bī͵rēkē| capital of Kiribati, on South Tarawa Island. Pop. 2,200.

**Bai·yin** |'bī'yin| industrial city in Gansu province, central China, NE of Lanzhou. Pop. 548,000.

**Ba·ja Cal·i·for·nia** |'bähä ˌkælə'fawrnyə| mountainous peninsula in NW Mexico, which extends S from the border with California and separates the Gulf of California from the Pacific Ocean. It consists of two states of Mexico: *Baja California* (capital, Mexicali) and *Baja California Sur* (capital, La Paz). Also called **Lower California**.

**Ba·ker Island** |'bakər| uninhabited island in the central Pacific, near the equator, claimed by the U.S. in 1857. Once a guano source, it is now a wildlife refuge.

**Ba·ker Lake** |'bakər| settlement in Nunavut, on the Thelon River W of Hudson Bay, home to the only inland Inuit community in Canada. Pop. 1,186.

**Ba·kers·field** |'bakərz͵fēld| industrial city in S central California, an oil industry center in the San Joaquin Valley. Pop. 174,820.

**Ba·ker Street** |'bakər| commercial street in W central London, England, S of Regent's Park, associated with the fictional detective Sherlock Holmes.

**Bakh·chi·sa·rai** |ˌbäkHCHisə'rī| town in S Ukraine, on the Crimean Peninsula. The palace of the khans there was restored by Potemkin while he was governor of Crimea.

**Bakh·ta·ran** |ˌbäkHtə'rän| (also called **Kermanshah**) commercial and industrial city in W Iran, in the Zagros Mts. Pop. 624,000.

**Ba·ku** |bä'kŏŏ| the capital of Azerbaijan, on the Caspian Sea. Pop. 1,780,000. It is an industrial port and a center of the oil industry.

**Ba·la·klava** |ˌbälə'klävə| (also **Balaclava**) village in S Ukraine, on the SW coast of the Crimean Peninsula. During the Crimean War, the famous Charge of the Light Brigade took place here. The so-called Balaklava helmet was first worn during that war.

**Ba·la·ko·vo** |ˌbälə'kawvə| city in W Russia, WNW of Saratov, E of the Volga River. Pop. 200,000.

**Ba·la·shi·kha** |ˌbälə'sHēkə| city in W Russia, NE of Moscow. Pop. 137,000.

**Bal·a·ton, Lake** |'bawlə͵tōn| large shallow lake in W central Hungary, situated in a resort and wine-producing region to the S of the Bakony Mts.

**Bal·boa** |bæl'bōə| town in S Panama, on the Gulf of Panama of the Pacific Ocean. Pop. 3,000. It was the administrative center for the U.S.-controlled Panama Canal Zone, and is at the W entrance of the canal.

**Bal·brig·gan** |bæl'brigən| port and resort town in E Ireland, N of Dublin. Pop. 8,000. Its textiles are famous.

**Bal·cones Escarpment** |bæl'kōnəs| geologic fault separating the plains of E Texas from highlands to the W. San Antonio, Austin, and Waco lie near or on it.

**Bald·win Park** |'bawldwən| city in SW California, a suburb E of Los Angeles. Pop. 69,330.

**Bâle** |bäl| French name for BASLE, Switzerland.

**Bal·e·ar·ic Islands** |ˌbælē'ærik| (also **the Balearics**) group of Mediterranean islands off the E coast of Spain, forming an autonomous region of that country, with four large islands (Majorca, Minorca, Ibiza, Formentera) and seven smaller ones. Capital: Palma (on Majorca).

**Ba·li** |'bälē; 'balē| mountainous island of Indonesia, to the E of Java; chief city, Denpasar. Pop. 2,856,000. It is noted for its beauty and the richness of its culture. □ **Balinese** *adj. & n.*

**Ba·li·ke·sir** |ˌbälikə'sir| city in NW Turkey, a textile center and capital of Balikesir province. Pop. 171,000.

**Ba·lik·pa·pan** |ˌbälik'pä͵pän| port and oil center in Indonesia, on E Borneo. Pop. 344,000.

**Bal·kan Mountains** |'bawlkən| (also called **Balkans**) range of mountains stretching across Bulgaria to the Black Sea. The highest peak is Botev Peak (7,793 ft./2,375 m.). □ **Balkan** *adj.*

**Bal·kans** |'bawlkənz| the countries occupying the part of SE Europe lying S of the Danube and Sava rivers, forming the

**Balkan Peninsula**, bounded by the Adriatic and Ionian seas in the W, the Aegean and Black seas in the E, and the Mediterranean in the south. At the crossroads of Europe and Asia, of Christianity and Islam, and of Byzantine and Western Roman Christianity, this mountainous region is noted for fierce ethnic and religious conflicts among its varied peoples—Greeks, Slavs, Turks, Albanians, and Gypsies. The peninsula was taken from the Byzantine Empire by the Ottoman Turks in the 14th and 15th centuries, and parts remained under Turkish control until 1912–13. After World War I the peninsula was divided among Greece, Albania, Bulgaria, and Yugoslavia (which broke up in 1991–3), with Turkey retaining only a small area including Constantinople (Istanbul). Balkan countries formed from the breakup of Yugoslavia include Slovenia, Croatia, Bosnia and Herzegovina, and Macedonia. □ **Balkan** adj.

**Balkh** |bawlk| historic town in N central Afghanistan, W of Mazar-e-Sharif. Pop. 7,000.

**Bal·la·rat** |'bælə,ræt| mining and sheep-farming center in Victoria, Australia. Pop. 64,980. It is the site of the discovery in 1851 of the largest gold reserves in Australia.

**Balls Bluff** |bawlz| historic locality on the Potomac River in NE Virginia, near Leesburg, site of an October 1861 Confederate victory.

**Bal·ly** |'bälē| (also **Bali**) industrial town in E India, N of Calcutta in West Bengal state. Pop. 182,000.

**Bal·ly·me·na** |,bælē'mēnə| town in Northern Ireland, to the N of Lough Neagh, in County Antrim. Pop. 28,000.

**Bal·mor·al Castle** |bæl'mawrəl| holiday residence of the British royal family, in NE Scotland, on the Dee River near Braemar.

**Bal·qash, Lake** |,bäl'käSH| (also **Balkhash, Balkash**) shallow salt lake in Kazakhstan, 350 mi./560 km. long.

**Bal·sas, Rio** |,rēō 'bawlsəs| river that flows 450 mi./725 km. through central Mexico, through Puebla, Guerrero, and Michoacán states, into the Pacific.

**Bal·tic Sea** |'bawltik| sea in N Europe. Nearly landlocked by Scandinavia, the Baltic states, and Germany, it is linked with the North Sea by the Kattegat strait and the Øresund channel.

**Bal·tic States** |'bawltik| **1** the republics of Estonia, Latvia, and Lithuania. **2** the ten members of the Council of Baltic States established in 1992: Denmark, Estonia, Finland, Germany, Latvia, Lithuania, Norway, Poland, Russia, and Sweden.

**Bal·ti·more** |'bawltə,mawr| historic industrial seaport, the largest city in Maryland, on Chesapeake Bay. Pop. 736,000.

**Bal·ti·more County** |'bawltə,mawr| county in N central Maryland, surrounding but not including the city of Baltimore. Towson is its seat. Pop. 692,134.

**Bal·ti·stan** |,bawltə'stæn| region of N Pakistan, in the Karakoram range of the Himalayas, to the S of K2. Also called **Little Tibet.**

**Ba·lu·chi·stan** |bə,lōōCHə'stæn| **1** a mountainous region of W Asia, which includes part of SE Iran, SW Afghanistan, and western Pakistan. **2** a province of western Pakistan. Capital: Quetta.

**Ba·ma·ko** |'bämə,kō| the capital of Mali, in the south of the country, an industrial port and historic cultural center on the Niger River. Pop. 646,000.

**Bam·berg** |'bæm,bərg| industrial port and commercial center on the Regnitz River in S Germany. It was once a renowned ecclesiastical center. Pop. 71,000.

**Ba·men·da** |bə'mendə| commercial and resort city in NW Cameroon. Pop. 138,000.

**Ba·mi·an** |,bämē'än| city in central Afghanistan. Pop. 8,000. Nearby are the remains of two colossal statues of Buddha and the ruins of the city of Ghulghuleh, which was destroyed by Genghis Khan c.1221.

**Ba·na·ba** |bə'näbə; 'bänəbə| island in the W Pacific, just S of the equator, to the W of the Gilbert Islands. Formerly within the Gilbert and Ellice Islands, the island has been part of Kiribati since 1979. Also called **Ocean Island.**

**Ba·nat** |'bän,ät| former province, now divided between Hungary and Romania, E of the Tisza River.

**Ban·bury** |'bænb(ə)rē; 'bæmb(ə)rē| commercial town in Oxfordshire, central England, noted for its market cross and for its cakes. Pop. 37,000.

**Ban·dar Ab·bas** |,bändər ə'bäs| (also **Benderabbas**) port city in S Iran, on the Strait of Hormuz at the mouth of the Persian Gulf. Pop. 250,000. It has long been one of the main ports of Iran.

**Ban·dar Lam·pung** |,bändər läm'pŏŏNG| city at the S tip of Sumatra, in Indonesia. Pop. 284,275. It was created in the 1980s as a result of the amalgamation of the city of Tanjungkarang and the nearby port of Telukbetung.

**Ban·dar Se·ri Be·ga·wan** |,bändər ,serē bəˈgä,wän| the capital of Brunei. Pop. 46,000.

**Ban·da Sea** |ˈbändə| sea in E Indonesia, between the central and S Moluccas Islands.

**Ban·dung** |ˈbän,dŏŏNG| industrial and cultural city in Indonesia. Pop. 2,056,900. Founded by the Dutch in 1810, it was the capital of the former Dutch East Indies.

**Banff** |bæmf| resort town in SW Alberta, in the Rocky Mts. W of Calgary. Pop. 5,688.

**Banff·shire** |ˈbæmfsHər; ˈbæmf,sHīr| former county of NE Scotland that became a part of Grampian region in 1975.

**Ban·ga·lore** |ˈbäNGgə,lawr| city in S central India, capital of the state of Karnataka. Pop. 2,651,000. It is a center of high-tech and other industries.

**Bang·ka** |ˈbæNGkä; ˈbäNGkä| (also **Banka**) island in Indonesia, SE of Sumatra, one of the world's foremost tin-producing centers. Chief town: Pangkalpinang.

**Bang·kok** |ˈbæNG,käk; bæNGˈkäk| industrial and commercial city, the capital and chief port of Thailand, on the Chao Phraya waterway, 25 mi./40 km. upstream from its outlet into the Gulf of Thailand. Pop. 5,876,000.

**Ban·gla·desh** |,bäNGgləˈdesH| republic of the Indian subcontinent, in the Ganges delta. Area: 55,813 sq. mi./143,998 sq. km. Pop. 107,992,140. Official language, Bengali. Capital and largest city: Dhaka. Long part of British India, then (1947–71) the E part of Pakistan, Bangladesh became independent in 1971. A densely populated, fertile agricultural low country, it is prone to repeated monsoonal flooding, and is one of the poorest countries in the world. □ **Bangladeshi** adj. & n.

Bangladesh

**Ban·gor¹** |ˈbæNGgər| industrial city in E central Maine, on the Penobscot River, formerly a lumbering center. Pop. 33,181.

**Ban·gor²** |ˈbæNG,gawr; ˈbæn,gawr; ˈbæNG-gər| resort town in Northern Ireland, E of Belfast on Belfast Lough. Pop. 71,000.

**Ban·gor³** |ˈbæNGgər; ˈbæNG,gawr| academic and industrial town in Gwynedd, N Wales, at the N end of the Menai Strait. Pop. 12,000.

**Ban·gui** |bäNGˈgē; ˈbäNG,gē| the capital of the Central African Republic, a port on the Ubangi River. Pop. 596,800.

**Ban·ja Lu·ka** |,bänyə ˈlŏŏkə| spa town in N Bosnia and Herzegovina. Pop. 143,000. It served as a base for Bosnian Serbs in their ethnic war against Bosnian Muslims in the 1990s.

**Ban·jar·ma·sin** |,bänjərˈmäsən| (also **Bandjarmasin**) a deepwater port and capital of the province of Kalimantan in Indonesia, on the island of Borneo. Pop. 480,700.

**Ban·jul** |ˈbæn,jŏŏl| the capital of the Gambia. Pop. 44,540. Until 1973 it was known as Bathurst.

**Banks Island** |bæNGks| westernmost island in the Arctic Archipelago of N Canada. Sparsely populated, it is home to abundant wildlife.

**Banks·town** |ˈbæNGks,town| city in Australia, a residential suburb WSW of Sydney, in New South Wales. Pop. 154,000.

**Ban·nock·burn** |ˈbænək,bərn; ,bænək-ˈbərn| village in central Scotland, S of Stirling, site of a Scottish victory over the English in 1314.

**Bann River** |bæn| longest (80 mi./130 km.) river of Northern Ireland, which flows through Lough Neagh and NW to the Atlantic. It is noted for salmon and eel fishing.

**Ban·ská Bys·tri·ca** |ˈbänkə ˈbistrit,sä| town in central Slovakia, at the confluence of the Hron and Bystrica rivers. Pop. 178,000.

**Ban·tam** |ˈbän,täm; ˈbæntəm| (also **Banten; Bantan**) ruined port town in Indonesia, on NW Java. The small domestic fowl known as "bantams" are named after it.

**Ban·try Bay** |ˈbæntrē| inlet of the N Atlantic in County Cork, SW Ireland, long used by fishing and naval fleets. It now has an oil terminal.

**Ban·tu·stan** |ˈbætŏŏ,stæn| name, often offensive, for any of the partially self-governing homelands reserved for black South Africans before 1994. Bophuthatswana was an example.

**Bao·ding** |ˈbowˈdiNG| city in Hebei province, E China, an agricultural distribution center on the Fu River. Pop. 483,000.

**Bao·ji** |'bow'jē| industrial city in Shaanxi province, central China, on the Wei River in the foothills of the Qin Ling Mts. Pop. 338,000.

**Bao·shan** |'bow'sнän| industrial city in Yunnan province, S China, between the Lancang and Nu rivers. Pop. 697,000. It is a major iron and steel center.

**Bao·tou** |'bow'tō| industrial city in Inner Mongolia, N China, on the Yellow River. Pop. 1,180,000.

**Ba·ra·cal·do** |,bärə'käldō| industrial city in N Spain, on the Nervion River. Pop. 105,000.

**Ba·ra·coa** |,bärə'kōə| port city in extreme E Cuba, on the N coast. Pop. 50,000. It is the oldest (1512) European settlement in Cuba.

**Ba·ra·ho·na** |,bärə'ōnə| port city in the SW Dominican Republic, on the Caribbean Sea. Pop. 158,000.

**Ba·ra·no·vi·chi** |bə'ränə,vесне| (also **Baranavichy**) industrial city in W Belarus. Pop. 163,000.

**Ba·ra·ta·ria Bay** |,bärə'tærēə| inlet of the Gulf of Mexico in SE Louisiana, S of New Orleans, associated with Jean Lafitte and other early 19th-century outlaws.

**Bar·ba·dos** |bär'bädəs| the most easterly of the Caribbean islands, a republic in the Windward Islands group. Area: 166 sq. mi./431 sq. km. Pop. 260,480. Official language, English. Capital: Bridgetown. Barbados became a British colony in the 1630s and remained British until 1966, when it gained independence. Tourism, sugar, and fishing are important to its economy. □ **Barbadian** adj. & n.

**Barbados**

**Bar·ba·ry** |'bärb(ə)rē| (also **Barbary States**) a former name for the Saracen countries of N and NW Africa, together with Moorish Spain. The area was noted between the 16th and 18th centuries as a haunt of pirates. Compare with MAGHRIB.

**Bar·ba·ry Coast**[1] |'bärb(ə)rē| former name for the Mediterranean coast of N Africa from Morocco to Egypt.

**Bar·ba·ry Coast**[2] |'bärb(ə)rē| historic district of central San Francisco, California, famed in the 19th century for its lawlessness.

**Bar·ber·ton** |'bärbərtən| city in NE Ohio, a suburb SW of Akron. Pop. 27,623.

**Bar·bi·can** |'bärbikən| section of E central London, England, NE of St. Paul's Cathedral, redeveloped after World War II bombing.

**Bar·bi·zon** |bärbə'zawN| village in the forest of Fontainebleau, N central France. It gave its name to a group of 19th-century landscape painters who worked here; they include Corot, Daubigny, and Millet.

**Bar·bu·da** |bär'bōōdə| see ANTIGUA AND BARBUDA. □ **Barbudan** adj. & n.

**Bar·ce·lo·na**[1] |,bärsə'lōnə| city on the coast of NE Spain, capital of Catalonia. Pop. 1,653,175. It is a large seaport and industrial city and a leading cultural center. It was the seat of the Republican government during the Spanish Civil War.

**Bar·ce·lo·na**[2] |,bärsə'lōnə| port and industrial city in NE Venezuela, on the Neveri River, near the Caribbean Sea. Pop. 222,000.

**Bar·ce·los** |bär'selōs| town in N Portugal, on the Cávado River. Pop. 5,000. The Barcelos cockerel is the national emblem.

**Bard·dha·man** |'bərdəmən; 'bärdəmən| city in NE India, in West Bengal state on the Damodar River. Pop. 245,000.

**Bar·de·jov** |'bärdəyawf| town in E Slovakia, on the Topla River, near the Polish border. Pop. 79,000. It is known for its hot springs.

**Bar·do·li·no** |,bärdə'lēnō| resort town in NE Italy, on the E shore of Lake Garda. Pop. 6,000. It is famous for its red wine.

**Ba·reil·ly** |bə'rälē| industrial city in N India, in Uttar Pradesh. Pop. 583,000.

**Ba·rents Sea** |'bærənts| part of the Arctic Ocean to the N of Norway and Russia, bounded to the W by Svalbard, to the N by Franz Josef Land, and to the E by Novaya Zemlya.

**Bar Harbor** |bär| resort town in S central Maine, on Mount Desert Island. Pop. 4,443.

**Ba·ri** |'bärē| industrial seaport on the Adriatic coast of SE Italy, capital of Apulia region. Pop. 353,030.

**Ba·ri·nas** |bə'rēnəs| commercial city in W Venezuela, the capital of Barinas state, a cattle- and oil-producing area. Pop. 154,000.

**Ba·ri·sal** |'bærə,säl| river port in S Bangladesh, on the Ganges delta. Pop. 180,010.

**Bar·king and Dag·en·ham** |'bärkıNG ən 'dægənəm| industrial borough of Greater London, England, N of the city center. Pop. 140,000.

**Bark·ly Tableland** |'bärklē| plateau region lying to the NE of Tennant Creek in Northern Territory, Australia.

**Bar·let·ta** |bär'letə| seaport and commercial center in SE Italy. Pop. 89,000. A famous duel between French and Italian knights took place near here in 1503.

**Bar·na·ul** |,bərnə'ōōl| the capital of Altai territory of S Russia, an industrial port on the Ob River. Pop. 603,000.

**Bar·ne·gat Bay** |'bärni,gæt; 'bärnigət| tidal body in SE New Jersey, shielded from the Atlantic by barrier islands, and the site of numerous resorts.

**Bar·net** |'bärnət| largely residential borough of N Greater London, England. Pop. 283,000.

**Barns·ley** |'bärnzlē| town in N England, a mining center in South Yorkshire. Pop. 217,300.

**Barn·sta·ble** |'bärnstəbəl| town in SE Massachusetts, on the SW part of Cape Cod. It is the commercial center for a resort area. Pop. 40,949.

**Ba·ro·da** |bə'rōdə| **1** former princely state of W India, now part of Gujarat. **2** former name (until 1976) for VADODARA.

**Ba·ros·sa Valley** |bə'raqsə| wine-producing region in Australia, N of Adelaide in South Australia.

**Ba·rot·se·land** |bə'rätsə,lænd| historic name for what is now the Western Province of Zambia. The Barotse people live in the area, along the Zambezi River.

**Bar·qui·si·me·to** |,bärkēsē'mätō| commercial city in NW Venezuela. Pop. 602,620.

**Bar·ra** |'bærə| small island toward the S end of the Outer Hebrides, Scotland, to the S of South Uist, from which it is separated by the Sound of Barra.

**Bar·rack·pore** |'bærək,pōr| (also **Barrackpur**) historic military town in NE India, in West Bengal state, N of Calcutta. Pop. 133,000.

**Bar·ra Man·sa** |,bärə 'mäNsə| industrial city in SE Brazil, NW of Rio de Janeiro. Pop. 165,000.

**Bar·ran·quil·la** |,bärən'kēə| the chief port of Colombia. Pop. 1,018,700. Founded in 1629, the city lies at the mouth of the Magdalena River, near the Caribbean Sea.

**Bar·ren Lands** |'bærən| name for tundra areas of northern Canada.

**Bar·rie** |'bærē| city in S Ontario, on Lake Simcoe, NW of Toronto. Pop. 62,728.

**Bar·row** |'bærō| city in N central Alaska, a commercial center on the Arctic Ocean. It is the northernmost U.S. city. Pop. 3,469. Nearby Point Barrow is the northernmost point in the U.S., at 71° 23′ N.

**Barrow-in-Furness** |'bærō ən 'fərnəs| industrial port city in Cumbria, NW England, on the Furness Peninsula. Pop. 74,000.

**Bar·stow** |'bär,stō| city in S central California, in the Mojave Desert NE of Los Angeles. Pop. 21,472.

**Bar·tles·ville** |'bärtlz,vil| city in NE Oklahoma, an oil industry center. Pop. 34,256.

**Bart·lett** |'bärtlət| town in SW Tennessee, a suburb NE of Memphis. Pop. 26,989.

**Ba·ry·saw** |bə'rēsəf| industrial city in central Belarus. Pop.147,000. Formerly **Borisov.**

**Bash·kiria** |bäsH'kirēə| autonomous republic in central Russia, W of the Urals. Pop. 3,964,000. Capital: Ufa. Also called **Bashkir Autonomous Republic, Bashkortostan.**

**Ba·sil·don** |'bæzldən| town in SE England. Pop. 157,500. It was developed as a new town (planned urban center) from 1949.

**Ba·si·li·ca·ta** |bə,zēlē'kätə| region of S Italy, lying between the 'heel' of Apulia and the 'toe' of Calabria. Capital: Potenza.

**Ba·sin and Range Province** |'bāsən ən 'rānj| largely arid intermountain region of the SW U.S., chiefly in Nevada, Utah, and California. The Great Basin and Death Valley are parts of the region.

**Basle** |bäl| commercial and industrial city on the Rhine in NW Switzerland. Pop. 171,000. French name **Bâle**, German name **Basel.**

**Basque Country** |bæsk| region of the W Pyrenees in both France and Spain, the homeland of the Basque people. French name **Pays Basque.**

**Basque Provinces** |bæsk| autonomous region of N Spain, on the Bay of Biscay. Capital: Vitoria.

**Bas·ra** |'bäsrə; 'äzrə| oil port of Iraq, on the Shatt al-Arab waterway. Pop. 616,700. It is a Shiite center with a long cultural history.

**Bas-Rhin** |bä 'ræN| department in NE France, between the Rhine River and the Vosges Mts. Area: 1,849 sq. mi./4,787 sq. km. Pop. 953,000. The capital and commerical center is Strasbourg.

**Bas·sein** |bəˈsān| port on the Irrawaddy delta in SW Burma. Pop. 144,100.

**Basse-Normandie** |ˌbäs ˌnawrmänˈdē| region of NW France, on the coast of the English Channel, including the Cherbourg Peninsula and the city of Caen.

**Basse·terre** |bäsˈter| the capital of St. Kitts and Nevis in the Leeward Islands, on the island of St. Kitts. Pop. 12,600.

**Basse-Terre** |bäs ˈter| the main island of the French overseas department of Guadeloupe, in the West Indies.

**Bass Strait** |bæs| channel separating Tasmania from the mainland of Australia.

**Ba·stia** |bästˈyä; ˈbästēə| the chief port of Corsica. Pop. 38,730.

**Bas·tille, the** |bäsˈtēl| (*hist.*) fortress and state prison in E Paris, France, near the present Place de la Bastille, built in the 14th century. The storming of the prison by revolutionaries on July 14, 1789, is considered to mark the beginning of the French Revolution. Demolition of the prison began the next day.

**Bas·togne** |bäˈstōn(yə)| town, SE Belgium. Pop. 11,000. It was the scene of heavy fighting during the Battle of the Bulge in World War II.

**Ba·su·to·land** |bəˈso͞otōˌlænd| former name (until 1966) for LESOTHO.

**Ba·ta** |ˈbätə| seaport in Equatorial Guinea. Pop. 17,000.

**Ba·taan** |bəˈtæn; bəˈtän| peninsula and province in the Philippines, on W Luzon, bounded by Manila Bay (E) and the South China Sea (W); scene of World War II battles and the infamous "Death March." Pop. 426,000.

**Ba·tal·ha** |bəˈtälyə| town in central Portugal. Pop. 3,000. Its Dominican abbey was built in 1388 in honor of Portugal's independence from Spain; Portuguese forces had defeated the Spanish in a battle nearby, in 1385.

**Ba·tan·gas City** |bəˈtäNGgəs| industrial and commercial port city in the Philippines, on SW Luzon. Pop. 144,000.

**Ba·tan Islands** |bəˈtän| the most northerly islands of the Philippines.

**Ba·ta·via** |bəˈtävēə; bəˈtävēə| former name (until 1949) for DJAKARTA, Indonesia. It derives from an earlier name for the Netherlands.

**Bath** |bæTH; bäTH| spa town in SW England, in Avon. Pop. 79,900. The town was founded by the Romans, who called it Aquae Sulis, and was a fashionable spa in the 18th century.

**Bath·urst Island** |ˈbæTHərst| island in the

Queen Elizabeth group in Nunavut, Canada, near which the North Magnetic Pole lies in the Arctic Ocean.

**Bat·man** |bätˈmän| city in SE Turkey, in Batman province on the Batman River, near its junction with the Tigris River. Pop. 147,000.

**Bat·na** |bətˈnä| industrial city in NE Algeria, SW of Constantine. Pop. 184,000.

**Bat·on Rouge** |ˌbætn ˈro͞oZH| the state capital of Louisiana, on the Mississippi River N of New Orleans. Pop. 219,530.

**Bat·tam·bang** |ˈbätəmˌbäNG| (also **Batdambang**) the capital of a province of the same name in W Cambodia, a commercial center in a rice-growing area. Pop. 551,860.

**Bat·ten·berg** |ˈbätnˌberg| village in Hesse, western Germany. The name was used for a branch of the British royal family; members married into the British royal family and their descendants later assumed the name Mountbatten.

**Bat·ter·sea** |ˈbætərsē| district of SW London, England, part of the borough of Wandsworth, on the S side of the Thames River, across from Chelsea.

**Bat·tery, the** |ˈbætərē| historic area at the S end of Manhattan Island, New York City.

**Bat·ti·ca·loa** |ˌbətikəˈlōə| city on the E coast of Sri Lanka. Pop. 42,900.

**Bat·tle** |ˈbætl| town in SE England, in East Sussex, actual site of the Battle of Hastings (1066). Pop. 6,000.

**Bat·tle Creek** |ˈbætl| city in S Michigan, noted as a cereal industry center. Pop. 53,540.

**Ba·tu·mi** |bəˈto͞omē| port city, capital of Adzharia, in the Republic of Georgia, on the Black Sea. Pop. 383,000.

**Ba·tu Pa·hat** |ˈbäto͞o ˈpäˌhät| (also called **Bandar Penggaram**) port town in Malaysia, on the Strait of Malacca in W Johor.

**Bat Yam** |ˈbät ˈyäm| city in central Israel, a suburb S of Tel Aviv, on the Mediterranean Sea. Pop. 142,000.

**Bau·chi** |ˈbowCHē| town in NE Nigeria, a tin mining center. Pop. 186,000. It is the capital of Bauchi state, part of a former kingdom of the same name.

**Bau·rú** |bow'ro͞o| commercial city in S Brazil, NW of São Paulo, in an agricultural region. Pop. 265,000.

**Ba·var·ia** |bəˈværēə| state of S Germany, formerly an independent kingdom. Capital: Munich. German name **Bayern**. □ **Bavarian** *adj. & n.*

**Bax·ter State Park** |ˈbækstər| preserve in N Maine that incorporates Mount

Katahdin and the N end of the Appalachian Trail.

**Ba·ya·mo** |bə'yämō| industrial and commercial city in SE Cuba, the capital of Granma province. Pop. 125,000. Bayamo was prominent in the 1890s revolt against Spanish rule.

**Ba·ya·món** |ˌbɪə'mōn| community in NE Puerto Rico, an industrial and residential suburb SW of San Juan. Pop. 202,103

**Bay Area** |bā| region around San Francisco Bay, in N central California. Oakland is the hub of the East Bay, San Jose of the South Bay.

**Bay City** |bā| industrial city in E Michigan, on the Saginaw River near Lake Huron. Pop. 38,936.

**Bay·ern** |'bīərn| German name for BAVARIA.

**Ba·yeux** |bī'yœ| market town in NW France, near the English Channel. Pop. 15,000. It was the first city liberated by the Allies after D-day, during World War II. It is famous for the medieval Bayeux tapestry, actually an embroidery, which recounts the story of the Norman Conquest of England in 1066.

**Bay·ko·nur** |ˌbīkə'noŏr| locality in central Kazakhstan, NE of Aral Sea. The Soviet Union maintained a missile- and rocket-testing site here.

**Bay of** for names beginning thus, see the other element, e.g., FUNDY, BENGAL, etc.

**Ba·yonne**[1] |ˌbā'ōn| port and industrial town in SW France, in the Basque region in the Pyrénées-Atlantiques. Pop. 42,000. In the 16th and 17th centuries, Bayonne produced cutlery; the word "bayonet" is derived from its name.

**Bay·onne**[2] |bā'yawn| industrial port city in NE New Jersey, on New York Bay. Pop. 61,444.

**Bay·ou Teche** |'bī,oŏ 'tesH| water route in S central Louisiana, at the heart of Cajun Country. Also called **the Teche**.

**Bay·ping** name formerly used in English for BEIJING (approximation of **Peiping**).

**Bay·reuth** |bī'roit; 'bī,roit| industrial and cultural city in Bavaria, S Germany. Pop. 73,000. The composer Richard Wagner is buried here, and festivals of his operas are held regularly.

**Bay State** |bā| nickname for MASSACHUSETTS.

**Bays·wa·ter** |'bāz,wawtər; 'bāz,wätər| residential district of W central London, England, N of Hyde Park.

**Bay·town** |'bā,town| city in SE Texas, an oil industry center E of Houston. Pop. 63,850.

**Beachy Head** |bēcHē 'hed| high chalk headland on the coast of East Sussex, SE England, on the English Channel, near which the French won a naval victory in 1690.

**Bea·con Hill** |'bēkən 'hil| historic neighborhood in downtown Boston, Massachusetts, on high ground N of the Boston Common.

**Bea·cons·field** |'bēkənz,fēld| town in S central England, in Buckinghamshire, NW of London, associated with the 19th-century politician and writer Benjamin Disraeli and with other literary figures. Pop. 11,000.

**Bea·gle Channel** |'bēgəl| channel through the islands of Tierra del Fuego at the S tip of South America, named for the ship in which Charles Darwin passed through in the 1830s.

**Beale Street** |bēl| historic commercial street in downtown Memphis, Tennessee, associated with black music and commerce.

**Beard·more Glacier** |bird,mawr| glacier in Antarctica, flowing from the Queen Maud Mts. to the Ross Ice Shelf, at the S edge of the Ross Sea.

**Bé·arn** |bā'ärn| former province in SE France, now part of the department of Pyrénées-Atlantique.

**Be·as** |'bē,äs| river of N India that rises in the Himalayas and flows through Himachal Pradesh to join the Sutlej River in Punjab. In ancient times called the Hyphasis, it marked the E limit of Alexander the Great's conquests.

**Beau·bourg** |bō'boŏr| see POMPIDOU CENTER, Paris, France.

**Beauce** |bōs| agricultural plain in N central France, SW of Paris. Its chief town is Chartres. A variety of crops are grown in its fertile soil, including wheat, corn, potatoes, barley, and oats.

**Beau·fort Sea** |'bōfərt| part of the Arctic Ocean lying to the N of Alaska and Canada.

**Beau·jo·lais** |ˌbōzHə'lā| wine-growing region in E central France, between Mâcon and Lyons W of the Saône River. The chief town is Villefrance-sur-Saône.

**Beau·mont** |'bō,mänt| industrial port in SE Texas, an oil industry center on the Neches River. Pop. 114,323.

**Beau·port** |bō'pawr| city in SE Quebec, a suburb on the Saint Lawrence River NE of Quebec City. Pop. 69,158.

**Beau·vais** |bō'vä| manufacturing town in N central France, N of Paris. Pop. 56,000. Beauvais had a renowned tapestry works, which were moved to Gobelins in 1940 after suffering damage in World War II. Its Gothic cathedral has the highest choir vault in the world.

**Bea·ver·ton** |'bēvərtən| city in NW Oregon, a suburb W of Portland, noted for its electronics industry. Pop. 53,310.

**Bech·u·a·na·land** |beCH'wänə,lænd| former British colony in southern Africa, now largely the nation of BOTSWANA. A section became part of present-day South Africa. *Bechuana* is an old name for the Tswana people.

**Bed·ford**[1] |'bedfərd| town in S central England, on the Ouse River, the county seat of Bedfordshire. Pop. 89,200.

**Bed·ford**[2] |'bedfərd| city in NE Texas, a suburb NE of Fort Worth. Pop. 43,762.

**Bed·ford·shire** |'bedfərd,SHir; 'bedfərd-SHər| county of S central England; county seat, Bedford.

**Bedford-Stuyvesant** |'bedfərd 'stīvəsənt| residential and commercial section of N Brooklyn, New York, home to one of the largest U.S. black communities.

**Bed·lam** |'bedləm| popular name for St. Mary of Bethlehem hospital, founded in London, England in 1247, and by the 14th century a well-known mental hospital.

**Bed·ling·ton** |'bedliNGtn| town in NE England, in Northumberland. Pop. 13,000. It gave its name to a breed of terrier.

**Bee·hive State** |'bē,hīv| nickname for UTAH.

**Beer·she·ba** |bir'SHēbə| historic commercial city in S Israel, on the N edge of the Negev desert. Pop. 138,100.

**Bei'an** |'bā'än| city in Heilongjiang province, NE China, in the foothills of the Xiao Hinggan Ling Mts. Pop. 205,000.

**Bei·hai** |'bā'hī| port city in Guangxi, S China, on the Gulf of Tonkin. Pop. 113,000. It is an industrial and fishing center.

**Bei·jing** |bā'jiNG; 'bā'zHiNG| the capital and second-largest city of China, in the NE of the country. Pop. 6,920,000. Beijing became the capital in 1421, at the start of the Ming period. The political and cultural center of China, it is also an industrial hub. Also called **Peking**; formerly called **Peiping**.

**Bei·ra** |'bārə| port on the coast of Mozambique, capital of Sofala province. Pop. 299,300.

**Bei·rut** |bā'rōot| the capital and chief port

of Lebanon. Pop. 1,500,000. The city was badly damaged during the Lebanese civil war of 1975–89. It has a long history as a commercial center and resort.

**Be·jaïa** |bə'jīə| (French name **Bougie**) port city in NE Algeria, on the Gulf of Bejaïa, an inlet of the Mediterranean Sea. Pop. 124,000. It has long been a political and academic center.

**Be·kaa** |bə'kä| (also **El Beqa'a**) a fertile valley in central Lebanon between the Lebanon and Anti-Lebanon Mts.

**Bel Air** |bel 'er; bel 'ær| affluent residential section of Los Angeles, California.

**Be·la·rus** |,byalə'rōōs; ,belə'rōōs| republic in eastern Europe. Area: 80,185 sq. mi./207,600 sq. km. Pop. 10,328,000. Official language, Belorussian. Capital and largest city: Minsk. Also called **Belorussia, White Russia**. Largely flat plains, with extensive marshes along the Dnieper River, Belarus is both agricultural and industrial. It was part of the Soviet Union 1921–91. □ **Belarussian** *adj. & n.* **Belorussian** *adj. & n.*

**Belarus**

**Be·la·ya River** |'byeləyə| river in the Bashkir Republic, E European Russia, flowing 700 mi./1,210 km. NW from the Ural Mts. to the Kama River.

**Be·la·ya Tser·kov** |'byeləyət'serkəf| (Ukrainian name **Bila Tserkva**) industrial city in Ukraine, S of Kiev. Pop. 200,500.

**Bel·cher Islands** |'belCHər| island group in SE Hudson Bay, in Nunavut, Canada.

**Be·lém** |bə'lem| city and port of N Brazil, at the mouth of the Amazon, capital of the state of Pará Pop. 1,244,640.

**Bel·fast** |'bel,fæst; bel'fæst| capital, largest city, and chief port of Northern Ireland. Pop. 280,970. Famed for its shipyards, the city suffered damage and population decline from the early 1970s as a result of sectarian violence.

**Bel·fort** |,bel'fawr| industrial city in E France, in the historically important

Belfort Gap between the Vosges and Jura mountains. Pop. 51,900.

**Bel·gaum** |bel'gowm| industrial city in W India, in the state of Karnataka. Pop. 326,000.

**Bel·gian Con·go** |'beljən 'käNGgō| former (1908–60) name for the Congo (formerly Zaire).

**Bel·gium** |'beljəm| low-lying republic in W Europe, on the S of the North Sea and English Channel. Area: 11,796 sq. mi./30,540 sq. km. Pop. 9,978,700 (1991); languages, Flemish and French (Walloon). Capital and largest city: Brussels. French name **Belgique**, Flemish name **België**. Belgium separated from the Netherlands in 1830. It suffered heavily in both world wars, but is one of the most industrial countries in Europe, as well as home to many European Union offices. □ **Belgian** adj. & n.

**Belgium**

**Bel·go·rod** |'byelgərət| industrial city in S Russia, on the Donets River close to the border with Ukraine. Pop. 306,000.

**Bel·grade** |'bel,gräd; bel'gräd| capital of Serbia and Yugoslavia, the industrial and commercial center and largest city of Serbia, on the Danube River. Pop. 1,168,450. Serbian name **Beograd**.

**Bel·gra·via** |bel'grävēə| fashionable district of London, England, S of Knightsbridge, noted for its diplomatic and literary associations.

**Be·li·tung** |bə'lē,tooNG| (also **Billiton**) Indonesian island in the Java Sea, between Borneo and Sumatra.

**Be·lize** |bə'lēz| country on the Caribbean coast of Central America. Area: 8,867 sq. mi./22,965 sq. km. Pop. 190,800. Languages, English (official), Creole, Spanish. Capital: Belmopan. Largest city: Belize City. Former name (until 1973) **British Honduras**. Belize, which became independent in 1981, relies on tourism and subsistence agriculture. Its people are largely of African extraction □ **Belizian** adj. & n.

**Belize**

**Be·lize City** |bə'lēz| the principal seaport and former capital (until 1970) of Belize. Pop. 46,000.

**Bell** |bel| city in SW California, a suburb SE of Los Angeles. Pop. 34,365.

**Bel·lary** |bə'lärē| industrial city in Karnataka state, S India. Pop. 245,800.

**Bel·leau Wood** |bel'ō| (French name **Bois de Belleau**) forest E of Paris, France, and just E of Château-Thierry, scene of a June 1918 victory by American forces over the Germans.

**Belle Glade** |bel| city in SE Florida, a sugarcane-producing hub. Pop. 16,177.

**Belle Isle, Strait of** |bel 'il| ocean passage between Newfoundland and Labrador, at the mouth of the Gulf of St. Lawrence in E Canada.

**Belle·ville**[1] |'bel,vil| section of E Paris, France. It is a working-class district famous for Père Lachaise cemetery, which contains the tombs of many famous people.

**Belle·ville**[2] |'bel,vil| industrial city in SW Illinois. Pop. 42,785.

**Belle·ville**[3] |'bel,vil| industrial township in NE New Jersey. Pop. 34,213.

**Belle·ville**[4] |'bel,vil| city in SE Ontario, near Lake Ontario. Pop. 37,243.

**Belle·vue**[1] |'bel,vyoo| city in E Nebraska. Pop. 30,982.

**Belle·vue**[2] |'bel,vyoo| historic municipal hospital in lower Manhattan, New York City.

**Bell·flow·er** |'bel,flow-ər| city in SW California, a suburb SE of Los Angeles. Pop. 61,815.

**Bell Gardens** |bel| unincorporated suburb E of Los Angeles, California. Pop. 42,355.

**Bel·ling·ham** |'beliNG,ham| industrial port city in NW Washington, on Bellingham Bay off Puget Sound. Pop. 52,179.

**Bel·lings·hau·sen Sea** |'beliNGz,howzən| part of the SE Pacific off the coast of Antarctica, bounded to the E and S by the Antarctic Peninsula and Ellsworth Land.

**Bel·lin·zo·na** |ˌbelənˈzōnə; ˌbeləntˈsōnə| historic resort town in S Switzerland, near the Italian border. Pop. 17,000.

**Bel·lo** |ˈbāyō| town in NW Colombia, just N of Medellín, of which it is a suburb.

**Bell·wood** |ˈbelˌwŏŏd| village in NE Illinois, a suburb W of Chicago. Pop. 20,421.

**Bel·mont¹** |ˈbelˌmänt| city in N central California, a suburb SE of San Francisco. Pop. 24,127.

**Bel·mont²** |ˈbelˌmänt| town in E Massachusetts, a suburb NW of Boston. Pop. 24,720.

**Bel·mo·pan** |ˌbelmōˈpæn| the capital of Belize. Founded in 1970 to succeed Belize City, it is one of the smallest capitals in the world. Pop. 3,850.

**Be·lo Ho·ri·zon·te** |ˌbalō ˌawreˈzawNNtē| city in E Brazil, capital of the state of Minas Gerais. Pop. 2,020,160. It is a center for regional mining and agricultural industries.

**Be·loit** |bəˈloit| industrial and academic city in SE Wisconsin. Pop. 35,573.

**Be·los·tok** |ˌbyeləˈstawk| Russian name for BIALYSTOK, Poland.

**Bel·sen** |ˈbelzən| village near Bergen, in Lower Saxony, NW Germany, site of a World War II Nazi concentration camp (also called **Bergen-Belsen**).

**Belts·ville** |ˈbelts,vil; ˈbeltsvəl| unincorporated village in central Maryland, just NE of Washington, D.C. Pop. 14,476. The U.S. Department of Agriculture has its chief experimental station here.

**Bel·tsy** |ˈbyeltsē| (Romanian name **Bălţi**) city in N central Moldova. Pop. 164,800.

**Belt·way, the** |ˈbelt,wā| circular highway around Washington, D.C., in Maryland and Virginia. The U.S. government is said to exist "inside the Beltway."

**Bel·ve·de·re, the** |ˈbelvə,dir| former court of the Vatican, in Rome, Italy, now a famous art museum.

**Be·mid·ji** |bəˈmijē| city in NW Minnesota, near the head of the Mississippi River. Pop. 11,245.

**Bemis Heights** |ˈbēməs| historic village in E New York, SE of Saratoga Springs, site of two 1777 Revolutionary War battles.

**Be·na·res** |bəˈnärəs| former name for VARANASI, India.

**Ben·be·cu·la** |ben'bekyŏŏlə| small island in the Outer Hebrides, Scotland, between North and South Uist and linked to them by causeways.

**Ben Bul·ben** |ben ˈbəlbən| small mountain in County Sligo, NW Ireland, at the SW foot of which, in Drumcliff, the poet W.B. Yeats is buried.

**Bend** |bend| city in central Oregon. Pop. 20,469.

**Ben·dery** |bənˈderē| former Russian name for TIGHINA, Moldova.

**Ben·di·go** |ˈbendiˌgō| commercial, and former gold-mining town in the state of Victoria, Australia. Pop. 57,430.

**Be·ne Be·raq** |bə,nä bəˈräk| city in central Israel, a suburb N of Tel Aviv, noted for its Talmudic schools. Pop. 127,000.

**Be·ne·lux** |ˈbenl,əks| collective name for Belgium, the Netherlands, and Luxembourg (an acronym of *Bel*gium, *Neth*erlands, and *Lux*embourg, especially with reference to their economic union.

**Ben·gal, Bay of** |ben'gawl; beNG'gawl| part of the Indian Ocean lying between India to the W and Burma and Thailand to the E.

**Ben·gal** |ben'gawl; beNG'gawl| region in the NE of the Indian subcontinent, containing the Ganges and Brahmaputra river deltas. In 1947 the province was divided into West Bengal, which has remained a state of India, and East Bengal, now Bangladesh. □ **Bengali** *adj. & n.*

**Beng·bu** |ˈbəNGˈbŏŏ| city in Anhui province, E China, an agricultural trade center. Pop. 623,000.

**Ben·gha·zi** |ben'gäzē| Mediterranean port in NE Libya. Pop. 485,400. It was the joint capital (with Tripoli) from 1951 to 1972.

**Beng·ku·lu** |beNG'kŏŏlŏŏ| port city in SW Sumatra, Indonesia. Pop. 173,000.

**Ben·gue·la** |ben'gwelə| port and railway terminal in Angola, on the Atlantic coast. Pop. 155,000.

**Ben·gue·la Current** |ben'gwelə| cold ocean current that flows from Antarctica N along the W coast of S Africa as far as Angola.

**Be·ni River** |ˈbānē| river that flows 1,000 mi./1,600 km. from central to N Bolivia, along the E of the Andes, into the Madeira River.

**Be·ni·cia** |bəˈnēsHə| city in N central California, N of San Francisco Bay. Pop. 24,437.

**Be·nin, Bight of** |bəˈnēn| wide bay on the coast of Africa N of the Gulf of Guinea, bordered by Togo, Benin, and SW Nigeria. Lagos is its chief port.

**Be·nin** |bəˈnēn| republic of W Africa, immediately W of Nigeria. Area: 43,483 sq. mi./112,622 sq. km. Pop. 4,883,000. Languages, French (official), West African languages. Capital: Porto Novo. Largest city:

**Benin**

Cotonou. The country, whose name recalls an earlier African kingdom, was conquered by the French in 1893 and became part of French West Africa. In 1960 it became fully independent. Cotton, cacao, oil, and subsistence farming are important. Former name (until 1975) DAHOMEY. □ **Beninese** *adj. & n.*

**Ben Nev·is** |ben 'nevəs| mountain in western Scotland. Rising to 4,406 ft./1,343 m., it is the highest mountain in the British Isles.

**Ben·ning·ton** |'beniNGtən| historic town in SW Vermont. Pop. 16,451.

**Be·no·ni** |bə'nōnē| city in South Africa, in the province of Gauteng, E of Johannesburg. Pop. 206,800. It is a gold-mining center.

**Ben·son·hurst** |'bensən,hərst| residential section of SW Brooklyn, New York.

**Ben·ton Harbor** |'bentn| industrial city in SW Michigan. Pop. 12,818.

**Bent's Fort** |bents| historic site in E central Colorado, NE of La Junta, on the Arkansas River and the former Santa Fe Trail.

**Be·nue River** |'bānwə| river that flows 870 mi./1,400 km. from N Cameroon into Nigeria, where it joins the Niger River.

**Ben·xi** |'ben'sHē| city in NE China, in the province of Liaoning. Pop. 920,000. It is a center for metal and other heavy industries.

**Be·o·grad** |'bāə,gräd| Serbian name for BELGRADE.

**Bep·pu** |'bepōō| resort city in SW Japan, on NW Kyushu, famed for its hot springs. Pop. 130,000.

**Ber·bera** |'bərbərə| port on the N coast of Somalia. Pop. 65,000.

**Berch·tes·ga·den** |berKHtəs,gädn| town in S Germany, in the Bavarian Alps close to the border with Austria. Pop. 8,186. Adolf Hitler's fortified retreat, the "Eagle's Nest," was here.

**Ber·dyansk** |bir'dyänsk| port city in SE Ukraine, on the Sea of Azov. Pop. 134,000.

**Be·rea** |bə'rēə| city in central Kentucky, home to Berea College. Pop. 9,126.

**Be·re·zi·na River** |bər'yazHinə| river that flows 370 mi./600 km. SE across Belarus to the Dnieper River. It was the scene of an 1812 retreat by Napoleon's armies, and of 1941 battles between German and Soviet forces.

**Be·rez·ni·ki** |bər'yawznəkē| port city on the Kama River in the W Urals, Russia, center of a chemical-processing complex. Pop. 201,000.

**Ber·ga·ma** |bər'gämə| commercial town in W Turkey, N of Izmir. Pop. 101,000. Ancient Pergamum, a cultural and political center under the Mysians and Romans, was here.

**Ber·ga·mo** |'bergə,mō| city in Lombardy, N Italy, in the foothills of the Alps. Pop. 118,000. It has historic upper and industrial lower sections.

**Ber·gen**[1] |'bergən| Flemish name for MONS, Belgium.

**Ber·gen**[2] |'bergən| seaport in SW Norway. Pop. 213,344. It is a center of the fishing and North Sea oil industries.

**Ber·gen·field** |,bərgən,fēld| suburban borough in NE New Jersey. Pop. 24,458.

**Ber·gen op Zoom** |'berKHən awp 'zōm| commercial town in the SW Netherlands, on the Zoom River and the Scheldt estuary. Pop. 47,000.

**Ber·ge·rac** |bərzHə'räk| wine-producing region in the Dordogne valley in SW France.

**Ber·ing Sea** |'beriNG| arm of the N Pacific lying between NE Siberia and Alaska, bounded to the S by the Aleutian Islands. It is linked to the Arctic Ocean by the Bering Strait.

**Ber·ing Strait** |'beriNG| narrow sea passage that separates the E tip of Siberia from Alaska and links the Arctic Ocean with the Bering Sea, about 53 mi./85 km. wide at its narrowest point. During the Ice Age, as a result of a drop in sea levels, the *Bering land bridge* formed between the two continents, allowing the migration of animals and dispersal of plants in both directions, including the earliest human arrivals in the Americas.

**Berke·ley** |'bərklē| city in W California, on San Francisco Bay, site of the University of California at Berkeley. Pop. 102,724.

**Berke·ley Springs** |'bərklē| (official name **Bath**) town in E West Virginia. Pop. 735. It is a famous spa.

**Berk·shire** |'bärksHər; 'bärk,sHir| county of S England, W of London; county seat, Reading.

**Berk·shire Hills** |'bərksHər| upland in W Massachusetts, noted as a resort area.

**Ber·lin** |bər'lin| the capital of Germany, an industrial, commercial, and cultural city on the Spree River, in the NE. The capital of the German Empire from 1871, it was divided into East Berlin and West Berlin after World War II. The former was the capital of East Germany, while Bonn became capital of West Germany. In 1990 Berlin was reunified. Pop. 3,102,500.

**Ber·lin Wall** |bər'lin| fortified and heavily guarded wall built in 1961 by the communist authorities on the boundary between East and West Berlin, chiefly to curb the flow of East Germans to the West. Regarded as a symbol of the division of Europe into the communist countries of the East and the democracies of the West, it was opened in November 1989 after the collapse of the communist regime in East Germany, and subsequently dismantled.

**Ber·me·jo River** |ber'mähō| river that flows 650 mi./1,045 km. SE from N Argentina to the Paraguay River, at the Paraguayan border.

**Ber·mu·da** |bər'myōōdə| (also **the Bermudas**) British crown colony, made up of about 150 small islands (20.5 sq. mi./53 sq. km.), about 650 mi./1,046 km. E of the coast of North Carolina. Pop. 58,000. Language, English. Capital: Hamilton. Inhabited since 1609, Bermuda now has internal self-government. Most of its people are of African extraction. Tourism, finance, fishing, and light industry are important. □ **Bermudan** adj. & n. **Bermudian** adj. & n.

**Bermuda**

**Ber·mu·da Hundred** |bər'myōōdə| locality SE of Richmond, Virginia, site of an 1864 Civil War battle.

**Ber·mu·da Tri·an·gle** |bər,myōōdə 'trī-,æNGgəl| area of the Atlantic between Florida, Bermuda, and Puerto Rico, the scene of many mysterious ship and aircraft disappearances.

**Bern** |bern; 'bərn| (also **Berne**) the capital of Switzerland since 1848, an industrial and administrative city in the W central part of the country. Pop. 134,620. □ **Bernese** adj. & n.

**Ber·nese Alps** |,bər'nēz; bər'nēs| (also **Bernese Oberland**) range of the Alps in central and W Switzerland. Finsteraarhorn (14,022 ft./4,274 m.), the Jungfrau, and the Eiger are here.

**Ber·ni·na Alps** |bər'nēnə| section of the Rhaetian Alps in S Switzerland and N Italy, reaching 13,284 ft./4,049 m. at Piz Bernina.

**Ber·ry** |be'rē| former province of central France; chief town, Bourges.

**Ber·wick·shire** |'berwik,sHir; 'beriksHər| former county of SE Scotland, on the border with England. It became a part of Borders region (now Scottish Borders) in 1975.

**Berwick-upon-Tweed** |'berik əpən 'twēd| town at the mouth of the Tweed River in NE England, close to the Scottish border. Pop. 13,000. It was ceded by Scotland to England in 1482.

**Ber·wyn** |'bərwən; 'bər,win| city in NE Illinois, a suburb W of Chicago. Pop. 45,426.

**Be·san·çon** |bəzän'sawN| the capital of Franche-Comté in NE France, a precision-industry center. Pop. 119,200.

**Bes·kids** |bes'kēdz| forested mountain range along the borders of Slovakia with Poland and the Czech Republic, reaching 5,659 ft./1,725 m. at Babia Góra, and noted for iron mining and resorts.

**Bes·sa·ra·bia** |,besə'räbēə| region in E Europe between the Dniester and Prut rivers, from 1918 to 1940 part of Romania. The major part of the region now is in Moldova, the remainder in Ukraine. □ **Bessarabian** adj. & n.

**Bes·se·mer** |'besəmər| city in N central Alabama, a steel and industrial center SW of Birmingham. Pop. 33,497.

**Beth·an·y** |'beTHənē| city in central Oklahoma, a suburb W of Oklahoma City. Pop. 20,075.

**Beth·el** |'beTHəl| city in SW Alaska, a fishing center. Pop. 4,674.

**Beth·el**² |'beTHəl| town in the Catskill Mts., SE New York. Pop. 3,693. It is the actual site of the 1969 Woodstock music festival.

**Beth·el**² |'beTHəl| ancient city of Palestine, N of Jerusalem in the West Bank, where in the biblical account Abraham built his first altar.

**Beth·el Park** |'beTHəl| borough in SW Pennsylvania, a suburb S of Pittsburgh. Pop. 33,823.

**Be·thes·da**¹ |bə'THezdə| in the Bible, a pool in Jerusalem with miraculous healing properties.

**Be·thes·da**² |bə'THezdə| affluent unincorporated suburb in central Maryland, N of Washington, D.C. It is home to the National Institutes of Health. Pop. 62,936.

**Beth·le·hem**¹ |'beTHli,hem; 'beTHlēəm| small town 5 mi./8 km. S of Jerusalem, in the Israeli-occipied West Bank. Pop. 14,000. It was the native city of King David and is the reputed birthplace of Jesus.

**Beth·le·hem**² |'beTHli,hem; 'beTHlēəm| industrial city in E Pennsylvania, on the Lehigh River. Pop. 71,428. It is a famed steelmaking center.

**Beth·sa·i·da** |beTH'sāədə| ancient city of Palestine, believed to have been near the Sea of Galilee, the birthplace of several followers of Jesus.

**Bet·ten·dorf** |'betn,dawrf| industrial city in SE Iowa, on the Mississippi River. It is one of the Quad Cities.

**Betws-y-Coed** |,betōōsə'koid| resort community in NW Wales, on the Conway River, noted for its scenery and as an outdoor center. Pop. 800.

**Bev·er·ly** |'bevərlē| industrial and resort city in NE Massachusetts. Pop. 38,195.

**Bev·er·ly Hills** |'bevərlē| largely residential city in California, on the NW side of the Los Angeles conurbation. Pop. 31,970. It is famous as the home of movie stars.

**Bex·ley** |'bekslē| borough of Greater London, England, comprising industrial and residential suburbs SE of the city. Pop. 211,000.

**Bé·ziers** |bā'zy| industrial town in S France, on the Orb River. Pop. 72,000. It is a communication center and a trade center for the wine industry.

**Bha·gal·pur** |'bägəl,pŏŏr| industrial and commercial city in Bihar, NE India, on the Ganges River. Pop. 262,000.

**Bha·rat** |'bərət| Hindi name for INDIA.

**Bhat·pa·ra** |bät'pärə| industrial city in West Bengal, E India, on the Hooghly River. Formerly an academic center, it now makes textiles and paper. Pop. 304,000.

**Bhav·na·gar** |bow'nəgər| industrial port in NW India, in Gujarat, on the Gulf of Cambay. Pop. 401,000. It was the capital of a former Rajput princely state of the same name.

**Bhi·lai·na·gar** |bi'lī,nəgər| (also **Bhilai**) industrial city in Madhya Pradesh, central India, a steel center. Pop. 399,000.

**Bho·pal** |bō'päl| city in central India, the capital of the state of Madhya Pradesh. Pop. 1,604,000. In December 1984 leakage of poisonous gas from an American-owned pesticide factory in the city caused the death of about 2,500 people.

**Bhu·ba·nes·war** |bŏŏbə'nəsHwər| administrative and industrial city in E India, capital of the state of Orissa. Pop. 412,000.

**Bhu·tan** |bŏŏ'tän; bŏŏtæn| kingdom on the SE slopes of the Himalayas, a protectorate of India. Area: 18,000 sq. mi./46,620 sq. km. Pop. 600,000. Languages, Dzongkha (official), Nepali. Capital: Thimphu. It is a country of subsistence farmers living in valleys and on the slopes of some of the highest mountains in the world. □ **Bhutanese** *adj. & n.*

Bhutan

**Bi·a·fra** |bē'æfrə; bē'äfrə| state proclaimed in 1967, when part of E Nigeria, inhabited chiefly by the Ibo people, sought independence from the rest of the country. In the ensuing civil war the new state's troops were overwhelmed by numerically superior forces, and by 1970 it had ceased to exist. □ **Biafran** *adj. & n.*

**Bi·ak** |'bē'äk| island off N Irian Jaya, Indonesia, scene of World War II battles. Air and naval facilities and fishing are important to its economy.

**Białys·tok** |'byowə,sHtawk| industrial city in NE Poland, close to the border with Belarus. Pop. 270,568. Russian name **Belostok**.

**Biar·ritz** |,bēə'rits| seaside resort in SW France, on the Bay of Biscay. Pop. 28,890.

**Bible Belt** |'bibəl ,belt| term for parts of the U.S. where fundamentalist Christianity is a major social force, especially in the upper S.

**Bid·de·ford** |'bidəfərd| industrial city in SW Maine. Pop. 20,710.

**Bie·le·feld** |'bēlə,felt| industrial city in North Rhine–Westphalia in western Germany. Pop. 322,130.

**Bielsko-Biala** |'byelskaw'byäwə| (German name **Bielitz**) industrial city in S Poland, on the Biala River. Pop. 181,000.

**Bien Hoa** |'byen 'hwä| industrial city in S Vietnam, N of Ho Chi Minh City. Pop. 314,000. A major U.S. airbase was here during the Vietnam War.

**Big Apple** |big 'æpəl| nickname for New York City.

**Big Bear Lake** |'big 'ber| reservoir and recreational center in S California, in the San Bernardino Mts. ENE of Los Angeles.

**Big Ben** |big 'ben| popular name for the bell, and also for the clock tower it hangs in, of the Houses of Parliament, in Westminster, London, England. Hung in 1859, Big Ben has become emblematic of Britain.

**Big Bend National Park** |big 'bend| U.S. national park in a bend of the Rio Grande, in the desert lands of S Texas on the border with Mexico, in which were discovered, in 1975, fossil remains of the pterosaur.

**Big Black River** |big 'blæk| river in Mississippi, flowing 330 mi./530 km. into the Mississippi River near Vicksburg.

**Big·horn Mountains** |'big,hawrn| range of the Rocky Mts. in Montana and Wyoming. The Bighorn River flows along its W side.

**Big Island** |big| popular name for the island of HAWAII.

**Big Mud·dy** |big 'mədē| popular name for the Missouri River, whose waters are much less clear than those of the Mississippi.

**Big Sioux River** |big 'sōō| river in South Dakota and Iowa, flowing 420 mi./680 km. into the Missouri River.

**Big Spring** |big 'spriNG| city in W Texas, an oil industry center NE of Midland. Pop. 23,093.

**Big Sur** |big 'sər| scenic locality in W central California, S of Monterey on the Pacific coast.

**Big Thick·et** |big 'THikit| forested area of E Texas, N of Beaumont, noted for its biological diversity.

**Bi·hac** |'beïhäCH| town in NW Bosnia and Herzegovina, near the Croatian border. Ruled by Turkey before 1878, it is largely Muslim. In 1993 it was the site of fierce fighting between the Muslim population and Bosnian government forces. Pop. 46,000.

**Bi·har** |bi'här| state in NE India. Pop. 86,339,000. Capital: Patna. □ **Bihari** adj. & n.

**Bi·ja·pur** |bi'jäpoor| largely Muslim city in Karnataka, SW India. Pop. 193,000.

**Bi·ka·ner** |,bikə'ner| historic city in Rajasthan, NW India, near the Thar Desert. Pop. 415,000.

**Bi·ki·ni** |bi'kēnē| atoll in the Marshall Islands, in the W Pacific, used by the U.S. between 1946 and 1958 as a site for testing nuclear weapons.

**Bi·las·pur** |bi'läs,poor| commercial city in Madhya Pradesh, central India. Pop. 234,000.

**Bil·bao** |bil'bow| seaport and industrial city in N Spain, in the Basque Country. Pop. 372,200.

**Bil·le·rica** |bil'rikə| town in NE Massachusetts, S of Lowell. Pop. 37,609.

**Bil·lings** |'biliNGz| commercial city in S central Montana. Pop. 81,151. It is Montana's largest city.

**Bil·lings·gate** |'biliNGz,gāt| London fish market dating from the 16th century. In 1982 the market moved to London's East End.

**Bi·loxi** |bə'ləksē| city in SE Mississippi, on the Gulf of Mexico. Pop. 46,319. It is a noted fishing and tourist center.

**Bim·i·ni** |'bimənē| (also **Biminis**) resort islands in the NW Bahamas. The legendary Fountain of Youth sought by Ponce de León was thought to be here.

**Bing·en** |'biNGen| (official name **Bingen am Rhein**) port city on the Rhine River in Rhineland-Palatinate, western Germany. Pop. 25,000.

**Bing·ham·ton** |'biNGəmtən| industrial city in S central New York, on the Susquehanna River near the Pennsylvania border. Pop. 53,008.

**Binh Dinh**[1] |'bin 'din| agricultural province of central Vietnam, on the South China Sea. Pop. 1.37 million. It was heavily bombed during the Vietnam War.

**Binh Dinh**[2] |'bin 'din| see AN NHON, Vietnam.

**Bio·ko** |bē'ōkō| island of Equatorial Guinea, in the E part of the Gulf of Guinea. Its chief town is Malabo, the capital of Equatorial Guinea. It was known as Fernando Póo until 1973, and from 1973 to 1979 as Macias Nguema.

**Bir Ha·cheim** |bir hä'KHäm| (Arabic name **Bir al Hakkayim**) oasis town in N Libya, SW of Tobruk, scene of World War II battles in 1942.

**Bir·ke·nau** |'birkə,now| village in S Poland, site of a Nazi concentration camp associated with nearby Auschwitz.

**Bir·ken·head** |'bərkən,hed| town in NW

England on the Mersey River opposite Liverpool. Pop. 116,000.

**Bir·ming·ham**[1] |'bərminɢ,hæm| industrial city in N central Alabama. Pop. 265,968.

**Bir·ming·ham**[2] |'bərminɢ,hæm| city in W central England, in West Midlands. Pop. 934,900. The second-largest British city, it is a center of heavy industry, high technology, and education. It is locally called Brum (a shortening of Brummagem).

**Bir·ming·ham**[3] |'bərminɢ,hæm; 'bərminɢəm| city in SE Michigan, a suburb N of Detroit. Pop. 19,997.

**Bis·bee** |'bizbē| resort city in SE Arizona, near the Mexican border. Pop. 6,288. It was formerly a noted mining center.

**Bis·cay, Bay of** |bis'kā| part of the N Atlantic between the N coast of Spain and the W coast of France, noted for its strong currents and storms.

**Bis·cayne Bay** |bis'kān| inlet of the Atlantic in SE Florida, S of Miami, noted for its islands and resorts.

**Bish·kek** |bisH'kek| the capital of Kyrgyzstan, an industrial and administrative city. Pop. 625,000. From 1926 to 1991 the city was named Frunze. Former name (until 1926) **Pishpek**.

**Bi·sho** |'bēsHō| town in southern South Africa, the capital of the province of Eastern Cape, situated near the coast to the NE of Port Elizabeth. Pop. (with East London) 270,130.

**Bis·kra** |'biskrə| city in N Algeria, between the Sahara Desert and the Aurès Mts. Pop. 129,000. An oasis, then a resort, it is now a growing commercial and industrial center.

**Bis·marck** |'bizmärk| the state capital of North Dakota. Pop. 49,256. A terminus of the Northern Pacific Railroad, it took the name of the German chancellor in recognition of German financial support to the railroad.

**Bis·marck Archipelago** |'bizmärk| island group in the W Pacific, part of Papua New Guinea. Held by Germany from 1884 to World War I, it includes New Britain, New Ireland, and several hundred other islands.

**Bis·marck Sea** |'bizmärk| arm of the Pacific NE of New Guinea and N of New Britain.

**Bis·sa·gos Islands** |bə'sägəs| group of islands off the coast of Guinea-Bissau, W Africa.

**Bis·sau** |bi'sow| port city, the capital and largest city of Guinea-Bissau. Pop. 125,000.

**Bis·triţa** |'bēstrit,sä| commercial city in N Romania. Pop. 87,000.

**Bi·thyn·ia** |bə'THinēə| region of NW Asia Minor (present-day Turkey) W of ancient Paphlagonia, bordering the Black Sea and the Sea of Marmara.

**Bi·to·la** |bə'tawlə| (also **Bitolj**, formerly **Monastir**) historic commercial city in S Macedonia. Pop. 76,000.

**Bit·ter·root Range** |'bitə,rōōt| part of the Rocky Mts. in W Montana and E Idaho.

**Bi·wa, Lake** |'bē,wä| largest lake in Japan, just N of Kyoto, in central Honshu. It is noted for its resorts, fishing, and pearl industry.

**Biysk** |bēsk| (also **Biisk**) industrial port city on the Biya River in Siberia, E Russia. Pop. 234,000.

**Bi·zer·ta** |bə'zərtə| (also **Bizerte**) a seaport on the N coast of Tunisia. Pop. 94,500.

**Black Belt** |'blæk 'belt| agricultural district in central Alabama and Mississippi, named for its rich soils.

**Black·burn** |'blækbərn| industrial town in NW England, in Lancashire. Pop. 132,800.

**Black Country** |blæk| district of the English Midlands with heavy industry.

**Black Earth** |blæk 'ərTH| see CHERNOZEM region.

**Black Forest** |blæk| hilly wooded region of SW Germany, lying to the E of the Rhine valley. German name **Schwarzwald**.

**Black·heath** |'blæk,hēTH| historic common and suburban district of S London, England, chiefly in Lewisham. Wat Tyler's rebels camped here in 1381.

**Black Hills** |blæk| range of mountains in E Wyoming and W South Dakota. The highest point is Harney Peak (7,242 ft./2,207 m.); the range also includes the sculptured granite face of Mount Rushmore.

**Black Mesa** |blæk| upland in NE Arizona, home to many of the Navajo. The Hopi live on extensions to the S.

**Black Mountain** |blæk| resort town in W North Carolina, noted as the former site of avant-garde Black Mountain College. Pop. 5,418.

**Black Mountains** |blæk| range of the Appalachian Mts. in W North Carolina. Mount Mitchell (6684 ft./2039 m.) is the high point.

**Black·pool** |'blæk,pōōl| seaside resort in Lancashire, NW England. Pop. 144,500.

**Black River** |blæk| river that flows 300 mi./480 km. SE through Missouri and Arkansas, along the E edge of the Ozark Plateau.

**Blacks·burg** |'blæks,bərg| town in SW Virginia, in the Appalachian Mts., home to Virginia Polytechnic Institute. Pop. 34,590.

**Black Sea** |blæk| tideless, highly saline, and almost landlocked sea bounded by Ukraine, Russia, Georgia, Turkey, Bulgaria, and Romania, and connected to the Mediterranean through the strait of Bosporus and the Sea of Marmara.

**Black·stone River** |'blæk,stōn| river that flows 50 mi./80 km. S through Worcester, Massachusetts to Pawtucket, Rhode Island, below which it is called the Seekonk River. The Blackstone Valley was a site of early U.S. industrial development.

**Black War·ri·or River** |blæk 'wawryər| river that flows 178 mi./287 km. across N Alabama to join the Tombigbee River. Tuscaloosa and the Birmingham area lie along its course.

**Bla·go·ev·grad** |,blä'gōəvgräd| spa town in SW Bulgaria, in the Pirin Mts. Pop. 86,000. Blagoevgrad is built on the ruins of an ancient Thracian town.

**Bla·go·vesh·chensk** |,bləgəv'yᴀsHcHinsk| transportation center and city in E Siberia, SE Russia, near the Chinese border. Pop. 208,000.

**Blaine** |blān| city in SE Minnesota, a suburb N of Minneapolis. Pop. 38,975.

**Blan·tyre** |blæn'tir| the chief commercial and industrial city of Malawi. Pop. 331,600 (with Limbe, a town 5 mi./8 km. SE of Blantyre).

**Blar·ney** |'blärnē| village in County Cork, S Ireland, just NW of Cork. Those who kiss the Blarney Stone, at its castle, are said to then possess the power to cajole.

**Blas·ket Islands** |'blæskit| island group off the Dingle Peninsula in SW Ireland, in County Kerry, uninhabited since 1953.

**Blen·heim** |'blenəm| village in S Germany, site of a victory by British and Austrian troops, led by the Duke of Marlborough, over the French in 1704. The Duke took the village's name for his country seat in Woodstock, England.

**Bli·da** |'blēdə| (Arabic name **El Boulaïda**) city in N Algeria, SW of Algiers, at the feet of the Atlas Mts. Pop. 191,000. It is a famed agricultural and horticultural center.

**Block Island** |bläk| resort island in S Rhode Island, in the Atlantic at the E end of Long Island Sound.

**Bloem·fon·tein** |'blōōm,fän,tān| the capital of Free State and judicial capital of South Africa. Pop. 300,150. An industrial center, it is also called **Mangaung**.

**Blois** |blə'wä| historic and commercial town in central France, in the Loire valley.

Pop. 52,000. Blois is the capital of the Loire-et-Cher department.

**Bloom·field** |'blōōm,fēld| township in NE New Jersey, an industrial suburb N of Newark. Pop. 45,061.

**Bloom·ing·ton**[1] |'blōōmiNGtən| commercial city in central Illinois. Pop. 51,972.

**Bloom·ing·ton**[2] |'blōōmiNGtən| city in S central Indiana, home to Indiana University and to a noted limestone industry. Pop. 60,633.

**Bloom·ing·ton**[3] |'blōōmiNGtən| city in SE Minnesota, a suburb S of Minneapolis. It is home to the huge Mall of America. Pop. 86,335.

**Blooms·bury** |'blōōmz,berē| area of central London noted for its large squares and gardens and for its associations with the literary and artistic circle called the Bloomsbury Group. The British Museum is located here.

**Blue·fields** |'blōō,fēldz| port on the Mosquito Coast of Nicaragua, situated on an inlet of the Caribbean Sea. Pop. 18,000.

**Blue·grass State** |'blōō,græs| nickname for KENTUCKY, referring to the Bluegrass Region, a rich central plateau famed for its horse farms.

**Blue Grotto, the** |blōō 'grätō| cavern on the N shore of the Isle of Capri, in the Bay of Naples, Italy. Half filled with water, the grotto is famous for the unusual blue light inside.

**Blue Mosque** |blōō 'mäsk| (also **Sultan Ahmet Mosque**) mosque in Istanbul, Turkey, with six minarets, built 1609–16, regarded as one of the finest in the world, and a widely known symbol of the region and the Islamic world.

**Blue Mountains**[1] |blōō| section of the Great Dividing Range in New South Wales, Australia.

**Blue Mountains**[2] |blōō| range of mountains in E Jamaica.

**Blue Mountains**[3] |blōō| range of mountains running from central Oregon to SE Washington State in the U.S.

**Blue Nile** |blōō 'nīl| one of the two principal headwaters of the Nile. Rising from Lake Tana in NW Ethiopia, it flows some 1,000 mi./1,600 km. SW then NW into Sudan, where it meets the White Nile at Khartoum.

**Blue Ridge Mountains** |'blōō ,rij| range of the Appalachian Mts. in the E U.S., stretching from S Pennsylvania to N Georgia. Mount Mitchell is the highest peak, rising to a height of 6,684 ft./2,037 m.

**Blue Springs** |blōō| city in W central

Missouri, a residential suburb E of Kansas City. Pop. 40,153.

**Blu·me·nau** |blōōmə'now| commercial city in S Brazil, in an agricultural area in Santa Caterina state. Pop. 231,000. The culture of its 19th-century German settlers still dominates.

**Blythe·ville** |'blīvəl| city in NE Arkansas. Pop. 22,906.

**Boa Vis·ta** |'bōə 'vēsHtə| town in N Brazil, capital of the state of Roraima. Pop. 130,426.

**Bobo-Dioulasso** |'bōbō,dyōōlä'sō| commercial and industrial city in SW Burkina Faso. Pop. 269,000. It is an agricultural market and rail center.

**Bob·ruysk** |bäb'rōōisk| (also **Babruysk, Bobruisk**) city in Belarus. Pop. 223,000. It is a port on the Berezina River and an industrial center.

**Bo·ca Ra·ton** |,bōkə rə'tōn| city in SE Florida, on the Atlantic N of Fort Lauderdale. A noted resort, it also has varied industries. Pop. 61,492.

**Bo·chum** |'bōkHōōm| industrial city in the Ruhr valley, North Rhine–Westphalia, western Germany. Pop. 398,580.

**Bo·den·see** |'bōdn,zā| German name for Lake Constance (see CONSTANCE, LAKE).

**Bodh·ga·ya** |,bōd'gīə| (also **Buddh Gaya**) a village in the state of Bihar, NE India, where the Buddha attained enlightenment.

**Bod·nath** |bōd'nät| site of a massive Buddhist stupa in Nepal, E of Kathmandu, the biggest in Nepal and one of the biggest in the world.

**Bo·drum** |bō'drōōm| resort town on the Aegean coast of W Turkey, site of the ancient city of Halicarnassus.

**Boe·o·tia** |be'ōsHə| department of central Greece, to the N of the Gulf of Corinth, and a region of ancient Greece of which the chief city was Thebes. □ **Boeotian** adj. & n.

**Bo·fors** |'bōfawrs| town in S central Sweden. The eponymous antiaircraft gun was made here in a factory owned by Alfred Nobel, founder of the Nobel prizes. Bofors is a major armaments center.

**Bo·ga·lu·sa** |,bōgə'lōōsə| city in SE Louisiana, on the Pearl River, a forest industry and agricultural center. Pop. 14,280.

**Bo·gaz·köy** |,bō,(g)äz'koi| village in central Turkey, E of Ankara, on the site of ancient Hattusas, the Hittite capital of the 15th–13th centuries B.C.

**Bo·gor** |'bō,gawr| resort town in Indonesia, on NW Java, S of Djakarta, famous for its botanical gardens. Pop. 271,000.

**Bo·go·tá** |,bōgə'taw; ,bōgəgə'tä| the capital of Colombia, situated in the E Andes at about 8,560 ft./2,610 m. Pop. 4,921,200. It was founded by the Spanish in 1538 on the site of a pre-Columbian center of the Chibcha culture. Official name **Santa Fé de Bogotá.**

**Bo Hai** |'bō 'hī| (also **Po Hai**) a large inlet of the Yellow Sea, on the coast of E China. Also called **Gulf of Chihli.**

**Bo·he·mia** |bō'hēmēə| region forming the W part of the Czech Republic. Formerly a Slavic kingdom, it became a province of the newly formed Czechoslovakia by the Treaty of Versailles in 1919. The term *Bohemian,* referring to a subculture that chooses not to live by the standards of the dominant culture, derives from the popular 19th-century association of Bohemia with the Gypsies. □ **Bohemian** adj. & n.

**Bo·he·mi·an Forest** |bō'hēmēən| wooded mountain range along the boundary between Germany and the Czech Republic. Its highest peak is Arber, in Bavaria: 4,780 ft./1,457 m.

**Bo·hol** |bō'hawl| island lying to the N of Mindanao in the central Philippines; chief town, Tagbilaran.

**Bois de Bou·logne** |,bwä də bōō'lōn| park in W Paris, France. Covering 2,137 acres/865 hectares, it was formerly a royal hunting ground. It now comprises wooded areas, restaurants, lakes, two racetracks, and gardens.

**Boi·se** |'boisē; 'boizē| the state capital of Idaho, an administrative and commercial city. Pop. 125,738.

**Bo·ka·ro Steel City** |bō'kärō 'stēl| steel-producing city in E India, in the coalfields of Bihar state. Pop. 416,000. It has one of Asia's largest steel plants.

**Bo·kha·ra** |bō'kHärə| see BUKHORO, Uzbekistan.

**Boks·burg** |'bäks,bərg| city in NE South Africa, a gold-mining center E of Johannesburg. Pop. 196,000.

**Bole** |bōl| (also called **Bortala**) Kazakh town in Xinjiang, NW China, N of the Tian Shan range. Pop. 141,000.

**Bo·ling·brook** |'bōliNGbrōōk| village in NE Illinois, a suburb SW of Chicago. Pop. 40,843.

**Bo·lí·var, Pi·co** |'pēkō ,bō'lē,vär| peak in W Venezuela, in the Cordillera de Mérida, near the Colombian border, the highest in the country: 16,411 ft./5,002 m. It is part of a mountain called La Columna.

**Bo·liv·ia** |bə'livēə| landlocked republic in South America. Area: 424,162 sq.

Bolivia

mi./1,098,580 sq. km. Pop. 6,420,800; languages, Spanish (official), Aymara, Quechua. Capital and largest city: La Paz; legal capital and seat of the judiciary, Sucre. An Inca country, then until 1825 a Spanish colony, Bolivia depends on agriculture in the Altiplano, oil and gas, and mining. Political instability has held back development. □ **Bolivian** *adj. & n.*

**Bo·lo·gna** |bə'lōn(y)ə| commercial and industrial city in N Italy, capital of Emilia-Romagna region. Pop. 411,800. Its university, which dates from the 11th century, is the oldest in Europe.

**Bol·ton** |'bōltn| historic industrial city in NW England, in Greater Manchester. Pop. 253,300.

**Bol·za·no** |bawlt'sänō| commercial and resort city in NE Italy, capital of the Trentino–Alto Adige region. Pop. 100,380. German name **Bozen**

**Bo·ma** |'bōmə| port city in W Congo (formerly Zaire), on the Congo River estuary. Pop. 246,000. It was the capital of the Belgian Congo before 1926.

**Bom·bay** |bäm'bā| port city on the W coast of India, capital of the state of Maharashtra. Pop. 9,990,000. Official name (from 1995) **Mumbai**. It is a center of textile and other industries.

**Bo·mu River** |'bōmoo| (also **M'Bomou**) river that flows 500 mi./800 km. from NE Congo (formerly Zaire), to join the Uele River in forming the Ubangi River. It forms part of the border between Congo and the Central African Republic.

**Bon, Cape** |bän| peninsula of NE Tunisia, extending into the Mediterranean Sea.

**Bon·aire** |bə'ner| one of the two principal islands of the Netherlands Antilles (the other is Curaçao); chief town, Kralendijk. Pop. 10,190.

**Bo·nam·pak** |bə'näm,päk| ruined city of the Maya, found in the 1940s in the jungles of E Chiapas state, SE Mexico.

Its frescoes give much detail on Maya life.

**Bo·nan·za Creek** |bə'nænzə| stream in the W central Yukon Territory, near Dawson, site of the 1896 discovery that set off the Klondike gold rush.

**Bon·di** |'bändē| coastal resort in New South Wales, Australia, a suburb of Sydney. It is noted for its beach and surfing.

**Bon·doc** |bawn'dawk| peninsula in the Philippines, on S Luzon, bounded by Mompog Pass (W) and Ragay Gulf (E).

**Bône** |bōn| former name for ANNABA, Algeria.

**Bon·gor** |bäNG'gawr| commercial town in SW Chad, across the Logone River from Cameroon. Pop. 195,000.

**Bo·nin Islands** |'bōnən| (Japanese name **Ogasawara-gunto**) volcanic island group of Japan in the NW Pacific, S of Tokyo.

**Bonn** |bän; bawn| industrial and university city in the state of North Rhine–Westphalia in Germany. Pop. 296,240. From 1949 until the reunification of Germany in 1990 Bonn was the capital of the Federal Republic of Germany.

**Bon·ne·ville Dam** |'bänə,vil| hydroelectric dam built in the 1930s on the Columbia River, E of Portland, Oregon.

**Bon·ne·ville Salt Flats** |'bänə,vil| desert in NW Utah, W of the Great Salt Lake, noted as the site of automotive speed trials.

**Boot·heel** portion of the state of Missouri in the southeast corner, jutting down between Arkansas and Tennessee, having the appearance on a map of a bootheel.

**Boo·thia, Gulf of** |'boōTHēə| gulf in the Canadian Arctic, between the Boothia Peninsula and Baffin Island, in Nunavut.

**Boo·thia Peninsula** |'boōTHēə| peninsula of N Canada, in Nunavut, situated between Victoria and Baffin islands.

**Boot Hill** |boōt| name for a cemetery in several cowboy towns, such as Dodge City, Kansas, or Deadwood, South Dakota.

**Boo·tle** |'boōtl| industrial port town in NW England, a suburb of Liverpool on the Mersey River. Pop. 71,000.

**Bo·phu·tha·tswa·na** |,bōpoōtät'swänə| former homeland established in South Africa for the Tswana people, now part of North-West and Mpumalanga provinces.

**Bora-Bora** |'bawrə 'bawrə| island of the Society Islands group in French Polynesia.

**Bo·rås** |boō'raws| industrial city in SW Sweden, a textile center. Pop. 101,770.

**Bor·deaux** |bawr'dō| port of SW France on the Garonne River, capital of Aquitaine. Pop. 213,270. It is a center of the wine trade.

**Bor·ders** |'bawrdərz| general term for the lands on either side of the England-Scotland border, and, since 1975, name of a local government region on the Scottish side.

**Bor·der States** those US states that were slave states but did not secede from the Union during the Civil War, including Delaware, Maryland, Kentucky, and Missouri.

**Bo·rin·quén** |,bawrin'kän| local (Arawakan) name for Puerto Rico. Also, **Boriquén**.

**Bor·neo** |'bawrnēō| large island of the Malay Archipelago, comprising Kalimantan (a region of Indonesia), Sabah and Sarawak (states of Malaysia), and Brunei. □ **Bornean** adj.

**Born·holm** |'bawrn,hō(l)m| Danish island in the Baltic Sea, SE of Sweden.

**Bor·no** |'bawrnō| (also **Bornu**) state in NE Nigeria, bordering Chad, Niger, and Cameroon. Much of the historic kingdom of Bornu occupied its agricultural plains.

**Bo·ro·bu·dur** |,bōrəbōō'dŏŏr| (also **Boroboedoer**) vast Buddhist temple complex in Indonesia, on central Java. Built in the 8th or 9th century, it is the biggest religious monument in SE Asia.

**Bo·ro·di·no** |,bərədē'naw| village in W Russia, W of Moscow. It was the site of a major battle between Russian and French troops during the Napoleonic Wars, before Napoleon occupied Moscow.

**Bo·ro·vets** |'bawrnō,(y)vets| ski resort in the Rila Mts. of W Bulgaria.

**Bor·ro·me·an Islands** |,bawrə'mēən| four small islands in Lake Maggiore, in N Italy. Isola Bella, the largest, is site of the 17th-century Borromeo Palace, with spectacular terraced gardens.

**Borscht Belt** |bawrSHt| popular name for region of the Catskill Mts., in SE New York, famed for its Jewish resorts.

**Bor·stal** |'bawrstəl| village in SE England, near Rochester, Kent, that gave its name to a system of reformatories for young offenders.

**Bo·ru·jerd** |,bōrōō'yerd| (also **Burujird**) city in W Iran, in the Zagros Mountains. Pop. 201,000.

**Bose** |bōs| city in Guangxi, S China, on the You River. Pop. 275,000.

**Bos·kop** |'baws,kawp| town in South Africa, in the North-West province, where a skull fossil was found in 1913. The fossil is undated and morphologically shows no primitive features. At the time this find was regarded as representative of a distinct "Boskop race" but is now thought to be related to the San-Nama (Bushman-Hottentot) types.

**Bos·nia** |'bäznēə| **1** short for BOSNIA AND HERZEGOVINA. **2** a region in the Balkans forming the larger, N part of Bosnia and Herzegovina. □ **Bosnian** adj. & n.

Bosnia

**Bos·nia and Her·ze·go·vi·na** |'bäznēə ən ,hərtsəgō'vēnə| (also **Bosnia–Herzegovina**) country in the Balkans, formerly a constituent republic of Yugoslavia. Area: 19,748 sq. mi./51,128 sq. km. Pop. 4,365,000. Capital and largest city: Sarajevo. Almost landlocked, Bosnia and Herzegovina was long dominated by the Ottoman Empire, then by Austria-Hungary. It was part of Yugoslavia 1918–92. Ethnic warfare since independence has severly damaged its economy.

**Bos·po·rus** |'bäsp(ə)rəs| (also **Bosphorus**) strait connecting the Black Sea with the Sea of Marmara, and separating Europe from the Anatolian peninsula of W Asia. Istanbul is located at its S end.

**Bos·ra** |'bäsrə| (also called **Busra esh-Sham**) village in SW Syria, near the border with Jordan, site of the ruined city of Bostra, which was important in Roman times.

**Bos·sier City** |'bōZHər| city in NW Louisiana, on the Red River, just NE of Shreveport. Pop. 52,721. It is an oil and gas industry center.

**Bos·ton¹** |'bawstən| commercial port town in E England, in Lincolnshire. Pop. 26,000. Puritans left here in 1633 for Massachusetts Bay.

**Bos·ton²** |'bawstən| the state capital and largest city in Massachusetts. Pop. 574,280. □ **Bostonian** adj. & n.

**Bos·worth Field** |'bäzwərTH| site in central England, near Market Bosworth, Leicestershire, scene of the last battle (1485) of the Wars of the Roses, in which the Yorkist king Richard III was defeated.

**Bot·a·ny Bay** |'bătn-ē| inlet of the Tasman Sea in New South Wales, Australia, just S of Sydney. It was the site of Captain James Cook's landing in 1770 and of an early British penal settlement.

**Bo·tev Peak** |'baw,tef| mountain in Bulgaria, highest peak in the Balkan Mts.: 7,793 ft./2,376 m.

**Both·nia, Gulf of** |'bäтHnēə| N arm of the Baltic Sea, between Sweden and Finland.

**Bo·to·sa·ni** |bätəSHän(yə)| market town in NE Romania, on the Moldavian Plain, near the Ukrainian border, capital of Botosani county. Pop. 120,000.

**Bot·swa·na** |bät'swänə| landlocked republic in southern Africa. Area: 231,800 sq. mi./600,360 sq. km. Pop. 1,300,000. Languages, Setswana and English. Capital and largest city: Gaborone. Arid tableland, much of it part of the Kalahari Desert, dominates Botswana, which was the British colony of Bechuanaland from 1885 until 1966. Herding, agriculture, and mining are important. □ **Botswanan** *adj. & n.*

**Botswana**

**Bot·trop** |'baw,trawp| industrial city in western Germany, N of Essen. Pop. 119,000. It was formerly a center of coal production.

**Boua·ké** |bwä'kä| (also **Bwake**) commercial city in central Côte d'Ivoire, a rail- and textile-industry center. Pop. 390,000.

**Bou·cher·ville** |'bōōSHər,vil| city in S Quebec, a suburb NE of Montreal. Pop. 33,796.

**Bouches-du-Rhône** |,bōōSH dY 'rōn| department in SE France, on the Thône delta. Area: 1,974 sq. mi./5,112 sq. km. Pop. 1,750,000. The capital city is Marseilles.

**Bou·gain·ville** |'bōōgən,vil; 'bōgən,vil| volcanic island in the S Pacific, the largest of the Solomon Islands.

**Boul·der** |'bōldər| city in N central Colorado, NW of Denver, home to the University of Colorado. Pop. 83,312.

**Bou·logne** |bōō'lawn(yə)| ferry port and fishing town in N France. Pop. 44,240. Full name **Boulogne-sur-Mer.**

**Bound·a·ry Waters** |'bownd(ə)rē| region of NE Minnesota, along the Ontario border, famed as a canoeing center.

**Boun·ti·ful** |'bowntəfəl| city in N Utah, a suburb N of Salt Lake City. Pop. 36,659.

**Bour·bon County** |'bərbən| county in N central Kentucky, in the Bluegrass region, birthplace of the American whiskey type.

**Bour·bon Island** |'bōōrbən; bōōr'bawn| former name for the French Indian Ocean island of RÉUNION. It gave its name to the bourbon rose.

**Bour·bon·nais** |,bōōrbə'nä| former duchy and province of central France; chief town, Moulins.

**Bourges** |bōōrZH| city and capital of the department of Cher, in central France. Pop. 80,000. An industrial and transportation center, it has a section with numerous Renaissance buildings.

**Bour·gogne** |bōōr'gawn(yə)| French name for BURGUNDY.

**Bourne·mouth** |'bawrnməтH; 'bōōrnməтH| resort on the S coast of England, a unitary council traditionally in Dorset. Pop. 154,400.

**Bourse** |bōōrs| (full name **Palais de la Bourse**) the stock exchange in Paris, France, on the Rue Vivienne.

**Bou·vet Island** |'bōōvə| uninhabited island in the S Atlantic, a former whaling station and dependency of Norway.

**Bow** |bō| (full name **St. Mary-le-Bow**) parish in E central London, England, in Cheapside, within the sound of whose bells the true Cockney is said to be born.

**Bow·ery** |'bow(ə)rē| street and district in lower Manhattan, New York City, historically associated with vagrant men and cheap hotels.

**Bow·ie** |'bōē| town in W central Maryland, a suburb NE of Washington, D.C. Pop. 37,589.

**Bowl·ing Green**[1] |bōliNG 'grēn| city in W central Kentucky. Pop. 40,641.

**Bowl·ing Green**[2] |bōliNG 'grēn| historic park in S Manhattan, New York City, just N of the Battery.

**Bow River** |bō| river that flows 315 mi./507 km. from the Rocky Mts. SE across Alberta to the South Saskatchewan River. Calgary lies on it.

**Boyne River** |boin| river in E Ireland that flows NE from the Bog of Allen to the Irish Sea near Drogheda, near which, in 1690, the Protestant army of William of Orange defeated Catholic supporters of James II.

**Boyn·ton Beach** |'bointən| resort city in SE Florida. Pop. 46,194.

**Boys Town** |boiz| village in E central Nebraska, just W of Omaha, famed as a home for troubled youth. Pop. 794.

**Boz·caa·da** |ˌbōzjə'dä| island off NW Turkey, in the Aegean Sea just S of the Dardanelles. As ancient **Tenedos**, it was a base for the Persian attack on Greece under Xerxes, and according to legend was the Greek base against nearby Troy.

**Boze·man** |'bōzmən| city in SW Montana. Pop. 22,660.

**Bra·bant** |brə'bænt| former duchy in W Europe, lying between the Meuse and Scheldt rivers. Its capital was Brussels. It is now divided into two provinces in two countries: North Brabant in the Netherlands, of which the capital is 's-Hertogenbosch; and Brabant in Belgium, of which the capital remains Brussels.

**Bra·den·ton** |'brādntən| city in SW Florida, noted as a resort and for citrus processing. Pop. 43,779.

**Brad·ford** |'brædfərd| industrial city, a longtime textile center, in N England, traditionally in Yorkshire. Pop. 449,100.

**Brae·mar** |brā'mär| historic village in NE Scotland, in the Grampian region, where the first Jacobite Rising began in 1715. It is famous for its summer Highland Games.

**Bra·ga** |'brägə| city in N Portugal, capital of a mountainous district of the same name. Pop. 90,535.

**Bra·gan·za** |brə'gäNs| city in NE Portugal, capital of a mountainous district of the same name. Pop. 16,550. It was the original seat of the Braganza dynasty. Portuguese name **Bragança**.

**Brah·ma·pu·tra Ri·ver** |ˌbrämə'pōŏtrə| river in S Asia, rising in the Himalayas and flowing 1,800 mi./2,900 km. through Tibet, NE India, and Bangladesh, to join the Ganges at its delta on the Bay of Bengal.

**Bră·i·la** |brə'ēlə| industrial city and port on the Danube, in E Romania. Pop. 236,300.

**Brain·tree** |'brān,trē| town in E Massachusetts, a suburb S of Boston. Pop. 32,836.

**Bramp·ton** |'bræmtən| city in S Ontario, an industrial and residential suburb W of Toronto. Pop. 234,445.

**Bran·den·burg** |'brændən,bərg| state of NE Germany. Capital: Potsdam. The modern state corresponds to the W part of the former Prussian electorate, of which the E part was ceded to Poland after World War II.

**Bran·den·burg Gate** |'brændən,bərg| only surviving city gate of Berlin (built

1788–91). It was designed as a triumphal arch commemorating the military successes of Prussia, especially of Frederick the Great (1712–86). After the construction of the Berlin Wall in 1961 it stood just behind the Wall in East Berlin. German name **Brandenburgertor**.

**Bran·don** |'brændən| city in SW Manitoba. Pop. 38,567.

**Bran·dy·wine Creek** |'brændē,wīn| historic stream in SE Pennsylvania and N Delaware, birthplace of the U.S. gunpowder industry.

**Bran·ford** |'brænfərd| town in S central Connecticut, a suburb E of New Haven. Pop. 27,603.

**Bran·son** |'brænsən| city in SW Missouri, on the Ozark Plateau, noted as a resort based on country music. Pop. 3,706.

**Brant·ford** |'bræntfərd| industrial city in S Ontario. Pop. 81,997.

**Bra·sí·lia** |brə'zilyə| the capital, since 1960, of Brazil. Pop. 1,601,100. Designed by Lúcio Costa in 1956, the city was located in the center of the country with the intention of drawing people away from the crowded coastal areas.

**Bra·şov** |brə'sHawv| second-largest city of Romania, an industrial and transportation center in the Carpathians. Pop. 352,640. It belonged to Hungary until after World War I, and was ceded to Romania in 1920. Hungarian name **Brassó**.

**Bras·só** |'bræsō| Hungarian name for BRAşOV, Romania.

**Bra·ti·sla·va** |ˌbrätə'slävə| the capital of Slovakia, an industrial port on the Danube River. Pop. 441,450. From 1526 to 1784 it was the capital of Hungary. German name **Pressburg**; Hungarian name **Pozsony**.

**Bratsk** |brätsk| city in central Siberia, E Russia, on the Angara River. Pop. 258,000.

**Brat·tle·bo·ro** |'brædl,bərə| town in SE Vermont, on the Connecticut River. Pop. 12,241.

**Braun·schweig** |'brown,sHfik| German name for BRUNSWICK.

**Bray**[1] |brā| village in S England, in Berkshire, on the Thames River, setting for the ballad "The Vicar of Bray," about 16th-century religious upheavals.

**Bray**[2] |brā| resort and port town in E Ireland, in County Wicklow, S of Dublin, on the Irish Sea. Pop. 25,000.

**Bra·zil** |brə'zil| the largest country in South America. Area: 3.29 million sq. mi./8.51 million sq. km. Pop. 146,825,475 (1991); language, Portuguese. Capital: Brasilia. Largest city: São Paulo. Portuguese name

BRAZIL

N

State/Territory boundary
■ Capital city

0   500   1000 km
0   250   500   750 miles

Boa
Vista ●
RORAIMA
AMAPÁ
Macapá ●
Belém ●
São Luís ●
Manaus ●
PARÁ
Fortaleza ●
MARANHÃO
Teresina ●
RÍO GRANDE
DO NORTE
CEARÁ
● Natal
AMAZONAS
PIAUI
PARAÍBA
João Pessoa ●
PERNAMBUCO ● Recife
ACRE
Río
Branco ●
Porto
Velho ●
RONDÔNIA
TOCANTINS
Palmas ●
● Maceió
ALAGOAS
Aracajú ●
SERGIPE
MATO
GROSSO
BAHIA
● Salvador
Cuiabá ●
GOIÁS
Brasília FD
Goiânia ●
MINAS GERAIS
MATO GROSSO
DO SUL
Belo Horizonte ●
ESPÍRITO
SANTO
Campo
Grande ●
SÃO
PAULO
Vitória ●
São
Paulo ●
RÍO DE JANEIRO
● Río de Janeiro
PARANÁ
Curitiba ●
SANTA
CATARINA
● Florianópolis
RÍO GRANDE
DO SUL
Pôrto Alegre ●

FD   FEDERAL DISTRICT

**Brasil.** The fifth-largest country in the world, Brazil was inhabited by Tupi and Guarani peoples, then colonized by the Portuguese, gaining independence in 1822. The N half lies in the Amazon basin, and the interior is largely undeveloped. Tropical and plains agriculture, mining, and industry are all important. The population is diverse. □ **Brazilian** *adj. & n.*

**Braz·os River** |'bræzəs| river that flows 840 mi./1350 km. SE across Texas, from the Panhandle to the Gulf of Mexico. The cities at its mouth are called collectively Brazosport.

**Braz·za·ville** |'bräzə,vil| the capital of the Republic of the Congo, an industrial port on the Congo River. Pop. 2,936,000. It was founded in 1880 by the French explorer Savorgnan de Brazza (1852–1905) and was

capital of French Equatorial Africa from 1910 to 1958.

**Brea** |breə| city in S California, an oil and industrial center E of Los Angeles. Pop. 32,873.

**Bread Bas·ket of Amer·ica** the Midwestern US states that are major producers of grain products.

**Brecon·shire** |'brekən,SHir; 'brekənSHər| (also **Brecknockshire**) a former county of S central Wales. It was divided between Powys and Gwent in 1974.

**Bre·da** |brä'dä; 'brädə| historic manufacturing town in the SW Netherlands. Pop. 124,800.

**Bre·genz** |'brägents| city in W Austria, on the E shores of Lake Constance. Pop. 27,240. It is the capital of the state of Vorarlberg.

**Breizh** |brezH| Breton name for BRITTANY.

**Bre·men** |'brämən; 'bremən| **1** state of NE Germany. Divided into two parts, which center on the city of Bremen and the port of Bremerhaven, it is surrounded by the state of Lower Saxony. **2** its capital, an industrial city linked by the Weser River to the port of Bremerhaven and the North Sea. Pop. 537,600.

**Brem·er·ha·ven** |'bremər,hävən| (formerly **Wesermünde**) seaport in NW Germany, on the North Sea coast N of Bremen. Pop. 131,000. Bremerhaven is one of the largest seaports and fishing centers in Europe. The first regular shipping service between the U.S. and Europe began here.

**Brem·er·ton** |'bremərtən| city in W central Washington, on Puget Sound, home to large naval shipyards. Pop. 38,142.

**Bren·ner Pass** |'brenər| Alpine pass at the border between Austria and Italy, on the route between Innsbruck and Bolzano, at an altitude of 4,450 ft./1,371 m.

**Brent** |brent| largely residential borough of NW Greater London, England. Pop. 226,000. Wembley stadium is here.

**Brent·ford** |'brentfərd| suburban community in S England, within the Greater London borough of Hounslow, N of the Thames River.

**Brent·wood**[1] |'brent,wŏŏd| town in SE England, a suburb in Essex, E of London. Pop. 51,000.

**Brent·wood**[2] |'brent,wŏŏd| affluent residential section of W Los Angeles, California.

**Brent·wood**[3] |'brent,wŏŏd| village in central Long Island, New York. Pop. 45,218.

**Bre·scia** |'bräshə| industrial city in Lombardy, in N Italy. Pop. 196,770.

**Bres·lau** |'bres,low| German name for Wrocław, Poland.

**Brest**[1] |brest| river port and industrial city in Belarus, situated close to the border with Poland. Pop. 268,800. A peace treaty between Germany and Russia was signed here in March 1918. Former name (until 1921) **Brest-Litovsk**. Polish name **Brześć nad Bugiem**.

**Brest**[2] |brest| port and naval base on the Atlantic coast of Brittany, in NW France. Pop. 153,100.

**Bre·tagne** |brə'tänyə| French name for Brittany.

**Bret·ton Woods** |'bretn| resort in the White Mts. of N central New Hampshire, noted as the site of United Nations conferences at the end of World War II.

**Bre·vard County** |brə'värd| county in E central Florida, on the Atlantic, the site of Cape Canaveral and large citrus and resort industries. Pop. 398,978.

**Bridge of Sighs** |'sīz| bridge across a canal in Venice, Italy, so called because prisoners were led across it between the Ducal Palace and the nearby prison. Italian name **Ponte dei Sospiri**.

**Bridge·port** |'brij,pawrt| industrial city in SW Connecticut, on Long Island Sound. Pop. 141,686.

**Bridge·town** |'brij,town| the capital of Barbados, a port on the S coast. Pop. 6,720.

**Brie** |brē| region in N France, E of Paris, between the Seine and the Marne rivers. The area is famous for its soft cheese.

**Brigh·ton** |'britn| resort town on the S coast of England, in East Sussex. Pop. 133,400. It was patronized by the Prince of Wales (later George IV), and is noted for its Regency architecture, as well as for its pleasure pier.

**Brigh·ton Beach** |'britn| section of S Brooklyn, New York, E of Coney Island, famed for its Jewish community, and now home to a large Russian immigrant population.

**Brin·di·si** |'brindizē| capital of Brindisi province, a port in SE Italy, on the Adriatic Sea. Pop. 93,000. It was the S terminus of the Appian Way, and a historic link between Italy and the E Mediterranean.

**Bris·bane** |'brizbən; 'briz,bān| the capital of Queensland, Australia, an industrial port on the E coast. Pop. 1,273,500.

**Bris·tol**[1] |'bristəl| industrial city and township in W central Connecticut. Pop. 60,640.

**Bris·tol**[2] |'bristəl| city in SW England. Pop. 370,300. Situated on the Avon River about 6 mi./10 km. from the Bristol Channel, it has been a leading port since the 12th century, and was key in the exploration and settling of North America.

**Bris·tol**[3] |'bristəl| industrial city in E Tennessee, adjoining Bristol, Virginia. Pop. 23,421.

**Bris·tol Channel** |'bristəl| wide inlet of the Atlantic between S Wales and the SW peninsula of England, narrowing into the estuary of the Severn River.

**Brit·ain** |'britn| the island containing England, Wales, and Scotland, and including the small adjacent islands. The name is broadly synonymous with Great Britain, but the longer form is more usual for the political unit. See also Great Britain. □ **British** *adj. & n.* **Britisher** *n.*

**Bri·tan·nia** Latin name of the Roman province, later applied as a literary term for the entire island of Britain or for the British Empire. Also used of the personification of Great Britain, depicted as a seated woman holding a trident and wearing a helmet.

**Brit·ish Ant·arc·tic Territory** |ˌbritish æntär(k)tik| that part of Antarctica claimed by Britain. Designated in 1962 from territory that was formerly part of the Falkland Islands Dependencies, it includes some 150,058 sq. mi./388,500 sq. km. of the continent of Antarctica as well as the South Orkney and South Shetland islands in the South Atlantic.

**Brit·ish Co·lum·bia** |ˌbritish kə'ləmbēə| province on the W coast of Canada. Area: 365,947 sq. mi./947,800 sq. km. Pop. 3,282,061. Capital: Victoria. Largest city: Vancouver. Formed in 1866 by the union of Vancouver Island (a former British colony) and the mainland area, then called New Caledonia, the province includes the Queen Charlotte Islands. Forest industries, tourism and recreation, fishing, mining, hydroelectric power, and manufacturing are all important.

**Brit·ish Gui·ana** |ˌbritish ˌgī'änə| name until 1966 for GUYANA.

**Brit·ish Hon·du·ras** |ˌbritish hän'd☉☉rəs| name until 1973 for BELIZE.

**Brit·ish In·dia** |ˌbritish 'indēə| that part of the Indian subcontinent administered by the British from 1765, when the East India Company acquired control over Bengal, until 1947, when India became independent and Pakistan was created. By 1850 British India was coterminous with India's boundaries in the W and N and by 1885 it included Burma in the E. The period of British rule was known as the Raj. See also INDIA.

**Brit·ish In·di·an Ocean Territory** |'british 'indēən 'ōsHən| British dependency in the Indian Ocean, comprising the islands of the Chagos Archipelago and (until 1976) some other groups now belonging to the Seychelles. Ceded to Britain by France in 1814, the islands became a separate dependency in 1965. There are no permanent inhabitants, but British and U.S. naval personnel occupy the island of Diego Garcia.

**Brit·ish Isles** |ˌbritish 'īlz| group of islands lying off the coast of NW Europe, from which they are separated by the North Sea or the English Channel. They include Britain, Ireland, the Isle of Man, the He-brides, the Orkney Islands, the Shetland Islands, the Scilly Isles, and the Channel Islands.

**Brit·ish North Amer·i·ca** |'british ˌnawrTH ə'merəkə| term for British possessions in North America after the U.S. gained independence. In 1867 most became parts of Canada.

**Brit·ish So·ma·li·land** |ˌbritish sə'mälēˌlænd| former British protectorate established on the Somali coast of E Africa in 1884. In 1960 it united with former Italian territory to form the independent republic of Somalia.

**Brit·ish Vir·gin Islands** |'british ˌvərjən| see VIRGIN ISLANDS.

**Brit·tany** |'britn-ē| region and former duchy of NW France, forming a peninsula between the Bay of Biscay and the English Channel. It was occupied in the 5th and 6th centuries by Celtic Britons fleeing the Saxons, and was not incorporated into France until 1532. The Breton language is still spoken widely here. French name **Bretagne**. Breton name **Breizh**. □ **Breton** adj. & n.

**Brive-la-Gaillard** |ˌbrēv lä gī'yär(d)| market town in SW France, E of Périgueux. Pop. 53,000.

**Brix·ton** |'brikstən| district of S London, England, in Lambeth borough, home to the major black community in the city.

**Br·no** |'bərnō| industrial city in the Czech Republic. Pop. 388,000. It is the capital of Moravia. German name **Brünn**.

**Broads** |brawdz| often **the Norfolk Broads** a network of shallow freshwater lakes, traversed by slow-moving rivers, in an area of Norfolk and Suffolk. They were formed by the gradual natural flooding of medieval peat diggings.

**Broad·stairs** |'brawd,sterz| coastal resort town in SE England, in the Isle of Thanet, Kent, associated with Charles Dickens, who lived here. Pop. 23,000.

**Broad·way** |'brawd,wā| street traversing the length of Manhattan, New York. It is famous for its theater district, and its name has become synonymous with the New York professional theater business. It is also known as the Great White Way, in reference to its brilliant illuminated theater marquees and other signs.

**Brock·en** |'bräkən| peak in the Harz Mts. of N central Germany, rising to 3,747 ft./1,143 m. It is noted for the phenomenon of the Brocken specter, a cloud effect, and for witches' revels that reputedly took place here on Walpurgis night.

**Brock·ton** |'bräktən| industrial city in SE Massachusetts, S of Boston, noted especially for shoe manufacture. Pop. 92,788.

**Bro·ken Ar·row** |'brōkən 'ærō| city in NE Oklahoma, a suburb SE of Tulsa. Pop. 58,043.

**Brok·en Hill**[1] |'brōkən| town in New South Wales, Australia. Pop. 23,260. It is a center of lead, silver and zinc mining.

**Brok·en Hill**[2] |brōkən| former name (1904–65) for KABWE, Zambia.

**Brom·berg** |'bräm,bərg| German name for BYDGOSZCZ, Poland.

**Brom·ley** |'brämlē| residential borough of SE Great London, England. Pop. 282,000. On the Kent border, it includes the site of the former Crystal Palace.

**Bronx, the** |bräNGks| largely residential and industrial borough in NE New York City. It is the only part of the city on the mainland, and is coextensive with Bronx County. Pop. 1,203,789. □ **Bronx-ite** n.

**Brook Farm** |'brʊk 'färm| historic commune that existed in the 1840s in West Roxbury, now a SW section of Boston, Massachusetts, associated with Margaret Fuller and other writers.

**Brook·field** |'brʊk,fēld| city in SE Wisconsin, a suburb W of Milwaukee. Pop. 35,184.

**Brook·ha·ven** |'brʊk,hāvən| town in E Long Island, New York, including Brookhaven, Stony Brook, and other villages. It is home to a noted nuclear laboratory. Pop. 407,779.

**Brook·lands** |'brʊklən(d)z| motor-racing circuit near Weybridge in Surrey, England, opened in 1907. During World War II the course was converted for aircraft manufacture.

**Brook·line** |'brʊk,līn| town in E Massachusetts, a suburb on the W side of Boston and almost surrounded by the city. Pop. 54,718.

**Brook·lyn** |'brʊklən| largely residential and the most populous borough of New York City, coextensive with Kings County, at the SW corner of Long Island. It is famed for its neighborhoods. Pop. 2,300,664. □ **Brooklynite** n.

**Brook·lyn Bridge** |'brʊklən| suspension bridge between S Manhattan and N Brooklyn, New York City. Completed in 1883, it was one of the period's engineering marvels, and is celebrated in art and literature.

**Brook·lyn Park** |'brʊklən| city in SE Min-

nesota, a suburb N of Minneapolis. Pop. 56,381.

**Brooks Range** |brʊks| mountain chain that lies across N Alaska. It is the NW extreme of the Rocky Mts., and the North Slope lies on its N.

**Bros·sard** |braw'sär| city in S Quebec, a suburb E of Montreal, across the Saint Lawrence River. Pop. 64,793.

**Brow·ard County** |'browərd| county in SE Florida, on the Atlantic, N of Miami. Fort Lauderdale is its seat. Pop. 1,255,488.

**Browns Ferry** |brownz| locality on the Tennessee River in N Alabama, site of a major nuclear power plant.

**Browns·ville**[1] |'brownz,vil| section of E Brooklyn, New York, noted in the early 20th century for its Jewish community, today a struggling inner-city neighborhood. Local name the 'Ville.

**Browns·ville**[2] |'brownz,vil| city in S Texas, on the Rio Grande and the Mexican border. Pop. 98,962.

**Bruce Peninsula** |brōōs| peninsula in S Ontario that extends NW across Lake Huron, separating Georgian Bay, to the N, from the main body.

**Bruges** |brōōzH| city in NW Belgium, capital of the province of West Flanders. Pop. 117,000. A center of the Flemish textile trade until the 15th century, it is a well-preserved medieval city surrounded by canals. Flemish name **Brugge**.

**Brug·ge** |'brykə; 'brōōgə| Flemish name for BRUGES, Belgium.

**Brum** |brəm| Brit. an informal name for the city of Birmingham, England, an abbreviation of the dialectical form of the city's name, **Brummagemo**.

**Bru·nei** |brōō'nī| oil-rich sultanate on the NW coast of Borneo. Area: 2,226 sq. mi./5,765 sq. km. Pop. 264,000. Languages, Malay, English, Chinese. Capital: Bandar Seri Begawan. Official name **Brunei Darussalam**. □ **Bruneian** adj. & n.

**Brunei**

**Bruns·wick**[1] |'brənzwik| **1** former duchy and state of Germany, mostly incorporated into Lower Saxony. German name **Braunschweig. 2** the capital of this former duchy, an industrial city in Lower Saxony, Germany. Pop. 259,130.

**Bruns·wick**[2] |'brənzwik| town in SW Maine, home to Bowdoin College. Pop. 20,906.

**Brus·sels** |'brəsəlz| the capital of Belgium and of the province of Brabant. Pop. 954,000. It is a major European commercial, financial, and administrative center. The headquarters of the European Commission is here. French name **Bruxelles**; Flemish name **Brussel**.

**Brux·elles** |brʏ(k)'sel| French name for BRUSSELS, Belgium.

**Bry·an** |'brīən| city in E central Texas. Pop. 55,002.

**Bry·ansk** |brē'änsk| industrial city in European Russia, SW of Moscow, on the Desna River. Pop. 456,000.

**Bryce Canyon** |brīs| region in S central Utah, site of a national park noted for spectacular rock formations.

**Brześć nad Bu·giem** |bə'zhesch näd 'boog,yem| Polish name for BREST, Belarus.

**Bu·bas·tis** |byoo'bæstəs| city of ancient N Egypt, in the Nile Delta, near present-day Zagazig. It has been much excavated.

**Bu·ca·ra·man·ga** |,bookərə'mänggə| commercial city in N central Colombia. Pop. 353,000. It is in a noted coffee- and tobacco-producing region.

**Bu·cha·rest** |'b(y)ooka,rest| the capital of Romania and former capital of Wallachia. Pop. 2,343,800. A cultural and industrial center, it was founded in the 14th century on the trade route between Europe and Constantinople. Romanian name **Bu·curești**.

**Bu·chen·wald** |'bookHən,wält| village in central Germany, near Weimar. It was the site of a Nazi concentration camp during World War II.

**Buck·eye State** |'bək,ī| nickname for OHIO.

**Buck·ing·ham Palace** |'bəkiNGem; 'bəkiNG,hæm| official residence of the British monarch, in central London, in Westminster, on the W of St. James's Park and just W of the Houses of Parliament.

**Buck·ing·ham·shire** |'bəkiNGəm,sHir; 'bəkiNGəmsHər| county of central England; county seat, Aylesbury. Abbreviation: **Bucks.**

**Bucks County** |bəks| county in SE Penn-

sylvania, on the Delaware River, noted for its affluent Philadelphia suburbs and its artists' colonies. Its seat is Doylestown. Pop. 541,174.

**Bu·cu·rești** |,bookoo'resHtē| Romanian name for BUCHAREST.

**Bu·da·pest** |'b(y)oodə,pest; 'boodə,pesHt| the capital, largest city, and commercial, industrial, and cultural center of Hungary. Pop. 2,000,000. The city was formed in 1873 by the union of the hilly city of Buda on the W bank of the Danube River with the low-lying city of Pest on the E.

**Bud·weis** |'boot,vīs| German name for ČESKÉ BUD JOVICE, Czech Republic. It gave this name to a type of beer.

**Bue·na Park** |,byoonə 'pärk| city in S California, SE of Los Angeles. Its tourist attractions include Knott's Berry Farm, a famous theme park. Pop. 68,784.

**Bue·na·ven·tu·ra** |,bwänəven't(y)oorə| the chief Pacific port of Colombia. Pop. 122,500.

**Bue·na Vis·ta** |,bwānə 'vēstə| village in N Mexico, in Coahuila state, near Saltillo, where U.S. forces under Zachary Taylor won a major battle against Mexican forces under Santa Anna in February 1847.

**Bue·nos Ai·res** |'bwänəs ,ærēz| the capital, largest city, commercial and industrial center, and chief port of Argentina, on the Plata River. Pop. 2,961,000.

**Buf·fa·lo** |'bəfə,lō| industrial city in W New York. Pop. 328,120. Situated at the E end of Lake Erie, it is a major port on the Great Lakes–St. Lawrence Seaway.

**Buf·fa·lo River** |'bəfə,lō| river that flows 132 mi./213 km. through the Ozark Plateau in NW Arkansas and is a designated national preserve.

**Bug River** |boog| (also **Western Bug River**) river (481 mi./774 km.) in E central Poland that rises in SW central Ukraine and flows into the Vistula River near Warsaw.

**Bu·gan·da** |b(y)oo'gændə| former kingdom in E Africa, now part of UGANDA. It was centered around Kampala, N of Lake Victoria.

**Bu·jum·bu·ra** |,boojəm'boorə| the capital of Burundi, at the NE end of Lake Tanganyika. Pop. 235,440. It was known as Usumbura until 1962.

**Bu·ka·vu** |boo'kävoo| town in E Congo (formerly Zaire), S of Lake Kivu. Pop. 210,000. A commercial and tourist center, it was formerly called Costermansville.

**Bu·kho·ro** |bə'kHärə| (also **Bukhara, Bokhara**) city in the central Asian republic of Uzbekistan. Pop. 246,200. In an extensive cotton-growing district, it is one of the oldest trade centers in central Asia, and is also noted for the production of karakul fleeces.

**Bu·ko·vi·na** |ˌbo͞okəˈvēnə| region of SE Europe in the Carpathians, divided between Romania and Ukraine. Formerly a province of Moldavia, it was ceded to Austria by the Turks in 1775. After World War I it was made part of Romania, the N part being incorporated into the Ukrainian SSR in World War II.

**Bu·la·wa·yo** |ˌbo͞oləˈwī,ō| industrial and commercial city in W Zimbabwe, the second-largest in the country. Pop. 620,940.

**Bul·gar·ia** |ˌbəlˈgerēə| republic in SE Europe, on the W shore of the Black Sea. Area: 42,840 sq. mi./110,912 sq. km. Pop. 8,798,000. Capital and largest city: Sofia. Language: Bulgarian. The Balkan Mts. traverse Bulgaria, which was Turkish-dominated from the 14th through the late 19th century. Independence was achieved in 1908. Agriculture has been joined since World War II by industry as economic mainstays. □ **Bulgarian** adj. & n. **Bulgar** n.

**Bulgaria**

**Bull·head City** |ˈbo͞ol,hed| city in NW Arizona, on the Colorado River, a resort and casino center. Pop. 21,951.

**Bull Run** |bo͞ol| small river in E Virginia, scene of two Confederate victories (also called the battles of Manassas), in 1861 and 1862, during the Civil War.

**Bun·bury** |ˈbənbərē| seaport and resort to the S of Perth in Western Australia. Pop. 24,000.

**Bun·combe County** |ˈbəngəm| county in the Blue Ridge Mts. of W North Carolina. Its seat is Asheville. Pop. 174,821. The term *bunkum* or *bunk* arose from a long, inconsequential speech made by the area's congressman in the 1820s.

**Bun·ker Hill** |ˌbəNGkər| hill in the Charlestown section of N Boston, Massa-

chusetts. The 1775 battle of Bunker Hill was actually fought on nearby Breed's Hill.

**Bur·bank** |ˈbər,baeNGk| city in S California, on the N side of Los Angeles. Pop. 93,640. It is a center of the film, television, and aerospace industries.

**Bur·gas** |bo͞orˈgäs| industrial port and resort in SE Bulgaria, on the Black Sea. Pop. 226,120.

**Bur·gen·land** |ˈbo͞orgən,länt| state of E Austria. Capital: Eisenstadt.

**Bur·gos** |ˈbo͞or,gōs| town in N Spain. Pop. 169,280. It was the capital of Castile during the 11th century, and the official seat of Franco's Nationalist government (1936-39).

**Bur·gun·dy** |ˈbərgəndē| region and former duchy of E central France, centered on Dijon. French name **Bourgogne**. □ **Burgundian** adj. & n.

**Bur·han·pur** |bərˈhän,po͞or| historic city in W central India, in Madhya Pradesh state. Pop. 173,000.

**Bur·ki·na Fa·so** |bo͞orˈkēnə ˈfäsō| (or **Burkina**) landlocked republic in W Africa, in the Sahel. Area: 105,870 sq. mi./274,200 sq. km. Pop. 9,271,000. Official language, French. Capital and largest city: Ouagadougou. A French protectorate from 1898, it became an autonomous republic within the French Community in 1958 and a fully independent republic in 1960. Its economy is based largely on subsistence farming. Former name (until 1984) UPPER VOLTA. □ **Burkinan** adj. & n. **Burkinabè** adj. & n.

**Burkina**

**Bur·lin·game** |ˈbərlən,gām| city in N central California, on San Francisco Bay, a suburb S of San Francisco. Pop. 26,801.

**Bur·ling·ton**[1] |ˈbərliNGtən| city in N central North Carolina, noted as a textile center. Pop. 39,498.

**Bur·ling·ton**[2] |ˈbərliNGtən| city in S Ontario, on Lake Ontario SW of Toronto. Pop. 129,600.

**Bur·ling·ton³** |'bərliNGtən| largest city in Vermont, in the NW part, on Lake Champlain. Pop. 39,127.

**Bur·ma** |'bərmə| country in SE Asia, on the Bay of Bengal. Area: 261,220 sq. mi./676,560 sq. km. Pop. 42,528,000. Language, Burmese. Capital and largest city: Rangoon (Yangon). Official name (since 1989) **Union of Myanmar**; also called **Myanmar**. In NW Indochina, Burma is dominated by the Irrawaddy River. It has a monsoonal climate, and grows rice, teak, and other forest and tropical crops. Mining and oil are also important. The army has controlled Burman politics since 1962. □ **Burmese** *adj. & n.* **Burman** *adj.*

**Burma**

**Bur·ma Road** |'bərmə| route linking Lashio in Burma to Kunming in China, covering 717 mi./1,154 km. Completed in 1939, it was built by the Chinese in response to the Japanese occupation of the Chinese coast, to serve as a supply route to the interior.

**Bur·na·by** |'bərnəbē| municipality in SW British Columbia, an industrial and residential center just E of Vancouver. Pop. 158,858.

**Burn·ley** |'bərnlē| industrial town in NW England, in Lancashire, N of Manchester. Pop. 89,000.

**Burns·ville** |'bərnz,vil| city in SE Minnesota, a suburb S of Minneapolis. Pop. 51,288.

**Bur·sa** |'bərsə| city in NW Turkey, capital of a province of the same name. Pop. 834,580. It was the capital of the Ottoman Empire 1326–1402.

**Burton-upon-Trent** |'bərtn ə,pän 'trent| town in W central England, in Staffordshire, on the Trent River NE of Birmingham. Pop. 59,600. It is noted for its breweries.

**Bu·run·di** |bə'rŏŏndē| central African republic, on the E side of Lake Tanganyika, to the S of Rwanda. Area: 10,747 sq.

mi./27,834 sq. km. Pop. 5,800,000. Languages, French and Kirundi. Capital and largest city: Bujumbura. Independent since 1962, Burundi has been torn by strife between its agricultural Hutu majority and the more urban Tutsi minority. □ **Burundian** *adj. & n.*

**Burundi**

**Bury** |'berē| industrial town in NW England, in Greater Manchester, noted for its textile and paper industries. Pop. 61,000.

**Bur·yat·ia** |bŏŏr'yätyə| (also **Buryat Republic**) an autonomous republic in SE Russia, between Lake Baikal and the Mongolian border. Pop. 1,049,000. Capital: Ulan-Ude.

**Bury Saint Ed·munds** |,berē sənt 'edmən(d)z| historic commercial town in SE England, in Suffolk. Pop. 31,000. The body of King (later Saint) Edmund was interred here in the 10th century, but *Bury* is the equivalent of *burg* or *borough*.

**Bu·shehr** |bŏŏsHer| (also **Bushire**) commercial port city in S Iran, on the Persian Gulf. Pop. 133,000.

**Butte** |byŏŏt| city in SW Montana, famed as a mining center. Pop. 33,336.

**Bu·tu·an** |bŏŏ'tŏŏ,än| commercial port city in the Philippines, on NE Mindanao. Pop. 172,000.

**Bu·zau** |bŏŏ'zow| industrial city in SE Romania, on the Buzau River, capital of Buzau county. Pop. 145,000.

**Buz·zards Bay** |'bəzərdz| inlet of the Atlantic in SE Massachusetts, just W of Cape Cod.

**Byb·los** |'biblə| ancient Mediterranean seaport, situated on the site of present-day Jebeil, to the N of Beirut in Lebanon. It became a thriving Phoenician city in the 2nd millennium B.C.

**Byd·goszcz** |'bidgawsH(CH)| industrial river port in N central Poland. Pop. 381,530. Twenty thousand of its citizens were massacred by Nazis in September 1939. German name **Bromberg**.

# Cc

**Ca·ba·na·tuan** |ˌkäbänäˈtwän| city in the Philippines, on central Luzon, N of Manila. Pop. 173,000.

**Ca·be·za Pri·e·ta** |kəˈbäzə prēˈātə| national wildlife refuge in SW Arizona, in the Sonoran Desert. The Cabeza Prieta Mts. give their name to the preserve, which is home to bighorn sheep and other species. Pop. 163,000.

**Ca·bi·mas** |käˈbēməs| industrial town in NW Venezuela, on the North shore of Lake Maracaibo. Pop. 166,000. It is an oil industry center.

**Ca·bin·da** |kəˈbində| 1 exclave of Angola at the mouth of the Congo River, separated from the rest of Angola by part of the Democratic Republic of Congo (formerly Zaire). 2 the capital of this area, an oil industry center. Pop. 163,000.

**Ca·bo·ra Bas·sa** |kəˌbawrə ˈbäsə| lake on the Zambezi River in W Mozambique. Its waters are enclosed by a dam and form part of a massive hydroelectric complex.

**Cab·ot Strait** |ˈkæbət| ocean passage between Newfoundland and Nova Scotia, linking the Gulf of Saint Lawrence with the Atlantic.

**Cá·ce·res** |ˈkäsəräs| walled city in W Spain, on the Cáceres River, capital of Cáceres province. Pop. 81,000.

**Cad·il·lac Mountain** |ˈkædlˌæk| peak on Mount Desert Island in SE Maine, within Acadia National Park. At 1,532 ft./467 m. it is the highest point on the U.S. E coast.

**Ca·diz** |kəˈdiz| city and port on the coast of SW Spain. Pop. 156,560. Founded by the Phoenicians, it was later a major center for journeys to the Americas.

**Caen** |käN| industrial city and river port in Normandy in N France, on the Orne River, capital of the region of Basse-Normandie. Pop. 115,620.

**Caer·nar·fon** |kärˈnärvən| (also **Caernarvon**) a town in NW Wales on the Menai Strait, the administrative center of Gwynedd. Pop. 9,400.

**Caer·nar·fon·shire** |kärˈnärvənsHər; kär-ˈnärvənsHir| (also **Caernarvonshire**) a former county of NW Wales, part of Gwynedd from 1974.

**Caer·phil·ly** |kärˈfilē| commercial town in S Wales, in Mid Glamorgan. Pop. 42,000. It gave its name to a kind of white cheese, and has a famous castle.

**Cae·sa·rea** |ˌsē zəˈrēə| ancient port on the Mediterranean coast of present-day Israel,

one of the principal cities of Roman Palestine.

**Cae·sa·rea Ma·za·ca** |ˌsēzəˈrēə ˈmæzəkə; ˌsezəˈrēə| former name for KAYSERI, Turkey.

**Cae·sa·rea Phil·ip·pi** |ˌsēzəˈrēə ˈfiləˌpī; ˌsezəˈrēə| city in ancient Palestine, on the site of the present-day village of Baniyas in the Golan Heights.

**Ca·ga·yan de Oro** |ˌkägəˈyän də ˈōrō| industrial port city in the Philippines, on NW Mindanao. Pop. 340,000.

**Ca·ga·yan Islands** |ˌkägəˈyän| group of seven small islands in the Sulu Sea in the W Philippines.

**Ca·glia·ri** |ˈkäl,yärē| the capital of Sardinia, a port on the S coast. Pop. 211,720.

**Cagnes-sur-Mer** |kän(yə) syr ˈmer| fishing port and resort in SE France, on the Riviera just W of Nice. Pop. 41,000.

**Ca·guas** |ˈkägwäs| commercial and industrial community in E central Puerto Rico, S of San Juan. Pop. 92,429.

**Ca·ho·kia** |kəˈhōkēə| village in SW Illinois, across the Mississippi River from St. Louis, Missouri. Pop. 17,550. The Cahokia Mounds, major pre-Columbian earthworks, are to the NE.

**Ca·hors** |käˈawr| industrial town, capital of the department of Lot in S central France. Pop. 21,000. It retains many medieval buildings.

**Cairn·gorm Mountains** |ˈkern,gawrm| (also the **Cairngorms**) a mountain range in N Scotland.

**Cairns** |ˈkernz| resort town in NE Australia, in NE Queensland. Pop. 64,000. It is one of the main sugar ports in Australia.

**Cai·ro**[1] |ˈkīrō| the capital of Egypt and the largest city in Africa, a port on the Nile near the head of its delta. Founded in the 10th century, it is an industrial, commercial, transportation, and cultural center. Pop. 13,300,000. Arabic name **Al Qahira**. □ **Cairene** adj.

**Cai·ro**[2] |ˈkārō| city in S central Illinois, at the junction of the Ohio and Mississippi rivers. Pop. 4,846.

**Caith·ness** |ˈkāTHnes| former county in the extreme NE of Scotland. It became part of Highland region in 1975.

**Ca·ja·mar·ca** |ˌkähəˈmärkə| commercial city in NW Peru, in the Andes. Pop. 93,000. It is in the middle of a mining district, and produces textiles and leather goods.

**Ca·jun Country** |'kajən| region of S Louisiana inhabited largely by Cajuns, descendants of 18th-century exiles from Acadia, now Nova Scotia.

**Ca·la·bar** |,kælə'bär| seaport in SE Nigeria. Pop. 126,000.

**Ca·la·bria** |kä'läbrēə| region of SW Italy, forming the "toe" of the Italian peninsula. Capital: Reggio di Calabria. □ **Calabrian** adj. & n.

**Ca·lais** |kæ'la| ferry port in N France. Pop. 75,840. Captured by Edward III in 1347 after a long siege, it remained an English possession until it was retaken by the French in 1558.

**Ca·lais, Pas de** French name for the Strait of Dover, connecting the English Channel and the North Sea.

**Ca·la·ma** |ko'lämə| city in N Chile, between the Andes Mts. and the Atacama Desert. Pop. 121,000. Nearby are the huge Chuquicamata copper mines.

**Ca·la·ma·ta** |,kælə'mätə; ,kälə'mätə| capital and principal trading port of Messinia prefecture, S Greece. Pop. 41,000. Greek name **Kalámai** or **Kalamáta**.

**Ca·lam·ba** |kä'lämbə| commercial and industrial town in the Philippines, on S Luzon, SE of Manila. Pop. 173,000.

**Că·lă·ra·și** |,kələ'räsH(ē)| city in SE Romania, capital of Călărași county. Pop. 76,000.

**Ca·la·ver·as County** |,kælə'verəs| largely rural county in E central California, in the Sierra Nevada, associated with the 1840s gold rush and the writing of Mark Twain.

**Cal·cut·ta** |kæl'kətə| port and industrial center in E India, capital of the state of West Bengal and the largest city in India. Pop. 10,916,000. It is situated on the Hooghly River near the Bay of Bengal. □ **Calcuttan** adj. & n.

**Cal·e·do·nia** |,kælə'dōnyə| Roman name for the N part of Britain, present-day SCOTLAND. □ **Caledonian** adj. & n.

**Cal·e·do·nian Canal** |,kælə'dōnyən| system of lochs and canals crossing Scotland from Inverness on the E coast to Fort William on the W. With canals built by Thomas Telford, it was opened in 1822. It traverses the Great Glen, part of its length being formed by Loch Ness.

**Ca·lex·i·co** |kə'leksikō| city in S California, across the border from Mexicali, Mexico. Pop. 18,633.

**Cal·ga·ry** |'kælgərē| commercial and industrial city in S Alberta, the largest in the province. Pop. 710,680.

**Ca·li** |'kälē| industrial city in W Colombia,

in the Cauca River valley. Pop. 1,624,400. An agricultural trade center, it was the reputed hub of cocaine traffic.

**Cal·i·cut** |'kæli,kət| seaport in the state of Kerala in SW India, on the Malabar Coast. Pop. 420,000. In the 17th and 18th centuries Calicut became a center of the textile trade with Europe. The cotton fabric known as calico originated here. Also called **Kozhikode**.

**Cal·i·for·nia** |,kælə'fawrnyə| see box. □ **Californian** adj. & n.

**Cal·i·for·nia, Gulf of** |,kælə'fawrnyə| arm

| California | |
|---|---|
| **Capital:** Sacramento | |
| **Largest city:** Los Angeles | |
| **Other cities:** Anaheim, Burbank, Long Beach, Oakland, Pasadena, San Diego, San Francisco, San Jose | |
| **Population:** 29,760,021 (1990); 32,666,550 (1998); 34,441,000 (2005 proj.) | |
| **Population rank (1990):** 1 | |
| **Rank in land area:** 3 | |
| **Abbreviation:** CA; Cal.; Calif. | |
| **Nickname:** The Golden State | |
| **Motto:** *Eureka* (Greek: 'I Have Found It') | |
| **Bird:** California valley quail | |
| **Fish:** California golden trout | |
| **Flower:** golden poppy | |
| **Tree:** California redwood | |
| **Song:** "I Love You, California" | |
| **Noted physical features:** Monterey Bay, San Diego Bay, San Francisco Bay; Lake Tahoe; Golden Gate Bridge; Big Sur; Cape Mendocino; Mohave Desert, Colorado Desert; San Andreas Fault; Palisade Glacier; Death Valley; Lassen Volcano | |
| **Tourist attractions:** RMS *Queen Mary*, Long Beach; Palomar Observatory; Disneyland, Anaheim; J. Paul Getty Museum, Malibu; Universal Studios, Hollywood; Los Angeles County Art Museum; San Diego Zoo; Knotts Berry Farm; Napa Valley; Monterey Peninsula; Fisherman's Wharf; Shasta Dam; Sutters Mill; Channel Islands, Kings Canyon, Lassen Volcanic, Redwood, Sequoia and Yosemite national parks; Alcatraz, Folsom Prison, San Quentin Prison | |
| **Admission date:** September 9, 1850 | |
| **Order of admission:** 31 | |
| **Name origin:** Named Alta ('upper') California by Spanish explorers moving north from Baja ('lower') California, the Mexican peninsula to the south. | |

of the Pacific separating the Baja California peninsula from mainland Mexico.

**Cal·i·for·nia Current** |ˌkælәˈfawrnyә| cold ocean current of the E Pacific that flows S along the W coast of North America.

**Cal·lao** |kәˈyow| the principal seaport of Peru. Pop. 369,770.

**Ca·lo·o·can** |ˌkälәˈoˌkän| (also **Kalookan**) city in the Philippines, on S Luzon, a suburb NW of Manila. Pop. 763,000.

**Cal·u·met City** |ˈkælyәˌmet| city in NE Illinois, a suburb S of Chicago, on the Indiana border. Pop. 37,840. The surrounding industrial region, in both states, is called the Calumet.

**Cal·va·dos** |ˈkælvәˌdōs| department in NW France, along the English Channel, in Basse-Normandie. Area: 2,143 sq.mi./ 5,548 sq. km. Pop. 618,000. The capital is Caen. An apple-growing area, it gave its name to a type of brandy.

**Cal·va·ry** |ˈkælvә(ә)rē| Latin name for the hill outside Jerusalem on which Jesus was crucified. The Greek name is **Golgotha**.

**Cal·y·don** |ˈkælәˌdän| ancient city in central Greece, near the coast of the Gulf of Patras. The legendary Calydonian boar hunt was the search for a savage boar sent by the goddess Artemis to destroy Calydon.

**Cam, River** |kæm| (ancient name **Granta**) river that flows 40 mi./65 km. NE from Essex, SE England, through Cambridge to join the Ouse River near Ely.

**Ca·ma·güey** |ˌkämәˈgwä; ˌkæmәˈgwä| commercial city in E Cuba, the capital of Camagüey province. Pop. 295,000. The surrounding region produces livestock and various crops.

**Ca·margue** |kәˈmärg| (also **the Camargue**) a region of the Rhône delta in SE France, characterized by numerous shallow salt lagoons. It is known for its white horses and as a nature reserve.

**Cam·a·ril·lo** |ˌkæmәˈrilō| city in SW California, W of Los Angeles. Pop. 52,303.

**Ca·mau Peninsula** |kәˈmow| (also called **Mui Bai Bung**) cape at the S end of Vietnam; marks the SE corner of the Gulf of Thailand.

**Cam·bay, Gulf of** |kæmˈbā| (also **Gulf of Khambat**) an inlet of the Arabian Sea on the Gujarat coast of W India, N of Bombay.

**Cam·bo·dia** |kæmˈbōdēә| country in SE Asia, in Indochina between Thailand and southern Vietnam. Area: 69,884 sq. mi./181,040 sq. km. Pop. 8,660,000. Language, Khmer. Capital and largest city: Phnom Penh. Also officially called the **Khmer Republic** (1970–75) and **Kam-**

Cambodia

puchea (1976–89). Remnant of a great Khmer empire, Cambodia was controlled by the French (1863–1953). During the Vietnam War it suffered U.S. bombing and incursions, followed by a civil war that led to massive atrocities under the Khmer Rouge (1975–79). The Mekong River and Tonlé Sap (lake) dominate this country, whose economy relies on agriculture and fishing. □ **Cambodian** adj. & n.

**Cam·brai** |känˈbre| industrial city in NW France, on the Escaut River in the Nord-Pas-de-Calais. Pop. 34,000. The Flemish version of the town's name, Kambryk, became the name of a linen or cotton fabric, in English cambric.

**Cam·bria** |ˈkämbrēә; ˈkæmbrēә| ancient name for WALES, which is mostly occupied by the **Cambrian Mountains**, a rugged upland that gave its name to geologic terminology. □ **Cambrian** adj.

**Cam·bridge**[1] |ˈkämbrij| city in E England, the county seat of Cambridgeshire. Pop. 101,000. Cambridge University is located here, and there are light industries. □ **Cantabrigian** adj. & n.

**Cam·bridge**[2] |ˈkämbrij| city in E Massachusetts, across the Charles River from Boston. Pop. 95,800. Harvard University and the Massachusetts Institute of Technology are here.

**Cam·bridge**[3] |ˈkämbrij| city in S Ontario, W of Toronto, a research and industrial center. Pop. 92,722.

**Cam·bridge·shire** |ˈkämbrij,sHir; ˈkämbrijsHәr| county of E England; county seat, Cambridge. Pop. 641,000.

**Cam·bu·luc** |ˌkämbōōˈlook| see BEIJING, China.

**Cam·den**[1] |ˈkæmdәn| borough of N central London, England, immediately N of Westminster. Pop. 170,000. Bloomsbury, Hampstead, and Highgate are among its constituent parts.

**Cam·den**[2] |ˈkæmdәn| industrial city in SW

New Jersey, across the Delaware River from Philadelphia, Pennsylvania. Pop. 87,492.

**Cam·e·lot** |ˈkæmə,lät| in Arthurian legend, the place where King Arthur, the Celtic hero of 5th-century England, had his court. Winchester is among sites suggested as having been Camelot.

**Cam·em·bert** |ˈkæməm,ber| village in the Orne department of Normandy, in NW France. It gave its name to the soft cheese.

**Cam·er·on Highlands** |ˈkæm(ə)rən| hill resort region in Pahang, Malaysia.

**Cam·er·oon** |ˌkæməˈrōōn| republic on the W coast of Africa, between Nigeria and Gabon. Area: 183,569 sq. mi./475,442 sq. km. Pop. 12,081,000. Languages, French, English, W African languages. Capital: Yaoundé Largest city: Douala. French name **Cameroun**. Controlled by the Germans, French, and English, Cameroon gained independence in 1960. It relies on tropical agriculture and forest products, along with oil. □ **Cameroonian** *adj. & n.*

**Cameroon**

**Cam·er·oon, Mount** |ˌkæməˈrōōn| active volcano in SW Cameroon, near the Atlantic Ocean. At 13,354 ft./4,070 m. it is the highest point in W Africa S of the Sahara.

**Ca·mi·no Re·al** |kəˈmē,nō räˈæl| name ("royal road") for various routes established by the Spanish during early settlement of the U.S. SW. Notable examples led from Mexico to San Francisco Bay and to Santa Fe, New Mexico.

**Cam·pa·gna di Ro·ma** |kämˈpänyə dē ˈrōmə| plain surrounding the city of Rome, in central Italy. It was a popular ancient residential area but was later abandoned because of unhealthy (malarial) conditions. It has been reclaimed and is now farmland.

**Cam·pa·nia** |kämˈpänēə| region of W central Italy. Capital: Naples. □ **Campanian** *adj. & n.*

**Camp·bell** |ˈkæmbəl| city in W central Cal-

ifornia, SW of San Jose, part of the Silicon Valley research and industrial complex. Pop. 36,048.

**Camp·bell·town** |ˈkæmbəl,town| city in Australia, in New South Wales, a suburb S of Sydney. Pop. 138,000.

**Camp Da·vid** |kæmp ˈdāvid| retreat in the Catoctin Mts. of Maryland, NW of Washington, D.C., used by U.S. presidents since the 1940s.

**Cam·pe·che** |kämˈpäCHə; kæmˈpēCHē| 1 state of SE Mexico, on the Yucatán Peninsula. Area: 19,626 sq. mi./50,812 sq. km. Pop.: 529,000. 2 its capital, a seaport on the Gulf of Mexico. Pop. 172,200.

**Cam·per·down** |ˈkämpər,down| (Dutch name **Camperduin**) village in the W Netherlands, on the North Sea. In a 1797 naval battle near here the British defeated Dutch forces.

**Cam·pi·na Gran·de** |kämˈpēnə ˈgrändē| commercial city in E Brazil, NW of Recife in Paraíba state. Pop. 326,000.

**Cam·pi·nas** |kämˈpēnəs| commercial city in SE Brazil, NW of São Paulo, a center for the coffee and high-tech industries. Pop. 835,000.

**Cam·po·bas·so** |ˌkämpōˈbäsō| city in central Italy, capital of Molise region. Pop. 51,300.

**Cam·po·bel·lo Island** |ˌkæmpəˈbelō| resort island in SW New Brunswick, off Eastport, Maine, noted as the vacation home of Franklin D. Roosevelt.

**Cam·po Gran·de** |ˈkämpōō ˈgrändē| city in SW Brazil, capital of the state of Mato Grosso do Sul. Pop. 489,000.

**Cam·pos** |ˈkämpōōs| (full name **Campos dos Goytacazes**) city in SE Brazil, on the Paraíba River, NE of Rio de Janeiro. Pop. 391,000. It is a sugar-producing and oil industry-servicing center.

**Cam Ranh Bay** |ˈkæm ˈrän| inlet of the South China Sea, southern central Vietnam. It has been a major base for France, Japan, the former Soviet Union, and the U.S., which had a major installation here during the Vietnam War.

**Camu·lo·du·num** |ˌkæmələˈdōōnəm| Roman name for COLCHESTER, England.

**Ca·na** |ˈkānə| biblical village in Galilee, N Israel, N of Nazareth, where Jesus performed his first miracle at a wedding. It was perhaps within present-day Kafr Kana, an Arab town (pop. 12,000).

**Ca·naan** |ˈkānən| the biblical name for the area of ancient Palestine W of the Jordan River, the Promised Land of the Israelites, who conquered and occupied it during the

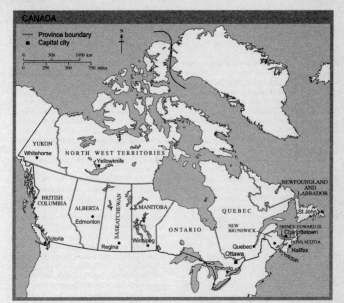

CANADA

- Province boundary
- ■ Capital city

0   500   1000 km
0   250   500   750 miles

YUKON
Whitehorse

NORTH WEST TERRITORIES
Yellowknife

BRITISH COLUMBIA

ALBERTA
Edmonton

SASKATCHEWAN

MANITOBA

Victoria

Regina

Winnipeg

ONTARIO

QUEBEC

NEWFOUNDLAND AND LABRADOR
St John's

NEW BRUNSWICK

PRINCE EDWARD IS.
Charlottetown

Quebec
Ottawa

NOVA SCOTIA
Halifax
Moncton

Toronto

latter part of the 2nd millennium B.C.
□ **Canaanite** *adj. & n.*

**Can·a·da** |'kænədə| the second-largest country in the world, covering N North America except for Alaska. Area: 3.85 million sq. mi./9.98 million sq. km. Pop. 27,296,859; Languages, English and French. Capital: Ottawa. Largest cities: Montreal, Calgary, Toronto. The object of a long power struggle between France and Britain, Canada became a dominion, essentially independent, in 1867. Its early economy was based on the fur trade. Today, mining, plains agriculture, fishing, hydropower, and heavy and light industry are all important. □ **Canadian** *adj. & n.*

**Ca·na·di·an River** |kə'nādēən| river that flows 900 mi./1,450 km. from E New Mexico across the Texas Panhandle and Oklahoma. Oklahoma City lies on it. It is also called the South Canadian River.

**Ca·na·di·an Shield** |kə'nādēən| massive plateau that occupies over two-fifths of the land area of Canada and is drained by rivers generally flowing into Hudson Bay. Extending N from the Great Lakes and including the Adirondacks of New York and the Arrowhead Region of Minnesota, it is

the oldest portion of the North American continent, being permanently elevated above sea level since the Precambrian Era. Also called **Laurentian Plateau.**

**Canal Zone** |kə'næl| see PANAMA CANAL.

**Ca·nar·ies Current** |kə'nerēz| cold ocean current in the North Atlantic that flows SW from Spain to meet equatorial waters near the Canary Islands.

**Ca·nar·sie** |kə'närsē| residential section of SE Brooklyn, New York, along Jamaica Bay, named for a local tribe.

**Ca·nary Islands** (also **the Canaries**; Spanish name **Islas Canarias**) group of islands in the Atlantic, off the NW coast of Africa, forming an autonomous region of Spain. Capital: Las Palmas. Pop. 1,557,530. The group includes the islands of Tenerife, Gomera, La Palma, Hierro, Gran Canaria, Fuerteventura, and Lanzarote.

**Ca·nav·er·al, Cape** |kə'næv(ə)rəl| cape on the E coast of Florida, known as Cape Kennedy from 1963 until 1973. It is the site of the John F. Kennedy Space Center, from which U.S. space missions are launched.

**Can·ber·ra** |'kænb(ə)rə| the capital of Australia and seat of the federal government, in Australian Capital Territory, an enclave of New South Wales. Pop. 310,000.

**Can·cún** |kæn'kōōn| beach resort in SE Mexico, on the NE coast of the Yucatán Peninsula. Pop. 27,500.

**Can·dia** |'kændēə| Venetian name for the Greek island of Crete, the city of Heraklion, and the part of the Aegean Sea that lies between the Cyclades and Crete. The ruins of the city of Knossos are near the modern city of Candia.

**Ca·nea** |kə'nēə| (also **Khaniá**) ancient city on Crete, in Greece. The modern city is a port and capital of Khaniá prefecture.

**Cang·zhou** |'zæNG'jō| city in Hebei province, E China, on the Grand Canal S of Tianjin. Pop. 303,000.

**Can·nae** |'kænē| battlefield in SE Italy, near Barletta. During the Second Punic War, in 216 B.C., Rome suffered one of its worst defeats here at the hands of Hannibal.

**Cannes** |kän; kæn| resort on the Mediterranean coast of France, in Alpes-Maritimes. Pop. 69,360. An international film festival is held here annually.

**Ca·no·as** |'kä'nōəs| city in S Brazil, a suburb N of Pôrto Alegre in Rio Grande do Sul state. Pop. 278,000.

**Ca·no·pus** |kə'nōpəs| resort city of ancient N Egypt, in the Nile Delta, E of Alexandria, near present-day Abu Qir (Aukir). It gave its name to canopic (burial) jars.

**Can·so, Strait of** |'kænsō| ocean passage between Cape Breton Island and the mainland of Nova Scotia, bridged since the 1950s. Also, the Canso Gut.

**Can·ta·bria** |kən'täbrēə| autonomous region of N Spain, between Asturias and the Basque provinces. Pop. 527,000. Capital: Santander. □ **Cantabrian** *adj. & n.*

**Can·ter·bury**[1] |'kæntər,berē| city in Kent, SE England, the seat of the Archbishop of Canterbury, head of the Church of England. Pop. 39,700. St. Augustine established a church and monastery here in 597. After the 1170 murder of Thomas à Becket, Canterbury became a place of medieval pilgrimage.

**Can·ter·bury**[2] |'kæntər,berē| region on the central east coast of South Island, New Zealand, including the Canterbury Plains.

**Can·ton and En·der·bury** |'kæntn ən 'endər,berē| two islands in Kiribati, in the Phoenix Islands group, that were held by the U.S. and the United Kingdom before 1980. Canton is also spelled **Kanton.**

**Can·ton**[1] |'kæn,tän| see GUANGZHOU, China.

**Can·ton**[2] |'kæntn| industrial city in NE Ohio. Pop. 84,161. The Professional Football Hall of Fame is in the city.

**Can·tons de l'Est** |kæn'tän də 'lest| French name for the EASTERN TOWNSHIPS, Quebec.

**Canyon de Chel·ly** |də 'sHä(lē)| national monument in NE Arizona, on the Navajo Indian Reservation, noted for cliff dwellings and other ruins.

**Can·yon·lands** |'kænyən,læn(d)z| region of SE Utah, many of whose noted rock formations are preserved in the Canyonlands National Park.

**Cap-de-la-Madeleine** |,käp də ,lä mäd 'len| industrial city in S Quebec, across the St. Maurice River from Trois-Rivières. Pop. 33,716.

**Cape Bret·on Island** |käp 'bretn| island forming the NE part of the province of Nova Scotia. It takes its name from the cape at its NE tip.

**Cape Che·lyus·kin** |cHel'yōōskən| cape on the Taimyr Peninsula, in Siberia, Russia. At 77° 45'N, it is the northernmost point on the Asian mainland.

**Cape Cod** |käd| sandy peninsula in SE Massachusetts. Forming an arm-shaped curve enclosing Cape Cod Bay, it includes many popular summer resorts. The Pilgrims landed on the N tip in November 1620, before proceeding to Plymouth.

**Cape Colony** |'kälənē| early name (1814–1910) for the former CAPE PROVINCE of South Africa.

**Cape Cor·al** |'kawrəl; 'kärəl| resort city in SW Florida, S of Fort Myers. Pop. 74,991.

**Cape Dor·set** |'dōrsit| Inuit community on an island off SW Baffin Island, in Nunavut. Remains found here gave their name to the Cape Dorset Culture of up to 2,500 years ago. Inuit name **Kinngait.**

**Cape Fear River** |'käp 'fir| river that flows 200 mi./320 km. across E North Carolina to enter the Atlantic near Wilmington, at Cape Fear.

**Cape Gi·rar·deau** |jə'rärdō| city in SE Missouri, on the Mississippi River. Pop. 34,438.

**Cape John·son Depth** |'jänsən 'depTH| the deepest point of the Philippine or Mindanao Trench, off the E coast of the Philippines, dropping to 34,440 ft./10,497 m. below sea level. It is named after the USS *Cape Johnson.*

**Cape May** |mā| resort city in extreme S New Jersey, on the Atlantic. Pop. 4,668.

**Cape Pi·ai** |pē'ī| cape in Malaysia at the tip of the Malay Peninsula, at 01° 16′ N the most southerly point of the Asian mainland.

**Cape Prov·ince** |ˈkāp ˈprävəns| former province of South Africa, containing the Cape of Good Hope. The area became a British colony in 1814; it was known as Cape Colony from then until 1910, when it joined the Union of South Africa. In 1994 it was divided into the provinces of Northern Cape, Western Cape, and Eastern Cape.

**Ca·per·na·um** |kəˈpərnēəm| biblical village on the N shore of the Lake of Galilee, on the site of present-day Kefar Nahum, Israel, a center of the work of Jesus and home to several of his disciples.

**Cape Ro·ca** |ˈrōkä| peninsula in Portugal, W of Lisbon, the westernmost point on the European mainland. Portuguese name **Cabo da Roca**.

**Cape Ta·ri·fa** |təˈrēfə| peninsula on the coast of S Spain. At 36° 00′ N, it is the southernmost point on mainland Europe.

**Cape Town** |ˈkāp ˌtown| the legislative capital of South Africa and administrative capital of the province of W Cape. Pop. 776,600. It is an historic port and an industrial center.

**Cape Ver·de** |ˌkāp ˈvərd| republic consisting of a group of ten islands in the Atlantic off the coast of Senegal, named after the most westerly cape of Africa. Area: 1,557 sq. mi./4,033 sq. km. Pop. 383,000. Languages, Portuguese, Creole. Capital: Praia. Largest city: Mindela. Previously uninhabited, the islands were settled by the Portuguese in the 15th century. In 1975, an independent republic was established. Farming, fishing, and salt extraction are important. □ **Cape Verdean** *adj. & n.*

**Cape Verde Islands**

**Cape Wrath** |ˌraтн; ˈräтн| headland at the NW tip of the mainland of Scotland.

**Cape York** |ˈyawrk| the northernmost point of the continent of Australia, on the Torres Strait at the tip of the sparsely populated Cape York Peninsula in Queensland.

**Cap-Haïtien** |käp ˈhäsнən| historic port city in N Haiti. Pop. 133,000. A former Haitian capital and the second-largest city in the country, it is associated with the early political leader Henri Christophe.

**Cap·i·tol Hill** |ˈkæpətl ˈhil| the region around the U.S. Capitol building in Washington, D.C. (often an allusive reference to the U.S. Congress itself).

**Cap·i·to·line** |ˈkæpətlˌin| (also **Capitoline Hill**) highest of the seven hills of Rome and historic center of the city, overlooking the Forum. Atop the hill is a complex of buildings on a site designed by Michelangelo. In the center is a famous equestrian statue of Marcus Aurelius.

**Cap·i·tol Reef National Park** |ˈkæpətl ˈrēf| preserve in S central Utah, noted for its fossils and rock formations.

**Cap·pa·do·cia** |ˌkæpəˈdōsнə| ancient region of central Asia Minor (present-day Turkey), between Lake Tuz and the Euphrates, N of Cilicia. It was an important center of early Christianity. □ **Cappadocian** *adj. & n.*

**Ca·pre·ra** |kəˈprärə| island off the NE coast of Sardinia, Italy. It was the home of the Italian nationalist leader Giuseppe Garibaldi, who is buried here.

**Ca·pri** |ˈkäprē; kəˈprē| island off the W coast of Italy, S of Naples; it has been a noted resort since ancient Roman times.

**Ca·pri·vi Strip** |kəˈprēvē| narrow strip of Namibia that extends toward Zambia from the NE corner of Namibia and reaches the Zambezi River.

**Cap·rock, the** |ˈkæpˌräk| escarpment in N Texas, separating the Llano Estacado from the central Texas prairies. The Llano Estacado itself is sometimes called the Caprock.

**Ca·rac·as** |kəˈrækəs; kəˈräkəs| the capital and largest city of Venezuela, in the N near the Caribbean. Pop. 1,824,890. It is the commercial, industrial, and cultural center of Venezuela.

**Ca·ra·vag·gio** |ˌkærəˈväjō| agricultural and industrial town in N Italy, on the Lombardy Plain. Pop. 14,000. The Mannerist painter Caravaggio was born here.

**Car·bon·dale** |ˈkärbənˌdäl| city in S central Illinois, a coal center and home to Southern Illinois University. Pop. 27,033.

**Car·cas·sonne** |ˌkärkəˈsawn| walled commercial city in SW France, the capital of Aude department, in Languedoc-Roussillon near the Spanish border. Pop. 45,000.

**Car·che·mish** |ˈkär,kemisн| ancient city on the upper Euphrates, NE of present-day Aleppo, Syria.

**Car·da·mom Mountains** |'kärdəməm; 'kärdə‚mäm| range of forested mountains in W Cambodia, along the Thai border, rising to 5,886 ft./1,813 m. at its highest point.

**Cár·de·nas** |kär'dānəs; 'kärdn-əs| industrial port in N central Cuba, E of Havana. Pop. 63,000.

**Car·diff** |'kärdəf| the capital of Wales, a seaport on the Bristol Channel. Pop. 272,600. Welsh name **Caerdydd**.

**Car·di·gan·shire** |'kärdəgənsHər; 'kärdəgən‚sHir| former county of SW Wales. It became part of Dyfed in 1974; the area became a county once more in 1996, as Ceredigion.

**Car·ia** |'kerēə| ancient region of SW Asia Minor, S of the Maeander River and NW of Lycia. □ **Carian** *adj. & n.*

**Ca·ri·a·ci·ca** |‚kärēə'sēkə| city in E Brazil, a suburb of Vitória, in Espírito Santo state. Pop. 252,000.

**Ca·rib·be·an National Forest** |‚kærə-'bēən; kə'ribēən| preserve in NE Puerto Rico, noted for its rainforest vegetation and wildlife. Also called **El Yunque**.

**Ca·rib·be·an Sea** |‚kærə'bēən; kə'ribēən| the part of the Atlantic lying between the Antilles and the mainland of Central and South America.

**Car·i·boo Mountains** |'kærə‚boo| range in E central British Columbia, part of the Rocky Mts., scene of an 1860s gold rush.

**Ca·rin·thia** |kə'rinTHēə| Alpine state of S Austria. Capital: Klagenfurt. German name **Kärnten**. □ **Carinthian** *adj. & n.*

**Car·lisle**[1] |kär'līl; 'kär‚līl| industrial and commercial town in NW England, the county seat of Cumbria. Pop. 99,800.

**Car·lisle**[2] |kär'līl; 'kär‚līl| historic borough in S Pennsylvania, SW of Harrisburg. Pop. 18,419. It is home to the Army War College.

**Car·low** |'kärlō| **1** county of the Republic of Ireland, in the province of Leinster. Pop. 41,000. **2** its capital, on the Barrow River. Pop. 11,000.

**Carls·bad**[1] |'kärlz‚bæd| city in SW California, on the Pacific coast N of San Diego. Pop. 63,126.

**Carls·bad**[2] |'kärls‚bät| see KARLOVY VARY, Czech Republic.

**Carls·bad**[3] |'kärlz‚bæd| city in SE New Mexico, on the Pecos River. Pop. 24,952. To the SW is Carlsbad Caverns, a vast cave complex.

**Car·ma·gno·la** |‚kärmən'yōlə| commune, in NW Italy, on the Po. Pop. 24,000. The carmagnole, a style of clothing worn by Piedmontese workmen and adopted by in-

surrectionists during the French Revolution in 1792, is thought to have taken its name from the village.

**Car·mar·then** |kar'märTHən| town in SW Wales, the administrative center of Carmarthenshire. Pop. 54,800. Welsh name **Caerfyrddin**.

**Car·mar·then·shire** |kər'märTHnsHər; ‚kär'märTHnsHir| county of S Wales; administrative center, Carmarthen. It was part of Dyfed between 1974 and 1996.

**Car·mel, Mount** |'kärməl| group of mountains near the Mediterranean coast in NW Israel, sheltering the port of Haifa. In the Bible it is the scene of the defeat of the priests of Baal by the prophet Elijah.

**Car·mel** |kär'mel| city in W central California, a resort on the Pacific S of Monterey. Pop. 4,239.

**Car·mi·chael** |'kär‚mīkəl| community in N central California, a suburb NE of Sacramento. Pop. 48,702.

**Car·na·by Street** |'kärnəbē| street in W central London, England, W of Soho, made famous in the 1960s as the center of the teenage fashion industry.

**Car·nac** |'kär‚næk| village in NW France, in Brittany, on the Atlantic coast. It is best known for its prehistoric stone monuments, huge standing stones aligned in long avenues or in semicircular or rectangular enclosures.

**Car·nat·ic** |‚kär'nætik| (also **Karnatic**) term sometimes applied to all of S India, but more usually used of the plains of the SE, to the E of the Eastern Ghats mountain range, where France and Britain struggled for control of India in the 18th century.

**Car·ne·gie Hall** |'kärnəgē 'hawl; kär'negē| famed concert hall in central Manhattan, New York City, traditionally the goal of any serious musician.

**Car·nic Alps** |'kärnik| (German name **Karnische Alpen**) range of the Alps on the border of S Austria and NE Italy, reaching 9,124 ft./2,781 m. at Monte Coglians (Hohe Warte).

**Car·nio·la** |‚kärn'yōlə; 'kärnē'ōlə| historic region of Slovenia on the border with Italy. After being occupied by Rome and then settled by Slovenes, it belonged to Austria and then was divided between Italy and Yugoslavia in 1919. Since 1947 it has been part of Yugoslavia and then Slovenia.

**Car·ol City** |'kærəl| suburban community in SE Florida, N of Miami. Pop. 53,331.

**Car·o·li·na**[1] |‚kærə'līnə| commercial and residential suburb E of San Juan, Puerto Rico. Pop. 162,404.

**Ca·ro·li·na**[2] |ˌkærə'lēnə| 17th-century English colony in SE North America, which eventually became North Carolina and South Carolina (the Carolinas).

**Car·o·line Islands** (also **the Carolines**) group of islands in the W Pacific Ocean, N of the equator, forming the Federated States of MICRONESIA.

**Car·ol Stream** |'kærəl| village in NE Illinois, a suburb W of Chicago. Pop. 31,716.

**Ca·ro·ni River** |ˌkärə'nē| river in E Venezuela that flows 550 mi./880 km. N from the Pacaraima Range to the Orinoco River. The Guri Reservoir is along it.

**Car·pa·thi·an Mountains** |kär'pāTHēən| (also **the Carpathians**) a mountain system extending SE from S Poland and the Czech Republic into Romania. See KARPATHOS.

**Car·pen·tar·ia, Gulf of** |'kärpən'terēə; 'kärpən'tærēə| large bay on the N coast of Australia, between Arnhem Land and the Cape York Peninsula.

**Car·ran·tuo·hill** |ˌkærən'tōōəl| highest peak in Ireland, in Macgillicuddy's Reeks, County Kerry, in the SW: 3,415 ft./1,041 m.

**Car·ra·ra** |kə'rärə| town in Tuscany in NW Italy, famous for the white marble quarried here since Roman times. Pop. 68,480. □ **Carrarese** *adj. & n.*

**Car·ri·a·cou** |ˌkærə'kōō| largest (13 sq. mi./21 sq. km.) island in the Grenadines, in the Windward Islands group in the West Indies. Pop. 5,000. Hillsborough is the chief town. Administered by Grenada, Carriacou has some agriculture and a tourist trade.

**Car·rick·fer·gus** |ˌkærək'fərgəs| historic port town in E Northern Ireland, NE of Belfast on Belfast Lough, in County Antrim. Pop. 31,000.

**Carrick-on-Shannon** |'kærik än 'sHænən| the county seat of Leitrim in the Republic of Ireland, on the Shannon River. Pop. 6,168.

**Car·ri·zo Plain** |kə'rēzō| lowland in W central California, along the San Andreas Fault, noted for its earthquakes and wildlife.

**Car·roll·ton** |'kærəltən| city in NE Texas, a suburb N of Dallas. Pop. 82,169.

**Car·son** |'kärsən| city in SW California, an industrial suburb S of Los Angeles. Pop. 83,995.

**Car·son City** |'kärsən| the state capital of Nevada, in the W, near the California line. Pop. 40,440. It was a famed 19th-century silver town, site of the Comstock Lode and later of a branch of the U.S. Mint.

**Car·ta·ge·na**[1] |ˌkärtə'hänə| port city, resort, and oil-refining center in NW Colombia, on the Caribbean Sea. Pop. 688,300.

**Car·ta·ge·na**[2] |ˌkärtə'hänə| port in SE Spain. Pop. 172,150. Originally named Mastia, it was refounded as Carthago Nova (New Carthage) by Hasdrubal in *c.*225 B.C., as a base for the Carthaginian conquest of Spain.

**Car·thage** |'kärTHij| ancient city on the coast of N Africa near present-day Tunis. Founded by the Phoenicians *c.*814 B.C., Carthage became a major force in the Mediterranean, and came into conflict with Rome in the Punic Wars. It was finally destroyed by the Romans in 146 B.C. □ **Carthaginian** *adj. & n.*

**Car·tier Islands** |ˌkärtē'ä| see ASHMORE AND CARTIER ISLANDS, Australia.

**Ca·ru·a·ru** |ˌkärōōə'rōō| city in NE Brazil, in Pernambuco state. Pop. 214,000. It is the commercial center of a farming and livestock-producing area.

**Cary** |'kærē| town in E central North Carolina, a commercial and research center. Pop. 43,858.

**Cas·a·blan·ca** |ˌkäsə'blänɡkə; 'kæsə 'blænɡkə| the largest city and commercial center of Morocco, a seaport on the Atlantic coast. Pop. 2,943,000.

**Ca·sa Gran·de** |'käsə 'grändē; 'grädä| city in S central Arizona, S of Phoenix. Pop. 19,082. It is named for nearby pre-Columbian ruins.

**Cas·cade Range** |kæs'kād| range of volcanic mountains in W North America, extending from S British Columbia through Washington and Oregon to N California. Its highest peak, Mount Rainier, rises to 14,410 ft./4,395 m. The range also includes the active volcano Mount St. Helens.

**Cas·co Bay** |'kæskō| inlet of the Atlantic in S Maine, known for its hundreds of islands and protected anchorages. Portland lies on it.

**Ca·ser·ta** |kə'zertə| commercial center in S central Italy, the capital of Caserta province. Pop. 70,000. Nearby is Caserta Vecchia, a medieval town.

**Cash·el** |'kæsHəl| town in S Ireland, in County Tipperary, dominated by the 200-ft./60-m. **Rock of Cashel**, seat of the kings of Munster in the 4th–12th centuries. A chapel now surmounts the Rock.

**Cash·mere** |'kæzH,mēr; 'kæsH,mir| see KASHMIR.

**Cas·per** |'kæspər| city in E central

Wyoming, on the North Platte River. Pop. 46,742. Oil is central to its economy.

**Cas·pi·an Sea** |'kæspēən| large landlocked salt lake, bounded by Russia, Kazakhstan, Turkmenistan, Azerbaijan, and Iran. It is the world's largest (143,524 sq. mi./370,992 sq. km.) body of inland water. Its surface lies 92 ft./28 m. below sea level.

**Cas·tal·ia** |kə'stālyə| spring on Mount Parnassus, in central Greece, that was sacred to Apollo and to the Muses; it was said to inspire those who bathed in it. □ **Castalian** adj.

**Ca·stel·lam·ma·re di Sta·bia** |käs,telə'märä dē 'stäbyə| fortified seaport in S Italy, on the Bay of Naples. Pop. 69,000.

**Cas·tel Gan·dol·fo** |,käs,tel gän'dawlfō| the summer residence of the pope, situated on the edge of Lake Albano near Rome.

**Cas·tel·li Ro·ma·ni** |käs,telē rō'mänē| region in the Alban Hills E of Rome, central Italy. The region is known for its vineyards and for the numerous castles belonging to popes and wealthy Italian families, including Castel Gandolfo.

**Cas·tel·lón de la Pla·na** |kästə(l)'yōn də lä 'plänə| seaport and industrial city in E Spain, on the Mediterranean Sea, and capital of Castellón province. Pop. 137,000.

**Cas·ter·bridge** |'kæstər,brij| name given by Thomas Hardy in his novels to DORCHESTER', the county seat of Dorset, SW England.

**Cas·tile** |kæ'stēl| region of central Spain, on the central plateau of the Iberian Peninsula, formerly an independent Spanish kingdom. The marriage of Isabella of Castile to Ferdinand of Aragon in 1469 linked these two powerful kingdoms and led eventually to the unification of Spain. □ **Castilian** adj. & n.

**Castilla–La Mancha** |kä'stē(l)yə lä 'mänchə| autonomous region of central Spain. Capital: Toledo.

**Castilla-León** |kä'stē(l)yə lā'ōn| autonomous region of N Spain. Capital: Valladolid.

**Cas·tle·bar** |,kæsəl'bär| the county seat of Mayo, in the Republic of Ireland. Pop. 6,070.

**Cas·tries** |kä'strē; 'kæs,trēs| capitol of the Caribbean island nation of St. Lucia, a seaport on the NW coast. Pop. 14,055.

**Cas·tro, the** |'kæstrō| popular name for a neighborhood of central San Francisco, California, noted as a center of gay politics and culture.

**Castrop-Rauxel** |'käs,trawp 'rowksəl| industrial city in the Ruhr district of western Germany. Pop. 79,000.

**Cat·a·li·na Island** |,kætl'ēnə| see SANTA BARBARA ISLANDS, California.

**Cat·a·lo·nia** |,kætl'ōnyə| autonomous region of NE Spain. Pop. 6,059,000. Capital: Barcelona. The region has a strong separatist tradition; the normal language for everyday purposes is Catalan, which has also won acceptance in recent years for various official purposes. Catalan name **Catalunya**; Spanish name **Cataluña**.

**Cat·a·mar·ca** |,kätə'märkə| mining and commercial town in NW Argentina, the capital of Catamarca province. Pop. 110,000.

**Ca·ta·nia** |kə'tänyə| seaport situated at the foot of Mount Etna, on the E coast of Sicily. Pop. 364,180.

**Ca·tan·za·ro** |,kätän(d)'zärō| chief town of the Calabria region of S Italy. Pop. 104,000. A commercial center, it is the capital of Catanzaro province.

**Ca·taw·ba River** |kə'tawbə; kə'täbə| river that flows 300 mi./480 km. from the Blue Ridge Mts. in North Carolina across much of South Carolina.

**Ca·thay** |kə'THā; kæ'THā| the name by which China was known to medieval Europe. Also called **Khitai**.

**Ca·the·dral City** |kə'THēdrəl| city in S California, a resort SE of Palm Springs. Pop. 30,085. It takes its name from a local canyon.

**Cath·er·ine, Mount** |'kæTH(ə)rin| (Arabic name **Jebel Katherina**) mountain at the S end of the Sinai Peninsula, NE Egypt, the highest point in the country: 8,652 ft./2,637 m. A monastery on its slopes is said to be on the site of the burning bush of *Genesis*.

**Ca·tons·ville** |'kätnz,vil| community in central Maryland, a suburb SW of Baltimore. Pop. 35,233.

**Cats·kill Mountains** |'kæt,skil| (also **the Catskills**) range of mountains in SE New York, W of the Hudson River, part of the Appalachian system. Among its many resorts are those of the Borscht Belt.

**Cau·ca River** |'kowkə| river in W Colombia that flows N for 800 mi./1,300 km. from the Andes to the Magdalena River.

**Cau·ca·sus** |'kawkəsəs| (also **Caucasia**) mountainous region of SE Europe, lying between the Black and the Caspian seas, in Georgia, Armenia, Azerbaijan, and SE Russia. Mount Elbrus, at 18,481 ft./5,642 m., is the highest point. The region has given its name to both language and racial categories. □ **Caucasian** adj. & n.

**Cau·very River** |'kawvərē| (also **Kaveri**) river in S India that flows 475 mi./764 km. from the Western Ghats to the Bay of Bengal. After the Ganges, it is India's most sacred river.

**Cav·an** |'kævən| **1** county of the NW Republic of Ireland, part of the old province of Ulster. Pop. 53,000. **2** its county seat. Pop. 3,330.

**Ca·vi·te** |kə'vētē| historic port city in the Philippines, on SW Luzon, SW of Manila. Pop. 92,000.

**Caw·dor** |'kawdər| village in N Scotland, in the Highlands near Nairn. Cawdor Castle figures in *Macbeth* by Shakespeare.

**Cawn·pore** |'kawn,pawr| another spelling for KANPUR, India.

**Ca·xi·as** |kä'sHēəs| commercial city in NE Brazil, on the Itapecuru River in Maranhão state. Pop. 134,000.

**Ca·xi·as do Sul** |'käsHēəs dōō 'sōōl| industrial city in S Brazil, in Rio Grande do Sul state. Pop. 263,000.

**Cay·enne** |kī'en| the capital and chief port of French Guiana. Pop. 41,600. It gave its name to a type of hot pepper.

**Cay·man Islands** |'kämən| (also **the Caymans**) group of three islands in the Caribbean Sea, S of Cuba. Pop. 31,930. Official language, English. Capital: George Town. A resort and financial center, the Caymans are a British dependency.

**Cayman Islands**

**Cay·u·ga, Lake** |kə'yōōgə; kā'(y)ōōgə| one of the Finger Lakes, in W central New York. Ithaca lies at its S end.

**Ce·a·nan·nus Mor** |,sēə'nænəs ,mawr| (also **Kells**) town in E Ireland, in County Meath, the source, in its monastery, of the *Book of Kells*, the famous illuminated gospel manuscript now in Dublin, and given the town's alternate name.

**Ce·a·rá** |,sāə'rä| state in NE Brazil, on the Atlantic coast. Pop. 6,363,000. Capital: Fortaleza.

**Ce·bu** |sābōō| **1** island of the S central

Philippines. **2** its chief city and port. Pop. 610,000.

**Ce·dar Falls** |'sēdər| city in NE Iowa, on the Cedar River. Pop. 34,298.

**Ce·dar Ra·pids** |'sēdər| industrial and commercial city in E central Iowa, on the Cedar River. Pop. 108,751.

**Ce·la·ya** |sā'līə| commercial city in W central Mexico, in Guanajuato state, in an agricultural area. Pop. 215,000.

**Cel·e·bes** |'selə,bēz| former name for SULAWESI, Indonesia.

**Cel·e·bes Sea** |'selə,bēz| part of the W Pacific between the Philippines and Sulawesi, bounded to the W by Borneo. It is linked to the Java Sea by the Makassar Strait.

**Ce·les·tial Empire** |sə'lesCHəl| old term for CHINA.

**Ce·lje** |'tselye| spa and industrial town in central Slovenia, on the Savinja River. Pop. 41,000.

**Cel·le** |'tselə; 'kælə| manufacturing city in N Germany, on the Aller River. Pop. 70,000.

**Cel·tic Sea** |'keltik; 'seltik| the part of the Atlantic between S Ireland and SW England.

**Cen·ten·ni·al State** |,sen'teneəl| nickname for COLORADO.

**Cen·tral Af·ri·can Republic** |'sentrəl ,æfrikən| republic in the Sahel of central Africa. Area: 241,313 sq. mi./625,000 sq. km. Pop. 3,113,000. Languages: French (official), Sango. Capital and largest city: Bangui. Formerly a French colony, it became a republic in 1958 and fully independent in 1960. Ranging from tropical forest to semidesert, it is essentially agricultural. Former name (until 1958) UBANGHI SHARI. In 1966–79 called the CENTRAL AFRICAN EMPIRE.

**Central African Republic**

**Cen·tral A·me·ri·ca** |,sentrəl ə'merəkə| the southernmost part of North America, linking the continent to South America and consisting of the countries of Guatemala, Belize, Honduras, El Salvador, Nicaragua, Costa Rica, and Panama. □ **Central American** *adj. & n.*

**Cen·tral Asia** |'sentrəl 'azhə| parts of the Asian land mass generally taken to include regions E of European Russia and W of China; much of the area is vast grasslands (steppes).

**Cen·tral Asian States** |'sentrəl 'azhən| association, formed in 1994, of the former Soviet Central Asian republics that are now independent Kazakhstan, Kyrgyzstan, and Uzbekistan.

**Cen·tral Eu·rope** |'sentrəl 'yŏŏrəp| loosely defined term for parts of Europe W of Eastern Europe, N of Southern Europe, and E of Western Europe, usually taken to include most of Germany, Switzerland, Austria, and sometimes the Czech Republic and parts of Poland.

**Cen·tral Park** |'sentrəl| large public park in the center of Manhattan, New York City. Created in the 1850s–70s, it was the model for U.S. urban parks.

**Cen·tral Valley** |'sentrəl| lowland of central California. In the N it is drained by the Sacramento River, and also called the Sacramento Valley. In the S, it is called the San Joaquin Valley after the major river here. It is a significant producer of agricultural products.

**Centre** |säntr| region of central France, including departments on the Loire River. Its capital is Orleans.

**Ceph·a·lo·nia** |‚sefə'lōnēə| Greek island in the Ionian Sea. Pop. 29,400. Greek name **Kefallinía**.

**Ce·ram** |'sä‚räm| (also **Seram; Serang**) island in E Indonesia, in the central Moluccas. Chief town: Masohi.

**Ce·ram Sea** |'sä‚räm| (also **Seram Sea**) the part of the W Pacific Ocean at the center of the Moluccas Islands.

**Ce·ra·sus** |'serəsəs| see GIRESUN, Turkey.

**Cer·ri·tos** |sə'rētəs| city in SW California, a suburb SE of Los Angeles. Pop. 53,240.

**Cer·ro de Pas·co** |'serō dä 'päskō| mining city in central Peru, in the Andes Mts. at 14,216 ft./4,333 m. Pop. 30,000. Once a key silver source, it today provides vanadium and other metals.

**Cer·ro Gor·do** |‚serō 'gawrdō| mountain pass in E Mexico, between Veracruz and Jalapa, scene of an 1847 victory by U.S. forces in the Mexican War.

**Cer·ro Ma·ra·vil·la** |'serō ‚märə'vēə| peak in the Cordillera Central of S Puerto Rico, near Ponce, site of a much-debated 1978

incident in which two independence activists were killed.

**Cer·tal·do** |cHer'täldō| village in central Italy, SW of Florence. Pop. 16,000. It was the childhood home of the poet Boccaccio.

**Ce·se·na** |cHa'zänə| agricultural and industrial town in N Italy. Pop. 90,000. Its Malatesta Library is one of the oldest monastic libraries extant.

**Če·ské Bu·dě·jo·vice** |'cHeska 'boodyə ‚yawvət‚sä| city in the S of the Czech Republic, on the Vltava River. Pop. 173,400. A tourist center, it is also noted for the production of beer. German name **Budweis**.

**Ce·ti·nje** |'tse‚tēnyə| historic town in Montenegro. Pop. 20,000. It was formerly the capital of Montenegro, and is a monastic center.

**Ceu·ta** |'THa‚ootə; 'sā‚ootə| Spanish exclave, a port and military post on the coast of N Africa, in Morocco. Pop. 67,615.

**Cé·vennes** |sä‚ven| mountain range on the SE edge of the Massif Central in France.

**Cey·han** |ja'hän| (ancient name **Pyramus**) river that flows 300 mi./480 km. S through central Turkey to the Gulf of Iskenderun in the Mediterranean Sea. The city of **Cey·han** (pop. 85,000) lies on its course.

**Cey·lon** |si'län; sā'län| former name (until 1972) for SRI LANKA.

**Cha·blais** |sHä'blä| former region in E France, S of Lake Geneva. It is now part of Haut-Savoie department.

**Cha·blis** |sHä'blē| village in central France, in Burgundy (Bourgogne), famous for its white wines.

**Cha·co** |'cHäkō| see GRAN CHACO, South America.

**Chad** |cHæd| landlocked republic in N central Africa. Area: 495,752 sq. mi./1,284,000 sq. km. Pop. 5,828,000. Official languages: French and Arabic. Capital and largest city: N'Djamena. Independent from France in 1960, Chad is dominated by the Sahara Desert in the N and the Lake Chad watershed, in the Sahel, in the S. Mining, agri-

**Chad**

culture, and herding are important. □ **Cha-dian** *adj. & n.*

**Chad, Lake** |ᴄHǽd| shallow lake on the borders of Chad, Niger, and Nigeria in N central Africa. Its size varies seasonally from *c.*4,000 sq. mi./10,360 sq. km. to *c.*10,000 sq. mi./25,900 sq. km.

**Cha·gos Archipelago** |'ᴄHägəs| island group in the Indian Ocean forming the British Indian Ocean Territory.

**Chal·ce·don** |'kælsə,dän| former city on the Bosporus in Asia Minor, now part of Istanbul, Turkey. The site was quarried for building materials, including chalcedony, during the construction of Constantinople by the Romans. Turkish name **Kadiköy**. □ **Chalcedonian** *adj. & n.*

**Chal·cid·i·ce** |kæl'sidesē| peninsula in N Greece, with three long headlands extending into the Aegean Sea SE of Thessaloníki.

**Chal·cis** |'kælsəs; 'kælkəs| the chief town of the island of Euboea, on the coast opposite mainland Greece. Pop. 44,800. Greek name **Khalkís**.

**Chal·dea** |kæl'dēə| ancient country of the Chaldeans, in what is now S Iraq. □ **Chaldean** *adj. & n.*

**Chal·leng·er Deep** |'ᴄHælənjər 'dēp| See MARIANA TRENCH, Pacific Ocean.

**Châlons-sur-Marne** |SHä'lawNsYr,märn| industrial and wine-making city and capital of the Marne department in NE France. Pop. 52,000.

**Chalon-sur-Saône** manufacturing city in E central France, at the junction of the Saône and Loire rivers. Pop. 56,000.

**Cham·bers·burg** |'ᴄHämbərz,bərg| historic borough in S Pennsylvania, SW of Harrisburg. Pop. 16,647.

**Cham·bé·ry** |SHäNbā'rē| commercial and administrative city in Savoie department, in E France. Pop. 55,600.

**Cham·bord** |SHäN'bawr| village in N central France, in the Loire valley. King Francis I built an immense Renaissance chateau here, sited in an enormous park.

**Cha·mi·zal, the** |'SHämə,zæl; ,chämē'säl| district divided between El Paso, Texas, and Ciudad Juarez, Mexico, on the Rio Grande, whose shifts have caused border disputes. Both countries maintain parks here.

**Cha·mo·nix** |SHämaw'nē| ski resort at the foot of Mont Blanc, in the Alps of E France. Pop. 9,255. Full name **Chamonix-Mont-Blanc**.

**Cham·pa** |'ᴄHämpə; 'ᴄHæmpə| former independent kingdom (2nd to *c.*14th centuries) in territory now in central and southern Vietnam; home of the Chams, related to Cambodians.

**Cham·pagne** |SHäN'pän(yə); sham'pän| region and former province of NE France, which now corresponds to the Champagne-Ardenne administrative region. The region is noted for the white sparkling wine first produced there in about 1700.

**Champagne-Ardenne** |SHäN,pän yär'den| region in NE France, comprising part of the Ardennes forest and the vine-growing area of Champagne.

**Cham·pagne Castle** |SHäN'pän| peak in the Drakensberg Range of NE South Africa, the highest in the country: 11,073 ft./3,375 m.

**Cham·paign** |SHæm'pän| city in E central Illinois, home to the University of Illinois. Pop. 63,502.

**Champigny-sur-Marne** |SHäNpēn'yē sYr ,märn| residential suburb SE of Paris, on the Marne River. Pop. 80,000. It was a battleground during the Franco-Prussian War.

**Cham·plain, Lake** |SHæm'plän| glacial lake in North America, to the E of the Adirondack Mts. It forms part of the border between New York and Vermont, and its N tip extends into Quebec. The Champlain Valley is noted for its scenery and history.

**Champs Ély·sées** |'SHäNz älē'zä| avenue in Paris, leading from the Place de la Concorde to the Arc de Triomphe. It is noted for its fashionable shops and restaurants.

**Chan·cel·lors·ville** |'ᴄHæns(ə)lərz,vil| historic locality in E central Virginia, W of Fredericksburg, site of a Civil War battle in May 1863.

**Chan Chan** |'ᴄHän 'ᴄHän| the capital of the pre-Inca civilization of the Chimu. Its extensive adobe ruins are situated on the coast of N Peru.

**Chan-chiang** |'ᴄHän jē'äNG| see ZHANG-JIANG, China.

**Chan·der·na·gore** |,ᴄHəndərnə'gōr| (also **Chandanaggar**) town in E India, in West Bengal state, a suburb N of Calcutta. Pop. 122,000.

**Chan·di·garh** |'ᴄHəndēgər| **1** Union Territory of NW India, created in 1966. **2** city in this territory. Pop. 503,000. The present city was designed in 1950 by Le Corbusier as a new capital for the Punjab and is now the capital of the states of Punjab and Haryana.

**Chan·dler** |'ᴄHændlər| city in S central Arizona, a suburb and resort SE of Phoenix. Pop. 90,533.

**Chan·dra·pur** |,ᴄHəndrə'pŏor| historic

city in central India, in Maharashtra state on the Irar River. Pop. 226,000.

**Chang** |CHäNG| (also **Ko Chang**) resort island, second-largest in Thailand, in the Gulf of Thailand.

**Chang'an** |'CHäNG'än| name of XI'AN, China, when it was the capital of the Han (206 B.C.–A.D. 220) and Sui (581–618) dynasties.

**Chang·chia·kow** |'jäNG'jē'ä'kō| see ZHANGJIAKOU, China.

**Chang·chun** |'CHäNG'CHŏŏn| industrial city in NE China, capital of Jilin province. Pop. 2,070,000. It is a center of vehicle and machinery production and of technical education.

**Chang·de** |'CHäNG'də| city and river port in Hunan province, SE central China, on the Yuan River. Pop. 301,000. It is an administrative and light industrial center.

**Chang Jiang** |'CHäNG jē'äNG| another name for the YANGTZE.

**Chang·kia·kow** |'jäNGjē'ä 'kō| see ZHANGJIAKOU.

**Chang·sha** |'CHäNG'SHä| the capital of Hunan province in E central China. Pop. 1,300,000.

**Chang·shu** |'CHäNG'SHŏŏ| town in Jiangsu province, E China, an industrial port near the mouth of the Yangtze River. Pop. 214,000.

**Ch'ang·won** |'CHäNG'wän| industrial city in S South Korea, on a bay off the Korea Strait. Pop. 482,000.

**Chang·zhi** |'CHäNG'jē| city in Shanxi province, E central China, W of Anyang. Pop. 317,000.

**Chang·zhou** |'CHäNG'jō| city in Jiangsu province, E China, on the Grand Canal N of Shanghai. Pop. 670,000.

**Chan·ia** |kän'yä| port on the N coast of Crete, capital of the island from 1841 to 1971. Pop. 47,340. Greek name **Khaniá**.

**Chan·nel Islands**[1] |'CHænl| another name for the SANTA BARBARA ISLANDS, California.

**Chan·nel Islands**[2] |'CHænl| group of islands in the English Channel off the NW coast of France, of which the largest are Jersey, Guernsey, and Alderney. Smaller islands include Sark, Herm, and Jethou. Pop. 146,000. Formerly part of the dukedom of Normandy, they have owed allegiance to England since 1066. French name **Îles Anglo-Normandes**.

**Chan·nel Tunnel** |'CHænl| rail tunnel under the English Channel, extending 31 mi./49 km. and linking England and France. The tunnel (popularly called the

**Channel Islands**

Chunnel) opened in 1994 after eight years of construction to link Holywell, near Folkestone, England, and Sangatte, near Calais, France.

**Chan·til·ly** |,shäntē'yē| town N of Paris, in N central France. Pop. 10,000. The town is noted for its chateau, which houses the Musée Condéc, a collection of medieval art; its racecourse; its fine lace; and its flavored whipped cream.

**Chao·hu** |'CHOw'hŏŏ| city in Anhui province, E China, on the E shore of Chao Lake (Chao Hu). Pop. 741,000.

**Chao Phra·ya** |CHOw 'priə| major waterway of central Thailand, formed by the junction of the Ping and Nan rivers.

**Chao·yang** |'CHOw'yäNG| city in Liaoning province, NE China, on the Daling River NE of Beijing. Pop. 328,000.

**Cha·pa·la, Lake** |CHə'pälə| largest (50 mi./80 km. long) lake in Mexico, in the W central states of Jalisco and Michoacán. It is a resort and fishing center.

**Chap·el Hill** |'CHæpəl| town in N central North Carolina, home to the University of North Carolina and to many research facilities. Pop. 38,719.

**Chap·pa·quid·dick Island** |,CHæpə-'kwidik| small resort island off the coast of Massachusetts, E of Martha's Vineyard, the scene of a car accident in 1969 involving Senator Edward Kennedy in which his assistant Mary Jo Kopechne drowned.

**Cha·pul·te·pec** |CHə'pŏŏltə,pek| hill ("Grasshopper Hill") in the major park of Mexico City, Mexico. It is the ancient seat of Aztec emperors, and is surmounted by a castle that was captured by U.S. forces in September 1847.

**Cha·rente** |SHä'räNt| river of W France, which rises in the Massif Central and flows 225 mi./360 km. W to enter the Bay of Biscay at Rochefort.

**Cha·ri River** |SHä'rē| (also **Shari**) river that flows 660 mi./1,060 km. through the Central African Republic, Chad, and Cameroon. Emptying into Lake Chad, it is the longest river in the African continent that drains internally.

**Cha·ri·kar** |ˈCHärē'kär| city in NE Afghanistan, in the Hindu Kush Mts., N of Kabul. Pop. 100,000.

**Char·ing Cross** |ˌCHæriNG 'kraws| district in central London, England, in the borough of Westminster, just SE of Trafalgar Square. Distances from London are measured from Charing Cross.

**Char·jew** |CHär'jōō| (also **Chardzhou** or **Charjui**) commercial city in E Turkmenistan, on the Amu Darya River. Pop. 166,000. It is a cotton-trade center.

**Char·le·roi** |ˌSHärlə'(r)wä| industrial city in SW Belgium. Pop. 206,200.

**Charles·bourg** |SHärl'bōōr| city in S Quebec, a suburb just NE of Quebec City. Pop. 70,788.

**Charles River** |CHärlz| river that flows 60 mi./100 km. through E Massachusetts, between Cambridge and Boston, to Boston Harbor.

**Charles·ton**¹ |ˈCHärlstən| historic port city in South Carolina, on the Ashley and Cooper rivers. Pop. 80,410. The bombardment in 1861 of Fort Sumter, in the harbor, by Confederate troops marked the beginning of the Civil War. Charleston is a commercial city and a center of tourism.

**Charles·ton**² |ˈCHärlstən| the state capital of West Virginia, an industrial city on the Kanawha River. Pop. 57,290.

**Charles·town**¹ |ˈCHärlz,town| neighborhood of N Boston, Massachusetts, N of the Charles River. Bunker Hill is here.

**Charles·town**² |ˈCHärlz,town| chief town of Nevis, in the federation of St. Kitts and Nevis, in the West Indies. Pop. 1,700. It is a port linked with Basseterre, on St. Kitts.

**Char·lotte** |ˈSHärlət| commercial city in S North Carolina, a major banking and financial center. Pop. 395,930.

**Char·lotte Ama·lie** |ˈSHärlət ə'mälyə| the capital of the U.S. Virgin Islands, a resort hub and port on the island of St. Thomas. Pop. 52,660.

**Char·lottes·ville** |ˈSHärləts,vil; ˈSHärlətsvəl| city in central Virginia, in the Blue Ridge Mts., home to the University of Virginia. Pop. 40,341. Monticello, the home of Thomas Jefferson, is nearby.

**Char·lotte·town** |ˈSHärlət,town| the capital and chief port of Prince Edward Island. Pop. 33,150.

**Char·tres** |ˈSHärt(rə)| city in N France.

Pop. 41,850. It is noted for its huge Gothic cathedral.

**Char·treuse** |SHär'trœz| (also **La Grande Chartreuse**) mountainous region in SE France. Its famous green and yellow liqueurs were first made in the monastery of La Grande Chartreuse, near Grenoble.

**Cha·ryb·dis** |kə'ribdes| in Greek mythology, a female monster thrown into the sea by Zeus. She landed across from Scylla and spewed out water, creating a whirlpool later identified with Galofalo, in the Strait of Messina, Sicily.

**Cha·teau·guay** |ˈSHætəgē; ˈSHætə,gä| city in S Quebec, a suburb SW of Montreal. Pop. 39,833.

**Cha·teau·roux** |SHätō'rōō| industrial city and capital of the department of Indre in N France, on the Indre River. Pop. 53,000.

**Chateau-Thierry** |SHæ,tō tye're| town in the Picardy region of N France, on the Marne River. Pop. 15,000. It was a major battlefield during World War I; there is a monument to the U.S. soldiers who took the town from German occupiers in 1918, and a military cemetery.

**Chat·ham**¹ |ˈCHætəm| port town in SE England, on the Medway River E of London, in Kent. Pop. 65,000. It was long a major naval base.

**Chat·ham**² |ˈCHætəm| city in S Ontario, E of Detroit, Michigan. Pop. 43,557.

**Chat·ham Islands** |ˈCHætəm| group of two islands, Pitt and Chatham islands, in the SW Pacific to the E of New Zealand, to which they belong.

**Chats·worth** |ˈCHæts,wərTH| estate, the seat of the Dukes of Devonshire, in N Derbyshire, N central England. It is one of the most famous and frequently visited British great houses.

**Chat·ta·hoo·chee River** |ˌCHætə'hōō-CHē| river that flows 435 mi./700 km. through Georgia, to the Florida border, where it continues as the Apalachicola River, into the Gulf of Mexico.

**Chat·ta·noo·ga** |ˌCHætn'ōōgə| city in SE Tennessee, on the Tennessee River near the Georgia border, a rail and industrial center. Pop. 152,466.

**Chau·bu·na·gun·ga·maug, Lake** |CHaw-,bənə'gəNGgə,mawg| small lake in S Massachusetts, S of Worcester, in the town of Webster. The full form of its name, Chargoggagoggmanchaugagoggchaubunagungamaugg, is said to be the longest American place name.

**Chau·diere River** |SHōd'yer| river that flows 120 mi./190 km. from the Maine border N through Quebec, emptying into the Saint Lawrence River opposite Quebec City.

**Chau·mont** |shō'mawn| manufacturing town and capital of the department of Haute-Marne in NE France. Pop. 29,000. Chaumont served as the headquarters of the U.S. Expeditionary Force in World War I.

**Chau·tau·qua** |shə'tawkwə| resort town in SW New York, on Chautauqua Lake, famed as the birthplace of a 19th-century popular education movement. Pop. 4,554.

**Cha·vin de Huán·tar** |chə'vēn dā 'wän-,tär| agricultural town in W central Peru near which are major pre-Columbian ruins, left by the pre-Inca Chavin culture of 3,000 years ago.

**Chea·dle** |'chēdl| (official name **Cheadle and Gatley**) industrial town in NW England, in Greater Manchester. Pop. 60,000.

**Cheap·side** |'chēp,sīd| historic commercial district in the city of London, England, near St. Paul's Cathedral.

**Che·bo·ksa·ry** |,chebäk'särē| city in W central Russia, on the Volga River, W of Kazan, capital of the autonomous republic of Chuvashia. Pop. 429,000.

**Chech·nya** |'chechnēə| (also **Chechenia**) autonomous republic in the Caucasus in SW Russia, on the border with Georgia. Pop. 1,290,000. Capital: Grozny. The republic declared itself independent of Russia in 1991; Russian troops invaded in 1994, but withdrew after the signing of a peace treaty in 1996. Also called **Chechen Republic**. ◻ **Chechen** adj. & n.

**Ched·dar** |'chedər| village in Somerset, SW England, that gave its name to the type of cheese. It is a center for tourists, especially those visiting nearby Cheddar Gorge in the Mendip Hills.

**Cheek·to·wa·ga** |,chēktə'wägə| town in W New York, an industrial suburb E of Buffalo. Pop. 99,314.

**Che·foo** |'jə'foo| see YANTAI, China.

**Che·ju** |'chə'joo| **1** island province of South Korea, S of the mainland in the North China Sea. Pop. 505,000. **2** its capital, a fishing port. Pop. 259,000.

**Che·kiang** |'jəjē'äNG| see ZHEJIANG, China.

**Che·lan, Lake** |shə'læn| recreational lake in N central Washington, in the Cascade Mts.

**Chelles** |shel| town in N France on the Marne River. The dating of prehistoric remains found here led to the designation "Chellean period" for that epoch in prehistory.

**Chelm** |KHelm; helm| industrial city in E Poland, the capital of Chelm county. Pop. 66,000.

**Chelm·no** |KHelmnō; helmnō| **1** industrial city in N central Poland, in the Vistula River valley. Pop. 22,000. **2** site of a Nazi concentration camp near Łodz, Poland.

**Chelms·ford** |'chelmsfərd| cathedral city in SE England, the county seat of Essex. Pop. 152,418.

**Chel·sea**¹ |'chelsē| fashionable residential district of London, England, on the N bank of the Thames River. The Kings Road here was a center of "Swinging London" of the 1960s.

**Chel·sea**² |'chelsē| industrial and commercial city in NE Massachusetts, just N of Boston. Pop. 28,710.

**Chel·sea**³ |'chelsē| fashionable residential section of S Manhattan, New York City, on the West Side.

**Chel·ten·ham** |'cheltn,əm| town in W England, in Gloucestershire. Pop. 85,900. It became a fashionable spa in the 19th century.

**Chel·ya·binsk** |&chel'yäbinsk| industrial city in S Russia, in a mining district on the E slopes of the Ural Mts. Pop. 1,148,000.

**Chem·nitz** |'kemnits| industrial city in eastern Germany, on the Chemnitz River. Pop. 310,000. Former name (1953–90) **Karl-Marx-Stadt**.

**Che·nab** |chə'näb| river of N India and Pakistan, which rises in the Himalayas and flows through Himachal Pradesh and Jammu and Kashmir, to join the Sutlej River in Punjab. It is one of the five rivers that gave Punjab its name.

**Chen-chiang** |'jənjē'äNG| see ZHENJIANG, China.

**Cheng·chow** |'jəNG'jō| see ZHENGZHOU, China.

**Cheng·de** |'chəNG'də| city in Hebei province, N China, on the Luan River. Pop. 247,000. It was the summer capital of the Manchu emperors.

**Cheng·du** |'chəNG'doo| the capital of Sichuan province in W central China. Pop. 2,780,000.

**Che·non·ceaux** |shənawN'sō| village in W central France, on the Cher River. It is famous for its romantic Renaissance chateau, whose arches span the Cher. During World War II the line separating occupied France from Vichy France ran through the Cher and thus through the chateau itself.

**Cheq·uers** |'CHekərz| estate in Buckinghamshire, central England, NW of London, since 1917 a country retreat for the British prime minister.

**Cher** |'sHer| river in central France, which rises in the Massif Central, flowing 220 mi./350 km. N to meet the Loire near Tours.

**Cher·bourg** |sHer'boŏr; 'sHer,boŏrg| seaport and naval base in Normandy, N France, formerly a key transatlantic harbor. Pop. 28,770.

**Che·re·po·vets** |,CHirəpə'vyets| industrial city in NW Russia, on the Rybinsk reservoir. Pop. 313,000.

**Cher·ka·sy** |CHir'käsē| port in central Ukraine, on the Dnieper River. Pop. 297,000. Russian name **Cherkassy**.

**Cher·kessk** |CHir'kesk| city in the Caucasus in S Russia, capital of the republic of Karachai-Cherkessia. Pop. 113,000.

**Cher·ni·hiv** |CHir'nēiv| port in N Ukraine, on the Desna River. Pop. 301,000. Russian name **Chernigov**.

**Cher·niv·tsi** |CHirnift'sē| city in W Ukraine, in the foothills of the Carpathians, close to the border with Romania; the economic hub of Bukovina. Pop. 257,000. It was part of Romania between 1918 and 1940. Russian name **Chernovtsy**; Romanian name **Cernăuţi**; German name **Czernowitz**.

**Cher·no·byl** |CHər'nōbəl| town near Kiev in Ukraine where, in April 1986, an accident at a nuclear power plant resulted in a serious escape of radioactive material and the subsequent contamination of parts of what are now Ukraine and Belarus, as well as other parts of Europe.

**Cher·no·zem** |,CHirnə'zHawm| semiarid regions in S Russia and N Kazakhstan that take their name from their fertile black soil, rich in humus. Also **Black Earth regions**.

**Cher·ra·pun·ji** |CHərə'poŏnjē| (also **Cherrapunjee**) commercial town in NE India, in Meghalaya state, on the S slope of the Khasi Hills. It is reputedly the wettest inhabited place in the world, with an average annual rainfall of 450 in./1,100 cm.

**Cher·ry Hill** |'CHerē| township in SW New Jersey, a suburb SE of Philadelphia, Pennsylvania. Pop. 69,359.

**Cher·so·nese** |'kərsə,nēz| ancient name for the Gallipoli Peninsula in Turkey. The name is also applied to other peninsulas, including the Crimea and the Malay Peninsula (the **Golden Chersonese**).

**Ches·a·peake** |'CHesə,pēk| port city in central Virginia, in the Hampton Roads area. Pop. 151,976.

**Ches·a·peake Bay** |'CHesə,pēk| large inlet of the North Atlantic on the E U.S. coast, extending 200 mi./320 km. inland through the states of Virginia and Maryland, and famed for the richness of its marine life.

**Chesh·ire** |'CHesHər; 'CHes,ir| county of W central England; county seat, Chester.

**Che·sil Beach** |'CHezəl| (also **Chesil Bank**) a shingle beach in S England, off the Dorset coast.

**Ches·ter**[1] |'CHestər| historic city in W England, the county seat of Cheshire. Pop. 115,000.

**Ches·ter**[2] |'CHestər| city in SE Pennsylvania, on the Delaware River SW of Philadelphia. Pop. 41,856.

**Ches·ter·field**[1] |'CHestər,fēld| industrial town in Derbyshire, central England. Pop. 99,700.

**Ches·ter·field**[2] |'CHestər,fēld| city in E central Missouri, a suburb W of St. Louis. Pop. 37,991.

**Chest·nut Hill**[1] |'CHes,nət| affluent suburban area W of Boston, Massachusetts, partly in Brookline, partly in Newton.

**Chest·nut Hill**[2] |'CHes,nət| affluent residential section of N Philadelphia, Pennsylvania.

**Che·tu·mal** |,CHätoŏ'mäl| port in SE Mexico, on the Yucatán Peninsula at the border with Belize, capital of the state of Quintana Roo. Pop. 40,000.

**Chev·i·ot Hills** |'CHevēət; 'CHēvēət| (also **the Cheviots**) a range of hills on the border between England and Scotland.

**Chevy Chase**[1] |'CHevē 'CHās| see OTTERBURN, England.

**Chevy Chase**[2] |'CHevē 'CHās| fashionable suburb N of Washington, D.C., in Montgomery County, Maryland. Pop. 8,559.

**Chey·enne** |sHī'æn; sHī'en| commercial city, the capital of Wyoming, in the SE. Pop. 50,008. Government, cattle, and tourism are central to its economy.

**Chey·enne River** |sHī'æn; sHī'en| river that flows 530 mi./850 km. from NE Wyoming into W South Dakota, joining the Missouri River at Lake Oahe.

**Chiai** |CHē'ē| (also **Chia-i**) city, W Taiwan, a distribution center for agricultural products from the surrounding region. Pop. 259,000.

**Chiang·mai** |CHē'äNG'mī| city in NW Thailand. Pop. 164,900.

**Chi·an·ti** |kē'äntē| region in Tuscany, in central Italy, NW of Siena, noted for its dry red wine.

**Chi·a·pas** |CHē'äpəs| state of S Mexico, bordering Guatemala. Area: 28,664 sq.

mi./74,211 sq. km. Pop. 3,204,000. Capital: Tuxtla Gutiérrez. Heavily Indian in population, Chiapas has long struggled with poverty and chafed at Mexican government control.

**Chi·ba** |'CHēbə| industrial city in Japan, on the island of Honshu, E of Tokyo. Pop. 829,470.

**Chi·ca·go** |SHə'kägō; SHe'kawgō| city in Illinois, on Lake Michigan. Pop. 2,783,730. Selected as a terminal for the Illinois and Michigan canal (1848), and for railroads to the E (1852), Chicago developed during the 19th century as a major grain market and food-processing center. It is the third-largest city in the U.S., and a major center of commerce, industry, culture, and education. □ **Chicagoan** *adj. & n.*

**Chi·chén It·zá** |CHi'CHen ēt'sä| site in central Yucatán, SE Mexico, a center of the Mayan empire until around the year 1200. Its pyramids, wells, temples, and other structures have been partly restored.

**Chich·es·ter** |'CHiCHəstər| city in S England, the county seat of West Sussex. Pop. 27,200.

**Chick·a·mau·ga Creek** |,CHikə'mawgə| stream that flows from NW Georgia into the Tennessee River, near Chattanooga, Tennessee. A brutal Civil War battle was fought along it in September 1863.

**Chi·cla·yo** |CHē'klīyō| commercial city in NW Peru, between the Andes and the Pacific, in an irrigated desert area. Pop. 426,000.

**Chi·co** |'CHēkō| city in N California, at the N end of the Sacramento Valley. Pop. 40,079.

**Chic·o·pee** |'CHikə,pē| city in S central Massachusetts, an industrial center on the N side of Springfield. Pop. 56,632.

**Chi·cou·ti·mi** |SHi'kōōtəmē| industrial city in SE Quebec, on the Saguenay River N of Quebec City. Pop. 62,670.

**Chiem, Lake** |kēm| in S Germany, SE of Munich, in a resort area. It is the largest lake in Bavaria (31 sq. mi./81 sq. km.).

**Chie·ti** |ke'etē| commercial town in central Italy on the Pescara River and capital of Chieti province. Pop. 57,000.

**Chi·feng** |'CHər'fəNG| (Mongolian name **Ulanhad**) city, Inner Mongolia, NE China. Pop. 392,000. It is a distribution center for agricultural products from the surrounding region.

**Chi·ga·sa·ki** |,CHēgä'säkē| resort and industrial city in E central Japan, on central Honshu. Pop. 202,000.

**Chih·li, Gulf of** |'jir'li; 'CHē'lē| see Bo Hai, China.

**Chi·hua·hua** |CHə'wäwə| **1** largest state of Mexico, in the N, bordering Texas and New Mexico. Area: 94,607 sq. mi./244,938 sq. km. Pop. 2,440,000. **2** its capital, the principal city of N central Mexico. Pop. 530,490.

**Chile** |'CHēlā; 'CHilē| republic occupying a long Pacific coastal strip in SW South America. Area: 292,132 sq. mi./756,622 sq. km. Pop. 13,232,000. Capital and largest city: Santiago. Language, Spanish. Part of the Inca empire, the country achieved independence from Spanish Peru in 1818. Much of the N is the mineral-rich Atacama Desert. In the S, grazing lands and forest predominate. Mining, agriculture, and fishing are important. □ **Chilean** *adj. & n.*

Chile

**Chil·lán** |CHē'yän| commercial city in S central Chile, in a rich agricultural valley NE of Concepción. Pop. 146,000.

**Chil·li·cothe** |,CHilə'käTHē; ,CHilə-'kawTHē| historic city in S central Ohio, an early capital of the state. Pop. 21,921.

**Chil·lon** |SHē'yawn| castle in Vaud, W Switzerland, at the E end of Lake Geneva. The Swiss patriot François Bonivard, hero of Byron's poem *The Prisoner of Chillon*, was kept here.

**Chil·pan·cin·go** |,CHēlpän'singō| city in SW Mexico, capital of the state of Guerrero. Pop. 120,000.

**Chil·tern Hills** |'CHiltərn| (also **the Chilterns**) range of chalk hills in S England, N of the Thames River and W of London.

**Chi·lung** |'jē'lōōNG| (also **Chi-lung;** also called **Keelung**) chief port and naval base of Taiwan, at the N tip of the island. Pop. 357,000. Shipbuilding, fishing, and chemicals are important industries.

**Chim·bo·ra·zo** |,CHimbə'räzō| the highest Andean peak in Ecuador, rising to 20,487 ft./6,310 m.

**Chim·bo·te** |CHĕm'bō,tā| industrial port city in W central Peru, on the Pacific N of Lima. Pop. 297,000. It is a major fishing center.

**Chim·kent** |SHim'kent| see SHYMKENT, Kazakhstan.

**Chi·na** |'CHīnə| country in E Asia, the third-largest and most populous in the world. Area: 3.7 million sq. mi./9.6 million sq. km. Pop. 1,151,200,000. Language, Chinese (Mandarin is official). Capital: Beijing. Largest city: Shanghai. Official name **People's Republic of China**. One of the oldest known cultures, China has been a republic since 1912, and a communist state since 1949. Almost all its people live in the E third of the country, the W being mostly arid and mountainous. Agriculture, mining, and manufacturing are all important. □ **Chinese** adj. & n.

**Chi·na, Republic of** |'CHīnə| official name for TAIWAN.

**Chi·na Sea** |'CHīnə| the part of the Pacific Ocean off the coast of China, divided at the island of Taiwan into the *East China Sea* at the N and the *South China Sea* at the S.

**Chi·na·town** |'CHīnə,town| generic term for a Chinese-dominated commercial district in any of various U.S. or Canadian cities. Noted examples are in San Francisco, New York, and Vancouver.

**Chin·co·teague Island** |'SHiNGkə,tēg; 'CHiNGkə,tēg| island N of Assateague Island and noted for its wild horses and much visited.

**Chin·dwin** |'CHin'dwin| river that rises in northern Burma and flows southwards for 500 mi./885 km. to meet the Irrawaddy.

**Chin Hills** |CHin| range of hills in W Burma, close to the borders with India and Bangladesh.

**Chin·ju** |'jin'jōō| commercial and industrial city in S South Korea. Pop. 330,000.

**Chin·kiang** |'jin'jäNG| see ZHENJIANG, China.

**Chi·no** |'CHēnō| city in SW California, an outer suburb E of Los Angeles. Pop. 59,682.

**Chi·non** |SHē'nawN| medieval town in W central France, in the Loire valley. Pop. 9,000. It is dominated by the ruins of its chateau, where Joan of Arc first presented herself to the Dauphin of France. The town produces fine wines.

**Chi·nook Belt** |SHə'nŏŏk; CHə'nŏŏk| term

CHINA

for region of the U.S. and Canada just E of the Rocky Mts., where warm *chinook* winds mitigate winter cold.

**Chi·os** |'kē,äs| Greek island in the Aegean Sea. Pop. 52,690. Greek name **Khios**. □ **Chian** *adj. & n.*

**Chi·pa·ta** |cHē'pätə| (formerly **Fort Jameson**) commercial town in E Zambia, near the Malawi border. Pop. 146,000.

**Chir·chik** |cHir'cHek| (also **Chirciq**) industrial city in NE Uzbekistan, NE of Tashkent. Pop. 157,000.

**Chi·ri·ca·hua Mountains** |,cHiri'käwə| range in SE Arizona, on the Mexican border, noted in the 19th century as controlled by Cochise and other Apache leaders.

**Chis·holm Trail** |'cHisəm| historic route over which 19th-century cowboys drove cattle 1,500 mi./2,400 km. N from Texas to Abilene and other Kansas cities reached by developing railroads.

**Chi·și·nău** |,kēsHə'now| the capital and largest city of Moldova. Pop. 665,000. Russian name **Kishinyov** or **Kishinev**.

**Chis·wick** |'cHizik| largely residential district of W London, England, N of the Thames River in the borough of Hounslow. It is associated with Alexander Pope, William Morris, and other cultural figures.

**Chi·ta** |cHi'tä| city in SE Siberia, Russia, on the Trans-Siberian Railway. Pop. 349,000.

**Chit·ta·gong** |'cHitə,gawNG| seaport in SE Bangladesh, on the Bay of Bengal. Pop. 1,566,070.

**Chi·tun·gwi·za** |,cHētooNG'gwēzə| city in NE Zimbabwe, a suburb SE of Harare. Pop. 274,000.

**Chka·lov** |cHə'käləf| former name (1938–57) for ORENBURG, Russia.

**Cho·be** |'cHōbä| district of N Botswana, site of a national park noted for its wildlife.

**Cho·fu** |'cHō,foo| city in E central Japan, on E central Honshu, a residential and industrial suburb of Tokyo. Pop. 198,000.

**Choi·seul** |sHwä'zœl| volcanic island in the Solomon Islands, E of Bougainville, a scene of fighting in World War II.

**Choi·sy** |sHwä'zē| (full name **Choisy-le-Roi**) commune, an industrial SE suburb of Paris, France. Pop. 38,000.

**Cho·lon** |'cHō'lawn| industrial and commercial district of Ho Chi Minh City, Vietnam. It was an important port before Saigon developed, and has long been heavily Chinese.

**Cho·lu·la** |cHō'loolə| (official name **Cholula de Rivadabia**) city in Puebla state, E central Mexico. Pop. 54,000. It is

famed for its Aztec pyramids, churches, and other historic sites.

**Chong·jin** |'cHəNG'jin| industrial port city on the NE coast of North Korea. Pop. 754,100.

**Chong·ju** |'cHəNG'joo| commercial and industrial city in W central South Korea, capital of N Chungchong province. Pop. 531,000.

**Chong·qing** |'cHooNG'cHiNG; 'cHooNG-'kiNG| (formerly **Chungking**) industrial city in Sichuan province, central China, on the Yangtze River. It produces steel, chemicals, textiles, and motorcycles. It was the capital of China from 1938 to 1945.

**Chon·ju** |'cHən'joo| commercial and industrial city in SW South Korea, capital of N Cholla province, in the heart of a rice-producing region. Pop. 563,000.

**Cho Oyu** |'cHō ō'yoo| peak in the Himalayas, on the Nepal-Tibet border, first climbed in 1954. 26,750 ft./8,150 m.

**Chor·ril·los** |cHō'rē-ōs| town in W central Peru, a resort and suburb S of Lima. Pop. 213,000.

**Cho·rzów** |'kō,zHoof| transportation and industrial center in S Poland. Pop. 133,000. It is in a mining region.

**Chotts** |sHäts| term, from the Arabic, for saline lakes, especially in Algeria and Tunisia. Their vicinity is used for herding.

**Christ·church** |'kris,cHərcH| commercial city, the largest on South Island, New Zealand. Pop. 303,400.

**Chris·ti·a·nia** |,kriscHē'ænēə; ,kristē'æ-nēə| (also **Kristiania**) former name (1624–1924) for OSLO, Norway.

**Chris·tian·sted** |'kriscHən,sted| resort town on Saint Croix Island in the U.S. Virgin Islands, once the capital of the Danish West Indies. Pop. 2,555.

**Christ·mas Island**[1] |'krisməs| island in the Indian Ocean 200 mi./350 km. S of Java, administered as an external territory of Australia since 1958. Pop. 1,275.

**Christ·mas Island**[2] |'krisməs| former name (until 1981) for KIRITIMATI, Kiribati.

**Chu·bu** |'cHō'boo| mountainous region of Japan, on the island of Honshu. Capital: Nagoya.

**Chu·gach Mountains** |'cHoo,gæcH; 'cHoo,gæsH| range of mountains, part of the Coast Ranges, in S Alaska. Anchorage lies at its feet, and it is noted for glaciers that flow S into the Gulf of Alaska.

**Chu·go·ku** |cHoo'gōkoo| region of Japan, on the island of Honshu. Capital: Hiroshima.

**Chuk·chi Sea** |'cHookcHē; 'cHəkcHē| part

of the Arctic Ocean lying between North America and Asia and to the N of the Bering Strait.

**Chu·la Vis·ta** |ˌCHOŌlə 'vistə| city in SW California, S of San Diego and near the Mexican border. Pop. 135,163.

**Chun·chon** |'CHOŌn'CHƏn| industrial city in NE South Korea, the capital of Kangwon province. Pop. 179,000.

**Chung·king** |CHƏNG'kiNG| see CHONG-QING, China.

**Chung·shan** |'jōONG'SHän| see ZHONG-SHAN, China.

**Chu·qui·sa·ca** |ˌCHOŌkē'säkə| former name (1539–1840) for SUCRE, Bolivia.

**Church·ill** |'CHƏRCHəl; 'CHƏr,CHil| settlement in NE Manitoba, a warm-weather port on Hudson Bay. Pop. 1,143.

**Church·ill Downs** |'CHƏr,CHil; 'CHƏrCHəl| horse-racing facility in Louisville, Kentucky, site of the annual Kentucky Derby.

**Church·ill River**[1] |'CHƏrCHəl; 'CHƏr,CHil| river that flows 600 mi./1,000 km. from the Canadian Shield across E Labrador to the Labrador Sea. Its high falls generate hydroelectric power. It was formerly called the Hamilton River.

**Church·ill River**[2] |'CHƏrCHəl; 'CHƏr,CHil| river that flows 1,000 mi./1,600 km. from N Saskatchewan across Manitoba to Hudson Bay at Churchill. It was important in the early fur trade.

**Chu·va·shia** |CHOŌ'väSHēə| autonomous republic in European Russia, E of Nizhni Novgorod. Pop. 1,340,000. Capital: Cheboksary. □ **Chuvash** adj. & n.

**Chu·xiong** |'CHOŌSHe'awNG| city in Yunnan province, S China, W of Kunming on a tributary of the Jinsha River. Pop 383,000.

**Chu·zhou** |'CHOŌ'jō| city in Anhui province, E China, NW of Nanjing. Pop. 370,000.

**Ci·bo·la** |'sibələ| legendary land of wealth, sometimes seven cities of gold, that enticed early Spanish explorers in the SW U.S. The name survives in various localities.

**Cic·ero** |'sisə,rō| town in NE Illinois, an industrial and residential suburb just W of Chicago. Pop. 67,436.

**Cien·fue·gos** |ˌsē-en'fwägōs| port city in S central Cuba, on Cienfuegos Bay in the Caribbean Sea, the capital of Cienfuegos province. Pop. 124,000.

**Ci·li·cia** |sə'liSHə| ancient region on the coast of SE Asia Minor, corresponding to the present-day province of Adana, Turkey. □ **Cilician** adj. & n.

**Ci·li·cian Gates** |se'liSHən| mountain pass in the Taurus Mts. of S Turkey, historically

forming part of a route linking Anatolia with the Mediterranean coast.

**Cim·ar·ron River** |'simə,rän; 'simə,rōn| river that flows 600 mi./1,000 km. from New Mexico across Oklahoma to the Arkansas River near Tulsa. The W Panhandle of Oklahoma was once known as the Territory of Cimarron.

**Cim·me·ri·an Bos·po·rus** |sə'mirēən 'bäspərəs| historical name for the Kerch Strait, which links the Sea of Azov and the Black Sea at the E of the Crimean Peninsula of the Ukraine. The Cimmerians, peoples from this region, overran Asia Minor (present-day Turkey) in the 7th century B.C.

**Cim·pu·lung** |kimpə'lōONG| commercial and resort town in central Romania, on the S slopes of the Transylvanian Alps. Pop. 40,000.

**Cin·cin·nati** |ˌsinsə'nætē| industrial city in SW Ohio, a port on the Ohio River. Pop. 364,000.

**Cinque Ports** |'siNGk 'pawrts| group of medieval ports in Kent and East Sussex, SE England, which were formerly allowed trading privileges in exchange for providing the bulk of England's navy. The five original Cinque Ports were Hastings, Sandwich, Dover, Romney, and Hythe; later Rye and Winchelsea were added.

**Ci·pan·go** |si'pæNGgō| (also **Zipango**) medieval name given to an island described by Marco Polo and thought to be Japan.

**Cir·cas·sia** |sər'kæSHə| historic region covering the area between the Black Sea, the Kuban River, and the Caucasus Mts., and roughly equivalent to the Krasnodar Territory in present-day SE Russia. □ **Circassian** adj. & n.

**Cir·cum·po·lar regions** |ˌsərkəm'pōlər| term for regions near or around a pole, used especially in describing areas and related peoples, such as the Inuit, of N Asia and N North America.

**Ci·re·bon** |'CHēre'bawn| industrial port city in Indonesia, on the N coast of W Java. Pop. 254,000.

**Ci·ren·ces·ter** |'siren,sestər; 'sisitər| town in Gloucestershire, SW England. Pop. 14,000. It was a major town in Roman Britain, when it was known as Corinium Dobunorum.

**Cis·al·pine Gaul** |sis'æl,pīn 'gawl| see GAUL.

**Cis·at·lan·tic** |sisət'læn(t)ik| on one's own side of the Atlantic; a term used chiefly by Europeans.

**Cis·kei** |'sis,kī| former homeland established in South Africa for the Xhosa people, now part of the province of Eastern Cape.

**Ci·teaux** |sē'tō| (Latin name **Cistercium**) village in E France, about 16 mi./26 km. SE of Dijon. The Cistercian order of Roman Catholic monks was founded here in 1098.

**Ci·thae·ron** |sə'THērən| (also **Kithairon**) mountain in Greece (4,623 ft./1,409 m.). It is the site of many events in Greek mythology.

**Cities of the Plain** see SODOM.

**Ci·ti·um** |'sēsH(ē)əm| (also called **Cition;** biblical name **Kittim** or **Chittim**) ancient city of SE Cyprus, on the site of present-day Larnaca. It was a Phoenician and Assyrian center.

**Ci·tlal·té·petl** |sēt,läl'tä,petl| the highest peak in Mexico, in the E of the country, N of the city of Orizaba. It rises to a height of 18,503 ft./5,699 m. and is an extinct volcano. Spanish name **Pico de Orizaba.** The name is from the Aztec and literally means 'star mountain.'

**Cit·rus Heights** |'sitrəs| community in N central California, a suburb NE of Sacramento. Pop. 107,439.

**City of Lon·don** |'ləndən| the part of London, England, within the ancient city boundaries and governed by the Lord Mayor and Corporation. It is noted as Britain's chief financial district. Also referred to as **the City.**

**Ciu·dad Bo·lí·var** |syōō'däd bō'lē,vär| city in SE Venezuela, a port on the Orinoco River. Pop. 225,850. Formerly called Angostura, it was renamed in 1846 to honor the country's liberator, Simón Bolívar.

**Ciu·dad del Es·te** |syōō'däd del 'estä| port city in SE Paraguay, on the Paraná River, near the Itaipu Dam. Pop. 134,000. Before 1989 it was called **Puerto Presidente Stroessner.**

**Ciu·dad Gua·ya·na** |syōō'däd gī'änə| (also **Santo Tomé de Guayana**) industrial city in E Venezuela, at the junction of the Caroní and Orinoco rivers. Pop. 543,000. It is a steel- and aluminum-producing center.

**Ciu·dad Juá·rez** |syōō'däd 'hwäres| (also **Juárez**) commercial and industrial city in Chihuahua state, N Mexico, across the Rio Grande from El Paso, Texas. Pop. 790,000.

**Ciu·dad Ma·de·ro** |syōō'däd mə'därō| city in E Mexico, a suburb and oil industry center just N of Tampico, in the state of Tamaulipas. Pop. 160,000.

**Ciu·dad Obre·gón** |syōō'däd ,ōbrä'gōn| commercial city in Sonora state, NW Mexico, in an irrigated farming district. Pop. 160,000.

**Ciu·dad Re·al** |syōō'däd rä'äl| agricultural market town in central Spain, between the Guadiana and Jablón rivers, and capital of Ciudad Real province. Pop. 475,000.

**Ciu·dad Tru·jil·lo** |syōō'däd trōō'hēyo| former name (1936–61) for SANTO DOMINGO, Dominican Republic.

**Ciu·dad Vic·to·ria** |syōō'däd vēk'tōryə| city in NE Mexico, capital of the state of Tamaulipas. Pop. 207,830.

**Ci·vi·ta·vec·chia** |,CHēvētə'vekēə| port on the W central coast of Italy, on the Tyrrhenian Sea. Pop. 51,000. Originally built as the chief port for Rome, it still serves in that role.

**Clack·man·nan** |klæk'mænən| (also **Clackmannanshire**) administrative region and former county of central Scotland; administrative center, Alloa.

**Clacton-on-Sea** |'klæktənän,sē| seaside resort in Essex, SE England, E of London. Pop. 40,000.

**Clair·vaux** |kler'vō| hamlet in NE France, near Ville-sous-la-Ferté, in the Aube department. The former Cistercian abbey here was founded 1115 by St. Bernard of Clairvaux.

**Clap·ham** |'klæpəm| residential district in SW London, England, in the borough of Wandsworth, noted for its major rail junction.

**Clare** |klær| county of the Republic of Ireland, on the W coast, in the province of Munster; county seat, Ennis. Pop. 91,000.

**Clare·mont** |'klær,mänt| city in SW California, a suburb and academic center E of Los Angeles. Pop. 32,503.

**Clark Fork River** |'klärk 'fôrk| river that flows 360 mi./580 km. from W Montana into E Idaho, into the Columbia River.

**Clarks·dale** |'klärks,dal| city in NW Mississippi, a Delta cotton center also associated with the development of blues music. Pop. 19,717.

**Clarks·ville** |'klärks,vil; 'klärksvəl| industrial and commercial city in N central Tennessee, on the Cumberland River. Pop. 75,494.

**Clear·field** |'klir,fēld| city in N Utah, SW of Ogden and Hill Air Force Base, which is central to its economy. Pop. 21,435.

**Clear Lake** |'klir 'lak| section of SE Houston, Texas, home to major U.S. space flight facilities and many of their workers.

**Clear·wa·ter** |'klir,wädər| city in W central

Florida, on the Gulf of Mexico, W of Tampa. It is a noted resort center. Pop. 98,784.

**Clear·wa·ter Mountains** |'klir,wawtər; 'klir,wätər| range in N Idaho, part of the Rocky Mts., noted for their forests and mining.

**Clee·thorpes** |'klē,THawrps| resort town in NE England, on the Humber estuary next to Grimsby, in Humberside. Pop. 67,000.

**Clem·son** |'klemsən| city in NW South Carolina, home to Clemson University. Pop. 11,096.

**Cle·o·pa·tra's Needle** |klēə'pætrəz 'nēdl| popular name for either of two ancient Egyptian obelisks, one on the Victoria Embankment in London, England, the other in Central Park, New York City.

**Clermont-Ferrand** |,kler,mawN fə'räN| industrial city in central France, capital of the Auvergne region, at the center of the Massif Central. Pop. 140,170.

**Cleve·land**[1] |'klēvlənd| former county on the North Sea coast of NE England, formed in 1974 from parts of Durham and North Yorkshire and replaced in 1996 by the unitary councils of Middlesbrough, Hartlepool, Stockton-on-Tees, and Redcar and Cleveland.

**Cleve·land**[2] |'klēvlənd| major port and industrial city in NE Ohio, on Lake Erie and the Cuyahoga River. Pop 505,600. It is a historic center of heavy industry, including oil, machinery, and metals.

**Cleve·land**[3] |'klēvlənd| city in SE Tennessee, NE of Chattanooga. Pop. 30,354.

**Cleve·land Heights** |'klēvlənd| city in NE Ohio, a residential suburb on the NE side of Cleveland. Pop. 54,052.

**Cleves** |klēvz| town in western Germany, between the Rhine River and the border with the Netherlands. Pop. 45,000. Its economy is based on tourism and manufacturing. German name **Kleve**.

**Clif·den** |'klifdən| coastal resort town in County Galway, W Ireland, near which Alcock and Brown landed after the first transatlantic airplane flight in 1919.

**Clif·ton**[1] |'kliftən| suburb of Bristol, SW England, site of a noted suspension bridge built by Isambard Brunel across the Avon Gorge.

**Clif·ton**[2] |'kliftən| industrial city in NE New Jersey, immediately W of Passaic. Pop. 71,742.

**Clinch River** |klinCH| river that flows 300 mi./480 km. from SW Virginia into Tennessee, where it passes the Norris Dam and

Oak Ridge before joining the Tennessee River.

**Clin·ton** |'klintən| city in E central Iowa, on the Mississippi River. Pop. 29,201.

**Clip·per·ton Island** |'klipərtən| uninhabited French island in the E Pacific, SW of Mexico. A phosphate source, it is named for an 18th-century English pirate.

**Clon·mac·noise** |,klänmək'noiz| village in W central Ireland, on the Shannon River, site of the ruins of a 6th-century monastery that was a major academic center.

**Clon·mel** |klän'mel| the county seat of Tipperary, in the Republic of Ireland. Pop. 14,500.

**Clo·vis**[1] |'klōvəs| city in central California, in the San Joaquin Valley, a suburb NE of Fresno. Pop. 50,323.

**Clo·vis**[2] |'klōvəs| agricultural city in E New Mexico. Pop. 30,954. The Clovis Culture of 10,000 years ago is named for artifacts found nearby.

**Cluj–Napoca** |'klōozH 'näpōkə| city in W central Romania. Pop. 321,850. It was founded in the 12th-century by German-speaking colonists; by the 19th century it belonged to Hungary and was the cultural center of Transylvania. The name was changed from Cluj in the mid-1970s to incorporate the name of a nearby ancient settlement. Also called **Cluj**; Hungarian name **Kolozsvár**; German name **Klausenburg**.

**Clu·ny** |klōo'nē| town in the Burgundy region of E France. Pop. 5,000. Cluny was once a leading religious center; its 12th-century abbey (now destroyed) was the largest in the world.

**Clu·tha River** |'klōoTHə| gold-bearing river at the S end of South Island, New Zealand. It flows 213 mi./338 km. to the Pacific Ocean.

**Clwyd** |'klōoəd| former county of NE Wales, replaced in 1996 by Denbighshire and Flintshire.

**Clyde** |klīd| river in W central Scotland that flows 106 mi./170 km. from the Southern Uplands to the Firth of Clyde, formerly famous for the shipbuilding industries along its banks, in the CLYDEBANK area.

**Clyde, Firth of** |,fərTH əv 'klīd| the estuary of the Clyde River in W Scotland.

**Clydes·dale** |'klīdz,dāl| valley of the upper Clyde River, in central Scotland, an agricultural district that gave its name to breeds of draft horses and dogs.

**Cni·dus** |'nīdəs| ancient Greek city of Asia Minor, in present-day SW Turkey, on Cape Krio in the Aegean Sea, N of Rhodes. It was noted for its artists and schools.

**Co·a·hui·la** |ˌkōə'wēlə| state of N Mexico, on the border with Texas. Area: 57, 930 sq. mi./149,982 sq. km. Pop. 1,971,000. Capital: Saltillo.

**Coast Mountains** |kōst| range that curves 1,000 mi./1,600 km. from British Columbia NW to Alaska, extending the line of the Cascade Mts. Mount Waddington (13,104 ft./3,994 m.) is the high point.

**Coast Rang·es** |kōst| name for various ranges that extend from S California along the Pacific coast to Alaska. Parallel to, and W of, the Coast Mts., they reach 19,524 ft./5,951 m. at Mount Logan, in the Yukon Territory.

**Coats Land** |'kōts ˌlænd| region of Antarctica, to the E of the Antarctic Peninsula.

**Co·at·za·co·al·cos** |kəˌwätsəkə'wälkōs| industrial port city in SE Mexico, on the Bay of Campeche in the Gulf of Mexico, in Veracruz state. Pop. 199,000. An oil industry center, it is at the mouth of the Coatzacoalcos River, which flows N across the Isthmus of Tehuantepec.

**Co·bán** |kō'bän| commercial city in central Guatemala, a coffee industry center in the highlands. Pop. 34,000.

**Cobb County** |käb| county in NW Georgia, containing many NW suburbs of Atlanta. Its seat is Marietta. Pop. 447,745.

**Cobh** |kōv| (formerly **Queenstown**) seaport and resort in County Cork, S Ireland, immediately S of Cork. Pop. 6,000.

**Co·burg** |'kō,bərg| city in S Germany, on the Itz River. Pop. 45,000. Between 1826 and 1918 it alternated with Gotha as the capital of Saxe-Coburg-Gotha.

**Co·cha·bam·ba** |ˌkōCHə'bämbə| industrial and commercial city in W central Bolivia, at the center of a rich agricultural region. Pop. 404,100.

**Co·chin** |kō'CHin| seaport and naval base on the Malabar Coast of SW India, in the state of Kerala. Pop. 504,000.

**Cochin-China** |ˈkōCHin'CHinə| the former name for the S region of what is now Vietnam. Part of French Indo-China from 1862, in 1946 it became a French overseas territory, then merged officially with Vietnam in 1949.

**Cock·aigne, land of** |kä'kān| (also **Cockayne**) in medieval English folklore, a land of luxurious idleness. The name has nothing to do with *cocaine*.

**Cock·er·mouth** |'käkərməTH; 'käkər,mowTH| commercial town in Cumbria, NW England, birthplace of William Wordsworth. Pop. 8,000.

**Co·co·nut Creek** |'kōkə,nət| city in SE Florida, a residential suburb NW of Fort Lauderdale. Pop. 27,485.

**Co·co·nut Grove** |'kōkə,nət| district of SW Miami, Florida, with a history as an arts colony and a thriving tourist trade.

**Co·co River** |'kō,kō| (formerly **Segovia**) river that flows 450 mi./720 km. from SW Honduras, forming much of the Honduras-Nicaragua border, into the Caribbean Sea.

**Co·cos Islands** |ˈkōkəs| group of twenty-seven small coral islands in the Indian Ocean, administered as an external territory of Australia since 1955. Pop. 603. The islands were discovered in 1609 by Captain William Keeling of the East India Company. Also called **Keeling Islands**.

**Cod·ring·ton** |'kädriNGtən| only settlement on the island of Barbuda, in Antigua and Barbuda, West Indies. Pop. 1,000.

**Co·dy** |'kōdē| city in NW Wyoming, associated with Buffalo Bill Cody, who lived here. Tourism is important to its economy. Pop. 7,897.

**Coeur d'Alene** |ˌkawr dl'än| commercial and resort city in NW Idaho, on Coeur d'Alene Lake, which is fed by the Coeur d'Alene River. Pop. 24,563.

**Co·gnac** |kawn'yäk; 'kōn,yæk| city in W France, on the Charentes River. Pop. 23,000. It is known for premium brandy, produced since the 17th century.

**Coi·hai·que** |koi'ikä| military and administrative city in the Aisén region of S Chile. Pop. 43,000. It is the chief town of S Chile.

**Coim·ba·tore** |'koimbə,tōōr| commercial and industrial city in the state of Tamil Nadu, in S India. Pop. 853,000.

**Co·im·bra** |kōō'imbrə| university city in central Portugal. Pop. 96,140.

**Col·ca Canyon** |'kōlkə| gorge in the Andes Mts. in S Peru, N of Arequipa. With sides rising to 14,300 ft./4,360 m., it is thought to be the deepest canyon in the world.

**Col·ches·ter** |'kōlCHəstər| commercial town in Essex, SE England. Pop. 82,000. It was prominent in Roman Britain, when it was known as Camulodunum.

**Col·chis** |'kälkəs| ancient region S of the Caucasus Mts. at the E end of the Black Sea. In classical mythology it was the goal of Jason's expedition for the Golden Fleece. Greek name **Kolkhis**.

**Col·ditz** |'kōldits| town in eastern Germany, SE of Leipzig. Its castle was used as a top-security prison for Allied prisoners during World War II.

**Cold Spring Harbor** |'kōld ,spriNG| village on the North Shore of Long Island, New York, in Huntington town, famed as a whaling port and today for biological research. Pop. 4,789.

**Cold·stream** |ˈkōld,strēm| town in SE Scotland, in the Borders region, where the Coldstream Guards were formed for a 1660 foray into England to restore Charles II to the throne.

**Cole·raine** |kōlˈrān; ˈkōl,rān| industrial port and university town in the N of Northern Ireland, on the Bann River in County Londonderry. Pop. 16,000.

**Co·li·ma** |kəˈlēmə| **1** a state of SW Mexico, on the Pacific coast. Area: 2,005 sq. mi./5,191 sq. km. Pop. 425,000. **2** its capital city. Pop. 58,000.

**Col·lege Park** |ˈkälij| city in central Maryland, just NE of Washington, D.C., home to the University of Maryland. Pop. 21,927.

**Col·lege Station** |ˈkälij| city in E central Texas, home to Texas A&M University. Pop. 52,456.

**Col·mar** |ˈkōl,mär| industrial port city on the Ill River, capital of the department of Haut-Rhin, NE France. Pop. 67,000. Also **Kolmar.**

**Co·logne** |kəˈlōn| industrial and university city in western Germany, in North Rhine–Westphalia. Pop. 956,690. Founded by the Romans and situated on the Rhine River, Cologne is notable for its medieval cathedral. German name **Köln.**

**Co·lo·ma** |kəˈlōmə| historic locality in NE California, on the American River NE of Sacramento, where gold was discovered in 1848 on John (Johann) Sutter's mill site, leading to the California gold rush.

**Co·lombes** |kôˈlawnb; kəˈlōm| industrial NW suburb of Paris, France, on the Seine River. Pop. 76,000.

**Co·lom·bia** |kəˈləmbēə| republic in the extreme NW of South America, having coastlines on both the Atlantic and the Pacific. Area: 440,365 sq. mi./1,140,105 sq. km. Pop. 34,479,000. Language, Spanish. Capital and largest city: Bogotá. Colombia was conquered by the Spanish in the early 16th

**Colombia**

century and achieved independence in 1819. Gran Colombia, as it was then known, has been reduced to the present-day boundaries. Largely in the Andes, with cities in the valleys, Colombia has an economy largely dependent on mining and agriculture. □ **Colombian** adj. & n.

**Co·lom·bo** |kəˈləmbō| the capital, largest city, and chief port of Sri Lanka. Pop. 615,000.

**Co·lón** |kəˈlōn| the chief port of Panama, at the Caribbean end of the Panama Canal. Pop. 140,900. It was founded in 1850 by the American William Aspinwall, after whom it was originally named.

**Co·lo·nia** |kəˈlōnyə| (official name **Colonia del Sacramento**) port and resort city in S Uruguay, across the Plate River from Buenos Aires, Argentina. Pop. 22,000.

**Col·o·ra·do** |,käləˈradō; ,käləˈrädō| see box.

---

### Colorado

**Capital/largest city:** Denver
**Other cities:** Arvada, Aurora, Boulder, Colorado Springs, Golden, Pueblo, Telluride
**Population:** 3,294,394 (1990); 3,970,971 (1998); 4,468,000 (2005 proj.)
**Population rank (1990):** 26
**Rank in land area:** 8
**Abbreviation:** CO; Colo.
**Nickname:** The Centennial State
**Motto:** *Nil sine Numine* ('Nothing without Providence')
**Bird:** lark bunting
**Flower:** columbine
**Tree:** blue spruce
**Song:** "Where the Columbines Grow"
**Noted physical features:** Black Canyon; Royal Gorge; Mount Elbert
**Tourist attractions:** Four Corners; Garden of the Gods; Continental Divide; Dinosaur, Great Sand Dunes, Black Canyon of Gunnison, and Colorado national monuments; Grand Mesa National Forest; Georgetown Loop Historic Mining Railroad Park, Cumbres & Toltec Scenic Railroad; Estes, Mesa Verde and Rocky Mountain national parks; Aspen Ski Resort
**Admission date:** August 1, 1876
**Order of admission:** 38
**Name origin:** Bestowed by the Spanish conquistadors (possibly by Cortez). It was the name of an imaginary island, an earthly paradise, in *Las Serges de Esplandian*, a Spanish romance written by Montalvo in 1510.

**Col·o·ra·do Desert** |ˌkälə'rædō; ˌkälə-'rädō| region of S California and N Baja California, Mexico. The Salton Sea, Palm Springs, and the Imperial Valley are here.

**Col·o·ra·do Plateau** |ˌkälə'rædō; ˌkälə-'rädō| region of arid uplands in the SW U.S., along the Colorado River, in Colorado, Utah, New Mexico, and Arizona, noted for its scenery.

**Col·o·ra·do River**[1] |ˌkälə'rædō; ˌkälə'rädō| river that rises in the Rocky Mts. of N Colorado and flows generally SW for 1,468 mi./2,333 km. to the Gulf of California, passing through the Grand Canyon.

**Col·o·ra·do River**[2] |ˌkälə'rædō; ˌkälə'rädō| river that flows 900 mi./1,450 km. E across Texas, from the Llano Estacado to the Gulf of Mexico. Austin lies on it.

**Col·o·ra·do Springs** |ˌkälə'rædō; ˌkälə-'rädō| city in central Colorado, S of Denver, at the foot of the Front Range of the Rocky Mts. A resort with many military installations, it is home to the U.S. Air Force Academy. Pop. 281,140.

**Co·los·sae** |kə'läsē| ancient city of Phrygia, Asia Minor, in present-day SW Turkey, near Denizli. Early Christians here (Colossians) were addressed in an epistle by Paul.

**Col·os·se·um** |ˌkälə'sēəm| amphitheater in Rome, begun by the Emperor Vespasian *c.* A.D. 75. It held 50,000 spectators, its sections connected by an elaborate network of stairs, and was the scene of various kinds of combat.

**Co·los·sus** |kə'läsəs| huge bronze statue of Helios, the sun-god, at Rhodes, in ancient Greece; one of the Seven Wonders of the World. Said to be more than 100 ft./30 m. tall, it was destroyed in an earthquake in 224 B.C.

**Col·ton** |'kōltn| city in SW California, immediately SW of San Bernardino. Pop. 40,213.

**Co·lum·bia, District of** |kə'ləmbēə| see DISTRICT OF COLUMBIA.

**Co·lum·bia**[1] |kə'ləmbēə| residential community in central Maryland, between Baltimore and Washington, D.C., planned and established in the 1960s. Pop. 75,883.

**Co·lum·bia**[2] |kə'ləmbēə| city in central Missouri, home to the University of Missouri. Pop. 69,101.

**Co·lum·bia**[3] |kə'ləmbēə| industrial city, the capital of South Carolina, in the central part. Pop. 98,052.

**Co·lum·bia River** |kə'ləmbēə| river in NW North America that rises in the Rocky Mts. of SE British Columbia, and flows 1,230 mi./1,953 km. generally SW into the U.S., where it winds across the COLUMBIA PLATEAU of central Washington, then turns W to form the Washington-Oregon border and enters the Pacific near Astoria, Oregon.

**Co·lum·bus**[1] |kə'ləmbəs| industrial city in W Georgia, on the Chattahoochee River, noted as a textile center. Pop. 179,278.

**Co·lum·bus**[2] |kə'ləmbəs| industrial city in S central Indiana. Pop. 31,802.

**Co·lum·bus**[3] |kə'ləmbəs| commercial, industrial, and university city, the capital of Ohio, in the central part. Pop. 632,910.

**Co·ma·ya·gua** |ˌkōmə'yägwə| historic city in W central Honduras, a former capital of the country. Pop. 36,000.

**Co·mil·la** |kə'milə| (also **Komilla**) city in E Bangladesh, SE of Dhaka. Pop. 165,000.

**Co·mi·no** |kə'mēnō| the smallest of the three main islands of Malta.

**Co·mi·tán** |ˌkōmē'tän| (official name **Comitán de Domínguez**) commercial city in Chiapas, S Mexico, near the Guatemalan border. Pop. 48,000.

**Com·mon·wealth, the** |'kämən,welTH| (official name **the Commonwealth of Nations**) association of nations and dependencies that were formerly part of the British Empire.

**com·mon·wealth** official designation of four U.S. states: Kentucky, Massachusetts, Pennsylvania, and Virginia.

**Com·mon·wealth of In·de·pen·dent States** (abbrev. **C.I.S.**) confederation of the former constituent republics of the Soviet Union, established in 1991. The member states are Armenia, Belarus, Kazakhstan, Kyrgyzstan, Moldova, Russia, Tajikistan, Turkmenistan, Ukraine, and Uzbekistan.

**Com·mun·ism Peak** |'kämyə,nizəm| highest peak in the Pamir Mts. of Tajikistan, rising to 24,590 ft./7,495 m. It was the highest mountain in the former Soviet Union. Former names **Mount Garmo** (until 1933) and **Stalin Peak** (until 1962).

**Co·mo, Lake** |'kōmō| lake in the foothills of the Alps in N Italy. The resort city of COMO (pop. 87,000) is at the SW end.

**Co·mo·do·ro Ri·va·da·via** |ˌkōmō'dawrō ˌrēvä'dävēə| port in S Argentina on the Atlantic coast of Patagonia. Pop. 124,000.

**Co·moé River** |ˌkōmō'ā| river that flows 475 mi./765 km. from Burkina Faso through Côte d'Ivoire, to the Gulf of Guinea. In NE Côte d'Ivoire, a national park along the river is noted for its wildlife.

**Com·o·rin, Cape** |'kämərin| cape at the S tip of India, in the state of Tamil Nadu.

Com•o•ros |'kämə,rōz; kə'mawrōz| republic consisting of a group of islands in the Indian Ocean, N of Madagascar. Area: 690 sq. mi./1,787 sq. km. Pop. 492,000. Languages, French (official), Arabic (official), Comoran Swahili. Capital: Moroni. Arab influence was dominant in the islands until, in the mid-19th century, they came under French control. In 1974 all but one (Mayotte) of the four major islands voted for independence. Plantation agriculture, producing foods, fibers, and essences, predominates. □ **Comoran** *adj. & n.*

Comoros

Com•piègne |kawn'pyen(yə)| city in N France on the Oise River. Pop. 45,000. The armistice that ended World War I was signed in the forest nearby on November 11, 1918; the armistice between France and Germany was signed on the same spot in 1940.

Comp•ton |'kämptən| industrial city in SW California, immediately S of Los Angeles. Pop. 90,454.

Com•stock Lode |'käm,stäk| historic gold and silver source in the Virginia Mts. of W Nevada, S of Reno, basis of a boom that lasted from the 1850s through the late-19th century.

Con•a•kry |'känəkrē| the capital, largest city, and chief port of Guinea, on Tombo Island in the Atlantic. Pop. 950,000.

Con•car•neau |,kōnkär'nō| port city in Finistère department, Brittany, NW France. Pop. 19,000. It is a fishing center and artists' retreat.

Con•cep•ci•ón |,kawnseps'yōn| industrial city in S central Chile, in a mining and agricultural district. Pop. 294,000.

Con•cord[1] |'käNGkərd; 'käNG,kawrd| city in N central California, NE of Oakland. Naval facilities are key to its economy. Pop. 111,348.

Con•cord[2] |'käNGkərd; 'käNG,kawrd| historic suburban town in E Massachusetts, on the Concord River. Pop. 17,080. Battles here and at Lexington in April 1775 marked the start of the Revolutionary War.

Con•cord[3] |'käNGkərd; 'käNG,kawrd| the state capital of New Hampshire, on the Merrimack River in the S central part. Pop. 36,006.

Con•cord[4] |'käNGkərd; 'käNG,kawrd| industrial city in S central North Carolina, a textile center. Pop. 27,347.

Con•corde, Place de la |'pläs də lä ,kawn-'kōrd| square adjoining the Tuileries, in Paris, France. Built in the late 18th century and originally called the Place Louis XV, it became the place of execution during the French Revolution; Louis XVI and Marie Antoinette were beheaded here.

Con•cor•dia |kən'kōrdēə| port city in NE Argentina, in a farming region of Entre Ríos province, on the Uruguay River and the border with Uruguay. Pop. 139,000.

Condé-sur-L'Escaut |kawn'däsyrles'kō| village in N France near the Belgian border. The name was attached to a branch of the royal house of Bourbon, and princes of Condé have played a major role in French history. The family owned the chateau at Chantilly.

Con•es•to•ga |,känə'stōgə| township in SE Pennsylvania, near Lancaster, birthplace of the Conestoga wagon that helped settle the western U.S. Pop. 3,470.

Co•ney Island |'kōnē| beach resort, amusement park, and residential district on the Atlantic coast in Brooklyn, New York.

Confederate States of America |kən-'fed(ə)rət 'stāts əv ə'merikə| (also **the Confederacy**) the eleven Southern states (Alabama, Arkansas, Florida, Georgia, Louisiana, Mississippi, North Carolina, South Carolina, Tennessee, Texas, and Virginia) that seceded from the United States in 1860–61, leading to the Civil War.

Con•go[1] |'käNGgō| (official name **Democratic Republic of Congo**; formerly **Zaïre**; also **Congo-Kinshasa**) equatorial country in central Africa with a short coastline on

Congo

the Atlantic. Area: 905,350 sq. mi./2.34 million sq. km. Pop. 38,473,000. Languages, French (official), Kongo, Lingala, Swahili, others. Capital and largest city: Kinshasa. A Belgian colony from 1885, it was the Belgian Congo 1908–60. Independence led to civil war. The dictator Mobutu Sese Seko, in power 1965–97, changed the name to Zaïre in 1971. Most of the country is in the Congo River basin, and is heavily forested. Copper and various minerals abound.

**Con·go²** |'käNGgō| (official name, **People's Republic of the Congo**; often **the Congo** or **Congo-Brazzaville**) equatorial country in Africa, with a short Atlantic coastline. Area: 132,046 sq. mi./342,000 sq. km. Pop. 2,351,000. Languages, French (official), Kikongo, and other Bantu languages. Capital and largest city: Brazzaville. Part of the former French Congo, the country, independent since 1960, is separated from the former Zaire by the Congo and Ubangi rivers. It produces oil, timber, coffee, and tobacco. □ **Congolese** *adj. & n.*

**Con·go River** |'käNGgō| major river of central Africa, which rises as the Lualaba to the S of Kisangani in N Congo (formerly Zaire) and flows 2,800 mi./4,630 km. in a great curve W, turning SW to form the border between the Congo and the Democratic Republic of Congo before emptying into the Atlantic. Also called **Zaire River**.

**Con·nacht** |'känawt| (also **Connaught**) province in the W of the Republic of Ireland, including Counties Sligo, Roscommon, Mayo, Leitrim, and Galway.

**Con·nect·i·cut** |kə'netikət| see box.

**Con·nect·i·cut River** |kə'netikət| longest river in New England, flowing 407 mi./655 km. from N New Hampshire, on the Quebec border, between New Hampshire and Vermont, then through W Massachusetts and central Connecticut, to Long Island Sound, on the Atlantic.

**Con·ne·ma·ra** |,känə'märə| mountainous coastal region of Galway, in the W of the Republic of Ireland.

**Con·roe** |'känrō| city in E Texas, a longtime lumber and oil center now a suburb N of Houston. Pop. 27,610.

**Con Son** |'kōn 'sōn| island in the South China Sea, off the S coast of Vietnam.

**Con·stance, Lake** |'känstən(t)s| lake in SE Germany on the N side of the Swiss Alps, at the meeting point of Germany, Switzerland, and Austria, forming part of the course of the Rhine River. German name **Bodensee**.

---

## Connecticut

**Capital:** Hartford
**Largest city:** Bridgeport
**Other cities:** New Haven, New London, Stamford, Waterbury
**Population:** 3,287,116 (1990); 3,274,069 (1998); 3,317,000 (2005 proj.)
**Population rank (1990):** 27
**Rank in land area:** 48
**Abbreviation:** CT; Conn.
**Nicknames:** The Constitution State; Nutmeg State; Land of Steady Habits; Blue Law State
**Motto:** *Qui Transtulit Sustinet* (Latin: 'He Who Transplanted Still Sustains')
**Bird:** American robin
**Flower:** mountain laurel
**Tree:** white oak
**Song:** "Yankee Doodle"
**Noted physical features:** Long Island Sound; Connecticut and Housatonic rivers
**Tourist attractions:** Mystic Seaport & Aquarium; Mark Twain House; Peabody Museum; Gillette Castle; U.S.S. *Nautilus* Memorial; Foxwoods Casino & Resort; Mohegan Sun Casino; Essex Steam Train.
**Admission date:** January 9, 1788
**Order of admission:** 5
**Name origin:** For the Connecticut River, from an Algonquian word translated 'long river place.'

---

**Con·stan·ţa** |kən'stäntsə| (also **Constanza**) the chief port of Romania, on the Black Sea. Pop. 349,000. Founded in the 7th century B.C. by the Greeks, it was under Roman rule from 72 B.C. Formerly called Tomis, it was renamed after the Roman emperor Constantine the Great in the 4th century.

**Con·stan·tine** |'känstən,tēn| commercial city in NE Algeria. Pop. 449,000. The capital of the Roman province of Numidia, it was destroyed in 311 but rebuilt by the Roman emperor Constantine the Great and given his name.

**Con·stan·ti·no·ple** |,kän,stæntə'nōpəl| the former name for Istanbul, Turkey, from A.D. 330 (when it was given its name by the Roman emperor Constantine the Great) to the capture of the city by the Turks in 1453.

**Con·sti·tu·tion State** |,känstə't(y)ōō-shən| informal name for CONNECTICUT.

**Con·ta·do·ra** |,käntə'dawrə| resort island in Panama, in the Pearl Islands, in the Gulf of Panama, that gave its name to a group of nations (Colombia, Panama, Venezuela, and Mexico) that sought, in 1983, to resolve Central American conflicts.

**Con·ta·gem** |ˌköntə'zHäm| city in Minas Gerais state, SE Brazil, an industrial suburb W of Belo Horizonte. Pop. 491,000.

**Con·ti·nen·tal Divide** |ˌkäntn'entl di'vīd| the main series of mountain ridges in W North America, chiefly the crests of the Rocky Mts., which form a watershed separating the rivers flowing E into the Atlantic or the Gulf of Mexico from those flowing W into the Pacific. Also called the **Great Divide**.

**Con·tra Cos·ta County** |ˌkäntrə 'kästə; 'kawstə| county in N central California, including many industrial and port cities along upper San Francisco Bay. Its seat is Martinez. Pop. 803,732.

**Con·way**[1] |'kän,wä| city in central Arkansas. Pop. 26,481.

**Con·way**[2] |'kän,wä| town in N central New Hampshire, a gateway to White Mt. resorts, noted especially for the village of North Conway. Pop. 7,940.

**Con·wy** |'känwē| (also **Conway**) commercial and resort town in NW Wales, in Gwynedd. Pop. 13,000.

**Cooch Be·har** |ˌkŏŏCH bə'här| (also **Koch Bihar**) commercial town in E India, in W. Bengal state. Pop. 71,000.

**Cook, Mount** |kŏŏk| the highest peak in New Zealand, in the Southern Alps on South Island, rising to a height of 12,349 ft./3,764 m. Maori name **Aorangi**.

**Cook County** |kŏŏk| county in NE Illinois, embracing Chicago and most of its closer suburbs. Pop. 5,105,067.

**Cook Inlet** |kŏŏk| inlet of the Gulf of Alaska, W of the Kenai Peninsula in S Alaska. Anchorage lies at its N end.

**Cook Islands** |kŏŏk| group of fifteen islands in the SW Pacific Ocean between Tonga and French Polynesia, which have the status of a self-governing territory in free association with New Zealand. Pop. 18,000. Languages, English (official), Rarotongan (a Polynesian language). Capital: Avarua, on Rarotonga.

**Cook Strait** |kŏŏk| the strait separating the North and South islands of New Zealand.

**Coon Rapids** |kŏŏn| city in SE Minnesota, on the Mississippi River N of Minneapolis. Pop. 52,978.

**Co·op·er·a·tive Republic of Guy·ana** |gī'änə| official name for GUYANA.

**Coo·pers·town** |'kŏŏpərz,town| resort village in central New York, on Otsego Lake,

site of the Baseball Hall of Fame. Pop. 2,180.

**Coos Bay** |kŏŏs| city in SW Oregon, on the Pacific coast. Pop. 15,076.

**Co·pa·ca·bana Beach** |ˌkōpəkə'bænə| resort on the Atlantic coast of Brazil, part of Rio de Janeiro.

**Co·pán** |kō'pän| ancient Mayan city, in W Honduras near the Guatemalan border, the southernmost point of the Mayan empire.

**Co·pen·ha·gen** |'kōpən,hägən| the capital and chief port of Denmark, a city occupying the E part of Zealand and N part of the island of Amager. Pop. 466,700. Danish name **København**.

**Co·pia·pó** |ˌkōpē'pō| industrial city in N Chile, on the S of the Atacama Desert. Pop. 79,000. It is a mining-industry center.

**Cop·ley Square** |'käplē| neighborhood in Back Bay, Boston, Massachusetts.

**Cop·per·belt** |'käpər,belt| a mining region of central Zambia with rich deposits of copper, cobalt, and uranium; chief town, Ndola.

**Cop·per Canyon** |'käpər| (Spanish name **Barranca del Cobre**) canyon in Chihuahua state, N Mexico, in the Sierra Madre Occidental. Named for the color of its walls, it is crossed by railroad and is a tourist attraction.

**Cop·per·mine** |'käpər,mīn| community in Nunavut, at the mouth of the Coppermine River on the Arctic Ocean. Pop. 1,116. Inuit name **Kugluktuk**.

**Co·quim·bo** |kō'kēmbō| port city in N Chile, in the Coquimbo region. Pop. 117,000. It is the port for La Serena, in a copper- and manganese-producing region.

**Cor·al Ga·bles** |ˌkawrəl 'gäbləz; ˌkärəl| resort and commercial city in SE Florida, just SW of Miami on Biscayne Bay. Pop. 40,091.

**Cor·al Sea** |ˌkawrəl; ˌkärəl| part of the W Pacific lying between Australia, New Guinea, and Vanuatu, the scene of a naval battle between U.S. and Japanese aircraft carriers in 1942.

**Cor·al Springs** |ˌkawrəl; ˌkärəl| residential city in SE Florida. Pop. 79,443.

**Cor·bières** |kawr'byer| wine-producing district in the S of the Languedoc region of France, between Narbonne and the Spanish border.

**Cor·co·va·do** |ˌkawrkə'vädŏŏ| peak rising to 2,310 ft./711 m. on the S side of Rio de Janeiro, Brazil. A gigantic statue of Christ, 131 ft./40 m. high, stands on its summit.

**Cor·cy·ra** |kawr'sīrə| ancient Greek name for CORFU.

**Cor·dil·le·ra Cen·tral** |'kawrdē'yerə sen-

'träl| name in several Spanish-speaking countries for the chief mountain range. There are such *cordilleras* in Peru, Colombia, the Dominican Republic, Puerto Rico, and the Philippines.

**Cór·do·ba¹** |'kawrdəbə| city in central Argentina, capital of Córdoba province. Pop. 1,198,000. It is a commercial center and the second-largest city in the country.

**Cór·do·ba²** |'kawrdəbə| commercial city in E central Mexico, in Veracruz state, in a coffee-, sugar-, and fruit-producing region. Pop. 131,000. An 1821 treaty signed here established Mexican independence.

**Cór·do·ba³** |'kawrdəbə| (also **Cordova**) city in Andalusia, S Spain. Pop. 309,200. Founded by the Carthaginians, it was under Moorish rule from 711 to 1236, and was renowned for its learning and for its architecture, particularly the Great Mosque. Spanish name **Córdoba.**

**Cor·fu** |kawr'foo| Greek resort island, one of the largest of the Ionian Islands, off the W coast. It was known in ancient times as Corcyra. Pop. 105,350. Greek name **Kérki·ra.**

**Cor·inth** |'kawrinTH; 'kärinTH| city on the N coast of the Peloponnese, Greece. Pop. 27,400. The modern city, built in 1858, is a little to the NE of the site of the prominent ancient city. Greek name **Kórinthos.** □ **Corinthian** *adj. & n.*

**Cor·inth, Gulf of** |'kawrinTH; 'kärinTH| inlet of the Ionian Sea extending between the Peloponnese and central Greece. Also called **Gulf of Lepanto.**

**Cor·inth, Isthmus of** |'kawrinTH; 'kärinTH| narrow neck of land linking the Peloponnese with central Greece and separating the Gulf of Corinth from the Saronic Gulf.

**Cor·inth Canal** |'kawrinTH; 'kärinTH| shipping channel across the narrowest part of the Isthmus of Corinth (a distance of 4 mi./ 6.4 km.). Opened in 1893, it links the Gulf of Corinth and the Saronic Gulf.

**Co·rin·to** |kə'rēntō| town in NW Nicaragua, the leading Pacific port in the country, exporting coffee, sugar, wood, and other products. Pop. 17,000.

**Cork** |kawrk| **1** largest (2,880 sq. mi./7,459 sq. km.) and second-most populous (410,000) county of the Republic of Ireland, in the SW in the province of Munster. **2** its county seat, a port on the Lee River and the second-largest city in the Republic. Pop. 127,000.

**Corn Belt** |kawrn| name for parts of the U.S. Midwest, especially Illinois and Iowa, where corn is a major crop.

**Cor·ner Brook** |kawrnər| industrial port city in W Newfoundland, a paper industry center. Pop. 22,410.

**Cor·ning** |'kawrninG| industrial city in S central New York, noted for glass production. Pop. 11,938.

**Corn Islands** |kawrn| (Spanish name **Islas de Maíz**) two small islands in the Caribbean Sea off E Nicaragua, used as a U.S. Marine base (1916–71).

**Corn·wall¹** |'kawrn,wawl; 'kawrnwəl| county occupying the extreme SW peninsula of England. Pop. 469,000. County town: Truro. It was a Celtic region with its own language, which survived until about 250 years ago, and customs. □ **Cornish** *adj. & n.*

**Corn·wall²** |'kawrn,wawl; 'kawrnwəl| city in E Ontario, a port on the Saint Lawrence River across from Massena, New York. Pop. 47,137.

**Co·ro** |'kōrō| (also **Santa Ana de Coro**) city in NW Venezuela, an oil center near the Paraguaná Peninsula. Pop. 125,000.

**Co·ro·man·del Coast** |,kawrə'mændl| the S part of the E coast of India, from Point Calimere to the mouth of the Krishna River.

**Co·ro·na¹** |kə'rōnə| city in SW California, an industrial and residential suburb SW of Riverside. Pop. 76,095.

**Co·ro·na²** |kə'rōnə| residential and commercial section of N Queens, New York City.

**Co·ro·nel** |,kawrə'nel| port city in S central Chile, S of Concepción. Pop. 83,000. It is a resort, and coal is mined in the area.

**Cor·pus Chris·ti** |,kawrpəs 'kristē| city, an industrial and fishing port in S Texas. Pop. 257,400. It is situated on Corpus Christi Bay, an inlet of the Gulf of Mexico.

**Cor·reg·i·dor** |kə'regə,dawr| island in the Philippines just S of the Bataan Peninsula on Luzon Island; scene of World War II battles and now a national shrine.

**Cor·rien·tes** |,kawrē'entäs| port city in NE Argentina, on the Paraná River across from Resistencia and near the Paraguayan border. Pop. 269,000.

**Corse** |kawrs| French name for CORSICA.

**Cor·si·ca** |'kawrsikə| mountainous island off the W coast of Italy, forming an administrative region of France. Pop. 249,740. Chief towns, Bastia (N department) and Ajaccio (S department). It was the birthplace of Napoleon I. French name **Corse.** □ **Corsican** *adj. & n.*

**Cor·si·ca·na** |ˌkawrsiˈkænə| city in E central Texas, an oil center. Pop. 22,911.

**Cor·ti·na d'Am·pez·zo** |kawrˈtēnə dämˈpetsō| popular winter resort town in NE Italy, in the Dolomites. Pop. 7,000. The 1956 Winter Olympics were held here.

**Ço·rum** |CHawˈrōōm| commercial city in N central Turkey, the capital of Çorum province. Pop. 117,000.

**Cor·val·lis** |kawrˈvæləs| city in W Oregon, on the Willamette River. Pop. 44,757. Oregon State University is here.

**Cor·vo** |ˈkawrvō| northernmost and smallest of the Azores Islands, part of Portugal. Area: 6.8 sq. mi./17.5 sq. km.

**Co·sen·za** |kōˈzentsə| market town in Calabria, S Italy, capital of Cosenza province. Pop. 105,000.

**Cos·ta Blan·ca** |ˌkōstə ˈblaNGkə| resort region on the Mediterranean coast of SE Spain.

**Cos·ta Bra·va** |ˌkōstə ˈbrävə| resort region to the N of Barcelona, on the Mediterranean coast of NE Spain.

**Cos·ta del Sol** |ˌkōstə del ˈsōl| resort region on the Mediterranean coast of S Spain.

**Cos·ta Do·ra·da** |ˌkōstə dōˈrädə| resort region, in Spain, on the E coast S of Barcelona, on the Mediterranean Sea.

**Cos·ta Mesa** |ˌkōstə ˈmäsə; ˌkästə| city in SW California, on the Pacific S of Los Angeles. Pop. 96,357.

**Cos·ta Ri·ca** |ˌkästə ˈrēkə; ˌkawstə| republic in Central America, on the Isthmus of Panama. Area: 19,707 sq. mi./51,022 sq. km. Pop. 3,301,210. Language: Spanish. Capital and largest city: San José. A former Spanish colony, Costa Rica achieved full independence in 1838. With temperate highlands and tropical lowlands, it produces timber, coffee, cacao, and sugar. Tourism is also important. □ **Costa Rican** adj. & n.

Costa Rica

**Co·ta·ba·to** |ˌkōtəˈbätō| port city in the Philippines, on W Mindanao, near the mouth of the Mindanao River. Pop. 127,000.

**Côte d'Azur** |ˌkōtdäˈzyr; ˌkōt dəˈzHŏŏr| coastal area of SW France, along the Mediterranean Sea. The area covered is roughly coterminous with the French Riviera and includes the towns of Cannes, Saint Tropez, Juan-les-Pins, and Antibes and the city of Nice. It also includes the principality of Monaco.

**Côte d'Ivoire** |ˌkōt dēˈvwär| (English name **Ivory Coast**) republic in W Africa, on the Gulf of Guinea. Area: 124,550 sq. mi./322,462 sq. km. Pop.: 12,000,000. Languages, French, W African languages. Capital: Yamoussoukro. Largest city: Abidjan. Controlled by the French from 1842, the country became independent in 1960. Largely savanna and tropical forest, it produces timber, coffee, cacao, bananas, rubber, and palm oil. It is one of the more developed and stable African states.

**Côte d'Or** |ˌkōt ˈdawr| department in central France, in Burgundy (Bourgogne), famous for its wines. Area: 3,385 sq. mi./8,763 sq. km. Pop. 494,000. The capital is Dijon.

**Co·ten·tin Peninsula** |ˌkōtäNˈtæN| region of NW France, in Normandy, that juts out into the English Channel. At its tip is the port city of Cherbourg.

**Co·to·nou** |ˌkōtōˈnōō; ˌkōtnˈŏŏ| largest city, chief port, and chief commercial and political center of Benin, on the coast of W Africa. Pop. 536,830.

**Co·to·paxi** |ˌkōtəˈpäksē| the highest active volcano in the world, rising to 19,142 ft./5,896 m. in the Andes of central Ecuador.

**Cots·wold Hills** |ˈkät,swōld; ˈkätswəld| (also **the Cotswolds**) range of limestone hills in SW England, largely in the county of Gloucestershire.

**Cott·bus** |ˈkät,bŏŏs| industrial city in SE Germany, in Brandenburg, on the Spree River. Pop. 123,320.

**Cot·tian Alps** |ˈkätēən| section of the W Alps on the border between SE France and NW Italy. The highest point is Mount Viso (12,634 ft./3,851 m.).

**Cot·ton Belt** |ˈkätn| region of the U.S. South where cotton is the historic main crop, especially parts of Georgia, Alabama, and Mississippi.

**Coun·cil Bluffs** |ˈkowntsəl| industrial and commercial city in SW Iowa, on the Missouri River opposite Omaha, Nebraska. Pop. 54,315.

**Cour·an·tyne River** |ˈkawrən,tīn| (Dutch

name **Corantijn**) river that flows 450 mi./725 km. N between Guyana and Suriname, into the Atlantic.

**Cour·be·voie** |ˌkŏŏrbə'vwä| industrial city and residential suburb, NW of Paris, France. Pop. 60,000.

**Cour·land** |'kŏŏr,länt; 'kŏŏrlənd| (also **Kurland**) historical name for region of W Latvia on the shores of the Baltic Sea.

**Cour·trai** |kŏŏr'trä| French name for KOR-TRIJK, Belgium.

**Cov·ent Garden** |ˌkəvənt 'gärdən| district in central London, England, originally the garden of the Abbey of Westminster. It was the site for 300 years of London's chief fruit and vegetable market, which in 1974 was moved to Battersea. Covent Garden is also famed as a home to theater and opera.

**Cov·en·try** |'kəvəntrē| industrial city in the W Midlands of England, the heart of the British auto industry. Pop. 292,600. The city center was destroyed in a November 1940 German air raid, and subsequently rebuilt.

**Co·vi·na** |kō'vēnə| city in SW California, a suburb E of Los Angeles. Pop. 43,207.

**Cowes** |kowz| town on the Isle of Wight, S England. Pop. 16,300. It is famous as a yachting center.

**Cox's Ba·zar** |ˌkäks(iz) bə'zär| port and resort town on the Bay of Bengal, near Chittagong, S Bangladesh. Pop. 29,600.

**Co·yo·a·cán** |ˌkoi-ōə'kän| municipality within the Federal District of Mexico, a suburb of Mexico City. Pop. 640,000. It has historic associations with Hernán Cortés, Trotsky, and Frida Kahlo.

**Co·zu·mel** |ˌkōsŏŏ'mel; 'kōzə,mel| resort island in the Caribbean, off the NE coast of the Yucatán Peninsula of Mexico.

**Cra·cow** |'krä,kŏŏf; 'kräk,ow| industrial and university city in S Poland, on the Vistula River. Pop. 750,540. It was the capital of Poland from 1320 until replaced by Warsaw in 1609. Polish name **Kraków**.

**Cra·io·va** |krī'ōvə| industrial city in SW Romania, in Oltenia. Pop. 300,030.

**Cran·ston** |'krænstən| industrial city in central Rhode Island, a suburb S of Providence. Pop. 76,060.

**Cra·ter Lake** |'krātər| lake filling a volcanic crater in the Cascade Range of SW Oregon. With a depth of more than 1,968 ft./600 m., it is the deepest lake in the U.S.

**Craw·ley** |'krawlē| town in SE England, in West Sussex, an industrial and residential suburb near Gatwick Airport. Pop. 87,000.

**Crays Mal·ville** |kremäl'vēl| site of the first commercial-style nuclear reactor, "Super-Phénis," near Lyons, in E France.

**Cré·cy** |krā'sē| (also **Crécy-en-Ponthieu**) village in N France, in Picardy. The English won their first great victory in the Hundred Years War here in 1346, with the defeat of King Philip VI by King Edward III and Edward, the Black Prince.

**Cre·mo·na** |krə'mōnə| commercial city in Lombardy, N Italy. Pop. 75,160. In the 16th–18th centuries the city was home to three renowned families of violinmakers: the Amati, the Guarneri, and the Stradivari.

**Crest·ed Butte** |'krestid 'bŏŏt| resort town in W central Colorado, a center for skiing and mountain biking. Pop. 878.

**Crete** |krēt| Greek island in the E Mediterranean. Pop. 536,980. Capital: Heraklion. It is noted for the remains of the Minoan civilization that flourished here in the 2nd millennium B.C. It fell to Rome in 67 B.C. and was subsequently ruled by Byzantines, Venetians, and Turks. Crete played an important role in the Greek struggle for independence from the Turks in the late 19th and early 20th centuries. Greek name **Kríti**. □ **Cretan** adj. & n.

**Cré·teil** |krā'tä| city, a SE suburb of Paris, France, on the Marne River. Pop. 82,000. It has some light industry.

**Crewe** |krŏŏ| industrial town and railway junction in Cheshire, W central England. Pop. 47,800.

**Cri·mea** |krī'mēə| (usu. **the Crimea**) a peninsula of Ukraine lying between the Sea of Azov and the Black Sea. It was the scene of the Crimean War in the 1850s. The majority of the population is Russian. □ **Crimean** adj.

**Crip·ple Creek** |'kripəl| city in central Colorado, W of Colorado Springs, scene of a gold-mining boom in the 1890s. Pop. 584.

**Croagh Pat·rick** |ˌkrō 'pætrik| mountain in W Ireland, near Westport, County Mayo, said to be where St. Patrick began his missionary work.

**Cro·a·tia** |krō'äsʜə| country in SE Europe, on the Adriatic Sea, formerly a constituent republic of Yugoslavia. Area: 21,838 sq. mi./56,538 sq. km. Pop. 4,760,000. Language, Croatian. Capital and largest city: Zagreb. Croatian name **Hrvatska**. After almost 1,000 years of Hungarian control, interrupted at times by Turkish power, Croatia in 1918 became part of what was later named Yugoslavia. Poor relations with neighboring Serbia were exacerbated by the Croatian alliance with Nazi Germany in 1941–45, and when Yugoslavia dissolved, strife ensued. Croatia produces coal, oil, grain, livestock, and timber. Coastal resorts are important. □ **Croatian** *adj. & n.* **Croat** *n.*

**Croatia**

**Cro-Magnon** |krōmän'yōN| cave in SW France, near Périgueux, where remains were found of an Upper Paleolithic prototype of Homo sapiens, or modern man. This population of early humans is now known as Cro-Magnon man.

**Cro•mar•ty Firth** |'krämərtē| inlet of the Moray Firth on the coast of Highland region; N Scotland.

**Cro•to•ne** |krə'tōnä| industrial town in Calabria, S Italy. Pop. 56,000. It was the site of an ancient Greek republic and the home of the mathematician Pythagoras.

**Cro•ton River** |'krōtn| short river in E New York, flowing into the Hudson River. It is the source of much New York City water.

**Crown Heights** |krown| neighborhood of N Brooklyn, New York, noted for its West Indian and Orthodox Jewish communities.

**Crown Point** |krown| resort town in NE New York, on Lake Champlain, scene of much 18th-century military action.

**Croy•don** |'kroiden| borough of S Greater London, England. Pop. 300,000. A light industrial and commercial center, it was the site of London's first (1915) airport.

**Cro•zet Islands** |krō'zä| group of five small islands in the S Indian Ocean, under French administration.

**Crys•tal Palace** |'kristl| iron and glass exhibition structure erected in Hyde Park, London, England, in 1851, then moved to Sydenham, near Croydon. It burned in 1936. The area around its Sydenham site is also called Crystal Palace.

**Ctes•i•phon** |'tesə,fän| ancient city on the Tigris near Baghdad, capital of the Parthian kingdom from *c.*224 and then of Persia under the Sassanian dynasty. It was taken

by the Arabs in 636 and destroyed in the 8th century.

**Cuauh•té•moc** |kwow'tämək| district of Mexico City, Mexico, named for the last Aztec emperor and incorporating most of the downtown area, including the Alameda and Zócalo.

**Cuau•tla** |'kwowtlə| commercial and resort city in Morelos state, S central Mexico. Pop. 120,000.

**Cu•ba** |'kyōōbə| republic in the Caribbean, the largest and westernmost of the islands of the West Indies, at the mouth of the Gulf of Mexico. Area: 42,820 sq. mi./110,860 sq. km. Pop. 10,977,000. Language, Spanish. Capital and largest city: Havana. A Spanish colony, Cuba was controlled by the U.S. from 1898, and became autonomous in 1934. After a 1959 revolution it became gradually a Soviet client state, and the U.S. enforced a trade embargo. Cuba produces sugar, tobacco, seafood, and some mine and industrial products. Tourism is regaining importance. □ **Cuban** *adj. & n.*

**Cuba**

**Cu•ban•go** |kōō'bäNGgō| Angolan name for the OKAVANGO River.

**Cu•ca•mon•ga** |,kōōkə'mäNGgə| see RANCHO CUCAMONGA, California.

**Cú•cu•ta** |'kōōkōō,tə| industrial and commercial city in N Colombia, near the Venezuelan border, in the Andes. Pop. 450,000.

**Cud•da•lore** |'kədl,awr| port in S India, on the Coromandel Coast of Tamil Nadu state, S of Pondicherry. Pop. 144,000.

**Cud•da•pah** |'kədəpə| commercial and industrial city in S central India, in Andhra Pradesh state. Pop. 121,000.

**Cuen•ca** |'kweNGkə| city in the Andes in S Ecuador. Pop. 239,900. Founded in 1557, it is known as the 'marble city' because of its many fine buildings.

**Cuer•na•va•ca** |,kwernə'väkə| highland resort town in central Mexico, capital of the state of Morelos. Pop. 400,000.

**Cu·ia·bá** |ˌkōōyəˈbä| river port in W central Brazil, on the Cuiabá River, capital of the state of Mato Grosso. Pop. 389,070.

**Cu·ia·bá River** |ˌkōōyəˈbä| river of W Brazil, which rises in the Mato Grosso plateau and flows for 300 mi./483 km. to join the São Lourenço River near the border with Bolivia.

**Cu·le·bra** |kōōˈläbrə| island community off the E coast of Puerto Rico, formerly a naval reserve, now a resort and wildlife preserve. Pop. 1,542.

**Cu·lia·cán Ro·sa·les** |ˌkōōlyəˈkän ˌrōˈsäləs| commercial city in NW Mexico, capital of the state of Sinaloa. Pop. 662,110.

**Cul·lo·den** |kəˈlädn| village in NE Scotland, near Inverness. At nearby Culloden Moor, in April 1746, English forces won the last pitched battle on British soil, ending the Jacobite uprising.

**Cul·ver City** |ˌkəlvər| city in SW California, W of Los Angeles, an industrial and filmmaking center. Pop. 38,793.

**Cu·mae** |ˈkyōōmē| ancient city in SW Italy, near Naples. It is believed to be the site of the earliest Greek colony in Italy or Sicily, founded around 750 B.C. The priestess called the Cumaean Sybil lived in a nearby cave. □ **Cumaean** *adj.*

**Cu·ma·ná** |ˌkōōmäˈnä| historic port city in NE Venezuela, capital of Sucre state, on the Manzanares River. Pop. 212,000. It is said to be the oldest European settlement in South America.

**Cum·ber·land** |ˈkəmbərlənd| former county of NW England. In 1974 it was united with Westmorland and part of Lancashire to form the county of Cumbria.

**Cum·ber·land Gap** |ˈkəmbərlənd| historic pass through the Appalachian Mts., from SW Virginia into SE Kentucky. In the 18th century it was the main route of the western settlement.

**Cum·ber·land River** |ˈkəmbərlənd| river that flows 690 mi./1,110 km. from the Cumberland Plateau in SE Kentucky across N Tennessee and back into Kentucky, where it joins the Ohio River near Paducah. Nashville lies along it.

**Cum·ber·nauld** |ˌkəmbərˈnawld| town in central Scotland, in North Lanarkshire, near Glasgow, for which it was built to house an expanding population. Pop. 48,760.

**Cum·bria** |ˈkəmbrēə| county of NW England. County town: Carlisle. Cumbria was an ancient British kingdom, and the name continued to be used for the hilly NW region of England containing the Lake Dis-

trict and much of the N Pennines. The county of Cumbria was formed in 1974, largely from the former counties of Westmorland and Cumberland. □ **Cumbrian** *adj. & n.*

**Cu·naxa** |kyōōˈnæksə| town of ancient Babylonia, NW of Babylon, near the Euphrates River, scene of a battle in 401 B.C. from which the events in the *Anabasis* of Xenophon followed.

**Cu·ne·ne** |kōōˈnänə| river of Angola, which rises near the city of Huambo and flows 156 mi./250 km. S as far as the border with Namibia, which then follows it W to the Atlantic.

**Cu·neo** |ˈkōōnēō| industrial and market town in N Italy, capital of Cuneo province. Pop. 56,000.

**Cu·per·ti·no** |ˌkōōpərˈtēnō| city in N central California, W of San Jose. It is part of the Silicon Valley complex. Pop. 40,263.

**Cu·ra·çao** |ˌk(y)ōōrəˈsow; ˌk(y)ōōrəˈsō| the largest island of the Netherlands Antilles, in the Caribbean Sea 37 mi./60 km. N of the Venezuelan coast. Pop. 144,100. Chief town: Willemstad.

**Cu·re·pipe** |kōōrˈpēp| resort town in W central Mauritius, in the highlands. Pop. 67,000.

**Cu·ria** |ˈkyōōrēə| the papal court and government departments in the Vatican City, Rome, Italy.

**Cu·ri·có** |ˌkōōrēˈkō| city in central Chile, in the agricultural Maule region. Pop. 104,000. It is the center of a wine-making district.

**Cu·ri·ti·ba** |ˌkōōrəˈtēbə| industrial and commercial city in S Brazil, capital of the state of Paraná. Pop. 1,315,035.

**Cur·ragh, the** |ˈkərə| plain in County Kildare, E Ireland, noted as a military training site and center for horse racing.

**Cur·zon Line** |ˈkərzən| line defining the Russian-Polish border, named for British foreign secretary Lord Curzon, who proposed it in 1919, and modified in later years.

**Cush** |kōōSH| (also **Kush**) ancient kingdom of the upper Nile valley, in Nubia (present-day Egypt and Sudan). It gave its name to the Cushitic peoples and languages.

**Cut·tack** |ˈkətək| industrial and commercial port city in E India, in Orissa state. Pop. 402,000. It is a historical and religious center.

**Cux·ha·ven** |kōōksˈhäfən| seaport in NW Germany, on the Elbe River. Pop. 60,000.

**Cuy·a·ho·ga River** |ˌkīəˈhōgə; kəˈhōgə| river that flows 80 mi./130 km. through N

Ohio, emptying into Lake Erie at Cleveland. The industrial suburb of **Cuyahoga Falls** (pop. 48,950) lies along it near Akron.

**Cuz·co** |'kōōskō| city in the Andes in S Peru. Pop. 275,000. It was the capital of the Inca empire until the Spanish conquest in 1533.

**Cwm·bran** |kōōm'brän| town in SE Wales, administrative center of Monmouthshire. Pop. 44,800.

**Cyc·la·des** |'siklə,dēz| large group of islands in the S Aegean Sea, regarded in antiquity as circling around the sacred island of Delos. The Cyclades form a department of modern Greece. Greek name **Kikládhes**.

**Cym·ru** |'kəmrē| Welsh name for WALES.

**Cy·press** |'sīprəs| city in S central California, a suburb SE of Los Angeles. Pop. 42,655.

**Cy·press Hills** |'sīprəs| forested upland in SW Saskatchewan and SE Alberta.

**Cy·prus** |'sīprəs| the third-largest Mediterranean island, a republic lying 50 mi./80 km. S of the Turkish coast. Area: 3,573 sq. mi./9,251 sq. km. Pop. 708,000. Languages, Greek and Turkish. Capital and largest city: Nicosia. An ancient Greek colony, Cyprus was controlled by Turkey 1571–1878, then by Britain until independence in 1960, which was preceded by Greek-Turkish fighting. In 1974 Turkish forces took over part of the island, but the Turkish Republic of Northern Cyprus has not been recognized. Fruit, wine, and clothing are among the products of Cyprus. □ **Cypriot** *adj. & n.*

Cyprus

**Cy·re·na·ica** |,sirə'nāekə| region of NE Libya, bordering on the Mediterranean Sea, settled by the Greeks *c.* 640 B.C. □ **Cyrenaic** *adj.*

**Cy·re·ne** |sī'rēnē| ancient Greek city in N Africa, near the coast in Cyrenaica. From the 4th century B.C. it was a great intellectual center.

**Cy·the·ra** |sə'THirə| (Greek name **Kithira**) a rocky island in S Greece, in the Aegean Sea off the coast of the Peloponnese.

**Czech·o·slo·va·kia** |,CHekəsləväkēə| former country in central Europe, now divided between the Czech Republic and Slovakia. Capital: Prague. □ **Czechoslovak** *n.* **Czechoslovakian** *adj. & n.*

Czechoslovakia

**Czech Republic** |CHek| country in central Europe, the W part of the former Czechoslovakia. Area: 30,461 sq. mi./78,864 sq. km. Pop. 10,298,700. Language, Czech. Capital and largest city: Prague. Comprising the former Bohemia, Moravia, and Silesia, the Czech Republic came into being in 1993. It has important heavy industry and mining sectors. Tourism is also important.

Czech Republic

**Czer·no·witz** |'CHernə,vits| German name for CHERNIVTSI, Ukraine.

**Czę·sto·cho·wa** |,CHenstə'kōvə| industrial city in S central Poland. Pop. 258,000. It is famous for the religious icon of the "Black Madonna" in its monastery, an object of pilgrimage.

# Dd

**Da·bro·wa Gór·ni·cza** |dawn'brawvə gŏŏr 'nēcHə| mining and manufacturing city in S Poland. Pop. 137,000.

**Dac·ca** |'däkə| another spelling for DHAKA, Bangladesh.

**Da·chau** |'dä,KHow| city in Bavaria, SW Germany, on the Amper River near Munich. Pop. 33,000. The Nazis operated a concentration camp here 1933–45.

**Dach·stein** |'däKH,SHtīn| **1**mountain range in central Austria, in the Salzkammergut resort area, with many mountain lakes and glaciers. **2** the highest peak in the range: 9,829 ft./2,996 m.

**Da·cia** |'dāsHə| ancient country of SE Europe in what is now NW Romania. It was annexed by Trajan in A.D. 106 as a province of the Roman Empire. □ **Dacian** adj. & n.

**Dade County** |dād| county in SE Florida, on the Atlantic coast, embracing Miami and many suburbs as well as much of the Everglades. Pop. 1,937,044. Formally **Miami-Dade County.**

**Da·dra and Na·gar Ha·ve·li** |də'drä ænd 'nəgər ə'velē| Union Territory in W India, on the Arabian Sea. Pop. 138,500. Capital: Silvassa.

**Dag·en·ham** |'dægənəm| see BARKING AND DAGENHAM, London, England.

**Dag·e·stan** |,dägə'stän| autonomous republic in SW Russia, on the western shore of the Caspian Sea. Pop. 1,823,000. Capital: Makhachkala.

**Da·ho·mey** |də'hōmē| former name (until 1975) for BENIN. It is an alternate name for the Fon, the chief ethnic group in Benin.

**Dai·qui·ri** |,dīke'rē| village in E Cuba, near Santiago de Cuba. U.S. troops landed here and at nearby Siboney in 1898, in the Spanish-American War. The rum drink is said to be named for the village.

**Dai·ren** |'dī'rən| former name for DALIAN.

**Da·kar** |'dä'kär| the capital of Senegal, a port on the Atlantic coast. Pop. 1,641,350. It is one of W Africa's major commercial and industrial centers.

**Dakh·la** |'däklə| (also **ad Dakhla**) port town in Western Sahara, on the Atlantic coast. Pop. 30,000. A Moroccan provincial capital, it was the chief center of the Spanish colony of Rio Oro, and was called **Villa Cisneros.**

**Da·ko·ta** |də'kōtə| former territory of the U.S., organized in 1889 into the states of North Dakota and South Dakota. □ **Dakotan** adj.

**Da·lar·na** |'dälər,nä| (formerly **Dalecarlia**) forested region in W central Sweden. Its people are known for their distinctive dialects and customs.

**Da Lat** |'dä 'lät| city in southern Vietnam. Pop. 87,000. It is a resort, a market town, and one of Vietnam's foremost educational centers.

**Da·le·car·lia** |,dälə'kärlēə| another name for DALARNA, Sweden.

**Dales, the** |dālz| (also **Yorkshire Dales**) series of valleys of small rivers in N England that drain through Yorkshire to the North Sea. Among them are Teesdale, Wensleydale, Wharfedale, and Airedale.

**Da·li** |'dä'lē| city in Yunnan, S China, on the W shore of Er Hai. It is a noted marble-producing center. Pop. 399,000.

**Da·lian** |'däl'yän| port and shipbuilding center on the Liaodong Peninsula in NE China, now part of the urban complex of Luda. Pop. 2,524,000. Former name **Dairen.**

**Dal·las** |'dæləs| commercial, industrial, and cultural city in NE Texas, noted as a center of the oil and banking industries. Pop. 1,006,877. Dallas–Fort Worth Airport is one of the largest in the world.

**Dalles, The** |dælz| (official name **The City of the Dalles**) inland port city in N central Oregon, on the Columbia River. Pop. 11,060.

**Dal·ma·tia** |dæl'māsHə| ancient region in what is now SW Croatia, comprising mountains and a narrow coastal plain along the Adriatic, together with offshore islands. It once formed part of the Roman province of Illyricum. □ **Dalmatian** adj. & n.

**Dal·ri·a·da** |dæl'rīədə| ancient Gaelic kingdom in northern Ireland whose people (the Scots) established a colony in SW Scotland from about the late 5th century. By the 9th century Irish Dalriada had declined, but the people of Scottish Dalriada gradually acquired dominion over the whole of Scotland.

**Dal·ton** |'dawltn| city in NW Georgia, a textile center. Pop. 21,761.

**Da·ly City** |'dālē| city in N central California, a suburb on the SW side of San Francisco. Pop. 92,311.

**Da·man and Diu** |də'män ən 'dēyŏŏ|

Union Territory in India, on the W coast N of Bombay. Pop. 101,400. Capital: Daman. It consists of the district of Daman and the island of Diu, and until 1987 was administered with Goa.

**Da·man·hur** |ˌdämən'hoŏr| (ancient name **Heliopolis Parva**) commercial and industrial city in N Egypt, in the Nile delta. Pop. 216,000.

**Da·ma·ra·land** |də'märə,lænd; 'dämərə,lænd| plateau region of central Namibia inhabited chiefly by the Damara and Herero peoples.

**Da·mas·cus** |də'mæskəs| the capital of Syria since the country's independence in 1946. Pop. 1,497,000. It has existed for over 4,000 years, and is the largest Syrian city, as well as the commercial and financial center.

**Da·ma·vand, Mount** |ˌdämə'vänd| peak in N Iran, in the Elburz range. It is the highest peak in Iran: 18,376 ft./5,601 m.

**Da·mi·et·ta** |ˌdæmē'etə| **1** the E branch of the Nile Delta, in N Egypt. **2** port at the mouth of the delta. Pop. 113,000. Arabic name **Dumyat**.

**Dan** |dæn| biblical city, the northernmost of the Holy Land, thought to have been just W of present-day Baniyas, Syria.

**Dan·a·kil Depression** |'dænə,kil| long low-lying desert region of NE Ethiopia and N Djibouti, between the Red Sea and the Great Rift Valley.

**Da Nang** |dä'näNG; də'næNG| port city in central Vietnam, on the South China Sea. Pop. 382,670. During the Vietnam War it was used as a U.S. military base. Former name **Tourane**.

**Da·na Point** |'dänə| city in SW California, on the Pacific coast. Pop. 31,896.

**Dan·bury** |'dæn,berē; 'dænb(ə)rē| city in W central Connecticut, formerly noted for its hat industry. Pop. 65,585.

**Dan·dong** |'dän'doŏNG| port in Liaoning province, NE China, near the mouth of the Yalu River, on the border with North Korea. Pop. 660,500. Former name **Antung**.

**Dane·law** |'dān,law| the part of N and E England occupied or administered by Danes from the late 9th century until after the Norman Conquest.

**Dan·ish West In·dies** |'dāniSH ,west 'indēz| former name for the U.S. Virgin Islands, held by Denmark 1754–1917.

**Dan·jiang·kou** |'dänje'äNG'kō| city in Hubei province, E central China, at the S end of the Danjiangkou Reservoir. Pop. 431,000.

**Dan·mark** |'dän,märk| Danish name for DENMARK.

**Dan River** |dæn| river that flows 180 mi./290 km. from SW Virginia into North Carolina, to the Roanoke River.

**Dan·ube River** |'dæn,yoŏb| river that rises in the Black Forest in SW Germany and flows about 1,700 mi./2,736 km. into the Black Sea. It is the second-longest river in Europe after the Volga; the cities of Vienna, Bratislava, Budapest, and Belgrade are situated on it. German name **Donau**. □ **Danubian** adj. & n.

**Da·nu·bi·an Principalities** |də'nyoŏbēən| the former European principalities of Moldavia and Wallachia. In 1861 they united to form the state of Romania.

**Dan·vers** |'dænvərz| town in NE Massachusetts, NE of Boston. Pop. 24,174.

**Dan·ville**[1] |'dæn,vil; 'dænvəl| city in N central California, NE of Oakland. Pop. 31,306.

**Dan·ville**[2] |'dæn,vil; 'dænvəl| city in E central Illinois. Pop. 33,828.

**Dan·ville**[3] |'dæn,vil; 'dænvəl| city in S Virginia, on the Dan River, noted for its tobacco and textile industries. Pop. 53,056.

**Dan·zig** |'däntsig| German name for GDAŃSK, Poland.

**Dão** |'däō; dow| river and wine-growing region in N central Portugal. The river (50 mi./80 km.) rises in the Serra de Lapa and flows SW into the Mondego River near Coimbra.

**Dap·sang** |däp'säNG| another name for K2.

**Da·qing** |'dä'CHiNG| (also **Taching**) major industrial city in NE China, in Heilongjiang province. Pop. 996,800.

**Dar·bhan·ga** |dər'bəNGgə| commercial city in NE India, in Bihar state. Pop. 218,000.

**Dar·da·nelles** |ˌdärdn'elz| narrow strait between European and Asiatic Turkey (called the Hellespont in classical times), linking the Sea of Marmara with the Aegean Sea. It is 38 mi./60 km. long. In 1915, it was the scene of an unsuccessful attack on Turkey by Allied troops (see GALLIPOLI).

**Dar es Sa·laam** |ˌdär ˌes sə'läm| (also **Daressalam**) the chief port and long the capital of Tanzania. Pop. 1,360,850. It was founded in 1866 by the sultan of Zanzibar. Although it retains some key functions, the capital is officially Dodoma, and the transition has been in progress through the 1990s.

**Dar·fur** |'där,foŏr| region in the W of Sudan. Until 1874 it was an independent kingdom.

**Dar·i·en, Gulf of** |ˌdærē'en| part of the Caribbean Sea between Panama and Colombia.

**Da·rién** |ˌdærē'en| sparsely populated province of E Panama. The name was formerly applied to the whole of the Isthmus of Panama.

**Dar·jee·ling** |där'jēliNG| (also **Darjiling**) hill station at an altitude of 7,054 ft./2,150 m. in W Bengal, NE India, near the Sikkim border. Pop. 73,090. The area is famous for its tea.

**Dark Continent** nickname for AFRICA, used esp. in the nineteenth century.

**Dar·khan** |'där,KHän| (also **Darhan**) industrial and mining city in N Mongolia, the second largest in the country, established in 1961. Pop. 80,100.

**Dar·ling River** |'därliNG| river of SE Australia, flowing 1,712 mi./2,757 km. in a generally SW course to join the Murray River.

**Dar·ling·ton** |'därliNGtən| industrial town in Durham, NE England. Pop. 96,700.

**Darm·stadt** |'därm,SHtät| city in Hesse, western Germany, a heavy industrial and European space agency center. Pop. 140,040.

**Dart·ford** |'därtfərd| town in Kent, SE England, an industrial and residential suburb E of London on the Thames River. Pop. 62,000.

**Dart·moor** |'därt,mawr| moorland district in Devon, SW England, that was a royal forest in Saxon times, now a national park. A famed prison is here.

**Dart·mouth**[1] |'därtməTH| port in Devon, SW England. Pop. 6,210. It is the site of the Royal Naval College.

**Dart·mouth**[2] |'därtməTH| city in S central Nova Scotia, across Halifax Harbour from Halifax. Pop. 67,798.

**Dar·win** |'därwən| the capital of Northern Territory, Australia, a remote military and tourist city on the Timor Sea. Pop. 73,300.

**Dash·howuz** |ˌdəsHə'wŌŌs| (formerly **Tashauz**) oasis city in N Turkmenistan, in the Amu Darya valley near the Uzbekistan border. Pop. 114,000.

**Da·tong** |'dä'tŌŌNG| industrial and mining city in N China, in Shanxi province. Pop. 1,090,000. The nearby Yungang caves are famed for their ancient stone carvings.

**Dau·gav·pils** |'dowgəv,pils| transportation center and commercial city in SE Latvia, on the Western Dvina River. Pop. 127,000. Former Russian name **Dvinsk**.

**Dau·lat·a·bad** |ˌdawlətə'bäd| (formerly **Deogiri**) historic town in W India, in Maharashtra state, NW of Aurangabad.

**Dau·phi·né** |ˌdawfē'nä| region and former province of SE France, in the Dauphiné Alps. Its capital was Grenoble.

**Da·van·ge·re** |'dəvəngərē| commercial and industrial city in S India, in Karnataka state. Pop. 287,000.

**Da·vao** |'dä,vow| seaport in the S Philippines, on the island of Mindanao. Pop. 850,000. Founded in 1849, it is the largest city on the island and the third-largest in the Philippines.

**Dav·en·port** |'dævən,pawrt| industrial city in SE Iowa, on the Mississippi River, one of the Quad Cities. Pop. 95,333.

**Da·vis** |'dävəs| academic and agricultural city in N central California, W of Sacramento. Pop. 46,209.

**Da·vis Mountains** |'dävəs| range in SW Texas, site of the Mount Locke observatory and several resorts.

**Da·vis Strait** |'dävəs| sea passage 400 mi./645 km. long separating Greenland from Baffin Island and connecting Baffin Bay with the Atlantic.

**Da·vos** |dä'vōs| resort and winter-sports center in E Switzerland. Pop. 10,500.

**Daw·son** |'dawsən| town in the W central Yukon Territory, on the Klondike and Yukon rivers, center of a gold rush after 1896.

**Da·xian** |'däsHē'än| (also **Dachuan**) city in Sichuan province, central China, on the Zhou River N of Chongqing. Pop. 218,000.

**Day·ton**[1] |'dätn| industrial city in W Ohio. Pop. 182,000. It was the home of the aviation pioneers the Wright brothers and is still a center of aerospace research.

**Day·ton**[2] |'dätn| city in SE Tennessee, famed as the site of the 1925 trial of John Scopes for teaching evolution. Pop. 5,671.

**Day·to·na Beach** |dā'tōnə| resort city in NE Florida, on the Atlantic coast. Pop. 61,921.

**Da·zu** |'däd'zŌŌ| important Buddhist archeological site, Sichuan province, central China, in the hills 100 mi./160 km. NW of Chongqing, with over 50,000 9th–13th century stone carvings.

**DDR** abbreviation for DEUTSCHE DEMOKRATISCHE REPUBLIK.

**Dead Sea** |ded| salt lake or inland sea in the Jordan valley, on the Israel–Jordan border. Its surface is 1,300 ft./400 m. below sea level.

**Dead·wood** |'ded,wŏŏd| city in W South Dakota, in the Black Hills, famed for its 1870s gold rush and Boot Hill cemetery. Pop. 1,830.

**Deal** |dēl| port and resort town in SE England, one of the Cinque Ports in Kent. Pop. 26,000. Julius Caesar is said to have landed here in his invasion of Britain in A.D.55.

**Dear·born** |'dir,bawrn; 'dirbərn| city in SE Michigan, on the SW side of Detroit, home to the Ford auto company and to Greenfield Village, a large historical restoration complex. Pop. 89,286.

**Death Valley** |deTH| desert basin, extending to 282 ft./86 m. below sea level, in SE California and SW Nevada, the lowest, hottest, and driest part of North America.

**Deau·ville** |'dō'vēl| resort town in Normandy, N France, on the English Channel. Long a fashionable resort, it has a famous casino and racetrack.

**De·bre·cen** |'debrət,sen| industrial and commercial city in E Hungary, in the Great Alföld. Pop. 217,290. It is the second-largest city in Hungary.

**De·cap·o·lis** |də'kæpələs| federation of ancient Greek cities in Palestine, mostly N and NE of the Sea of Galilee, formed under Roman protection in the 1st century B.C. Damascus was the most important.

**De·ca·tur**[1] |də'kātər| industrial city in N Alabama, on the Tennessee River. Pop. 48,761.

**De·ca·tur**[2] |də'kātər| industrial and commercial city in central Illinois. Pop. 83,885.

**Dec·can** |'dekən| triangular plateau in S India, bounded by the Malabar Coast in the W, the Coromandel Coast in the E, and by the Vindhaya Mts. and the Narmada River in the N.

**Ded·ham** |'dedəm| town in E Massachusetts, a suburb SW of Boston. Pop. 23,782.

**Dee**[1] |dē| river in NE Scotland, which rises in the Grampian Mts. and flows E past Balmoral Castle to the North Sea at Aberdeen.

**Dee**[2] |dē| river that rises in North Wales and flows past Chester and into the Irish Sea.

**Deep South** |'dēp 'sowTH| parts of the SE U.S. regarded as most embodying Southern traditions. Mississippi, Alabama, and South Carolina are regarded as at its heart. See also SOUTH, THE.

**Deer·field** |'dir,fēld| historic town in NW Massachusetts, on the Connecticut River. Pop. 5,018. It suffered major Indian attacks in 1675 and 1704.

**Deer·field Beach** |'dir,fēld| resort city in SE Florida, N of Fort Lauderdale. Pop. 46,325.

**De·fense, la** |,lä dä'fäNs| business complex just W of Paris, France. Ultramodern, sleek buildings and sculptures characterize the area.

**De·hi·wa·la** |,dähē'wələ| resort town on the W coast of Sri Lanka. Pop. 174,000. It has one of the best-regarded zoos in Asia.

**Deh·ra Dun** |'dərə 'dōon| city in N India, in a valley at the foot of the Himalayas in Uttar Pradesh state. Pop. 270,000. The Indian military academy and a noted forestry research institute are here.

**De Kalb** |di'kælb| industrial city in N central Illinois. Pop. 34,925.

**De·la·no** |də'länō| agricultural city in S central California. Pop. 22,762.

**Del·a·ware** |'delə,wær| see box.

**Del·a·ware River** |'delə,wær| river of the NE U.S. Rising in the Catskill Mts. in New York State, it flows some 280 mi./450 km. S to N Delaware, where it meets the Atlantic at Delaware Bay. For much of its length it forms the E border of Pennsylvania.

**Delft** |delft| town in the Netherlands, in the province of South Holland. Pop. 89,400. The home of the painters Pieter de Hooch and Jan Vermeer, it is noted for its pottery.

**Del·hi** |dele| Union Territory in N central

---

### Delaware

**Capital:** Dover
**Largest city:** Wilmington
**Other cities:** Brookside, Claymont, Edgemoor, Newark, Smyrna
**Population:** 666,168,000 (1990); 743,603 (1998); 800,000 (2005 proj.);
**Population rank (1990):** 46
**Rank in land area:** 49
**Abbreviation:** DE; Del.
**Nicknames:** First State; Diamond State; Blue Hen State
**Motto:** 'Liberty and Independence'
**Bird:** blue hen chicken
**Fish:** weakfish
**Flower:** peach blossom
**Tree:** American holly
**Song:** "Our Delaware"
**Noted physical features:** Delaware Bay, Rehoboth Bay
**Tourist attractions:** E.I. du Pont de Nemours; Ft. Christina Monument, Holy Trinity (Old Swedes) Church; Hagley Museum, Winterthur Museum and Gardens; Rehoboth Beach; Dover Downs International Speedway
**Admission date:** December 7, 1787
**Order of admission:** 1
**Name origin:** Name first given to the river by Capt. Samuel Argall, who explored it in 1610, for Lord De La Warr, early governor of Virginia; then used of the Lenni-Lenape Indians, and finally of the state.

India, containing the cities of Old and New Delhi. Pop. 7,175,000. *Old Delhi*, a walled city on the Jumna River, was made the capital of the Mogul Empire in 1638 by Shah Jahan (1592–1666). *New Delhi*, the capital of India, was built 1912–29 to replace Calcutta as the capital of British India.

**Del·mar·va Peninsula** |del'märvə| region comprising part of *Dela*ware, the Eastern Shore of *Mary*land, and part of *Virg*inia. Chesapeake Bay lies to the W.

**Del·men·horst** |'delmən,hawrst| industrial city in NW Germany, near Bremen. Pop. 76,000.

**De·los** |'dē,läs| small Greek island in the Aegean Sea, regarded as the center of the Cyclades. Now virtually uninhabited, in classical times it was considered to be sacred to Apollo, and according to legend was the birthplace of Apollo and Artemis. Greek name **Dhílos**. □ **Delian** *adj. & n.*

**Del·phi** |'del,fī| one of the most important religious sanctuaries of ancient Greece, dedicated to Apollo and situated on the lower S slopes of Mount Parnassus above the Gulf of Corinth. Thought of as the "navel" of the earth, it was the seat of the Delphic Oracle, whose riddling responses to a wide range of questions were delivered by Apollo's priestess, the Pythia. Greek name **Dhelfoí**. □ **Delphic** *adj.*

**Del·ray Beach** |'del,rā| resort city in SE Florida, N of Fort Lauderdale. Pop. 47,181.

**Del Rio** |del 'rēō| city in SW Texas, on the Rio Grande. Pop. 30,705.

**Del·ta, the** |'deltə| region in N Mississippi, lying between the Yazoo and Mississippi rivers, famed for its cotton and for blues music. Also called the **Yazoo Delta** or **Mississippi Delta**.

**Del·ta** |'deltə| municipality in SW British Columbia, SE of Vancouver. Pop. 88,978.

**De·me·rara**[1] |,demə'rærə| former Dutch colony in South America, now part of Guyana.

**De·me·rara**[2] |,demə'rærə| river of N Guyana. Rising in the Guiana Highlands, it flows about 200 mi./320 km. N to the Atlantic.

**Demp·ster Highway** |'dempstər| road opened in 1979 to connect the Yukon Territory with the Mackenzie delta, in the Northwest Territories. It is the only highway in Canada to cross the Arctic Circle.

**De·na·li** |də'nälē| another name for MOUNT MCKINLEY, Alaska, and the name of the national park that surrounds it.

**Den·bigh·shire** |'denbēsHər; 'denbēsHir| county of N Wales; administrative center, Ruthin. It was divided between Clwyd and Gwynedd between 1974 and 1996.

**Den Haag** |dən 'häg| Dutch name for the HAGUE.

**Den Hel·der** |dən 'heldər| chief North Sea naval base of the Netherlands, opposite the island of TEXEL. Pop. 62,000.

**Den·i·son** |'denəsən| city in N Texas, on the Red River. Pop. 21,505.

**De·niz·li** |,deniz'lē| commercial city in SW Turkey, capital of Denizli province. Pop. 203,000. Ruins of ancient Laodicea ad Lycum, nearby, draw tourists.

**Den·mark** |'den,märk| (official name **Kingdom of Denmark**; Danish name **Danmark**) country in N Europe, in Scandinavia, on the Jutland peninsula and neighboring islands, between the North and Baltic seas. Area: 16,631 sq. mi./43,075 sq. km. Pop. 5,100,000. Language, Danish. Capital and largest city: Copenhagen. Denmark emerged as a separate country during the Viking period (10th–11th centuries). It is both industrial and agricultural; dairying is important, as is tourism. Greenland and the Faeroe Islands are overseas territories. □ **Danish** *adj.* **Dane** *n.*

Denmark

**Den·mark Strait** |'den,märk| arm of the N Atlantic Ocean between Iceland and Greenland.

**Den·pa·sar** |dən'päs,är| the chief city of the island of Bali, Indonesia, a seaport on the S coast. Pop. 261,200.

**Den·ton** |'dentn| commercial and educational city in NE Texas. Pop. 66,270.

**D'En·tre·cas·teaux Islands** |,däNtrəkäs-'tō| island group in SE Papua New Guinea, off the SE coast of New Guinea, of which the largest are Goodenough, Fergusson, and Normanby islands.

**Dents du Mi·di** |,däN dY mē'dē| mountain group in SE France, in the W Alps, between the Rhône River at Martigny and Mont

Blanc. The highest point is Dent du Midi (10,695 ft./3,260 m.).

**Den·ver** |'denvər| the state capital and largest city of Colorado. Pop. 467,600. Situated at an altitude of 5,280 ft./1,608 m. on the E side of the Rocky Mts., Denver developed in the 1870s as a silver-mining town. The "Mile-High City" is now an administrative, industrial, and commercial center, the metropolis of the mountain region.

**De·o·la·li** |ˌdaō'lälē| commercial and resort town in W India, in Maharashtra state. Pop. 51,000.

**Der·bent** |dyir'byent| city in S Russia, in Dagestan on the W shore of the Caspian Sea. Pop. 80,000.

**Der·by** |'därbē; 'dərbē| industrial city in the Midlands of England, on the Derwent River. Pop. 214,000.

**Der·by·shire** |'därbē,SHir; 'därbēSHər| county of N central England; county seat, Matlock.

**Der·ry** |'derē| see LONDONDERRY, Northern Ireland.

**Der·went** |'dərwənt| name of four short rivers in N and N central England, in Cumbria, Derbyshire, Durham and Northumberland, and Yorkshire. **Derwent Water** is a lake on the first of these, in the Lake District in Cumbria.

**Des·er·et** |ˌdezə'ret| name proposed in the 1840s by Mormon settlers for what became Utah.

**Des Moines** |də 'moin| the state capital and largest city of Iowa. Pop. 193,200.

**Des·na River** |dyiz'nä| river (550 mi./885 km.) in W Russia and Ukraine, rising E of Smolensk and flowing into the Dnieper River near Kiev.

**De So·to** |də 'sōtō| city in NE Texas, a suburb S of Dallas. Pop. 30,544.

**Des Plaines** |des 'plänz| city in NE Illinois, a suburb NW of Chicago. Pop. 53,223. O'Hare International Airport is on its S side.

**Des·sau** |'des,ow| industrial city in Germany, on the Mulde River, in Anhalt about 70 mi./112 km. SW of Berlin. Pop. 95,100. The famed Bauhaus design institute was here 1925–32.

**Det·mold** |'det,mawlt| city and capital of North Rhine–Westphalia, in NW Germany. Pop. 67,000. A resort on the N edge of the Teutoburg Forest, it is also a manufacturing center.

**De·troit** |di'troit; 'dē,troit| industrial city and Great Lakes port in SE Michigan. Pop. 1,028,000. Its metropolitan area is the cen-

ter of the U.S. automobile industry. It is popularly known as either **Motor City** or **Motown.**

**Deut·sche De·mo·kra·tische Re·pub·lik** |'doiCHə ˌdemōkrätisHə ˌräpōō'blēk| German name for the former state of East Germany.

**Deutsch·land** |'doiCH,länt| German name for GERMANY.

**De·va** |'dāvə| market town in W central Romania, on the Mures River. Pop. 77,000.

**De·ven·ter** |'dāvəntər| industrial city in E Netherlands, on the IJssel River. Pop. 68,000.

**Dev·il's Island** |'devəlz| rocky island off the coast of French Guiana, used 1852–1953 as a penal settlement, especially for political prisoners.

**Dev·il's Tower** |'devəlz| rock column in NE Wyoming, a national monument on the Belle Fourche River. It is 865 ft./264 m. high.

**Dev·on** |'devən| (also **Devonshire**) a county of SW England; county seat, Exeter.

**Dev·on Island** |'devən| southernmost of the Queen Elizabeth Is., in the Arctic Archipelago of Nunavut. It has some plant and animal life.

**Dews·bu·ry** |'dyezHnəf| (also **East Cape**) textile-manufacturing town in N England, near Leeds. Pop. 50,000.

**De·yang** |'də'yæNG| industrial city in Sichuan province, central China, N of Chengdu. Pop. 768,000.

**Dez·ful** |dez'fōōl| (also **Desful; Disful**) commercial town in W Iran, on the Dez River. Pop. 181,000.

**Dezh·nev, Cape** |'dyezHnəf| (also **East Cape**) cape at E end of Chukchi Peninsula, E Russia, projecting into the Bering Strait.

**De·zhou** |'də'jō| city in Shandong province, E China, on the Grand Canal NW of Jinan. Pop. 283,000.

**Dhah·ran** |dä'rän; ˌdähə'rän| oil town in E Saudi Arabia. Pop. 74,000. It was an Allied forces port and military base during the Persian Gulf War.

**Dha·ka** |'däkə| (also **Dacca**) the capital and largest city of Bangladesh, a commercial center in the Ganges delta. Pop. 3,637,890.

**Dhan·bad** |'dänbäd| city in Bihar, NE India, center of a coal-mining district. Pop. 818,000.

**Dha·ram·sa·la** |därm'sälə| (also **Dharmshala**) hill resort in N India, in Himachal Pradesh state. Pop. 17,000. The Dalai Lama's Tibetan government-in-exile is here.

**Dhar·war** |där'wär| textile-manufacturing city in S India, in Karnataka state, twinned with Hubli. Pop. 648,000.

**Dhau·la·gi·ri** |ˌdowlə'girē| mountain massif in the Himalayas, in Nepal, with six peaks, rising to 26,810 ft./8,172 m. at its highest point.

**Dhel·foi** |ᴛHel'fē| Greek name for DELPHI.

**Dhí·los** |'ᴛHē,laws| Greek name for DELOS.

**Dhu·lia** |'dōōlēə| (also **Dhule**) ndustrial city in W India, in Maharashtra state, NE of Bombay. Pop. 278,000.

**Di·ab·lo Canyon** |dē'æblō| nuclear power plant site in SW California, near San Luis Obispo, controversial because it was built over a geologic fault.

**Di·a·man·ti·na River** |ˌdīəmən'tēnə| intermittent river in E central Australia, flowing 560 mi./890 km. from central Queensland to South Australia.

**Dia·mond Head** |'dī(ə)mənd| an extinct volcano (761 ft./232 m.) overlooking the port of Honolulu on the Hawaiian island of Oahu.

**Di·as·po·ra, the** |dī'æsp(ə)rə| from a Greek term for 'scattering,' the world outside historical Palestine, into which the Jews were dispersed from the 6th century B.C.

**Die·go Gar·cia** |dē,ägō gär'sēə| the largest island of the Chagos Archipelago in the middle of the Indian Ocean, site of a strategic Anglo-American naval base established in 1973.

**Dien Bien Phu** |ˌdyen ,byen 'fōō| village in NW Vietnam, in 1954 the site of a French military post that was captured by the Vietminh after a 55-day siege, effectively ending French power in the region.

**Di·eppe** |dē'ep| channel port in N France, from which ferries run to Newhaven and other English ports. Pop. 36,600. In August 1942, it was the scene of an unsuccessful British-Canadian commando raid.

**Dig·by** |'digbē| port town in W Nova Scotia, off the Bay of Fundy. Pop. 2,311.

**Di·jon** |dē'ᴢHawN| industrial city in E central France, the former capital of Burgundy. Pop. 151,640.

**Di·li** |'dilē| seaport on the Indonesian island of Timor, which was (until 1975) the capital of the former Portuguese colony of East Timor. Pop. 60,150.

**Di·mi·tov·grad** |di'mētrəf,grät| industrial town in W Russia, NW of Samara. Pop. 133,000.

**Di·naj·pur** |di'näj,pōōr| commercial city in NW Bangladesh, capital of Dinajpur district. Pop. 128,000.

**Di·na·ric Alps** |də'nærik| mountain range in the Balkan peninsula, running parallel to the Adriatic coast from Slovenia in the NW, through Croatia, Bosnia, and Montenegro, to Albania in the SE. The Karst region is here.

**Din·digul** |'dindi,gəl| commercial town in S India, in Tamil Nadu state. Pop. 182,000. It is noted for its cheroots.

**Din·gle** |'diNGgəl| port town in SW Ireland, at the W end of the **Dingle Peninsula**, on the N side of **Dingle Bay**, in County Kerry. Pop. 1,300. It is the westernmost town in Europe.

**Di·o·mede Islands** |'dīə,mēd| two islands in the Bering Strait. Big Diomede belongs to Russia, and Little Diomede belongs to the United States. They are separated by the International Date Line.

**Di·re·da·wa** |'dērä'dowə| industrial and commercial city in E Ethiopia, on the rail line from Addis Ababa to Djibouti. Pop. 165,000.

**Dis·ko** |'diskō| island with extensive coal deposits on the W coast of Greenland. Its chief settlement is Godhavn.

**Dis·mal Swamp** |'dizməl| wetland in SE Virginia and NE North Carolina, famed in legend and history. Also, **Great Dismal Swamp.**

**Dis·ney·land** |'diznē,lænd| amusement park in Anaheim, California, opened in 1955.

**Dis·ney World** |'diznē ,wərld| amusement park in Lake Buena Vista, SW of Orlando, Florida, opened in 1971. Formally **Walt Disney World.**

**Dis·pu·ra** |dis'pōōrə| (also **Dispur**) city in NE India, capital of Assam state.

**Dis·trict of Co·lum·bia** |kə'ləmbēə| (abbrev.: **D.C.**) federal district of the U.S., coextensive with the city of WASHINGTON, on the Potomac River between Virginia and Maryland. Created in 1790, it had its Virginia components (now Arlington County and Alexandria) returned to that state in 1846.

**Dis·tri·to Fe·de·ral** |dēs'trētō ,fädə'räl| (abbrev. **D.F.**; English name **Federal District**) governmental district of Mexico, surrounding and including Mexico City. Pop. 8.2 million.

**Diu** |'dēōō| a constituent part of Daman and Diu Union Territory, W India, comprising mainly an island and port town of the same name.

**Di·vi·nó·po·lis** |jēvē'nawpōlēs| commercial city in SE Brazil, in Minas Gerais state. Pop. 172,000.

**Dix·ie** |'diksē| popular name for the U.S. South, especially the pre-Civil War South. Also **Dixieland**.

**Di·yar·ba·kir** |di,yärbä'kir| commercial city in SE Turkey, capital of a province of the same name. Pop. 381,100. It has a large Kurdish community.

**Dja·ja·pu·ra** |,jäyä'pŏŏrə| see JAYAPURA, Indonesia.

**Dja·kar·ta** |jə'kärtə| (also **Jakarta**) the capital and largest city of Indonesia, situated in NW Java. Pop. 8,222,500. Former name (until 1949) **Batavia**. It is the commercial, cultural, and administrative center of Indonesia.

**Djam·bi** |'jämbē| (also **Jambi**) port city in Indonesia, on SE Sumatra. Pop. 340,000.

**Djer·ba** |'jərbə; 'jerbə| (also **Jerba**) resort island in the Gulf of Gabès off the coast of Tunisia.

**Dji·bou·ti** |jə'bŏŏtē| (also **Jibuti**) **1** republic on the NE coast of Africa, on the Gulf of Aden. Area: 9,003 sq. mi./23,310 sq. km. Pop. 441,000. Languages, Arabic (official), French (official), Somali and other Cushitic languages. It is largely desert. **2** its capital, a port that handles much Ethiopian trade. Pop. 290,000. □ **Djiboutian** *adj. & n.*

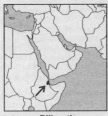

Djibouti

**DMZ** abbreviation for Demilitarized Zone, a strip of land separating North and South Korea, intended to keep the hostile forces apart. A similar zone was also in use during the Vietnam War, separating North and South Vietnam.

**Dnie·per River** |(də)'nēpər| river of E Europe, rising in Russia W of Moscow and flowing S some 1,370 mi./2,200 km. through Ukraine to the Black Sea. Ukrainian name **Dnipro**.

**Dnies·ter River** |(də)'nēstər| river of E Europe, rising in the Carpathian Mts. in W Ukraine and flowing 876 mi./1,410 km. to the Black Sea near Odessa. Russian name **Dnestr**, Ukrainian name **Dnister**.

**Dni·pro·dzer·zhinsk** |(də),nyeprədzir-'zhinsk| industrial city and river port in Ukraine, on the Dnieper River. Pop. 283,600. Former name (until 1936) **Kamenskoye**.

**Dni·pro·pe·trovsk** |(də),neyprōpə'trawf-sk| industrial city and river port in Ukraine, on the Dnieper River. Pop. 1,187,000. It was known as Yekaterinoslav (Ekaterinoslav) until 1926.

**Do·brich** |'dawbrēcH| city in NE Bulgaria, the center for an agricultural region. Pop. 115,800. It was formerly called Tolbukhin (1949–91).

**Dob·ru·ja** |'dawbrŏŏ,jä| district in E Romania and NE Bulgaria on the Black Sea coast, bounded on the N and W by the Danube River.

**Do·dec·a·nese** |dō'dekə,nēz| group of twelve major and many smaller Greek islands in the SE Aegean, of which the largest is Rhodes.

**Dodge City** |däj| city in SW Kansas. Pop. 21,129. Established in 1872 as a railhead on the Santa Fe Trail, it rapidly gained a reputation as a rowdy frontier town.

**Do·do·ma** |'dōdəmə| the official capital of Tanzania, in the center of the country. Pop. 203,830. See also DAR ES SALAAM

**Do·do·na** |də'dōnə| ancient town in NW Greece. It was the site of an early oracle of Zeus, believed to originate when a dove landed in an oak tree here; believers interpreted the rustling of the leaves and other sounds to divine Zeus's message.

**Dog·ger Bank** |'dawgər 'bæNGk| submerged sandbank in the North Sea, about 70 mi./115 km. off the NE coast of England. It is an important fishing zone.

**Dog·patch** |'dawg,pæcH| home of Li'l Abner and others in the comic strip of Al Capp, a fictional setting somewhere in the Ozark Plateau.

**Do·ha** |'dōhə| the capital of Qatar; pop. 300,000.

**Dol·drums** |'dōldrəmz| area of the earth, just N of the equator and near the trade winds, where seas give birth to hurricanes but may also be characterized by extended periods of calm.

**Dollard-des-Ormeaux** |dō'lärdəzor'mō| city in S Quebec, a residential suburb SW of Montreal. Pop. 46,922.

**Dol·o·mite Mountains** |'dōlə,mīt; 'dälə-,mīt| (also **the Dolomites**) range of the Alps in N Italy, so named because the characteristic rock of the region is dolomitic limestone. Marmolada, at 10,965 ft./3,342 m., is the high point.

**Do·lo·res Hi·dal·go** |də'lōrəs ē'dälgō| historic commercial city in central Mexico, in Guanajuato state. Pop. 40,000. Here Father Miguel Hidalgo issued the 1810 declaration (the *Grito de Hidalgo*) initiating the Mexican war of independence.

**Dom, the** |dōm| mountain in the Mischabelhörner group of the Pennine Alps, in S Switzerland. It is the highest mountain entirely in Switzerland: 14,911 ft./4,545 m.

**Dome of the Rock** Islamic shrine in E Jerusalem, surrounding the rock on which Abraham is said to have prepared to sacrifice his son Isaac, and from which Muhammad ascended into heaven. It is built on Mt. Moriah, sacred to Jews as the site of the Temple of Solomon.

**Dom·i·ni·ca** |,dämə'nēkə; də'minikə| mountainous island commonwealth in the West Indies, the loftiest of the Lesser Antilles and the northernmost and largest (290 sq. mi./751 sq. km.) of the Windward Islands. Pop. 71,790. Languages, English (official), Creole. Capital and largest community: Roseau. Tropical crops are important. The island came into British possession at the end of the 18th century, becoming independent in 1978. □ **Dominican** *adj. & n.*

**Dominica**

**Do·mi·ni·can Republic** |də'minikən| country in the Caribbean occupying the E part of the island of Hispaniola. Area: 18,704 sq. mi./48,442 sq. km. Pop. 7,770,000. Language, Spanish. Capital and largest city: Santo Domingo. The Dominican Republic is the former Spanish colony of Santo Domingo. It was proclaimed a republic in 1844. The mountainous country relies on agriculture, mining, light industry, and tourism. □ **Dominican** *adj. & n.*

**Dom·re·my** |'dawⁿrä'mē| (also called **Domremy-la-Pucelle**) village in NE France, SW of Nancy, on the Meuse River. It is the birthplace of Joan of Arc.

**Dominican Republic**

**Don, River**[1] |dän| river in N England that rises in the Pennines and flows 70 mi./112 km. E to join the Ouse shortly before it, in turn, joins the Humber.

**Don, River**[2] |dän| river in Scotland that rises in the Grampians and flows 82 mi./131 km. E to the North Sea at Aberdeen.

**Do·nau** |'dȯ,now| German name for the DANUBE River.

**Don·bas** |'dän,bæs| Ukrainian name for DONETS BASIN.

**Don·bass** |dən'bäs; 'dän,bæs| Russian name for DONETS BASIN.

**Don·cas·ter** |'däⁿGkəstər| industrial town and rail center in N England, formerly part of Yorkshire. Pop. 284,300.

**Don·e·gal** |,däni'gawl; ,dəni'gawl| county in the extreme NW of the Republic of Ireland, part of the old province of Ulster. Pop. 128,000. Capital: Lifford.

**Do·nets** |də'n(y)ets| river in E Europe, rising near Belgorod in S Russia and flowing SE for some 630 mi./1,000 km. through Ukraine before re-entering Russia and joining the Don near Rostov.

**Do·nets Basin** |də'n(y)ets| coal-mining and industrial region of SE Ukraine, stretching between the valleys of the Donets and lower Dnieper rivers. Ukrainian name **Donbas**.

**Do·netsk** |də'n(y)etsk| the leading city of the Donets Basin in Ukraine. Pop. 1,117,000. The city was called **Yuzovka** from 1872 until 1924, and **Stalin** or **Stalino** from 1924 until 1961.

**Dong-nai River** |'dawⁿG 'ni| (also **Don-nai**) river in Vietnam that flows 300 mi./483 km. from S central Vietnam to join the Saigon River below Ho Chi Minh City.

**Dong·ting, Lake** |'dȯⁿG 'tiⁿG| (Chinese name **Dongting Hu**) lake in Hunan province, E central China, the second-largest freshwater lake in China; area 1,089 sq. mi./2,820 sq. km.

**Dong·ying** |'dȯⁿG 'yiⁿG| city in Hebei

province, E China, near the mouth of the Yellow River, in an area rich in oil. Pop. 540,000.

**Don Mills** |'dän 'milz| planned industrial, commercial, and residential community in North York, Ontario, just NE of Toronto.

**Don·ner Pass** |'dänər| site in the Sierra Nevada of NE California where some members of an 1844 emigrant party survived a blizzard partly by eating the dead.

**Don·ny·brook** |'dänē,brŏŏk| suburb to the SE of Dublin, Ireland, scene (1204–1855) of an annual fair famous for its fighting and riotous behavior.

**Don River** |dän| river in Russia that rises near Tula, SE of Moscow, and flows for a distance of 1,224 mi./1,958 km. to the Sea of Azov.

**Doon River** |dŏŏn| short river in SW Scotland, in the Strathclyde region, celebrated in the poetry of Robert Burns. It flows through **Loch Doon**, a widening, and into the Firth of Clyde.

**Doone Valley** |dŏŏn| valley in N Devon, SW England, N of Exmoor, Somerset, setting for the events in R.D. Blackmore's popular novel *Lorna Doone.*

**Door·nik** |'dawrnik| Flemish name for TOURNAI, Belgium.

**Door Peninsula** |dawr| resort region of NE Wisconsin, lying between Green Bay and Lake Michigan.

**Dor·ches·ter**[1] |'dawrCHəstər; 'dawr,CHes-tər| town in S England, the county seat of Dorset. Pop. 14,000.

**Dor·ches·ter**[2] |'dawrCHəstər; 'dawr,CHes-tər| residential section of Boston, Massachusetts, S of downtown.

**Dor·dogne**[1] |dawr'dōn(ye)| department of SW France. It contains caves that have yielded abundant remains of early humans and their artifacts and art, such as that at Lascaux.

**Dor·dogne**[2] |dawr'dōn(ye)| river of W France that rises in the Auvergne and flows 297 mi./472 km. W to meet the Garonne and form the Gironde estuary.

**Dor·drecht** |'dawr,drekHt| industrial city and river port in the Netherlands, near the mouth of the Rhine (there called the Waal), 12 mi./20 km. SE of Rotterdam. Pop. 110,500. Also called **Dort.**

**Do·ris** |'dawrəs| ancient name for a mountainous district in central Greece. It was home to the Dorians, one of the four main groups of ancient Greeks.

**Dor·set** |'dawrsət| county of SW England; county seat, Dorchester. Pop. 645,000. It is central to the writings of Thomas Hardy.

**Dort·mund** |'dawrt,mŏŏnt| industrial city and canal port in NW Germany, in North Rhine-Westphalia, a center for steel and brewing. Pop. 601,000.

**Dor·val** |dawr'väl| city in S Quebec, a suburb W of Montreal and home to its older airport. Pop. 17,249.

**Dos Her·ma·nas** |,dōs er'mänəs| industrial commune in SW Spain, SE of Seville. Pop. 77,000.

**Do·than** |'dōTHən| city in SE Alabama, near the Florida line. Pop. 53,589.

**Dou·ai** |dwe; dŏŏ'a| industrial and commercial town in NW France, on the Scarpe River near Lille. Pop. 44,000. Douai was the center of the textile trade in the Middle Ages.

**Dou·a·la** |dŏŏ'älə| the chief port and largest city of Cameroon. Pop. 1,200,000.

**Doubs River** |dŏŏ| river (270 mi./435 km.) that rises in the Jura Mts., E France, flows NE, becoming part of the French-Swiss border, flows into Switzerland , and then turns W to return to France, finally joining the Saône River.

**Doug·las** |'dəgləs| resort town, the capital of the Isle of Man, in the Irish Sea. Pop. 22,210.

**Doun·reay** |dŏŏn'rā| village in extreme N Scotland, in Caithness, site of two now inactive nuclear breeder reactors and of an experimental wave-power station in the Pentland Firth.

**Dou·ro** |'dō,rŏŏ| river of the Iberian Peninsula, rising in central Spain and flowing W for 556 mi./900 km/ through Portugal to the Atlantic near Oporto. Spanish name **Duero.**

**Do·ver**[1] |'dōvər| the state capital of Delaware. Pop. 23,500.

**Do·ver**[2] |'dōvər| ferry port in Kent, SE England, on the English Channel. Pop. 34,300. It is mainland Britain's nearest point to the Continent, being only 22 miles (35 km) from Calais, France.

**Do·ver**[3] |'dōvər| industrial city in SE New Hampshire. Pop. 25,042.

**Do·ver, Strait of** |'dōvər| sea passage between England and France, connecting the English Channel with the North Sea. At its narrowest it is 22 mi./35 km. wide.

**Down** |down| one of the Six Counties of Northern Ireland, formerly an administrative area; chief town, Downpatrick. Pop. 339,000.

**Down East** |down 'ēst| name for NE New England and/or the Maritime Provinces, deriving from an old term for sailing downwind, to the E.

**Dow·ners Grove** |'downərz| village in NE Illinois, a suburb W of Chicago. Pop. 46,858.

**Dow·ney** |'downē| city in SW California, an industrial suburb SE of Los Angeles. Pop. 91,444.

**Down·ing Street** |'downiNG| street in central London, England, in Westminster, next to Whitehall. The official residence of the British prime minister is at 10 Downing St., and other key residences and offices are here as well.

**Down·pat·rick** |ˌdown'pætrik| town in SE Northern Ireland, the seat of County Down. Pop. 8,000. It is associated with St. Patrick, who was long thought to have been buried here along with Saints Columba and Brigid.

**Downs** |downz| region of chalk hills in S England, forming parallel ranges. The **North Downs** are in Surrey and Kent, the **South Downs** in Sussex.

**Down Under** nickname for Australia and New Zealand.

**Doyles·town** |'doilz,town| township in SE Pennsylvania, noted for its museums. Pop. 14,510.

**Dra·chen·fels Mountain** |'dräKHən,fels| hill in the Siebengebirge, near Bonn, S Germany, rising 1,053 ft./321 m. The legendary character Siegfried is supposed to have slain a dragon here.

**Dra·kens·berg Mountains** |'dräkənz-ˌbərg| range of mountains in southern Africa, stretching in a NE–SW direction for 700 mi./1,126 km. through Lesotho and parts of South Africa. The highest peak is Thabana Ntlenyana (11,425 ft./3,482 m.).

**Drake Passage** |drāk| area of ocean, noted for its violent storms, connecting the South Atlantic with the South Pacific and separating the S tip of South America (Cape Horn) from the Antarctic Peninsula.

**Drakes Bay** |drāks| inlet of the Pacific Ocean, NW of San Francisco, California, visited by Francis Drake in 1579.

**Dra·ma** |'drämə| department in N Greece. Area: 1,339 sq. mi./3,468 sq. km. Pop. 97,000. Its capital is Drama.

**Dram·men** |'drämən| seaport in SE Norway, on an inlet of Oslofjord. Pop. 51,900.

**Dran·cy** |dräNsē| industrial town, a NE suburb of Paris, France. Pop. 61,000. During World War II there was a Nazi internment camp here.

**Dra·va River** |'drävə| (also **Drave**), river that rises in N Italy and flows 456 mi./725 km. through S Austria, Slovenia, and Croa-

tia to join the Danube near Osijek. It forms part of the border between Hungary and Croatia.

**Dres·den** |'drezdən| city in eastern Germany, the capital of Saxony, on the Elbe River. Pop. 485,130. Famous for its baroque architecture and china industry, it was almost totally destroyed by Allied bombing in 1945.

**Dri·na River** |'drēnə| river, 285 mi./459 km. long, that flows into the Sava River W of Belgrade, Serbia. It constitutes part of the border between Bosnia and Herzegovina and Serbia.

**Drobeta-Turnu Se·ve·rin** |drō'bätə 'tōōrnōō ˌsävə'rēn| industrial port city in SW Romania, on the Danube River. Pop. 116,000.

**Dro·ghe·da** |'draw-ədə; 'droiədə| port city in the NE Republic of Ireland, in Louth. Pop. 23,000. In 1649 the inhabitants were massacred after refusing to surrender to Oliver Cromwell's forces. The Battle of the Boyne was fought nearby in 1690.

**Drôme** |drōm| department in SE France. Area: 2,520 sq. mi./6,525 sq. km. Pop. 414,000. The capital is Valence.

**Drott·ning·holm** |'drootniNG,hō(l)m| the winter palace of the Swedish royal family, on an island to the W of Stockholm.

**Drouzh·ba** |'drooZHbə| (also **Druzba**) resort town on the Black Sea coast of Bulgaria, N of Varna. Also called **Sveti Konstantin**.

**Drum·cliff** |ˌdrəm'klif| see BEN BULBEN, Ireland.

**Drum·mond·ville** |'drəmənd,vil| industrial city in S Quebec, E of Montreal. Pop. 35,462.

**Dru·ry Lane** |'droorē| street in central London, England, NE of Covent Garden, site since 1663 of the most famous British theaters, and thus a term for the theater itself.

**Druze, Je·bel** |'jebəl 'drooz| (also **Jebel ed Druz**) **1** region in S Syria, home of the Druze, E of the Sea of Galilee, on the border with N Jordan. **2** mountain in this area: 5,900 ft./1,800 m.

**Dry Tor·tu·gas** |ˌdrī tawr'tōōgəz| island group in SW Florida, W of Key West, noted for its wildlife and for Fort Jefferson, built during the Civil War. Also **the Tortugas** or **Tortugas Keys**.

**Duar·te, Pi·co** |'pēkō 'dwärtə| (formerly **Monte Trujillo**) peak in the Cordillera Central of the central Dominican Republic, at 10,417 ft./3,175 m. said to be the highest in the Caribbean.

**Du·bai** |dŌŌ'bī| **1** member state of the United Arab Emirates. Area: 1,506 sq. mi./3,900 sq. km. Pop. 674,100. **2** its capital city, a port on the Persian Gulf. Pop. 265,700.

**Dub·lin** |'dəblin| **1** the capital and largest city of the Republic of Ireland, an industrial port on the Irish Sea at the mouth of the Liffey River. Pop. 477,700. It is a cultural center associated with writers including Jonathan Swift, Oscar Wilde, and James Joyce. Irish name **Baile Átha Cliath**. **2** the most populous county in Ireland, including the city and many suburbs. Pop. 1,024,000. □ **Dubliner** *n*.

**Du·brov·nik** |dŌŌ'brawvnik| port and resort on the Adriatic coast of Croatia. Pop. 66,100. A major medieval port, famed for its architecture, it was damaged during a Serbian siege in 1991. Italian name (until 1918) **Ragusa**.

**Du·buque** |də'byŌŌk| industrial and commercial city in NE Iowa, on the Mississippi River. Pop. 57,546.

**Dud·ley** |'dədlē| industrial and commercial city in the West Midlands of England, near Birmingham. Pop. 187,000.

**Duf·fel** |'dəfəl| town in S Belgium. Pop. 7,000. The coarse woolen cloth known as *duffel* originated here.

**Du·four·spit·ze** |də'fŌŌr'sHpitsə| second-highest peak in the Alps and the highest in Switzerland: 15,203 ft./4,634 m. It is in the Monta Rosa group of the Pennine Alps, on the Swiss-Italian border.

**Dug·way** |'dəg,wā| community in NW Utah, in the Great Salt Lake Desert, site of an Army range where chemical and biological weapons have been tested. Pop. 1,761.

**Duis·burg** |'dYs,berk; 'd(y)ŌŌz,bərg| industrial city in NW Germany, in North Rhine-Westphalia. Pop. 537,440. It is the largest inland port in Europe, at the Rhine-Ruhr junction.

**Du·luth** |də'lŌŌTH| port in NE Minnesota, at the western end of Lake Superior. Pop. 92,800. With its neighbor Superior, Wisconsin, it is a leading grain- and ore-exporting port.

**Dum·bar·ton** |,dəm'bärtn| town in Scotland on the Clyde W of Glasgow, in West Dunbartonshire. Pop. 21,960.

**Dum·bar·ton Oaks** |'dəm,bärtn 'ōks| historic site in Washington, D.C., an estate at which plans for the United Nations were formulated in a 1944 meeting.

**Dum Dum** |'dəm ,dəm| city in NE India, in West Bengal state, near Calcutta. Pop. 41,000. The "dum-dum" bullet was first made here while the city was headquarters for British artillery.

**Dum·fries** |,dəm'frēs| market town in SW Scotland, administrative center of Dumfries and Galloway region. Pop. 32,130.

**Dum·fries and Gal·lo·way** |'dəm'frēs ən 'gælə,wā| administrative region in SW Scotland, formed in 1975; administrative center, Dumfries.

**Dum·fries·shire** |,dəm'frēsHər; ,dəm'frē ,sHir| former county of SW Scotland, which became part of Dumfries and Galloway region in 1975.

**Dum·yat** |dŌŌm'yät| Arabic name for DAMIETTA, Egypt.

**Du·na·új·vá·ros** |'dŌŌnow,värōsH| industrial town in central Hungary, on the Danube River. Pop. 60,000.

**Dun·bar·ton·shire** |dəm'bärtnsHər; dəm-'bärtn,sHir| (also **Dumbartonshire**) administrative region and former county of W central Scotland, on the Clyde, divided into *East Dunbartonshire* and *West Dunbartonshire*.

**Dun·dalk**[1] |,dən'daw(l)k| the county seat of Louth, in the Republic of Ireland, a port on the E coast. Pop. 25,800.

**Dun·dalk**[2] |'dən,dawk| community in N central Maryland, a port and suburb just SE of Baltimore. Pop. 65,800.

**Dun·dee** |dən'dē| industrial port and university city in E Scotland, on the N side of the Firth of Tay. Pop. 165,500.

**Dun·e·din**[1] |dən'ēdən| resort city in W Florida, on the Gulf of Mexico W of Tampa. Pop. 34,012.

**Dun·e·din**[2] |dən'ēdən| industrial port city on South Island, New Zealand. Pop. 113,900.

**Dun·ferm·line** |dən'fərmlən| industrial city in Fife, central Scotland, near the Firth of Forth. Pop. 55,000.

**Dun·gar·van** |dən'gärvən| town on the S coast of the Republic of Ireland, the administrative center of Waterford. Pop. 6,920.

**Dunge·ness** |,dənjə'nes; 'dənjə,nes| locality in NW Washington, on the Olympic Peninsula, that gave its name to a kind of crab.

**Dun·hua** |'dŌŌn'hwä| industrial city in Jilin province, NE China, on the Mudan River NW of Yanji. Pop. 450,000.

**Dun·huang** |'dŌŌn'hwäNG| town in Gansu province, NW China, on the old Silk Road near the site of the earliest known Buddhist cave shrines in China (4th century A.D.).

**Dun·kirk** |dən'kərk; 'dən,kərk| (French name **Dunkerque**) port in N France, on the English Channel. Pop 71,070. It was the scene of the evacuation to Britain in 1940 of 335,000 Allied troops who were rescued by warships, requisitioned civilian ships, and a host of small boats, under constant attack by German aircraft.

**Dun Laoghaire** |ˌdən 'lirē| ferry port and resort town in the Republic of Ireland, on Dublin Bay just SE of Dublin. Pop. 54,715. Earlier names **Dunleary** and (1820–1921) **Kingstown**.

**Dun•net Head** |'dənət 'hed| headland on the N coast of Scotland, between Thurso and John o'Groats. It is the most northerly point on the British mainland.

**Dun•si•nane** |dən'sinən; 'dənsəˌnān| hill in central Scotland, in Tayside, in the Sidlaw Hills, the scene of the final defeat of Macbeth in the play of Shakespeare, based on events of the year 1054.

**Dun•sta•ble** |'dənstəbəl| historic industrial town in S England, N of the Chiltern Hills in Bedfordshire, at the junction of the ancient Watling Street and Icknield Way. Pop. 31,000.

**Du•que de Ca•xi•as** |'dookē dē kä'sHēəs| city in SE Brazil, a suburb of Rio de Janeiro. Pop. 1,352,160.

**Dura-Europos** |'doorə yoo'rōpəs| ancient city of Syria, on the Euphrates River, E of Palmyra. Founded in the 3rd century B.C., it was abandoned about 550 years later.

**Du•ran•go** |d(y)oo'ræNGgō| **1** state of N central Mexico. Area: 47,579 sq. mi./123,181 sq. km. Pop. 1,352,000. **2** its capital city. Pop. 414,000. Full name **Victoria de Durango**.

**Dur•ban** |'dərbən| seaport and resort in South Africa, on the coast of KwaZulu/Natal. Pop. 1,137,380. Former name (until 1835) **Port Natal**.

**Dü•ren** |'dyrən| industrial city and transportation center in W Germany, on the Ruhr River. Pop. 83,000.

**Durg** |doorg| commercial town in central India, in Madhya Pradesh state. Pop. 151,000. It is twinned with Bhilainagar.

**Dur•ga•pur** |'doorgəˌpoor| industrial city in NE India, in the state of West Bengal. Pop. 415,990.

**Dur•ham**[1] |'dərəm; 'doorəm| **1** city on the Wear River, in NE England. Pop. 85,800. It is famous for its 11th-century cathedral, which contains the tomb of the Venerable Bede, and its university. **2** (also **County Durham**) a county of NE England. Pop. 590,000. County town, Durham.

**Dur•ham**[2] |'dərəm; 'doorəm| industrial and academic city in N central North Carolina, noted for its tobacco business and as the home of Duke University. Pop. 136,611.

**Dur•rës** |'doorəs| port and resort in Albania, on the Adriatic coast. Pop. 72,000. Italian name **Durazzo**.

**Du•shan•be** |d(y)oo'sHäm‚bä| industrial city, the capital of Tajikistan. Pop. 602,000. Former name (1929–61) **Stalinabad**.

**Düs•sel•dorf** |'dysəlˌdawrf| industrial, commercial, and cultural city of NW Germany, on the Rhine, capital of North Rhine-Westphalia. Pop. 577,560.

**Dust Bowl** |'dəs(t)ˌbōl| popular name for parts of the U.S. Great Plains where 1930s windstorms blew topsoil across a wide area. Kansas, Oklahoma, and N Texas were at its center.

**Dutch East In•dies** |'dəCH ēst 'indēz| former name (until 1949) for INDONESIA.

**Dutch•ess County** |'dəCHəs| county in SE New York, E of the Hudson River, traditionally agricultural but increasingly suburban. Its seat its Poughkeepsie. Pop. 259,462.

**Dutch Gui•a•na** |'dəCH gē'änə| former name (until 1948) for SURINAME.

**Dutch New Gui•nea** |ˌdəCH n(y)oo 'ginē| former name (until 1963) for IRIAN JAYA, Indonesia.

**Du•yun** |'doo'yoon| agricultural and industrial city in Guizhou province, S China, on the Longtou River SE of Guiyang. Pop. 392,000.

**Dvi•na River** |d(ə)vē'nä| river (634 mi./1,020 km.) that rises in Russia's Valai Hills and flows SW across Belarus and Latvia into the Gulf of Riga.

**Dy•fed** |'dəvēd| former county of SW Wales 1974–96, comprising the former counties of Cardiganshire, Carmarthenshire, and Pembrokeshire.

**Dzaud•zhi•kau** |(d)zow'jēkō| former name (1944–54) for VLADIKAVKAZ, Russia.

**Dzer•zhinsk** |jer'zHinsk| city in W central Russia, W of Nizhni Novgorod. Pop. 286,000. Former name **Chernorechye** (until 1919) and **Rastyapino** (1919–29).

**Dzier•zo•niów** |jer'zHawnyoof| (German name **Reichenbach**) manufacturing town, in SW Poland. Pop. 38,000. It is known for its textiles.

**Dzun•ga•ria** |zooNG'gærēə| (also **Junggar** or **Junggar Basin**) sparsely populated semidesert region of Xinjiang, NW China, between the Tien Shan and Altai Shan ranges.

# Ee

**Ea·gan** |'ēgən| city in SE Minnesota, a suburb just S of Saint Paul. Pop. 47,409.

**Ea·gle Pass** |'ēgəl| city in SW Texas, on the Rio Grande. Pop. 20,651.

**Ea·ling** |'ēliNG| residential borough of W Greater London, England. Pop. 264,000. It is noted as the longtime center of the British film industry.

**East, the** |'ēst| countries to the E of Europe. See NEAR EAST, MIDDLE EAST, and FAR EAST. In the 20th century, communist countries from the Soviet Union have also been referred to as the East.

**East Af·ri·ca** |ēst 'æfrikə| the E part of the African continent, especially the countries of Kenya, Uganda, and Tanzania.

**East An·glia** |ēst 'æNGglēə| region of E England consisting of the counties of Norfolk, Suffolk, and parts of Essex and Cambridgeshire.

**East Ben·gal** |,ēst ben'gäl| the part of the former Indian province of Bengal that was ceded to Pakistan in 1947, forming the greater part of the province of East Pakistan. It gained independence as Bangladesh in 1971.

**East Ber·lin** |,ēst bər'lin| the E half of the city of Berlin (divided in 1945) and, until German reunification in 1990, part of the German Democratic Republic. It was separated from West Berlin in 1961 by the Berlin Wall.

**East·bourne** |'ēst,bawrn| resort town on the S coast of England, in East Sussex. Pop. 78,000.

**East Chi·ca·go** |ēst sHə'kägō; sHə'kawgō| industrial port city in NW Indiana, on Lake Michigan SE of Chicago, Illinois. Pop. 33,892.

**East Chi·na Sea** see CHINA SEA.

**East Co·ker** |,ēst 'kōkər| village in SW England, in Somerset, S of Yeovil, the ancestral home and burial place of the poet T.S. Eliot.

**East End** |ēst 'end| the part of London, England, east of the City as far as the Lea River, including the Docklands. □ **East Ender** *n.*

**Eas·ter Island** |'ēstər| (Polynesian name **Rapa Nui**) island in the SE Pacific, W of Chile. Pop. 2,000. It has been administered by Chile since 1888. The island, first settled by Polynesians in about A.D. 400, is famous for its monolithic statues of human heads, believed to date from the period 1000–1600.

**East·ern bloc** the nations of eastern and central Europe that were under Soviet domination from the end of World War II until the collapse of the Soviet communist system in 1989-91, usually considered to include Poland, East Germany, Czechoslovakia, Hungary, Romania, Bulgaria, and Yugoslavia.

**East·ern Cape** -|'ēstərn| province of SE South Africa, formerly part of the Cape province. Pop. 6,504,000. Capital: Bisho.

**East·ern Desert** |'ēstərn| another name for the ARABIAN DESERT, Egypt.

**East·ern Eur·ope** |'ēstərn 'yŏŏrəp| portion of the European landmass lying east of Germany and the Alps and west of the Ural Mountains. It includes the former Eastern bloc countries of Poland, the Czech Republic and Slovakia (formerly as Czechoslovakia), Hungary, Romania, and Bulgaria, as well as the Baltic republics of Estonia, Latvia, and Lithuania, and the former Soviet republics of Belarus and Ukraine, along with Russia west of the Urals.

**East·ern Hemisphere** |'ēstərn| the half of the earth containing Europe, Asia, and Africa.

**East·ern Shore** |'ēstərn| region of E Maryland on the Delmarva Peninsula, on the E side of Chesapeake Bay.

**East·ern Townships** |'ēstərn| region of SE Quebec, E of Montreal, settled in the 19th century by English speakers, but today mostly French-speaking. French name **Cantons de l'Est**, also **Estrie**.

**East·ern Trans·vaal** |'ēstərn trænz'väl| former province of NE South Africa, formerly part of Transvaal, and now MPUMALANGA. Capital: Nelspruit.

**East Flan·ders** |ēst 'flændərz| province of N Belgium. Pop. 1,336,000. Capital: Ghent. See also FLANDERS.

**East Fri·sian Islands** |ēst 'frizHən| see FRISIAN ISLANDS, Germany.

**East Ger·many** |ēs(t) 'jərmənē| (official name **German Democratic Republic**) former independent nation created in 1949 from the area of Germany occupied by the Soviet Union after World War II. It was reunited with West Germany after the fall of its communist government in 1990. German name **Deutsche Demokratische Republik**.

**East Hamp·ton** |ĕst 'hæmptən| resort town in E Long Island, New York, noted for its artists' colony. Pop. 16,132.

**East Har·lem** |ĕst 'härləm| neighborhood of Harlem, in N Manhattan, New York City. Parts of it have been called Italian Harlem and Spanish Harlem, reflecting local ethnic history.

**East Hart·ford** |ĕst 'härtfərd| industrial town in central Connecticut, across the Connecticut River from Hartford. Pop. 50,452.

**East In·dies** |ĕst 'indēz| **1** the islands of SE Asia, especially the Malay Archipelago. **2** (*archaic*) the whole of SE Asia to the east of and including India. □ **East Indian** *adj.* & *n.*

**East Kil·bride** |ˌĕst kil'brīd| town in W central Scotland, in South Lanarkshire. Pop. 81,400.

**East Lan·sing** |ĕst 'lænsiNG| city in S central Michigan, home to Michigan State University. Pop. 50,677.

**East Liv·er·pool** |ĕst 'livərpōōl| city in E Ohio, on the Ohio River, famed for its ceramics industry. Pop. 13,654.

**East Lon·don** |ĕst 'ləndən| industrial port and resort in South Africa, on the Eastern Cape coast. Pop. 270,130.

**East Los An·ge·les** |ˌĕst laws 'ænjələs| community in SW California, a largely Hispanic suburb on the E side of Los Angeles. Pop. 126,379.

**East Lo·thi·an** |ˌĕs(t) 'lōTHēən| administrative region and former county of E central Scotland.

**East·main River** |'ĕst,mān| river in W central Quebec that flows 470 mi./760 km. into Hudson Bay. The Eastmain region was an early fur trade center, and is today the site of major hydroelectric developments.

**East New York** |ˌĕst n(y)ōō 'yawrk| largely residential section of E Brooklyn, New York City.

**Eas·ton** |'ēstən| industrial city in E Pennsylvania, on the Lehigh and Delaware rivers. Pop. 26,276.

**East Orange** |ĕst 'är(i)nj; 'awr(i)nj| city in NE New Jersey, a suburb NW of Newark. Pop. 73,552.

**East Pak·i·stan** |'ēs(t) ˌpækə'stæn| former part of Pakistan, bounded by India to the N, W, and E and by Burma to the SE; the largely Muslim Indian state of East Bengal before 1947, it became Bangladesh in 1971.

**East Point** |'ĕst 'point| city in NW Georgia, a residential and industrial suburb S of Atlanta. Pop. 34,402.

**East·port** |'ēst,pawrt| maritime city in E Maine, on an island in Passamaquoddy Bay Pop. 1,965. It is the easternmost U.S. city.

**East Prov·i·dence** |ĕst 'prävədəns| city in E Rhode Island, an industrial and commercial suburb across the Seekonk River from Providence. Pop. 50,380.

**East Prus·sia** |ĕst 'prəshə| the NE part of the former kingdom of Prussia, on the Baltic coast, later part of Germany and divided after World War II between the Soviet Union (now Russia) and Poland.

**East Ri·ding of York·shire** |ĕst 'ridiNG əv 'yawrksHər; 'yawrk,sHir| administrative region in NE England, formerly one of the traditional ridings or divisions of the county of Yorkshire.

**East River** |'ĕst| strait running from Long Island Sound to Upper New York Bay, in New York City, separating Manhattan and the Bronx from Brooklyn and Queens.

**East Saint Louis** |ĕst sānt 'lōōwəs| city in SW Illinois, an industrial and commercial center across the Mississippi River from Saint Louis. Pop. 40,944.

**East Si·be·ri·an Sea** |ˌĕst sī'birēən| part of the Arctic Ocean lying between the New Siberian Islands and Wrangel Island, to the N of E Siberia.

**East Side** |'ĕst 'sīd| part of Manhattan, New York City, lying between the East River and Fifth Avenue. The **Upper East Side,** S of East Harlem, is generally affluent. The **Lower East Side,** below 14th Street, is famed as home to immigrants.

**East Sus·sex** |ĕst 'səsiks| county of SE England. Pop. 671,000. County town, Lewes.

**East Ti·mor** |ĕst 'tē,mawr; tē'mawr| the E part of the island of Timor in the S Malay Archipelago; chief town, Dili. Formerly a Portuguese colony, the region declared itself independent in 1975. In 1976 it was invaded by Indonesia, which annexed and claimed it as the 27th state of Indonesia, a claim that has never been recognized by the

**East Timor**

United Nations. Since then the region has been the scene of bitter fighting and of alleged mass killings by the Indonesian government and military forces.

**East·wood** |'ēst,wŏod| mining village in central England, in Nottinghamshire, the birthplace of the writer D.H. Lawrence.

**East York** |ēst 'yawrk| residential borough in S Ontario, immediately N of Toronto. Pop. 102,696.

**Eau Claire** |ō 'kler| industrial city in W central Wisconsin. Pop. 58,856.

**Eb·bw Vale** |'ebŏo| industrial town in S Wales, in Gwent, N of Cardiff. Pop. 9,000. Once a noted coal- and steel-producing center, it now has light industries.

**Eb·la** |'eblə| city in ancient Syria, to the SW of Aleppo. It became very powerful in the mid-3rd millennium B.C., when it dominated a region corresponding to present-day Lebanon, N Syria, and SE Turkey.

**Ebo·ra·cum** |i'bawrəkəm| Roman name for YORK, England.

**Ebro River** |abrō| the principal river of NE Spain, rising in the mountains of Cantabria and flowing 570 mi./910 km. SE into the Mediterranean Sea.

**Eca·te·pec de Mo·re·los** |ā,kātə'pec 'dā mə'rālōs| industrial city in central Mexico, a suburb NE of Mexico City in the state of Mexico. Pop. 1,218,000.

**Ec·bat·a·na** |ek'bætn-ə| see HAMADAN, Iran.

**Ech Chlef** |,esH shə'lef| (also **Ech Chéliff** or **Chlef**) industrial and commercial town in N Algeria, on the Chéliff River SW of Algiers. Pop. 130,000.

**Ec·ua·dor** |'ekwə,dawr| equatorial republic in South America, on the Pacific coast. Area: 109,484 sq. mi./270,670 sq. km. Pop. 11,460,100. Languages, Spanish (official), Quechua. Capital and largest city: Quito. Stretching from coastal plains to the Andes and Amazonian jungles, Ecuador is largely agricultural, and produces oil. The Gala-

**Ecuador**

pagos Islands are an external territory. □ **Ecuadorean** adj. & n.

**Edam** |'ēdəm| market town in the Netherlands, to the NE of Amsterdam, noted for its cheese. Pop. 24,840.

**Ed·dy·stone Rocks** |'edēstōn| rocky reef off the coast of Cornwall, England, 14 mi./22 km. SW of Plymouth. It was the site of the earliest lighthouse (1699) built on rocks fully exposed to the sea.

**Ede**[1] |'ādə| industrial city in E Netherlands. Pop. 96,000.

**Ede**[2] |'a,dā| industrial town in SW Nigeria, NE of Ibadan, in a predominantly Yoruba region. Pop. 271,000.

**Eden** |'ēdn| biblical paradise, the original garden abode of Adam and Eve. It is usually located in the EUPHRATES River valley, but has sometimes been placed as far E as the Araks River, on the Turkey-Armenia border.

**Eden Prai·rie** |'ēdn| city in SE Minnesota, a suburb SW of Minneapolis. Pop. 39,311.

**Edes·sa** |i'desə| (also **Edhessa** or **Vodena**) commercial city in NE Greece. Pop. 18,000. It was the ancient seat of kings of Macedonia.

**Edge·hill** |'ej,hil| (also **Edge Hill**) locality in central England, on the Warwickshire-Oxfordshire border, NW of Banbury, where the first major battle of the English Civil War was fought in 1642.

**Edge·wood** |'ej,wŏod| community in NE Maryland, noted for its U.S. arsenal. Pop. 23,903.

**Edi·na** |ē'dīnə| city in SE Minnesota, a suburb SW of Minneapolis. Pop. 46,070.

**Ed·in·burg** |'edn,bərg| city in S Texas, in the Rio Grande Valley. Pop. 29,885.

**Ed·in·burgh** |'edn,bərə| the capital of Scotland, lying on the S shore of the Firth of Forth. Pop. 421,200. The city grew up around an 11th-century castle built by Malcolm III, which dominates the landscape. It is an administrative, commercial, and cultural center.

**Edir·ne** |a'dirnə| (ancient name **Adrianopolis**) historic commercial city in European Turkey, NW of Istanbul. Pop. 102,000. It is the capital of Edirne province.

**Ed·mond** |'edmənd| city in central Oklahoma, a residential suburb and oil industry center N of Oklahoma City. Pop. 52,315.

**Ed·monds** |'edmən(d)z| city in W central Washington, on Puget Sound, a suburb N of Seattle. Pop. 30,744.

**Ed·mon·ton** |'edməntən| the capital of Alberta, on the North Saskatchewan River E of the Rockies. Pop. 703,070. It is an oil and petrochemical center.

**Edo** |'edō| (also **Yedo**) former name (until 1868) of Japan's capital, Tokyo.

**Edom** |'ēdəm| (also **Seir**) ancient land S of the Dead Sea. According to the Bible, its people were descendants of Esau. Its capital was Petra (in present-day Jordan). Edom was later the Roman Idumaea. □ **Edomite** *adj. & n.*

**Ed·ward, Lake** |'edwərd| lake on the border between Uganda and the Democratic Republic of Congo (former Zaire), linked to Lake Albert by the Semliki River.

**Ed·wards Air Force Base** |'edwərdz| facility in S central California, NE of Los Angeles and on the W of the Mojave Desert, noted as a center for air and space experimentation.

**Ed·wards Plateau** |'edwərdz| highland region of SW Texas, between the Llano Estacado and the Balcones Escarpment, noted for its ranchlands.

**Ee·lam** |'ē,läm| the proposed homeland of the Tamil people of Sri Lanka, for which the Tamil Tigers separatist group have been fighting since the early 1980s.

**Efa·te** |ä'fätä| (also **Vaté**; formerly **Sandwich Island**) island in central Vanuatu, site of the capital, Vila.

**Ega·di Islands** |'ä,gädē| group of small islands in the Mediterranean Sea off the W coast of Sicily, in Italy. The principal islands are Marettimo, Favignana, Levanzo, and Stagnone.

**Eger** |'egər| spa town in the N of Hungary, noted for the 'Bull's Blood' red wine produced in the surrounding region. Pop. 63,365.

**Eg·mont, Mount** |'eg,mänt| volcanic peak in North Island, New Zealand, rising to a height of 8,260 ft./2,518 m. Maori name **Taranaki**.

**Egypt** |'ējəpt| republic in northeasternmost Africa, bordering on the Mediter-

**Egypt**

ranean Sea. Area: 386,900 sq. mi./1.0 million sq. km. Pop. 53,087,000. Official language, Arabic. Capital and largest city: Cairo. Mostly desert in the W, Egypt is dominated in the E by the Nile River and its delta. Known to history for over 5,000 years, it was conquered by the Arabs in A.D. 642. Agriculture, petroleum, and textiles are important industries today. □ **Egyptian** *adj. & n.*

**Eh·ren·breit·stein** |,ärən'brīt,SHtīn| former town, now part of Koblenz, in western Germany. Its powerful fortress was built c. A.D. 1000.

**Ei·fel** |'īfəl| plateau in western Germany, N of the Moselle River and E of the Ardennes, forming the NW part of the Rhenish Slate Mts. It is composed of limestone and is a generally barren region, with a history of mining.

**Eif·fel Tower** |'īfəl| iron tower, 984 ft./300 m. tall, in Paris, France, constructed for the 1889 World's Fair and since then the unofficial symbol of Paris. A popular tourist attraction, it also has a meteorological station and broadcasting antennae.

**Ei·ger** |'īgər| mountain peak in the Bernese Alps in central Switzerland, which rises to 13,101 ft./3,970 m.

**Ei·lat** |ä'lät| (also **Elat**) the southernmost city in Israel, a port and resort at the head of the Gulf of Aqaba. Pop. 36,000. Founded in 1949 near the ruins of biblical Elath, it is Israel's only outlet to the Red Sea.

**Eind·ho·ven** |'īnt,hōvən| industrial city in the S of the Netherlands. Pop. 193,000. It is a major producer of electrical and electronic goods.

**Eire** |'erə| the Gaelic name for Ireland, the official name of the Republic of Ireland from 1937 to 1949.

**Ei·se·nach** |'īzə,näKH| resort and industrial town in central Germany. Pop. 51,000.

**Ei·sen·hüt·ten·stadt** |'īzən,hYtn,SHtät| industrial and trade city in eastern Germany, on the Oder River near the Polish border. Pop. 49,000.

**Ei·sen·stadt** |'īzən,SHtät| city in E Austria, capital of the state of Burgenland and historic seat of the Esterházy family. Pop. 10,500.

**Eis·rie·sen·welt** |'īs,rēzən,velt| cave system in the Tennen massif, S of Salzburg, Austria. It is believed to be the largest system of ice caves in the world: 25 mi./40 km. long.

**Eka·te·rin·burg** |yi'kætərən,bərg| (also **Yekaterinburg**) industrial city in central Russia, in the E foothills of the Urals. Pop.

1,372,000. In 1924–91 it was known as **Sverdlovsk**.

**Eki·bas·tuz** |ˌekēˈbäsˌto͞os| coal-mining town in E Kazakhstan, SW of Pavlodar. Pop. 93,000.

**El Aaiún** |ˌel īˈo͞on| Arabic name for LA'Y-OUN, Western Sahara.

**El Ala·mein** |ˌelˈæləˌmän| (also **Alamein**) historic town in N Egypt, on the road along the Mediterranean coast W of Alexandria, where British forces stopped a German advance in 1942.

**Elam** |ˈēləm| ancient state in SW Iran, E of the Tigris, established in the 4th millennium B.C. Susa was one of its chief cities. □ **Elamite** adj. & n.

**Ela·zig** |eläˈzi| commercial city in E central Turkey, E of the upper Euphrates River. Pop. 205,000. It is the capital of Elazig province.

**El·ba** |ˈelbə| small island off the W coast of Italy, famous as the place of Napoleon's first exile (1814–15).

**El·ba·san** |ˌelbäˈsän| industrial and commercial town in central Albania. Pop. 83,000.

**El·be River** |ˈelbə; elb| river of central Europe, flowing 720 mi./1,159 km. from the Czech Republic through Germany, past Dresden, Magdeburg, and Hamburg, to the North Sea.

**El·bert, Mount** |ˈelbərt| mountain in Colorado, to the E of the resort town of Aspen. Rising 14,431 ft./4,399 m., it is the highest peak in the Rocky Mts.

**El·blag** |ˈelblawNGk| seaport city in N Poland, on the Elblag River near the Baltic Sea, SE of Gdańsk. Pop. 125,000.

**El·brus, Mount** |elˈbro͞os; 'el,bro͞os| peak in the Caucasus Mts., on the border between Russia and Georgia. Rising to 18,481 ft./5,642 m., it is the highest mountain in Europe.

**El·burz Mountains** |elˈbo͞orz| mountain range in NW Iran, close to the S shore of the Caspian Sea. Damavand is the highest peak, rising to 18,386 ft./5,604 m.

**El Ca·jon** |ˌel kəˈhōn| city in SW California, a suburb E of San Diego. Pop. 88,693.

**El Cap·i·tan** |ˌel ˌkæpiˈtæn| peak in Yosemite National Park, California, famed for its sheer walls rising over 3,000 ft./1,000 m. above its base.

**El Cen·tro** |el ˈsentrō| city in S California, commercial center of the Imperial Valley. Pop. 31,384.

**El·che** |ˈelCHä| town in the province of Alicante in SE Spain. Pop. 181,200.

**El Djem** |el ˈjem| town in E Tunisia, noted for its well-preserved Roman amphitheater.

**El Do·ra·do** |ˌel dəˈrädō; dəˈrädō| land of wealth in legends of early American exploration, named for a ruler, perhaps somewhere in modern Colombia, who was said to be inaugurated with gold dust.

**Elea** |ˈēlēə| (also known as **Velia**) ancient town in S Italy, founded by Greeks in 536 B.C. It was the home of the Eleatic school of philosophers, led by Parmenides. □ **Eleatic** adj. & n.

**Elek·tro·stal** |el,yektrəˈstäl| industrial city in W Russia, E of Moscow. Pop. 153,000.

**El·e·phan·ta Island** |ˌelə'fæntə| (Hindu name **Gharapuri**) small island in W India, in Bombay Harbor, Maharashtra state. It is known for its centuries-old caves with carvings and sculptures.

**El·e·phant Pass** |ˈeləfənt| narrow strip of land at the N end of Sri Lanka, linking the Jaffna peninsula with the rest of the island.

**Eleu·sis** |əˈlyo͞osis| ancient city in E Greece, NW of Athens, on the site of present-day Elévsis. It was the home of the Eleusinian Mysteries, which celebrated the goddess Demeter, and the birthplace of the playwright Aeschylus.

**Eleu·thera** |əˈlo͞oTHərə| island in the central Bahamas, over 100 mi./160 km. long. Settled by the British in the 1640s, it has a pop. of 9,000.

**El Faiyum** |ˌel fäˈ(y)o͞om| (also **Fayum** or **Al Fayyum**) historic oasis town in N Egypt, SW of Cairo. Pop. 244,000. It now has many light industries.

**El Fer·rol** |ˌel ferˈrawl| seaport in NW Spain, on the Atlantic. Pop. 87,000. Spain's most important naval base is here.

**El·gin¹** |ˈeljin| industrial city in NE Illinois, W of Chicago, formerly noted for its watch manufacturing. Pop. 77,010.

**El·gin²** |ˈelgin| historic town in NE Scotland, a commercial and religious center in the Moray district of the Grampian region. Pop. 19,000.

**El·gon, Mount** |ˈel,gän| extinct volcano on the border between Kenya and Uganda, rising to 14,178 ft./4,321 m.

**Elis** |ˈēlis| ancient city in SW Greece, on the Kyllini Peninsula. It was famous for its temple of Zeus at Olympia and for a time controlled the Olympian games.

**Elis·a·beth·ville** |əˈlizəbəTH,vil| former name (until 1966) for LUBUMBASHI, Congo (formerly Zaire).

**Elis·ta** |əˈlistə| city in SW Russia, capital of the autonomous republic of Kalmykia. Pop. 85,000.

**Eliz·a·beth** |ə'lizəbəтн| industrial port city in NE New Jersey, on Newark Bay. Pop. 110,002.

**El Ja·di·da** |el 'jädēdə| (formerly **Mazagan**) port and resort town in N Morocco, on the Atlantic coast SW of Casablanca. Pop. 119,000.

**Elk·hart** |'el,kärt| industrial city in N Indiana, a rail center long noted for manufacture of musical instruments. Pop. 43,627.

**Elk Hills** |elk| range in S central California, near Bakersfield, site of an oil reserve involved in the 1920s Teapot Dome scandal.

**Elles·mere Island** |'elz,mir| the northernmost and third-largest island of the Canadian Arctic.

**Elles·mere Port** |'elz,mir| industrial port in NW England, in Cheshire, on the estuary of the Mersey River. Pop. 65,800.

**El·lice Islands** |'eləs| former name for TU-VALU.

**El·li·cott City** |'elikət| historic community in N central Maryland, W of Baltimore, primarily a residential suburb. Pop. 41,396.

**El·lis Island** |'eləs| island in New York Bay that from 1892 until 1943 served as an entry point for immigrants to the U.S., and later (until 1954) as a detention center for deportees. It is now a museum site and the focus of a territorial dispute between New York and New Jersey,

**El·lo·ra** |ə'lawrə| (also **Elura**) a village in W India, in Maharashtra state, NW of Aurangabad. It is known for its rock temples.

**Ells·worth Land** |'elzwərтн| plateau region of Antarctica between the Walgreen Coast and Palmer Land. It rises at the Vinson Massif, the highest point in Antarctica, to 16,863 ft./5,140 m.

**El Ma·hal·la el Ku·bra** |,el mə'hælə 'el 'kōōbrə| industrial city in N Egypt, in the Nile Delta W of the Damietta branch. Pop. 400,000.

**El Man·su·ra** |,el män'sŏŏrə| (also **Al Mansurah**) industrial city in NE Egypt, in the Nile Delta, on the Damietta branch. Pop. 362,000. It is a cotton trade center.

**Elm·hurst**[1] |'elm,hərst| city in NE Illinois, W of Chicago. Pop. 42,029.

**Elm·hurst**[2] |'elm,hərst| largely residential section of N Queens, New York City, noted for the diversity of its population.

**El Min·ya** |el 'minyə| (also **Al Minya**) industrial city in N central Egypt, on the Nile River. Pop. 203,000.

**El·mi·ra** |el'mīrə| industrial city in S central New York, near the Pennsylvania line. Pop. 33,724.

**El Mis·ti** |el 'mēstē| dormant volcano in S Peru, rising to 19,031 ft./5,822 m. NE of Arequipa. It has been important in Inca and Peruvian religion and legend.

**El Mon·te** |el 'mäntē| city in SW California, a suburb E of Los Angeles. Pop. 106,209.

**El Mor·ro** |el 'mawrō| historic fortress in San Juan, Puerto Rico, begun in 1539. Also **Morro Castle.**

**El Ni·ño** |el 'nēnyō| popular name for a complex of climate fluctuations in the equatorial regions of the Pacific, especially cyclical warming of ocean currents off the NW shores of South America. The name is from the Spanish for the infant Jesus, as effects intensify around Christmas.

**El Nor·te** |el 'nawrtä| common term used in Mexico and elsewhere in Latin America to refer to the US; Spanish "the North."

**El Obeid** |,el ə'bād| (also **Al Ubayyid**) desert city in central Sudan, in the Kordofan region, where local foces under the Mahdi defeated the British in 1883.

**El Paso** |el 'pæsō| industrial city in W Texas, on the Rio Grande, across from Ciudad Juárez, Mexico. Pop. 515,342.

**El Qa·hi·ra** |'kähərə| variant spelling of Al Qahira, the Arabic name for CAIRO, Egypt.

**El Sal·va·dor** |el 'sælvä,dawr| republic in Central America, on the Pacific coast. Area: 8,260 sq. mi./21,393 sq. km. Pop. 5,048,000. Language, Spanish. Capital and largest city: San Salvador. Independent from Spain in 1821, El Salvador is dominated by volcanic ranges and subtropical valleys. Coffee, cotton, and sugar are the chief products. □ **Salvadorean** adj. & n.

El Salvador

**El·si·nore** |'elsə,nawr| port on the NE coast of the island of Zealand, Denmark. Pop. 56,750. It is the site of the 16th-century Kronborg Castle, which is the setting for Shakespeare's *Hamlet.* Danish name **Helsingør.**

**Els·tree** |'el,strē| village in SE England, in

Hertfordshire, NW of London. Pop. 5,000. It is a center of the British film industry.

**El Ta·jín** |ˌel təˈhēn| archaeological site in E central Mexico, in Veracruz state, noted for its Totonac Pyramid of the Niches.

**El To·ro** |el ˈtawrō| suburban community in SW California, SE of Los Angeles, formerly site of a Marine air base. Pop. 62,685.

**El Uq·sur** |el ˈooksoŏr| (also **Al Uqsur**) Arabic name for Luxor, Egypt.

**Ely, Isle of** |ˈēlē| former county of England extending over the N part of present-day Cambridgeshire. Before widespread drainage it formed a fertile 'island' in the surrounding fenland.

**Ely¹** |ˈēlē| cathedral city in the fenland of Cambridgeshire, SE England, on the Ouse River. Pop. 9,100.

**Ely²** |ˈēlē| city in E central Nevada, a famed mining center. Pop. 4,756.

**Elyr·ia** |əˈlirēə| industrial city in N Ohio, W of Cleveland. Pop. 56,746.

**Ely·sée Palace** |ˌālēˈzā| official residence (since 1873) of the president of France, in Paris. Built in 1718, it was once the property of the Marquise de Pompadour, mistress of King Louis XV.

**Ely·si·um** |əˈlizhəm| (also **Elysian Fields**) in ancient Greek myth, a land far to the W, or in the underworld, where heroes lived happily after death. □ **Elysian** *adj.*

**El Yunque** popular name for the Caribbean National Forest.

**Em·den** |ˈemdən| port in NW Germany, on the North Sea in the estuary of the Ems River. Pop. 51,000. The city's development was encouraged by the industrial growth of the Ruhr Valley and by the construction of the Dortmund-Ems Canal.

**Emei Shan** |ˈəmˈā ˈsHän| (formerly **O-mei Shan**) mountain in Sichuan province, S central China, SW of Chengdu. A sacred Buddhist site, it has many temples and images.

**Em·er·ald Coast** |ˈem(ə)rəld| name given to part of the coast of Brittany, NW France. It includes the towns of Dinard, Paramé, Saint-Briac, and Saint-Lunaire.

**Em·er·ald Isle** poetic name for Ireland.

**Eme·sa** |ˈeməsə| city in ancient Syria, on the Orontes River on the site of present-day Homs. It was famous for its temple to the sun god Elah-Gabal.

**Emi Kous·si** |ˈä'mē ˈkoōsē| volcanic mountain in the Sahara, in N Chad, rising to 11,202 ft./3,415 m., the highest peak in the Tibesti Mts.

**Emilia-Romagna** |əˈmēlyə rōˈmänyə| region of N Italy. Capital: Bologna.

**Em·ma·us¹** |əˈmäəs| ancient town, NW of Jerusalem, probably now Imwas, in Israeli-occupied Jordan. Judas Maccabeus won a notable victory here in 166 B.C.

**Em·ma·us²** |əˈmäəs| borough in E Pennsylvania, S of Allentown, noted as the home of Rodale Press, exponent of organic farming. Pop. 11,157.

**Em·men** |ˈemən| industrial city in the NE Netherlands. Pop. 93,000.

**Em·men·tal** |ˈemən,täl| valley of the Emme River, in W central Switzerland. The region gives its name to the characteristic Swiss cheese.

**Emo·na** |iˈmōnə| Roman name for Ljubljana, Slovenia.

**Em·pire State** nickname for New York.

**Em·pire State Building** |ˈem,pīr ˈstāt| office building in Manhattan, New York City. At 1,454 ft./443 m., it was the tallest building in the world from 1931 until 1971.

**Em·po·ria** |emˈpawrēə| commercial city in E central Kansas, associated with William Allen White and his Emporia *Gazette*, which he published 1895–1944. Pop. 25,512.

**Empty Quarter** another name for the Rub' al Khali, Saudi Arabia.

**Ems River** |ems; emz| river (208 mi./335 km.), rising in the Teutoburger Wald of NW Germany and flowing into the North Sea near Emden. The Dortmund-Ems Canal runs parallel to the river.

**En·ci·ni·tas** |ˌensiˈnētəs| city in SW California, a suburb NW of San Diego. Pop. 55,386.

**En·der·bury Island** |ˈendər,berē| see Canton and Enderbury, Kiribati.

**En·der·by Land** |ˈendərbē| part of Antarctica claimed by Australia.

**En·field** |ˈen,fēld| residential and industrial borough of N Greater London, England. Pop. 249,000. It gave its name to the Enfield rifle.

**En·ga·dine** |ˌenGɡəˈdēn| valley of the Inn River in E Switzerland, in the Rhaetian Alps. Noted for its beauty and climate, the region has many resorts, including Saint Moritz and Pontresina.

**Eng·land** |ˈinG(g)lənd| country forming the largest and southernmost part of Great Britain and of the United Kingdom, and containing the capital, London. Area: 50,397 sq. mi./130,478 sq. km. Pop. 46,170,000. □ **English** *adj. & n.*

**Eng·lish Channel** |ˈinG(g)lisH| (French name **la Manche**) the sea channel separating S England from N France. It is 22 mi./35 km. wide at its narrowest point. A

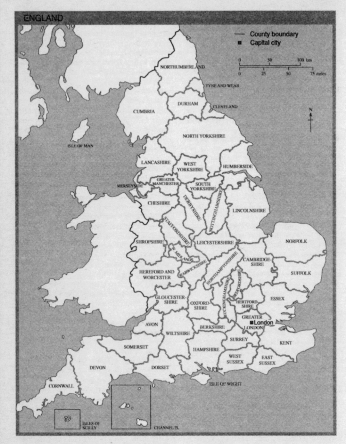

ENGLAND

— County boundary
■ Capital city

NORTHUMBERLAND

TYNE AND WEAR

DURHAM   CLEVELAND

CUMBRIA

NORTH YORKSHIRE

ISLE OF MAN

LANCASHIRE   WEST YORKSHIRE   HUMBERSIDE

GREATER MANCHESTER   SOUTH YORKSHIRE

MERSEYSIDE

CHESHIRE   DERBYSHIRE   NOTTINGHAMSHIRE   LINCOLNSHIRE

STAFFORDSHIRE

SHROPSHIRE   LEICESTERSHIRE   NORFOLK

WEST MIDLANDS

HEREFORD AND WORCESTER   WARWICKSHIRE   NORTHAMPTONSHIRE   CAMBRIDGESHIRE   SUFFOLK

GLOUCESTERSHIRE   OXFORDSHIRE   BUCKINGHAMSHIRE   HERTFORDSHIRE   ESSEX

AVON   BERKSHIRE   GREATER LONDON   ■London

WILTSHIRE   SURREY   KENT

SOMERSET   HAMPSHIRE   WEST SUSSEX   EAST SUSSEX

DEVON   DORSET

CORNWALL   ISLE OF WIGHT

ISLES OF SCILLY   CHANNEL IS.

N

0   50   100 km

0   25   50   75 miles

railway tunnel beneath it linking England and France was opened in 1994 (the Channel Tunnel).

**Enid** |'ēnid| city in N central Oklahoma, home to Vance Air Force Base. Pop. 45,309.

**Eni·we·tok** |ˌenəˈwēˌtäk| (also **Enewetak**) uninhabited island in the North Pacific, one of the Marshall Islands. Cleared of its native population, it was used by the U.S. as a testing ground for nuclear weapons from 1948 to 1954.

**En·nis** |'enəs| county seat of Clare, in the Republic of Ireland. Pop. 14,000.

**En·nis·kil·len** |ˌenəˈskilən| county seat of

Fermanagh, Northern Ireland. Pop. 10,000. Former spelling *Inniskilling*.

**En·sche·de** |'enskəˌdä| industrial and university city in the E Netherlands. Pop. 147,000.

**En·se·na·da** |ˌensəˈnädə| city in NW Mexico, in Baja California state, on the Pacific. Pop. 260,000. It is a cruise ship port and industrial center.

**En·teb·be** |enˈtebə; enˈtebē| town in S Uganda, on the N shore of Lake Victoria. Pop. 42,000. It was the capital of Uganda during the period of British rule, from 1894 to 1962.

**Entre-deux-Mers** |'äNtrədœ'mer| region in SW France, between the Dordogne and the Garonne rivers. The area is noted for its wines.

**En·u·gu** |a'nōōgōō| industrial city in SE Nigeria, capital of the state of Enugu. Pop. 293,000. In a coal producing-region, it was the capital of BIAFRA.

**Éper·nay** |ˌāpər'ne| town in NE France, on the Marne River. Pop. 28,000. Many well-known makers of champagne are head-quartered here, and tourists come to visit the wine caves.

**Eph·e·sus** |'efəsəs| ancient Greek city on the W coast of Asia Minor, in present-day Turkey, noted in ancient times as site of the temple of Diana, one of the Seven Wonders of the World. It was an important center of early Christianity; St. Paul preached here and St. John is said to have lived here.

**Eph·ra·ta** |'efrətə| historic borough in SE Pennsylvania, SW of Reading, settled by German pietists and now a tourist and crafts center. Pop. 12,133.

**Ep·i·dau·rus** |'epəˌdawrəs| ancient Greek city and port on the NE coast of the Pelo-ponnese. Greek name **Epídhavros**.

**Epi·nal** |ˌāpē'näl| manufacturing town, capital of the department of Vosges in E France, on the Moselle River. Pop. 40,000.

**Epi·rus** |i'pīrəs| **1** coastal region of NW Greece. Capital: Ioánnina. Greek name **Ipiros**. **2** an ancient country of which the modern region corresponds to the SW part, extending N to Illyria and E to Macedonia and Thessaly.

**Ep·ping** |'epiNG| town in SE England, a residential suburb NE of London, in Essex. Pop. 11,000. **Epping Forest,** now a park, is what remains of the former Waltham For-est, a royal preserve that included all of Essex.

**Ep·som** |'epsəm| town in Surrey, SE Eng-land. Pop. 68,500. Its natural mineral wa-ters were used in the production of the purgative known as Epsom salts. The an-nual Derby and Oaks horse races are held at Epsom Downs.

**equa·tor, the** |ə'kwātər| imaginary line around the earth, equidistant from the poles and having a latitude of 0°. It divides the earth into N and S hemispheres. The equator is generally thought of as a zone (the *equatorial* regions) of great heat.

**Equa·to·ri·al Gui·nea** |ˌekwə'tawrēəl 'ginē| republic in W Africa on the Gulf of Guinea, comprising several offshore islands and a coastal settlement between Camer-

**Equatorial Guinea**

oon and Gabon. Area: 10,830 sq. mi./ 28,051 sq. km. Pop. 426,000. Languages, Spanish (official), local Niger–Congo lan-guages, pidgin. Capital: Malabo (on the is-land of Bioko). Formerly a Spanish colony, the country became fully independent in 1968. It is the only independent Spanish-speaking state in Africa. Cacao, coffee, and timber are its chief exports. □ **Equatorial Guinean** adj. & n.

**Er·e·bus, Mount** |'erəbəs| volcanic peak on Ross Island, Antarctica. Rising to 12,452 ft./3,794 m., it is the world's most southerly active volcano.

**Erech** |'ē,rek| biblical name for URUK, Iraq.

**Er·furt** |'er,fŏŏrt| industrial city in central Germany, capital of Thuringia. Pop. 205,000.

**Erie, Lake** |'irē| one of the five Great Lakes of North America, between Canada and the U.S. It is linked to Lake Huron by the De-troit River and to Lake Ontario by the Welland Canal and by the Niagara River, which is its only natural outlet. Cleveland and Buffalo lie on its shores.

**Erie** |'irē| industrial port city in extreme NW Pennsylvania, on Lake Erie. Pop. 108,718.

**Erie Canal** |'irē| historic canal that con-nected the Hudson River at Albany, in E New York, with the Niagara River and the Great Lakes. Opened in 1825, it spurred the growth of New York City. Today it is chiefly recreational.

**Erin** |'erən| archaic poetic or literary name for Ireland.

**Er·i·trea** |ˌerə'trēə; ˌerə'trāə| independent state in NE Africa, on the Red Sea. Area: 36,183 sq. mi./93,769 sq. km. Pop. 3,500,000. Language, Tigray and Cushitic languages. Capital and largest city: Asmara. Half Muslim, half Christian, Eritrea sepa-rated fully from Ethiopia in 1993. Agricul-ture and mining are important. □ **Eritrean** adj. & n.

Eritrea

**Er·lan·gen** |'er,läNGən| industrial city in S Germany, on the Regnitz River. Pop. 102,000.

**Er·na·ku·lum** |ər'näkələm| city in S India, in Kerala state, near Kochi. Its Jewish community is thought to date back to the 2nd or 3rd century.

**Erne** |'ərn| river that flows 72 mi./115 km. from N Republic of Ireland into Northern Ireland, to the Atlantic at Donegal Bay. Along its route are two widenings, Upper and Lower Lough Erne, between which the town of Enniskillen lies.

**Erode** |i'rōd| cotton-processing city in S India, in Tamil Nadu state. Pop. 357,000.

**Er·ro·man·go** |,erō'mäNGgō| (also **Erromanga**) volcanic island in S Vanuatu, noted for its coral formations and bays.

**Ery·man·thus** |,ere'mænTHəs| mountain group in S Greece, in NW Peloponnesus. According to Greek mythology, the mountains were the home of the Erymanthian boar captured by Hercules.

**Erz·ge·bir·ge** |'ertsgə,birgə| range of mountains on the border between Germany and the Czech Republic. Also called the **Ore Mountains**.

**Er·zin·can** |,erzin'jän| (also **Erzinjan**) historic town in E central Turkey, in agricultural Erzincan province. Pop. 91,000.

**Er·zu·rum** |,erzə'rŏŏm| commercial city in NE Turkey, capital of mountainous Erzurum province. Pop. 242,000.

**Es·bjerg** |'esbyer| port in Denmark, on the W coast of Jutland. Pop. 82,000. It has ferry links with Britain and the Faroe Islands.

**Es·ca·na·ba** |,eskə'näbə| port city in the Upper Peninsula of NW Michigan, on Lake Michigan. Pop. 13,659.

**Es·caut** |es'kō| French name for the SCHELDT River.

**Es·con·di·do** |,eskən'dēdō| commercial city in SW California, N of San Diego. Pop. 108,635.

**Es·co·ri·al, el** |,el ,eskawr'yäl| 16th-century building complex in central Spain, NW of Madrid, comprising a palace, a monastery, a church, and the mausoleums of several Spanish sovereigns.

**Es·dra·e·lon** |,ezdrə'elən| (also called **Plain of Jezreel**) plain in N Israel that separates Galilee (N) from Samaria (S).

**Eskil·stu·na** |'eskil,stynə| industrial city in SE Sweden, between Lakes Hjälmaren and Mälaren, W of Stockholm. Pop. 90,000.

**Es·ki·se·hir** |,eskiSHə'hir| industrial and spa city in W central Turkey, the capital of Eskisehir province. Pop. 413,000.

**Es·me·ral·das** |,esmə'räldəs| port city in NW Ecuador, the capital of Esmeraldas province. Pop. 99,000.

**Es·pa·ña** |es'pänyə| Spanish name for SPAIN.

**Es·pí·ri·to San·to** |esH'pērətŏŏ 'säNtŏŏ| state of E Brazil, on the Atlantic coast. Capital: Vitória.

**Es·pi·ri·tu San·to** |es'pērətŏŏ 'säntō| volcanic island in NW Vanuatu, the largest in the country. Largely agricultural, it was the site of U.S. bases during World War II.

**Es·poo** |'espō| (Swedish name **Esbo**) city in S Finland; a W suburb of Helsinki. Pop. 173,000. It is the second-largest city in Finland.

**Es·qui·pu·las** |,eske'pŏŏləs| town in SE Guatemala, near the border with Honduras. Pop. 19,000. Noted for the image of the "Black Christ of Esquipulas" in its church, the town is a center of pilgrimage.

**Es·sa·oui·ra** |,esə'wirə| (formerly **Mogador**) port city in SW Morocco, on the Atlantic coast. Pop. 54,000.

**Es·sen** |'esən| industrial city in the Ruhr valley, in NW Germany. Pop. 627,000. It is home to the Krupp steelworks.

**Es·se·qui·bo** |,esə'kwēbō| river in Guyana, rising in the Guiana Highlands and flowing about 600 mi./965 km. N to the Atlantic.

**Es·sex** |'esiks| county of E England, NE of London. Pop. 1,496,000. County town, Chelmsford.

**Ess·ling·en** |'esliNGən| industrial city in SW Germany, on the Neckar River near Stuttgart. Pop. 91,000.

**Es·sone** |e'sawn| department S of Paris in the Île-de-France, in N central France. Pop. 1,084,000. The capital is Evry.

**Es·te** |'estä| agricultural town in NE Italy. Pop. 17,000. Many Roman ruins are in the area.

**Es·te·rel** |,ester'el| mountainous region in S France, along the coasts of the departments of Var and Alpes-Maritimes. Its highest point is Mont Vinaigre (2,020 ft./616 m.).

**Es•tes Park** |'estēz| resort town in N central Colorado, a gateway to Rocky Mountain National Park. Pop. 3,184.

**Es•to•nia** |e'stōnēə| Baltic republic on the S coast of the Gulf of Finland. Area: 17,420 sq. mi./45,100 sq. km. Pop. 1,591,000. Languages, Estonian (official), Russian. Capital and largest city: Tallinn. Dominated by Russia for over two centuries, Estonia regained independence in 1991. Flat and characterized by forests and wetlands, it has a maritime and forest-industry economy. □ **Estonian** *adj. & n.*

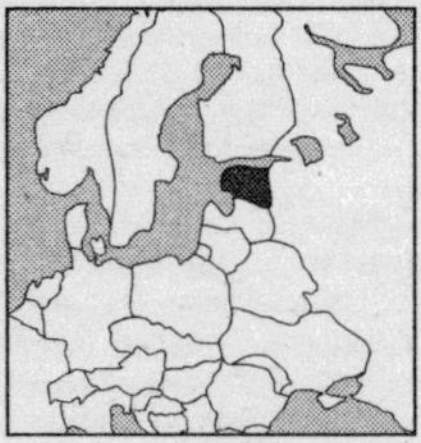

**Estonia**

**Es•to•ril** |,ēsHtə'ril| resort on the Atlantic coast of Portugal, W of Lisbon. Pop. 25,000.

**Es•tre•ma•du•ra** |,isHtrəmə'do͝orə| coastal region and former province of W central Portugal.

**Es•trie** |'estrē| see EASTERN TOWNSHIPS, Quebec.

**Esz•ter•gom** |'estər,gōm| historic town and river port on the Danube in Hungary, NW of Budapest. Pop. 30,000.

**Eta•wah** |ā'täwə| commercial town in N India, in Uttar Pradesh state, SE of Agra. Pop. 124,000.

**Ethi•o•pia** |,ēTHē'ōpēə| landlocked republic in NE Africa. Area: 472,432 sq. mi./1.22 million sq. km. Pop. 45,892,000. Languages, Amharic (official), several other Afro-Asiatic languages. Capital and largest city: Addis Ababa. Former name **Abyssinia**. The oldest independent African country, Ethiopia was dominated by Italy in 1935–41. Most of its people are subsistence farmers, who struggle against repeated droughts. Separatist struggles in Eritrea and Tigray have characterized recent decades. □ **Ethiopian** *adj. & n.*

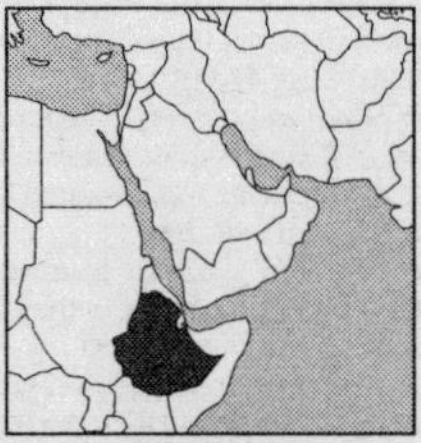

**Ethiopia**

**Et•na, Mount** |'etnə| volcano in E Sicily, rising to 10,902 ft./3,323 m. It is the highest and most active volcano in Europe.

**Eto•bi•coke** |i'tōbə,kōk| city in S Ontario, an industrial and residential center W of Toronto. Pop. 309,993.

**Etoile, Place de l'** |,pläs də ,lā'twäl| circular intersection in Paris, in N central France. Twelve avenues meet at L'Etoile, at one end of the Champs Elysées. In the center is the Arc de Triomphe, constructed in 1806 by Napoleon I to commemorate his military victories. The Tomb of the Unknown Soldier rests at the base of the Arc.

**Eton** |'ētn| town in SE England, in Buckinghamshire, N across the Thames River from Windsor, and W of London, noted as the home of Eton College, the famous school for boys. Pop. 4,000.

**Eto•sha Pan** |ē'tōsHə 'pæn| depression in the plateau of N Namibia, filled with salt water and having no outlets, extending over an area of 1,854 sq. mi./4,800 sq. km.

**Etre•tat** |,ātrə'tä| town in NW France, in Normandy, on the English Channel N of Le Havre. It is noted for its beaches and for its dramatic white cliffs.

**Etru•ria** |i'tro͝orēə| ancient state of W Italy, situated between the Arno and Tiber rivers and corresponding approximately to present-day Tuscany and parts of Umbria. It was the center of the Etruscan civilization, which flourished in the middle centuries of the 1st millennium B.C. □ **Etruscan** *adj. & n.*

**Eu•boea** |yo͞o'bēə| island of Greece in the W Aegean Sea, separated from the mainland by only a narrow channel at its capital, Chalcis. Greek name **Évvoia**.

**Eu•clid** |'yo͞oklid| city in NE Ohio, an industrial and residential suburb NE of Cleveland. Pop. 54,875.

**Eu•gene** |yo͞o'jēn| city in W central Oregon, on the Willamette River. An industrial and commercial center, it is also home to the University of Oregon. Pop. 112,659.

**Eu•phra•tes** |yo͞o'frātēz| river of SW Asia

that rises in the mountains of E Turkey and flows 1,700 mi./2,736 km. through Syria and Iraq to join the Tigris, forming the Shatt al-Arab waterway. The two rivers define MESOPOTAMIA.

**Eur·a·sia** |yŏŏ'rāzHə| term used to describe the total continental land mass of Europe and Asia combined. □ **Eurasian** *adj.*

**Eure** |œr| **1** department in NW France, in Haute-Normandie. Pop. 514,000. The capital is Evreux. **2** river in NW France, rising in the Perche Hills and flowing NW for 142 mi./225 km. to the Seine River near Rouen.

**Eu·re·ka** |yŏŏ'rēkə| port city in NW California, on Humboldt Bay off the Pacific, a noted lumbering center. Pop. 27,025.

**Eu·ro Dis·ney** |'yŏŏrō 'diznē| (also called **Disneyland Paris**) theme park, in Marne-la-Valée, 19 mi./30 km. E of Paris, in N central France, opened in 1992. The park is modeled on Disney's U.S. parks.

**Eu·ro·land** |'yŏŏrō,lænd| popular term for the eleven European nations that in 1998 initiated use of the *euro,* a common currency.

**Eu·rope** |'yŏŏrəp| continent of the N hemisphere, separated from Africa to the S by the Mediterranean Sea and from Asia to the E roughly by the Dardanelles, Sea of Marmara, and the Bosporus, the Black Sea, the Caucasus Mts., the Caspian Sea, and the Ural Mts. Area: 3.8 million sq. mi./9.9 million sq. km. Europe contains approximately 10 percent of the world's population. Europe consists of the W part of the land mass of which Asia forms the E (and far greater) part, and includes the British Isles, Iceland, and most of the Mediterranean islands. Its recent history has been dominated by the decline of European states from their former colonial and economic pre-eminence, the emergence of the European Union among the wealthy democracies of W Europe, and the collapse of the Soviet Union with consequent changes of power in central and E Europe. □ **European** *adj. & n.*

**Eu·ro·pe·an Com·mu·ni·ty** |,yŏŏrə'pēən| (abbreviated **EC**) organization of W European countries, formed in 1967 by merging the earlier European Economic Community (EEC) and other bodies for purposes of economic and political integration. It was superseded in 1993 by the EUROPEAN UNION.

**Eu·ro·poort** |'yŏŏrə,pawrt| major European port in the Netherlands, near Rotterdam, created in 1958.

**Eus·ca·di** |,ŭskä'dē| (also known as **Basque Country** and, in French, **Pays Basque**) the territory on both sides of the Pyrénées, in France and Spain, occupied by the Basque people, including the Basque Provinces of N Spain and most of Pyrénées-Atlantique department in SW France.

**Eux·ine Sea** |'yŏŏksin; 'yŏŏk,sīn| ancient name (in Latin **Pontus Euxinus**) for the BLACK SEA.

**Ev·ans·ton** |'evənstən| city in NE Illinois, a suburb just N of Chicago, home to Northwestern University and to various industries. Pop. 73,233.

**Ev·ans·ville** |'evənz,vil| industrial port city in SW Indiana, on the Ohio River. Pop. 126,272.

**Ev·er·est, Mount** |'ev(ə)rəst| mountain in the Himalayas, on the border between Nepal and Tibet. Rising to 29,028 ft./8,848 m., it is the highest mountain in the world; its summit was first reached in 1953 by New Zealander Edmund Hillary and Nepalese Tenzing Norgay.

**Ev·er·ett¹** |'ev(ə)rət| industrial city in NE Massachusetts, just N of Boston. Pop. 35,701.

**Ev·er·ett²** |'ev(ə)rət| industrial port city in NW Washington, N of Seattle, noted for its huge Boeing aircraft-assembly plant. Pop. 69,961.

**Ev·er·glades** |'evər,glädz| vast area of marshland and coastal mangrove in S Florida, part of which is protected as a national park.

**Evian-les-Bains** |ā'vyän lā 'bæn| resort and spa in E France, on Lake Geneva. Pop. 6,000. Its bottled mineral water is popular around the world.

**Évo·ra** |'evərə| commercial center and city in S Portugal, capital of Évora district. Pop. 35,000.

**Evreux** |ā'vrœ| industrial town, capital of Eure department, in Haute-Normandie, in NW France. Pop. 51,000.

**Ex·e·ter¹** |'eksətər; 'egzətər| the county seat of Devon, SW England, on the Exe River. Pop. 101,000. Exeter was founded by the Romans, who called it Isca.

**Ex·e·ter²** |'eksətər; 'egzətər| historic town in SE New Hampshire, home to the Phillips (Exeter) Academy. Pop. 12,481.

**Ex·moor** |'ek,smŏŏr; 'ek,smawr| area of moorland in N Devon and W Somerset, SW England, rising to 1,706 ft./520 m. at

Dunkery Beacon. The area is designated a national park.

**Ex·tre·ma·du·ra** |ˌestrəmə'doͻrə| autonomous region of W Spain, on the border with Portugal. Capital: Mérida. Spanish name **Estremadura.**

**Ex·u·ma Cays** |ig'zoͻmə 'kĕz; ik'soͻmə| group of some 350 small islands in the Bahamas.

**Eyre, Lake** |ær; er| Australia's largest salt lake, in South Australia.

# Ff

**Fa·en·za** |fäˈenzə| town in Emilia-Romagna, N Italy. Pop. 54,000. It gave its name to the type of pottery known as faience.

**Fair·banks** |ˈfærˌbæŋks| second-largest city in Alaska, in the central part, near the junction of the Chena and Tanana rivers. With a mining history, it is now chiefly commercial. Pop. 30,843.

**Fair·born** |ˈfærˌbawrn| city in SW Ohio, NE of Dayton. In a farm area, it is also adjacent to Wright-Patterson Air Force Base. Pop. 31,300.

**Fair·fax County** |ˈfærfæks| county in NE Virginia that incorporates many suburbs of Washington, D.C. Pop. 818,584.

**Fair·field**[1] |ˈfærˌfēld| city in N central California, an agricultural processing center. Pop. 77,211.

**Fair·field**[2] |ˈfærˌfēld| residential town in SW Connecticut, with many suburban villages. Pop. 53,418.

**Fair·field**[3] |ˈfærˌfēld| city in SW Ohio, N of Cincinnati. Pop. 39,729.

**Fair Isle** |ˈfær ˈīl| one of the Shetland Islands of Scotland, lying about halfway between Orkney and the main Shetland group. It gave its name to a knitting style.

**Fair·mount Park** |ˈfærmänt| park in Philadelphia, Pennsylvania, noted as the site of the 1876 U.S. Centennial Exposition.

**Fai·sa·la·bad** |ˌfīˈsäləˌbäd| industrial city in Punjab, Pakistan. Pop. 1,092,000. Until 1979 it was known as Lyallpur.

**Faiz·a·bad** |ˈfīzəˌbäd| commercial and industrial city in N India, in Uttar Pradesh state. Pop. 178,000.

**Fa·laise** |fäˈlāz| market town in Normandy, NW France. Pop. 8,000. Heavy fighting occurred here after the Allied D-Day invasion in June 1944.

**Fal·kirk** |ˈfawlˌkərk| town in central Scotland, administrative center of Falkirk region. Pop. 37,000. Edward I defeated the Scots here in 1298.

**Falk·land Islands** |ˈfawklənd| (also **the Falklands**) group of islands in the South Atlantic, forming a British Crown Colony. Pop. 2,121. Capital: Stanley (on East Falkland). In 1982 Argentina, which calls the islands **Las Malvinas**, and Britain fought a brief war for control.

**Falk·land Islands Dependencies** |ˈfawklənd| overseas territory of the U.K. in the South Atlantic, consisting of the South Sandwich Islands and South Georgia, which is administered from the Falkland Islands.

**Falkland Islands**

**Fall·ing·wa·ter** |ˈfawliNGˌwawtər; ˈfawliNGˌwätər| house designed by Frank Lloyd Wright that stands over Bear Run, a stream in SW Pennsylvania, near the Maryland line.

**Fall Line** |fawl| in the U.S., imaginary line between the points at which rivers drop from the PIEDMONT into the Atlantic coastal plain. Many eastern industrial cities lie on the Fall Line.

**Fall River** |fawl| industrial city in SE Massachusetts, a longtime textile center associated with the Lizzie Borden legend. Pop. 92,703.

**Falls Road** |fawlz| road in the Catholic neighborhoods of Belfast, Northern Ireland, parallel to the Shankill Road, which passes through Protestant neighborhoods to the S.

**Fal·mouth**[1] |ˈfælməTH| historic port town in SW England, in Cornwall. Pop. 18,000. The westernmost port on the N of the English Channel, it is a yachting and shipbuilding center.

**Fal·mouth**[2] |ˈfælməTH| commercial town in SE Massachusetts, on the SW of Cape Cod. The Woods Hole ocean science complex is here. Pop. 27,960.

**Fal·ster** |ˈfälstər| Danish island in the Baltic Sea, S of Zealand.

**Fa·ma·gus·ta** |ˌfäməˈgōōstə| historic city in Turkish-occupied E Cyprus. Pop. 8,000. Important during the Crusades, it is a ferry port and resort.

**Far·al·lon Islands** |ˈfærəˌlän| small, uninhabited island group in the Pacific Ocean just W of San Francisco, California. Also, the **Farallones**.

**Far East** |ˈfär ˈēst| informal term for China, Japan, and other countries of E Asia. □ **Far Eastern** *adj.*

**Fare·well, Cape**[1] |fərˈwel| the southernmost point of Greenland. Danish name **Kap Farvel**.

**Fare·well, Cape**[2] |fərˈwel| the northernmost point of South Island, New Zealand. The cape was named by Captain James Cook as the last land sighted before he left for Australia in March 1770.

**Far·go** |ˈfärgō| largest city in North Dakota, in the SE part, across the Red River of the North from Moorhead, Minnesota. Pop. 74,111.

**Fa·ri·da·bad** |fəˈrēdəˌbäd| industrial city in N India, S of Delhi, in the state of Haryana. Pop. 614,000.

**Farm Belt** the states of the Midwest that are noted particularly for their agricultural production: Iowa, Kansas, Minnesota, Nebraska, North Dakota, and South Dakota.

**Farm·ing·ton** |ˈfärmiNGtən| city in NW New Mexico, an energy industry center. Pop. 33,997.

**Farn·bor·ough** |ˈfärnb(ə)rə| town in S England, in Hampshire. Pop. 48,000. Noted as a center of aviation, it is the site of an annual air show.

**Farne Islands** |färn| group of seventeen small islands off the coast of Northumberland, NE England, noted for their wildlife.

**Fa·ro** |ˈfärōō| seaport on the S coast of Portugal, capital of the Algarve. Pop. 32,000.

**Far·oe Islands** |ˈfærō; ˈferō| (also **Faeroe Islands** or **the Faroes**) a group of islands in the N Atlantic between Iceland and the Shetland Islands, belonging to Denmark but partly autonomous. Pop. 44,000; languages, Faroese (official), Danish. Capital: Tórshavn. □ **Faroese** *adj. & n.*

**Far·ra·ka Barrage** dam on the Ganges River, on the border between India and Bangladesh, completed in 1975.

**Far·rukh·a·bad** |fəˈrookəˌbäd| commercial city in N India, in Uttar Pradesh state. Pop. 208,000 (with neighboring Fategarh).

**Fars** |färs| an area in SW Iran roughly equivalent to the ancient province of Pars, the nucleus of the Persian Empire.

**Far West** |ˈfär ˈwest| the regions of North America in the Rocky Mts. and along the Pacific coast.

**Fa·sho·da** |fəˈsHōdə| village in SE Sudan, on the White Nile River, that gave its name to an 1898 confrontation between France

and Great Britain over African territory. After the "Fashoda Incident" was resolved, the village's name was changed to Kodok.

**Fast·net** |ˈfæs(t)nət| rocky islet off the SW coast of Ireland.

**Fá·ti·ma** |fəˈtēmə| village in W central Portugal, NE of Lisbon. Pop. 5,000. It became a center of Roman Catholic pilgrimage after the reported sighting here in 1917 of the Virgin Mary.

**Faw** |faw| (also called **Al Faw; Fao**) port city in SE Iraq, near the Persian Gulf.

**Fay·ette·ville**[1] |ˈfäət,vil; ˈfäətvəl| commercial city in NW Arkansas, home to the University of Arkansas. Pop. 42,099.

**Fay·ette·ville**[2] |ˈfäət,vil; ˈfäətvəl| commercial city in S central North Carolina. Fort Bragg and other military installations are central to its economy. Pop. 75,695.

**Fed·er·al Way** |ˈfed(ə)rəl| city in W central Washington, a suburb lying between Seattle and Tacoma. Pop. 67,554.

**Fei·ra de San·ta·na** |ˈfärə dä sänˈtänə| commercial and industrial city in NE Brazil, in Bahia state, NW of Salvador. Pop. 393,000. It is a beef industry center.

**Feld·berg Mountain** |ˈfeltberg| mountain peak in Baden-Wurttemberg, SW Germany. It is the highest peak in the Black Forest (4,898 ft./1,493 m.).

**Fe·lix·stowe** |ˈfelik,stō| port on the E coast of England, in Suffolk. Pop. 23,000.

**Fen·no·scan·dia** |,fenəˈskændēə| land mass in NW Europe comprising Scandinavia, Finland, and the adjacent area of NE Russia.

**Fens, the** |fenz| (also **Fen Country** or **Fenland**) low-lying wetlands in E England, principally in Lincolnshire, reclaimed since the 17th century for agricultural use. The Wash lies N and E.

**Fen·way, the** |ˈfen,wā| park system incorporating wetlands in Boston, Massachusetts. Nearby is Fenway Park, the famous baseball stadium.

**Fer·ga·na** |,färgəˈnä| **1** administrative subdivision in E Uzbekistan. Pop. 2,226,000. **2** (formerly **Novy Margelan** and **Skobelev**) its capital, a city in the Fergana Valley. Pop. 183,000.

**Fer·ma·nagh** |fərˈmænə| one of the Six Counties of Northern Ireland, formerly an administrative area. Pop. 51,000; chief town, Enniskillen.

**Fer·nan·do de No·ro·nha** |fərˈnändōō dē nawˈrōnyə| territory of NE Brazil, a group of volcanic islands in the S Atlantic, NE of Natal. Long used as a penal colony, it is now in part a national park.

**Fer·nan·do Póo** |fər'nændō 'pō| former name (to 1973) for the island of Bioko, Equatorial Guinea.

**Fer·ney** |fer'nə| (also called **Ferney-Voltaire**) village in E France, near the Swiss border. The French philosopher Voltaire lived here.

**Fern Hill** |'fərn 'hil| farm at Llangain, near Carmarthen, SW Wales, in Dyfed, setting of a well-known poem ("Fern Hill") by Dylan Thomas.

**Fer·ra·ra** |fə'rärə| city in N Italy, capital of a province of the same name. Pop. 141,000. Ferrara grew to prominence in the 13th century under the rule of the Este family.

**Fer·tile Cres·cent** |'fərtl 'kresənt| crescent-shaped area of fertile land in the Middle East extending from the E Mediterranean coast through the valley of the Tigris and Euphrates rivers to the Persian Gulf. It was the center of the Neolithic development of agriculture (from 7000 B.C.), and the cradle of the Assyrian, Sumerian, and Babylonian civilizations.

**Fer·tő Tó** |'fertœ'tō| Hungarian name for the Neusiedler See.

**Fez** |fez| (also **Fès**) historic city in N Morocco, founded in 808. Pop. 564,000. A textile center, it gave its name to the hat style.

**Fez·zan** |fe'zæn| (Arabic name **Fazzan**) historic desert and oasis region of SW Libya, known to Europeans since pre-Roman times.

**Fi·an·a·ran·tsoa** |,fëänärän'tsōə| town in E central Madagascar, a noted academic center in an agricultural area. Pop. 124,000.

**Fie·so·le** |'fyäzə,la| tourist center and village outside Florence, in central Italy, on a hill overlooking the city. Pop. 4,000.

**Fife** |fïf| administrative region and former county of E central Scotland; administrative center, Glenrothes.

**Fi·ji** |'fëjē| republic in the S Pacific consisting of a group of some 840 islands, of which about a hundred are inhabited. Area: 7,078 sq. mi./18,333 sq. km. Pop. 800,000. Languages, English (official), Fijian, Hindi. Capital and largest community: Suva, on Viti Levu. Independent since 1970, Fiji is peopled chiefly by Polynesians and Indians. Subsistence agriculture and the export of sugar, copra, and spices dominate the economy. □ **Fijian** *adj. & n.*

**Fíl·ip·poi** |'fēlepē| Greek name for Philippi.

**Fill·more, the** |'fil,mawr| popular name for a neighborhood of San Francisco, California, W of downtown, that was central to 1960s youth culture.

**Find·horn** |'find,hawrn| village in N Scotland, in the Grampian region W of Elgin, site of a noted New Age agricultural community.

**Find·lay** |'fin(d)lē| industrial city in NW Ohio. Pop. 35,675.

**Fin·gal's Cave** |'fiNGgəlz| cave on the island of Staffa in the Inner Hebrides, Scotland, noted for the basaltic pillars that form its cliffs. It is said to have been the inspiration for Mendelssohn's overture *The Hebrides*.

**Fin·ger Lakes** |'fiNGgər| region of central New York named for its series of narrow glacial lakes that lie parallel in a N–S orientation. Canandaigua, Keuka, Seneca, and Cayuga are among the better known. Farms and resorts surround the lakes.

**Fin·is·tère** |,fēnē'ster| department of Brittany, in NW France. Pop. 839,000. The capital is Quimper. It is the westernmost department in France.

**Fin·is·terre, Cape** |,fēnē'ster| promontory of NW Spain, forming the westernmost point of the mainland. The shipping forecast area *Finisterre* covers part of the Atlantic off NW Spain, W of the Bay of Biscay.

**Fin·land** |'finlənd| republic on the Baltic Sea, between Sweden and Russia. Area: 130,608 sq. mi./338,145 sq. km. Pop. 4,999,000. Languages, Finnish and Swedish. Capital and largest city: Helsinki.

Fiji

Finland

Finnish name **Suomi**. Heavily forested and with thousands of islands, Finland has been dominated by Russia during much of its history. Wood, paper, and manufacturing industries are important. □ **Finnish** *adj.* **Finn** *n.*

**Fin·land, Gulf of** |'finlənd| arm of the Baltic Sea between Finland and Estonia, extending E to St. Petersburg in Russia.

**Fin·ster·aar·horn Mountain** |,finster'är-,hawrn| highest peak in the Bernese Alps, in Switzerland: 14,022 ft./4,274 m.

**Fire Island** |fīr| barrier island on the S shore of Long Island, New York, site of numerous small resort communities.

**Fi·ren·ze** |fe'rentsä| Italian name for FLOR-ENCE.

**Fi·ro·za·bad** |fir'ōzə,bäd| commercial and industrial town in N central India, in Uttar Pradesh state. Pop. 271,000.

**First World** |'fərst 'wərld| see THIRD WORLD.

**Fish River** |fiSH| river that flows 300 mi./480 km. from central Namibia into the Orange River at the border with South Africa.

**Fitch·burg** |'fiCH,bərg| city in N central Massachusetts, NW of Boston, noted especially for its plastics industry. Pop. 41,194.

**Fitz·roy, Cer·ro** |'särō 'fēts,roi| (English name **Fitzroy Mountains**) range in Patagonia, on the border of S Argentina and S Chile, rising to 11,073 ft./3,375 m.

**Fiu·me** |'fyŏōmä| Italian name for RIJEKA, Croatia.

**Flag·staff** |'flæg,stæf| city in N central Arizona, near the San Francisco Peaks, home to Lowell Observatory and the University of Northern Arizona. Pop. 45,857.

**Flam·bor·ough Head** |'flæm,b(ə)rə| rocky promontory on the E coast of England, in the East Riding of Yorkshire.

**Fla·min·i·an Way** |fləminēən 'wä| (in Latin **Via Flaminia**) ancient road in Italy that led N from Rome to Rimini, extending more than 200 mi./322 km.

**Flan·ders** |'flændərz| region in the SW part of the Low Countries, now divided between Belgium (where it forms the provinces of East and West Flanders), France, and the Netherlands. It was a powerful medieval principality and the scene of prolonged fighting during the World War I. □ **Flemish** *adj.* **Fleming** *n.*

**Flat·bush** |'flæt,bŏŏSH| residential and commercial section of central Brooklyn, New York.

**Flat·head Range** |'flæt,hed| range of the Rocky Mts. in NW Montana. The **Flathead River,** which flows through the area, is a tributary of the Clark Fork River, and an important recreational resource.

**Fleet Street** |'flēt ,strēt| street in central London, England, along which the offices of British national newspapers were located until the mid-1980s. The term is used to refer to the British press.

**Flens·burg** |'flents,bŏŏrg; 'flenz,berg| industrial seaport in NW Germany, on the Flensburg fjord of the Baltic Sea. Pop. 87,000. Before 1867 it belonged to Denmark. It is Germany's northernmost city.

**Flevo·land** |'flävō,länt| province of the Netherlands, created in 1986 from land reclaimed from the Zuider Zee during the 1950s and 1960s.

**Flin·ders Island** |'flindərz| the largest island in the Furneaux group, in the Bass Strait between Tasmania and mainland Australia.

**Flin·ders Ranges** |'flindərz| mountain range in South Australia state, Australia.

**Flint** |flint| industrial city in SE Michigan, an auto industry center since the Buick Company was established here in 1903. Pop. 140,761.

**Flint·shire** |'flintsHir| county of NE Wales; administrative center, Mold. It was part of Clwyd from 1974 to 1996.

**Flod·den** |'flädn| (also **Flodden Field**) battle site in N England, near Branxton, Northumberland and the Scottish border, where English forces in 1513 defeated the Scots, inflicting devastating losses.

**Flor·ence**[1] |'flawrəns| industrial and commercial city in NW Alabama, on the Tennessee River E of Muscle Shoals. Pop. 36,426.

**Flor·ence**[2] |'flawrəns| city in W central Italy, the capital of Tuscany, on the Arno River. Pop. 408,000. Florence was a leading center of the Italian Renaissance from the 14th to the 16th centuries, especially under the rule of the Medici family during the 15th century. Italian name **Firenze**. □ **Florentine** *adj. & n.*

**Flor·ence**[3] |'flawrəns| commercial city in NE South Carolina. Pop. 29,813.

**Flo·ren·cia** |flaw'rensēə| commercial town in S Colombia, the capital of Caquetá department, in an agricultural area. Pop. 108,000.

**Flo·res** |'flawrəs| the largest of the Lesser Sunda Islands in Indonesia.

**Flo·ri·a·nó·po·lis** |,flawrēə'nawōpŏŏlis| city in S Brazil, on the Atlantic coast, capital of the state of Santa Catarina. Pop. 293,000.

**Flor·i·da** |'flawrədə; 'flärədə| see box. □ **Floridian** *adj. & n.*

**Flor·i·da Keys** |'flawrədə; 'flärədə| chain of small islands off the tip of the Florida peninsula. Linked to each other and to the mainland by a series of causeways and bridges forming the Overseas Highway, the islands extend SW over 100 mi./160 km. Key Largo, the longest, is closest to the mainland, and the highway extends as far as Key West.

**Flor·is·sant** |'flawrəsənt| historic city in E central Missouri, NW of St. Louis. Pop. 51,206.

**Flush·ing**[1] |'fləSHiNG| port in the SW Netherlands. Pop. 44,000. Dutch name **Vlissingen**.

---

### Florida

**Capital:** Tallahassee

**Largest city:** Jacksonville

**Other cities:** Clearwater, Daytona Beach, Ft. Lauderdale, Hialeah, Miami, Orlando, St. Petersburg, Tampa

**Population:**    12,937,926    (1990); 14,915,980 (1998); 16,279,000 (2005 proj.)

**Population rank (1990):** 4

**Rank in land area:** 22

**Abbreviation:** FL; Fla.

**Nickname:** Sunshine State

**Motto:** 'In God We Trust'

**Bird:** mockingbird

**Fish:** largemouth bass (freshwater); Atlantic sailfish (saltwater)

**Flower:** orange blossom

**Trees:** sabal palmetto palm (cabbage palm)

**Song:** "Old Folks at Home" (also known as "Swanee River")

**Noted physical features:** Apalachee, Biscayne, Waccasassa bays; Cape Canaveral, Cape Sable; Gulf of Mexico; Atlantic Ocean; Rainbow Springs, Silver Springs; Everglades and Okefenokee swamps

**Tourist attractions:** Walt Disney World, Epcot Center, Disney-MGM Studios; Universal Studios; Marine Land; Miami Beach; Ringling Bros. Museum of Circus; Everglades National Park; Cypress Gardens; Busch Gardens

**Admission date:** March 3, 1845

**Order of admission:** 27

**Name origin:** Named *Pascua Florida* ('Flowery Easter') by Juan Ponce de Leon.

---

**Flush·ing**[2] |'fləSHiNG| commercial and residential section of N Queens, New York City, noted for its diverse population.

**Fly River** |fli| longest river in Papua New Guinea, flowing 750 mi./1,200 km. from the border with Irian Jaya, Indonesia into the Gulf of Papua. It is noted for its wide estuary and its crocodiles.

**Fly·over** jocular term for the central US between the east and west coast metropolitan regions, esp. between New York City and Los Angeles. This disparaging reference to the majority of the country and its population is said to have been promulgated by frequent-flying executives of the broadcast industry.

**Foc·sani** |fōk'sHän(yə)| industrial city in E central Romania, in the foothills of the Transylvanian Alps. Pop. 99,000.

**Fog·gia** |'fawjə| industrial town in SE Italy, in Apulia. Pop. 160,000.

**Fog·gy Bot·tom** |'fawgē 'bätəm| low-lying part of the District of Columbia, along the Potomac River, home to the U.S. State Department, which is sometimes also called Foggy Bottom.

**Fo·go** |'fōgō| island in S Cape Verde. São Filipe is its chief town.

**Folke·stone** |'fōkstən| seaport and resort in Kent, on the SE coast of England. Pop. 44,000. The English terminal of the Channel Tunnel is at Cheriton, nearby.

**Fol·som**[1] |'fōlsəm| city in N central California, NE of Sacramento. Pop. 29,802.

**Fol·som**[2] |'fōlsəm| village in NE New Mexico that gave its name to an ancient culture whose artifacts, especially spear points, were found here.

**Fond du Lac** |'fändl,æk; 'fänjə,læk| industrial and commercial city in SE Wisconsin, on Lake Winnebago. Pop. 37,757.

**Fon·se·ca, Gulf of** |fän'säkə| inlet of the Pacific Ocean in W Central America. El Salvador lies on its N, Honduras on its E, and Nicaragua on its S.

**Fon·taine·bleau** |,fawNten'blō; 'fäntn,blō| town, SE of Paris, in N central France. Pop. 20,000. In the Renaissance chateau in its vast forest, King Louis XIV revoked the Edict of Nantes and Napoleon I signed his first abdication.

**Fon·tana** |fän'tænə| city in SW California, a steel center E of Los Angeles. Pop. 87,535.

**Fon·te·noy** |fawNt'nwä| village in SW Belgium. The French won a celebrated victory over English, Irish, Dutch, and Hanoverian troops here in 1745.

**Foo·chow** |'fōō'CHow| see FUZHOU, China.

**For·bid·den City**[1] |fər'bidn| area of Beijing, China containing the former imperial palaces, to which entry was forbidden to all except the members of the imperial family and their servants.

**For·bid·den City**[2] |fər'bidn| name given to Lhasa, Tibet.

**Ford·ham** |'fawrdəm| section of the central Bronx, New York City, that takes its name from Fordham University.

**For·est Hills** |'fawrəst; 'färəst| affluent residential section of central Queens, New York City, associated with the U.S. Open (tennis), played here until 1978.

**For·far** |'fawrfər| town in E Scotland, administrative center of Angus region. Pop. 13,000. It is noted for its castle, the meeting place in 1057 of an early Scottish Parliament and the home of several Scottish kings.

**For·far·shire** |'fawrfər‚SHir; 'fawfərSHər| former name (from the 16th century until 1928) for ANGUS, Scotland.

**For·lì** |fawr'lē| industrial town in NE Italy. Pop.110,000. It is the capital of Forlì province.

**For·men·te·ra** |‚fawrmen'tārə| small island in the Mediterranean, S of Ibiza. It is the southernmost of the Balearic Islands of Spain.

**For·mo·sa** |fawr'mōsə| former (Portuguese) name for TAIWAN. □ **Formosan** adj.

**For·ta·le·za** |‚fawrtlāzə| port and resort city in NE Brazil, on the Atlantic coast, capital of the state of Ceará. Pop. 1,769,000.

**Fort Ben·ning** |'beniNG| military installation in W Georgia, outside Columbus, a center of infantry training.

**Fort Bragg** |bræg| military installation in central North Carolina, outside of Fayetteville, a center for airborne training.

**Fort Col·lins** |'kälinz| commercial and industrial city in N central Colorado, home to Colorado State University. Pop. 87,758.

**Fort-de-France** |‚fawrdə'fräNs| the capital of Martinique. Pop. 102,000. □ **Foyalais** adj. & n.

**Fort Dix** |diks| military installation in S central New Jersey, major U.S. training center during World War II.

**Fort Dodge** |däj| commercial and mining city in NW Iowa. Pop. 25,894.

**Forth** |fawrTH| river of central Scotland, rising on Ben Lomond and flowing E through Stirling into the North Sea.

**Forth, Firth of** |'ferTH əv; 'fōrTH| the estuary of the Forth River, spanned by a cantilever railway bridge (opened 1890) and a road suspension bridge (1964).

**Fort Hood** |hŏŏd| military installation in central Texas, near Killeen, an armored training center.

**Fort Knox** |näks| U.S. military reservation in Kentucky, famous as the site of the depository (built in 1936) that holds the bulk of U.S. gold bullion in its vaults.

**Fort La·my** |‚fawr lə'mē| former name (until 1973) for N'DJAMENA, Chad.

**Fort Lau·der·dale** |'lawdər‚däl| resort, commercial, and industrial city in SE Florida, N of Miami. Pop. 149,377.

**Fort Lee** |lē| commercial and residential borough in NE New Jersey, across the Hudson River from New York City. Pop. 31,997.

**Fort Mc·Hen·ry** |mik'henrē| historic site in the harbor of Baltimore, Maryland, scene of an 1812 British siege that inspired Francis Scott Key to write "The Star Spangled Banner."

**Fort My·ers** |'mīərz| resort and commercial city in SW Florida. Pop. 45,206.

**Fort Peck Dam** |‚fawrt 'pek| dam on the Missouri River in NE Montana, built in 1940, that created Fort Peck Lake, the largest reservoir in the state.

**Fort Pierce** |piərs| resort and port city in E central Florida. Pop. 36,830.

**Fort Sill** |sil| military installation in SW Oklahoma, N of Lawton. A cavalry base in the 19th century, it now is an artillery training center.

**Fort Smith** |smiTH| industrial city in W Arkansas, on the Arkansas River. Pop. 72,798.

**Fort Sum·ter** |'səmtər| historic site in the harbor of Charleston, South Carolina. Confederate forces fired on U.S. troops here in April 1861, beginning the Civil War.

**Fort Wayne** |wān| industrial and commercial city in NE Indiana. Pop. 173,072.

**Fort Wil·liam** |'wilyəm| town in W Scotland, on Loch Linnhe near Ben Nevis. Pop. 11,000.

**Fort Worth** |fawrt 'wərTH| industrial and commercial city in N Texas, W of Dallas. Pop. 447,619.

**forty-ninth parallel** |'fawrtē‚ninTH 'pærə‚lel| the parallel of latitude 49° N of the equator, especially as forming the boundary between Canada and the U.S. W of the Lake of the Woods, Minnesota.

**Fo·shan** |'fōshän| (formerly **Fatshan**; **Namhoi**) industrial city in Guangdong province, S China, SW of Guangzhou, known for its silk and porcelain. Pop. 303,000.

**Fosse Way** |'fäs wā| ancient road in Britain. It ran from Axminster to Lincoln, via Bath and Leicester (about 200 mi./320 km.), and marked the limit of the first stage of the Roman occupation (mid-1st century A.D.)

**Foth·er·in·gay** |'fäTHəriNG,gä; 'fäTHərNG-,hä| village in Northamptonshire, S England, on the Nene River, scene of the birth of Richard III and the execution of Mary, Queen of Scots.

**Foun·tain of Youth** |'fowntn əv 'yo͞oTH| see under BIMINI, Bahamas.

**Foun·tain Valley** |'fowntn| city in SW California, a suburb SE of Los Angeles. Pop. 53,691.

**Four Cor·ners** |fawr 'kawrnərz| point where Arizona, New Mexico, Colorado, and Utah meet. The only such site in the U.S., it is surrounded by Navajo and Ute reservations.

**Fourth World** |'fawrTH 'wərld| term used to designate the poorest countries in the THIRD WORLD, especially Asian, Latin American, and African states.

**Fou·ta Djal·lon** mountainous district in W Guinea, in a Fulani homeland. The headstreams of the Niger and Senegal rivers are here.

**Fox·bor·ough** |'fäks,bərō| suburban town in E Massachusetts, SW of Boston, site of Foxborough (Shaeffer) Stadium. Pop. 14,637.

**Foxe Basin** |fäks| shallow inlet of the Atlantic in Nunavut, Canada, between Baffin Island and the mouth of Hudson Bay.

**Fox·woods** |'fäks,wo͝odz| gambling resort on the Mashantucket Pequot reservation in the town of Ledyard, in SE Connecticut, N of New London.

**Fra·ming·ham** |'främiNG,hæm| industrial and commercial town in E Massachusetts. Pop. 64,994.

**Fran·ca** |'fräNkə| industrial and commercial city in S Brazil, in São Paulo state, in a coffee-, diamond-, and livestock-producing area. Pop. 267,000.

**France** |fræns| republic in W Europe. Area: 211,208 sq. mi./547,026 sq. km. Pop. 56,556,000. Language, French. Capital and largest city: Paris. French name **République française**, abbrev. **RF**. The Gaul of the Roman period, France emerged in the Middle Ages, and has been a major European power since the 16th century. It is industrial and agricultural, but is perhaps best known for its cultural strengths. □ **French** *adj. & n.*

**Franche-Comté** |,fränshkawN'tä| region of E France, in the N foothills of the Jura Mts.

**Fran·cis·town** |'frænsəs,town| industrial and commercial town in NE Botswana, in a mining area. Pop. 65,000.

**Fran·co·nia** |fræNG'kōnēə| medieval duchy of S Germany, inhabited by the Franks.

**Fran·co·nia Notch** |frä&ng'kōnēə 'näCH| valley in the White Mts. of N New Hampshire, noted for its scenery, including the Old Man of the Mountains, the famous rock formation.

**Fran·ken·thal** |'fräNkən,täl| industrial city in western Germany, NW of Mannheim. Pop. 47,000.

**Frank·fort** |'fræNGkfərt| the state capital of Kentucky. Pop. 25,968.

**Frank·furt** |'fräNGk,fo͝ort; 'fræNGkfərt| commercial city in western Germany, in Hesse. Pop. 654,000. The headquarters of the Bundesbank is here. Full name **Frankfurt am Main**.

**Frank·lin Mountains** |'fræNGklən| range in the W Northwest Territories, E of the Mackenzie River.

**Franz Jo·sef Land** |,fräns 'jōsəf| group of islands in the Arctic Ocean, discovered in 1873 by an Austrian expedition and annexed by the USSR in 1928.

**Fra·scati** |fräs'kätē| town in central Italy. Pop. 20,000. A popular summer resort since the Roman era, it is known for its white wine.

**Fra·ser** |'fräzər; 'fräzHər| river of British Columbia. It rises in the Rocky Mts. and flows in a wide curve 850 mi./1,360 km. into the Strait of Georgia, just S of Vancouver.

**Fray Ben·tos** |fri 'bäntaws| port and meat-packing center in W Uruguay. Pop. 20,000.

**Fred·er·ick** |'fred(ə)rik| city in N Maryland. Fort Detrick is nearby. Pop. 40,148.

**Fred·er·icks·burg**¹ |'fred(ə)riks,bərg| resort city in central Texas, in the Hill Country. Pop. 6,934.

**Fred·er·icks·burg**² |'fred(ə)riks,bərg| historic commercial city in NE Virginia, on the Rappahannock River. Pop. 19,027.

**Fred·er·ic·ton** |'fred(ə)riktən| the capital of New Brunswick, in the SW, on the St. John River. Pop. 46,466. The city was founded in 1785 by United Empire Loyalists, colonists who left the U.S. after the Revolutionary War.

**Fred·er·iks·berg** |'freTHrigz,ber| W suburb of Copenhagen, Denmark. Pop. 86,000.

**Free·port**¹ |'frē,pawrt| port city in the N Bahamas, on Grand Bahama Island. Pop.

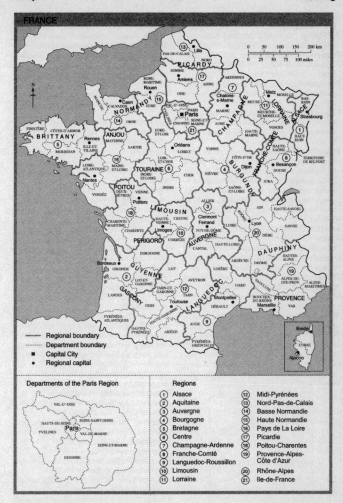

FRANCE

**Regional boundary**
**Department boundary**
■ **Capital City**
● **Regional capital**

**Departments of the Paris Region**

VAL-D'OISE
HAUTS-DE-SEINE SEINE-SAINT-DENIS
Paris
YVELINES VAL-DE-MARNE
SEINE-ET-MARNE
ESSONNE

**Regions**

1. Alsace
2. Aquitaine
3. Auvergne
4. Bourgogne
5. Bretagne
6. Centre
7. Champagne-Ardenne
8. Franche-Comté
9. Languedoc-Roussillon
10. Limousin
11. Lorraine
12. Midi-Pyrénées
13. Nord-Pas-de-Calais
14. Basse Normandie
15. Haute Normandie
16. Pays de La Loire
17. Picardie
18. Poitou-Charentes
19. Provence-Alpes-Côte d'Azur
20. Rhône-Alpes
21. Ile-de-France

27,000. It is a resort and commercial center.

**Free·port**[2] |'frē‚pawrt| commercial and industrial city in NW Illinois. Pop. 25,840.

**Free·port**[3] |'frē‚pawrt| commercial village in Hempstead town, Long Island, New York. Pop. 39,894.

**Free States** |'frē 'stāts| in U.S. history, those states in which slavery was not legal before the Civil War.

**Free·town** |'frē‚town| the capital and chief port of Sierra Leone. Pop. 505,000.

**Frei·berg** |'frī‚berg| industrial center and rail junction in eastern Germany, in the foothills of the Ore Mts. Pop. 51,000. It is in a mining region.

**Frei·burg** |'frī,boŏrk; 'fri,bərg| industrial city in SW Germany, in Baden-Württemberg, on the edge of the Black Forest. Pop. 194,000. Full name **Freiburg im Breisgau.**

**Fre·man·tle** |'frē,mæntl| the principal port of Western Australia, part of the Perth metropolitan area. Pop. 24,000.

**Fre·mont** |'frē,mänt| industrial and commercial city in N central California, S of Oakland off San Francisco Bay. Pop. 173,339.

**French Com·mu·ni·ty** |'frencH kə-'myōōnətē| (French name **Communauté française**) organization established in 1958 linking France with overseas territories and departments, as well as with seven former African colonies. It ceased to have practical importance by the early 1960s.

**French Con·go** |,frencH 'käNGō| early name for FRENCH EQUATORIAL AFRICA, now the People's Republic of Congo.

**French Equa·to·ri·al Af·ri·ca** |frencH ,ekwə'tawrēəl 'æfrikə| former federation of French territories in W central Africa (1910–58). Previously called French Congo, its constituent territories were Chad, Ubangi Shari (now the Central African Republic), Gabon, and Middle Congo (now the Republic of the Congo).

**French Gui·a·na** |frencH gē'änə| overseas department of France, in N South America. Area: 35,126 sq. mi./90,976 sq. km. Pop. 96,000. Capital: Cayenne. A low, tropical land, it produces timber, rum, and fish.

**French Guiana**

**French Indo·china** |'frencH,indō'cHīnə| former French colonial territory of SE Asia, comprising the present countries of Vietnam, Cambodia, and Laos.

**French Pol·y·ne·sia** |frencH ,pälə'nēzHə|

overseas territory of France in the South Pacific. Pop. 200,000. Capital: Papeete (on Tahiti). French Polynesia comprises the Society Islands, the Gambier Islands, the Tuamotu Archipelago, the Tubuai Islands, and the Marquesas. It became an overseas territory of France in 1946, and was granted partial autonomy in 1977.

**French So·ma·li·land** |frencH sə'mäle-,lænd| former name (until 1967) for DJI-BOUTI.

**French South·ern and Ant·arc·tic Ter·ritories** |'frencH 'səTHərn ənd ænt'är(k)-tik| overseas territory of France, comprising Adélie Land in Antarctica, and the Kerguelen and Crozet archipelagos and the islands of Amsterdam and St. Paul in the S Indian Ocean.

**French Sudan** former name for MALI.

**French West Af·ri·ca** |frencH west æfrikə| former federation of French territories in NW Africa (1895–1959). Its constituent territories were Senegal, Mauritania, French Sudan (now Mali), Upper Volta (now Burkina Faso), Niger, French Guinea (now Guinea), the Côte d'Ivoire, and Dahomey (now Benin).

**Fres·nil·lo** |frez'nēyō| city in N central Mexico, in Zacatecas state, in a silver-mining region. Pop. 75,000. It has a noted mining school.

**Fres·no** |'freznō| city in central California, in the San Joaquin Valley, in an agricultural and oil-producing area. Pop. 354,202.

**Fri·bourg** |frē'boōr| (in German **Freiburg**) canton in W Switzerland, on a plateau in the foothills of the Alps. Area: 644 sq. mi./1,672 sq. km. Pop. 204,000. The area is agricultural.

**Frie·drichs·ha·fen** |'frēdriкHs'häfən| industrial and port city in S Germany, on the Lake of Constance. Pop. 52,000.

**Friend·ly Islands** |'fren(d)lē| another name for TONGA.

**Fries·land**[1] |'frēs,länt| the W part of the ancient region of Frisia.

**Fries·land**[2] |'frēs,länt| N province of the Netherlands, bounded to the W and N by the IJsselmeer and the North Sea. Capital: Leeuwarden.

**Fri·sia** |'frizHə; 'frēzHə| ancient region of NW Europe. It consisted of the Frisian Islands and parts of the mainland corresponding to the present-day provinces of Friesland and Groningen in the Netherlands and the regions of Ostfriesland and Nordfriesland in NW Germany. □ **Frisian** adj. & n.

**Fri·sian Islands** |'frizHən; 'frēzHən| chain of islands lying off the coast of NW Europe, extending from the IJsselmeer in the Netherlands to Jutland. The islands consist of three groups: the *West Frisian Islands* form part of the Netherlands, the *East Frisian Islands* form part of Germany, and the *North Frisian Islands* are divided between Germany and Denmark.

**Fri·u·li** |'frē-ळॆ,lē; frē'ळॆlē| historic region of SE Europe now divided between Slovenia and the Italian region of Friuli-Venezia Giulia. A Rhaeto-Romance dialect is spoken locally. □ **Friulian** *adj. & n.*

**Friuli–Venezia Giu·lia** |'frē-ळॆ,lē və-'netsēə 'jळॆlyə; frē'ळॆlē| region in NE Italy, on the border with Slovenia and Austria. Capital: Trieste.

**Fro·bi·sher Bay** |'frōbishər| inlet of the Atlantic at the S end of Baffin Island, in Nunavut. Iqaluit, the town at its head, was formerly also called Frobisher Bay.

**Front Range** |frənt| easternmost range of the Rocky Mts., chiefly in Colorado, reaching 14,270 ft./4,349 m. at Grays Peak. Pikes Peak is also here.

**Frun·ze** |'frळnzə| former name (1926–91) for BISHKEK, Kyrgyzstan.

**Fu·chu** |'fळCHळ| industrial and residential city in E central Japan, on Honshu, a suburb of Tokyo. Pop. 209,000.

**Fuer·te·ven·tu·ra** |,fwertəvän'tळərə| second-largest of the Canary Islands, belonging to Spain, in the Atlantic. Area:655 sq. mi./1,722 sq. km. Its chief town is Puerto del Rosario.

**Fu·jai·rah** |fळ'jīrə| (also **Al Fujairah**) **1** one of the seven member states of the United Arab Emirates. Pop. 76,000. **2** its capital.

**Fu·ji, Mount** |'fळjē| dormant volcano in the Chubu region of Japan. Rising to 12,385 ft./3,776 m., it is Japan's highest mountain, with a symmetrical, conical, snow-capped peak. Its last eruption was in 1707. Regarded by the Japanese as sacred, it has been celebrated in art and literature for centuries. Also called **Fujiyama**.

**Fu·jian** |'fळjēən| (formerly **Fukien**) mountainous province, SE China, across the Taiwan Strait from Taiwan. Pop. 27.49 million. Capital: Fuzhou.

**Fu·ji·sa·wa** |,fळjē'säwä| city and resort town in central Japan on E Honshu, a suburb SW of Tokyo. Pop. 350,000.

**Fu·kui** |fळ'kळē| industrial city in W central Japan, on central Honshu. Pop. 253,000.

**Fu·ku·o·ka** |,fळkळ'ōkä| industrial city and port in S Japan, capital of Kyushu island. Pop. 1,237,000.

**Fu·ku·shi·ma** |,fळkळ'sHēmə; fळ'kळ-sHēmə| main commercial city of NE Japan, on N Honshu. Pop. 278,000.

**Fu·ku·ya·ma** |,fळkळ'yämä| industrial and commercial port in W Japan, on SW Honshu. Pop. 366,000.

**Ful·da** |'foolda| headwater of the Weser River, in western Germany. It flows 137 mi./218 km. to join the Werra River, forming the Weser.

**Ful·ham** |'foolam| district of W London, England, part of the borough of **Hammersmith and Fulham**.

**Fu·ling** |'foo'liNG| city in Sichuan province, central China, on the Yangtze River at its junction with the Wu River. Pop. 986,000.

**Ful·ler·ton** |'foolərtən| city in SW California, SE of Los Angeles. Pop. 114,144.

**Fu·na·ba·shi** |,foonä'bäsHē| city in central Japan, on E Honshu, a residential and industrial suburb of Tokyo. Pop. 533,000.

**Fu·na·fu·ti** |,f(y)ळonä'f(y)ळotē| the capital of Tuvalu, situated on an island of the same name. Pop. 2,500.

**Fu·nan** |'foo'nän| former kingdom of SE Asia (1st to 6th centuries) in territory occupied by much of present-day Cambodia and southern Vietnam.

**Fun·chal** |foon'sHäl| the capital and chief port of Madeira, on the S coast of the island. Pop. 110,000.

**Fun·dy, Bay of** |'fəndē| arm of the Atlantic extending between the Canadian provinces of New Brunswick and Nova Scotia. It is subject to fast-running tides, the highest in the world, which reach 50–80 ft./12–15 m. and are used to generate electricity.

**Fur·neaux Islands** |'fərnō| group of Australian islands off the coast of NE Tasmania, in the Bass Strait. The largest is Flinders Island.

**Fur·ness** |'fərnəs| peninsular region of NW England, W of Morecambe Bay in Cumbria. The chief town is BARROW-IN-FURNESS.

**Fur Seal Islands** another name for the PRIBILOF ISLANDS.

**Fürth** |fyrt| industrial city in S Germany, suburb of Nuremberg, on the Rednitz and Pegnitz rivers. Pop. 105,000.

**Fu·shun** |'foo'sHळon| coal-mining city in NE China, in the province of Liaoning. Pop. 1,330,000.

# Gg

**Ga·bès** |'gäb,es; gäb'es| (also **Qabis**) industrial seaport in E Tunisia. Pop. 99,000.

**Ga·bon** |gä'bawN| equatorial republic in W Africa, on the Atlantic coast. Area: 103,386 sq. mi./267,667 sq. km. Pop. 1,200,000. Languages, French (official), Fang, other African languages. Capital and largest city: Libreville. A French territory from 1888 to 1958, Gabon became independent in 1960. Oil, timber, and minerals are important to its economy. □ **Gabonese** *adj. & n.*

**Gabon**

**Ga·bo·rone** |,gäbə'rōnä| the capital of Botswana, in the S of the country near the border with South Africa. Pop. 133,000.

**Ga·bro·vo** |'gäbrō,vō| industrial city in central Bulgaria, on the Yantra River. Pop. 88,000. Bulgaria's chief textile center, it is situated on an approach to the Shipka Pass through the Balkan Mts.

**Ga·dag** |'gədəg| commercial town in SW India, in Karnataka state. Pop. 134,000 (with neighboring Betgeri).

**Gads·den** |'gædzdən| industrial city in NE Alabama. Pop. 42,523.

**Gads·den Purchase** |'gædzdən| area in New Mexico and Arizona, near the Rio Grande. Extending over 30,000 sq. mi./77,700 sq. km., it was purchased from Mexico in 1853 by the American diplomat James Gadsden (1788-1858), with the intention of ensuring a southern railroad route to the Pacific.

**Gael·tacht** |'gāl,täxt| (**the Gaeltacht**) region of Ireland in which the vernacular language is Irish, particularly in Connacht.

**Gaf·sa** |'gæfsə| (Arabic name **Qafsah**; Roman name **Capsa**) oasis and industrial town in W central Tunisia. Pop. 71,000. It gave its name to the Paleolithic Capsian culture.

**Gaines·ville** |'gānz,vil; 'gänzvəl| city in N

central Florida, home to the University of Florida. Pop. 84,770.

**Gai·thers·burg** |'gāTHərz,bərg| city in central Maryland, a residential and corporate center NW of Washington, D.C. Pop. 39,542.

**Ga·la·pa·gos Islands** |gə'läpəgəs; gə-'læpəgəs| Pacific archipelago on the equator, about 650 mi./1,045 km. W of Ecuador, to which it belongs. Pop. 9,750. Spanish name **Archipiélago de Colón**. The islands are noted for their abundant wildlife, including giant tortoises and many other endemic species. They were the site of Charles Darwin's observations of 1835, which helped him to form his theory of natural selection.

**Ga·laţi** |gə'läts| industrial city in E Romania, a river port on the lower Danube. Pop. 324,000.

**Ga·la·tia** |gə'lāsHə| ancient region in central Asia Minor (present-day Anatolian Turkey), settled by invading Gauls (the Galatians) in the 3rd century B.C. It later became a province of the Roman Empire. □ **Galatian** *adj. & n.*

**Gales·burg** |'gālz,bərg| commercial and industrial city in W central Illinois. Pop. 33,530.

**Ga·li·cia**[1] |gə'lisHə| region of E central Europe, north of the Carpathian Mountains. A former province of Austria, it now forms part of SE Poland and W Ukraine. Hasidic Judaism developed here. □ **Galician** *adj. & n.*

**Ga·li·cia**[2] |gə'lisHə| autonomous region and former kingdom of NW Spain. Capital: Santiago de Compostela. □ **Galician** *adj. & n.*

**Gal·i·lee, Sea of** |'gælə,lē| lake in N Israel. The River Jordan flows through it from N to S. Also called **Lake Tiberias, Lake Kinneret**.

**Gal·i·lee** |'gælə,lē| N region of ancient Palestine, W of the Jordan River, associated with the ministry of Jesus. It is now part of Israel. □ **Galilean** *adj. & n.*

**Gal·le** |gäl; gæl| seaport on the SW coast of Sri Lanka. Pop. 77,000.

**Gal·li·po·li** |gə'lipəlē| (Turkish name **Gallibolu**) peninsula in European Turkey, between the Dardanelles and the Aegean Sea, scene of a bloody and unsuccessful Allied attack on Turkish positions in 1915-16, during World War I.

**Gal·lo·way** |'gælə,wā| area of SW Scotland consisting of the two former counties of Kirkcudbrightshire and Wigtownshire, and now part of Dumfries and Galloway region.

**Gal·ves·ton** |'gælvəstən| port in Texas, SE of Houston. Pop. 59,070. It is situated on Galveston Bay, an inlet of the Gulf of Mexico.

**Gal·way** |'gawl,wā| **1** county of the Republic of Ireland, on the W coast in the province of Connacht. Pop. 180,000. **2** its county seat, a seaport at the head of Galway Bay. Pop. 51,000.

**Gal·way Bay** |'gawl,wā| inlet of the Atlantic on the W coast of Ireland.

**Gam·bia** |'gæmbēə; 'gämbēə| (also **the Gambia**) a country on the coast of W Africa. Area: 4,363 sq. mi./11,295 sq. km. Pop. 900,000. Languages, English (official), Malinke and other indigenous languages. Capital: Banjul. A narrow strip on the Gambia River, within the territory of Senegal (with which it has been politically joined at times), Gambia relies on tourism, fishing, and agriculture to sustain its economy. See also SENEGAMBIA. □ **Gambian** adj. & n.

Gambia

**Gam·bia River** |'gæmbēə; 'gämbēə| river of W Africa that rises near Labé in Guinea and flows 500 mi./800 km. through Senegal and Gambia to the Atlantic at Banjul.

**Gam·bier Islands** |'gæm,bir| group of coral islands in the S Pacific, forming part of French Polynesia.

**Gän·că** |gän'jä| industrial city in Azerbaijan. Pop. 281,000. The city was formerly called Elizavetpol (1804–1918) and Kirovabad (1935–89). Russian name **Gyandzha**.

**Gan·der** |'gændər| town on the island of Newfoundland, on Lake Gander. Pop. 10,339. Its airport served the first regular transatlantic flights, during World War II.

**Gan·dhi·na·gar** |,gərdi'nəgər| city in W India, capital of the state of Gujarat. Pop. 122,000.

**Gan·ga** |'gəNGge| Hindi name for the GANGES River.

**Gan·ga·na·gar** |'əNGgə,nəgər| commercial town in NW India, in Rajasthan state, near the border with Pakistan. Pop. 161,000.

**Gan·ges** |'gæn,jēz| river of N India and Bangladesh, which rises in the Himalayas and flows some 1,678 mi./2,700 km. SE to the Bay of Bengal, where it forms the world's largest delta. The river is regarded by Hindus as sacred. Hindi name **Ganga**. □ **Gangetic** adj.

**Gang·tok** |'gəng,tawk| city in N India, in the foothills of the Kanchenjunga mountain range, capital of the state of Sikkim. Pop. 25,000.

**Gan·su** |'gän'sōō| (also **Kansu**) a province of NW central China, between Mongolia and Tibet. Pop. 22.37 million. Capital: Lanzhou. This narrow, mountainous province forms a corridor through which the Silk Road passed.

**Gao** |gow| port town in NE Mali, on the Niger River. Pop. 40,000.

**Gap** |gäp| tourist center, manufacturing town, and capital of the Hautes-Alpes department in SE France, in the foothills of the Dauphiné Alps. Pop. 36,000.

**Gard** |gär| department in S France, in the lower Rhône Valley. Area: 2,260 sq. mi./5,853 sq. km. Pop. 585,000. The capital is Nîmes.

**Gar·da, Lake** |'gärdə| largest lake in Italy, in the NE, between Lombardy and Venetia.

**Gar·de·na** |gär'dēnə| city in SW California, an industrial suburb S of Los Angeles. Pop. 49,847.

**Gar·den City** |'gärdn| commercial village in Hempstead town, Long Island, New York. Pop. 21,686. The historic air facility Roosevelt Field was here.

**Gar·den Grove** |'gärdn| city in SW California, an industrial and residential suburb SE of Los Angeles. Pop. 143,050.

**Gar·den State** |'gärdn| informal name for NEW JERSEY.

**Gar·land** |'gärlənd| city in NE Texas, an industrial and residential suburb on the NE side of Dallas. Pop. 180,650.

**Garmisch-Partenkirchen** |'gärmisH ,pärtn,kirkHən| resort town in S Germany, in the Bavarian Alps near Oberammergau. Pop. 27,000. It hosted the 1936 Winter Olympic Games.

**Gar·mo, Mount** |'gärmō| former name

(until 1933) for COMMUNISM PEAK, Kyrgyzstan.

**Ga·ronne** |gä'rawn| river of SW France, which rises in the Pyrenees and flows 400 mi./645 km. NW through Toulouse and Bordeaux to join the Dordogne at the Gironde estuary.

**Ga·roua** |gə'rōōə| river port in N Cameroon, on the Bénoué River. Pop. 78,000.

**Gary** |'gærē| industrial port city in NW Indiana, a steel center on Lake Michigan SE of Chicago. Pop. 116,646.

**Gas·co·ny** |'gæskənē| region and former province of SW France, in the N foothills of the Pyrenees. It was held by England between 1154 and 1453. French name **Gascogne**. □ **Gascon** adj. & n.

**Gaspé Peninsula** |gæs'pā| region of SE Quebec between the Saint Lawrence River and New Brunswick. Fishing, agriculture, and tourism are important to its economy.

**Ga·stein·er Valley** |gä'sHtīnər| (also called **Gasteintal**) river valley in the Hohe Tauern range, W Austria. It is known for its scenery and for the spas of Bad Hofgastein and Badgastein.

**Gas·to·nia** |gæ'stōnēə| industrial city in SW North Carolina, a noted textile center. Pop. 54,732.

**Gat·chi·na** |'gächinə| city in NW Russia. Pop. 84,000. It is the site of a former imperial palace, built in the late 18th century and a favorite residence of the czars.

**Gates·head** |'gāts,hed| industrial town in NE England, on the S bank of the Tyne River opposite Newcastle. Pop. 196,000.

**Gath** |gæTH| biblical city in Philistia, E of present-day Ashdod, Israel, the home of the giant Goliath.

**Gat·i·neau** |ˌgætn'ō| city in SW Quebec, a largely French-speaking suburb across the Ottawa River from Ottawa, Ontario. Pop. 92,284.

**Ga·tun Lake** |gə'tōōn| (Spanish name **Lago Gatún**) lake in Panama, created by the damming of the Chagres River during construction of the Panama Canal. The Gatun Locks control passage on the Canal.

**Gat·wick** |'gætwik| international airport in SE England, to the S of London in West Sussex.

**Gau·ha·ti** |gow'hätē| industrial city in NE India, in Assam, a river port on the Brahmaputra. Pop. 578,000.

**Gaul** |gawl| (Latin name **Gallia**) ancient region of Europe, corresponding to modern France, Belgium, the S Netherlands, SW Germany, and N Italy. The area S of the Alps was conquered in 222 B.C. by the Romans, who called it *Cisalpine Gaul*. The area N of the Alps, known as *Transalpine Gaul*, was taken by Julius Caesar between 58 and 51 B.C. □ **Gallic** adj.

**Gaunt** |gawnt| former name for GHENT, Belgium.

**Gau·teng** |'gow,teNG| province of NE South Africa, formerly part of Transvaal. Capital: Johannesburg. Former name (until 1995) **Pretoria-Witwatersrand-Vereeniging**.

**Ga·var·nie** |ˌgävär'nē| village in SW France, in the central Pyrenees. Nearby are a waterfall (1,385 ft./422 m.) and a huge natural amphitheater, the Cirque de Gavarnie.

**Gäv·le** |'yevlə| seaport in E central Sweden, on the Gulf of Bothnia, N of Stockholm. Pop. 89,000. It is the capital of Gävleborg county.

**Ga·ya** |gə'yä| city in NE India, in the state of Bihar S of Patna. Pop. 291,000. It is a place of Hindu pilgrimage.

**Ga·zan·ku·lu** |ˌgäzən'kōōlōō| former homeland established in South Africa for the Tsonga people, now part of the provinces of Northern province and Mpumalanga.

**Ga·za Strip** |'gäzə; 'gæzə| strip of territory in Palestine, on the SE Mediterranean coast, including the town of Gaza. Pop. 748,000. Administered by Egypt from 1949, and occupied by Israel from 1967, it became a self-governing Palestinian enclave under an agreement with Israel in 1994 and elected its own legislative council in 1996.

**Ga·zi·an·tep** |ˌgäzēän'tep| commercial and industrial city in S Turkey, near the border with Syria. Pop. 603,000. Former name (until 1921): **Aintab**.

**Gdańsk** |gə'dänsk; gə'dænsk| (German name **Danzig**) industrial port and shipbuilding center in N Poland, on an inlet of the Baltic Sea. Pop. 465,000. Disputed between Prussia and Poland during the 19th century, it was a free city under a League of Nations mandate from 1919 until 1939, when it was annexed by Nazi Germany, precipitating hostilities with Poland and the outbreak of World War II. In the 1980s the Gdańsk shipyards were the site of the activities of the Solidarity movement, which eventually led to the collapse of the communist regime in Poland in 1989.

**GDR** abbreviation for GERMAN DEMOCRATIC REPUBLIC.

**Gdy·nia** |gə'dinēə| port and naval base in

N Poland, on the Baltic Sea NE of Gdań sk. Pop. 251,000.

**Gee•long** |jēˈlawNG| port and oil-refining center on the S coast of Australia, in the state of Victoria. Pop. 126,000.

**Ge•hen•na** |gəˈhenə| biblical name for Hinnom, a valley near Jerusalem where children were burned in sacrifice to Moloch and other gods. Gehenna came to signify torment and misery.

**Ge•jiu** |ˈgəjēˈo͞o| (also **Geju**)a tin-mining city in S China, near the border with Vietnam. Pop. 384,000.

**Ge•la** |ˈjälə| port and industrial center in S Sicily, S Italy. Pop. 72,000.

**Gel•der•land** |ˈgeldər,lænd| province of the Netherlands, on the border with Germany. Capital: Arnhem. Formerly a duchy, the province was variously occupied by the Spanish, the French, and the Prussians until 1815.

**Gel•sen•kir•chen** |,gelzənˈkirKHən| industrial city in western Germany, in North Rhine-Westphalia NE of Essen. Pop. 294,000.

**Gems•bok National Park** |ˈgemz,bäk| preserve in SW Botswana and an adjoining part of South Africa, in the Kalahari Desert. It is noted for its dunes and wildlife.

**Ge•ne•ral San Mar•tín** |,KHänäˈräl ,sän märˈtēn| (also **San Martín**) city in E Argentina, a NW suburb of Buenos Aires. Pop. 408,000.

**Ge•ne•ral San•tos** |,KHänäˈräl ˈsäntōs| (also called **Dadiangas**) port city in the Philippines, on S Mindanao, on Saragani Bay. Pop. 250,000.

**Ge•ne•ral Sar•mien•to** |,KHänäˈräl ,särˈmyentō| (also **Sarmiento** or **San Miguel**) city in E Argentina, a suburb W of Buenos Aires, in a cattle-producing district. Pop. 647,000.

**Gen•e•see River** |,jenəˈsē; ˈjenə,sē| river that flows 144 mi./232 km. from NW Pennsylvania through W New York, into Lake Ontario at Rochester.

**Ge•ne•va** |jəˈnēvə| city in SW Switzerland, on Lake Geneva. Pop. 167,000. It is the headquarters of international bodies such as the Red Cross, various organizations of the United Nations, and the World Health Organization. French name **Genève**. It was the site of the Geneva Conventions (1846–1949), which established rules for the conduct of war, and was the headquarters of the League of Nations (1920–46).

**Ge•ne•va, Lake** |jəˈnēvə| lake in SW central Europe, between the Jura Mts. and the Alps. Its S shore forms part of the border between France and Switzerland. French name **Lac Léman**.

**Genk** |KHeNGk| (also **Genck**) town in NE Belgium. Pop. 61,000.

**Gen•oa** |ˈjenəwə| seaport on the NW coast of Italy, capital of Liguria region. Pop. 701,000. It was the birthplace of Christopher Columbus. Italian name **Genova**. □ **Genoese** adj. & n.

**Gent** |KHent| Flemish name for GHENT, Belgium.

**George, Lake** |jawrj| resort lake in NE New York, NE of Albany, near the Vermont line, scene of many 18th-century military actions.

**Georges Bank** |ˈjawrjəz| underwater rise in the Atlantic, between Massachusetts and Nova Scotia, site of important U.S. and Canadian fishing zones.

**George•town**[1] |ˈjawrj,town| the capital of Guyana, a port at the mouth of the Demerara River. Pop. 188,000.

**George•town**[2] |ˈjawrj,town| affluent section of NW Washington, D.C., home to government officials, shopping districts, and Georgetown University.

**George Town**[1] |ˈjawrj ,town| the capital of the Cayman Islands, on the island of Grand Cayman. Pop. 12,000.

**George Town**[2] |ˈjawrj ,town| the chief port of Malaysia and capital of the state of Penang, on Penang island. Pop. 219,000. It was founded in 1786 by the British East India Company. Also called **Penang**.

**Geor•gia, Strait of** |ˈjawrjə| ocean passage between Vancouver Island and the mainland of British Columbia and Washington.

**Geor•gia**[1] |ˈjawrjə| a republic of SE Europe, on the E shore of the Black Sea. Area: 26,905 sq. mi./69,700 sq. km. Pop. 5,500,000 (1994). Languages, Georgian (official), Russian, and Armenian. Capital and largest city: Tbilisi. A medieval kingdom, Georgia was dominated by Russia in the 19th–20th centuries, regaining inde-

Georgia

pendence in 1991. It is both agricultural and industrial. □ **Georgian** *adj. & n.*

**Geor·gia²** |'jawrjə| see box. □ **Georgian** *adj. & n.*

**Geor·gian Bay** |'jawrjən| inlet of Lake Huron, in central Ontario, separated from the rest of the lake by the Bruce Peninsula.

**Ge·ra** |'gärä| industrial city in eastern central Germany, in Thuringia. Pop. 127,000.

**Ger·ald·ton** |'jerəl(d)tən| seaport and resort on the W coast of Australia, to the N of Perth. Pop. 24,000.

**Ger·man Dem·o·cratic Republic** official name for the former state of East Germany.

**Ger·man East Af·ri·ca** |'jərmən ɛst 'æfrikə| former German protectorate in East Africa (1891–1918), corresponding to present-day Tanzania, Rwanda, and Burundi.

**Ger·man South West Af·ri·ca** |'jərmən ,sowTH west 'æfrikə| former German protectorate in SW Africa (1884–1918), corresponding to present-day Namibia.

**Ger·man·town** |'jərmən,town| historic residential section of NW Philadelphia, Pennsylvania, scene of a 1777 battle.

---

## Georgia

**Capital/largest city:** Atlanta
**Other cities:** Albany, Athens, Augusta, Columbus, Macon, Marietta, Savannah, Augusta, Sparta
**Population:** 6,478,216 (1990); 7,642,207 (1998); 8,413,000 (2005 proj.)
**Population rank (1990):** 11
**Rank in land area:** 24
**Abbreviation:** GA; Ga.
**Nicknames:** Empire State of the South; Peach State; Goober State; Peachtree State
**Motto:** 'Wisdom, Justice, Moderation'
**Bird:** brown thrasher
**Fish:** largemouth bass
**Flower:** Cherokee rose
**Tree:** live oak
**Song:** "Georgia"
**Noted physical features:** Warm Springs; Okefenokee Swamp; Brasstown Bald Peak
**Tourist attractions:** Andersonville National Cemetery; Fort Frederica, Fort Pulaski and Ocmulgee national monuments
**Admission date:** January 2, 1788
**Order of admission:** 4
**Name origin:** Named by early settler James Oglethorpe for King George II of England, who in 1732 granted Oglethorpe a royal charter to the land.

---

**Ger·many** |'jərmənē| republic in central Europe. Area: 137,838 sq. mi./357,000 sq. km. Pop. 78,700,000. Language, German. Capital and largest city: Berlin; seat of government, Bonn. German name **Deutschland**. Ranging from N coastal plains to the Alps, Germany unified in the mid-19th century, and became a world power in the 20th. Divided, after World War II, into WEST GERMANY and EAST GERMANY, it was reunified in 1990. It is an industrial and economic power, which also has a strong agricultural sector and an important cultural position. □ **German** *adj. & n.*

**Ger·mis·ton** |'jərməstən| city in South Africa, in the province of Gauteng, SE of Johannesburg. Pop. 134,000. It is the site of a large gold refinery, which serves the Witwatersrand gold-mining region.

**Ge·ro·na** |hä'rōnə| industrial city in NE Spain, on the Oñar River, NE of Barcelona. Pop. 67,000. It is the capital of Gerona province.

**Ge·ta·fe** |he'täfä| industrial and market center in central Spain, near Madrid. Pop. 135,000.

**Geth·sem·a·ne** |,geTH'semənē| biblical garden, between Jerusalem and the Mount of Olives, the scene of the agony of Jesus and his betrayal.

**Get·tys·burg** |'getēz,bərg| historic agricultural and commercial borough in S central Pennsylvania, scene of a critical Civil War battle in July 1863. Pop. 7,025.

**Gey·sir** |'gäsir| (also **Great Geysir**) hot spring in SW Iceland, active in the 1890s, that gave its name to the term *geyser*.

**Ge·zi·ra, El** |,el jə'zērə| (also **Al Jazirah**) region of central Sudan, S of Khartoum, between the White Nile and Blue Nile, a center of irrigated agriculture.

**Gha·da·mis** |gə'dämis| (also **Ghadames** or **Ghudamis**) oasis town in W Libya, on the Algerian border and near the Tunisian border. Pop. 52,000.

**Gha·ga·ra Ri·ver** |gə'gärə; 'gägərə| (also **Gogra**; Nepalese **Karnali**) river in S central Asia that flows 570 mi./900 km. from SW Tibet through Nepal into India, where it joins the Ganges River.

**Gha·na** |'gänə| republic of W Africa, with its S coastline on the Atlantic. Area: 92,100 sq. mi./238,537 sq. km. Pop. 16,500,000. Languages, English (official), W African languages. Capital and largest city: Accra. Known as the Gold Coast 1874–1957, Ghana was the first British African colony to gain independence. It produces cacao,

GERMANY

--- State boundary (Länder)
■ Capital city

0  50  100  150 km
0  25  50  75  100 miles

N

SCHLESWIG-HOLSTEIN

Kiel

BREMEN

MECKLENBURG-WEST POMERANIA

Hamburg
Schwerin
HAMBURG

Bremen

BRANDENBURG

LOWER SAXONY

Berlin
Potsdam
BERLIN

Hanover

Magdeburg

SAXONY-ANHALT

NORTH RHINE-WESTPHALIA

Düsseldorf

SAXONY

Dresden

Erfurt

THURINGIA

HESSE

RHINELAND-PALATINATE

Wiesbaden

Mainz

Saarbrücken

SAARLAND

Stuttgart

BAVARIA

BADEN-WÜRTTEMBERG

Munich

coffee, coconuts, timber, and other crops.
□ **Ghanaian** *adj. & n.*

**Gha·ry·an** |gär'yän| city in NW Libya, S of
Tripoli. Pop. 118,000.

**Ghats** |gawts| two mountain ranges in cen-
tral and S India. Known as *the Eastern Ghats*
and *the Western Ghats,* they run parallel to
the coast on either side of the Deccan
plateau.

**Gha·zi·a·bad** |'gäzēə,bäd| city in N India,
in Uttar Pradesh E of Delhi. Pop. 461,000.

**Ghaz·ni** |'gäznē| commercial city in E cen-

Ghana

tral Afghanistan, SW of Kabul. Pop. 33,000. It is famous for sheepskin coats.

**Ghent** |gent| city in Belgium, capital of the province of East Flanders. Pop. 230,200. Founded in the 10th century, it became the capital of the medieval principality of Flanders. It was formerly known in English as Gaunt (surviving in names, e.g., John of Gaunt). Flemish name **Gent**.

**Ghet·to** |'getō| term for a section of a city where residents of a particular race or ethnic identity are forced to live. The term was first used for a site in 16th-century Venice, Italy (*ghetto is the Italian word for 'foundry'*).

**Giant's Cause·way** |'jīənts 'kawz,wā| formation of basalt columns, dating from the Tertiary period, on the N coast of Northern Ireland. It was once believed to be the end of a road made by a legendary giant to STAFFA in the Inner Hebrides, where there is a similar formation.

**Gib·e·on** |'gibēən| biblical town, NW of Jerusalem in the present-day West Bank, whose inhabitants, the Gibeonites, allied themselves with the Israelites under Joshua.

**Gi·bral·tar** |jə'brawltər| British dependency near the S tip of the Iberian Peninsula, at the E end of the Strait of Gibraltar. Area: 2.26 sq. mi./5.86 sq. km. Pop. 28,000. Languages, English (official), Spanish. Occupying a site of great strategic importance, Gibraltar consists of fortified town and military base at the foot of a rocky headland, the **Rock of Gibraltar**. Britain captured it during the War of the Spanish Succession in 1704 and is responsible for its defense, external affairs, and internal security. □ **Gibraltarian** *adj. & n.*

**Gibraltar**

**Gi·bral·tar, Strait of** |jə'brawltər| channel between the S tip of the Iberian Peninsula and N Africa, forming the only outlet of the Mediterranean Sea to the Atlantic. It is some 38 mi./60 km. long and varies in width from 15 mi./24 km. to 25 mi./40 km. at its W extremity.

**Gib·son Desert** |'gibsən| desert region in Western Australia, to the SE of the Great Sandy Desert.

**Gies·sen** |'gēsən| industrial city and rail junction in central Germany, on the Lahn River. Pop. 72,000.

**Gi·fu** |'gē,fōō; gē'fōō| industrial city in central Japan, on the island of Honshu, noted for paper production. Pop. 410,000.

**Gi·jón** |hē'hōn| port and industrial city in N Spain, on the Bay of Biscay. Pop. 260,000.

**Gi·la River** |'hēlə| river that flows 645 mi./1,045 km. from New Mexico across S Arizona to the Colorado River. Phoenix is in its valley.

**Gil·bert and El·lice Island** |'gilbərt ən(d) 'elis| former British colony (1915–75) in the central Pacific, consisting of two groups of islands: the Gilbert Islands, now a part of Kiribati, and the Ellice Islands, now Tuvalu.

**Gil·boa, Mount** |gil'bōə| mountain in NE Israel, in the Samarian highlands above the plain of Esdraelon, where in the biblical account Saul was defeated by the Philistines and killed himself.

**Gil·git** |'gilget| commercial town in the NW Himalayas, controlled by Pakistan, capital of the Gilgit region. Pop. 44,000.

**Gil·ling·ham** |'jiliNGəm| residential town on the Medway estuary SE of London, England. Pop. 94,000.

**Gil·roy** |'gil,roi| agricultural city in W central California, noted for its garlic production. Pop. 31,487.

**Gin·za, the** |'genzə| shopping and entertainment district of Tokyo, Japan.

**Gi·re·sun** |,gērə'sōōn| port city in NE Turkey, on the Black Sea. Pop. 68,000. The capital of Giresun province, it was the ancient Cerasus, whose name, from a famous local product, is the source of the word *cherry*.

**Gi·ronde** |zHē'rawNd| **1** estuary in SW France, formed at the junction of the Garonne and Dordogne rivers, N of Bordeaux, and flowing NW for 45 mi./72 km. into the Bay of Biscay. **2** a department in Aquitaine, SW France. Pop. 1,213,000. Capital, Bordeaux.

**Gis·borne** |'gizbərn| port and resort on the E coast of North Island, New Zealand. Pop. 31,000.

**Gi·te·ga** |gē'tāgə| commercial town in central Burundi, E of Bujumbura. Pop. 102,000.

**Giur·giu** |'jōōrjōō| port city in S Romania, on the Danube River. Pop. 72,000. Giurgiu is linked by bridge with Ruse, Bulgaria.

**Gi·za** |'gēzə| suburban city SW of Cairo in N Egypt, on the W bank of the Nile, site of the Pyramids and the Sphinx. Pop. 2,156,000. Also called **El Giza**; Arabic name **Al Jizah**.

**Gji·ro·ka·stër** |,gyĕrō'kästər| historic city in S Albania, on the Drino River. Pop. 25,000.

**Gla·cier Bay National Park** |'glasHər| preserve in SE Alaska, on the Pacific coast. Extending over an area of 4,975 sq. mi./12,880 sq. km, it contains the terminus of the Grand Pacific Glacier.

**Glad·beck** |'glät,bek| industrial city in W Germany, in the Ruhr district. Pop. 80,000.

**Gla·mor·gan** |glə'mawrgən| former county of S Wales.

**Glar·ner Alps** |'glärnər| (also **Glarner Alps**) range in the Alps, in NE Switzerland between Lake Lucerne and the Rhine River. Glärnissch (9,560 ft./2,914 m.) has one of the steepest faces in the Alps. The commune of Glarus, at the foot of Glärnisch, is the capital of Glarus canton.

**Glas·gow** |'glæz,gō; 'glæsgō| largest city in Scotland on the Clyde River. Pop. 655,000. Formerly a major shipbuilding center and still an important commercial and cultural center. □ **Glaswegian** adj. & n.

**Glas·ton·bury** |'glæstənb(ə)rē; 'glæstən,berē| town in Somerset, SW England. Pop. 7,000. It is the legendary burial place of King Arthur and Queen Guinevere and the site of a ruined abbey held by legend to have been founded by Joseph of Arimathea.

**Glen Canyon** see POWELL, LAKE.

**Glen·coe** |glen'kō| valley in W Scotland, in the Highlands SE of Fort William, scene of a 1692 massacre of Jacobite Macdonald clansmen by soldiers of the Protestant William III.

**Glen·dale**[1] |'glen,dāl| city in S central Arizona, a residential and commercial suburb NW of Phoenix. Pop. 148,134.

**Glen·dale**[2] |'glen,dāl| city in SW California, a commercial and residential suburb N of Los Angeles. Pop. 180,038.

**Glen·da·lough** |'glendə,läKH| (also **Vale of Glendalough**) valley in Wicklow, SE Ireland, noted for its beauty and for its cluster of medieval religious ruins.

**Glen·do·ra** |glen'dawrə| city in SW California, a suburb NE of Los Angeles. Pop. 47,828.

**Glen·ea·gles** |glen'ēgəlz| valley in E Scotland, SW of Perth, site of a noted hotel and golfing center.

**Glen Gar·ry** |glen'gærē| valley in W Scotland, in the Highlands N of Fort William, that gave its name to the *glengarry,* a characteristic Scottish cap.

**Glen More** |glen 'mawr| another name for the GREAT GLEN of Scotland.

**Glen·roth·es** |glen'räTHəs| town in E Scotland, administrative center of Fife region. Pop. 39,000.

**Glit·ter·tind** |'glitər,tin| mountain in Norway, in the Jotunheim range. Rising to 8,104 ft./2,470 m., it is the highest peak in the country.

**Gli·wi·ce** |gli'vĕtsə| mining and industrial city in S Poland, near the border with the Czech Republic. Pop. 214,000.

**Glom·ma river** |'glawmə| longest river in Norway (365 mi./590 km.), rising in the SE and flowing S to the Skagerrak at Frederikstad.

**Glouces·ter**[1] |'glästər; 'glawstər| city in SW England, the county seat of Gloucestershire. Pop. 92,000. It was founded by the Romans, who called it Glevum, in A.D. 96.

**Glouces·ter**[2] |'glästər; 'glawstər| city in NE Massachusetts, on Cape Ann, a famed fishing and resort center. Pop. 28,716.

**Glouces·ter·shire** |'glästərshər; 'glawstərshər| county of SW England. Pop. 521,000; county seat, Gloucester.

**Glynde·bourne** |'glin(d),bawrn| estate in SE England, near Lewes, East Sussex, scene of a famed summer opera festival.

**Gniez·no** |gə'nyeznaw| historic town in W central Poland. Pop. 70,000. It was the first capital of Poland and the site of royal coronations until 1320.

**Goa** |'gōə| state on the W coast of India. Capital: Panaji. Formerly a Portuguese territory, it was seized by India in 1961. It formed a Union Territory with Daman and Diu until 1987, when it was made a state. □ **Goan** adj. & n. **Goanese** adj. & n.

**Go·bi Desert** |'gōbē| barren plateau of S Mongolia and N China. Covering over 500,000 sq. mi./1.2 million sq. km., it is noted for its fossils.

**Go·da·va·ri** |gō'dävərē| river in central India that rises in the state of Maharashtra and flows about 900 mi./1,440 km. SE across the Deccan plateau to the Bay of Bengal.

**God·havn** |'gōTH,hown| (Inuit name **Qeqertarsuaq**) town in W Greenland, on the S coast of the island of Disko.

**Go·doy Cruz** |gōdoi krōōs| city in W Argentina, S of Mendoza. Pop. 180,000. It is a wine-making center.

**Godt·håb** |'gawt,hawp| former name (until 1979) for NUUK, Greenland.

**Godwin-Austen, Mount** |'gädwin 'awstən| former name for K2.

**Go·ge·bic Range** |gō'gēbik| range of iron-bearing hills in the W Upper Peninsula of Michigan and adjacent parts of Wisconsin.

**Goi·â·nia** |goi'änyə| city in S central Brazil, capital of the state of Goiás. Pop. 998,000. Founded as a new city in 1933, it replaced Goiás as state capital in 1942.

**Goi·ás** |goi'äs| state in S central Brazil. Capital: Goiânia.

**Go·lan Heights** |'gō,län 'hīts| range of hills on the border between Syria and Israel, NE of the Sea of Galilee. Formerly under Syrian control, the area was occupied by Israel in 1967 and annexed in 1981. Negotiations for the withdrawal of Israeli troops from the region began in 1992.

**Gol·con·da** |gäl'kändə| historic ruined city in S central India, in Andhra Pradesh state. It was famous for its diamonds.

**Gold Beach** |gōld| name given to the W section of the beach at Normandy where British troops landed on D-day in June 1944. It lies E of Arromanches.

**Gold Coast**[1] |'gōld 'cōst| term for any of various affluent residential or resort districts in the U.S., either in a city like New York or Chicago or along an actual coast, such as that S of Miami, Florida.

**Gold Coast**[2] |'gōld 'cōst| resort region on the E coast of Australia, to the S of Brisbane.

**Gold Coast**[3] |'gōld 'cōst| former name (until 1957) for GHANA.

**Gol·den** |'gōldən| city in N central Colorado, NW of Denver, a mining, brewing, and academic center. Pop. 13,116.

**Gol·den Gate** |'gōldən 'gæt| deep channel connecting San Francisco Bay, California, with the Pacific Ocean, spanned by the Golden Gate suspension bridge (completed 1937).

**Gol·den Horde** |'gōldən 'hawrd| (also **Kipchak Empire**) Mongol empire of the 14th century, centered along the Volga River, with its capital at Sarai, at first near present-day Astrakhan, later near present-day Volgograd. It controlled much of what is now Russia.

**Gol·den Horn** |'gōldən 'hawrn| curved inlet of the Bosporus forming the harbor of Istanbul. Turkish name **Haliç**.

**Gol·den Sands** |'gōldən 'sændz| (Bulgarian name **Zlatni Pyasuti**) resort town in E Bulgaria, on the Black Sea N of Varna.

**Gol·den State** |'gōldən 'stāt| nickname for CALIFORNIA.

**Gol·den Tri·an·gle** |'gōldən 'trī,æ ngəl| region in SE Asia covering parts of Burma, Laos, and Thailand, a major source of opium and heroin.

**Golds·boro** |'gōldz,bərō| city in E North Carolina, a noted tobacco center. Pop. 40,709.

**Gol·go·tha** |'gälgəTHə; gäl'gäTHə| Greek name, from the Hebrew for skull, for CALVARY.

**Go·ma·ti River** |'gawmətē| river in N India, in Uttar Pradesh state, that flows 500 mi./800 km. from the foothills of the Himalayas to join the Ganges River near Varanasi.

**Go·mel** |gaw'm(y)el| Russian name for HOMEL, Belarus.

**Gó·mez Pa·la·cio** |'gōmes pä'läseō| commercial and industrial city in N Mexico, in Durango state, in an agricultural region. Pop. 233,000.

**Go·mor·rah** |gə'mawrə| see SODOM, biblical city.

**Go·na·ïves** |,gōnä'ēv| port town in W Haiti, on the Gulf of Gonâve. Pop. 63,000. The independence of Haiti from France was proclaimed here in 1804.

**Gon·dar** |'gawndər| (also **Gonder**) commercial city in NW Ethiopia, in Amhara province. Pop. 112,000. An historic center for both Christians and Jews (Falashas), it was the capital of Ethiopia before 1855.

**Gond·wa·na·land** |gän'dwänə,lænd| (also **Gondwana**) supercontinent thought to have existed in the S hemisphere before breaking apart into Africa, South America, Antarctica, Australia, the Arabian Peninsula, and the Indian subcontinent.

**Good Hope, Cape of** |gŏŏd 'hōp| mountainous promontory S of Cape Town, South Africa, near the S extremity of Africa. Sighted toward the end of the 15th century by Bartolomeu Dias, it was rounded for the first time by Vasco da Gama in 1497.

**Good·win Sands** |'gŏŏdwin 'sændz| area of sandbanks in the Strait of Dover, SE England. Often exposed at low tide, the sandbanks are a hazard to shipping.

**Go·rakh·pur** |'gawrək,pŏŏr| industrial city in NE India, in Uttar Pradesh near the border with Nepal. Pop. 490,000.

**Go·raz·de** |gə'räzHdə| predominantly Muslim town in E Bosnia and Herzegovina that was attacked repeatedly by Bosnian Serbs in 1993–94 in the ethnic fighting that followed the breakup of Yugoslavia in 1991. Pop. 17,000.

**Gor·bals** |'gawrbəlz| district of Glasgow, Scotland, on the south bank of the Clyde

River, formerly noted for its slums and tenement buildings.

**Gor·di·um** |'gawrdēəm| ancient city of Asia Minor (now NW Turkey), the capital of Phrygia in the 8th and 9th centuries B.C. Alexander the Great here cut the Gordian knot.

**Go·rée Island** |gaw'rā| (French name Île de Gorée) island near Dakar, Senegal, held by various European powers for centuries, and noted as an embarkation point for slaves.

**Gö·reme** |'gawrəmə| valley in Cappadocia in central Turkey, noted for its cave dwellings hollowed out of the soft tufa rock. In the Byzantine era these contained hermits' cells, monasteries, and more than 400 churches.

**Gor·gan** |'gawr'gawn| (formerly **Aster·abad; Astarabad**) town in NE Iran, in the NE foothills of the Elburz Mts. Pop. 162,000.

**Gor·gon·zo·la** |ˌgawrgən'zōlə| village in N Italy, NE of Milan, known for its rich, veined cheese. Pop. 16,000.

**Gori** |'gōrē| industrial city in central Republic of Georgia, on the Kura River. Pop. 62,000.

**Go·ri·zia** |gə'rētsyə| town in NE Italy, NW of Trieste. Pop. 39,000. It is the capital of Gorizia province.

**Gor·ky** |'gawrkē| former name (1932–91) for NIZHNI NOVGOROD, Russia.

**Gor·litz** |'gœr,litz| industrial town in E Germany, on the Neisse River, E of Dresden at the Polish border. Pop. 70,000.

**Gor·lov·ka** |'gawrləfkə| industrial city in SE Ukraine, in the Donets Basin. Pop. 338,000.

**Gorno-Altai** |'gawrnəäl'tī| autonomous republic in S central Russia, on the border with Mongolia. Pop. 192,000. Capital: Gorno-Altaisk.

**Gor·zow Wiel·ko·pol·ski** |'gōzHŏŏf ˌvyelkə'pawlskē| transportation and trade center in W Poland, on the Warthe River. Pop. 121,000.

**Go·saint·han** |ˌgō,sin'tän| (also called **Xi·xabangma Feng**) peak in the Himalayas in S Tibet near Nepal. It is the highest peak entirely within China: 26,287 ft./ 8,012 m.

**Go·shen** |'gōsHən| fertile area of NE ancient Egypt, E of the Nile delta, where the biblical Jacob and his descendants lived on land granted by the pharaoh before the Exodus.

**Gos·port** |'gäs,pawrt| port town in S England, on Portsmouth Harbour in Hamp-

shire. Pop. 70,000. It is a former naval port, now a yachting center.

**Gö·ta·land Canal** |'yœtə,länd| 240-mi./386-km. system of lakes, rivers, and canals in S Sweden, connecting Göteborg and Stockholm. The canals, incorporating 58 locks, make up half the system's length. Built in 1832, they reach a height of 300 ft./91 m.

**Gö·te·borg** |'yœtə,bawr(yə)| Swedish name for GOTHENBURG.

**Go·tha** |'gōtə| city in central Germany, in Thuringia. Pop. 58,000. From 1640 until 1918 it was the residence of the dukes of Saxe-Gotha and Saxe-Coburg-Gotha.

**Go·tham**[1] |'gōtəm| village in Nottinghamshire, England. It is associated with the folk tale *The Wise Men of Gotham*, in which the inhabitants of the village demonstrated cunning by feigning stupidity.

**Go·tham**[2] |'gäTHəm| nickname for New York City, used originally in satires by Washington Irving. □ **Gothamite** *n.*

**Goth·en·burg** |'gäTHən,bərg| seaport in SW Sweden, on the Kattegat strait. Pop. 433,000. It is the second-largest city in Sweden. Swedish name **Göteborg**.

**Got·land** |'gawt,länt; 'gät,lænd| island and province (including neighboring smaller islands) of Sweden, in the Baltic Sea. Pop. 57,000. Capital: Visby.

**Go·to Is·lands** |'gōtō| (also called **Goto·retto**) island group in SW Japan, in the East China Sea off W Kyushu.

**Göt·ting·en** |'gœtiNGən| town in N central Germany, on the Leine River. Pop. 124,000. It is noted for its university.

**Gou·da** |'gŏŏdə| market town in the Netherlands, just NE of Rotterdam. Pop. 66,000. It is noted for its cheese.

**Gough Island** |gawf; gäf| island in the S Atlantic, S of Tristan da Cunha. In 1938 it became a dependency of the British Crown Colony of St. Helena.

**Go·ver·na·dor Va·la·da·res** |ˌgŏŏvərnə'dawr ˌvälə'däris| industrial and commercial city in SE Brazil, in Minas Gerais state. Pop. 231,000.

**Go·zo** |'gawdzō| Maltese island, to the NW of the main island of Malta.

**Grace·land** |'gräsländ; 'grās,lænd| home and burial place of Elvis Presley, a major tourist attraction in Memphis, Tennessee.

**Gra·cias a Di·os, Cape** |'gräsēäs ä'dēaws| cape forming the easternmost extremity of the Mosquito Coast in Central America, on the border between Nicaragua and Honduras. Its name in Spanish means thanks (be) to God. It was so named by

Columbus, who, becalmed off the coast in 1502, was able to continue his voyage with the arrival of a following wind near this point.

**Gra·ham Land** |'grääm| the N part of the Antarctic Peninsula, the only part of Antarctica lying outside the Antarctic Circle. Discovered in 1831–2 by the English navigator John Biscoe (1794–1843), it now forms part of British Antarctic Territory, but is claimed also by Chile and Argentina.

**Gra·ian Alps** |'grään; 'grïən| W range of the Alps, along the French-Italian border S of Mont Blanc. It reaches 13,323 ft./4,061 m. at Gran Paradiso, in Italy.

**Gram·pi·an** |'græmpēən| former local government region in NE Scotland, dissolved in 1996.

**Gram·pi·an Mountains**[1] |'græmpēən| mountain range in SE Australia, in Victoria. It forms a large part of the Great Dividing Range at its W extremity.

**Gram·pi·an Mountains**[2] |'græmpēən| mountain range in N central Scotland. Its S edge forms a natural boundary between the Highlands and the Lowlands.

**Gra·na·da**[1] |grə'nädə| city in Nicaragua, on the NW shore of Lake Nicaragua. Pop. 89,000. Founded by the Spanish in 1523, it is the oldest city in the country.

**Gra·na·da**[2] |grə'nädə| city in Andalusia in S Spain. Pop. 287,000. Founded in the 8th century, it became the capital of the Moorish kingdom of Granada in 1238. It is the site of the Alhambra.

**Gran·by** |'grænbē| city in S Quebec, E of Montreal. Pop. 42,804.

**Gran Ca·na·ria** |,gräNGkə'näryə| volcanic island off the NW coast of Africa, one of the Canary Islands of Spain. Its chief town, Las Palmas, is the capital of the Canaries.

**Gran Cha·co** |grän 'CHäcō| (also **Chaco**) a lowland plain in central South America, extending from S Bolivia through Paraguay to N Argentina.

**Gran Co·lom·bia** |,grän kə'lōmbēə| country formed in NW South America in 1819, from lands liberated from Spanish rule. It comprised present-day Colombia, Venezuela, Panama, and Ecuador, and dissolved in 1830.

**Grand Ba·ha·ma** |bə'hämə; bə'hämə| fourth-largest island in the Bahamas, in the NW. Freeport is its chief town. Grand Bahama is a tourist center.

**Grand Banks** |grænd 'bæŋks| submarine plateau of the continental shelf off the SE coast of Newfoundland, Canada. It is a meeting place of the warm Gulf Stream and the cold Labrador Current; this promotes the growth of plankton, making the waters an important feeding area for fish.

**Grand Canal**[1] |,grand kə'næl| series of waterways in E China, extending from Beijing S to Hangzhou, a distance of 1,060 mi./1,700 km. Its original purpose was to transport rice from the river valleys to the cities. Its construction proceeded in stages between 486 B.C. and A.D. 1327.

**Grand Canal**[2] |grand kə'næl| the main waterway of Venice, Italy. It is lined on each side by fine palaces and spanned by the Rialto Bridge.

**Grand Can·yon** |grand 'kænyən| deep gorge in Arizona, formed by the Colorado River. It is about 277 mi./440 km. long, 5 to 15 mi./8 to 24 km. wide, and, in places, 6,000 ft./1,800 m. deep. The area was designated a national park in 1919.

**Grand Canyon of the Snake** another name for HELL'S CANYON.

**Grand Cou·lee Dam** |grænd 'koolē| dam on the Columbia River in E central Washington, completed in 1942.

**Grande Com·o·ro** |,gränd kaw'mawr| largest·island of the Comoros, off the NW coast of Madagascar. Pop. 233,500. Chief town (and capital of the Comoros), Moroni.

**Grande-Terre** |gräND'ter| second largest of the islands that make up the French department of Guadeloupe, in the E West Indies. The department's largest town, Point-à-Pitre, is here.

**Grand Forks** |'grænd 'fawrks| city in NE North Dakota, on the Red River of the North and the Minnesota line. Pop. 49,425.

**Grand Island** |grænd ,īlənd| commercial and industrial city in S central Nebraska. Pop. 39,386.

**Grand Junction** |græn(d) 'jəNGkSHən| city in W Colorado, at the junction of the Colorado (formerly the Grand) and Gunnison rivers. Pop. 29,034.

**Grand Port·age** |grænd 'pawrtij| historic locality in NE Minnesota, on Lake Superior, where early traders began a portage around the falls of the Pigeon River.

**Grand Prairie** |grænd 'prärē| industrial city in NE Texas, between Dallas and Fort Worth. Pop. 99,616.

**Grand Pré** |'græn 'prä| historic locality in W central Nova Scotia, on the Minas Basin, scene of the 1755 expulsion of Acadians recounted in *Evangeline.*

**Grand Rapids** |grænd 'ræpədz| industrial

city in SW Michigan, on the Grand River, noted for its furniture production. Pop. 189,126.

**Grand Strand** |grænd 'strænd| name for the NE coast of South Carolina, site of many resorts including Myrtle Beach.

**Grand Te•ton National Park** |grænd 'tē-,tän| preserve in NW Wyoming, just S of Yellowstone National Park, named for the highest of its peaks. Jackson Hole is here.

**Gran•ite State** |'grænit| nickname for NEW HAMPSHIRE.

**Gran Sas•so d'Ita•lia** |grän 'säsō dē'tälyə| limestone massif in E central Italy, in the Apennine range. Its highest peak is the Corno Grande (9,554 ft./2,914 m.). It has the only glacier in the Apennines.

**Gran•ta** |'græntə| alternate name for the Cam River, England.

**Gras•mere** |'græs,mir| village in Cumbria, NW England, beside a small lake of the same name. Pop. 1,000. William and Dorothy Wordsworth lived here.

**Grasse** |gräs| town near Cannes in SE France, center of the French perfume industry. Pop. 42,000.

**Graves** |gräv| district in the department of Gironde, SW France, extending from the banks of the Garonne River to S of Bordeaux. It is known for its wines.

**Graves•end** |gräv'zend| (official name **Gravesham**) industrial town in SE England, in the Thames estuary E of London, in Kent. Pop. 90,000. It is the burial place of Pocahontas.

**Grave•yard of the At•lan•tic** nickname for CAPE HATTERAS, noted for the many shipwrecks that have occurred near it.

**Grays Harbor** |grāz 'härbər| inlet of the Pacific Ocean in W Washington, just S of the Olympic Peninsula, a noted fishing and lumbering area.

**Graz** |gräts| industrial city in S Austria, on the Mur River, capital of the state of Styria. Pop. 232,000. It is the second-largest city in Austria.

**Great Aus•tra•lian Bight** |aw'strālyən 'bīt| wide bay on the S coast of Australia, part of the S Indian Ocean.

**Great Bar•rier Reef** |'bærēər| coral reef in the W Pacific, off the coast of Queensland, Australia. It extends for about 1,250 mi./2,000 km., roughly parallel to the coast, and is the largest coral reef in the world.

**Great Basin** |'bāsən| arid region of the western U.S. between the Sierra Nevada and Rocky Mts., including most of Nevada and parts of the adjacent states. Death

Valley and the Great Salt Lake are within the Basin.

**Great Bear Lake** fourth-largest North American lake, in the Northwest Territories, Canada. It drains into the Mackenzie River via the Great Bear River.

**Great Brit•ain** |grāt 'britn| England, Wales, and Scotland considered as a unit. The name is also often used loosely to refer to the United Kingdom. Wales was politically incorporated with England in the 16th century, and in 1604 James I, the first king of both England and Scotland, was proclaimed 'King of the Great Britain'; this name was adopted at the Union of the English and Scottish Parliaments in 1707. In 1801 Great Britain was united with Ireland (from 1921, only Northern Ireland) as the United Kingdom.

**Great Dis•mal Swamp** |'dizməl| (also **Dismal Swamp**) an area of swampland in SE Virginia and NE North Carolina.

**Great Divide** popular name for the CONTINENTAL DIVIDE in the western U.S.

**Great Di•vi•ding Range** mountain system in E Australia. Curving roughly parallel to the coast, it extends from E Victoria to N Queensland. Also called **Great Divide**.

**Great•er An•til•les** |än'tilēz| see ANTILLES.

**Great•er Lon•don** |'ləndən| metropolitan area comprising central London and the surrounding regions. It is divided administratively into the City of London, thirteen inner London boroughs, and nineteen outer London boroughs. Pop. 6,379,000.

**Great•er Man•ches•ter** |'mæn,CHestər; 'mænCHəstər| metropolitan county of NW England including the city of Manchester and adjacent areas. Pop. 2,445,000.

**Great•er Sun•da Islands** |'soondə| see SUNDA ISLANDS.

**Great Falls** |fawlz| industrial city in N central Montana, on the Missouri River. Pop. 55,097.

**Great Glen** |glen| large fault valley in Scotland, extending from the Moray Firth SW for 60 mi./37 km. to Loch Linnhe, and containing Loch Ness. Also called **Glen More**.

**Great In•di•an Desert** |'indēən| another name for the THAR DESERT.

**Great Lakes** |grāt lāks| group of five large interconnected lakes in central North America, consisting of Lakes Superior, Michigan, Huron, Erie, and Ontario, and constituting the largest area of fresh water in the world. Lake Michigan is wholly within the U.S., and the others lie on the Canada–U.S. border. Connected to the Atlantic by the St. Lawrence Seaway, the Great Lakes form an important commercial waterway.

**Great Lakes–St. Law·rence Seaway** |'lawrəns| waterway in North America that flows 2,342 mi./3,768 km. from near Duluth, Minnesota through the Great Lakes and along the course of the St. Lawrence River to the Atlantic. A number of artificial sections bypass rapids in the river. It is open along its entire length to oceangoing vessels; it was inaugurated in 1959.

**Great Plain** see ALFOLD.

**Great Plains** vast area of plains to the E of the Rocky Mts. in North America, extending from the valley of the Mackenzie River in Canada to S Texas. The North Slope of Alaska is considered an extension of the Plains. Areas closer to the Rockies and of higher elevation are called the High Plains.

**Great Rift Valley** large system of rift valleys in E Africa and the Middle East, forming the most extensive such system in the world and running for some 3,000 mi./4,285 km. from the Jordan valley in Syria, along the Red Sea into Ethiopia, and through Kenya, Tanzania, and Malawi into Mozambique. It is marked by a chain of lakes and a series of volcanoes, including Mount Kilimanjaro.

**Great St. Ber·nard Pass** |'sänt bər'närd| see ST. BERNARD PASS.

**Great Salt Lake** salt lake in N Utah, W of Salt Lake City, in the Great Basin. With an area of some 1,000 sq. mi./2,590 sq. km., it is the largest salt lake in North America.

**Great Sand Sea** area of desert in NE Africa, on the border between Libya and Egypt.

**Great Sandy Desert**[1] large tract of desert in N central Western Australia.

**Great Sandy Desert**[2] another name for the RUB' AL KHALI, chiefly in Saudi Arabia.

**Great Slave Lake** fifth-largest (11,030 sq. mi./28,568 sq. km.) North American lake, in the Northwest Territories. The deepest lake in North America, it reaches 2,015 ft./615 m. The Mackenzie River flows out of it.

**Great Smoky Mountains** |'smōkē| (also **Smoky Mountains** or **Smokies**) range of the Appalachian Mts. in SW North Carolina and E Tennessee. A noted tourist attraction, they are named for a frequent haze.

**Great Vic·to·ria Desert** |vik'tawrēə| desert region of Australia, which straddles the boundary between Western Australia and South Australia.

**Great Wall of Chi·na** former defensive wall in N China, extending 4,187 mi./6,700 km. from Gansu province to Yellow Sea NE of Beijing. The first wall was constructed by unifying existing smaller walls during the Qin dynasty c.210 B.C., and the present wall dates largely from the Ming dynasty (1368–1644). The intent was to keep nomadic invaders, chiefly Mongols, from attacking.

**Great Whale River** |(h)wāl| (French name **Grande Rivière de la Baleine**) river that flows 365 mi./590 km. W across NW Quebec to Hudson Bay, subject of recent controversy over power development.

**Great White Way** nickname for the theater district of BROADWAY, New York City.

**Great Zim·ba·bwe** |zim'bäbwə| complex of stone ruins in a fertile valley in Zimbabwe, about 175 mi./270 km. S of Harare, discovered by Europeans in 1868. They are the remains of a city that was the center of a flourishing civilization in the 14th and 15th centuries. The circumstances of its decline and abandonment are unknown.

**Greece** |grēs| republic in SE Europe, on the Aegean, Mediterranean, and Ionian seas. Area: 50,488 sq. mi./130,714 sq. km. Pop. 10,269,000. Language, Greek. Capital and largest city: Athens. Official name: **The Hellenic Republic.** Greek name: **Ellás.** A great power and center of culture in the 5th century B.C., Greece passed through two thousand years of eclipse and domination by Macedonians, Romans, Turks, and others before gaining independence in 1830. It is now both agricultural and industrial, and its cultural history draws visitors. □ **Greek** adj. & n.

Greece

**Gree·ley** |'grēlē| agricultural and commercial city in N central Colorado. Pop. 60,536.

**Green Bay** |'grēn 'bā| industrial port city in NE Wisconsin, on Green Bay, an inlet of Lake Michigan. Pop. 96,466.

**Green Gab·les** |'grēn 'gābəlz| home of the fictional Anne of Green Gables, on Prince Edward Island. Sites identified with her story are now tourist attractions.

**Green·land** |'grēnlənd| largest island (840,325 sq. mi./2.2 million sq. km.) in the world, lying to the NE of North America and mostly within the Arctic Circle. Pop. 55,000. Capital: Nuuk (Godthåb). Danish name **Grønland**; called in Inuit **Kalaallit Nunaat**. □ **Greenlander** n.

Greenland

**Green·land Sea** |'grēnlənd| sea that lies between the E coast of Greenland and the Svalbard archipelago, forming part of the Arctic Ocean.

**Green Mountains** |grēn| range of the Appalachians that extends N to S through Vermont, reaching 4,393 ft./1,340 m. at Mount Mansfield.

**Green Mountain State** |grēn| nickname for VERMONT.

**Green·ock** |'grēnək| port in W central Scotland, on the Firth of Clyde. Pop. 55,000.

**Green River** |grēn| river that flows 730 mi./1,130 km. from Wyoming through Colorado and Utah, into the Colorado River.

**Greens·boro** |'grēnz,bərə| city in N central North Carolina. Pop. 183,521. Textiles are its best-known manufacture.

**Green·ville**[1] |'grēn,vil; 'grēnvəl| city in NW Mississippi, in the Delta. Pop. 45,226.

**Green·ville**[2] |'grēn,vil; 'grēnvəl| industrial city in NW South Carolina. Pop. 58,282.

**Green·wich**[1] |'grenicH; 'grēn| town in SW Connecticut, on Long Island Sound. Pop. 58,441. It is chiefly an affluent New York suburb.

**Green·wich**[2] |'grenicH; 'grēn,wicH| London borough on the S bank of the Thames, the original site of the Royal Greenwich Observatory. Pop. 201,000. The prime meridian (0° longitude) is here, and Green-

wich Time is the standard from which times around the world are determined.

**Green·wich Village** |'grenicH 'vilij; 'grenij| district of New York City on the Lower West Side of Manhattan, traditionally associated with writers, artists, and musicians.

**Greifs·wald** |'grifs,fält| port and manufacturing city in NE Germany, near the Baltic Sea. Pop. 66,000.

**Gre·na·da** |grə'nädə| republic in the West Indies, consisting of the island of Grenada (the southernmost of the Windward Islands) and the S Grenadine Islands. Area: 133 sq. mi./345 sq. km. Pop. 94,800. Languages, English (official), English Creole. Capital: St. George's. Colonized by the French and British, Grenada became independent in 1974. Agriculture and tourism are important to its economy. □ **Grenadian** adj. & n.

Grenada

**Gren·a·dine Islands** |,grenə'dēn| (also **the Grenadines**) a chain of small islands in the Caribbean, part of the Windward Islands. They are divided administratively between ST. VINCENT AND THE GRENADINES and GRENADA.

**Gre·no·ble** |grə'nawbl(ə)| industrial, resort, and academic city in SE France, in the Dauphiné Alps. Pop. 154,000.

**Gresh·am** |'gresHəm| city in NW Oregon, a suburb E of Portland. Pop. 68,235.

**Gret·na Green** |'gretnə 'grēn| village in Scotland just N of the English border, near Carlisle, formerly a popular place for runaway couples from England to be married without the parental consent required in England for people under a certain age.

**Gri·mal·di Caves** |gri'mäldē| resort village near Ventimiglia, NW Italy, at the French border. Prehistoric remains, including human skeletons, have been found in caves here.

**Grims·by** |'grimzbē| fishing port in NE England, on the S of the Humber estuary.

Pop. 89,000. Official name **Great Grimsby.**

**Grin·del·wald** |'grindəl,vält| Alpine resort in S central Switzerland, in the Jungfrau region of the Bernese Alps. Pop. 4,000.

**Gri·qua·land** |'grēkwə,lænd| former territory of S South Africa, created in 1862 by the mixed-race Griquas and annexed to the Cape Province in 1879–80. Kokstad and Kimberly are the chief towns in the area.

**Gris-Nez, Cape** |grē 'nā| headland, N France, extending into the Strait of Dover 15 mi./24 km. SW of Calais. It is the point in France closest to Great Britain.

**Gri·sons** |grē'zawN| mountainous canton in SW Switzerland. Pop. 170,000. Its capital is Chur. The canton includes several popular ski resorts, including Saint Moritz and Davos.

**Grod·no** |'grawdnə| Russian name for HRODNA, Belarus.

**Gro·ning·en** |'grōniNGən| commercial and industrial city in the N Netherlands, capital of a province of the same name. Pop. 169,000.

**Gros·se·to** |grō'sātō| market center and capital of Grosseto province, W central Italy, in the Maremma coastal region. Pop. 71,000.

**Gross·glock·ner** |'grōs,glawknər| the highest mountain in Austria, in the E Tyrolean Alps, rising to 12,457 ft./3,797 m.

**Grot·on** |'grätn| town in SE Connecticut, on the Thames River and Long Island Sound. Pop. 45,144. It is noted for the manufacture of submarines.

**Group of Sev·en** name given to seven leading industrial nations, as when they meet to discuss international policy. Members are the U.S., Japan, Germany, France, the United Kingdom, Italy, and Canada. They are also called the **G-7** or **G7.**

**Groz·ny** |'grawznē; 'gräznē| city in SW Russia, near the border with Georgia, capital of Chechnya. Pop. 401,000.

**Gru·dziadz** |'grōō,jawnts| port and industrial city in N central Poland, on the Vistula River. Pop. 100,000.

**Gru·yère** |grĭ'yer; grē'yer| village in W Switzerland, SW of Fribourg. The well-known hard cheese was first made here.

**Gryt·vi·ken** |'grit,vēkən| the chief settlement on the island of South Georgia, in the South Atlantic, a former whaling station.

**Gstaad** |gə'sHtät| winter-sports resort in W Switzerland.

**Gua·da·la·ja·ra**¹ |,gwädl-ə'härə| second-largest city in Mexico, an industrial, com-

mercial, and arts center and the capital of the state of Jalisco, in the W central part. Pop. 2,847,000.

**Gua·da·la·ja·ra**² |,gwädl-ə'härə| commercial city in central Spain, to the NE of Madrid, the capital of Guadalajara province. Pop. 67,000.

**Gua·dal·ca·nal** |,gwädlkə'næl| island in the W Pacific, the largest of the Solomon Islands. Pop. 71,000. During the World War II it was the scene of the first major U.S. offensive against the Japanese (August 1942).

**Gua·dal·quiv·ir** |,gwädlki'vir| river of Andalusia in S Spain. It flows for 410 mi./657 km. through Cordoba and Seville to reach the Atlantic NW of Cadiz.

**Gua·da·lu·pe Hi·dal·go** |'gwädl-ōōp(ä)hi-'dälgō| name for part of present-day GUSTAVO MADERO, central Mexico. The Basilica de Guadalupe, a shrine to Our Lady of Guadalupe, and the object of pilgrimages since the 1550s, is here.

**Gua·da·lu·pe Mountains** |'gwädl,ōōp; ,gwädl'ōōpē| range in W Texas and S New Mexico. Guadalupe Peak (8,749 ft./2,668 m.) is the highest point in Texas. The Carlsbad Caverns are in the New Mexico section.

**Gua·de·loupe** |,gwädl'ōōp| group of islands in the Lesser Antilles, forming an overseas department of France. Pop. 387,000 (1991). Languages, French (official), French Creole. Capital: Basse-Terre. □ **Guadeloupian** adj. & n.

Guadeloupe

**Gua·dia·na** |gwä'dyänə| river of Spain and Portugal. Rising in a plateau region SE of Madrid, it flows SW for some 360 mi./580 km., entering the Atlantic at the Gulf of Cadiz. For the last part of its course it forms the border between Spain and Portugal.

**Gual·la·ti·ri** |,gwäyə'tirē| volcano in N Chile, in the Andes along the Bolivian border. At 19,892 ft./6,063 m., it is the highest active volcano in South America.

**Guam** |gwäm| the largest and southernmost of the Mariana Islands, administered as an unincorporated territory of the U.S. Pop. 133,152. Languages, English (official), Austronesian languages. Capital: Agaña. Guam was ceded to the U.S. by Spain in 1898. □ **Guamanian** *adj. & n.*

Guam

**Gua·na·ba·ra Bay** |ˌgwänəˈbärə| (also **Rio de Janeiro Bay**) inlet of the S Atlantic in SE Brazil. Rio de Janeiro lies on its SW.

**Gua·na·cas·te** |ˌgwänəˈkästə| region of NW Costa Rica, E of the Cordillera de Guanacaste, that draws tourists to Pacific resorts and wildlife preserves.

**Gua·na·jua·to** |ˌgwänəˈhwätō| **1** state of central Mexico. Area: 11,777 sq. mi./30,491 sq. km. Pop. 3,890,000. **2** its capital city. Pop. 45,000. The city developed as a silver-mining and silver-working center after 1558.

**Guang·dong** |ˈgwäNGˈdo͝oNG| (also **Kwangtung**) a province of S China, on the South China Sea. Pop. 63.64 million. Capital: Guangzhou (Canton).

**Guang·xi Zhuang** (formerly **Kwangsi**) autonomous region, S China, on the border with Vietnam. Pop. 39.46 million. Capital: Nanning.

**Guang·zhou** |ˈgwäNGˈjō| (also **Kwangchow**) a city in S China, the capital of Guangdong province. Pop. 3,918,000. It is one of the leading industrial and commercial centers of S China. Also called **Canton**.

**Guan·tá·na·mo Bay** |gwänˈtänəˌmō| bay on the SE coast of Cuba. It is the site of a U.S. naval base established in 1903, the source of U.S. and Cuban disputes in recent decades. The city of **Guantanamo**, pop. 200,000, is to the W.

**Gua·po·ré** |ˌgwäpəˈrä| river that flows NW for 1,090 mi./1,745 km. from SW Brazil, forming much of the Brazil-Bolivia border, to the Mamoré River.

**Gua·ru·lhos** |gwäˈro͞olyo͞os| industrial and

commercial city in SE Brazil, a suburb NE of São Paulo. Pop. 973,000.

**Gua·te·ma·la** |ˌgwäteˈmälə| republic in Central America, bordering on the Pacific and with a short coastline on the Caribbean Sea. Area: 42,056 sq. mi./108,889 sq. km. Pop. 10,621,200. Language, Spanish. Capital and largest city: Guatemala City. A Mayan land, Guatemala was a Spanish colony 1523–1828. It has a largely agricultural economy. □ **Guatemalan** *adj. & n.*

Guatemala

**Gua·te·ma·la City** |ˌgwätəˈmälə| the capital of Guatemala. Pop. 1,167,000. Situated at an altitude of 4,920 ft./1,500 m. in the central highlands, the city was founded in 1776 to replace the former capital, Antigua Guatemala, which was destroyed by an earthquake in 1773. The largest Central American city, it is an industrial and commercial center.

**Gua·via·re River** |gwävˈyärä| river that flows 650 mi./1,040 km. E from the Andes in Colombia to join the Orinoco River at the Venezuelan border.

**Gua·ya·quil** |ˌgwīəˈkēl| industrial city in Ecuador, the country's principal port and second-largest city. Pop. 1,877,000.

**Guay·mas** |ˈgwīmäs| port city in NW Mexico, in Sonora state, on the Gulf of California. Pop. 87,000. It is a resort and the port for Hermosillo, to the N.

**Guay·na·bo** |gwiˈnäbō| community in NE Puerto Rico, a suburb S of San Juan. Pop. 73,385.

**Guelph** |gwelf| industrial and academic city in S Ontario. Pop. 87,976.

**Guer·ni·ca** |ˈgerˈnēkə| town in Vizcaya, one of the Basque Provinces of N Spain, to the E of Bilbao. Pop. 18,000. Formerly the seat of a Basque parliament, it was bombed in 1937, during the Spanish Civil War, by German planes in support of Franco, an event depicted in a famous painting by Picasso. Full name **Guernica y Luno**.

**Guern·sey** |ˈgərnzē| island in the English

Channel, to the NW of Jersey. Pop. 59,000. Capital: St. Peter Port. It is the second-largest of the Channel Islands.

**Guer·re·ro** |gə'rerō| state of SW central Mexico, on the Pacific coast. Area: 24,828 sq. mi./64,281 sq. km. Pop. 2,622,000. Capital: Chilpancingo.

**Gui·a·na** |gē'änə| region in N South America, bounded by the Orinoco, Negro, and Amazon rivers and the Atlantic. It now comprises Guyana, Suriname, French Guiana, and the Guiana Highlands.

**Gui·a·na Highlands** |gē'änə 'hīləndz| mountainous plateau region of N South America, lying between the Orinoco and Amazon River basins, largely in SE Venezuela and northern Brazil. Its highest peak is Roraima (9,094 ft./2,774 m.).

**Guild·ford** |'gildfərd| largely residential cty in S England, in Surrey. Pop. 63,000.

**Gui·lin** |'gwē'lin| (also **Kweilin**) a city in S China, on the Li River, in the autonomous region of Guangxi Zhuang. Pop. 552,000.

**Gui·ma·rães** |ˌgēmə'rīNSH| city in NW Portugal. Pop. 48,000. It was the first capital of Portugal.

**Guin·ea** |'ginē| republic on the W coast of Africa. Area: 94,962 sq. mi./245,857 sq. km. Pop. 6,909,300. Languages, French (official), Fulani, Malinke, and other languages. Capital and largest city: Conakry. Part of the medieval Fulani empire, Guinea was a French colony before independence in 1958. Mining and agriculture are central to its economy. See also GUINEA-BISSAU and EQUATORIAL GUINEA. □ **Guinean** *adj. & n.*

**Guinea**

**Guin·ea, Gulf of** |'ginē| large inlet of the Atlantic along the S coast of West Africa.

**Guinea-Bissau** |ˌginēbi'sow| republic on the W coast of Africa, between Senegal and Guinea. Area: 13,953 sq. mi./36,125 sq. km. Pop. 1,000,000. Languages, Portuguese (official), W African languages, Creoles. Capital and largest city: Bissau. A Portuguese colony and slave trade center, Guinea-Bissau gained independence in 1974. Fishing and tropical agriculture are key to its economy.

**Guinea-Bissau**

**Gui·púz·coa** |gē'pŏŏTHkəwə| smallest of the three Basque provinces in N Spain. Pop. 676,000. The capital is San Sebastian.

**Guise** |gēz| town in N France. Pop. 7,000. It gave its name to the dukes of Guise, the ruins of whose 16th-century castle still exist.

**Gui·yang** |'gwē'yäng| (also **Kweiyang**) an industrial city in S China, capital of Guizhou province. Pop. 1,490,000.

**Gui·zhou** |'gwē'jō| (also **Kweichow**) mountainous province of S China. Pop. 32.4 million. Capital: Guiyang.

**Gu·ja·rat** |ˌgŏŏjə'rät| state in W India, with an extensive coastline on the Arabian Sea. Capital: Gandhinagar. Formed in 1960 from the N and W parts of the former state of Bombay, it is one of the most industrialized parts of the country. □ **Gujarati** *adj. & n.*

**Guj·ran·wa·la** |'gŏŏjrən'wälə| city in Pakistan, in Punjab province, NW of Lahore. Pop. 597,000. It was the birthplace of the Sikh ruler Ranjit Singh, and was an important center of Sikh influence in the early 19th century.

**Guj·rat** |gŏŏj'rät| city in Pakistan, in Punjab province, N of Lahore. Pop. 154,000.

**Gu·lag Archipelago** |'gŏŏˌläg| name given to the chain of forced-labor camps (gulags) that operated in Russia 1918–1956. Alexander Solzhenitsyn, the Russian Nobelist, wrote a book under this title, documenting the existence of the gulag and the horrific conditions there.

**Gul·bar·ga** |ˌgŏŏlbər,gä| city in S central India, in the state of Karnataka. Pop. 303,000. Formerly the seat of the Bahmani kings of the Deccan (1347–c.1424), it is now a center of the cotton trade.

**Gulf of Aden, Gulf of Boo·thia** |'adn,

'bŏŏTHēə| for entries beginning thus, see under the other name element, e.g., ADEN, GULF OF; BOOTHIA, GULF OF.

**Gulf In·tra·coast·al Water·way** route that allows sheltered boat passage along the coast of the Gulf of Mexico between Key West, Florida, and Brownsville, Texas.

**Gulf·port** |'gəlf,pawrt| city in S Mississippi, on the Gulf of Mexico W of Biloxi. Pop. 40,775.

**Gulf States**[1] |'gəlf| the states bordering on the Persian Gulf (Iran, Iraq, Kuwait, Saudi Arabia, Bahrain, Qatar, the United Arab Emirates, and Oman).

**Gulf States**[2] |'gəlf| the states of the U.S. bordering on the Gulf of Mexico (Florida, Alabama, Mississippi, Louisiana, and Texas).

**Gulf Stream** |'gəlf| warm ocean current that flows from the Gulf of Mexico N along the American coast toward Newfoundland, continuing across the Atlantic Ocean toward NW Europe as the North Atlantic Drift.

**Gul·ja** |'gŏŏljə| see YINING, China.

**Gun·ni·son River** |'gənəsən| river that flows 180 mi./290 km. through W Colorado to the Colorado River. It is noted for its "Black Canyon."

**Gun·tur** |gŏŏn'tŏŏr| historic commerical city in E India, in Andhra Pradesh. Pop. 471,000.

**Gup·ta Em·pire** |'gŏŏptə| empire of the Hindu Gupta dynasty (4th to 6th centuries) in territory roughly equivalent to present-day N India.

**Gur·kha** |'gŏŏrkə; 'gərkə| (also **Gorkha**) area in E central Nepal known for its fighting men, many of whom served with distinction in the British and Indian armies.

**Gu·ryev** |'gŏŏryəf| (also known as **Atyraū**) **1** administrative subdivision in Kazakhstan. Pop. 447,000. **2** its capital, a seaport town. Pop. 157,000.

**Gus·ta·via** |gŏŏst'ävyə| capital of the French island of Saint-Barthélémy, in the Leeward Islands, West Indies.

**Gu·ters·loh** |'gȳtərz,lō| industrial city in NW Germany. Pop. 84,000.

**Guy·ana** |gī'änə| country on the NE coast of South America. Area: 83,082 sq. mi./214,969 sq. km. Pop. 737,950. Languages, English (official), English Creole, Hindi. Capital and largest city: Georgetown. Official name **Cooperative Republic of Guyana**. Occupied by the British

Guyana

1796–1966, and known as British Guiana, Guyana produces sugar, rice, bauxite, timber, and fish. Its interior is largely tropical forest. □ **Guyanese** *adj. & n.*

**Guy·enne** |gē'en| (also **Guienne**) region and former province of S France, stretching from the Bay of Biscay to the SW edge of the Massif Central.

**Gwa·li·or** |'gwälē,awr| industrial city in Gwalior district in Madhya Pradesh, central India. Pop. 693,000. Noted for its 6th-century fortress.

**Gwent** |gwent| former county of SE Wales, formed in 1974 from most of Monmouthshire, part of Breconshire, and Newport, and dissolved in 1996.

**Gwe·ru** |'gwārŏŏ| (formerly **Gwelo**) city in central Zimbabwe. Pop. 128,000. It is a commercial and rail center in a mining district.

**Gwyn·edd** |'gwinəTH| **1** county of NW Wales, formed in 1974 from Anglesey, Caernarfonshire, part of Denbighshire, and most of Merionethshire and re-formed in 1996 with a smaller area; administrative center, Caernarfon. **2** a former principality of North Wales. Powerful in the mid-13th century under Llewelyn, it was subjugated by the English forces of Edward I in 1282.

**Gyan·dzhe** |gyän'jä| Russian name for GĂNCĂ, Azerbaijan.

**Györ** |dyœr| (German **Raab**) city in NW Hungary near the border with Slovakia. Pop. 131,000. It is a transportation hub and an industrial center.

**Gyum·ri** |'gyŏŏmrē| industrial city in NW Armenia, close to the border with Turkey. Pop. 123,000. Founded as a fortress in 1837, the city was destroyed by an earthquake in 1926 and again in 1988. It was formerly called Aleksandropol (1840–1924) and Leninakan (1924–91). Russian name **Kumayri**.

# Hh

**Haar·lem** |ˈhärləm| city in the Netherlands, near Amsterdam. Pop. 148,000. It is the capital of the province of North Holland and the center of the Dutch bulb industry.

**Haar·lem·mer·meer** |ˈhärləmərˌmēr| (also known as **Hoofddorp**) city in W Netherlands, built on land reclaimed from the Harlem Meer, a branch of the Zuider Zee. Pop. 98,000.

**Ha·bi·ki·no** |hä'bēkēˌnō| city in W central Japan, on S Honshu, SSE of Osaka. Pop. 115,000.

**Habs·burg** |ˈhäps,boŏrk; ˈhæps,bərg| castle in N Switzerland, near the Aare River. Built c. 1030, it was the family seat of the counts of Habsburg, whose descendants ruled various countries, including Germany and Austria, for nearly 700 years.

**Ha·chi·no·he** |ˌhäCHē'nōhä| industrial and commercial port city in N Japan, on N Honshu. Pop. 241,000.

**Ha·chi·o·ji** |ˌhäCHē'ōjē| industrial city in E central Japan, on E central Honshu, W of Tokyo. Pop. 466,000. It is noted for its silk-weaving

**Hack·en·sack** |ˈhækən,sæk| city in NE New Jersey, E of Paterson. Pop. 37,049.

**Hack·ney** |ˈhæk,nē| industrial and residential borough of NE London, England, just N of Tower Hamlets. Pop. 164,000. It probably gave its name to the *hackney* or *hack*, a horse-drawn cab.

**Ha·da·no** |hä'dänō| commercial city in E central Japan, on central Honshu, SW of Tokyo. Pop. 156,000.

**Ha·dhra·maut** |ˌhädrə'mawt| narrow region on the S coast of Yemen, separating the Gulf of Aden from the desert land of the S Arabian peninsula.

**Ha·dri·an's Wall** |ˈhädrēənz| defensive wall across N England, from the Solway Firth in the W to the mouth of the Tyne River in the E, built by the Romans in the 2nd century to protect against attacking N tribes.

**Hae·ju** |ˈhī'jōō| industrial port city in SW North Korea, on the Yellow Sea. Pop. 195,000.

**Ha·fun, Cape** |hä'fōōn| (Arabic name **Ras Hafun**) peninsula in NE Somalia, on the Indian Ocean. At 51° 23′ E, it is the easternmost point in Africa.

**Ha·gen** |ˈhägən| industrial city in NW Germany, in North Rhine-Westphalia. Pop. 214,000.

**Ha·gers·town** |ˈhägərzˌtown| city in NW Maryland. Pop. 35,445.

**Ha·gia So·phi·a** |ˈhäjēə sō'fēə| (also **Saint Sophia**) domed monument of Byzantine architecture in Istanbul, Turkey, built as a Christian church in the 6th century, converted to a mosque in 1453, and a museum since 1935.

**Hague** |hāg| (**The Hague**) the seat of government and administrative center of the Netherlands, on the North Sea coast, capital of the province of South Holland. Pop. 444,000. The International Court of Justice is based here. Dutch name **Den Haag**; also called **'s-Gravenhage**.

**Hai·fa** |ˈhīfə| the chief port of Israel, in the NW on the Mediterranean coast. Pop. 248,000.

**Haight-Ash·bury** |ˈhāt'asH,berē| residential and commercial section of central San Francisco, California, associated with youth culture of the 1960s.

**Hai·kou** |ˈhī'kō| industrial seaport, S China, capital and largest city of the island province of Hainan. Pop. 280,000.

**Ha'il** |hīl| (also **Hail; Hayel**) city in NW Saudi Arabia, on the pilgrimage route from Iraq to Mecca. Pop. 177,000.

**Hai·lar** |ˈhī'lär| market town, Inner Mongolia, NE China, on the Hailar River W of the Da Hinggang Mts. Pop. 185,000.

**Hai·nan** |ˈhī'nän| island province, S China, between the South China Sea and Gulf of Tonkin. Pop. 6.42 million. Capital: Haikou.

**Hai·naut** |a'nō| province of S Belgium, N of the Ardennes. Pop. 77,000. Capital: Mons.

**Hai·phong** |ˈhī'fawNG| industrial port in northern Vietnam, on the delta of the Red River in the Gulf of Tonkin. Pop. 783,000. It was damaged during the Vietnam War.

**Hai River** |hī| (Chinese name **Hai He**) river in E China that flows 677 mi./1,090 km. from the Taihang Shan range to the Bo Hai E of Tianjin.

**Hai·ti** |ˈhātē| republic in the Caribbean, occupying the W third of the island of Hispaniola. Area: 10,718 sq. mi./27,750 sq. km. Pop. 7,041,000. Official languages, Haitian Creole, French. Capital and largest city: Port-au-Prince. A French colony 1697–1804, Haiti gained independence through a slave rebellion. A series of dictatorships and U.S. domination have charac-

Haiti

terized its history. Tropical fruits and baux-ite are leading products, but the country is poor. Its culture is strongly African. □ **Hai-tian** *adj. & n.*

**Hajj** |häj| (also **Hadj**) the pilgrimage to Mecca, Saudi Arabia, that each Muslim is required to make once in a lifetime. JEDDAH is a major port on the pilgrimage, which also flows through the airports of Arabia.

**Ha·ko·da·te** |ˌhäkōˈdätä| port in N Japan, on the S tip of the island of Hokkaido. Pop. 307,000.

**Ha·ko·ne** |häˈkōnä| mountain resort in E central Japan, on E central Honshu. Pop. 19,000. It is in the center of Fuji-Hakone-Izu National Park, in an area famous for its hot springs and scenic beauty.

**Ha·lab·ja** |häˈlobzHə| (also **Alabja**) Kurdish town in NE Iraq, close to the Iranian border, where thousands died during a gas attack by Iraqi planes in 1988.

**Ha·le·a·ka·la** |ˌhälä,äkəˈlä| dormant volcano on E Maui, Hawaii that draws many visitors.

**Hales·o·wen** |ˌhālˈzōən| engineering town in the West Midlands of England, W of Birmingham. Pop. 58,000.

**Ha·liç** |häˈlēcH| Turkish name for GOLDEN HORN.

**Hal·i·car·nas·sus** |ˌhælikärˈnæsəs| ancient Greek city on the SW coast of Asia Minor, at what is now the Turkish city of Bodrum. It was the birthplace of the historian Herodotus and the site of the Mausoleum of Halicarnassus, one of the Seven Wonders of the World.

**Hal·i·fax**[1] |ˈhæləˌfæks| industrial town in N England, on the Calder River, formerly in Yorkshire. Pop. 77,000.

**Hal·i·fax**[2] |ˈhæləˌfæks| historic port city, the capital of Nova Scotia. Pop.114,455. It is Canada's principal ice-free port on the Atlantic coast.

**Hal·lan·dale** |ˈhælənˌdäl| resort city in SE Florida, N of Miami. Pop. 30,996.

**Hal·le** |ˈhälə| city in east central Germany, on the Saale River, in Saxony-Anhalt. Pop. 303,000. HALLE-NEUSTADT (pop. 91,000) is just NE.

**Hall·stadt** |ˈhäl,sHtät| (also **Hallstatt**) village in W central Austria. Graves from as early as c. 1000 B.C. have been discovered here. The site gave its name to the Hallstadt culture of the Iron Age.

**Hal·ma·he·ra** |ˌhälmə'herə| the largest of the Molucca Islands of Indonesia.

**Halm·stad** |ˈhälm,städ| seaport in SW Sweden, on the Kattegat, capital of Halm-stad county. Pop. 81,000.

**Häl·sing·borg** |ˈhelsiNG,bawr(yə)| Swedish name for HELSINGBORG.

**Ha·ma** |ˈhämä| (also **Hamah**) an industri-al city in W Syria, on the Orontes River. Pop. 229,000. It was the center of an Ara-maean kingdom in the 11th century B.C. Much of the modern city was destroyed during an unsuccessful uprising against the government in 1982.

**Ha·ma·dan** |ˌhämä'dän| commercial city in W Iran, in the Zagros Mts. between Tehran and Bakhtaran. Pop. 350,000. It is on the site of the ancient city of Ecbatana, which became the capital of the kingdom of Media in the 6th century B.C.

**Ha·ma·matsu** |ˌhämä'matsōō| industrial city on the S coast of the island of Honshu, Japan. Pop. 535,000.

**Ham·burg**[1] |ˈhäm,bŏŏrg| industrial port city in N Germany, on the Elbe River. Pop. 1,669,000. Founded by Charlemagne in the 9th century, and largely destroyed by bombing during World War II, it is now the largest port in Germany, with extensive shipyards.

**Ham·burg**[2] |ˈhæm,bərg| town in W New York, containing suburbs S of Buffalo. Pop. 53,735.

**Ham·burg·er Hill** |ˈhæm,bərgər| name given to mountain in central Vietnam, near the border with Laos, where hundreds of American soldiers were killed in a 1969 assault during the Vietnam War.

**Ham·den** |ˈhæmdən| town in S central Connecticut, a residential and industrial suburb on the N side of New Haven. Pop. 52,434.

**Hä·meen·lin·na** |ˌhämän'linä| (Swedish name **Tavastehus**) industrial city in SW Finland, on Lake Vanajavesi. Pop. 43,000.

**Ha·meln** |ˈhäməln| (also **Hamelin**) a town in NW Germany, in Lower Saxony, on the Weser River. Pop. 57,000. A medieval mar-ket town, it is the setting of the legend of the Pied Piper of Hamelin.

**Ham·hung** |'häm'hŏoNG| industrial city in E North Korea. Pop. 775,000. It was the center of government of NE Korea during the Yi dynasty of 1392–1910.

**Ha·mi** |'hä'mē| (also called **Kumul**) city and oasis in Xinjiang, NW China, on the trade route SE from Ürümqi. Pop. 275,000.

**Ham·il·ton**[1] |'hæməl,tən| the capital of Bermuda. Pop. 1,100.

**Ham·il·ton**[2] |'hæməl,tən| township in W central New Jersey, containing suburbs on the SE side of Trenton. Pop. 86,553.

**Ham·il·ton**[3] |'hæməl,tən| city on North Island, New Zealand. Pop. 149,000.

**Ham·il·ton**[4] |'hæməl,tən| industrial city in SW Ohio, N of Cincinnati. Pop. 61,368.

**Ham·il·ton**[5] |'hæməl,tən| port and industrial city in S Ontario, Canada, at the W end of Lake Ontario. Pop. 318,499.

**Ham·il·ton**[6] |'hæməl,tən| town in South Lanarkshire, S Scotland, near Glasgow. Pop. 50,000.

**Hamm** |häm| industrial city in NW Germany, in North Rhine-Westphalia, on the Lippe River. Pop. 180,004.

**Ham·mer·fest** |'hæmər,fest| ice-free port in N Norway, on North Kvaløy island. Pop. 7,000. It is the northernmost town in Europe.

**Ham·mer·smith** |'hæmər,smiTH| industrial and residential district of W London, England, now part of the borough of **Hammersmith and Fulham** (pop. 136,000), on the N side of the Thames. BBC television is based here.

**Ham·mond** |'hæmənd| industrial port city in NW Indiana, on Lake Michigan, SE of Chicago, Illinois. Pop. 84,236.

**Hamp·shire** |'hæmpsHər; 'hæmp,sHir| county on the coast of S England. Pop. 1,512,000; county seat, Winchester.

**Hamp·stead** |'hæm(p),sted| residential suburb of NW London, England, part of the borough of Camden. **Hampstead Heath** is one of the best-known parks in London.

**Hamp·ton**[1] |'hæm(p)tən| district of the borough of Richmond upon Thames, in W Greater London, England, N of the Thames River. **Hampton Court** is a 16th-century palace used by monarchs from Henry VIII through George II.

**Hamp·ton**[2] |'hæm(p)tən| historic city in SE Virginia, in the Hampton Roads complex, on Chesapeake Bay. Pop. 133,793.

**Hamp·ton Roads** |'hæm(p)tən| deep-water estuary 4 mi./6 km. long, formed by the James River where it joins Chesapeake Bay, on the Atlantic coast in SE Virginia.

The ports of Newport News and Hampton are situated on it.

**Hamp·tons, the** |'hæm(p)tənz| cluster of resort villages in E Long Island, New York, including Southampton, East Hampton, and Amagansett.

**Ha·nau** |'hä,now| (full name **Hanau am Main**) river port and industrial city in central Germany, E of Frankfurt on the Main River. Pop. 84,000.

**Han·dan** |'hän'dän| industrial city in S Hebei province, E China, a communications and transportation hub on the Fuyang River N of Anyang. Pop. 1,110,000.

**Han·ford** |'hænfərd| government reservation in Richland, SE Washington, former U.S. plutonium-production site.

**Hang·zhou** |'häNG'jō| (also **Hangchow**) the capital of Zhejiang province in E China, situated on Hangzhou Bay, an inlet of the Yellow Sea, at the S end of the Grand Canal. Pop. 2,589,500.

**Han·ni·bal** |'hænəbəl| port city in NE Missouri, on the Mississippi River. Pop. 18,004. It is noted as the boyhood home of Mark Twain.

**Ha·noi** |hæ'noi| the capital of Vietnam, an industrial city on the Red River in the N of the country. Pop. 1,090,000. It was the capital of French Indochina from 1887 to 1946, and of North Vietnam before the reunification of North and South Vietnam.

**Han·o·ver**[1] |hä'nōvər| **1** industrial city in NW Germany, on the Mittelland Canal. Pop. 517,000. It is the capital of Lower Saxony. German name **Hannover**. **2** a former state and province in northern Germany. In 1714 the Elector of Hanover succeeded to the British throne as George I, and from then until the accession of Victoria (1837) the same monarch ruled both Britain and Hanover. □ **Hanoverian** adj. & n.

**Han·o·ver**[2] |'hæn,ōvər| town in W central New Hampshire, on the Connecticut River. Pop. 9,212. It is home to Dartmouth College.

**Han River** |hän| **1** (Chinese name **Han Shui**) river of E China that flows 952 mi./1,532 km. SE from SW Shaanxi province to the Yangtze River in Hubei province. **2** (Chinese name **Han Jiang**) river in S China, rising in SE Fujian province and flowing 210 mi./338 km. S to the South China Sea at Shantou in Guangdong province.

**Han·se·at·ic League** |,hænsē'ætik| association of N German port cities on the Baltic Sea, founded in the 13th century to enhance trade. Lübeck was its center, and

Hamburg and Bremen major partners. Non-German cities as far away as London and Novgorod were associates. It declined by the 17th century. Member cities were known as **Hanse towns.**

**Han·zhong** |ˈhänˈjo͞oNG| city in Shaanxi province, central China, SW of Xi'an on the N bank of the Han River. Pop. 420,000.

**Ha·ran** |häˈrän| (also **Harran:** ancient name **Charan** or **Carrhae**) historic city in SE Turkey, in Urfa province, near the Syrian border. On Mesopotamian trade routes, it was the scene of several important battles in antiquity.

**Ha·rap·pa** |həˈräpə| ancient city of the Indus valley civilization (c. 2600–1700 B.C.), in N Pakistan. The site of the ruins was discovered in 1920.

**Ha·ra·re** |həˈrärä| the capital, largest city, and commercial center of Zimbabwe. Pop. 1,184,000. Former name (until 1982) **Salisbury**.

**Har·bin** |ˈhärbin; härˈbin| the capital of Heilongjiang province in NE China, an industrial city and rail center on the Songhua River. Pop. 3,597,000.

**Har·dang·er Fjord** |härˈdäNGər| fjord on the SW coast of Norway, extending inland for 75 mi./120 km. It is Norway's second-largest fjord.

**Har·dwar** |ˈhär,dwär| city in Uttar Pradesh, N India, on the Ganges River. Pop. 189,000. It is a place of Hindu pilgrimage.

**Har·fleur** |ärˈflœr| town in N France, at the mouth of the Seine River on the English Channel. Pop. 10,000. Formerly a flourishing port, it lost its importance as its harbor silted up.

**Har·gei·sa** |härˈgäsə| (also **Hargeysa**) commercial city in NW Somalia, former capital of British Somaliland. Pop. 400,000.

**Har·in·gey** |ˈhæriNG,gä| industrial and residential borough of NE London, England, just N of Hackney. Pop. 187,000. Highgate and Tottenham are among its districts.

**Har·lan County** |ˈhärlən| county in the Cumberland Mts. of SE Kentucky, famed scene of strife between coal miners and mine owners. Pop. 36,574.

**Har·lech** |ˈhärlekH| village on the W coast of Wales, in Gwynedd. It is noted for the ruins of its 13th-century castle.

**Har·lem** |ˈhärləm| district of New York City, situated to the N of 96th Street in NE Manhattan. It has long had a large black population, and from the 1920s was noted for its musical and night life. The literary and artistic movement known as the Harlem

Renaissance flourished here after World War I. □ **Harlemite** n.

**Har·ley Street** |ˈhärlē| street in central London, England, where many eminent physicians and surgeons have consulting rooms.

**Har·lin·gen** |ˈhärlinjən| city in S Texas, NW of Brownsville. Pop. 48,735. It is the hub of a vegetable-producing region.

**Har·low** |ˈhärlō| town in W Essex, SE England, N of London. Pop. 80,000.

**Har·ney Peak** |ˈhärnē| peak in the Black Hills of SW South Dakota. At 7,242 ft./2,209 m., it is the highest in the U.S. E of the Rocky Mts.

**Har·pers Ferry** |ˈhärpərz| town in Jefferson County, West Virginia, at the confluence of the Potomac and Shenandoah rivers. Pop. 308. In October 1859 John Brown and a group of abolitionists briefly captured a Federal arsenal here, hoping to spur a slave rebellion.

**Har·ris** |ˈhæris| the S part of the island of Lewis and Harris in the Outer Hebrides of Scotland, famous for its tweeds.

**Har·ris·burg** |ˈhærəs,bərg| the state capital of Pennsylvania, on the Susquehanna River in the central part. Pop. 52,376. The nearby nuclear power station at Three Mile Island suffered a serious accident in 1979.

**Har·ri·son·burg** |ˈhærisən,bərg| commercial and academic city in N Virginia, in the Shenandoah Valley. Pop. 30,707.

**Har·rods·burg** |ˈhærədz,bərg| historic city in central Kentucky. Pop. 7,335. Established in 1774, it was the first English settlement W of the Allegheny Mts.

**Har·ro·gate** |ˈhærə,gät| town in N England, in N Yorkshire, N of Leeds. Pop. 69,000. It is a noted spa.

**Har·row** |ˈhærō| largely residential borough of NW Greater London, England. Pop. 194,000. The Harrow School was founded here in 1572. □ **Harrovian** adj. & n.

**Hart·ford** |ˈhärtfərd| the state capital of Connecticut, on the Connecticut River in the central part. Pop. 139,739. An industrial city, it is also an insurance center.

**Har·tle·pool** |ˈhärtlē,poōl| port on the North Sea coast of NE England, in Cleveland. Pop. 92,000.

**Har·wich** |ˈhærij; ˈhæriCH| ferry port in Essex, on the North Sea coast of SE England. Pop. 17,000.

**Ha·ry·a·na** |,härēˈänə| state of N India. Pop. 16.32 million. Capital: Chandigarh. It was formed in 1966, largely from Hindi-speaking parts of the former state of Punjab.

**Harz Mountains** |härtz| range of mountains in central Germany, the highest of which is the Brocken. The mountains figure in much folklore.

**Has·selt** |'häsəlt| city in NE Belgium, on the Demer River, capital of the province of Limburg. Pop. 67,000.

**Has·tings**[1] |'hästiNGz| resort and residential town in SE England, in East Sussex, one of the Cinque Ports, on the English Channel. Pop. 75,000. The Battle of Hastings (1066) was fought nearby at BATTLE.

**Has·tings**[2] |'hästiNGz| industrial city in New Zealand, on North Island, near Napier. Pop. 58,000.

**Ha·to Rey** |'ätō'rā| district of central San Juan, Puerto Rico, site of much of the Commonwealth's business activity.

**Hat·ter·as, Cape** |'hætərəs| peninsula in E North Carolina. The treacherous waters around it have been called "the Graveyard of the Atlantic."

**Hat·ties·burg** |'hætēz,bərg| industrial, commercial, and academic city in SE Mississippi. Pop. 41,882.

**Hat·tu·sa** the capital of the ancient Hittite Empire, situated in present-day central Turkey about 22 mi./35 km. E of Ankara.

**Hau·sa·land** |'howsə,lænd| historical name for the highland regions of N Nigeria that were home to the Hausa people and language before the 19th century. Kano was the chief town.

**Haute-Garonne** |,ōtgä'rōn| department in S France, in the Midi-Pyrénées region. Pop. 926,000. The capital city is Toulouse.

**Haute-Normandie** |,ōt,nawrmäN'dē| region of N France, on the coast of the English Channel, including the city of Rouen.

**Haute-Saône** |,ōt'sōn| department in E France, in the Franche-Comté region. Pop. 230,000. The area is largely agricultural. The capital is Vesoul.

**Haute-Vienne** |,ōt'vyen| department in central France, in the Limousin region. Pop. 354,000. The capital city is Limoges.

**Haut-Rhin** |ō'reN| department in E France, in the Alsace region. Pop. 671,000. The capital city is Colmar.

**Hauts-de-Seine** |,ōdə'sen| department in central France, in the Île-de-France region. Pop. 1,392,000. The capital city is Nanterre.

**Ha·va·na** |,hə'vænə| the capital and chief port of Cuba, on the N coast. Pop. 2,160,000. It was founded in 1519, and is an industrial center with a tourist industry beginning to recover from isolation since the 1959 Cuban revolution. Spanish name **La Habana**.

**Hav·ant** |'hævənt| engineering town in SE Hampshire, England. Pop. 50,000.

**Ha·va·su, Lake** |'hævə,sōō| reservoir and recreational site on the Colorado River between Arizona and SE California. **Lake Havasu City** (pop. 24,363), in Arizona, is home to the reconstructed 19th-century London Bridge.

**Ha·ver·hill** |'hav(ə)rəl| industrial city in NE Massachusetts, on the Merrimack River. Pop. 51,418.

**Ha·ver·ing** |'havəriNG| easternmost borough of Greater London, England, N of the Thames River. Pop. 224,000. It is mostly residential.

**Ha·waii** |hə'wä(y)ē| see box. □ **Hawaiian** *adj. & n.*

**Ha·worth** |'haw-wərTH| town in N Eng-

---

### Hawaii

**Capital/largest city:** Honolulu

**Other cities:** Aiea, Kailua, Kaneohe, Pearl City

**Population:** 1,108,229 (1990);1,193,001 (1998); 1,342,000 (2005 proj.)

**Population rank (1990):** 41

**Rank in land area:** 43

**Abbreviation:** HI; Haw.

**Nicknames:** Aloha State; Paradise of the Pacific

**Motto:** *Ua mau ke ea o ka aina i ka pono* (Hawaiian: 'The Life of the Land is Perpetuated in Righteousness')

**Bird:** nene or Hawaiian goose

**Fish:** humuhumunukunukuapuaa

**Flower:** pua aloalo (hibiscus)

**Tree:** kukui or candlenut

**Song:** "Hawaii Ponoi"

**Noted physical features:** Halawa, Kamohio, Kaneohe, Kawaihae, Kiholo, Mamala, Maunalua, Pohue, Waiagua bays; Waikiki Beach; Waimea Canyon; Aua, Kaiwi, Kalohi, Pailolo channels; Kilauea and Punchbowl craters; Kau Desert; Pearl Harbor; Diamond Head; Iao and Manoa valleys; Haleakala, Kilauea, Mauna Kea, Mauna Loa volcanos

**Tourist attractions:** Lahaina; Haleakala National Park; Hawaiian volcanos; Pearl Harbor; *U.S.S. Arizona* Memorial

**Admission date:** August 21, 1959

**Order of admission:** 50

**Name origin:** Possibly derived from the native Polynesian word meaning 'homeland.'

land, in W Yorkshire, N of Halifax, noted as the home of the Brontë sisters, the writers.

**Haw·thorne** |'haw,THawrn| city in SW California, an industrial suburb S of Los Angeles. Pop. 71,349.

**Hay·mar·ket Square** |'hā,märkət| historic site in Chicago, Illinois, site of an 1886 bombing during a labor demonstration.

**Hay·ward** |'hāwərd| city in N central California, S of Oakland on San Francisco Bay. Pop. 111,498.

**Heard and Mc·Don·ald Island** |hərd ænd mik'dänld| group of uninhabited islands in the S Indian Ocean, administered by Australia since 1947 as an external territory.

**Heart** |härt| commercial and industrial city in W Afghanistan. Pop. 177,000.

**Heath·row** |'hēTHrō| international airport situated 15 mi./25 km. W of the center of London, England, in the borough of Hillingdon.

**He·bei** |'hə'bā| (also **Hopeh**) a province of NE central China. Pop. 61.08 million. Capital: Shijiazhuang.

**Heb·ri·des** |'hebrə,dēz| group of about 500 islands off the NW coast of Scotland. Also called **Western Isles**. The **Inner Hebrides** include the islands of Skye, Mull, Jura, Islay, Iona, Coll, Eigg, Rhum, Staffa, and Tiree. The Little Minch separates this group from the **Outer Hebrides**, which include the islands of Lewis and Harris, North and South Uist, Benbecula, Barra, and the isolated St. Kilda group. Norse occupation has influenced the language, customs, and place names, although most of the present-day population have Celtic affinities and Gaelic is still spoken on several of the islands. □ **Hebridean** adj. & n.

**He·bron** |'hēbrən| Palestinian city on the West Bank of the Jordan. Pop. 75,000. As the home of Abraham it is a holy city of both Judaism and Islam. Israeli forces withdrew from all but a small part of the city in 1997.

**Heer·len** |'herlən| industrial city and transportation center in the SE Netherlands, near Maastricht. Pop. 95,000.

**He·fei** |'hə'fā| (also **Hofei**; formerly **Luchow**) an industrial city in E China, capital of Anhui province. Pop. 1,541,000.

**He·gang** |'hə'gäNG| city in Heilongjiang province, NE China, NE of Harbin. Pop. 650,000.

**Hei·del·berg** |'hīdl,bərg| city in SW Germany, on the Neckar River, in Baden-Württemberg. Pop. 139,000. Its famed university received its charter in 1386 and is the oldest in Germany.

**Heil·bronn** |'hīl,brän| industrial city in SW Germany, a port on the Neckar River, in Baden-Württemberg. Pop. 117,000.

**Hei·long Jiang** |'hī'lōōNG jē'äNG| see AMUR RIVER, China.

**Hei·long·jiang** |'hī'lōōNG jē'äNG| (formerly **Heilungkiang**) province of NE China, on the Russian border, the most northerly Chinese province. Pop. 35.22 million. Capital: Harbin.

**He·jaz** |he'jæz| (also **Hijaz**) coastal region of W Saudi Arabia, extending along the Red Sea. Mecca and Medina are here.

**Hek·la** |'heklə| intermittently active volcano in SW Iceland, rising to 4,840 ft./1,491 m.

**Hel·e·na** |'helənə| the state capital of Montana, a former mining center, in the W central part. Pop. 24,569.

**Hel·go·land** |'helgə,lænd| German name for HELIGOLAND.

**Hel·i·con , Mount** |'helə,kän| mountain in Boeotia, central Greece, to the N of the Gulf of Corinth, rising to 5,741 ft./1,750 m. It was believed by the ancient Greeks to be the home of the Muses.

**Hel·i·go·land** |'helə,gō,lænd| small island in the North Sea off the coast of Germany, one of the North Frisian Islands. The island was Danish from 1714 until seized by the British navy in 1807 and later ceded officially to Britain. In 1890 it was returned to Germany. German name **Helgoland**.

**He·li·op·o·lis[1]** |,helē'äpələs| ancient Egyptian city situated near the apex of the Nile delta at what is now Cairo. It was the original site of the obelisks known as Cleopatra's Needles.

**He·li·op·o·lis[2]** |,helē'äpələs| ancient Greek name for BAALBEK, Lebanon.

**Hel·las** |'heləs| Greek name for GREECE.

**Hel·les·pont** |'helə,spänt| the ancient name for the Dardanelles, after the legendary Helle, who fell into the strait and was drowned while escaping with her brother Phrixus from their stepmother, Ino, on a golden-fleeced ram.

**Hell's Canyon** |helz| chasm in Idaho, cut by the Snake River and forming the deepest gorge in the U.S. Flanked by the Seven Devils Mts., the canyon drops to a depth of 7,900 ft./2,433 m.

**Hell's Kit·chen** |helz| former neighborhood in W Manhattan, New York City, noted for its violence. Times Square is nearby. The area is now called Clinton.

**Hel·mand** |'helmənd| the longest river in Afghanistan. Rising in the Hindu Kush, it flows 700 mi./1,125 km., generally SW, before emptying into marshland near the Iran–Afghanistan border.

**Hel·sing·borg** |'helsiNG,bawr(yə)| port in S Sweden, on the Øresund opposite Elsinore in Denmark. Pop. 109,000. Swedish name **Hälsingborg**.

**Hel·sing·fors** |'helsiNG,fawrz| Swedish name for HELSINKI, Finland.

**Hel·sing·ør** |,helsiNG'œr| Danish name for ELSINORE.

**Hel·sin·ki** |,hel'siNGkē| the capital, largest city, and cultural center of Finland, an industrial port in the S on the Gulf of Finland. Pop. 492,000. Swedish name **Helsingfors**.

**Hel·ve·tia** |hel'vēsHə| Latin name for SWITZERLAND.

**Hel·wan** |hel'wän| (also **Hilwan**) industrial city in N Egypt, a suburb S of Cairo and E of the Nile River. Pop. 328,000.

**Hem·el Hemp·stead** |,heməl'hem(p)sted| town in SE England, in Hertfordshire. Pop. 80,000.

**Hem·et** |'hemet| city in S California, SE of Riverside, in an agricultural area. Pop. 36,094.

**Hemp·stead** |'hem(p),sted| town in W Long Island, New York, on the E boundary of Queens, New York City. Pop. 725,639. Hempstead, Rockville Centre, Levittown, and many other suburban villages are here.

**He·nan** |hə'nän| (also **Honan**) a province of N central China. Pop. 85.51 million. Capital: Zhengzhou.

**Hen·der·son** |'hendərsən| city in SE Nevada, SE of Las Vegas, home to a large chemical industry. Pop. 64,942.

**Heng·e·lo** |'heNGə,lō| industrial town in the Netherlands, near the German border. Pop. 76,000.

**Heng·yang** |'həNG'yäNG| city in Hunan province, SE China, on the Xiang River S of Changsha. Pop. 616,000. It is a transportation and industrial center.

**Hen·ley** |'henlē| (also **Henley-on-Thames**) town in SE England, in Oxfordshire, on the Thames River. Pop. 10,000. It is famous as the home of an annual rowing regatta begun in 1839.

**He·rak·li·on** |hə'ræklēən| the capital of Crete, a port on the N coast of the island. Pop. 117,000. Greek name **Iráklion**.

**Hé·rault** |a'rō| department in S France, in the Languedoc region. Pop. 795,000. The capital is Montpellier.

**Her·cu·la·ne·um** |,hərkyə'lānēəm| ancient Roman town, near Naples, on the lower slopes of Vesuvius. The volcano's eruption in A.D. 79 buried it deeply under volcanic ash, along with Pompeii, and thus largely preserved it until its accidental rediscovery by a well digger in 1709.

**Her·e·ford** |'herəfərd| city in W central England, administrative center of Herefordshire, on the Wye River. Pop. 50,000.

**Here·ford and Worce·ster** |'herəfərd ən 'wŏŏstər| former county of W central England, formed in 1974 from the counties of Herefordshire and Worcestershire, which were reinstated in 1998.

**Here·ford·shire** |'herəfərd,sHir; 'herəfərd-sHər| county of W central England, between 1974 and 1998 part of the county of Hereford and Worcester.

**Her·ford** |'her,fawrt| manufacturing city in NW Germany, on the Werre River. Pop. 62,000.

**Her·mit·age, the¹** |'hərmətij| famed art museum in Saint Petersburg, Russia. It is housed in an adjunct to the Winter Palace constructed in 1764 by Catherine the Great, who started its collection.

**Her·mit·age, the²** |'hərmətij| estate, the home of Andrew Jackson, in central Tennessee, NE of Nashville.

**Her·mon, Mount** |'hərmən| the S part of the Anti-Lebanon range on the Syria-Lebanon border.

**Her·mo·sillo** |,ermō'sēyō| city in NW Mexico, an agricultural trade center and capital of the state of Sonora. Pop. 449,000.

**Herne** |hern| port and industrial city in NW Germany, NE of Essen, on the Rhine-Herne Canal. Pop. 179,000.

**Her·ning** |'herniNG| manufacturing city in Jutland, central Denmark. Pop. 57,000. It is an important textile center.

**Her·shey** |'hərsHē| village in SE Pennsylvania, created by Hershey, the chocolate manufacturer. Pop. 11,860. It is a popular tourist destination.

**Her·stal** |'her,stäl| industrial city in E Belgium. Pop. 38,000. The birthplace of Pepin II, it is now a center of the armament industry.

**Her·ten** |'hertn| manufacturing city in NW Germany, N of Essen. Pop. 70,000.

**Hert·ford** |'härtfərd| the county seat of Hertfordshire, England. Pop. 21,000.

**Hert·ford·shire** |'härtfərd,sHir; 'härtfərd-sHər| county of SE England, one of the Home Counties, NW of London. Pop. 952,000; county seat, Hertford.

**Her·ze·go·vi·na** |,hertsə'gōvənə| (also **Hercegovina**) a region in the Balkans forming the S part of BOSNIA AND HERZEGOVINA and separated from the Adriatic by part of Croatia. Its chief town is Mostar. □ **Herzegovinian** *adj. & n.*

**Her·zliy·ya** |ˌhɛrtsəˈlēyə| (also **Hertseliya; Herzliya; Herzlia**) resort city in central Israel. Pop. 84,000. It was named after the founder of Zionism, Theodor Herzl.

**Hes·pe·ria** |heˈspirēə| city in S California, a suburb N of San Bernardino. Pop. 50,418.

**Hes·per·i·des, Garden of the** |heˈsperə ˌdēz| in Greek myth, land where the daughters of Atlas guarded a tree with golden apples, at the westernmost extreme of the world; the garden is conflated with the mythical Islands of the Blessed, or Western Islands, a vision of paradise.

**Hesse** |ˈhes(ə)| state of western Germany. Pop. 5,600,000. Capital: Wiesbaden. German name **Hessen**. □ **Hessian** *adj. & n.*

**He·ze** |ˈhəˈzə| (also called **Caozhou**) city and transportation center in W Shandong province, E China, S of the Yellow River. Pop. 1,017,000.

**Hi·a·le·ah** |ˌhīəˈlēə| city in SE Florida, a largely Hispanic suburb NW of Miami. Pop. 188,004.

**Hib·bing** |ˈhibiNG| city in NE Minnesota, a mining center in the Mesabi Range. Pop. 18,046.

**Hi·ber·nia** |hīˈbərniə| Latin and literary name for Ireland. □ **Hibernian** *adj. & n.*

**Hick·o·ry** |ˈhik(ə)rē| city in W central North Carolina, noted for its furniture industry. Pop. 28,301.

**Hicks·ville** |ˈhiks,vil| village in central Long Island, New York, the commercial hub of a suburban area. Pop. 40,174.

**Hi·dal·go** |ēˈdälgō| state of S Mexico. Pop. 1,881,000. Capital: Pachuca de Soto. Mountainous Hidalgo was long a mining center.

**Hi·ga·shi·hi·ro·shi·ma** |heˈgäsHēheˈrōsHēmä| city in W Japan, on SW Honshu, E of Hiroshima. Pop. 94,000.

**Hi·ga·shi·ku·ru·me** |heˈgäsHēkoōˈroōmä| city in E central Japan, on E central Honshu, a residential suburb of Tokyo. Pop. 114,000.

**Hi·ga·shi·mat·su·ya·ma** |heˈgäsHēmätsoōˈyämä| city in E central Japan, on E central Honshu, a suburb of Tokyo. Pop. 84,000.

**Hi·ga·shi·mu·ra·ya·ma** |heˈgäsHēmoōrä ˈyämä| city in E central Japan, on E central Honshu, NW of Tokyo. Pop. 134,000.

**Hi·ga·shi·o·sa·ka** |heˈgäsHēˈōsäkä| city in W central Japan, on S Honshu, a residential and industrial suburb E of Osaka. Pop. 518,000.

**Hi·ga·shi·ya·ma·to** |heˈgäsHēyäˈmätō|

city in E central Japan, on E central Honshu, N of Shinjuku. Pop. 75,000.

**High·gate** |ˈhī,gāt| largely residential district of NE London, England, part of the borough of Haringey, NE of Hampstead Heath, noted especially for its cemetery.

**High·lands** |ˈhīlən(d)z| region of N Scotland, traditionally the mountainous areas N of a line from Dumbarton in the SW to Stonehaven, near Aberdeen, in the NE. It included the Hebrides and other islands to the W. The present-day **Highland** administrative region covers approximately the N half of Scotland.

**High Plains** see GREAT PLAINS.

**High Point** |ˈhī,point| industrial city in N central North Carolina. Pop. 69,496. Furniture and tobacco are central to its economy.

**High Wy·combe** |hīˈwikəm| industrial town in S England, in Buckinghamshire. Pop. 70,000. It is noted especially for its furniture.

**Hi·güey** town, in the E Dominican Republic, the capital of La Altagracia province. Pop. 84,000.

**Hi·ko·ne** |hiˈkōnä| city in central Japan, on S Honshu, on the E shore of Lake Biwa. Pop. 100,000.

**Hil·den** |ˈhildən| manufacturing city in NW Germany, SE of Düsseldorf. Pop. 55,000.

**Hil·des·heim** |ˈhildəs,hīm| industrial city in Lower Saxony, NW Germany. Pop. 106,000.

**Hill Country** region of S central Texas, NW of San Antonio and the Balcones Escarpment, with many recreational resources.

**Hil·le·rød** |ˈhilə,rœTH| industrial and tourist town in Denmark. Pop. 33,000. It is the site of the notable 17th-century Frederiksborg Castle.

**Hil·ling·don** |ˈhiliNGdən| residential and industrial borough of W Greater London, England. Pop. 226,000. Heathrow Airport is here.

**Hills·bo·ro** |ˈhilz,bərō| commercial and industrial city in NW Oregon. Pop. 37,520.

**Hi·lo** |ˈhēlō| port community in Hawaii, on the N coast of the island of Hawaii. Pop. 37,808.

**Hil·ton Head Island** |ˈhiltn ˈhed| resort island in S South Carolina, one of the Sea Islands.

**Hil·ver·sum** |ˈhilvərsəm| town in the Netherlands, in North Holland province, near Amsterdam. Pop. 85,000. It is the center of the Dutch radio and television network.

**Hi·ma·chal Pra·desh** |hə'mäCHəl prə 'deSH| mountainous state in N India. Pop. 44.82 million. Capital: Simla.

**Hi·ma·la·yas** |,himə'lāəz; hi'mäl(ə)yəz| a vast mountain system in S Asia, extending 1,500 mi./2,400 km. from Kashmir eastward to Assam. It covers most of Nepal, Sikkim, and Bhutan and forms part of the N boundary of the Indian subcontinent. The Himalayas consist of a series of parallel ranges rising up from the Ganges basin to the Tibetan plateau, at over 9,840 ft./3,000 m. above sea level, and include the Karakoram, Zaskar, and Ladakh ranges. The backbone is the Great Himalayan Range, the highest mountain range in the world, with several peaks rising to over 25,000 ft./7,700 m., the highest being Mount Everest. □ **Himalayan** *adj.*

**Hi·ma·may·lan** |,hēmä'mī,län| town in the Philippines, on W Negros, on Panay Gulf. Pop. 81,000.

**Hi·me·ji** |hē'mäjē| industrial city in W central Japan, on S Honshu, WNW of Kobe. Pop. 454,000.

**Hin·den·burg** |'hindən,bərg| former German name (1915–45) for ZABRZE, Poland.

**Hin·den·burg Line** |'hindən,bərg| defensive line established by Germany along its borders with France and Belgium during World War I. Fortifications stretched from Lille SE to Metz.

**Hin·du Kush** |'hindŏŏ'kŏŏSH| range of high mountains in N Pakistan and Afghanistan, forming a W continuation of the Himalayas. Several peaks exceed 20,000 ft./6,150 m., the highest being Tirich Mir.

**Hin·du·stan** |,hindŏŏ'stæn| *hist.* the Indian subcontinent in general, more specifically that part of India N of the Deccan, especially the plains of the Ganges and Jumna rivers.

**Hin·nom** |'hin,äm; 'hinəm| see GEHENNA, biblical site.

**Hi·no** |hēnō| city in E central Japan, on E central Honshu, a residential suburb W of Tokyo. Pop. 166,000.

**Hip·po·crene** |'hipə,krēn; ,hipə'krēnē| spring on Mount HELICON that was, according to Greek mythology, created by Pegasus and considered sacred to the Muses and a source of inspiration.

**Hip·po Re·gi·us** |'hipō 'rējēəs| see ANNABA, Algeria.

**Hi·ra·ka·ta** |,hērä'kätä| city in W central Japan, on S Honshu, near Osaka. Pop. 391,000.

**Hi·ra·tsu·ka** |hē'räts(ə)kä| commercial city

in E central Japan, on E central Honshu, SW of Yokohama. Pop. 246,000.

**Hi·ro·sa·ki** |,hērō'säkē| city in N Japan, on N Honshu, S of Aomori. Pop. 175,000.

**Hi·ro·shi·ma** |,hirə'SHēmə; hə'rōSHəmə| city on the S coast of the island of Honshu, W Japan, capital of Chugoku region. Pop. 1,086,000. It was the target of the first atomic bomb, which was dropped by the United States on August 6, 1945 and resulted in the deaths of about one third of the city's population of 300,000.

**His·pan·io·la** |,hispən'yōlə| island of the Greater Antilles in the Caribbean. After its European discovery by Columbus in 1492, Hispaniola was colonized by the Spanish, who ceded the W part (now Haiti) to France in 1697. The eastern part became the Dominican Republic.

**His·sar·lik** |,hisər'lik| see TROY, ancient city.

**Hi·ta·chi** |hē'täCHē| industrial city in E central Japan, on the E coast of Honshu, NE of Mito. Pop. 202,000.

**Hi·va Oa** |,hēvä 'ōä| volcanic island in the Marquesas Islands, French Polynesia. The commercial center of the Marquesas, it is also the site of the grave of artist Paul Gauguin.

**Hka·ka·bo Ra·zi** |kä'käbō 'räzē| peak in N Burma on an outlier of the Himalayas, on the frontier with China. It is the highest peak in Burma: 19,295 ft./5,881 m.

**Ho·bart** |'hō,bärt| the capital and chief port of Tasmania, Australia. Pop. 127,000.

**Ho·bo·ken** |'hō,bōkən| industrial city in NE New Jersey, on the Hudson River opposite New York City. Pop. 33,397.

**Ho Chi Minh City** |,hōCHē'min| (former name, before 1975: **Saigon**) city and port on the S coast of Vietnam; pop. 3,016,000. It was the capital of the French colony of Cochin China, established in Vietnam in the 19th century, becoming capital of South Vietnam in the partition of 1954. After the communist victory in the Vietnam War, it was renamed. The largest Vietnamese city, it is an industrial center on the Saigon River.

**Ho Chi Minh Trail** |,hōCHē'min| a covert system of trails along Vietnam's W frontier, a major supply route for North Vietnamese forces during the Vietnam War.

**Ho·dei·da** |hō'dädə| the chief port of Yemen, on the Red Sea. Pop. 246,000. Arabic name **Al-Hudayda**.

**Hoek van Hol·land** |,hŏŏk vän 'hawlänt| Dutch name for HOOK OF HOLLAND.

**Hof** |hōf; hawf| town in S Germany, on the Saale River, near the Czech border. Pop.

53,000. Before Germany's reunification in 1990, Hof was a major checkpoint for travelers between East and West Germany.

**Hof·burg** |'hōfbŏórk; 'hawf,bŏŏrg| complex of buildings in Vienna, Austria, including the former imperial palace. It was the seat of government for the emperors of Germany until 1806 and for the rulers of Austria until 1918.

**Ho·fei** |'hə'fā| see HEFEI, China.

**Ho·fu** |'hōfŏŏ| city in W Japan, on SW Honshu, SW of Hiroshima. Pop. 118,000.

**Hog·gar Mountains** |'hägər; hə'gär| mountain range in the Saharan desert of S Algeria, rising to a height of 9,573 ft./2,918 m. at Tahat. Also called **Ahaggar Mountains**.

**Ho·hen·lin·den** |,hōən'lindən| village in S Germany, E of Munich. A French victory here in 1800 over the Austrians helped pave the way to the Peace of Lunéville in 1801.

**Ho·hen·zol·lern** |'hōənt,sälərn| former province of Germany, now part of the state of Baden-Württemberg. The Hohenzollern family ruled the region as emperors of Germany 1871–1918. After 1945 it became part of the state of Württemberg-Hohenzollern, and in 1952 it took its present name.

**Ho·he Tau·ern Mountains** |,hōə'towərn| range in the E Alps, S Austria. The highest peak is Grossglockner: 12,457 ft./3,797 m.

**Hoh·hot** |'hə'hawt| (also **Huhehot**) the capital of Inner Mongolia autonomous region, NE China. Pop. 1,206,000. Former name (until 1954) **Kweisui**.

**Hok·kai·do** |hä'kidō| the most northerly of the four main islands of Japan, constituting an administrative region. Pop. 5,644,000. Capital: Sapporo.

**Hol·guín** |awl'gēn| commercial city in NE Cuba, the capital of Holguín province. Pop. 246,000. Gibara, its port, is to the N.

**Hol·land¹** |'hälənd| **1** another name for the NETHERLANDS. **2** former province of the Netherlands, comprising the coastal parts of the country. It is now divided into **North Holland** and **South Holland**

**Hol·land²** |'hälənd| city in SW Michigan, noted for its Dutch heritage. Pop. 30,745.

**Hol·lan·dia** |hä'lændēə| former name for JAYAPURA, Indonesia.

**Hol·ly Springs** |'hälē| historic city in N Mississippi. Pop. 7,261.

**Hol·ly·wood¹** |'hälē,wŏŏd| resort and retirement city in SE Florida, N of Miami, on the Atlantic. Pop. 121,697.

**Hol·ly·wood²** |'hälē,wŏŏd| district of Los Angeles, the principal center of the American film and television industry.

**Ho·lon** |'hō,län; KHaw'lawn| manufacturing town in W central Israel, part of the Tel Aviv-Jaffa metropolitan area. Pop. 164,000.

**Hol·royd** |'hawl,roid| city in SE Australia, in New South Wales, a residential suburb of Sydney. Pop. 79,000.

**Hol·stein** |'hōl,SHtīn| former duchy of the German kingdom of Saxony, situated in the S part of the Jutland peninsula. A duchy of Denmark from 1474, it was taken by Prussia in 1866 and incorporated with the neighboring duchy of Schleswig as the province of Schleswig-Holstein.

**Hol·y·head** |'hälē,hed| port on Holy Island in Wales, off Anglesey. Pop. 13,000. It is the chief port for ferries between Great Britain and Ireland.

**Ho·ly Island** |'hōlē| another name for LINDISFARNE, England.

**Ho·ly Land** |'hōlē'lænd| region on the E shore of the Mediterranean, in what is now Israel and Palestine, revered by Christians as the place in which Christ lived and taught, by Jews as the land given to the people of Israel, and by Muslims.

**Hol·yoke** |'hōlē,ōk; 'hō(l),yōk| industrial city in W central Massachusetts, NW of Springfield. Pop. 43,704.

**Ho·ly Ro·man Em·pire** |,hōlē ,rōmən 'empīr| empire that was proclaimed in A.D. 800 and formally dissolved in 1806. Established by the papacy to ensure secular rule in Europe, it gradually became a rival centered in Germany, and later in Austria. Its boundaries were in constant flux.

**Hol·y·rood** |'hälē,rŏŏd| 16th-century palace, the official residence of the British monarch in Edinburgh, Scotland.

**Ho·ly See** |'hōlē 'sē| the papal court, or governing center of the Roman Catholic Church, thus often taken as synonymous with the VATICAN CITY.

**Home Counties** |'hōm| the English counties surrounding London, into which London has extended. They comprise chiefly Essex, Kent, Surrey, and Hertfordshire.

**Ho·mel** |haw'm(y)el| industrial city in SE Belarus. Pop. 506,000. Russian name **Gomel**.

**Home·stead** |'hōm,sted| agricultural and suburban city in SE Florida, SW of Miami. Pop. 28,866.

**Homs** |hawmz| (also **Hims**) industrial city in western Syria, on the Orontes River. Pop. 537,000. It was named in 636 by the Muslims and occupies the site of ancient Emesa.

**Ho·nan** |'hō'nän| see HENAN, China.

**Hon•du•ras** |hän'd(y)ŏŏrəs| republic of Central America, bordering on the Caribbean Sea and with a short coastline on the Pacific. Area: 43,294 sq. mi./112,088 sq. km. Pop. 5,294,000. Language, Spanish. Capital and largest city: Tegucigalpa. See also BRITISH HONDURAS. A Spanish colony for over 300 years, Honduras gained independence in 1821. It is primarily agricultural, much of its land undeveloped. Bananas and other tropical crops grow in the lowlands, coffee in the highlands. □ **Honduran** adj. & n.

**Hon•fleur** |awn'flœr| port and resort on the Normandy coast, NW France, on the Seine estuary. Pop. 8,000.

**Hong Kong** |'häNG'käNG; 'hawNG,kawNG| (Chinese name **Xianggang**) special administrative region governed by China, on its SE coast, formerly (until 1997) a British dependency. Area: 414 sq. mi./1,071 sq. km. Pop. 5,900,000. Official languages, English and Cantonese. Capital: Victoria. The area comprises Hong Kong Island, which was ceded by China in 1841, the Kowloon peninsula, ceded in 1860; and the New Territories, additional areas of the mainland that were leased for 99 years in 1898. Hong Kong has become one of the world's major financial and manufacturing centers, with the third-largest container port in the world.

Hong Kong

**Hong•shui** |'həNG,SHwē| (Chinese name **Hongshui He**; formerly **Hungshui River**) river, S China, flowing 900 mi./1,448 km. S and E from EYunnan to join theYou River near Guiping to form the Xi.

**Ho•ni•a•ra** |,hōnē'ärə| port and the capital of the Solomon Islands, on the NW coast of the island of Guadalcanal. Pop. 35,000.

**Hon•o•lu•lu** |,hän-l-'lōō,lōō; ,hōn-l'ōō,lōō| the state capital and principal port of Hawaii, on the SE coast of the island of Oahu. Pop. 365,272.

**Hon•shu** |'hänSHŌŌ| the largest (89,184 sq. mi./230,897 sq. km.) of the four main islands of Japan. Pop. 99,254,000. Tokyo is the chief city.

**Hood, Mount** |'hŏŏd| peak in the Cascade Range in NW Oregon, E of Portland. At 11,239 ft./3,426 m. it is the highest point in the state.

**Hoogh•ly** |'hŏŏg,lē| (also **Hugli**) the most westerly of the rivers of the Ganges delta, in West Bengal, India. It flows for 120 mi./192 km. into the Bay of Bengal and is navigable to Calcutta.

**Hook of Holland** |'hälənd| cape and port of the Netherlands, nearThe Hague, linked by ferry to the British isles. Dutch name **Hoek van Holland**.

**Hoorn** |hawrn| city in the Netherlands, on an inlet of the IJsselmeer. Pop. 58,000. It is a popular yachting center and agricultural market.

**Hoo•sier State** |'hŏŏZHər| nickname for INDIANA.The meaning of *Hoosier* is unclear.

**Ho•peh** |'hō'bä; 'hō'pä| see HEBEI, China.

**Ho•reb, Mount** |'hawr,eb| biblical mountain in Sinai, probably identical with Mount SINAI.

**Hor•liv•ka** |'hawrlivkə| industrial city in SE Ukraine, in the Donets Basin. Pop. 338,000. Russian name **Gorlovka**.

**Hor•muz, Strait of** |'hawrməz;hawr'mōōz| strait linking the Persian Gulf with the Gulf of Oman, which leads to the Arabian Sea, and separating Iran from the Arabian Peninsula. It is of strategic and economic importance as a waterway through which sea traffic to and from the oil-rich states of the Gulf must pass.

**Hor•muz** |'hawrməz; hawr'mōōz| (also **Ormuz**) an Iranian island at the mouth of the Persian Gulf, in the Strait of Hormuz. It is the site of an ancient city, which was an important center of commerce in the Middle Ages.

**Horn, Cape** |'hawrn| the southernmost point of South America, on a Chilean island S of Tierra del Fuego. The region is notorious for its storms, and until the opening of the Panama Canal in 1914 constituted the only sea route between the Atlantic and Pacific. Also called **the Horn**.

**Horn of Af•ri•ca** |'æfrikə| peninsula of NE Africa, comprising Somalia and parts of Ethiopia. It lies between the Gulf of Aden and the Indian Ocean. Also called **Somali Peninsula**.

**horse latitudes** |hawrs| belt of light winds about 30° from the equator in both the N and the S hemispheres, between the westerlies (closer to the equator) and trade winds. Sailing vessels often were becalmed here.

**Hor·sens** |'hawrsəns| port on the E coast of Denmark, situated at the head of Horsens Fjord. Pop. 55,000.

**Hos·pet** |'hōsH,pet| commercial town in S India, in Karnataka state, E of Hubli. Pop. 135,000.

**Hos·pi·ta·let** |,ōspētä'let| (also **Hospitalet de Llobregat**) city and S suburb of Barcelona, in NE Spain. Pop. 269,000.

**Ho·tan** |'haw'tän| (formerly **Khotan**) town in Xinjiang, NW China, an oasis in the foothills of the Kunlun Shan range, on the caravan route on the S edge of the Taklimakan Desert. Pop. 121,000.

**Hot Springs** spa city in central Arkansas. Pop. 32,462.

**Hou·ma** |'hōmə| city in SE Louisiana, in the Cajun Country, SW of New Orleans. Pop. 30,495.

**Houns·low** |'hownz,lō| largely residential borough of W Greater London, England, N of the Thames River. Pop. 193,000.

**Hou·sa·ton·ic River** |,hōōsə'tänik| river that flows 130 mi./210 km. from the Berkshire Hills in W Massachusetts through Connecticut, to Long Island Sound.

**Hous·ton** |'(h)yōōstən| industrial port and the largest city in Texas, linked to the Gulf of Mexico by the Houston Ship Canal, a major oil industry and transshipment center. Pop. 1,630,553. Since 1961 it has been the headquarters for U.S. space research and manned space flight; it is the site of NASA's Johnson Space Center.

**Hove** |'hōv| resort town on the S coast of England, adjacent to Brighton. Pop. 67,000.

**How·land Island** |'howlənd| uninhabited island in the central Pacific, near the equator, held by the U.S. It is a wildlife refuge.

**How·rah** |'howrə| (also **Haora**) heavy industrial city and rail center in E India, on the Hooghly River opposite Calcutta. Pop. 947,000.

**Howth** |hōтн| suburban district of E Dublin, Ireland, a port and resort whose hill dominates the N side of Dublin Bay.

**Hoya** |'hoiə| city in E central Japan, on E central Honshu, a residential suburb of Tokyo. Pop. 95,000.

**Hra·dec Krá·lo·vé** |'hrädets 'krälə,ve| town in the N Czech Republic, capital of East Bohemia region on the Elbe River. Pop. 162,000. German name **Königgrätz**.

**Hrod·na** city in W Belarus, on the Neman River near the borders with Poland and

Lithuania. Pop. 277,000. Russian name **Grodno**.

**Hsin·chu** |'sHin'cHōō| (also **Hsin-chu**) port on the NW coast of Taiwan. Pop. 293,000. The city is an important computer and electronics center.

**Hsü-chou** |'sHY'jō| see XUZHOU, China.

**Hua·cho** |'wäcHō| port city in W central Peru, NW of Lima. Pop. 51,000.

**Huai·bei** |'hwī'bā| industrial city in N Anhui province, E China, SW of Xuzhou. Pop. 1,308,000.

**Huai·hua** |'hwī'hōōä| city in Hunan province, S central China, on a bend of the Wu River. Pop. 436,000.

**Huai·nan** |'hwī'nän| city in the province of Anhui, in E central China, in a mining district. Pop. 1,228,000.

**Huai·yin** |'hwī'yin| city in Jiangsu province, E China, on the Grand Canal N of Yangzhou, and E of Hongze Lake. Pop. 391,000.

**Hua·lla·ga** |wä'yägä| river in central Peru, one of the headwaters of the Amazon. Rising in the central Andes, it flows, generally NE for 700 mi./1,100 km. and emerges into the Amazon Basin at Lagunas.

**Huam·bo** |'wämbō| city in the mountains in W Angola. Pop. 400,000. Founded in 1912, it was known by its Portuguese name of Nova Lisboa until 1978.

**Huan·ca·yo** |wäNG'kīō| commercial city in S central Peru, on the Mantaro River, in a mining district of the Andes. Pop. 97,000.

**Huang Hai** |'hwäNG'hī| Chinese name for the YELLOW SEA.

**Huang He** |'hwäNG'hə| (also **Huang Ho**) see YELLOW RIVER, China.

**Huang·pu** |'hwäNG'pōō| (formerly **Whampoa**) port and industrial city in S Guangdong province, S China, on an island in the Pearl River. Economically tied to Guangzhou (Canton) to its W, it is the site of a military academy founded by the Kuomintang party.

**Huang Shan** |'hwäNG'sHän| (English name **Yellow Mountains**) mountain range in S Anhui province, E China, to the S of the Yangtze River. Its cloud-swept landscape has been popular with Chinese poets and painters.

**Huang·shan** |'hwäNG'sHän| town in S Anhui province, E China, situated N of the Huang Shan range. Pop. 151,000.

**Huang·shi** |'hwäNG'sHē| (formerly **Hwangshih**) industrial city in Hubei province, E central China, on the Yangtze River S of Wuhan. Pop. 458,000. It has iron and steel and other heavy industries.

**Huá·nu·co** |'wänoͦ,kō| commercial city in central Peru, on the Huallaga River in the Andes. Pop. 73,000. It is the capital of Huánuco province, and the ancient Temple of Kotosh is nearby.

**Hua·ráz** |wä'räs| commercial and resort city in W Peru, the capital of Ancash department. Pop. 44,000. HUASCARÁN national park is just W.

**Huas·ca·rán** |wäskä'rän| extinct volcano in the Peruvian Andes, W central Peru, rising to 22,205 ft./6,768 m. It is the highest peak in Peru.

**Hub, the** |həb| popular nickname for Boston, Massachusetts, the "Hub of the Universe."

**Hu·bei** |'hoͦ'ba| (formerly **Hupeh**) province of E central China, mountainous in the N and traversed by the Yangtze River in the S. Pop. 53.97 million. Capital: Wuhan.

**Hub·li** |'hoͦbli| (also **Hubli-Dharwad**) industrial city and rail junction in SW India. Pop. 648,000. It was united with the adjacent city of Dharwad in 1961.

**Hud·ders·field** |'hədərs,fēld| town in N England, formerly in Yorkshire. Pop. 149,000. It is an historic textile center.

**Hud·din·ge** |'hədiNGə| city in E Sweden, a suburb S of Stockholm. Pop. 76,000.

**Hud·son Bay** |'hədsən| body of water in NE Canada. It is the largest inland sea in the world (over 475,000 sq. mi./1.23 million sq. km.) and is connected to the N Atlantic via the Hudson Strait.

**Hud·son River** |'həd,sən| major river of E North America, which rises in the Adirondack Mts. and flows S for 350 mi./560 km. past Albany, where it is connected via the Erie Canal, and into the Atlantic at New York City.

**Hué** |hoͦ'a; (h)wä| industrial port city in central Vietnam, the former (1802–1945) capital. Pop. 219,000.

**Hue·co Mountains** |'wäkō| range in S New Mexico and W Texas, near El Paso, rising to 6,717 ft./2,049 m.

**Huel·va** |'welvə| industrial city and port in S Spain, near the Portuguese border; capital of Huelva province. Pop. 144,000.

**Hues·ca** |'weskə| marketing and industrial town in NE Spain, at the base of the Pyrenees, the capital of Huesca province. Pop. 50,000.

**Hui·zhou** |'hwē'jō| port city in Guangdong province, S China, on the Dong River to the east of Guangzhou (Canton). Pop. 161,000.

**Hull¹** |həl| (official name **Kingston-upon-**

Hull) city and port in NE England, at the junction of the Hull and Humber rivers. Pop. 252,000.

**Hull²** |həl| industrial and administrative city in SW Quebec, across the Ottawa River from Ottawa, Ontario. Pop. 60,707.

**Hum·ber** |'həmbər| estuary in NE England, flowing 38 mi./60 km. E from the junction of the Rivers Ouse and Trent to the North Sea. It has the major port of Hull on its N bank and is spanned by the world's largest suspension bridge, opened in 1981 and having a span of 4,626 ft./1,410 m.

**Hum·ber·side** |'həmbər,sīd| former county of NE England, formed in 1974 from parts of the East and West Ridings of Yorkshire and the N part of Lincolnshire. It was dissolved in 1996.

**Humboldt Current** |'həm,bōlt| another name for the PERUVIAN CURRENT.

**Hum·boldt River** |'həm,bōlt| river that flows 300 mi./480 km. across N Nevada, disappearing in the NW into a basin called the Humboldt Sink.

**Hu·nan** |'hoͦ'nän| province of E central China. Pop. 60.66 million. Capital: Changsha. □ **Hunanese** *adj. & n.*

**Hu·ne·doa·ra** |'hoͦnä,dwärä| industrial city in W central Romania. Pop. 86,000.

**Hun·ga·ry** |'həNGgə,rē| republic in central Europe. Area: 35,934 sq. mi./93,033 sq. km. Pop. 10,600,000. Language, Hungarian (Magyar). Capital and largest city: Budapest. Hungarian name **Magyarország**. Settled by the Magyars in the 9th century, Hungary came under the Habsburgs in the 17th century, and gained independence in 1918. It was a communist state from the end of World War II until 1989. Once chiefly agricultural, it is increasingly industrial. □ **Hungarian** *adj. & n.*

Hungary

**Hun·jiang** |'hoͦNGjē'äNG| industrial city in Jilin province, NE China, near the border with North Korea. Pop. 694,000.

**Hun·ting·don·shire** |'hǝntiNGdǝn,sHir; 'hǝtiNGdǝnsHǝr| former county of SE England. It became part of Cambridgeshire in 1974.

**Hun·ting·ton**[1] |'hǝntiNGtǝn| town in N Long Island, New York, containing Huntington, Cold Spring Harbor, and other largely residential villages. Pop. 191,474.

**Hun·ting·ton**[2] |'hǝntiNGtǝn| industrial city in West Virginia, on the Ohio River. Pop. 54,840.

**Hun·ting·ton Beach** |'hǝntiNGtǝn| city in S California, on the Pacific coast, to the S of Long Beach. Pop. 181,519.

**Hunts·ville**[1] |'hǝnts,vil| city in N Alabama. Pop. 159,789. It is a center for space exploration and solar energy research.

**Hunts·ville**[2] |'hǝnts,vil| city in E Texas, N of Houston. Pop. 27,925.

**Hu·ron, Lake** |'(h)yŏŏrǝn; '(h)yŏŏr,än| the second-largest (24,361 sq. mi./63,096 sq. km.) of the five Great Lakes of North America, between Ontario and Michigan. Georgian Bay is its NE extension, separated by the Bruce Peninsula of Ontario.

**Hur·ri·cane Alley** |'hǝrǝ,kän| popular term for areas of the U.S. and Caribbean, such as Florida and the Gulf Coast, especially prone to hurricanes.

**Hutch·in·son** |'hǝCHǝn,sǝn| city in S central Kansas. Pop. 39,308.

**Hu·zhou** |'hŏŏ'jŏ| (formerly **Wuxing**) city in N Zhejiang province, E China, W of Shanghai and S of Tai Lake. Pop. 218,000.

**Hvar** |hvär| island, part of Bosnia and Herzegovina, in the Adriatic Sea off the Dalmatian coast. It was a popular tourist destination before the Balkan wars of the 1990s.

**Hwan·ge** |'(h)wäNGgä| town in W Zimbabwe. Pop. 39,000. Nearby is the Hwange National Park, established as a game reserve in 1928. Fomer name (until 1982) **Wankie**.

**Hy·an·nis** |hi'ænis| commercial village, in SE Massachusetts, on Cape Cod, in a resort area. Pop. 14,120.

**Hyde Park**[1] |hid| the largest British royal park, in W central London. Its Serpentine and Speakers' Corner are well-known to visitors.

**Hyde Park**[2] |hid| town in SE New York, on the Hudson River N of Poughkeepsie, associated with the family of Franklin D. Roosevelt. Pop. 21,320.

**Hy·der·a·bad**[1] |'hid(ǝ)rǝ,bäd| **1** commercial and university city in central India, capital of the state of Andhra Pradesh. Pop. 3,005,000. **2** former large princely state of S central India, divided in 1956 among Maharashtra, Mysore, present-day Karnataka, and Andhra Pradesh.

**Hy·der·a·bad**[2] |'hid(ǝ)rǝ,bäd| commercial and industrial city in SE Pakistan, in the province of Sind, on the Indus River. Pop. 1,000,000.

**Hy·dra** |'hidrǝ| island in Greece, in the S Aegean Sea, off the E coast of Peloponnese. It is mostly rocky and barren.

**Hy·met·tus** |hi'metǝs| mountain ridge SE of Athens, Greece, reaching 3,366 ft./1,026 m, and noted for its marble.

**Hy·pha·sis** |'hifǝsis| ancient Greek name for the BEAS River, India.

# Ii

**Ia·şi** |'yäsHĕ| commercial and industrial city in E Romania. Pop. 338,000. From 1565 to 1859 it was the capital of the principality of Moldavia. German name **Jassy**.

**Iba·dan** |ē'bädän; ē'bädn| the second largest city of Nigeria, a commercial center 100 mi./160 km. NE of Lagos. Pop. 1,295,000.

**Iba·gué** |ˌēbə'gā| city in W central Colombia, capital of Tolima department. Pop. 334,000. An Andes market center, it is also noted for its music conservatory and festivals.

**Iba·ra·ki** |ē'bärəkē; ˌēbä'räkē| city in W central Japan, on S Honshu, near Osaka. Pop. 254,000.

**Ibar·ra** |ē'bärə| historic city in N Ecuador, the capital of Imbabura province, N of Quito. Pop. 81,000. It is a center for commerce and folk arts.

**Ibe·ri·an Peninsula** |ī'birēən| the extreme SW peninsula of Europe (ancient **Iberia**, land of the Iberes), containing present-day Spain and Portugal. It was colonized by Carthage before the Third Punic War (149–146 B.C.), after which it came increasingly under Roman influence. It was invaded by the Visigoths in the 4th–5th centuries A.D. and by the Moors in the 8th century.

**Ibi·za** |ĭ'bēzä| **1** the westernmost of the Balearic Islands of Spain. **2** its capital city and port. Pop. 25,000. □ **Ibizan** *adj. & n.*

**Ica** |'ēkä| commercial city in SW Peru, on the Ica River, the capital of Ica department. Pop. 109,000. Its name is also that of a pre-Incan culture that flourished nearby.

**Ice·land** |'īslənd| an island republic in the N Atlantic. Area: 39,714 sq. mi./102,820 sq. km. Pop. 300,000. Language, Icelandic. Capital and largest city: Reykjavik. Icelandic name **Ísland** (meaning 'iceland').

Settled by Vikings in the 9th century, Iceland was ruled by Norway, then Denmark, until 1944. Volcanically active, it relies on geothermal energy, fishing, and mining. □ **Icelandic** *adj.* **Icelander** *n.*

**Ichi·ha·ra** |ē'CHē,härə| industrial city in E central Japan, on central Honshu, SE of Tokyo. Pop. 258,000.

**Ichi·ka·wa** |ē'CHē,käwə| industrial city in W central Japan, on E Honshu, NE of Tokyo. Pop. 437,000.

**Ichi·no·mi·ya** |ˌēCHē'nōmēə| industrial city in central Japan, on S central Honshu, NW of Nagoya. Pop. 262,000.

**Ichun** |'ē'CHo͞on| see YICHUN, China.

**Ick·nield Way** |'ik,nēld| ancient pre-Roman track that crosses S England in a wide curve from Wiltshire on the S coast to Norfolk, on the E coast.

**Ida** |'īdə| mountain in central Crete, associated in classical times with the god Zeus. Rising to 8,058 ft./2,456 m., it is the highest peak on the island.

**Ida·ho** |'īdə,hō| see box.

| Idaho |
|---|
| **Capital/largest city:** Boise |
| **Other cities:** Idaho Falls, Lewiston, Moscow, Pocatello, Twin Falls |
| **Population:** 1,006,749 (1990); 1,228,684 (1998); 1,480,000 (2005 proj.) |
| **Population rank (1990):** 42 |
| **Rank in land area:** 14 |
| **Abbreviation:** ID; Ida. |
| **Nicknames:** Gem State; Light on the Mountain |
| **Motto:** *Esto perpetua* (Latin: 'May it endure forever') |
| **Bird:** mountain bluebird |
| **Fish:** cutthroat trout |
| **Flower:** syringa |
| **Tree:** Western white pine |
| **Song:** "Here We Have Idaho" |
| **Noted physical features:** Moyie, Shoshone and Upper Mesa falls; Hooper, Lavahot and Soda springs; Borah Peak |
| **Tourist attractions:** Sun Valley; Continental Divide; Brownlee Dam, Oxbow Dam; Craters of the Moon National Park; Hells Canyon; Shoshone Falls; River of No Return Wilderness Area; Redfish Lake |
| **Admission date:** July 3, 1890 |
| **Order of admission:** 43 |
| **Name origin:** Said to be a coined name with the invented meaning 'gem of the mountains.' Another theory suggests *Idaho* may be a Kiowa Apache term for the Comanche. |

Iceland

**Ida·ho Falls** |'idə,hō| city in SE Idaho, on the Snake River. Pop. 43,929.

**Idi·ta·rod River** |i'ditə,räd| river in W Alaska, scene of a 1908 gold rush. It is on the route of the Iditarod dog sled race, which goes from Anchorage to Nome.

**Id·lib** |'id,lib| commercial town in NW Syria, SW of Aleppo. Pop. 100,000. Ancient Ebla lay to the S.

**Id·u·mae·a** |,id(y)ŏŏ'mēə| another name for ancient EDOM.

**Ie·per** |ēpər| Flemish name for YPRES, Belgium.

**If** |ēf| small island off the S coast of France, 2 mi./3 km. from Marseilles. On it is the Château d'If, a famous fortress prison.

**Ife** |'efä| industrial city in SW Nigeria. Pop. 241,000. It was a center of the Yoruba kingdom from the 14th to the 17th centuries. It ceded to Morocco in 1969.

**If·ni** |'ifnē| former overseas province of Spain, on the SW coast of Morocco, ceded to Morocco in 1969.

**Igua·çu** |,ēgwə'sŏŏ| river of S Brazil. It rises in the Serra do Mar in SE Brazil and flows W for 800 mi./1,300 km. to the Paraná River, which it joins shortly below the noted Iguaçu Falls. Spanish name **Iguazú**

**Igua·la** |ē'gwälə| (official name **Iguala de la Independencia**) historic city in S Mexico, in Guerrero state. Pop. 83,000. In a mining region, it was the scene of a noted 1821 announcement of independence.

**IJs·sel** |'isəl| river in the E Netherlands, flowing 72 mi./115 km. N to the IJsselmeer.

**IJs·sel·meer** |'isəl,mer| shallow lake in the NW Netherlands, created in 1932 by the building of a dam across the entrance to the old Zuider Zee. Large areas have since been reclaimed as polders.

**Ika·ría** |,ēkə'rēə| (also **Icaria**) island of Greece, part of the Southern Sporades group, in the Aegean Sea, named for the mythical figure Icarus, who flew too close to the sun and fell into the sea.

**Ike·da** |ē'kädə| city in W central Japan, on S Honshu, an industrial and residential suburb N of Osaka. Pop. 104,000.

**Ike·ja** |ē'käjə| industrial town in SW Nigeria, just NW of Lagos. Murtala Muhammad International Airport is here. Pop. 60,000.

**Ik·san** |'ēk,sän| commercial city in SW South Korea, in an agricultural region. Pop. 323,000.

**Ila** |'ēlə| commercial town in SW Nigeria, in an agricultural area. Pop. 233,000.

**Île-de-France** |,ēl də fräNs| region of N central France, incorporating the city of Paris and surrounding departments.

**Ile de la Ci·té** |,ēl də lä sē'tä| island in the Seine River, in Paris, France. The site of the first settlement in Paris and later the center of the Roman colony, it is now the site of the cathedral of Notre-Dâme and other historic buildings and government offices.

**Ile·sha** |ē'lashə| city in SW Nigeria, an agricultural trade center. Pop. 342,000.

**Il·hé·us** |ēl'yaŏŏs| port city in E Brazil, in S Bahia state. Pop. 224,000. It is historically the leading cacao exporting center in Brazil.

**Ili·gan** |ē'lē'gän| industrial port city in the Philippines, on W central Mindanao, on Iligan Bay. Pop. 227,000.

**Ili River** |'ēlē| river in central Asia, formed in NW Xinjiang, China, by the conjunction of the Tekes and Künes rivers, whose headwaters rise in the Tian Shan range. It flows 590 mi./950 km. W and NW to the S end of Lake Balkash in Kazakhstan.

**Il·i·um** |'ilēəm| the alternative name for ancient TROY, especially the 7th-century B.C. Greek city.

**Il·li·nois** |,ilə'noi; ,ilə'noiz| see box.

---

### Illinois

**Capital:** Springfield
**Largest city:** Chicago
**Other cities:** Aurora, Bloomington, Decatur, Elgin, Peoria, Rockford
**Population:** 11,430,602 (1990); 12,045,326 (1998); 12,266,000 (2005 proj.)
**Population rank (1990):** 6
**Rank in land area:** 25
**Abbreviation:** IL; Ill.
**Nicknames:** Prairie State; Land of Lincoln
**Motto:** 'State Sovereignty, National Union'
**Bird:** cardinal
**Fish:** bluegill
**Flower:** violet
**Tree:** white oak
**Song:** "Illinois"
**Noted physical features:** Shawnee Hills; Charles Mound
**Tourist attractions:** Chicago; Abraham Lincoln home and tomb; Lincoln Trail; Starved Rock State Park; Shawnee National Forest; Illinois State Museum
**Admission date:** December 3, 1818
**Order of admission:** 21
**Name origin:** From the French collective noun for the Illini or Inini Indians, whose name is from an Algonquin word meaning 'men' or 'warriors.'

**Il·li·nois River** |ˌiləˈnoi; ˌiləˈnoiz| river that flows 273 mi./440 km. SW through Illinois to the Mississippi River.

**Il·lyr·ia** |iˈlirēə| ancient region along the E coast of the Adriatic Sea, including Dalmatia and what is now Montenegro and N Albania. □ **Illyrian** *adj. & n.*

**Ilo·cos** |ēˈlōkōs| region in the Philippines, on NW Luzon. Pop. 4.22 million. Ilocos Norte and Ilocos Sur are two of the four provinces in the region.

**Ilo·i·lo** |ˌēlōˈēlō| port on the S coast of the island of Panay in the Philippines. Pop. 310,000.

**Ilo·rin** |ēˈlawren| industrial city in W Nigeria. Pop. 390,000. In the 18th century it was the capital of a Yoruba kingdom that was eventually absorbed into a Fulani state in the early 19th century.

**Ima·ba·ri** |ˌēmäˈbärē| industrial port city in W Japan, on the NW coast of Shikoku. Pop. 123,000.

**Im·bros** |ˈēm,braws| Turkish island in the NE Aegean Sea, near the entrance to the Dardanelles. Turkish name **Imroz.**

**Im·pe·ra·triz** |ēm,perəˈtrēs| commercial city in NE Brazil, on the Tocantins River in Maranhão state. Pop. 228,000. It ships regional farm and forest products.

**Im·pe·ri·al Valley** |imˈpirēəl| irrigated section of the Colorado Desert, in SE California, site of a major agricultural industry.

**Im·phal** |ˈimp,häl| the capital of the state of Manipur in the far NE of India, lying close to the border with Burma. Pop. 157,000. It was the scene of an important victory in 1944 by Anglo-Indian forces over the Japanese.

**Im·roz** |imˈrawz| Turkish name for IMBROS.

**Inch·cape Rock** |ˈinCH,kāp| (also **Bell Rock**) sandstone reef in the North Sea, off the mouth of the Tay River in Scotland, subject of a ballad by Robert Southey.

**In·chon** |ˈin,CHän| industrial port on the W coast of South Korea, on the Yellow Sea near Seoul. Pop. 1,818,000. It is the site of a U.S. amphibious landing in the Korean War (1950).

**In·de·pend·ence** |ˌindəˈpendəns| historic suburban city in NW Missouri, E of Kansas City. Pop. 112,301.

**In·dia** |ˈindēə| republic of S Asia, occupying most of the Indian subcontinent, on the Indian Ocean. Area: 1.23 million sq. mi./3.18 million sq. km. Pop. 859,200,000. Languages, Hindi, English, fourteen others including Bengali, Gujarati, Marathi, Tamil, Telugu, Urdu. Capital: New Delhi. Largest cities: Bombay (Mumbai), Calcut-

ta. Hindi Name **Bharat.** Settled since at least the 3rd millennium B.C., India has been dominated by Aryans, Muslims, and Europeans, especially the British. It achieved independence from the U.K. in 1947, then split into Hindu (India) and Muslim (Pakistan) states. Although 83% Hindi, India still has the third-largest Muslim community in the world. Many Indians are subsistence farmers, but mining and industry are also important. □ **Indian** *adj. & n.*

**In·di·ana** |ˌindēˈænə| see box.

**In·di·an·ap·o·lis** |ˌindēəˈnæp(ə)ləs| the capital and largest city of Indiana. Pop. 741,952. A commercial and industrial center, it is also noted as host to the annual Indianapolis 500 motor race (held in Speedway, a city enclosed by Indianapolis).

**In·di·an Ocean** |ˈindēən| the ocean to the S of India and neighboring Asia, extending from the E coast of Africa to the East Indies and Australia.

**In·di·an subcontinent** |ˈindēən| the part of Asia S of the Himalayas that forms a peninsula extending into the Indian Ocean,

---

### Indiana

**Capital/largest city:** Indianapolis
**Other cities:** Bloomington, Evansville, Ft. Wayne, Gary, Hammond, Lafayette, South Bend, Terre Haute
**Population:** 5,544,159 (1990); 5,899,195 (1998); 6,215,000 (2005 proj.)
**Population rank (1990):** 14
**Rank in land area:** 38
**Abbreviation:** IN; Ind.
**Nickname:** Hoosier State
**Motto:** 'The Crossroads of America'
**Bird:** cardinal
**Flower:** peony
**Tree:** tulip tree (yellow poplar)
**Song:** "On the Banks of the Wabash, Far Away"
**Noted physical features:** Wyandotte Cave; Greensfort Top Mountain; Indiana Dunes
**Tourist attractions:** Lincoln Boyhood National Monument; New Harmony; Indian mounds
**Admission date:** December 11, 1816
**Order of admission:** 19
**Name origin:** A Latinized or Spanish form of *Indian* meaning 'land of the Indians'; used in 1768 by the Philadelphus Trading Company for territory ceded to them by the Iroquois.

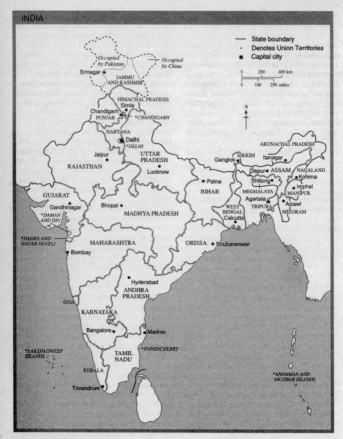

INDIA

—— State boundary
• Denotes Union Territories
■ Capital city

0    200      400 km
0   100    250 miles

N

*Occupied by Pakistan*    *Occupied by China*
Srinagar    JAMMU AND KASHMIR

HIMACHAL PRADESH
Chandigarh    Simla
PUNJAB    *CHANDIGARH*
HARYANA
■ Delhi
*DELHI*
Jaipur    UTTAR PRADESH    ARUNACHAL PRADESH
RAJASTHAN    Lucknow    Gangtok  SIKKIM    Itanagar
Dispur  ASSAM    NAGALAND
Patna    Shillong    ● Kohima
GUJARAT    BIHAR    Agartala  MEGHALAYA    Imphal
Gandhinagar    WEST    TRIPURA    MANIPUR
*DAMAN AND DIU*    Bhopal    BENGAL    Aizawl
MADHYA PRADESH    Calcutta    MIZORAM
*DADRA AND NAGAR HAVELI*
MAHARASHTRA    ORISSA  ● Bhubaneswar
● Bombay

● Hyderabad
ANDHRA PRADESH
GOA
KARNATAKA
Bangalore ●    ● Madras
*LAKSHADWEEP ISLANDS*    TAMIL NADU    *PONDICHERRY*
KERALA    *ANDAMAN AND NICOBAR ISLANDS*
● Trivandrum

between the Arabian Sea and the Bay of Bengal. Historically forming the whole territory of greater India, the region is now divided among India, Pakistan, and Bangladesh. Geologically, the Indian subcontinent is a distinct unit, formerly part of the ancient supercontinent of Gondwanaland. As a result of continental drift it became joined to the rest of Asia, perhaps as recently as 40 million years ago, in a collision that created the Himalayas.

**In·dies** |ˈindēz| archaic term for the EAST INDIES.

**In·di·gir·ka** |ˌindəˈgirkə| river of far E Siberia, which flows N for 1,112 mi./1,779 km. to the Arctic Ocean, where it forms a wide delta.

**In·dio** |ˈindēˌō| desert city in S California, SE of Palm Springs. Pop. 36,793.

**In·di·ra Gan·dhi Canal** |inˈdirə ˈgändē| canal in NW India, bringing water to the Thar Desert of Rajasthan from the Harike Barrage on the Sutlej River. The canal, which is 406 mi./650 km. long, was completed in 1986. Former name **Rajasthan Canal**.

**In·do·chi·na** |ˌindōˈCHīnə| (also **Indo-China**) the peninsula of SE Asia containing Burma, Thailand, Malaysia, Laos, Cambodia, and Vietnam; especially, the part of this area consisting of Laos, Cambodia, and Vietnam, which was a French dependency (FRENCH INDOCHINA) from 1862 to 1954. □ **Indochinese** *adj. & n.*

**In·do·ne·sia** |ˌində'nēzнə; ˌində'nēsнə| SE Asian republic consisting of many islands in the Malay Archipelago. Area: 735,638 sq. mi./1.90 million sq. km. Pop. 184,300,000. Languages, Indonesian (Bahasa Indonesia: official), Malay, Balinese, Chinese, Javanese, others. Capital and largest city: Djakarta (on Java). Former name **Dutch East Indies**. Controlled by the Dutch for two centuries before 1949, Indonesia is predominantly agricultural. Rice, rubber, palm oil, timber, tin, other metals, and oil and gas are all important products. □ **Indonesian** *adj. & n.*

**Indonesia**

**In·dore** |in'dawr| manufacturing city of Madhya Pradesh in central India. Pop. 1,087,000.

**In·dus** |'indəs| river of S Asia, about 1,800 mi./2,900 km. in length, flowing from Tibet through Kashmir and Pakistan to the Arabian Sea. Along its valley an early civilization flourished from *c.*2600 to 1760 B.C., whose economic wealth was derived from sea and land trade with the rest of the Indian subcontinent.

**In·gle·wood** |'iNGgəl,wood| city in SW California, an industrial and residential suburb S of Los Angeles. Pop. 109,602.

**In·gol·stadt** |'iNGgəl,sнtät| industrial and commercial city in SW Germany, on the Danube River. Pop. 107,000.

**In·gu·she·tia** |ˌiNGgoo'sнēsнə| (also **Ingush Republic**) autonomous republic of Russia, N of Georgia. Until the breakup of the Soviet Union in 1991, it was united with Chechnya. Its capital is Nazran.

**In·ker·man** |'iNGkərmən| village in Ukraine, near the mouth of the Chernaya

River E of Sevastopol. The Russians were defeated by English and French forces here in a battle (1854) during the Crimean War.

**In·land Empire** |'inlənd| popular name for highland agricultural regions of central Washington, E of the Cascade Range.

**In·land Sea** |'inlənd| arm of the Pacific, enclosed by the Japanese islands of Honshu, Shikoku, and Kyushu. Its chief port is Hiroshima.

**In·land Water·way** another name for ATLANTIC INTRACOASTAL WATERWAY or GULF INTRACOASTAL WATERWAY.

**In·ner Mon·go·lia** |mäNG'gōlyə| (Chinese name **Nei Monggol**) autonomous region of N China, on the border with Mongolia. Pop. 21.46 million. Capital: Hohhot.

**In·nis·free** |ˌinisн'frē| island in County Sligo, NW Ireland, in Lough Gill, that is the setting for a well-known poem by W.B. Yeats.

**Inn River** |in| river in W Europe that rises in the Rhaetian Alps of Switzerland and flows 320 mi./508 km. through the Austrian Tyrol past Innsbruck into S Germany, where it flows into the Danube River at Passau.

**Inns·bruck** |'ins,brook| resort and industrial city in W Austria, capital of Tyrol. Pop. 115,000.

**In·side Passage** |'in,sīd| water route from Seattle, Washington, to Alaska, passing through islands in Washington, British Columbia, and SE Alaska.

**Inter-American Highway** |ˌintərə'merəkən| name for the section of the PAN-AMERICAN HIGHWAY between the U.S.-Mexico border (at Nuevo Laredo, Mexico) and Panama City, Panama.

**In·ter·la·ken** |'intər,läkən| the chief town of the Bernese Alps in central Switzerland, on the Aare River between Lakes Brienz and Thun. Pop. 5,000.

**In·ter·mon·tane Region** |ˌintərmän'tān| (also **Intermountain Region**) term for the mountain and basin regions lying between the Rocky Mts. and the mountains of the U.S. W coast.

**In·ter·na·tion·al Date Line** |ˌin(t)ər-'næsнənl| imaginary line at 180° longitude, halfway around the earth from Greenwich, England. Points immediately W are 12 hours ahead of Greenwich Mean Time, points immediately E 12 hours behind. In the Pacific, the line bends in various places to avoid dividing populations.

**In·tra·coast·al Wa·ter·way** see ATLANTIC

INTRACOASTAL WATERWAY; GULF INTRA-COASTAL WATERWAY.

**In·va·lides, Hôtel des** |ŏ'tel dez ,änvä'lēd| building complex in Paris, France. Originally built as a home for aged soldiers by King Louis XIV, it is now a military museum. The sarcophagus of Napoleon I rests beneath the classical dome.

**In·ver·car·gill** |,invər'kärgil| city in New Zealand, capital of Southland region, South Island. Pop. 52,000.

**In·ver·ness** |,invər'nes| city in N Scotland, administrative center of Highland region, at the mouth of the Ness River. Pop. 41,000.

**In·yo Mountains** |'inyō| range in E central California that includes Mount Whitney, at 14,495 ft./4,418 m. the highest point in the U.S. outside Alaska.

**Io·án·ni·na** |yō'änēnə| department in NW Greece. Pop. 157,000. The capital is Ioánnina.

**Iona** |ī'ōnə| small island in the Inner Hebrides, Scotland, off the W coast of Mull. It is the site of a monastery founded by St. Columba in about 563.

**Io·nia** |ī'ōnēə| in classical times, the central part of the W coast of Asia Minor, which had long been inhabited by Hellenic people (the Ionians) and was again colonized by Greeks from the mainland from about the 8th century B.C. □ **Ionian** *adj. & n.*

**Io·ni·an Islands** |ī'ōnēən| chain of about forty Greek islands off the W coast of mainland Greece, in the Ionian Sea, including Corfu, Cephalonia, Ithaca, and Zakinthos.

**Io·ni·an Sea** |ī'ōnēən| the part of the Mediterranean Sea between W Greece and S Italy, at the mouth of the Adriatic.

**Io·wa** |'īəwə| see box. □ **Iowan** *adj. & n.*

**Io·wa City** |'īəwə| city in E Iowa. Pop. 59,738. Founded in 1838, it was the state capital until replaced by Des Moines in 1858. The University of Iowa is here.

**Ip·a·ne·ma** |,ipə'nēmə| beachfront section of S Rio de Janeiro, Brazil, just SW of Copacabana.

**Ipi·ran·ga** |,ēpē'räNGgə| stream and district SE of central São Paulo, Brazil, site where Brazilian independence from Portugal was declared in 1822.

**Ipoh** |'ēpō| the capital of the state of Perak in W Malaysia. Pop. 383,000. It replaced Taiping as state capital in 1937.

**Ips·wich** |'ip,swicH| the county seat of Suffolk, E England, a port and industrial center on the estuary of the Orwell River. Pop. 116,000.

---

## Iowa

**Capital/largest city:** Des Moines

**Other cities:** Cedar Rapids, Davenport, Dubuque, Perry, Sioux City, Waterloo

**Population:** 2,776,755 (1990); 2,862,447 (1998); 2,941,000 (2005 proj.)

**Population rank (1990):** 30

**Rank in land area:** 26

**Abbreviation:** IA; Ia.

**Nicknames:** The Hawkeye State; Corn State

**Motto:** 'Our Liberties We Prize and Our Rights We Will Maintain'

**Bird:** eastern goldfinch

**Flower:** wild rose

**Tree:** oak

**Song:** "The Song of Iowa"

**Tourist attractions:** Amana Colonies; first apple orchard; Little Brown Church; Herbert Hoover National Historical Site; Effigy Mounds National Monument

**Admission date:** December 28, 1846

**Order of admission:** 29

**Name origin:** For the Iowa River, which was named for the Iowa Indians of Siouan linguistic stock; the name is a French version of the Dakota name for the tribe, said to mean 'the sleepy ones.'

---

**Iqa·lu·it** |ē'kälōōit| (formerly **Frobisher Bay**) capital of Nunavut Territory, Canada, in S Baffin Island. Pop. 3,552.

**Iqui·que** |ē'kēkä| port city in N Chile, in the Tarapacá region. Pop. 149,000. It exports nitrates from the Atacama Desert as well as fish.

**Iqui·tos** |ē'kētōs| city in NE Peru, a port on the Amazon River. Pop. 252,000. It is a commercial, oil industry, and cultural center in the tropical rainforest.

**Irá·kli·on** |ē'räklē,awn| Greek name for HERAKLION, Crete.

**Iran** |i'rän; i'ræn; ī'ræn| republic in the Middle East, between the Caspian Sea and the Persian Gulf. Area: 636,539 sq. mi./1.65

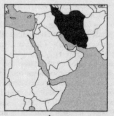

Iran

million sq. km. Pop. 54,600,000. Languages, Farsi (Persian) (official), Azerbaijani, Kurdish, Arabic, others. Capital and largest city: Tehran. Successor to Persia, Iran took its current name in 1935. Its monarchy was overthrown in 1979, and a theocratic Islamic republic established. Oil, textiles, and foods are major products in this largely desert country. □ **Iranian** *adj. & n.*

**Ira·pua·to** |ˌērə'pwätō| commercial city in central Mexico, in Guanajuato state. Pop. 265,000. Its region is famous for flower, fruit, and vegetable production.

**Iraq** |i'räk; i'ræk; I'ræk| republic in the Middle East, on the Persian Gulf. Area: 169,300 sq. mi./438,317 sq. km. Pop. 17,583,450. Language, Arabic (minorities speak Kurdish and Turkoman). Capital and largest city: Baghdad. The site of ancient Mesopotamia, Iraq was conquered by Arabs in the 7th century. After centuries of domination by the Turks and then the British, it gained independence in 1932. Its economy relies heavily on oil. Wars with its neighbors Iran and Kuwait and strife with Kurdish and Marsh Arab minorities have characterized recent decades. □ **Iraqi** *adj. & n.*

Iraq

**Ir·bid** |ir'bid; 'irbid| commercial city in N Jordan, N of Amman on the Jordan River. Pop. 170,000. It is an administrative and cultural center in a grain-producing region.

**Ir·bil** |'ər,bēl; 'ir,bēl| see ARBIL, Iraq.

**Ire·land, Republic of** |'īrlənd| country comprising approximately four-fifths of Ireland. Area: 27,146 sq. mi./70,282 sq. km. Pop. 3,523,400. Languages, Irish (official), English. Capital and largest city: Dublin. Also called **Irish Republic**. Comprising 26 of the 32 counties of Ireland, the Republic separated itself from British rule gradually in 1921–37. Its traditional pastoral and agricultural economy is shifting toward light industry. Tourism is important. □ **Irish** *adj. & n.*

**Ire·land** |'īrlənd| island of the British Isles, lying W of Great Britain. Approximately four-fifths of the area (32,327 sq. mi./83,694 sq. km.) of Ireland forms the Republic of Ireland, with the remainder forming NORTHERN IRELAND.

**Iri·an Ja·ya** |'ir,ēän 'jīə| province of E Indonesia comprising the W half of the island of New Guinea together with the adjacent small islands. Pop. 1.83 million. Capital: Jayapura. Until its incorporation into Indonesia in 1963 it was known as Dutch New Guinea. Also called **West Irian**.

**Irish Republic** |'irish| see IRELAND, REPUBLIC OF.

**Irish Sea** |'irish| the sea separating Ireland from England and Wales.

**Ir·kutsk** |ir'kōōtsk| industrial and cultural city of Siberia, near the W shore of Lake Baikal in E Russia. Pop. 635,000.

**Iron·bot·tom Sound** |'ī(ə)rn,bätəm| name given by U.S. forces in 1942 to the waters N of Guadalcanal, in the Solomon Islands. Especially around Savo Island, the ocean floor here was considered to be covered with sunken ships.

**Iron Cur·tain** |ˌī(ə)rn| cold war dividing line between the Soviet Union and its satellites and the West, defined by Winston Churchill in 1946 as extending from eastern Germany in the N to Trieste, on the Italy-Yugoslavia border, in the S.

**Iron Gate** |ī(ə)rn| gorge through which a section of the Danube River flows, forming part of the boundary between Romania and Serbia. Navigation was improved by means of a ship canal constructed through it in 1896. Romanian name **Porţile de Fier**, Serbo-Croat name **Gvozdena Vrata**.

**Ir·ra·wad·dy** |ˌirə'wädē| the principal river of Burma, 1,300 mi./2,090 km. long. It flows in a large delta into the E part of the Bay of Bengal.

**Ir·tysh** |ir'tish| river of central Asia, which rises in the Altai Mts. in N China and flows W into NE Kazakhstan, where it turns NW into Russia, joining the Ob River near its mouth. Its length is 2,655 mi./4,248 km.

**Iru·ma** |ē'rōōmə| city in E central Japan, on E central Honshu, a residential and industrial suburb NW of Tokyo. Pop. 138,000. It is noted for cultivation of green tea.

**Irún** |ē'rōōn| river port and industrial town in N Spain, on the Bidassoa River. Pop. 54,000.

**Ir·ving** |'ərviNG| industrial city in NE Texas, between Dallas and Fort Worth. Pop. 155,037.

**Ir·ving·ton** |'erviNGtən| industrial and res-

**IRELAND**

- ── International boundary
- ── Provincial boundary
- ⋯⋯ County boundary
- ■ Capital city

0 — 50 — 100 km
0 — 25 — 50 miles

N

DONEGAL • Lifford
U L S T E R

SLIGO • Sligo
MONAGHAN • Monaghan
LEITRIM
Carrick on Shannon • Cavan
CAVAN

MAYO • Castlebar
ROSCOMMON
CONNAUGHT
Longford
LONGFORD • Roscommon
Mullingar
WESTMEATH
MEATH • Navan
LOUTH • Dundalk

GALWAY • Galway
Tullamore
OFFALY
Naas
KILDARE
DUBLIN • Dublin
LEINSTER

CLARE • Ennis
Port Laoise
LAOIS
WICKLOW • Wicklow

Limerick
LIMERICK
TIPPERARY
Kilkenny
CARLOW • Carlow
KILKENNY
WEXFORD

Tralee •
MUNSTER
Clonmel •
WATERFORD
Wexford •

KERRY
CORK
Dungarvan

• Cork

idential township in NE New Jersey, on the W side of Newark. Pop. 61,010.

**Is·chi·a** |'iskēə| resort island in the Tyrrhenian Sea off the W coast of Italy, about 16 mi./26 km. W of Naples. The 'Emerald Isle' is noted for its hot springs.

**Ise** |'ēsə| city in central Honshu, Japan, on Ise Bay. Pop. 104,000. Former name (until 1956) **Ujiyamada**.

**Isère River** |ē'zer| river in E France that rises in the Alps near Val d'Isère and flows 180 mi./290 km., meeting the Rhône River near Valence.

**Iser·lohn** |ˌēzər'lōn| commercial and industrial city in western Germany. Pop. 93,000. In the 19th century it was the most populous city in Westphalia.

**Ise·sa·ki** |ˌēsa'säke| city in N central Japan, on central Honshu, NW of Tokyo. Pop. 116,000.

**Ise·yin** |ē'sāin| commercial and industrial town in SW Nigeria, N of Ibadan. Pop. 192,000. In a tobacco-growing region, it also has noted textile industries.

**Is·fa·han** |ˌisfə'hän| (also **Esfahan, Ispahan**) historic industrial city in central Iran, the country's third-largest city. Pop.

1,127,000. It was the capital of Persia from 1598 until 1722.

**Ish·i·ka·ri River** |ˌēsHēˈkärē| river in N Japan, on W Hokkaido, that flows 225 mi./362 km. from the interior of Hokkaido to Ishikari Bay on the Sea of Japan; second-longest river in Japan.

**Ishim River** |iˈshim| river (1,330 mi./2,140 km.) in N central Kazakhstan and W Asian Russia. It rises in the central steppes of Kazakhstan and flows N to the Irtysh at Ust-Ishim.

**Ishi·no·ma·ki** |ˌēsHēnōˈmäkē| commercial and fishing port in NE Japan, on the NE coast of Honshu. Pop. 122,000.

**Isis** |ˈisis| local and poetic name for the Thames River, in S England, especially in and around Oxford.

**Is·ken·de·run** |ˌiskendəˈrōōn| port and naval base in S Turkey, on the Mediterranean coast. Pop. 159,000. Formerly named Alexandretta, it lies on or near the site of Alexandria ad Issum, founded by Alexander the Great in 333 B.C.

**Is·lam·a·bad** |isˈlämə,bäd| the capital of Pakistan, a modern planned city in the N of the country, which replaced Rawalpindi as capital in 1967. Pop. 201,000.

**Is·la Mu·je·res** |ˈeslä mōōˈhärəs| island in SE Mexico, in the Gulf of Mexico off Quintana Roo state. It is a popular resort.

**Is·lay** |ˈīlə; ˈī,lā| island that is the southernmost of the Inner Hebrides, Scotland, S of Jura.

**Isle of Wight** |ˈwīt| see WIGHT, ISLE OF.

**Isle Roy·ale** |īl ˈroiəl| island in Michigan, in W Lake Superior, near Grand Portage, Minnesota, part of a national park and noted for its wildlife.

**Is·ling·ton** |ˈizliNGtən| residential and industrial borough of N London, England. Pop. 155,000. Sadler's Wells Theatre is here.

**Is·mai·lia** |ˌizmāəˈlēə| (Arabic name **Al Is·mailiyah**) port city in NE Egypt, on the Suez Canal, halfway between Port Said and Suez. Pop. 247,000.

**Is·ra·el** |ˈizrēəl; ˈizrāəl| country in the Middle East, on the Mediterranean Sea. Area: 8,022 sq. mi./20,770 sq. km. Pop. 4,600,000. Languages, Hebrew (official), English, Arabic. Capital (not recognized as such by the U.N.), Jerusalem; most embassies in Tel Aviv. Established in 1948 as a Jewish homeland in part of British-controlled Palestine, Israel has been in continual conflict with its Arab neighbors, and today occupies territories taken in war, in-

Israel

cluding the WEST BANK and Syrian GOLAN HEIGHTS. Irrigated agriculture, industry, tourism, and the support of Jews in the DIASPORA are key to the well-being of Israel. See also PALESTINE. □ **Israeli** adj. & n.

**Issyk-Kul, Lake** |ˌisikˈkōōl| (also **Issiq Köl**) lake in NE Kyrgyzstan, in a mountain range at 5,279 ft./1,609 m., site of several ancient cultures.

**Is·tan·bul** |ˌistänˈbōōl| historic port, the largest city in Turkey, on the Bosporus, lying partly in Europe, partly in Asia. Pop. 7,309,000. Formerly the Roman city of Constantinople (330–1453), it was built on the site of the ancient Greek city of Byzantium. It was captured by the Ottoman Turks in 1453 and was the capital of Turkey from that time until 1923. Istanbul has long been a commercial and religious center.

**Is·tria** |ˈestrēə| (also **Istrian Peninsula**) mountainous peninsula jutting into the N Adriatic Sea and belonging to Croatia and Slovenia. The peninsula is primarily agricultural. The NW section, including Trieste, belongs to Italy.

**Ita·bu·na** |ˌētəˈbōōnə| city in E Brazil, in Bahia state. Pop. 185,000. It is a center for cacao and cattle industries.

**Ita·i·pú Dam** |ēˈtīpōō| dam on the Paraná River between SW Brazil and E Paraguay, operational since 1984. One of the largest hydroelectric projects in the world, it impounds the huge **Itaipú Reservoir.**

**Ital·ian East Af·ri·ca** former African possessions of Italy, including Eritrea, Ethiopia, and Italian Somaliland (now part of Somalia).

**It·aly** |ˈitl-ē| republic in S Europe. Area: 116,348 sq. mi./301,225 sq. km. Pop. 57,746,160. Language, Italian. Capital and largest city: Rome. Italian name **Italia**. Successor to Rome, Italy achieved unification in the 19th century. In addition to its rich cultural heritage, it has a strong industrial

ITALY

— Region boundary
■ Capital city

0    50    100    150    200 km
0    25    50    75    100 miles

N

base. The agricultural S is less prosperous. Sicily and Sardinia are the largest Italian islands in the Mediterranean. □ **Italian** *adj. & n.*

**Ita·mi** |ĕ'tämē| city in W central Japan, on S Honshu, a residential suburb N of Osaka. Pop. 186,000.

**Ita·na·gar** city in the far NE of India, N of the Brahmaputra River, capital of the state of Arunachal Pradesh. Pop. 17,000.

**Ith·a·ca¹** |'ɪтнəkə| island off the W coast of Greece in the Ionian Sea, the legendary home of Odysseus.

**Ith·a·ca²** |'ɪтнəkə| academic city in central New York, at the S end of Cayuga Lake, home to Cornell University. Pop. 29,541.

**Itsu·ku·shi·ma** |ˌēts(ōō)'kōō'sHēmä| (also called **Miyajima**) island in W Japan, in the Inland Sea, off SW Honshu. It is noted for its beauty and its historic and sacred buildings.

**Ivano-Frankovsk** |ē͵vänōfräNG'kawfsk| (formerly known as **Stanislav**) industrial city in W Ukraine. Pop. 220,000.

**Iva·no·vo** |i'vänəvə| textile city in W Russia, NE of Moscow, capital of Ivanovo Oblast. Pop. 482,000.

**Ivo·ry Coast** |'ɪv(ə)rē| English name for CÔTE D'IVOIRE.

**Ivry-sur-Seine** |ē͵vrēsʏr'sen| industrial SE suburb of Paris, France. Pop. 56,000.

**Iwa·ki** |ē'wäkē| industrial city in NE Japan, on the E coast of Honshu, between Sendai and Mito. Pop. 356,000.

**Iwa·ku·ni** |ˌēwä'kōōnē| industrial city in W Japan, on the SW coast of Honshu. Pop. 110,000.

**Iwo** |'ēwō| commercial city in SW Nigeria, NE of Ibadan, in a cacao producing area. Pop. 262,000.

**Iwo Ji·ma** |ˌiwə 'jēmə| largest of the Volcano Islands in the W Pacific, 760 mi./1,222 km. S of Tokyo. During World War II it was the heavily fortified site of a Japanese airbase, and its attack and capture in 1944–45 was one of the bloodiest campaigns in the Pacific. It was returned to Japan in 1968.

**Izal·co** |ē'sälkō| volcano in W El Salvador, N of Sonsonate, that rises to 7,828 ft./2,386 m. Long called the Lighthouse of the Pacific, it last erupted in 1966 but is active.

**Izhevsk** |'ē͵zHevsk| industrial city in central Russia, capital of the republic of Udmurtia. Pop. 642,000. Former name (1984–87) **Ustinov**.

**Iz·ma·il** |ˌēzmä'yēl| (also known as **Ismayil**) city in Ukraine, on the N side of the Danube Delta near the Black Sea. Pop. 95,000.

**Iz·mir** |iz'mir| seaport and naval base in W Turkey, on an inlet of the Aegean Sea. Pop. 1,757,000. It is the third-largest city in Turkey. Former name **Smyrna**.

**Iz·mit** |iz'mit| port city in NW Turkey, on the Gulf of Izmit, an inlet of the Sea of Marmara. Pop. 257,000.

**Iz·ta·cal·co** |ˌēstə'kälkō| (also **Ixtacalco**) industrial city, a constituent of the Distrito Federal, just S of Mexico City, Mexico. Pop. 448,000.

**Iz·tac·ci·huatl** |ˌēstäk'sē͵wätl| (also **Ixtaccihuatl**) dormant volcano in central Mexico, reaching 17,342 ft./5,286 m. Neighbor to POPOCATÉPETL, it is SE of Mexico City, from which it can be seen in clear weather.

**Iz·ta·pa·la·pa** |ˌēstəpə'läpə| (also **Ixtapalapa**) community in central Mexico, a constituent of the DISTRITO FEDERAL, SE of downtown Mexico City. Pop. 1,490,000.

**Izu·mi** |ē'zōōmē| city in W central Japan, on S Honshu, a residential and industrial suburb S of Osaka. Pop. 138,000.

# Jj

**Ja·bal·pur** |'jəbəl,pŏŏr| industrial city and military post in Madhya Pradesh, central India. Pop. 760,000.

**Ja·blon·ec nad Ni·sou** |'yäblō,nets ,näd 'nĕ,sŏŏ| city in the N central Czech Republic. Pop. 88,000. It is a center of the Bohemian glassmaking industry.

**Ja·blo·ni·ca Pass** (also known as **Tatar Pass** or **Delatyn Pass**) pass through the E Carpathian Mts., Ukraine, SW of Kolomyya.

**Ja·bo·a·tão** |,ZHäb,wätowN| commercial city in NE Brazil, in Pernambuco state, a suburb W of Recife. Pop. 487,000.

**Ja·ca·rei** |,ZHäkəräyĕ| industrial and commercial city in SE Brazil, E of São Paulo. Pop. 168,000.

**Jack·son**[1] |'jæksən| industrial city in S central Michigan. Pop. 37,446.

**Jack·son**[2] |'jæksən| industrial and commercial city, the capital of Mississippi, in the central part, on the Pearl River. Pop. 196,637.

**Jack·son**[3] |'jæksən| commercial city in W Tennessee. Pop. 48,949.

**Jack·son Heights** |,jæksən 'hīts| commercial and residential section of N Queens, New York City.

**Jack·son Hole** |,jæksən 'hōl| valley on the Snake River in NW Wyoming, partly in Grand Teton National Park. It is a fashionable resort.

**Jack·son·ville**[1] |'jæksən,vil| industrial city and port in NE Florida. Pop. 635,230.

**Jack·son·ville**[2] |'jæksən,vil| city in SE North Carolina, a service town for nearby Camp Lejeune and other military facilities. Pop. 30,013.

**Ja·én** |hä'än| market and manufacturing city in S Spain. Pop. 106,000.

**Jaf·fa** |'jäfə; 'yäfə| city and port on the Mediterranean coast of Israel, forming a S suburb of Tel Aviv and since 1949 united with Tel Aviv. Pop. (with Tel Aviv) 355,000. Inhabited since prehistoric times, Jaffa was a Byzantine bishopric until captured by the Arabs in 636; later, it was a stronghold of the Crusaders. Hebrew name **Yafo**; biblical name **Joppa**.

**Jaff·na** |'jäfnə| city and port on the Jaffna Peninsula at the N tip of Sri Lanka. Pop. 129,000.

**Jag·ga·nath** (also **Juggernaut**) see PURI, India.

**Jai·pur** |'jī,pŏŏr| cultural and industrial city in W India, the capital of Rajasthan. Pop. 1,455,000.

**Ja·kar·ta** |jə'kärtə| another spelling for DJAKARTA, Indonesia.

**Ja·lal·a·bad** |jə'lälə,bäd| city in E Afghanistan, E of Kabul, near the border with Pakistan. Pop. 61,000.

**Ja·lan·dhar** |'jələndər| (formerly **Jullundur**) industrial and commercial city in N India, in Punjab state. Pop. 520,000.

**Ja·la·pa** |hä'läpä| (also **Xalapa**) commercial city in E central Mexico, capital of the state of Veracruz, in an agricultural area. Pop. 288,000. Full name **Jalapa Enríquez**.

**Jal·gaon** |jäl,gown| commercial city in W central India, in Maharashtra state. Pop. 242,000.

**Ja·lis·co** |hä'lĕskō| state of W central Mexico, on the Pacific coast. Area: 31,223 sq. mi./80,836 sq. km. Pop. 5,279,000. Capital: Guadalajara.

**Jal·na** |'jälnə| town in W central India, in Maharashtra state, SW of Aurangabad. Pop. 175,000.

**Ja·mai·ca**[1] |jə'mākə| island republic in the Caribbean, SE of Cuba. Area: 4,230 sq. mi./10,956 sq. km. Pop. 2,314,480. Language, English. Capital and largest city: Kingston. Colonized by the Spanish from the 15th century, and seized by the British in 1655, Jamaica gained independence in 1962. Its economy relies on bauxite extraction, agriculture, and tourism. □ **Jamaican** adj. & n.

**Jamaica**

**Ja·mai·ca**[2] |jə'mākə| commercial and residential section of E central Queens, New York City.

**Jam·bi** |'jämbĕ| (also **Djambi**) commercial city in Indonesia, on S Sumatra, on the Hari River. Pop. 340,000.

**James Bay** |'jāmz| shallow S arm of Hudson Bay, Canada, once a fur trading center, now the focus of disputes over hydroelectric projects.

**James River**¹ |,jāmz| (also **Dakota River**) river that flows 700 mi./1,100 km. from North Dakota through South Dakota, into the Missouri River.

**James River**² |,jāmz| river that flows 340 mi./550 km across E Virginia, past Richmond and into the Tidewater region, into Hampton Roads. Colonial Jamestown was on its estuary.

**James•town**¹ |'jāmz,town| city in SW New York, on Lake Chautauqua. It is both industrial and a resort service center. Pop. 34,681.

**James•town**² |'jāmz,town| the capital and chief port of the Atlantic island of St. Helena. Pop. 1,500.

**James•town**³ |'jāmz,town| British settlement established on the James River in Virginia in 1607, abandoned when the colonial capital was moved to Williamsburg at the end of the 17th century.

**Jam•mu** |'jəmoo| town in NW India. Pop. 206,000. It is the winter capital of the state of Jammu and Kashmir.

**Jam•mu and Kash•mir** |'jəmoo; 'kæsн,mir| mountainous state of NW India at the W end of the Himalayas, formerly part of Kashmir. Pop. 7.72 million. Capitals: Srinagar (in summer) and Jammu (in winter).

**Jam•na•gar** |jäm'nəgər| port and walled city in the state of Gujarat, W India. Pop. 325,000.

**Jam•shed•pur** |'jämsнed,poŏr| industrial city in the state of Bihar, NE India. Pop. 461,000.

**Janes•ville** |'jānz,vil| industrial city in S Wisconsin, on the Rock River. Pop. 52,133.

**Jan May•en** |'yän 'mīən| barren and virtually uninhabited island in the Arctic Ocean between Greenland and Norway, annexed by Norway in 1929.

**Ja•pan, Sea of** |jə'pæn| the sea between Japan and the mainland of Asia.

**Ja•pan** |jə'pæn| country in E Asia, occupying a chain of islands in the Pacific roughly parallel with the E coast of the Asian mainland. Area: 145,931 sq. mi./377,815 sq. km. Pop. 122,626,000. Language, Japanese. Capital and largest city: Tokyo. Japanese name **Nippon** (Land of the Rising Sun). In existence from around the 6th century B.C., Japan became a modern state in the late 19th century. It has few natural resources, but has made itself an industrial and commercial power. Expansionist

Japan

drives of the early 20th century came to an end with the Japanese loss in World War II. □ **Japanese** adj. & n.

**Ja•pan Current** |jə'pæn| (also **Japanese Current**) another name for KUROSHIO.

**Ja•pu•rá River** |,zнäpoŏ'rä| (Colombian name **Caquetá**) river that flows 1,750 mi./2,815 km. from SW Colombia into Brazil, to join the Amazon River.

**Jar•row** |'jərō| town in NE England, on the Tyne estuary. Pop. 31,000. From the 7th century until the Viking invasions its monastery was a center of Northumbrian Christian culture. Its name is also associated with hunger marches to London by the unemployed during the Depression of the 1930s.

**Jär•ven•pää** |'yärven,pä| town in S Finland, notes as home to the composer Sibelius. Pop. 32,000.

**Jas•sy** |yäsн| German name for IAŞI, Romania.

**Jaun•pur** |'jown,poŏr| commercial city in NE India, in Uttar Pradesh state. Pop. 136,000.

**Ja•va** |'jävə| volcanic island in the Malay Archipelago, forming part of Indonesia. Pop. 112.16 million. Heavily forested and agricultural, with most of the population of Indonesia, Java is noted for its cultural history. □ **Javan** adj. & n. **Javanese** adj. & n.

**Ja•va•ri River** |,zнävä'rē| (Peruvian name **Yavari**) river that flows NE for 500 mi./810 km. from E Peru along the Peru-Brazil border, to the Amazon River.

**Ja•va Sea** |'jävə| sea in the Malay Archipelago of SE Asia, surrounded by the islands of Borneo, Java, and Sumatra.

**Ja•ya•pu•ra** |,jäyä'poŏrä| (also **Djajapura**) port city in Indonesia, capital of Irian Jaya province on W New Guinea. Pop. 46,000.

**Ja•zi•rah, al** |,æl jä'zērä| region in Iraq, NW of Baghdad, in the Tigris-Euphrates valley; an important trading center in both ancient and medieval times.

**Jeb·el Mu·sa** |'jebəl'mōōsə| mountain in N Morocco, just W of Ceuta; 2,790 ft./850 m. With the Rock of Gibraltar, it is one of the Pillars of Hercules, flanking the Strait of Gibraltar.

**Jef·fer·son City** |'jefərsən| commercial and industrial city, the capital of Missouri. Pop. 35,481.

**Je·hol** former province of NE China, now divided among Inner Mongolia, Hebei, and Liaoning.

**Je·le·nia Gó·ra** |yə'lenyä 'gawrä| industrial and commercial city in SW Poland. Pop. 93,000.

**Jel·ga·va** |'yelgəvä| (also **Yelgava**) historic commercial city in S Latvia, on the Lielupe River. Pop. 75,000.

**Je·mez Mountains** |'hāmes| range in N New Mexico, NW of Santa Fe, site of Valle Grande, an enormous caldera. Chicoma Peak (11,950 ft./3,642 m.) is the high point.

**Je·na** |'yänə| university town in central Germany, in Thuringia. Pop. 101,000. It was the scene of a battle (1806) in which Napoleon defeated the Prussians. It is noted as a manufacturing center for optical and precision instruments.

**Je·rez** |ha'res; ha'reᴛʜ| town in Andalusia, Spain. Pop. 184,000. It is the center of the sherry (from *jerez*) making industry. Full name **Jerez de la Frontera**.

**Jer·i·cho** |'jerə,kō| town in Palestine, in the West Bank N of the Dead Sea. It has been occupied from at least 9000 B.C. According to the Bible, Jericho was a Canaanite city destroyed by the Israelites after they crossed the Jordan into the Promised Land; its walls were flattened by the shout of the army of Joshua and the blast of the trumpets. Occupied by the Israelis since the Six Day War of 1967, in 1994 Jericho was the first area given partial autonomy under the PLO-Israeli peace accord.

**Jer·sey** |'jərzē| the largest (45 sq. mi./116 sq. km.) of the Channel Islands of Britain. Pop. 83,000. Capital: St. Helier.

**Jer·sey City** |'jərzē| industrial city in NE New Jersey, on the Hudson River opposite New York City. Pop. 228,537.

**Je·ru·sa·lem** |jə'rōōs(ə)ləm; jə'rōōz(ə)-ləm| the holy city of the Jews, sacred also to Christians and Muslims, lying in the Judaean hills about 20 mi./30 km. from the Jordan River. Pop. 562,000. The city was captured from the Canaanites by King David of the Israelites, who made it his capital. As the site of the Temple, built by Solomon (957 B.C.), it also became the center of the Jewish religion. Since then it has shared the troubled history of the area—destroyed by the Babylonians in 586 B.C. and by the Romans in A.D. 70, and fought over by Saracens and Crusaders in the Middle Ages. From 1947 the city was divided between the states of Israel and Jordan until the Israelis occupied the whole city in June 1967 and proclaimed it the capital of Israel. It is revered by Christians as the place of Christ's death and resurrection, and by Muslims as the site of the Dome of the Rock.

**Jer·vis Bay Territory** |'järvis| territory on Jervis Bay on the SE coast of Australia. Incorporated in 1915 as a sea outlet for the Australian Capital Territory, it separated from the Capital Territory in 1988.

**Jes·sore** |je,'sawr| commercial city in SW Bangladesh, on the Bhairab River. Pop. 176,000.

**Jew·ish Republic** |'jōōiSH| autonomous oblast in extreme E Russia, in the basins of the Biro and Bidzhan rivers. Pop. 212,000. Although it was intended as a home for Jews, only a small percentage of its population is Jewish.

**Jez·re·el** see ESDRAELON.

**Jhang Sa·dar** (also called **Jhang-Maghiana**) commercial town in central Pakistan, W of Lahore. Pop. 196,000.

**Jhan·si** |'jänse| city in the state of Uttar Pradesh, N India. Pop. 301,000.

**Jhe·lum** |'jäləm| river that rises in the Himalayas and flows through the Vale of Kashmir into Punjab, where it meets the Chenab River. In ancient times it was called by the Greek name Hydaspes.

**Jia·ling River** |jē'ä'liNG| (Chinese name **Jialing Jiang**) river, central China, rising in the area around the S Gansu-Shaanxi border and flowing 600 mi./965 km. S through Sichuan to the Yangtze River at Chongqing.

**Jia·mu·si** |jē'ä'mōō'sē| city in Heilongjiang province, NE China, on the Sungari River NE of Harbin. Pop. 493,000.

**Jiang·men** |jē'äNG'men| city in Guangdong province, S China, on a branch of the Pearl River SW of Guangzhou (Canton). Pop. 231,000.

**Jiang·su** |jē'äNG'sōō| (also **Kiangsu**) a province of E China. Pop. 67,006,000. Capital: Nanjing. It includes much of the Yangtze delta.

**Jiang·xi** |jē'äNG'sē| (also **Kiangsi**) a province of SE China. Pop. 37,710,000. Capital: Nanchang.

**Jiao·zu·o** |jē'owd'zwō| city in Henan

province, E central China, NW of Zhengzhou. Pop. 409,000.

**Jia·xing** |jē'ä'sHĭNG| (formerly **Kashing**) city in Zhejiang province, E China, on the Grand Canal SW of Shanghai. Pop. 697,000.

**Ji·ca·ril·la Mountains** |ˌhēkə'rēə| range in S central New Mexico, reaching 8,200 ft./2,500 m. at Jicarilla Mt.

**Jid·dah** |'jidə| (also **Jeddah**) seaport on the Red Sea coast of Saudi Arabia, near Mecca. It is the Saudi administrative capital. Pop. 1,400,000.

**Ji·lin** |'jē'lin| (also **Kirin**) **1** a province of NE China. Pop. 24,660,000. Capital: Changchun. **2** an industrial city in Jilin province. Pop. 2,252,000.

**Ji·nan** |'ji'nän| (also **Tsinan**) city in E China, the capital of Shandong province. Pop. 2,290,000.

**Jing·de·zhen** |'jĭNG'də'jen| (formerly **Fowliang**) city in Jiangxi province, SE China, E of Poyang Lake. Pop. 281,000. It has been a porcelain center since the Han dynasty, reaching its height during Sung times.

**Jin·zhou** |'jin'jō| city in Liaoning province, NE China, near the Gulf of Liaodong at the N end of the Bo Hai. Pop. 569,000.

**Ji·pi·ja·pa** |ˌhēpē'häpə| commercial town in W Ecuador, a noted center for Panama-hat production. Pop. 32,000.

**Jiu·jiang** |jē'ōōjē'äNG| city in N Jiangxi province, E central China, on the Yangtze River, N of Poyang Lake and SE of Wuhan. Pop. 291,000. Bricks, tiles, and textiles are produced.

**Ji·xi** |'jē'sHē| city in Heilongjiang province, NE China, on the Muling River E of Harbin. Pop. 684,000.

**João Pes·soa** |'zHownpe'sōwə| resort and industrial city in NE Brazil, on the Atlantic coast, capital of the state of Paraíba. Pop. 484,000.

**Jo·burg** |'jō,bərg| informal name for JO-HANNESBURG, South Africa.

**Jodh·pur** |'jädpər; 'jäd,pŏŏr| **1** city in W India, in Rajasthan. Pop. 649,000. **2** a former princely state of India, now part of Rajasthan.

**Jod·rell Bank** |'jädrəl| scientific site in Cheshire, NW England, home to the Nuffield Radio Astronomy Laboratory, with one of the world's largest radio telescopes.

**Jog·ja·kar·ta** |ˌjawkjə'kärtə| variant spelling of YOGYAKARTA, Indonesia.

**Jo·han·nes·burg** |jō'hänəs,bərg; jō'hænəs,bərg| city in South Africa, the capital of the province of Gauteng. Pop. 1,916,000. It is the largest city in South Africa and the center of its gold-mining industry.

**Jo·han·nis·berg** |yō'hänis,berg| village in central Germany, near the Rhine River. Best known for its wine, it is also a health resort.

**John Day River** |'jän 'dā| river that flows 280 mi./450 km. across N Oregon to join the Columbia River E of The Dalles.

**John o'Groats** |ˌjän ə'grōts| village at the extreme NE point of the Scottish mainland.

**John·son City** |'jänsən| industrial city in NE Tennessee, part of a complex with Bristol and Kingsport. Pop. 49,381.

**John·ston Atoll** |'jänstən| atoll in the central Pacific, SW of Hawaii, controlled by the U.S. and used for military operations.

**Johns·town** |'jänz,town| industrial city in SW Pennsylvania, SE of Pittsburgh, noted as the site of a devastating 1889 flood. Pop. 28,134.

**Jo·hor** |jə'hawr| (also **Johore**) state of Malaysia, at the southernmost point of mainland Asia, joined to Singapore by a causeway. Pop. 2.1 million. Capital: Johor Baharu.

**Jo·hor Ba·ha·ru** |jə'hawr 'bähə,rōō| the capital of the state of Johor in Malaysia. Pop. 329,000.

**Jo·li·et** |ˌjōlē'et| industrial and commercial city in NE Illinois. Pop. 76,836.

**Jo·lo** |'hō,lō| (also called **Sulu**) **1** island in the Philippines, chief island in the Sulu Archipelago, between the Sulu Sea and the Celebes Sea. **2** its chief town. Pop. 53,000.

**Jones·bo·ro** |'jōnz,bərō| city in NE Arkansas. Pop. 46,535.

**Jones·town** |'jōnz,town| former religious settlement in the jungle of Guyana, established by Reverend Jim Jones with some 1,000 followers, almost all of whom died in a mass suicide in late 1978.

**Jön·kö·ping** |'yœn,sHœpĭNG| industrial city in S Sweden, at the S end of Lake Vättern. Pop. 111,000.

**Jon·quière** |ˌzHawn'kyär| industrial city in S Quebec, on the Saguenay River just W of Chicoutimi. Pop. 57,993.

**Jop·lin** |'jäplən| industrial and commercial city in SW Missouri. Pop. 40,961.

**Jop·pa** biblical name for JAFFA.

**Jor·dan** |'jawrdn| country in the Middle East, east of the Jordan River. Area: 35,475 sq. mi./89,206 sq. km. Pop. 4,000,000. Language, Arabic. Capital and largest city: Amman. Official name **Hashemite King-**

**dom of Jordan**. In an area dominated by successive empires for centuries, Jordan gained independence from Britain in 1946. In 1948–49 it took over the WEST BANK, but lost it to Israel in 1967. The country is now home to many Palestinian refugees. Mining and tourism are important to its economy. □ **Jordanian** *adj. & n.*

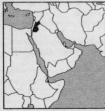

**Jordan**

**Jor·dan River** |'jawrdn| river flowing S for 200 mi./320 km. from the Anti-Lebanon Mts. through the Sea of Galilee into the Dead Sea. John the Baptist baptized Christ in the Jordan. It is regarded as sacred not only by Christians but also by Jews and Muslims.

**Jor·na·da del Muer·to** |hawr'nädə del 'mwer,tō| desert region in S New Mexico, near White Sands, famed as the "journey of death" for the difficulties it presented early travelers.

**Josh·ua Tree National Park** |'jäshəwə| preserve in S California, noted for its desert plant and animal life.

**Jo·tun·heim** |'yōtn,häm| **1** mountain range in S central Norway. Its highest peak is Glittertind 8,110 ft./2,472 m. **2** in Norse mythology, a part of the universe inhabited by giants.

**Juan de Fu·ca Strait** |'(h)wän də 'fyōōkə| ocean passage between Vancouver Island, British Columbia, and the Olympic Peninsula of Washington.

**Juan Fer·nan·dez Islands** |'hwän fer'nän,däs| group of three almost uninhabited islands in the Pacific Ocean 400 mi./640 km. W of Chile.

**Juan-les-Pins** |,zHwäenlä'peN| resort on the S coast of France, part of Antibes, on the Riviera, between Nice and Cannes, known for its fine beaches.

**Juá·rez** |'hwär,es| another name for CIUDAD JUÁREZ, Mexico.

**Juà·zei·ro do Nor·te** |,zHwä'särōō dōō 'nawrtä| city in NE Brazil, in Ceará state,

an agricultural processing center. Pop. 186,000.

**Ju·ba** |'jōōbə| capital of the S region of Sudan, on the White Nile. Pop. 100,000.

**Jub·ba** |'jōōbə| (also **Juba**) a river in E Africa, rising in the highlands of central Ethiopia and flowing S for about 1,000 mi./1,600 km. through Somalia to the Indian Ocean. The surrounding territory was formerly known as **Jubaland**.

**Ju·daea** |jōō'dēə| the S part of ancient Palestine, corresponding to the former kingdom of Judah. The Jews returned to the region after the Babylonian Captivity, and in 165 B.C. the Maccabees again established it as an independent kingdom. It became a province of the Roman Empire in 63 B.C., and was subsequently amalgamated with Palestine. Also spelled **Judea**. □ **Judaean** *adj. & n.*

**Juiz de Fo·ra** |'zHwēz dē 'fawrə| industrial city in E Brazil, in Minas Gerais state, a textile-producing and rail center. Pop. 386,000.

**Ju·juy** |hōō'hwē| (official name **San Salvador de Jujuy**) historic city in extreme NW Argentina, capital of Jujuy province. Pop. 183,000. It processes sugar and other crops and has many manufacturers.

**Ju·lian Alps** |'jōōlyən| Alpine range in W Slovenia and NE Italy, rising to a height of 9,395 ft./2,863 m. at Triglav.

**Jul·lun·dur** |'jələndər| see JALANDHAR, India.

**Jum·na** |'jəmnə| river of N India, which rises in the Himalayas and flows in a large arc S and SE, through Delhi, joining the Ganges below Allahabad. Its source (Yamunotri) and its confluence with the Ganges are both Hindu holy places. Hindi name **Yamuna**.

**Ju·na·ghad** |jōō'nägəd| (also **Junagarh**) commercial town in W India, in Gujarat state. Pop. 167,000.

**Jun·dial** |,zHōōndyä'e| industrial city in S Brazil, in São Paulo state. Pop. 286,000.

**Ju·neau** |'jōōnō| the capital of Alaska, a seaport on an inlet of the Pacific in the S panhandle. Pop. 26,751.

**Jung·frau** |'yōōNG,frow| mountain in the Swiss Alps, 13,642 ft./4,158 m. high.

**Ju·no Beach** |'jōōnō| name given to one of three sections of the beach on the Normandy coast, NW France, that was the landing site for British troops on D-day in June 1944. It is centered around the village of Courseulles sur Mer.

**Ju·ra¹** |'jōōrə| system of mountain ranges on the border of France and Switzerland.

It has given its name to the Jurassic period, when most of its rocks were laid down.

**Ju•ra²** |'joͮorə| island of the Inner Hebrides, Scotland, N of Islay and S of Mull, separated from the W coast of Scotland by the Sound of Jura.

**Ju•rong** |'joͮo'rawNG| industrial town, developed since the 1970s, in SW Singapore. Much of the Singapore workforce is employed here.

**Ju•ruá River** |zhoͮor'wä| river that flows 1,500 mi./2,400 km. from E Peru through NW Brazil, into the Amazon River.

**Jut•land** |'jət,lənd| peninsula of NW Europe, forming the mainland of Denmark together with the N German state of Schleswig-Holstein. Danish name **Jylland**.

**Ju•ven•tud, Isla de la** |'ēslä ,dä ,lä ,hoͮovän 'toͮod| (English name **Isle of Youth**; formerly **Isle of Pines**) island off SW Cuba, in the Caribbean Sea. Pop. 71,000. Long a source of jurisdictional disputes between Cuba and the U.S., it has been a resort and prison colony. It was renamed in 1978 and has many facilities dedicated to youth.

**Jyl•land** |'yɣ,län| Danish name for JUT-LAND.

**Jy•väs•ky•lä** |'yɣväs,kylä| industrial port city in central Finland. Pop. 67,000.

# Kk

**K2** |'ka'tōō| the highest mountain in the Karakoram range, on the border between Pakistan and China. It is the second highest peak in the world, rising to 28,250 ft./8,611 m. It was discovered in 1856 and named K2 because it was the second peak to be surveyed in the Karakoram range. It was also formerly known as Mount Godwin-Austen after Col. H. H. Godwin-Austen, who first surveyed it. Also called **Dapsang**.

**Kaa·ba** |'käbə| (also **Caaba**) a shrine within the Great Mosque at Mecca, Saudi Arabia, the focal point of the Muslim haj, or pilgrimage.

**Ka·ba·le·ga Falls** |ˌkäbəˈlagə| waterfall on the lower Victoria Nile near Lake Albert, in NW Uganda. Former name **Murchison Falls**.

**Kabardino-Balkaria** |ˌkəbərˈdyēnəbawl'kärēə| autonomous republic of SW Russia, on the border with Georgia. Pop. 768,000. Capital: Nalchik. Also called **Kabarda-Balkar Republic**.

**Ka·bul** |'käbəl; 'kä‚bŏŏl| the capital of Afghanistan. Pop. 700,000. It is situated in the NE of the country, with a strategic position commanding the mountain passes through the Hindu Kush, especially the Khyber Pass. It was capital of the Mogul Empire 1504–1738 and in 1773 replaced Kandahar as capital of an independent Afghanistan.

**Ka·bwe** |'käb‚wä| mining town in central Zambia, to the N of Lusaka. Pop. 167,000. It is the site of a cave that has yielded human fossils associated with the Upper Pleistocene period. Former name (1904–65) **Broken Hill**.

**Ka·by·lia** |kä'bēlyə| name for regions of the Atlas Mts. in Algeria that are occupied by the Kabyle, a Berber people.

**Ka·chin** |ˌkäˈCHĬn| state in N Burma, on the frontier with China and India. Pop. 804,000. Capital: Myitkyina.

**Ka·di·köy** |kä'dəkœi| Turkish name for CHALCEDON.

**Ka·do·ma** |ˌkä'dōmä| city in W central Japan, on S Honshu, an industrial and residential suburb N of Osaka. Pop. 142,000.

**Kae·song** |'gä'sawNG| commercial and industrial city in S North Korea, on the 38th Parallel (the South Korean border). Pop. 346,000. An ancient city, it was the scene of armistice talks at the end of the Korean War.

**Ka·fue River** |kä'fōōə| river that flows 600 mi./965 km. from N Zambia across the country to the Zambezi River. Kafue National Park lies in its floodplains.

**Ka·ge·ra River** |kä'gärä| river that flows 250 mi./400 km. from NW Tanzania, along the Rwanda and Uganda borders, into Lake Victoria. It is the farthest headwater of the Nile River.

**Ka·go·shi·ma** |kägō'sHēmə| city and port in Japan. Pop. 537,000. Situated on the S coast of Kyushu, on the Satsuma Peninsula, it is noted for its porcelain (Satsuma ware).

**Ka·ho·o·la·we** |ˌkä‚hō-ō'läwä| island in Hawaii, SW of Maui, formerly used as a military range.

**Kah·ra·man·ma·raş** historic commercial city in central Turkey, capital of Kahramanmaraş province. Pop. 228,000. It was a Hittite center in the 9th century B.C.

**Kai·bab Plateau** |'kī‚bæb| highland region of NW Arizona, N of the Grand Canyon, and adjoining S Utah.

**Kai·feng** |'kī'fəNG| city in Henan province, E China, on the Yellow River. Pop. 693,000. One of the oldest cities in China, as Bianliang it was the Chinese capital from A.D. 907 to A.D. 1127.

**Kai Islands** |'kī| island group in Indonesia, in the SE Moluccas, in the Banda Sea between Ceram Island (NW) and the Aru Islands (E).

**Kai·las** |kī'läs| (also called **Kangrinboqê Feng**) peak, SW Tibet; the highest peak in the Kailas, or Gangdisê, Mts.: 22,027 ft./6,714 m. It is near the headwaters of the Indus and Brahmaputra rivers and is sacred to Hindus.

**Kai·lua** |kī'lōōə| community in SE Oahu, Hawaii, on the Pacific NE of Honolulu. Pop. 36,818.

**Kai·pa·ro·wits Plateau** |kī'pärəwits| highland region in S central Utah, N of Lake Powell.

**Kair·ouan** |ker'wän| city in NE Tunisia. Pop. 72,000. It is a Muslim holy city and a place of pilgrimage.

**Kai·sers·lau·tern** |ˌkīzərz'lowtərn| industrial city in western Germany, in Rhineland-Palatinate. Pop. 101,000.

**Ka·ki·na·da** |ˌkäki'nädə| (formerly **Cocanada**) commercial port city in SE India, on the Bay of Bengal in Andhra Pradesh state. Pop. 327,000.

**Ka·ko·ga·wa** |ˌkäkŏ'gäwä| industrial city in W central Japan, on S Honshu, W of Kobe. Pop. 240,000.

**Ka·laal·lit Nu·naat** |kä'lä(t)lēt nōo'nät| Inuit name for GREENLAND.

**Ka·la·ha·ri Desert** |ˌkälə'härē| high, vast, arid plateau in southern Africa N of the Orange River. It comprises most of Botswana with parts in Namibia and South Africa.

**Kal·a·ma·ta** |ˌkälə'mätə| see CALAMATA, Greece.

**Kal·a·ma·zoo** |ˌkæləmə'zōō| industrial and commercial city in SW Michigan. Pop. 80,277.

**Kal·gan** |'kæl'gæn| Mongolian name for ZHANGJIAKOU, China.

**Kal·goor·lie** |kæl'gŏorlē| gold-mining town in Western Australia, focus of a gold rush in the 1890s. Pop. 11,000.

**Ka·li·man·tan** |ˌkälē'män,tän| region of Indonesia, comprising the S part of the island of Borneo.

**Kalinin** |kə'lēnen| former name (1931–91) for TVER, Russia.

**Ka·li·nin·grad** |kə'lēnen,grəd| **1** port on the Baltic Sea, capital of the Russian region of Kaliningrad. Pop. 406,000. It was known by its German name of Königsberg until 1946, when it was ceded to the Soviet Union and renamed in honor of Soviet President Mikhail Kalinin. Its port is ice-free all year round and is a major naval base. **2** region of Russia, an exclave on the Baltic coast of E Europe. Capital: Kaliningrad. It is separated from Russia by the territory of Lithuania, Latvia, and Belarus.

**Ka·lisz** |'kälɛsн| industrial city in central Poland. Pop. 106,000.

**Kal·mar** |'käl,mär| port in SE Sweden, on the Kalmar Sound opposite Öland. Pop. 56,000.

**Kalmar Sound** |'käl,mär| narrow strait between the mainland of SE Sweden and the island of Öland, in the Baltic Sea.

**Kal·my·kia** |kæl'mikēə| autonomous republic in SW Russia, on the Caspian Sea. Pop. 325,000. Capital: Elista. Official name **Republic of Kalmykia-Khalmg Tangch**.

**Ka·lu·ga** |kə'lōōgə| industrial city and river port in European Russia, on the Oka River SW of Moscow. Pop. 314,000.

**Kal·yan** |kəl'yän| commercial and industrial city on the W coast of India, in the state of Maharashtra, NE of Bombay. Pop. 1,014,000.

**Ka·ma River** |'kämə| river (1,128 mi./1,805 km.) in Russia that rises in the central Ural Mts. and flows to the Volga River near Kazan.

**Ka·ma·ku·ra** |ˌkämä'kŏo,rä| historic town in E central Japan, on E central Honshu. Pop. 174,000. It is noted chiefly as a religious center.

**Ka·mar·ha·ti** |ˌkämər'hätē| industrial city in NE India, in West Bengal state, a suburb of Calcutta. Pop. 266,000.

**Kam·chat·ka** |kəm'cнätkə| vast mountainous peninsula of the NE coast of Siberian Russia, separating the Sea of Okhotsk from the Bering Sea; chief port, Petropavlovsk.

**Ka·men·skoye** |'käminskəyə| former name (until 1936) for DNIPRODZERZHINSK, Ukraine.

**Kamensk-Uralsky** |'käminsk ŏo'rälskyē| industrial city in central Russia, in the E foothills of the Urals. Pop. 208,000.

**Ka·menz** |'kä,ments| industrial city in E Germany, on the Schwarze Elster River. Pop. 19,000.

**Ka·mien·na Gó·ra** |kä'myenä 'gŏorə| (German name **Landshut**) industrial and commercial center in W Poland. Pop. 93,000.

**Kam·loops** |'kæm,lŏops| city in S central British Columbia, an administrative, commercial, and transportation center. Pop. 67,057.

**Kam·pa·la** |käm'pälə| the capital of Uganda. Pop. 773,000. It is situated on the N shores of Lake Victoria and replaced Entebbe as capital when the country became independent in 1963.

**Kam·pu·chea** |ˌkämpə'cнēə; ˌkæmpə 'cнēə| former name (1976–89) for CAMBODIA. □ **Kampuchean** adj. & n.

**Ka·nan·ga** |kə'näNggə| (formerly **Luluabourg**) commercial city in S central Congo (formerly Zaire), on the Lulua River. Pop. 372,000. It is in an agricultural and diamond-mining area.

**Ka·na·ta** |kə'nætə| city in SE Ontario, an industrial and residential suburb W of Ottawa. Pop. 37,344.

**Ka·na·wha River** |kə'naw-wə; kə'noi| river in W central West Virginia that connects the New River with the Ohio River. Charleston and other industrial centers lie along it.

**Ka·na·za·wa** |ˌkänä'zäwä| port city in central Japan, on central Honshu. Pop. 443,000. An agricultural, industrial, and tourist center, it was once the seat of powerful feudal lords.

**Kan·chen·jun·ga** |ˌkəncнən'jŏoNggə| (also **Kangchenjunga** or **Kinchinjunga**) a mountain in the Himalayas, on the border between Nepal and Sikkim. Rising to a height of 28,209 ft./8,598 m., it is the world's third-highest mountain.

**Kan·chi·pu·ram** |kən'CHēpərəm| (formerly **Conjeeveram**) city in S India, in Tamil Nadu state, W of Madras. Pop. 171,000. An ancient city with many temples, it is one of the most sacred Hindu towns in India.

**Kan·da·har** |,kəndə'här| city in S Afghanistan. Pop. 225,000. It was Afghanistan's first capital after independence (1748), until being replaced by Kabul in 1773.

**Kan·dy** |'kændē| city in Sri Lanka. Pop. 104,000. It was the capital (1480–1815) of the former independent kingdom of Kandy and contains one of the most sacred Buddhist shrines, the Dalada Maligava (Temple of the Tooth). □ **Kandyan** *adj. & n.*

**Ka·ne·o·he** |,känä'ōhā| community in E Oahu, Hawaii, a largely residential suburb NE of Honolulu. Pop. 35,448.

**Kan·gar** |'käNG,gär| the capital of the state of Perlis in N Malaysia, near the W coast of the Malay Peninsula. Pop. 13,000.

**Ka·Ngwa·ne** |käNG'(g)wänä| former homeland established in South Africa for the Swazi people, now part of the province of Mpumalanga.

**Kan·ka·kee** |,kæNGkə'kē| city in NE Illinois, on the Kankakee River. Pop. 27,575.

**Kan·kan** |kän'kän| commercial town in E central Guinea, a rail center and port on the Milo River. Pop. 100,000.

**Ka·no** |'känō| commercial, industrial, and cultural city in N Nigeria. Pop. 553,000.

**Kan·pur** |'kän,pŏŏr| (also **Cawnpore**) industrial city in Uttar Pradesh, N India, on the Ganges River. Pop. 2,100,000.

**Kan·sas** |'kænzəs| see box. □ **Kansan** *adj. & n.*

**Kan·sas City** |,kænzəs| each of two adjacent cities in the U.S., at the junction of the Missouri and Kansas rivers, one in NE Kansas (pop. 149,767) and the other in NW Missouri (pop. 435,146). Together they are an industrial, commercial, and rail complex.

**Kan·su** |'kän'sŏŏ| see GANSU, China.

**Kan·to** |'käntō| region of Japan, on the island of Honshu. Capital: Tokyo.

**Kao·hsiung** |'gowsHē'ŏŏNG| the chief port of Taiwan, on the SW coast. Pop. 1,390,000.

**Ka·pa·chi·ra Falls** waterfall on the Shire River in S Malawi. Former name **Murchison Rapids**.

---

### Kansas

**Capital:** Topeka
**Largest city:** Wichita
**Other cities:** Kansas City, Lawrence, Leavenworth, Overland Park, Salina
**Population:** 2,477,574 (1990); 2,629,067 (1998); 2,668,000 (2005 proj.)
**Population rank (1990):** 32
**Rank in land area:** 15
**Abbreviation:** KS; Kans.
**Nicknames:** Sunflower State; Wheat State; Breadbasket of America; Jayhawk State
**Motto:** *Ad Astra per Aspera* (Latin: 'To the Stars Through Difficulties')
**Bird:** western meadowlark
**Flower:** sunflower
**Tree:** cottonwood
**Song:** "Home on the Range"
**Noted physical features:** Great Plains, Osage Plains; Mount Sunflower
**Tourist attractions:** Eisenhower Center; Fort Riley, Fort Scott; Haskell Institute Indian Training School; Leavenworth Penitentiary; Tuttle Creek Reservoir
**Admission date:** January 29, 1861
**Order of admission:** 34
**Name origin:** For the Kansas River, the name of which first applied to Indians living along it; the name is a Siouan word, *Kansa,* translated 'people of the south wind.'

---

**Kap Far·vel** |,kæp 'fär,vel| Danish name for Cape FAREWELL, Greenland.

**Ka·pi·la·vas·tu** |,kəpilə'vəstŏŏ| town and principality of ancient India; birthplace of the Buddha (c.563 B.C.); in present-day Nepal.

**Ka·pos·var** |'kawpōSH,vär| commercial city in SW Hungary. Pop. 74,000. It is the capital of Somogy county.

**Kara-Bogaz Gol** |kä'rä bə'gäz'gawl| (also **Garabogazkol**) shallow salt lake in NW Turkmenistan, an inlet of the Caspian Sea separated by dike in the 1970s. Chemical industries are important in the area.

**Karachai-Cherkessia** autonomous republic in the N Caucasus, SW Russia. Pop. 436,000. Capital: Cherkessk. Official name **Karachai-Cherkess Republic.**

**Ka·ra·chi** |kə'räCHē| major city and port in Pakistan, capital of Sind province. Pop. 6,700,000. Situated on the Arabian Sea, it was the capital of Pakistan 1947–59 before being replaced by Rawalpindi.

**Ka·ra·fu·to** |ˌkärä'foõtō| the Japanese name for the S part of the island of Sakhalin.

**Ka·ra·gan·da** |ˌkärə'gändə| Russian name for QARAGHANDY, Kazakhstan.

**Ka·raj** |kä'räj| city in N Iran, to the west of Tehran. Pop. 442,000.

**Kar·a·ko·ram** |ˌkärə'kawrəm| great mountain system of central Asia, extending over 300 mi./480 km. SE from NE Afghanistan to Kashmir and forming part of the borders of India and Pakistan with China. One of the highest mountain systems in the world, it consists of a group of parallel ranges, forming a W continuation of the Himalayas, with many peaks over 26,000 ft./7,900 m., the highest being K2. Virtually inaccessible, it also contains the highest passes in the world, at elevations over 16,000 ft./4,900 m., including Karakoram Pass and Khardungla Pass.

**Kar·a·ko·rum** |ˌkärə'kawrəm| ancient city in central Mongolia, now ruined, which was the capital of the Mongol Empire, established by Genghis Khan in 1220. The capital was moved to Khanbaliq (modern Beijing) in 1267, and Karakorum was destroyed by Chinese forces in 1388.

**Ka·ra Kul, Lake** |ˌkärä 'kool| (also **Qara Kul**) lake in E Tajikistan, in the Pamirs plateau.

**Ka·ra Kum** |ˌkärə 'koom| desert in central Asia, to the E of the Caspian Sea, covering much of Turkmenistan. Russian name **Karakumy**.

**Ka·ra Sea** |'kärə| arm of the Arctic Ocean off the N coast of Russia, bounded to the E by the islands of Severnaya Zemlya and to the W by Novaya Zemlya.

**Ka·ra·wan·ken Alps** |ˌkärə'väNGkən| (Italian name **Caravanche**) range of the E Alps along the Austria-Slovenia border, rising to 7,341 ft./2,238 m. at Hochstule.

**Kar·ba·la** |'kärbələ| city in S Iraq. Pop. 185,000. A holy city for Shiite Muslims, it is the site of the tomb of Husayn, grandson of Muhammad, who was killed here in A.D. 680.

**Ka·re·lia** |kə'rēlyə| region of NE Europe on the border between Russia and Finland. Following Finland's declaration of independence in 1917, part of Karelia became a region of Finland and part an autonomous republic of the Soviet Union. After the Russo-Finnish war of 1939–40 the greater part of Finnish Karelia was ceded to the Soviet Union. The remaining part of Karelia constitutes a province of eastern Finland. □ **Karelian** adj. & n.

**Ka·ren State** |kə'ren| state in SE Burma,

on the border with Thailand. Capital: Paan. Inaugurated in 1954 as an autonomous state of Burma, it was given the traditional Karen name of Kawthoolay in 1964, but reverted to Karen after the 1974 constitution limited its autonomy. Starting in 1995 a rebel army, the Karen National Union, engaged in armed conflict with the Burmese government in an attempt to gain independence. Also called **Kawthoolay**, **Kawthulei**.

**Ka·ri·ba, Lake** |kə'rēbə| artificial lake on the Zambia–Zimbabwe border in central Africa. It was created by the damming of the Zambezi River by the Kariba Dam, and is the chief source of hydroelectric power for Zimbabwe and Zambia.

**Ka·ri·ba Dam** |kə'rēbə| concrete arch dam on the Zambezi River, 240 mi./385 km. downstream from the Victoria Falls. It was built in 1955–59.

**Ka·ri·ya** |kä'rēyä| industrial city in central Japan, on central Honshu, SE of Nagoya. Pop. 120,000.

**Karl-Marx-Stadt** |'kärl 'märks ˌSHtät| former name (1953–90) for CHEMNITZ, Germany.

**Kar·lo·vac** |'kärlə,väts| industrial town in NW Croatia, on the Kupa River. Pop. 60,000.

**Kar·lo·vy Va·ry** |'kärlōvē 'värē| spa town in the W Czech Republic. Pop. 56,000. It is famous for its alkaline thermal springs. German name **Karlsbad**.

**Karls·kro·na** |ˌkärl'skroonə| seaport and fishing center in SE Sweden, on the Baltic Sea, capital of Belkinge province. Pop. 59,000.

**Karls·ru·he** |'kärls,rooə| industrial town and port on the Rhine in western Germany. Pop. 279,000.

**Karl·stad** |'kärl,städ| industrial town in central Sweden, on the N shore of Lake Vänern. Pop. 76,000.

**Kar·nak** |'kär,næk| village in Egypt on the Nile, now largely amalgamated with Luxor. It is the site of the N complex of monuments of ancient Thebes, including the great temple of Amun.

**Kar·nal** |kər'näl| historic city in NW India, in Haryana state. Pop. 176,000.

**Kar·na·ta·ka** |ˌkär'nätəkə| state in SW India. Pop. 44.82 million. Capital: Bangalore. Former name (until 1973) **Mysore**.

**Kärn·ten** |'kernten| German name for CARINTHIA, Austria.

**Ka·roo, the** |kə'roo| (also **Karroo**) elevated semidesert plateau in South Africa, used for grazing.

**Kár·pa·thos** |'kärpə,THaws| island in Greece, in the Aegean Sea between Crete and Rhodes. Pop. 5,000. Its largest town is Karpathos.

**Kars** |kärs| city in NE Turkey, in Kars province. Pop. 78,000. A historic Armenian city, Kars is noted for its crafts.

**Kar·shi** |'kärsHē| (also **Qarshi**; formerly **Bek-Budi**) transportation center in SE Uzbekistan. Pop. 168,000.

**Karst** |kärst| (in Slovenian **Kras**) limestone region near Trieste in Slovenia, noted for its geologic formations. Its name is used by geologists to describe similar limestone regions elsewhere.

**Ka·sai River** |kä'sī| (also **Cassai**) river that flows 1,100 mi./1,800 km. from central Angola through S and central Congo (formerly Zaire), into the Congo River. In its lower 500 mi./800 km. it is an important trade route.

**Ka·shan** |kä'sHän| oasis town in central Iran, N of Isfahan. Pop. 155,000. It has long been noted for its carpets.

**Ka·shi** |'kä'sHē| (also called **Kashgar**) chief commercial city of W Xinjiang, NW China, on the Kashgar River. Pop. 175,000. It is a fertile oasis on the former Silk Road.

**Ka·shi·wa** |kä'sHēwä| city in E central Japan, on E central Honshu, NE of Tokyo. Pop. 305,000.

**Kash·mir, Vale of** |'kæsH,mir; kæsH'mir| Himalayan valley in Jammu and Kashmir, N India, on the Jhelum River and lakes, noted for its beauty.

**Kash·mir** |'kæsH,mir; kæsH'mir| region on the N border of India and NE Pakistan. Formerly a state of India, it has been disputed between India and Pakistan since partition in 1947, with sporadic outbreaks of fighting. The NW part is controlled by Pakistan, most of it forming the state of Azad Kashmir, while the remainder is incorporated into the Indian state of Jammu and Kashmir. Formerly spelled **Cashmere**. □ **Kashmiri** *adj. & n.*

**Kas·sa·la** |'käsə,lə| (also **Kasala**) historic commercial town in E Sudan, near the Eritrean border. Pop. 146,000.

**Kas·sel** |'käsəl| industrial city in central Germany, in Hesse. Pop. 197,000. It was the capital of the kingdom of Westphalia (1807–13) and of the Prussian province of Hesse-Nassau (1866–1944).

**Kas·ser·ine Pass** |'käsə,rēn| historic site near the township of Al-Qasrayn, N central Tunisia. A gap in an extension of the Atlas Mts., it was fought over by German and American forces in February 1943.

**Ka·su·gai** |kä'soōgī| industrial city in central Japan, on S central Honshu, a suburb N of Nagoya. Pop. 267,000.

**Ka·su·ka·be** |,käs(oō)'käbə| city in E central Japan, on E central Honshu, N of Tokyo. Pop. 189,000.

**Ka·sur** |kä'soōr| city in Punjab province, NE Pakistan. Pop. 155,000.

**Ka·tah·din, Mount** |kə'tädn| (also **Ktaadn**) peak in N central Maine, in Baxter State Park. At 5,267 ft./1,606 m., it is the highest point in the state. The N end of the Appalachian Trail is here.

**Ka·tan·ga** |kə'tæNGgə| former name (until 1972) for SHABA, Congo (formerly Zaire).

**Ka·thi·a·war** |,kätē'wär| peninsula on the W coast of India, in the state of Gujarat, separating the Gulf of Kutch from the Gulf of Cambay.

**Kath·man·du** |,kätmæn'doō| (also **Katmandu**) historic city, the capital of Nepal. Pop. 419,000. It is situated in the Himalayas at an altitude of 4,450 ft./1,370 m.

**Kat·mai National Park** |'kæt,mī| preserve in SW Alaska, on the Alaska Peninsula, noted for its volcanic activity and wildlife.

**Ka·to·wi·ce** |,kätə'vētsə| city in SW Poland. Pop. 349,000. It is the industrial center of the Silesian coal-mining region.

**Ka·tsi·na** |'kätsēnə| commercial and industrial city in N Nigeria, near the Niger border and NW of Kano. Pop. 182,000. It was the capital of the Kingdom of Katsina, part of HAUSALAND.

**Kat·te·gat** |'kætə,gæt; 'kät.ə,gät| strait, 140 mi./225 km. in length, between Sweden and Denmark. It is linked to the North Sea by the Skagerrak and to the Baltic Sea by the Øresund.

**Kau·ai** |'kow,ī| island in the state of Hawaii, separated from Oahu by the Kauai Channel; chief town, Lihue.

**Kau·nas** |'kownəs| industrial city and river port in southern Lithuania, at the confluence of the Viliya and Neman rivers. Pop. 430,000. It was the capital of Lithuania 1918–40.

**Ka·vál·la** |kä'välä| port on the Aegean coast of NE Greece. Pop. 57,000. Originally a Byzantine city and fortress, it was Turkish until 1912, when it was ceded to Greece.

**Ka·ve·ri** |'kävərē| see CAUVERY River, India.

**Ka·wa·goe** |kä'wägō,ā| city in E central Japan, on E central Honshu, NW of Tokyo. Pop. 305,000.

**Ka·wa·gu·chi** |,käwä'gōōcHē| industrial city in E central Japan, on E central Honshu, a suburb N of Tokyo. Pop. 439,000.

**Ka·wa·sa·ki** |ˌkäwəˈsäkē| industrial city on the SE coast of the island of Honshu, Japan. Pop. 1,174,000.

**Kaw·thoo·lay** |ˌkawⲦⲎʘʘˈlä| (also **Kawthulei**) former name (1964–74) for KAREN STATE, Burma.

**Kay·se·ri** |ˈkīsərē| city in central Turkey, capital of a province of the same name. Pop. 421,000. Known as Kayseri since the 11th century, it was formerly called Caesarea Mazaca and was the capital of Cappadocia.

**Ka·zakh·stan** |kəzäkˈstän| (also spelled **Kazakstan**) republic in central Asia, on the S border of Russia, extending from the Caspian Sea E to the Altai Mts. and China. Area: 1.05 million sq. mi./2.72 million sq. km. Pop.: 16,899,000. Languages, Kazakh (official), Russian. Capital: Aqmola (Akmola). Largest city: Almaty. A Turkic homeland later dominated by Mongols, Kazakhstan eventually was absorbed into the Russian Empire. In 1991 it gained independence as the Soviet Union dissolved. Rich in reources, the country is characterized by nomadic pastoralism, crops including cotton and grains, and growing industry. □ **Kazakh** *adj. & n*

Kazakhstan

**Ka·zan** |kəˈzän(yə)| port on the Volga River to the E of Nizhni Novgorod in Russia, capital of the autonomous republic of Tatarstan. Pop. 1,103,000.

**Ka·zan·luk** |ˌkäzänˈlək| (also **Kazanlik**) industrial city in central Bulgaria, near the Valley of the Roses. Pop. 62,000.

**Kaz·bek** |kəzˈbyek| extinct volcano in Georgia, in the central Caucasus Mts., rising over the Daryal Pass. Height: 16,558 ft./5,056 m.

**Kear·ny** |ˈkärnē| industrial town in NE New Jersey, on Newark Bay, just W of Jersey City. Pop. 34,874.

**Keb·ne·kai·se** |ˌkebneˈkīsə| the highest peak in Sweden, in the N of the country, rising to a height of 6,962 ft./2,117 m.

**Ke·dah** |ˈkedə| state of NW Malaysia, on the W coast of the Malay Peninsula. Pop. 1,413,000. Capital: Alor Setar.

**Ke·di·ri** |kəˈdirē| city in Indonesia, on E Java. Pop. 250,000. It is famous for handicrafts such as batik.

**Kee·ling Islands** |ˈkēliNG| another name for COCOS ISLANDS.

**Kee·lung** |ˈkēˈlooNG| see CHILUNG, Taiwan.

**Keene** |kēn| city in SW New Hampshire. Pop. 22,430.

**Ke·fal·lin·ía** |ˌkefälēˈnēä| Greek name for CEPHALONIA.

**Kef·la·vik** |ˈkyeblə,vēk; ˈkeflə,vik| fishing port in SW Iceland. Pop. 8,000. Iceland's international airport is located nearby.

**Ke·lang** |kəˈläNG| (also called **Port Kelang**; also **Klang**) port city in Malaysia, on the Strait of Malacca in Selangor state. Pop. 368,000. It is Malaysia's busiest international port.

**Ke·lan·tan** |kəˈlän,tän| state of N Malaysia, on the E coast of the Malay Peninsula. Pop. 1,220,000. Capital: Kota Baharu.

**Kells** |kelz| see CEANNANUS MOR, Ireland.

**Kelmscott** |ˈkelmskət; ˈkelm,skät| (also **Kelmscot**) village in Oxfordshire, S England, longtime home of the writer and designer William Morris, and associated with the Arts and Crafts movement of the late 19th century.

**Ke·low·na** |kiˈlōnə| city in S British Columbia, on Okanagan Lake, in an agricultural and resort area. Pop. 75,950.

**Ke·me·ro·vo** |ˈkyemə,rōvə; ˈkyemərə,vō| industrial city in S central Russia, to the E of Novosibirsk. Pop. 521,000.

**Ke·nai Peninsula** |ˈkē,nī| region in S Alaska, in the Gulf of Alaska just S of Anchorage.

**Ken·dal** |ˈkendəl| resort town in Cumbria, NW England, in the Lake District. Pop. 24,200.

**Ken·il·worth** |ˈkenl,wərⲦⲎ| commercial town in central England, in Warwickshire, SW of Coventry. Pop. 17,000. It is associated with the novels of Walter Scott.

**Ke·ni·tra** |kəˈnētrə| (formerly **Port Lyautey**) river port city in N Morocco, NE of Rabat and near the Atlantic coast, on the Sebou River. Pop. 293,000.

**Ken·ne·bec River** |ˈkenə,bek| river that flows 150 mi./240 km. through W central Maine to the Atlantic. Waterville, Augusta, and Bath lie on it.

**Ken·ner** |ˈkenər| city in SE Louisiana, a suburb W of New Orleans. Pop. 72,033.

**Ken·ne·wick** |ˈkenə,wik| city in SE Washington, on the Columbia River. The nuclear industry at nearby Hanford has been central to its economy. Pop. 42,155.

**Ke·no·sha** |kə'nōSHə| industrial port city in SE Wisconsin, on Lake Michigan. Pop. 80,352.

**Ken·sing·ton** |'kensiNGtən; 'kenziNGtən| fashionable residential district in central London, England, part of the borough of Kensington and Chelsea. Pop. 128,000.

**Kent[1]** |kent| county on the SE coast of England. Pop.: 1,486,000; county seat, Maidstone. □ **Kentish** adj. & n.

**Kent[2]** |kent| city in NE Ohio, home to Kent State University. Pop. 28,835.

**Ken·tucky** |kən'təkē| see box. □ **Kentuckian** adj. & n.

**Ken·ya, Mount** |'kenyə; 'kēnyə| mountain in central Kenya, just S of the equator, rising to a height of 17,058 ft./5,200 m. The second-highest mountain in Africa, it gave its name to the country Kenya.

**Ken·ya** |'kenyə; 'kēnyə| equatorial republic in E Africa, on the Indian Ocean. Area: 225,047 sq. mi./582,646 sq. km. Pop. 25,016,000. Languages, Swahili (official), English (official), Kikuyu. Capital and largest city: Nairobi. Peopled largely by Bantu speakers, Kenya came under British domination in the early 20th century, and gained independence in 1963. Tea and coffee are important products, and tourism is also important. Most of the N is sparsely populated semidesert. □ **Kenyan** adj. & n.

Kenya

**Ke·o·kuk** |'kēə,kək| city in SE Iowa, on the Mississippi River. Pop. 12,451.

**Ke·ra·la** |'kerələ| state on the coast of SW India. Pop. 29,010,000. Capital: Trivandrum. It was created in 1956 from the former state of Travancore-Cochin and part of Madras. □ **Keralite** adj. & n.

**Kerch** |'kerCH| city in S Ukraine, the chief port and industrial center of the Crimea, at the E end of the Kerch Peninsula. Pop. 176,000.

---

### Kentucky

**Official name:** Commonwealth of Kentucky
**Capital:** Frankfort
**Largest city:** Louisville
**Other cities:** Bowling Green, Covington, Lexington, Paducah
**Population:** 3,685,296 (1990); 3,936,499 (1998); 4,098,000 (2005 proj.)
**Population rank (1990):** 23
**Rank in land area:** 37
**Abbreviation:** KY; Ky.
**Nicknames:** Bluegrass State; Dark and Bloody Ground
**Motto:** 'United We Stand, Divided We Fall'
**Bird:** cardinal
**Fish:** bass
**Flower:** goldenrod
**Tree:** Kentucky coffee tree
**Song:** "My Old Kentucky Home"
**Noted physical features:** Bluegrass Basin; Mammoth Cave; Land Between the Lakes; Cumberland Gap; Cumberland Plateau; Black Mountain
**Tourist attractions:** Birthplace of Abraham Lincoln; Fort Knox; Mammoth Cave National Park; Kentucky Derby; Churchill Downs; Wilderness Trail
**Admission date:** June 1, 1792
**Order of admission:** 15
**Name origin:** Named when the territory was established as a county of Virginia in 1776, from a Wyandot word *ken-tah-teh,* meaning 'land of tomorrow.'

---

**Ker·gue·len Islands** |'kərgə,lən; ,kergä 'len| group of islands in the S Indian Ocean, comprising the island of Kerguelen and some 300 small islets, forming part of French Southern and Antarctic Territories.

**Kér·ki·ra** |'kerkirə| modern Greek name for CORFU.

**Kerk·ra·de** |'kərk,rädə| mining town in the S Netherlands, on the German border. Pop. 53,000. An international music competition is held here every four years.

**Ker·mad·ec Islands** |kər'madek| group of uninhabited islands in the W South Pacific, N of New Zealand, administered by New Zealand since 1887.

**Ker·man** |kər'män| (formerly called **Carmana**) historic desert city in SE Iran. Pop. 312,000.

**Ker·man·shah** |kər,män'SHä| another name for BAKHTARAN, Iran.

**Ker·ry** |'kerē| county of the Republic of Ireland, on the SW coast in the province of

Munster. Pop. 122,000; county seat, Tralee.

**Ker·u·len River** |'kerə,len| (also called **Herlen**) river of NE Mongolia and NE China. Rising in the Hentiyn Nuruu range NE of Ulan Bator, Mongolia, it flows 785 mi./1,263 km. S and E to Hulun Lake in Heilongjiang province, China.

**Kes·te·ven** |kes'tēvən| one of three administrative divisions of Lincolnshire, England before the local government reorganization of 1974, now administered as the districts of North and South Kesteven.

**Kes·wick** |'kezik| market and resort town on the shores of Derwent Water in Cumbria, NW England. Pop. 6,000.

**Ket River** |'ket| river (842 mi./1,355 km) in SE Russia. It rises N of Krasnoyarsk and flows W into the Ob River at Kolpashevo.

**Ketch·i·kan** |'keCHi,kæn| city in SE Alaska, on Revillagigedo Island in the Alexander Archipelago. Pop. 8,263.

**Ket·ter·ing** |'ketəriNG| city in SW Ohio, an industrial and residential suburb SE of Dayton. Pop. 60,569.

**Kew Gardens** |'kyōō| the Royal Botanic Gardens at Kew, in Richmond, SW London, England.

**Key Largo** |'kē 'lär,gō| resort island off the S coast of Florida, the S and the longest of the Florida Keys.

**Key·stone State** |'kē,stōn| nickname for PENNSYLVANIA.

**Key West** |'kē 'west| resort city in southern Florida, at the S tip of the Florida Keys. Pop. 24,832. It is the southernmost city in the U.S. outside Hawaii.

**Kha·ba·rovsk** |kə'bärərəfsk| industrial city in Siberian Russia, on the Amur River and the Chinese border. Pop. 608,000.

**Kha·kas·sia** |kə'käsyə| autonomous republic in S central Russia. Pop. 569,000. Capital: Abakan.

**Kha·li·stan** |,kälə'stän| the name given by Sikh nationalists to a proposed independent Sikh state, created chiefly from Indian territory.

**Khal·kís** |KHäl'kēs| Greek name for CHALCIS.

**Khan·ba·lik** |,känbä'lēk| see BEIJING, China.

**Kha·niá** |KHän'yä| Greek name for CHANIA, Crete.

**Khan·ka, Lake** |'käNGkə| lake that lies on the boundary between China and Primorsky Krai, SE Russia, N of Vladivostok. Most of the lake lies in Russia.

**Kha·rag·pur** |'kərəg,pŏōr| industrial town

in NE India, in West Bengal state, W of Calcutta. Pop. 280,000.

**Kharg Island** |'kärg| small island at the head of the Persian Gulf, site of Iran's principal deep-water oil terminal.

**Khar·kiv** |'KHärkəf| (formerly **Kharkov**) industrial and commercial city in NE Ukraine, in the Donets basin. Pop. 1,618,000. It was the capital of Soviet Ukraine 1919–34, before Kiev.

**Khar·toum** |kär'tŏōm| the capital of Sudan, situated at the junction of the Blue Nile and the White Nile. Pop. 925,000. Originally a 19th-century military garrison, it now has administrative and industrial zones.

**Khas·ko·vo** |'käskə,vō| capital city of Khaskovo province, central Bulgaria. Pop. 95,000. It processes tobacco.

**Khay·lit·sa** |'kī,lētsə| township 25 mi./40 km. SE of Cape Town, South Africa. Pop. 190,000. It was built in 1983 for African workers from several nearby squatter camps.

**Kha·zar·ia** |kə'zärēə| ancient region of SE Russia, important for its strategic location along trade routes between the Black and Caspian seas.

**Kher·son** |kHer'sawn| industrial and oil port in S Ukraine, on the Dnieper estuary near the Black Sea. Pop. 361,000.

**Khe Sanh** |'kā'sän| site, in N central Vietnam, of one of the costliest battles of the Vietnam War.

**Khi·os** |'kHē,aws| Greek name for CHIOS.

**Khi·va** |'kHēvä| (ancient name **Chorasmia**) former khanate on the left bank of the Amu Darya River, in what is now NW Uzbekistan. The region is largely desert. Its capital is the oasis town of Khiva.

**Khmel·nit·sky** |kHmel'nitskē| (also **Khmelnytskyy**) industrial city in W Ukraine, SW of Kiev. Pop. 241,000.

**Khmer Republic** |kə'mer| former official name (1970–75) for CAMBODIA.

**Khon Kaen** |'kawn 'kän| town in E central Thailand, on the Korat Plateau, NE of Bangkok. Pop. 131,000.

**Kho·per River** |kHə'pyawr| river (625 mi./1,010 km.) in SW Russia. It rises SW of Penza and flows into the Don River.

**Khor·ram·shahr** |,kawrəm'sHhər| oil port on the Shatt al-Arab waterway in W Iran. It was almost totally destroyed during the Iran-Iraq War of 1980–88. Former name (until 1924) **Mohammerah**.

**Khudzhand** |kHŏō'jät| (also **Khodzhent**; formerly **Leninabad**; earlier, **Khojend**) town in NW Tajikistan, on the Syr Darya

River. Pop. 165,000. It is a textile center and one of the oldest towns in central Asia.

**Khul·na** |'kо̄о̄lnä| industrial city in S Bangladesh, on the Ganges delta. Pop. 601,000.

**Khun·je·rab Pass** |'kənjə,rəb| high-altitude pass through the Himalayas, on the Karakoram highway at a height of 16,088 ft./4,900 m., linking China and Pakistan.

**Khu·ze·stan** |‚KHо̄о̄zHi'stän| province in SW Iraq. Pop. 3,176,000. Capital: Ahvaz. It is rich in oil fields.

**Khy·ber Pass** |'kībər| mountain pass in the Hindu Kush, on the border between Pakistan and Afghanistan at a height of 3,520 ft./1,067 m. The pass was once of great commercial and strategic importance, the route by which successive invaders entered India, and was garrisoned by the British intermittently between 1839 and 1947.

**Kiang·si** |jëäNG'ë| see JIANGXI, China.

**Kiang·su** |jë'äNG'sо̄о̄| see JIANGSU, China.

**Kid·der·min·ster** |'kidər,minstər| town in W central England, in Worcestershire, on the Stour River. Pop. 51,000. It is known for its carpets.

**Kid·ron** |'kidrən; ki'drо̄n| valley in the Israeli-occupied West Bank, and an intermittent stream flowing through it from East Jerusalem to the Dead Sea, both mentioned in the Bible.

**Kiel** |kël| naval port in N Germany, capital of Schleswig-Holstein, on the Baltic Sea coast at the E end of the Kiel Canal. Pop. 247,000.

**Kiel Canal** |kël| waterway, 61 mi./98 km. in length, in NW Germany, running W from Kiel to Brunsbüttel at the mouth of the Elbe. It connects the North Sea with the Baltic and was constructed in 1895 to provide the German navy with a shorter route between these two seas. German name **Nord-Ostsee Kanal**.

**Kiel·ce** |'kyeltsə| heavy industrial city in S Poland. Pop. 214,000.

**Ki·ev** |'kë,ef; 'kë,ev| capital of Ukraine, an industrial city and port on the Dnieper River. Pop. 2,616,000. Founded in the 8th century, and the medieval capital of Kievan Rus, it became capital of the Ukrainian Soviet Socialist Republic in 1934. In 1991 it became capital of independent Ukraine.

**Ki·ga·li** |ki'gäle| the capital of Rwanda, a commercial city E of Lake Kivu. Pop. 234,000.

**Ki·go·ma** |kë'gōmä| port town in W Tanzania, on Lake Tanganyika. It has rail connections to Dar es Salaam, and has been a trade center for centuries, transshipping goods from central Africa.

**Ki·klá·dhes** |ki'kläTHis| Greek name for the CYCLADES.

**Ki·lau·ea** |‚kēlow'äə| volcano with a crater roughly 5 mi./8 km. long by 3 mi./5 km. broad on the island of Hawaii, on the eastern flanks of Mauna Loa at an elevation of 4,090 ft./1,247 m.

**Kil·dare** |kil'dær; kil'der| county of the Republic of Ireland, in the E, in the province of Leinster. Pop. 123,000; county seat, Naas.

**Kil·i·man·ja·ro, Mount** |‚kiləmən'järō| extinct volcano in N Tanzania. It has twin peaks, the higher of which, Kibo 19,340 ft./5,895 m., is the highest mountain in Africa.

**Kil·ken·ny** |kil'kenë| **1** county of the Republic of Ireland, in the SE, in the province of Leinster. Pop. 74,000. **2** its county seat. Pop. 9,000.

**Kil·lar·ney** |ki'lärnë| town in the SW of the Republic of Ireland, in County Kerry, famous for the beauty of the nearby lakes and mountains. Pop. 7,000.

**Kil·leen** |ki'lēn| city in E central Texas. Pop. 63,535. Nearby Fort Hood is key to its economy.

**Kil·ling Fields, the** name given to all or parts of Cambodia under the Khmer Rouge regime (1975–79), which was responsible for the deaths of a million or more Cambodians.

**Kil·mar·nock** |kil'märnək| town in W central Scotland, administrative center of East Ayrshire. Pop. 44,000.

**Kim·ber·ley**[1] |'kimbərlë| (also **the Kimberleys**) plateau region in the far N of Western Australia. A mining and cattle-rearing region, it was the scene of a gold rush in 1885.

**Kim·ber·ley**[2] |'kimbərlë| city in South Africa, in the province of Northern Cape. Pop. 167,000. It has been a diamond-mining center since the early 1870s.

**Kim·chaek** |'kēm'cHæk| (formerly **Somgjin**) industrial port city in E North Korea, on the Sea of Japan. Pop. 281,000.

**Kin·a·ba·lu, Mount** |‚kēn'äbälо̄о̄| mountain in the state of Sabah in E Malaysia, on the N coast of Borneo. Rising to 13,431 ft./4,094 m., it is the highest peak of Borneo and of SE Asia.

**Kin·car·dine·shire** |kin'kärdnsHər; kin 'kärdn,SHir| former county of E Scotland. In 1975 it became part of Grampian region and in 1996 part of Aberdeenshire.

**Kings Canyon National Park** |'kiNGz

'kænyən| national park in the Sierra Nevada, California, to the N of Sequoia National Park. Established in 1940, it preserves groves of ancient sequoia trees, including some of the largest in the world.

**Kings County** county in New York state coextensive with the borough of Brooklyn.

**King's Lynn** |'kiNGz 'lin| (also **Lynn Regis** or **Lynn**) port and market town in E England, near the Wash and the mouth of the Ouse. Pop. 37,000.

**Kings•port** |'kiNGz,pawrt| industrial city in NE Tennessee, part of a complex with Johnson City and Bristol. Pop. 36,365.

**Kings•ton**¹ |'kiNGstən| the capital, largest city, and chief port of Jamaica. Pop. 538,000. Founded in 1693, it became capital in 1870.

**Kings•ton**² |'kiNGstən| historic city in SE New York, on the Hudson River. Pop. 23,095.

**Kings•ton**³ |'kiNGstən| industrial port in SE Ontario, on Lake Ontario, at the head of the St. Lawrence River. Pop. 56,597.

**Kingston-upon-Hull** |'kiNGstənə,pän 'həl| official name for HULL, England.

**Kings•ton upon Thames** |'kiNGztən ə ,pawn 'temz| industrial and commercial borough of SW Greater London, England. Pop. 130,000.

**Kings•town** |'kiNG,stown| the capital and chief port of St. Vincent and the Grenadines, in the West Indies. Pop. 26,000.

**King Wil•liam Island** |kiNG 'wilyəm| island in the Arctic Archipelago of Nunavut, Canada. Gjoa Haven, in the history of the Northwest Passage, is on the S shore.

**Kin•ki** |'kinkē| region of Japan, on the island of Honshu. Capital: Osaka. Kyoto, Kobe, and Nara are here.

**Kinross-shire** |kin'rawssHər; kin'raws ,sHir| former county of E central Scotland.

**Kin•sale** |kin'sāl| historic port and resort town in SW Ireland, in S County Cork. Off **Old Head of Kinsale**, a cape to the S, the *Lusitania* was sunk in 1915.

**Kin•sha•sa** |kin'sHäsə| the capital, largest city, and industrial center of the Democratic Republic of Congo (formerly Zaire), a port on the Congo River, in the SW. Pop. 3,804,000. Founded in 1881 by the explorer Sir Henry M. Stanley, it became the capital of Zaire in 1960. Former name (until 1966) **Léopoldville.**

**Kin•ston** |'kinz,tən| industrial and commercial city in E North Carolina. Pop. 25,295. Tobacco is central to its economy.

**Kin•tyre** |kin'tīr| peninsula on the W coast of Scotland, to the W of Arran, extending S for 40 mi./64 km. into the North Channel and separating the Firth of Clyde from the Atlantic. Its S tip is the Mull of Kintyre.

**Kir•ghi•zia** |kir'gēzHə| another name for KYRGYZSTAN.

**Ki•ri•ba•ti** |,kirə'bätē; 'kirə,bæs| republic in the SW Pacific including the Gilbert Islands, the Line islands, the Phoenix Islands, and Banaba (Ocean Island). Area: 277 sq. mi./717 sq. km. Pop. 71,000. Official languages, English and I-Kiribati (local Austronesian language): Capital: Bairiki (on Tarawa). The Micronesian islands were dominated by Britain 1892–1975. Phosphate mining was formerly the main economic base; today tuna fishing and copra are important. □ **Kiribatian** *adj. & n.*

**Kiribati**

**Ki•rin** |'kē'rin| see JILIN province, China.

**Ki•ri•ti•ma•ti** |kə'risməs| island in the Pacific Ocean, one of the Line Islands of Kiribati. Pop. 3,000. The largest atoll in the world, it was discovered by Captain James Cook on Christmas Eve, 1777 and was British until it became part of an independent Kiribati in 1979. Former name (until 1981) **Christmas Island.**

**Kirk•cal•dy** |kə(r)'kawdē| industrial town and port in Fife, SE Scotland, on the N shore of the Firth of Forth. Pop. 47,000.

**Kirk•cud•bright** |kə(r)'kōōbrē| town in Dumfries and Galloway, SW Scotland, on the Dee River. Pop. 3,000.

**Kirk•cud•bright•shire** |kə(r)'kōōbrēsHər; kə(r)'kōōbrē,sHir| former county of SW Scotland. It became part of the region of Dumfries and Galloway in 1975.

**Kirk•land** |'kərklənd| city in W central Washington, a suburb NE of Seattle. Pop. 40,052.

**Kir•kuk** |kir'kōōk| industrial city in N Iraq, center of the oil industry in that region. Pop. 208,000.

**Kirk•wall** |'kərkwəl; 'kər,kwawl| port in the

Orkney Islands, Scotland. Pop. 6,000. Situated on the island of Mainland, it is the chief town of the islands.

**Ki·rov** |'kē,rawf| former name (1934–92) for VYATKA, Russia.

**Ki·ro·va·bad** |ˌkērəvə'bät| former name (1935–89) for GÄNCÄ, Azerbaijan.

**Ki·ro·vo·hrad** |ˌkērəvə'hräd| industrial city in central Ukraine, on the Ingul River, capital of Kirovohrad oblast. Pop. 274,000. Former name **Kirovograd**.

**Ki·ru·na** |'kērōō,nä| the northernmost town of Sweden, in the Lapland iron-mining region. Pop. 26,000.

**Kir·yu** |'kiryōō; kir'yōō| city in N central Japan, on central Honshu, NNW of Tokyo. Pop. 126,000. It has been a major center of silk production since the 8th century.

**Ki·san·ga·ni** |ˌkēsän'gänē| city in the northernmost part of the Democratic Republic of Congo (formerly Zaire), on the Congo River. Pop. 373,000. Former name (until 1966) **Stanleyville**.

**Kish** |'kiSH| major city of ancient Mesopotamia, on a former channel of the Euphrates River. Its ruins lie E of those of Babylon, and E of present-day Hillah, Iraq.

**Ki·shi·nev** |'kiSHi,nef| Russian name for CHIŞINĂU, Moldova.

**Ki·shi·wa·da** |ˌkēsHē'wädä| city in W central Japan, on S Honshu, an industrial and residential suburb S of Osaka. Pop. 189,000.

**Kis·ka Island** |'kiskə| island in the Aleutian Islands, in SW Alaska. Site of naval facilities, it was occupied by the Japanese during World War II.

**Kis·sim·mee** |ki'simē| resort and agricultural city in central Florida. Pop. 30,050.

**Ki·ta·kyu·shu** |kē'täkyōō,SHōō| industrial port in S Japan, a steelmaking center on the N coast of Kyushu. Pop. 1,026,000.

**Kitch·e·ner** |'kiCHənər| city in SE Ontario. Pop. 168,282. Settled by German Mennonites in 1806, it is an industrial and university center.

**Kitt Peak** |'kit| peak in the Quinlan Mts., in S Arizona, site of a large observatory complex.

**Kit·ty Hawk** |'kitē,hawk| resort town on the Outer Banks, on the Atlantic coast of North Carolina. Pop. 1,973. It was near here, in Kill Devil Hills, in 1903, that the Wright Brothers made the first powered airplane flight.

**Kit·we** |'kē,twä| city in the Copperbelt mining region of N Zambia. Pop. 338,000.

**Kitz·bühel** |'kits,byōō(ə)l| town in the Tyrol, W Austria. Pop. 8,000. It is a popular winter resort center.

**Ki·vu, Lake** |'kēvōō| lake in central Africa, on the border between the Democratic Republic of Congo (formerly Zaire) and Rwanda.

**Ki·zil Ir·mak** |ˌki'zil ir'mäk| (ancient name **Halys**) longest river of Turkey, flowing 715 mi./1,150 km. in a great curve through central Anatolia to the Black Sea.

**Klad·no** |'klædnaw| industrial city in the NW Czech Republic. Pop. 72,000.

**Kla·gen·furt** |'klägən,fŏŏrt| city in S Austria, capital of Carinthia. Pop. 89,000.

**Klai·pe·da** |'klīpədə| industrial city, the chief port of Lithuania, on the Baltic Sea. Pop. 206,000. Former name (1918–23 and 1941–44, when under German control) **Memel**.

**Klam·ath Mountains** |'klæməTH| ranges in SW Oregon and N California, through which the **Klamath River** flows to the Pacific.

**Klau·sen·burg** |'klowzen,bŏŏrk| German name for CLUJ-NAPOCA, Romania.

**Klerks·dorp** |'klerks,dawrp| commercial city in South Africa, in North-West Province, SW of Johannesburg. Pop. 239,000.

**Klon·dike** |'klän,dīk| tributary of the Yukon River, in Yukon Territory, NW Canada, which rises in the Ogilvie Mts. and flows 100 mi./160 km. W to join the Yukon at Dawson. It gave its name to the surrounding region, which became famous when gold was found in nearby Bonanza Creek in 1896, touching off the Klondike Gold Rush of 1897–98.

**Klos·ters** |'klawstərz| Alpine winter-sports resort in E Switzerland, near Davos and the Austrian border.

**Knights·bridge** |'nīts,brij| district in the West End of London, England, to the S of Hyde Park, noted for its fashionable and expensive shops, including Harrods Department Store.

**Knos·sos** |'näsəs| the principal city of Minoan Crete, the remains of which are on the N coast. The site was occupied from Neolithic times until c. 1200 B.C. Excavations from 1899 onwards revealed the remains of what became known as the Palace of Minos.

**Knox·ville** |'näks,vil; 'näksvəl| industrial city on the Tennessee River, in E Tennessee. Pop. 165,121. The early 19th-century state capital, it is home to the University of Tennessee.

**Ko·be** |'kōbä| industrial port in central

Japan, on the island of Honshu. Pop. 1,477,000. The city was severely damaged by an earthquake in 1995.

**Kø•ben•havn** |ˌkœbən'hown| Danish name for COPENHAGEN.

**Ko•blenz** |'kō,blents| (also **Coblenz**) manufacturing city in western Germany, at the confluence of the Moselle and Rhine rivers. Pop. 110,000.

**Ko•chi** |'kōCHē| commercial port in W Japan, on the S coast of Shikoku. Pop. 317,000.

**Kocs** |'kōCH| village in NW Hungary. The English word "coach" for a horse-drawn carriage is derived from its name.

**Ko•dai•ra** |kō'dī| city in E central Japan, on E central Honshu, a suburb E of Tokyo. Pop. 164,000.

**Ko•di•ak Island** |'kōdē,æk| island in the Gulf of Alaska, in SW Alaska, noted for its wildlife and sites of early European settlement.

**Ko•dor** |kōdawr| see FASHODA.

**Ko•fu** |'kōfōō| industrial city in central Japan, on Honshu, W of Tokyo. Pop. 201,000. It was the seat of powerful feudal lords.

**Ko•hi•ma** |'kōhēmə| city in the far NE of India, capital of the state of Nagaland. Pop. 53,000.

**Koil** |koil| see ALIGARH, India.

**Ko•kand** |kō'känt| (Uzbek name **Qŭqon**) city in E Uzbekistan, a rail and trade center. Pop. 175,000.

**Ko•ko•mo** |'kōkə,mō| industrial city in N central Indiana. Pop. 44,962.

**Ko•la Peninsula** |'kōlə| peninsula on the NW coast of Russia, separating the White Sea from the Barents Sea. The port of Murmansk lies on its N coast.

**Kol•ha•pur** |'kōlə,pŏŏr| industrial city in the state of Maharashtra, W India. Pop. 405,000.

**Kol•khis** Greek name for COLCHIS.

**Köln** |'kœln| German name for COLOGNE.

**Ko•lozs•vár** |'kōlōzh,vär| Hungarian name for CLUJ–NAPOCA, Romania.

**Kol•we•zi** |kōl'wäzē| industrial city in SE Congo (formerly Zaire), in the Shaba region. Pop. 545,000. It is a mining center.

**Ko•ly•ma** |ˌkälē'mä| river of far E Siberia, which flows approximately 1,500 mi./2,415 m. N to the Arctic Ocean.

**Ko•man•dor•ski Islands** |ˌkəmən'dawrskyē| island group in extreme E Russia, off the E Kamchatka Peninsula. The Danish explorer Vitus Bering died (1741) at Bering Island here, and U.S. naval forces defeated the Japanese nearby in 1943.

**Ko•ma•ti River** |ˌkō'mätē| (also **Rio Incomati**) river that flows 500 mi./800 km. from the Drakensberg Range in South Africa, through Swaziland, South Africa, and Mozambique, to the Indian Ocean N of Maputo.

**Ko•mi** |'komē| autonomous republic of NW Russia. Pop. 1,265,000. Capital: Syktyvkar.

**Ko•mo•do** |kə'mōdō| island in Indonesia, in the Lesser Sunda Islands, between Sumbawa and Flores, home to the komodo dragon, the largest species of lizard.

**Kom•pong Som** |ˌkawm,pawNG sawm| (also **Kampong Som**; formerly **Sihanoukville**) port city in S Cambodia, on the Gulf of Thailand. Pop. 75,000. It is the principal deepwater port and commercial center of Cambodia, and has resort trade.

**Kom•so•molsk** |ˌkämsə'mawlsk| industrial city in the far E of Russia, on the Amur River. Pop. 318,000. It was built in 1932 by members of the Komsomol, the Soviet communist youth organization. Also called **Komsomolsk-on-Amur**.

**Ko•na Coast** |'kōnə| name for part of the SW coast of the island of Hawaii, noted for its resorts and coffee production.

**Kong** |'kawNG| 18th-century kingdom of W Africa whose name survives in a region and town in E central Côte d'Ivoire.

**Kon•go** |'känGgō| former kingdom in W central Africa, in the area of the Congo River. It was established in the 14th century and declined under Portuguese influence until absorbed into what is now Angola and Congo (formerly Zaire).

**Kö•nig•grätz** |'kōnik,grets| German name for HRADEC KRÁLOVÉ, Czech Republic.

**Kö•nigs•berg** |'kœniks,berk| German name for KALININGRAD, Russia.

**Kon•ya** |kawn'yä| commercial city in SW central Turkey. Pop. 513,000. An ancient Phrygian settlement, it became the capital of the Seljuk sultans toward the end of the 11th century.

**Koo•te•nai River** |'kŏŏtn-,ā| (also **Kootneya**) river that flows 450 mi./720 km. from SE British Columbia into Montana and Idaho, then back into British Columbia, where it joins the Columbia River.

**Kor•do•fan** |ˌkawrdə'fæn| region of central Sudan. El Obeid is the chief town.

**Ko•rea** |kə'rēə| region of E Asia forming a peninsula between the Sea of Japan and the Yellow Sea, now divided into the countries of North Korea and South Korea.

**Ko•rea Bay** |kə'rēə| arm of the Yellow Sea

along the coast of NW North Korea. The Yalu River enters the sea here.

**Ko·rea Strait** |kə'rēə| channel between the Sea of Japan, to the N, and the East China Sea, to the S. South Korea lies to the NW, Japan to the SE. In the middle is the Japanese island of Tsushima; waters to the SE of the island are called Tsushima Strait.

**Kó·rin·thos** |'körin,ᴛʜaws| Greek name for CORINTH.

**Ko·ri·ya·ma** |,kawrē'yämä| industrial city in NE Japan, on N central Honshu, S of Fukushima. Pop. 315,000.

**Ko·ror** |'kawr,awr| (also **Oreor**) capital of the Republic of Palau, in the W Pacific, on Koror Island (pop. 10,000).

**Kort·rijk** |'kawr,trīk| city in W Belgium, a textile center in West Flanders. Pop. 76,000. French name **Courtrai**.

**Ko·rup National Park** |'kawrəp| national park in W Cameroon, on the border with Nigeria. It was established in 1961 to protect a large area of tropical rainforest.

**Kos** |kaws; käs| (also **Cos**) a Greek island in the SE Aegean, one of the Dodecanese group.

**Kos·ci·us·ko, Mount** |,käzē'əskō| peak in SE Australia, in the Great Dividing Range in SE New South Wales. Rising to 7,234 ft./2,228 m., it is the highest mountain in Australia.

**Ko·shi·ga·ya** |kō'sʜēgäyä| city in E central Japan, on E central Honshu, a suburb N of Tokyo. Pop. 285,000.

**Ko·ši·ce** |'kōsʜētse| industrial city in S Slovakia. Pop. 235,000.

**Ko·so·vo** |'kawsə,vō| autonomous province of Serbia. Capital: Priština. It borders on Albania and the great majority of the people are of Albanian descent. Unrest, spurred by opposition to Serbian rule, gripped the region in the late 1990s. □ **Kosovar** adj. & n.

**Kos·rae** |'kaws,rī| island in the Caroline Islands, constituting a state in the Federated States of Micronesia. Pop. 7,000.

**Kos·tro·ma** |kə,strä'mä| industrial city in European Russia, on the Volga River to the NW of Nizhni Novgorod. Pop. 280,000.

**Ko·ta** |'kōtə| industrial city in Rajasthan state, in NW India, on the Chambal River. Pop. 536,000.

**Ko·ta Ba·ha·ru** |'kōtə 'bähə,bōō| city in Malaysia, on the east coast of the Malay Peninsula, the capital of the state of Kelantan. Pop. 219,000.

**Ko·ta Ki·na·ba·lu** |'kōtə ,kinəbə'lōō| port in Malaysia, on the N coast of Borneo, capital of the state of Sabah. Pop. 56,000.

**Kot·ka** |'kätkə| port on the S coast of Finland. Pop. 57,000.

**Ko·tor** |'kō,tawr| (also **Cattaro**) seaport and commercial center in Montenegro, on the Gulf of Kotor. Pop. 22,000.

**Kot·ze·bue** |'kätsə,bōō| city in NW Alaska, on Kotzebue Sound. Pop. 2,751.

**Kou·rou** |kōō'rōō| town on the N coast of French Guiana. Pop. 11,000. Nearby is a satellite-launching station of the European Space Agency.

**Kov·rov** |kəv'rawf| industrial town in W Russia E of Moscow. Pop. 162,000. It is a railroad junction.

**Kow·loon** |'kow'lōōn| densely populated peninsula on the SE coast of China, forming part of Hong Kong. It is separated from Hong Kong Island by Victoria Harbour.

**Kra, Isthmus of** |'krä| the narrowest part of the Malay Peninsula, forming part of S Thailand.

**Kra·gu·je·vac** |'krägōōyə,väts| city in central Serbia. Pop. 147,000. It was the capital of Serbia 1818–39.

**Kraj·i·na** |krä'yēnə| predominantly Serbian region of E Croatia that attempted to secede following Croatia's separation from Yugoslavia in 1991.

**Kra·ka·toa** |,krækə'tōə| (also **Krakatau**) small volcanic island in Indonesia, lying between Java and Sumatra, scene of an eruption in 1883 that destroyed most of the island and is the most powerful explosion in recorded history.

**Kra·ków** |'krä,kōōf; 'kräk,ow| Polish name for CRACOW.

**Kra·lje·vo** |'krälye,vō| industrial and market town in central Serbia, near the confluence of the Ibar and Morava rivers. Pop.122,000.

**Kra·ma·torsk** |,krämə'tawrsk| industrial city and transportation hub in E Ukraine, in the Donets Basin. Pop. 201,000.

**Kras·no·dar** |,kräsnə'där| industrial port on the lower Kuban River in SW Russia, in a wheat growing area near the Black Sea. Pop. 627,000. It was known before 1922 as Yekaterinodar (Ekaterinodar).

**Kras·no·yarsk** |,kräsnə'yärsk| port and rail center on the Yenisei River in central Siberian Russia. Pop. 922,000. Some 40 mi./64 km. N of the city was a secret Soviet reactor used to produce military materials.

**Kre·feld** |'krä,felt| industrial port city, a textile center, on the Rhine in western Germany, in North Rhine-Westphalia. Pop. 246,000.

**Kre·men·chuk** |,kremen'cʜōōk| industrial city in E central Ukraine, on the Dnieper River. Pop. 238,000. Russian name **Kremenchug**.

**Krem•lin, the** |'kremlən| citadel in Moscow, Russia, on RED SQUARE. A walled complex built over several hundred years and containing churches and palaces, it is the seat of the Russian government and was earlier the seat of the government of the Soviet Union.

**Krish•na River** |'krisHnə| (also **Kistna**) river that rises in the Western Ghats of S India and flows 805 mi./1,288 km. to the Bay of Bengal.

**Kris•tian•sand** |'krisCHən,sæn(d)| ferry port on the S coast of Norway, in the Skagerrak. Pop. 66,000.

**Kris•tian•stad** |'krisCHən,städ| industrial and commercial town in SE Sweden, on the Helge River, capital of Kristianstad county. Pop. 72,000.

**Krí•ti** |'krētē| Greek name for CRETE.

**Kri•voy Rog** |kryi'voi 'rawk| Russian name for KRYVY RIH, Ukraine.

**Krk** |kərk| largest island of Croatia, in the Adriatic Sea. Pop. 13,000. It is a resort area with several small towns.

**Kron•stadt**[1] |'krōn,SHtät| German name for BRAŞOV, Romania.

**Kron•stadt**[2] |'krōn,SHtät| (also **Kronshtadt**) port city on Kotlin Island, W Russia, W of Saint Petersburg. Pop. 45,000. The fortress here was built by Peter the Great and was important in Russia's strategic defense system, especially during the siege of Leningrad in World War II.

**Kru Coast** |'krōō| section of the coast of Liberia to the NW of Cape Palmas, inhabited by the Kru people.

**Kru•ger National Park** |'krōōgər| preserve in South Africa, in Mpumalanga, on the Mozambique border. It was originally a game reserve established in 1898 by South African President Paul Kruger.

**Kru•gers•dorp** |'krōōgərz,dawrp| industrial town in Gauteng province, NE South Africa, W of Johannesburg, in a region where gold, asbestos, and uranium are mined. Pop. 196,000.

**Kru•se•vac** |'krōōsHe,väts| industrial town in S central Serbia, near the confluence of the Rasina and Morava rivers. Pop. 133,000.

**Kry•vy Rih** |kri'vē 'riKH| industrial city in S Ukraine, at the center of an iron-ore-mining region. Pop. 717,000. Russian name **Krivoy Rog**.

**Kua•la Lum•pur** |,kwälə 'lōōm,pŏŏr| the capital of Malaysia, in the SW of the Malay Peninsula. Pop. 1,145,000. It is a major commercial center in the middle of a rubber-growing and tin-mining region.

**Kua•la Treng•ga•nu** |'kwälə təreNG 'gänōō| (also **Kuala Terengganu**) the capital of the state of Trengganu in Malaysia, on the E coast of the Malay Peninsula at the mouth of the Trengganu River. Pop. 229,000.

**Kuan•tan** |'kwän,tän| the capital of the state of Pahang in Malaysia, on the E coast of the Malay Peninsula. Pop. 199,000.

**Ku•ban River** |kŏŏ'bän| river (584 mi./934 km.) in S Russia. It rises in the Greater Caucasus Mts. and flows into the Sea of Azov.

**Ku•ching** |'kŏŏCHiNG| port in Malaysia, on the Sarawak River near the NW coast of Borneo, capital of the state of Sarawak. Pop. 148,000.

**Kui•by•shev** |'kŏŏēbəsHəf| former name (1935–91) for SAMARA, Russia.

**Ku•li•ko•vo** |,kŏŏli'kawvə| plain in SW Russia, near the source of the Don River. A major battle here in 1380 was important in freeing Russia from Mongol domination.

**Ku•ma•ga•ya** |,kŏŏmä'gäyä| industrial city in E central Japan, on E central Honshu, NW of Tokyo. Pop. 152,000.

**Ku•ma•mo•to** |,kŏŏmə'mōtō| industrial and commercial city in S Japan, on the W coast of Kyushu island. Pop. 579,000.

**Ku•ma•no•vo** |kŏŏ'mänawvō| city in N Macedonia, NE of Skopje, in a tobacco-growing region. Pop. 136,000. It is the scene of a Serbian victory over the Turks in 1912.

**Ku•ma•si** |kŏŏ'mäsi| commercial city in S Ghana. Pop. 376,000. It is the capital of the Ashanti region.

**Ku•may•ri** |'kŏŏ,mīrē| Russian name for GYUMRI, Armenia.

**Kum•ba•ko•nam** |,kŏŏmbə'kōnəm| (also **Combaconum**) commercial city in S India, in Tamil Nadu state. Pop. 151,000. Noted for its many Hindu temples, it is a center of Brahmanism and a pilgrimage site.

**Kun•lun Shan** |'kŏŏn'lŏŏn 'SHän| range of mountains in W China, on the N edge of the Tibetan plateau, extending E for over 1,000 mi./1,600 km. from the Pamir Mts. Its highest peak is Muztag, which rises to 25,338 ft./7,723 m.

**Kun•ming** |'kŏŏn'miNG| industrial city in SW China, capital of Yunnan province, on Lake Dianchi. Pop. 1,612,000.

**Kuo•pio** |'kwawpē,aw| resort and industrial city in S Finland, capital of Kuopio province. Pop. 81,000.

**Ku·ra River** |kə'rä; 'koorə| river that flows 940 mi./1,510 km. from NE Turkey through Georgia and Azerbaijan, into the Caspian Sea. It is important for irrigation, hydroelectric power, and navigation.

**Kur·di·stan** |ˌkoͅodə'stæn; 'kərdəˌstæn| extensive region in the Middle East S of the Caucasus, the traditional home of the Kurdish people. The area includes large parts of E Turkey, N Iraq, W Iran, E Syria, Armenia, and Azerbaijan. The creation of the separate state of Kurdistan, proposed by the Allies after World War I, has long been opposed by Iraq, Iran, Syria, and Turkey. Following persecution of the Kurds by Iraq in the aftermath of the Gulf War of 1991, certain areas designated safe havens were established for the Kurds in N Iraq, although these havens are not officially recognized as a state.

**Ku·re** |'koorä| city in S Japan, a shipbuilding center on the S coast of Honshu, near Hiroshima. Pop. 217,000.

**Kur·gan** |koor'gän| city in central Russia, commercial center for an agricultural region. Pop. 360,000.

**Ku·rile Islands** |'k(y)oor,ēl; kyoo'rēl| (also **Kuril Islands** or **the Kurils**) chain of 56 islands between the Sea of Okhotsk and the N Pacific, stretching from the S tip of the Kamchatka Peninsula of Russia to the NE corner of the Japanese island of Hokkaido. The islands were given to Japan in exchange for the N part of Sakhalin island in 1875, but were returned to the Soviet Union in 1945. They are the subject of dispute between Russia and Japan.

**Kur·nool** |kar'nool| (also **Karnul**) commercial town in S India, in Andhra Pradesh state. Pop. 275,000.

**Ku·ro·shio** |koor'ōsheō| warm current flowing in the Pacific NE past Japan and toward Alaska. Also called **Japanese Current, Japan Current**.

**Kursk** |koorsk| industrial city in SW Russia. Pop. 430,000. It was the scene of an important Soviet victory over the Germans in World War II.

**Ku·ruk·shet·ra** |ˌkoorook'sHätrə| city in N India, in Haryana state. Pop. 81,000. It is a Hindu pilgrimage site.

**Kur·ze·me** |'koorzə,ma| (also **Kurland**) former province in W Latvia, along the Baltic Sea and the SW shore of the Gulf of Riga. It is an agricultural, wooded region.

**Kuş·a·da·si** |ˌkoosHädä'si| resort town on the Aegean coast of western Turkey. Pop. 32,000.

**Ku·shi·ro** |koo'sHērō| fishing port and industrial city in N Japan, on the SE coast of Hokkaido. Pop. 206,000.

**Küss·nacht** |'kYs,näKHt| village in N central Switzerland, E of Lucerne. Pop. 8,000. According to legend, William Tell shot the Austrian bailiff Gessler nearby.

**Ku·ta·i·si** |ˌkoͅotä'ēsē| industrial city in central Georgia. Pop. 236,000. One of the oldest cities in Transcaucasia, it has been the capital of various kingdoms, including Colchis and Abkhazia.

**Kutch, Gulf of** |'kəcH| inlet of the Arabian Sea on the W coast of India.

**Kutch, Rann of** |'kəcH| vast salt marsh in the NW of the Indian subcontinent, on the shores of the Arabian Sea, extending over the boundary between SE Pakistan and the state of Gujarat in NW India.

**Ku·wait** |kə'wät| country on the Arabian Peninsula, on the NW coast of the Persian Gulf. Area: 6,880 sq. mi./17,818 sq. km. Language, Arabic. Capital: Kuwait City. With a history as a fishing and trading sheikhdom, Kuwait since the 1930s has become one of the world's leading oil producers. Iraqi claims on the area led to the 1990–91 occupation and resulting Gulf War. □ **Kuwaiti** *adj. & n.*

Kuwait

**Ku·wait City** |kə'wät| port on the Persian Gulf, the capital city of Kuwait. Pop. 150,000.

**Kuz·bass** |kooz'bäs| another name for KUZNETS BASIN of Russia.

**Kuz·nets Basin** |kooz'nyetsk| (also **Kuznetsk**) industrial region of S Russia, in the valley of the Tom River, between Tomsk and Novokuznetsk. The region is rich in iron and coal deposits. Also called **Kuzbass**.

**Kwa·ja·lein** |'kwäjələn; 'kwäjə,län| largest atoll in the Marshall Islands, in the W central Pacific. During World War II it was fought over by U.S. and Japanese forces.

**Kwa Nde·be·le** |ˌkwändə'bälä| former

homeland established in South Africa for the Ndebele people, now part of the province of Mpumalanga.

**Kwan·do River** |'kwändō| (also **Cuando** or **Linyanti**) river that flows 500 mi./800 km. from central Angola, along the Angola-Zambia border, into the Caprivi Strip of Namibia, and along the N border of Botswana, where the Chobe River extends its course to the Zambezi River.

**Kwang·chow** |'gwäNG'jō| see GUANGZHOU, China.

**Kwang·cho·wan** |'gwäNG'jō'wän| (Chinese name **Zhanjiang**) former French territory in Guangdong province, S China. Leased for 99 years in 1898, it was returned in 1945.

**Kwang·ju** |'gawNG'jōō| industrial city in SW South Korea. Pop. 1,145,000.

**Kwang·si** |'gwäNG'SHē| see GUANGXI, China.

**Kwang·tung** |'gwäNG'ŏŏNG| see GUANGDONG, China.

**Kwan·tung** |'gwän'dŏŏNG| (Japanese name **Kanto**) former territory, S Liaoning province, NE China, on the Liaodong Peninsula. Leased by China to Russia in 1898, the area was under Japanese control from 1905 to 1945. Dairen (now Dalian) and Port Arthur (now Lüshun) were part of Kwantung.

**KwaZulu/Natal** |kwaä'zŏŏlŏŏnä'täl| province of E South Africa, on the Indian Ocean. Capital: Pietermaritzburg. Formerly called Natal, it became one of the new provinces of South Africa following the democratic elections of 1994. See also NATAL².

**Kwa·Zu·lu** |kwä'zŏŏlŏŏ| former homeland established in South Africa for the Zulu people, now part of the province of KwaZulu/Natal. The general area was formerly known as Zululand.

**Kwei·chow** |'gwä'jō| see GUIZHOU, China.

**Kwei·lin** |'kgä'lin| see GUILIN, China.

**Kwei·yang** |'gwä'yäNG| see GUIYANG, China.

**Kyo·ga, Lake** |'kyōgə| (also **Kioga**) shallow lake in S central Uganda, on the Victoria Nile River, N of Lake Victoria, to which it was once joined.

**Kyong·ju** |'kyawNG'jōō| historic city in SE South Korea. Pop. 274,000. It was the cap-

ital of the Silla dynasty for a millennium, to A.D. 935, and is a tourist center today.

**Kyo·to** |kē'ōtō| industrial city in central Japan, on the island· of Honshu. Pop. 1,461,000. Founded in the 8th century, it was the imperial capital from 794 until 1868, and has many noted buildings and sites.

**Ky·re·nia** |kə'rēnēə| historic port in N central Cyprus, N of Nicosia. Turkish forces landed here in 1974 in their invasion of the island.

**Kyr·gyz Republic** |kir'gēz| another name for KYRGYZSTAN.

**Kyr·gyz·stan** |,kirgə'stän| mountainous republic in central Asia, on the NW border of China. Area: 76,640 sq. mi./198,500 sq. km. Pop. 4,448,000. Official language, Kyrgyz. Capital and largest city: Bishkek. Also called **Kirghizia; Kyrgyz Republic**. Under Russian control 1864–1991, Kyrgyzstan has an economy based on agriculture, mining, and hydropower production. □ **Kyrgyz** *adj. & n.* **Kirgis** *adj. & n.*

**Kyrgyzstan**

**Kyu·shu** |kē'yŏŏSHŏŏ| the most southerly of the four main islands of Japan, constituting an administrative region. Pop. 13,296,000. Capital: Fukuoka.

**Kyu·sten·dil** |,kyŏŏsten'dil| market city in SW Bulgaria, near the Serbian border. Pop. 55,000. Famed for its mineral springs, it is also a spa.

**Ky·zyl** |ki'zil| city in S central Russia, on the Yenisei River, capital of the republic of Tuva. Pop. 80,000.

**Ky·zyl Kum** |ki'zil kŏŏm| arid desert region in central Asia, extending E from the Aral Sea to the Pamir Mts. and covering part of Uzbekistan and S Kazakhstan.

# Ll

**La·bé** |lä'ba| commercial town in W central Guinea, in the Fouta Djallon region. It is predominantly Fulani and an Islamic center. Pop. 110,000.

**La Belle Province** |lä'bel| nickname for QUEBEC (French, literally 'the Beautiful Province').

**Lab·ra·dor** |'læbrə,dawr| coastal region of E Canada, which forms the mainland part of the province of Newfoundland and Labrador. Largely on the barren Canadian Shield, it has mining and fishing centers.

**Lab·ra·dor Current** |'læbrə,dawr 'kərənt| cold ocean current that flows S from the Arctic Ocean along the NE coast of North America. It meets the warm Gulf Stream in an area off the coast of Newfoundland that is noted for its dense fogs.

**Lab·ra·dor Peninsula** |'læbrə,dawr| broad peninsula of E Canada, between Hudson Bay, the Atlantic, and the Gulf of St. Lawrence. Consisting of the Ungava Peninsula and Labrador, it contains most of Quebec and the mainland part of the province of Newfoundland and Labrador. Also called **Labrador-Ungava**.

**Lab·ra·dor Sea** |'læbrə,dawr| section of the Atlantic between Labrador and S Greenland, noted for its icebergs.

**La·bu·an** |lə'bōōən| Malaysian island off the N coast of Borneo. Pop. 26,000. Capital: Victoria.

**Lac·ca·dive Islands** |'lækədīv| one of the groups of islands forming the Indian territory of Lakshadweep in the Indian Ocean.

**La·ce·dae·mon** |,læsə'dēmən| see SPARTA, Greece. □ **Lacedaemonian** adj. & n.

**La Ce·i·ba** |lä 'säbä| seaport on the Caribbean coast of Honduras. Pop. 68,000.

**La Chaux-de-Fonds** |ləsHōd(ə)'fawN| commune in W Switzerland, in the Jura Mts., NW of Bern. Pop. 36,000. It is a major watch-manufacturing center.

**La·chine** |lə'sHEn| industrial city in S Quebec, just SW of Montreal, site of a canal that in the 1820s opened the upper Saint Lawrence River to commerce.

**Lach·lan** |'läklən| river of New South Wales, Australia, which rises in the Great Dividing Range and flows some 920 mi./1,472 km. to join the Murrumbidgee River near the border with Victoria.

**Lack·a·wan·na** |,lækə'wänə| industrial city in W New York, on Lake Erie and the W side of Buffalo. Pop. 20,585.

**Lac Lé·man** |'läklə'mäN| French name for Lake Geneva (see GENEVA, LAKE), Switzerland.

**La·co·ni·a** |lə'kōnēə| (also **Lakonia**) modern department and ancient region of Greece, in the SE Peloponnese. Throughout the classical period the region was dominated by its capital, Sparta. □ **Laconian** adj. & n.

**La Co·ru·ña** |läkaw'rōōnyä| (also **Corunna**) port in NW Spain. Pop. 251,000. It was the point of departure for the Spanish Armada in 1588 and the site of a battle in 1809 in the Peninsular War, at which British forces under Sir John Moore defeated the French.

**La Crosse** |lə'kraws| industrial and commercial city in W Wisconsin, on the Mississippi River. Pop. 51,003.

**La·dakh** |lə'däk| high-altitude region of NW India, Pakistan, and China, containing the Ladakh and Karakoram mountain ranges and the upper Indus valley; chief town, Leh (in India).

**Lad·o·ga, Lake** |'lædəgə| lake in NW Russia, NE of St. Petersburg, near the border with Finland. It is the largest lake in Europe, with an area of 6,837 sq. mi./17,700 sq. km.

**La·dy·smith** |'lädē,smiTH| town in E South Africa, in KwaZulu/Natal, scene of famous siege by Boer forces in 1899–1900.

**Lae** |lä| industrial seaport on the E coast of Papua New Guinea, the country's second-largest city. Pop. 81,000.

**La·fay·ette**[1] |,läfē'et| industrial and commercial city in NW Indiana. Pop. 43,764.

**La·fay·ette**[2] |,läfē'et; lə'faət| city in S Louisiana, an oil industry center in the Cajun Country. Pop. 94,440.

**La·gash** |'lä,gæsH| (also **Shirpurla**) ancient Sumerian city in present-day S Iraq, between the Tigris and Euphrates rivers.

**La·gos** |'lä,gäs; 'lä,gōs| the chief city of Nigeria, a port on the Gulf of Guinea. Pop. 1,347,000. Originally a center of the slave trade, it became capital of the newly independent Nigeria in 1960. It was replaced as capital by Abuja in 1991.

**La Grande River** |lə'gränd; lə 'grænd| river that flows 500 mi./800 km. across central Quebec to Hudson Bay. It is the site of huge, and controversial, power projects.

**La Guai·ra** |lä'gwirə| port city in N Venezuela, on the Caribbean Sea. Pop.

24,000. It is the port for Caracas, just S, and the leading port of the country, with an international airport and cruise ship facilities.

**La Ha·bra** |lə 'häbrə| city in SW California, SE of Los Angeles. Pop. 51,266.

**La·hai·na** |lə'hinə| resort and agricultural community in W Maui, Hawaii. Pop. 9,073.

**La·hore** |lə'hawr| commercial city, the capital of Punjab province and second largest city of Pakistan, situated near the border with India. Pop. 3,200,000.

**Lah·ti** |'lätē| industrial city and lake port in S Finland, at the S end of Lake Päijänne. Pop. 93,000.

**Lai·bach** |'lībäKH| German name for LJUBLJANA, Slovenia.

**La Jol·la** |lə'hoiə| resort and institutional section of N San Diego, California, on the Pacific Ocean.

**Lake Al·bert, Lake Bai·kal &**, etc. for lakes, see the other element in the place name, e.g., ALBERT, BAIKAL, SUPERIOR, etc.

**Lake Charles** |'CHär(ə)lz| industrial port city in SW Louisiana, on the Calcasieu River. Pop. 70,580.

**Lake District** |lak| region of lakes and mountains in Cumbria, NW England, noted for its resorts and associated with artists and writers, including English poets Wordsworth, Coleridge, and Southey (the Lake Poets).

**Lake·hurst** |'lākhərst| borough in E central New Jersey, site of a naval facility associated with the 1937 crash of the dirigible *Hindenburg*.

**Lake·land**[1] |'laklənd| another term for the LAKE DISTRICT, England.

**Lake·land**[2] |'læklənd| city in central Florida, noted for its resorts and its citrus industry. Pop. 70,576.

**Lake Lou·ise** |lə'wēz| resort in SW Alberta, in the Rocky Mts., noted for the beauty of the lake that gives it its name.

**Lake of the Ozarks** |'ō,zärks| lake in central Missouri, a noted recreational resource created by a dam built in 1931.

**Lake of the Woods** |wo͞odz| lake on the border between Canada and the U.S., to the W of the Great Lakes. It is bounded to the W by Manitoba, to the N and E by Ontario, and to the S by Minnesota. See also NORTHWEST ANGLE.

**Lake Plac·id** |'plæsid| resort village in the Adirondack Mts., in NE New York, site of Olympic competition in 1932 and 1980. Pop. 2,485.

**Lake·wood**[1] |'lāk,wo͝od| city in SW Cali-

fornia, a suburb SE of Los Angeles. Pop. 73,557.

**Lake·wood**[2] |'lāk,wo͝od| city in N central Colorado, a suburb on the W side of Denver. Pop. 126,481.

**Lake·wood**[3] |'lāk,wo͝od| city in NE Ohio, a suburb W of Cleveland, on L. Erie. Pop. 59,718.

**Lak·shad·weep Islands** |lək'sHäd,wēp| group of islands off the Malabar Coast of SW India, constituting a Union Territory in India. Pop. 52,000. Capital: Kavaratti. The group consists of the Laccadive, Minicoy, and Amindivi islands.

**La La·gu·na** |lä lə'gōōnə| university town and tourist center on Tenerife, in the Spanish Canary Islands. Pop. 117,000.

**La Lou·vière** |lə lōō'vyer| industrial city in SW Belgium, in the province of Hainaut W of Charleroi. Pop. 76,000.

**La Man·cha** |lə 'mänCHə| flat, arid plateau in S central Spain, once part of New Castile and now mostly in the region of Castilla-La Mancha. Cervantes wrote *Don Quixote* while imprisoned in La Mancha.

**Lam·ba·ré·né** |,lämbə'rānä| town in W central Gabon, on the Ogooué River, SE of Libreville, longtime base of the missionary doctor Albert Schweitzer. Pop. 15,000.

**Lam·beth** |'læmbəTH| borough of inner London, England, on the S bank of the Thames. Pop. 220,000. **Lambeth Palace** is the London residence of the Archbishop of Canterbury, ecclesisastical head of the Church of England.

**La·mía** |la'mēə| (formerly known as **Zitu-ni**) historic market city in E central Greece. Pop. 44,000.

**Lam·mer·muir Hills** |'læmər,myo͝or| (also **Lammermoor**) low range of hills in SE Scotland, in East Lothian and the Borders.

**Lam·pe·du·sa** |,lämpə'do͞osə| island in the Mediteranean Sea between Malta and N Africa, administered by Italy. It is the largest of the Pelagian group. Pop. 4,000.

**La·nai** |lə'nī| island in Hawaii, W of Maui. It is primarily agricultural, with some resorts.

**Lan·ark·shire** |'lænərk,sH(i)ər; 'lænərk-sHər| former county of SW central Scotland, now divided into the administrative regions of **North Lanarkshire** and **South Lanarkshire**.

**Lan·ca·shire** |'læNGkə,sHir; 'læNGkəsHər| county of NW England, on the Irish Sea. Pop. 1,365,000; administrative center, Preston.

**Lan·cas·ter**[1] |'læNG,kæstər; 'læNGkəstər| city in SW California, NE of Los Angeles, on the edge of the Mojave Desert. Pop. 97,291. Edwards Air Force Base is nearby.

**Lan·cas·ter**[2] |'læ NGkəstər; 'læ NG,kæstər| city in Lancashire, NW England, on the estuary of the Lune River. Pop. 44,000. It was the county seat of Lancashire until 1974. □ **Lancastrian** adj. & n.

**Lan·cas·ter**[3] |'læ NG,kæstər; 'læ NGkəstər| city in SE Pennsylvania, primarily a commercial center for the Pennsylvania Dutch Country. Pop. 55,551.

**Lan·chow** |'län'CHow| see LANZHOU, China.

**Landes** |'lændz| department in SW France, along the Atlantic coast in Aquitaine. Pop. 331,000. The main economic activities are forestry, agriculture, and tourism. The capital is Mont-de-Marsan.

**Land of the Ris·ing Sun** popular name for Japan, a rough translation of *Nippon*, derived from a Chinese name for the island nation.

**Land's End** |'læn(d)z 'end| rocky promontory in SW Cornwall, which forms the westernmost point of England and Britain. The approximate distance by road from Land's End to Britain's northeastermost point at John o'Groats in Scotland is 876 mi./1,400 km.

**Lands·hut** |'länts,hoŏt| industrial city in S Germany, on the Isar River NE of Munich. Pop. 60,000.

**Lang·fang** |'lä NG'fä NG| city in Hebei province, E China, between Beijing and Tianjin. Pop. 533,000.

**Lang·ley** |'læ NGlē| community in NE Virginia, just NW of Washington, D.C., home to the Central Intelligence Agency.

**Lan·gue·doc** |lä NNG'dawk; ,læ NGgə'däk| former province of S France, which extended from the Rhône valley to the N foothills of the E Pyrenees. Its name derives from *langue d'oc*, the term for the form of medieval French spoken in the South, the predecessor of modern Provencal.

**Languedoc-Roussillon** |lä NNG'dawk ,roōsē'yawn| region of S France, on the Mediterranean coast, extending from the Rhône delta to the border with Spain.

**L'Anse aux Mead·ows** |,læns ō 'medōz| historic site in NW Newfoundland, where remains of Viking settlement dating from about A.D. 1000, possibly the legendary VINLAND, have been found.

**Lan·sing** |'lænsi NG| industrial city, the capital of Michigan. Pop. 127,321.

**Lan·tau** |'län'dow| island of Hong Kong, to the W of Hong Kong Island and form-

ing part of the New Territories. Chinese name **Tai Yue Shan**.

**La·nús** |lä'noōs| city in E Argentina, an industrial suburb S of Buenos Aires. Pop. 467,000.

**Lan·za·ro·te** |,länsə'rōtä| one of the Canary Islands of Spain, the most easterly of the group; chief town, Arrecife. A series of volcanic eruptions in about 1730 dramatically altered the island's landscape, creating an area of volcanic cones in the SW known as the 'Mountains of Fire.'

**Lan·zhou** |'læn'zHoō| (also **Lanchow**) industrial city in N China, on the upper Yellow River, capital of Gansu province. Pop. 1,480,000.

**Laois** |lēsH; läsH| (also **Laoighis, Leix**) county of the Republic of Ireland, in the province of Leinster. Pop. 53,000; county seat, Portlaoise. Former name **Queen's County**.

**Laon** |län| historic commercial town, capital of Aisne department, N France. Pop. 29,000. It formerly served as the capital of France (8th–10th centuries).

**Laos** |lows; 'lä,ōs; 'lä,äs| landlocked country in SE Asia, in Indochina. Area: 91,464 sq. mi./236,800 sq. km. Pop. 4,279,000. Language, Laotian. Capital and largest city: Vientiane. A kingdom from the 14th century, dominated by the French 1898–1949, Laos underwent a 25-year civil war, and is now a communist republic. Most of its people are subsistence farmers, and many of its resources are undeveloped. □ **Laotian** adj. & n. **Lao** adj. & n.

Laos

**La Pal·ma** |lə 'pälmə| one of the Canary Islands of Spain, the most northwesterly in the group. It is the site of an astronomical observatory.

**La Paz**[1] |lə 'päs; lə 'päz| the capital of Bolivia, an industrial city in the NW near the border with Peru. Pop. 711,000. (The judicial capital is Sucre.) Situated in the Andes at an altitude of 12,000 ft. (3,660 m), La Paz is the highest capital city in the world.

**La Paz**² |lə 'päs| city in Mexico, near the S tip of the Baja California peninsula, capital of the state of Baja California Sur. Pop. 100,000.

**La Pé•rouse Strait** |,lä pə'rōōs| (also **Soya Strait**) strait separating Hokkaido, N Japan, from Sakhalin Island, Russia. The Sea of Okhotsk lies to the E, the Sea of Japan to the W.

**Lap•land** |'læp,lænd; 'læplənd| region of N Europe that extends from the Norwegian Sea to the White Sea and lies mainly within the Arctic Circle. It consists of the N parts of Norway, Sweden, and Finland, and the Kola Peninsula of Russia. It is inhabited by a nomadic people, the Lapps or Laplanders.

**La Pla•ta** |lə 'plætə; lə 'plätə| port in Argentina, on the Plate River (Río de la Plata) SE of Buenos Aires. Pop. 640,000.

**Lap•tev Sea** |'læp,tef; 'læp,tev| part of the Arctic Ocean that lies to the N of Russia between the Taymyr Peninsula and the New Siberian Islands.

**Lapu-Lapu** |,läpōō 'läpōō| (formerly **Opon**) city in the Philippines, on the NW coast of Mactan. Pop. 146,000.

**L'Aqui•la** |'läkwēlə| city in the Abruzzi region of E central Italy. Pop. 68,000. It is a summer resort.

**Lar•a•mie** |'lerə,mē| industrial and resort city in SE Wyoming. Pop. 26,687. It was settled in 1868, during construction of the Union Pacific Railroad.

**La•re•do** |lə'rädō| industrial port city in S Texas, across the Rio Grande from Nuevo Laredo, Mexico. Pop. 122,899.

**Lar•go** |'lär,gō| resort city in W central Florida, on the SW side of Clearwater. Pop. 65,674.

**La Rio•ja**¹ |,lä rē'ōhä| commercial city in NW Argentina, the capital of La Rioja province, in the Andes. Pop. 105,000.

**La Rio•ja**² |,lä rē'ōhä| autonomous region of N Spain, in the wine-producing valley of the Ebro River. Capital: Logroño.

**La•ris•sa** |lə'risə| city in Greece, the chief town of Thessaly. Pop. 113,000. Greek name **Lárisa**.

**Lar•ka•na** |lär'känə| commercial city in S central Pakistan, N of Karachi. Pop. 275,000.

**Lar•na•ca** |'lärnəkə| historic port city in SE Cyprus, in the Greek-controlled zone. Pop. 44,000. On the site of ancient Citium, it is an industrial and resort center.

**La Ro•chelle** |,lä raw.'sнel| port on the At-

lantic coast of W France. Pop. 74,000. It was a 17th-century Huguenot stronghold.

**La Roche-sur-Yon** |lä 'rawsнsyr'yawn| capital of the department of the Vendèe in W France. Pop. 49,000. It is an agricultural and transportation center.

**La Ro•ma•na** |lə rō'mänə| port city in the SE Dominican Republic. Pop. 133,000. It has an airport and cruise ship facilities, and is a resort center.

**La Salle** |lə 'sæl| city in S Quebec, a residential and industrial suburb SW of Montreal. Pop. 73,804.

**La Sca•la** |lä 'skälə| opera house, built 1776–78, in Milan, Italy, long famed the largest and most prestigious in the world.

**Las•caux** |lä'skō; læs'kō| village in SW France, in the Périgord region, site of a cave with famed Paleolithic paintings and drawings. The cave was closed to the public in 1963 in order to preserve the art.

**Las Cru•ces** |läs'krōōsəs| city in S New Mexico, on the Rio Grande. Pop. 62,126.

**La Se•re•na** |lä sä'ränä| historic city in N central Chile, a coastal resort and the capital of Coquimbo province. Pop. 120,000. Chilean independence was declared here in 1818.

**Las Pal•mas** |läs 'pälməs| port and resort on the N coast of the island of Gran Canaria, capital of the Canary Islands. Pop. 372,000. Full name **Las Palmas de Gran Canaria**.

**La Spe•zia** |lä'spetsēə| industrial port in NW Italy. Pop. 103,000. Since 1861 it has been Italy's chief naval station.

**Las•sen Peak** |'læsən| (also **Mount Lassen**) dormant volcano in the Cascade Range, in N California. It rises to 10,457 ft./3,187 m.

**Las Ve•gas** |läs 'vägəs| city in S Nevada. Pop. 258,295. It is noted for its casinos and nightclubs, and is the center of one of the fastest-growing metropolitan areas in the U.S.

**Lat•a•kia** |,lätə'kēə| seaport on the coast of W Syria, opposite the NE tip of Cyprus. Pop. 293,000.

**La Tène** |lä'ten| site near Lake Neuchâtel in Switzerland where ancient Celtic artifacts were found, giving a name to the second phase of the European Iron Age, from the 5th century B.C. to the Roman conquest.

**Lat•er•an** |'lætərən| complex in SE Rome, Italy, including the cathedral church of Rome. Formerly the residence of the popes, it is associated with several ecclesiastical councils and treaties.

**Lat·in A·mer·i·ca** |ˌlætn əˈmerikə| the parts of the American continent where Spanish or Portuguese is the main national language (i.e., Mexico and, in effect, the whole of Central and South America including many of the Caribbean islands).
□ **Latin American** adj. & n.

**Lat·in Quarter** |ˈlætn ˈkwawrtər| section of Paris, France, on the Left Bank (S side) of the Seine River) and centered around the Sorbonne. It has attracted students, writers, and intellectuals for centuries.

**La·ti·um** |ˈlāsh(ē)əm| ancient region of W central Italy, W of the Apennines and S of the Tiber River. Settled during the early part of the 1st millennium B.C. by a branch of the Indo-European people known as the Latini, it had become dominated by Rome by the end of the 4th century B.C.; it is now part of the modern region of Lazio.

**La·tur** |lāˈtōōr| town in S central India, in Maharashtra state, NW of Hyderabad. Pop. 197,000.

**Lat·via** |ˈlætvia| republic on the E shore of the Baltic Sea, between Estonia and Lithuania. Area: 24,947 sq. mi./64,589 sq. km. Pop. 2,693,000. Language, Latvian (Lettish). Capital and largest city: Riga. Long dominated by Poland, Sweden, or Russia. Latvia was independent 1918–40, then became a constituent of the Soviet Union. Independence was regained in 1991. Farming and commerce are essential to its economy. □ **Latvian** adj. & n.

**Latvia**

**Laugh·lin** |ˈläklən; ˈläflən| community in S Arizona, across the Colorado River from Bullhead City, Arizona. Pop. 4,791. It is a gambling resort.

**Laun·ces·ton** |ˈlawnsəstən| city in N Tasmania, Australia, on the Tamar estuary, the second-largest city of the island. Pop. 67,000.

**Laur·a·sia** |lawˈrāzHə| supercontinent thought to have existed in the N hemisphere before breaking up into North America, Greenland, Europe, and most of Asia (excluding the Indian subcontinent and the Arabian Peninsula).

**Lau·rel** |ˈlawrəl| city in central Maryland, a largely residential center between Washington, D.C. and Baltimore. Pop. 19,438.

**Lau·ren·tian Plateau** |lawˈrenCHən| another name for the CANADIAN SHIELD. The Laurentian Mountains are a resort area in S Quebec, NW of Montreal.

**Lau·sanne** |lōˈzän| resort town in SW Switzerland, on the N shore of Lake Geneva. Pop. 123,000. It is headquarters for the International Olympic Committee.

**La·val**[1] |läˈväl| industrial center and capital city of the department of Mayenne, in NW France. Pop. 53,000. It is noted for its linen products.

**La·val**[2] |läˈväl| city in S Quebec, a suburb on the Île Jésus, just N of Montreal. Pop. 314,398.

**La Ve·ga** |lä ˈvāgə| commercial city in the central Dominican Republic, the capital of La Vega province. Pop. 73,000.

**La Ven·ta** |lä ˈväntə| village in SE Mexico, in mangrove swamps in W Tabasco state, site of major Olmec archaeological finds. The La Venta culture of 2,500 years ago takes its name from the vicinity.

**Law·rence** |ˈlawrəns; ˈlärəns| city in NE Kansas, home to the University of Kansas. Pop. 65,608. It was the scene of bloody fighting before and during the Civil War.

**Law·ton** |ˈlawtn| city in SW Oklahoma. Pop. 80,561. Fort Sill is just N.

**La'youn** |liˈōōn| (also **Laayoune**) the capital of Western Sahara, on the Atlantic coast. Pop. 97,000. Arabic name **El Aaiún**.

**Lay·ton** |ˈlātn| city in N Utah, S of Ogden. Pop. 41,784.

**La·zio** |ˈlätsēō| administrative region of W central Italy, on the Tyrrhenian Sea, including the ancient region of Latium. Capital: Rome.

**Lead·ville** |ˈledˌvil| historic mining city in central Colorado. Pop. 2,629. At 10,190 ft./3,108 m., it is the highest U.S. city.

**Leam·ing·ton Spa** |ˌlemiNGtən ˈspä| town in central England, in Warwickshire, SE of Birmingham. Pop. 57,000. Noted for its saline springs, it was granted the status of royal spa after a visit by Queen Victoria in 1838. Official name **Royal Leamington Spa**.

**Leav·en·worth** |ˈlevən,wərTH| city in NE Kansas, on the Missouri River. Several noted prisons are in or near the city, which also has military facilities. Pop. 38,495.

**Leb·a·non**[1] |ˈlebənən; ˈlebə,nän| republic

in the Middle East, NE of Israel, with a coastline on the Mediterranean Sea. Area: 4,037 sq. mi./10,452 sq. km. Pop. 2,700,000. Language, Arabic. Capital and largest city: Beirut. Successor to ancient Phoenicia, long dominated by the Turks, later the French, Lebanon gained independence in 1943. Its commercial and tourist economy suffered severe damage during civil war in the 1980s. □ **Lebanese** *adj. & n.*

**Lebanon**

**Leb·a·non**² |'lebənən; 'lebə,nän| industrial city in SE Pennsylvania, in the Pennsylvania Dutch Country. Pop. 24,800.

**Leb·a·non Mountains** |'lebənən; 'lebə,nän| range of mountains in Lebanon. Running parallel to the Mediterranean coast, it rises to 10,022 ft./3,087 m. at Qornet es Saouda. It is separated from the Anti-Lebanon Mts., on the border with Syria, by the Bekaa Valley.

**Le Bour·get** |lə boŏr'zHā| town in N central France, 25 mi./40 km. N of Paris. It was the site of Le Bourget airport, now closed, where Charles Lindbergh landed after his solo transatlantic flight in May 1927.

**Le·bo·wa** |lə'bŏə| former homeland established in South Africa for the North Sotho people, now part of Northern Province.

**Lec·ce** |'lācHā| ancient market town in SE Italy, capital of Lecce province. Pop. 102,000. It is noted for its Baroque architecture.

**Lec·co** |'lakō| town on Lake Lecco, a SE branch of Lake Como, in N Italy. Pop. 46,000.

**Leeds** |lēdz| industrial city in N England, formerly in Yorkshire. Pop. 674,000. It developed as a wool town in the Middle Ages, becoming a center of the clothing trade in the Industrial Revolution.

**Lee's Summit** |,lēz| industrial city in NW Missouri, SE of Kansas City. Pop. 46,418.

**Leeu·war·den** |'lā,värdn| market town in N Netherlands, capital of Friesland province. Pop. 85,000.

**Lee·ward Islands** |'lēwərd; 'lŏŏərd| group of islands in the West Indies, constituting the N part of the Lesser Antilles. The group includes Guadeloupe, Antigua, St. Kitts, and Montserrat. *Leeward* refers to the islands' situation farther downwind (in terms of the prevailing southeasterly winds) than the Windward Islands.

**Lef·ko·sia** |,lefkə'sēyə| Greek name for NICOSIA, Cyprus, and the name of the district surrounding the city.

**Left Bank** |'left 'bæNGk| district of the city of Paris, France, on the S bank of the Seine River. The site of educational and arts institutions including the Sorbonne and the Académie des Beaux-Arts, as well as the surrounding Latin Quarter, it is an area noted for its intellectual and artistic life. French name **Rive Gauche.**

**Le·gaz·pi** |lə'gäspē| (also **Legaspi**) port city in the Philippines, on SE Luzon, on Albay Gulf. Pop. 121,000. It is at the base of the active Mayon Volcano.

**Leg·horn** |'leg,hawrn| another name for LIVORNO, Italy.

**Leg·ni·ca** |leg'nētsə| textile center and manufacturing town, capital of Legnica county, in SW Poland. Pop. 105,000. German name **Liegnitz.**

**Leh** |lä| town in Jammu and Kashmir, N India, to the E of Srinagar near the Indus River. Pop. 9,000. It is the chief town of the Himalayan region of Ladakh, and the administrative center of Ladakh district.

**Le Ha·vre** |lə 'häv(rə)| industrial port in N France, on the English Channel at the mouth of the Seine. Pop. 197,000.

**Le·high River** |'lē,hī| river that flows 103 mi./166 km. through E Pennsylvania, to the Delaware River. The Lehigh Valley is heavily industrial, with Bethlehem and Allentown among its centers.

**Leices·ter** |'lestər| industrial city in central England, on the Soar River, the county seat of Leicestershire. Pop. 271,000. It was founded as a Roman settlement on the Fosse Way (AD 50–100).

**Leices·ter·shire** |'lestərsHir; 'lestərsHər| county of central England. Pop. 860,000; county seat, Leicester.

**Lei·den** |'līdn| (also **Leyden**) city in the W Netherlands, 9 mi./15 km. NE of The Hague. Pop. 112,000. It is the site of the country's oldest university, founded in 1575.

**Lein·ster** |'lenstər| province of the Republic of Ireland, in the SE, comprising twelve counties centered on Dublin.

**Leip·zig** |'līpsig| industrial city in E central Germany. Pop. 503,000. A publishing and music center, it is associated with J. S. Bach, who is buried here.

**Lei·ria** |la'rēə| town in central Portugal. Capital of Leiria district, on the Liz River. Pop. 28,000.

**Leith** |lēTH| former port city in SE Scotland, now part of Edinburgh.

**Lei·trim** |'lētrəm| county of the Republic of Ireland, in the province of Connacht. Pop. 25,000; county seat, Carrick-on-Shannon.

**Lei·zhou Peninsula** |'lā'jō| (formerly **Luichow Peninsula**) peninsula in S Guangdong province, S China, across the Hainan Strait from Hainan Island. The former French territory of Kwangchowan was on the E coast.

**Le Mans** |lə 'män; lə 'män(z)| industrial town in NW France. Pop. 148,000. It is the site of a famed motor-racing circuit, on which a 24-hour endurance race is held each summer.

**Lem·berg** |'lem,bərg| German name for LVIV, Ukraine.

**Lem·nos** |'lem,näs; 'lemnəs| Greek island in the N Aegean Sea, off NW Turkey; chief town, Kástron. Greek name **Límnos**.

**Le·na** |'lānə| river in Siberia, which rises in the mountains on the W shore of Lake Baikal and flows for 2,750 mi./4,400 km. into the Laptev Sea. It is famous for the goldfields in its basin.

**Le·nin·a·kan** |lə,nēnə'kän| former name (1924–91) for GYUMRI, Armenia.

**Len·in·grad** |'lenən,græd| former name (1924–91) for ST. PETERSBURG, Russia. The German siege of Leningrad (1941–44) was one of the most destructive in history.

**Lenin Peak** |'lenin| (formerly **Kaufman Peak**) mountain in the Trans Alai Range, between Kyrgyzstan and Tajikistan. It was the second-highest peak in the former Soviet Union (23,405 ft./7,134 m.) and is the highest in the Trans Alai.

**Len·ox** |'lenəks| resort town in W Massachusetts, in the Berkshire Hills. Pop. 5,069. Tanglewood, the noted summer music complex, is here.

**Lens** |läns| industrial city in N France. Pop. 38,000.

**Leom·in·ster** |'lemənstər| industrial city in N central Massachusetts. Pop. 38,145.

**Le·ón¹** |lā'ōn| industrial city in Guanajuato state, central Mexico. Pop. 872,000.

**Le·ón²** |lā'ōn| industrial and university city

in W Nicaragua, the second-largest city in the country. Pop. 159,000.

**Le·ón³** |lā'ōn| city in N Spain. Pop. 146,000. It is the capital of the province and former kingdom of León, now part of Castilla-León region.

**Le·o·nine City** |'lēə,nīn| the part of Rome, Italy in which the Vatican stands, walled and fortified by Pope Leo IV.

**Lé·o·pold·ville** |'lēə,pōlkd,vil; 'laə,pold,vil| former name (until 1966) for KINSHASA, Congo (formerly Zaire).

**Le·pan·to, Gulf of** |lə'pänto; lə'pæntō| another name for the Gulf of Corinth (see CORINTH, GULF OF), Greece.

**Le·pon·tine Alps** |li'pän,tīn; 'lepən'tīn| range of the central Alps on the Italian-Swiss border, just N of the Italian lake district, reaching 11,683 ft./3,563 m. at Monte Leone. The range extends into central Switzerland.

**Lep·tis Mag·na** |'leptəs 'mægnə| ancient seaport and trading center on the Mediterranean coast of N Africa, near present-day Al Khums in Libya. Founded by the Phoenicians, it became one of the three chief cities of Tripolitania and was later a Roman colony under Trajan.

**Lé·ri·da** |lārēdä| industrial city in NE Spain, on the Segre River, capital of Lérida province. Pop. 119,000. The surrounding area is agricultural.

**Ler·wick** |'lərwik| the capital of the Shetland Islands, Scotland, on the island of Mainland. Pop. 7,000. The most northerly town in the British Isles, it is a fishing center and a service port for the oil industry.

**Les Abymes** |lā zä'bēm| town on Grand-Terre, in Guadeloupe, in the West Indies. Pop. 63,000. The department's international airport is here.

**Les Baux-de-Provence** |lā'bō də prō-'väns| village in Bouches-du-Rhône department, SE France. A tourist attraction atop a hill, it gave its name to the mineral bauxite.

**Les·bos** |'lez,bäs| Greek island in the E Aegean, off the coast of NW Turkey. Pop. 104,000; chief town, Mytilene. Its artistic golden age of the late 7th and early 6th centuries B.C. produced the poets Alcaeus and Sappho. Greek name **Lésvos**.

**Les Cayes** |lā 'kä| (also **Cayes** or **Aux Cayes**) port city in SW Haiti, on the Caribbean Sea. Pop. 38,000.

**Le·so·tho** |lə'sōōtō; lə'sōtō| landlocked mountainous kingdom forming an enclave within South Africa. Area: 11,717 sq. mi./30,335 sq. km. Pop. 1,816,000. Official

Lesotho

languages, Sesotho and English. Capital and largest city: Maseru. Formerly Basutoland, and independent since 1966, Lesotho sends many of its workers to South Africa. Agriculture and handicrafts are also important.

**Les·ser An·til·les** |'lesər æn'tilēz| see ANTILLES.

**Les·ser Sun·da Islands** |'lesər 'səndə; 'soondə| see SUNDA ISLANDS.

**Lés·vos** |'lez,vaws| Greek name for LESBOS.

**Leth·bridge** |'leTHbrij| city in S Alberta, on the Oldman River. It is an industrial, academic, and research center. Pop. 60,974.

**Lethe** |'lēTHē| in Greek mythology, river of the underworld. When the dead drank its waters, they forgot their life on earth.

**Le·ti·cia** |lə'tēsyə| town and river port at the S tip of Colombia, on the upper reaches of the Amazon on the border with Brazil and Peru. Pop. 24,000.

**Leu·ven** |'lœvən| historic university town in Belgium, E of Brussels. Pop. 85,000. It was the capital of Brabant (11th–15th century). French name **Louvain**.

**Levallois-Perret** |lə,väwäpə'rā| industrial and residential suburb NW of Paris, France. Pop. 54,000.

**Le·vant** |lə'vænt| historical term for the E part of the Mediterranean with its islands and coastal regions, from the French *levant,* 'rising' (in reference to the sun).

**Le·ver·ku·sen** |'lāvər,koozən| industrial city in western Germany, in North Rhine-Westphalia, on the Rhine River N of Cologne. Pop. 161,000.

**Levis-Lauzon** |lä,vēlō'zawN| industrial city in S Quebec, across the Saint Lawrence River from Quebec City. Pop. 39,452.

**Lev·it·town** |'levət,town| village in central Long Island, New York, developed after World War II. Pop. 53,286. It was noted for its "cookie-cutter" houses. There were also Levittowns in New Jersey, Pennsylvania, and Puerto Rico.

**Lew·es** |'looəs| town in S England, NE of Brighton, the county seat of East Sussex. Pop. 15,000.

**Lew·is** |'looəs| the northern part of the island of Lewis and Harris in the Outer Hebrides, Scotland.

**Lew·is and Clark Trail** |'looəs ən 'klärk| (official name **Lewis and Clark National Historic Trail**) route of the Lewis and Clark expedition, which in 1804–06 explored the Louisiana Purchase from St. Louis, Missouri to the Pacific Coast.

**Lew·is and Har·ris** |'looəs ənd 'hærəs| (also **Lewis with Harris**) the largest and northernmost island of the Outer Hebrides in Scotland; chief town, Stornoway. The island, which is separated from the mainland by the Minch, consists of a N part, Lewis, and a smaller and more mountainous S part, Harris.

**Lew·i·sham** |'looəsHəm| largely residential borough of SE Greater London, England, S of the Thames River. Pop. 215,000.

**Lew·is·ton**[1] |'looəstən| industrial city in NW Idaho, on the Snake River. Pop. 28,082.

**Lew·is·ton**[2] |'looəstən| industrial city in SW Maine, on the Androscoggin River opposite Auburn. Pop. 39,757.

**Lex·ing·ton**[1] |'leksiNGtən| historic commercial city in central Kentucky. Pop. 225,366. It is a noted horse-breeding center.

**Lex·ing·ton**[2] |'leksiNGtən| residential town NW of Boston, Massachusetts. Pop. 28,974. It was the scene in 1775 of the first battle in the Revolutionary War.

**Ley·te** |'lātē; 'lātä| island in the central Philippines. Pop. 1,362,000; chief town, Tacloban.

**Ley·te Gulf** |'lātē; 'lātä| inlet of the Philippine Sea, E Philippines, between Leyte and Samar. A Japanese fleet was destroyed here during World War II, in 1944.

**Le·zhë** |'lazHə| (also **Lesh**; ancient name **Lissus**; Italian name **Alessio**) historic town in NW Albania, the burial place of the national hero Skanderbeg.

**Lha·sa** |'läsə| the capital of Tibet. Pop. 140,000. It is situated in the N Himalayas at an altitude of 11,800 ft./3,600 m., on a tributary of the Brahmaputra. The historic center of Tibetan Buddhism, it was the seat of the Dalai Lama until a Chinese takeover in 1959.

**Lian·yun·gang** |lē'än'yyn'gäNG| deepwater port in Jiangsu province, E China, on the Yellow Sea. Pop, 354,000. It is a special economic zone in a mining and agricultural region.

**Liao River** |lēˈow| river in NE China, rising in Inner Mongolia and flowing 864 mi./1,390 km. through Liaoning province to the Gulf of Liaodong at the N end of the Bo Hai.

**Liao·dong Peninsula** |lēˈowˈdŌŌNG| peninsula in NE China, which extends S into the Yellow Sea between Bo Hai and Korea Bay.

**Liao·ning** |lēˈowˈniNG| province in NE China, separated on the E from North Korea by the Yalu River. Pop. 39,460,000. Capital: Shenyang. An important industrial region, it is a leading producer of iron, steel, coke, and chemicals.

**Liao·yang** |lēˈowˈyäNG| city in Liaoning province, NE China, SE of Shenyang. Pop. 493,000. An agricultural distribution center with light industries, it was the site of a Japanese victory (1904) during the Russo-Japanese War.

**Liao·yuan** |lēˈowyYˈen| city in Jilin province, NE China, in the Jilin Hada Ling mountains to the S of Changchun. Pop. 378,000.

**Li·ard River** |ˈlē‚ärd; lēˈärd| river that flows 570 mi./920 km. from the Yukon Territory through British Columbia and the Northwest Territories to the Mackenzie River.

**Li·be·rec** |ˈlēbə‚rets| industrial city in the N central Czech Republic. Pop. 48,000. The city is a center of textile manufacturing, especially woolens.

**Li·be·ria** |līˈbirēə| republic on the Atlantic coast of W Africa. Area: 37,757 sq. mi./97,754 sq. km. Pop. 2,639,000. Languages, English (official), English-based pidgin. Capital and largest city: Monrovia. Founded in 1822 for freed U.S. slaves, Liberia gained independence in 1847. Civil war in 1980–96 severely damaged its econ-

Liberia

omy, which is based on mining and other extractive industries. □ **Liberian** *adj. & n.*

**Lib·er·ty Island** |ˈlibərtē| island in New York Bay, off Jersey City, New Jersey, site, since 1885, of the Statue of Liberty.

**Li·bre·ville** |ˈlēbrə‚vil| the capital of Gabon, a port on the Atlantic coast at the mouth of the Gabon River. Pop. 352,000.

**Lib·ya** |ˈlibēə| country in North Africa, on the Mediterranean, with most of its S in the Sahara Desert. Area: 685,786 sq. mi./1.78 million sq. km. Pop. 4,714,000. Capital and largest city: Tripoli. Part of Roman and Turkish empires, later controlled by Italy, Libya gained independence in 1951. Oil, discovered in 1959, is key to its economy. □ **Libyan** *adj. & n.*

Libya

**Lib·yan Desert** |ˈlibēən| name for the NE Sahara Desert, W of the Nile in Egypt, Libya, and NW Sudan. In Egypt it is also called the Western Desert.

**Lich·field** |ˈliCH‚fēld| town in central England, in Staffordshire N of Birmingham. Pop. 26,000. It was the birthplace of lexicographer Samuel Johnson.

**Li·di·ce** |ˈlēd(y)ət‚sä| village, 5 mi./8 km. W of Kladno, in the Czech Republic. In June 1942 Nazis killed all the male inhabitants, sent the women to concentration camps and the children to German institutions, then destroyed the entire village in retaliation for the assassination of a high Nazi official.

**Li·dingö** |ˈlē‚deNGŒ| island suburb of Stockholm in Sweden, in the NE of the city. Pop. 38,000.

**Li·do** |ˈlēdō| **1** an island reef off the coast of NE Italy, in the N Adriatic. It separates the Lagoon of Venice from the Gulf of Venice. Full name **Lido di Malamocco. 2** (also **the Lido**) a town and beach resort in NE Italy, on the Lido reef opposite Venice. Pop. 21,000.

**Liech·ten·stein** |ˈliKHtən‚sHtīn| small (62 sq. mi./160 sq. km.) independent principality in the Alps, between Switzerland and Austria. Pop. 28,880; official language, German. Capital and largest town: Vaduz. Created in 1719 and independent since 1866, Liechtenstein is economically integrated with Switzerland. Finance and tourism are important. □ **Liechtensteiner** n.

**Liechtenstein**

**Li·ège** |lē'ezн| **1** province of E Belgium. Formerly ruled by independent prince-bishops, it became a part of the Netherlands in 1815 and of Belgium in 1830. Flemish name **Luik. 2** its capital city, an industrial port on the Meuse River. Pop. 195,000.

**Lie·pā·ja** |'lyepäyə| seaport in Latvia, on the Baltic Sea. Pop. 115,000. It has a naval base as well as a commercial harbor.

**Lif·fey** |'life| river of E Ireland, which flows for 50 mi./80 km. from the Wicklow Mts. to Dublin Bay. The city of Dublin is situated at its mouth.

**Lif·ford** |'lifərd| the county seat of Donegal, in the NW Republic of Ireland. Pop. 1,500.

**Li·gu·ria** |lə'gyŏŏrēə| coastal region of NW Italy, which extends along the Mediterranean coast from Tuscany to the border with France. Capital: Genoa. In ancient times Liguria extended as far as the Atlantic seaboard. □ **Ligurian** adj. & n.

**Li·gur·i·an Alps** |li'gyŏŏrēən| spur of the Alps extending from the Maritime Alps along the French border into NE Italy, to the Apennines. The **Ligurian Sea** is the section of the Mediterranean just to the S.

**Li·ka·si** |li'käsē| (formerly **Jadotville**) mining city in SE Congo (formerly Zaire), in the Shaba region. Pop. 280,000. The region produces copper and cobalt.

**Lille** |'lēl| industrial city in N France, a textile and technology center near the border with Belgium. Pop. 178,000.

**Lil·le·ham·mer** |'lilə,hämər| resort town and capital of Oppland county, S Norway.

Pop. 23,000. The 1994 Winter Olympics were held here.

**Li·long·we** |lə'lawnGwä| commercial city, founded as the capital of Malawi in 1975. Pop. 234,000.

**Li·ma**¹ |'līmə| industrial city in NW Ohio, N of Dayton. Pop. 45,549.

**Li·ma**² |'lēmə| the capital of Peru. Pop. 5,706,000. Founded in 1535 by Francisco Pizarro, it was the capital of the Spanish colonies in South America until the 19th century. Today it is an industrial center with a Pacific port at Callao.

**Li·mas·sol** |,lēmə'sawl| port on the Greek-controlled S coast of Cyprus, on Akrotiri Bay. Pop. 143,000.

**Lim·be** |'limbä| (formerly **Victoria)** port and resort town in SW Cameroon, on the Atlantic coast W of Douala. Pop. 45,000. It is a former colonial capital.

**Lim·burg** |'lim,bərg| former duchy of Lorraine, divided in 1839 between Belgium and the Netherlands. It now forms a province of NE Belgium (capital, Hasselt) and a province of the SE Netherlands (capital, Maastricht). French name **Limbourg.**

**Li·mei·ra** |lē'märə| city in S Brazil, in São Paulo state. Pop. 230,000. It is a commercial and processing center in an area known for orange production.

**Lim·er·ick** |'lim(ə)rik| **1** county of the Republic of Ireland, in the W in the province of Munster. Pop. 162,000. **2** its county seat, on the Shannon River. Pop. 52,000.

**Lím·nos** |'lēmnaws| Greek name for **Lemnos.**

**Li·moges** |lə'mōzн| city in W central France, the principal city of Limousin. Pop. 136,000. Famous in the late Middle Ages for enamel work, it has been noted since the 18th century for the production of porcelain.

**Li·món** |lē'mōn| port on the Caribbean coast of Costa Rica. Pop. 75,000. Also called **Puerto Limón.**

**Li·mou·sin** |lēmŏŏ'zen| region and former province of central France, centered on Limoges.

**Lim·po·po** |lim'pōpō| river of SE Africa. Rising as the Crocodile River near Johannesburg, it flows 1,100 mi./1,770 km. in a sweeping curve to the N and E to meet the Indian Ocean in Mozambique, N of Maputo. For much of its course it forms South Africa's boundary with Botswana and Zimbabwe.

**Li·na·res**¹ |lē'närās| commercial city in S central Chile, in the Maule region, in an agricultural district. Pop. 76,000.

**Li·na·res²** |lē'närās| industrial town in S Spain, in a silver- and lead-mining area. Pop. 57,000.

**Lin·coln¹** |'liNGkən| city in E England, the county seat of Lincolnshire. Pop. 82,000. It was founded by the Romans as Lindum Colonia.

**Lin·coln²** |'liNGkən| the state capital of Nebraska. Pop. 191,972. The second-largest Nebraska city, it is a university and commercial center.

**Lin·coln·shire** |'liNGkən,SHir; 'liNGkən-SHər| county on the E coast of England. Pop. 574,000; county seat, Lincoln. The former N part of the county, included in Humberside 1974–96, is now divided into *North Lincolnshire* and *North East Lincolnshire*.

**Lin·den** |'lindən| industrial city in NE New Jersey, S of Elizabeth, noted for its oil refineries. Pop. 36,701.

**Lin·dis·farne** |'lindəs,färn| small island off the coast of Northumberland, in the Farne Islands. Linked to the mainland by a causeway exposed only at low tide, it is the site of a church and monastery founded by St. Aidan in 635. Also called **Holy Island**.

**Lind·sey** |'linzē| one of three administrative divisions of Lincolnshire before the local government reorganization of 1974 (the others were Holland and Kesteven), comprising the N part of the county.

**Line Islands** |lin| group of eleven islands in the central Pacific, straddling the equator S of Hawaii. Eight of the islands, including Kiritimati (Christmas Island), form part of Kiribati; the remaining three (Jarvis, Palmyra, and Kingman Reef) are uninhabited dependencies of the U.S.

**Lin·fen** |'lin'fən| city in Shanxi province, E central China, on the Fen River S of Taiyuan. Pop. 187,000.

**Lin·ga·yen** |,liNGgä'yen| **1** inlet of the South China Sea, in central Luzon, the Philippines. **2** port town in the Philippines, central Luzon, on the Lingayen Gulf. Pop. 79,000.

**Lin·hai** |'lin'hi| city in Zhejiang province, E China, NW of Jiaojiang on the Ling River. Pop. 1,012,000.

**Lin·he** |'lin'hə| city in Inner Mongolia, N China, W of Baotou near the bend of the Yellow River. Pop. 347,000.

**Lin·kö·ping** |'lin'CHœ'piNG| industrial town in SE Sweden. Pop. 122,000. It was a noted cultural and ecclesiastical center in the Middle Ages.

**Lin·lith·gow** |lin'liTHgō| historic town in central Scotland, in West Lothian. Pop. 10,000. Its palace, home to Scottish kings and birthplace of Mary, Queen of Scots, is now a ruin.

**Lin·qing** |'lin'CHiNG| city in Shandong province, E China, on the Grand Canal, W of Jinan. Pop. 124,000.

**Lin·yi** |'lin'yē| city in Shandong province, E China, on the Yi River, SE of Jinan. Pop. 325,000.

**Linz** |lin(t)s| industrial city in N Austria, on the Danube River, capital of the state of Upper Austria. Pop. 203,000.

**Lip·a·ri Islands** |'lipərē| group of seven volcanic resort islands in the Tyrrhenian Sea, off the NE coast of Sicily, and in Italian possession. Believed by the ancient Greeks to be the home of Aeolus, the islands were formerly known as the Aeolian Islands.

**Li·petsk** |'lēpitsk| industrial city in SW Russia, on the Voronezh River. Pop. 455,000.

**Li·piz·za** |'lēpētsə| (Slovenian name **Lipica**) village in Slovenia, a horse breeding center since Roman times. It gave its name to the white Lipizzaner horses.

**Lip·pe** |'lipə| former state in N central Germany, since 1947 part of the state of North Rhine-Westphalia. Its capital was Detmold.

**Lis·bon** |'lizbən| the capital and chief port of Portugal, an industrial and cultural center on the Atlantic coast at the mouth of the Tagus River. Pop. 678,000. Much of the city was rebuilt after a 1755 earthquake. Portuguese name **Lisboa**.

**Lis·burn** |'lizbərn| town in County Antrim, Northern Ireland, to the SW of Belfast, on the border with County Down. Pop. 40,000.

**Lis·doon·var·na** |lis'dŌŌn,värnə| spa town in the Republic of Ireland, in County Clare. Pop. 600.

**Li·shui** |'lē'SHwē| city in Zhejiang province, SE China, NW of Wenzhou on a tributary of the Ou River. Pop. 303,000.

**Li·sieux** |lēz'yŒ| town in Calvados, N France. Pop. 25,000. It is the site of a shrine of Saint Theresa of Lisieux, who was canonized in 1925.

**Litch·field** |'liCH,fēld| historic town in NW Connecticut. Pop. 8,365.

**Lith·u·a·nia** |,liTHə'wānēə| republic on the SE shore of the Baltic Sea. Area: 25,183 sq. mi./65,200 sq. km. Pop. 3,765,000. Languages, Lithuanian (official), Russian. Capital and largest city: Vilnius. Long tied to Poland, Lithuania was dominated by Russia in the 18th–20th centuries, regaining independence in 1991. Traditionally agricultural, it has since 1940 become increasingly industrial. □ **Lithuanian** *adj. & n.*

**Lithuania**

**Lit·tle A·mer·i·ca** |ə'merikə| name given five former U.S. exploration bases in Antarctica between 1929 and 1958. All were on or near the Bay of Whales in the Ross Sea.

**Lit·tle Ar·a·rat** |'ærə,ræt| see ARARAT, MOUNT.

**Lit·tle Belt** channel between the Kattegat and the Baltic Sea that separates the mainland of Denmark from Fyn Island.

**Lit·tle Big·horn River** |,litl 'big,hawrn| river in N Wyoming and SE Montana, scene of the 1876 defeat of George Custer's cavalry by Cheyenne and Sioux warriors.

**Lit·tle Mis·sou·ri River** |mə'zo͝ore| river that flows 560 mi./900 km. from Wyoming through Montana and the Dakotas, to the Missouri River.

**Lit·tle Rock** |'litl ,räk| the capital of Arkansas, an industrial city on the Arkansas River. Pop. 175,795.

**Lit·tle Rus·sia** |'rəSHə| term formerly applied chiefly to the Ukraine, but also to neighboring regions in historic RUTHENIA.

**Lit·tle St. Ber·nard Pass** |,sänt bə(r)-'närd| see ST. BERNARD PASS.

**Lit·tle Ti·bet** |tə'bet| another name for BALTISTAN.

**Lit·tle·ton** |'lidltən| industrial city in N central Colorado, S of Denver. Pop. 33,685.

**Liu·zhou** |le'o͞o'jo| (also **Liuchow**) an industrial city in S China, in Guangxi Zhuang province NE of Nanning. Pop. 740,000.

**Liv·er·more** |'livər,mawr| city in N central California, E of Oakland, noted as home to the Lawrence Livermore nuclear laboratory. Pop. 56,741.

**Liv·er·pool** |'livər,po͞ol| industrial port city in NW England, on the E side of the mouth of the Mersey River. Pop. 448,000. Liverpool developed as a port in the 17th cen-

tury with the import of cotton from America and the export of textiles produced in Lancashire and Yorkshire, and in the 18th century became an important center of shipbuilding and engineering.

**Liv·ing·stone** |'liviNGstən| former name for MARAMBA, Zambia.

**Li·vo·nia¹** |lə'vo͞oneə| region on the E coast of the Baltic Sea, N of Lithuania, comprising most of present-day Latvia and Estonia. German name **Livland**. □ **Livonian** *adj. & n.*

**Li·vo·nia²** |lə'vo͞oneə| industrial city in SE Michigan, W of Detroit. Pop. 100,850.

**Li·vor·no** |lə'vawr,no| port in NW Italy, in Tuscany, on the Ligurian Sea. Pop. 171,000. It is the site of the Italian Naval Academy. Also called **Leghorn**.

**Liz·ard, the** |'lizərd| promontory in SW England, in Cornwall. Its S tip, Lizard Point, is the southernmost point of the British mainland.

**Lju·blja·na** |lē,o͞oblē'änə| the capital of Slovenia. Pop. 267,000. The city was founded (as Emona) by the Romans in 34 B.C. Long the capital of Illyria, it is a modern industrial city. German name **Laibach**.

**Llan·dud·no** |hlän'didno| resort town in Conwy, N Wales, on the Irish Sea. Pop. 14,000.

**Lla·nel·li** |hlä'nehlē| industrial port in S Wales, in Dyfed, on Carmarthen Bay, a former center of steel and tin manufacturing. Pop. 73,000.

**Llan·gol·len** |hlä'gawhlən| resort town in NE Wales, in Clwyd. Pop. 3,000. A tourist center, it is home to the annual international *eisteddfod* (arts festival).

**Llano Es·ta·ca·do** |'yäno ,estə'kädo| (also **Staked Plain**) high section of the Great Plains in the Texas Panhandle and SE New Mexico.

**Lla·nos** |'yänos| vast grassy plains or savannas in tropical South America, especially in the Orinoco River basin. They are known as the home of cattle-tending *llaneros*, South American cowboys.

**Lo·bam·ba** |lo'bämbə| village in W central Swaziland, SE of Mbabane, that is the royal and legislative capital of the kingdom.

**Lo·bi·to** |lo'beto| seaport and natural harbor on the Atlantic coast of Angola. Pop. 150,000.

**Lo·car·no** |lo'kärno| resort in S Switzerland, at the N end of Lake Maggiore. Pop. 14,000.

**Lock·er·bie** |'läkərbē| town in SW Scotland, in Dumfries and Galloway. Pop. 4,000. In 1988 the wreckage of a Pan Am jetliner, bound for NewYork, but destroyed by a terrorist bomb, crashed on the town, killing all those on board and eleven people on the ground.

**Lock·port** |'läk,pawrt| city in W New York, NE of Buffalo, on the Erie Canal route. Pop. 24,426.

**Lo·cris** |'lōkrəs| region in the central part of ancient Greece, eventually divided into parts. It was a very early state, probably predating the arrival of the Phocians.

**Lod** |lōd| (also **Lydda**) historic city in central Israel, SE of Tel Aviv. Pop. 51,000.

**Lo·di**[1] |'lawdē| city in N central California, N of Stockton, in the San Joaquin Valley. Pop. 51,874.

**Lo·di**[2] |'lō'dī| town in N Italy, SE of Milan. Pop. 42,000. French troops led by Napoleon defeated Austrian troops here in 1796.

**Łódź** city in central Poland. Pop. 842,000.

**Lo·fo·ten Islands** |'lōfōtn| island group off the NW coast of Norway. They are situated within the Arctic Circle, SW of the Vesterålen group.

**Lo·gan, Mount** |'lōgən| mountain in the SW Yukon Territory, in Kluane National Park, near the border with Alaska. Rising to 19,850 ft./6,054 m., it is the highest peak in Canada and the second-highest peak in North America.

**Lo·gan** |'lōgən| city in N Utah, in an agricultural area. Pop. 32,762.

**Lo·gro·ño** |lō'grōnyō| market town in N Spain, on the Ebro River, capital of La Rioja region. Pop. 127,000.

**Loire** |lə'wär| longest river of France. It rises in the Massif Central and flows 630 mi./1,015 km. N and W to the Atlantic at St. Nazaire. Its valley is noted for its historic chateaus.

**Lo·ja** |'lōhä| commercial and university city in S Ecuador, the capital of Loja province. Pop. 94,000.

**Lol·land** |'law,län| Danish island in the Baltic Sea, to the S of Zealand and W of Falster.

**Lo·mas de Za·mo·ra** |'lōmäs dä sə-'mawrə| city in E Argentina, an industrial suburb S of Buenos Aires. Pop. 573,000.

**Lom·bard Street** |'läm,bärd| street in the financial district of London, England, containing many leading banks.

**Lom·bar·dy** |'läm,bärdē; 'lämbərdē| region of N central Italy, between the Alps and the Po River. Capital: Milan. Italian name **Lombardia**. □ **Lombard** *adj. & n.*

**Lom·bok** |'läm,bäk| volcanic island of the Lesser Sunda group in Indonesia, between

Bali and Sumbawa. Pop. 2,500,000; chief town, Mataram.

**Lo·mé** |'lōmä| the capital and chief port of Togo, on the Gulf of Guinea. Pop. 450,000.

**Lo·mond, Loch** |läk 'lōmənd; läкн| lake in W central Scotland, to the NW of Glasgow. The largest freshwater lake in Scotland, it is the subject of songs and folklore.

**Lom·poc** |'läm,päk| city in SW California, NW of Santa Barbara. Pop. 37,649. Its economy relies on agriculture and government installations.

**Lon·don**[1] |'ləndən| industrial and commercial city in S Ontario, on the Thames River to the N of Lake Erie. Pop. 303,165.

**Lon·don**[2] |'ləndən| the capital of the United Kingdom, situated in SE England on the River Thames. Pop. 6,379,000. London was settled as a river port and trading center, called Londinium, shortly after the Roman invasion of A.D. 43, and since the Middle Ages has been a leading world city. Devastated by the Great Plague (1665–66) and the Fire of London (1666), the city was rebuilt in the late 17th century. Damage during World War II again led to substantial reconstruction. It is divided administratively into the City of London, known as the Square Mile, which is the British financial center, and thirty-two boroughs of Greater London. It is the seat, at Westminster, of the British government. □ **Londoner** *n.*

**Lon·don Bridge** |'ləndən| name of several successive bridges over the River Thames in London, England, beginning with a wood structure of the 10th century. The stone bridge of the 1830s was moved in 1968 to Lake Havasu City, Arizona, where it is a tourist attraction.

**Lon·don·der·ry** |'ləndən,derē| **1** one of the Six Counties of Northern Ireland, formerly an administrative area. Pop. 187,000. **2** its chief town, a port city on the Foyle River near the N coast. Pop. 63,000. It was formerly called Derry, a name still used by many. In 1613 it was granted to the City of London for colonization and became known as Londonderry.

**Lon·dri·na** |lōn'drēnə| commercial city in S Brazil, in Paraná state, in an agricultural area. Pop. 413,000.

**Lone Star State** |'lōn ,stär| nickname for TEXAS, whose flag contains one star.

**Long Beach** |'lawNG ,bēcH| port and resort city in S California, just S of Los Angeles. Pop. 429,433.

**Long Branch** |'lawNG ,bræncH| city in E central New Jersey, on the Atlantic, long a noted summer resort. Pop. 28,658.

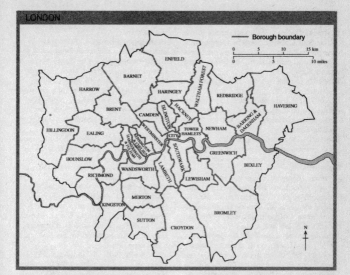

LONDON

——— Borough boundary

0 5 10 15 km
0 5 10 miles

ENFIELD

BARNET

HARROW

HARINGEY

WALTHAM FOREST

REDBRIDGE

HAVERING

BRENT

CAMDEN

ISLINGTON

HACKNEY

BARKING & DAGENHAM

HILLINGDON

EALING

WESTMINSTER

KENSINGTON & CHELSEA

TOWER HAMLETS

CITY

NEWHAM

HAMMERSMITH & FULHAM

HOUNSLOW

SOUTHWARK

GREENWICH

BEXLEY

RICHMOND

WANDSWORTH

LAMBETH

LEWISHAM

KINGSTON

MERTON

SUTTON

CROYDON

BROMLEY

N

**Long·champs** |lôn'shän| famed racetrack in Paris, France, in the Bois de Boulogne, long a resort for the fashionable.

**Long·ford** |'lawNGfərd| **1** county in the central Republic of Ireland, in the province of Leinster. Pop. 30,000. **2** its county seat. Pop. 6,000.

**Long Island** |lawNG 'ilənd| island of New York State, extending E of Manhattan for 118 mi./210 km. roughly parallel to the coast of Connecticut, from which it is separated by Long Island Sound. Its W tip, comprising the New York boroughs of Brooklyn and Queens, is separated from Manhattan and the Bronx by the East River. To the E are suburban NASSAU COUNTY and SUFFOLK COUNTY.

**Long Island City** |lawNG 'ilənd| section of Queens, New York City, across the East River from Manhattan, and both industrial and residential.

**Long·mont** |'lawNG,mänt| city in N Colorado, an agricultural and industrial center. Pop. 51,555.

**Lon·gueuil** |lawNG'gäl| city in S Quebec, an industrial suburb across the St. Lawrence River from Montreal. Pop. 129,874.

**Long·view**[1] |'lawNG,vyōō| city in E Texas, in an oil-producing area. Pop. 70,311.

**Long·view**[2] |'lawNG,vyōō| port city in SW

Washington, on the Cowlitz and Columbia rivers. Pop. 31,499.

**Long·yan** |'lŏŏNG'yän| industrial and agricultural city in Fujian province, SE China, NW of Xiamen. Pop. 386,000.

**Look·out Mountain** |'lŏŏk,owt| Appalachian ridge on the Cumberland Plateau in Alabama, Georgia, and Tennessee, where near Chattanooga it was the scene of a November 1863 Civil War battle.

**Loop, the** |lŏŏp| commercial district at the center of Chicago, Illinois, named for the railway tracks that circle around part of it.

**Lop Nor** |'lŏp 'nawr| (also **Lop Nur**) dried-up salt lake in the arid basin of the Tarim River in NW China, used since 1964 for nuclear testing.

**Lo·rain** |law'rān| port city in N central Ohio, on Lake Erie W of Cleveland. Pop. 71,245.

**Lor·ca** |'lawrkə| market town in Murcia, SE Spain, on the Guadalentin River. Pop. 67,000.

**Lord Howe Island** |lawrd 'how| volcanic island in the SW Pacific off the E coast of Australia, administered as part of New South Wales. Pop. 320.

**Lord's** |lawrdz| cricket ground in St. John's Wood, N London, England, headquarters since 1814 of the Marylebone Cricket Club

(MCC), the sport's unofficial governing body.

**Lo·re·lei** |'lawrə,lī| rock cliff on the Rhine River S of Coblenz, western Germany, in legend the home of a siren whose song lures boatmen to destruction. The cliff is noted for its echo.

**Lo·re·to** |lə'rātō| town in E Italy, near the Adriatic coast to the S of Ancona. Pop. 11,000. It is the site of the 'Holy House', said to be the home of the Virgin Mary and to have been brought from Nazareth by angels in 1295.

**Lo·rient** |lawr'yäɴ| shipbuilding port in NW France, on the S coast of Brittany. Pop. 62,000.

**Lor·raine** |law'ren; lə'rān| region of NE France, between Champagne and the Vosges mountains. The modern region corresponds to the southern part of the medieval kingdom of Lorraine (from the ancient name **Lotharingia**), which extended from the North Sea to Italy.

**Los Al·a·mos** |laws 'æləmōs| community in N New Mexico, on the Pajarito Plateau. Pop. 11,455. It has been a center for nuclear research since the 1940s, when it was built to be the site of the development (in the Manhattan Project) of the first nuclear bombs.

**Los An·ge·les**[1] |laws 'ænjələs| city on the Pacific coast of S California, the second-largest city in the U.S. Pop. 3,485,398. Founded by the Spanish in 1781, it developed after the arrival of the Southern Pacific Railroad and the discovery of oil in 1894. It has become a major center of industry, filmmaking, and television in the 20th century, its metropolitan area having expanded to include towns such as Beverly Hills, Hollywood, Santa Monica, and Pasadena. **Los Angeles County** is the largest in the U.S.: pop. 8,863,164.

**Los An·ge·les**[2] |laws'ænjələs| city in S central Chile, a processing center in the agricultural Bío-Bío River valley. Pop. 142,000.

**Los Gat·os** |laws 'gætəs| city in N central California, SW of San Jose. Pop. 27,357.

**Los Mo·chis** |laws 'mōchēs| commercial city in W Mexico, in Sinaloa state. Pop. 163,000.

**Lost Colony** see ROANOKE ISLAND.

**Los Te·ques** |laws 'tākes| commercial and resort city in N Venezuela, the capital of Miranda state. Pop. 141,000.

**Lot** |lawt| river of S France, which rises in the Auvergne and flows 300 mi./480 km. W to meet the Garonne SE of Bordeaux.

**Lo·thi·an** |'lōthēən| former local government region in central Scotland, now divided into *East Lothian, Midlothian,* and *West Lothian.*

**Louang·phra·bang** |'lwäɴɢprä'bäɴɢ| variant spelling of LUANG PRABANG, Laos.

**Lough·bor·ough** |'ləfb(ə)rə| town in Leicestershire, England, on the River Soar N of Leicester. Pop. 46,000.

**Lou·is·bourg** |'lōōəs,bərg| historic town in E Cape Breton Island, Nova Scotia, captured by British and New England forces during 18th-century fighting. Pop. 1,261.

**Lou·i·si·ade Archipelago** |lōō,ēzē| island group in extreme SE Papua New Guinea. Tagula is the largest island.

**Lou·i·si·ana** |lə,wēzē'ænə; ,lōō(ə)zē'ænə| see box. ☐ **Louisianan** adj. & n.

**Lou·i·si·ana Purchase** |lə,wēzē'ænə; ,lōō(ə)zē'ænə| region W of the Mississippi River, bought from France by the U.S. in 1803. Including most of the present-day U.S. N of Texas and E of the Continental Divide, it was explored by the Lewis and Clark expedition.

**Lou·is·ville** |'lōōi,vil| industrial city and river port in N Kentucky, on the Ohio River across from Indiana. Pop. 269,063. It is the

---

### Louisiana

**Capital:** Baton Rouge

**Largest city:** New Orleans

**Other cities:** Alexandria, Lafayette, Lake Charles, Shreveport

**Population:** 4,219,973 (1990); 4,368,967 (1998); 4,535,000 (2005 proj.)

**Population rank (1990):** 21

**Rank in land area:** 31

**Abbreviation:** LA; La.

**Nicknames:** Pelican State; Bayou State

**Motto:** 'Union, Justice, and Confidence'

**Bird:** Eastern brown pelican

**Flower:** magnolia

**Tree:** bald cypress

**Songs:** "Give Me Louisiana"; "You Are My Sunshine"

**Noted physical features:** Head of the Passes; coastal marshlands; Mississippi Delta; Gulf of Mexico; Five Islands Salt Domes; Driskill Mountain

**Tourist attractions:** New Orleans (French Quarter, Bourbon Street, Mardi Gras festival); Bayou Country

**Admission date:** April 30, 1812

**Order of admission:** 18

**Name origin:** Named in 1682 to honor France's King Louis XIV by French explorer Robert Cavelier, Sieur de La Salle.

site, at Churchill Downs, of the annual Kentucky Derby horse race.

**Lourdes** |lŏŏrdz| town in SW France, at the foot of the Pyrenees. Pop. 17,000. It has been a major place of Roman Catholic pilgrimage since 1858, when a young peasant girl, Marie Bernarde Soubirous (St. Bernadette), claimed to have had a series of visions of the Virgin Mary in a grotto here.

**Lou·ren·ço Mar·ques** |lō'ränsōō mär-'käsн| former name (until 1976) for MAPUTO, Mozambique.

**Louth** |lowтн; lowтн| county of the Republic of Ireland, on the E coast in the province of Leinster. Pop. 91,000; county seat, Dundalk.

**Lou·vain** |lŏŏ'veN| French name for LEUVEN, Belgium.

**Louvre, the** |'lŏŏv(rə)| art museum in Paris, France. Housed in a Renaissance palace, the museum is one of the largest in the world, with such famous works as the *Mona Lisa* and the *Venus de Milo*.

**Love Canal** |'ləv| section of Niagara Falls, New York that was evacuated after 1970s exposure that chemical wastes underlay its residential neighborhood. It has been partially reoccupied.

**Love·land** |'ləvkænd; 'ləvlənd| city in N central Colorado, between Denver and Fort Collins. Pop. 37,352.

**Low Countries** general term for the Netherlands, Belgium, and Luxembourg. French name **Pays-bas.**

**Low·ell** |'lōəl| city in NE Massachusetts, on the Concord and Merrimack rivers, developed after 1822 as a planned textile community, based on textile manufacturing. Pop. 103,439.

**Low·er Aus·tria** |'awstreə| state of NE Austria. Pop. 1,481,000. Capital: St. Pölten. German name **Niederösterreich.**

**Low·er Cal·i·for·nia** |ˌkælə'fawrnyə| another name for BAJA CALIFORNIA, Mexico.

**Low·er Can·a·da** |'kænədə| the mainly French-speaking region of Canada around the lower St. Lawrence River, in what is now S Quebec. It was a British colony under this name in 1791–1841. See also UPPER CANADA.

**Low·er East Side** |'lōər ˌest 'sīd| district of SE Manhattan, New York City, famed as home to immigrants, especially Jews, from the 1880s through the early 20th century.

**Low·er Egypt** |'ējipt| see UPPER EGYPT.

**Low·er Forty-eight States** term for the 48 contiguous United States, excluding Alaska and Hawaii.

**Low·er Hutt** |'hət| city in New Zealand, NE of Wellington. Pop. 64,000. It is the site of the Prime Minister's official residence, Vogel House.

**Low·er Sax·o·ny** |'sæksənē| state of NW Germany. Pop. 7,238,000. Capital: Hanover. It corresponds to the NW part of the former kingdom of Saxony. German name **Niedersachsen.**

**Lowes·toft** |'lō(ə),stawft| fishing port and resort town on the North Sea coast of E England, in NE Suffolk. Pop. 60,000. It is the most easterly English town.

**Loy·al·ty Islands** |'loi(ə)ltē| group of islands in the SW Pacific, forming part of the French overseas territory of New Caledonia. Pop. 18,000.

**Lu·a·la·ba** |ˌlŏŏə'läbə| river of central Africa, which rises near the S border of the Democratic Republic of Congo (formerly Zaire) and flows N for about 400 mi./640 km., joining the Lomami to form the Congo River.

**Lu·an·da** |lə'wändə| the capital of Angola, a port on the Atlantic coast. Pop. 2,250,000.

**Luang Pra·bang** |lŏŏ'äNG prə'bäNG| (also **Louangphrabang**) city in NW Laos, on the Mekong River. Pop. 44,000. It was the royal residence and Buddhist religious center of Laos until the end of the monarchy in 1975.

**Lu·ang·wa River** |lŏŏ'äNGwə| river that flows 500 mi./800 km. from NE Zambia, to form part of the Zambia-Mozambique border, before emptying into the Zambezi River.

**Lu·an·shya** |lŏŏ'änsнä| industrial city in central Zambia, near the border with Congo (formerly Zaire). It is in a region producing copper, uranium, peanuts, and other crops. Pop. 146,000.

**Lub·bock** |'ləbək| commercial and industrial city in NW Texas, an agricultural processing hub. Pop. 186,206.

**Lü·beck** |'lγbek| historic port city in N Germany, on the Baltic coast of Schleswig-Holstein. Pop. 211,000. It was a leading city in the Hanseatic League (14th–19th centuries).

**Lub·lin** |'lŏŏblən; 'lŏŏ,blēn| manufacturing city in E Poland. Pop. 351,000.

**Lu·bum·bashi** |ˌlŏŏbŏŏm'bäshē| city in the SE of the Democratic Republic of Congo (formerly Zaire), near the border with Zambia, capital of the mining region of Shaba. Pop. 739,000. Former name (until 1966) **Elisabethville.**

**Luc·ca** |'lŏŏkə| city in N Italy, a noted silk-

and olive-producing center in Tuscany, W of Florence. Pop. 86,000.

**Lu·ce·na** |lōō'sänä| commercial city in the Philippines, on S Luzon. Pop. 151,000.

**Lu·cerne, Lake** |lōō'sərn| (also **Lake of Lucerne**) lake in central Switzerland, surrounded by the four cantons of Lucerne, Nidwalden, Uri, and Schwyz. Also called **Lake of the Four Cantons**; German name **Vierwaldstättersee**.

**Lu·cerne** |lōō'sərn| resort city on the W shore of Lake Lucerne, in central Switzerland. Pop. 59,000. German name **Luzern**.

**Lu·chow** |'lōō'jō| **1** see HEFEI, China. **2** see LUZHOU, China.

**Luck·now** |'lək,now| city in N India, capital of the state of Uttar Pradesh. Pop. 1,592,000. The former capital of Oudh, it is noted for its crafts industries.

**Lü·da** |'lY'dä| industrial center and port on the SE tip of the Liaodong Peninsula in Liaoning province, NE China, consisting of the cities of Dalian and Lüshun. Pop. 1,630,000.

**Lü·den·scheid** |'lYdensHīt| industrial city in western Germany. Pop. 76,000.

**Ludh·i·a·na** |,lōōdē'änə| industrial and commercial city in NW India, in Punjab, SE of Amritsar. Pop. 1,012,000.

**Lud·low** |'lədlō| commercial and tourist town in W England, in Shropshire. Pop. 9,000.

**Lud·wigs·burg** |'lōōdviks,bŏŏrk| transportation center and industrial city in SW Germany. Pop. 79,000.

**Lud·wigs·ha·fen** |,lōōdviks'häfen| industrial river port in W central Germany, SW of Mannheim, on the Rhine in the state of Rhineland-Palatinate. Pop. 165,000.

**Lu·ga·no** |lōō'gänō| resort and financial town in S Switzerland, on the N shore of Lake Lugano. Pop. 26,000.

**Lu·go** |'lōōgō| walled city and trade center in NW Spain, on the Minho River. Pop. 87,000. It is the capital of Lugo province, in an agricultural region.

**Lu·hansk** |lōō'hänsk| industrial city in E Ukraine, in the Donets Basin. Pop. 501,000. Former name **Voroshilovgrad**. Russian name **Lugansk**.

**Lui·chow Peninsula** |lə'wēCHow| see LEIZHOU PENINSULA, China.

**Luik** |loik| Flemish name for LIÈGE, Belgium.

**Lu·leå** |'lōōlə,aw| seaport in N Sweden, on the Gulf of Bothnia, capital of Norrbotten county. Pop. 68,000.

**Lund** |lŏŏnd| city in SW Sweden, just NE of Malmö. Pop. 88,000. Its university was founded in 1666.

**Lun·dy** |'ləndē| granite island in the Bristol Channel, off the coast of N Devon, SW England.

**Lü·ne·burg Heath** |'lYne,bŏŏrg| sandy heath between the Elbe and Aller rivers in N Germany. Part of it is a military training site, and part is a nature preserve. German name **Lüneberger Heide**.

**Lu·nen** |'lōōnən| manufacturing city in N central Germany on the Lippe River. Pop. 86,000.

**Luo·yang** |lə'waw'yäNG| industrial city in Henan province, E central China, on the Luo River. Pop. 1,160,000. It was founded in the 12th century B.C. in the Zhou (Chou) dynasty and was the capital of several subsequent dynasties.

**Lu·que** |'lōōka| historic city in S Paraguay. Pop. 84,000. A capital of the country in the 19th century, it is now a suburb of Asunción.

**Lu·sa·ka** |lōō'säkə| the capital of Zambia, an industrial city and transportation center in an agricultural area. Pop. 982,000.

**Lu·sa·tia** |lōōsäsHə| region of E Germany and SW Poland. Upper, or South, Lusatia is largely agricultural; Lower Lusatia, in the N, is forested. The inhabitants of the region have periodically sought independence. □ **Lusatian** adj. & n.

**Lü·shun** |'lY'sHoon| (formerly **Port Arthur**) port on the Liaodong Peninsula, NE China, now part of the urban complex of Lüda. It was leased by Russia as a Pacific naval port in 1898 and seized by the Japanese in 1904.

**Lu·si·ta·nia** |,lōōsə'tānēə| ancient Roman province in the Iberian Peninsula, corresponding to modern Portugal. □ **Lusitanian** adj. & n.

**Lu·te·tia** |lōō'tēsH(ē)ə| Roman name for the settlement that became PARIS, France.

**Lu·ton** |'lōōtn| industrial town to the NW of London, England, formerly in Bedfordshire. Pop. 167,000.

**Lutsk** |lōōtsk| (Polish name **Luck**) river port and industrial city in NW Ukraine, on the Styr River. Pop. 210,000.

**Lüt·zen** |'lYtsən| town in S central Germany. It was the site of a Napoleonic victory, in 1813, over Russian and Prussian forces.

**Lux·em·bourg**[1] |'ləksəm,bərg| **1** country in W Europe, between Belgium, Germany, and France. Area: 999 sq. mi./2,586 sq. km. Pop. 378,000. Languages, Luxembourgish, French, and German. An independent grand duchy since 1815, Luxembourg has had close ties with Belgium and the Netherlands. Iron and steel are key to its economy. **2** its capital, a commercial, cultural, and industrial center. Pop. 76,000. It is the seat of the European Court of Justice. **3** a province of SE Belgium, until 1839 a province of the Grand Duchy of Luxembourg. Capital: Arlon. □ **Luxembourger** *n.*

**Luxembourg**

**Lux·em·bourg**[2] |'ləksəm,bərg| **1** the **Luxembourg Gardens**, a park in Paris, France, on the Left Bank, near the Sorbonne. **2** the **Palace of Luxembourg**, a palace in the Luxembourg Gardens, built in 1615–20. It now houses the French Senate.

**Lux·or** |'lək,sawr; 'lŏŏk,sawr| city in E Egypt, on the E bank of the Nile. Pop. 142,000. It is the site of the S part of ancient Thebes and contains the ruins of the temple built by Amenhotep III and of monuments erected by Ramses II. Arabic name **El Uqsur**.

**Lu·zhou** |'lŏŏ'jō| (formerly **Luchow**) city in Sichuan province, central China, on the Yangtze River SW of Chongqing. Pop. 263,000.

**Lu·zon** |lŏŏ'zän; lŏŏ'zawn| the most northerly and the largest (40,420 sq. mi./104,688 sq. km.) island in the Philippines. Its chief towns are Quezon City and Manila, the national capital.

**Lviv** |lə'vēŏŏ; lə'vēf| industrial and commercial city in W Ukraine, near the border with Poland. Pop. 798,000. Russian name **Lvov**.

**Ly·all·pur** |'līəl,pŏŏr| former name (until 1979) for FAISALABAD, Pakistan.

**Ly·ce·um, the** |lī'sēəm| gymnasium and garden near ancient Athens, Greece, where Aristotle taught his philosophy.

**Ly·cia** |'lishə| ancient region on the coast of SW Asia Minor (present-day SW Turkey), between Caria and Pamphylia. □ **Lycian** *adj. & n.*

**Lyd·ia** |'lidēə| ancient region of W Asia Minor (present-day W Turkey), S of Mysia and N of Caria. It became a powerful kingdom in the 7th century B.C., but in 546 was absorbed into the Persian Empire. □ **Lydian** *adj. & n.*

**Lyme** |līm| town in SE Connecticut, on the Connecticut River, which gave its name to Lyme disease. Pop. 1,949.

**Lynch·burg** |'linch,bərg| city in W central Virginia, near the Blue Ridge Mts. Pop. 66,049.

**Lynn** |lin| city in NE Massachusetts, on Massachusetts Bay NE of Boston, noted for its shoe and other industries. Pop. 81,245.

**Ly·ons** |lyawN| industrial and commercial city and river port in SE France, at the confluence of the Rhône and Saône rivers. Pop. 422,000. The Roman Lugdunum, it was an important city of Gaul. Its cuisine is famous. French name **Lyon**.

# Mm

**Maas** |'mäs| Dutch name for the MEUSE River.

**Maas·tricht** |mä'striкнt| industrial city in the Netherlands, capital of the province of Limburg, on the Maas (Meuse) River near the Belgian and German borders. Pop. 117,000. The Treaty of the European Union was signed here in 1992.

**Ma·cao** |mə'kow| (Portuguese name **Macau**) Portuguese dependency, SE China, on the Pearl River estuary opposite Hong Kong. Area: 6.5 sq. mi./17 sq. km. Pop. 467,000. Capital: Macao City. Comprising Macao peninsula and two neighboring islands, the colony was established as a trading settlement in 1557. Tourism, gambling, and fishing are its economic mainstays. It is due to return to Chinese control in 1999. □ **Macanese** adj. & n.

**Macao**

**Ma·ca·pá** |ˌmäkä'pä| town in N Brazil, on the Amazon delta, capital of the state of Amapá. Pop. 167,000.

**Ma·cau** |mə'kow| see MACAO.

**Mac·cles·field** |'mækəlz,fēld| industrial town in W England, in Cheshire. Pop. 48,000. Once a silk industry center, it now has various manufactures.

**Mac·Don·nell Ranges** |mək'dänl| series of mountain ranges extending W from Alice Springs in Northern Territory, Australia. The highest peak is Mount Liebig: 4,948 ft./1,524 m.

**Mac·e·do·nia**[1] |ˌmæsə'dōnēə| ancient country in SE Europe, at the N end of the Greek peninsula. In the 4th century B.C. it was a kingdom that under Philip II and Alexander the Great became a great empire. The region is now divided among Greece, Bulgaria, and the republic of Macedonia.

**Mac·e·do·nia**[2] |ˌmæsə'dōnēə| landlocked republic in the Balkan peninsula. Area: 9,932 sq. mi./25,713 sq. km. Pop. 2,038,000. Language, Macedonian. Capital: Skopje. Formerly a constituent republic of Yugoslavia, Macedonia became independent after a referendum in 1991. It is both agricultural and industrial. □ **Macedonian** adj. & n.

**Macedonia**

**Mac·e·do·nia**[3] |ˌmæsə'dōnēə| region in the northeast of modern Greece. Pop. 2,263,000. Capital: Thessaloníki.

**Mac·eió** |ˌmäsä'ō| port in E Brazil, on the Atlantic coast. Pop. 700,000. It is the capital of the state of Alagoas.

**Ma·ce·ra·ta** |ˌmäcнä'rätä| agricultural and industrial town in E central Italy, capital of the province of Macerata. Pop. 44,000.

**Mac·gil·li·cud·dy's Reeks** |mə'giləkədēz 'rēks| range of hills in County Kerry, SW Ireland. It rises to 3,415 ft./1,041 m. at Carrantuohill, highest point in Ireland.

**Ma·cha·la** |mä'CHälä| commercial town in S Ecuador, capital of El Oro province, in an agricultural area. Pop. 144,000.

**Ma·chi·da** |mä'CHēdä| city in E central Japan, on E central Honshu, an industrial and residential suburb SW of Tokyo. Pop. 349,000.

**Ma·chi·li·pat·nam** |məCH'lēpətnəm| port city in E India, in Andhra Pradesh state, on the Bay of Bengal. Pop. 159,000.

**Ma·chu Pic·chu** |ˈmäcHōō 'pikcHōō| fortified Inca town in the Andes in Peru. It is famous for its dramatic position, high on a steep-sided ridge. It contains a palace, a temple to the sun, and extensive cultivation terraces. Rediscovered in 1911, it was named after the mountain that rises above it.

**Ma·ci·as Ngue·ma** |mä'sēäs əNG'wämä|

former name (1973–79) for Bioko, Equatorial Guinea.

**Mac·kay** |mə'kā| port in NE Australia, on the coast of Queensland. Pop. 40,000.

**Mac·ken·zie Mountains** | mə'kenzē| range of the N Rocky Mts., chiefly along the border between the Yukon Territory and the Northwest Territories.

**Mac·ken·zie River** | mə'kenzē| the longest river in Canada, flowing 1,060 mi./1,700 km. NW from the Great Slave Lake in the Northwest Territories to its delta and mouth on the Beaufort Sea.

**Mack·i·nac, Straits of** | 'makə,naw| passage between Lakes Huron and Michigan, crossed since 1957 by the Mackinac Bridge. The Upper Peninsula of Michigan lies to the N, and historic Mackinac Island lies just to the E.

**Ma·con** |'mākən| industrial and commercial city in central Georgia, on the Ocmulgee River. Pop. 106,612.

**Mâ·con** |'mäkən| town, the capital of Saône-et-Loire department, E central France, on the Saône River. Pop. 39,000. At the center of a wine-producing region, it is also a transportation hub and an industrial center.

**Mac·quar·ie River** | mə'kwerē| river in New South Wales, Australia, rising on the W slopes of the Great Dividing Range and flowing 600 mi./960 km. NW to join the Darling River, of which it is a headwater.

**Mac·tan** |mäk'tän| island in the Philippines, off the E coast of Cebu. The Portuguese navigator Ferdinand Magellan was killed here in 1521.

**Mad·a·gas·car** |,mædə'gæskər| island country in the Indian Ocean, off the E coast of Africa. Pop. 12,016,000. Official languages, Malagasy and French. Capital: Antananarivo. The fourth-largest island in the world, Madagascar resisted colonization until the French took control in 1896. Independent as the Malagasy Republic in 1960, it changed its name back in 1975. Its

Madagascar

predominantly agricultural people are a mix of African, Polynesian, and Arab.
□ **Madagascan** *adj. & n.*

**Ma·dei·ra**¹ |mə'derə| river in NW Brazil, which rises on the Bolivian border and flows about 900 mi./1,450 km. to meet the Amazon E of Manaus. It is navigable to large ocean-going vessels as far as Pôrto Velho. □ **Madeiran** *adj.*

**Ma·dei·ra**² |mə'derə| island in the Atlantic off NW Africa, the largest of the Madeiras, a group that constitutes an autonomous region of Portugal. Pop. 270,000. Capital: Funchal. Encountered by the Portuguese in 1419, the islands are known for the fortified wine produced here, and have agricultural and crafts industries.

**Ma·de·leine, Isles de la** |'el dä lä mawd-'len| (English name **Magdalen Islands**) island group in SE Quebec, in the Gulf of St. Lawrence N of Prince Edward Island.

**La Ma·de·leine** |lə mæ'dlen| church in Paris, France. Begun in 1806 by Napoleon, it has the form and shape of a Greek temple, with 52 Corinthian columns running around the exterior. The church is unusual in having no windows.

**Ma·dhya Pra·desh** |'mädē prə'desH| state in central India, the largest (171,261 sq. mi./443,446 sq. km.) Indian state, formed in 1956. Pop. 66.14 million. Capital: Bhopal.

**Mad·i·son** |'mædəsən| the state capital of Wisconsin, an industrial and university city in the central part, largely on Lakes Mendota and Monona. Pop. 191,262.

**Mad·i·son Avenue** |'mædəsən| street in Manhattan, New York City, associated with the advertising industry, which has many offices here.

**Mad·i·son Square** |'mædəsən| park in Manhattan, New York City, at the S end of Madison Ave. The original **Madison Square Garden**, the famous sports arena, was here. Today the arena is on 34th Street.

**Ma·di·un** |mädē'yŏon| (also **Madioen**) industrial and commercial municipality in Indonesia, on E Java, W of Surabaya. Pop. 170,000.

**Ma·dras** |'mædrəs| **1** industrial seaport on the SE coast of India, capital of Tamil Nadu. Pop. 3,795,000. Official name (since 1995) **Chennai. 2** former name (until 1968) for the state of Tamil Nadu.

**Ma·drid** |mə'drid| the capital and largest city of Spain. Pop. 2,985,000. Situated on a high plateau in the center of the country, it replaced Valladolid as capital in 1561. It is an industrial and cultural center.

**Ma·du·ra** |'mæjərə| agricultural island of Indonesia, off the NE coast of Java. Its chief town is Pamekasan. Pop. 952,000.

**Ma·du·rai** |mədə'rī| historic city in Tamil Nadu in S India. Pop. 952,000.

**Mae·an·der** |mē'(y)ændir| ancient name for the MENDERES River, Turkey.

**Mae·ba·shi** |mä'ēbäsHē| (also **Maye-bashi**) city in N central Japan, on central Honshu. Pop. 286,000. It is noted for silk-worm growing and silk production.

**Mael·strom, the** |'mäl,sträm| powerful current and whirlpool that passes through a channel in the Norwegian Sea off the NW coast of Norway, in the Lofoten Islands.

**Maf·e·king** |'mæfə,kiNG| (also **Mafikeng**) a town in South Africa, in North-West Province, scene of an 1899–1900 siege during which a British force outlasted Boer attackers.

**Ma·fe·teng** |mäfə'teNG| town in W Lesotho, in an agricultural district SW of Maseru. Pop. 206,000.

**Ma·ga·dan** |məgä'dän| port and naval base in E Siberia, Russia, on the Sea of Okhotsk. Pop. 154,000.

**Ma·ga·dha** |'məgädä| ancient kingdom of NE India (7th century B.C.–A.D. 325) on territory within present-day Bihar state.

**Ma·ga·di, Lake** |mäg'ädē| salt lake in the Great Rift Valley, in S Kenya, with extensive deposits of sodium carbonate and other minerals.

**Mag·da·le·na** |,mægdə'lēnə| the principal river of Colombia, rising in the Andes and flowing N for about 1,000 mi./1,600 km. to enter the Caribbean at Barranquilla.

**Mag·de·burg** |'mægdə,bərg| industrial city in Germany, the capital of Saxony-Anhalt, a port on the Elbe River and linked to the Rhine and Ruhr by the Mittelland Canal. Pop. 290,000.

**Ma·gel·lan, Strait of** |mə'jelən| passage separating Tierra del Fuego and other islands of Chile and Argentina from mainland South America, connecting the Atlantic and Pacific.

**Ma·gen·ta** |mə'jen(t)ə| commune in N Italy, W of Milan. Pop. 23,000. French and Sardinian armies defeated Austrian forces here in 1859. In honor of the victory, the town's name was given to a reddish-purple dye.

**Mag·giore, Lake** |mə'jawrē| the second-largest of the lakes of N Italy, extending into S Switzerland. It is surrounded by mountains and has many resorts along its shores.

**Ma·ghrib** |'mæ,grib| (also **Maghreb**) Arabic name for the region of N and NW Africa

between the Atlantic and Egypt, comprising the coastal plain and Atlas Mtns. of Morocco, together with Algeria, Tunisia, and sometimes also Libya, forming a well-defined zone bounded by sea or desert. Moorish Spain was also considered part of this region during the Arab rule here. Compare with BARBARY.

**Ma·gi·not Line** |,mä(d)zHē'nō ,līn| line of defensive fortifications, completed in 1936, along France's NW frontier, extending from Switzerland to Luxembourg. In World War II, although the defenses held, the Germans went around its end through Belgium, and conquered France.

**Mag·na Grae·cia** |'mægnə 'grāsH(ē)ə| term for ancient Greek port colonies in present-day S Italy, excluding Sicily. Chief cities included Tarentum (now Tarento), Crotona (Crotone), Cumae, and Sybaris.

**Mag·ne·sia** |mæg'nēzHə| the name of two ancient cities in Lydia, in Asia Minor, now part of Turkey: Magnesia on the Maeander, the site of a temple to Artemis Leukophryne, and Magnesia at Sipulus, near modern MANISA.

**mag·net·ic pole** |mæg,netik 'pōl| either of two places on earth where a compass needle will dip vertically. The South Magnetic Pole is in Antarctica, the North Magnetic Pole near Bathurst Island in the Arctic Archipelago of Canada. The location of each fluctuates.

**Mag·ni·to·gorsk** |məg'n(y)itä'gōrsk| industrial city, a metallurgical center in S Russia, on the Ural River close to the border with Kazakhstan. Pop. 443,000.

**Mag·no·lia State** nickname for MISSISSIPPI.

**Mag·ya·ror·szág** |'mädyär,awr,säg; 'mäj,är,awr'säg| Hungarian name for HUNGARY.

**Ma·ha·bad** |mää'bäd| city in NW Iran, near the Iraqi border, with a chiefly Kurdish population. Pop. 63,000. In 1941–46 it was the center of a Soviet-supported Kurdish republic.

**Ma·ha·jan·ga** |mä'zäNGgä| port city in NW Madagascar, on the Mozambique Channel of the Indian Ocean. Pop. 122,000.

**Ma·ha·na·di River** |mä'hänədē| river in central India, flowing 550 mi./885 km. from the Eastern Ghats to the Bay of Bengal.

**Ma·ha·rash·tra** |,mä(h)ə'räsHtrə| state in W India bordering on the Arabian Sea, formed in 1960 from the SE part of the former Bombay State. Pop. 78,750,000. Capital: Bombay. □ **Maharashtrian** adj. & n.

**Ma·ha·we·li** |,mä(h)ə'welē| the largest river in Sri Lanka. Rising in the central highlands, it flows 206 mi./330 km. to the Bay of Bengal near Trincomalee.

**Mahe** |,mə'hä| largest island of the Seychelles. Pop. 63,000. Victoria, the capital, is here. The economy relies on fishing, tourism, and agriculture.

**Ma·hi·lyow** |məgi'lyawf| industrial city and railway center in E Belarus, on the Dnieper River. Pop. 363,000. Russian name **Mogilev**.

**Mahon** |mə'hon; mə'hōn| (also **Port Mahón**) the capital of the island of Minorca in the Balearic Islands of Spain, a port on the SE coast. Pop. 22,000.

**Ma·ho·ning River** |mə'hōniNG| river in E Ohio and NW Pennsylvania whose valley was the 19th-century hub of the U.S. steel industry.

**Ma·hore** |mə'hōr; mə'hawr| another name for the French Indian Ocean island group of **Mayotte**.

**Maid·en·head** |'mädn,hed| industrial town in Berkshire, S England, W of London on the Thames River. Pop. 60,000.

**Maid·stone** |'mäd,stōn| town in SE England, on the River Medway, the county seat of Kent. Pop. 133,000.

**Mai·du·gu·ri** |mi'dōōgərē| commercial and industrial town in NE Nigeria, near Lake Chad. Pop. 282,000.

**Mai·kop** |mi'kawp| city in SW Russia, capital of the republic of Adygea. Pop. 120,000.

**Main** |män| river of Germany that rises in N Bavaria and flows 310 mi./500 km. W, through Frankfurt, to meet the Rhine at Mainz.

**Maine**[1] |män| historic region and former province in NW France, S of Normandy and E of Brittany. It comprises the present departments of Mayenne and Sarthe and parts of the departments of Loire-et-Cher, Eure-et-Loir, and Orne. The commercial center is Le Mans. The Maine River, 8 mi./13 km. long, formed by the confluence of the Sarthe and Mayenne rivers near Angers, flows into the Loire River.

**Maine**[2] |män| see box.

**Main·land** |'män,lænd| in Scotland: **1** (also called **Pomona**) the largest (178 sq. mi./460 sq. km.) of the Orkney Islands. Chief town: Kirkwall. Scapa Flow and Skara Brae are here. **2** the largest (225 sq. mi./580 sq. km.) of the Shetland Islands. Chief town: Lerwick.

**Main Line** |'män,lïn| popular name for a series of affluent suburbs W of Philadel-

| **Maine** |
|---|
| **Capital:** Augusta |
| **Largest city:** Portland |
| **Other cities:** Auburn, Bangor, Brunswick, Lewiston |
| **Population:** 1,227,928 (1990); 1,244,250 (1998); 1,285,000 (2005 proj.) |
| **Population rank (1990):** 38 |
| **Rank in land area:** 39 |
| **Abbreviation:** ME |
| **Nickname:** Pine Tree State |
| **Motto:** *Dirigo* (Latin: 'I direct') |
| **Bird:** chickadee |
| **Fish:** landlocked salmon |
| **Flower:** white pine cone and tassel |
| **Tree:** Eastern white pine |
| **Song:** "State of Maine Song" |
| **Noted physical features:** Casco; Penobscot, Passamaquoddy bays; Desert of Maine Sand Dunes; Mount Katahdin |
| **Tourist attractions:** Acadia National Park; Allagash Wilderness Waterway; Old Orchard Beach; West Quoddy Head lighthouse |
| **Admission date:** March 15, 1820 |
| **Order of admission:** 23 |
| **Name origin:** For the former province of Maine in western France; also reflects an older reference to the mainland as distinct from the offshore islands. |

phia, Pennsylvania, along the old Pennsylvania Railroad main line.

**Mainz** |mïn(t)s| commercial city in W Germany, capital of Rhineland-Palatinate, situated at the confluence of the Rhine and Main rivers. Pop. 183,000. Johannes Gutenberg built the first printing press here c.1448.

**Mai·po River** |'mïpō| river that flows 155 mi./250 km. W from the Chilean Andes, near Santiago, to the Pacific. Its valley is a noted wine-producing center.

**Maj·da·nek** |mï'dänek| (also **Maidanek**) village near Lublin, SE Poland, site of a major Nazi death camp during World War II.

**Ma·jor·ca** |mə'jawrkə| the largest of the Balearic Islands. Pop. 614,000. Capital: Palma. Spanish name **Mallorca**. □ **Majorcan** *adj.*

**Ma·kas·sar Strait** |mə'käsər| stretch of water separating the islands of Borneo and Sulawesi and linking the Celebes Sea in the N with the Java Sea in the S. Makassar is also the former name of Ujung Padang, Indonesia.

**Ma·ka·ti** |mä'kätē| town just SE of Manila,

the Philippines, a residential and high-tech industrial suburb of the capital. Pop. 453,000.

**Ma·kga·di·kga·di Pans** |mə,gædē,gædē| extensive area of salt pans in N central Botswana, a game preserve.

**Ma·khach·ka·la** |məkhəchkä'lä| port in SW Russia, on the Caspian Sea, capital of the autonomous republic of Dagestan. Pop. 327,000. Former name (until 1922) **Port Petrovsk**.

**Ma·ke·yev·ka** |mə'käyef(v)kæ(ə)| (also **Makeevka**) industrial city and coal-mining center in E Ukraine, NE of Donetsk. Pop. 424,000.

**Mak·kah** |'mekä| Arabic name for MECCA, Saudi Arabia.

**Mal·a·bar Coast** |'mælə,bär| the S part of the W coast of India, including the coastal region of Karnataka and most of the state of Kerala.

**Ma·la·bo** |'mælə,bō| seaport, the capital of Equatorial Guinea, on the island of Bioko. Pop. 10,000. Former name **Santa Isabel**.

**Ma·la·bon** |mälä'bōn| (also called **Ta-nong**) industrial and commercial port town in the Philippines, on S Luzon, just N of Manila. Pop. 278,000.

**Ma·la·ca·nang Palace** official residence of the president of the Philippines, in Manila, SW Luzon, on the Pasig River.

**Ma·lac·ca, Strait of** |mə'läkä| the channel between the Malay Peninsula and the Indonesian island of Sumatra, an important sea passage linking the Indian Ocean to the South China Sea. The ports of Melaka and Singapore lie on this strait.

**Ma·la·ga** |'mäləgə| seaport and resort on the Andalusian coast of S Spain. Pop. 525,000. Spanish name **Málaga**.

**Mal·a·gasy Republic** |'mælə'gæsē| former name (1960–75) for MADAGASCAR.

**Ma·lang** |mä'läNG| commercial and industrial city in Indonesia, on E Java, S of Surabaya. Pop. 695,000.

**Mä·la·ren** |'melären| lake in SE Sweden, extending inland from the Baltic Sea. The city of Stockholm is situated at its outlet.

**Ma·la·tya** |mä'lätyä| (ancient name **Me-litene**) historic city in E central Turkey, capital of Malatya province. Pop. 282,000. It is an important agricultural region.

**Ma·la·wi, Lake** |mə'läwē| another name for Lake Nyasa (see NYASA, LAKE).

**Ma·la·wi** |mə'läwē| landlocked republic of S central Africa, in the Great Rift Valley. Area: 45,764 sq. mi./118,484 sq. km. Pop. 8,796,000. Official languages, English and Nyanja. Capital: Lilongwe. Largest city:

Blantyre. From 1891 to 1964 it was Nyasaland, under British control. Largely agricultural, it depends on Mozambique for access to overseas trade. □ **Malawian** adj. & n.

**Malawi**

**Ma·laya** |mə'lāə| former country in SE Asia, consisting of the S part of the Malay Peninsula and some adjacent islands (originally including Singapore), now forming the W part of the federation of Malaysia and known as West Malaysia. The area was colonized by the Dutch, Portuguese, and the British, who eventually became dominant; the several Malay states federated under British control in 1896. Malaya was occupied by the Japanese 1941–45. The country became independent in 1957, the federation expanding to become Malaysia in 1963.

**Ma·lay Archipelago** |'mā,lä| an extended group of islands, including Sumatra, Java, Borneo, the Philippines, and New Guinea, lying between SE Asia and Australia. They

constitute the bulk of the area formerly known as the East Indies.

**Ma·lay Peninsula** |'mā,lā| peninsula in SE Asia separating the Indian Ocean from the South China Sea. It extends approximately 700 mi./1,100 km. S from the Isthmus of Kra and comprises the S part of Thailand and the whole of Malaya (West Malaysia).

**Ma·lay·sia** |mə'lāzHə| country in SE Asia, on the Malay Peninsula (West Malaysia) and N Borneo (East Malaysia). Area: 127,369 sq. mi./329,758 sq. km. Pop. 18,294,000. Language, Malay. Capital and largest city: Kuala Lumpur. A historic Malay kingdom was later dominated by Hindus, Muslims, the Dutch, the Portuguese, and the British. Independent since 1963, it is largely agricultural, exporting forest products, rubber, tin, palm oil, and oil. □ **Malaysian** *adj. & n.*

**Mal·den** |'mawldən| city in E Massachusetts, a suburb just N of Boston. Pop. 53,884.

**Mal·dives** |'mawldīvz; 'mawldēvz| (also **Maldive Islands**) republic consisting of a chain of coral islands in the Indian Ocean SW of Sri Lanka. Area: 115 sq. mi./298 sq. km. Pop. 221,000. Language, Maldivian (Sinhalese). Capital and largest settlement: Malé. Long under Arab influence, and a British colony 1887–1965, the Maldives depend on fishing, tourism, and tropical fruits for income. □ **Maldivian** *adj. & n.*

**Mal·don** |'mawldən| commercial town in SE England, on the Blackwater River estuary in E Essex. Pop. 15,000. A battle against

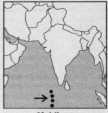

**Maldives**

the Danes here in A.D.991 gave rise to a famous Anglo-Saxon poem.

**Ma·lé** |māl| the capital and largest atoll of the Maldives. Pop. 55,000.

**Ma·le·gaon** |mä'lāgown| city in W India, in Maharashtra NE of Bombay. Pop. 342,000.

**Ma·li** |'mälē| landlocked republic in W Africa, S of Algeria. Area: 479,024 sq. mi./1.24 million sq. km. Pop. 8,706,000. Languages, French (official), others main-

**Mali**

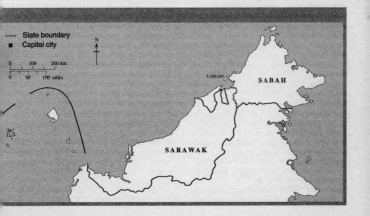

ly of the Mande group. Capital and largest city: Bamako. Former name (until 1960) **French Sudan**. Largely in the Sahara and Sahel, Mali takes its name from a medieval trade empire. It became independent from France in 1959. Agriculture, fishing, and extractive industries are key to its economy. □ **Malian** *adj. & n.*

**Mal•i•bu** |'mælə,bσσ| resort community, part of Los Angeles, on the Pacific coast of S California. It is noted for its beaches, for its elaborate oceanview residences, and as the home of the J. Paul Getty Museum.

**Ma•lin•che** |mä'lēnCHä| dormant volcano in central Mexico, on the border of Tlaxcala and Puebla: 14,636 ft./4,461 m.

**Ma•lin•di** |mä'lēndē| port city in SE Kenya, on the Indian Ocean. Pop. 51,000. It is a former Portuguese colonial capital, and earlier was an Arab trade center.

**Ma•lines** |mə'lēn| French name for MECHELEN, Belgium.

**Mal•lor•ca** |mə'yawrkə| Spanish name for MAJORCA, Balearic Islands.

**Mal•mai•son** |,mälmä'zawn| chateau, now a museum in Rueil-Malmaison, a W suburb of Paris, France. Built in 1669, it was the favorite home of the Empress Josephine, the first wife of Napoleon I. She died here in 1814.

**Mal•mé•dy** |'mälmādē| tourist and industrial town in E Belgium, in the Ardennes, scene of heavy fighting and a massacre of captured Americans in 1944. Pop. 10,000.

**Malmö** |'mäl,mö| port and industrial city in SW Sweden, on the Øresund opposite Copenhagen. Pop. 234,000.

**Ma•lo•los** |mä'lōlōs| commercial town in the Philippines, on SW Luzon, N of Manila. Pop. 125,000. It was the capital of the Philippine Republic proclaimed by revolutionaries in 1898.

**Mal•pla•quet** |'mælplæ,ket| village in N France, on the border with Belgium. In 1709 British and Austrian troops won a victory there over the French in a major battle of the War of the Spanish Succession.

**Mal•ta** |'mawltə| island republic in the central Mediterranean, about 60 mi./100 km. S of Sicily. Area: 122 sq. mi./316 sq. km. Pop. 356,000. Official languages, Maltese and English. Capital and chief settlement: Valletta. Important to maritime peoples since the Phoenicians, Malta was held by the British 1814–1964. As its naval importance has declined, tourism has grown. □ **Maltese** *adj. & n.*

**Mal•vern Hills** |'mawlvərn| (also **the Malverns**) range of limestone hills in W

**Malta**

England, in Herefordshire and Worcestershire. The highest point is Worcestershire Beacon (1,394 ft./425 m.).

**Mal•vi•nas, Islas** | mäl'vēnəs| Argentinian name for the FALKLAND ISLANDS.

**Mam•moth Cave National Park** |'mæməɵH| preserve in W central Kentucky, site of the largest known cave system. It consists of over 300 mi./480 km. of charted passageways and contains spectacular rock formations.

**Ma•mo•ré River** |məmσσ'rä| river that flows 600 mi./970 km. from central Bolivia to the border with W Brazil. It joins the Beni River to form the Madeira River.

**Ma•mou•tzu** the capital (since 1977) of the French Indian Ocean territory of Mayotte (Mahore). Pop. 12,000.

**Man, Isle of** |'il əv 'mæn| island in the Irish Sea that is a British Crown possession having home rule, with its own legislature (the Tynwald) and judicial system. Pop. 70,000. Capital: Douglas. The island was part of the Norse kingdom of the Hebrides in the Middle Ages, passing into Scottish hands in 1266; the English gained control in the early 15th century. Its ancient Gaelic language, Manx, is still occasionally used for ceremonial purposes. □ **Manx** *adj. & n.*

**Ma•na•do** |mä'nädō| commercial port in Indonesia, on NE Sulawesi. Pop. 217,000.

**Ma•na•gua** |mə'nägwə| the capital, commercial and industrial center, and largest city of Nicaragua. Pop. 682,000. The city was devastated by an earthquake in 1972, and damaged further during the civil strife of the late 1970s.

**Ma•na•ma** |mə'nämə| seaport capital of Bahrain, a center for oil refining and finance. Pop. 140,000.

**Ma•na Pools National Park** |'mänä 'pσσlz| national park and wildlife habitat in N Zimbabwe, in the Zambezi valley NE of Lake Kariba, established in 1963.

**Ma·nas·sas** |mə'næsəs| see BULL RUN, Virginia.

**Ma·naus** |mä'nows| city in NW Brazil, capital of the state of Amazonas. Pop. 1,012,000. It is the principal commercial center of the upper Amazon region.

**Manche, la** |mawnSH,lä| French name for the ENGLISH CHANNEL.

**Manche** |mawnSH| department in NW France, coextensive with the Cotentin Peninsula, Normandy. Pop. 480,000. The region is largely agricultural. The main towns are Cherbourg and the capital, Saint Lô.

**Man·ches·ter**[1] |'mænCHəstər| industrial city in NW England. Pop. 397,000. Founded in Roman times, it developed in the 18th and 19th centuries as a center of the English textile industry, and is an important industrial and trade center, with access to the sea via the Manchester Ship Canal. □ **Mancunian** adj. & n.

**Man·ches·ter**[2] |'mænCHəstər| largest city in New Hampshire, on the Connecticut River in the S part. It is an industrial center long noted for textile production. Pop. 99,567.

**Man·chou·li** |'män'CHŏŏ'lē| see MANZHOULI, China.

**Man·chu·kuo** |män'CHŏŏkwaw| (also **Manzhouguo**) country created 1932 by the invading Japanese in NE China. Claimed to be a Manchu state, it was in fact a puppet, and was abolished in 1945.

**Man·chu·ria** |mæn'CHŏŏrēə| mountainous region forming the NE portion of China, now comprising the provinces of Jilin, Liaoning, and Heilongjiang. In 1932 it was declared an independent state by Japan and renamed Manchukuo; it was restored to China in 1945. □ **Manchurian** adj. & n.

**Man·da·lay** |'mændəlā| port on the Irrawaddy River in central Burma. Pop. 533,000. Founded in 1857, it was the capital until 1885 of the Burmese kingdom. It is an important Buddhist religious center.

**Man·da·lu·yong** |,mändälŏŏ'yawNG| industrial town in the Philippines, on S Luzon, a suburb of Manila. Pop. 245,000.

**Man·fre·do·nia** |mänfre'dônyä| seaport in SE Italy, on the Gulf of Manfredonia. Pop. 59,000.

**Man·hat·tan**[1] |mæn'hætn| commercial city in NE Kansas. Pop. 37,712. Fort Riley is just to the W.

**Man·hat·tan**[2] |mæn'hætn| island near the mouth of the Hudson River, forming the best-known borough of the City of New York. The site of the original Dutch settlement of New Amsterdam (1625), it was taken by the British in 1664. Manhattan, coextensive with New York County, is the commercial and cultural center of New York City. Pop. 1,487,526. □ **Manhattanite** n.

**Ma·ni·ca·land** |mə'nēkə,länd| goldmining province of E Zimbabwe. Capital: Mutare.

**Man·i·coua·gan River** |mæne'kwägən| river that flows 280 mi./450 km. from central Quebec to the Saint Lawrence River. It is the site of huge hydroelectric power plants, and a reservoir that fills a circular meteorite impact zone 60 mi./100 km. in diameter.

**Ma·ni·la** |mə'nilə| the capital, chief port, and financial and industrial center of the Philippines, on the island of Luzon. Pop. 1,599,000. Founded in 1571, it was an important trade center of the Spanish until taken by the U.S. in 1898.

**Ma·ni·pur** |'mænə,pŏŏ(ə)r| state in the far E of India, E of Assam, on the border with Burma. Pop. 1.83 million. Capital: Imphal.

**Ma·ni·sa** |,mäne'sä| (ancient name **Magnesia**) historic commercial city in W Turkey, capital of Manisa province. Pop. 158,000. Its area produces minerals, cotton, and other crops.

**Man·i·to·ba** |,mænə'tōbə| prairie province of central Canada, noted for its many lakes and rivers, with a coastline on Hudson Bay. Area: 250,947 sq. mi./649,950 sq. km. Pop. 1,091,942. Capital and largest city: Winnipeg. The area was part of Rupert's Land from 1670 until it was transferred to Canada by the Hudson's Bay Company and became a province in 1870. Farming, mining, and manufacturing are all important. □ **Manitoban** adj. & n.

**Man·i·tou·lin Island** |,mänə'tŏŏlēn| island in Ontario, in N Lake Huron. At 1,068 sq. mi./2,766 sq. km., it is the largest lake island in the world. It has numerous fishing and resort villages.

**Man·i·za·les** |,mäne'zäläs| commercial city in W central Colombia, in the Andes, the capital of Caldas department. Pop. 327,000. It is a center for the coffee industry.

**Man·ka·to** |män'kätō| city in S central Minnesota, in an agricultural and quarrying district. Pop. 31,477.

**Man·nar, Gulf of** |mən'när| inlet of the Indian Ocean lying between NW Sri Lanka and the S tip of India. It lies to the S of Adam's Bridge, which separates it from the Palk Strait.

**Man·nar** |mən'när| **1** island off the NW

coast of Sri Lanka, linked to India by the chain of coral islands and shoals known as Adam's Bridge. **2** a town on this island. Pop. 14,000.

**Man·ner·heim Line** |'mänərhām; 'mænərhīm| fortifications erected by Finland across the Karelian isthmus during the Finnish-Russian War. Begun in 1939 and never completed, the fortifications extended 80 mi./129 km. from the Gulf of Finland to Lake Ladoga.

**Mann·heim** |'mæn,hīm| industrial port at the confluence of the Rhine and the Neckar in Baden-Württemberg, SW Germany. Pop. 315,000.

**Ma·no** |'mæ,nō| river of W Africa. It rises in NW Liberia and flows 200 mi./320 km. to the Atlantic, forming for part of its length the boundary between Liberia and Sierra Leone.

**Man·re·sa** |män'räsä| industrial city in NE Spain, on the Cardoner River. Pop. 66,000.

**Mans, Le** |lə 'mawn| see LE MANS, France.

**Mans·field, Mount** |'mænz,fēld| peak in N Vermont, at 4,393 ft./1,340 m. the highest in the state and in the Green Mts.

**Mans·field**[1] |'mæns,fēld| industrial town in central England, N of Nottingham. Pop. 72,000. Sherwood Forest is to the E.

**Mans·field**[2] |'mæns,fēld| industrial city in N central Ohio. Pop. 50,627.

**Man·ta** |'mæntə| port city in W Ecuador, NW of Guayaquil. Pop. 126,000. Its name is also that of an ancient culture of the area.

**Man·te·ca** |män'tēkæ| city in central California, in the San Joaquin Valley, in an agricultural area. Pop. 40,773.

**Man·ti·nea** |mände'nä(y)ä| city of ancient Greece, in E Arcadia. It was the scene of three major battles, including one in the Peloponnesian War.

**Man·tua** |'mænCHwə| (Italian name **Mantova**) town in N Italy. Pop. 54,000. It is an agricultural, industrial, and tourist center. It was an important cultural center during the Renaissance. □ **Mantuan** *adj. & n.*

**Ma·nus** |'mänōōs| largest island in the Admiralty Islands, N Papua, New Guinea, in the Manus administrative district. Volcanic and hilly, it has coconut plantations but is largely uninhabited.

**Man·za·nil·lo**[1] |,mänzä'nēyō| port city in SE Cuba, on the Caribbean Sea. Pop. 98,000. It exports sugar, tobacco, and other regional crops.

**Man·za·nil·lo**[2] |,mänzä'nēyō| commercial city in SW Mexico, in Colima state. Pop. 68,000. It is a leading Pacific port and a resort.

**Man·zhou·li** |män'zHōlē| (formerly **Manchouli**) city in Inner Mongolia, NE China, on the Russian and near the Mongolian border. Pop. 120,000.

**Man·zi·ni** |män'zēnē| (formerly **Bremersdorp**) industrial city in central Swaziland. Pop. 19,000. It was a colonial capital before 1902.

**Ma·pu·to** |mə'pōōtō| the capital and chief port of Mozambique, on the Indian Ocean in the S of the country. Pop. 1,098,000. Founded as a Portuguese fortress in the late 18th century, it became the capital of Mozambique in 1907. Former name (until 1976) **Lourenço Marques**.

**Mar·a·cai·bo** |,merə'kībō| city and port in NW Venezuela, situated on the channel linking the Gulf of Venezuela with Lake Maracaibo. Pop. 1,401,000. Founded in 1571, the city expanded rapidly after the discovery of oil in the region in 1917.

**Mar·a·cai·bo, Lake** |,märə'kībō| lake in NW Venezuela, the largest (5,120 sq. mi./13,261 sq. km.) in South America, linked by a narrow channel to the Gulf of Venezuela and the Caribbean Sea.

**Ma·ra·cay** |märə'kī| industrial and commercial city in N Venezuela, capital of Aragua state. Pop. 354,000. It is a cattle industry center.

**Ma·ra·di** |'mərädē| industrial and commercial town in S Niger, near the Nigerian border. Pop. 113,000.

**Ma·rais, le** |lə mä'rā| section of Paris, France, on the Right Bank of the Seine. An old section of narrow streets and ancient buildings, the once run-down Marais, home to Paris's Jewish community, has been largely restored and has become fashionable. At its center is the Place des Vosges.

**Ma·ra·jó** |,märä'zHō| island in NE Brazil, at the mouth of the Amazon, with the Pará River on its SE side. Flat and over 150 mi./240 km. long, it is used for cattle raising and has prehistoric sites.

**Ma·ram·ba** |mə'rämbə| city in S Zambia, about 3 mi./5 km. from the Zambezi River and the Victoria Falls. Pop. 95,000. Formerly called Livingstone, it was the capital of Northern Rhodesia from 1911 until Lusaka succeeded it in 1935.

**Ma·ra·nhão** |,märän'yown| state of NE Brazil, on the Atlantic coast. Pop. 4,930,000. Capital: São Luís.

**Ma·ra·ñón** |,märän'yōn| river of N Peru, which rises in the Andes and flows 1,000 mi./1,600 km., forming one of the principal headwaters of the Amazon.

**Mar·a·thon** |'merə,ᴛʜän| village and plain in SE Greece, NE of Athens. In 490 B.C. the Athenians and Plataeans defeated a Persian army here, and the messenger Pheidippides ran 20 mi./32 km. to Athens to bring the news.

**Mar·be·lla** |mär'bäə| resort town on the Costa del Sol of S Spain, in Andalusia. Pop. 81,000.

**Mar·ble·head** |'märbəlhed| coastal town in NE Massachusetts, a noted yachting and fishing port. Pop. 19,971.

**Mar·burg** |'märbərg| (officially **Marburg an der Lahn**) **1** city in the state of Hesse, in west central Germany. Important in the history of Protestantism, it draws tourists and has light industries. Pop. 71,000. **2** German name for **Maribor**, Slovenia.

**Marche**[1] |'märcʜ| agricultural region of central France, on the NW edge of the Massif Central, comprising the department of Creuse and parts of the departments of Haut-Vienne, Indre, and Charente. Guèret is the chief town.

**Marche**[2] |'märcʜ| (also **the Marches**) region in E central Italy, between the Apennine Range and the Adriatic Sea. Pop. 1,436,000. The area is hilly or mountainous, and farming is the chief industry.

**Mar·co Po·lo Bridge** |'märkō 'pōlō| marble bridge spanning the Yongding River at Lugouqiao, 9 mi./14 km. SW of Beijing, China. In July 1937 a clash between Japanese and Chinese troops here marked the beginning of the Second Sino-Japanese War (1937–45).

**Mar del Pla·ta** |,mär dəl 'plätə| fishing port and resort in Argentina, on the Atlantic coast S of Buenos Aires. Pop. 520,000.

**Ma·ren·go** |mə'reɴɢgō| village near Turin, NW Italy. In 1800 Napoleon I defeated an Austrian army here.

**Mar·ga·ri·ta** |,märgə'rētə| island in the Caribbean Sea, off the coast of Venezuela. Visited by Columbus in 1498, it was used as a base by Simón Bolívar in 1816 in the struggle for independence from Spanish rule.

**Mar·gate** |'mär,gāt| port and resort town in SE England, E of London in the Isle of Thanet, Kent. Pop. 53,000.

**Mar·gi·lan** |,märge'län| (also **Margelan**) town in E Uzbekistan, adjacent to the city of Kokand. Pop. 125,000. It is an important silk center.

**Ma·ri** |'märē| ancient city on the W bank of the Euphrates, in Syria, near the Iraqi border. Its period of greatest importance was from the late 19th to the mid 18th centuries B.C.; the vast palace of the last king, Zimri-Lin, has yielded an archive of 25,000 cuneiform tablets, which are the principal source for the history of N Syria and Mesopotamia at that time.

**Ma·ri·ana Islands** |,merē'ænə; ,märē'änə| (also **the Marianas**) a group of islands in the W Pacific, comprising Guam and the Northern Marianas. Visited by Magellan in 1521, the islands were colonized by Spain in 1668. Guam was ceded to the U.S. in 1898 and the remaining islands were sold to Germany in the following year. Administered by Japan after World War I, they became part of the Pacific Islands Trust Territory, administered by the U.S., in 1947. In 1975 the Northern Marianas voted to establish a commonwealth in union with the U.S., and became self-governing three years later. See also GUAM; NORTHERN MARIANAS

**Ma·ria·nao** |,märēə'now| city in NW Cuba, a residential suburb W of Havana. Pop. 134,000. It has resort beaches and some industry.

**Ma·ri·ana Trench** |,merē'ænə; ,märē'änə| ocean trench to the SE of the Mariana Islands in the W Pacific, with the deepest known ocean depth (36,201 ft./11,034 m. at the Challenger Deep).

**Ma·rián·ské Lázně** |,märē'änske 'läznye| (also **Marienbad**) spa town in W Bohemia, Czech Republic. Pop. 15,000. World-famous for its healing springs, it was popular with writers.

**Ma·ri Auton·o·mous Republic** |'märē| another name for MARI EL, Russia.

**Ma·rib** |'märib| ancient city, now in ruins, in E Yemen, E of Sana'a. It was one of the chief cities of the kingdom of Sheba (c. 1000 B.C.)

**Ma·ri·bor** |'märēbōr| industrial city in NE Slovenia, on the Drava River near the border with Austria. Pop. 104,000. German name **Marburg**.

**Mar·i·co·pa County** |,meri'cōpə| county in S central Arizona. Its seat is Phoenix, which, with nearby suburbs, is home to more than half of all Arizonans. Pop. 2,122,101.

**Ma·rie Byrd Land** |mä'rē 'bərd| region of Antarctica bordering the Pacific, between Ellsworth Land and the Ross Sea.

**Ma·ri El** |mə'rē 'el| autonomous republic in European Russia, E of Moscow and N of the Volga. Pop. 754,000. Capital: Yoshkar-Ola. Also called **Mari Autonomous Republic**.

**Mar·ien·bad** German name for MARIÁNSKÉ LÁZNĚ.

**Ma·ri·ki·na** |ˌmärēˈkēnä| (also **Mariquina**) commercial town in the Philippines, on S Luzon, E of Manila. Pop. 310,000.

**Ma·rí·lia** |ˈmärēlyə| commercial and agricultural city in SE Brazil, in W São Paulo state. Pop. 178,000.

**Ma·rin County** |märˈən| county in NW California, across the Golden Gate from San Francisco. Many affluent suburbs are here. Pop. 230,096.

**Ma·rin·gá** |ˈmärēn,gä| commercial city in SE Brazil, in Paraná state. Pop. 269,000. Coffee is among its agricultural products.

**Mar·i·on**[1] |ˈmærēən| industrial city in E central Indiana. Pop. 32,618.

**Mar·i·on**[2] |ˈmærēən| industrial city in N central Ohio. Pop. 34,075.

**Mar·i·time Alps** |ˈmærə,tim| section of the Alps, in NW Italy and SW France. The highest peak is Punta Argentera (10,817 ft./3,297 m.)

**Mar·i·time Provinces** |ˈmærə,tīm| (also **the Maritimes**) the Canadian provinces of New Brunswick, Nova Scotia, and Prince Edward Island, with coastlines on the Gulf of St. Lawrence and the Atlantic. These provinces, with Newfoundland and Labrador, are also known as the Atlantic Provinces.

**Ma·ri·tsa** |məˈritsə| river of S Europe, which rises in the Rila Mts. of SW Bulgaria and flows 300 mi./480 km. S to the Aegean Sea. It forms part of the border between Bulgaria and Greece and that between Greece and European Turkey. Its ancient name is the Hebros or Hebrus. Turkish name **Meriç**; Greek name **Évros**.

**Ma·ri·u·pol** |märēˈo͞opōl| industrial port on the S coast of Ukraine, on the Sea of Azov. Pop. 517,000. Former name (1948–89) **Zhdanov**.

**Marl** |märl| industrial and mining center in western Germany, in the Ruhr district. Pop. 90,000.

**Marl·bor·ough** |ˈmärlbərō| industrial city in E central Massachusetts. Pop. 31,813.

**Mar·ma·ra, Sea of** |ˈmärmərə| small sea in NW Turkey. Connected by the Bosporus to the Black Sea and by the Dardanelles to the Aegean, it separates European Turkey from Anatolia. In ancient times it was known as the Propontis.

**Marne** |ˈmärn| river of E central France, which rises in the Langres plateau N of Dijon and flows 328 mi./525 km. N and W to join the Seine near Paris. Its valley was the scene of two important battles in World War I. The first (September 1914) halted and repelled the German advance on Paris; the second (July 1918) ended the final German offensive.

**Ma·roua** |ˈmäro͞oä| town in N Cameroon, S of L. Chad. Pop. 143,000. It is the trade center for a large region.

**Mar·que·sas Islands** |märˈkäsäz| group of volcanic islands in the S Pacific, forming part of French Polynesia. Pop. 8,000. The islands were annexed by France in 1842. The largest is Hiva Oa, on which the French painter Gauguin spent the last years of his life.

**Mar·quette** |märˈket| port city in the Upper Peninsula of Michigan, on Lake Superior. Pop. 21,977.

**Mar·ra·kesh** |ˌmerəˈkeSH| (also **Marrakech**) industrial and tourist city in W Morocco, in the foothills of the High Atlas Mts. Pop. 602,000. It was founded in 1062 as the capital of the Muslim Almoravid dynasty. It was the capital of Morocco until 1147, and again 1550–1660.

**Mar·sa·la** |märˈsälə| seaport in Sicily, S Italy, on the Mediterranean Sea. Pop. 81,000. It gave its name to a sweet red wine.

**Mar·seilles** |märˈsä| industrial city and port on the Mediterranean coast of S France. Pop. 808,000. French name **Marseille**. The second-largest city in France, settled in the 6th century B.C. as the Greek Massilia, it was the chief port for the French colonization of Algeria.

**Mar·shall Islands** |ˈmärSHəl| republic consisting of two chains of islands in the NW Pacific. Area: 70 sq. mi./181 sq. km. Pop. 43,420. Languages, English (official), local Austronesian languages. Capital: Majuro. Formerly controlled by the Germans and Japanese, the Marshalls were administered by the U.S. in 1947–86, then entered into free association with the U.S. Tourism is important. Kwajalein, Bikini, and Eniwetok have all been used for nuclear or

**Marshall Islands**

other military tests. □ **Marshallese** *adj. & n.*

**Mars•ton Moor** |'märstən ,mawr| moor in N England, just W of York, site of the largest battle (1644) of the English Civil War, a victory for Parliamentarians under Thomas Fairfax and Oliver Cromwell.

**Mar•ta•ban, Gulf of** |'märtə,bän| inlet of the Andaman Sea, a part of the Indian Ocean, on the coast of SE Burma E of Rangoon.

**Mar•tha's Vineyard** |'märTHəz 'vinyərd| resort island in the Atlantic off the coast of Massachusetts, to the S of Cape Cod; its chief town is Edgartown.

**Mar•ti•nez** |mär'tēnez| industrial port in N central California, on Suisun Bay, N of Oakland. Pop. 31,808.

**Mar•ti•nique** |,märtn'ēk| French island in the West Indies, in the Lesser Antilles. Pop. 360,000. Capital: Fort-de-France. □ **Martiniquan** *adj. & n.* **Martinican** *adj. & n.*

**Martinique**

**Ma•ry** |mə'rē| commercial city in SE Turkmenistan, in a natural gas- and cotton-producing area. Pop. 95,000. It was formerly called **Merv**, and is near the site of the ancient Merv, a town of great historical and religious importance.

**Mar•y•land** |'merələnd| see box. □ **Marylander** *n.*

**Ma•sa•da** |mə'sädə| site in Israel of the ruins of a palace and fortification built by Herod the Great on the SW shore of the Dead Sea in the 1st century B.C. It was a Jewish stronghold in the Zealots' revolt against the Romans (A.D. 66–73) and was the scene in A.D. 73 of mass suicide by the Jewish defenders when the Romans breached the citadel after a siege of nearly two years.

**Ma•san** |'mä,sän| port city in SE South Korea, on an inlet of the Western Channel (the Korea Strait). Pop. 497,000. It is the center of a free-trade zone, with textile and other industries.

---

**Maryland**

**Capital:** Annapolis
**Largest city:** Baltimore
**Other cities:** Bethesda, Columbia, Frederick, Hagerstown
**Population:** 4,781,468 (1990); 5,134,808 (1998); 5,467,000 (2005 proj.)
**Population rank (1990):** 19
**Rank in land area:** 42
**Abbreviation:** MD; Md.
**Nicknames:** Old Line State; Free State
**Motto:** *Fatti maschii, parole femine* (Italian: 'Manly deeds, womanly words')
**Bird:** Baltimore oriole
**Fish:** rockfish or striped bass
**Flower:** black-eyed Susan
**Tree:** white oak
**Song:** "Maryland, My Maryland"
**Noted physical features:** Chesapeake Bay; Pocoson Swamp; Great Valley, Hagerstown Valley; Backbone Mountain
**Tourist attractions:** Fort McHenry; Antietam National Battlesite; U.S. Naval Academy; Camp David Presidential Retreat
**Admission date:** April 28, 1788
**Order of admission:** 7
**Name origin:** For Queen Henrietta Maria (1609-99), wife of Charles I of England.

---

**Ma•sa•ya** |mä'säyä| commercial and industrial city in W Nicaragua, the capital of Masaya province, SE of Managua. Pop. 80,000.

**Mas•ba•te** |mäs'bätä| island, noted as a mining district, in the central Philippines. Pop. 599,000. The chief town is Masbate.

**Mas•ca•rene Islands** |,mæskə'rēn| (also **the Mascarenes**) group of three islands in the W Indian Ocean, E of Madagascar, comprising Réunion, Mauritius, and Rodrigues.

**Ma•se•ru** |'mæzə,rōō| the capital of Lesotho, situated on the Caledon River near the border with the province of Free State in South Africa. Pop. 367,000.

**Mash•had** |mə'sHäd| (also **Meshed**) city in NE Iran, close to the border with Turkmenistan. Pop. 1,463,000. The burial place in A.D. 809 of the Abbasid caliph Harun ar-Rashid and in 818 of the Shiite leader Ali ar-Rida, it is a holy city of the Shiite Muslims. It is the second-largest city in Iran, and is noted for its textiles.

**Ma•sho•na•land** |mə'sHōnəlænd| area of N Zimbabwe, occupied by the Shona people. A former province of S Rhodesia, it is now divided into the three provinces of Mashonaland East, West, and Central.

**Ma·son City** |ˌmāsn| industrial city in N central Iowa. Pop. 29,040.

**Mason-Dixon Line** |ˈmāsnˈdiksən| boundary between Maryland and Pennsylvania, named for its two 1760s surveyors. By extension, it is popularly considered the boundary between the U.S. North and South.

**Mas·sa·chu·setts** |ˌmæsəˈCHo͞osəts| see box.

**Mas·sa·chu·setts Bay** |ˌmæsəˈCHo͞osəts| inlet of the Atlantic between Cape Cod and Cape Ann, in E Massachusetts. Boston Harbor is an inlet of Massachusetts Bay.

**Mas·sa·wa** |məˈsäwə| (also **Mitsiwa**) the chief port of Eritrea, on the Red Sea. Pop. 27,000. It serves as an outlet for Ethiopian trade.

**Mas·sif Central** |məˈsēf ˌsänˈträl| mountainous plateau in S central France. Covering almost one-sixth of the country, it rises to a height of 6,188 ft./1,887 m. at Puy de Sancy in the Auvergne.

**Mas·sil·lon** |ˈmæsələn| city in NE Ohio, S of Akron. Pop. 31,007.

**Ma·su·ria** |məˈzoŏrēə| low-lying forested lakeland region of NE Poland. Formerly part of East Prussia, it was assigned to Poland after World War I. Also called **Masurian Lakes**. □ **Masurian** adj.

**Ma·ta·be·le·land** |ˌmätəˈbäləˌlænd| former province of Southern Rhodesia, lying between the Limpopo and Zambezi rivers and occupied by the Matabele people. It is now divided into the two Zimbabwean provinces of Matabeleland North and South.

**Ma·ta·di** |māˈtädē| commercial city in W Congo (formerly Zaire), on the Congo River 80 mi./130 km. from the Atlantic. Pop. 173,000. It is the chief port of Congo.

**Mat·a·gor·da Bay** |ˌmætəˈgôrdə| inlet of the Gulf of Mexico in SE Texas, at the mouth of the Colorado River.

**Mat·a·mo·ros** |mätäˈmôrōs| (also **Heroica Matamoros**) commercial city in NE Mexico, in Tamaulipas state, across the Rio Grande from Brownsville, Texas. Pop. 303,000.

**Mat·a·nus·ka Valley** |ˌmætəˈno͞oskə| agricultural region in S central Alaska, NE of Anchorage.

**Ma·tan·zas** |məˈtänzəs| port city in N Cuba, capital of Matanzas province, E of Havana. Pop. 114,000. Once a pirate center, it now exports sugar and other crops.

**Ma·ta·ram** |ˈmätäräm| former Muslim sul-

---

| **Massachusetts** |
|---|
| **Official name:** Commonwealth of Massachusetts |
| **Capital/largest city:** Boston |
| **Other cities:** Agawam, Brockton, Cambridge, Holyoke, New Bedford, Pittsfield, Springfield, Worcester |
| **Population:** 6,016,425 (1990); 6,147,132 (1998); 6,310,000 (2005 proj.) |
| **Population rank (1990):** 13 |
| **Rank in land area:** 44 |
| **Abbreviation:** MA; Mass. |
| **Nicknames:** (Old) Bay State; Old Colony State; Puritan State; Baked Bean State |
| **Motto:** *Ense petit placidam sub libertate quietem* (Latin: 'By the sword we seek peace, but peace only under liberty') |
| **Bird:** chickadee |
| **Fish:** cod |
| **Flower:** mayflower (also called ground laurel or trailing arbutus) |
| **Tree:** American elm |
| **Song:** "All Hail to Massachusetts" |
| **Noted physical features:** Buzzard's Bay; Cape Ann, Cape Cod; Mount Greylock |
| **Tourist attractions:** Boston (many historic and cultural sites); Walden Pond; Plymouth Rock; Cape Cod National Seashore; Old Sturbridge Village |
| **Admission date:** February 6, 1788 |
| **Order of admission:** 6 |
| **Name origin:** From Algonquian (Natick) Indian words *massa* meaning 'great' and *wachuset* meaning 'hill,' probably referring to the Blue Hills near Boston, then used of the Indians living near them, and later of the bay. |

---

tanate in the Malay Archipelago. At its most powerful (17th century), it controlled most of Java.

**Ma·te·ra** |māˈtärä| town in S Italy, capital of Matera province. Pop. 55,000. It is an agricultural and industrial center.

**Ma·thu·ra** |ˈmətərə| (formerly **Muttra**) city in N India, in Uttar Pradesh state. Pop. 233,000. It is the reputed birthplace of the Hindu god Krishna.

**Mat·ma·ta** |mätmäˈtä| village in SE Tunisia, in the Matmata hills S of Gabés, noted for its cave dwellings.

**Ma·to Gros·so** |ˌmäto͞o ˈgrōso͞o| high plateau region of SW Brazil, forming a watershed between the Amazon and Plate river systems. The region is divided into two states, *Mato Grosso* (Pop. 2,020,000; Capital: Cuiabá) and MATO GROSSO DO SUL.

**Ma·to Gros·so do Sul** |ˈmäto͞o ˈgrōso͞o|

state of SW Brazil, on the borders with Bolivia and Paraguay. Pop. 1,780,000. Capital: Campo Grande.

**Ma·tsu** |'mätsōō| island, SE China, off the coast of Fujian province, E of Fuzhou. Under the control of the Nationalist government on Taiwan after the fall of the mainland, it was subjected (with Quemoy) to periodic shelling during the 1950s.

**Ma·tsu·ba·ra** |mä'tsōōbärä| city in W central Japan, on S Honshu, an industrial and residential suburb S of Osaka. Pop. 136,000.

**Ma·tsu·do** |mä'tsōōdō| city in E central Japan, on E central Honshu, a suburb of Tokyo. Pop. 456,000.

**Ma·tsue** |mät'sōōä| (also **Matsuye**) port city in W Japan, on SW Honshu. Pop. 143,000.

**Ma·tsu·mo·to** |mä'tsōōmōtō| commercial city in central Japan, on central Honshu, NE of Nagoya. Pop. 201,000.

**Ma·tsu·shi·ma islands** |mä'tsōōsHēmä| group of islands in Japan, in Matsushima Bay, N Honshu. The soft volcanic rock of these hundreds of small islands has been worn into fantastic shapes by the sea.

**Ma·tsu·ya·ma** |,mätsōō'yämə| city in Japan, the capital and largest city of the island of Shikoku. Pop. 443,000.

**Mat·ter·horn** |'mædər,haw(ə)rn| mountain in the Pennine Alps, on the border between Switzerland and Italy. Rising to 14,688 ft./4,477 m., it was first climbed in 1865 by the English mountaineer Edward Whymper. French name **Mont Cervin**; Italian name **Monte Cervino**.

**Ma·tu·rín** |mätōō'rēn| commercial city in NE Venezuela, capital of Monagas state. Pop. 207,000.

**Mauá** |mæōō'ä| city in SE Brazil, a suburb SE of São Paulo. Pop. 345,000.

**Maui** |'mowē| the second-largest of the Hawaiian islands, lying to the NW of the island of Hawaii.

**Mau·na Kea** |,mownə 'kāə| extinct volcano on the island of Hawaii, in the central Pacific. Rising to 13,796 ft./4,205 m., it is the highest peak in the Hawaiian islands. The summit is the site of several large astronomical telescopes.

**Mau·na Loa** |,mownə 'lōə| active volcano on the island of Hawaii, to the S of Mauna Kea, rising to 13,678 ft./4,169 m. The volcano Kilauea is situated on its flanks.

**Mau·re·ta·nia** |,mawrə'tānēə| ancient region of N Africa, corresponding to the N part of Morocco and W and central Algeria. Originally occupied by the Moors

(Latin *Mauri*) and conquered by the Arabs in the 7th century. □ **Mauretanian** *adj. & n.*

**Mau·ri·ta·nia** |,mawrə'tānēə| republic in W Africa with a coastline on the Atlantic. Area: 398,107 sq. mi./1.03 million sq. km. Pop. 2,023,000. Languages, Arabic (official), French. Capital and largest city: Nouakchott. Mauritania was a center of Berber power in the 11th and 12th centuries, at which time Islam became established in the region. Later, nomadic Arab tribes became dominant, while on the coast European nations, especially France, established trading posts. Controlled by the French from 1902, Mauritania achieved independence in 1961. Its people are largely nomadic pastoralists; fishing and mining are also important. □ **Mauritanian** *adj. & n.*

**Mauritania**

**Mau·ri·tius** |maw'risHəs| island republic in the Indian Ocean, about 550 mi./850 km. E of Madagascar. Area: 788 sq. mi./2,040 sq. km. Pop. 1,105,740. Languages, English (official), French Creole, Indian languages. Capital and largest city: Port Louis. Held by the Portuguese, Dutch, French, and British, Mauritius gained independence in 1968. Its economy is centered on sugar. □ **Mauritian** *adj. & n.*

**Ma·ya·güez** |mīyä'gwäz| industrial port in W Puerto Rico, on the Mona Passage. Pop. 83,010.

**Mauritius**

**Ma·yenne** |mä'yen| **1** department of NW France. Pop. 278,000. **2** river in W France, a headwater of the Maine.

**May·er·ling** |'mīerliNG| village in E Austria, in the Vienna Woods. Crown Prince Rudolf and Baroness Maria Vetsera died in unexplained circumstances in a hunting lodge here in January 1889.

**May·fair** |'mā,fæ(ə)r| fashionable and opulent district in the West End of London, England.

**May·kop** |mī'kawp| (also **Maikop**) industrial town in S Russia, in the N foothills of the Caucasus Mts. Pop. 120,000.

**May·nooth** |mə'nōōTH| village in Country Kildare, in the Republic of Ireland. Pop. 1,300. It is the site of St. Patrick's College, founded in 1795, the academic center of Irish Catholicism.

**Mayo** |'māō| county in the NW Republic of Ireland, in the province of Connacht. Pop. 111,000; county seat, Castlebar.

**Ma·yon Volcano** |mä'yōn| active volcano in the Philippines, on SE Luzon. It is considered to be one of the most perfect cones on Earth.

**Ma·yotte** |mä'yawt| island to the E of the Comoros in the Indian Ocean. Pop. 94,000. Languages, French (official), local Swahili dialect. Capital: Mamoutzu. When the Comoros became independent in 1974, Mayotte remained an overseas territory of France. Also called **Mahore**.

**Mayotte**

**Mazar-e-Sharif** |mə'zärēsHə'rēf| industrial city in N Afghanistan. Pop. 131,000. The city, whose name means 'tomb of the saint', is the reputed burial place of Ali, son-in-law of Muhammad.

**Ma·za·tlán** |mäsät'län| seaport and resort city in Mexico, on the Pacific coast in the state of Sinaloa. Pop. 314,000. Founded in 1531, it developed as a center of Spanish trade with the Philippines.

**Ma·zo·via** |mə'zōvēə| ancient principality in Poland, E of the Vistula River. At one time semi-independent, it was incorporated into Poland by the early 16th century.

**Mba·bane** |əmbä'bänä| the administrative capital of Swaziland, a resort in the high veld. Pop. 38,000.

**Mban·da·ka** |əmbän'däkä| (formerly **Co·quilhatville**) commercial and industrial city in N Congo (formerly Zaire), a port on the Congo River. Pop. 166,000.

**Mbe·ya** |əm'bāä| commercial town in S Tanzania, NW of Lake Malawi. Pop. 93,000. It is a former gold-mining center.

**Mbuji-Mayi** |əm'bōōjē māyē; 'miē| (formerly **Bakwanga**) commercial city in S central Congo (formerly Zaire). Pop. 603,000. It is a famed diamond-mining center.

**Mc·Al·len** |mə'kælən| city in S Texas, in the agricultural Rio Grande valley. Pop. 84,021.

**Mc·Kees·port** |mə'kēzpōrt| city in SW Pennsylvania, an industrial suburb SE of Pittsburgh. Pop. 26,016.

**Mc·Kin·ley, Mount** |mə'kinlē| mountain in S central Alaska. Rising to 20,110 ft./6,194 m., it is the highest peak in North America. Also called **Denali**, it is in Denali National Park.

**Mead, Lake** |mēd| largest U.S. reservoir, in SE Nevada, created after 1933 by the Hoover Dam on the Colorado River.

**Mead·ow·lands, the** |'medō,lændz| entertainment and sports complex in NE New Jersey, in the meadows of the Hackensack River, NW of New York City.

**Meath** |mēTH| county in the E part of the Republic of Ireland, in the province of Leinster. Pop. 106,000; county seat, Navan.

**Meaux** |mō| industrial city in N France, on the Marne River. Pop. 45,000.

**Mec·ca** |,mekə| city in W Saudi Arabia, an oasis town in the Red Sea region of Hejaz, E of Jiddah, considered by Muslims to be the holiest city of Islam. Pop. 618,000. The birthplace in A.D. 570 of the prophet Muhammad, it was the scene of his early teachings before his emigration (the Hegira) to Medina in 622. On his return to Mecca in 630 it became the center of the new Muslim faith. It is the site of the Great Mosque and the Kaaba, and is a center of Islamic ritual, including the hajj pilgrimage. The city is closed to non-Muslims. Arabic name **Makkah**.

**Me·che·len** |'mäkHələn| city in N Belgium, N of Brussels. Pop. 75,000. It is noted for its cathedral and for Mechlin lace. French name **Malines**.

**Meck·len·burg** |'meklən,bərg| former

state of NE Germany, on the Baltic coast, now part of Mecklenburg–West Pomerania.

**Meck·len·burg-West Pomerania** |'mek-lən,bərg| state of NE Germany, on the coast of the Baltic Sea. Pop. 2,100,000. Capital: Schwerin. It consists of the former state of Mecklenburg and the W part of Pomerania.

**Me·dan** |mā,dän| city in Indonesia, in NE Sumatra near the Strait of Malacca. Pop. 1,730,000. It was established as a trading post by the Dutch in 1682 and became a leading commercial center.

**Me·de·llín** |mādə'yēn| city in E Colombia, the second-largest city in the country. Pop. 1,581,000. A major center of coffee production, it has in recent years gained a reputation as the hub of the Colombian drug trade.

**Med·ford**[1] |'medfərd| city in NE Massachusetts, a suburb just NW of Boston. Pop. 57,407.

**Med·ford**[2] |'medfərd| commercial city in SW Oregon, in an agricultural area near the California line. Pop. 46,951.

**Me·dia** |'mēdēə| ancient region of Asia to the SW of the Caspian Sea, corresponding approximately to present-day Azerbaijan, NW Iran, and NE Iraq. The region is roughly the same as that inhabited today by the Kurds. Originally inhabited by the Medes, the region was conquered in 550 B.C. by Cyrus the Great of Persia. □ **Median** adj.

**Med·i·cine Bow Mountains** |'medəsin bō| range of the Rocky Mts., extending the Front Range of Colorado into S Wyoming.

**Med·i·cine Hat** |'medəsən ,hæt| commercial and industrial city in SE Alberta, on the South Saskatchewan River. Pop. 43,625.

**Me·di·na** |mə'dēnə| city in W Saudi Arabia, around an oasis some 200 mi./320 km. N of Mecca. Pop. 500,000. Medina was the refuge of Muhammad's infant Muslim community from its removal from Mecca in A.D. 622 until its return there in 630. It was renamed Medina, meaning 'city', by Muhammad and made the capital of the new Islamic state until it was superseded by Damascus in 661. It is Muhammad's burial place and the site of the first Islamic mosque, constructed around his tomb. It is considered by Muslims to be the second-most holy city after Mecca, and a visit to the prophet's tomb at Medina often forms a sequel to the formal pilgrimage to Mecca. Arabic name **Al Madinah**.

**Med·i·ter·ra·nean Sea** |,medətə'rānēən| almost landlocked sea between S Europe, the N coast of Africa, and SW Asia. It is connected with the Atlantic by the Strait of Gibraltar, with the Red Sea by the Suez Canal, and with the Black Sea by the Dardanelles, the Sea of Marmara, and the Bosporus.

**Me·doc** |'mā,däk| district in Aquitaine, in SW France, NW of Bordeaux between the Bay of Biscay and the Gironde River estuary. It contains some of France's most famous vineyards. The main towns are Pauillac and Lesparre.

**Mee·rut** |'mārət| industrial and commercial city in N India, in Uttar Pradesh NE of Delhi. Pop. 850,000. It was the scene in 1857 of the first uprising against the British in the Indian Mutiny.

**Meg·a·lóp·o·lis** |,megə'läpələs| city in ancient SE Greece, founded by citizens from many other cities for defense against Sparta. The name means 'large city.'

**Mé·ga·ra** |'megərə| city of E central Greece, on the Gulf of Saronica. The philosopher Euclid founded the Megarian school of philosophy (5th century B.C.). □ **Megarian** adj.

**Megh·a·la·ya** |,māgə'läə| state in the extreme NE of India, on the N border of Bangladesh. Pop. 1,761,000. Capital: Shillong. It was created in 1970 from part of Assam.

**Me·gid·do** |mi'gi'dō| ancient city of NW Palestine, situated to the SE of Haifa in present-day Israel. Founded in the 4th millennium B.C., it controlled an important route linking Syria and Mesopotamia with the Jordan valley, Jerusalem, and Egypt. Its commanding location made the city the scene of many battles throughout history. It is believed to be the site referred to by the biblical name *Armageddon* (possibly meaning 'hill of Megiddo') in Revelation 16.

**Meis·sen** |'mīsən| city in E Germany, in Saxony, on the Elbe River NW of Dresden. Pop. 39,000. It is famous for its porcelain.

**Mei·xian** city in Guangdong province, S China, on the Mei River, NW of Shantou. Pop. 749,000.

**Me·ke·le** |'mākələ| city in N Ethiopia, the capital of Tigray province. Pop. 62,000.

**Mek·nès** |mek'nes| historic commercial city in N Morocco, in the Middle Atlas Mts. W of Fez. Pop. 120,000. In the 17th century it was the residence of the Moroccan sultan.

**Me·kong** |'mā'kawNG| river of SE Asia, which rises in Tibet and flows SE and S for 2,600 mi./4,180 km. through S China,

Laos, Cambodia, and Vietnam to its extensive delta on the South China Sea. It forms much of the boundary between Laos and its W neighbors Burma and Thailand.

**Me·la·ka** |mä'läkä| (also **Malacca**) **1** state of Malaysia, on the SW coast of the Malay Peninsula, on the Strait of Malacca. **2** its capital and chief port. Pop. 88,000. It was conquered by the Portuguese in 1511 and played an important role in the development of trade between Europe and the East, especially China.

**Mel·a·ne·sia** |ˌmelə'nēzʜə| region of the W Pacific to the S of Micronesia and W of Polynesia. It contains the Bismarck Archipelago, the Solomon Islands, Vanuatu, New Caledonia, Fiji, and the intervening islands, and is the area of earliest human settlement in the Pacific. □ **Melanesian** adj. & n.

Melanesia

**Mel·bourne**[1] |'melbərn| the capital of Victoria, SE Australia, on the Bass Strait opposite Tasmania. Pop. 2,762,000. It became state capital in 1851 and was capital of Australia 1901–27. It is a major port and commercial center and the second-largest city in Australia.

**Mel·bourne**[2] |'melbərn| resort city in E central Florida, just S of Cape Canaveral. Pop. 59,646.

**Me·li·lla** |mə'lēyə| Spanish exclave on the Mediterranean coast of Morocco. Pop. (with Ceuta) 57,000. It was occupied by Spain in 1497.

**Me·li·to·pol** |ˌmelə'tawpəl| industrial city in S Ukraine, on the Sea of Azov. Pop. 176,000.

**Me·los** |'mēläs| Greek island in the Aegean Sea, in the SW of the Cyclades group. It was the center of a flourishing civilization in the Bronze Age and is the site of the discovery in 1820 of a Hellenistic marble statue of Aphrodite, the *Venus de Milo*. □ **Melian** adj. & n.

**Mel·rose** |'mel,rōz| town in S Scotland, in

the Borders region, on the Tweed River, site of Melrose Abbey, a ruin known for its beauty and associations with Walter Scott.

**Me·lun** |mə'lən| industrial town in N central France, SE of Paris; capital of the Seine-et-Marne department. Pop. 36,000.

**Me·mel** |'mäməl| **1** former district of East Prussia. Centered on the city of Memel (Klaipeda). It became an autonomous region of Lithuania in 1924. In 1938 it was taken by Germany, but it was restored to Lithuania by the Soviet Union in 1945. See also Klajpeda. **2** the Neman River in its lower course (see Neman).

**Mem·phis**[1] |'mem(p)fəs| ancient city of Egypt, whose ruins are situated on the Nile just S of Cairo. It is thought to have been founded as the capital of the Old Kingdom of Egypt by Menes, the ruler of the first Egyptian dynasty, who united the kingdoms of Upper and Lower Egypt. Associated with the god Ptah, it remained one of Egypt's principal cities even after Thebes was made the capital of the New Kingdom, and is the site of the pyramids of Saqqara and Giza and the Sphinx.

**Mem·phis**[2] |'mem(p)fəs| river port on the Mississippi in the extreme SW of Tennessee. Pop. 610,337. Founded in 1819, it was a major cotton trading center just N of the Mississippi Delta, and today is a commercial and medical hub. It is the scene of the 1968 assassination of Martin Luther King, and the home and burial place of Elvis Presley.

**Men·ai Strait** |'me,nī| channel separating Anglesey from the mainland of NW Wales, noted for two bridges built 1819–26 and 1846–50.

**Men·de·res** |mende'res| river of SW Turkey. Rising in the Anatolian plateau, it flows for some 240 mi./384 km., entering the Aegean Sea S of the Greek island of Samos. Known in ancient times as the Maeander, and noted for its winding course, it gave its name to the verb *meander*.

**Men·dip Hills** |'mendip| (also **the Mendips**) a range of limestone hills in SW England.

**Men·do·ci·no** |ˌmendə'sēnō| resort community in NW California, on the Pacific coast. **Cape Mendocino**, the westernmost point in the state, is farther to the N.

**Men·do·za** |men'dōzə| city in W Argentina, in the foothills of the Andes at the center of a wine-producing region. Pop. 122,000.

**Men·lo Park**[1] |'menlō| city in N central California, an industrial and commercial suburb S of San Francisco. Pop. 28,040.

**Men·lo Park** |'menlō| historic community in central New Jersey, in Edison Township, NE of New Brunswick. It was the scene of the laboratory, and many inventions, of Thomas Edison.

**Me·nor·ca** |mə'nawrkə| Spanish name for MINORCA, in the Balearic Islands.

**Men·ton** |mawn'tōn| resort town in SE France, near the Italian border on the French Riviera. Pop. 29,000.

**Me·ra·no** |mā'ränō| tourist and health resort in NE Italy, NW of Bolzano, on the S slope of the Alps. Pop. 33,000.

**Mer·ced** |mər'sed| city in central California, an agricultural processing hub in the San Joaquin Valley. Pop. 56,216.

**Mer·cia** |'mərsH(ē)ə| former kingdom of central England. It was established by invading Angles in the 6th century A.D. in the border areas between the new Anglo-Saxon settlements in the east and the Celtic regions in the west. □ **Mercian** *adj. & n.*

**Mer·iç** |me'rēcH| Turkish name for the MARITSA River.

**Mé·ri·da**[1] |'mērēdə| city in SE Mexico, capital of the state of Yucatán. Pop. 557,000. It is a major agricultural trade center.

**Mé·ri·da**[2] |'mērēdə| historic city in W Spain, on the Guadiana River, capital of Extremadura region and formerly of Roman Lusitania. Pop. 50,000.

**Mé·ri·da**[3] |mā'rēdə| city in W Venezuela, in the N Andes, S of Lake Maracaibo, the capital of Mérida province. Pop. 168,000. It is a religious and tourist center.

**Mer·i·den** |'merədən| industrial city in S central Connecticut. Pop. 59,479.

**Me·rid·i·an** |mə'ridēən| city in E Mississippi, a commercial, transportation, and military center. Pop. 41,036.

**Mer·i·on·eth·shire** |,merē'änəTHSHir| former county of NW Wales. It became a part of Gwynedd in 1974.

**Mer·lo** |'mərlō| town in E Argentina, a suburb W of Buenos Aires. Pop. 390,000.

**Mer·oe** |'merōwē| ancient city on the Nile, in present-day Sudan NE of Khartoum. Founded in *c.* 750 B.C., it was the capital of the ancient kingdom of Cush from *c.* 590 B.C. until it fell to the invading Aksumites in the early 4th century A.D. □ **Meroitic** *adj. & n.*

**Mer·ri·mack River** |'merə,mæk| river that flows 110 mi./180 km. from New Hampshire through E Massachusetts to the Atlantic. Its valley, site of Manchester, Con-

cord, and Nashua, New Hampshire, and Lowell, Lawrence, and Haverhill, Massachusetts, is often considered the birthplace of American industry.

**Mer·sa Ma·truh** |',mərsə mə'trōō| naval and resort town on the Mediterranean coast of Egypt, W of Alexandria. Pop. 113,000.

**Mer·sey** |'mərzē| river in NW England, which rises in the Peak District of Derbyshire and flows 70 mi./112 km. to the Irish Sea near Liverpool.

**Mer·sey·side** |'mərzē,sīd| metropolitan county of NW England; its chief city is Liverpool. Pop. 1,377,000.

**Mer·sin** |mer'sēn| industrial port in S Turkey, on the Mediterranean SW of Adana. Pop. 422,000.

**Mer·thyr Tyd·fil** |',mərTHər 'tidvil| industrial town in S Wales, in a historic mining area. Pop. 59,000.

**Mer·ton** |'mərtən| largely residential borough of SW Greater London, England. Pop. 162,000. The tennis center at Wimbledon is here.

**Merv** |'merv| earlier name for MARY, and name of the ancient city nearby.

**Me·sa** |'māsə| city in S central Arizona, an industrial and residential suburb E of Phoenix. Pop. 288,091.

**Me·sa·bi Range** |mə'säbē| low hills in NE Minnesota, site of one of the largest iron sources in the world. Hibbing is a regional mining center.

**Me·sa Ver·de** |'māsə 'verdē| high plateau in S Colorado, in a national park with the remains of many prehistoric cliff dwellings.

**Mes·o·a·mer·i·ca** |'mezōə'merəkə| (also **Meso-America**) the central region of America, from central Mexico to Nicaragua, especially as a region of ancient civilizations and native cultures before the arrival of Europeans. □ **Mesoamerican** *adj. & n.*

**Me·so·lón·gi·on** |,mesō'lōNGyin| Greek name for MISSOLONGHI.

**Mes·o·po·ta·mia** |,mesəpə'tāmēə| ancient region of SW Asia in present-day Iraq, lying between the Tigris and Euphrates rivers ; its name derives from Greek *mesos* ('middle') + *potamos* ('river'). Its alluvial plains were the site of the early civilizations of Akkad, Sumer, Babylonia, and Assyria. □ **Mesopotamian** *adj. & n.*

**Mes·quite** |me'skēt| city in NE Texas, an industrial and commercial suburb on the E side of Dallas. Pop. 101,484.

**Mes·se·nia** |mäs'sēnēə| division of ancient

Greece in the SW Peloponnese, a center of Mycenaean culture.

**Mes•si•na** |məˈsēnə| industrial port city in NE Sicily. Pop. 275,000. Founded in 730 B.C. by the Greeks, it is situated on the Strait of Messina.

**Mes•si•na, Strait of** |məˈsēnə| channel separating the island of Sicily from the 'toe' of Italy. It forms a link between the Tyrrhenian and Ionian seas. The strait, which is 20 mi./32 km. in length and 2.5 to 12 mi./4 to 19 km. wide, is noted for the strength of its currents. It is traditionally identified as the location of the legendary sea monster Scylla and the whirlpool Charybdis.

**Me•ta River** |ˈmātə| river that flows 650 mi./1,050 km. from central Colombia to the NE, forming part of the Colombia-Venezuela boundary, into the Orinoco River.

**Met•air•ie** |ˈmetərē| community in SE Louisiana, the largest residential suburb of New Orleans, on its NW side. Pop. 149,428.

**Me•te•o•ra** |məˈtäōrä| group of monasteries in N central Greece, in Thessaly. The monasteries, built between the 12th and the 16th centuries, are perched on the summits of curiously shaped rock formations.

**Me•trop•o•lis** |məˈträpələs| see THERA.

**Metz** |mets| historic industrial city in Lorraine, NE France, on the Moselle River. Pop. 124,000. Once the capital of Frankish Austrasia, it has more recently been an iron and steel center.

**Meu•don** |məˈdōn| town, a suburb of Paris, in N central France. Pop. 49,000.

**Meuse** |ˈmyo͞oz| river of W Europe, which rises in NE France and flows 594 mi./950 km. through Belgium and the Netherlands to the North Sea S of Dordrecht. Flemish and Dutch name **Maas**.

**Mex•i•cali** |ˌmeksəˈkælē| the capital of the state of Baja California, in NW Mexico, adjacent to Calexico, California. Pop. 602,000.

**Mex•i•co, Gulf of** |ˈmeksəkō| extension of the W Atlantic. Bounded in a sweeping curve by the U.S. to the N, by Mexico to the W and S, and by Cuba to the SE, it is linked to the Atlantic by the Straits of Florida and to the Caribbean Sea by the Yucatán Channel.

**Mex•i•co, State of** |ˈmeksəkō| (Spanish name **México**) state in central Mexico, surrounding the Distrito Federal. Area: 8,245 sq. mi./21,355 sq. km. Pop. 9,816,000. Capital: Toluca.

**Mex•i•co, Valley of** |ˈmeksəkō| basin in central Mexico, the site of Mexico City and

the Distrito Federal. Its many shallow lakes have been largely drained, and the valley is now densely populated.

**Mex•i•co** |ˈmeksəkō| republic in North America, with extensive coastlines on the Gulf of Mexico and the Pacific Ocean, bordered by the U.S. to the N. Area: 756,200 sq. mi./1.96 million sq. km. Pop. 81,140,920. Language, Spanish. Capital and largest city: Mexico City. The center of the Mayan and Aztec civilizations, it was conquered by Spain in the 1520s, gaining independence in 1821. In the early 19th century it lost much territory to the U.S. Today it has 31 states and a federal district, and is both agricultural and industrial, with an important oil industry and much cross-border trade with the U.S. Tourism is important. ▫ **Mexican** adj. & n.

**Mex•i•co City** |ˈmeksəkō| the capital of Mexico. Pop. 13,636,000. Founded in about 1300 as the Aztec capital Tenochtitlán, it was destroyed in 1521 by the Spanish conquistador Cortés, who rebuilt it as the capital of New Spain. A financial, cultural, and commercial center, it is one of the most populous cities in the world.

**Mez•zo•gior•no** |ˈmetsōˈj(ē)awrnō| term for the S part of Italy from Abruzzi and Campania S, and including Sicily and Sardinia. The name in Italian means 'midday,' and refers to the strength of the sun in the region. See also MIDI.

**Mi•ami** |mīˈæmē| port city on the coast of SE Florida. Pop. 358,548. Its subtropical climate and miles of beaches make this and the resort island of Miami Beach, separated from the mainland by Biscayne Bay, a year-round holiday resort. Miami is also a major Hispanic commercial and cultural center.

**Mi•ami Beach** |mīˈæmē| city in SE Florida, on the Atlantic, across Biscayne Bay from Miami. It is a famous resort, known recently especially for its South Beach (Art Deco) district. Pop. 92,639.

**Mich•i•gan, Lake** |ˈmiSHigən| one of the five Great Lakes of North America. Bordered by Michigan, Wisconsin, Illinois, and Indiana, it is the only one of the Great Lakes to lie wholly within the U.S. Chicago is at its SW corner.

**Mich•i•gan** |ˈmiSHigən| see box, p. 233. ▫ **Michigander** n.

**Mi•cho•a•cán** |ˌmēCHōäˈkän| mountainous state of W Mexico, on the Pacific coast. Pop. 3,534,000. Capital: Morelia.

**Mi•chu•rinsk** |məˈCHo͞orənsk| transporta-

MEXICO

— — — State boundary
■ Capital city

0   200   400 km
0   100   200   300 miles

1 AGUASCALIENTES
2 GUANAJUATO
3 QUERÉTARO DE ARTEAGA
4 HIDALGO
5 MEXICO
6 DISTRITO FEDERAL
7 MORELOS
8 TLAXCALA

## Michigan

**Capital:** Lansing
**Largest city:** Detroit
**Other cities:** Ann Arbor, Bay City, Flint, Grand Rapids, Marquette, Muskegon, Saginaw
**Population:** 9,295,297 (1990); 9,817,242 (1998); 9,763,000 (2005 proj.)
**Population rank (1990):** 8
**Rank in land area:** 11
**Abbreviation:** MI; Mich.
**Nicknames:** Wolverine State; Water Wonderland; Upper Peninsula often referred to as the Land of Hiawatha
**Motto:** *Si quaeris peninsulam amoenam, circumspice* (Latin: 'If you seek a pleasant peninsula, look about you')
**Bird:** robin
**Fish:** brook trout
**Flower:** apple blossom
**Tree:** white pine
**Song:** "Michigan, My Michigan"
**Noted physical features:** Saginaw Bay, Lake St. Clair; Mackinac Straits
**Tourist attractions:** Mackinac Bridge; Soo Canal, Sault Ste. Marie Canal; Holland Tulip Festival; Isle Royale National Park; Greenfield Village
**Admission date:** January 26, 1837
**Order of admission:** 26
**Name origin:** Named in 1805 apparently for Lake Michigan, itself named from an Indian word, possibly Chippewa *Michigama*, meaning 'great lake.'

tion center and industrial city in W Russia, SE of Moscow. Pop. 109,000.

**Mi·cro·ne·sia, Federated States of** |ˌmɪkrəˈnēʒHə| group of associated island states comprising the 600 islands of the Caroline Islands, in the W Pacific to the N of the equator. Area: 271 sq. mi./701 sq. km. Pop. 108,000. Languages, English (official), Austronesian languages. Capital: Palikir (on Pohnpei). The group, which includes the islands of Yap, Kosrae, Truk, and Pohnpei, was administered by the U.S. as part of the Pacific Islands Trust Territory from 1947 and entered into free association with the U.S. as an independent state in 1986. Subsistence agriculture and fishing are important. □ **Micronesian** *adj. & n.*

**Mi·cro·ne·sia** |ˌmɪkrəˈnēʒHə| region of the W Pacific to the N of Melanesia and N and W of Polynesia. It includes the Mariana, Caroline, and Marshall island groups, and Kiribati.

**Mid-Atlantic Ridge** |ˌmidətˈlæn(t)ik ˈrij| submarine ridge that lies under the Atlantic, from Iceland in the N to near Antarctica in the S. It roughly parallels the outlines of the continents to either side, and is considered to mark where continental plates are separating, allowing new crustal

**Micronesia**

material to rise. The islands of Iceland, the Azores, Ascension, St. Helena, and Tristan da Cunha are situated on it.

**Mid-Atlantic States** term for the US states between New England and the South that are on or near the Atlantic coast, usually including New York, New Jersey, and Pennsylvania, and sometimes also Delaware and Maryland.

**Mid·dle A·mer·i·ca** |'midəl ə'merəkə| general name for the region that includes Mexico and the countries of Central America, and usually also the West Indies.

**Mid·dle At·lan·tic** |'midəl ; ət'læn(t)ik| region of the U.S., generally including New Jersey, Pennsylvania, and Delaware, and often also New York and Maryland.

**Mid·dle East** |'midəl 'ēst| extensive area of SW Asia and N Africa, stretching from the shores of the W Mediterranean to Pakistan and including the Arabian Peninsula. □ **Middle Eastern** adj.

**Mid·dle Passage** |'midəl 'pæsij| historical term for the route taken by slave ships from W Africa to the Americas.

**Mid·dles·brough** |'midəlzbrə| port in NE England, the county seat of Celeveland, on the estuary of the Tees River. Pop. 141,000.

**Mid·dle·sex** |'midəl,seks| former county of SE England, to the NW of London. In 1965 it was divided among Hertfordshire, Surrey, and Greater London.

**Mid·dle·town**[1] |'midəltown| commercial and industrial city in central Connecticut, on the Connecticut River S of Hartford, home to Wesleyan University. Pop. 42,762.

**Mid·dle·town**[2] |'midəltown| industrial city in SW Ohio, between Cincinnati and Dayton. Pop. 46,029.

**Mid Gla·mor·gan** |'mid glə'mawrgən| former county of South Wales formed in 1974 from parts of Breconshire, Glamorgan, and Monmouthshire and dissolved in 1996.

**Mi·di** |mē'dē| term for the S of France. The name in French means 'midday' and refers

to the strength of the sun in the region. See also MEZZOGIORNO.

**Mid·i·an** |'midēən| biblical name for a region of the NW Arabian Peninsula, home of the Midianites, enemies of the Israelites. Situated E of the Gulf of Aqaba, it may have been the equivalent of present-day Madian, Saudi Arabia.

**Midi-Pyrénées** |,midēpērə'nā| region of S France, between the Pyrenees and the Massif Central, centered on Toulouse.

**Mid·land**[1] |'midlənd| city in central Michigan, best known as home to the Dow Chemical Company. Pop. 38,053.

**Mid·land**[2] |'midlənd| city in W Texas, an oil industry center in the Permian Basin. Pop. 89,443. Its sister city is Odessa.

**Mid·lands, the** | 'midləndz| general name for inland counties of central England, from just NW of London (Buckinghamshire) N to Nottinghamshire and W to West Midlands.

**Mid·lo·thi·an** |mid'lōTHēən| administrative region and former county of central Scotland; administrative center, Dalkeith.

**Midnight Sun, Land of the** |'midnit 'sən| popular term for Arctic regions where the sun remains above the horizon through the night in midsummer, especially for N Norway.

**Mid·way Islands** |'midwā| two small islands with a surrounding coral atoll, in the central Pacific in the W part of the Hawaiian chain. The islands were annexed by the U.S. in 1867 and remain a U.S. territory and naval base. They were the scene in 1942 of the Battle of Midway, in which the U.S. Navy repelled a Japanese invasion fleet, sinking four aircraft carriers.

**Mid·west** |'mid'west| the region of N states of the U.S. from Ohio W through the Dakotas. □ **Midwestern** adj. **Midwesterner** n.

**Mid·west City** |'mid'west| city in central Oklahoma, a suburb just E of Oklahoma City. Tinker Air Force Base is nearby. Pop. 52,267.

**Mi·ko·nos** |'mēkōnōs| Greek name for MYKONOS.

**Mi·lan** |mə'län| industrial city in NW Italy, capital of Lombardy region. Pop. 1,432,000. A politically powerful city in the past, particularly from the 13th to the 15th centuries. Milan today is a leading fashion, finacial, cultural, and commercial center. Italian name **Milano**. □ **Milanese** adj. & n.

**Mi·le·tus** |mī'lētəs| ancient city of the Ionian Greeks in SW Asia Minor. In the 7th and 6th centuries B.C. it was a powerful port, from which more than sixty colonies were founded on the shores of the Black Sea and in Italy and Egypt. It was the home of the pre-Socratic philosophers Thales, Anaximander, and Anaximenes.

**Mil·ford** |ˌmilfərd| city in SW Connecticut, a suburb W of New Haven. Pop. 49,938.

**Mil·ford Ha·ven** |ˈmilfərd ˈhāvən| (Welsh name **Aberdaugleddau**) historic industrial port in SW Wales, in Dyfed. Pop. 14,000. It is today a major oil port and refinery center.

**Milk River** |ˈmilk| river that flows 625 mi./1,000 km. through NW Montana and S Alberta, into the Missouri River. It is the northwesternmost part of the Missouri-Mississippi system.

**Mill·ville** |ˈmil,vil| city in S New Jersey, across the Maurice River from Vineland. It is a longtime glass industry center. Pop. 25,992.

**Mí·los** |ˈmēlōs| Greek name for MELOS.

**Mil·ton Keynes** |ˈmiltən| residential and academic town in Buckinghamshire, S central England. Pop. 172,000.

**Milvian Bridge** see SAXA RUBRA.

**Mil·wau·kee** |milˈwawkē| industrial port city in SE Wisconsin, on the W shore of Lake Michigan. Pop. 628,088. It is noted for its brewing industry and German culture.

**Mi·na·ma·ta** |ˌmēˈnämätä| industrial city in SW Japan, on SW Kyushu, S of Kumamoto, scene of a 1960s mercury poisoning episode. Pop. 35,000.

**Mi·nas Bas·in** |ˈmīnəs| inlet of the Bay of Fundy in W central Nova Scotia, scene of some of the most extreme tides in the world.

**Mi·nas Ge·rais** |ˈmēnə ZHēˈrīs| state of SE Brazil. Pop. 15.73 million. Capital: Belo Horizonte. It has major deposits of iron ore, coal, gold, and diamonds.

**Mi·na·ti·tlán** |ˌmēnätēˈtlän| industrial port in E Mexico, in Veracruz state, on the Coatzacoalcos River. Pop. 200,000. It is an oil industry center.

**Minch** |minCH| (also **the Minch**) a channel of the Atlantic, between the mainland of Scotland and the Outer Hebrides. The N stretch is called the *North Minch*, the S stretch, W of Skye, is called the *Little Minch*. Also called **the Minches**.

**Min·da·nao** |ˌmindəˈnäō| the second largest (39,400 sq. mi./102,000 sq. km.) island in the Philippines, in the SE of the group. Pop. 14.30 million. Its chief town is Davao.

**Min·den** |ˈminden| industrial city and transportation center in NW Germany, on the Weser River and the Midland Canal. Pop. 75,000.

**Min·do·ro** |minˈdōrō| island in the Philippines, situated to the SW of Luzon.

**Min·gre·lia** |minˈgrēlēyə| lowland region in the Republic of Georgia, bordering on the Black Sea. Its major products are tea and grapes. Poti is the main port. The area corresponds to the former country of Colchis.

**Mi·nho** |ˈmēnyōō| Portuguese name for the MIÑO River.

**Min·i·coy Islands** |ˈminəkoi| one of the groups of islands forming the Indian territory of Lakshadweep in the Indian Ocean.

**Min·ne·ap·o·lis** |ˌminēˈæpələs| industrial city and port on the Mississippi River in SE Minnesota. Pop. 368,383, the largest city in the state. It is adjacent to the state capital, St. Paul; the two are referred to as the *Twin Cities.* Minneapolis is the major agricultural processing center of the upper Midwest and is a commercial and technological center.

**Min·ne·so·ta** |ˌminəˈsōtə| see box. ◻ **Minnesotan** *adj. & n.*

**Min·ne·so·ta River** |ˌminəˈsōtə| river that

---

### Minnesota

**Capital:** St. Paul

**Largest city:** Minneapolis

**Other cities:** Bloomington, Duluth, Rochester, St. Cloud

**Population:** 4,375,099 (1990); 4,725,419 (1998); 5,005,000 (2005 proj.)

**Population rank (1990):** 20

**Rank in land area:** 12

**Abbreviation:** MN; Minn.

**Nicknames:** North Star State; Gopher State; Bread and Butter State

**Motto:** *L'Etoile du Nord* (French: 'The North Star')

**Bird:** common loon

**Fish:** walleye

**Flower:** moccasin flower; pink and white lady's slipper

**Tree:** Norway (red) pine

**Song:** "Hail! Minnesota"

**Noted physical features:** Big Bog; Northwest Angle; Minnehaha Falls; Eagle Mountain

**Tourist attractions:** Paul Bunyan Monument; Pipestone and Grand Portage national monuments; Voyageurs' National Park; Kensington Rune Stone

**Admission date:** May 11, 1858

**Order of admission:** 32

**Name origin:** For the Minnesota River; from the Siouan word *Menesota,* meaning "cloudy water," or possibly "water reflecting cloudy skies."

flows 320 mi./530 km. through Minnesota, to join the Mississippi River just S of the Twin Cities.

**Mi•ño** |mēˈnyō| river that rises in NW Spain and flows S to the Portuguese border, which it follows before entering the Atlantic N of Viana do Castelo. Portuguese name **Minho**.

**Mi•nor•ca** |məˈnawrkə| most easterly of the Balearic Islands of Spain, in the W Mediterranean Sea. Pop. 59,000. The secondlargest of the Balearic chain at 271 sq. mi./702 sq. km., it is largely agricultural, and is a popular tourist destination.

**Mi•not** |ˈmīnät| commercial and industrial city in N central North Dakota. Pop. 34,544.

**Minsk** |ˈminsk| the capital of Belarus, an industrial city in the central region of the country. Pop. 1,613,000.

**Miq•ue•lon** |ˈmēk,län| see ST. PIERRE AND MIQUELON.

**Mi•ra•bel** |ˌmērəˈbel| city in S Quebec, a suburb NW of Montreal, and site of its international airport. Pop. 17,971.

**Mir•a•flor•es** |ˌmərəˈflawrez| residential suburb of Lima, W central Peru, a beach resort just S of the city. Pop. 87,000.

**Mir•za•pur** |ˈmərzäpōōr| city in N India, in Uttar Pradesh state. Pop. 169,000. It includes the Hindu pilgrimage center, Vindhhyachal.

**Mi•sha•wa•ka** |miˈSHäwawkə| industrial city in NE Indiana, on the E side of South Bend. Pop. 42,608.

**Mi•shi•ma** |mēˈSHēmä| resort city in E central Japan, on central Honshu, NE of Shizuoka. Pop. 105,000.

**Mis•kolc** |ˈmiSHkōlts| industrial and university city in NE Hungary. Pop. 191,000.

**Mis•ra•tah** |mēsˈrätə| (also **Misurata**) oasis and port city in NW Libya, on the Mediterranean Sea E of Tripoli. Pop. 178,000.

**Mis•sion•ary Ridge** |ˈmiSHə,nerē| historic site SE of Chattanooga, Tennessee, on the Georgia line, scene of a November 1863 Civil War battle following that at nearby Lookout Mt.

**Mis•sis•sau•ga** |ˌmisiˈsawgə| city in S Ontario, on the W shore of Lake Ontario. Pop. 463,388. It is an industrial and residential SW suburb of Toronto.

**Mis•sis•sip•pi** |ˌmisəˈsipē| see box. □ **Mississippian** adj. & n.

**Mis•sis•sip•pi River** |ˌmisəˈsipē| major river of the U.S., which rises in N Minnesota near Bemidji and Lake Itasca and flows S to a delta in Louisiana on the Gulf of Mexico. With its chief tributary, the Mis

---

### Mississippi

**Capital/largest city:** Jackson
**Other cities:** Biloxi, Gulfport, Greenville, Hattiesburg, Meridian, Tupelo
**Population:** 2,573,216 (1990); 2,752,092 (1998); 2,908,000 (2005 proj.)
**Population rank (1990):** 31
**Rank in land area:** 32
**Abbreviation:** MS; Miss.
**Nickname:** The Magnolia State
**Motto:** *Virtute et armis* (Latin: 'By valor and arms')
**Bird:** mockingbird
**Fish:** largemouth bass or black bass
**Flower:** magnolia blossom
**Tree:** magnolia
**Song:** "Go, Mississippi"
**Noted physical features:** Yazoo Basin Delta; Tennessee Hills and Loess Bluffs; Black Prairie, Jackson Prairie; Mississippi River; Woodall Mountain
**Tourist attractions:** Natchez Trace; Vicksburg National Military Park; Gulf Islands National Seashore
**Admission date:** December 10, 1817
**Order of admission:** 20
**Name origin:** For the Mississippi River; from Algonquian *meeche* or *mescha*, meaning 'great,' and *cebe*, meaning 'river, water,' thus 'great river.'

---

souri, it is 3,710 mi./5,970 km. long, and drains over one-third of the U.S. The Ohio River flows into it at Cairo, Illinois. It has been a major route for transportation since the 17th century, and remains important for commercial shipping, forming a major portion of the border of 10 states. Important cities along the Mississippi include Minneapolis and St. Paul, Minnesota; Dubuque and Davenport, Iowa; St. Louis, Missouri; Memphis, Tennessee; and Baton Rouge and New Orleans, Louisiana.

**Mis•so•lon•ghi** |ˌmisəˈlawNGē| city in W Greece, on the N shore of the Gulf of Patras. Pop. 11,000. It is noted as the place where the poet Byron, who had joined the fight for Greek independence from the Turks, died of malaria in 1824. Greek name **Mesolóngion**.

**Mis•sou•la** |məˈsōōlə| commercial city in W Montana, on the Clark Fork River. Pop. 42,918.

**Mis•sou•ri** |məˈzŏŏrē| see box, p. 237. □ **Missourian** adj. & n.

**Mis•sou•ri River** |məˈzŏŏrē| a major river of the U.S., one of the main tributaries of the Mississippi. It rises in the Rocky Mts.

## Missouri

**Capital:** Jefferson City
**Largest city:** St. Louis
**Other cities:** Columbia, Kansas City, Springfield, St. Joseph
**Population:** 5,117,073 (1990); 5,438,559 (1998); 5,718,000 (2005 proj.)
**Population rank (1990):** 15
**Rank in land area:** 21
**Abbreviation:** MO; Mo.
**Nicknames:** The Show Me State; Mother of the West
**Motto:** *Salus populi suprema lex esto* (Latin: 'The welfare of the people shall be the supreme law')
**Bird:** bluebird
**Flower:** hawthorn blossom
**Tree:** flowering dogwood
**Song:** "Missouri Waltz"
**Noted physical features:** Big Spring; Till Plains, Osage Plains; Ozark Plateau; Taum Sauk Mountain
**Tourist attractions:** Branson; Osage Dam
**Admission date:** August 10, 1821
**Order of admission:** 24
**Name origin:** For the Missouri River; the name was that of an Indian tribe that lived near the mouth of the river.

in Montana and flows 2,315 mi./3,736 km. through the Dakotas, Nebraska, Iowa, Kansas, and Missouri to meet the Mississippi just N of St. Louis. A major transportation route, dammed for Great Plains agriculture, it is popularly called the Big Muddy.

**Mi·ta·ka** |mē'täkä| city in E central Japan, on E central Honshu, a suburb W of Tokyo. Pop. 166,000.

**Mi·ti·lí·ni** |ˌmitə'lēnē| Greek name for MYTILENE.

**Mit·la** |'mētlə| ancient city in S Mexico, to the E of the city of Oaxaca, now a noted archaeological site. Believed to have been established as a burial site by the Zapotecs, it was eventually overrun by the Mixtecs in about A.D. 1000.

**Mi·to** |'mētō| city in E central Japan, a prefectural capital in central Honshu. Pop. 235,000. It contains one of the greatest landscape gardens in Japan.

**Mit·tel·land Canal** |'mitəlländ| canal in NW Germany, which was constructed between 1905 and 1930. It is part of an inland waterway network linking the Rhine and Elbe rivers.

**Mix·co** |'mēsнkō| city in S central Guatemala, a suburb just W of Guatemala City. Pop. 413,000.

**Mi·ya·ji·ma** |mēyä'jēmə| earlier name for ITSUKUSHIMA.

**Mi·ya·za·ki** |mē'yäzäkē| port and resort city in SW Japan, on SE Kyushu. Pop. 288,000. A great Shinto shrine dedicated to the first emperor of Japan is here.

**Mi·zo·ram** |mə'zawrəm| state in the far NE of India, lying between Bangladesh and Burma. Pop. 686,000. Capital: Aizawl. Separated from Assam in 1972, it was administered as a Union Territory in India until 1986, when it became a state.

**Mla·da Bo·les·lav** |əm'lädä 'bawləzläf| (German name **Jungbunzlau**) industrial city in the N central Czech Republic. Pop. 48,000.

**Mma·ba·tho** |mäbätō| the capital of North-West Province in South Africa, near the border with Botswana. Pop. 28,000. It was the capital of the former homeland of Bophuthatswana.

**Mo·ab** |'mōæb| the ancient kingdom of the Moabites, situated to the E of the Dead Sea, in present-day Jordan. □ **Moabite** *adj. & n.*

**Mo·bile** |'mō,bēl| industrial port city on the coast of S Alabama. Pop. 196,278. It is situated at the head of Mobile Bay, an inlet of the Gulf of Mexico.

**Mo·cha** |'mōkə| (also **Mokha**) port in SW Yemen, on the Red Sea coast. Pop. 6,000. It gave its name to a type of coffee once exported from here.

**Mo·de·na** |'mōdənə| industrial city in N Italy, NW of Bologna. Pop. 117,000.

**Mo·des·to** |mə'destō| city in N central California, in the San Joaquin Valley, an agricultural processing and wine-making center. Pop. 164,730.

**Mo·doc Plateau** |'mōdäk| volcanic highland in N California and S Oregon, former home of the Modoc people.

**Moers** |mœrz| industrial city in western Germany, in North Rhine–Westphalia. Pop. 105,000.

**Moe·sia** |'mēsнə| ancient country and Roman province in SE Europe, corresponding to parts of modern Bulgaria and Serbia.

**Mog·a·di·shu** |ˌmōgə'dēsнoo͞| the capital of Somalia, a port on the Indian Ocean. Pop. 377,000. Also called **Muqdisho;** Italian name **Mogadiscio.**

**Mo·gi das Cru·zes** |'mōzнē däz 'kroozes| industrial city in SE Brazil, an iron and steel industry center E of São Paulo. Pop. 262,000.

**Mo·gi·lyov** |mägi'lyawf| (also **Mogilev**) Russian name for MAHILYOW.

**Mo·gol·lon Plateau** |məgē'ōn; mōgə'yōn| highland region of E central Arizona. Its S boundary is the **Mogollon Rim**, an escarpment also called the Mogollon Mts., but not to be confused with a range of that name in New Mexico.

**Mo·gul Empire** |'mōgəl| (also **Moghul** or **Mughal**) Muslim empire in N and central India, established in the 16th century, and expanded until the 18th. It declined until the British abolished it in 1857.

**Mo·hács** |'mōhäCH| river port and industrial town on the Danube in S Hungary, close to the borders with Croatia and Serbia. Pop. 21,000. It was the site of a battle in 1526 in which the Hungarians were defeated by a Turkish force, as a result of which Hungary became part of the Ottoman Empire.

**Mo·ham·me·rah** |mə,hämä'rä| former name (until 1924) for KHORRAMSHAHR, Iran.

**Mo·hawk River** |'mō,hawk| river that flows 140 mi./230 km. across central New York, joining the Hudson River above Albany. The Mohawk Valley is the site of much of the Erie Canal, and has long been a transportation corridor.

**Mohenjo-Daro** |mō'henyō'därō| ancient city of the civilization of the Indus valley (c. 2600–1700 B.C.), now a major archaeological site in Pakistan, SW of Sukkur.

**Mo·ja·ve Desert** |mō'hävē| (also **Mohave**) desert in S California, to the SE of the Sierra Nevada and N and E of Los Angeles.

**Mo·jo·ker·to** |mōjō'kertō| (also **Modjokerto**) industrial town in Indonesia, on E Java, SW of Surabaya. Pop. 100,000.

**Mok·po** |'mäk,pō| port city in extreme SW South Korea. Pop. 253,000.

**Mol·dau** |'mawl,dow| German name for the VLTAVA River.

**Mol·da·via** |mäl'dävēə| 1 a former principality of SE Europe. Formerly a part of the Roman province of Dacia, it came under Turkish rule in the 16th century. In 1861 Moldavia united with Wallachia to form Romania. 2 another name for MOLDOVA.

**Mol·do·va** |mäl'dōvə| landlocked republic in SE Europe, between Romania and Ukraine. Area: 13,017 sq. mi./33,700 sq. km. Pop. 4,384,000. Languages, Moldavian (official), Russian. Capital and largest city: Chişinău. Also called **Moldavia**. Part of Romania, then (1940–91) a republic of the Soviet Union, Moldova is a fertile agri-

Moldava

cultural country. □ **Moldovan** adj. & n. **Moldavian** adj. & n.

**Mol·do·vea·nu** |,mōdōl'vyänōō| mountain peak in Romania, in the Transylvanian Alps SE of Sibiu. It is the highest peak in Romania (8,346 ft./2,544 m.).

**Mo·line** |'mō'lēn| city on the Rock and Mississippi rivers in NW Illinois, one of the Quad Cities and home to a noted farm machinery industry. Pop. 43,202.

**Mo·li·se** |mō'lēzä| region of E Italy, on the Adriatic coast. Pop. 336,000. Capital: Campobasso.

**Mo·lo·kai** |,mōlō'kī| island of Hawaii, E of Oahu, site of numerous resorts.

**Mo·lo·tov** |'mälə,tawf| former name (1940–57) for PERM, Russia.

**Mo·luc·cas Islands** |mō'ləkəz| island group in Indonesia, between Sulawesi and New Guinea; chief city, Amboina. Settled by the Portuguese in the early 16th century, the islands were taken a century later by the Dutch. They were formerly known as the Spice Islands. Indonesian name **Maluku**. □ **Moluccan** adj. & n.

**Mom·ba·sa** |mōm'bäsä| seaport and industrial city in SE Kenya, on the Indian Ocean. Pop. 465,000. It is the leading port and second-largest city of Kenya.

**Mo·na** |'mōnə| ancient and literary name for either the island of ANGLESEY, Wales, or the Isle of MAN.

**Mon·a·co** |'mänəkō| principality forming an enclave (0.75 sq. mi./1.95 sq. km.) within French territory, on the Mediterranean coast near the Italian border. Pop. 30,000; official language, French. Capital: Monaco-Ville. Ruled by the Grimaldi family since 1297, and the smallest sovereign state, except for the Vatican, Monaco relies on tourism and its casinos for income. □ **Monacan** adj. & n. **Monégasqu** adj. & n.

**Mo·nad·nock, Mount** |mə'näd,näk| isolated peak in SW New Hampshire whose name stands for any mountain of its type.

**Monaco**

**Mon·a·ghan** |'mänə,hæn| **1** county of the Republic of Ireland, part of the old province of Ulster. Pop. 51,000. **2** its county seat. Pop. 6,000.

**Mo·na Passage** |'mōnə| ocean passage between Puerto Rico and the Dominican Republic, leading from the Atlantic into the Caribbean Sea, and noted for its difficult waters.

**Mo·nash·ee Mountains** |mə'näSHē| range of the N Rocky Mts. in SE British Columbia, reaching 10,560 ft./3,219 m. at Hallam Peak.

**Mön·chen·glad·bach** |,mənKHen'glädbäk| industrial city in NW Germany. Pop. 263,000. It is the site of the NATO headquarters for N Europe.

**Mon·clo·va** |mäNG'klōva| industrial city in NE Mexico, in Coahuila state. Pop. 178,000. It is an iron and steel center.

**Monc·ton** |'məNGktən| commercial and academic city in SE New Brunswick, on the Petitcodiac River. Pop. 57,010.

**Mo·nem·va·sía** |,mōnemvä'sēä| (also known as **Monembasia**) village in S Greece, on a small island off the coast of Laconia, in the Peloponnese. It is known for its wine, called malmsey or malvasia.

**Mon·go·lia** |mäNG'gōlēə| republic of E Asia, between Siberian Russia and China. Area: 604,480 sq. mi./1.56 million sq. km. Pop. 2,184,000. Language, Mongolian.

**Mongolia**

Capital and largest city: Ulan Bator. Center of the former Mongol Empire, it was later a Chinese province (Outer Mongolia, to distinguish it from Inner Mongolia). It has great mineral resources, but most of its people remain nomadic pastoralists. □ **Mongolian** *adj. & n.*

**Mon·mouth·shire** |'mänməTHSHi(ə)r| county of SE Wales, on the border with England; administrative center, Cwmbran. The major part of it was part of Gwent 1974–96.

**Mo·no Lake** |'mōnō| saline lake in E central California, near the Nevada line, noted for its rock formations, many exposed when local waters were diverted to the Los Angeles area.

**Mo·non·ga·he·la River** |mä,nängä'hēlä| river that flows 128 mi./206 km. from West Virginia into W Pennsylvania, to Pittsburgh, where it joins the Allegheny River to form the Ohio River. Its valley is highly industrial.

**Mon·roe** |mən'rō| industrial and commercial city in N central Louisiana, in a natural gas producing area. Pop. 54,909.

**Mon·ro·via¹** |mən'rōvēə| industrial city in SW California, NE of Los Angeles. Pop. 35,761.

**Mon·ro·via²** |mən'rōvēə| the capital and chief port of Liberia. Pop. 500,000. Founded in 1822 for resettled American slaves, it was later named for President James Monroe.

**Mons** |mawnz| industrial town in S Belgium, capital of the province of Hainaut. Pop. 92,000. It was the scene in August 1914 of the first major battle of World War I between British and German forces. Flemish name **Bergen**.

**Mon·tana** |män'tænə| see box, p. 240. □ **Montanan** *adj. & n.*

**Mont·au·ban** |mäntə'bän| market center in S France, capital of the Tarn-et-Garonne department in the Midi-Pyrénées. Pop. 53,000.

**Mont Blanc** |,mawn 'bläNGk| peak in the Alps on the border between France and Italy, rising to 15,771 ft./4,807 m. The highest peak in the Alps and in W Europe, it was first climbed in 1786.

**Mont Ce·nis** |mōn sə'nē| (Italian name **Monte Cenisio**) Alpine pass linking Modane, France, and Susa, Italy. The nearby Mont Cenis Tunnel, opened 1871, was the first major tunnel through the Alps. It links Modane and Bardonnecchia, Italy.

**Mont Cer·vin** |mawn ser'ven| French name for the MATTERHORN.

**Mont·clair** |mänt'klär| township in NE

---

**Montana**

**Capital:** Helena

**Largest city:** Billings

**Other cities:** Bozeman, Butte, Great Falls, Missoula

**Population:** 799,065 (1990); 880,453 (1998); 1,006,000 (2005 proj.)

**Population rank (1990):** 44

**Rank in land area:** 4

**Abbreviation:** MT; Mont.

**Nickname:** Treasure State; Big Sky Country

**Motto:** *Oro y Plata* (Spanish: 'Gold and Silver')

**Bird:** Western meadowlark

**Fish:** black-spotted (cutthroat) trout

**Flower:** bitterroot

**Tree:** Ponderosa pine

**Song:** "Montana"

**Noted physical features:** Great Falls; Granite Peak

**Tourist attractions:** Continental Divide; Custer Cemetery; Glacier and Yellowstone national parks

**Admission date:** November 8, 1889

**Order of admission:** 41

**Name origin:** From Latin *montana*, meaning 'mountainous region.'

---

New Jersey, an affluent suburb NW of Newark. Pop. 37,729.

**Mon·te Al·bán** |'mōnte äl'bän| ancient city, now in ruins, in Oaxaca, S Mexico. Occupied from the 8th century B.C., it was a center of the Zapotec culture from about the 1st century B.C. to the 8th century A.D.

**Mon·te Car·lo** |män(t)ē 'kär,lō| resort in Monaco, forming one of the four communes of the principality. Pop. 12,000. It is famous as a gambling center.

**Mon·te Cas·si·no** |,män(t)ā kə'sē,nō| hill in central Italy near the town of Cassino, the site of the principal monastery of the Benedictines, founded by St. Benedict *c.*529.

**Mon·te Cer·vi·no** |,män(t)ā ser'vēnō| Italian name for the MATTERHORN.

**Mon·te Cris·to** |,män(t)ā 'kristō| uninhabited Italian island in the Tyrrhenian Sea, S of Elba, associated with the novel *The Count of Monte Cristo* by Alexandre Dumas.

**Mon·te·go Bay** |mən'tē,gō| free port and beach resort on the N coast of Jamaica. Pop. 82,000.

**Mon·té·li·mar** |,mänta lē'mär| manufacturing town in Dauphiné, SE France, noted for nougat production. Pop. 31,000.

**Mon·te·ne·gro** |,mäntə'ne,grō| mountainous, landlocked republic in the Balkan peninsula. Area: 5,335 sq. mi./13,812 sq. km. Pop. 632,000. Official language, Serbo-Croat. Capital: Podgorica. Long tied to Serbia, Montenegro remains a nominal constituent of the much reduced Yugoslavia. Its economy is based on livestock raising, agriculture, mining, and iron and steel. □ **Montenegrin** *adj. & n.*

**Mon·te·rey** |,mäntə'rā| city and fishing port on the coast of central California, founded by the Spanish in the 18th century. Pop. 31,954. The harbor is the site of the Monterey Bay Aquarium, and of Cannery Row, featured in the writing of John Steinbeck.

**Mon·te·ría** |,mäntə'rēä| commercial city in N Colombia, a port on the Sinú River and capital of Córdoba department. Pop. 266,000.

**Mon·ter·rey** |,mäntə'rā| city in NE Mexico, capital of the state of Nuevo León and the third largest city in Mexico. Pop. 2,522,000. It is an iron and steel and heavy industrial center.

**Mon·te Sant'An·gel·o** |'mäntəsæn'tænjəlō| commune in SE Italy. Pop. 15,000. The archangel Michael is said to have appeared at a grotto here; a 5th-century sanctuary at the site has long been a pilgrimage destination.

**Mon·tes Cla·ros** |,mōnCHēz 'klärōs| industrial and agricultural city in E Brazil, in Minas Gerais state. Pop. 271,000.

**Mon·te·vid·eo** |,mäntəvə'dāō| the capital and chief port of Uruguay, on the Plate River. Pop. 1,360,000. It is the commercial and financial center of Uruguay.

**Mon·te·zu·ma, Halls of** |,mäntə'zōōmə| in the U.S. Marine anthem, Mexico City, especially CHAPULTEPEC, as a scene of Marine activity.

**Mont·gom·ery** |mən(t)'gəm(ə)rē| the state capital of Alabama, an industrial and commercial city on the Alabama River. Pop. 187,106.

**Mont·gom·ery County** |mən(t)'gəm(ə)rē| county in central Maryland, containing many suburbs on the N side of Washington, D.C. Rockville is its seat. Pop. 757,027.

**Mont·gom·ery·shire** | mən(t)'gəmrēsHir; mən(t)'gəmrēsHīər| former county of central Wales. It became a part of Powys in 1974.

**Mon·ti·cel·lo** |,mäntə'cHelō| historic estate just SE of Charlottesville, in central Virginia, the home of Thomas Jefferson.

**Mont·mar·tre** |ˌmän'märtrə| district in N Paris, on a hill above the Seine, much frequented by artists in the late 19th and early 20th centuries when it was a separate village. Topped by the basilica of Sacré Coeur, it is the site of the Moulin Rouge and the Place Pigalle.

**Mont·par·nasse** |ˌmänpär'näs| district of Paris, on the left bank of the River Seine. Frequented in the late 19th century by writers and artists, it is traditionally associated with Parisian cultural life.

**Mont·pe·lier** |ˌmän(t)'pēlyər| the state capital of Vermont, in the N central part on the Winooski River. Pop. 8,247.

**Mont·pel·lier** |ˌmänpəl'yā| city in S France, near the Mediterranean coast, capital of Languedoc-Roussillon. Pop. 211,000. A medical school and university, world famous in medieval times, was founded here in 1221.

**Mont·re·al** |ˌmäntrē'awl| port city on the St. Lawrence River in S Quebec. Pop. 1,017,666. Founded in 1642, it was under French rule until 1763; almost two-thirds of its current population are French-speaking. Montreal, one of the largest French cities in the world, is an industrial, commercial, and cultural center. French name **Montréal**.

**Mon·treuil** |mōn'troi| town, an E suburb of Paris, France. Pop. 95,000. It has a variety of light industries.

**Mon·treux** |mən'trō| resort town in SW Switzerland, at the E end of Lake Geneva. Pop. 20,000. Since the 1960s it has hosted annual festivals of jazz and television.

**Mont St. Mi·chel** |ˌmawn ˌsän mē'sHel| rocky prominence off the coast of Normandy, NW France. An island only at high tide, it is surrounded by sandbanks and linked to the mainland by a causeway. It is crowned by a medieval Benedictine abbey-fortress.

**Mont·ser·rat** |ˌmäntsə'rät| island in the Caribbean, one of the Leeward Islands.

**Montserrat**

Pop. 12,000. Capital: Plymouth. It was colonized by Irish settlers in 1632 and is now a British dependency. Since 1995, it has been severely affected by the ongoing eruption of the Soufrière Hills volcano, causing the evacuation of the S part of the island, including Plymouth. ☐ **Montserratian** adj. & n.

**Mon·u·ment Valley** |'mänyəmənt| region of NE Arizona and S Utah, W of the Four Corners, whose scenery has been the backdrop for many movies.

**Mon·za** |'mäntsä| industrial city in N Italy, NE of Milan, a textile and motor-racing center. Pop. 123,000.

**Moon, Mountains of the** |mōōn| see RUWENZORI, Uganda.

**Mo·o·rea** |mōē'räyä| (formerly **Eimeo**) volcanic island in Windward (E) group of the Society Islands, French Polynesia. Tourism is important on this mountainous island.

**Moor·head** |'mo͝or(ə)r,hed| commercial city in W Minnesota, a transportation hub across the Red River of the North from Fargo, North Dakota. Pop. 32,295.

**Moose·head Lake** |'mo͝oshed| largest lake in Maine, in the W central section. Small resorts lie along its forested shores.

**Moose Jaw** |'mo͝os ,jaw| city in S central Saskatchewan, a transportation and processing center W of Regina. Pop. 33,593.

**Mo·rad·a·bad** |mə'rədäbäd| city and railway junction in N India, in Uttar Pradesh. Pop. 417,000.

**Mor·ar, Loch** |'mawrər| loch in W Scotland. At 1,017 ft./310 m., it is Scotland's deepest.

**Mo·ra·va** |'mawrävä| river (240 mi./385 km.) that flows SW through the Czech Republic, forming part of its border with Slovakia, into the Danube River.

**Mo·ra·via** |mə'rāvēə| region of the Czech Republic, situated S of the Sudeten Mts., between Bohemia in the W and the Carpathians in the E; chief town, Brno. A province of Bohemia from the 11th century, it was made an Austrian province in 1848, becoming a part of Czechoslovakia in 1918. ☐ **Moravian** adj. & n.

**Mo·ra·vi·an Gate** |mə'rāvēyən| historic pass in the N Czech Republic, between the E end of the Sudeten Mts. and the W end of the Carpathian Mts.

**Mor·ay** |'mərē| (also **Morayshire**) administrative region and former county of N Scotland, bordered on the N by the Moray Firth; administrative center, Elgin.

**Mor·ay Firth** |'mərē| deep inlet of the

North Sea on the NE coast of Scotland. Inverness is near its head.

**Mor·bi·han** |mawrbē'yän| department in Brittany, NW France, on the Atlantic. Pop. 620,000. The capital is Vannes.

**Mord·vin·ia** |mawrd'vēnēə| (also **Mordovia**) autonomous republic in European Russia, SE of Nizhni Novgorod. Pop. 964,000. Capital: Saransk.

**More·cambe Bay** |'môrkəm| inlet of the Irish Sea, on the NW coast of England between Cumbria and Lancashire.

**Mo·re·lia** |mō'ralyä| city in central Mexico, capital of the state of Michoacán. Pop. 490,000. Founded in 1541, it was known as Valladolid until 1828.

**Mo·re·los** |mō'rālōs| state of central Mexico, to the W of Mexico City. Pop. 1,195,000. Capital: Cuernavaca.

**Mo·re·no Valley** |mə'rānō| city in SW California, a suburb just E of Riverside. Pop. 118,779.

**Mor·gan·town** |'môrgən,town| commercial city in N West Virginia, home to West Virginia University. Pop. 25,879.

**Mo·ri·ah, Mount** |mə'rīyä| biblical name for the hill in present-day E Jerusalem on which the Temple of Solomon was built. It may also be the place where Abraham was to sacrifice his son Isaac.

**Mo·rio·ka** |môrē'ōkə| industrial and commercial city in NE Japan, on N Honshu. Pop. 235,000.

**Mo·roc·co** |mə'räkō| kingdom in NW Africa, with coastlines on the Mediterranean Sea and Atlantic. Area: 177,184 sq. mi./458,730 sq. km. Pop. 25,731,000. Languages, Arabic (official), Berber, Spanish, French. Capital: Rabat. Largest city: Casablanca. Conquered by the Arabs in the 7th century, later controlled by the Portuguese, Spanish, and French, Morocco regained independence in 1956. Mining, agriculture, tourism, and fishing are important. □ **Moroccan** adj. & n.

Morocco

**Mo·ro Gulf** | 'mō,rō| inlet of the N Celebes Sea, SW of Mindanao in the Philippines.

**Mo·rón** |'mō,rawn| city in E Argentina, a suburb SW of Buenos Aires. Pop. 642,000.

**Mo·ro·ni** |mə'rōnē| the capital of Comoros, on the island of Grande Comoré Pop. 22,000.

**Mor·ris Jes·up, Cape** |'mawrəs 'jesəp| northernmost (83° 38′ N) point of land in the world, at the N tip of Greenland, 439 mi./706 km. from the North Pole.

**Mor·ro Castle** |'mawrō| name for two forts in Cuba, in the harbors of Havana and Santiago de Cuba. The fort in Santiago was attacked and taken by U.S. troops in 1898, during the Spanish-American War.

**Mos·cow**[1] |'mäs,kow| city in NW Idaho, home to the University of Idaho. Pop. 18,519.

**Mos·cow**[2] |'mäs,kow| the capital of Russia, an industrial and cultural hub at the center of the vast plain of European Russia, on the Moskva River. Pop. 9,000,000. First mentioned in medieval chronicles in 1147, it soon became the chief city of the increasingly powerful Muscovite princes. Moscow became the capital when Ivan the Terrible proclaimed himself the first czar of Russia in the 16th century. Peter the Great moved his capital to St. Petersburg in 1712, but after the Bolshevik Revolution of 1917 Moscow was made the capital of the USSR and seat of the new Soviet government, with its center in the Kremlin, the fortress that was the citadel of the medieval city. Russian name **Moskva**. □ **Muscovite** adj. & n.

**Mo·selle** |mō'zel| (also **Moselle**) river of W Europe, which rises in the Vosges Mts. of NE France and flows 346 mi./550 km. NE through Luxembourg and Germany to meet the Rhine at Koblenz.

**Mo·shi** |'mōsHē| commercial city in N Tanzania, just S of Mount Kilimanjaro, in a coffee-growing region. Pop. 95,000.

**Mos·kva** |'mäskvə| Russian name for Moscow.

**Mos·qui·to Coast** |mə'skētō| sparsely populated coastal strip of swamp, lagoon, and tropical forest comprising the Caribbean coast of Nicaragua and NE Honduras, occupied by the Miskito people after whom it is named.

**Mos·so·ró** |mōsō'raw| city in NE Brazil, in Rio Grande do Norte state, a salt and mining center. Pop. 192,000.

**Most** |mawst| industrial city and rail junction in the NW Czech Republic, near the German border. Pop. 71,000.

**Mos·ta·ga·nem** |mawstägä'nem| commercial port city in NW Algeria, on the Mediterranean Sea, E of Oran. Pop. 115,000.

**Mo·star** |'mōstär| predominantly Muslim city in central Bosnia and Herzegovina. Pop. 110,000. It was nearly destroyed in 1992–93 by Serb and Croat forces trying to eliminate the Muslim presence in the city.

**Mo·sto·les** |'mōstōles| city in central Spain, SW of Madrid. Pop. 176,000.

**Mo·sul** |mō'sōol| city in N Iraq, on the Tigris River, opposite the ruins of Nineveh. Pop. 571,000. It gives its name to muslin, a cotton fabric first produced here.

**Moth·er Lode** |'məTHər| popular name for the area, on the W of the Sierra Nevada in N central California, where much of the gold sought after 1848 in local rivers is thought to have come.

**Motor City** (also **Motown**) nickname for Detroit, the center of the US automobile industry.

**Mo·town** |'mō,town| see DETROIT, Michigan.

**Moul·mein** |'mōol,män| port in SE Burma, capital of the state of Mon . Pop. 220,000.

**Moun·dou** |'mōondōo| commercial city in S Chad. Pop. 281,000.

**Mountain State** |'mowntn| nickname for WEST VIRGINIA.

**Mountain States** |'mowntn| region of the U.S. comprising states that contain part of the Rocky Mts. New Mexico, Colorado, Wyoming, Utah, Idaho, and Montana are generally considered Mountain States.

**Moun·tain View** |'mowntn| city in N central California, near the S end of San Francisco Bay, part of the Silicon Valley complex. Pop. 67,460.

**Mount Ararat, Mount Carmel**, etc. see ARARAT, MOUNT; CARMEL, MOUNT, etc.

**Mount Des·ert Island** |'mownt'dəsərt| island in the Atlantic in SE Maine, site of Bar Harbor and other resorts. Most of the island is in Acadia National Park.

**Mount Isa** |'mownt'izə| lead- and silver-mining town in NE Australia, in W Queensland. Pop. 24,000.

**Mount Ver·non**[1] |'mownt 'vərnən| city in SE New York, a suburb on the N side of the Bronx, New York City. Pop. 67,153.

**Mount Ver·non**[2] |'mownt 'vərnən| property in NE Virginia, about 15 mi./24 km. from Washington D.C., on a site overlooking the Potomac River. Built in 1743, it was the home of George Washington from 1747 until his death in 1799. It remains a popular tourist attraction, and is the site of Washington's grave.

**Mourne Mountains** |mōrn| range of hills in SE Northern Ireland, in County Down. Slieve Donard (2,796 ft./853 m.) is the high point in the province.

**Mo·zam·bique** |,mōzæm'bēk| republic on the E coast of southern Africa. Area: 308,760 sq. mi./799,380 sq. km. Pop. 16,142,000. Languages, Portuguese (official), Bantu languages. Capital and largest city, Maputo. Controlled by Portugal for over 400 years before independence in 1975, Mozambique relies chiefly on subsistence agriculture, with some mining. □ **Mozambican** adj. & n.

**Mozambique**

**Mo·zam·bique Channel** |,mōzæm'bēk| arm of the Indian Ocean separating the E coast of mainland Africa from the island of Madagascar.

**Mpu·ma·lan·ga** |,əmpōomə'läNGä| province of NE South Africa, formerly East Transvaal. Capital: Nelspruit.

**Mu·dan·jiang** |'mōo'dän'yäNG| city in Heilongjiang province, NE China, on the Mudan River, SE of Harbin. Pop. 572,000.

**Mu·fu·li·ra** |,mōofōolē'rä| industrial and commercial city in N central Zambia, on the border of Congo (formerly Zaire), in a copper-mining area. Pop. 153,000.

**Mühl·haus·en** |'myōolhowzən| German name for MULHOUSE, France.

**Mühl·haus·en in Thü·ring·en** |'myōolhowzən in 'tyōoriNGən| manufacturing city in Thuringia, in central Germany, on the Unstrut River. Pop. 44,000.

**Mu·ka·che·ve** |,mōoka'cHōvə| (also **Mu·kachevo**; Hungarian name **Munkács**) historic industrial town in the W Ukraine. Pop. 88,000. It has changed hands repeatedly since the 9th century.

**Mu·kal·la** |mōo'kælə| port on the S coast of Yemen, in the Gulf of Aden. Pop. 154,000.

**Muk·den** |'mo͝okdən| former name for SHENYANG, China.

**Mul·ha·cén** |mo͞olä'THän| mountain in S Spain, SE of Granada, in the Sierra Nevada range. Rising to 11,424 ft./3,482 m., it is the highest mountain in the country.

**Mül·heim** |'myo͝olhīm| industrial city in western Germany, in North Rhine-Westphalia, SE of Essen. Pop. 117,000. Full name **Mülheim an der Ruhr.**

**Mul·house** |mo͞o'lo͞oz| industrial city in NE France, in Alsace. Pop. 110,000. It was a free imperial city until it joined the French Republic in 1798. In 1871, after the Franco-Prussian War, the city became part of the German Empire until it was reunited with France in 1918. German name **Mühlhausen.**

**Mull** |məl| large island of the Inner Hebrides; chief town, Tobermory. It is separated from the coast of Scotland near Oban by the Sound of Mull.

**Mul·lin·gar** |ˌmələn'gär| the county seat of Westmeath, in the Republic of Ireland. Pop. 14,000.

**Mul·tan** |məl'tän| commercial city in Punjab province, E central Pakistan. Pop. 980,000.

**Mün·chen** |mo͝onKHən| German name for MUNICH.

**Mun·cie** |'mənsē| industrial city in E central Indiana, noted as home to Ball Company, maker of glass containers, and as the 'Middletown' of sociological literature. Pop. 71,035.

**Mun·ger** |'məngər| (also **Monghyr**) city in E India, in Bihar state. Pop. 150,000. It has one of the largest cigarette factories in India.

**Mu·nich** |'myo͝onək| city in SE Germany, capital of Bavaria. Pop. 1,229,000. Munich is noted for the architecture of the medieval city center and as an artistic and cultural center. German name **München.**

**Mun·kács** |'myo͞oNGkäCH| Hungarian name for MUKACHEVE.

**Mun·ster** |'mənstər| village in NE France, SW of Strasbourg, in the Haut-Rhin. The village gave its name to the well-known cheese.

**Mun·ster**² |'mənstər| province of the Republic of Ireland, in the SW of the country, comprising Counties Cork, Clare, Kerry, Tipperary, Limerick, and Waterford.

**Mün·ster** |'myo͝onstər| industrial port city in NW Germany. Pop. 250,000. It was formerly the capital of Westphalia; the Treaty of Westphalia, ending the Thirty Years War, was signed here in 1648.

**Muq·di·sho** alternate form of MOGADISHU, Somalia.

**Mur River** |myo͝or| river that rises in the E part of the Hohe Tauern and flows 279 mi./170 km. through Austria and Slovenia, draining into the Drava River.

**Mu·ra·no** |mo͝or'änō| N suburb of Venice, Italy, on five small islands in the Lagoon of Venice. It is famous for its colorful glass.

**Mur·chi·son Falls** |mərCHəsən| former name for KABALEGA FALLS, Uganda.

**Mur·chi·son Rapids** |'mərCHəsən| former name for KAPACHIRA FALLS, Malawi.

**Mur·cia** |'mərSHə| **1** autonomous region in SE Spain. In the Middle Ages, along with Albacete, it formed an ancient Moorish kingdom. **2** its capital, an industrial city on the Segura River. Pop. 329,000.

**Mu·res River** |'mo͝oresH| (in Hungarian **Maros**) river (470 mi./755 km.) that rises in the Carpathians in Romania and flows W into Hungary, meeting the Tisza at Szeged.

**Mur·frees·boro** |mərfrēz'bərō| commercial city in central Tennessee, SE of Nashville. A Civil War battle fought near here (January 1863) is also called the battle of Stones River.

**Mur·gab river** |mo͝or'gäb| (also **Morghab; Murghab**) river in NW Afghanistan and SE Turkmenistan, flowing 600 mi./965 km. from the W Hindu Kush to the Kara-Kum desert, where it disappears into the sand.

**Mur·mansk** |mo͝or'mænsk| port in NW Russia, on the N coast of the Kola Peninsula, in the Barents Sea. Pop. 472,000. It is the largest city N of the Arctic Circle and its port is ice-free throughout the year.

**Mu·rom** |'mo͝orəm| port and transportation center in W Russia. Pop. 127,000. First mentioned in in 862, it is one of the oldest Russian cities.

**Mu·ro·ran** |mo͝o'rörän| industrial port city in N Japan, on SW Hokkaido. Pop. 118,000.

**Mur·ray River** |mərē| the principal river of Australia, which rises in the Great Dividing Range in New South Wales and flows 1,610 mi./2,590 km. generally NW, forming part of the border between the states of Victoria and New South Wales, before turning S in South Australia to empty into the Indian Ocean SE of Adelaide.

**Mur·rum·bidg·ee** |ˌmərəm'bijē| river of SE Australia, in New South Wales. Rising in the Great Dividing Range, it flows 1,099 mi./1,759 km. W to join the Murray, of which it is a major tributary.

**Mu·ru·roa** |ˌmo͝oro͞o'röə| remote South Pacific atoll in the Tuamotu archipelago, in French Polynesia, used as a nuclear testing site from 1966.

**Mu·sa·la, Mount** |myoŏsä'lə| (also **Mou·salla**) the highest peak in Bulgaria, in the Rila Mountains, rising to 9,596 ft./ 2,925 m.

**Mu·sa·shi·no** |moŏ'sä,sHēnō| city in E central Japan, on E central Honshu, a suburb of Tokyo. Pop. 139,000.

**Mus·cat** |'məskät| (also **Masqat**) the capital of Oman, a port on the SE coast of the Arabian Peninsula. Pop. 41,000.

**Mus·cat and Oman** |'məsket| former name (until 1970) for OMAN.

**Mus·cle Shoals** |'məsəl| industrial city in NW Alabama, on the Tennessee River, near the Wilson Dam and the former site of the Mussel (or Muscle) Shoals shallows. Pop. 9,611.

**Mus·co·vy** |məs'kōvē| **1** medieval principality in W central Russia, centered on Moscow, which formed the nucleus of present-day Russia. Founded in the late 13th century by Daniel, son of Alexander Nevsky, Muscovy gradually expanded despite Tartar depredations, finally overcoming the Tartars in 1380. Princes of Muscovy became the rulers of Russia; in 1472 Ivan III completed the unification, overcoming rivalry from the principalities of Novgorod, Tver, and Vladimir and adopted the title "Ruler of all Russia." In 1547 Ivan IV (Ivan the Terrible) became the first czar of the new empire, and made Moscow its capital. **2** archaic name for Russia. □ **Muscovite** adj. & n.

**Mu·shin** |'moŏ'sHin| industrial city in SW Nigeria, a suburb NW of Lagos. Pop. 294,000.

**Mus·ke·gon** |məs'kēgən| industrial port in W Michigan, on Lake Michigan. Pop. 40,283.

**Mus·ko·gee** |məs'skōgē| commercial city in E central Oklahoma, on the Arkansas River. Pop. 37,708.

**Mus·tique** |mə'stēk| small resort island in the N Grenadines, in the Caribbean to the S of St. Vincent.

**Mu·ta·re** |moŏ'tärə| industrial town in the E highlands of Zimbabwe. Pop. 70,000. Former name (until 1982) **Umtali**.

**Mu·zaf·far·a·bad** |moŏ'zəfərə'bäd| town in NE Pakistan, the administrative center of Azad Kashmir.

**Mu·zaf·far·na·gar** |moŏ'zəfərnəgər| commercial town in N India, in Uttar Pradesh state, N of Delhi. Pop. 248,000.

**Mu·zaf·far·pur** |moŏ'zəfərpoŏr| town in

NE India, in Bihar state, N of Patna. Pop. 240,000.

**Muz·tag** |muz'tag; moŏz'tag| **1** (also **Ulugh Muztagh**) peak in W China on the Tibet-Xinjiang border near the Karamiran Pass; the highest peak in the Kunlun Shan Mts.: 25,338 ft./7,723 m. **2** (also **Muztagh**) peak in W China, S Xinjiang region near the Kashmir border: 23,885 ft./7,282 m. high.

**Muz·ta·ga·ta** |moŏz,tägä'tä| (also **Muztagh Ata**) peak in the Muztagata range, in Xinjiang, W China, near the Tajikistan border: 24,757 ft./7,546 m. high.

**Mwan·za** |'mwänzä| commercial city in N Tanzania, a port on Lake Victoria, in an agricultural area. Pop. 260,000.

**Mwe·ru, Lake** |'mwärōō| (also **Moero**) lake on the border of Zambia and Congo (formerly Zaire), W of Lake Tanganyika. The Luapula River flows through this fishing resource.

**Myan·mar, Union of** official name of BURMA.

**My·ce·nae** |mī'sēnē| ancient city in Greece, situated near the coast in the NE Peloponnese, the center of the late Bronze Age Mycenaean civilization. The capital of King Agamemnon, it was at its most prosperous c. 1400–1200 B.C.; systematic excavation of the site began in 1840. □ **Mycenaean** adj. & n.

**Myit·kyi·na** |myitCHē'nä| town in N Burma, capital of Kachin state, near the Chinese border. Pop. 56,000.

**My·ko·la·yiv** |,mikō'läyēv| industrial city in S Ukraine, on the Southern Bug river near the N tip of the Black Sea. Pop. 508,000. Russian name **Nikolaev**.

**Myk·o·nos** |'mikə,näs| Greek island in the Aegean, one of the Cyclades. Greek name **Míkonos**.

**My Lai** |'mē'lī| village in Son My district, central Vietnam, S of Quang Ngai, site of a 1968 massacre of Vietnamese civilians by U.S. troops during the Vietnam War.

**My·men·singh** |'mīmən'siNG| port on the Brahmaputra River in central Bangladesh. Pop. 186,000.

**Myr·tle Beach** |'mərtəl| resort city in NE South Carolina, the hub of the part of the Atlantic coast called the Grand Strand. Pop. 24,848.

**My·sia** |'mīsHēə| ancient region of NW Asia Minor (present-day NW Turkey), on the Mediterranean coast S of the Sea of Marmara. □ **Mysian** adj. & n.

**My·sore** |mī'sōr| **1** city in the Indian state of Karnataka. Pop. 480,000. It was the cap-

# Nn

**Naas** |näs| county seat of Kildare in the central Republic of Ireland, in Leinster. Pop. 11,000.

**Na·be·rezh·nye Chel·ny** |nəbir'ezнniyə cнil'nē| (formerly **Brezhnev**; earlier, **Chelny**) city in W Russia, on the Kama River. Pop. 514,000.

**Na·beul** |nə'bŏŏl| (also **Nabul**) resort town in NE Tunisia, on the Cape Bon peninsula. Pop. 39,000.

**Nab·lus** |'näbləs| commercial city, largely Palestinian, in the Israeli-occupied West Bank, N of Jerusalem. Pop. 120,000. It is near the site of ancient Shechem.

**Na·ca·la** |nä'kälə| deepwater port on the E coast of Mozambique. Pop. 104,000. It is linked by rail with landlocked Malawi.

**Nac·og·do·ches** |näkə'dōcнes| historic city in E Texas, on the Angelina River. Pop. 30,872.

**Na·di·ad** |nədē'äd| commercial and industrial town in W India, in Gujarat state. Pop. 170,000.

**Na·fud** |næ'fŏŏd| (also **Nefud; An Nafud**) desert region in N Saudi Arabia, in a large oval depression surrounded by curiously-shaped sandstone outcrops.

**Na·ga** |'nägä| (formerly **Nueva Caceres**) commercial city in the Philippines, on SE Luzon. Pop. 115,000. It was one of the earliest Spanish settlements.

**Na·ga·land** |'nägə,lænd| state in the far NE of India, on the border with Burma. Pop. 1,216,000. Capital: Kohima. It was created in 1962 from parts of Assam. The Naga Hills straddle the India-Burma border.

**Na·ga·no** |nä'gänō| commercial and industrial city in central Japan, on central Honshu. Pop. 347,000. It is the site of a major Buddhist shrine.

**Na·ga·o·ka** |nägä'ōkä| industrial city in N central Japan, on central Honshu. Pop. 186,000.

**Na·ga·sa·ki** |,nägə'säkē| city and port in SW Japan, on the W coast of Kyushu island. Pop. 445,000. A center of shipbuilding, it is the Japanese port nearest to China, and in 1639–1854 was the only Japanese port open (on the island of Dejima) to foreign trade. It was the target of the second atomic bomb dropped by the United States, on August 9, 1945.

**Na·ger·coil** |'nägərkoil| industrial city in S India, in Tamil Nadu state. Pop. 189,000. The southernmost city in India, it is an important Christian center in a mainly Hindu area.

**Nagorno-Karabakh** |nə',gawrnə,kerə-'bäk| region of Azerbaijan in the S foothills of the Caucasus. Pop. 192,000. Capital: Xankändi. Formerly a Persian khanate, it was absorbed into the Russian Empire in the 19th century, later becoming an autonomous region of the Soviet Union, within Azerbaijan. Fighting between Azerbaijan and Armenia began in 1985, with the majority Armenian population desiring to be separated from Muslim Azerbaijan and united with Armenia; the region declared unilateral independence in 1991, and most Azeris have now left the area.

**Na·go·ya** |nə'goiə| city in central Japan, a center of heavy industry on the S coast of the island of Honshu, capital of Chubu region. Pop. 2,155,000.

**Nag·pur** |,näg'pŏŏr| city in central India, in the state of Maharashtra. Pop. 1,622,000. The former center of the Gond dynasty, it is now an administrative and commercial center.

**Nags Head** |'nægs hed| resort town in E North Carolina, in the Outer Banks. Pop. 1,838.

**Na·ha** |'nähä| industrial port in S Japan, capital of Okinawa island. Pop. 305,000.

**Na·ha·vand** |nähə'vænd| (also **Nehavand**) commercial town in W Iran, S of Hamadan. Pop. 59,000. The Arabs defeated the Persians here c.641, marking the de facto end of the Persian Empire.

**Na·huel Hua·pí** |nä'welwä'pē| lake in W central Argentina, in the Andes near the Chilean border. The ski resort of San Carlos de Bariloche lies on its S, and the lake and surrounding national park are also popular.

**Nairn·shire** |'nærnsнēr; 'nærnsнir| former county of NE Scotland, on the Moray Firth. It was part of the Highland region in 1975–96

**Nai·ro·bi** |nī'rōbē| the capital of Kenya. Pop. 1,346,000. It is situated on the central Kenyan plateau at an altitude of 5,500 ft./1,680 m., and is an administrative, commercial, light industrial, and tourist center.

**Na·jaf** |'näjäf| (also **An Najaf**) city in S Iraq, on the Euphrates. Pop. 243,000. It contains the shrine of Ali, the prophet Muhammad's son-in-law, and is a holy city for the Shiite Muslims.

**Na·khi·che·van** |ˌnäkəCHəˈvän| see NAX-ÇIVAN, Azerbaijan.

**Na·khod·ka** |nəˈkawtkə| port and naval base in extreme E Russia, on the Sea of Japan E of Vladivostok. Pop. 163,000. It is the E terminus of the Trans-Siberian Railroad.

**Na·khon Pa·thom** |nəkawn päˈtəm| city in SW Thailand, NW of Bangkok. Pop. 45,000. The most sacred Buddhist shrine in Thailand is here.

**Na·khon Rat·cha·si·ma** |nəkawn räCHə-sēmä| (also **Khorat; Korat**) commercial city in NE Thailand, on the Takhong River. Pop. 204,000.

**Na·ku·ru** |nəˈkŏŏrŏŏ| industrial city in W Kenya. Pop. 163,000. Nearby is Lake Nakuru, famous for its spectacular flocks of flamingos.

**Nal·chik** |ˈnälCHik| city in the Caucasus, SW Russia, capital of the republic of Kabardino-Balkaria. Pop. 237,000.

**Na·man·gan** |ˌnämənˈgän| city in E Uz-bekistan, an agricultural processing center near the border with Kyrgyzstan. Pop. 312,000.

**Na·ma·qua·land** |nəˈmäkwəˌlænd| region in SW Africa, the homeland of the Nama people. **Little Namaqualand** lies immediately to the S of the Orange River and is in the South African province of Northern Cape, while **Great Namaqualand** lies to the N of the river, in Namibia.

**Na·men** |ˈnämən| Flemish name for NAMUR, Belgium.

**Na·mib Desert** |ˈnämib| desert of SW Africa. It extends for 1,200 mi./1,900 km. along the Atlantic coast, from the Curoca River in SW Angola through Namibia to the border between Namibia and South Africa.

**Na·mib·ia** |nəˈmibēə| republic in SW Africa, on the Atlantic. Area: 318,382 sq. mi./824,292 sq. km. Pop. 1,834,000. Languages, English, Bantu and Khoisan languages, Afrikaans. Capital and largest city:

Namibia

Windhoek. Formerly controlled by Germany, then South Africa, and known as South West Africa, Namibia gained independence in 1990. Largely desert, it has an economy based on livestock raising, fishing, and mining. □ **Namibian** adj. & n.

**Nam·po** |ˈnämˈpō| (also **Chinnampo**) industrial city in W North Korea, SW of Pyongyang, for which it is the port. Pop. 691,000.

**Nam·pu·la** |nämˈpŏŏlə| commercial city in NE Mozambique, capital of Nampula province. Pop. 203,000.

**Na·mur** |nəˈmŏŏr| **1** province in central Belgium. It was the scene of the last German offensive in the Ardennes in 1945. Flemish name **Namen**. **2** the capital of this province, at the junction of the Meuse and Sambre rivers. Pop. 103,000.

**Na·nai·mo** |nəˈnīˌmō| lumbering port on the E coast of Vancouver Island in British Columbia. Pop. 60,129.

**Nan·chang** |nänˈCHäNG| industrial city in SE China, capital of Jiangxi province. Pop. 1,330,000.

**Nan·cy** |ˈnænsē| industrial and cultural city in NE France, chief town of Lorraine. Pop. 102,000.

**Nan·ded** |ˈnänded| (also **Nander**) commercial city in central India, in Maharashtra state. Pop. 309,000. It is an important Sikh pilgrimage site.

**Nan·ga Par·bat** |ˈnəNGgə ˈpərbət| mountain in N Pakistan, highest peak in the W Himalayas. It rises to 26,660 ft./8,126 m.

**Nan·jing** |nænˈjiNG| (formerly **Nanking**) industrial city and capital of Jiangsu province, E China, on the Yangtze River. Pop. 3,682,000. It was the capital of China from 1368 to 1421 and from 1912 to 1937. The bloody Japanese capture of the city (1937) during the Second Sino-Japanese War is known as the "rape of Nanking."

**Nan·ning** |ˈnänˈdziNG| industrial city, the capital of Guangxi Zhuang autonomous region in S China. Pop. 1,070,000.

**Nan·terre** |nänˈter| industrial city, capital of the Hauts-de-Seine department, and a W suburb of Paris, in N central France. Pop. 96,000.

**Nantes** |nänt| historic port city in W France, on the Loire, chief town of Pays de la Loire region. Pop. 252,000.

**Nan·tong** |ˈnänˈtŏŏNG| (formerly **Nantung**) port city in Jiangsu province, E central China, near the mouth of the Yangtze River. Pop. 343,000. It is a special economic zone and textile center.

**Nan·tuck·et** |nænˈtəkət| island off the

coast of Massachusetts, S of Cape Cod and E of Martha's Vineyard. It was an important whaling center in the 18th and 19th centuries. It is now a summer resort.

**Nan·yang** |ˈnänˈyäNG| city in Henan province, E central China, on the Bai River, SW of Zhengzhou. Pop. 304,000.

**Na·pa** |ˈnæpə| commercial city in N central California, the hub of the wine-making Napa Valley. Pop. 61,842.

**Na·per·ville** |ˈnäpərˌvil| city in NE Illinois, an outer suburb W of Chicago, with many high-technology businesses. Pop. 85,351.

**Na·pier** |ˈnäpēər| seaport on Hawke Bay, North Island, New Zealand. Pop. 52,000.

**Na·ples**[1] |ˈnäpəlz| resort city in SW Florida, on the Gulf of Mexico. Pop. 19,505.

**Na·ples**[2] |ˈnäpəlz| port city on the W coast of Italy, capital of Campania region. Pop. 1,206,000. It was formerly the capital of the kingdom of Naples and Sicily (1816–60). Italian name **Napoli**. □ **Neapolitan** adj. & n.

**Na·po·li** |ˈnäpōlē| Italian name for NAPLES[2].

**Na·ra** |ˈnärä| city in central Japan, on the island of Honshu. Pop. 349,000. It was the first capital of Japan (710–784) and an important center of Japanese Buddhism.

**Na·ra·shi·no** |näräˈsHēnō| city in E central Japan, on E central Honshu, an industrial suburb E of Tokyo. Pop. 151,000.

**Na·ra·yan·ganj** |nəˈräyən͵gənj| river port in Bangladesh, on the Ganges delta SE of Dhaka. Pop. 406,000.

**Nar·bonne** |närˈbawn| city in S France, in Languedoc-Roussillon, just inland from the Mediterranean. Pop. 47,000. It was founded by the Romans in 118 B.C. as the capital of Gallia Narbonensis, and was a prosperous medieval port until its harbor silted up in the 14th century.

**Na·ri·ta** |näˈrētə| city in E central Japan, on E central Honshu. Pop. 87,000. The Tokyo International Airport is here.

**Nar·ma·da** |nərˈmədə| river that rises in Madhya Pradesh, central India, and flows generally W for 778 mi./1,245 km. to the Gulf of Cambay. It is regarded by Hindus as sacred.

**Nar·ra·gan·sett Bay** |͵nerəˈgænsit| inlet of the Atlantic in S and central Rhode Island. Providence, Newport, and many resorts lie on it.

**Nar·va** |ˈnärvə| industrial city in NE Estonia, on the Narva River. Pop. 82,000. It is a major textile-manufacturing center.

**Nar·vik** |ˈnär͵vik| ice-free port on the NW coast of Norway, N of the Arctic Circle.

Pop. 19,000. It is an iron-ore exporting center.

**Nase·by** |ˈnäzbē| village in central England, in Northamptonshire, scene of the last major battle (1645) of the English Civil War, in which Parliamentary armies won a conclusive victory.

**Nash·ua** |ˈnæsHəwə| industrial city on the Merrimack River in S New Hampshire. Pop. 79,662.

**Nash·ville** |ˈnæsH͵vil| the state capital of Tennessee. Pop. 488,374. It is a financial and commercial center, also known for its music industry, and is the site of Opryland U.S.A. (an entertainment complex) and the Country Music Hall of Fame.

**Na·sik** |ˈnäsik| (also **Nashik**) city in W India, in Maharashtra, on the Godavari River NE of Bombay. Pop. 647,000.

**Nas·sau**[1] |ˈnä͵saw| port on the island of New Providence, capital of the Bahamas and a resort and financial center. Pop. 172,000.

**Nas·sau**[2] |ˈnä͵saw| former duchy of western Germany, centered on the small town of Nassau, from which a branch of the House of Orange arose. It corresponds to parts of the present-day states of Hesse and Rhineland-Palatinate.

**Nas·sau County** |ˈnä͵saw| county in central Long Island, New York, immediately E of Queens and home to many New York suburbs. Pop. 1,287,348.

**Nas·ser, Lake** |ˈnäsər| lake in SE Egypt created in the 1960s by the building of two dams on the Nile at Aswan.

**Na·tal**[1] |nəˈtäl| port on the Atlantic coast of NE Brazil, capital of the state of Rio Grande do Norte. Pop. 606,000.

**Na·tal**[2] |nəˈtäl| former province of South Africa, on the E coast. Having been a Boer republic and then a British colony, it acquired internal self-government in 1893 and became a province of the Union of South Africa in 1910. The province was renamed KwaZulu/Natal in 1994.

**Natch·ez** |ˈnæcHiz| historic port city on the Mississippi River in SW Mississippi. Pop. 19,460. The **Natchez Trace**, leading from here to Nashville, Tennessee, was a 19th-century route for riverboatmen returning N from trips to New Orleans.

**Na·tion·al City** |ˈnæsHənəl| city in SW California, S of San Diego, site of numerous naval facilities. Pop. 54,249.

**Na·tion·al·ist Chi·na** term once used for the Chinese government established on Taiwan after 1949, for many years the only Chinese government recognized by the US.

**Na·tion·al Road** |'næsHənəl| historic highway that in the early 19th century led from Maryland through the Appalachian Mts., to St. Louis, Missouri. It was once the major route for W expansion.

**NATO** |'nātō| acronym for the NORTH ATLANTIC TREATY ORGANIZATION.

**Nat·ron, Lake** |'nātrən| lake in N Tanzania, on the border with Kenya, containing large deposits of salt and soda.

**Na·u·cal·pan de Jua·rez** |now'kälpän dä 'hwäres| industrial city in central Mexico, a suburb on the NW side of Mexico City. Pop. 773,000.

**Nau·cra·tis** |'nawkrətis| ancient Greek commercial city in N Egypt, SE of present-day Damanhur.

**Nau·ga·tuck** |'nawgə,tək| industrial borough in SW Connecticut, on the Naugatuck River next to Waterbury. Pop. 30,625.

**Nau·plia** |'nawplēə| (also called **Na**) port on the Gulf of Argolis in S Greece. Pop. 11,000. It was the first capital of independent Greece. The ruins of the ancient city of Tiryns are nearby.

**Na·u·ru** |nä'ōōrōō| island republic in the SW Pacific, near the equator. Area: 8 sq. mi./21 sq. km. Pop. 10,000. Languages, Nauruan (an Austronesian language) and English; no official capital. Independent since 1968, it has the world's richest deposits of phosphates. □ **Nauruan** *adj. & n.*

**Nauru**

**Na·vad·wip** |nəvəd'vēp; nəvəd'wēp| (also **Nabadwip**; formerly **Nadia**) commercial and industrial city in E India, in West Bengal state. Pop. 155,000. It is a noted Hindu educational center.

**Nav·an** |'nævən| the county seat of Meath, in the Republic of Ireland. Pop. 3,000.

**Na·va·ri·no** |,nævə'rēnō| (Greek name **Pylos**) seaport in SW Peloponnese, Greece. Nearby are the ruins of an ancient Mycenaean city. In 1827 Greeks and their allies defeated Turkish and Egyptian naval forces here.

**Na·varre** |nə'vär| autonomous region of N Spain, on the border with France. Capital: Pamplona. It represents the S part of the former kingdom of Navarre, which was conquered by Ferdinand in 1512 and attached to Spain, while the N part passed to France in 1589 through inheritance by Henry IV. Spanish name **Navarra**.

**Na·vas·sa Island** |nä'väsə| island in the Caribbean Sea W of Haiti, held by the U.S. and used as a Coast Guard base.

**Na·vo·joa** |nä'vōhōä| commercial city in NW Mexico, in Sonora state, an agricultural processing center. Pop. 83,000.

**Na·vo·tas** |nä'vōtä| (also **Nabotas**) port town in the Philippines, on S Luzon. Pop. 187,000. It is the largest fishing port in the Philippines.

**Nav·pak·tos** |'näfpäktōs| (in Italian **Lepanto**) port in central Greece, on the Gulf of Corinth. In the Battle of Lepanto, in 1571, Christian naval forces under Don John of Austria defeated those of the Ottoman Empire.

**Na·wab·ganj** |nə'wäbgənj| commercial city in W Bangladesh, NW of Rajshahi. Pop. 121,000.

**Nax·çi·van** |nəkēCHi'vän| **1** predominantly Muslim Azerbaijani autonomous republic, situated on the borders of Turkey and N Iran and separated from the rest of Azerbaijan by a narrow strip of Armenia. Pop. 300,000. Russian name **Nakhichevan**. **2** the capital city of this republic. Pop. 51,000.

**Nax·os** |'näksōs| Greek island in the S Aegean, the largest (165 sq. mi./428 sq. km.) of the Cyclades. Pop. 14,000. It is associated with the legend of Theseus and Ariadne.

**Na·ya·rit** |,nīyä'rēt| state of W Mexico, the Pacific coast. Area: 10,420 sq. mi./26,979 sq. km. Pop. 816,000. Capital: Tepic.

**Naz·a·reth** |'næzərəTH| historic town in lower Galilee, in present-day N Israel. Pop. 39,000. Mentioned in the Gospels as the home of Mary and Joseph, it is closely associated with the childhood of Jesus and is a center of Christian pilgrimage.

**Naz·ca** |'näskä| (also **Nasca**) city and province in SW Peru, noted for the artifacts of a pre-Incan civilization, especially the huge "Nazca lines" on the desert floor. Pop. 23,000.

**N'Dja·me·na** |ənjä'mänə| the capital of Chad. Pop. 531,000. Former name (1900–1973) Fort Lamy. It is a communications, agricultural processing, and university center.

**Ndo·la** |ən'dōlə| commercial city in the Copperbelt region of central Zambia. Pop. 376,000.

**Neagh, Lough** |'läk 'na| shallow lake in Northern Ireland, the largest (147 sq. mi./382 sq. km.) freshwater lake in the British Isles.

**Ne·an·der·thal** |nē'ændər,tawl| valley E of Düsseldorf, in western Germany, where remains of the first fossil to be identified as belonging to *Homo sapiens*, or modern man, were found in 1856; the skeleton was called Neanderthal man.

**Near East** |,nēr 'ēst| (**the Near East**) a term originally applied to the Balkan states of SE Europe, but now generally applied to the countries of SW Asia between the Mediterranean and India (including the Middle East), especially in historical contexts. □ **Near Eastern** *adj.*

**Near Islands** |nēr| island group at the W end of the Aleutian Islands, in SW Alaska. Attu is one of the Near Islands.

**Neath** |nēTH| industrial town in S Wales on the Neath River. Pop. 49,000. Welsh name **Castell-Nedd.**

**Neb·li·na, Pico da** see PICO DA NEBLINA, Brazil.

**Ne·bo, Mount** |'nēbō| biblical mountain, identified with a peak in N central Jordan, NE of the Dead Sea, from which Moses viewed the Promised Land. Pisgah is an alternate name, or the name of one part of Mount Nebo.

**Ne·bras·ka** |nə'bræskə| see box. □ **Nebraskan** *adj. & n.*

**Neck·ar** |'nekär| river of western Germany, which rises in the Black Forest and flows 228 mi./367 km. N and W through Stuttgart to meet the Rhine at Mannheim.

**Ne·der·land** |'nādər,lænd| Dutch name for the NETHERLANDS.

**Nee·nah** |'nēnə| city in E Wisconsin, on the Fox River, a flour and paper-milling center. Pop. 23,219.

**Ne·gri Sem·bi·lan** |'nāgərē səm'bēlən| state of Malaysia, on the SW coast of the Malay Peninsula. Pop. 724,000. Capital: Seremban.

**Neg·ev** |'ne,gev| (also **the Negev**) an arid region forming most of S Israel, between Beersheba and the Gulf of Aqaba, on the Egyptian border. Large areas are irrigated for agriculture.

**Ne·gom·bo** |nā'gawm,bō| port and resort on the W coast of Sri Lanka, N of Colombo. Pop. 61,000.

---

### Nebraska

**Capital:** Lincoln
**Largest city:** Omaha
**Other cities:** Fremont, Grand Island, Hastings, North Platte, Scottsbluff
**Population:** 1,578,385 (1990); 1,662,719 (1998); 1,761,000 (2005 proj.)
**Population rank (1990):** 36
**Rank in land area:** 16
**Abbreviation:** NE; Neb. or Nebr.
**Nickname:** Cornhusker State; Tree Planters' State
**Motto:** 'Equality Before the Law'
**Bird:** Western meadowlark
**Flower:** goldenrod
**Tree:** cottonwood
**Song:** "Beautiful Nebraska"
**Noted physical features:** Badlands; Sand Hills, Drift Hills, Loess Hills; Chimney Rock; Ogalla Aquifer
**Tourist attractions:** Boys' Town; Scott's Bluff and Agate Fossil Beds national monuments
**Admission date:** March 1, 1867
**Order of admission:** 37
**Name origin:** From the Oto Indian word *nebrathka*, meaning 'flat water,' applied to both the Platte and Nebraska rivers.

---

**Neg·ril** |'negril| resort township near the W end of Jamaica, noted for its beaches.

**Ne·gro, Rio** |'rēō 'nāgrō| see RIO NEGRO.

**Ne·gros** |'nāgrōs| island in the Visayan group, the fourth-largest of the Philippines. Pop. 3,182,000; chief city, Bacolod.

**Nei·jiang** |'nā'jyæNG| river port and rail center in Sichuan province, central China, on the Tuo River, W of Chongqing. Pop. 310,000.

**Neis·se¹** |'nīsə| river in central Europe, which rises in the N of the Czech Republic and flows over 140 mi./225 km. generally N, forming the S part of the border between Germany and Poland (the Oder–Neisse Line) and joining the Oder River NE of Cottbus. German name **Lausitzer Neisse**; Polish name **Nysa Luzycka.**

**Neis·se²** |'nīsə| river of S Poland, which rises near the border with the Czech Republic and flows 120 mi./195 km. generally NE, through the town of Nysa, joining the Oder River SE of Wrocław. German name **Glatzer Neisse.** Polish name **Nysa Klodzka.**

**Nei·va** |'nävä| commercial city in S central

Colombia, on the Magdalena River, the capital of Huila department. Pop. 233,000.

**Nejd** |nejd| arid plateau region in central Saudi Arabia, N of the Rub' al Khali desert, at an altitude of about 5,000 ft./1,500 m. It is home to many Bedouins, who gather in its oases.

**Nel•lore** |ne'lawr| port city in SE India, in Andhra Pradesh, on the Penner River. Pop. 316,000. Situated close to the mouth of the river, it is one of the chief ports of the Coromandel Coast.

**Nel•son** |'nelsən| port in New Zealand, on the N coast of South Island. Pop. 47,000.

**Nel•son River** |'nelsən| river that flows 400 mi./640 km. across E Manitoba, to Hudson Bay. Once a fur trade route, it is now an important source of hydroelectric power.

**Nels•pru•it** |nels'proit| town in E South Africa, the capital of the province of Mpumalanga, situated on the Crocodile River to the W of Kruger National Park. Pop. 62,000.

**Ne•man** |'nemən| river of E Europe, which rises S of Minsk in Belarus and flows 597 mi./955 km. W and N to the Baltic Sea. Its lower course, which forms the boundary between Lithuania and the Russian enclave of Kaliningrad, is called the Memel. Lithuanian name **Nemunas**, Belorussian name **Nyoman**.

**Ne•mea** |'nēmēə| city of ancient Greece, in N Argolis. A great Temple of Zeus was located here. It was home to the Nemean Games, which drew participants from all over Greece and which took place in the second and fourth years of each Olympiad. □ **Nemean** adj.

**Ne•mi, Lake** |'nāmē| lake in the Alban Hills, central Italy, SE of Rome. In ancient times there were a temple and a grove to Diana nearby.

**Ne•mours** |nə'mŏōr| town, SE suburb of Paris, in N central France. Pop. 12,000.

**Nen River** |'nən| (Chinese name **Nen Jiang**; formerly **Nonni River**) river, NE China, the chief tributary of the Sungari. It flows 740 mi./1,190 km. S from the Da Hinggan Ling mountains to the Sungari W of Harbin.

**Ne•nets** |ne'nets| autonomous region in N Russia, comprising the tundra coast N of the Komi Republic. Pop. 55,000. Its people, the Nenets, are also known as Samoyeds.

**Ne•o•sho River** |nē'ōsHō| (also, **Grand River**) river that flows 460 mi./740 km. from central Kansas through NE Oklahoma, into the Arkansas River.

**Ne•pal** |ˌnaˈpäl| mountainous landlocked kingdom in S Asia, in the Himalayas (and including Mount Everest). Area: 56,849 sq. mi./147,181 sq. km. Pop. 19,406,000. Language, Nepali. Capital and largest city: Kathmandu. Conquered by the Gurkhas in the 18th century, Nepal has since remained independent. It exports clothing, carpets, leather, and grain. □ **Nepalese** adj. & n.

**Nepal**

**Ne•pe•an** |ni'pēən| city in SE Ontario, a research and industrial center on the SW side of Ottawa. Pop. 107,627.

**Ne•se•bur** |ne'sebər| historic town in E Bulgaria, on the Black Sea. Pop. 9,000. The ancient Mesembria, it now draws tourists.

**Loch Ness** |'lawk 'nes| deep lake in NW Scotland, in the Great Glen. Forming part of the Caledonian Canal, it is 24 miles (38 km) long, with a maximum depth of 755 ft. (230 m). It is well known as home to an aquatic monster whose existence has been disputed for centuries.

**Neth•er•lands** |'neTHərlən(d)z| **1** kingdom in W Europe, on the North Sea. Area: 14,412 sq. mi./37,313 sq. km. Pop. 15,010,000. Language, Dutch. Capital: Amsterdam; seat of government, The Hague. Dutch name **Nederland**. Also called **Holland**. Independent since 1648, the Netherlands has been a leading colonial power. Low and densely populated, it has a maritime and industrial economy. **2**

**Netherlands**

*hist.* the Low Countries. □ **Netherlander** *n.* **Netherlandish** *adj.*

**Neth·er·lands An·til·les** |'neᴛнərlən(d)z æn'tilēz| two widely separated groups of islands in the Caribbean, in the Lesser Antilles. Capital: Willemstad, on Curaçao. Pop. 189,000. The southernmost group, just off the N coast of Venezuela, comprises Bonaire and Curaçao, and until 1986 also included Aruba. The N group comprises St. Eustatius, St. Martin, and Saba. The islands were visited in the 16th century by the Spanish and were settled by the Dutch in the mid-17th century. In 1954 they were granted self-government and became an autonomous region of the Netherlands.

**Netherlands Antilles**

**Ne·tza·hual·có·yotl** |nāt,säwäl'kō,yōtl| (also **Ciudad Netzahualcóyotl**) city in central Mexico, in México state, a suburban part of the Mexico City area. Pop. 1,255,000.

**Neu·bran·den·burg** |noi'brändənbərg| industrial city in NE Germany. Pop. 88,000.

**Neu·châ·tel, Lake** |nōōsнä'tel| the largest lake lying wholly within Switzerland, situated at the foot of the Jura Mts. in W Switzerland.

**Neu·châ·tel** |,nōōsнə'tel| canton in the Jura Mts. of W Switzerland. Pop. 161,000. Its capital is Neuchâtel.

**Neuilly-sur-Seine** |noi'yēsərsän| city, a suburb of Paris, in N central France. Pop. 64,000. Primarily a wealthy residential community, Neuilly also has some industry. The American Hospital of Paris is here.

**Neu·mün·ster** |noi'mōōnster| industrial city and transportation center in NW Germany, N of Hamburg. Pop.81,000.

**Neun·kir·chen** |noin'kirkhən| industrial city in NW Germany. Pop. 52,000.

**Neu·quén** |neōō'kän| city in W Argentina, the capital of Neuqén province. Pop. (with nearby Plottier) 183,000. On the Neuquén River, it is a port and agricultural processing center.

**Neu·sie·dler See** |'noi,zēdlər,zā| shallow lake in the steppe region between E Austria and NW Hungary. Hungarian name **Fertö Tó.**

**Neuss** |nois| industrial city and canal port in western Germany, on the Rhine River, W of Düsseldorf. Pop. 148,000.

**Neu·stadt an der Wein·stras·se** |'noisнtät än der 'vīnsнträsə| industrial city and wine center in western Germany, W of the Rhine River and SW of Mannheim. Pop. 53,000.

**Neus·tria** |'nōōstreə| in France, during the Merovingian dynasty (6th–8th centuries), the western portion of the kingdom of the Franks. It consisted of the area around the Seine and the Loire rivers and lands to the north.

**Neu·tral Zone** |'nōōtrəl 'zōn| area between N Saudi Arabia and SE Iraq, W of Kuwait, that formerly had no recognized sovereignty but is now divided, roughly equally, between Saudi Arabia and Iraq.

**Ne·va** |'nyēvə| river in NW Russia that flows 46 mi./74 km. W from Lake Ladoga to the Gulf of Finland, passing through St. Petersburg. Alexander Nevsky took his name from this river after defeating the Swedes here in 1240.

**Ne·va·da** |nə'vædə| see box. □ **Nevadan** *adj. & n.*

| Nevada | | |
| --- | --- | --- |
| **Capital:** Carson City | | |
| **Largest city:** Las Vegas | | |
| **Other cities:** Reno | | |
| **Population:** 1,201,833 (1990); 1,746,898 (1998); 2,070,000 (2005 proj.) | | |
| **Population rank (1990):** 39 | | |
| **Rank in land area:** 7 | | |
| **Abbreviation:** NV; Nev. | | |
| **Nickname:** Silver State; Sagebrush State | | |
| **Motto:** 'All for Our Country' | | |
| **Bird:** mountain bluebird | | |
| **Fish:** Lahontan cutthroat trout | | |
| **Flower:** sagebrush | | |
| **Tree:** single-leaf pinon; bristlecone pine | | |
| **Song:** "Home Means Nevada" | | |
| **Noted physical features:** Great Basin; Gypsum Cave; Sonoran Desert; Lake Mead; Columbia Plateau; Boundary Peak | | |
| **Tourist attractions:** Las Vegas; Comstock Lode; Davis and Hoover dams; Tule, Punch Bowl, and Steam Boat hot springs | | |
| **Admission date:** October 31, 1864 | | |
| **Order of admission:** 36 | | |
| **Name origin:** From the Spanish word *nevada*, meaning 'snow-covered,' shortened from Sierra Nevada, the mountain range in western Nevada along the California border. | | |

**Never-Never** |'nevər'nevər| **1** the unpopulated desert country of the interior of Australia; the remote outback. **2 (Never-Never Land** or **Country)** a region of Northern Territory, Australia, SE of Darwin; chief town, Katherine.

**Ne·vers** |nə'ver| city in central France, on the Loire. Pop. 44,000. It was capital of the former province of Nivernais.

**Ne·ves** |'nevis| city in SE Brazil, an industrial suburb NE of Rio de Janeiro and just N of Niterói, on Guanabara Bay. Pop. 151,000.

**Ne·vis** |'nēvis| one of the Leeward Islands in the Caribbean, part of St. Kitts and Nevis. Pop. 9,000. Capital: Charlestown. □ **Nevisian** adj. & n.

**Nev·sky Pros·pekt** |'nevskē 'prawspekt| main thoroughfare in Saint Petersburg, Russia, along which are ranged the Winter Palace, the Hermitage, and other buildings of historic and architectural interest.

**New Al·ba·ny** |n(y)ōō 'awlbənē| industrial city in S Indiana, across the Ohio River from Louisville, Kentucky Pop. 36,322.

**New Am·ster·dam** |n(y)ōō 'æm(p)stər ,dæm| former name for NEW YORK CITY.

**New·ark**[1] |'n(y)ōō,ärk| city in NW Delaware, home to the University of Delaware. Pop. 25,098.

**New·ark**[2] |'n(y)ōōwərk| industrial port city in N New Jersey, the largest city in the state. Pop. 275,221.

**New·ark**[3] |'n(y)ōōwərk| industrial and commercial city in central Ohio. Pop. 44,389.

**New Bed·ford** |n(y)ōō 'bedfərd| industrial port city in SE Massachusetts, on Buzzards Bay, a famed 19th-century whaling center. Pop. 99,922.

**New Bern** |'n(y)ōō 'bərn| historic commercial city in E North Carolina. Pop. 17,363.

**New Braun·fels** |n(y)ōō 'brownfəlz| city in S central Texas. Pop. 27,334.

**New Brit·ain**[1] |'n(y)ōō 'britən| industrial city in central Connecticut, noted for its hardware manufacturing. Pop. 75,491.

**New Brit·ain**[2] |'n(y)ōō 'britən| mountainous island in the South Pacific, largest of the Bismarcks and part of Papua New Guinea, lying off the NE coast of New Guinea. Pop. 312,000. Capital: Rabaul.

**New Bruns·wick**[1] |,n(y)ōō 'brənz,wik| city in central New Jersey, on the Raritan River, home to Rutgers, the state university. Pop. 41,711.

**New Bruns·wick**[2] |,n(y)ōō 'brənz,wik| maritime province on the SE coast of Canada. Area: 28,355 sq. mi./73,440 sq. km. Pop.

723,900. Capital: Fredericton. Largest city: St. John. Settled in the early 17th century by the French, the area was ceded to Britain in 1713. New Brunswick, created in 1784 from Nova Scotia, became one of the original four provinces in the Dominion of Canada in 1867. Tourism, fishing, mining, and forest industries are important.

**New·burgh** |'n(y)ōō,bərg| historic industrial city in SE New York, on the Hudson River. Pop. 26,454.

**New·bury·port** |'n(y)ōōbərēpawrt| historic port city, now chiefly residential, in NE Massachusetts, at the mouth of the Merrimack River. Pop. 16,317.

**New Cal·e·do·nia** |,n(y)ōō ,kælə'dōnēə| island in the South Pacific, E of Australia. Pop. 178,000. Capital: Nouméa. Since 1946 it has formed, with its dependencies, a French overseas territory. It was inhabited by Melanesians for at least 3,000 years before the French annexed the island in 1853, and after the discovery of nickel in 1863 it assumed some economic importance for France. There has been a movement for independence in recent years. □ **New Caledonian** adj. & n.

**New Caledonia**

**New·cas·tle** |'n(y)ōō,kæsəl| industrial port on the SE coast of Australia, in New South Wales. Pop. 262,000.

**Newcastle-under-Lyme** |'n(y)ōō,kæsəl ,əndər līm| industrial town in Staffordshire, W central England, just SW of Stoke-on-Trent. Pop. 117,000.

**Newcastle-upon-Tyne** |'n(y)ōō,kæsəl ə,pän 'tīn| industrial city in NE England, a port on the River Tyne. Pop. 263,000. It was long famed for its coal.

**New·chwang** |'nōō'CHWäNG; 'nyōō-'CHWäNG| see YINGKOU, China.

**New Del·hi** |,n(y)ōō 'delē| see DELHI, India.

**New Eng·land** |,n(y)ōō 'iNG(g)lənd| area in the NE U.S., comprising the states of

Maine, New Hampshire, Vermont, Massachusetts, Rhode Island, and Connecticut. The name was originally applied to the region by the English explorer John Smith in 1614. □ **New Englander** n.

**New Forest** |ˌn(y)o͞o 'fawrəst| area of heath and woodland in S Hampshire, S England. It has been reserved as Crown property since 1079, originally as a royal hunting area, and is noted for its ponies.

**New·found·land** |'n(y)o͞ofən(d)lən(d)| island off the E coast of Canada, at the mouth of the St. Lawrence River. Area: 43,359 sq. mi./112,300 sq. km. A British colony from the 16th century, in 1949 it was united with Labrador (as Newfoundland and Labrador) to form a province of Canada. Fishing, forest industries, mining, and oil are important to the economy. □ **Newfoundlander** n.

**New·found·land and Lab·ra·dor** |'n(y)o͞ofən(d)lən(d) ænd 'læbrə,daw(ə)r| province of Canada, comprising the island of Newfoundland and the Labrador coast of the Ungava Peninsula. Area: 156,649 sq. mi./404,517 sq. km. Pop. 568,474. Capital: St. John's. Newfoundland was united with Labrador and joined the Dominion of Canada in 1949. The provincial economy relies on fishing, mining, and forest industries.

**New France** term for French colonial area in the New World.

**New·gate** |'n(y)o͞o,gāt| former prison in London, England, at the W gate to the City, on a site today occupied by the Central Criminal Court. It was notorious for its unsanitary conditions. It burned during a 1780 riot.

**New Geor·gia** |ˌn(y)o͞o 'jawrjə| volcanic island group in the W central Solomon Islands. **New Georgia Sound**, along the N side, was called "the Slot" by Americans during World War II, when the area saw heavy fighting with Japanese forces.

**New Gra·na·da** |ˌn(y)o͞o grə'nädə| (Spanish name **Nuevo Granada**) former Spanish colony, a viceroyalty, roughly comprising present-day Colombia, Panama, Ecuador, and Venezuela. Colombia and Panama were called New Granada 1819–58.

**New Guin·ea** |ˌn(y)o͞o 'ginē| island in the W S Pacific, off the N coast of Australia, the second-largest (305,000 sq. mi./790,000 sq. km.) island in the world (after Greenland). It comprises two political divisions; the W half is part of Irian Jaya, a province of Indonesia, the E half forms part of Papua New Guinea. □ **New Guinean** adj. & n.

**New·ham** |'n(y)o͞oəm| industrial and residential borough of E London, England. Pop. 200,000. In the docklands area of London, it incorporates East Ham and West Ham.

**New Hamp·shire** |ˌn(y)o͞o 'hæm(p)sHər| see box.

**New Ha·ven** |'n(y)o͞ohāvən| industrial city in S central Connecticut, on Long Island Sound, home to Yale University. Pop. 130,474.

**New·ha·ven** |ˌn(y)o͞o'hāvən| port town in S England, in East Sussex, a terminus for ferries across the English Channel. Pop. 10,000.

**New Heb·ri·des** |ˌn(y)o͞o 'hebrədēz| former name (until 1980) for VANUATU.

**New Hope** |'no͞o 'hōp| borough in SE Pennsylvania, on the Delaware River, a well-known tourist destination and artists' colony. Pop. 1,400.

**New Ibe·ria** |ˌn(y)o͞o i'birēə| city in S Louisiana, on the Bayou Teche in Cajun Country, in a salt- and oil-producing area. Pop. 31,828.

**New Ire·land** |ˌn(y)o͞o 'iərlənd| island in the South Pacific, part of Papua New Guinea, lying to the N of New Britain. Pop. 87,000. Capital: Kavieng.

---

### New Hampshire

**Capital:** Concord
**Largest city:** Manchester
**Other cities:** Dover, Nashua, Portsmouth
**Population:** 1,109,252 (1990); 1,185,048 (1998); 1,281,000 (2005 proj.)
**Population rank (1990):** 40
**Rank in land area:** 46
**Abbreviation:** NH; N.H.
**Nickname:** Granite State
**Motto:** 'Live Free or Die'
**Bird:** purple finch
**Flower:** purple lilac
**Tree:** white birch
**Song:** "Old New Hampshire"
**Noted physical features:** Lake Winnipesaukee; White Mountains
**Tourist attractions:** Great Stone Face; Mount Washington; Kinsman's Notch, Pinkham Notch, Crawford Notch, and Franconia Notch
**Admission date:** June 21, 1788
**Order of admission:** 9
**Name origin:** Named by Capt. John Mason (1586-1636) to honor the county of Hampshire, England; he received a grant to a portion of the territory later occupied by the colony and state.

## New Jersey

**Capital:** Trenton
**Largest city:** Newark
**Other cities:** Atlantic City, Camden, Jersey City, Paterson
**Population:** 7,730,188 (1990); 8,115,011 (1998); 8,392,000 (2005 proj.)
**Population rank (1990):** 9
**Rank in land area:** 47
**Abbreviation:** NJ; N.J.
**Nickname:** Garden State
**Motto:** 'Liberty and Prosperity'
**Bird:** Eastern goldfinch
**Flower:** purple violet
**Tree:** red oak
**Noted physical features:** Palisades, Sandy Hook; Delaware Bay; Cape May
**Tourist attractions:** Atlantic City; Jersey shore; Delaware Water Gap
**Admission date:** December 18, 1787
**Order of admission:** 3
**Name origin:** For the island of Jersey in the English Channel; probably named by James, Duke of York, for his friend, Sir George Carteret, who was born on Jersey and was its principal royal defender during the English Commonwealth.

## New Mexico

**Capital:** Santa Fe
**Largest city:** Albuquerque
**Other cities:** Las Cruces, Los Alamos, Roswell
**Population:** 1,515,069 (1990); 1,736,931 (1998); 2,016,000 (2005 proj.)
**Population rank (1990):** 37
**Rank in land area:** 5
**Abbreviation:** NM; N.M. or N. Mex.
**Nickname:** Land of Enchantment
**Motto:** Crescit Eundo (Latin: 'It Grows as it Goes')
**Bird:** roadrunner
**Fish:** cutthroat trout
**Flower:** yucca
**Tree:** pinon
**Song:** "O, Fair New Mexico"
**Noted physical features:** Tularosa Basin; Jornada de Muerto Desert; Wheeler Peak
**Tourist attractions:** Carlsbad Caverns; Four Corners; Butte and Elephant dams; Los Alamos National Laboratory
**Admission date:** January 6, 1912
**Order of admission:** 47
**Name origin:** Named by the Spanish explorer Francisco de Ilbarra in 1562 for the country of Mexico, of which it was a territory until the end of the Mexican War (1846-48).

**New Jer•sey** |ˌn(y) oo 'jərzē| see box.
◻ **New Jerseyan** n.

**New Lon•don** |ˌn(y)oo 'ləndən| industrial port city in SE Connecticut, across the Thames River from Groton and on Long Island Sound. Pop. 28,540.

**New Mad•rid** |ˌn(y)oo mə'drid| commercial city in SE Missouri, on the Mississippi River, in the center of an area devastated by an 1811 earthquake along the **New Madrid Fault.**

**New•mar•ket** |'n(y)oomärkət| town in Suffolk, SE England, a famed horse racing center. Pop. 16,000.

**New Mex•i•co** |ˌn(y)oo 'meksəkō| see box.
◻ **New Mexican** adj. & n.

**New Or•leans** |ˌn(y)oo 'awrlənz; ˌnoo or-'lēnz| river port in SE Louisiana, the largest city in the state, on the Mississippi; a major shipping and industrial center and tourist destination. Pop. 496,938. It was founded by the French in 1718; ceded to Spain in 1763, it was ceded back to France in 1803, then sold to the U.S. in the Louisiana Purchase. It is noted for its annual Mardi Gras celebrations and for its association with the development of jazz.

**New Plym•outh** |ˌn(y)oo 'plimərH| port in New Zealand, on the W coast of North Island. Pop. 49,000.

**New•port**[1] |'n(y)oo,pawrt| historic port city in S Rhode Island, on Rhode Island, famed as a resort and home to naval facilities. Pop. 28,277.

**New•port**[2] |'n(y)oo,pawrt| industrial town and port in S Wales, on the Bristol Channel. Pop. 130,000. Welsh name **Casnewydd.**

**New•port Beach** |'n(y)oo,pawrt| resort, residential, and industrial city in SW California, SE of Los Angeles. Pop. 66,643.

**New•port News** |'n(y)oo,pawrt| city in SE Virginia, at the mouth of the James River on the Hampton Roads estuary. Pop. 170,045. Settled around 1620, it is a major seaport and shipbuilding center.

**New Prov•i•dence** |n(y)oo 'prawvidəns| island in the central Bahamas, site of the capital, Nassau. Pop. 172,000. It is home to most of the people of the Bahamas.

**New Que•bec** |n(y)oo kwi'bek| (French name **Nouveau-Québec**) vast, lightly populated district of N Quebec, between Labrador and Hudson Bay, that was part of the Northwest Territories before 1912.

**New River** |n(y)oo 'rivər| river that flows 320 mi./515 km. from North Carolina through Virginia and into West Virginia, where it enters the Kanawha River.

**New Ro•chelle** |ˌn(y)ōō rə'sHel; rō'sHel| city in SE New York, a suburb NE of New York City, on Long Island Sound. Pop. 67,265.

**New•ry** |'n(y)ŏŏrē| industrial port town in the SE of Northern Ireland, in County Down. Pop. 19,000.

**New Si•be•ri•an Islands** |ˌn(y)ōō sī'bērēən| group of uninhabited islands in E Siberia, Russia, in the Arctic Ocean. They are divided into two parts by the Sannikov Strait.

**New South Wales** |ˌn(y)ōō ˌsoᴡᴛʜ 'wālz| state of SE Australia. Pop. 5,827,000. Capital: Sydney. First colonized from Britain in 1788, it was federated with the other states of Australia in 1901. Agriculture and mining are important.

**New Spain** |ˌn(y)ōō 'spān| former Spanish viceroyalty established in Central and North America in 1535, centered on present-day Mexico City. It comprised all the land under Spanish control N of the Isthmus of Panama, including parts of the S U.S. It also came to include the Spanish possessions in the Caribbean and the Philippines. The viceroyalty was abolished in 1821, when Mexico achieved independence.

**New Territories** |ˌn(y)ōō 'terə,tawrēz| part of Hong Kong along the S coast of mainland China, lying to the N of the Kowloon peninsula, also including the islands of Lantau, Tsing Yi, and Lamma. It comprises 92 percent of the land area of Hong Kong.

**New•ton** |'n(y)ōōtn| city in E Massachusetts, a residential and industrial suburb on the Charles River, W of Boston. Pop. 82,585.

**New•town•ab•bey** |'n(y)ōōtn'æbē| suburban town in E Northern Ireland, on Belfast Lough, just NE of Belfast, in County Antrim. Pop. 73,000.

**New West•min•ster** |n(y)ōō ,wes(t)'minstər| port city in SW British Columbia, a suburb E of Vancouver. Pop. 43,585.

**New World** |ˌn(y)ōō 'wərld| North and South America regarded collectively in relation to Europe, Asia, and Africa, especially after the early voyages of European explorers.

**New York** |'n(y)ōō 'yawrk| see box. □ **New Yorker** n.

**New York City** |ˌn(y)ōō 'yawrk| largest U.S. city, in the SE of New York State, a port on the Atlantic coast at the mouth of the Hudson River. Pop. 7,322,564. The city is situ-

---

### New York

**Capital:** Albany
**Largest city:** New York
**Other cities:** Binghamton, Buffalo, Islip, Rochester, Syracuse
**Population:** 17,990,455 (1990); 18,175,301 (1998); 18,250,000 (2005 proj.)
**Population rank (1990):** 3
**Rank in land area:** 27
**Abbreviation:** NY; N.Y.
**Nickname:** The Empire State; Excelsior State
**Motto:** *Excelsior* (Latin: 'Ever upward')
**Bird:** bluebird
**Fish:** brook or speckled trout
**Flower:** rose
**Tree:** sugar maple
**Song:** "I Love New York"
**Noted physical features:** Adirondack Mountains; Finger Lakes; Hudson Valley; Niagara Falls; Mohawk Valley
**Tourist attractions:** New York City (many sites); Baseball Hall of Fame; Fire Island
**Admission date:** July 26, 1788
**Order of admission:** 11
**Name origin:** For James, Duke of York and Albany (1633-1701), later King James II of England; name applied from 1664 as Yorkshire, to the territory east of the Hudson, later as New York, as distinct from New Jersey.

---

ated mainly on islands and comprises five boroughs: Manhattan, Brooklyn, the Bronx (on the mainland), Queens, and Staten Island. Manhattan is the economic and cultural heart of the city, with world-famous art galleries, museums, and theaters, the headquarters of many major corporations, and the Wall Street financial district. The Hudson River and Manhattan Island were discovered by European explorers in 1609, and in 1626 Dutch colonists are said to have purchased Manhattan Island from local Indians for merchandise traditionally valued at $24, establishing a settlement here that they called New Amsterdam. In 1664 it was captured by the British, who renamed it in honor of the Duke of York (later King James II). Because of the island's small area and population density Manhattan has been built upward, with many tall buildings that give it its characteristic skyline. □ **New Yorker** n.

**New Zea•land** |ˌn(y)ōō 'zēlənd| island country in the S Pacific about 1,200 mi./1,900 km. E of Australia. Area: 103,455 sq. mi./267,844 sq. km. Pop. 3,434,950. Languages, English (official), Maori. Capital: Wellington. Maori name **Aotearoa**. Maoris lived in the islands before the Dutch arrived in 1642. The British took control in 1840, and independence came in 1931. Agriculture, especially livestock raising and mining, form the backbone of the economy. □ **New Zealander** *n.*

**New Zealand**

**Ne·ya·ga·wa** |näyä'gäwä| city in W central Japan, on S Honshu, a suburb N of Osaka. Pop. 257,000.

**Ney·sha·bur** |näsHä'boŏr| (also **Nishapur**) historic commercial and cultural city in NE Iran, W of Mashhad. Pop. 136,000. In an agricultural region, it was a center of Persian life. The poet Omar Khayyam was born and is buried here.

**Nga·li·e·ma, Mount** |əNG,gäle'ämä| Congolese name for Mount Stanley (see STANLEY, MOUNT).

**Nga·mi·land** |əNG'gämē,lænd| region in NW Botswana, N of the Kalahari Desert. It includes the Okavango marshes and Lake Ngami.

**Ngo·ron·go·ro** |,əNGawrōNG'gōrō| extinct volcanic crater in the Great Rift Valley in NE Tanzania, 126 sq. mi./326 sq. km. in area.

**Nha Trang** |'nyä'träNG| commercial port city in southern Vietnam, Pop. 216,000. It is one of the main cultural, religious, and educational centers of Vietnam.

**Ni·ag·a·ra Falls** |nī'æg(ə)rə| **1** the waterfalls on the Niagara River, consisting of two principal parts separated by Goat Island: the Horseshoe Falls adjoining the W (Canadian) bank, which fall 158 ft./47 m., and the American Falls adjoining the E bank, which fall 167 ft./50 m. They are a popular tourist attraction, long a noted destination for honeymooners. In 1859 Charles Blondin was the first to walk across the gorge on a tightrope and in 1901 Annie Edson Taylor was the first person to go over

the falls in a barrel. **2** city in upper New York State situated on the E bank of the Niagara River beside the Falls. Pop. 61,840. **3** city in S Ontario, on the W bank of the Niagara River beside the Falls. Pop. 75,399.

**Ni·ag·a·ra River** |nī'æg(ə)rə| river of North America, flowing northward for 35 miles (56 km) from Lake Erie to Lake Ontario, and forming part of the border between Canada and the U.S. The Niagara Falls are halfway along its course. It is a major source of hydroelectric power.

**Nia·mey** |'nyä,mā| the capital of Niger, a commercial city and port on the Niger River. Pop. 410,000.

**Ni·caea** |nī'sēə| ancient city in Asia Minor, on the site of present-day Iznik, Turkey, which was important in Roman and Byzantine times. It was the site of two ecumenical councils of the early Christian Church (in 325 and 787).

**Nic·a·ra·gua, Lake** |nikə'rägwə| lake near the W coast of Nicaragua, the largest (3,100 sq. mi./8,029 sq. km.) lake in Central America. Granada is on its NW shore.

**Nic·a·ra·gua** |nikə'rägwə| the largest country in Central America, a republic with a coastline on both the Atlantic and the Pacific. Area: 46,448 sq. mi./120,254 sq. km. Pop. 3,975,000. Language, Spanish. Capital and largest city: Managua. A Spanish colony, Nicaragua gained full independence in 1838. Coffee, cotton, bananas, sugar, and meat are leading products. □ **Nicaraguan** *adj. & n.*

**Nicaragua**

**Nice** |nēs| resort city on the French Riviera, near the border with Italy. Pop. 346,000. Annexed from Italy in 1860, it is the capital of Alpes-Maritimes department.

**Nic·o·bar Islands** |'nikəbär| see ANDAMAN AND NICOBAR ISLANDS, India.

**Nic·o·me·dia** |,nikə'mēdēə| ancient city of Asia Minor, on the site of Izmit, NW Turkey. It was the capital of the Byzantine Empire before Byzantium.

**Nic·o·sia** |ˌnikəˈsēə| the capital of Cyprus. Pop. 186,000. Since 1974 it has been divided into Greek and Turkish sectors.

**Nie·der·ö·ster·reich** |ˈnēdəˈrōstərˌräik| German name for LOWER AUSTRIA.

**Nie·der·sach·sen** |ˈnēdərˌzäksən| German name for LOWER SAXONY.

**Ni·ger** |ˈnijər| landlocked republic in West Africa, on the S edge of the Sahara. Area: 489,378 sq. mi./1.27 million sq. km. Pop. 7,909,000. Languages, French (official), Hausa, and other W African languages. Capital and largest city: Niamey. Part of French West Africa from 1922, it became fully independent in 1960. Its people are overwhelmingly pastoral, although mining is also important.

**Niger**

**Ni·ge·ria** |nīˈjirēə| republic on the coast of W Africa, bordered by the Niger River to the N. Area: 356,805 sq. mi./923,768 sq. km. Pop. 88,514,500. Languages, English (official), Hausa, Ibo, Yoruba, and others. Capital: Abuja. Largest city: Lagos. The most populous country in Africa, Nigeria was controlled by the British from the 19th century until independence in 1960. Traditionally focused on agriculture, fishing, and forest industries, Nigeria has since the 1960s become a major oil producer. □ **Nigerian** adj. & n.

**Ni·ger River** |ˈnijər| river in NW Africa, which rises on the NE border of Sierra Leone and flows 2,550 mi./4,100 km. NE to Mali, then SE through W Niger and Nigeria, before turning S into the Gulf of Guinea.

**Ni·i·ga·ta** |nēˈgätä| industrial port in central Japan, on the NW coast of the island of Honshu. Pop. 486,000.

**Ni·i·ha·ma** |ˈnēhämä| fishing port in W Japan, on N Shikoku. Pop. 129,000.

**Ni·i·hau** |ˈnēhow| island in Hawaii, SW of Kauai, whose residents are all native Hawaiians.

**Ni·i·za** |ˈnēzä| city in central Japan, on Honshu, a suburb of Tokyo. Pop. 139,000.

**Nij·me·gen** |ˈnäˌmägən| industrial town in the E Netherlands, S of Arnhem. Pop. 146,000.

**Nik·ko** |ˈnēkkō| historic city and mountain resort in N central Japan, on central Honshu, in Nikko National Park. Pop. 20,000.

**Ni·ko·la·ev** |ˌnikəˈläyəf| Russian name for MYKOLAYIV, Ukraine.

**Ni·ko·pol** |nēˈkawpōl| industrial city in S Ukraine, on the Dnieper River. Pop. 158,000.

**Nile** |nīl| river in E Africa, the longest river in the world, which rises in E central Africa near Lake Victoria and flows 4,160 mi./6,695 km. generally N through Uganda, Sudan, and Egypt to empty through a large delta into the Mediterranean. See also BLUE NILE, ALBERT NILE, VICTORIA NILE, WHITE NILE.

**Nil·gi·ri Hills** |ˈnilgərē| range in S India, in W Tamil Nadu, rising to 8,648 ft./2,636 m. at Doda Betta. They form a branch of the Western Ghats.

**Ni·ló·po·lis** |niˈlawpəlis| city in SE Brazil, a suburb NW of Rio de Janeiro. Pop. 155,000.

**Nîmes** |nēm| city in S France, capital of the Gard department. Pop. 134,000. It is noted for its many well-preserved Roman ruins and for its textile industry; the fabric *denim* takes its name from Nimes.

**Nim·rud** |nimˈrood| modern name of an ancient Mesopotamian city on the E bank of the Tigris S of Nineveh, near present-day Mosul, Iraq. It was the capital of Assyria 879–722 B.C. The city was known in biblical times as Calah; the modern name arose through association in Islamic mythology with the biblical figure of Nimrod.

**Nin·e·veh** |ˈninəvə| ancient city on the E bank of the Tigris, opposite present-day Mosul, Iraq. It was the oldest city of the Assyrian empire, and its capital, until it was destroyed by a coalition of Babylonians and Medes in 612 B.C.

**Nigeria**

**Ning·bo** |'nɪNG'bō| (formerly **Ningpo**) port city in Zhejiang province, E China, at the junction of the Fenghua, Tong, and Yuyao rivers. Pop. 1,090,000. A special economic zone, it is a oil-refining, shipbuilding, and fishing center.

**Ning·xia** (formerly **Ningsia**) autonomous region, N central China. Area: 25,492 sq. mi./66,000 sq. km. Pop. 4,660,000. Capital: Yinchuan. It is an agricultural province on the Loess Plateau.

**Niort** |nyawr| commercial and industrial town in W France, capital of Deux-Sèvres department. Pop. 59,000.

**Nip·i·gon, Lake** |'nipigän| lake in NW Ontario, NE of Thunder Bay, used largely for recreational purposes.

**Nip·is·sing, Lake** |'nipəsiNG| lake in E central Ontario. The city of North Bay is on its shore.

**Nip·pon** |ni'pän| old name for Japan (from the Chinese, 'land of the Rising Sun'). □ **Nipponese** *adj. & n.*

**Nip·pur** |ni'pŏŏr| ancient city of Babylonia and Sumeria, in SE present-day Iraq, on a former course of the Euphrates River. It was occupied more than 4,000 years ago.

**Niš** |nēSH| (also **Nish**) historically dominant industrial city in SE Serbia, on the Nišava River near its confluence with the Morava. Pop. 175,000.

**Ni·shi·no·mi·ya** |'nēSHē'nōmēyə| industrial port city in W central Japan, on S Honshu. Pop. 427,000.

**Ni·te·rói** |,nētä'roi| industrial port on the coast of SE Brazil, on Guanabara Bay opposite the city of Rio de Janeiro. Pop. 455,000.

**Ni·tra** |nyĕt'rä| agricultural market town in W Slovakia, on the Nitra River. Pop. 90,000. It is the site of the oldest church and castle in the country, dating from c. 830.

**Niue** |nē'ŏŏa| island territory of New Zealand in the S Pacific, to the E of Tonga. Pop. 2,200. Languages, English (official),

**Niue**

local Austronesian. Capital: Alofi. Annexed in 1901, the island achieved self-government in free association with New Zealand in 1974. Niue is the world's largest coral island.

**Ni·ver·nais** |nĕver'nä| former duchy and province of central France. Its capital was the city of Nevers.

**Ni·zam·a·bad** |nē'zäməbäd| commercial city in central India, in Andhra Pradesh state. Pop. 241,000.

**Nizh·ne·var·tovsk** |nizHnē'värtəfsk| city in W Siberia, Russia. Pop. 246,000. It is near one of the world's largest oil fields.

**Nizh·ni Nov·go·rod** |'nizHnē 'nawv-,gərəd| industrial river port in European Russia, on the Volga. Pop. 1,443,000. Between 1932 and 1991 it was named Gorky after the writer Maxim Gorky, who was born here.

**Nizh·ni Ta·gil** |'nizHnē tə'gil| industrial and metal-mining city in central Russia, in the Urals N of Ekaterinburg. Pop. 440,000.

**Nkong·sam·ba** |əNGkawNG'sämbə| (also **N'Kongsamba**) commercial city in SW Cameroon, NW of Yaounde. It is a tourist center near Mount Nlonako. Pop. 85,000.

**No·be·o·ka** |nō'bēōkə| industrial and commercial port city in SW Japan, on SE Kyushu. Pop. 131,000.

**Nob Hill** |näb| commercial district of N San Francisco, California, long noted for the homes of the wealthy ("nobs").

**No·da** |'nōdä| commercial and industrial city in E central Japan, on E central Honshu. Pop. 114,000.

**No·gal·es** |nə'gäläs| commercial city in NW Mexico, in Sonora state, on the U.S. border across from Nogales, Arizona. Pop. 106,000.

**No·ginsk** |nō'ginsk| manufacturing city in W Russia, E of Moscow. Pop. 123,000.

**Nome** |nōm| city in W Alaska, on the S coast of the Seward Peninsula. Pop. 3,500. Founded in 1896, it was a center of the Alaskan gold rush.

**non·aligned na·tions** term for those independent nations that were not formally allied with either of the two Cold War superpowers, the United States and the Soviet Union; examples: India and Egypt.

**Non·tha·bu·ri** |'nōn'tə'bŏŏrē| (also **Nondaburi**) town in S Thailand, a suburb N of Bangkok. Pop. 248,000.

**Noot·ka Island** |'nŏŏtkə| island in SW British Columbia, off SW Vancouver Island, noted for its native culture.

**Nord·kapp** |'nawrkäp| Norwegian name for NORTH CAPE.

**Nord·kyn** |'nawrdkin| promontory on the N coast of Norway, to the E of North Cape. At 71° 8′ N, it is the northernmost point of the European mainland, North Cape being on an island.

**Nord-Pas-de-Calais** |nawr'pädəkä'le| region of M France, on the border with Belgium.

**Nordrhein-Westfalen** |'nawrtrīn,vest-'fälən| German name for NORTH RHINE–WESTPHALIA.

**Nor·folk**[1] |'nawrfək| county on the E coast of England, E of the Wash. Pop. 737,000; county seat, Norwich.

**Nor·folk**[2] |'nawrfək| industrial and naval port city in SE Virginia, on Hampton Roads. Pop. 261,229.

**Nor·folk Island** |'nawrfək| island in the Pacific, off the E coast of Australia, administered since 1913 as an external territory of Australia. Pop. 1,912. Discovered by Captain James Cook in 1774, it was used from 1788 to 1814 as a penal colony.

**Norfolk Islands**

**Nor·ge** |'nawrgə| Norwegian name for NORWAY.

**Nor·ic Alps** |'nōrik ælps| range of the E Alps in S Austria, along the borders of Styria and Carinthia, reaching 8,006 ft./2,440 m. at Eisenhut.

**Nor·i·cum** |'nawrikəm| ancient Roman province, a Celtic homeland S of the Danube River in present-day Austria and Bavaria.

**No·rilsk** |nə'rēlsk| city in N Siberia, Russia, within the Arctic Circle and the northernmost city in Russia. Pop. 173,000. It was founded as a prison camp and is thought to be the coldest city in the world.

**Nor·mal** |'nawrməl| town in central Illinois, home to Illinois State University (originally a *normal*, or teachers', school). Pop. 40,023.

**Nor·man** |'nawrmən| city in central Oklahoma, S of Oklahoma City, home to the University of Oklahoma. Pop. 80,071.

**Nor·man·dy** |'nawrməndē| former province of NW France with its coastline on the English Channel, now divided into the two regions of Lower Normandy (Basse-Normandie) and Upper Normandy (Haute-Normandie); chief town, Rouen. Farming and orcharding are key to the economy of Normandy, which was the historic home to the Normans who invaded England in 1066, and which was the scene of the D-Day landings in June, 1944. □ **Norman** *adj. & n.*

**Norr·kö·ping** |'nawr,shōpiNG| industrial city and seaport on an inlet of the Baltic Sea in SE Sweden. Pop. 121,000.

**North Af·ri·ca** |,nawrTH 'æfrəkə| the N part of the African continent, especially the countries bordering the Mediterranean and the Red seas. □ **North African** *adj. & n.*

**North·al·ler·ton** |nawr'THælərtən| town in the N of England, the administrative center of North Yorkshire. Pop. 14,000.

**North Amer·i·ca** |,nawrTH ə'merəkə| continent comprising the N half of the American land mass. Connected to South America by the Isthmus of Panama. It contains Canada, the United States, Mexico, and the countries of Central America. □ **North American** *adj. & n.*

**North·amp·ton**[1] |nawr'THæm(p)tən| town in S central England, on the Nene River, the county seat of Northamptonshire. Pop. 178,000.

**North·amp·ton**[2] |nawr'THæm(p)tən| industrial and commercial city in W central Massachusetts, on the Connecticut River. It is home to Smith College. Pop. 29,289.

**North·amp·ton·shire** |nawr'THæm(p)-tən,shi(ə)r| county of central England. Pop. 569,000; county seat, Northampton.

**North At·lan·tic Drift** |,nawrTH ət'læn-(t)ik| continuation of the Gulf Stream across the Atlantic and along the coast of NW Europe, where it has a significant warming effect on the climate.

**North At·lan·tic Ocean** |,nawrTH ət-'læn(t)ik| see ATLANTIC OCEAN.

**North At·lan·tic Treaty Organization** |,nawrTH ət'læn(t)ik 'trētē ,awrgənə'zā-sHən| (also **NATO**) military association of European and North American nations, formed in 1949 to guard against perceived Soviet expansionism. Its headquarters are in Brussels, Belgium. In the 1990s some former Soviet bloc nations were invited to join NATO.

**North Bay** |,nawrTH 'bā| city in E central

Ontario, a commercial and transportation hub on Lake Nipissing. Pop. 55,405.

**North Ca·na·di·an River** |ˌnawrTH kə-'nādēən| (also **Beaver River**) river that flows 800 mi./1,300 km. from NE New Mexico through Texas and Oklahoma, to the Canadian River. Oklahoma City lies on it.

**North Cape** |ˌnawrTH 'kāp| promontory on Magerøya, an island off the N coast of Norway. North Cape is the northernmost point of the world accessible by road. Norwegian name **Nordkapp**.

**North Car·o·li·na** |ˈnawrTH ˌkerə'linə| see box. □ **North Carolinian** adj. & n.

**North Channel** |ˌnawrTH 'CHænəl| the stretch of sea separating SW Scotland from

---

### North Carolina

**Capital:** Raleigh
**Largest city:** Charlotte
**Other cities:** Durham, Fayetteville, Greensboro, Greenville, High Point, Winston-Salem
**Population:** 6,628,637 (1990); 7,546,493 (1998); 8,227,000 (2005 proj.)
**Population rank (1990):** 10
**Rank in land area:** 28
**Abbreviation:** NC; N.C, N. Car.
**Nickname:** Tarheel State
**Motto:** *Esse quam videri* (Latin: 'To be rather than to seem')
**Bird:** cardinal
**Fish:** channel bass
**Flower:** dogwood blossom
**Tree:** pine
**Song:** "The Old North State"
**Noted physical features:** Outer Banks; Cape Fear, Cape Hatteras, Cape Lookout; Pamlico Sound; Dismal Swamp; Mount Mitchell
**Tourist attractions:** Great Smoky Mountain National Park (with Tennessee); Cape Lookout; Cape Hatteras; Wright Brothers National Memorial
**Admission date:** November 21, 1789
**Order of admission:** 12
**Name origin:** For Charles I of England, who called the territory *Carolana*, "land of Charles," in a 1629 land grant to Sir Robert Heath; the area had already been named *Carolina* in 1562 by French explorer Jean Ribaut to honor Charles IX, king of France; *Carolina* was used from 1663. The northern portion of the origininal Carolina came to be called 'North Carolina' after the colony was divided in 1729.

---

Northern Ireland and connecting the N Irish Sea to the Atlantic.

**North Charles·ton** |ˌnawrTH 'CHärəlstən| city in SE South Carolina, a residential suburb with naval facilities. Pop. 70,218.

**North Chi·ca·go** |ˌnawrTH SHi'kawgō| industrial city in NE Illinois, on Lake Michigan just S of Waukegan. Pop. 34,978.

**North Country**[1] |'nawrTH 'kəntrē| in England, traditional term for areas N of the River Humber.

**North Country**[2] |'nawrTH 'kəntrē| in New York state, areas N of the Mohawk and Hudson rivers, extending to the St. Lawrence valley and Lake Ontario.

**North Da·ko·ta** |'nawrTH də'kōdə| see box. □ **North Dakotan** adj. & n.

**North·east** region of the US, usually thought to include the six New England states, New Jersey, and the eastern portions of New York State and Pennsylvania.

**North·east King·dom** nickname for the region including the three most northerly counties of Vermont.

---

### North Dakota

**Capital:** Bismarck
**Largest city:** Fargo
**Other cities:** Grand Forks, Minot
**Population:** 638,800 (1990); 638,244 (1998); 677,000 (2005 proj.)
**Population rank (1990):** 47
**Rank in land area:** 19
**Abbreviation:** ND; N.D, N. Dak.
**Nickname:** Flickertail State; Sioux State; Land of the Dakotas; Peace Garden State
**Motto:** 'Liberty and Union, Now and Forever, One and Inseparable'
**Bird:** western meadowlark
**Fish:** northern pike
**Flower:** wild prairie rose
**Tree:** American elm
**Song:** "North Dakota Hymn"
**Noted physical features:** Williston Basin; The Slope; Red River Valley; Little Missouri National Grasslands; White Butte
**Tourist attractions:** Garrison Dam; Theodore Roosevelt National Park
**Admission date:** November 2, 1889
**Order of admission:** 39
**Name origin:** For the Dakota (Sioux) Indian confederation, in whose language the word means 'allies,' referring to the friendly compact that joined seven smaller tribes. The original Dakota Territory was divided into north and south regions in 1889.

**North·east Passage** |ˌnawrTH'ēst 'pæsij| passage for ships along the N coast of Europe and Asia, from the Atlantic to the Pacific via the Arctic Ocean, sought for many years as a possible trade route to the East. It was first navigated in 1878–79 by the Swedish explorer Baron Nordenskjöld.

**North Equa·to·ri·al Current** |ˌnawrTH ˌekwə'tawrēəl 'kerənt| ocean current that flows W across the Pacific just N of the equator.

**North·ern Neck** region in E Virginia between the Potomac and Rappahannock rivers, a tidewater peninsula.

**North·ern Cape** |'nawrTHərn 'kāp| largest (139,700 sq. mi./362,000 sq. km.) province of South Africa, in the SW, formerly part of Cape Province. Pop. 749,000. Capital: Kimberley. Northern Cape is largely Karoo scrubland.

**North·ern Cir·cars** |'nawrTHərn ser'kärz| former name for the coastal region of E India between the Krishna River and Orissa, now in Andhra Pradesh.

**north·ern hem·i·sphere** the half of the earth that is N of the equator.

**North·ern Ire·land** |ˌnawrTHərn 'ī(ə)rlənd| province of the United Kingdom occupying the NE part of Ireland. Area: 1,944 sq. mi./5,032 sq. km. Pop. 1,570,000. Capital and largest city: Belfast. Northern Ireland, which comprises six of the nine historic counties of Ulster, was established as a self-governing province in 1920, having refused to be part of the Irish Free State. It has long been dominated by Unionist parties, which represent the Protestant majority. Many members of the Roman Catholic minority favor union with the Republic of Ireland. Discrimination against Catholics led to violent conflicts and (from 1969) the presence of British army units in an attempt to keep the peace. Terrorism and sectarian violence by paramilitary groups representing both sides of the conflict continued into the late 1990s. Industry in Belfast and agriculture are key to the local economy.

**North·ern Ma·ri·an·as, Commonwealth of the** |'nawrTHərn märē'änəs| self-governing territory in the W Pacific, comprising the Mariana Islands with the exception of the southernmost, Guam. Area: 184 sq. mi./477 sq. km. Pop. 43,345. Languages, English (official), Austronesian languages. Capital: Chalan Kanoa (on Saipan). The Northern Marianas are constituted as a self-governing commonwealth

**Northern Mariana Islands**

in union with the United States. Military bases are important to their economy.

**North·ern Province** |'nawrTHərn| province of N South Africa, formerly part of Transvaal. Capital: Pietersburg. Mining and farming are important.

**North·ern Rho·de·sia** |ˌnawrTHərn rō-'dēZHə| former name (until 1964) for ZAMBIA.

**North·ern Territory** |ˌnawrTHərn 'terəˌtawrē| state of N central Australia. Pop. 158,000. Capital: Darwin. The territory was annexed by the state of South Australia in 1863, and administered by the Commonwealth of Australia from 1911. It became a self-governing territory in 1978 and a full state in 1995. Mining is important.

**North Fri·sian Islands** |nawrTH 'frizHən| see FRISIAN ISLANDS.

**North Island** |nawrTH 'īlənd| the northern of the two main islands of New Zealand, separated from South Island by Cook Strait. Area: 44,180 sq. mi./114,383 sq. km. Pop. 2,553,000.

**North Ko·rea** |nawrTH kə'rēə| republic in E Asia, occupying the N part of the peninsula of Korea. Area: 46,558 sq. mi./120,538 sq. km. Pop. 22,227,000. Language, Korean. Capital and largest city: Pyongyang. Official name **Democratic People's Republic of Korea**. Formed when Korea was partitioned in 1948, North Korea is an in-

**North Korea**

creasingly isolated communist state. Industry and mining are important, as is agriculture, although famine is a recurrent problem. □ **North Korean** *adj. & n.*

**North Lit·tle Rock** |nawrᴛн 'litəl räk| city in central Arkansas, an industrial center across the Arkansas River from Little Rock. Pop. 61,741.

**North Os·se·tia** |nawrᴛн aw'sēshə| autonomous republic of Russia, in the Caucasus on the border with Georgia. Pop. 638,000. Capital: Vladikavkaz. Since 1994 it has been called Alania. See also OSSETIA.

**North Platte River** |nawrᴛн 'plat| river that flows 620 mi./960 km. from N Colorado across Wyoming and Nebraska, to the Platte River. Its valley was part of the Oregon Trail.

**North Rhine-Westphalia** |,nawrᴛн 'rīn,west'fälyə| the most populous state of Germany, in the W. Area: 13,159 sq. mi./ 34,070 sq. km. Pop. 17,104,000. Capital: Düsseldorf. German name **Nordrhein-Westfalen**.

**North Sea** |'nawrᴛн 'sē| shallow arm of the Atlantic lying between the mainland of Europe and the coast of Britain, important for its oil and gas deposits and for its fishing grounds.

**North Slope** |nawrᴛн 'slōp| name for regions of Alaska N of the Brooks Range, extending to the Arctic Ocean. Sparsely populated, it is the scene of much oil exploration and extraction.

**North Syd·ney** |nawrᴛн 'sidnē| town in SE Australia, in New South Wales, a commercial and industrial suburb N of Sydney. Pop. 50,000.

**North Ton·a·wan·da** |nawrᴛн ,tänə'wändə| industrial city in W New York, on the Niagara River N of Buffalo, at the W end of the historic Erie Canal. Pop. 34,989.

**North·um·ber·land** |nawr'ᴛнəmbərlən(d)| county in NE England, on the Scottish border. Pop. 301,000; county seat, Morpeth.

**North·um·ber·land Strait** |nawr'ᴛнəmbərlənd| ocean passage in the Gulf of St. Lawrence, separating Prince Edward Island from New Brunswick and Nova Scotia.

**North·um·bria** |nawr'ᴛнəmbrēə| **1** area of NE England comprising the counties of Northumberland, Durham, and Tyne and Wear. **2** an ancient Anglo-Saxon kingdom in NE England extending from the Humber to the Forth. □ **Northumbrian** *adj. & n.*

**North Vi·et·nam** |nawrᴛн vē,et'näm| former communist republic in SE Asia, in the N part of Vietnam, created in 1954 when Vietnam was partitioned; after defeating noncommunist South Vietnam in the Vietnam War, it declared a reunited, socialist republic (1976).

**North·west An·gle** |,nawrᴛн'west 'æŋgəl| forested region of N Minnesota, separated from the rest of the state and the U.S. by Lake of the Woods. It is the northernmost part of the contiguous U.S.

**North-West Fron·tier Province** |,nawrᴛн'west frən'tēr| province of western Pakistan, on the border with Afghanistan. Pop. 12,290,000. Capital: Peshawar.

**Northwest Passage** |,nawrᴛн'west 'pæsəj| sea passage along the N coast of the American continent, through the Canadian Arctic from the Atlantic to the Pacific. It was sought for many years as a possible trade route; it was first navigated in 1903–06 by Roald Amundsen, but has no commercial value.

**North-West Province** |,nawrᴛн'west| province of N South Africa, formed in 1994 from the NE part of Cape Province and SW Transvaal. Pop. 3,349,000. Capital: Mmabatho.

**North·west Territories** |,nawrᴛнwest 'terə,tawrēz| territory of NW Canada, between Yukon Territory and Nunavut. Capital: Yellowknife. Much of it consists of sparsely inhabited forests and tundra. The Northwest Territories, then including the land that is now Nunavut, was ceded by Britain to Canada in 1870. Nunavut became a separate territory in 1999.

**North·west Territory** |,nawrᴛнwest 'terə,tawrē| region and former territory of the U.S. lying E of the Mississippi and N of the Ohio rivers. It was acquired in 1783 after the Revolutionary War and now forms the states of Indiana, Ohio, Michigan, Illinois, Wisconsin, and part of Minnesota. Also called the **Old Northwest**.

**North York** |,nawrᴛн 'yawrk| city in S Ontario, a largely residential suburb N of Toronto. Pop. 562,564.

**North York·shire** |,nawrᴛн 'yawrk,sнir| county in NE England. Pop. 699,000; administrative center, Northallerton. It was formed in 1974 from parts of the former North, East, and West ridings of Yorkshire. The city of York is here.

**Nor·walk**[1] |'nawrwawk| city in SW California, a suburb SE of Los Angeles. Pop. 94,279.

**Nor·walk**[2] |'nawrwawk| industrial city in SW Connecticut, on Long Island Sound. Pop. 78,331.

**Nor·way** |'nawrwā| mountainous European kingdom, on the N and W coastline of Scandinavia. Area: 125,098 sq. mi./323,878 sq. km. Pop. 4,249,830. Language, Norwegian. Capital and largest city: Oslo. Norwegian name **Norge**. Norway gained independence, after longtime domination by either Denmark or Sweden, in 1905. Maritime and forest industries have been supplemented, since the 1960s, by North Sea oil. □ **Norwegian** *adj. & n.*

Norway

**Nor·we·gian Sea** |nawr'wējən| sea that lies between Iceland and Norway and links the Arctic Ocean with the NE Atlantic.

**Nor·wich**[1] |'nawr(w)icH| industrial city in SE Connecticut, on the Thames River. Pop. 37,391.

**Nor·wich**[2] |'nawr(w)icH| commercial and university city in E England, the county seat of Norfolk. Pop. 121,000.

**Nos·sob River** |'nŏsäb| (also **Nosop**) river that flows 500 mi./800 km. from Namibia across the Kalahari Desert into Botswana, where it forms part of the border with South Africa and empties into the Auob River.

**Notre-Dame** |'nŏtrə 'däm| cathedral church of Paris, France, on the Ile de la Cité In 1163 Pope Alexander III laid the cornerstone for the church, built in early Gothic style, and most of the construction was completed within 30 years. During the French Revolution the church became a "Temple of Reason," and many of the sculptures on the façade were destroyed. Restoration was undertaken in 1845 by Viollet-le-Duc.

**No·tre Dame Mountains** |'nŏdər 'däm; 'nŏtrə 'däm| Appalachian range in S Quebec, extending S of the St. Lawrence River into the Gaspé Peninsula, where they include the Shickshock Mts.

**Not·ting·ham** |'nätiNG,hæm| industrial city in E central England, the county seat of Nottinghamshire. Pop. 261,000.

**Not·ting·ham·shire** |'nätiNGəm,SHi(ə)r|

county in central England. Pop. 981,000; county seat, Nottingham.

**Not·ting Hill** |'nätiNG 'hil| residential area of N central London, England, N of Holland Park, a center of the city's West Indian population.

**Nouad·hi·bou** |,nwäde'boo| the principal port of Mauritania, on the Atlantic coast at the border with Western Sahara. Pop. 22,000. Former name **Port-Étienne**.

**Nouak·chott** |nw'äkSHät| the capital of Mauritania, on the Atlantic coast. Pop. 850,000 .

**Nou·méa** |noo'mäə| the capital of the island and French overseas territory of New Caledonia. Pop. 65,000. Former name **Port de France**.

**Nouvelle-Calédonie** |voo'velkə'lädōnē| French name for NEW CALEDONIA.

**No·va Igua·çu** |'nawvä ,ēgwä'soo| city in SE Brazil, an industrial suburb NW of Rio de Janeiro. Pop. 801,000.

**No·va Lis·boa** |,nŏvə liz'bōə| former name (until 1978) for HUAMBO, Angola.

**No·va·ra** |nō'värə| agricultural and industrial town in N Italy, capital of Novara province. Pop. 103,000.

**No·va Sco·tia** |,nŏvə 'skōsHə| **1** a peninsula on the SE coast of Canada, projecting into the Atlantic and separating the Bay of Fundy from the Gulf of St. Lawrence. **2** a province of E Canada, comprising the peninsula of Nova Scotia and the adjoining Cape Breton Island. Area: 21,425 sq. mi./ 55,490 sq. km. Pop. 899,942. Capital and largest city: Halifax. Settled by the French as ACADIA, it changed hands several times befor being controlled by the British in 1713. One of the original four provinces in Canada in 1867, it has maritime, iron and steel, and lumber industries, and tourism is important. □ **Nova Scotian** *adj. & n.*

**No·va·to** |nə'vätō| city in NW California, N of San Francisco. Pop. 47,585.

**No·va·ya Zem·lya** |,nŏvəyə ,zem'l(y)ä| two large uninhabited islands in the Arctic Ocean off the N coast of Siberian Russia. The name means 'new land.'

**Nov·go·rod** |'nawv,gərəd| commercial city in NW Russia, on the Volkhov River at the N tip of Lake Ilmen. Pop. 232,000. Russia's oldest city, it was settled by the Varangian chief Rurik in 862 and ruled by Alexander Nevsky between 1238 and 1263, when it was an important center of medieval E Europe.

**No·vi Pa·zar** |'nŏvē pə'zär| historic commercial city in Serbia, on a tributary of the Ibar River. Pop. 86,000.

**No·vi Sad** |'nōvē 'säd| industrial city in Serbia, on the Danube River, capital of the autonomous province of Vojvodina. Pop. 179,000.

**No·vo·cher·kassk** |ˌnōvəCHər'käsk| industrial city in W Russia, NE of Rostov. Pop. 188,000.

**No·vo Ham·bur·go** |'nōvŏŏ æm'bŏŏrgŏŏ| industrial and commercial city in S Brazil, in Rio Grande do Sul state. Pop. 207,000. It was settled by Germans in the 19th century.

**No·vo·kuz·netsk** |ˌnōvəkŏŏz'n(y)etsk| industrial city in the Kuznets Basin in S central Siberian Russia. Pop. 601,000.

**No·vo·mos·kovsk** |ˌnōvəmä'kawfsk| industrial city in W Russia, S of Moscow. Pop. 146,000.

**No·vo·ros·siysk** |nōvərə'sēsk| naval base and seaport in SW Russia, on the Black Sea coast. Pop. 190,000.

**No·vo·si·birsk** |ˌnōvəsi'bərsk| industrial city and rail center in central Siberian Russia, to the W of the Kuznets Basin, on the Ob River. Pop. 1,443,000.

**Noy·on** |nwæ'yæn| industrial and commercial town in N France. Pop. 15,000. In 768 Charlemagne was crowned King of the Franks here.

**Nu·bia** |'nŏŏbēə| ancient region of S Egypt and northern Sudan, including the Nile valley between Aswan and Khartoum and the surrounding area. Much of Nubia is now covered by the waters of Lake Nasser, formed by the building of the two dams at Aswan. Nubia fell under ancient Egyptian rule from the time of the Middle Kingdom, soon after 2000 B.C., and from about the 15th century B.C. was ruled by an Egyptian viceroy. The country was Egyptianized, and trade (especially in gold) flourished. By the 8th century B.C., however, as Egypt's centralized administration disintegrated, an independent Nubian kingdom emerged, and for a brief period extended its power over Egypt. Nubians constitute an ethnic minority group in present-day Egypt. The **Nubian Desert** lies between the Nile and the Red Sea. □ **Nubian** adj. & n.

**Nu·e·ces River** |nŏŏ'āsəs| river that flows 315 mi./515 km. from central Texas into the Gulf of Mexico at Nueces Bay. The city of Corpus Christi is at its mouth.

**Nue·va San Sal·va·dor** |'nwävə sæn 'sælvədawr| (also **Santa Tecla**) city in SW El Salvador, a suburb W of San Salvador in coffee-growing country. Pop. 96,000. It was established after an 1850s earthquake destroyed San Salvador.

**Nue·vo La·re·do** |'nwävō lə'rädō; nŏŏ'ävō| commercial city in E Mexico, in Tamaulipas state, across the Rio Grande from Laredo, Texas. Pop. 218,000. It is a rail and road terminus and international trade center.

**Nue·vo Le·ón** |'nwävō lā'ōn; nŏŏ'ävō| state of NE Mexico, on the border with the U.S. Area: 25,077 sq. mi./64,924 sq. km. Pop. 3,086,000. Capital: Monterrey.

**Nu·ku'a·lo·fa** |ˌnŏŏkŏŏə'lōfə| the capital of Tonga, situated on the island of Tongatapu. Pop. 30,000.

**Nu·ku Hi·va** |'nŏŏkŏŏ 'hēvə| largest (127 sq. mi./329 sq. km.) of the Marquesas Islands, in French Polynesia. It is mountainous and has several good harbors.

**Nu·kus** |nŏŏ'kŏŏs| industrial city in S Uzbekistan, on the right bank of the Amu Darya River. Pop. 180,000.

**Null·ar·bor Plain** |'nəlärbər| vast arid plain in SW Australia, stretching inland from the Great Australian Bight. It contains no surface water, has sparse vegetation, and is almost uninhabited.

**Nu·ma·zu** |nŏŏ'mäzŏŏ| industrial port city in central Japan, on central Honshu. Pop. 212,000.

**Nu·mid·ia** |nŏŏ'midēə| ancient kingdom, later a Roman province, situated in N Africa in an area N of the Sahara corresponding roughly to present-day Algeria. □ **Numidian** adj. & n.

**Nu·na·vut** territory in N Canada, comprising the eastern part of the original Northwest Territories and including most of the islands of the Arctic Archipelago. It is the homeland of the Inuit people.

**Nun·a·wa·ding** |'nənəwə,diNG| city in Australia, in Victoria, a suburb E of Melbourne. Pop. 91,000.

**Nun·ea·ton** |nə'nētən| industrial city in central England, in Warwickshire, a textile center. Pop. 82,000.

**Nu·ni·vak Island** |'nŏŏnəvæk| island in the Bering Sea, in SW Alaska, home to Inuit hunters and fishermen and to much wildlife.

**Nür·bur·gring** |'nyŏŏrbərgriNG| auto racetrack in Nürburg, Rhineland-Palatinate, W central Germany.

**Nu·rem·berg** |'nŏŏr(ə)m,bərg| commercial, industrial, and cultiral city in S Germany, in Bavaria. Pop. 497,000. In the 1930s Nazi Party congresses and annual rallies were held in the city, and in 1945–46 it was the scene of the Nuremberg trials, in which Nazi war criminals faced an international tribunal. German name **Nürnberg**.

**Nu·ri·stan** |no͝orə'stæn| mountainous region of NE Afghanistan, scene of heavy fighting during the Soviet occupation of the 1980s.

**Nürn·berg** |nyern,berg| German name for NUREMBERG.

**Nut·meg State** |'nətmeg| nickname for CONNECTICUT.

**Nuuk** |'no͝ok| capital of Greenland, a port on the Davis Strait. Pop. 12,000. It was known by the Danish name Godthåb until 1979.

**Nyan·za** |nē'ænzə| agricultural province of NW Kenya; pop. 3.89 million. Its capital is Kisumu. The Bantu term *nyanza* is also an element in the names of several major African lakes.

**Nya·sa, Lake** |'nyäsä| lake in E central Africa, the third largest lake in Africa. About 360 mi./580 km. long, it forms most of the E border of Malawi with Mozambique and Tanzania. Also called **Lake Malawi**.

**Nya·sa·land** |'nyäsəlænd| former name (until 1966) for MALAWI.

**Nyi·regy·há·za** |'nyērej 'häzaw| commercial and industrial city in E Hungary. Pop. 115,000.

**Ny·kø·ping** |'no͝ocho͝opēNG| port in SE Sweden, on the Baltic Sea, capital of Södermanland county. Pop. 66,000.

**Nym·phen·burg** |'nimpfenbərg| complex of palaces in Munich, S Germany (Bavaria). The Nymphenburg chateau was built in the late 17th century. A porcelain factory was later established here.

**Ny·sa** |'nisə| Polish name for the NEISSE River.

**Ny·stad** |'no͝ostäd| Swedish name for UUSIKAUPUNKI.

# Oo

**Oahe, Lake** |ō'wähē| reservoir NW of Pierre, South Dakota, in the Missouri River, created since 1963 by the huge, earthen Oahe Dam.

**Oa·hu** |ō'wähōō| the third-largest of the Hawaiian islands. Its principal community, Honolulu, is the state capital of Hawaii. The U.S. naval base at Pearl Harbor is here.

**Oak·land** |'ōklənd| industrial port city on the E side of San Francisco Bay in N California. Pop. 372,242.

**Oak Park** |ōk 'pärk| village in NE Illinois, a largely residential suburb W of Chicago. Pop. 53,648.

**Oak Ridge** |'ōk ,rij| city in E Tennessee, on the Clinch River, established in 1942 as part of U.S. nuclear development, and still a research and industrial center. Pop. 27,310.

**Oak·ville** |'ōk,vil| port city in S Ontario, on L. Ontario SW of Toronto, an industrial and residential suburb. Pop. 114,670.

**Oa·xa·ca** |wä'häkə| **1** state of S Mexico. Area: 36,289 sq. mi./93,952 sq. km. Pop. 3,022,000. **2** its capital city, an historic cultural and commercial center. Pop. 213,000. Full name **Oaxaca de Juárez**.

**Ob** |äb| the principal river of the W Siberian lowlands and one of the largest rivers in Russia. Rising in the Altai Mts., it flows generally N and W for 3,481 mi./5,410 km. before entering the Gulf of Ob (or Ob Bay), an inlet of the Kara Sea, a part of the Arctic Ocean.

**Oban** |'ōbən| port and tourist resort on the W coast of Scotland, in Argyll and Bute, opposite the island of Mull. Pop. 8,000.

**Ober·am·mer·gau** |,ōbər'ämərgow| village in the Bavarian Alps of SW Germany. Pop. 5,000. It is the site of the most famous of the few surviving passion plays, which has been performed by the villagers every tenth year (with few exceptions) since 1634 as a result of a vow made during an epidemic. The villagers divide the parts among themselves and are responsible also for the production, music, costumes, and scenery.

**Ober·hau·sen** |'ōbər,howzən| industrial city in western Germany, in the Ruhr valley in North Rhine–Westphalia. Pop. 225,000.

**Ober·land** |'ōbər,lænd| in German, generic term for mountainous or upland region. It appears in such German or Swiss names as Bernese Oberland.

**Ober·lin** |'ōberlin| city in N central Ohio, home to Oberlin College. Pop. 8,191.

**Ober·ö·ster·reich** |,ōbə,röstər,räik| German name for UPPER AUSTRIA.

**Obi·hi·ro** |ōbē'hērō| city in N Japan, on N central Hokkaido, E of Sapporo. Pop. 167,000.

**Obi Islands** |'ōbē| (also called **Ombi Islands**) island group in Indonesia, in the N central Moluccas, in the Ceram Sea between Halmahera (N) and Ceram (S).

**Ocala** |ō'kälə| industrial and resort city in N central Florida. Pop. 42,045.

**Oc·ci·dent, the** |'awksidənt| literary term for Europe, America, or both, as distinct from the ORIENT. It derives from the Latin word for 'setting' (used of the sun). □ **Occidental** adj. & n.

**Oce·an·ia** |,ōshē'ænēə| (also **Oceanica**) the islands of the Pacific and adjacent seas, variously defined. Also, **Oceanica**. □ **Oceanian** adj. & n.

**Ocean Island** |'ōshən| another name for BANABA, Kiribati.

**Ocean·side** |'ōshənsīd| residential and commercial city in SW California, N of San Diego. Nearby Camp Pendleton, a Marine base, is central in its life. Pop. 128,398.

**Ocean State** |'ōshən| nickname for RHODE ISLAND.

**Ocho Ri·os** |'ōchō 'rēōs| resort town in N Jamaica, a port on the Caribbean Sea, famed for its waterfalls. Pop. 8,000.

**Ocra·coke Island** |'ōkrəkōk| barrier island in E North Carolina, part of the Outer Banks. Fishing and resort trade are central to its economy.

**Oda·wa·ra** |ōdä'wärə| city in E central Japan, on E central Honshu, SW of Tokyo. Pop. 193,000.

**Oden·se** |'ōdənsə| industrial port in E Denmark, on the island of Fyn. Pop. 178,000.

**Oder** |'ōdər| river of central Europe that rises in the mountains in the W of the Czech Republic and flows N through W Poland to meet the Neisse River, then continues N forming the N part of the border between Poland and Germany before flowing into the Baltic Sea. This border between Poland and Germany, known as the Oder–Neisse Line, was adopted at the Potsdam Conference in 1945. Czech and Polish name **Odra**.

**Odes·sa¹** |ō'desə| city in SW Texas, with its neighbor Midland an oil industry center in the Permian Basin. Pop. 89,699.

**Odes·sa**² |ō'desə| city and naval, industrial, and resort port on the S coast of Ukraine, on the Black Sea. Pop. 1,106,000. Ukrainian name **Odesa**.

**Odra** |'ōdər| Polish name for the ODER River.

**Of·fa·ly** |'awfələ| county in the central part of the Republic of Ireland, in the province of Leinster. Pop. 58,000; county seat, Tullamore.

**Of·fa's Dyke** |'awfəz 'dīk| series of earthworks along the England-Wales border, attributed to Offa, 8th-century king of Mercia, whose aim was to mark the boundary established in wars with the Welsh.

**Of·fen·bach** |'awfən,bäk| (also **Offenbach am Main**) industrial city in W Germany, on the Main River. Pop. 116,000.

**Oga·den** |ō'gäden| (**the Ogaden**) desert region in SE Ethiopia, largely inhabited by Somali nomads. It has been claimed by successive governments of neighboring Somalia.

**Oga·ki** |ō'gäkē| city in central Japan, on central Honshu, W of Gifu. Pop. 148,000.

**Ogal·lala Aq·ui·fer** vast groundwater resource under eight U.S. states, used esp. for crop irrigation. It stretches from southern South Dakota to W Texas and E New Mexico.

**Og·bo·mo·sho** |,ōgbō'mōsHō| city and agricultural market in SW Nigeria, N of Ibadan. Pop. 661,000. Its people are largely Yoruba.

**Og·den** |'ägdən| industrial and military city in N Utah, N of Salt Lake City. Pop. 63,909.

**Og·dens·burg** |'ägdənz,berg| industrial city in N New York, on the St. Lawrence River. Pop. 13,521.

**Ogo·oué River** |ōgō'wä| (also **Ogowe**) river that flows 560 mi./900 km. from the SW Congo across Gabon to the Gulf of Guinea in the Atlantic. It is key to Gabon's economy.

**O'Hare In·ter·na·tion·al Airport** |ō'her ,intər'naSHənl| facility in NE Illinois, NW of Chicago, on the S side of Des Plaines. It is one of the busiest airports in the world.

**Ohio** |ō'hīō| see box. □ **Ohioan** adj. & n.

**Ohio River** |ō'hīō| river that flows 980 mi./1,580 km. from Pittsburgh, Pennsylvania, where it is formed by the Allegheny and Monongahela rivers, through the E Midwest to join the Mississippi River at Cairo, Illinois. Now heavily industrial and a route of commerce, it was a key corridor of 19th-century W expansion.

---

## Ohio

**Capital/Largest city:** Cleveland
**Other cities:** Akron, Canton, Cincinnati, Dayton, Toledo, Youngstown
**Population:** 10,847,115 (1990); 11,209,493 (1998); 11,428,000 (2005 proj.)
**Population rank (1990):** 7
**Rank in land area:** 34
**Abbreviation:** OH; O.
**Nickname:** Buckeye State
**Motto:** 'With God, All Things Are Possible'
**Bird:** cardinal
**Flower:** scarlet carnation
**Tree:** buckeye
**Song:** "Beautiful Ohio"
**Noted physical features:** Ohio River; Lake Erie
**Tourist attractions:** Pro Football Hall of Fame; Rock and Roll Hall of Fame
**Admission date:** March 1, 1803
**Order of admission:** 17
**Name origin:** Named for the river, which itself was named by French explorers after similar words in several Indian languages; the name is from the Iroquoian *oheo*, 'beautiful,' *ohion-hiio*, 'beautiful river,' or possibly Wyandot *ohezuh*, 'great; fair to look upon.'

---

**Ohrid, Lake** |'ōkrēd| lake in SE Europe, on the border between Macedonia and Albania.

**Oil Rivers** |oil| general term for the delta of the Niger River, in S Nigeria.

**Oise River** |wäz| river in S Belgium and N France, rising in the Ardennes Mts. and flowing 189 mi./302 km. SW, meeting the Seine River near Pointoise.

**Oi·ta** |'awē,tä| commercial and industrial port city in SW Japan, on NE Kyushu. Pop. 409,000.

**Ojai** |'ōhī| city in SW California, NW of Los Angeles, a resort and artists' colony. Pop. 7,613.

**Oka River** |ō'kä| **1** river (530 mi./853 km. long) in S central Russia. It flows N from the Sayan Mts. into the Angara River. **2** river (919 mi./1,479 km. long) in W Russia, rising in Kursk oblast and flowing into the Volga River at Nizhny Novgorod; it is the main tributary of the Volga.

**Oka·na·gan, Lake** |ōkə'nägən| lake in S British Columbia, noted for its resorts and for Ogopogo, a rumored marine inhabitant.

**Oka·ra** |ō'kärə| commercial city in NE Pakistan, in Punjab province. Pop. 154,000.

**Oka·van·go** river of SW Africa that rises in central Angola and flows 1,000 mi./1,600 km. SE to Namibia, where it turns E to form part of the border between Angola and Namibia before entering Botswana, where it drains into the extensive Okavango marshes of Ngamiland. Also called **Cuban·go**.

**Oka·ya·ma** |ˈōkäˈyämä| industrial city and major railroad junction in SW Japan, on the SW coast of Honshu. Pop. 594,000.

**Oka·za·ki** |ˈōkäˈzäkē| city in central Japan, on S central Honshu, S of Nagoya. Pop. 307,000.

**O.K. Cor·ral** |ˈōˈka kəˈræl| see TOMBSTONE, Arizona.

**Okee·cho·bee, Lake** |ˌōkəˈCHōbē| lake in S Florida. Fed by the Kissimmee River from the N, it drains into the Everglades in the S, this drainage being controlled by embankments and canals. It forms part of the Okeechobee Waterway, which crosses the Florida peninsula from W to E, linking the Gulf of Mexico with the Atlantic.

**Oke·fe·no·kee Swamp** |ˌōkəfəˈnōkē| extensive area of swampland in SE Georgia and NE Florida, associated with the cartoon character Pogo.

**Okhotsk, Sea of** |əˈkätsk| inlet of the N Pacific on the E coast of Russia (Siberia), between the Kamchatka Peninsula and the Kurile Islands. Magadan is the chief port here.

**Oki·na·wa** |ōkiˈnäwä| an island group of Japan, in the S Ryukyu Islands. Pop. 1,222,000. Capital: Naha. Controlled after World War II by the U.S., the islands were returned to Japan in 1972, but many U.S. military facilities remain. □ **Okinawan** *adj. & n.*

**Ok·la·ho·ma** |ˌōkləˈhōmə| see box. □ **Oklahoman** *adj. & n.*

**Ok·la·ho·ma City** |ˌōkləˈhōmə| the capital of Oklahoma and largest city in the state, an industrial and commercial center. Pop. 444,719. It expanded rapidly after the discovery in 1928 of underlying oil fields.

**Öland** |ˈȫˌländ| narrow island in the Baltic Sea off the SE coast of Sweden, the largest in the country, separated from the mainland by Kalmar Sound. Pop. 26,000.

**Ola·the** |ōˈlaTHə| industrial city in NE Kansas, SW of Kansas City. Pop. 63,352.

**Old Bai·ley** |ˌōld ˈbälē| name for the Central Criminal Court of London, England, originally in a courtyard (*bailey*) of the city walls, since 1906 on the site of NEWGATE prison.

**Old Cas·tile** |ōld kæˈstēl| former province

---

### Oklahoma

**Capital/largest city:** Oklahoma City
**Other cities:** Lawton, Norman, Tulsa
**Population:** 3,145,585 (1990); 3,346,713 (1998); 3,491,000 (2005 proj.)
**Population rank (1990):** 28
**Rank in land area:** 20
**Abbreviation:** OK; Okla.
**Nickname:** Sooner State; Boomer State
**Motto:** *Labor omnia vincit* (Latin: 'Labor conquers all things')
**Bird:** scissor-tailed flycatcher
**Fish:** white (sand) bass
**Flower:** mistletoe
**Tree:** redbud
**Song:** "Oklahoma!"
**Noted physical features:** Panhandle; Black Mesa
**Tourist attractions:** American Indian Hall of Fame; National Cowboy Hall of Fame
**Admission date:** November 16, 1907
**Order of admission:** 46
**Name origin:** From Choctaw *okla*, 'people,' and *humma* or *homma*, 'red,' thus, 'land of the red people.'

---

in N Spain, now part of N Castile. It comprises the modern provinces of Avila, Burgos, Cantabria, La Rioja, Palencia, Segovia, Soria, and Valladolid.

**Old Del·hi** |ōld ˈdelē| see DELHI, India.

**Ol·den·burg** |ˈōldən,bərg| market town and industrial center of NW Germany, on the Hunte River, W of Bremen. Pop. 146,000.

**Old·ham** |ˈōld,hæm| industrial town in NW England, NE of Manchester. Pop. 100,000.

**Old Sar·um** |ˌōld ˈserəm| ancient hill city in S England, in Wiltshire, just N of Salisbury (New Sarum). Fortified since the Iron Age, it had a cathedral, then declined until, in the early 19th century, it was a classic "rotten borough," represented in Parliament although it had almost no inhabitants.

**Ol·du·vai Gorge** |ˈawldə,vī ˈgawrj| gorge in N Tanzania, 30 mi./48 km. long and up to 300 ft./90 m. deep. Its exposed strata contain numerous fossils (especially hominids) spanning the full range of the Pleistocene period.

**Old World** |ōld wər(ə)ld| Europe, Asia, and Africa, regarded collectively as the part of the world known before the discovery of the Americas. Compare with NEW WORLD.

**Ole·nek River** |əliˈnyōk| river (1,350

m./2,175 km.) in Russia that rises in the central Siberian plateau and flows NE to the Laptev Sea.

**Olé·ron, Ile d'** |ˌēldawlăˈrawn| resort island in the Bay of Biscay, off the W coast of France. It is the largest island in the Bay of Biscay: 66 sq. mi./171 sq. km. The main towns are Saint-Pierre and Le Château.

**Olin·da** |ōˈlində| historic city in E Brazil, in Pernambuco state, just N of Recife. Pop. 341,000. A Portuguese colonial capital and longtime cultural center, it also has many nearby beaches.

**Ol·ives, Mount of** |ˈawlǝvz| the highest point in the range of hills to the E of Jerusalem, in the West Bank. It is a holy place for both Judaism and Christianity and is frequently mentioned in the Bible. The Garden of Gethsemane is nearby.

**Olo·mouc** |ˈawlawmōts| historic industrial city on the Morava River in N Moravia, in the Czech Republic. Pop. 106,000.

**Olon·ga·po** |ō‚lawNGgǝˈpō| port city in the Philippines, on central Luzon. Pop. 193,000.

**Olsz·tyn** |ˈawlsHtən| city in N Poland, in the lakeland area of Masuria. Pop. 164,000. Founded in 1348 by the Teutonic Knights, it was a part of Prussia between 1772 and 1945. German name **Allenstein**.

**Olt River** |awlt| river (348 mi./557 km.) in S Romania that rises in the Carpathian Mts. and flows S, meeting the Danube River at Turnu Măgurele.

**Ol·te·nia** |awlˈtēnēǝ| region of S Romania, the W part of Wallachia.

**Olym·pia¹** |ǝˈlimpēǝ| plain in Greece, in the western Peloponnese. In ancient times it was the site of the chief sanctuary of the god Zeus, the place where the original Olympic Games were held.

**Olym·pia²** |ǝˈlimpēǝ| the capital of the state of Washington, a port on Puget Sound. Pop. 33,840.

**Olym·pic Peninsula** |ǝˈlimpik| region of NW Washington, on the Pacific and Juan de Fuca Strait. The Olympic Mts. and Olympic National Park are here.

**Olym·pus, Mount¹** |ǝˈlimpǝs| mountain in Cyprus, in the Troodos range. Rising to 6,400 ft./1,951 m., it is the highest peak on the island.

**Olym·pus, Mount²** |ǝˈlimpǝs| mountain in N Greece, at the E end of the range dividing Thessaly from Macedonia; height 9,570 ft./2,917 m. It was the abode of the gods in Greek mythology.

**Olyn·thus** |ōˈlintHǝs| ancient city in NE Greece, on the peninsula of Chalcidice. It was the head of the Chalcidian League, formed to oppose the hegemony of Athens and Sparta.

**Omagh** |ōˈmä| town in Northern Ireland, principal town of County Tyrone. Pop. 15,000.

**Oma·ha** |ˈōmǝ‚hä| largest city in Nebraska, an industrial and market center in the E, on the Missouri River. Pop. 335,795.

**Oma·ha Beach** |ˈōmǝ‚hä| name used during the D-Day landing in June 1944 for one part of the Norman coast where U.S. troops landed. It is at the mouth of the Vire River, at the village of Saint-Laurent-sur-Mer, NW of Bayeux.

**Oman, Gulf of** |ōˈmän| inlet of the Arabian Sea, N of Oman, connected by the Strait of Hormuz to the Persian Gulf.

**Oman** |ōˈmän| country at the E corner of the Arabian Peninsula. Area: 82,030 sq. mi./212,458 sq. km. Pop. 1,600,000. Language, Arabic. Capital and largest city: Muscat. The sultanate, a regional power in the 19th century, when it was known as Muscat and Oman, is now an oil producer. □ **Omani** adj. & n.

**Oman**

**Om·dur·man** |ˌawmdǝrˈmän| city in central Sudan, on the Nile opposite Khartoum. Pop. 229,000. In 1898 it was the site of a battle that marked the final British defeat of local Mahdist forces.

**Ome** |ˈōmä| city in central Japan, on Honshu, W of Tokyo. Pop. 126,000.

**O-mei Shan** |ˈōmä ˈsHän| see EMEI SHAN, China.

**Omi·ya** |ōwˈmēyä| city in E central Japan, on E central Honshu, a suburb N of Tokyo. Pop. 404,000.

**Omo·lon River** |ǝmǝˈlawn| river (715 mi./1,150 km.) in E Russia. Rising in the Kolyma Mts., it flows into the Kolyma River.

**Omsk** |awmsk| industrial city in S central Russia, a port on the Irtysh and Om rivers. Pop. 1,159,000.

**Omu·ta** |'ōmळōtä| industrial city in SW Japan, on W Kyushu. Pop. 150,000.

**On·do** |'awndō| commercial city in SW Nigeria, NE of Lagos, capital of Ondo state. Pop. 150,000.

**One·ga, Lake** |ə'negə| lake in NW Russia, near the border with Finland, the second-largest (3,710 sq. mi./9,609 sq. km.) European lake, after Lake LADOGA..

**Onei·da** |ō'nīdə| city in central New York, near Oneida Lake, noted for its silverware industry, a legacy of a 19th-century religious community. Pop. 10,850.

**Onit·sha** |ō'nēcHə| industrial and commercial city in S Nigeria, a port on the Niger River. Pop. 328,000.

**Ono·mi·chi** |ōnōmēcHē| city in W Japan, on SW Honshu, W of Okayama. Pop. 97,000. It has noted Buddhist temples.

**On·tar·io, Lake** |awn'terēō| the smallest and most easterly of the Great Lakes, lying on the U.S.–Canadian border between Ontario and New York State.

**On·tar·io**[1] |awn'terēō| commercial city in SW California, E of Los Angeles, in an agricultural area. Pop. 133,179.

**On·tar·io**[2] |awn'terēō| province of E Canada, between Hudson Bay and the Great Lakes. Area: 412,581 sq. mi./1.069 million sq. km. Pop. 9,914,200. Capital and largest city: Toronto. Settled by the French and English in the 17th century, ceded to Britain in 1763, Ontario (formerly Upper Canada) became one of the original four provinces in the Dominion of Canada in 1867. It is agricultural and industrial, and Ottawa and Toronto conduct much of the administration and business of Canada. □ **Ontarian** *adj. & n.*

**Oost·en·de** |ō'stendə| Flemish name for OSTEND, Belgium.

**OPEC** |'ōpek| acronym for the **Organization of Petroleum Exporting Countries,** founded in 1960 and based in Vienna, Austria. Members are Algeria, Gabon, Indonesia, Iran, Iraq, Kuwait, Libya, Nigeria, Qatar, Saudi Arabia, the United Arab Emirates, and Venezuela.

**Ophir** |'ōfər| country of riches, especially gold and precious stones, mentioned in the Bible. It may have been in the SE Arabian Peninsula, or in E Africa.

**Opo·le** |aw'pawle| (in German **Oppeln**) industrial port city in S Poland, on the Oder River. Pop. 127,000.

**Opor·to** |ō'pawrtळ| the principal city and port of N Portugal, near the mouth of the Douro River, famous for port wine. Pop. 311,000. Portuguese name **Porto**.

**Ora·dea** |aw'rädyä| industrial city in W Romania, near the border with Hungary. Pop. 222,000.

**Oradour-sur-Glane** |awrə'dळrsळrglän| village in W central France, near Limoges, site of a World War II massacre. In June 1944, just after D-day, Nazis murdered the entire populace of approximately 700 persons, with the exception of a few who escaped, and then burned the entire village. The burned remains have been left as a reminder; a new village has developed nearby.

**Oral** |'awrəl| (former Russian name **Uralsk**) market city in NW Kazakhstan, on the Ural River. Pop. 207,000.

**Oran** |aw'rän| port on the Mediterranean coast of Algeria, an industrial center and the second-largest Algerian city. Pop. 664,000.

**Or·ange**[1] |'awrənj| city in SW California, SE of Los Angeles in an agricultural area. Pop. 110,658.

**Or·ange**[2] |'awrənj| town in S France, on the Rhône, home of the ancestors of the Dutch royal house.

**Or·ange County** |'awrənj| county in SW California, between Los Angeles and San Diego. Santa Ana, its seat, is one of many cities here. Pop. 2,410,556.

**Or·ange Free State** |'awrənj 'frē ˌstät| area and former province in central South Africa, to the north of the Orange River. First settled by Boers after the Great Trek, the area became a province of the Union of South Africa in 1910 and in 1994 became one of the new provinces of South Africa. The province was renamed **Free State** in 1995.

**Or·ange River** |'awrənj| the longest river in South Africa, which rises in the Drakensberg Mts. in NE Lesotho and flows generally W for 1,155 mi./1,859 km. to the Atlantic, forming the border between Namibia and South Africa in its lower course.

**Ora·ni·en·burg** |aw'ränēənbərg| city in NE Germany, on the Havel River. It was the site of one of the earliest Nazi concentration camps. Pop. 29,000.

**Oran·je·stad** |aw'ränyəstät| the capital of the Dutch island of Aruba in the Caribbean. Pop. 25,000.

**Ora·şul Stalin** former name for BRAŞOV, Romania.

**Or·du** |'awrdळ| (ancient name **Cotyora**) port city in N Turkey, the capital of Ordu province, on the Black Sea. Pop. 102,000.

**Or·dzho·ni·kid·ze** |ˌawrjäni'kijə| former

name (1954–93) for VLADIKAVKAZ, Russia.

**Öre·bro** |awrə'brōō| industrial city in S central Sweden. Pop. 121,000.

**Or·e·gon** |'awrə,gän; 'awrə,gən| see box.
□ **Oregonian** adj. & n.

**Or·e·gon Trail** |'awrə,gän; 'awrə,gən| pioneer route across the W U.S., from Independence, Missouri, to Fort Vancouver in the Willamette Valley of W Oregon Territory, some 2,000 mi./3,000 km. in length. It was used chiefly from 1842–1860 by settlers moving W.

**Orekhovo-Zuyevo** |,ər'yəKHəvə'zōōyəvə| industrial city in W Russia, E of Moscow, on the Klyazma River. Pop. 137,000.

**Orel** |aw'rel| historic industrial city in SW Russia, S of Moscow on the Oka and Orlik rivers. Pop. 342,000.

**Orem** |'ōrəm| city in N central Utah, a suburb of Provo. Pop. 67,561.

**Ore Mountains** |'aw(ə)r| English name for the ERZGEBIRGE, in Germany and the Czech Republic.

**Oren·burg** |'ōrən,bərg| industrial and commercial city in S Russia, on the Ural River. Pop. 552,000. It was known as Chkalov from 1938 to 1957.

**Oren·se** |aw'rensä| city in NW Spain, on the Miño River, in an agricultural region, capital of Orense province. Pop. 106,000.

---

### Oregon

**Capital:** Salem
**Largest city:** Portland
**Other cities:** Eugene, Medford, Portland
**Population:** 2,842,321 (1990); 3,281,974 (1998); 3,613,000 (2005 proj.)
**Population rank (1990):** 29
**Rank in land area:** 9
**Abbreviation:** OR; Ore., Oreg.
**Nickname:** Beaver State
**Motto:** 'The Union'
**Bird:** Western meadowlark
**Fish:** chinook salmon
**Flower:** Oregon grape
**Tree:** Douglas fir
**Song:** "Oregon, My Oregon"
**Noted physical features:** Coos Bay; Marble Hills Caves; Cascade Range and Mount Hood
**Tourist attractions:** Columbia River Gorge; Crater Lake National Park; Sea Lion Caves
**Admission date:** February 14, 1859
**Order of admission:** 33
**Name origin:** Possibly from a former name of the Columbia River; the exact origin of the name is in dispute.

---

**Øre·sund** |'əresən| narrow channel between Sweden and the Danish island of Zealand. It connects the Kattegat (N) with the Baltic Sea. Also called **the Sound**.

**Organization of African Unity** |,awrgənə'zäsHən əv 'æfrəkən 'yōōnədē| (abbreviated **OAU**) organization founded in 1963 for cooperation among independent African states. It now has over 50 members and is headquartered in Addis Ababa, Ethiopia.

**Organization of American States** |,awrgənə'zäsHən əv ə'merəkən stäts| (abbreviated **OAS**) organization founded in 1948 to promote political and economic cooperation among states of North America, South America, and the Caribbean. Cuba was denied participation in 1962. Headquarters are in Washington, D.C.

**Ori·ent, the** |'awrēənt| literary name for countries of E Asia, or of all of Asia. Originally it referred to the Near East. It derives from the Latin term for 'rising' (used of the sun). □ **Oriental** adj. & n.

**Oril·lia** |ō'rilyə| city in S Ontario, on Lake Simcoe N of Toronto. Pop. 25,925.

**Ori·no·co** |,awrə'nōkō| river in N South America, which rises in SE Venezuela and flows 1,280 mi./2,060 km., entering the Atlantic through a vast delta. For part of its length it forms the border between Colombia and Venezuela.

**Oris·sa** |aw'risə| state in E India, on the Bay of Bengal. Pop. 31,510,000. Capital: Bhubaneswar.

**Ori·za·ba** |,ōrē'säbə| commercial and resort city in E central Mexico, in Veracruz state. Pop. 114,000. Nearby is the **Pico de Orizaba**, or CITLALTÉPETL, the highest peak in the country.

**Ork·ney Islands** |'awrknē| (also **Orkney** or **the Orkneys**) a group of more than 70 islands off the NE tip of Scotland, constituting an administrative region of Scotland. Pop. 19,000; chief town, Kirkwall. Colonized by the Vikings in the 9th century, they came into Scottish possession (together with Shetland) in 1472, having previously been ruled (together with Shetland) by Norway and Denmark.

**Or·kon River** |'awrkän| (also **Orkhon**) river in N Mongolia, flowing 698 mi./1,123 km. from the N edge of the Gobi Desert until it joins the Selenga River near the Russian border.

**Or·lan·do** |awr'lændō| city in central Florida. Pop. 164,693. It is a popular tourist destination, situated near the John F. Kennedy Space Center and Disney World.

**Or·lé·a·nais** |awrläə'ne| region and former

province of N central France, centered around Orléans.

**Orl·é·ans, Île d'** |ˌēldawrlaˈän| historic residential and resort island in the St. Lawrence River in S Quebec, just NE of Quebec City.

**Orl·e·ans** |ˈawrlē(ə)nz| commercial city in central France, on the Loire, capital of Loiret department. Pop. 108,000. In 1429 it was the scene of Joan of Arc's first victory over the English during the Hundred Years War. French name **Orléans**.

**Or·ly** |ˈawrˈlē| SW suburb of Paris, in N central France, site of an international airport.

**Or·moc** |awrˈmäk| (also called **MacArthur**) commercial port city in the Philippines, on W Leyte. Pop. 129,000. It was a Japanese military base during World War II, until captured by U.S. troops in 1944.

**Or·mond Beach** |ˈawrmənd| resort city in NE Florida, N of Daytona Beach. Pop. 29,721.

**Orne River** |awrn| river (95 mi./152 km.) in NW France, rising in the Orne department and flowing through Calvados, past Caen into the English Channel.

**Oro·no** |ˈōrə,nō| town in E central Maine, on the Penobscot River N of Bangor, home to the University of Maine. Pop. 10,573.

**Oron·tes** |awˈrawntēz| river in SW Asia that rises near Baalbek in N Lebanon and flows 355 mi./571 km. through W and N Syria before turning W through S Turkey to enter the Mediterranean. It is an important source of water for irrigation, especially in Syria.

**Or·re·fors** |awrreˈfawrs| town in SE Sweden, NW of Kalmar, noted for its crystal and glassware.

**Or·sha** |ˈawrsHə| city in NE Belarus. Pop. 112,000. It is a rail and industrial center.

**Orsk** |awrsk| industrial city in S Russia, in the Urals on the Ural River near the border with Kazakhstan. Pop. 271,000.

**Oru·mi·yeh** |ˌoo,roōˈmēyə| (also **Uru·miyeh**) **1** shallow salt lake in NW Iran, W of Tabriz. **2** city in NW Iran. Pop. 357,000. According to tradition, the religious leader Zoroaster was born here.

**Oru·ro** |awˈroōrō| city in W Bolivia. Pop. 183,000. It is the center of an important mining region.

**Or·vie·to** |awrˈvyätō| town in Umbria, central Italy. Pop. 22,000. It lies at the center of a wine-producing area.

**Osage River** |ōˈsäj| river that flows 360 mi./580 km. through Missouri to the Missouri River. The Lake of the Ozarks is along it.

**Osa·ka** |ōˈsäkə| port and commercial and industrial city in central Japan, on the island of Honshu, capital of Kinki region. Pop. 2,642,000. It is the third-largest Japanese city.

**Osa·sco** |ooˈsäskoo| city in S Brazil, a suburb W of São Paulo. Pop. 622,000.

**Osh** |awsH| city in W Kyrgyzstan, near the border with Uzbekistan. Pop. 236,000. It was an important post on an ancient trade route to China and India.

**Osh·a·wa** |ˈäsHəwə| city in Ontario, on the shore of Lake Ontario E of Toronto. Pop. 174,010. It is the center of the Canadian automobile industry.

**Osh·kosh** |ˈäsHkäsH| industrial city in E central Wisconsin, on L. Winnebago. Pop. 55,006.

**Osho·gbo** |ōˈsHōgbō| commercial and industrial city in SW Nigeria, NE of Ibadan. Pop. 421,000.

**Osi·jek** |ˈōsēyek| industrial city in E Croatia, on the Drava River. Pop. 105,000.

**Öskemen** |ˈawskemən| ( formerly **Ust-Kamenogosk**) industrial city in NE Kazakhstan, on the Irtysh River. Pop. 330,000.

**Os·lo** |ˈäz,lō| the capital, largest city, and chief port of Norway, on the S coast at the head of Oslofjord. Pop. 458,000. Founded in the 11th century, it was known as Christiania (or Kristiania) from 1624 until 1924.

**Os·na·brück** |äsnəbroōk| industrial city in NW Germany, in Lower Saxony. Pop. 165,000.

**Osor·no** |ōsˈawrnō| commercial city in S Chile, in the lake resort district. Pop. 117,000. It is home to many descendants of German immigrants.

**Os·sa, Mount**[1] |ˈäsə| mountain in Thessaly, NE Greece, south of Mount Olympus, rising to a height of 6,489 ft./1,978 m. In Greek mythology the giants piled Mount Ossa onto Mount Pelion in an attempt to reach Olympus and destroy the gods.

**Os·sa, Mount**[2] |ˈäsə| the highest mountain on the island of Tasmania, rising to a height of 5,305 ft./1,617 m.

**Os·se·tia** |äˈsēsHə| region of the central Caucasus. It is divided by the boundary between Russia and Georgia into two parts, North Ossetia (now Alania) and South Ossetia, and between 1989 and 1992 was the scene of ethnic conflict.

**Os·si·ning** |ˈawsəninG| town in SE New York, on the Hudson River, noted as the home of Sing Sing prison. Pop. 34,124.

**Os·tend** |äˈstend| port on the North Sea coast of NW Belgium, in West Flanders. Pop. 68,000. It is a major ferry port. Flemish name **Oostende**; French name **Ostende**.

**Os·tia** |'ästēə| ancient city and harbor that was situated on the W coast of Italy at the mouth of the Tiber River; siltation eventually left it several miles inland. It was the first colony founded by ancient Rome and was a major port and commercial center.

**Ostra·va** |'awstrəvə| industrial city in the Moravian lowlands of the NE Czech Republic. Pop. 328,000. It is in the coalmining region of Silesia.

**Os·we·go** |äs'wēgō| industrial port city in N central New York, on Lake Ontario and the Oswego River. Pop. 19,195.

**Ota** |'ōtə| industrial city in N central Japan, on central Honshu, NE of Tokyo. Pop. 140,000.

**Ota·go** |ō'tägō| region of New Zealand, on the SE coast of South Island. Dunedin is the chief setlement.

**Ota·ru** |ō'tä,rōō| industrial and commercial port city in N Japan, on W Hokkaido. Pop. 163,000.

**Otran·to, Strait of** |aw'träntō| channel linking the Adriatic Sea with the Ionian Sea and separating the 'heel' of Italy from Albania.

**Otsu** |'ōtsōō| industrial port city in central Japan, on S Honshu, E of Kyoto. Pop. 260,000.

**Ot·ta·wa** |'ätə,wä| the federal capital of Canada, in SE Ontario on the Ottawa River. Pop. 313,987. Founded in 1827, it was named Bytown until 1854.

**Ot·ta·wa River** |'ätə,wä| river that flows 700 mi./1,100 km. through E Canada, forming much of the border between Ontario and Quebec, into the St. Lawrence River.

**Ot·ter·burn** |'ätər,bərn| village in N England, in Northumberland, scene of a 1388 Scottish victory over the English, celebrated in the ballads "Chevy Chase" and "Otterburn."

**Ot·to·man Empire** |'ätəmən 'em,pī(ə)r| Muslim empire of the Turks, established in 1299 and finally dissolved in 1922. In the 16th century it dominated the E Mediterranean and much of SE Europe.

**Ouach·i·ta Mountains** |'wäSHitaw| low range in W Arkansas and E Oklahoma, S of the Ozark Plateau. Magazine Mt., at 2,753 ft./840 m., is the high point in Arkansas.

**Ouach·i·ta River** |'wäSHitaw| river that flows 600 mi./970 km. across W Arkansas and into N Louisiana, where it is known in part as the Black River and empties into the Red River.

**Oua·ga·dou·gou** |,wägə'dōōgōō| the capital of Burkina Faso, a commercial and administrative city, formerly capital of the Mossi empire. Pop. 634,000.

**Ou·de·naar·de** |,awdən'ärdə| town in East Flanders, Belgium, site of a British and Austrian victory over French troops in 1708. Pop. 27,000.

**Oudh** |awd| (also **Audh** or **Awadh**) region of N India. In 1877 it joined with Agra and in 1902 it formed the United Provinces of Agra and Oudh. This was renamed Uttar Pradesh in 1950.

**Oues·sant** |we'sän| (also **Ushant**) island 10 mi./16 km. off the coast of Brittany, in NW France. Its lighthouse marks the S entrance to the English Channel.

**Oui·dah** |'wēdə| (also **Whydah** or **Wida**) port town in S Benin, W of Cotonou on the Gulf of Guinea. Pop. 32,000. In the 17th–19th centuries it was a major slaveexporting center.

**Ouj·da** |ōō'jdä| (also **Oudjda**) commercial city in NE Morocco, near the Algerian border, in a mining district. Pop. 357,000.

**Ou·lu** |'aw,lōō| city in central Finland, on the W coast, capital of a province of the same name. Pop. 101,000. Swedish name **Uleåborg**.

**Ouro Prê·to** |'ōrōō 'prätōō| historic city in E Brazil, in Minas Gerais state. Pop. 62,000. A cultural and former gold rush town, it draws tourists.

**Ouse** |ōōz| name of several English rivers (especially the **Great Ouse**), which rises in Northamptonshire and flows 160 mi./257 km. E then northward through East Anglia to the Wash near King's Lynn.

**Out·back, the** |'owt ,bæk| popular name for isolated, sparsely populated, rural areas of Australia.

**Out·er Banks** |'owtər 'bænks| series of barrier islands on the Atlantic coast in E North Carolina. It is noted for its resorts, and for the older culture of inhabitants called "Bankers."

**Out·er Mon·go·lia** |'owdər mäNG'gōlēyə| see MONGOLIA.

**Ou·tre·mont** |'ōōtrə,mänt| residential city in S Quebec, across Mount Royal from downtown Montreal. Pop. 22,935.

**Ov·am·bo·land** |ō'væmbō,lænd| semiarid region of N Namibia, the homeland of the Ovambo people.

**Over·ijs·sel** |,ōvər'äsəl| province of the E central Netherlands, N of the IJssel River, on the border with Germany. Pop. 1,026,000. Capital: Zwolle.

**Over·land Park** |'ōvər,lænd| city in NE

**Oviedo** Kansas, a commercial and residential suburb SW of Kansas City. Pop. 111,790.

**Ovie·do** |aw'vyedō| industrial city in NW Spain, capital of the Asturias region and Oviedo province. Pop. 203,000.

**Owa·ton·na** |ˌōwə'tänə| commercial city in SE Minnesota, in a dairy farming region. Pop. 19,386.

**Owen·do** |ō'wendō| village in NW Gabon, on the Gabon River just SE of Libreville, for which it is the deepwater port, and just upstream from the Atlantic.

**Ow·ens·boro** |'ōwənzˌbərō| industrial port city in NW Kentucky, on the Ohio River. Pop. 53,549.

**Owen Stan·ley Range** |'ōwən 'stænlē| mountains extending SE to NW across New Guinea Island, Papua New Guinea, reaching 13,363 ft./4,073 m. at Mount Victoria.

**Owens Valley** |'ōwənz| valley of the Owens River, in E central California, between the Sierra Nevada and the Inyo Mts., the source since 1913 of much of the water supply for Los Angeles.

**Ox·ford**[1] |'äksfərd| industrial and cultural city in central England, on the Thames River, the county seat of Oxfordshire. Pop. 109,000. Oxford University is here.

**Ox·ford**[2] |'äksfərd| town in N central Mississippi, home to the University of Mississippi and associated with novelist William Faulkner. Pop. 9,984. See also YOKNAPATAWPHA COUNTY.

**Ox·ford·shire** |'äksfərdˌSHi(ə)r| county of S central England. Pop. 554,000; county seat, Oxford.

**Ox·nard** |'äksˌnärd| city in SW California, in an agricultural area NW of Los Angeles, on the Pacific coast. Pop. 142,216.

**Ox·us** |'äksəs| ancient name for the AMU DARYA River.

**Ox·y·rhyn·chus** |ˌäksə'riNGkəs| archaeological site in NE Egypt, on the Nile River S of El Faiyum, where many important papyri have been recovered. The present-day village of Al-Bahnasa (or Behnesa) is here.

**Oya·ma** |ō'yäˌmä| industrial city in N central Japan, on central Honshu, N of Tokyo. Pop. 148,000.

**Oyo** |'ōyō| commercial and agricultural city in SW Nigeria, N of Ibadan. Pop. 226,000.

**Oys·ter Bay** |'oistər| town in central Long Island, New York, containing Hicksville, Farmingdale, Oyster Bay, and other suburban villages. Pop. 292,657.

**Oz** nickname for AUSTRALIA.

**Ozark Mountains** |'ō,zärk| (also **the Ozarks**) heavily forested highland plateau dissected by rivers, valleys, and streams, lying between the Missouri and Arkansas rivers and within the states of Missouri, Arkansas, Oklahoma, Kansas, and Illinois. The Ozarks are noted for their rural culture.

# Pp

**Paarl** |pärl| town in SW South Africa, in the province of Western Cape, NE of Cape Town. Pop. 71,000. It is at the center of a noted wine-producing region.

**Pa·chu·ca de So·to** |pə'CHŏŏkə di 'sōtō| (officially **Pachuca de Soto**) city in Mexico, capital of the state of Hidalgo. Pop. 179,000.

**Pa·cif·i·ca** |pə'sifikə| city in N central California, a suburb just S of San Francisco, on the Pacific. Pop. 37,670.

**Pa·cif·ic Crest Trail** |pə'sifik| recreational trail that extends from the Mexican to the Canadian border, through California, Oregon, and Washington, following mountain ridges for 2,600 mi./4,200 km.

**Pa·cif·ic Islands, Trust Territory of the** |pə'sifik| United Nations trusteeship established in 1947 under U.S. administration, and dissolved in 1994. It included the Caroline, Marshall, and Mariana islands, today all components of the Marshall Islands, the Northern Mariana Islands, the Federated States of Micronesia, or Palau.

**Pa·cif·ic Ocean** |pə'sifik| the largest of the world's oceans, lying between North and South America to the E and Asia and Australasia to the W, and occupying roughly one-third of the surface of the earth. The explorer Magellan named it for its relatively calm weather. See also SOUTH SEA.

**Pa·cif·ic Rim** |pə'sifik| the countries and regions bordering the Pacific Ocean, especially the nations of E Asia that experienced rapid economic growth in the 1980s and 1990s.

**Pa·dang** |'päd,äNG| seaport of Indonesia, the largest city on the W coast of Sumatra. Pop. 481,000.

**Pad·ding·ton** |'pädiNGtən| largely residential district of W central London, England, known for its railroad station, which serves W England and Wales.

**Pa·der·born** |'pädərbawrn| agricultural market and industrial city in Germany, E of Münster. Pop. 126,000. The Holy Roman Empire was born here in a meeting between Charlemagne and Pope Leo III in 799.

**Pad·ma** |'pädmə| river of S Bangladesh, formed by the confluence of the Ganges and the Brahmaputra in the Ganges delta near Rajbari.

**Pa·do·va** |'pädōvə| Italian name for PADUA.

**Pad·re Island** |'pädrä| barrier island in S Texas, on the Gulf of Mexico, noted for its resorts and its wildlife. It is 113 mi./183 km. long.

**Pad·ua** |'päjŏŏə| historic industrial and commercial city in NE Italy. Pop. 218,000. Italian name **Padova**.

**Pa·du·cah** |pə'd(y)ŏŏkə| historic commercial city in W Kentucky, on the Ohio River near the mouth of the Tennessee River. Pop. 27,256.

**Paes·tum** |'pestəm| ancient city in S Italy, on the Gulf of Salerno. It was founded in the 6th century B.C. by Greek colonists.

**Pa·ga·lu** |pə'gälŏŏ| former name (1973–79) for ANNOBÓN, Equatorial Guinea.

**Pa·gan** |'pägən| town in Burma, situated on the Irrawaddy SE of Mandalay. It is the site of an ancient city that was the capital of a powerful Buddhist dynasty the 11th–13th centuries.

**Pa·go Pa·go** |,pägō 'pägō| chief port of American Samoa, on Tutuila Island. Pop. 4,000. Fagatogo, the territorial capital, is just to the E.

**Pa·hang** |pə'hæNG| mountainous forested state of Malaysia, on the E coast of the Malay Peninsula. Capital: Kuantan.

**Paign·ton** |'pān(t)ən| resort town in SW England, on the S coast of Devon. Pop. 41,000.

**Paint·ed Desert** | 'päntəd| region of NE Arizona noted for its colorful eroded landscapes.

**Pais·ley** |'päzlē| town in central Scotland, to the W of Glasgow, administrative center of Renfrewshire. Pop. 75,000. A center of handweaving by the 18th century, it became famous for its distinctive shawls.

**Pak·i·stan** |'pækə,stæn| republic in the NW of the Indian subcontinent. Area: 310,522 sq. mi./803,943 sq. km. Pop. 115,588,000. Languages, Urdu (official), Punjabi, Sindhi, Pashto. Capital: Islamabad. Largest city: Karachi. Created in 1947 from Indian territory as an Islamic nation, Pakistan lost East Pakistan (as the new Bangladesh) in 1972. Predominantly agricultural, it has growing industry. □ **Pakistani** *adj. & n.*

**Pak·se** |päk'sä| (also **Pakxe**) largest town in S Laos, on the Mekong River. Pop. 25,000. The 7th-century ruins of the

**Pakistan**

ancient Khmer capital of Wat Phou lie to the S.

**Pa·lat·i·nate** |pə'lætnət| name given to two regions of Germany during the Holy Roman Empire: the Rhenish or Lower Palatinate, now part of Rhineland-Palatinate, and the Upper Palatinate, now in NE Bavaria.

**Pal·a·tine** |'pælə,tīn| village in NE Illinois, a suburb NW of Chicago. Pop. 39,253.

**Pa·lau** |pə'law| (also called **Belau**) island republic in the W Pacific, in the Caroline Islands. Area: 188 sq. mi./488 sq. km. Pop. 16,400. Capital: Koror (to be replaced by Babelthuap). Held by Spain, Germany, and the U.S. before 1994, the islands have an economy based on fishing and tourism.

**Pa·la·wan** |pə'lawən| long, narrow, mountainous island in the W Philippines, separating the Sulu Sea from the South China Sea; chief town, Puerto Princesa.

**Pale, the** |pāl| **1 English Pale** or **Irish Pale** the part of Ireland controlled by the British from the 11th century until the 16th century, when complete control was achieved. **2 Jewish Pale** parts of Poland in which Jews were traditionally allowed to live.

**Pa·lem·bang** |pälem'bäNG| historic commercial city in Indonesia, in the SE part of the island of Sumatra, a port on the Musi River. Pop. 1,141,000.

**Pa·len·cia** |pə'lensēə| industrial city in NW Spain, site of the first Spanish university (1208), and capital of Palencia province. Pop. 77,000.

**Pa·len·que** |pə'leNGkə| site of a former Mayan city in N Chiapas, SE Mexico, SE of present-day Villahermosa. The well-preserved ruins of the city, which existed from about A.D. 300 to 900, include notable examples of Mayan architecture and extensive hieroglyphic texts.

**Pa·ler·mo** |pə'lər,mō| the capital of the Italian island of Sicily, an industrial port on

the N coast. Pop. 734,000. It was founded by the Phoenicians in the 8th century B.C.

**Pal·es·tine** |'pælə,stīn| territory in the Middle East on the E coast of the Mediterranean Sea. It has had many changes of frontier and status in the course of history, and contains several places that are sacred to Christians, Jews, and Muslims. In biblical times Palestine comprised Israel and Judah. The land was controlled at various times by the Egyptian, Assyrian, Persian, and Roman empires before being conquered by the Arabs in A.D. 634. It remained in Muslim hands, except for the period during the Crusades (1098–1197), until World War I, being part of the Ottoman Empire from 1516 to 1918. The name Palestine was used as the official political title for the land W of the Jordan mandated to Britain in 1920. In 1948 the state of Israel was established in what was traditionally Palestine, but the name continued to be used in the context of the struggle for territory and political rights of displaced Palestinian Arabs. Agreements from 1993 and subsequently between Israel and the Palestine Liberation Organization gave limited autonomy to the Gaza Strip and the West Bank and set up the Palestine National Authority and a police force. □ **Palestinian** adj. & n.

**Pa·les·tri·na** |,pælə'strēnə| agricultural market town in central Italy. Pop. 14,000. It is built on the site of a town, Praeneste, that was a summer resort for wealthy residents of ancient Rome.

**Pal·ghat** |'pälgät| (also **Pulicat; Palakkad**) commercial town in SE India, in Kerala state. Pop. 180,000. It commands a major pass through the Western Ghats.

**Pa·li·kir** |,pälē'kir| capital of the Federated States of Micronesia, on Pohnpei. It succeeds nearby Kolonia.

**Pal·i·sades, the** |,pælə'sādz| (also **Palisades of the Hudson**) cliffs that line the W side of the Hudson River, in New Jersey and New York, across from New York City and N to Newburgh, New York.

**Palk Strait** |pälk| inlet of the Bay of Bengal separating N Sri Lanka from the coast of Tamil Nadu in India. It lies to the N of Adam's Bridge, which separates it from the Gulf of Mannar.

**Pall Mall** |,päl 'mäl| street in central London, England, in Westminster, N of St. James's Park, noted for its clubs and as a resort of high society. It gave its name to the term *mall*.

**Pal·ma** |'pälmə| the capital of the Balearic

Islands of Spain, an industrial port and resort on the island of Majorca. Pop. 309,000. Full name **Palma de Mallorca**.

**Pal·mas** |'pälməs| town in central Brazil, on the Tocantins River, capital of the state of Tocantins. Pop. 6,000.

**Palm Bay** |pälm| residential city in E central Florida, just SW of Melbourne. Pop. 62,632.

**Palm Beach** |pälm| fashionable resort town in SE Florida, on a barrier island between the Atlantic and Lake Worth (a lagoon). Pop. 9,814.

**Palm·dale** |'pälmdäl| city in SW California, a suburb N of Los Angeles, near Edwards Air Force Base. Pop. 68,842.

**Pal·mer·ston North** |',pä(l)mərstən 'nawrTH| commercial city in the SW part of North Island, New Zealand. Pop. 69,000.

**Pal·met·to State** |päl'metō| nickname for SOUTH CAROLINA.

**Pal·mi·ra** |'pälmīrə| city in W Colombia, in Valle del Cauca department, an agricultural commerce and research center. Pop. 175,000.

**Palm Springs** |,pä(l)m 'spriNGz| resort city in the Colorado Desert of S California, E of Los Angeles, noted for its hot mineral springs and affluent lifestyle. Pop. 40,181.

**Pal·my·ra**[1] |päl'mīrə| town in W New York, SE of Rochester, noted as the early home of Joseph Smith, Mormon church founder. Pop. 7,690.

**Pal·my·ra**[2] |päl'mīrə| ancient city of Syria, an oasis in the Syrian desert NE of Damascus on the site of present-day Tadmur.

**Pal·my·ra Atoll** |'pälmīrə| atoll in the central Pacific, part of the Line Islands and formerly part of Hawaii, but excluded at statehood in 1959.

**Pa·lo Al·to** |'pælō 'æltō| city in W California, S of San Francisco. Pop. 55,900. It is a noted center for electronics and computer technology, and the residential center for nearby Stanford University.

**Pal·o·mar, Mount** |'pælə,mär| mountain in S California, NE of San Diego, rising to a height of 6,126 ft./1,867 m. It is the site of a noted astronomical observatory.

**Pa·los** |'pälōs| former seaport in SW Spain. Pop. 7,000. Christopher Columbus sailed from here on his first voyage to the New World, in 1492.

**Pa·lu** |'pälōō| city in Indonesia, on W Sulawesi. Pop. 299,000.

**Pa·mir Mountains** |pə'mir| (also **the Pamirs**) mountain system of central Asia, centered in Tajikistan and extending into Kyrgyzstan, Afghanistan, Pakistan, and W China. The highest peak in the Pamirs, Communism Peak in Tajikistan, rises to 24,590 ft./7,495 m.

**Pam·li·co Sound** |'pæmli,kō| inlet of the Atlantic in E North Carolina, inside the Outer Banks islands. Albemarle Sound is to its N.

**Pam·pas** |'pämpəz| (also **Pampa**) wide treeless plains of South America, in central Argentina and S Uruguay. Humid and grass-covered, they are used for cattle and grain production.

**Pam·phyl·ia** |pæm'filyə| ancient coastal region of S Asia Minor, between Lycia and Cilicia, to the E of the modern port of Antalya, Turkey. □ **Pamphylian** adj. & n.

**Pam·plo·na** |pæm'plōnə| industrial city in N Spain, capital of the former kingdom and modern region of Navarre. Pop. 191,000. It is noted for the fiesta of San Fermin, held in July, which is celebrated with the running of bulls through the streets of the city.

**Pa·na·ji** |pə'näjē| (also **Panjim**) city in W India, a port on the Arabian Sea. Pop. 85,000. It is the capital of the state of Goa.

**Pan·a·ma** |'pænə,mä| republic in Central America, in the Isthmus of Panama. Area: 29,773 sq. mi./77,082 sq. km. Pop. 2,329,330. Language, Spanish. Capital and largest city: Panama City. A Spanish colony, Panama became part of Colombia in 1821, and gained independence in 1903. The U.S. controlled the Canal Zone, splitting the country, until 1979. Panama is primarily agricultural, with Canal-based business also important. □ **Panamanian** adj. & n.

Panama

**Pan·a·ma, Isthmus of** |'pænə,mä| (formerly the **Isthmus of Darien**) in the narrowest sense, the site of the Panama Canal. More broadly, all the territory of Panama, or the entire region connecting North and South America.

**Pan·a·ma Canal** |'pænə,mä kə'næl| canal

about 50 mi./80 km. long, across the Isthmus of Panama, connecting the Atlantic and Pacific. Its construction, begun by Ferdinand de Lesseps in 1881 but abandoned in 1889, was completed by the U.S. between 1904 and 1914. Control of the canal by the U.S. is due to be ceded to Panama in 1999. The surrounding territory, the (Panama) Canal Zone, was administered by the U.S. until 1979, when it was returned to Panama.

**Pan·a·ma City**[1] |'pænə‚mä| port city in NW Florida, a resort center in the Panhandle. Pop. 34,378.

**Pan·a·ma City**[2] |'pænə‚mä| the capital of Panama, situated on the Pacific coast (the Gulf of Panama) close to the Panama Canal. Pop. 585,000.

**Pan-American Highway** |‚pæn'æmerə‚kən| road system initiated in the 1920s to link nations of the W hemisphere from Alaska to Chile. Gaps remain in Panama and Colombia. The **Inter-American Highway** is the section from the Texas-Mexico border S to Panama City.

**Pan·a·mint Range** |'pænəmint| mountain range in E central California, W of Death Valley, noted for its high walls and deep canyons.

**Pa·nay** |pə'nī| island in the Visayas group, in the central Philippines; chief town, Iloilo.

**Pan·chiao** |'pæn'CHiow| (also **Pan-ch'iao**; formerly **Pankiao**) city in N Taiwan, a suburb SW of Taipei. Pop. 544,000.

**Pan·dhar·pur** |'pəndər‚po͝or| town in W central India, in Maharashtra state. Pop. 64,000. It is a Hindu pilgrimage site.

**Pa·ne·ve·žys** |pänyə‚və'ZHēz| industrial city in Lithuania, NE of Kaunas. Pop. 132,000.

**Pan·gaea** |pæn'jēə| name for earth's hypothetical single land mass prior to its separation into distinct continents between 300 and 200 million years ago.

**Pan·han·dle** |'pæn‚hæ(d)əl| popular name for part of any of various U.S. states that projects from its main body. Examples are those in SE Alaska, NW Florida, N Texas, and W Oklahoma.

**Pa·ni·ha·ti** |pänē'hätē| industrial and commercial city in NE India, in West Bengal state, a suburb N of Calcutta. Pop. 275,000.

**Pa·ni·pat** |'pänēpət| historic town in NW India, in Haryana state, N of Delhi. Pop. 191,000.

**Pan·mun·jom** |'pan'mo͝on'jawm| village in the demilitarized zone between North and South Korea. It was here that the armistice ending the Korean War was signed on July 27, 1953. International talks have been held here since.

**Pan·no·nia** |pə'nōnēə| ancient country of S Europe lying S and W of the Danube, in present-day Austria, Hungary, Slovenia, and Croatia.

**Pan·ta·nal** |päntä'näl| vast region of tropical swampland in the upper reaches of the Paraguay River in SW Brazil.

**Pan·tel·le·ria** |‚pæn(t)ələ'rēə| volcanic Italian island in the Mediterranean, situated between Sicily and the coast of Tunisia. It was used as a place of exile by the ancient Romans, who called it Cossyra. Pop. 7,000.

**Pan·the·on, the** |'pænTHē‚än| secular temple in Paris, France. Constructed 1759–89 in the classical style, it contains the tombs of many illustrious French writers, including Voltaire and Victor Hugo.

**Pa·pal States** |'päpəl ‚stāts| the temporal dominions formerly (756–1870) belonging to the Pope, in central Italy. See also VATICAN CITY.

**Pa·pe·e·te** |‚päpä'ātā| the capital of French Polynesia, situated on the NW coast of Tahiti. Pop. 24,000.

**Paph·la·go·nia** |‚pæflə'gōnēə| ancient region of N Asia Minor (present-day Turkey), on the Black Sea coast between Bithynia and Pontus, to the N of Galatia. □ **Paphlagonian** adj. & n.

**Pa·phos** |'pa‚fŏs| historic port and resort town in SW Cyprus. Pop. 29,000. According to Greek legend, the goddess Aphrodite was born on the waves near here.

**Pap·ua** |'päpo͝oə| the SE part of the island of New Guinea, now part of the independent state of Papua New Guinea.

**Pap·ua New Guinea** country in the W Pacific comprising the E half of the island of New Guinea together with some neighboring islands. Area: 178,772 sq. mi./462,840 sq. km. Pop. 3,530,000. Languages, English (official), Tok Pisin, and several hundred Austronesian and Papuan languages.

**Papua New Guinea**

Capital and largest city: Port Moresby. Formed administratively in 1949, under Australian control, Papua New Guinea gained independence in 1975. It is largely agricultural, with mining also important. □ **Papua New Guinean** *adj. & n.*

**Pa·rá** |pe'rä| **1** name for the E mouth of the Amazon River, also at the mouth of the Tocantins River, in N Brazil. **2** state in N Brazil, on the Atlantic coast at the delta of the Amazon. Pop. 5,182,000. Capital: Belém. It is a region of dense rainforest.

**Pa·ra·cel Islands** |‚pärə'sel| (also the **Paracels**) group of about 130 small barren coral islands and reefs in the South China Sea to the SE of the Chinese island of Hainan. The islands are claimed by both China and Vietnam.

**Paracel Islands**

**Par·a·dise** |'perə‚dīs| suburban community in SE Nevada, just S of Las Vegas. Pop. 124,682.

**Par·a·guay** |'perə‚gwī| landlocked republic in central South America. Area: 157,108 sq. mi./406,752 sq. km. Pop. 4,120,000. Languages, Spanish (official), Guarani. Capital and largest city: Asunción. Independent of Spanish rule in 1811, Paraguay has warred with its neighbors in 1865–70 and 1932–35. Ranching, agriculture, and textiles are leading industries. □ **Paraguayan** *adj. & n.*

**Par·a·guay River** |'perə‚gwī| river that

**Paraguay**

flows 1,584 mi./2,549 km. from the Mato Grosso of W Brazil into Paraguay, and into the Paraná River. It is navigable by larger vessels as far as Concepción.

**Pa·ra·í·ba** |pärä'ēbä| state of E Brazil, on the Atlantic coast. Pop. 3,201,000. Capital: João Pessoa.

**Pa·ra·mar·i·bo** |‚perə'merə‚bō| the capital of Suriname, a port on the Atlantic coast. Pop. 201,000.

**Par·a·mount** |'perə‚mownt| city in SW California, a suburb SE of Los Angeles. Pop. 47,669.

**Pa·ram·us** |pə'ræməs| borough in NE New Jersey, a commercial and residential suburb NE of Paterson. Pop. 25,101.

**Pa·ra·ná¹** |'pärä'nä| river port in E Argentina, on the Paraná River. Pop. 276,000.

**Pa·ra·ná²** |‚pärä'nä| state of S Brazil, on the Atlantic coast. Pop. 8,443,000. Capital: Curitiba.

**Pa·ra·ná³** |‚pärä'nä| river of South America, which rises in SE Brazil and flows some 2,060 mi./3,300 km. S to the Plate River estuary in Argentina. For part of its length it forms the SE border of Paraguay.

**Pa·ra·na·guá** |'päränäg'wä| port city in SE Brazil, in Paraná state. Pop. 108,000. It is a coffee-exporting center.

**Pa·ra·ña·que** |‚pärə'nyäkä| commercial and residential town in the Philippines, on S Luzon, S of Manila. Pop. 308,000.

**Par·bha·ni** |'pərbənē| commercial town in central India, in Maharashtra state. Pop. 190,000.

**Par·du·bi·ce** |'pärdōō‚bitsē| industrial city in the N central Czech Republic, on the Elbe River. Pop. 96,000.

**Pa·ra·í·ba River** |pär'äbə| river that flows 650 mi./1,050 km. across S Brazil, from São Paulo state through Rio de Janeiro state, to the Atlantic at Campos. Its valley is a key agricultural region.

**Pa·ri·cu·tin** |pä'rēkōōtēn| volcano in W central Mexico, in Michoacán state, that appeared in 1943 and grew until 1952, burying a village and being studied closely by scientists.

**Par·is¹** |'pærəs| the capital of France, on the Seine River. Pop. 2,175,000. Paris was held by the Romans, who called it Lutetia, and from the 5th century by the Franks, and was established as the capital in 987. It was organized into three parts, the Île de la Cité (an island in the Seine), the Right Bank, and the Left Bank, during the reign of Philippe-Auguste (1180–1223). The city's neoclassical architecture dates from modernization in the Napoleonic era; this continued under Napoleon III, when the bridges and boulevards of the modern city were built. Famous landmarks are the Eiffel Tower, the Louvre, and Notre-Dame cathedral. Paris is a world cultural and administrative center. □ **Parisian** adj. & n.

**Par·is**[2] |'pĕrəs| commercial city in NE Texas. Pop. 24,699.

**Park Avenue** |'pärk| commercial and residential street in Manhattan, New York City, regarded as emblematic of worldly success.

**Par·kers·burg** |'pärkərzbərg| industrial city in NW West Virginia, on the Ohio River. Pop. 33,862.

**Park Range** |'pärk| range of the Rocky Mts. in S Wyoming and N Colorado, W of the Front Range. It is noted for its resorts.

**Par·lia·ment Hill** |'pärlə,mənt| locality in Ottawa, Ontario, site of the chief buildings and offices of the government of Canada.

**Par·ma**[1] |'pärmə| **1** province of N Italy, S of the Po River in Emilia-Romagna. **2** its capital. Pop. 194,000. Founded by the Romans, it became a bishopric in the 9th century A.D. and capital of the duchy of Parma and Piacenza in about 1547.

**Par·ma**[2] |'pärmə| city in NE Ohio, a residential and industrial suburb S of Cleveland. Pop. 87,876.

**Par·na·í·ba** |pärnä'ĕbä| commercial city in NE Brazil, in N Piauí state, on the Parnaíba River near the Atlantic. Pop. 128,000.

**Par·nas·sus, Mount** |pär'năsəs| mountain in central Greece, just N of Delphi, rising to a height of 8,064 ft./2,457 m. Held to be sacred by the ancient Greeks, as was the spring of Castalia on its S slopes, it was associated with Apollo and the Muses and regarded as a symbol of poetry. Greek name **Parnassós**. □ **Parnassian** adj. & n.

**Pa·ros** |'păr,äs| Greek island in the S Aegean, in the Cyclades. It is noted for the translucent white Parian marble that has been quarried here since the 6th century B.C. □ **Parian** adj. & n.

**Par·ral** |päh'räl| (official name **Hidalgo del Parral**) city in N Mexico, in Chihuahua state, a mining center. Pop. 91,000.

**Par·ra·mat·ta** |perə'mätə| city in SE Australia, in New South Wales, an industrial suburb W of Sydney. Pop. 132,000. It is one of the oldest settlements in Australia.

**Parsippany–Troy Hills** |pär'sĕpənĕtrōi| commercial and residential township in N New Jersey. Pop. 48,478.

**Par·the·non** |'pärTHə,nän| see the ACROPOLIS, Athens, Greece.

**Par·thia** |'pärTHēə| ancient Asian kingdom SE of the Caspian Sea. At its height, it ruled

an empire that stretched from the Euphrates to the Indus. □ **Parthian** adj. & n.

**Pas, The** |'pä| commercial town in W Manitoba, on the Saskatchewan River. Pop. 6,166.

**Pas·a·de·na**[1] |,păsə'dēnə| industrial city in S California, in the San Gabriel Mts/ NE of Los Angeles. Pop. 131,591. It is the site of the Rose Bowl football stadium.

**Pas·a·de·na**[2] |,păsə'dēnə| industrial port city in SE Texas, on the E side of Houston. Pop. 119,363.

**Pa·sar·ga·dae** |pə'särgə,dē| ruined city of ancient Persia, capital of Cyrus the Great; it was NE of present-day Shiraz, Iran.

**Pa·say** |'päsī| commercial city in the Philippines, on S Luzon, just S of Manila. Pop. 374,000.

**Pas·ca·gou·la** |,păskə'gōōlə| industrial port city in SE Mississippi, a shipbuilding center on the Gulf of Mexico. Pop. 25,899.

**Pas de Ca·lais** |pädkä'le| **1** department in NW France, on the English Channel. Pop. 1,433,000. The capital is Arras. **2** French name for the **Strait of Dover** (21 mi./34 km. wide), which connects the English Channel and the North Sea.

**Pa·sig** |'päsig| commercial town in the Philippines, on S Luzon, E of Manila. Pop. 395,000.

**Pa·so Ro·bles** |,păsō 'rōbəlz| (official name **El Paso de Robles**) resort and agricultural city in W central California. Pop. 18,583.

**Pas·sa·ic** |pə'sāik| industrial city in NE New Jersey, on the Passaic River. Pop. 58,041.

**Pas·sa·ma·quod·dy Bay** |,păsəmə 'kwädē| (also **Quoddy Bay**) inlet of the Bay of Fundy at the border of Maine and New Brunswick, noted for its powerful tides.

**Pas·sau** |'päs,ow| town in S Germany at the confluence of the Danube, the Inn, and the Ilz rivers. Pop. 51,000. It has an annual trade fair.

**Pass·chen·dae·le** |'päsHən,dälə| village in W Belgium. During World War I the British Ypres advance of 1917 was halted here after bloody fighting.

**Pas·so Fun·do** |'päsō'fōōndōō| city in S Brazil, in Rio Grande do Sul state. Pop. 147,000. It is the commercial center of an agricultural region.

**Pas·to** |'pästō| historic commercial city in SW Colombia, the capital of Nariño department, in an agricultural district. Pop. 303,000.

**Pat·a·go·nia** |,pătə'gōnēə| region of South America, in S Argentina and Chile. Consisting largely of a dry barren plateau, it extends from the Colorado River in central Argentina to the Strait of Magellan and from the Andes to the Atlantic coast. □ **Patagonian** *adj. & n.*

**Pa·ta·li·pu·tra** |ˌpätäli'pŏŏtrə| ancient name for PATNA, India.

**Pa·tan** |'pätən| town in W India, in Gujarat state, NW of Ahmadabad. Pop. 120,000. It is noted for its Jain temples.

**Pat·er·son** |'pætərsən| historic industrial city in NE New Jersey, on the Passaic River. It is famed for its silk and other manufactures. Pop. 140,891.

**Pa·than·kot** |pə'tänkōt| commercial city in W India, in Punjab state Pop. 147,000.

**Pa·ti·a·la** |ˌpətē'älə| (also **Puttiala**) commercial and industrial city in NW India, in Punjab state. Pop. 269,000.

**Pat·mos** |'pæt,maws| Greek island in the Aegean Sea, one of the Dodecanese group. It is believed that St. John was living here in exile when he had the visions described in the book of Revelation.

**Pat·na** |'pətnə| city in NE India, on the Ganges, capital of the state of Bihar. Pop. 917,000. Important in ancient times, it had become deserted by the 7th century but was refounded in 1541 by the Moguls and became a viceregal capital. Former name **Pataliputra**.

**Pa·tras** |'pätrəs| industrial port in the NW Peloponnese, W Greece, on the Gulf of Patras. Pop. 155,000. Taken by the Turks in the 18th century, it was the site in 1821 of the outbreak of the Greek war of independence. It was finally freed in 1828. Greek name **Pátrai**.

**Pat·ta·ya** |pə'tīyə| beach resort on the coast of S Thailand, SE of Bangkok.

**Pátz·cua·ro** |'pätskwärō| city in W central Mexico, in Michoacán state, a commercial and resort center on Lake Pátzcuaro. Pop. 42,000.

**Pau** |pō| resort and industrial town in the Aquitaine region of SW France, capital of the department of Pyrénées-Atlantique. Pop. 84,000.

**Pauil·lac** |pō'yäk| commune in the Médoc region of Aquitaine, in SW France, near Bordeaux. Pauillac is noted for its wines and produces some of the greatest red wines in France.

**Pa·via** |pə'vēə| university city in N Italy, capital of Pavia province. Pop. 80,000.

**Pav·lo·dar** |pävlä'där| **1** administrative district in NE Kazakhstan. Pop. 957,000. **2** its capital, a city on the Irtysh River. Pop. 337,000.

**Paw·tuck·et** |pə'təkət| industrial city in NE Rhode Island, on the Blackstone River, NE of Providence, site of pioneering metal and textile plants. Pop. 72,644.

**Pays-Bas** French name for the LOW COUNTRIES.

**Pays Basque** |'päz 'bæsk| French name for BASQUE COUNTRY.

**Pays de la Loire** |päd lä'l wär| region of W France centered on the Loire valley. Nantes is the chief city.

**Pa·zar·dzhik** |päzärjēk| spa town and industrial center in central Bulgaria, on the Maritsa River. Pop. 138,000.

**Pea·body** |'pē,bədē| industrial city in NE Massachusetts. Pop. 47,039.

**Peace River** |pēs| river that flows 1,194 mi./1,923 km. from N British Columbia into Alberta, to the Slave River. Its valley is noted for grain production.

**Peach State** |pēCH| nickname for the U.S. state of GEORGIA.

**Peak District** |'pēk ',distrik(t)| limestone plateau in Derbyshire, N central England, at the S end of the Pennines, rising to 2,088 ft./636 m. at Kinder Scout.

**Pearl Harbor** |'pərl 'härbər| harbor on the island of Oahu, in Hawaii, the site of American Pacific Fleet headquarters, where a surprise attack on December 7, 1941 by Japanese carrier aircraft inflicted heavy damage and brought the U.S. into World War II.

**Pearl River**[1] |pərl| river of S China, flowing from Guangzhou (Canton) S to the South China Sea and forming part of the delta of the Xi River. Its lower reaches widen to form the Pearl River estuary, the inlet between Hong Kong and Macao.

**Pearl River**[2] |pərl| river that flows 485 mi./780 km. across central Mississippi to form part of the border with Louisiana. It empties into the Gulf of Mexico.

**Pea·ry Land** |'pirē| mountainous region on the Arctic coast of N Greenland.

**Peb·ble Beach** |'peb(ə)l| resort on the Monterey Peninsula, in W central California, site of a famous golf course.

**Peć** |peCH| (also **Pech**) market town in SW Serbia, near the Albanian border. Pop. 111,000.

**Pe·chen·ga** |pə'CHengə| region of NW Russia, lying W of Murmansk on the border with Finland. Formerly part of Finland, it was ceded to the Soviet Union in 1940. It was known by its Finnish name, Petsamo, from 1920 until 1944.

**Pe·cho·ra** |pə'CHawrə| river of N Russia,

which rises in Urals and flows some 1,125 mi./1,800 km. N and E to the Barents Sea.

**Pe·con·ic Bay** |pə'känik| inlet of the Atlantic Ocean in the East End of Long Island, New York, separating the North Fork and South Fork of the island.

**Pe·cos River** |'pā,kōs| river that flows 925 mi./1,490 km. from N New Mexico through W Texas, to the Rio Grande.

**Pécs** |pāCH| industrial city in SW Hungary. Pop. 172,000, formerly the capital of the S part of the Roman province of Pannonia.

**Pee Dee River** |'pē,dē| river that flows 230 mi./370 km. through North Carolina and South Carolina, to an inlet on the Atlantic S of the Grand Strand.

**Peeks·kill** |'pēkskil| commercial city in SE New York, on the Hudson River. Pop. 19,536.

**Pee·ne·mun·de** |,pānə'mo͝ondə| village in NE Germany, on a small island just off the Baltic coast. During World War II it was the chief site of German rocket research and testing.

**Pe·gu** |pe'go͞o| city and river port of S Burma, on the Pegu River NE of Rangoon. Pop. 150,000. Founded in 825 as the capital of the Mon kingdom, it is a center of Buddhist culture.

**Pei·ching** variant spelling of BEIJING, China.

**Pei·ping** former name for BEIJING, China.

**Pei·pus, Lake** |'pīpəs| (also called **Lake Chudo**) lake in E Estonia, on the Russian border. It drains into the Narva River.

**Pe·ka·long·an** |pəkä'lawngən| (also **Pecalongan**) industrial and commercial city in Indonesia, on N Java. Pop. 243,000.

**Pe·kan·ba·ru** |pe'känbär͞oo| (also **Pakanbaru**) port and oil town in Indonesia, on central Sumatra. Pop. 399,000.

**Pe·king** (also **Pekin**) former spelling of BEIJING, China.

**Pe·la·gi Islands** |pe'läjē| (also **Pelagian**; Italian name **Isole Pelagie**) three islands in the Mediterranean Sea, S of Sicily and held by Italy: Lampedusa, Linosa, and Lampione.

**Pe·lée, Mount** |pə'lā| volcano on the island of Martinique, in the Caribbean. Its eruption in 1902 destroyed the island's then capital St. Pierre, killing its population of some 30,000.

**Pe·le·lieu** |,pālə'lē͞oo| island in S Palau, in the W Pacific, noted for the fierce battle fought here between Japanese and American forces in 1944.

**Pe·li·on** |'pēlēən| wooded mountain in Greece, near the coast of SE Thessaly, rising to 5,079 ft./1,548 m. It was held in Greek mythology to be the home of the centaurs, and the giants were said to have piled Pelion onto Mount Ossa in their attempt to reach heaven and destroy the gods.

**Pel·la** |'pelə| ancient capital of Greek Macedonia, the birthplace of Alexander the Great in 356 B.C.

**Pel·ly Mountains** |'pelē| range in the S central Yukon Territory. The **Pelly River** flows N of the range to the Yukon River.

**Pel·o·pon·nese** |,peləpə'nēsəs| (**the Peloponnese**; also **Peloponnesus**) the mountainous S peninsula of Greece, connected to central Greece by the Isthmus of Corinth. Greek name **Pelopónnisos**.

**Pe·lo·tas** |pe'lōtæs| city in S Brazil, in Rio Grande do Sul state, a canal port and beef industry center. Pop. 277,000.

**Pem·ba¹** |'pembə| seaport in N Mozambique, on the Indian Ocean. Pop. 41,000. Formerly **Porto Amelia**.

**Pem·ba²** |'pembə| island off the coast of Tanzania, in the W Indian Ocean N of Zanzibar, noted for clove production.

**Pem·broke** |'pem,brōk| port in SW Wales, in Pembrokeshire. Pop. 16,000. It was a Norman stronghold from the 11th century, and was long a naval dockyard center. Welsh name **Penfro**.

**Pem·broke Pines** |'pembrōk| city in SE Florida, a residential suburb NW of Miami. Pop. 65,452.

**Pem·broke·shire** |'pəmbrookSHər| county of SW Wales; administrative center, Haverfordwest. It was part of Dyfed from 1974 to 1996.

**Pe·nang** |pə'næNG| (also **Pinang**) **1** island of Malaysia, situated off the W coast of the Malay Peninsula. In 1786 it was ceded to the East India Company as a British colony. Known as Prince of Wales Island until 1867, it united with Malacca and Singapore in a union of 1826, which in 1867 became the British colony called the Straits Settlements. It joined the federation of Malaya in 1948. **2** a state of Malaysia, consisting of this island and a coastal strip on the mainland. Capital: George Town (also called Penang, on Penang island). The mainland strip was united with the island in 1798 as part of the British colony.

**Pen·de·li·kón Mountain** |,pendelē'kōn| mountain in E central Greece, NE of Athens. Height: 3,639 ft./1,109 m.

**Pend Oreille, Lake** |pändə'rā| lake in N Idaho, noted for its trout fishing. The **Pend Oreille River** flows from its N end into

Washington and British Columbia, to the Columbia River.

**Pen·in·su·la, the** |pə'nins(ə)lə| the Iberian Peninsula in SW Europe, comprising Spain and Portugal. A phase of the Napoleonic Wars was fought here, in which the combined forces of Spain, Portugal, and Britain successfully repulsed the French.

**Pen·nine Hills** |'pen͵ĭn| (also **Pennine Chain** or **the Pennines**) range of hills in N England, extending from the Scottish border S to the Peak District in Derbyshire. Its highest peak is Cross Fell in Cumbria, which rises to 2,930 ft./893 m.

**Penn·syl·va·nia** |͵pensəl'vānyə| see box. □ **Pennsylvanian** *adj. & n.*

**Penn·syl·va·nia Avenue** |͵pensəl'vānyə| street in Washington, D.C. along whose route are the White House (at number 1600) and Capitol Hill.

---

## Pennsylvania

**Official name:** Commonwealth of Pennsylvania
**Capital:** Harrisburg
**Largest city:** Philadelphia
**Other cities:** Allentown, Bethlehem, Erie, Hershey, Pittsburgh, Scranton
**Population:** 11,881,643 (1990); 12,001,451 (1998); 12,281,000 (2005 proj.)
**Population rank (1990):** 5
**Rank in land area:** 33
**Abbreviation:** PA; Pa., Penn., Penna.
**Nickname:** Keystone State; Quaker State
**Motto:** 'Virtue, Liberty, and Independence'
**Bird:** ruffed grouse
**Fish:** brook trout
**Flower:** mountain laurel
**Tree:** eastern hemlock
**Noted physical features:** Appalachian Mountains; Allegheny Front and Allegheny Mountains; Great Valley; Piedmont Plateau, Pocono Mountains
**Tourist attractions:** Gettysburg Battle Site; Philadelphia: Liberty Bell, Independence Hall; Valley Forge
**Admission date:** December 2, 1787
**Order of admission:** 2
**Name origin:** Named in 1681 in charter for the land granted by Charles II of England, to honor Admiral Sir William Penn (1621-70), father of William Penn (1644-1718), who received the royal charter and was the founder of Pennsylvania.

---

'vānyə| popular name, from a corruption of *Deutsch*, for areas in E Pennsylvania settled and dominated by Germans. Lancaster is often considered the chief city.

**Pe·nob·scot River** |pə'näbskät| river that flows 350 mi./560 km. through central Maine, into Penobscot Bay on the Atlantic. Bangor lies on it, and its upper reaches are lumbering and recreational areas.

**Pen·rith** |'penriTH| city in SE Australia, in New South Wales, a suburb W of Sydney. Pop. 150,000.

**Pen·sa·cola** |͵pensə'kōlə| industrial and port city in NW Florida, in the Panhandle near the Alabama line. It is a naval center. Pop. 58,165.

**Pen·ta·gon, the** |'pen(t)ə͵gän| building in Arlington County, N Virginia, across the Potomac River from Washington, D.C. It is home to the U.S. Defense Department.

**Pent·land Firth** |'pentlənd firTH| channel separating the Orkney Islands from the N tip of mainland Scotland. It links the North Sea with the Atlantic.

**Pen·za** |'penzə| city in S central Russia. Pop. 548,000. Situated on the Sura River, a tributary of the Volga, it is an industrial and transportation center.

**Pen·zance** |pen'zæns| resort and port town in SW England, on the S coast of Cornwall near Land's End. Pop. 20,000.

**People's Republic of China** |'pēpəlz rē 'pəblik| official name (since 1949) of CHINA.

**Pe·o·ria** |pē'ôrēə| river port and industrial city in central Illinois, on the Illinois River. Pop. 113,504. The city developed around a fort built by the French in 1680.

**Pe·rak** |'perək| state of Malaysia, on the W side of the Malay Peninsula. Capital: Ipoh. It is a major tin-mining center.

**Perche** |persH| former province in N France. Its territory is now divided among the Orne, Eure-et-Loir, and Eure departments. Its capitals were Nogent-le-Rotrou and Mortagne. The breed of draft horses known as Percherons came from Perche.

**Pe·rei·ra** |pə'rârə| commercial city in W central Colombia, capital of Risaralda department, in the agricultural Cauca River valley. Pop. 336,000.

**Père Lachaise** |perlä'sHeyz| cemetery in BELLEVILLE¹, in Paris, France, resting place for many French and other notables.

**Per·ga·mum** |'pərgəməm| city in ancient Mysia, in W Asia Minor (present-day W Turkey), to the N of Izmir on a rocky hill close to the Aegean coast. The capital in the 3rd and 2nd centuries B.C. of the Attalid dynasty, it was one of the greatest of the Hellenistic cities and was famed for its cultural institutions, especially its library, which was second only to that at Alexandria. □ **Pergamene** *adj. & n.*

**Pé·ri·gord** |pārē'gawr| area of SW France, in the SW Massif Central. It became a part of Navarre in 1470, and of France in 1670.

**Pe·ri·gueux** |pārē'gŏo| commercial city, capital of the Dordogne department in SW France. Pop. 33,000. It is particularly famous for its foods, especially its pâtés.

**Per·lis** |'pɔrlǝs| the smallest state of Malaysia and the most northerly of those on the Malay Peninsula. Pop. 188,000. Capital: Kangar.

**Perm** |pǝrm| industrial city in Russia, in the W foothills of the Ural Mts. Pop. 1,094,000. Former name (1940–57) **Molotov**.

**Per·mi·an Basin** |'pǝrmēǝn| region of W Texas, a major oil and gas source in which the cities of Midland and Odessa are production centers.

**Per·nam·bu·co** |,pernǝm'bŏo,kŏo| state of E Brazil, on the Atlantic coast. Pop. 7,123,000. Capital: Recife (also formerly called Pernambuco).

**Per·nik** |'pernik| industrial city in W Bulgaria, in a coal-mining region. Pop. 121,000.

**Per·pi·gnan** |pärpēn'yän| city in S France, in the NE foothills of the Pyrenees, close to the border with Spain. Pop. 108,000. A former fortress town, it was the capital of the old province of Roussillon.

**Per·rier** |,perē'yä| spring at Vergèze, S France, SW of Nîmes. Its name is given to the effervescent water that is bottled and sold commercially.

**Per·sep·o·lis** |pǝr'sepǝlǝs| city in ancient Persia, to the NE of present-day Shiraz. It was founded in the late 6th century B.C. by Darius I as the ceremonial capital of Persia under the Achaemenid dynasty. The city is noted for ruins including functional and ceremonial buildings and cuneiform inscriptions in Old Persian, Elamite, and Akkadian.

**Per·sia** |'pɔrzhǝ| former country of SW Asia, now called Iran. The ancient kingdom of Persia, corresponding to the modern district of Fars in SW Iran, became in the 6th century B.C. the domain of the Achaemenid dynasty. Under Cyrus the Great in the 6th century B.C. Persia became the center of a powerful empire that included all of W Asia, Egypt, and parts of E Europe; the empire, defied by the Greeks in the Persian Wars of the 5th century B.C., was eventually overthrown by Alexander the Great in 330 B.C. The country was subsequently ruled by a succession of dynasties until it was conquered by the Muslim Arabs between A.D. 633 and 651. Taken by the Mongols in the 13th century, Persia was ruled by the Kajar dynasty from 1794 until 1925, when Reza Khan Pahlavi became shah. It was renamed Iran in 1935. □ **Persian** *adj. & n.*

**Per·sian Gulf** |,pǝrzhǝn 'gǝlf| arm of the Arabian Sea, to which it is connected by the Strait of Hormuz and the Gulf of Oman. It extends NW between the Arabian Peninsula and the coast of SW Iran. Also called **Arabian Gulf**; informally **the Gulf**.

**Per·sian Gulf States** |,pǝrzhǝn 'gǝlf| see GULF STATES.

**Perth**[1] |pǝrTH| the capital of the state of Western Australia, on the Indian Ocean. Pop. 1,019,000 (including the port of Fremantle). Founded by the British in 1829, it developed rapidly after the discovery in 1890 of nearby gold.

**Perth**[2] |pǝrTH| town in E Scotland, at the head of the Tay estuary. Pop. 41,000. The administrative center of Perth and Kinross region, it was the capital of Scotland from 1210 until 1452.

**Perth Am·boy** |'pǝrTH 'æm,boi| historic industrial city in NE New Jersey, on the Raritan River and across the Arthur Kill from Staten Island, New York. Pop. 41,967.

**Perth·shire** |'pǝrTHSHīr; 'pǝrTHSHǝr| former county of central Scotland. It became a part of Tayside region in 1975 and of Perth and Kinross in 1996.

**Pe·ru**[1] |pǝ'rŏo| commercial city in N central Indiana, on the Wabash River. Pop. 12,843.

**Pe·ru**[2] |pǝ'rŏo| republic in South America, on the Pacific coast, traversed throughout its length by the Andes. Area: 496,414 sq. mi./1.28 million sq. km. Pop. 22,048,000. Official languages, Spanish and Quechua. Capital and largest city: Lima. The center

Peru

of the Inca empire, Peru was controlled by Spain 1532–1824. Its economy relies chiefly on agriculture, mining, and fishing. □ **Peruvian** adj. & n.

**Pe·ru·gia** |pə'rōōjə| historic university city in central Italy, the capital of Umbria. Pop. 151,000. It flourished in the 15th century as a center of the Umbrian school of painting. A papal possession from 1540, it became a part of united Italy in 1860.

**Pe·ru·vi·an Current** |pə'rōōvēən| cold ocean current that moves N from the S Pacific along the coast of Chile and Peru before turning W into the South Equatorial Current.

**Per·vo·uralsk** |pirvə'rälsk| city in central Russia, near Yekaterinburg. Pop. 129,000.

**Pe·sa·ro** |'päzärō| port and resort town on the Foglia River in E central Italy, in the Marche district and capital of Pesaro province. Pop. 90,000.

**Pes·ca·do·res** |,peskə'dōrēz| (Chinese name **P'eng-hu Ch'ün-tao**) group of 64 small Taiwanese islands in the Taiwan Strait, between Taiwan and China. Pop. 120,000. The largest and most populous island is Penghu.

**Pe·sca·ra** |pes'kärä| tourist resort and seaport in E central Italy, on the Pescara River, capital of Pescara province. Pop. 129,000.

**Pe·sha·war** |pə'sHäwər| the capital of North-West Frontier Province, in Pakistan. Pop. 555,000. Mentioned in early Sanskrit literature, it is one of Pakistan's oldest cities. Under Sikh rule from 1834, it was occupied by the British between 1849 and 1947. Situated near the Khyber Pass on the border with Afghanistan, it is of strategic and military importance.

**Pest** |pest| **1** county in central Hungary. Pop. 954,000. Its capital is Budapest. **2** town on the W bank of the Danube River, since 1873 a component, with the town of Buda, of Budapest.

**Pe·tach Tik·va** |'petək 'tikvə| (also **Petah Tikva; Petah Tiqwa**) industrial city in W central Israel, E of Tel Aviv. Pop. 152,000. It was founded in the late 19th century as one of the first modern agricultural Jewish settlements in Palestine.

**Pe·ta·ling Ja·ya** |pə'täliNG 'jīə| industrial city in SW Malaysia, SW of Kuala Lumpur. Pop. 208,000.

**Pet·a·lu·ma** |,petəl'ōōmə| city in NW California, a suburb and poultry-producing center N of San Francisco. Pop. 43,184.

**Pe·ta·re** |pe'tärä| city in N Venezuela, a suburb E of Caracas. Pop. 338,000.

**Pe·ter·bor·ough**[1] |'pētər,bərə| industrial

city in E central England, formerly in Cambridgeshire. Pop. 149,000. An old city with a 12th-century cathedral, it has been developed as a planned urban center since the late 1960s.

**Pe·ter·bor·ough**[2] |'pētər,bərō| city in E Ontario, on the Trent Canal E of Toronto. Pop. 68,371.

**Pe·ters·burg** |'pēdərz,bərg| industrial and commercial city in SE Virginia, S of Richmond, scene of heavy fighting in the Civil War. Pop. 38,386.

**Pe·tra** |'petrə| ancient city of SW Asia, in present-day Jordan. The city, which lies in a hollow surrounded by cliffs, is accessible only through narrow gorges. Its extensive ruins include temples and tombs hewn from "rose-red" sandstone cliffs.

**Pet·ri·fied Forest** |'petrəfīd| highland area of E central Arizona, noted for its agates and plant fossils. It is now a national park.

**Pet·ro·dvo·rets** |pitrədvə'ryets| (formerly **Leninsk**; earlier, **Peterhof**) port and resort city in W Russia, on the S bank of Neva River. Pop. 81,000. The Peterhof, the Tsarist summer palace, is here.

**Pet·ro·grad** |'petrə,gräd| former name (1914–24) for ST. PETERSBURG, Russia.

**Pe·tro·li·na** |petrō'lēnä| city in E central Brazil, in Pernambuco state, a port on the São Francisco River, across from Juàzeiro, Bahia. Pop. 175,000.

**Pet·ro·pav·lovsk**[1] |,petrə'pæv,lawfsk| (also **Petropavl**) industrial and commercial city in N Kazakhstan, on the Trans-Siberian Railroad. Pop. 248,000.

**Pet·ro·pav·lovsk**[2] |,petrə'pævlawfsk| Russian fishing port and naval base on the E coast of the Kamchatka Peninsula in E Siberia. Pop. 245,000. Full name **Petropavlovsk-Kamchatsky**.

**Pe·tró·po·lis** |pə'träpələs| historic resort city in SE Brazil, in hills N of Rio de Janeiro. Pop. 294,000. It was the longtime summer capital of the emperor of Brazil.

**Pet·ro·za·vodsk** |,petrəsə'vätsk| city in NW Russia, on Lake Onega, capital of the republic of Karelia. Pop. 252,000.

**Pet·sa·mo** |'petsə,mō| former Finnish name (1920–44) for PECHENGA, Russia.

**Pforz·heim** |'fawrts,(h)īm| city in SW Germany, on the edge of the Black Forest. Pop. 116,000. It was an important medieval trade center and is now the center of Germany's jewelry and watch-making industries.

**Phan Thiet** |'pän 'tyet| port city in southern Vietnam, E of Ho Chi Minh City. Pop. 151,000.

**Pha·ros** |'fe͞aws| peninsula, formerly an island, in Alexandria, Egypt, site of a lighthouse built in the 3rd century B.C. that was one of the Seven Wonders of the Ancient World. An earthquake destroyed it in the 14th century.

**Pharr** |fär| city in S Texas, in the agricultural Rio Grande valley. Pop. 32,921.

**Phar·sa·lus** |fär'sӓləs| town in E central Greece; nearby, on the Pharsalian Plain, Julius Caesar decisively defeated Pompey the Great in 48 B.C.

**Phil·a·del·phia** |ˌfiləˈdelfēə| the chief city of Pennsylvania, an industrial port on the Delaware River. Pop. 1,585,577. Established as a Quaker colony by William Penn and others in 1681, it was the site in 1776 of the signing of the Declaration of Independence and in 1787 of the adoption of the Constitution of the United States, and was the U.S. capital from 1790 to 1800. It is now the second largest city on the E coast, and a major commercial and cultural center. □ **Philadelphian** *adj. & n.*

**Phil·ip·pi** |fə'lipē| city in ancient Macedonia, the scene in 42 B.C. of two battles in which Mark Antony and Octavian defeated Brutus and Cassius, the assassins of Julius Caesar. Its ruins lie close to the Aegean coast in NE Greece, near the port of Kaválla (ancient Neapolis). Greek name **Fílippoi**.

**Phil·ip·pines** |ˌfiləˈpēnz| republic in SE Asia consisting of an archipelago of over 7,000 islands separated from the Asian mainland by the South China Sea. Area: 115,875 sq. mi./300,000 sq. km. Pop. 60,685,000. Official languages, Pilipino (Tagalog) and English. Capital and largest city: Manila. Controlled by Spain 1565–1898, the islands were then held by the U.S. until 1946. Their economy is based on agriculture, mining, timbering, and various manufactures. □ **Philippine** *adj.* **Filipino** *adj. & n.*

**Phil·ip·pine Sea** |ˌfiləˈpēn| section of the

**Phillipines**

W Pacific on the E of the Philippine Islands, and extending N to Japan. During World War II several major battles, including that at LEYTE GULF, were fought here.

**Phil·ip·pop·o·lis** |ˌfiliˈpäpōlis| ancient Greek name for PLOVDIV, Bulgaria.

**Phi·lis·tia** |fə'listēə| ancient land of the Philistines, a seafaring people who in biblical times occupied the coast of Palestine. Their chief cities were Gaza, Ashkelon, Ashdod, Gath, and Ekron. After defeat by the Israelites around 1000 B.C., Philistia declined.

**Phnom Penh** |pə'nawm 'pen| the capital of Cambodia, a port at the junction of the Mekong and Tonlé Sap rivers. Pop. 920,000. It became the capital of a Khmer kingdom in the mid-15th century. Between 1975 and 1979 the Khmer Rouge forced a great many of its population (then 2.5 million) to leave the city and resettle in the country.

**Pho·caea** |fō'sēə| ancient city of Asia Minor, in present-day NW Turkey, on the Aegean Sea on the site of Foça. It was a maritime power from about 3,000 to about 2,500 years ago.

**Pho·cis** |'fōsəs| ancient district in central Greece, N of the Gulf of Corinth, that included the site of the Delphic oracle, as well as Mount Parnassus.

**Phoe·ni·cia** |fə'nishə| ancient country on the shores of the E Mediterranean, corresponding to modern Lebanon and the coastal plains of Syria. It consisted of a number of city-states, including Tyre and Sidon, and was a flourishing center of Mediterranean trade and colonization during the early part of the 1st millennium B.C. □ **Phoenician** *adj. & n.*

**Phoe·nix** |'fēniks| industrial and commercial city, the state capital of Arizona. Pop. 983,403. Its dry climate makes it a popular winter resort and retirement location.

**Phoe·nix Islands** |'fēniks| group of eight islands lying just S of the equator in the W Pacific. They form a part of Kiribati.

**Phoe·nix Park** |'fēniks| public park in Dublin, Ireland, W of the city center, along the Liffey River, associated with literary figures as well as with sensational 1882 political murders.

**Phryg·ia** |'frijēə| ancient region of W central Asia Minor (present-day Turkey) to the S of Bithynia. Centered on the city of Gordium, it dominated Asia Minor after the decline of the Hittites in the 12th century B.C., reaching the peak of its power in the 8th century under King Midas. It was eventually absorbed into the kingdom of Lydia in the 6th century B.C. □ **Phrygian** *adj. & n.*

**Phu·ket** |ˌpoō'ket| **1** an island of Thailand, situated at the head of the Strait of Malacca off the W coast of the Malay Peninsula. **2** a port at the S end of Phuket island, a major resort center and outlet to the Indian Ocean. Pop. 24,000.

**Pia·cen·za** |pyä'CHen(t)sə| commune in N Italy, on the Po River, SE of Milan, capital of Piacenza province. Pop. 103,000. It is an agricultural and industrial center.

**Piatra-Neamţ** |'pyäträ'nyäms| industrial city in NE Romania. Pop. 116,000.

**Piauí** |'pyawē| state of NE Brazil, on the Atlantic coast. Pop. 2,581,000. Capital: Teresina.

**Pic·ar·dy** |'pikərdē| region and former province of N France, centered on the city of Amiens. It was the scene of heavy fighting in World War I. French name **Picardie**.

**Pic·ca·dil·ly** |ˌpikə,dilē| street in central London, England, extending from Hyde Park E to Piccadilly Circus, noted for its fashionable shops, hotels, and restaurants.

**Pic du Mi·di** |pēk doō 'mēdē| (also **Pic du Midi de Bigorre**) mountain peak (9,409 ft./2,868 m.) in the W central Pyrenees, in SW France.

**Pick·er·ing** |'pik(ə)riNG| town in S Ontario, NE of Toronto on Lake Ontario, site of a major nuclear power development. Pop. 68,631.

**Pi·co da Ne·bli·na** |'pēkō dä 'nəblēnä| mountain in NW Brazil, close to the border with Venezuela. Rising to 9,888 ft./3,014 m., it is the highest peak in Brazil.

**Pi·co de Ane·to** |'pēkō dä ä'netō| highest peak in the Pyrenees, in N Spain. Height: 11,168 ft./3,404 m.

**Pi·co de Ori·za·ba** |'pēkō dä ōrē'zäbä| another name for CITLALTÉPETL, Mexico.

**Pi·co Ri·ve·ra** |ˌpēkō ri'verə| city in SW California, an industrial suburb E of Los Angeles. Pop. 59,177.

**Pied·mont**[1] |'pēd,mänt| region of NW Italy, in the foothills of the Alps. Capital: Turin. Dominated by Savoy from 1400, it became a part of the kingdom of Sardinia in 1720. It was the center of the movement for a united Italy in the 19th century. Italian name **Piemonte**. □ **Piedmontese** *n. & adj.*

**Pied·mont**[2] |'pēd,mänt| in the U.S., highland areas between the Appalachian Mts. and the Atlantic coast. The Piedmont ends at the Fall Line, where rivers drop to the coastal plain.

**Pi·e·ria** |pī'irēä| in ancient Greece, the name for a plain in Macedonia where the Muses were born. □ **Pierian** *adj.*

**Pierre** |pē'e(ə)r| the capital of South Dakota, a commercial city on the Missouri River. Pop. 12,906.

**Pie·tar·saa·ri** |'pyetär,säri| industrial and port city in W Finland, on the Gulf of Bothnia. Pop. 20,000.

**Pie·ter·mar·itz·burg** |ˌpētər'merəts,bərg| industrial city in E South Africa, the capital of KwaZulu/Natal. Pop. 229,000.

**Pie·ters·burg** |'pētərz,bərg| town in N South Africa, the capital of Northern Province. Pop. 55,000. In 1994 it took the official name Polokwane.

**Pi·galle** |pi'gäl| area of Paris, France, on the Right Bank, near Montmartre. The Place Pigalle is noted for its disreputable bars and nightspots.

**Pig Island** |pig| nickname for New Zealand, said to be so named because of the pigs left here by Captain Cook.

**Pigs, Bay of** |'pigz| bay on the SW coast of Cuba, scene of an unsuccessful attempt in 1961 by U.S.-backed Cuban exiles to invade the country and overthrow the regime of Fidel Castro.

**Pikes Peak** |'pīks| mountain in the Front Range of the S Rocky Mts., near Colorado Springs, Colorado. At 14,110 ft./4,300 m., it has long been a guide for travelers on the plains.

**Pik Po·be·dy** |'pēk pä'byedē| mountain in E Kyrgyzstan, close to the border with China. Rising to a height of 24,406 ft./7,439 m., it is the highest peak in the Tien Shan range.

**Pil·co·ma·yo River** |ˌpilkə'mäyō| river that flows 1,000 mi./1,600 km. from the Andes of W Bolivia, along the Argentina-Paraguay border, and joins the Paraguay River at Asunción, Paraguay.

**Pillars of Her·cu·les** |'hərkyəlēz| two promontories at the E end of the Strait of Gibraltar. Calpe is today known as the Rock of Gibraltar. Abyla is either Mount Acho or the Jebel Musa, in Morocco. Said to have been pushed into place by Hercules, the Pillars were long thought of as the end of the known world.

**Pil·sen** |'pilzən| industrial city in the W part of the Czech Republic. Pop. 173,000. It is noted for the production of lager (pilsener) beer. Czech name **Plzeň**.

**Pilt·down** |'pilt,down| hamlet in SE England, in East Sussex, scene of the 1912 "discovery" of Piltdown Man, shown in the 1950s to be a hoax.

**Pim·li·co**[1] |'pimli,kō| residential district in central London, England, N of the River Thames in Westminster, adjacent to Belgravia.

**Pim·li·co**[2] |'pimli,kō| neighborhood in NW Baltimore, Maryland, site of a famous horseracing track, home to the Preakness.

**Pi·nar del Rio** |pē'när del 'rēō| city in W Cuba, capital of Pinar del Rio province. Pop. 101,000. It is a tobacco industry center.

**Pi·na·tu·bo, Mount** |,pinə'tōōbō| volcano on the island of Luzon, in the Philippines. It erupted in 1991, killing more than 300 people and destroying the homes of more than 200,000.

**Pin·dus Mountains** |'pindəs| range of mountains in W central Greece, stretching from the border with Albania S to the Gulf of Corinth. The highest peak is Mount Smolikas, which rises to 8,136 ft./2,637 m. Greek name **Píndhos**.

**Pine Barrens** |'pīn| region of S New Jersey, lightly populated and characterized by sandy soils, stunted conifer forests, and numerous small rivers.

**Pine Bluff** |'pīn| industrial city in SE Arkansas, on the Arkansas River, site of a large arsenal. Pop. 57,140.

**Pine Ridge** |'pīn| village in SW South Dakota, headquarters for the Pine Ridge Indian Reservation. Pop. 2,596.

**Pines, Isle of**[1] |'pīnz| see JUVENTUD, ISLA DE LA, Cuba.

**Pines, Isle of**[2] |'pīnz| (French name **Île des Pins**) island in the S Pacific, off SE New Caledonia, long a French penal colony, now a resort.

**Ping·ding·shan** |'ping'ding'shæn| city in Henan province, E central China, S of Zhengzhou. Pop. 843,000.

**Ping·tung** |'ping'dəng| (also **P'ing-tung**) city, SW Taiwan, E of Kaohsiung. Pop. 213,000. It is an industrial and food-processing center in an agricultural region.

**Ping·xiang** |'ping'siäng| city in Jiangxi province, SE China, in the foothills of the Luoxiao Shan range, SE of Changsha. Pop. 1,305,000.

**Pink·ham Notch** |'piNGkəm| valley in the White Mts. of N New Hampshire, just E of the Presidential Range. It is a recreational center.

**Pinsk** |'pinsk| city, a shipping and manufacturing center, in SW Belarus. Pop. 122,000.

**Pi·ra·ci·ca·ba** |pēräsē'käbä| city in SE Brazil, in São Paulo state. Pop. 303,000. In an agricultural region. It is a processing and academic center.

**Pi·rae·us** |pī'rāəs| the chief port of Athens, Greece, situated on the Saronic Gulf 5 mi./8 km. SW of the city. Pop. 183,000. Greek name **Piraiévs** or **Piraiéus**.

**Pi·sa** |'pēzə| industrial city in N Italy, in Tuscany, on the Arno River. Pop. 101,000. It is noted for the 'Leaning Tower of Pisa', a circular bell tower that leans about 17 ft./5 m. from the perpendicular over its height of 181 ft./55 m.

**Pis·cat·a·way** |'pi'skætə,wā| suburban township in central New Jersey, across the Raritan River from New Brunswick. Pop. 47,089.

**Pis·gah** |'pizgə| see Mount NEBO.

**Pish·pek** |pisH'pek| former name (until 1926) for BISHKEK, Kyrgyzstan.

**Pi·sid·ia** |pə'sidēə| ancient region of Asia Minor (present-day Turkey), between Pamphylia and Phrygia. It was incorporated into the Roman province of Galatia in 25 B.C. □ **Pisidian** *adj. & n.*

**Pis·mo Beach** |'pízmō| city in SW California, S of San Luis Obispo, a resort center in an oil producing area. Pop. 7,669.

**Pi·sto·ia** |pēs'tōyä| city at the foot of the Apennine Range in N central Italy, NW of Florence. Pop. 90,000. It is the capital of Pistoia province.

**Pit·cairn Islands** |'pit,kärn| British dependency comprising a group of volcanic islands in the S Pacific, E of French Polynesia. The only settlement is Adamstown, on Pitcairn Island, the chief island of the group. Pop. 54. Pitcairn Island was discovered in 1767, and remained uninhabited until settled in 1790 by mutineers from HMS *Bounty*. The island is named after the midshipman who first sighted the islands.

**Pitcairn Island**

**Pi·teş·ti** |pe'tesHt| industrial town and rail junction in an oil-producing area of S Romania, on the Argeş River, NW of Bucharest. Pop. 163,000.

**Pitt Island** |pit| see CHATHAM ISLANDS, New Zealand.

**Pitts•burg** |'pitsbərg| industrial port city in N central California, on Suisun Bay NE of Oakland. Pop. 47,564.

**Pitts•burgh** |'pits,bərg| industrial city in SW Pennsylvania, at the junction of the Allegheny and Monongahela rivers (forming the Ohio River). Pop. 369,879. The city, originally named Fort Pitt, was founded in 1758 on the site of a French settlement. An important center of steel production for many years, its economic base has shifted to transportation services and high technology.

**Pitts•field** |'pitsfēld| industrial city in W Massachusetts, on the Housatonic River. It is the commercial center of the Berkshire Hills. Pop. 48,622.

**Piu•ra** |'pyōōrä| commercial city in NW Peru, the capital of Piura department. Pop. 324,000. In a coastal desert, it is a processing center for an irrigated agricultural district.

**Pla•cen•tia Bay** |plə'senCHə| inlet of the Atlantic in SE Newfoundland, site of early European settlement and 20th-century naval activity.

**Plain•field** |'plānfēld| industrial city in NE New Jersey. Pop. 46,567.

**Plain of Jars** |'plän| plain in central Laos where over 300 jars, about 1,500 to 2,000 years old and 3 ft./1m.-10 ft./3 m. tall, are scattered; their origin and function are unknown. The plain was the scene of heavy fighting during the Vietnam War.

**Plain of Reeds** |'plän| swampy region of southern Vietnam, N of the Mekong Delta.

**Plains of A•bra•ham** |plänz əv 'äbrəhæm| plateau beside the city of Quebec, overlooking the St. Lawrence River. It was the scene in 1759 of a battle in which the British army under General Wolfe, having scaled the heights above the city under cover of darkness, surprised and defeated the French. The battle led to British control over Canada.

**Plains States** the US states dominated by the GREAT PLAINS, generally including North and South Dakota, Nebraska, and Kansas, and sometimes Iowa and Missouri.

**Pla•no** |'plänō| city in NE Texas, an industrial and commercial suburb NE of Dallas. Pop. 128,713.

**Plan•ta•tion** |plæn'tāsHən| city in SE Florida, a residential suburb W of Fort Lauderdale. Pop. 66,692.

**Plas•sey** |'plæsē| village in NE India, in West Bengal, NW of Calcutta. It was the scene in 1757 of a battle in which a small British army under Robert Clive defeated the forces of the nawab of Bengal, establishing British supremacy in Bengal.

**Pla•taea** |plə'tēə| ancient city of Greece. The Greeks defeated the Persians here in 479 B.C. Repeatedly captured and sacked, it was rebuilt by Alexander the Great.

**Plate, River** |'plät| wide estuary on the Atlantic coast of South America between Argentina and Uruguay, formed by the confluence of the Paraná and Uruguay rivers. The cities of Buenos Aires and Montevideo lie on its shores. Spanish name **Río de la Plata.**

**Platte River** |'plæt| river that is formed by the North Platte and South Platte rivers in SW Nebraska, and flows 310 mi./500 km. to the Missouri River near Omaha.

**Platts•burgh** |'plætsbərg| city in NE New York, on Lake Champlain, a papermaking center and the site of battles in the 18th and 19th centuries. Pop. 21,255.

**Pleas•an•ton** |'plesəntən| city in N central California, a suburb SE of Oakland. Pop. 50,553.

**Plei•ku** |'plä'kōō| (also **Play Cu**) commercial city in the central highlands of Vietnam. Pop. 126,000.

**Plen•ty, Bay of** |'plentē| region of North Island, New Zealand, extending around the bay of the same name. The port of Tauranga is situated on it.

**Ple•ven** |'plevən| industrial city in N Bulgaria, NE of Sofia. Pop. 168,000. An important fortress town and trading center of the Ottoman Empire, it was taken from the Turks by the Russians in the Russo-Turkish War of 1877, after a siege of 143 days.

**Plock** |plōtsk| port in central Poland, capital of Plock county, on the Vistula River. Pop. 123,000.

**Plo•ieş•ti** |plō'yesHt| oil-refining city in central Romania, N of Bucharest. Pop. 254,000.

**Plov•div** |'plōvdif| industrial and commercial city in S Bulgaria. Pop. 379,000. Known to the ancient Greeks as Philippopolis and to the Romans as Trimontium, it assumed its present name after World War I, and is the second-largest Bulgarian city.

**Ply•mouth**[1] |'pliməTH| port and naval base in SW England, on the Devon coast. Pop. 239,000. In 1620 it was the scene of the Pilgrims' departure to North America in the *Mayflower.*

**Ply•mouth**[2] |'pliməTH| resort town in SE Massachusetts, on the Atlantic coast S of Boston. Pop. 45,608. The site in 1620 of the landing of the Pilgrims, it was the earliest permanent European settlement in New England.

**Ply·mouth**[3] |'plimǝTH| city in SE Minnesota, a suburb NW of Minneapolis. Pop. 50,889.

**Ply·mouth**[4] |'plimǝTH| the capital of the island of Montserrat in the Caribbean. Pop. 3,500. It was abandoned following the eruption of the Soufrière Hills volcano from 1995.

**Ply·mouth Rock** |,plimǝTH 'räk| granite boulder at Plymouth, Massachusetts, onto which the Pilgrims are said to have stepped from the *Mayflower*.

**Pl·zeň** |'pǝl,zen| Czech name for PILSEN.

**Po** |pō| longest river of Italy. It rises in the Alps near the border with France and flows 415 mi./668 km. eastward to the Adriatic. Turin is on the Po, Milan in its valley.

**Po·ca·tel·lo** |,pōkǝ'telō| industrial and commercial city in SE Idaho. Pop. 46,080.

**Po·co·no Mountains** |'pōkǝ,nō| range in NE Pennsylvania, noted for its resorts.

**Pod·go·ri·ca** |'pädgǝ,rētsǝ| industrial city, the capital of Montenegro. Pop. 118,000. It was under Turkish rule from 1474 until 1878. Between 1946 and 1993 it was named Titograd in honor of Yugoslav leader Marshal Tito.

**Po·do·lia** |pǝ'dōlēǝ| former region, now in W Ukraine, between the Southern Bug and Dniester rivers. It has belonged to Lithuania, Poland, Turkey, Austria, and Russia.

**Po·dolsk** |pǝ'dǝlsk| industrial and technological city in Russia, S of Moscow. Pop. 209,000.

**Po·dunk** |'pō,dǝNGk| in the U.S., an insignificant rural place, perhaps originally from a Connecticut Indian locality name.

**Po Hai** |'bō 'hī| see BO HAI, China.

**P'o·hang** |'pō'häNG| industrial port city in SE South Korea, on the Sea of Japan. Pop. 509,000. It is a steel industry center.

**Pohn·pei** |'pänpā| (formerly **Ponape**) volcanic island, forming with surrounding atolls one of the four Federated States of MICRONESIA. Pop. 33,000. Kolonia, the capital, is here.

**Pointe-à-Pitre** |,pwäntǝpē'trǝ| the chief port and commercial capital of the French island of Guadeloupe in the West Indies. Pop. 26,000.

**Pointe-Noire** |,pwänt'nwär| the chief seaport of the Republic of Congo, an industrial city and oil terminal on the Atlantic coast. Pop. 576,000.

**Point Pe·lée National Park** |'pēlē| preserve in SW Ontario, on the W end of Lake Erie, at the southernmost point on the mainland of Canada.

**Pois·sy** |,pwæ'sē| commune in N France, on the Seine River NW of Paris. Pop. 37,000. The Villa Savoye (1929–30), by Le Corbusier, is an important example of the International Style of architecture.

**Poi·tiers** |,pwätyā| city in W central France, the chief town of Poitou-Charentes region and capital of the former province of Poitou. Pop. 82,000.

**Poi·tou** |pwä'tōō| former province of W central France, now united with Charente to form the region of Poitou-Charentes. Formerly part of Aquitaine, it was held by the French and English in succession until it was finally united with France at the end of the Hundred Years War.

**Poitou-Charentes** |pwä'tōōSHä'rät| region of W France, on the Bay of Biscay, centered on Poitiers.

**Po·kha·ra** |'pōkǝrǝ| city in central Nepal, NW of Kathmandu. Pop. 95,000.

**Po·land** |'pōlǝnd| republic in central Europe with a coastline on the Baltic Sea. Area: 117,599 sq. mi./304,463 sq. km. Pop. 38,183,000. Language, Polish. Capital and largest city: Warsaw. Polish name **Polska**. A nation since the 11th century, Poland was a regional power in the 16th century, but has since suffered domination by Russia, Germany, and other neighbors. It has an industrial economy; agriculture and mining are also important. □ **Polish** *adj.* **Pole** *n.*

Poland

**Po·land Spring** |'pōlǝnd| former spa in the town of Poland, in SW Maine, known today for its bottled water.

**Po·lish Corridor** |'pōlisH| former name for a region of Poland that extended N to the Baltic coast and separated East Prussia from the rest of Germany, granted to Poland after World War I to ensure Polish access to the coast. Its annexation by Germany in 1939, and the German invasion of the rest of Poland, was the beginning of World War II. After the war the area was restored to Poland.

**Polokwane** see PIETERSBURG.

**Po·lon·na·ru·wa** |pōlō'nərōōwä| town in NE Sri Lanka. Pop. 12,000. Succeeding Anuradhapura in the 8th century as the capital of Ceylon, it became an important Buddhist center in the 12th century. It was subsequently deserted until a modern town was built here in the 20th century.

**Pol·ska** |'pōlskä| Polish name for POLAND.

**Pol·ta·va** |pəl'tävə| industrial and agricultural city in E central Ukraine. Pop. 317,000.

**Pol·y·ne·sia** |ˌpälə'nēzНə| region of the central Pacific, lying to the E of Micronesia and Melanesia and containing the easternmost of the three great groups of Pacific islands, including Hawaii, the Marquesas Islands, Samoa, the Cook Islands, and French Polynesia. □ **Polynesian** adj. & n.

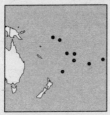

Polynesia

**Pom·er·a·nia** |ˌpämə'rānēə| region of N Europe, extending along the S shore of the Baltic Sea between Stralsund in NE Germany and the Vistula River in Poland. The region was controlled variously by Germany, Poland, the Holy Roman Empire, Prussia, and Sweden, until the larger part was restored to Poland in 1945, the western portion becoming a part of the German state of Mecklenburg–West Pomerania.

**Po·mo·na** |pə'mōnə| industrial and commercial city in SW California, in an agricultural area E of Los Angeles. Pop. 131,723.

**Pom·pa·no Beach** |ˌpämpə,nō| resort city in SE Florida, N of Fort Lauderdale, on the Atlantic. Pop. 72,411.

**Pom·peii** |päm'pā| ancient city in W Italy, SE of Naples. It was buried by an eruption of Mount Vesuvius in 79 AD; excavations of the site began in 1748, revealing well-

preserved remains of buildings, mosaics, furniture, and the personal possessions of inhabitants.

**Pom·pi·dou Center** | pawNpē'dōō| (also **Centre Pompidou**; informally known as **Beaubourg**), cultural center in Paris, France, on the Right Bank (N of the Seine River). Most of the building, which opened in 1977, is occupied by the National Museum of Modern Art.

**Pon·ca City** |'päNGkə| industrial city in N central Oklahoma, an oil-industry center. Pop. 26,359.

**Ponce** |'päns| industrial port in S Puerto Rico, on the Caribbean Sea. Pop. 159,151.

**Pon·di·cher·ry** |ˌpändə'cHerē| **1** Union Territory of SE India, on the Coromandel Coast, formed from several widely separated former French territories and incorporated into India in 1954. Pop. 789,000. **2** its capital city. Pop. 203,000.

**Pon·ta Del·ga·da** |ˌpäntə del'gädə| resort and port on the island of São Miguel in the Portuguese Azores. Pop. 21,000.

**Pon·ta Gros·sa** |'pöntä 'grösä| commercial city in S Brazil, in Paraná state. Pop. 253,000. It processes farm and forest products of the region.

**Pont-Aven** |pawntə'ven| village in Brittany, NW France, associated with Paul Gauguin and other late-19th-century French artists.

**Pont·char·train, Lake** |'pänCHər,trän| shallow lake in SE Louisiana, N of New Orleans and Metairie, noted for its long causeway and as a seafood producer.

**Pont du Gard** |pawn dyōō 'gär| Roman aqueduct built C.A.D.14 across the Gard River in S France to supply water to Nîmes. It consists of three tiers of arches and is 900 ft./270 m. long and 160 ft./50 m. high.

**Pon·te Vec·chio** |'pönte 'veCHō| bridge in Florence, Italy, over the Arno River. Built in the 14th century, the shop-lined structure is the only Florentine bridge to survive World War II.

**Pon·te·ve·dra** |ˌpöntä,vädrä| port in NW Spain, capital of Pontevedra province. Pop. 75,000.

**Pon·ti·ac** |'päntēæk| industrial city in SE Michigan, NW of Detroit, an auto-industry center. Pop. 71,166.

**Pon·ti·a·nak** |ˌpäntē'änək| seaport in Indonesia, on the W coast of Borneo at the delta of the Kapuas River. Pop. 305,000.

**Pon·tine Marshes** |'pän,tēn ,märsHəz| area of marshland in W Italy, on the Tyrrhenian coast S of Rome. It became infested with malaria in ancient times, and it was not until 1928 that an extensive scheme to drain the marshes was begun. Several new towns have since been built in the region, which is now a productive agricultural area. Italian name **Agro Pontino**.

**Pon·tus** |ˈpäntəs| ancient region of N Asia Minor, on the Black Sea coast N of Cappadocia. It reached its height between 120 and 63 B.C. under Mithridates VI, when it dominated the whole of Asia Minor; by the end of the 1st century B.C. it had been defeated by Rome and absorbed into the Roman Empire.

**Pon·tus Eux·i·nus** ancient Greek name for the BLACK SEA.

**Poole** |poōl| port and resort town on the S coast of England, in Dorset, just W of Bournemouth. Pop. 131,000.

**Poo·na** |ˈpoōnə| (also **Pune**) industrial city in Maharashtra, W India, in the hills SE of Bombay. Pop. 1,560,000. A Maratha capital, it became a military and administrative center under British rule.

**Po·pa·yán** |ˌpōpəˈyän| historic cultural city in SW Colombia, the capital of Cauca department. Pop. 204,000.

**Po·po·ca·té·petl** |ˌpōpəˈkætəpetəl| active volcano in Puebla state, Mexico, SE of Mexico City, which rises to 17,887 ft./5,452 m. It is one of twin peaks (the other is Ixtaccihuatl) visible from the city in clear weather.

**Por·ban·dar** |pōrˈbəndər| port town in W India, in Gujarat state. Pop. 160,000. Mohandas Gandhi, father of Indian independence, was born here.

**Por·cu·pine River** |ˈpawrkyəpīn| river that flows 450 mi./720 km. from the Yukon Territory into NE Alaska, to the Yukon River.

**Po·ri** |ˈpawrē| industrial port in SW Finland, on the Gulf of Bothnia. Pop. 76,000.

**Por·tage**[1] |ˈpawrtij| port city in NW Indiana, on L. Erie E of Gary. Pop. 29,060.

**Por·tage**[2] |ˈpawrtij| city in SW Michigan, a suburb S of Kalamazoo. Pop. 41,042.

**Port Ar·thur**[1] |ˈärTHər| former name (1898–1905) for LÜSHUN, China.

**Port Ar·thur**[2] |ˈärTHər| city in SE Texas, an oil industry center on the Neches and Sabine rivers near the Gulf Coast. Pop. 58,724.

**Port-au-Prince** |ˌpawrtōˈprins| the capital of Haiti, a port on the W coast of Hispaniola. Pop. 1,255,000. Founded by the French in 1749, it became capital of the new republic in 1806.

**Port Blair** |ˈblär| port city on the S tip of South Andaman Island, India, in the Bay

of Bengal. Pop. 75,000. It is the capital of the Andaman and Nicobar Islands.

**Port Co·quit·lam** |kōˈkwitləm| industrial and commercial city in SW British Columbia, on the Fraser River E of Vancouver. Pop. 36,773.

**Port de France** |fræns| former name for NOUMÉA, in French New Caledonia.

**Port Dick·son** |ˈdiksən| port and resort town in Malaysia, on the Strait of Malacca, SW of Seremban. Pop. 48,000.

**Port Eliz·a·beth** |əˈlizə,beTH| port city in South Africa, on the coast of the province of Eastern Cape. Pop. 853,000. Settled by the British in 1820, it is now an auto manufacturing city and beach resort.

**Port-Étienne** |ˌpōrtāˈtyen| former name for NOUADHIBOU, Mauritania.

**Port-Gentil** |ˈpōr ˌzhänˈta| the principal port city of Gabon, on the Atlantic coast S of Libreville. Pop. 76,000.

**Port Har·court** |ˈhär,kawrt| principal port of SE Nigeria, an industrial city on the Gulf of Guinea at the E edge of the Niger delta. Pop. 371,000.

**Port Hed·land** |ˈhedlənd| seaport on the NW coast of Western Australia. Pop. 14,000.

**Port Hue·ne·me** |wīˈnēmē| industrial and military port city in SW California, NW of Los Angeles. Pop. 20,319.

**Port Hu·ron** |ˈhyoōrən; ˈhyoōrän| industrial port city in SE Michigan, on Lake Huron and the St. Clair River. Pop. 33,694.

**Por·ți·le de Fier** |pōrˈtselede ˈfyer| Romanian name for the IRON GATE.

**Port·land, Isle of** |ˈpawrtlənd| rocky limestone peninsula on the S coast of England, in Dorset. Its southernmost tip is known as the Bill of Portland or Portland Bill. The peninsula is quarried for its building stone.

**Port·land**[1] |ˈpawrtlənd| largest city in Maine, on Casco Bay off the Atlantic, in the SW part. It is an industrial, commercial, and tourist center. Pop. 64,358.

**Port·land**[2] |ˈpawrtlənd| industrial port city in NW Oregon, on the Willamette River near its confluence with the Columbia River. Pop. 437,319. Founded in 1845, it developed as a supply center in gold rushes of the 1860s and 1870s, and as a lumber port. It is the largest city in Oregon.

**Port·laoi·se** |pawrtˈlēshə| (also **Port-laoighise**) the county seat of Laois, in the S central Republic of Ireland. Pop. 9,000.

**Port Lou·is** |pawrˈlwē| the capital of Mauritius, a port on the NW coast. Pop. 144,000.

**Port Moo·dy** |ˈmoōdi| city in SW British

Columbia, an industrial port on Burrard Inlet, just E of Vancouver. Pop. 17,712.

**Port Mores·by** |'mōrzbē| the capital of Papua New Guinea, situated on the S coast of the island of New Guinea, on the Coral Sea. Pop. 193,000.

**Port Na·tal** former name (until 1835) for DURBAN, South Africa.

**Por·to** |'pōr,tōō| Portuguese name for OPORTO.

**Pôr·to Ale·gre** |'pawrtōō ä'ləgre| major port and commercial city in SE Brazil, capital of the state of Rio Grande do Sul. Pop. 1,263,000. It is situated on the Lagoa dos Patos, a lagoon separated from the Atlantic by a sandy peninsula.

**Por·to·bel·lo Road** |pawrtō'bälō| street in W central London, England, N of Notting Hill, noted for its open-air market.

**Por·to·fi·no** |pawrtō'fēnō| village, a resort in NW Italy, SE of Genoa. Pop. 600. Its picturesque port attracts visitors.

**Port-of-Spain** |'pawrdəv'spän| the capital of Trinidad and Tobago, a port on the NW coast of the island of Trinidad. Pop. 46,000.

**Por·to No·vo** |'pawrtō 'nō,vō| the capital of Benin, a port on the Gulf of Guinea close to the border with Nigeria. Pop. 179,000. It was a center of the Portuguese slave trade in the 17th century.

**Pôr·to Vel·ho** |'pawrtōō 'velyōō| city in W Brazil, capital of the state of Rondônia, in a mining and lumbering district. Pop. 286,000.

**Por·to·vie·jo** |pawrtōvē'ähō| commercial city in W Ecuador, on the Portoviejo River NW of Guayaquil, in an agricultural district. Pop. 201,000.

**Port Pe·trovsk** former name (until 1922) for MAKHACHKALA, Russia.

**Port Pirie** |'pirē| port city on the coast of South Australia, on the Spencer Gulf N of Adelaide, in a mining district. Pop. 15,000.

**Port Roy·al** |'rōyäl| port town in SE Jamaica, on the peninsula enclosing Kingston harbor. A notorious buccaneering center, it was destroyed by a 1692 earthquake. In 1907 another quake occurred. It continues to be used for shipyards.

**Port-Royal** |',pawrt 'roiäl| abbey for women, later also a boys' school, founded in 1204, W of Paris, in N central France. It was moved to Paris in 1626. A center of Jansenism, the abbey was closed by papal bull in 1704.

**Port Said** |si'ēd| port city in Egypt, on the Mediterranean coast at the N end of the Suez Canal. Pop. 461,000. It was founded in 1859 at the start of the construction of

the Suez Canal, and is today both an industrial center and a resort.

**Port Saint Lu·cie** |'lōōsē| resort and retirement city in E central Florida. Pop. 55,866.

**Ports·mouth**[1] |'pawrtsməTH| port city and naval base on the S coast of England, formerly in Hampshire. Pop. 175,000. A naval dockyard was established here in 1496.

**Ports·mouth**[2] |'pawrtsməTH| historic port city in SE New Hampshire, on the Piscataqua River off the Atlantic. Pop. 25,925.

**Ports·mouth**[3] |'pawrtsməTH| commercial and naval city in SE Virginia, on Hampton Roads W of Norfolk. Pop. 103,907.

**Port Su·dan** |sōō'dæn| the chief port city of Sudan, on the Red Sea. Pop. 207,000.

**Port Town·send** |'townzənd| historic port city in NW Washington, on the Olympic Peninsula. Pop. 7,001.

**Por·tu·gal** |'pōrCHəgəl| republic occupying the W part of the Iberian peninsula in SW Europe. Area: 35,563 sq. mi./92,072 sq. km. Pop. 10,393,000. Language, Portuguese. Capital and largest city: Lisbon. Portugal broke from Spain in the 12th century, and was a colonial power in the 15th–16th centuries. Today, agriculture, tourism, mining, and some industry are important. □ **Portuguese** adj. & n.

**Portugal**

**Por·tu·guese India** |,pōrCHəgēz| former Portuguese colonial possessions in India, comprising Goa, Daman and Diu, and Dadra and Nagar-Haveli. By 1961 all had been repossessed by India.

**Port Vi·la** |vē'lä| see VILA, Vanuatu.

**Po·sa·das** |pō'sädäs| industrial and commercial city in NE Argentina, on the Paraná River opposite Encarnación, Paraguay. Pop. 220,000.

**Po·sen** |'pōzən| German name for POZ-NAŃ, Poland.

**Po·ten·za** |pō'tentsä| market town in S Italy, capital of Basilicata region. Pop. 68,000.

**Po·to·mac** |pəˈtōmək| river of the E U.S., which rises in the Appalachian Mts. in West Virginia and flows about 285 mi./459 km., into Chesapeake Bay on the Atlantic coast. Washington, D.C. is on the Potomac.

**Po·to·sí** |pəˈtōsē| mining city in S Bolivia. Pop. 112,000. Situated at an altitude of about 13,780 ft./4,205 m., it is one of the highest cities in the world.

**Pots·dam** |ˈpäts,dæm| city in eastern Germany, the capital of Brandenburg, just SW of Berlin on the Havel River. Pop. 95,000. It is the site of the rococo Sans Souci palace built for Frederick the Great of Prussia in 1745–47.

**Pot·ter·ies, the** |ˈpätərēz| industrial district in central England, in N Staffordshire, in the Trent River valley. The ceramic industry in Stoke-on-Trent and other "Five Towns" peaked here at the end of the 18th century.

**Potts·town** |ˈpätstown| industrial borough in SE Pennsylvania, on the Schuylkill River NW of Philadelphia. Pop. 21,381.

**Potts·ville** |ˈpätsvil| industrial and commercial city in SE Pennsylvania, on the Schuylkill River NW of Philadelphia. Pop. 16,603.

**Pough·keep·sie** |pəˈkipsē| industrial city in SE New York, on the Hudson River, noted as the home of Vassar College. Pop. 28,844.

**Pow·der River** |ˈpowdər| river that flows 485 mi./780 km. from NE Wyoming into S Montana, to the Yellowstone River.

**Pow·ell, Lake** |ˈpowel| reservoir on the Colorado River in S Utah, formed since the 1960s by the Glen Canyon Dam. The lake inundated famed Glen Canyon.

**Pow·ys** |ˈpäəs| county of E central Wales, on the border with England, formed in 1974 from the former counties of Montgomeryshire, Radnorshire, and most of Breconshire. Pop. 116,000; administrative center, Llandrindod Wells. Its name is that of a former Welsh kingdom.

**Po·yang Lake** |ˈpōyaNG| (Chinese name **Poyang Hu**) lake in Jiangxi province, SE central China; the largest freshwater lake in China; 1,383 sq. mi./3,583 sq. km. It is linked to the Yangtze River, for which it serves as an overflow reservoir.

**Po·za Ri·ca** |ˈpōzä ˈrēkä| (official name **Poza Rica de Hidalgo**) city in E central Mexico, an oil industry center in Veracruz state. Pop. 152,000.

**Poz·nań** |ˈpōz,næn| city in NW Poland. Pop. 590,000. An area of German colonization since the 13th century, it was under German control almost continuously until World War I, and was overrun by the Germans again in 1939. It was severely damaged during World War II. German name **Posen**.

**Po·zsony** |ˈpōzhōnē| Hungarian name for BRATISLAVA, Slovakia.

**Poz·zuo·li** |pōtˈtswawlē| seaport on the Bay of Naples, W Italy. Pop. 65,000. It has extensive Roman ruins and is a tourist center.

**Prades** |präd| village in S France, SW of Perpignan, site of a music festival founded by Pablo Casals, who settled here in 1939 in protest against the Franco government in Spain.

**Pra·do, the** |ˈprädō| national art gallery in Madrid, Spain, established in 1815 and housing a famed collection of Spanish art, as well as art from other countries.

**Prague** |präg| the capital of the Czech Republic, in the NE on the Vltava River. Pop. 1,212,000. Czech name **Praha**. Prague was the capital of Czechoslovakia from 1918 until the partition of 1993. The capital of Bohemia from the 14th century, it was the scene of much religious conflict. In 1618 Protestant citizens threw Catholic officials from the windows of Hradčany Castle, an event, known as the **Defenestration of Prague**, which contributed to the outbreak of the Thirty Years War. Modern Prague is an industrial and cultural center, noted for its beauty.

**Praia** |ˈprīə| the capital of Cape Verde, a port on the island of São Tiago. Pop. 62,000.

**Prai·rie du Chien** |ˈprərē də ˈsHēn| historic commercial city in SW Wisconsin, near the mouth of the Wisconsin River on the Mississippi River. Pop. 5,659.

**Pra·to** |ˈprätō| city in Tuscany, N Italy, NW of Florence. Pop. 167,000.

**Pres·cott** |ˈpres,kät| historic city in W central Arizona, a mining and tourist center. Pop. 26,455.

**Pres·i·den·tial Range** |,prezədenCHl| range in the White Mts., in N New Hampshire, including Mount Washington, at 6,288 ft./1,918 m. the highest peak in the NE U.S.

**Pre·šov** |ˈpresHaw| market town in E Slovakia, on the Torysa River. Pop. 88,000.

**Press·burg** |ˈpres,bərg| German name for BRATISLAVA, Slovakia.

**Pres·ton** |ˈprestən| industrial city in NW England, the administrative center of Lancashire, on the Ribble River. Pop. 126,000. It was the site in the 18th century of the first English cotton mills.

**Prest•wick** |'prest,wik| resort town to the S of Glasgow in South Ayrshire, SW Scotland, the site of an international airport. Pop. 14,000.

**Pre•to•ria** |prə'tawrēə| the administrative capital of South Africa, in Gauteng province. Pop. 1,080,000. Founded in 1855, it is an industrial and university city.

**Prib•i•lof Islands** |'pribə,lawf| (also **Fur Seal Islands**) group of four islands in the Bering Sea, off the coast of SW Alaska. First visited in 1786 by the Russian explorer Gavriil Loginovich Pribylov, they came into U.S. possession after the purchase of Alaska in 1867.

**Pri•lep** |'prēlep| commercial and industrial city in S Macedonia. Pop. 100,000.

**Prime Me•rid•i•an, the** |prīm mə'ridēən| 0° longitude, which runs through Greenwich, England. Other longitudes are based on it. See also INTERNATIONAL DATE LINE.

**Pri•mor•sky Krai** |prē'mōrski krī| krai (administrative territory) in the far SE of Siberian Russia, between the Sea of Japan and the Chinese border. Pop. 2,281,000. Capital: Vladivostok.

**Prince Al•bert** |'prints 'älbərt| industrial and commercial city in central Saskatchewan. Pop. 34,181.

**Prince Ed•ward Island** |,prins 'edwərd| island in the Gulf of St. Lawrence, in E Canada, the country's smallest (2,185 sq. mi./5,660 sq. km.) province. Capital and largest city: Charlottetown. Explored and colonized by the French, it was ceded to the British in 1763. It became a province of Canada in 1873. Fishing and tourism are important industries. A bridge to mainland New Brunswick was opened in 1997.

**Prince George** |'prints 'jōrj| city in central British Columbia, a transportation and commercial hub on the Fraser River. Pop. 69,653.

**Prince George's County** |'prints 'jōrjəz| county in S central Maryland, site of many SE suburbs of Washington, D.C. Pop. 729,268.

**Prince of Wales Island**[1] |'prints əv 'wälz| largest island in the Alexander Archipelago, in SE Alaska. It is the home of the Haida people.

**Prince of Wales Island**[2] |'prints əv 'wälz| an island in the Canadian Arctic, in Nunavut, NW of the Boothia Peninsula.

**Prince of Wales Island**[3] |'prints əv 'wälz| former name for PENANG, Malaysia.

**Prince Ru•pert** |prints 'rōōpərt| industrial port city in W central British Columbia, on Chatham Sound and the Inside Passage. Pop. 16,620.

**Prince•ton** |'prinstən| historic academic borough in W central New Jersey, home to Princeton University. Pop. 12,016.

**Prince Wil•liam Sound** |'prints 'wilyəm| inlet of the Pacific in S central Alaska, scene of a huge 1989 oil tanker spill. Cordova and Valdez are the main ports.

**Prin•ci•pe Island** |'prin(t)səpə| volcanic island in the Gulf of Guinea, W Africa, that constitutes part of the nation of São Tomé and Príncipe. Pop. 5,000.

**Pri•pyat** |'prēpyət.| (also **Pripet**) river of NW Ukraine and S Belarus, which rises in Ukraine near the border with Poland and flows some 440 mi./710 km. E through the Pripyat Marshes to join the Dnieper River N of Kiev.

**Priš•ti•na** |'prēsHtēnä| city in S Serbia, the capital of the autonomous province of Kosovo. Pop. 108,000. The capital of medieval Serbia, it was under Turkish control from 1389 until 1912.

**Priz•ren** |'prizren| market town in Kosovo, S Serbia, near the Albanian border. Pop. 135,000.

**Pro•bo•ling•go** |,prōbō'liNGō| (also **Prabalingga; Perobolinggo**) port city in Indonesia, on NE Java, SE of Surabaya. Pop. 177,000.

**Pro•ko•pyevsk** |prə'kawpyəfsk| coal-mining city in S Russia, in the Kuznets Basin industrial region to the S of Kemerovo. Pop. 274,000.

**Prom•ised Land** |'prämisd| in the Bible, land promised to the Jews by God, and viewed by their leader, Moses, from Mt. Pisgah, at the end of his life.

**Prom•on•to•ry Mountains** |'präməntōrē| short range that forms a peninsula in the N Great Salt Lake, in N Utah. The first transcontinental railroad passed through Promontory, N of the range. Today trains pass Promontory Point, at the S end, via a causeway across the lake.

**Pro•pon•tis** |prə'päntəs| ancient name for the Sea of Marmara (see MARMARA, SEA OF).

**Pro•vence** |prō'väns| former province of SE France, on the Mediterranean coast E of the Rhône. Settled by the Greeks in the 6th century B.C., the area around Marseilles became, in the 1st century B.C., part of the Roman colony of Gaul. It was united with France in 1481 and is now part of the region of Provence–Alpes–Côte d'Azur. The language and culture of Provence are distinctive. □ **Provencal** adj. & n.

**Provence-Alpes-Côte d'Azur** |prə'vän-sälpkōtdä'zyōr| mountainous region of SE France, on the border with Italy and including the French Riviera. Pop. 4,258,000. Marseilles is the chief city.

**Prov·i·dence** |'prävə,dens| the state capital of Rhode Island, a port on the Atlantic coast. Pop. 160,728. It was founded in 1636 as a haven for religious dissenters by Roger Williams (1604–83), who had been banished from the colony at Plymouth, Massachusetts. It developed in the 18th century as a major port for trade with the West Indies, and is today an industrial and financial center.

**Prov·i·dence Plan·ta·tions** |'prävə,dens| the mainland portion of the state of Rhode Island.

**Prov·ince·town** |'prävən,stown| port town in SE Massachusetts, a famed resort and artists' community at the N tip of Cape Cod. Pop. 3,561.

**Pro·vo** |'prōvō| industrial and commercial city in N central Utah, S of Salt Lake City. It is home to Brigham Young University. Pop. 86,835.

**Prud·hoe Bay** |',prōōdō| inlet of the Arctic Ocean on the N coast of Alaska. Since 1968 it has been a major center of Alaskan oil production.

**Prus·sia** |'prəsHə| former kingdom of Germany. Originally a small country on the SE shores of the Baltic, under Frederick the Great it became a major European power controlling much of modern NE Germany and Poland. After the Franco-Prussian War of 1870–71 it became the center of Bismarck's new German Empire, but following Germany's defeat in World War I the Prussian monarchy was abolished. Its nucleus was an area E of the Vistula, taken in the 13th century by the Teutonic Knights and passing in 1618 to the electors of Brandenburg. The kingdom of Prussia was proclaimed in 1701, with its capital at Berlin. □ **Prussian** adj. & n.

**Prut** |'prōōt| (also **Pruth**) river of SE Europe, which rises in the Carpathian Mts. in S Ukraine and flows SE for 530 mi./850 km., joining the Danube near Galaţi in Romania. For much of its course it forms the border between Romania and Moldova.

**Pskov** |pskôf| ancient city in W Russia, in an agricultural area SW of Saint Petersburg. Pop. 206,000.

**Pu·call·pa** |pōō'kīpä| commercial town in E Peru, capital of Ucayali department, a port on the Ucayali River. Pop. 153,000.

**Pu·ch'on** |pōō'cHawn| (also **Puchon**) industrial and agricultural city in NW South Korea, W of Seoul. Pop. 779,000.

**Pue·bla** |'pweblə| **1** state of S central Mexico. Pop. 4,118,000. **2** its capital city. Pop. 1,055,000. The fourth-largest Mexican city, an industrial center, it lies at the edge of the central plateau. Full name **Puebla de Zaragoza**.

**Pueb·lo** |'pweblō| industrial city in S central Colorado, on the Arkansas River at the foot of the Front Range of the Rocky Mts. Pop. 98,640.

**Puer·to Bar·rios** |'pwertō 'bärēōs| port city in E Guatemala, on the Bay of Amatique in the Caribbean Sea. Pop. 29,000. The capital of Izabal department, it was long a key banana-export center.

**Puer·to Ca·bel·lo** |kä'vāyō| historic industrial port city in N Venezuela, W of Caracas. Pop. 129,000. It exports fruit and ores and has oil and chemical facilities.

**Puer·to Cor·tés** |kawr'tās| port in NW Honduras, on the Caribbean coast at the mouth of the Ulua River. Pop. 40,000.

**Puer·to Es·con·di·do** |eskän'didō| resort town in S Mexico, on the Pacific coast in Oaxaca state. Pop. 8,000.

**Puer·to Montt** |mawnt| port city in S central Chile, on the Gulf of Ancud off the Pacific. Pop. 131,000. It has resort and fishing trade, and is the S terminus of Chilean railroads.

**Puer·to Pla·ta** |'plætə| resort town and cruise port in the Dominican Republic, on the N coast (the Amber Coast). Pop. 96,000.

**Puer·to Prin·ce·sa** |pren'sesə| commercial town in the Philippines, on E central Palawan. Pop. 92,000.

**Puer·to Ri·co** |'pwertō 'rikō, 'pawrtō| island of the Greater Antilles, in the Caribbean. Area: 3,460 sq. mi./8,959 sq. km. Pop. 3,522,040. Official languages, Spanish and English. Capital and largest city: San Juan. One of the earliest Spanish settlements in the New World, it was ceded

Puerto Rico

to the U.S. in 1898 after the Spanish-American War, and in 1952 it became a commonwealth in voluntary association with the U.S., with full powers of local government. Its economy, based on manufacturing, agriculture, and tourism, is highly dependent on the U.S. □ **Puerto Rican** *adj. & n.*

**Puer·to Ri·co Trench** |ˌpwertō 'rikō| ocean trench extending in an E–W direction to the N of Puerto Rico and the Leeward Islands. It reaches a depth of 28,397 ft./9,220 m.

**Puer·to Val·lar·ta** |väyärtə| resort and port city in W Mexico, on the Pacific in Jalisco state. Pop. 94,000. It is noted for its fishing, yachting, and hotel facilities.

**Pu·get Sound** |ˌpyōōjət| island-filled inlet of the Pacific on the coast of Washington State in the U.S. It is linked to the ocean by the Strait of Juan de Fuca and is overlooked by the city of Seattle, which is situated on its E shore.

**Pu·glia** |ˈpōōlyä| Italian name for APULIA.

**Pu·la** |ˈpōōlə| port, industrial center, and resort town in W Croatia, on the Adriatic Sea, on the S tip of the Istrian Peninsula. Pop. 62,000.

**Pull·man** |ˈpōōlmən| commercial city in SE Washington, on the Palouse River, home to Washington State University. Pop. 23,478.

**Pun·jab** |ˈpən,jäb| (also **the Punjab**) region of NW India and Pakistan, a wide, fertile plain traversed by the Indus and the five tributaries that gave the region its name. □ **Punjabi** *adj. & n.*

**Pu·no** |ˈpōōnō| commercial city in SE Peru, the capital of Puno department, on Lake Titicaca. Pop. 100,000. It is a tourist and cultural center.

**Punt** |pōōnt| land visited by Egyptian traders as early as the 15th century B.C., probably the coast of present-day Eritrea and Djibouti

**Pun·ta Are·nas** |ˈˌpōōntə ə'rānəs| port in S Chile, on the Strait of Magellan. Pop. 114,000.

**Pun·ta del Es·te** |del 'ästä| resort city in S Uruguay, in Maldonado department, E of the mouth of the Rio de la Plata. Pop. 8,000. It has been the scene of international conferences.

**Punx·su·taw·ney** |ˌpəNGksə'tawni| borough in W central Pennsylvania, noted as the home of Punxsutawney Phil, a groundhog whose movements are closely observed by the media each February 2.

**Pu·qi** town in Hubei province, E central China, SW of Wuhan. Pop. 413,000.

**Pur·cell Mountains** |ˈpərsəl| range of the N Rocky Mts. in SE British Columbia, E of the Selkirk Mts.

**Pu·ri** |ˈpōōrē| (also called **Jagannath; Juggernaut**) port city in E India, in Orissa state. Pop. 125,000. It is the center of worship of the Hindu god Jagannath.

**Pur·nia** |ˈpōōrnēä| (also **Purnea**) commercial town in E India, in Bihar state. Pop. 137,000.

**Pu·rus River** |pə'rōōs| river that flows NE for 2,100 mi./3,400 km. from the Andes in E Peru into NW Brazil, where it joins the Amazon.

**Pu·san** |ˌpōō'sän| port city on the SE coast of South Korea. Pop. 3,798,000. A center of heavy industry, it is the second-largest South Korean city.

**Push·kar Lake** |ˈpōōsHker| lake in NW India, in E central Rajasthan state. It is a religious site with the only temple in India dedicated to the Hindu god Brahma.

**Push·kin** |ˈpōōsH,kin| (formerly **Detskoye Selo** and, earlier, **Tsarskoye Selo**) residential and resort suburb of Saint Petersburg, Russia. The site was given by Peter the Great to his wife as a summer residence. After the 1917 Revolution, it became known as Detskoye Selo ('children's village') and was a health resort. In 1937 it was renamed Pushkin, for the poet.

**Put·u·ma·yo River** |ˌpōōtə'mīō| river that flows 1,000 mi./1,610 km. from the Andes in SW Colombia, along the borders with Ecuador and Peru, into NW Brazil, where it joins the Amazon.

**PWV** *abbrev. for* Pretoria–Witwatersrand–Vereeniging, former South African province, now GAUTENG.

**Pya·ti·gorsk** |ˌpitē'görsk| (also **Piatigorsk**) spa in W Russia, on the Kuma River, NW of Grozny, Chechnya. Pop. 129,000. The city also has some mineral waters.

**Pyong·yang** |ˈpyawNG'yæNG| the capital of North Korea, on the Taedong River. Pop. 2,000,000. The oldest city on the Korean peninsula, it was first mentioned in records of 108 B.C. It developed as an industrial city during the Japanese occupation of 1910–45.

**Pyr·e·nees** |ˈpirə,nēz| range of mountains extending along the border between France and Spain from the Atlantic coast to the Mediterranean. Its highest peak is the Pico de Aneto in northern Spain, which rises to a height of 11,168 ft./3,404 m. □ **Pyrenean** *adj. & n.*

# Qq

**Qa·ra·ghan·dy** |kärə'gändə| industrial city in E Kazakhstan, at the center of a major coal-mining region. Pop. 613,000. Russian name **Karaganda**.

**Qa·tar** |'kä,tär| sheikhdom occupying a peninsula on the W coast of the Persian Gulf. Area: 4,416 sq. mi./11,437 sq. km. Pop. 402,000. Language, Arabic. Capital and largest city: Doha. The country was a British protectorate from 1916 until 1971, when it became independent. Oil is the chief source of revenue. □ **Qatari** *adj. & n.*

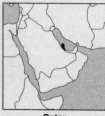

Qatar

**Qat·ta·ra Depression** |kə'tärə| extensive, low-lying, and largely impassable area of desert in NE Africa, to the W of Cairo, that falls to 436 ft./133 m. below sea level.

**Qaz·vin** |käz'vēn| (also **Kazvin; Kasbin**) industrial and commercial city in NW Iran, NW of Tehran. Pop. 279,000.

**Qena** |'kēnə| (also **Kena**; ancient name **Caene**) town in S central Egypt, on the Nile River, in an agricultural area. Pop. 137,000.

**Qi·lian Shan** |'CHi'lyän 'SHän| mountain range in N China, on the border between Gansu and Qinghai provinces, rising to a height of 19,114 ft./5,826 m.

**Qing·dao** |'CHĕNG'dow| port in E China, in Shandong province on the Yellow Sea coast. Pop. 2,040,000.

**Qing·hai** |'CHĬNG'hĭ| (also **Tsinghai**) mountainous province in N central China. Pop. 4,457,000. Capital: Xining.

**Qing·hai Lake** |'CHĔNG'hĭ| (Chinese name **Qinghai Hu**) salt lake in Qinghai province, N central China; the largest lake in the country. Area: 1,770 sq. mi./4,583 sq. km.

**Qin·huang·dao** |'CHĭn'hwäNG'dow| industrial port in Hebei province, NE China, on the Bo Hai near the Liaoning border. Pop. 448,000. A special economic zone, it

is linked by pipeline to the oil fields at Daqing.

**Qin·zhou** |'CHĕn'jō| city in Guangxi, S China, on an inlet of the Gulf of Tonkin, S of Nanning. Pop. 944,000.

**Qi·qi·har** |'CHĕ'CHĕ'här| port on the Nen River, in Heilongjiang province, NE China. Pop. 1,370,000.

**Qi·shon** |'kĭSHən| (also **Kison; Kishon**) river in N Israel that flows 45 mi./72 km., from near Mount Gilboa to the Mediterranean Sea at Haifa.

**Qi·tai·he** |'CHĕ'tĭ'hə| industrial city in Heilongjiang province, NE China, E of Harbin near the Russian border. Pop. 327,000.

**Qom** |'kōm| (also **Qum** or **Kum**) industrial city in central Iran. Pop. 780,000. It is a holy city and center of learning and pilgrimage for Shiite Muslims.

**Qos·ta·nay** |kəstə'nĭ| (also known as **Kustanay**) **1** administrative subdivision in N Kazakhstan. Pop. 1,074,000. **2** its capital city, a mining and agricultural center. Pop. 234,000.

**Quad Cities** |kwäd| industrial complex on the Mississippi River, composed of Davenport and Bettendorf, SE Iowa, and Moline and Rock Island, NW Illinois. A second Quad Cities, in N Alabama on the Tennessee River, consists of Florence, Sheffield, Tuscumbia, and Muscle Shoals.

**Quai d'Orsay** |'kä dawr'sä| riverside street on the Left (S) Bank of the Seine in Paris. The French ministry of foreign affairs has its headquarters in this street.

**Quang Tri** |'kwæNG 'trē| province in central Vietnam, NW of Hue. The center of the Demilitarized Zone (DMZ) during the Vietnam War, it suffered heavy deforestation by U.S. forces.

**Quan·ti·co** |'kwäntə,kō| town in NE Virginia, on the Potomac River, SW of Washington, D.C. Pop. 670. Nearby are major Marine and FBI training centers.

**Quan·zhou** |'CHwæn'jō| city in Fujian province, SE China, NE of Xiamen. Pop. 444,000. It was one of the great Chinese ports during the Middle Ages.

**Qua·tre Bras** |'kätrə 'brä| village in central Belgium, SE of Brussels, site of an 1815 battle in which the English under Wellington defeated French troops.

**Que·bec¹** |k(w)ə'bek| province in E Canada. Area: 594,860 sq. mi./1.67 million sq. km. Pop. 6,845,700. Settled by the French in 1608, it was ceded to the British in 1763, and became one of the original four provinces in the Dominion of Canada in 1867. The majority of its residents are French-speaking and its culture remains predominantly French. It has some political independence from the rest of Canada, and is the focal point of the French-Canadian nationalist movement. Varied manufacturing, mining, forest industries, fishing, hydropower, and tourism are all important. French name **Québec**. □ **Québecois** adj. & n. **Quebecer** n.

**Que·bec²** |k(w)ə'bek| (also **Quebec City**) the capital of Quebec province, a port on the St. Lawrence River. Pop. 167,517. Founded on the site of a Huron village (Stadacona) in 1608, it is Canada's oldest city. It was a center of the struggle between the French and British for control of North America and it was captured by a British force in 1759 after the battle of the Plains of Abraham. It became capital of Lower Canada (later Quebec) in 1791.

**Qued·lin·burg** |'kfedlinbərg| historic industrial and market city in central Germany. Pop. 29,000.

**Queen Char·lotte Islands** |'sHärlət| group of more than 150 islands off the W coast of Canada, in British Columbia, noted for fishing and lumbering.

**Queen City** nickname for CINCINNATI, Ohio.

**Queen Eliz·a·beth Islands** |ə'lizə,beTH| name for all islands in the Arctic Archipelago of Canada N of the Parry Channel (approximately 74° N). Mostly unpopulated, and often ice-covered, they were formerly called the Parry Islands.

**Queen Maud Land** |mowd| part of Antarctica bordering the Atlantic, claimed since 1939 by Norway.

**Queens** |kwēnz| largest and second most populous borough of New York City, coextensive with Queens County, at the W end of Long Island. Pop. 1,951,598. It is noted for its diverse populace and residential and light industrial neighborhoods.

**Queen's County** |kwēnz| former name for County LAOIS, Ireland.

**Queens·land** |'kwēnzlənd| state comprising the NE part of Australia. Pop. 2,922,000. Capital: Brisbane. Established in 1824 as a penal settlement, Queensland was constituted a separate colony in 1859, having previously formed part of New South Wales, and was federated with the other states of Australia in 1901. Agricul-

ture and mining are key to the economy. □ **Queenslander** n.

**Queens·ton** |'kwēnztən| historic locality, now in Niagara-on-the-Lake, E Ontario, just N of Niagara Falls, site of fighting in the War of 1812.

**Quel·i·ma·ne** |kelē'mänə| (also **Quilimane** or **Kilimane**) port town in E central Mozambique, near the Indian Ocean on the Quelimane River. Pop. 146,000.

**Que·luz** |ke'lōōsH| town in central Portugal, N of Lisbon. Pop. 44,000. Its 18th-century palace was a royal residence.

**Que·moy** |ki'moi| island group, SE China, off the coast of Fujian province, E of Xiamen. Under the control of the Nationalist government on Taiwan after the communist takeover of the mainland, it was subjected to periodic shelling during the 1950s.

**Que·ré·ta·ro** |kə'retə,rō| **1** state of central Mexico. Area: 4,422 sq. mi./11,449 sq. km. Pop. 1,044,000. **2** its capital city, an industrial and tourist center. Pop. 454,000. In 1847 it was the scene of the signing of the treaty ending the U.S.-Mexican war.

**Quet·ta** |'kwetə| city in western Pakistan, the capital of Baluchistan province. Pop. 350,000.

**Quet·zal·te·nan·go** |ketsälte'näNGō| city in SW Guatemala, capital of Quetzaltenango department. Pop. 246,000. It is an industrial center and the second-largest Guatemalan city.

**Que·zon City** |'kāsōn| city on the island of Luzon in the N Philippines, on the outskirts of Manila. Pop. 1,667,000. It was established in 1940 and from 1948 to 1976 was the capital of the Philippines.

**Qu·fu** |'CHōō'fōō| small town in Shandong province in E China, where Confucius was born in 551 BC and lived for much of his life.

**Quib·dó** |kēb'dō| town in W Colombia, the capital of Chocó department. Pop. 119,000. It is a mining and tropical agriculture center.

**Qui·be·ron** |kēb'rôn| **1** peninsula in Brittany, NW France. **2** fishing port and resort at its tip. Pop. 5,000.

**Quil·mes** |'kēlmes| industrial city in E Argentina, a suburb SE of Buenos Aires. Pop. 509,000.

**Qui·lon** |kwē'lōn| (also **Kollam**) commercial port in SW India, on the Malabar Coast in Kerala state. Pop. 362,000.

**Quil·pué** |kēl'pwä| commercial and resort city in central Chile, E of Valparaiso. Pop. 107,000.

**Quin·cy**[1] |'kwinsē| industrial and commercial city in W central Illinois, on the Mississippi River. Pop. 39,681.

**Quin·cy**[2] |'kwinsē| historic industrial city in E Massachusetts, on Boston Harbor, just SE of Boston, a noted shipbuilding center. Pop. 84,985.

**Qui Nhon** |kwē 'nyawn| (also **Quy Nhon**) industrial and commercial city in SE Vietnam, on the South China Sea. Pop. 202,000. A naval station and military base during the Vietnam War, it was the center of heavy fighting.

**Quin·ta·na Roo** |kēn'tänä 'rōō| state of SE Mexico, on the Yucatán Peninsula. Area: 19,394 sq. mi./50,212 sq. km. Pop. 494,000. Capital: Chetumal.

**Quir·i·nal** |'kwirənəl| one of the seven original hills on which Rome was built. The Quirinal Palace, built for the Pope, has been home to kings, and now is home to the president of Italy.

**Qui·to** |'kētō| the capital and educational and cultural center of Ecuador. Pop. 1,401,000. It is situated in the Andes just S of the equator, at an altitude of 9,350 ft./2,850 m.

**Qui·vi·ra** |kɪ'vērä| legendary land of wealth, somewhere in what is now the U.S. SW, sought by Spanish adventurers. The 1540 Coronado expedition followed rumors as far as Great Bend, Kansas.

**Qum·ran** |kōōm'ræn| region on the W shore of the Dead Sea, in the West Bank. The Dead Sea scrolls were found (1947–56) in caves at nearby Khirbet Qumran, the site of an ancient Jewish (probably Essene) settlement.

**Qwa·qwa** |'kwäkwə| (also **QwaQwa**) former homeland established in South Africa for the South Sotho people, in the Drakensberg Mts. in what is now Free State province.

**Qy·zyl·or·da** |kə,silər'dä| (also **Kzyl-Orda**) **1** administrative subdivision in S Kazakhstan, E of the Aral Sea. Pop. 665,000. **2** its capital. Pop. 158,000.

# Rr

**Ra·bat** |rə'bät| the capital of Morocco, an industrial port on the Atlantic coast. Pop. 1,220,000. It was founded as a fort in the 12th century by the Almohads, and is today an administrative and textile center.

**Ra·baul** |rä'bowl| the chief town and port of the island of New Britain, in Papua New Guinea. Pop. 17,000.

**Ra·ci·bórz** |rä'CHēbŏŏsн| (German name **Ratibor**) industrial port town in S Poland, on the Oder River. Pop. 62,000.

**Ra·cine** |rə'sēn; rä'sēn| industrial city in SE Wisconsin, on Lake Michigan. Pop. 84,298.

**Ră·dă·u·ţi** |‚rədə'ŏŏtsē| industrial town in N Romania, in Bukovina. Pop. 31,000.

**Rad·nor·shire** |'rædnərsнiər; sнər; rædnərsнir| former county of E Wales. It became part of Powys in 1974.

**Ra·dom** |'rä‚dawm| industrial city in central Poland. Pop. 228,000.

**Rae Ba·re·li** |ri bə'rä‚lē| city in N central India, in Uttar Pradesh state, SSE of Lucknow. Pop. 130,000.

**Rae·tia** |'rē‚sнēə| (also **Rhaetia**) ancient Roman province, S of the Danube River in what is now E Switzerland and part of the Tyrol.

**Ra·gu·sa**[1] |rə'gŏŏsə| Italian name (until 1918) for **Dubrovnik**, Croatia. It is the probable source of the word *argosy*, referring to large and richly-freighted merchant ships of the 16th century.

**Ra·gu·sa**[2] |rə'gŏŏsə| industrial town in SE Sicily, S Italy, capital of Ragusa province. Pop. 69,000.

**Rah·way** |'raw‚wā| industrial city in NE New Jersey, SW of Elizabeth. Pop. 25,325.

**Ra·ia·tea** |‚rīə'tāə| volcanic island, the largest in the Leeward group of the Society Islands, French Polynesia. It has been thought the homeland from which Polynesian migrations spread across the Pacific.

**Rai·chur** |'rīcHər| commercial town in S central India, in Karnataka state. Pop. 171,000.

**Rain·bow Bridge** |'rānbō| bridge of natural rock, the world's largest, in S Utah, just N of the border with Arizona. Its span is 278 ft./86 m.

**Rai·nier, Mount** |‚rā'nēr| volcanic peak in the SW of Washington State in the U.S. Rising to a height of 14,410 ft./4,395 m., it is the highest peak in the Cascade Range.

**Rainy River** |'rā‚nē| short river that flows W along the Minnesota-Ontario border, past International Falls and into the Lake of the Woods. One of its sources is Rainy Lake, also on the border.

**Rai·pur** |'rī‚pawr| city in central India, in Madhya Pradesh, an agricultural processing center. Pop. 438,000.

**Ra·jah·mun·dry** |‚räjə'mŏŏndrē| commercial and industrial city in E central India, in Andhra Pradesh state. Pop. 404,000,

**Ra·ja·sthan** |'räjə‚stän| state in W India, on the Pakistani border. Pop. 43.88 million. Capital: Jaipur. The W part of the state consists largely of the Thar Desert and is sparsely populated. □ **Rajasthani** *adj. & n.*

**Ra·ja·sthan Canal** |'räjə‚stän| former name for the **Indira Gandhi Canal**, India.

**Raj·kot** |'räj‚kŏt| administrative city in Gujarat, W India, in an agricultural area. Pop. 556,000.

**Raj·pu·ta·na** |‚räjpə'tänə| ancient region of India consisting of a collection of princely states ruled by dynasties. Following independence from Britain in 1947, they united to form the state of Rajasthan, parts also being incorporated into Gujarat and Madhya Pradesh.

**Raj·sha·hi** |‚räj'sнä‚hē| industrial port on the Ganges River in W Bangladesh. Pop. 325,000.

**Ra·leigh** |'rawlē; 'rälē| the state capital of North Carolina, a research and industrial center in a tobacco growing region. Pop. 207,951.

**Ra·mat Gan** |rə'mät 'gän| industrial city in W central Israel, adjacent to Tel Aviv. Pop. 122,000.

**Ram·bouil·let** |‚ränbŏŏ'yä| town in N France, in the Forest of Rambouillet. Pop. 25,000. The chateau here, formerly a royal residence, is now the summer home of the French president, and a conference center.

**Ra·mil·lies** |'rämē‚yē| village in central Belgium, site of a 1706 battle in which English troops defeated French forces.

**Ram·pur** |'ræm‚pŏŏr| town in N India, in Uttar Pradesh state. Pop. 243,000. It is noted for a collection of rare manuscripts and Mogul miniature paintings.

**Ran·ca·gua** |‚rän'kägwə| historic city in central Chile, capital of the Libertador General Bernardo O'Higgins region. Pop. 190,000. Copper mining, manufacturing, and agriculture are important here.

**Ran·chi** |'ræncHē| industrial and educational city in Bihar, NE India. Pop. 598,000.

**Ran·cho Cor·do·va** |'ræn,CHō 'kawr-,dəvə| industrial suburb in N central California, NE of Sacramento. Pop. 48,731.

**Ran·cho Cu·ca·mon·ga** |'ræn,CHō ,kōō-kə'mäNGə| (also **Cucamonga**) city in SW California, a residential and industrial suburb E of Los Angeles. Pop. 101,409.

**Rand** |rænd| also **the Rand** another name for WITWATERSRAND, South Africa.

**Ran·ders** |'rænərz| port of Denmark, on the Randers Fjord on the E coast of the Jutland peninsula. Pop. 61,000.

**Rand·olph** |'ræn,dawlf| town in E Massachusetts, a suburb S of Boston. Pop. 30,093.

**Rand·stad** |'ränd,städ| urban region in the NW of the Netherlands that stretches in a horseshoe shape from Dordrecht and Rotterdam to Utrecht and Amersfoort via The Hague, Leiden, Haarlem, and Amsterdam. The majority of the people of the Netherlands live in this area.

**Range·ley Lakes** |'rānj,lē| resort region in W Maine, near the New Hampshire line, noted for Rangeley, Mooselookmeguntic, and other lakes and the Mahoosuc Range, which stands just S.

**Ran·goon** |ræNG'gōōn| the capital of Burma, a port in the Irrawaddy delta. Pop. 2,459,000. For centuries a Buddhist religious center, it is the site of the Shwe Dagon Pagoda, built over 2,500 years ago. The modern city was established by the British in the mid-19th century and became capital in 1886. Burmese name **Yangon.**

**Rang·pur** |'rəNG,pawr| city in NW Bangladesh. Pop. 221,000. It is noted for its cotton carpets.

**Rann of Kutch** see KUTCH, RANN OF, India.

**Ra·pal·lo** |rə'pä,lō| seaport and resort in NW Italy, on the Riviera, on the Gulf of Genoa. Pop. 27,000.

**Ra·pa Nui** |,rä,pä 'nōō,ē| Polynesian name for EASTER ISLAND.

**Rap·id City** |'ræ,pid| city in SW South Dakota, commercial center for Black Hills and Mount Rushmore tourism. Pop. 54,523.

**Rap·pa·han·nock River** |,ræpə'hænək| river that flows 210 mi./340 km. across E Virginia, into the Tidewater region. Fredericksburg lies on it, the Northern Neck to the N.

**Rar·i·tan River** |'rærə,tən| short river in central New Jersey that flows past New Brunswick and Perth Amboy, into Raritan Bay, an arm of New York Bay and the Atlantic.

**Rar·o·ton·ga** |,rärə'tawNGə| mountainous island in the S Pacific, the chief island of the Cook Islands. Its chief town, Avarua, is the capital of the Cook Islands. □ **Rarotongan** adj. & n.

**Ras al Khai·mah** |'räs ,el'kämə| **1** one of the seven member states of the United Arab Emirates. Pop. 144,000. It joined the UAE in 1972, after the British withdrawal from the Persian Gulf. **2** its capital, a port on the Gulf. Pop. 42,000.

**Ra·shid** |rə'sHēd| (formerly **Rosetta**) port city in N Egypt, E of Alexandria at the Rashid (Rosetta) branch of the delta of the Nile River. Pop. 52,000. The Rosetta stone, key to deciphering Egyptian hieroglyphics, was found here in 1799.

**Rasht** |ræsHt| (also **Resht**) commercial and industrial city in N Iran, near the Caspian Sea. Pop. 341,000.

**Rath·lin Island** |'ræTH,lin| island in the North Channel, off County Antrim, Northern Ireland, associated with ancient connections between Ireland and Scotland.

**Ra·tin·gen** |'rätiNG,ən| industrial city in NW Germany, N of Dusseldorf. Pop. 91,000.

**Rat Islands** |'ræt| island group in the Aleutian Islands, in SW Alaska. Lying between the Near and Andreanof islands, they include Amchitka and Kiska.

**Rat·lam** |,rət'läm| (also **Rutlam**) commercial city in W central India, in Madhya Pradesh state. Pop. 196,000.

**Ra·ton** |rə'tōn| commercial city in NE New Mexico, at the Colorado border. It grew below Raton Pass, which was key in the development of the Santa Fe Trail and Santa Fe Railroad.

**Ra·ven·na** |rə'venə| city near the Adriatic coast in N central Italy. Pop. 137,000. It became the capital of the Western Roman Empire in 402 and then of the Ostrogothic kingdom of Italy, afterward serving as capital of Byzantine Italy. It is noted for its ancient mosaics dating from the early Christian period. The oil industry and tourism are important today.

**Ra·vens·brück** |,rävenz'brōōk| village in Brandenburg, NE Germany, N of Berlin. The Nazis maintained a concentration camp here during World War II.

**Ra·vi** |'rä,vē| river in the N of the Indian subcontinent, one of the headwaters of the Indus, which rises in the Himalayas in Himachel Pradesh, NW India, and flows 450 mi./725 km. generally SW into Pakistan, where it empties into the Chenab River just N of Multan.

**Ra·wal·pin·di** |,räwəl'pindē| industrial city

in Punjab province, N Pakistan, in the foothills of the Himalayas. Pop. 955,000. A former military station, it was the interim capital of Pakistan, 1959–67, during the construction of Islamabad.

**Raw·son** |'rawsən| port town in S Argentina, in Patagonia, on the Atlantic coast, capital of Chubut province. Pop. 19,000.

**Read·ing**[1] |'rediNG| the county seat of Berkshire, in S England, on the Kennet River near its junction with the Thames. Pop. 123,000.

**Read·ing**[2] |'rediNG| industrial and commercial city in SE Pennsylvania, on the Schuylkill River. Pop. 78,380.

**Re·ci·fe** |re'sēfē| port and resort city on the Atlantic coast of NE Brazil, capital of the state of Pernambuco. Pop. 1,298,000. Former name **Pernambuco**.

**Reck·ling·hau·sen** |,rəkliNG'howzən| industrial city in NW Germany, S of Münster. Pop. 126,000.

**Red Bank** |'rəd| resort and commercial borough in E New Jersey. Pop. 10,636.

**Red·bridge** |'red,brij| largely residential borough of NE Greater London, England. Pop. 221,000. On the Essex border, it includes much of Epping Forest.

**Red China** term used of mainland China, in reference to its communist government.

**Red Deer** |'red,dir| industrial city in central Alberta, an oil industry center between Edmonton and Calgary. Pop. 58,134.

**Red·ding** |'rədiNG| commercial and resort city in N California, at the N end of the Sacramento Valley. Pop. 66,462.

**Red·ditch** |'rediCH| industrial town in W central England, a Birmingham suburb in Worcestershire. Pop. 77,000.

**Red Hook** |'red| industrial port section of Brooklyn, New York, on New York Bay across from Governor's Island.

**Red·lands** |'redlənz| commercial and resort city in S California, near the San Bernardino Mts. Pop. 60,394.

**Red·mond** |'redmənd| city in W central Washington, a suburb NE of Seattle, noted as the home of the Microsoft corporation. Pop. 35,800.

**Re·don·do Beach** |,rə'dändō| city in SW California, a largely residential suburb on Santa Monica Bay, S of Los Angeles. Pop. 60,167.

**Red River**[1] |'red| river in SE Asia, which rises in S China and flows 730 mi./1,175 km. generally SE through N Vietnam to the Gulf of Tonkin. Chinese name **Yuan Jiang**. Vietnamese name **Song Hong**.

**Red River**[2] |'red| **1** river in the S U.S., a tributary of the Mississippi, which rises in N Texas and flows 1,222 mi./1,966 km. generally SE, forming part of the border between Texas and Oklahoma, and enters the Mississippi in Louisiana. Also called **Red River of the South**. **2** river in the N U.S. and Canada, which rises in North Dakota and flows 545 mi./877 km. N, forming for most of its length the border between North Dakota and Minnesota, before entering Manitoba, passing Winnipeg, and emptying into Lake Winnipeg. Also called **Red River of the North**.

**Red Sea** |red| long, narrow nearly landlocked sea separating Africa from the Arabian Peninsula. It is linked to the Indian Ocean in the S by the Bab el Mandab and Gulf of Aden and to the Mediterranean in the N by the Suez Canal.

**Red Square** |red| large public square in Moscow, Russia, bounded on one side by the Kremlin and on another by Saint Basil's cathedral.

**Red·wood City** |'red,wŏŏd| port city in N central California, on SW San Francisco Bay, now part of the Silicon Valley complex. Pop. 66,072.

**Reel·foot Lake** |'rēl,fŏŏt| lake in the NW corner of Tennessee, near the Mississippi River, formed during the 1811 earthquake centered on nearby New Madrid, Missouri.

**Re·gens·burg** |'rāgəmz,bərg| port city, a tourist and industrial center in SE Germany, at the confluence of the Danube and Regen rivers. Pop. 123,000.

**Reg·gio di Ca·la·bria** |'red,jō ,dē ,kä'läbrēä| port at the S tip of the 'toe' of Italy, on the Strait of Messina, capital of Calabria region. Pop. 183,000. The original settlement was founded about 720 B.C. by Greek colonists as Rhegion (Latin, Rhegium).

**Reg·gio Emi·lia** |,ā'mēlyə| industrial city in N Italy. Pop. 130,000. It is capital of a province of the same name (also called **Reggio Emilia**) in Emilia-Romagna.

**Re·gi·na** |rə'jīnə| the capital of Saskatchewan, situated in the center of the wheat-growing plains of S central Canada. Pop. 179,178. It was the administrative headquarters of the Northwest Territories until 1905, and is today a wheat, oil, and steel center.

**Re·ho·vot** |ri'hō,vŏt| (also **Rehovoth; Rehoboth**) industrial town in central Israel, SW of Ramala. Pop. 85,000.

**Reich** |rīk| German word for 'state or nation', used for particular German governments. The First Reich was the Holy

Roman Empire; the Second Reich was the German Empire (1871–1919); the Third Reich was the Nazi regime (1933–1945).

**Rei·chen·bach** |'rīkHən,bäk| waterfall in SW Switzerland, with five cascades dropping more than 200 ft./61 m.

**Reich·stag, the** |'rīkH,stäg| historic name for the lower house of the German parliament. Hitler charged that communists had set a major fire that destroyed most of the Reichstag in 1933; the Nazis won the next election, starting their rise to power. The Reichstag was abolished in 1949, but its restored building stands in the Tiergarten park in Berlin.

**Reims** |rēmz| (also **Rheims**) city of N France, chief town of Champagne-Ardenne region. Pop. 185,000. It was the traditional coronation place of most French kings and is noted for its 13th-century Gothic cathedral and as the center of the champagne industry.

**Re·ma·gen** |'rämä,gən| town in western Germany, on the Rhine River, where the Allies first crossed the Rhine, taking the Ludendorff Bridge, in 1945.

**Rem·scheid** |'rem,SHīt| industrial city in NW Germany, E of Düsseldorf. Pop. 124,000.

**Ren·do·va** |,ren'dōvə| island in the W central Solomon Islands, off the coast of New Georgia, the scene of 1943 fighting between U.S. and Japanese forces.

**Ren·frew·shire** |'renfrōō,SHir; SHər| administrative region and former county of W central Scotland, on the Firth of Clyde, divided into *Renfrewshire* and *East Renfrewshire*.

**Rennes** |ren| industrial and educational city in NW France. Pop. 204,000. It was established as the capital of a Celtic tribe, the Redones, later becoming the capital of the ancient kingdom of Brittany.

**Re·no** |'rēnō| city in W Nevada, on the Truckee River. Pop. 133,850. It is noted as a gambling resort and was long the scene of many quick marriages and divorces.

**Ren·ton** |'rentən| city in W central Washington, a residential and industrial suburb SE of Seattle, on Lake Washington. Pop. 41,688.

**Re·pub·li·can River** |,ri'pəblikən| river that flows 445 mi./715 km. from NE Colorado through S Nebraska and into Kansas, where it joins the Smoky Hill River to form the Kansas River.

**Re·search Tri·an·gle Park** |'rē,sərCH 'trīæNG,gəl| research complex in central

North Carolina, between Durham, Raleigh, and Chapel Hill, created in the 1950s by Duke and North Carolina State universities and the University of North Carolina.

**Re·sis·ten·cia** |,rāsis'tensēə| city in NE Argentina, capital of Chaco province, across the Paraná River from Corrientes. Pop. 291,000. It exports agricultural produce and has some industries.

**Re·și·ta** |'re,SHētsä| industrial city in the foothills of the Transylvanian Alps, W Romania, capital of Caraș-Severin county. Pop. 110,000.

**Res·ton** |'restən| planned residential and commercial community in N Virginia, NW of Washington, D.C., established in the 1960s. Pop. 48,556.

**Re·thondes** |,rə'tawn| village in N France, near Compiègne. The armistice that ended World War I was signed here on November 11, 1918, and Hitler demanded that the French surrender in 1940 be signed in the same railway car.

**Re·thym·non** |'re.THēm,nawn| port on the N coast of Crete. Pop. 18,000. Greek name **Réthimnon**.

**Ré·u·nion** |rē'yōōnyən| volcanically active, subtropical island in the Indian Ocean E of Madagascar, one of the Mascarene Islands. Pop. 597,000. Capital: Saint-Denis. A French possession since 1638, the island became an administrative region of France in 1974.

**Réunion**

**Re·us** |'re,ōōs| commercial and industrial town in NE Spain. Pop. 88,000. It has an international airport.

**Reut·ling·en** |'roitliNG,ən| industrial city in western Germany, S of Stuttgart. Pop. 106,000.

**Re·vere** |rə'vir| suburban city in E central Massachusetts, on Massachusetts Bay NE of Boston, famed for its beach. Pop. 42,786.

**Re·vil·la·gi·ge·do Islands** |rə,viləgə 'gēdō| (also **Revilla Gigedo**) island group in the Pacific off the W coast of Mexico, part of Colima state. Socorro is the largest.

**Reyes, Point** |'rāz| promontory in NW California, N of Drakes Bay, in Marin County, noted for its winds, fog, and wildlife.

**Reyk·ja·vik** |'rākyə,vik| the capital and oldest and largest city of Iceland, a port on the W coast. Pop. 98,000. It is the northernmost capital in the world.

**Rey·no·sa** |,rā'nōsə| commercial city in NE Mexico, in Tamaulipas state, across the Rio Grande from Hidalgo, Texas. Pop. 266,000. Agriculture and oil are important in the area.

**Rhein** |rīn| German name for the RHINE River.

**Rhein·gau** |'rīn,gow| wine-growing region in central Germany, on the Rhine River. It produces what are considered Germany's best white wines.

**Rhein·land** |'rīn,länd| German name for the RHINELAND.

**Rheinland-Pfalz** |'rīn,länd,fälts| German name for the state of RHINELAND-PALATINATE.

**Rhine** |rīn| river in W Europe that rises in the Swiss Alps and flows for 820 mi./1,320 km. to the North Sea, forming part of the German–Swiss border, before flowing through Germany, along the French border, and the Netherlands. On its course it flows through major cities including Basle (the head of navigation), Mannheim, Mainz, Cologne, and Düsseldorf. The Rhine is central to German culture and tourism, but has serious pollution problems today. German name **Rhein**; French name **Rhin**.

**Rhine·land** |'rīn,länd| the region of western Germany through which the Rhine flows, especially the part to the W of the river. German name **Rheinland**.

**Rhineland-Palatinate** |'rīnləndpə'lætənāt| state of western Germany. Pop. 3,702,000. Capital: Mainz. German name **Rheinland-Pfalz**.

**Rhode Island** see box. □ **Rhode Islander** *n.*

**Rhodes** |rōdz| **1** Greek island in the SE Aegean, off the Turkish coast, the largest of the Dodecanese and the most easterly island in the Aegean. Pop. 98,000. Greek name **Ródhos. 2** its capital, a port on the northernmost tip. Pop. 42,000. It was founded *c.*408 B.C. and was the site of the Colossus of Rhodes, one of the Seven Wonders of the Ancient World.

**Rho·de·sia** |rō'dēzHə| the former name of

---

### Rhode Island

**Capital/largest city:** Providence
**Other cities:** Cranston, Kingston, East Providence, Newport, Pawtucket, Warwick, Woonsocket
**Population:** 1,003,464 (1990); 988,480 (1998); 1,012,000 (2005 proj.)
**Population rank (1990):** 43
**Rank in land area:** 50
**Abbreviation:** RI; R.I.
**Official name:** State of Rhode Island and Providence Plantations
**Nickname:** Ocean State; Little Rhody
**Motto:** 'Hope'
**Bird:** Rhode Island Red chicken
**Flower:** violet
**Tree:** red maple
**Song:** "Rhode Island"
**Noted physical features:** Narragansett Bay; Block Island Sound; Jerimoth Hill; Point Judith
**Tourist attractions:** Newport; Block Island
**Admission date:** May 29, 1790
**Order of admission:** 13
**Name origin:** For Rhode Island in Narragansett Bay, which Italian explorer Giovanni da Verrazano is said to have named for its likeness to the Mediterranean isle of Rhodes, off the coast of Turkey.

---

a large territory in south central Africa that was divided into Northern Rhodesia (now Zambia) and Southern Rhodesia (now Zimbabwe). The region was developed by Cecil Rhodes through the British South African Company, which administered it until Southern Rhodesia became a self-governing British colony in 1923 and Northern Rhodesia a British protectorate in 1924. From 1953 to 1963 Northern and Southern Rhodesia were united with Nyasaland (now Malawi) to form the Federation of Rhodesia and Nyasaland. The name Rhodesia was adopted by Southern Rhodesia when Northern Rhodesia left the Federation in 1963 to become the independent republic of Zambia; Rhodesia became independent Zimbabwe in 1979. □ **Rhodesian** *adj. & n.*

**Rhod·o·pe Mountains** |'rä,dəpē| mountain system in the Balkans, SE Europe, on the border between Bulgaria and Greece, rising to a height of over 6,600 ft./2,000 m. and including the Rila Mts. in the NW.

**Rhond·da** |'ründə| urbanized district of S Wales, which extends along the valleys of the Rhondda Fawr and Rhondda Fach rivers. It was formerly noted as a coal-mining area.

**Rhône** |rōn| river in SW Europe that rises in the Swiss Alps and flows 505 mi./812 km., through Lake Geneva into France, then to Lyons, Avignon, and the Mediterranean W of Marseilles, where it forms a wide delta that includes the Camargue.

**Rhône-Alpes** |'rōnälp| region of SE France, extending from the Rhône valley to the borders with Switzerland and Italy and including much of the former duchy of Savoy.

**Rhum** |rōom| (also **Rum**) island in the Inner Hebrides of Scotland, to the S of Skye, a nature reserve.

**Ri•al•to**[1] |rē'æl,tō| city in SW California, a suburb W of San Bernardino. Pop. 72,388.

**Ri•al•to**[2] |rē'æl,tō| island in Venice, containing the old mercantile quarter of medieval Venice. The Rialto Bridge, completed in 1591 and lined with shops, crosses the Grand Canal between Rialto and San Marco islands. It gives its name to lively commercial zones including the theater district of central Manhattan, New York City.

**Ri•au Archipelago** |'rē,aw| island group in Indonesia, off the SE end of the Malay Peninsula, at the entrance to the Strait of Malacca.

**Ri•bei•rão Prê•to** |'rēbə,rown 'prā,tōō| city in SE Brazil, in São Paulo state. Pop. 453,000. It is an agricultural center in a coffee-producing region.

**Rich•ard•son** |'riCHərdsən| city in NE Texas, a suburb on the NE side of Dallas. Pop. 74,840.

**Rich•field** |'riCH,fēld| city in SE Minnesota, a suburb S of Minneapolis. Pop. 35,710.

**Rich•land** |'riCHlənd| city in SE Washington, on the Columbia and Yakima rivers near Kennewick and Pasco, with which it has been a service center for the Hanford nuclear reservation. Pop. 32,315.

**Rich•mond**[1] |'riCHmənd| city in SW British Columbia, a suburb just S of Vancouver. Pop. 126,624.

**Rich•mond**[2] |'riCHmənd| industrial port city in N central California, on E San Francisco Bay, just N of Berkeley. Pop. 87,425.

**Rich•mond**[3] |'riCHmənd| industrial city in E central Indiana. Pop. 38,705.

**Rich•mond**[4] |'riCHmənd| residential borough of Greater London, England, on the Thames. Pop. 155,000. It contains Hampton Court Palace and the Royal Botanic Gardens at Kew. Full name **Richmond-upon-Thames**.

**Rich•mond**[5] |'riCHmənd| the state capital of Virginia, a port on the James River. Pop. 203,056. During the American Civil War it was the Confederate capital after July 1861. It is a tobacco, heavy industry, and educational center.

**Rich•mond County** |'riCHmənd| see STATEN ISLAND.

**Ri•deau Canal** |,ri'dō| waterway in E Ontario, created in the 1820s, linking Ottawa and the Ottawa River with Kingston and Lake Ontario.

**Rie•sen•ge•bir•ge Mountains** |'rēzənGə ,bərgə| mountain range on the border between SW Poland and the N Czech Republic, part of the Sudetes Mts.

**Rif Mountains** |'rif| (also **Er Rif**) mountain range of N Morocco, running parallel to the Mediterranean for about 180 mi./290 km. E from Tangier. Rising to over 7,000 ft./2,250 m., it forms a W extension of the Atlas Mts. The mountains are a noted retreat of Berber tribes.

**Ri•ga** |'rēgə| industrial port on the Baltic Sea, capital and largest city of Latvia. Pop. 915,000. It was a 13th-century hub of the Hanseatic League.

**Right Bank** |'rit 'bæNk| district of the city of Paris, France, to the N of the Seine River. The historic home to commerce and the middle class of Paris, the area contains the Champs Élysées and the Louvre. French name **Rive Droite**.

**Ri•je•ka** |ri'yekə| industrial port on the Adriatic coast of Croatia. Pop. 168,000. Before 1918 it was the chief Austro-Hungarian naval base. Italian name **Fiume**.

**Ri•la Mountains** |'rē,lä| range in W Bulgaria, forming the westernmost extent of the Rhodope Mts. It is the highest range in Bulgaria, rising to 9,596 ft./2,925 m. at Mount Musala.

**Ri•mi•ni** |'rēminē| port and resort on the Adriatic coast of NE Italy. Pop. 131,000. It is a cultural center associated with the medieval Malatesta family.

**Ri•mou•ski** |,ri'mōōskē| industrial port city in SE Quebec, on the Saint Lawrence River NE of Quebec City. Pop. 30,873.

**Ring of Fire** |'riNG ,əv 'fir| term for the volcanically and seismically active regions around the Pacific, including the Andes Mts., the Aleutian Islands, the Japanese and Philippine islands, and many other island and continental zones.

**Ri•o•bam•ba** |'rē,ō'bämbə| historic city in central Ecuador, capital of Chimborazo province. Pop. 96,000. It is an industrial and commercial center. The first Ecuadorian constitution was drawn up here in 1830.

**Rio Bran·co** |'bräNG,kōō| city in W Brazil, a rubber industry center and capital of the state of Acre. Pop. 197,000.

**Rio Cla·ro** |'klä,rōō| industrial and commercial city in SE Brazil, in São Paulo state. Pop. 153,000.

**Río Cuar·to** |'kwär,tō| commercial city in central Argentina, on the Cuarto River in Córdoba province. Pop. 139,000.

**Rio de Ja·nei·ro** |,dä zHə'nerō| **1** state of E Brazil, on the Atlantic coast. Pop. 12.78 million. **2** (also **Rio**) its capital. Pop. 5,481,000. The chief port of Brazil, it was the capital from 1763 until 1960, when it was replaced by Brasília. Its skyline is dominated by two rocky peaks: Sugar Loaf Mts. to the E and Corcovado, with its statue of Christ, to the S. A leading financial, cultural, and tourist center, Rio is noted for its Copacabana and Ipanema beach resorts, and its annual Carnival.

**Río de Oro** |dä 'aw,rō| arid region on the Atlantic coast of NW Africa, forming the S part of Western Sahara. It was united with Saguia el Hamra in 1958 to form the province of Spanish Sahara (now Western Sahara).

**Rio Gran·de** |'rēō 'grænd; 'grändə| river of North America that rises in the Rocky Mts. of SW Colorado and flows 1,880 mi./3,030 km. generally SE to the Gulf of Mexico, forming the U.S.–Mexico border from El Paso, Texas to the sea. Mexican name **Rio Bravo (del Norte)**.

**Rio Gran·de do Nor·te** |'grän,dä dōō 'nawr,tä| semiarid state of NE Brazil, on the Atlantic coast. Pop. 2,414,000. Capital: Natal.

**Rio Gran·de do Sul** |'grän,dä ,dōō 'sōōl| state of Brazil, on the Atlantic coast at the southern tip of the country, on the border with Uruguay. Pop. 9,135,000. Capital: Pôrto Alegre.

**Rí·o·ha·cha** |,rēyō'äCHə| historic port town in N Colombia, on the Caribbean Sea. Pop. 126,000. Coal, gold, and pearls have all been important local products.

**Rio Mu·ni** |'m(y)ōōnē| the part of Equatorial Guinea that lies on the mainland of W Africa, consisting largely of lowlands along the Mbini River. Its chief town is Bata.

**Rio Ne·gro** |'näg,rō| river of South America, which rises as the Guainía in E Colombia and flows for about 1,400 mi./2,255 km. through NW Brazil before joining the Amazon near Manaus.

**Río Pie·dras** |'pyädräs| academic and

commercial section of San Juan, Puerto Rico, home to the University of Puerto Rico.

**Rio Ran·cho** |'rænCHō| city in N central New Mexico, a residential and industrial suburb NW of Albuquerque. Pop. 32,505.

**Rip·on** |'ripän| historic city in E Wisconsin, home to Ripon College and regarded as the birthplace of the Republican party. Pop. 7,241.

**Ri·shon le-Ziyyon** |,rē'sHawn,lətsē'yawn| (also **Rishon Le-Zion; Rishon Lezion; Rishon le Tsiyon**) mainly residential city in W Israel, S of Tel Aviv. Pop. 160,000.

**Rish·ra** |'risHrə| town in E India, in West Bengal state, N of Calcutta. Pop. 103,000.

**Ri·sing Sun, Land of the** |'rīziNG'sən| name for Japan, a translation of Chinese NIPPON.

**Riv·er·side** |'rivər,sīd| industrial and residential city in S California, in an orange-growing region E of Los Angeles. Pop. 226,505.

**Ri·vi·era** |,rivē'erə| Mediterranean coastal region from Marseilles, France, E to La Spezia, Italy, famed for its beauty and climate, and scene of many famed resorts. See also CÔTE D'AZUR.

**Ri·vi·era Beach** |,ri'virə| resort and industrial city in SE Florida, N of West Palm Beach. Pop. 27,639.

**Riv·ne** |'rivnə| industrial city in W Ukraine, NE of Lviv. Pop. 233,000. Russian name **Rovno**.

**Ri·yadh** |rē'yäd| the capital and comercial center of Saudi Arabia. Pop. 2,000,000. Situated on a high plateau in the center of the country, it has extensive new suburbs.

**Road Town** |'rōd| the capital of the British Virgin Islands, on the island of Tortola. Pop. 6,000.

**Ro·a·noke** |'rōə,nōk| industrial city in W central Virginia, a rail center in the Shenandoah Valley. Pop. 96,397.

**Ro·a·noke Island** |'rōə,nōk| island in E North Carolina, E of Croatan Sound, inside the Outer Banks, scene of the first English settlement in America, the "Lost Colony," established in 1585, which disappeared mysteriously by 1591.

**Ro·a·noke River** |'rōə,nōk| river that flows 410 mi./660 km. from SW Virginia, across North Carolina, to Albemarle Sound. Roanoke, Virginia and Roanoke Rapids, North Carolina along its course.

**roar·ing for·ties** |'rōriNG 'fawr,tēz| (**the roaring forties**) stormy ocean tracts between latitudes 40° and 50° S.

**Rob·ben Island** |,räbən| island in Table

Bay, off Cape Town, South Africa. Formerly a military reservation, then a prison colony that held Nelson Mandela among others, it is now a resort.

**Rob·in·son Cru·soe Island** |'räbin,sən 'krōō,sō| (also **Mas á Tierra**) island in the JUAN FERNANDEZ group off W Chile, associated with Alexander Selkirk, the model for the protagonist of the Defoe novel, who was marooned here in 1704.

**Ro·ca·ma·dour** |rō'kämä,dawr| medieval pilgrimage village, built into a cliff in SW France, in Quercy. Pilgrims climbed the 223 stone steps to the tomb of Saint Amadour as part of their trek to Santiago de Compostela. The site is now a popular tourist attraction.

**Roch·dale** |'räCH,däl| industrial town in NW England, N of Manchester. Pop. 97,000. A textile center, it was the birthplace in 1844 of the British cooperative movement.

**Roche·fort** |'rōSH,fawr| (also called **Rochefort-sur-Mer**) industrial port in W France, on the Charente River S of La Rochelle, formerly an important naval base. Pop. 27,000.

**Roch·es·ter¹** |'räCHəstər| town on the Medway estuary SE of London, England. Pop. 24,000.

**Roch·es·ter²** |'räCHəstər| industrial city in SE Minnesota, home to the famed Mayo Clinic, established in 1889. Pop. 70,475.

**Roch·es·ter³** |'räCHəstər| city in NW New York State, on Lake Ontario, a manufacturing center noted for its photographic and optical industries. Pop. 231,636.

**Roch·es·ter Hills** |'rä,CHestər| residential and industrial city in SE Michigan, just NE of Pontiac. Pop. 61,766.

**Rock·all** |'räk,awl| rocky islet in the N Atlantic, about 250 mi./400 km. NW of Ireland. It was formally annexed by Britain in 1955 but has since become the subject of territorial dispute among Britain, Denmark, Iceland, and Ireland.

**Rock·e·fel·ler Center** |'räkə,felər| business building complex in midtown Manhattan, New York City. Radio City Music Hall is here.

**Rock·ford** |'räkfərd| industrial city in N central Illinois, on the Rock River. Pop. 139,426.

**Rock·hamp·ton** |räk'hæmptən| port on the Fitzroy River, in Queensland, NE Australia. Pop. 56,000. It is the center of Australia's largest beef-producing area.

**Rock Hill** |'räk| industrial city in N South Carolina. Pop. 41,643.

**Rock Island** |'räk| industrial city in NW Illinois, on the Mississippi River, one of the Quad Cities. It is noted for its arsenal. Pop. 40,552.

**Rock·land County** |'räk,lən(d)| largely suburban county in SE New York, on the W side of the Hudson River and the New Jersey line. Pop. 265,475.

**Rock of Gi·bral·tar** |,ji'brältər| see GIBRALTAR.

**Rock·port** |'räk,pärt| town in NE Massachusetts, a resort and fishing community on Cape Ann. Pop. 7,482.

**Rock, the** nickname for ALCATRAZ.

**Rock·ville** |'räk,vil| city in central Maryland, a residential suburb with many government offices, NW of Washington, D.C. Pop. 44,835.

**Rocky Mount** |'rä,ke| industrial city in E central North Carolina, a tobacco industry center. Pop. 48,997.

**Rocky Mountains** |,räke| (also **the Rockies**) the chief mountain system of North America, which extends from the U.S.–Mexico border to the Yukon Territory of N Canada. It separates the Great Plains from the W intermountain and coastal states and forms the Continental Divide. Several peaks rise to over 14,000 ft./4,300 m., the highest being Colorado's Mount Elbert at 14,431 ft./4,399 m.

**Ró·dhos** |'rōdōs| Greek name for RHODES.

**Rod·ri·guez** |,räd'rēgəs| (also **Rodrigues**) mountainous island in the W Indian Ocean, NE of Mauritius, of which it is a dependency. Pop. 35,000. Fishing and tourism are important here.

**Roe·se·la·re** |,rōōsə'lärə| textile manufacturing town in NW Belgium, in West Flanders. Pop. 58,000. French name **Roulers**.

**Rogue River** |'rōōZH| river that flows 200 mi./320 km. W across S Oregon, to the Pacific. In an agricultural area, it is noted for its fishing.

**Rohn·ert Park** |'rōnərt| city in NW California, a suburb N of San Francisco. Pop. 36,326.

**Roh·tak** |'rōtək| commercial town in NW India, in Haryana state. Pop. 216,000.

**Ro·ma** |'rōmə| Italian name for ROME.

**Ro·ma·gna** |rō'mänyə| historic region, formerly under papal control, in N central Italy, on the Adriatic Sea. Its territory is now part of several Italian regions: Emilia-Romagna, Marche, and Tuscany.

**Ro·man Empire** |'rōmən| areas controlled by Rome during the time of its emperors, from the 1st century B.C. until its collapse in A.D. 476. Its greatest extent was from Armenia and Mesopotamia in the E to Iberia in the W, and from Britain in the N to N Africa in the S. In A.D. 395 it was divided into the EASTERN EMPIRE and WESTERN EMPIRE.

**Ro•ma•nia** |rō'mānēə| (also **Rumania**) republic in SE Europe with a coastline on the Black Sea. Area: 88,461 sq. mi./229,027 sq. km. Pop. 23,276,000. Language, Romanian. Capital and largest city: Bucharest. The Dacia of Roman times, the country was later Wallachia and Moldavia, independent from the Ottoman Empire in 1878. From 1945 to 1989 it was a communist state. With sizable Hungarian, Gypsy, and German communities, it has an economy based on industry, mining, oil and gas, and some agriculture. □ **Romanian** *adj. & n.*

**Romania**

**Rome**[1] |rōm| industrial city in NW Georgia, on the Coosa River. Pop. 30,326.

**Rome**[2] |rōm| (Italian name **Roma**) the capital of Italy and of the Lazio region, situated on the Tiber River about 16 mi./25 km. inland from the Tyrrhenian Sea. Pop. 2,791,000. Italian name **Roma**. According to tradition the city was founded by Romulus (after whom it was named) in 753 B.C. on the Palatine Hill; as it grew it spread to the other six hills of Rome (Aventine, Caelian, Capitoline, Esquiline, and Quirinal). Rome was ruled by kings until the expulsion of Tarquinius Superbus in 510 B.C. led to the establishment of the Roman Republic. By the mid-2nd century B.C. Rome had subdued all of Italy and had come to dominate the W Mediterranean and the Hellenistic world in the E, acquiring the first of the overseas possessions that became the ROMAN EMPIRE. By the time of the empire's fall in the 5th century A.D. the city was overshadowed politically by Constantinople, but emerged as the seat of the papacy and as the spiritual capital of Western Christianity. In the 14th and 15th centuries Rome became a center of the Re-

naissance. It remained part of the Papal States until 1871, when it was made the capital of a unified Italy. Today it is a center of culture, finance, fashion, and international organizations. □ **Roman** *adj. & n.*

**Rome**[3] |rōm| industrial city in central New York, on the Mohawk River. Pop. 44,350.

**Ron•ces•val•les** |,rawnsəs'välyāz| (in French **Roncevaux**) mountain pass in the Pyrenees, between Pamplona, Spain and Saint-Jean-Pied-de-Port, France. Part of Charlemagne's army was defeated here in 788; the feats and death of one of his nobles, Roland, are celebrated in the *Chanson de Roland*.

**Ron•champ** |,rawn'sHän| commune in E central France, near the Swiss and German borders. A massive, free-standing chapel designed by French architect Le Corbusier was erected here in 1950–55.

**Ron•dô•nia** |rawn'dō,nyə| state of NW Brazil, in the Amazon basin on the border with Bolivia. Pop. 1,131,000. Capital: Pôrto Velho.

**Rong•e•lap** |'rawNGə,læp| atoll in the W Pacific, in the N Marshall Islands at the NW end of the Ratak group, E of Bikini. It was evacuated in the 1980s because of contamination from 1950s nuclear tests at ENI-WETOK.

**Roo•se•velt Island** |'rōzə,velt| (formerly **Blackwell's Island** and **Welfare Island**) residential island in the East River, New York City, between Manhattan and Queens.

**Roo•se•velt Roads** |'rōzə,velt| (official name **Atlantic Fleet Weapons Training Facility**) naval reserve on the E coast of Puerto Rico.

**Roquefort-sur-Soulzhon** |rōk'fawrsŏŏr ,sŏŏl'zawn| village in S France, in the S foothills of the Massif Central. It is famous for its blue-veined cheese, which is aged in limestone caves.

**Ro•rai•ma** |raw'rīmə| **1** mountain in the Guiana Highlands of South America, at the junction of the borders of Venezuela, Brazil, and Guyana. Rising to 9,094 ft./2,774 m., it is the highest peak in the range. **2** state of N Brazil, on the borders with Venezuela and Guyana. Pop. 216,000. Capital: Boa Vista.

**Ro•sa•rio** |rō'särēō| inland port on the Paraná River in E central Argentina. Pop. 1,096,000. An outlet for Pampas agriculture, it is also industrial.

**Ros•com•mon** |räs'kämən| **1** county in the N central part of the Republic of Ireland, in the province of Connacht. Pop. 52,000. **2** its county seat. Pop. 18,000.

**Ro·seau** |ˌrōˈzō| the capital of the island commonwealth of Dominica, in the Caribbean. Pop. 16,000.

**Rose·mead** |ˈrōzˌmēd| city in SW California, a residential suburb E of Los Angeles. Pop. 51,638.

**Rose·ville**¹ |ˈrōzˌvil| city in NE California, a suburb NE of Sacramento. Pop. 44,685.

**Rose·ville**² |ˈrōzˌvil| city in SE Michigan, a suburb N of Detroit. Pop. 51,412.

**Rose·ville**³ |ˈrōzˌvil| city in SE Minnesota, a suburb N of St. Paul. Pop. 33,485.

**Ros·kil·de** |ˈrawsˌkilə| port in Denmark, on the island of Zealand, W of Copenhagen. Pop. 49,000. It was the seat of Danish kings from *c.*1020 and the capital of Denmark until 1443.

**Ross and Crom·ar·ty** |ˈräs ˈkrawmərˌtē| former county of N Scotland, stretching from the Moray Firth to the North Minch. In 1975 it became part of the Highland region. Dingwall is the chief town.

**Ross·lare** |ˌräsˈler| ferry port on the SE coast of the Republic of Ireland, in County Wexford.

**Ross Sea** |ˈraws| large arm of the Pacific forming a deep indentation in the coast of Antarctica. At its head is the Ross Ice Shelf, the world's largest body of floating ice, which is approximately the size of France. On the E shores of the Ross Sea lies Ross Island, which is the site of Mount Erebus and of Scott Base, an Antarctic station established by New Zealand in 1957.

**Ros·tock** |ˈrästäk| industrial port on the Baltic coast of NE Germany. Pop. 244,000.

**Ros·tov** |rəsˈtawf| port and industrial city in SW Russia, on the Don River near its entry into the Sea of Azov. Pop. 1,025,000. The city is built around a fortress erected by the Turks in the 18th century. Full name **Rostov-on-Don**.

**Ros·well**¹ |ˈräzˌwel| city in NW Georgia, a suburb N of Atlanta. Pop. 47,923.

**Ros·well**² |ˈräzˌwel| agricultural and military city in SE New Mexico, the scene of a mysterious crash in July 1947. Controversy has surrounded claims by some investigators that the crashed object was a UFO. Pop. 44,654.

**Ro·ta** |ˈrōtə| island in the W Pacific, in the S Northern Mariana Islands, NE of Guam. Pop. 2,000. The scene of heavy World War II fighting and of an important U.S. air base, it now draws tourists.

**Roth·er·ham** |ˈräTHərəm| industrial town in N England, a steel center formerly in South Yorkshire. Pop. 247,000.

**Ro·to·rua** |ˌrōtōˈrōōə| city and health resort on North Island, New Zealand, on the SW shore of Lake Rotorua. Pop. 54,000. It lies at the center of a region of thermal springs and geysers.

**Rot·ter·dam** |ˈrätərˌdæm| city in the Netherlands, at the mouth of the Meuse River, 15 mi./25 km. inland from the North Sea. Pop. 582,000. It is one of the world's largest ports, with extensive shipbuilding, oil refining, and petrochemical industries. See also EUROPOORT.

**Rott·weil** |ˈrawtˌwil; ˈrawtˌvil| town in SW Germany, on the Neckar River, SW of Stuttgart. It gave its name to Rottweiler dogs, formerly used here by drovers.

**Rou·baix** |ˌrōōˈbā| industrial town in N France, near Lille on the Belgian border. Pop. 98,000. It is part of one of the most important textile-manufacturing regions in France.

**Rou·en** |ˈrwän| port on the Seine River in NW France, chief town of Haute-Normandie. Pop. 105,000. Rouen was in English possession from the time of the Norman Conquest until captured by the French in 1204, and again 1419–49; in 1431 Joan of Arc was tried and burned at the stake there. The modern city is an industrial and tourist center.

**Rouge, River** |ˈrōōZH| short river with several branches in and around Detroit, Michigan.

**Rou·lers** |rōōˈlers| French name for ROE-SELARE, Belgium.

**Round Rock** |ˈrownd| city in central Texas, a suburb N of Austin. Pop. 30,923.

**Rous·sil·lon** |ˌrōōsēˈyawn| former province of S France, on the border with Spain in the E Pyrenees, now part of Languedoc-Roussillon. Part of Spain until 1659, Roussillon retains many of its Spanish characteristics; Catalan is widely spoken.

**Route 128** |rōōt wən ˈtwen(t)ē ˌyāt; rowt| highway that circles Boston, Massachusetts in the N, W, and S, noted for its complex of high-technology industries.

**Route 66** |rōōt ˈsikstē siks; rowt| former interstate highway from Chicago, Illinois to Santa Monica, California, designated in 1926 and today supplanted by such newer routes as Interstates 40 and 44.

**Rouyn-Noranda** |ˈrōō,win,naw'rændə| industrial city in SW Quebec, center of a major mining district. Pop. 26,448.

**Ro·va·nie·mi** |ˈrōvä,nyəmē| the principal town of Finnish Lapland, just S of the Arctic Circle. Pop. 33,000.

**Rov·no** |'rawvnə| Russian name for RIVNE, Ukraine.

**Rox·burgh·shire** |'rawksbərə,SHər; SHir| former county in S Scotland, now part of the Scottish Borders region. Hawick is the chief town.

**Rox·bury** |'rawksbə,rē| district of Boston, Massachusetts, today the center of the city's black community.

**Roy·al, Mount** |'roiyəl| hill in Montreal, Quebec, rising to 763 ft./233 m. Topped by recreational parks, it dominates the city and gives it its name.

**Roy·al Gorge** |'roiyəl| (also the **Grand Canyon of the Arkansas**) steep defile on the Arkansas River in S central Colorado, near Cañon City, a noted tourist attraction.

**Roy·al Oak** |'roiyəl| city in SE Michigan, a residential and industrial suburb NW of Detroit. Pop. 65,410.

**Ruan·da-Urundi** |,rōō'wändə,ōō'rōōndē| former Belgian and United Nations trust territory, now the nations of RWANDA and BURUNDI.

**Rub' al Kha·li** |'rəb ,äl'kälē| vast desert in the Arabian peninsula, extending from central Saudi Arabia S to Yemen and E to the United Arab Emirates and Oman. It is also known as the Great Sandy Desert or Empty Quarter.

**Ru·bi·con River** |'rōōbi,kawn| small river that flows into the Adriatic Sea in NE Italy near San Marino that marked the ancient boundary between Cisalpine Gaul and Italy. In 49 B.C. Julius Caesar led his army across it into Italy, breaking the law forbidding a general to lead an army out of his province, and so committing himself to war against the Senate and Pompey. The ensuing civil war resulted in victory for Caesar after three years.

**Rub·tsovsk** |,rōōp'tsawfsk| city in W Siberia, S Russia. Pop. 172,000.

**Ru·by Mountains** |'rōō,bē| range in NE Nevada, noted for its alpine scenery.

**Rud·ny** |'rōōdnē| (also **Rudnyy**) city in NW Kazakhstan, on the Tobol River. Pop. 128,000. It is in an iron-mining region.

**Ru·fisque** |rōō'fēsk| port city in W Senegal, a suburb E of Dakar. Pop. 112,000.

**Rug·by** |'rəgbē| commercial and engineering town in central England, on the Avon River in Warwickshire. Pop. 60,000. Rugby School, where the game of rugby was developed in the early 19th century, was founded here in 1567.

**Rü·gen** |'rōō,gən| island in the Baltic Sea off the NE coast of Germany, to which it is linked by a causeway. It forms part of the state of Mecklenburg–West Pomerania.

**Ruhr** |'rōōr| region of coal mining and heavy industry in North Rhine–Westphalia, western Germany. It is named after the Ruhr River, which flows through it, meeting the Rhine near Duisburg.

**Ru·iz, Ne·va·do del** |,ne'vädō ,del ,rōō-'wēs| active volcano in Tolima department, W central Colombia, in the Cordillera Central of the Andes: 17,720 ft./5,400 m.

**Ru·me·lia** |rōō'mēlyə| (also **Roumelia**) the territories in Europe that formerly belonged to the Ottoman Empire, including Macedonia, Thrace, and Albania.

**Run·corn** |'rəNGkərn| industrial town in NW England, on the Mersey River and canals in Cheshire. Pop. 65,000.

**Run·ny·mede** |'rənē,mēd| meadow on the S bank of the River Thames near Windsor, in Surrey, England. It is associated with the Magna Carta, signed by King John in 1215 here or nearby.

**Ru·pert's Land** |'rōōpərts| (also **Prince Rupert's Land**) historic region of N and W Canada, roughly corresponding to what are now Manitoba, Saskatchewan, Yukon, Alberta, and S parts of the Northwest Territories and Nunavut. It was granted in 1670 by Charles II to the Hudson's Bay Company and named after Prince Rupert, the first governor of the Company; it was purchased by Canada in 1870.

**Ruse** |'rōōsə| (also **Rousse**) industrial city and the principal river port of Bulgaria, on the Danube. Pop. 210,000. Turkish during the Middle Ages, it was captured by Russia in 1877 and ceded to Bulgaria. Former name **Ruschuk**.

**Rush·more, Mount** |'rəSH,mawr| mountain in the Black Hills of South Dakota, near Rapid City, noted for its giant relief carvings of four U.S. presidents—Washington, Jefferson, Lincoln, and Theodore Roosevelt—carved (1927–41) under the direction of the sculptor Gutzon Borglum.

**Rus·sia** |'rəSHə| republic in E Europe and N Asia, the largest country in the world. Area: 6.6 million sq. mi./17.1 million sq. km. Pop. 148,930,000. Official language, Russian. Capital and largest city: Moscow. Official name **Russian Federation**. Russia developed from medieval Muscovy into a great empire by the 18th century. After the revolution of 1917, it became the largest constituent of the Soviet Union, which broke up in 1991. A land of vast distances and numerous national groups, Russia is a leading industrial and agricultural state engaged in adjusting to life after communism. □ **Russian** *adj. & n.*

**Russia**

**Rus·sian Federation** |ˈrəsHən| official name for RUSSIA.

**Rus·ta·vi** |ˌrˌo͞oˈstävē| industrial city in the Republic of Georgia, on the Kura River. Pop. 160,000.

**Rust Belt** |ˈrəst ˈbelt| popular name for regions of the U.S. NE and Midwest where heavy industry has declined. Steel-producing cities in Pennsylvania and Ohio are at its center.

**Rus·ton** |ˈrəstən| commercial city in N Louisiana. Pop. 20,027.

**Ru·the·nia** |ro͞oˈTHēnyə| region of central Europe on the S slopes of the Carpathian Mts., now forming the Transcarpathian region of W Ukraine. Formerly part of the Austro-Hungarian Empire, it was divided among Poland, Czechoslovakia, and Romania. Gaining independence for a single day in 1938, it was occupied by Hungary and in 1945 ceded to the Soviet Union, becoming part of Ukraine. □ **Ruthenian** *adj. & n.*

**Rut·land**[1] |ˈrətlənd| county in the E Midlands, the smallest (153 sq. mi./396 sq. km.) county in England; county seat, Oakham. Between 1974 and 1997 it was part of Leicestershire.

**Rut·land**[2] |ˈrətlənd| industrial and commercial city in S central Vermont. Pop. 18,230.

**Ru·wen·zo·ri** |ˌro͞owənˈzawrē| mountain range in central Africa, on the Uganda–Congo (formerly Zaire) border between Lake Edward and Lake Albert, rising to 16,765 ft./5,110 m. at Margherita Peak on Mount Stanley. The range is generally thought to be the 'Mountains of the Moon' mentioned by Ptolemy, and as such the supposed source of the Nile.

**Rwan·da** |rəˈwändə| landlocked republic in central Africa, to the N of Burundi and the S of Uganda. Area: 10,173 sq. mi./26,338 sq. km. Pop. 7,403,000. Official languages, Rwanda (a Bantu language) and French. Capital and largest city: Kigali. Official name **Rwandese Republic**. Dominated by Germany, then Belgium, from the late 19th century, Rwanda became independent in 1962. Densely populated and mainly agricultural, it has seen repeated bloodshed between its Hutu majority and Tutsi minority. □ **Rwandan** *adj. & n.* **Rwandese** *adj. & n.*

**Rwanda**

**Rya·zan** |ˌrēəˈzän(yə)| industrial city in European Russia, a port on the Oka River SE of Moscow. Pop. 522,000.

**Ry·binsk** |ˈribyinsk| city in NW Russia, a port on the Volga River. Pop. 252,000. It was formerly known as Shcherbakov (1946–57) and, in honor of former President Yuri Andropov of the Soviet Union, as Andropov (1984–89).

**Ryb·nik** |ˈribnik| transportation center and industrial town in S Poland. Pop. 140,000.

**Ry·dal** |ˈrīdl| village in NW England, in the Lake District in Cumbria, on Rydal Water. It is the site of Rydal Mount, longtime home of the poet Wordsworth.

**Ryde** |rīd| resort town in S England, in the Isle of Wight, on Spithead Channel, SW of Portsmouth. Pop. 25,000.

**Rye**[1] |rī| resort town in SE England, in East Sussex. Pop. 4,000. Once one of the later CINQUE PORTS, it has more recently been associated with writers and artists.

**Rye**[2] |rī| city in SE New York, a suburb on Long Island Sound, N of New York City. Pop. 14,936.

**Ry·sy** |ˈrisē| peak in the Tatra Mts., the highest in Poland: 8,197 ft./2,499 m.

**Ryu·kyu Islands** |rēˈo͞o,kyo͞o| chain of islands in the W Pacific, stretching for about

600 mi./960 km. from the S tip of the island of Kyushu, Japan, to Taiwan. The
largest island is Okinawa. Part of China in
the 14th century, the archipelago was in-
corporated into Japan by 1879 and was held
under U.S. military control between 1945
and 1972.

**Rze•szow** |'zHe,sHo͞of| industrial town in
SW Poland, capital of Rzeszow county, on
the Wislik River. Pop. 153,000.

# Ss

**Saa·le** |'zälǝ; 'sälǝ| river of E central Germany. Rising in N Bavaria near the border with the Czech Republic, it flows 265 mi./425 km. N to join the Elbe near Magdeburg.

**Saa·nich** |'sänicH| municipality in SW British Columbia, on Vancouver Island, a suburb on the NW side of Victoria. Pop. 95,577.

**Saar** |sär; zär| **1** river of W Europe. Rising in the Vosges Mts. in E France, it flows 150 mi./240 km. N to join the Mosel River in Germany, just E of the border with Luxembourg. French name **Sarre**. **2** the Saarland.

**Saar·brück·en** |zär'brykǝn; sär'brookǝn| industrial city in W Germany, the capital of Saarland, on the Saar River close to the border with France. Pop. 362,000.

**Saar·land** |'zär,länt; 'sär,lænd| state of W Germany, on the border with France. Pop. 1,077,000. Capital: Saarbrücken. Rich in coal and iron-ore and long dominated by France, the area became a German state in 1957.

**Sa·ba**[1] |'säbǝ| ancient kingdom in SW Arabia, famous for its trade in gold and spices; the biblical Sheba.

**Sa·ba**[2] |'säbǝ; 'säbǝ| island in the Netherlands Antilles, in the Caribbean. Pop. 1,130. The smallest island in the group, it is to the NW of St. Kitts.

**Sa·ba·dell** |säbä'del| manufacturing city in NE Spain, near Barcelona, on the Ripoll River. Pop. 184,000. It is a leading textile center.

**Sa·bah** |'säbä| state of Malaysia, comprising the N part of Borneo and some offshore islands. Capital: Kota Kinabalu. A British protectorate from 1888, it joined Malaysia in 1963.

**Sab·ha** |'säb,hä| oasis town in W central Libya, in the Sahara Desert. Pop. 113,000.

**Sa·bine River** |sǝ'bēn| river that flows 360 mi./580 km. from E Texas to form the border with Louisiana, reaching the Gulf of Mexico at Sabine Pass.

**Sa·ble Island** |'säbǝl| island in SE Nova Scotia, in the Atlantic 175 mi./285 km. SE of Halifax. It has been called the Graveyard of the Atlantic for the many shipwrecks that have occurred nearby.

**Sab·ra·tha** |'sabrǝTHǝ| (also **Sabrata**) one of the three ancient Phoenician cities of Tripolitania, near present-day Tripoli, Libya.

**Sab·ze·var** |,sæbzǝ'vär| commercial city in NE Iran. Pop. 148,000.

**Sach·sen** |'zäksǝn| German name for SAXONY.

**Sachsen-Anhalt** |'zäksǝn'än,hält| German name for SAXONY-ANHALT.

**Sac·ra·men·to** |,sækrǝ'mentō| the capital of California, on the Sacramento River to the NE of San Francisco. Pop. 369,365.

**Sac·ra·men·to Mountains** |,sækrǝ'mentō| range in S New Mexico and W Texas. The Jicarilla, Sierra Blanca, and Guadalupe mountains are all considered part of the Sacramentos.

**Sac·ra·men·to River** |,sækrǝ'mentō| river of N California, which rises near the border with Oregon and flows 380 mi./611 km. S to San Francisco Bay, through the Central Valley.

**Sa·do Island** |'sädō| island in N central Japan, in the Sea of Japan off the W coast of Honshu.

**Sa·fed Koh Mountains** |sä'fed 'kō| (also **Safid Koh, Sefid Koh**) mountain range in E Afghanistan, on border with Pakistan; the Khyber Pass crosses a spur of the range.

**Sa·fi** |'säfē| (also **Saffi**) industrial port city in W central Morocco, on the Atlantic coast. Pop. 262,000.

**Sa·ga** |'sägä| industrial city in SW Japan, on W Kyushu. Pop. 170,000.

**Sa·ga·mi·ha·ra** |sä,gämē'härǝ| industrial city in E central Japan, on E central Honshu. Pop. 532,000.

**Sa·ga·mi Sea** |sä'gämē| inlet of the N Pacific, off the SE coast of Honshu, S central Japan.

**Sagar** |'sägǝr| (also **Saugor**) commercial town in central India, in Madhya Pradesh state. Pop. 257,000.

**Sag Harbor** |sæg| resort village in E Long Island, New York, famous as a 19th-century whaling port. Pop. 2,134.

**Sag·i·naw** |'sægǝ,naw| industrial and commercial city in E central Michigan, on the Saginaw River. Pop. 69,512.

**Sag·ue·nay River** |,sægǝ'nā| river that flows 110 mi./180 km. through S Quebec, from the Lac Saint-Jean to the St. Lawrence River. Chicoutimi and Jonquière are among industrial cities along it.

**Sa·guia el Ham·ra** |'sägeǝ el '(h)ämrǝ| intermittent river in the N of the Western

Sahara. It flows into the Atlantic W of La'youn. The name is also used for the region through which it flows. A territory of Spain from 1934, it united with Río de Oro in 1958 to become a part of Spanish Sahara.

**Sa·gun·to** |säˈgōōntō| seaport city in E Spain, on the Mediterranean Sea. Pop. 19,000. The capture by Hannibal in 219 B.C. of this Roman outpost began the Second Punic War.

**Sa·ha·ra Desert** |səˈherærə; səˈhärə| (also **the Sahara**) vast desert in N Africa, extending from the Atlantic in the W to the Red Sea in the E, and from the Mediterranean and the Atlas Mts. in the N to the Sahel in the S. The largest desert in the world, it covers an area of about 3,500,000 sq. mi./9,065,000 sq. km, almost one-third of Africa. In recent years it has been extending S into the Sahel. □ **Saharan** adj.

**Sa·ha·ran·pur** |səˈhärən,pŏŏr| commercial and industrial city in N India, in Uttar Pradesh state. Pop. 374,000.

**Sa·hel** |səˈhel| vast semiarid region of N Africa, to the S of the Sahara, which forms a transitional zone at the S of the desert and comprises the northern part of the region known as the Sudan. The Sahel covers about one-fifth of Africa. □ **Sahelian** adj. & n.

**Sa·hi·wal** |ˈsähēwäl| commercial city in E central Pakistan, SW of Lahore. Pop. 151,000.

**Sai·da** |sīˈdä| Arabic name for SIDON, Lebanon.

**Sai·gon** |sīˈgän| name before 1975 for HO CHI MINH CITY, Vietnam.

**Saint Al·bans** |sənt ˈawlbənz| city in Hertfordshire, SE England. Pop. 56,000. It developed around an abbey, which was founded in Saxon times on the site of the martyrdom in the 3rd century of St. Alban, a Christian Roman from the nearby Roman city of Verulamium.

**Saint Al·bert** |sänt ˈælbərt| city in central Alberta, a suburb on the NW side of Edmonton. Pop. 42,146.

**Saint An·drews** |sänt ˈændrōōz| town in E Scotland, in Fife, on the North Sea. Pop. 14,000. It is noted for its university, founded in 1410, and its championship golf courses.

**Saint Au·gus·tine** |sänt ˈawgə,stēn| historic port city in NE Florida, SE of Jacksonville, near the Atlantic coast. Founded by the Spanish in 1565, it is often called "the oldest city in America." Pop. 11,692.

**Saint-Bar·thé·le·my** |seN ˌbärtälˈmē| (familiarly **St. Bart's**) resort island in the West Indies, in the Leeward Islands. Pop. 5,000. Gustavia is its capital. St. Bart's is a dependency of Guadeloupe, which is to the SE.

**Saint Ber·nard Pass** |ˌsänt bərˈnärd| either of two passes across the Alps in S Europe. The *Great St. Bernard Pass*, on the border between SW Switzerland and Italy, rises to 8,100 ft./2,469 m. The *Little St. Bernard Pass*, on the French–Italian border SE of Mont Blanc, rises to 7,178 ft./2,188 m. They are named after the hospices founded on their summits in the 11th century by the French monk St. Bernard.

**Saint Cath·e·rines** |sänt ˈkæTH(ə)rənz| industrial and commercial city in S Ontario, on Lake Ontario NW of Niagara Falls. Pop. 129,300.

**Saint Charles** |sänt CHärlz| historic commercial city in E central Missouri, on the Missouri River. Pop. 54,555.

**St. Chris·to·pher and Nevis, Federation of** |sänt ˈkristəfər ən ˈnevəs| see ST. KITTS AND NEVIS.

**Saint Clair River** |sənt ˈklær| short river that flows from Lake Huron, forming the boundary between Michigan and Ontario, into Lake Saint Clair, which in turn is drained into Lake Erie by the Detroit River.

**Saint Cloud** |sänt ˈklowd| industrial and commercial city in E central Minnesota, on the Mississippi River NW of Minneapolis. Pop. 48,812.

**Saint-Cloud** |seNˈklōō| residential and resort W suburb of Paris, in N central France. It has a famous racetrack.

**Saint Croix** | sänt ˈkroi| island in the Caribbean, the largest of the U.S. Virgin Islands. Pop. 50,000; chief town, Christiansted. Purchased by Denmark in 1753, it was sold to the U.S. in 1917.

**Saint Croix River**[1] |sänt ˈkroi| river that flows 75 mi./120 km. from E Maine to form the boundary with New Brunswick, before entering Passamaquoddy Bay. The first French settlement in North America was established in 1604 on Dochet Island, near its mouth.

**Saint Croix River**[2] |sänt ˈkroi| river that flows 164 mi./265 km. from NW Wisconsin to form part of the boundary with Minnesota, before emptying into the Mississippi River.

**Saint-Cyr-l'Ecole** |ˌsæNˈsirläˈkōl| commune in N France, 3 mi./5 km. W of Versailles, site of a famed military school (founded 1808).

**Saint David's** |sənt ˈdävidz| city near the coast of SW Wales, in Pembrokeshire. Pop.

1,800. Its 12th-century cathedral houses the shrine of St. David, the patron saint of Wales. Welsh name **Tyddewi**.

**Saint-Denis**[1] |ˌsæn dəˈnē| municipality in France, now an industrial N suburb of Paris. Pop. 91,000.

**Saint-Denis**[2] |ˌsæn dəˈnē| the capital of the French island of Réunion, a port on the N coast. Pop. 122,000.

**Sainte-Anne-de-Beaupré** |seNT,ändəbō-ˈprā| city in S Quebec, on the St. Lawrence River NE of Quebec City, site of a shrine that is the object of many pilgrimages. Pop. 3,146.

**Sainte-Foy** |seNT ˈfwä| city in S Quebec, a suburb just SW of Quebec City. Pop. 71,133.

**Saint Eli·as Mountains** |ˌsänt əlˈīəs| section of the Coast Ranges in SE Alaska and the neighboring Yukon Territory. Mount Logan, the highest point in Canada, is here, along with other high peaks and numerous glaciers.

**Saint Émi·lion** |seNT āmēˈlyōN| town in the Gironde department of SW France, on the Dordogne River, that gave its name to a group of Bordeaux wines.

**Saint-Étienne** |seNT āˈtyen| city in S central France, the capital of Loire department, SW of Lyons. Pop. 202,000. It is one of the leading French heavy industry centers.

**Saint Eu·sta·ti·us** |ˌsänt yooˈstāsHəs| small volcanic island in the Caribbean, in the Netherlands Antilles. Pop. 2,000. Dutch name **Sint Eustatius**; locally, **Statia**.

**Saint Fran·cis River** |ˌsänt ˈfränsis| river that flows 425 mi./685 km. from SE Missouri into E Arkansas, emptying into the Mississippi River near Helena.

**Saint Gall** |ˌsänt ˈgawl| (in German **Sankt Gallen**) town in NE Switzerland, capital of Saint Gall canton. Pop. 73,000. It has a famous abbey, founded by Saint Gall in the 7th century, with a renowned collection of medieval manuscripts; the abbey was a major center of learning during the Middle Ages.

**Saint George** |ˌsänt ˈjawrj| historic resort city in SW Utah, near the Arizona line. Pop. 28,502.

**Saint George's** |ˌsänt jȯrjiz| the capital of Grenada in the West Indies, a port in the SW of the island. Pop. 36,000.

**St. George's Channel** |ˌsänt jȯrjiz| channel between S Wales and SE Ireland, linking the Irish Sea with the Celtic Sea (the Atlantic Ocean).

**Saint-Germain** |ˌseNZHərˈmeN| **1** section of Paris, France, on the Left Bank (S of the Seine). A colorful quarter of narrow streets and cafes, it was the favorite haunt of postwar intellectuals and writers. In recent years it has become increasingly fashionable. **2** church of Saint-Germain-des-Prés, in the district. There has been a church on this spot since the 6th century, but the oldest parts of the present church date from the 11th century.

**Saint-Germain-en-Laye** |ˌseNZHərˈmenäNˈlā| residential and resort suburb W of Paris, in N central France. Pop. 42,000. The town has a notable promenade. A treaty of 1919 signed here dissolved the Austro-Hungarian Empire.

**St. Gott·hard Pass** |ˌsänt ˈgätərd| seN gəˈtär| mountain pass in the Alps in S Switzerland, situated at an altitude of 6,916 ft./2,108 m. It is named after a former chapel and hospice (14th century), dedicated to an 11th-century bishop of Hildesheim in Germany.

**St. He·le·na** |ˌsänt həˈlēnə| solitary island in the South Atlantic, a British dependency. Pop. 6,000. Capital: Jamestown. It was administered by the East India Company from 1659 until 1834 when it became a British colony. Ascension, Tristan da Cunha, and Gough Island are dependencies of St. Helena. It is famous as the place of Napoleon's exile (1815–21) and death. □ **St. Helenian** adj. & n.

St Helena

**St. Hel·ens, Mount** |ˌsänt ˈhelənz| active volcano in SW Washington, in the Cascade Range, rising to 8,312 ft./2,560 m. A dramatic eruption in May 1980 reduced its height by several hundred meters and spread volcanic ash and debris over a large area.

**St. Hel·ens** |sənt ˈhelənz| industrial town in NW England, in Merseyside NE of Liverpool. Pop. 175,000.

**St. Hel·ier** |sənt ˈhelyer| the capital of Jersey, in the Channel Islands of Britain, situated on the S coast. Pop. 28,000.

**Saint-Hubert** |ˌseNt Yʹber| city in S Quebec, a suburb across the St. Lawrence River from Montreal. Pop. 74,027.

**Saint Ives** |sənt ʹīvz| in England: **1** fishing port and resort town in the SW, in Cornwall. Pop. 11,000. Its arts colony is well known. **2** commercial town in the SE, in Cambridgeshire. Pop. 15,000. The nursery rhyme riddle pertains to the latter.

**Saint James's Palace** |sənt ʹjāmzəz| former residence of the British royal family, in Westminster, London, from 1697 until BUCKINGHAM PALACE replaced it in the 19th century. The **Court of St. James** is the official term for the British court, to which ambassadors are accredited.

**Saint-Jean, Lac** |ˌlä seNʹzHäN| lake in S central Quebec, NW of Quebec City. Drained by the Saguenay River, it is the site of many resorts.

**Saint-Jean-de-Luz** |seNʹzHäNdəʹlyz| town, SW France, on the Bay of Biscay near the Spanish border. Pop. 13,000. Formerly a fishing village, it is now primarily a resort.

**Saint-Jean-sur-Richelieu** |seN,zHäNsyr-,rēsHəlʹyœ| commercial city in S Quebec, SE of Montreal. Pop. 37,607.

**St. John**[1] |sänt ʹjän| island in the Caribbean, smallest of the three principal islands of the U.S. Virgin Islands. Pop. 3,504.

**St. John**[2] |sänt ʹjän| (usu. **Saint John**) largest city in New Brunswick, an industrial port on the Bay of Fundy at the mouth of the St. John River. Pop. 74,969.

**St. John's**[1] |sänt ʹjänz| the capital of Antigua and Barbuda, on the NW coast of Antigua. Pop. 36,000.

**St. John's**[2] |sänt ʹjänz| the capital of Newfoundland, a port on the SE coast of the island. Pop. 95,770. One of the oldest European settlements in North America, it was inhabited seasonally by the British from 1583.

**Saint Joseph** |sänt ʹjōzef| port city in NW Missouri, an industrial and commercial hub on the Missouri River. Pop. 71,852.

**St. Kil·da** |sənt ʹkildə| small island group of the Outer Hebrides of Scotland, in the Atlantic 40 mi./64 km. W of Lewis and Harris. The islands are now uninhabited and are a nature reserve.

**St. Kitts and Nevis** |sänt ʹkits ən(d) ʹnevəs| country in the Caribbean consisting of two adjoining islands in the Leeward Islands. Area: 101 sq. mi./261 sq. km. Pop.

**St Kitts**

44,000. Languages, English (official), Creole. Capital and largest town: Basseterre (on St. Kitts). Official name **Federation of St. Christopher and Nevis**. Colonized by Britain from 1623, the islands became fully independent in 1983. Tourism, sugar, and some light industry sustain the economy. □ **Kittitian** *adj. & n.* **Nevisian** *adj. & n.*

**Saint Law·rence Island** |sänt ʹlawrəns| island in W Alaska, in the Bering Sea. Most of its few inhabitants are Inuit.

**St. Law·rence River** |sänt ʹlawrəns| river of North America, which flows for some 750 mi./1,200 km. from Lake Ontario along the border between Canada and the U.S. to the Gulf of St. Lawrence on the Atlantic coast. The Thousand Islands, Montreal, and Quebec City lie along it. See also GREAT LAKES–ST. LAWRENCE SEAWAY.

**St. Law·rence Seaway** |sänt ʹlawrəns| see GREAT LAKES–SAINT LAWRENCE SEAWAY.

**Saint-Lô** |seNʹlō| town, capital of the Manche department, in Normandy, NW France. Pop. 23,000. It was almost completely destroyed during the Allied invasion during World War II and has since been rebuilt.

**Saint-Louis** |ˌseNləʹwē| port city in NW Senegal, on St.-Louis Island in the Senegal River delta, near the Mauritanian border. Pop. 126,000. It is a former colonial capital of both Senegal and Mauritania.

**St. Lou·is** |sänt ʹlo͞oəs| historic port city in E Missouri, on the Mississippi just S of its confluence with the Missouri. Pop. 396,685. Founded by the French as a furtrading post in the 1760s, it passed to the Spanish, the French again, and finally in 1803 to the U.S. as part of the Louisiana Purchase. It was long the gateway to settlement of the Louisiana Purchase and other western regions.

**Saint Lou·is Park** |sänt ʹlo͞oəs| city in SE Minnesota, a suburb SW of Minneapolis. Pop. 43,787.

**St. Lu•cia** |sänt 'lo͞osHə| country in the West Indies, one of the Windward Islands. Area: 238 sq. mi./616 sq. km. Pop. 133,310. Languages, English (official), French Creole. Capital and largest town: Castries. France and Britain disputed control of St. Lucia for over 200 years until France yielded in 1814. Independence came in 1979. Tourism, agriculture, and light industries sustain the economy. □ **St. Lucian** adj. & n.

**St Lucia**

**St. Ma•lo** |seNmä'lō| walled town and port on the N coast of Brittany, in NW France. Pop. 49,000.

**Saint Marks** |sänt 'märks| see SAN MARCO.

**St. Mar•tin** |sänt 'märtn| small island in the Caribbean, one of the Leeward Islands. Pop. 32,000. The S section is administered by the Dutch, forming part of the Netherlands Antilles; the larger N section is part of the French overseas department of Guadeloupe. Dutch name **Sint Maarten.**

**Saint Mar•tin•ville** |sänt 'märtin,vil| city in S Louisiana, a Cajun Country center on the Bayou Teche. Pop. 7,137.

**Saint-Maur-des-Fosses** |seN,mawrdə-faw'sä; ,sän'mawrdäfä'sə| industrial city, a suburb of Paris, in N central France, on the Marne River. Pop. 81,000.

**Saint Mau•rice, Rivière** |,seN maw'rēs; sänt 'mawrəs| river that flows 325 mi./525 km. through S Quebec, emptying into the St. Lawrence River at Trois-Rivières. Industrial cities along it include Shawinigan and Grand-Mère. Its valley is called **La Mauricie.**

**Saint-Mihiel** |,seNmē'yel| commune in NE France. Pop. 5,000. Fighting independently for the first time in World War I, U.S. troops took the village from the Germans in September 1918.

**St. Mo•ritz** |sänt 'mawrits| resort and winter sports center in SE Switzerland.

**St.-Nazaire** |,seNnä'zär| naval and industrial port city in NW France, on the Atlantic

at the mouth of the Loire River. Pop. 66,000.

**St. Ni•co•las** |seN ,nēkaw'lä| French name for SINT-NIKLAAS, Belgium.

**St. Paul** |sänt 'pawl| the state capital of Minnesota, a commercial and university city on the Mississippi adjacent to Minneapolis, with which it forms the Twin Cities. Pop. 272,235.

**Saint Paul's Cathedral** |sənt pawlz| cathedral on Ludgate Hill, in central London, England, built by Christopher Wren 1675–1711. It often serves as a symbol of London, or of England.

**Saint Pe•ter Port** |sänt 'pētər| town, the commercial and administrative center of Guernsey, in the British Channel Islands. Pop. 16,000.

**Saint Pe•ter's** |sänt 'pētərz| principal and largest Christian church in the world, the seat of the Catholic faith, in the Vatican City, in Rome, Italy. The current building dates from the 16th century; the famous dome follows a design by Michelangelo.

**St. Pe•ters•burg**[1] |sänt 'pētərz,bərg| resort and industrial city in W Florida, on the Gulf of Mexico. Pop. 238,630.

**St. Pe•ters•burg**[2] |sänt 'pētərz,bərg| city and seaport in NW Russia, in the delta of the Neva River, on the E shores of the Gulf of Finland. Pop. 5,035,000. Former names **Petrograd** (1914–24) and **Leningrad** (1924–91). Founded in 1703 by Peter the Great, it was the capital of Russia from 1712 until the Russian Revolution. During World War II, as Leningrad, it was subjected to a siege that lasted from 1941 to 1944. A city of waterways and bridges, it is an industrial and cultural center.

**St. Pierre and Miq•ue•lon** |sänt 'pir ən(d) 'mikə,län| group of eight small islands in the North Atlantic, off the S coast of Newfoundland. Pop. 6,390. An overseas territory of France, the islands form the last remaining French possession in North America. Fishing is key to the economy.

**St Pierre & Miquelon**

**Saint Pöl·ten** |sänt 'pöltən| see SANKT PÖLTEN.

**Saint-Quentin** |ˌseNkäN'teN| industrial commune in N France, on the Somme River. Pop. 62,000.

**Saint-Remy-de-Provence** |ˌseNrä'mēdə-praw'väNs; ˌsænrä'mēdə'prō'väns| town in SE France, about 15 mi./24 km. NE of Arles. A popular tourist destination, it is known for its Roman ruins and its association with the artist Van Gogh.

**Saint So·phia** |sänt sə'fēə| see HAGIA SOPHIA, Istanbul, Turkey.

**Saint Thom·as** |sänt 'täməs| industrial city in S Ontario, just N of Lake Erie. Pop. 29,990.

**St. Thom·as** |sänt 'täməs| resort island in the Caribbean, the second-largest of the U.S. Virgin Islands, to the E of Puerto Rico. Pop. 48,170; chief town, Charlotte Amalie. Settled by the Dutch in 1657, it passed nine years later to the Danes, who sold it to the U.S. in 1917.

**St.-Tropez** |ˌseNtraw'pe; sän,trō'pe| fishing port and resort on the Mediterranean coast of S France, SW of Cannes. Pop. 6,000.

**St. Vin·cent, Cape** |sänt 'vinsənt| headland in SW Portugal, at the SW tip of the country. It was the site of a sea battle in 1797 in which the British fleet defeated the Spanish. Portuguese name **São Vincente**.

**St. Vin·cent and the Gren·a·dines** |sänt 'vinsənt; ˌgrenə'dēnz| island state in the Windward Islands in the Caribbean, consisting of the mountainous island of St. Vincent and some of the Grenadines. Area: 150 sq. mi./389 sq. km. Pop. 108,000. Languages, English (official), English Creole. Capital and largest town: Kingstown. Controlled by Britain 1783–1979, the islands have an economy based on agriculture and tourism. □ **Vincentian** *adj. & n.*

St Vincent & Grenadines

**Sai·pan** |sī'pæn| the largest of the islands comprising the Northern Marianas in the W Pacific.

**Sa·ïs** |'sā-is| ancient city of N Egypt, on the old Canopic branch of the Nile River delta. It was the capital of Lower Egypt.

**Sa·kai** |'säk,ī| industrial city in Japan, on Osaka Bay just S of the city of Osaka. Pop. 808,000.

**Sa·kha, Republic of** |'säkə| official name for YAKUTIA, Russia.

**Sa·kha·lin** |ˌsäkə'lēn; ˈsækə,lēn| Russian island in the Sea of Okhotsk, off the coast of E Russia and separated from it by the Tartar Strait. Pop. 709,000. Capital: Yuzhno-Sakhalinsk. From 1905 to 1946 it was divided into a N part held by Russia, and a S part (Karafuto), occupied by Japan.

**Sa·kur·a** |sə'kᴏᴏrə| city in E central Japan, on E central Honshu, N of Chiba. Pop. 145,000.

**Sa·la·do, Río** |ˌrēō sə'läTHō| (also **Río Salado del Norte**) river that flows 1,250 mi./2,010 km. across N Argentina, from the Andes, to join the Paraná River at Santa Fe. Its lower course has been channeled for irrigation. Argentina has several smaller rivers also called Río Salado.

**Sa·la·man·ca** |ˌsælə'mäNGkə| industrial and agricultural city in W Spain, in Castil-la-León. Pop. 186,000.

**Sal·a·mis** |'sæləməs| island in the Saronic Gulf in Greece, to the W of Athens. The strait between the island and the mainland was the scene in 480 B.C. of a crushing defeat of the Persian fleet under Xerxes I by the Greeks under Themistocles.

**Sa·lang Pass** |sä'läNG| high-altitude route across the Hindu Kush in Afghanistan. A road and tunnel were built by the Soviet Union during the 1960s to improve military and commercial access to Kabul.

**Sa·la·vat** |sə'lävät| city in Bashkortostan, W Russia, S of Ufa. Pop. 152,000.

**Sa·lé** |sä'la| industrial port city in N Morocco, on the Atlantic, NE of Rabat. Pop. 580,000. It was once home to the Sallee Rovers, a group of Barbary pirates.

**Sa·lem¹** |'saləm| industrial city in Tamil Nadu in S India. Pop. 364,000.

**Sa·lem²** |'saləm| port city in NE Massachusetts, on the Atlantic coast N of Boston. Pop. 38,091. It was the scene in 1692 of a notorious series of witchcraft trials. Tourism is important today.

**Sa·lem³** |'saləm| the capital of Oregon, an industrial city on the Willamette River SW of Portland. Pop. 107,786.

**Sa·ler·no** |sə'lernō| port on the W coast of Italy, on the Gulf of Salerno SE of Naples. Pop. 151,000.

**Sal·ford** |'sawlfərd| industrial city in NW

England, in Greater Manchester. Pop. 218,000.

**Sa·li·na** |sə'lī:nə| industrial and commercial city in central Kansas. Pop. 42,303.

**Sa·li·nas** |sə'lēnəs| city in W central California, a commercial center in the agriculturally important Salinas Valley. Pop. 108,777.

**Salis·bury**¹ |'sawlz,berē; 'sawlzbərē| market city in S England, in the Salisbury Plain in Wiltshire. Pop. 35,000. It is noted for its 13th-century cathedral, whose spire, at 404 ft./123 m. ĩs the highest in England. Its diocese is known as Sarum, an old name for the city.

**Salis·bury**² |'sawlz,berē; 'sawlzbərē| industrial city in W central North Carolina. Pop. 23,087.

**Salis·bury**³ |'sawlz,berē; 'sawlzbərē| former name (until 1982) for HARARE, Zimbabwe.

**Salm·on River** |'sæmən| river that flows 425 mi./685 km. through central Idaho. With its branches, it is noted as a salmon breeding and river sports resource.

**Sa·lon·i·ca** |sə'länikə; ,sælə'nēkə| another name for THESSALONÍKI, Greece.

**Sal·op** |'sæləp| another name for SHROPSHIRE, England. It was the official name of the county 1974–80. □ **Salopian** adj. & n.

**Sal·ta** |'sältə| commercial city in NW Argentina, capital of Salta province. Pop. 370,000. It ships agricultural products.

**Sal·ti·llo** |säl'tē(y)ō| industrial and university city in N Mexico, capital of the state of Coahuila, in the Sierra Madre SW of Monterrey. Pop. 441,000.

**Salt Lake City** | sawlt| the capital and largest city of Utah, situated near the SE shore of the Great Salt Lake. Pop. 159,936. Founded in 1847 by Brigham Young, the city is the world headquarters of the Church of Latter-Day Saints (Mormons). It is a center of high-tech industry.

**Sal·to** |'sältō| city in NW Uruguay, capital of Salto department, on the Uruguay River across from Concordia, Argentina. Pop. 93,000. It is a commercial and transportation center.

**Sal·ton Sea** |'sawltn| salt lake in SE California, created in the dry **Salton Sink** by a 1905 diversion of the Colorado River. It is a recreational resource and wildlife refuge.

**Sal·va·dor** |,sælvə'dawr; 'sælvə,dawr| port on the Atlantic coast of E Brazil, capital of the state of Bahia. Pop. 2,075,000. Founded in 1549, it was the capital of the Portuguese colony until 1763, when the seat of

government was transferred to Rio de Janeiro. Former name **Bahia**.

**Sal·ween** |'sæl,wēn| river of SE Asia, which rises in Tibet and flows for 1,500 mi./2,400 km. SE and S through Burma to the Gulf of Martaban, an inlet of the Andaman Sea.

**Salz·burg** |'zälts,boŏrk| city in W Austria, near the border with Germany, the capital of a state of the same name; pop. 144,000. It is noted for its annual music festivals, one dedicated to the composer Mozart, who was born here in 1756.

**Salz·git·ter** |'zälts,gitər| industrial city in Germany, in Lower Saxony SE of Hanover. Pop. 115,000.

**Salz·kam·mer·gut** |'zält,skämər,goŏt| resort area of lakes and mountains in the states of Salzburg, Upper Austria, and Styria, in W Austria.

**Sa·mar** |'sä,mär| island in the Philippines, situated to the SE of Luzon. It is the third-largest island of the group. The island-enclosed **Samar Sea** lies to the W.

**Sa·ma·ra** |sə'märə| industrial city and river port in SW Russia, situated on the Volga at its confluence with the Samara River. Pop. 1,258,000.

**Sa·mar·ia** |sə'mærēə| **1** an ancient city of central Palestine, founded in the 9th century B.C. as the capital of the northern Hebrew kingdom of Israel. The ancient site is in the modern West Bank, NW of Nablus. **2** the region of ancient Palestine around this city, between Galilee in the N and Judaea in the S. □ **Samaritan** adj. & n.

**Sam·a·rin·da** |,sæmə'rində| commercial city in Indonesia, capital of East Kalimantan, in E Borneo. Pop. 265,000.

**Sa·mar·kand** |'sæmər,kænd| (also **Samarqand**) city in E Uzbekistan. Pop. 370,000. One of the oldest cities of Asia, it was founded in the 3rd or 4th millennium B.C. It grew to prominence as a center of the silk trade, situated on the Silk Road, and in the 14th century became the capital of Tamerlane's Mongol Empire.

**Sa·mar·ra** |sə'märə| city in Iraq, a Shiite center on the Tigris River N of Baghdad. Pop. 62,000.

**Sam·bal·pur** |'səmbəl,poŏr| city in E central India, NW of Cuttack in Orissa state. Pop. 193,000.

**Sam·bhal** |'səmbəl| commercial city in N India, in Uttar Pradesh state. Pop. 150,000.

**Sam·ni·um** |'sæmnēəm| ancient country in what is now central Italy, comprising Abruzzi and part of Campania. It was conquered by Rome in 290 B.C. □ **Samnite** adj. & n.

**Sa·moa** |sə'mōə| **1** group of islands in Polynesia, divided between American Samoa and the state of Samoa. **2** (also **Western Samoa**) independent state comprising a group of nine islands in the SW Pacific. Area: 1,098 sq. mi./2,842 sq. km. Pop. 160,000. Languages, Samoan and English. Capital, Apia. Controlled by Germany, then New Zealand, Samoa became independent in 1962. It exports coconut products and other foods and spices. See also AMERICAN SAMOA. □ **Samoan** *adj. & n.*

**Sa·mos** |'sämaws| Greek island in the Aegean, close to the coast of W Turkey.

**Sam·o·thrace** |'sæmə,THräs; ,sæmə 'THräsē| island in NE Greece, in the Aegean Sea. The island's peak, at 5,577 ft.,/1,700 m., is the tallest of any Aegean island. The statue *Victory of Samothrace*, popularly known as *Winged Victory*, found here, is now in the Louvre in Paris.

**Sam·sun** |säm'sōon| historic port city in N Turkey, the capital of Samsun province. Pop. 304,000. The leading Turkish port on the Black Sea, it is also a tobacco-industry center.

**Sana'a** |sæn'ä| (also **Sanaa**) the capital of Yemen. Pop. 500,000. A handicrafts center claimed to be the oldest city in the world, it is noted for its huge medina (walled city).

**Sa·nan·daj** |,sänən'däj| a mostly Kurdish city in NW Iran, in the Zagros Mts. Pop. 244,000.

**San An·dre·as Fault** |,sæn æn'drēəs| fault line extending for some 600 mi./965 km. through coastal California. Seismic activity is common along its course, caused by two crustal plates sliding past each other. The city of San Francisco lies close to the fault, and such movement caused the devastating earthquake of 1906 and a further convulsion in 1989.

**San An·drés** |,sæn æn'drāəs| resort island in the Caribbean Sea, E of Nicaragua but part of an archipelago held by Colombia. Pop. 40,000. Tourism and duty-free commerce are important.

**San An·ge·lo** |sæn 'ænjələ| commercial and industrial city in W central Texas. Pop. 84,474.

**San An·to·nio** |sæn än'tōnē,ō| industrial, commercial, and military city in S central Texas. Pop. 935,933. It is the site of the Alamo.

**San Ber·nar·di·no** |,sæn ,bərnə(r)'dēnō| industrial and commercial city in S California, E of Los Angeles. Pop. 164,164. It is the seat of **San Bernardino County**, the largest (20,064 sq. mi./51,966 sq. km.) in the U.S. The **San Bernardino Mountains** lie mostly N of the city.

**San Ber·nar·do** |,sän ber'närdō| industrial and commercial city in central Chile, in Maipo province, S of Santiago. Pop. 188,000.

**San Bru·no** |sæn 'brōonō| city in N central California, a suburb on San Francisco Bay, S of San Francisco. Pop. 38,961.

**San Car·los** |sæn 'kärlōs| **1** city in the Philippines, on central Luzon. Pop. 125,000. **2** port city in the Philippines, on E Negros. Pop. 106,000.

**San Car·los de Ba·ri·lo·che** |sæn 'kawrlōs də ,bärē'lōCHä| ski resort in the Andes of Argentina, on the shores of Lake Nahuel Huapi. Pop. 48,000.

**San·chi** |'sänCHi| village in central India, in Madhya Pradesh state, site of the best-preserved Buddhist monuments in India.

**San·chung** |'sæn'jōONG| (also **San·ch'ung**) city in N Taiwan, W of Taipei and N of Panchiao. Pop. 382,000.

**San Cle·men·te** |,sæn klə'mentē| city in SW California, on the Pacific SE of Los Angeles, noted as the home of Richard Nixon. Pop. 41,100.

**San Cris·to·bal** |,sänkrē'stōbäl| (also **Makira** or **San Cristoval**) volcanic island in the S Solomon Islands, SE of Guadalcanal.

**San Cris·tó·bal**[1] |,sän krē'stōbäl| historic commercial city in the S Dominican Republic, in an agricultural area. Pop. 88,000.

**San Cristóbal**[2] |,sänkrē'stōbäl| industrial and commercial city in W Venezuela, the capital of Táchira state. Pop. 221,000.

**Sanc·ti Spí·ri·tus** |'säNGktē 'spērē,tōōs| historic commercial city in W central Cuba, the capital of Sancti Spíritus province. Pop. 86,000.

**San·da·kan** |,sändä'kän| commercial port city in Malaysia, on NE Borneo. Pop. 157,000.

**San·dal·wood Island** |'sændəl,wōod| another name for SUMBA, Indonesia.

**Sand Hills** |sænd| large plains area of W central Nebraska, noted as a ranching district.

**Sand·hills** |'sænd,hilz| (also **Sand Hills**) line of low, sandy hills lying across the Carolinas and Georgia, at the boundary of the coastal plain and the Piedmont.

**Sand·hurst** |'sænd,hərst| town in S central England, in Berkshire, original home to the British Royal Military College, now at Camberley, in Surrey.

**San·dia Mountains** |sæn'dēə| range in

central New Mexico, rising to 10,678 ft./3,255 m. at Sandia Peak, near Albuquerque.

**San Di·e·go** |săn dē'ägō| industrial, institutional, and retirement city and naval port on the Pacific coast of S California, just N of the border of Mexico. Pop. 1,110,549. It was founded as a mission in 1769.

**San·dring·ham** |'săndriNGəm| village in SE England, in Norfolk, NE of King's Lynn, site of one of the holiday retreats of the British royal family.

**San·dus·ky** |sən'dəskē; săn'dəskē| industrial port city in N Ohio, on Lake Erie at Sandusky Bay. Pop. 29,764.

**Sand·wich**[1] |'săn(d)wiCH| resort town in SE England, in Kent, one of the CINQUE PORTS. Pop. 4,000.

**Sand·wich**[2] |'săn(d)wiCH| town in SE Massachusetts, on Cape Cod, a resort with a history of glassmaking. Pop. 15,489.

**Sand·wich Islands** |'săn(d)wiCH| former name for HAWAII.

**Sandy** |'săndē| city in N central Utah, a residential and commercial suburb S of Salt Lake City. Pop. 75,058.

**Sandy Hook** |'săndē 'hŏŏk| peninsula in NE New Jersey, S of New York City, separating Raritan Bay from the Atlantic. It is noted for its lighthouse, beaches, and forts.

**Sandy·mount** |,săndē,mownt| residential SE section of Dublin, Ireland, the birthplace of the poet W.B. Yeats. Nearby **Sandy·cove**, to the E of Dun Laoghaire, is associated with the writer James Joyce.

**San Fer·nan·do**[1] |,săn fər'năndō| port city in E Argentina, just N of Buenos Aires. Pop. 145,000.

**San Fer·nan·do**[2] |,săn fər'năndō| **1** commercial port town in the Philippines on N central Luzon, NW of Baguio. Pop. 85,000. **2** industrial town in the Philippines, on central Luzon, NW of Manila. Pop. 158,000.

**San Fer·nan·do**[3] |,săn fər'năndō| (formerly **Isla de León**) port city in S Spain. Pop. 82,000. It has a naval academy and an arsenal.

**San Fer·nan·do Valley** |,săn fər'năndō| (popularly **the Valley**) irrigated district NW of downtown Los Angeles, California, comprising city neighborhoods and nearby suburbs.

**San·ford** |'sănfərd| resort and commercial city in N central Florida. Pop. 32,387.

**San Fran·cis·co** |,săn frən'siskō; frän 'siskō| historic city and seaport on the coast of California, situated on a peninsula between the Pacific and San Francisco Bay. Pop. 723,959. It is a major center of com-

merce, finance, industry, and culture. Founded as a mission by Mexican Jesuits in 1776, it was taken by the U.S. in 1846. The fine natural harbor of San Francisco Bay is entered by the channel known as the Golden Gate. The city suffered severe damage from an earthquake in 1906, and has been frequently shaken by less severe earthquakes. □ **San Franciscan** *adj. & n.*

**San Fran·cis·co Peaks** |,săn frən'siskō; frän'siskō| mountain group in N Arizona, N of Flagstaff, including Humphreys Peak, at 12,633 ft./3,851 m. the highest point in the state.

**San Ga·bri·el Mountains** |săn 'gābrēəl| range in S California, on the N of (and partly in) the city of Los Angeles. Mount San Antonio, at 10,080 ft./3,105 m., is the high point. The Mount Wilson observatory is here. The city of **San Gabriel** (pop. 37,120) is a suburb E of Los Angeles.

**San Gi·mi·gna·no** |,săn jēmē'nyänō| medieval town in central Italy. Pop. 7,000. Set atop a hill, the walled town, with its 14 towers, is a major tourist attraction.

**San·gli** |'säNGgli| commercial town in W India, in Maharashtra state. Pop. 364,000.

**San·gre de Cris·to Mountains** |,săNGgrē də 'kristō| range in S Colorado and N New Mexico, an extension of the Front Range of the Rocky Mts. The Pecos and Canadian rivers rise here.

**San·i·bel Island** |'sănəbəl| resort island in SW Florida, SW of Fort Myers, famed among seashell collectors.

**San Isi·dro** |,săn ē'sēTHrō| city in E Argentina, a suburban part of the Buenos Aires area. Pop. 299,000.

**San Ja·cin·to River** |,săn jə'sin,tō| river in SE Texas that flows into Galveston Bay, E of Houston. The 1836 battle that won Texas independence from Mexico was fought on its bank.

**San Joa·quin River** |,săn wä'kēn| river that flows 350 mi./560 km. from S central California, to join the Sacramento River and enter San Francisco Bay. The agricultural and oil producing lands surrounding it are known as the San Joaquin Valley, part of the Central Valley.

**San Jo·se** |,săn (h)ō'zā; ə'zā| city in W California, to the S of San Francisco Bay. Pop. 782,248. It is the largest city in Silicon Valley, a center of high-tech industries.

**San Jo·sé** |,sän haw'sā; ,săn hō'zā| the capital and chief port of Costa Rica. Pop. 319,000.

**San Juan**[1] |,săn 'wän| city in W Argentina,

the capital of San Juan province, in the E Andes. Pop. 353,000. It produces foods and wines.

**San Juan**² |ˌsæn ˈwän| the capital and chief port of Puerto Rico, a commercial and tourist center on the N coast. Pop. 437,745.

**San Juan Cap·is·tra·no** |ˌsæn ˈwän ˌkæpəs ˈtränō| city in SW California, between Los Angeles and San Diego, site of a 1776 mission to which migrating swallows famously return each March 19. Pop. 26,183.

**San Juan Hill**¹ |ˌsän ˈhwän| hill near Santiago de Cuba, E Cuba, scene of a July 1898 battle in the Spanish-American War.

**San Juan Hill**² |ˌsæn ˈ(h)wän| former neighborhood in Manhattan, New York City, where the cultural complex of Lincoln Center now stands.

**San Juan Islands** |ˌsæn ˈ(h)wän| island group in NW Washington, N of Puget Sound and S of the Strait of Georgia. San Juan and Orcas are the largest islands in the group.

**San Juan Mountains** |ˌsæn ˈ(h)wän| range of the Rocky Mts. in SW Colorado and N New Mexico, source of the Rio Grande, which here flows through the agricultural San Juan Valley.

**Sankt Pöl·ten** |zänkt ˈpœltn| industrial city and transportation center in N central Austria, capital of Lower Austria. Pop. 49,000.

**San·ku·ru River** |sänGˈkōōrōō| river that flows 750 mi./1,200 km. from the S central Congo (formerly Zaire) into the Kasai River. In its upper third it is called the Lubilash River.

**San Le·an·dro** |ˌsæn lēˈændrō| city in N central California, a suburb on the SE side of Oakland, in an agricultural area. Pop. 68,223.

**San Lo·ren·zo** |ˌsän lōˈrenzō| industrial and commercial city in central Paraguay, just E of Asunción. Pop. 133,000.

**San Lu·cas, Ca·bo** |ˌkävō ˈsän ˈlōōkäs| (English name **Cape San Lucas**) cape at the S end of Baja California, Mexico, on the W of the mouth of the Gulf of California, noted for its scenery and as a resort.

**San Lu·is Obis·po** |ˌsæn ˌlōōəs əˈbispō| city in W central California, in an agricultural area NW of Los Angeles. Pop. 41,958.

**San Lu·is Pot·o·sí** |ˌsän lōōˌēs ˌpōtəˈsē| **1** state of N central Mexico. Area: 24,360 sq. mi./63,068 sq. km. Pop. 2,002,000. **2** its capital, an industrial and silver-mining city. Pop. 526,000.

**San Mar·co** |sän ˈmärkō| one of the two large islands that make up Venice, in NE Italy. It is also the name of that city's famous square, the Piazza San Marco, dominated by the Byzantine Cathedral of San Marco.

**San Mar·cos**¹ |sæn ˈmärkəs| city in SW California, a suburb N of San Diego. Pop. 38,974.

**San Mar·cos**² |sæn ˈmärkəs| city in S central Texas, S of Austin. Pop. 28,743.

**San Ma·ri·no**¹ |ˌsæn mäˈrēnō| city in SW California, a suburb NE of Los Angeles. Pop. 12,959.

**San Ma·ri·no**² |ˌsæn mäˈrēnō| republic forming a small (23.5 sq. mi./61 sq. km.) enclave in Italy, near Rimini. Pop. 23,000. Language, Italian. Capital: the town of San Marino. Perhaps Europe's oldest state, claiming to have been independent almost continuously since its foundation in the 4th century, it is said to be named after Marino, a Dalmatian stonecutter who fled here to escape the persecution of Christians under Diocletian. Agriculture and crafts are the backbone of the economy.

**San Marino**

**San Ma·teo** |ˌsæn məˈtāō| commercial and industrial city in N central California, on San Francisco Bay S of San Francisco. Pop. 85,486.

**San Mi·guel** |ˌsän mēˈgel| industrial and commercial city in E El Salvador, on the Pan-American Highway. Pop. 183,000.

**San Mi·guel de Allen·de** |ˌsän mēˈgel dä äˈyendə| city in central Mexico, in Guanajuato state. Pop. 49,000. It is a commercial and tourist center, and has a noted arts colony.

**San Mi·guel de Tu·cu·mán** |ˌsän ˈmēgel də ˌtōōkōōˈmän| (also **Tucumán**) historic city in N Argentina, the capital of Tucumán province. Pop. 622,000. It is a sugar industry center. Argentine independence was proclaimed here in 1816.

**San Ni·co·lás** |ˌsän ˌnēkōˈläs| (official name **San Nicolás de los Arroyos**) industrial and commercial city in central

Argentina, on the Paraná River, SE of Rosario. Pop. 115,000.

**San Ni·co·lás de los Gar·za** |ˌsän ˌnēkō ˈläs dä lōs ˈgärsä| city in N Mexico, in Nuevo León state, a suburb N of Monterrey. Pop. 437,000.

**San Pab·lo**¹ |sæn ˈpäblō| city in N central California, on San Pablo Bay N of Oakland. Pop. 25,158.

**San Pab·lo**² |sän ˈpäblō| commercial city in the Philippines, on S Luzon. Pop. 162,000.

**San Pe·dro** |sæn ˈpēdrō; ˈpädrō| section of S Los Angeles, California, on San Pedro Bay, site of the city's harbor facilities.

**San Pe·dro de Ma·co·rís** |sän ˈpädrō dä ˌmäkōˈrēs| industrial port city in the SE Dominican Republic, capital of San Pedro de Macorís province. Pop. 124,000. It is a famous producer of baseball players.

**San Pe·dro Su·la** |sän ˈpädrō ˈsoōlä| second-largest city in Honduras, an industrial and commercial center near the Caribbean coast. Pop. 326,000.

**San Quen·tin** |sæn ˈkwentn| site in Marin County, NW California, across the Golden Gate from San Francisco, where a famous state prison is located.

**San Ra·fael** |sæn rəˈfel| city in NW California, on San Rafael Bay, N of San Francisco. Pop. 48,404.

**San Re·mo** |sän ˈrämō| resort on the Riviera, in NW Italy, on the Ligurian Sea. Pop. 64,000. It is also a major flower market.

**San Sal·va·dor**¹ |sän ˌsälväˈdawr; sæn ˈsælvəˌdawr| (also **Watlings**) island in the SE Bahamas, believed to be the site where Columbus first landed in the New World in 1492. Pop. 2,000.

**San Sal·va·dor**² |sän ˌsälväˈdawr; sæn ˈsælvəˌdawr| the capital of El Salvador, a trade and light industrial center. Pop. 423,000.

**San Sal·va·dor**³ |sän ˌsälväˈdawr; sæn ˈsælvəˌdawr| see JUJUY.

**San Sebastián** |ˌsän säbästˈyän| port and resort in N Spain, in the Basque Country, on the Bay of Biscay close to the border with France. Pop. 174,000.

**San Sim·e·on** |sæn ˈsimēən| community in W central California, on the Pacific coast, site of the Hearst Estate, a noted tourist attraction.

**Sans Sou·ci** |ˌsän soōˈsē| see POTSDAM.

**San·ta Ana**¹ |ˌsæntə ˈænə| industrial and commercial city in S California, SE of Los Angeles. Pop. 293,742. To the E are the

**Santa Ana Mountains,** source of the hot, dry Santa Ana winds.

**San·ta Ana**² |ˌsäntə ˈänə| city in El Salvador, in an agricultural region close to the border with Guatemala. Pop. 202,000.

**San·ta Ana**³ |ˌsäntə ˈ| highest volcano in El Salvador, SW of the city of Santa Ana. It rises to 7,730 ft./2,381 m.

**San·ta Bar·ba·ra** |ˌsæntə ˈbärb(ə)rə| resort city in California, on the Pacific coast NW of Los Angeles. Pop. 85,571.

**San·ta Bar·ba·ra Islands** |ˌsæntə ˈbärb(ə)rə| (also **Channel Islands**) island group in SW California, off the Pacific coast. Santa Catalina (also called Catalina) is a tourist destination.

**San·ta Ca·ta·ri·na** |ˌsäntä ˌkätäˈrēnə| state of S Brazil, on the Atlantic coast. Pop. 4,538,000. Capital: Florianópolis.

**San·ta Clara**¹ |ˌsæntə ˈklærə| city in N central California, a longtime fruit-producing center now at the heart of Silicon Valley. Pop. 93,613.

**San·ta Clara**² |ˌsäntä ˈklärä| commercial and industrial city in central Cuba, the capital of Villa Clara province. Pop. 217,000.

**San·ta Clar·i·ta** |ˌsæntə kləˈrētə| city in SW California, a suburb NW of Los Angeles. Pop. 110,642.

**San·ta Co·lo·ma de Gra·ma·net** |ˌsäntä kōˈlōmä dä ˌgrämäˈnet| commune in NE Spain, a suburb of Barcelona. Pop. 132,000.

**San·ta Cruz**¹ |ˌsäntä ˈkroōs| industrial and commercial city in the central region of Bolivia. Pop. 695,000.

**San·ta Cruz**² |ˌsæntə ˈkroōz| resort and academic city in W central California, on Monterey Bay. Pop. 49,040.

**San·ta Cruz**³ |ˌsäntä ˈkroōs| port and the chief city of the island of Tenerife, in the Canary Islands. Pop. 192,000. Full name **Santa Cruz de Tenerife**.

**San·ta Cruz Islands** |ˌsæntə ˈkroōz| island group in the SE Solomon Islands, in the SW Pacific, scene of an October 1942 naval battle between U.S. and Japanese forces.

**San·ta Fe**¹ |ˈsäntä ˈfä| city in N Argentina, a port on the Salado River near its confluence with the Paraná. Pop. 395,000.

**San·ta Fe**² |ˌsæntə ˈfä| the capital of New Mexico. Pop. 55,859. It was founded as a mission by the Spanish in 1610. From 1821 until the arrival of the railroad in 1880 it was the terminus of the Santa Fe Trail. Taken by U.S. forces in 1846 during the Mexican War, it became the capital of New Mexico in 1912. It is today an administrative and tourist center.

**San•ta Fe Trail** |ˌsæntə ˈfā| historic route, established in the 1820s, from St. Louis, Missouri, to Santa Fe, New Mexico. Merchants and settlers used it until the Santa Fe Railroad was built in the 1870s.

**San•ta Is•a•bel Island** |ˌsæntə ˈizäˌbel| mountainous island in the central Solomon Islands, in the SW Pacific. Pop. 14,000.

**San•ta Lu•cia Range** |ˌsæntə lōōˈsēə| range in W central California, part of the Coast Ranges, noted for its resorts and wineries.

**San•ta Ma•ria**[1] |ˌsäntə mäˈrēə| commercial, industrial, and military city in S Brazil, in Rio Grande do Sul state. Pop. 218,000.

**San•ta Ma•ria**[2] |ˌsæntə məˈrēə| commercial city in SW California, in an agricultural area. Pop. 61,284.

**San•ta Mar•ta** |ˌsäntə ˈmärtə| historic port city in N Colombia, the capital of Magdalena department. Pop. 286,000.

**San•ta Mon•i•ca** |ˌsæntə ˈmänikə| resort city on the coast of SW California, just W of Los Angeles. Pop. 86,905.

**San•tan•der** |ˌsänˌtänˈder| industrial port in N Spain, on the Bay of Biscay, capital of Cantabria. Pop. 194,000.

**San•ta•rém**[1] |ˌsäntəˈrem| commercial city in N Brazil, in Pará state, a port on the Amazon River. 243,000.

**San•ta•rém**[2] |ˌsäntəˈrem| town in central Portugal, capital of Santaém province, on the Tagus River, NE of Lisbon. Pop. 15,000.

**San•ta Ro•sa** |ˌsæntə ˈrōzə| commercial city in NW California, in an agricultural area N of San Francisco. Pop. 113,313.

**San•tee River** |sænˈtē| river that flows 140 mi./230 km. through E South Carolina, to the Atlantic.

**San•ti•a•go** |ˌsäntēˈägō| the capital and largest city of Chile, situated to the W of the Andes in the central part of the country. Pop. 5,181,000. It is the industrial and cultural center of Chile.

**San•ti•a•go de Com•pos•te•la** |ˌsäntēˈägō dä ˌkawmpōˈstälä| city in NW Spain, capital of Galicia. Pop. 106,000. The remains of St. James the Great (Spanish *Sant Iago*) are said to have been brought there after his death; it is an important place of pilgrimage.

**San•ti•a•go de Cu•ba** |ˌsäntēˈägō dä ˈkōōbä| industrial port on the coast of SE Cuba, the second-largest city on the island. Pop. 433,000.

**San•ti•a•go del Es•te•ro** |ˌsäntēˈägō del äˈstärō| city in N central Argentina, the capital of Santiago del Estero province. Pop. 264,000. One of the oldest cities in Ar-

gentina, it is a spa and agricultural trade center.

**San•ti•a•go de los Ca•ba•lle•ros** |ˌsäntēˈägō dä lōs ˌkäbäˈyärōs| commercial city in the N central Dominican Republic, an agricultural trade center. Pop. 365,000.

**San•to An•dré** |ˌsäntōō änˈdre| city in S Brazil, an industrial and commercial suburb of São Paulo. Pop. 625,000.

**San•to Do•min•go** |ˌsäntō dōˈmiNGgō| the capital and largest city of the Dominican Republic, a port on the S coast. Pop. 2,055,000. Founded in 1496 by the brother of Christopher Columbus, it is the oldest European settlement in the Americas. From 1936 to 1961 it was called Ciudad Trujillo.

**San•to Do•min•go de los Co•lo•ra•dos** |ˌsäntō dōˈmiNGgō dälōs ˌkōlawˈrädōs| commercial city in NW Ecuador, in Pichincha province on the W of the Andes. Pop. 114,000. Its name derives from the local Colorados Indians.

**San•to•ri•ni** |ˌsæntōˈrēnē| another name for THERA, Greece.

**San•tos** |ˈsæntōōs| industrial port on the coast of Brazil, SE of São Paulo. Pop. 429,000.

**San•tur•ce** |sänˈtōōrsä| commercial and residential district of San Juan, Puerto Rico, with noted beaches.

**São Ber•nar•do do Cam•po** |sōwN berˈnärdō dōō ˈkämpōō| city in SE Brazil, an industrial suburb SE of São Paulo. Pop. 659,000.

**São Ca•e•ta•no do Sul** |sōwN kiˈtänōō dōō sōōl| city in SE Brazil, a commercial suburb SE of São Paulo. Pop. 141,000.

**São Car•los** |sōwN ˈkärlōs| commercial and industrial city in SE Brazil, in NW São Paulo state. Pop. 175,000.

**São Fran•cis•co** |sōwN fränˈsēskō| river of E Brazil. It rises in Minas Gerais and flows for 1,990 mi./3,200 km. N then E, meeting the Atlantic to the N of Aracajú.

**São Gon•ça•lo** |sōwN ˈgōNˈsälōō| city in SE Brazil, an industrial and commercial suburb E of Rio de Janeiro, on Guanabara Bay. Pop. 721,000.

**São João de Me•ri•ti** |sōwN ˈ ZHwOwN də ˈmirēˈtē| city in SE Brazil, a largely residential suburb NW of Rio de Janeiro. Pop. 425,000.

**São Jo•sé do Rio Prê•to** |sōwN ZHōˈzä dōō ˈrēō ˈpretōō| commercial and industrial city in SE Brazil, in São Paulo state. Pop. 323,000.

**São Jo•sé dos Cam•pos** |ˌsōwN ZHōˈzä dōōSH ˈkämpōs| industrial and commercial city in SE Brazil, in São Paulo state. Pop. 486,000.

**São Le·o·pol·do** |ˌsowɴ ˌlāōˈpōldōō| industrial city in S Brazil, in Rio Grande do Sul state. Pop. 168,000.

**São Lu·ís** |ˌsowɴ ləˈwēs| port in NE Brazil, on the Atlantic coast, capital of the state of Maranhão. Pop. 695,000.

**Saône** |sōn| river of E France, which rises in the Vosges Mts. and flows 298 mi./480 km. SW to join the Rhône at Lyons.

**São Pau·lo** |ˌsowɴ ˈpowlōō| **1** state of S Brazil, on the Atlantic coast. Pop. 31.55 million. **2** its capital. Pop. 9,700,000. It is the largest city in Brazil and second-largest in South America, and is the financial, industrial, and institutional center of Brazil.

**São Tia·go** |ˌsowɴ ˈtyägōō| (also **Santiago**) largest (383 sq. mi./992 sq. km.) island of Cape Verde. Pop. 176,000. Praia, the capital, is here. Agriculture is central to the economy.

**São To·mé and Prín·ci·pe** |ˌsowɴ təˈmä ən(d) ˈprinsəpə| country consisting of two main islands and several smaller ones in the Gulf of Guinea. Pop. 120,000. Languages, Portuguese (official), Portuguese Creole. Capital São Tomé. The islands were settled by Portugal from 1493 and became independent in 1975.

Sao Tome & Principe

**São Vi·cen·te, Cabo de** |ˈkabōō dä sowɴ vēˈsäɴtē| Portuguese name for Cape St. Vincent (see ST. VINCENT, CAPE).

**São Vi·cen·te** |ˌsowɴ vēˈsäɴtē| historic resort city in SE Brazil, a suburb of Santos, on an Atlantic island in São Paulo state. Pop. 280,000.

**São Vi·cen·te Island** |ˌsowɴ vēˈsäɴtē| island in NW Cape Verde, in the Windward group. Pop. 51,000. Fishing and mining are important here.

**Sa·pe·le** |səˈpälä| port city in S Nigeria, in the Niger River delta. Pop. 123,000. It is a timber industry center.

**Sap·po·ro** |säˈpawrō| city in N Japan, capital of the island of Hokkaido, a manufacturing and winter sports center. Pop. 1,672,000.

**Saq·qa·ra** |səˈkärə| (also **Sakkara**) archaeological site in N Egypt, just S of Cairo, near the Nile River, noted for its ancient ruins and burial structures.

**Sar·a·gos·sa** |ˌsærəˈgawsə| industrial city in N Spain, capital of Aragon, situated on the Ebro River. Pop. 614,000. The ancient settlement here was taken in the 1st century B.C. by the Romans, who called it Caesaraugusta (from which the modern name is derived). Spanish name **Zaragoza**.

**Sa·rai** |säˈrī| former city in SW Russia, E of the lower Volga River, near Leninsk. In the 13th–15th centuries it was the capital of the Mongol state, the Empire of the Golden Horde.

**Sa·ra·je·vo** |ˌsärəˈyävō| industrial city, the capital of Bosnia and Herzegovina. Pop. 200,000. Taken by the Austro-Hungarians in 1878, it became a center of Slav opposition to Austrian rule. It was the scene in June 1914 of the assassination by a Bosnian Serb of Archduke Franz Ferdinand, the heir to the Austrian throne, an event that triggered the outbreak of World War I. The city suffered severely from the ethnic conflicts that followed the breakup of Yugoslavia in 1991, and was beseiged by Bosnian Serb forces in the surrounding mountains from 1992 to 1994.

**Sar·a·nac Lakes** |ˈsærəˌnæk| group of resort lakes in NE New York, in the Adirondack Park, site of a pioneering tuberculosis sanatorium.

**Sa·ransk** |səˈränsk| city in European Russia, capital of the autonomous republic of Mordvinia, to the S of Nizhni Novgorod. Pop. 316,000.

**Sar·a·so·ta** |ˌsærəˈsōtə| resort city in SW Florida, on Sarasota Bay off the Gulf of Mexico, long noted as a winter base for circuses. Pop. 50,961.

**Sa·ras·va·ti River** |ˈsärəs,vətē| (also **Saraswati**) river in W India, flowing 120 mi. /195 km., from E of Palanpur in S Rajasthan state to Little Rann of Kutch, in Gujarat state.

**Sar·a·to·ga** |ˌsærəˈtōgə| agricultural city in W central California, SW of San Jose. Pop. 28,061.

**Sar·a·to·ga Springs** |ˈsærəˈtōgə| city in E New York, N of Albany, a spa noted for horse racing and for two battles fought nearby during the American Revolution. Pop. 25,001.

**Sa·ra·tov** |sə'rätəf| industrial city in SW Russia, on the Volga River N of Volgograd. Pop. 909,000.

**Sa·ra·wak** |sə'räwä(k)| state of Malaysia, comprising the NW part of Borneo. Pop. 1,669,000. Capital: Kuching.

**Sar·din·ia** |sär'dinēə| large (9,305 sq. mi./24,090 sq. km.) Italian island in the Mediterranean Sea to the W of Italy. Pop. 1,664,000. Capital: Cagliari. In 1720 it was joined with Savoy and Piedmont to form the kingdom of Sardinia; the kingdom formed the nucleus of the Risorgimento, becoming part of a unified Italy under Victor Emmanuel II of Sardinia in 1861. Italian name **Sardegna**.

**Sar·dis** |'särdəs| ancient city of Asia Minor, the capital of Lydia, whose ruins lie near the W coast of modern Turkey, to the NE of Izmir.

**Sar·gas·so Sea** |sär'gæsō| region of the W Atlantic between the Azores and the Caribbean, so called because of the prevalence in it of floating sargasso seaweed. It is the breeding place of eels from the rivers of Europe and E North America, and is known for its usually calm conditions.

**Sar·go·dha** |sər'gōdə| market city and rail junction in N central Pakistan. Pop. 294,000.

**Sarh** |sär| (formerly **Fort-Archambault**) city in S Chad, on the Chari River. Pop. 130,000. It is a cotton industry center.

**Sa·ri** |'särē| commercial and industrial port city in N Iran, near the Caspian Sea. Pop. 168,000.

**Sark** |särk| one of the British Channel Islands, lying to the E of Guernsey. A tourist destination, it has its own parliament.

**Sar·ma·tia** |sär'mäsHə| ancient region to the N of the Black Sea, extending originally from the Urals to the Don and inhabited by Slavic peoples. The term has also been used to refer to Poland. □ **Sarmatian** adj. & n.

**Sar·nath** |sär'nät| Buddhist shrine in N India, in Uttar Pradesh state, E of Varanasi. According to legend, Buddha gave his first sermon here, c.528 B.C.

**Sar·nia** |'särnēə| (offiical name **Sarnia-Clearwater**) industrial port in S Ontario, on Lake Huron and the St. Clair River. It is a major oil-industry center. Pop. 74,376.

**Sa·ron·ic Gulf** |sə'ränik| inlet of the Aegean Sea on the coast of SE Greece. Athens and the port of Piraeus lie on its N shores.

**Sarre** |sär| French name for the SAAR.

**Sarthe** |särt| **1** department in W France.

Pop.514,000. **2** river in NW France that flows 178 mi./285 km. S from the department of Orne past Le Mans to Angers, where it meets the Loir and the Mayenne rivers.

**Sar·um** |'særəm| old name for Salisbury, England, still used as the name of its diocese. See also OLD SARUM.

**Sa·se·bo** |'säsä‚bō| commercial and industrial port city in SW Japan, on W Kyushu. Pop. 245,000.

**Sas·katch·e·wan** |sə'skæCHəwən| prairie province of central Canada. Area: 251,866 sq. mi./652,330 sq. km. Pop. 994,000. Capital: Regina. Largest city: Saskatoon. Administered by the Hudson's Bay Company before 1870, it became part of the Northwest Territories, then, in 1905, a province. It is a major producer of grains.

**Sas·katch·e·wan River** |sə'skæCHəwən| river of Canada. Rising in two headstreams, the North and South Saskatchewan, in the Rocky Mts., it joins and flows E for 370 mi./596 km. to Lake Winnipeg. Its waters continue via the Nelson River to Hudson Bay.

**Sas·ka·toon** |‚sæskə'tōon| industrial city in S central Saskatchewan, in the Great Plains on the South Saskatchewan River. Pop. 186,060. It is the largest city in the province.

**Sas·sa·ri** |'säsəre| administrative and trade center in NW Sardinia, Italy, capital of Sassari province. Pop. 120,000.

**Sa·tsu·ma** |sæt'sōomə; 'sätsə‚mä| former province of SW Japan. It comprised the major part of the SW peninsula of Kyushu, also known as the Satsuma Peninsula.

**Sa·tu Ma·re** |'sätōo 'märə| transportation junction and city in NW Romania, capital of Satu Mare county, on the Someş River near the Hungarian border. It is the original home of the Satmar sect of Orthodox Jews. Pop. 138,000.

**Sau·di Ara·bia** |'sowdē ə'räbēə; 'sawdē| kingdom in SW Asia occupying most of the

Saudi Arabia

Arabian Peninsula. Area: 829,996 sq. mi./2.15 million sq. km. Pop. 15,431,000. Language, Arabic. Capital and largest city: Riyadh. Administrative capital: Jeddah. Largely desert, it is the birthplace of Islam in the 7th century. An independent kingdom since 1932, it was revolutionized in 1938 by the discovery of oil. Mecca, the Islamic holy city, draws millions of visitors annually. □ **Saudi Arabian** adj. & n. **Saudi** adj. & n.

**Sau·gus** |'sawgəs| town in E Massachusetts, a suburb N of Boston that was the site of the first U.S. ironworks (1646). Pop. 25,549.

**Sault Sainte Ma·rie** |ˌsoo ˌsänt mə'rē| each of two North American river ports that face each other across the falls of the St. Mary's River, between Lakes Superior and Huron. The N port (pop. 72,822) lies in Ontario, while the S port (pop. 14,700) is in Michigan. The region is popularly known as **the Soo**.

**Sau·mur** |sō'mYr| town in W central France, on the Loire River, in a wine-producing region. Pop. 32,000.

**Sau·sa·li·to** |ˌsawsə'lētō| city in NW California, across the Golden Gate from San Francisco. It is residential and has an artists' colony. Pop. 7,152.

**Sau·ternes** |sō'tern; sō'tərn| region in SW France, S of Bordeaux, known for its sweet white wines.

**Sa·va River** |'sävä| river (580 mi./930 km.) that rises in the Julian Alps of W Slovenia and flows SE through Croatia and Serbia to the Danube at Belgrade.

**Sa·vai'i** |sə'vī-ē| (also **Savaii**) mountainous volcanic island in the SW Pacific, the largest (700 sq. mi./1,813 sq. km.) of the Samoan islands.

**Sa·van·nah** |sə'vænə| industrial port in Georgia, just S of the border with South Carolina, on the Savannah River close to its outlet on the Atlantic. Pop. 137,560. It is noted for its 18th-century town design and architecture.

**Sa·vann·ah River** |sə'vænə| river that flows 315 mi./506 km., mostly along the border of Georgia and South Carolina, to reach the Atlantic near Savannah. Augusta, Georgia, lies on its course.

**Sa·van·na·khet** |sə,vänə'ket| (also **Savannaket**) town in S Laos, on the Mekong River at the border with Thailand. Pop. 51,000. It is a center for Thai-Lao trade.

**Sa·vo Island** |'sävō| volcanic island in the central Solomon Islands, in the SW Pacific, across Ironbottom Sound N of Guadal-

canal. Its waters were the scene of a defeat of U.S. naval forces by the Japanese in 1942.

**Sa·vo·na** |sə'vōnə| seaport in NW Italy, on the Gulf of Genoa, capital of Genoa province. Pop. 67,000.

**Sa·von·lin·na** |'sävawn,lẽnnə| resort town in SE Finland, noted for its opera festival. Pop. 29,000.

**Sa·voy** |sə'voi| area of SE France bordering on NW Italy, a former duchy ruled by the counts of Savoy from the 11th century. In 1720 it was joined with Sardinia and Piedmont to form the kingdom of Sardinia, but in 1861, when Sardinia became part of a unified Italy, Savoy was ceded to France. French name **Savoie**. □ **Savoyard** adj. & n.

**Sa·voy Theatre** |sə'voi| theater in London, England, famed especially for its presentations of operettas of Gilbert and Sullivan, whose devotees came to be called Savoyards. The name was repeated in such other sites as the Savoy Ballroom in Harlem, New York City.

**Sa·vu Sea** |'sävoo| part of the Indian Ocean that is encircled by the Indonesian islands of Sumba, Flores, Savu, and Timor, N of Australia.

**Sa·watch Range** |sə'wäCH| range of the Rocky Mts. in central Colorado that includes Mount Elbert, at 14,433 ft./4,399 m., the highest peak in the state and in the entire Rocky Mt. system.

**Saw·tooth Range** |'sawtōoTH| range of the N Rockies in S central Idaho, noted for its jagged peaks. It is a noted recreational area.

**Sa·xa Ru·bra** |ˌsæksə 'rōōbrə| town in ancient Etruria, N of Rome, Italy. In A.D. 312 the Emperor Constantine here defeated a rival, Maxentius, who drowned while crossing the Milvian Bridge. Legend holds that a sign then appeared in the sky that led Constantine to accept Christianity and to become emperor of the Western as well as of the Eastern Roman Empire.

**Sax·o·ny** |'sæksənē| **1** state in eastern central Germany. Its capital is Dresden. Pop. 5,000,000. **2** region and former kingdom of Germany, including the present-day states of Saxony in the SE, Saxony-Anhalt in the center, and Lower Saxony in the NW. German name **Sachsen**.

**Saxony-Anhalt** |'säksənē'änhält| state of Germany, on the plains of the Elbe and the Saale rivers. Pop. 2,823,000. Capital: Magdeburg. It corresponds to the former duchy of Anhalt and the central part of the former kingdom of Saxony. German name **Sachsen-Anhalt**.

**Sa·ya·ma** |sä'yämä| resort town and industrial center in E central Japan, on E central Honshu. Pop. 157,000.

**Sayre·ville** |'saər,vil; 'servil| industrial and residential borough in E New Jersey. Pop. 34,986.

**Sa·zan** |'sä,zän| (Italian name **Saseno**) island in SW Albania, in Vlorë Bay off the Gulf of Otranto (the Adriatic Sea). It was held by the Italians as a naval base 1914–47, and later used by Soviet and Chinese submarines.

**Sca·fell Pike** |'skaw,fel| mountain in the Lake District of NW England, in Cumbria. Rising to a height of 3,210 ft./978 m., it is the highest peak in England.

**Scan·di·na·via** |,skændə'nāvēə| **1** large peninsula in NW Europe, occupied by Norway and Sweden. It is bounded by the Arctic Ocean in the N, the Atlantic in the W, and the Baltic Sea in the S and E. **2** a cultural region consisting of the countries of Norway, Sweden, and Denmark and sometimes also of Iceland, Finland, and the Faroe Islands. □ **Scandinavian** adj. & n.

**Scapa Flow** |,skæpə 'flō| strait in the Orkney Islands, N Scotland. It was an important British naval base, especially in World War I. The German High Seas Fleet was interned here after its surrender, and was scuttled in 1919 as an act of defiance against the terms of the Versailles peace settlement.

**Scar·bor·ough**[1] |'skärb(ə)rə| fishing port and resort on the coast of North Yorkshire, England. Pop. 38,000.

**Scar·bor·ough**[2] |'skärb(ə)rə| industrial and residential city in S Ontario, part of metropolitan Toronto. Pop. 524,598.

**Scars·dale** |'skärz,dāl| residential town in SE New York, an affluent suburb of New York City. Pop. 16,987.

**Schaff·hau·sen** |SHäf'howzən| canton in N Switzerland, N of the Rhine River. Pop. 72,000. Its capital is Schaffhausen.

**Schaum·burg** |'SHawm,bərg| residential and industrial village in NE Illinois, a suburb NW of Chicago. Pop. 68,586.

**Scheldt** |skelt| river of N Europe. Rising in N France, it flows 270 mi./432 km. through Belgium and the Netherlands to the North Sea. Also called **Schelde**; French name **Escaut**.

**Sche·nec·ta·dy** |skə'nektədē| industrial city in E New York, NW of Albany. Pop. 65,566. It is a center of electrical and related industries.

**Schip·hol** |'SHip,ōl| see AMSTELVEEN, Netherlands.

**Schles·wig** |'SHles,viKH| former Danish duchy, in the S part of the Jutland peninsula. Taken by Prussia in 1866, it was incorporated with the neighboring duchy of Holstein as the province of Schleswig-Holstein. The N part of Schleswig was returned to Denmark in 1920 after a plebiscite held in accordance with the Treaty of Versailles.

**Schleswig-Holstein** |'SHles,viKH 'hōl ,SHtīn| state of NW Germany, occupying the S part of the Jutland peninsula. Pop. 2,649,000. Capital: Kiel.

**Schmal·kal·den** |'SHmäl,käldən| town in central Germany. Pop. 18,000. It has been a center of metalworking since the Middle Ages. In 1531 Protestant princes met here to form the Schmalkaldic League to fight against the Holy Roman Empire.

**Schön·brunn, Palace of** |'SHœn,broon| palace in Vienna, Austria, built in the late 17th–early 18th centuries as the summer residence of the Austrian emperor. In the Austrian Baroque style, it is graced by extensive gardens.

**Schuyl·kill River** |'skool,kil; 'skookəl| river that flows 130 mi./210 km. through E Pennsylvania, joining the Delaware River at Philadelphia.

**Schwa·ben** |'SHfäbən| German name for SWABIA.

**Schwä·bisch Gmünd** |'SHfebiSH 'gmʏnt| (also **Gmünd**) industrial city in SW Germany, to the E of Stuttgart. Pop. 56,000.

**Schwarz·wald** |'SHfärts,vält| German name for the BLACK FOREST.

**Schwein·furt** |'SHfīn,foort| industrial city in S Germany, in Bavaria. Pop. 55,000.

**Schweiz** |'SHfīts| German name for SWITZERLAND.

**Schwe·rin** |SHfä'rēn| industrial and commercial city in NE Germany, capital of Mecklenburg–West Pomerania, on the SW shore of Lake Schwerin. Pop. 126,000.

**Schwyz** |'SHfēts| city in central Switzerland, to the E of Lake Lucerne, capital of a canton of the same name. Pop. 13,000. The canton was one of the three original (13th-century) members of the Swiss Confederation, to which it gave its name.

**Scil·ly Isles** |'sili| (also **Isles of Scilly** or **the Scillies**) group of about 140 small islands (of which five are inhabited) off the SW tip of England. Pop. 3,000. Capital: Hugh Town (on St. Mary's). □ **Scillonian** adj. & n.

**Scone** |skoon| ancient Scottish settlement N of Perth, where the kings of medieval

Scotland were crowned on the Stone of Destiny. It is believed to be on the site of a Pictish capital.

**Sco•pus, Mount** |'skōpəs| peak in Israel, N of Jerusalem. It has long been of strategic importance in the defense of the city.

**Scores•by Sound** |'skawrzbē| inlet of the Greenland Sea in E central Greenland, noted for its fjords.

**Sco•tia** |'skōsHə| literary name for Scotland, from medieval Latin.

**Scot•land** |'skätlənd| country forming the northernmost part of Great Britain and of the United Kingdom. Area: 29,805 sq. mi./77,167 sq. km. Pop. 4,957,300. Capital: Edinburgh. Largest city: Glasgow. Peopled by Celts who resisted Roman and later English domination, Scotland finally became part of the United Kingdom in 1707. It produces textiles, timber, whisky, and foods. North Sea oil and tourism are also important. □ **Scottish** adj. **Scot** n.

**Scot•land Yard** |'skätlənd| headquarters of the London Metropolitan Police, in England, originally in Great Scotland Yard, off Whitehall in Westminster, later in two different locations called New Scotland Yard.

**Scot•tish Borders** |'skätisH| administrative region of S Scotland; administrative center, Melrose.

**Scotts•bluff** |'skäts,bləf| commercial city in W Nebraska. Pop. 13,711. It is named for a nearby promontory that was a pioneer landmark.

**Scotts•dale** |'skäts,dāl| city in S central Arizona, a suburb E of Phoenix. Pop. 130,069. Taliesin West, the architectural school of Frank Lloyd Wright, is here.

**Scran•ton** |'skræntn| industrial city in NE Pennsylvania, a steel center in the anthracite-mining region. Pop. 81,805.

**Scroo•by** |'skrŏŏbē| village in central England, in N Nottinghamshire, the original home of several of the Pilgrims.

**Scun•thorpe** |'skən,THawrp| industrial town in NE England, in North Lincolnshire. Pop. 60,000.

**Scu•ta•ri¹** |'skŏŏtərē| Italian name for SHKODËR, Albania.

**Scu•ta•ri²** |'skŏŏtərē| former name for Üsküdar, near Istanbul, Turkey, site of a British army hospital in which Florence Nightingale worked during the Crimean War.

**Scyth•ia** |'siTHēə| ancient region of SE Europe and Asia. The Scythian Empire, which existed between the 8th and 2nd centuries B.C., was centered on the N shores of the Black Sea and extended from S Russia to the border of Persia. □ **Scythian** adj. & n.

**Sea Islands** |'sē| chain of islands off the Atlantic coast of N Florida, Georgia, and South Carolina. They include many resorts and nature preserves, and are noted for their African-derived Gullah culture.

**Seal Beach** |'sēl| city in SW California, just SE of Long Beach. Pop. 25,098.

**Sea•ly•ham** |'sēlēəm| location in S Wales, in Dyfed, S of Fishguard, that gave its name to a breed of terrier.

**Sea of Azov, Sea of Galilee, etc.** see AZOV, SEA OF; GALILEE, SEA OF; etc.

**Sears Tower** |sirz| office building in Chicago, Illinois, formerly the tallest occupied structure in the world, at 1,454 ft./443 m.

**SEATO** |'sētō| see SOUTHEAST ASIA TREATY ORGANIZATION.

**Se•at•tle** |sē'ætəl| port and industrial city in the state of Washington, on the E shore of Puget Sound. Pop. 516,259. First settled in 1852, it is now the largest city in the NW U.S. Aircraft manufacturing, commerce, and tourism are important.

**Se•bas•to•pol** |sə'bæstə,pōl| fortress and naval base in Ukraine, near the S tip of the Crimea. Pop. 361,000. The focal point of military operations during the Crimean War, it fell to Anglo-French forces in September 1855 after a year-long siege. Russia and Ukraine have recently disputed control and use of its harbor. Ukrainian and Russian name **Sevastopol**.

**Se•bring** |'sēbriNG| city in S central Florida. Pop. 8,900. In an agricultural area, it is a famed home to sports car racing.

**Se•cau•cus** |si'kawkəs| industrial town in NE New Jersey. Pop. 14,061. It is noted for its warehouses and outlet stores.

**Sec•ond City** nickname for CHICAGO.

**Se•cun•der•a•bad** |si'kəndərə,bäd; si 'kəndərə,bäd| (also **Sikandarabad**) city in S central India, in Andhra Pradesh state. Pop. 136,000. Once one of the largest British military stations in India, it is now a major Indian army base.

**Se•da•lia** |si'dālyə| industrial and commercial city in W central Missouri. Pop. 19,800.

**Se•dan** |sə'dän| town in NE France, on the Meuse River. Pop. 22,000. The decisive battle of the Franco-Prussian War took place here in 1870; the French defeat led to the end of the Second Empire. The town has been a textile center since the 16th century.

**Se·do·na** |si'dōnə| resort city in N central Arizona, a popular New Age center. Pop. 7,720.

**Se·go·via** |sə'gōvēə| city in N central Spain, NE of Madrid. Pop. 58,000. Taken by the Moors in the 8th century, it was reclaimed by Castile in 1079, and was long a royal residence.

**Sei·kan Tunnel** |'sā,kän| rail tunnel in Japan, joining the islands of Honshu and Hokkaido. Completed in 1988, it is the longest underwater tunnel in the world: 32.3 mi./51.7 km.

**Seine** |sān; sen| river of N France. Rising N of Dijon, it flows NW for 473 mi./761 km., through the cities of Troyes and Paris to the English Channel near Le Havre.

**Sekondi-Takoradi** |'sekən'dē ,täkə'rädē| joint city and industrial seaport in SW Ghana, on the Gulf of Guinea. It is capital of the W region of Ghana, and one of the most important W African ports. Pop. 615,000.

**Se·lang·or** |sə'läNGɔor| state of Malaysia, on the W coast of the Malay Peninsula. Capital: Shah Alam.

**Sel·borne** |'sel,bawrn| village in S England, in Hampshire, the home of 18th-century naturalist Gilbert White.

**Selebi-Phikwe** |sə'läbē'pē,kā| mining town in E Botswana, S of Francistown. Pop. 40,000.

**Se·len·ga River** |,siliNG'gä| river in Mongolia and Russia, flowing 980 mi./1,568 km. from NW Mongolia to Lake Baikal in Russia.

**Se·leu·cia** |sə'lōōSHə| ancient city on the Tigris River, just S of present-day Baghdad, Iraq, a capital of the Seleucid Empire from the 4th century B.C. to the 2nd century A.D.

**Sel·kirk Mountains** |'sel,kərk| range of the Rocky Mts. in British Columbia, between the Monashees (W) and the Purcells (E).

**Sel·kirk·shire** |'sel,kərkSHər; 'säl,kərk-,SHīr| former county of SE Scotland. It was made a part of Borders region (now Scottish Borders) in 1975.

**Sel·la·field** |'selə,fēld| the site of a nuclear power station and reprocessing plant on the coast of Cumbria in NW England. It was the scene in 1957 of a fire that caused a serious escape of radioactive material. Former name (1947–81) **Windscale.**

**Sel·ma** |'selmə| industrial city in S central Alabama, on the Alabama River. Pop. 23,755.

**Se·ma·rang** |sə'mär,äNG| port and commercial and industrial city in Indonesia, on the N coast of Java. Pop. 1,249,000.

**Se·mei** |'semä| (also **Semey**) industrial city and river port in E Kazakhstan, on the Irtysh River close to the border with Russia. Pop. 339,000. Founded in the 18th century, it was known as Semipalatinsk until 1991.

**Se·me·ru** |sə'merōō| (also called **Mahemeru; Mahameroe**) volcanic peak in Indonesia, at the E end of the island of Java and the island's highest point: 12,060 ft./3,676 m.

**Se·mi·pa·la·tinsk** |,semēpə'lätinsk| former name (until 1991) for SEMEI, Kazakhstan.

**Sem·me·ring Pass** |'semməriNG| mountain pass in the E Alps of Austria that connects the states of Styria and Lower Austria. The Semmeringbahn, built 1848–54, was the first major mountain railroad in Europe.

**Sen·dai** |sen'dī| industrial and university city in Japan, near the NE coast of Honshu. Pop. 918,000. It is the capital of the region of Tohoku.

**Sen·e·ca Falls** |'senikə| town in W central New York, W of Cayuga Lake. Pop. 9,384. It was the scene in 1848 of the first women's rights convention in the U.S.

**Sen·e·ca Lake** |'senikə| largest of the Finger Lakes in W central New York. Geneva is on its N, Watkins Glen on its S.

**Sen·e·gal** |,seni'gawl| republic on the coast of W Africa. Area: 75,984 sq. mi./196,722 sq. km. Pop. 7,632,000. Languages, French (official), Wolof, and other W African languages. Capital and largest city: Dakar. Part of the medieval Mali Empire, Senegal was controlled by the French before independence in 1959. Largely rural and semidesert, it almost encloses the Gambia. □ **Senegalese** adj. & n.

**Sen·e·gal River** |,seni'gawl| (also **Sénégal**) river of W Africa whose headstreams

Senegal

are in the Fouta Djallon of N Guinea. It flows 680 mi./1,088 km., through Mali and then along the Senegal-Mauritania border, to the Atlantic at St.-Louis, Senegal.

**Sen·e·gam·bia** |ˌseni'gämbēə| **1** region of W Africa consisting of the Senegal and Gambia rivers and lands between them, mostly in Senegal and W Mali. **2** short-lived (1982–89) confederation of Senegal and the Gambia. □ **Senegambian** *adj. & n.*

**Seoul** |sōl| the capital of South Korea, in the NW of the country on the Han River. Pop. 10,628,000. It was the capital of the Yi dynasty from the late 4th century until 1910, when Korea was annexed by the Japanese. Extensively developed under Japanese rule, it became the capital of South Korea after the partition of 1945. It is a world industrial, financial, and commercial center.

**Se·quoia National Park** |si'kwoiə| preserve in the Sierra Nevada of California, E of Fresno. It was established in 1890 to protect groves of giant sequoia trees, of which the largest, the General Sherman Tree, is though to be between 3,000 and 4,000 years old.

**Se·raing** |sənreN| industrial town in Belgium, on the Meuse River just SW of Liège. Pop. 61,000.

**Ser·am·pore** |'serəm,pawr| (also **Serampur; Shrirampur**) industrial town in E India, West Bengal state. Pop. 137,000. It originated as a Danish settlement in the 18th century.

**Ser·bia** |'sərbēə| republic in the Balkan Peninsula, part of Yugoslavia. Area: 34,129 sq. mi./88,361 sq. km. Pop. 9,660,000. Language, Serbo-Croat. Capital and largest city: Belgrade. Serbian name **Srbija.** Independent by the 6th century, Serbia was dominated by the Turks from the 14th century until 1878. From World War I until 1991, it was the dominant partner in Yugoslavia; today only Montenegro remains in the Yugoslav confederation with Serbia. Recent decades have seen strife with neighboring Croatia and Bosnia, and within Serbia with the nominally autonomous regions of Kosovo (largely Albanian) and Vojvodina (largely Hungarian). □ **Serbian** *adj. & n.* **Serb** *n.*

**Se·rem·ban** |sə'rembən| the capital of the state of Negri Sembilan in Malaysia, in the SW of the Malay Peninsula. Pop. 136,000.

**Ser·en·dib** |'serən,dib| see SRI LANKA.

**Ser·en·ge·ti** |ˌserən'getē| vast plain in Tanzania, to the W of the Great Rift Valley. In 1951 the Serengeti National Park was cre-

ated to protect the area's large numbers of wildebeest, zebra, and Thomson's gazelle.

**Ser·gi·pe** |serzHēpē| state in E Brazil, on the Atlantic coast. Pop. 1,492,000. Capital: Aracajú.

**Ser·gi·yev Po·sad** |sir'gyāyif pä'säd| (formerly **Zagorsk**) industrial town in W Russia, NE of Moscow. Pop. 115,000.

**Ser·pu·khov** |ser'pōŏkəf| industrial city in W Russia, S of Moscow, on the Oka River. Pop. 145,000.

**Ses·tos** |'sestōs| ancient town in present-day European Turkey, on the N side of the Dardanelles narrows opposite ABYDOS. The Persian king Xerxes attempted to bridge the strait here to attack Greece in the 5th century B.C.

**Sète** |set| (formerly **Cette**) town in S France, in Languedoc, on the Mediterranean Sea. Pop. 42,000. It is a major commercial and fishing port and a shipping center, with canals running through the town.

**Sé·tif** |sä'tēf| commercial and industrial city in NE Algeria. Pop. 170,000. It was a center of a 1945 uprising against French colonial rule.

**Se·tú·bal** |sə'tōōbəl| port and industrial town on the coast of Portugal, S of Lisbon. Pop. 84,000.

**Se·vas·to·pol** |se'västə,pōl| Russian name for SEBASTOPOL, Ukraine.

**Sev·en Hills** |'sevən| original site of the city of Rome, Italy. The hills are the Aventine, Caelian, Capitoline, Esquiline, Palatine, Quirinal, and Viminal. According to legend, the city was founded by Romulus on the Palatine hill in 753 B.C. The name Seven Hills has since been applied to prominences in such cities as San Francisco, California, and to regions like the Siebengebirge of Germany.

**Sev·en Wonders of the World** (also **Seven Wonders of the Ancient World**) traditional list of the most spectacular man-made structures in the world, dating from the 2nd century and usually comprising the Pyramids of Egypt; the Hanging Gardens of Babylon; the Mausoleum of Halicarnassus; the Temple of Diana at Ephesus; the Colossus of Rhodes; the statue of Zeus at Olympia; and the Pharos at Alexandria.

**Sev·ern** |'sevərn| river of SW Britain. Rising in central Wales, it flows NE, then S, in a broad curve for some 180 mi./290 km. to its mouth on the Bristol Channel. The estuary is spanned by a suspension bridge N of Bristol, opened in 1966, and a second bridge a few miles to the S, opened in 1996.

**Se·ver·na·ya Zem·lya** |'syevirnəyə zemlē

'ä| group of uninhabited islands in the Arctic Ocean off the N coast of Russia, to the N of the Taimyr Peninsula.

**Se·ve·ro·do·netsk** |ˌsyevirədə'netsk| city in SE Ukraine, NW of Lugansk. Pop. 132,000.

**Se·ve·rod·vinsk** |ˌsyevirəd'vinsk| industrial port in NW Russia, on the White Sea coast W of Archangel. Pop. 250,000.

**Se·vier River** |sə'vir| river that flows 325 mi./525 km. through central Utah, irrigating the E edge of the Great Basin.

**Se·ville** |sə'vil| industrial port city in S Spain, the capital of Andalusia, on the Guadalquivir River. Pop. 683,000. A leading cultural center of Moorish Spain, it was reclaimed by the Spanish in 1248, and rapidly became prominent as a center of trade with the colonies of the New World. Spanish name **Sevilla**.

**Sè·vres** |'sevrə| town and SW suburb of Paris, in N central France. Pop. 22,000. Sèvres produced fine porcelains especially during the 18th and 19th centuries.

**Sew·ard Peninsula** |'sōōərd| region of NW Alaska on the Bering Strait and the Chukchi Sea. Nome lies on its S coast.

**Sey·chelles** |sā'sHel(z)| (also **the Seychelles**) republic consisting of a group of about ninety islands in the SW Indian Ocean, about 600 mi./1,000 km. NE of Madagascar. Land area: 175 sq. mi./453 sq. km. Pop. 69,000. Languages, French Creole (official), English, French. Capital: Victoria (on Malé island). Uninhabited but known to Arab traders, the islands were annexed by France in the 18th century. The British took control during the Napoleonic Wars. Independence came in 1976. Tourism, fishing, and copra and spice production are important. □ **Seychellois** *adj. & n.*

Seychelles

**Sey·han** |sā'hän| river that flows 350 mi./560 km. through central Turkey to the Mediterranean Sea. Adana is on its course.

**Sfax** |sfæks| (also **Safaqis**) port on the E coast of Tunisia. Pop. 231,000. It is a center for the region's phosphate industry.

**'s Graven·hage** Dutch name for THE HAGUE.

**Shaan·xi** |'sHän'sHē| (also **Shensi**) mountainous province of central China. Pop. 32,880,000. Capital: Xi'an. It is the site of the earliest settlements of the ancient Chinese civilizations.

**Sha·ba** |'sHäbə| copper-mining region of SE Congo (formerly Zaire). Capital: Lubumbashi. Former name (until 1972) **Katanga**. The most populous Congolese region, and a major cobalt producer, it has been subject to repeated secessionist pressures.

**Shah Alam** |'sHä 'äläm| the capital of the state of Selangor in Malaysia, near the W coast of the Malay Peninsula. Pop. 24,000.

**Shah·ja·han·pur** |ˌsHäjə'hän,poor| commercial city in N central India, in Uttar Pradesh state. Pop. 260,000. It was founded by and named for the Mogul emperor Shah Jahan (1647).

**Shak·er Heights** |'sHäkər| city in NE Ohio, an affluent suburb E of Cleveland. Pop. 30,831.

**Shakh·ty** |'sHäkti| coal-mining city in SW Russia, in the Donets Basin NE of Rostov. Pop. 227,000.

**Shan** |sHän| state in E central Burma. Pop. 3,719,000. Its people are mostly Shans, whose Shan States flourished in much of this area between the 12th and 16th centuries.

**Shan·dong** |'sHän'dooNG| (formerly **Shantung**) province in E China, on the Yellow Sea. Pop. 84,890,000. Capital: Jinan. It is a leading industrial and agricultural province.

**Shan·dong Peninsula** |'sHän'dooNG| peninsula in E Shandong province, NE China, separating the Bo Hai from the Yellow Sea. It is the largest peninsula in China.

**Shang·hai** |'sHæNG,hī; sHæNG'hī| city on the E coast of China, a port on the estuary of the Yangtze. Pop. 7,780,000. Opened for trade with the W in 1842, Shanghai contained until World War II areas of British, French, and American settlement. It was the site in 1921 of the founding of the Chinese Communist Party. It is now China's most populous city.

**Shang·qiu** |'sHänCHē'ōō| city in NE Henan province, E China, SE of Zhengzhou. Pop. 165,000. It was the site of a Northern Song (Sung) dynasty imperial residence.

**Shangri-La** |ˌSHæNGgrəˈlä| Tibetan utopia in the 1933 novel *Lost Horizon* by James Hilton. The name has been applied to various retreats from worldly care, notably CAMP DAVID, the presidential resort in Maryland.

**Shan·kill Road** |ˈSHæNGkil| road in the Protestant neighborhoods of Belfast, Northern Ireland, parallel to Falls Road, which passes through Roman Catholic neighborhoods to the N.

**Shan·non** |ˈSHænən| the longest river of Ireland. It rises in County Leitrim near Lough Allen and flows 240 mi./390 km. S and W to its estuary on the Atlantic. Near its mouth, W of Limerick, is the international airport also called Shannon.

**Shan·si** |ˈSHänˈSHē| see SHANXI, China.

**Shan·tou** |ˈSHänˈtō| port in the province of Guangdong in SE China, on the South China Sea at the mouth of the Han River. Pop. 860,000. It was designated a treaty port in 1869. Former name **Swatow**.

**Shan·tung** |ˈSHänˈdəNG| see SHANDONG, China.

**Shan·tung Peninsula** |ˈSHänˈdəNG| see SHANDONG PENINSULA, China.

**Shan·xi** |ˈSHänˈSHē| (also **Shansi**) a province of N central China, to the S of Inner Mongolia. Pop. 28,760,000. Capital: Taiyuan.

**Shao·guan** |ˈSHowˈgwän| city in Guangdong province, S China, on the Bei River N of Guangzhou (Canton). Pop. 350,000.

**Shao·xing** |ˈSHowˈSHiNG| commercial city in Zhejiang province, E China, in a rice-growing region on the Grand Canal SE of Hangzhou. Pop. 180,000.

**Shao·yang** |ˈSHowˈyäNG| city in Hunan province, SE central China, SW of Changsha. Pop. 247,000. It is a coal- and iron-mining center.

**Shar·jah** |ˈSHärjə| **1** one of the seven member states of the United Arab Emirates. Pop. 400,000. Arabic name **Ash Shariqah**. **2** its capital city, on the Persian Gulf. Pop. 125,000.

**Sharm al-Sheikh** |ˈSHärm ælˈSHäk| (also **Ras Nasrani**) cape at the S of the Sinai Peninsula, NE Egypt. Its commanding position on the Gulf of Aqaba led to fighting between Egyptian and Israeli forces in 1956 and 1967. Israel occupied it 1967–82.

**Shar·on** |ˈSHærən| fertile coastal plain in Israel, lying between the Mediterranean Sea and the hills of Samaria.

**Sha·shi** |ˈSHäˈSHē| inland port and commercial center in Hubei province, E central China, on the Yangtze River W of Wuhan. Pop. 281,000.

**Shas·ta, Mount** |ˈSHæstə| peak in N California, the highest point (14,162 ft./4,317 m.) in the Cascade Range within the state. Recreational Shasta Lake lies on its S.

**Shatt al-Arab** |ˈSHæt æl ˈærəb| river of SW Asia, formed by the confluence of the Tigris and Euphrates and flowing 120 mi./195 km. through SE Iraq to the Persian Gulf. Its lower course forms the border between Iraq and Iran.

**Sha·win·i·gin** |SHəˈwinəgən| industrial city in S Quebec, on the St.-Maurice River N of Trois-Rivières. Pop. 19,931.

**Shaw·mut Peninsula** |ˈSHawmət| promontory on which the city of Boston, Massachusetts was founded in the 1630s. Beacon Hill is the only survivor of the three that gave the settlement its early name, Trimountaine.

**Shaw·nee**[1] |SHawˈnē; SHäˈnē| city in NE Kansas, a suburb SW of Kansas City. Pop. 37,993.

**Shaw·nee**[2] |SHawˈnē; SHäˈnē| industrial city in central Oklahoma, in an oil- and gas-producing region. Pop. 26,017.

**She·ba** |ˈSHēbə| the biblical name of Saba, in SW Arabia. The queen of Sheba visited King Solomon in Jerusalem (1 Kings 10).

**She·boy·gan** |SHiˈboigən| industrial city in E Wisconsin, a port on Lake Michigan. Pop. 49,676.

**Shef·field** |ˈSHefˌēld| industrial city in N England, formerly in Yorkshire. Pop. 500,000. Sheffield is famous for the manufacture of cutlery and silverware and for the production of steel.

**Shel·ton** |ˈSHeltn| industrial city in SW Connecticut. Pop. 35,418.

**Shen·an·do·ah National Park** |ˌSHenən-ˈdōə| national park in the Blue Ridge Mts. of N Virginia, to the SE of the Shenandoah River.

**Shen·an·do·ah River** |ˌSHenənˈdōə| river of Virginia, rising in two headstreams, one on each side of the Blue Ridge Mts., and flowing some 150 mi./240 km. N to join the Potomac at Harpers Ferry, West Virginia. Its valley is famed for its beauty and Civil War history.

**Shen·si** |ˈSHenˈSHē| see SHAANXI, China.

**Shen·yang** |ˈSHenˈyäNG| city in NE China. Pop. 4,500,000. An important Manchurian city between the 17th and early 20th centuries, it is now the capital of the province of Liaoning. Former name **Mukden**.

**Shen·zhen** |ˈSHenˈjen| industrial city in S China, just N of Hong Kong. Pop. 875,000.

**Shep·herd's Bush** |ˈʃHɛpərdz| largely residential district of W London, England, W of Kensington, noted as the site of BBC television studios.

**Sher·brooke** |ˈʃHər,brŏŏk| commercial and industrial city in S Quebec, in the Eastern Townships E of Montreal. Pop. 76,429.

**Sher·i·dan** |ˈʃHɛrədn| city in N central Wyoming. Pop. 13,900.

**Sher·man** |ˈʃHərmən| commercial and industrial city in NE Texas. Pop. 31,601.

**'s Her·to·gen·bosch** |sɛr,tôkHən,baws| commercial city in the S Netherlands, the capital of North Brabant. Pop. 92,000.

**Sher·wood Forest** |ˈʃHər,wŏŏd| former forest that covered much of Nottinghamshire, central England, associated with legends of Robin Hood. A few remnants are preserved.

**Shet·land Islands** |ˈʃHɛtlənd| (also **Shetland** or **the Shetlands**) group of about 100 islands off the N coast of Scotland, NE of the Orkneys, constituting the administrative region of Shetland. Pop. 22,000; chief town, Lerwick. Together with the Orkney Islands the Shetland Islands became a part of Scotland in 1472, having previously been ruled by Norway and Denmark. Noted for the production of knitwear, they have provided in the late 20th century a base for the North Sea oil and gas industries. □ **Shetlander** n.

**Shi·bam** |ʃHiˈbäm| commercial town in SE Yemen. A fortress town, it is noted for the height of its houses, which have from six to nine stories.

**Shick·shock Mountains** |ˈʃHik,ʃHäk| (French name **Monts Chic-Chocs**) range of the Appalachian Mts. that extends NE through the Gaspé Peninsula of Quebec.

**Shi·ga·tse** |ʃHiˈgätse| see XIGAZÊ, China.

**Shi·he·zi** |ʃHiˈhəd'zə| city in Xinjiang, NE China, in the N foothills of the Tian Shan mountains, W of Ürümqi. Pop. 300,000.

**Shi·jia·zhuang** |ˈʃHêjêˈäjöŏˈäNG| industrial city in NE China, capital of Hebei province. Pop. 1,320,000.

**Shi·ko·ku** |ʃHiˈkôkŏŏ| the smallest (7,260 sq. mi./18,795 sq. km.) of the four main islands of Japan, constituting an administrative region. Pop. 4,195,000. Capital: Matsuyama. It is divided from Kyushu to the W and S Honshu to the N by the Inland Sea.

**Shi·li·gu·ri** |ʃHiˈlē,gŏŏrē| town in E India, in West Bengal state, SSE of Darjeeling. Pop. 227,000.

**Shil·le·lagh** |ʃHəˈlälē| village in SE Ireland,

in County Wicklow, that gave its name to a cudgel made from a kind of oak or blackthorn that grows locally.

**Shil·long** |ʃHəˈlawNG| city in the far NE of India, capital of the state of Meghalaya. Pop. 131,000.

**Shi·loh**[1] |ˈʃHilō| biblical place where the Ark of the Covenant was kept after Canaan was conquered. Present-day Khirbat Saylun, in the Israeli-occupied West Bank N of Jerusalem, is on the site.

**Shi·loh**[2] |ˈʃHilō| historic site in SW Tennessee, near Pittsburg Landing on the Tennessee River, scene of a major Civil War battle in April 1862.

**Shi·ma·ba·ra** |ʃHiˈmä,bärä| (also **Simabara**) city in SW Japan, on the Shimabara Peninsula on NW Kyushu. Pop. 45,000.

**Shi·mi·zu** |ʃHiˈmēzŏŏ| port city in E central Japan, on the S coast of central Honshu. Pop. 242,000.

**Shi·mo·da** |ʃHiˈmōdä| port city in E central Japan, in central Honshu. Pop. 30,000. The first U.S. consulate to Japan was opened here in 1856.

**Shi·mo·no·se·ki** |ˈʃHimōnō,sekē| industrial port city in W Japan, at the extreme SW of Honshu. Pop. 263,000.

**Ship·ka Pass** |ˈʃHipkä| pass through the Balkan Mts., central Bulgaria, near which Russian and Bulgarian forces won a major victory over the Turks in 1878.

**Ship·rock** |ˈʃHipräk| eroded volcanic feature that stands above the desert in NW New Mexico near the Four Corners. It was sacred to the Navajo and a landmark for travelers.

**Shi·raz** |ʃHiˈräz| city in S central Iran. Pop. 965,000. It is noted for the school of miniature painting based here between the 14th and 16th centuries, and for the manufacture of carpets and wine.

**Shire River** |ˈʃHir,ä| (also **Shiré**) river that flows 250 mi./400 km. from Lake Malawi in Malawi into Mozambique, where it joins the Zambezi River. The **Shire Highlands** on the E side in Malawi, are a fertile agricultural area.

**Shi·shou** |ˈʃHiˈʃHō| city in Hubei province, E central China, on the Yangtze River S of Shashi. Pop. 558,000.

**Shit·tim** |ˈʃHitəm| biblical land, E of Jericho, where the Israelites stopped before reaching the Promised Land.

**Shi·yan** |ˈʃHiˈyän| city in N Hubei province, E central China, on the Wudang Shan range W of the Danjiangkou Reservoir. Pop. 274,000.

**Shi·zu·o·ka** |,ʃHizŏŏˈōkä| port on the S

coast of the island of Honshu in Japan. Pop. 472,000.

**Shko·dër** |'sHKōdər| city in NW Albania, near the border with Montenegro. Pop. 82,000. Italian name **Scutari**.

**Shkum·bin River** |sHKŏŏm'bin| river that flows across central Albania, from near Lake Ohrid, past Elbasan, to the Adriatic Sea. It divides the country between Gheg speakers to the N and Tosk speakers to the S.

**Sho·la·pur** |'sHōlə,pŏŏr| city in W India, a textile center on the Deccan plateau in the state of Maharashtra. Pop. 604,000.

**Show Me State** |'sHō mē| nickname for MISSOURI.

**Shreve·port** |'sHrēv,pawrt| industrial city in NW Louisiana, on the Red River near the border with Texas. Pop. 198,525. Founded in 1839, it grew rapidly after the discovery of oil and gas in the region in 1906.

**Shrews·bury** |'sHrōōz,bərē| town in W England, the county seat of Shropshire, on the Severn River near the border with Wales. Pop. 59,000.

**Shrop·shire** |'sHräp,sHər| county of W England, on the border with Wales. Pop. 402,000; county seat, Shrewsbury. Also called **Salop**.

**Shuang·ya·shan** |'sHŏŏäNG'yä'sHän| city in Heilongjiang province, NE China, NE of Harbin and S of the Sungari (Songhua) River. Pop. 386,000.

**Shu·bra el Khei·ma** |'sHŏbrä el 'kämä| (also **Shubra al-Khayma**) city in NE Egypt, an industrial suburb N of Cairo. Pop. 812,000.

**Shu·men** |'sHŏŏ,men| industrial and cultural city in NE Bulgaria. Pop. 126,000.

**Shym·kent** |cHim'kent| (also **Chimkent**) **1** former administrative district of Kazakhstan, now called South Kazakhstan. Pop. 1,879,000. **2** its capital, an industrial city N of Tashkent. Pop. 438,000.

**Sia·chen Glacier** |'syäcHin| glacier in the Karakoram Mts. in NW India, at an altitude of some 17,800 ft./5,500 m. Extending over 44 mi./70 km., it is one of the world's longest glaciers.

**Si·al·kot** |sē'äkōt| industrial city in the province of Punjab, in Pakistan. Pop. 296,000.

**Si·am, Gulf of** |sī'æm| former name for the Gulf of Thailand (see THAILAND, GULF OF).

**Si·am** |sī'æm| former name (until 1939) for THAILAND. □ **Siamese** adj. & n.

**Siau·liai** |'sHow'lä| manufacturing city in N Lithuania, NW of Kaunas. Pop. 149,000.

**Ši·be·nik** |'sHēbenĕk| industrial city and port in Croatia, on the Adriatic coast. Pop. 41,000.

**Si·be·ria** |sī'birēə| vast region of Russia, including some three-quarters of the republic and extending from the Urals to Kamchatka in the Pacific and from the Arctic coast to the N borders of Kazakhstan, Mongolia, and China. It was occupied by the Russians in successive stages from 1581 when a Cossack expedition ousted the Tartar khanate of Sibir, which gave the region its name. After the opening in 1905 of the Trans-Siberian Railway, Siberia became more accessible and attracted settlers from European Russia. Noted for the severity of its winters, it was traditionally used as a place of exile; it is now a major source of minerals and hydroelectric power. □ **Siberian** adj. & n.

**Si·biu** |'sēbyŏŏ| industrial city in central Romania. Pop. 188,000.

**Si·bo·ney** |,sēbō'nā| town in E Cuba, in Santiago de Cuba province, with nearby Daiquiri the landing place of U.S. troops in 1898, during the Spanish-American War.

**Si·bu·yan** |,sēbŏŏ'yän| island in the central Philippines, in the Sibuyan Sea S of Luzon.

**Si·chuan** |'sī'cHwän| (also **Szechuan** or **Szechwan**) province of W central China. Pop. 107,220,000. Capital: Chengdu. Surrounded by mountains, it is largely agricultural. □ **Sichuanese** adj. & n.

**Si·ci·lia** |sē'cHēlyä; sī'silyə| Italian name for SICILY.

**Sic·i·lies, Kingdom of the Two** |'sisilēz| unification under one crown of Sicily and S Italy (the kingdom of Naples, or lands S of the Papal States), first effected in 1442, and last official in 1816–60.

**Sic·i·ly** |'sisilē| island, the largest (9,929 sq. mi./25,706 sq. km.) in the Mediterranean, off the SW tip of Italy. Pop. 5,197,000. Capital and largest city: Palermo. It is separated from the Italian mainland by the Strait of Messina and its highest point is the volcano Mount Etna. Settled successively by Phoenicians, Greeks, and Carthaginians, it became a Roman province in 241 B.C. after the first Punic War. It was conquered toward the end of the 11th century by the Normans, who united the island with S Italy as the kingdom of the Two Sicilies. Conquered by Charles of Anjou in 1266, the island subsequently passed to the House of Aragon. It was reunited with S Italy in 1442. The kingdom was claimed in 1816 by the Spanish Bourbon King Ferdinand, but was liberated in 1860 by Garibaldi and incorporated into the new state of Italy. Italian name **Sicilia**. ◻ **Sicilian** *adj. & n.*

**Si·di bel Ab·bès** |'sēdē bel ä'bes| commercial and industrial town in N Algeria, to the S of Oran. Pop. 186,000. It is the former home of the French Foreign Legion.

**Si·don** |'sīdn| port city in Lebanon, on the Mediterranean coast S of Beirut. Pop. 38,000. Founded in the 3rd millennium B.C., it was a Phoenician seaport and city-state. Arabic name **Saida**.

**Sid·ra, Gulf of** |'sidrə| (also **Gulf of Sirte**) broad inlet of the Mediterranean on the coast of Libya, between Benghazi and Misratah.

**Sie·ben·ge·bir·ge Mountains** |'sēbengebērge| mountain range in western Germany, on the Rhine River, SE of Bonn. The highest peak is the Grosser Olberg (1,509 ft./460 m.). The scenic region attracts many tourists.

**Sie·gen** |'sēgen| industrial town in western Germany, on the Sieg River, in an iron-producing region. Pop. 111,000.

**Sieg·fried Line** |'sēg,frēd| line of defensive fortification built in western Germany before World War II, facing the French Maginot Line and extending from the Swiss border on the S to Cleve on the N, generally parallel to the Rhine River. Allied forces first broke through the line in late 1944.

**Si·em Re·ap** |,sēəm 'reəp| town in NW Cambodia, on the Siem Reap River The ruins of the ancient city of Angkor are just to the N.

**Si·e·na** |sē'enə| commercial and cultural city in W central Italy, in Tuscany. Pop. 58,000. In the 13th and 14th centuries it was the center of a flourishing school of art. Its central square is the venue for the noted Palio horse race. ◻ **Sienese** *adj. & n.*

**Si·er·ra Le·one** |sē'erə lē'onē| republic on the coast of W Africa. Area: 27,709 sq. mi./71,740 sq. km. Pop. 4,239,000. Languages, English (official), English Creole, Temne, and other W African languages. Capital and largest city: Freetown. Coastal areas were controlled by the British from the late 18th century, inland areas in 1896. Independence came in 1961. Agriculture and mining are both important. ◻ **Sierra Leonean** *adj. & n.*

**Si·er·ra Mad·re** |sē'erə 'mädrə| mountain system in Mexico, extending from the border with the U.S. in the N to the S border with Guatemala. Regarded as an extension of the Rocky Mts., it reaches 18,697 ft./5,699 m. at CITLALTÉPETL, SE of Mexico City.

**Si·er·ra Ma·es·tra** |sē'erä mä'esträ| mountain range in SE Cuba, reaching 6,470 ft./1,972 m. at Pico Turquino. Forested and rich in minerals, the mountains are famous as the base of 1950s rebels under Fidel Castro.

**Si·er·ra Ne·va·da**[1] |sē'erə nə'vädə| mountain range in E California. Rising sharply from the Great Basin in the E, it descends more gently to California's Central Valley in the W. Its highest peak is Mount Whitney, which rises to 14,495 ft./4,418 m.

**Si·er·ra Ne·va·da**[2] |sē'erə nə'vädə| mountain range in S Spain, in Andalusia, SE of Granada. Its highest peak is Mulhacén, which rises 11,424 ft./3,482 m.

**Si·er·ra Ne·va·da de Mé·ri·da** |sē'erə nə-'vädə de 'meridä| (also **Cordillera de Mérida**) range of the Andes Mts. in NW Venezuela, reaching 16,420 ft./5,000 m. at Pico Bolívar, the highest peak in the country.

**Si·er·ra Ne·va·da de San·ta Mar·ta** |sē-'erə nə'vädə de 'sæntə 'märtə| mountain range in N Colombia, near the Caribbean Sea and the Venezuela border, reaching 19,020 ft./5,797 m. at Pico Cristóbal Colón, the highest peak in the country.

**Si·ghi·şoa·ra** |,sēgə'sHwärə| industrial and resort city in central Romania, in Transylvania. Pop. 38,000.

**Sig·ma·ring·en** |'sigmä,riNGən| city in SW Germany, on the Danube River. Pop. 16,000. Its castle became the home of the Hohenzollerns, rulers of Germany, in 1535.

**Si·ha·nouk·ville** |sē'hänʊʊk,vil| see KOMPONG SOM, Cambodia.

**Si·kang** |'sHē'käNG| former province (1928–55) in S China, now divided between Tibet and Sichuan.

**Si·king** |'sHē'kiNG| former name for XI'AN, China.

**Sik·kim** |'sikim| state of NE India, in the E Himalayas between Bhutan and Nepal, on the border with Tibet. Pop. 405,000. Cap-

Sierra Leone

ital: Gangtok. After British rule it became an Indian protectorate, becoming a state of India in 1975. □ **Sikkimese** *adj. & n.*

**Sil·ches·ter** |'sil,CHestər| village in Hampshire, S England, SW of Reading. It is the site of an important town of pre-Roman and Roman Britain, known to the Romans as Calleva Atrebatum.

**Si·le·sia** |sī'lēzhə| region of central Europe, centered on the upper Oder valley, now largely in SW Poland. It was partitioned at various times among the states of Prussia, Austria–Hungary, Poland, and Czechoslovakia. It is known for its coal deposits and forests. □ **Silesian** *adj. & n.*

**Sil·i·con Valley** |'silikən; 'silikän| name given to an area between San Jose and Palo Alto in Santa Clara County, California, noted for its computer and electronics industries.

**Silk Road** |'silk| (also **Silk Route**) ancient caravan route linking Xi'an in central China with the E Mediterranean. Skirting the N edge of the Taklimakan Desert and passing through Turkestan, it covered a distance of some 4,000 mi./6,400 m. It was established during the period of Roman rule in Europe, and took its name from the silk that was brought W from China. It was also the route by which Christianity spread E. A railway (completed in 1963) follows the Chinese part of the route, from Xi'an to Urumqi.

**Si·lo·am** |sī'lōəm| biblical spring and pool just SE of Jerusalem, from which water was drawn through a tunnel to the city.

**Sil·ver Spring** |'silvər| residential and commercial suburb in central Maryland, just N of Washington, D.C. Pop. 76,046.

**Sil·ver State** |'silvər| nickname for NEVADA.

**Sim·birsk** |sim'birsk| city in European Russia, a port on the Volga River SE of Nizhni Novgorod. Pop. 638,000. Between 1924 and 1992 it was called Ulyanovsk, in honor of Lenin (Vladimir Ilich Ulyanov), who was born here in 1870.

**Sim·coe, Lake** |'simkō| recreational lake in S Ontario, N of Toronto, in an agricultural area.

**Sim·fer·o·pol** |,simfə'rawpəl| city in the Crimea, Ukraine. Pop. 349,000. It was settled by the Tartars in the 16th century, when it was known as Ak-Mechet, and was seized in 1736 by the Russians.

**Si·mi Valley** |se'mē| city in SW California, a residential suburb NW of Los Angeles. Pop. 100,217.

**Sim·la** |'simlə| resort city in NE India, cap-

ital of the state of Himachal Pradesh. Pop. 110,000.

**Sim·plon** |'sim,plawn| pass in the Alps in S Switzerland, consisting of a road built by Napoleon 1801–5 at an altitude of 6,591 ft./2,028 m. and a railway tunnel (built in 1922) that links Switzerland and Italy.

**Simp·son Desert** |'sim(p)sən| desert in central Australia, situated between Alice Springs and the Channel Country to the E.

**Si·nai** |'sī,nī| (**the Sinai**) arid mountainous peninsula in NE Egypt, extending into the Red Sea between the Gulf of Suez and the Gulf of Aqaba. It was occupied by Israel between 1967 and 1982, when it was fully restored to Egypt following the Camp David agreement. In the S is Mount Sinai, where, according to the Bible, Moses received the Ten Commandments. □ **Sinaitic** *adj.*

**Si·na·loa** |,sēnə'lōə| state on the Pacific coast of Mexico. Area: 22,529 sq. mi./58,328 sq. km. Pop. 2,211,000. Capital: Culiacán Rosales.

**Sin·ce·le·jo** |,sēnsä'lähō| commercial city in N Colombia, the capital of Sucre department. Pop. 168,000.

**Sind** |sind| province of SE Pakistan, traversed by the lower reaches of the Indus. Pop. 21.68 million. Capital: Karachi.

**Si·nes** |'sēnisH| industrial port in SW Portugal, the birthplace of the explorer Vasco da Gama. Pop. 10,000.

**Sin·ga·pore** |'siNG(g)ə,pawr| republic in SE Asia consisting of the island of Singapore (linked by a causeway to the S tip of the Malay Peninsula) and some fifty-four smaller islands. Area: 239 sq. mi./618 sq. km. Pop. 3,045,000. Official languages, Malay, Chinese, Tamil, and English. Capital and largest city: Singapore City. An East India Company trading post from 1819, ruled by the British from 1867, Singapore gained independence in 1965, after two years as part of Malaysia. Long a commercial and naval hub, it remains a financial

**Singapore**

and trade center. □ **Singaporean** *adj. & n.*

**Si·ning** |'sē'niNG| see XINING, China.

**Sin·kiang** |'siNG'kyæNG| see XINJIANG, China.

**Si·nop** |sē'nōp| (ancient name **Sinope**) historic port town in N Turkey, the capital of Sinop province. Pop. 26,000. Founded by Ionian Greeks in the 8th century B.C., it was the birthplace of Diogenes, the Cynic philosopher.

**Sint Maar·ten** |sint 'märtin| Dutch name for ST. MARTIN, in the Antilles.

**Sint-Niklaas** |sint 'nēkläs| industrial town in N Belgium, SW of Antwerp. Pop. 68,000. French name **St. Nicolas**.

**Sin·tra** |'sintrə| (also **Cintra**) historic town in W Portugal, in a mountainous area NW of Lisbon. Pop. 20,000.

**Sin·ui·ju** |'sHi'nwē'jōō| industrial port city in North Korea, on the Yalu River near its mouth on the Yellow Sea. Pop. 500,000.

**Sioux City** |sōō| commercial and industrial city in NW Iowa, on the Missouri and Big Sioux rivers. Pop. 80,505.

**Sioux Falls** |sōō| largest city in South Dakota, a commercial and industrial center in the SE, on the Big Sioux River. Pop. 100,814.

**Si·ping** |'sə'piNG| city in Jilin province, NE China, SW of Changchun near Liaoning province. Pop. 317,000.

**Si·ra·cu·sa** |ˌsirə'kōōzə| Italian name for SYRACUSE.

**Sir·dar·yo** |sirdär'yō| river of central Asia. Rising in two headstreams in the Tien Shan mountains in E Uzbekistan, it flows for some 1,380 miles (2,220 km) W and NW through southern Kazakhstan to the Aral Sea. Russian name **Syr-Darya**.

**Si·ret River** |sē'ret| river (280 mi./448 km.) in Ukraine and Romania, rising in the Carpathian Mts. and flowing S to meet the Danube River near Galaţi.

**Sir·mio·ne** |sēr'myōnā| (formerly **Sermione**) resort and historic port on Sirmione Peninsula, N Italy, on the S shore of Lake Garda.

**Sis·ki·you Mountains** |'siski,yōō| forested range of the Klamath Mts. in NW California and SW Oregon.

**Sis·op·hon** |'sē'sō'pən| commercial town in W Cambodia, in a forested area near the border with Thailand.

**Sis·sing·hurst** |'sisiNG,hərst| estate in SE England, in Kent, noted in the 20th century as a literary retreat owned by Harold Nicolson and Victoria Sackville-West.

**Sis·tine Chapel** |'si,stēn| chapel in the Vat-

ican City, built by Pope Sixtus V, and best known for its ceiling, painted by Michelangelo.

**Sit·ka** |'sitkə| city in the Panhandle of SW Alaska, on Baranof Island. A historic trade center, it draws tourists. Pop. 8,588.

**Sit·tang** |'si,tāNG| river of S Burma. Rising in the Pegu Mts., it flows some 350 mi./560 km. S into the Bay of Bengal at the Gulf of Martaban.

**Sit·twe** |'sitwē| port and rice-milling center in W Burma. Pop. 108,000.

**Si·vas** |si'väs| (ancient name **Sebaste** or **Sebastea**) historic city in central Turkey, the capital of Sivas province, on the Kizil Irmak River. Pop. 222,000. Important under the Romans and Byzantines, it is industrial and commercial.

**Si·vash Sea** |si'væsH| (also known as **Putrid Sea**) area of marshes and salt lagoons in S Ukraine, in the N and NE Crimea.

**Si·wa·lik Hills** |si'wälik| range of foothills in the S Himalayas, extending from NE India across Nepal to Sikkim.

**Six Counties** |'siks| the counties of Northern Ireland: Antrim, Down, Armagh, Londonderry, Tyrone, and Fermanagh. Along with Cavan, Donegal, and Monaghan, now in the Irish Republic, they formed historic Ulster.

**Sjæl·land** |'sHe,län| Danish name for ZEALAND.

**Skag·er·rak** |'skægə,ræk| (also **the Skagerrak**) strait separating S Norway from the NW coast of Denmark. It links the Baltic Sea (SE) to the North Sea via the Kattegat.

**Skag·way** |'skæg,wā| city in SW Alaska, in the Panhandle. Pop. 692. A cruise ship port, it was a gateway to the 1897–98 Klondike gold rush.

**Skå·ne** |'skōne| (also known as **Scania**) historic province of S Sweden, now divided between Malmöhus and Kristianstad counties. It was formerly held by Denmark.

**Ska·ra Brae** |ˌskerə 'brä| Stone Age settlement on Mainland, in the Orkney Islands of Scotland, one of the leading prehistoric sites of N Europe.

**Skee·na River** |'skēnə| river that flows 360 mi./580 km. through central British Columbia to the Pacific.

**Skel·e·ton Coast** |'skeltən| arid coastal area in Namibia. Comprising the N part of the Namib Desert, it extends from Walvis Bay in the S to the border with Angola.

**Skel·ligs, the** |'skeligz| three rocky islands

off County Kerry, SW Ireland, formerly a noted pilgrimage site.

**Ski·a·thos** |'skĭə,THäs| Greek island in the Aegean Sea, the most westerly of the Northern Sporades group. Greek name **Skíathos**.

**Skid Row** |'skid 'rō| term for a marginal city district where alcoholics and drifters congregate. The original was Skid Road, where loggers gathered, in Seattle, Washington.

**Sko·kie** |'skōkē| residential and industrial village in NE Illinois, a suburb NW of Chicago. Pop. 59,432.

**Skop·je** |'skawpye; 'skawpyä| the capital of the republic of Macedonia, in the N on the Vardar River. Pop. 440,000. Founded by the Romans, it was controlled by the Turks for over 500 years before World War I.

**Skye** |'skī| mountainous island of the Inner Hebrides, recently linked to the W coast of Scotland by a bridge; chief town, Portree. It is the largest and most northerly island of the group.

**Sky·ros** |'skē,raw| island, largest of the Northern Sporades, in Greece, in the Aegean Sea.

**Slave Coast** |slāv| name given by Europeans to the coastal region of W Africa roughly from present-day Togo to the Niger River delta. This was the primary source of slaves in the 16th–19th centuries.

**Sla·vo·nia** |slä'vōnēə| historic region in Croatia. It was originally part of the Roman province of Pannonia, became a Slavic state, and was later dominated by Turkey.

**Slav·yansk** |'slävyänsk| (also **Slovyansk**) industrial city in E Ukraine, N of Donetsk. Pop. 137,000.

**Sleepy Hollow** |'slēpē| town in SE New York, E of the Hudson River and N of Tarrytown. It is associated with the writings of Washington Irving.

**Sli·dell** |slĭ'del| city in SE Louisiana, NE of New Orleans, noted as a center for science related to space exploration. Pop. 24,124.

**Sli·go** |'slīgō| **1** county of the Republic of Ireland, in the W in the province of Connacht. Pop. 55,000. **2** its county seat, a seaport on Sligo Bay, an inlet of the Atlantic. Pop. 17,000.

**Sli·ven** |'slēven| commercial city in E central Bulgaria, in the foothills of the Balkan Mts. Pop. 150,000.

**Slot, the** |'slät| name given in World War II by U.S. forces to New Georgia Sound, in the central Solomon Islands. Japanese

forces trying to defend Guadalcanal were seen as coming consistently down this passage from the NW.

**Slough** |sləf| industrial town in S central England, in Berkshire, W of London. Pop. 97,000.

**Slo·va·kia** |slō'väkēə| republic in central Europe. Area: 18,940 sq. mi./49,035 sq. km. Pop. 5,268,935. Language, Slovak. Capital and largest city: Bratislava. Slovak name **Slovensko**. Independent of Hungary in 1918, Slovakia joined Bohemia and Moravia to form Czechoslovakia, then became independent in 1993. Agricultural until World War II, it is increasingly industrial. □ **Slovak** adj. & n. **Slovakian** adj. & n.

**Slovakia**

**Slo·ve·nia** |slō'vēnēə| nearly landlocked republic in SE Europe, formerly a constituent republic of Yugoslavia. Area: 7,822 sq. mi./20,251 sq. km. Pop. 1,962,000. Language, Slovene. Capital and largest city: Ljubljana. Slavic since the 6th century, Slovenia was part of the Austrian Empire before 1919, when it was made part of what became Yugoslavia. In 1991 it became independent. Mineral-based industries and tourism are important. □ **Slovene** adj. & n.

**Słupsk** |'slo͞opsk| industrial city in N Poland, on the Slupia River. It is the capital of Słupsk county. Pop. 101,000.

**Slovinia**

**Smith·field**[1] |'smiTH,fēld| part of London, England, just NW of the City, noted as a site of meat and horse markets, scene of the annual Bartholomew Fair, and execution place.

**Smith·field**[2] |'smiTH,fēld| town in S Virginia, in the Tidewater, famed for its ham production. Pop. 4,686.

**Smith·so·ni·an Institution** foundation for scientific research, established in 1838 and based in Washington, D.C. It operates over a dozen museums and institutes in Washington and other cities.

**Smith·town** |'smiTH,town| residential town on the North Shore of Long Island, New York. Pop. 113,406.

**Smoky Hill River** |'smōkē 'hil| river that flows 540 mi./870 km. from Colorado across Kansas. Its valley was long a route for W migration.

**Smo·lensk** |smō'lensk| industrial city in E European Russia, on the Dnieper River close to the border with Belarus. Pop. 346,000.

**Smyr·na** |'smirnə; 'smərnə| ancient city on the W coast of Asia Minor, on the site of present-day Izmir, Turkey.

**Snake River** |'snāk| river of the NW U.S. Rising in Yellowstone National Park in Wyoming, it flows for 1,038 mi./1,670 km. through Idaho into the state of Washington, where it joins the Columbia River. Irrigation systems made its valley an important agricultural area.

**Sneek** |snāk| town in the Netherlands, a water-sports center with a large yachting harbor. Pop. 29,000.

**Snow·don** |'snōdən| mountain in NW Wales. Rising to 3,560 ft./1,085 m., it is the highest mountain in Wales. Welsh name **Yr Wyddfa**.

**Snow·do·nia** |snō'dōnēə| massif region in NW Wales, forming the heart of the Snowdonia National Park. Its highest peak is Snowdon.

**So·chi** |'sōCHē| Black Sea port and resort in SW Russia, in the W foothills of the Caucasus, close to the border with Georgia. Pop. 339,000.

**So·ci·e·ty Islands** |sə'sī,itē| group of islands in the S Pacific, forming part of French Polynesia. Pop. 163,000.

**So·co·tra** |sə'kōtrə| island in the Arabian Sea near the mouth of the Gulf of Aden. Capital: Tamridah. It is administered by Yemen.

**Sö·der·täl·je** |sədər'telyə| industrial W suburb of Stockholm, Sweden, on the Södertälje Canal. Pop. 82,000.

**Sod·om** |'sädəm| city of biblical Palestine, one of the Cities of the Plain, probably S of the Dead Sea, destroyed along with neighboring Gomorrah because of the wickedness of its inhabitants.

**So·fia** |sō'fēə| the capital, largest city, and industrial and cultural center of Bulgaria. Pop. 1,221,000. An ancient Thracian settlement, it became a province of Rome in the first century A.D. It was held by the Turks between the late 14th and late 19th centuries and became the capital of Bulgaria in 1879.

**Sogne Fjord** |'sawnə| fjord on the W coast of Norway. The longest and deepest fiord in the country, it extends inland for some 125 mi./200 km., with a maximum depth of 4,291 ft./1,308 m. Norwegian name **Sognafjorden**.

**So·ho**[1] |'sō,hō| commercial and entertainment district in the West End of London, England, around Soho Square, noted for its night life and long an immigrant quarter.

**So·Ho**[2] |'sō,hō| district of S Manhattan, New York City, famed for its artist-occupied industrial lofts and galleries. Its name derives from *So*uth of *Ho*uston Street.

**Sois·sons** |swäsawN| agricultural and industrial city in N France, on the Aisne River. Pop. 30,000. Settled by the Romans and an early religious center, it has been the site of many battles.

**So·ka** |'sōkä| city in E central Japan, on E central Honshu, a suburb NE of Tokyo. Pop. 206,000.

**So·ko·to** |sō'kōtō| industrial and commercial city in NW Nigeria, capital of Sokoto state, in a region once part of the Muslim Fulani Empire. Pop. 181,000.

**So·le·dad** |'sōlə,dæd| city in the Salinas Valley of W central California, home to a noted state prison. Pop. 7,146.

**So·lent** |'sōlənt| (also **the Solent**) channel between the NW coast of the Isle of Wight and the mainland of S England.

**So·leure** |sawlœr| French name for SOLOTHURN, Switzerland.

**So·li·hull** |,sōlə'həl| industrial and residential town in the West Midlands of England, forming part of the Birmingham metropolitan area . Pop. 95,000.

**So·li·kamsk** |səli'kämsk| town in central Russia, in the W foothills of the Ural Mts. Pop. 110,000.

**So·ling·en** |'zōliNGən; 'sōliNGən| industrial city in western Germany, in the Ruhr Valley, E of Düsseldorf. Pop. 166,000.

**Sol·o·mon Islands** |'säləmən| (also **the Solomons**) country consisting of a group

**Solomon Islands**

of islands in the SW Pacific, to the E of New Guinea. Area: 10,643 sq. mi./27,556 sq. km. Pop. 326,000. Languages, English (official), Pidgin, local Austronesian languages. Capital: Honiara (on Guadalcanal). Divided between Britain and Germany in the 19th century, with Australia replacing Germany in 1920, the islands became independent in 1978. They are sparsely populated and chiefly agricultural. The N part of the chain is part of Papua New Guinea. □ **Solomon Islander** *n.*

**So·lo·thurn** |'zōlə,toorn| **1** canton in NW Switzerland, in the Jura Mts. Pop. 227,000. French name **Soleure**. **2** its capital, a town on the Aare River. Pop. 15,000.

**So·lu·tré** |sôlətrā| (also called **Solutré-Pouilly**), village in E central France, in Burgundy. The area is known for its white wines. A site containing a rock shelter and a prehistoric burial, discovered here in 1867, gave a name to the Solutrean phase of the Paleolithic era.

**Sol·way Firth** |'sawlwä| inlet of the Irish Sea, separating Cumbria (in England) from Dumfries and Galloway (in Scotland).

**So·ma·lia** |sə'mälyə| republic in the Horn of Africa, NE Africa. Area: 246,294 sq. mi./637,657 sq. km. Pop. 8,041,000. Official languages, Somali and Arabic. Capital and largest city: Mogadishu. Controlled in parts by Britain and Italy, Somalia became

**Somalia**

independent in 1960. Civil war has beset the largely agricultural country since 1988. □ **Somali** *adj. & n.*

**So·ma·li Peninsula** |sə'mälē| another name for the HORN OF AFRICA.

**Som·er·set** |'səmər,set| county of SW England, on the Bristol Channel. Pop. 459,000; county seat, Taunton.

**Som·er·ville** |'səmər,vil| industrial and residential city in E Massachusetts, a suburb immediately NW of Boston. Pop. 76,210.

**Somme** |'sawm| river of N France. Rising E of Saint-Quentin, it flows 153 mi./245 km. through Amiens to the English Channel NE of Dieppe. The area around it was the scene of heavy fighting in World War I.

**Som·nath** |'sōmnät| (also called **Patan Somnath; Patan; Prabhas Patan**) port town in W central India, in Gujarat state. It is famous in Hindu mythology as the spot where Krishna was accidentally killed by a hunter's arrow.

**Song·hai Empire** |säNG'gī| (also **Songhay**) Berber, later Muslim, empire that flourished in the 8th–16th centuries along the Niger River. It was centered in present-day Mali, around Gao.

**Song·hua River** |'səNG'hwä| (Chinese name **Songhua Jiang**) see SUNGARI River, China.

**Song·nam** |'səNG'näm| city in NW South Korea, a suburb SE of Seoul. Pop. 869,000.

**So·no·ma County** |sə'nōmə| county in NW California, famed for its wineries and agriculture. Pop. 388,222.

**So·no·ra** |sə'nawrə| state of NW Mexico, on the Gulf of California. Area: 70,317 sq. mi./182,052 sq. km. Pop. 1,822,000. Capital: Hermosillo.

**So·no·ra Desert** |sə'nawrə| arid region of North America, comprising much SE California and SW Arizona in the U.S. and, in Mexico, much of Baja California and the W part of Sonora. The Mojave and Colorado deserts in California are extensions.

**Soo, the** |'soo| popular name for the region around and including the twin cities of Sault Ste. Marie, in Michigan and Ontario, from a pronunciation of *sault,* French for 'rapid.'

**Soo·chow** |'soo'chow| see SUZHOU, China.

**Soon·er State** |'soonər| nickname for OKLAHOMA, which was settled in part in the 1890s by those who arrived *sooner* than the official opening day for land claims.

**So·rac·te** |saw'räktē| isolated mountain in central Italy, NE of Rome. Height:

2,267ft./691 m. In ancient times there was a temple of Apollo at the top, and the mountain was mentioned in the poetry of Horace and Ovid.

**Sor·bonne, the** |sawr'bən; sawr'bawn| seat of the faculty of arts and letters of the University of Paris, in Paris, in N central France. The Sorbonne opened in 1253 on the Left Bank (S side of the Seine River) as a school of theology. It became part of the University of Paris in 1808.

**So·ro·ca·ba** |ˌsawrō'käbä| industrial and commercial city in S Brazil, in São Paulo state. Pop. 431,000.

**Sor·ren·to** |sə'rentō| resort town on the W coast of central Italy, on a peninsula separating the Bay of Naples, which it faces, from the Gulf of Salerno. Pop. 17,000.

**Sos·no·wiec** |saw'snōv,yets| industrial and mining town in SW Poland, W of Cracow. Pop. 259,000.

**Sou·fri·ère**[1] |ˌsoofrē'yər| dormant volcano on the French island of Guadeloupe in the Caribbean. Rising to 4,813 ft./1,468 m., it is the highest peak in the Lesser Antilles.
**Sou·fri·ère**[2] |ˌsoofrē'yər| active volcanic

peak on the island of St. Vincent in the Caribbean. It rises to a height of 4,006 ft. (1,234 m).

**Sousse** |soos| (also **Susah, Susa**) port and resort on the E coast of Tunisia. Pop. 125,000.

**South, the** in the U.S., term with several definitions, most commonly the eleven states of the 1861–65 Confederacy: Alabama, Arkansas, Florida, Georgia, Louisiana, Mississippi, North Carolina, South Carolina, Tennessee, Texas, and Virginia. □ **Southern** *adj.* **Southerner** *n.*

**South Af·ri·ca** |ˌsowTH 'æfrəkə| republic occupying the southernmost part of the continent of Africa. Area: 471,625 sq. mi./1.22 million sq. km. Pop. 36,762,000. Languages, English, Afrikaans, Zulu, Xhosa, and others. Administrative capital: Pretoria; seat of legislature: Cape Town; judicial capital: Bloemfontein; largest city: Johannesburg. Settled and then fought over at the end of the 19th century by the Dutch and English, South Africa achieved self-government (by the white minority) in 1910. From 1948 its policy of

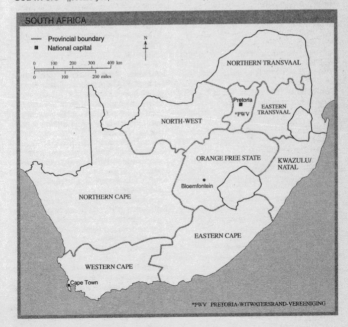

SOUTH AFRICA

----- Provincial boundary
■ National capital

0   100   200   300   400 km
0        100        200 miles

N

NORTHERN TRANSVAAL

Pretoria
•PWV   EASTERN TRANSVAAL

NORTH-WEST

ORANGE FREE STATE

KWAZULU/ NATAL

Bloemfontein

NORTHERN CAPE

EASTERN CAPE

WESTERN CAPE

Cape Town

*PWV PRETORIA-WITWATERSRAND-VEREENIGING

racial separation (apartheid) brought increasing international isolation, which receded as apartheid collapsed after 1990. Majority (African) rule was achieved in 1994. Its mining, agriculture, and industry make South Africa one of the most prosperous African nations. □ **South African** *adj. & n.*

**South Amer•i•ca** |‚sowTH ə'merikə| continent comprising the S half of the American land mass, connected to North America by the Isthmus of Panama. It includes the Falkland Islands, the Galapagos Islands, and Tierra del Fuego. (See also AMERICA.) □ **South American** *adj. & n.*

**South•amp•ton**[1] |‚sowTH'(h)æm(p)tən| industrial city and seaport on the S coast of England, formerly in Hampshire. Pop. 194,000. It lies at the end of Southampton Water, an inlet of the English Channel opposite the Isle of Wight.

**South•amp•ton**[2] |‚sowTH'(h)æm(p)tən| resort and residential town in SE New York, at the E end of Long Island. Pop. 44,976.

**South At•lan•tic Ocean** |sowTH æt'læntik| see ATLANTIC OCEAN.

**South Aus•tra•lia** |‚sowTH aws'trālyə| state comprising the S central part of Australia. Area: 380,069 sq. mi./984,000 sq. km. Pop. 1,454,000. Capital: Adelaide. Constituted as a semi-independent colony in 1836, it became a Crown Colony in 1841 and was federated with the other states of Australia in 1901. Irrigated agriculture is important.

**South Bank** |'sowTH| district of London, England, across the Thames River from Parliament, developed since the 1950s as an arts center.

**South Beach** |'sowTH| fashionable resort district of Miami Beach, Florida, noted for its Art Deco buildings.

**South Bend** |'sowTH| industrial city in N Indiana. Pop. 105,511. The university community of Notre Dame is just N of the city.

**South Bos•ton** |'sowTH| residential district of E Boston, Massachusetts, noted for its Irish working-class community. Familiarly, **Southie.**

**South Car•o•li•na** |‚sowTH ‚kerə'līnə| see box. □ **South Carolinean** *adj. & n.*

**South Chi•na Sea** |'sowTH 'CHīnə| see CHINA SEA.

**South Da•ko•ta** |‚sowTH də'kōtə| see box, p. 347. □ **South Dakotan** *adj. & n.*

**South Dum Dum** |'sowTH 'dəm dəm| city in NE India, in West Bengal, near Calcutta. Pop. 231,000.

---

### South Carolina

**Capital/largest city:** Columbia
**Other cities:** Charleston, Greenville, North Charleston, Spartanburg
**Population:** 3,486,703 (1990); 3,835,962 (1998); 4,033,000 (2005 proj.)
**Population rank (1990):** 25
**Rank in land area:** 40
**Abbreviation:** SC; S. Car.
**Nickname:** Palmetto State
**Motto:** *Animis opibusque parati* ("Prepared in mind and resources")
**Bird:** Carolina wren
**Fish:** striped bass
**Flower:** Carolina jessamine (yellow jasmine)
**Tree:** palmetto
**Song:** "Carolina"
**Noted physical features:** Piedmont Plateau; Sassafras Mountain
**Tourist attractions:** Hilton Head Island; Myrtle Beach; Saluda Dam; Fort Sumter; Cypress Gardens
**Admission date:** May 23, 1788
**Order of admission:** 8
**Name origin:** For *Carolina,* see at *North Carolina.* The southern portion of the original Carolina colony came to be called 'South Carolina' after the colony was divided in 1729.

---

**Southeast Asia Treaty Organization** (abbrev. **SEATO**) a defense alliance that existed between 1954 and 1977 for countries of SE Asia and part of the SW Pacific, to further a US policy of containing communism. Its members were Australia, Britain, France, New Zealand, Pakistan, the Philippines, Thailand, and the US.

**Southend-on-Sea** |'sowTH‚end‚än'sē| resort town in Essex, England, on the Thames estuary E of London. Pop. 154,000.

**South Equa•to•ri•al Current** |‚sowTH ‚ēkwä'tawrēəl| ocean current that flows W across the Pacific just S of the equator.

**South•ern Alps** |'səTHərn 'ælps| mountain range in South Island, New Zealand. Running roughly parallel to the W coast, it extends almost the entire length of the island. At Mount Cook, its highest peak, it rises to 12,349 ft./3,764 m.

**south•ern hem•i•sphere** the half of the earth that is S of the equator.

**South•ern Ocean** |'səTHərn| the expanse of ocean surrounding Antarctica. Also **Antarctic Ocean.**

**South•ern Pines** |'səTHərn 'pīnz| resort

---

### South Dakota

**Capital:** Pierre
**Largest city:** Sioux Falls
**Other cities:** Aberdeen, Rapid City, Sioux Falls, Watertown
**Population:** 696,004 (1990); 738,171 (1998); 810,000 (2005 proj.)
**Population rank (1990):** 45
**Rank in land area:** 17
**Abbreviation:** SD; S.D., S. Dak.
**Nickname:** Coyote State
**Motto:** 'Under God the People Rule'
**Bird:** ring-necked pheasant
**Fish:** walleye
**Flower:** American pasque
**Tree:** Black Hills spruce (white spruce)
**Song:** "Hail, South Dakota"
**Noted physical features:** Black Hills; Missouri River; Lake Oahe
**Tourist attractions:** Mt. Rushmore National Memorial; Wounded Knee; Oahe Dam; Homestake Mine; Badlands and Wind Cave national parks
**Admission date:** November 2, 1889
**Order of admission:** 40
**Name origin:** For *Dakota* see at *North Dakota*. The original Dakota Territory was divided into north and south regions in 1889.

---

town in S central North Carolina, noted for its golf courses. Pop. 9,129.

**South•ern Rho•de•sia** |'sǝᴛʜǝrn rō 'dēzʜyä| see ZIMBABWE.

**South•field** |'sowᴛʜ'fēld| residential and industrial city in SE Michigan, a suburb NW of Detroit. Pop. 75,728.

**South Gate** |'sowᴛʜ ,gāt| industrial city in SW California, SE of Los Angeles. Pop. 86,284.

**South Geor•gia** |'sowᴛʜ 'jawrjǝ| barren island in the South Atlantic, situated 700 mi./1,120 km. E of the British Falkland Islands, of which it is a dependency. It was first explored in 1775 by Captain James Cook, who named the island after George III.

**South Gla•mor•gan** |'sowᴛʜ glæ'mawrgǝn| former county of S Wales, on the Bristol Channel, dissolved in 1996.

**South Had•ley** |'sowᴛʜ 'hædlē| town in W Massachusetts, on the Connecticut River N of Springfield, noted as home to Mount Holyoke College. Pop. 16,685.

**South Island** |'sowᴛʜ| the more southerly and larger (58,406 sq. mi./151,215 sq. km.) of the two main islands of New

Zealand, separated from North Island by Cook Strait. Pop. 882,000.

**South Ko•rea** |'sowᴛʜ kaw'rēyǝ| republic in E Asia, occupying the S part of the peninsula of Korea. Area: 38,340 sq. mi./99,263 sq. km. Pop. 42,793,000. Language, Korean. Capital and largest city: Seoul. Official name **Republic of Korea**. Formed in 1948, when Korea was partitioned along the 38th parallel, South Korea has a strong agricultural sector but is primarily an emerging industrial power. □ **South Korean** *adj. & n.*

**South Korea**

**South Ork•ney Islands** |'sowᴛʜ 'awrknē| group of uninhabited islands in the South Atlantic, lying to the NE of the Antarctic Peninsula. Discovered in 1821, they are administered as part of the British Antarctic Territory.

**South Os•se•tia** |'sowᴛʜ ō'sēsʜǝ| autonomous region of Georgia, situated in the Caucasus on the border with Russia. Capital: Tskhinvali. (See also OSSETIA.)

**South Pass** |'sowᴛʜ| valley in the Wind River Mts. of SW Wyoming that was a major route for settlers moving W through the Rockies in the 19th century.

**South Platte River** |'sowᴛʜ 'plæt| river that flows 425 mi./685 km. from the Rocky Mts. in Colorado, through Denver, and across Colorado to Nebraska, where it joins the North Platte to form the Platte.

**South Pole** |'sowᴛʜ 'pōl| 90° S, the southernmost point on earth. It is on a plateau in central Antarctica, and was first reached in 1911 by Roald Amundsen. See also MAGNETIC POLE.

**South•port** |'sowᴛʜ,pawrt| resort and suburban town in NW England, on the Irish Sea coast n of Liverpool. Pop. 91,000.

**South Sand•wich Islands** |'sowᴛʜ 'sæn ,(d)wicʜ| group of uninhabited volcanic islands in the South Atlantic, lying 300 mi./480 km. SE of South Georgia. They are administered from the British Falkland Islands.

**South Sea** |'sowTH| (also **South Seas**) historical name for the S Pacific, whose various islands have been called the **South Sea Islands**.

**South Shet·land Islands** |'sowTH 'sHetlənd| group of uninhabited islands in the South Atlantic, lying N of the Antarctic Peninsula. Discovered in 1819, they are administered as part of the British Antarctic Territory.

**South Shields** |'sowTH 'sHēldz| industrial port on the coast of NE England, at the mouth of the Tyne opposite North Shields. Pop. 87,000.

**South Side** |sowTH sīd| area S of central Chicago, Illinois, in the 20th century home to the largest U.S. black community.

**South Vi·et·nam** |'sowTH vē'etnäm| former republic in SE Asia, established in the southern part of Vietnam in 1954. After its defeat in the Vietnam War, it was reunited with North Vietnam to form Vietnam.

**South·wark** |'səTHərk| borough of SE London, England, on the Thames River. Pop. 196,000. Residential and industrial, it is noted as the former site of the Globe Theatre.

**South West Af·ri·ca** former name for NAMIBIA.

**South York·shire** |,sowTH 'yawrksHər| metropolitan county of N England. Pop. 1,249,000. Sheffield is the major city.

**So·vi·et Union** |'sōvē,et| former federation of communist republics occupying the N half of Asia and part of E Europe. Capital: Moscow. Full name **Union of Soviet Socialist Republics**. Created from the Russian Empire in the aftermath of the 1917 Russian Revolution, the Soviet Union was the largest country in the world. It comprised fifteen republics: Russia, Belarus, Ukraine, Georgia, Armenia, Moldova, Azerbaijan, Kazakhstan, Kyrgyzstan, Turkmenistan, Tajikistan, Uzbekistan, and the three Baltic states (annexed in 1940). After World War II, in which it was invaded by Germany and sustained some 20 million casualties, the Soviet Union emerged as a superpower in rivalry with the U.S., leading to the Cold War. Decades of repression and economic failure eventually led to attempts at liberalization and economic reform under President Mikhail Gorbachev during the 1980s. This resulted, however, in a resurgence of nationalist feeling in the republics. The USSR was formally dissolved in 1991, some of its constituents joining a looser confederation, the Commonwealth of Independent States. □ **Soviet** *adj.*

**So·we·to** |sə'wetō| largely residential city, formerly several townships, in South Africa SW of Johannesburg. Pop. 597,000. In 1976 demonstrations against the compulsory use of Afrikaans in schools resulted in violent police activity and the deaths of hundreds here. The name is from *So(uth) We(stern) To(wnships)*. □ **Sowetan** *adj. & n.*

**Spa** |spä| town in E Belgium, SE of Liège. Pop. 10,000. It has been celebrated since medieval times for the curative properties of its mineral springs, and its name became generic.

**Spain** |spān| kingdom in SW Europe, occupying the greater part of the Iberian Peninsula. Area: 194,959 sq. mi./504,750 sq. km. Pop. 39,045,000. Languages, Spanish (official), Catalan. Capital and largest city: Madrid. Spanish name **España**. Dominated in various periods by Carthaginians, Romans, Visigoths, and Moors, Spain became a great power under the Habsburgs by the 16th century, and controlled one of the largest colonial empires. In the 19th century the empire largely dissolved. Modern Spain retains its agricultural base, but is also heavily industrial in some regions. □ **Spanish** *adj. & n.*

**Span·dau** |'spæn,dow| industrial district of Berlin, Germany; its 16th-century fortress was more recently a prison, and several condemned Nazi war criminals, including Rudolph Hess, were held here after the Nuremberg trials.

**Span·ish Amer·i·ca** |'spænisH| the parts of America once colonized by the Spanish and in which Spanish is still generally spoken, including most of Central and South America (except Brazil) and part of the Caribbean.

**Span·ish Main** the former name for the NW coast of South America between the Orinoco River and Panama, and adjoining parts of the Caribbean Sea.

**Span·ish Sa·ha·ra** former name (1958–75) for WESTERN SAHARA.

**Span·ish Steps** famous stairs in Rome, Italy, built 1721–25 to connect the Piazza di Spagna with the church of the Trinità Dei Monti.

**Span·ish Town** second-largest town in Jamaica, W of Kingston; it is a former capital of Jamaica. Pop. 110,000.

**Sparks** |spärks| commercial city in W Nevada, NE of Reno. Pop. 53,367.

**Spar·ta** |'spärtə| city (modern Greek name **Spartí**) in the S Peloponnese in Greece, capital of the department of Laconia. Pop. 13,000. It was a powerful city-state in the 5th century B.C., defeating its rival Athens in the Peloponnesian War to become the leading city of Greece. The ancient Spartans (also called Lacedaemonians) were renowned for the military organization of their state and for their rigorous discipline, courage, and austerity. □ **Spartan** adj. & n.

**Spar·tan·burg** |'spärtən,bərg| industrial and commercial city in NW South Carolina. Pop. 43,467.

**Spey** |spā| river of E central Scotland. Rising in the Grampian Mts. E of the Great Glen, it flows 108 mi./171 km. NE to the North Sea.

**Spey·er** |'sHpīər| river port and industrial center in SW Germany, on the Rhine River. Pop. 44,000.

**Sphinx, the** colossal desert structure near Giza, N Egypt, with a lion's body and the head of a man. A funerary monument, it dates from the 3rd millennium B.C.

**Spice Islands** |'spīs| former name for the MOLUCCA ISLANDS.

**Spit·head** |,spit'hed| channel between the NE coast of the Isle of Wight and the mainland of S England. It offers sheltered access to Southampton Water (the inlet of the Solent) and deep anchorage. It has long been a naval anchorage.

**Spits·ber·gen** |'spits,bərgən| Norwegian island in the Svalbard archipelago, in the Arctic Ocean N of Norway; principal settlement, Longyearbyen.

**Split** |split| port city in S Croatia, on the Adriatic coast. Pop. 189,000. An industrial and resort center, it contains the ruins of the palace of the Roman emperor Diocletian (3rd century A.D.). Ancient name **Spalatum**.

**Spo·kane** |spō'kæn| industrial and commercial city in E Washington, in the Inland Empire, at the falls of the Spokane River, near the border with Idaho. Pop. 177,196.

**Spo·le·to** |spə'lātō| town in Umbria, in central Italy. Pop. 38,000. It was one of Italy's principal cities from the 6th to the 8th century A.D. It is a cultural center, the site of an annual arts festival.

**Spoon River** |'spo͞on| river that flows 160 mi./260 km. through central Illinois, associated with the verse of Edgar Lee Masters.

**Spor·a·des** |'spawrə,dēz| two groups of Greek islands in the Aegean Sea. The *Northern Sporades*, which lie close to the E coast of mainland Greece, include the islands of Euboea, Skiros, Skiathos, and Skopelos. The *Southern Sporades*, situated off the W coast of Turkey, include Rhodes and the other islands of the Dodecanese.

**Spot·syl·va·nia County** |ˌspätsil'vānēə| rural county in NE Virginia, scene of Civil War battles including Fredericksburg and Spotsylvania Court House.

**Sprat·ly Islands** |'sprætlē| group of small islands and coral reefs in the South China Sea, between Vietnam and Borneo. Dispersed over a distance of some 600 mi./965 km., the islands are variously claimed by China, Taiwan, Vietnam, the Philippines, and Malaysia. There are nearby undersea oil deposits.

**Spratley Islands**

**Spree River** |'sHprā| river (247 mi./400 km.) in E Germany, rising in mountains near the Czech border and flowing N to join the Havel River at Spandau.

**Spring·dale** |'spriNG,dāl| commercial and agricultural city in NW Arkansas. Pop. 29,941.

**Spring·field**[1] |'spriNG,fēld| industrial and commercial city, the capital of Illinois, in the central part. Pop. 105,227.

**Spring·field**[2] |'spriNG,fēld| industrial city in SW Massachusetts, on the Connecticut River. Pop. 156,983.

**Spring·field**[3] |'spriNG,fēld| industrial and commercial city in SW Missouri, on the N edge of the Ozark Mts. Pop. 140,494.

**Spring Green** |'spriNG 'grēn| town in S Wisconsin, NW of Madison, noted as the site of Taliesin, the home and studio of Frank Lloyd Wright. Pop. 1,343.

**Spring·hill** |'spriNG,hil| town in N central Nova Scotia, formerly a noted coal-mining center. Pop. 4,373.

**Springs** |spriNGz| industrial city in NE South Africa, in Gauteng province, in a coal-, gold-, and uranium-producing region. Pop. 158,000.

**Square Mile** informal name for the financial district of London, England.

**Squaw Valley** |'skwaw| resort in NE California, on Lake Tahoe, site of the 1960 Winter Olympics.

**Sreb·re·ni·ca** |ˌsrebrə'nētsə| town in E Bosnia and Herzegovina, in a mining area. It was a target of "ethnic cleansing" by Serbian forces in the fighting between Muslims and Serbs that followed the breakup of Yugoslavia in 1991.

**Sri Lanka** |ˌsrē 'läNGkə; ˌsHrē,läNGkə| island republic off the SE coast of India. Area: 24,895 sq. mi./64,453 sq. km. Pop. 17,194,000. Languages, Sinhalese (official), Tamil, English. Capital and largest city: Colombo. Former name (until 1972) **Ceylon**. Arabic name **Serendib**. With a history of over 2,000 years, Ceylon was dominated by colonial powers from the 16th century, and annexed by Britain in 1815. Since independence in 1972 there has been friction, often open warfare, between the government and Tamil separatists. Sri Lanka is largely agricultural. □ **Sri Lankan** *adj. & n.*

**Sri Lanka**

**Sri·na·gar** |srē'nägər; ˌsHrē'nägər| city in NW India, the summer capital of the state of Jammu and Kashmir, on the Jhelum River in the foothills of the Himalayas. Pop. 595,000.

**Staf·fa** |'stæfə| small uninhabited island of the Inner Hebrides of Scotland, W of Mull. It is the site of Fingal's Cave and is noted for its basalt columns.

**Staf·ford** |'stæfərd| industrial and commercial town in central England, the county seat of Staffordshire, to the S of Stoke-on-Trent. Pop. 62,000.

**Staf·ford·shire** |'stæfərd,sHər| county of central England. Pop. 1,020,000; county seat, Stafford.

**Sta·gi·ra** |stä'jirə| town in NE Greece, on the E Chalcidice Peninsula. The philosopher Aristotle was born here in 384 B.C.

**Staked Plain** |stäktplän| another name for LLANO ESTACADO.

**Sta·kha·nov** |stä'känŏv| mining city in SE Ukraine, S of the Donets River. Pop. 112,000.

**Sta·lin·grad** |'stälən,græd| former name (1925–61) for VOLGOGRAD, Russia. In the 1942–43 battle of Stalingrad, Soviet forces wore down and defeated Nazi armies.

**Sta·lin Peak** |'stälən| former name (1933–62) for COMMUNISM PEAK.

**Stam·boul** |stæm'bōōl| archaic name for ISTANBUL, Turkey.

**Stam·ford** |'stæmfərd| commercial city in SW Connecticut, on Long Island Sound. Pop. 108,056. It is noted for its corporate headquarters.

**Stand·ing Rock** |'stændiNG| Sioux Indian reservation that straddles the North Dakota–South Dakota border, W of the Missouri River.

**Stan·ley, Mount** |'stænlē| mountain in the Ruwenzori range in central Africa, on the border between the Democratic Republic of Congo (formerly Zaire) and Uganda. Its highest point, Margherita Peak, which rises to 16,765 ft./5,110 m., is the third-highest in Africa. African name **Mount Ngaliema**.

**Stan·ley** |'stænlē| (also **Port Stanley**) the chief port and town of the British Falkland Islands, on the island of East Falkland. Pop. 1,557.

**Stan·ley·ville** |'stænlē,vil| former name (1882–1966) for KISANGANI.

**Sta·ra Za·go·ra** |stärä zä'gawrä| industrial city in E central Bulgaria. Pop. 188,000. A former Thracian settlement, it was held by the Turks from 1370 until 1877, then destroyed by them during the Russo-Turkish War. It has since been rebuilt as a modern planned city.

**Starn·ber·ger See** |'sHtärnbergər 'zä| (formerly **Würmsee**) lake in Bavaria, Germany, surrounded by summer palaces of the region's aristocracy and public parks and beaches. It is a popular vacation area.

**Sta·ry Os·kal** |stäri ä'skōl| (also **Staryy Oskal**) industrial and mining city in W Russia, W of Voronezh. Pop. 184,000.

**State College** borough in central Pennsylvania, in the Nittany Valley, home to Pennsylvania State University. Pop. 38,923.

**Stat·en Island** |stætn| island borough of New York City, in the SW across New York Bay from Manhattan. Pop. 378,977. It is coextensive with Richmond County.

**Staun·ton** |'stæn(t)ən| city in N central Virginia, in the Shenandoah Valley. Pop. 24,461.

**Sta·vang·er** |stə'væNGər| seaport in SW Norway. Pop. 98,000. It is an important center servicing offshore oil fields in the North Sea.

**Stav·ro·pol¹** |stäv'rawpəl; stäv'rōpəl| former name (until 1964) for TOGLIATTI, Russia.

**Stav·ro·pol²** 1 krai (administrative territory) in S Russia, in the N Caucasus. 2 its capital city. Pop. 324,000.

**Steam·boat Springs** |'stēm,bōt| resort city in NW Colorado, a famed skiing center. Pop. 6,695.

**Stei·er·mark** |'sHtīər,märk| German name for STYRIA.

**Stel·len·bosch** |'stelən,baws; 'stelən,bōOSH| university town in Cape province, SW South Africa, just E of Cape Town. Pop. 74,000.

**Sten·dal** |sten'däl; stæn'däl| city and rail junction in central Germany, in Saxony-Anhalt. Pop. 76,000. Its name was adopted by the French writer Marie Henry Beyle (Stendhal).

**Ste·pa·na·kert** |stepänä'kert| Russian name for XANKÄNDI.

**Steppes, the** |steps| region of extensive flat grasslands in W central Asia, particularly in central Kazakhstan. The term is also used of such areas as the ALFOLD, in Hungary.

**Ster·ling Heights** |'stərliNG 'hīts| city in SE Michigan, a residential and industrial suburb N of Detroit. Pop. 117,810.

**Ster·li·ta·mak** |,stirlitä'mäk| industrial city in S Russia, on the Belaya River to the N of Orenburg. Pop. 250,000.

**Stet·tin** |sHte'tēn| German name for SZCZECIN.

**Steu·ben·ville** |'stōōbən,vil| industrial city in E Ohio, on the Ohio River. Pop. 22,125.

**Ste·ven·age** |'stēvənij| industrial town in Hertfordshire, SE England. Pop. 75,000.

**Ste·vens Point** |'stēvənz| industrial and commercial city in central Wisconsin, on the Wisconsin River. Pop. 23,006.

**Stew·art Island** |'stōōərt| island of New Zealand, off the S coast of South Island, from which it is separated by the Foveaux Strait; chief settlement, Oban.

**Steyr** |'sHtīər| industrial city in N Austria. Pop. 39,000.

**Sti·kine River** |sti'kēn| river that flows 335 mi./540 km. across British Columbia to the Pacific.

**Still·wa·ter** |'stil,wätər| city in N central Oklahoma, home to Oklahoma State University. Pop. 36,676.

**Still·well Road** |'stilwel| World War II military highway that connected NE India with China by way of Burma. It was 1,044 mi./1,680 km. long.

**Stil·ton** |'stiltən| village in SE England, in Cambridgeshire, which gave its name to a cheese made in Leicestershire and first sold here at the Bell Inn.

**Stir·ling** |'stərliNG| university town in central Scotland, on the Forth River, administrative center of Stirling region. Pop. 28,000.

**Stock·bridge** |'stäk,brij| resort town in W Massachusetts, in the Berkshire Hills. Pop. 2,408. Tanglewood estate, site of a famed summer music festival, is here.

**Stock·holm** |'stäk,hō(l)m| the capital of Sweden, a port on the E coast, situated on the mainland and on numerous adjacent islands. Pop. 674,000. It is the largest city and the economic and cultural center of the country.

**Stock·port** |'stäk,pawrt| industrial town in NW England, in Greater Manchester. Pop. 130,000.

**Stock·ton** |'stäktən| industrial city in N central California, a port on the San Joaquin River. Pop. 210,943.

**Stockton-on-Tees** |'stäktən än 'tēz| industrial town in NE England, a port on the Tees River near its mouth on the North Sea. Pop. 170,000. The town developed after the opening in 1825 of the Stockton and Darlington Railway, the first passenger rail service in the world.

**Stoke-on-Trent** |'stōk än 'trent| city on the Trent River in W central England, formerly part of Staffordshire. Pop. 245,000. It has long been the center of the Staffordshire pottery industries.

**Stoke Po·ges** |'stōk 'pōjis| village in S central England, in Buckinghamshire N of Slough, whose churchyard is the burial place of Thomas Grey and the presumed setting for his "Elegy Written in a Country Church Yard."

**Stone·henge** |'stōn,henj| megalithic monument in SW England, on Salisbury Plain in Wiltshire. Its standing stones, whose origin and purpose are debated, are often taken as a symbol of England.

**Stone Mountain** |'stōn| granite mass E of Atlanta, Georgia, site of the Confederate National Monument, created (1917–67) to a design by Gutzon Borglum.

**Stones River** see MURFREESBORO.

**Ston·ey Creek** |'stōnē| suburban city in S Ontario, on Lake Ontario next to Hamilton. Pop. 49,968.

**Stony Brook** |'stōnē| resort and academic village in E Long Island, New York. Pop. 13,726.

**Stor·mont** |'stawr,mänt| suburb to the E of Belfast, Northern Ireland, seat of the Northern Irish parliament (suspended since 1972), and thus a term for British rule in the province.

**Stor·no·way** |'stawrnə,wā| port on the E coast of Lewis, in the Outer Hebrides of Scotland. Pop. 6,000. The administrative center of the Western Isles, it is noted for the manufacture of Harris tweed.

**Story·ville** |'stawrē,vil| former entertainment district of New Orleans, Louisiana, closed in 1917 but associated with the early development of jazz music.

**Stour** |stōr| **1** river of central England that rises W of Wolverhampton and flows SW through Stourbridge and Kidderminster to meet the Severn at Stourport-on-Severn. **2** river of S England that rises in W Wiltshire and flows SE to meet the English Channel E of Bournemouth.

**Stowe** |stō| town in N central Vermont, a noted skiing and resort center. Pop. 3,433.

**Straits Settlements** |strāts| former British Crown Colony in SE Asia. Established in 1867, it comprised Singapore, Penang, and Malacca, and later included Labuan, Christmas Island, and the Cocos Islands. It was disbanded in 1946.

**Stral·sund** |'strälsənd| resort town and fishing port in N Germany, on the Baltic coast opposite the island of Rügen. Pop. 72,000.

**Stran·raer** |stræn'rär| port and market town in SW Scotland, in Dumfries and Galloway. Pop. 10,000. It is the terminus of a ferry service from Larne, in Northern Ireland.

**Stras·bourg** |'sträs,bōōrg| industrial and commercial city in NE France, in Alsace, close to the border with Germany. Pop. 256,000. Annexed by Germany in 1870, it was returned to France after World War I. It is the headquarters of the Council of Europe and of the European Parliament.

**Strat·ford¹** |'strætfərd| industrial town in SW Connecticut, E of Bridgeport, former home to the American Shakespeare Festival. Pop. 49,389.

**Strat·ford²** |'strætfərd| city in S Ontario, on the Avon River, noted for its summer Shakespeare Festival. Pop. 27,666.

**Stratford-upon-Avon** |,strætfərd,əpän 'ävän| town in Warwickshire, central England, on the Avon River. Pop. 20,000. Famous as the birth and burial place of

William Shakespeare, it is the site of the Royal Shakespeare Theatre.

**Strath·clyde** |straTH'klīd| former local government region in W central Scotland, dissolved in 1996. It took its name from a Celtic kingdom of the 5th–11th centuries, centered on Dumbarton.

**Strom·bo·li** |'strämbōlē| volcanic island in the Mediterranean, the most north-easterly of the Lipari Islands, NE of Sicily. Its volcano has been in a state of continual mild eruption throughout history.

**Stru·ma River** |'strōomä| river that rises in the Vitosha Mts. of Bulgaria and flows 216 mi./346 km. through Greece, draining into the Aegean Sea near Thessaloniki.

**Stur·bridge** |'stərbrij| town in S central Massachusetts, noted for its historical recreation Old Sturbridge Village. Pop. 7,775.

**Stutt·gart** |'stŏŏt,gärt| industrial and commercial city in western Germany, the capital of Baden-Württemberg, on the Neckar River. Pop. 592,000. It is an auto manufacturing center.

**Stym·pha·lis, Lake** |stim'falis| lake in NE Peloponnese, Greece. In Greek mythology, Hercules slew the man-eating birds, the Stymphalians, here.

**Styr·ia** |'stirēə| mountainous state of SE Austria. Pop. 1,185,000. Capital: Graz. German name **Steiermark**.

**Styx** |stiks| in Greek mythology, river of the underworld, over which Charon ferried the souls of the dead. □ **Stygian** adj.

**Su·bic Bay** |'sŏŏbik| inlet of the South China Sea in the Philippines, off central Luzon. A large U.S. naval facility here, closed in 1992, has become an industrial zone.

**Sub·lime Porte** |sə'blīm 'pawrt| name for the court of the sultan in Constantinople, the capital of the Ottoman Empire (present-day Istanbul, Turkey). It refers to the "imperial gate" leading to the sultan's audience chamber.

**Su·bo·ti·ca** |,sŏŏbə'tētsə| industrial city and transportation center in Serbia, near the Hungarian border. Pop. 102,000.

**sub-Sa·har·an Af·ri·ca** the part of Africa to the south of the Sahara Desert, beginning with the southern regions of Mali, Niger, Chad, and Sudan and extending south to South Africa.

**Su·cea·va** |sŏŏ'CHyävə| industrial town in NE Romania, in the E foothills of the Carpathian Mts., capital of Suceava county. Pop. 106,000.

**Sü·chow** |'sŏŏ'CHow| see XUZHOU.

**Su·cre** |'sŏŏ,krā| historic city, the judicial capital and seat of the legislature of Bolivia. Pop. 131,000. It is situated in the Andes, at an altitude of 8,860 ft./2,700 m. Named Chuquisaca by the Spanish in 1539, the city was renamed in 1825 in honor of Antonio José de Sucre, the first president of Bolivia.

**Su·dan** |sŏŏ'dæn| (also **the Sudan**) 1 republic in NE Africa, S of Egypt, with a coastline on the Red Sea. Area: 967,940 sq. mi./2.51 million sq. km. Pop. 25,855,000. Languages, Arabic (official), Dinka, Hausa, and others. Capital and largest city: Khartoum. Ruled by the Arabas from the 13th century, by Egypt from 1822, Sudan revolted in the 1880s and finally achieved independence in 1956, after a period of British dominance. Largely agricultural, it has suffered from struggles between the Islamic central government and separatist S provinces. 2 vast region of N Africa, extending across the width of the continent from the S edge of the Sahara to the tropical equatorial zone in the S. □ **Sudanese** adj. & n.

Sudan

**Sud·bury** |'səd,bərē| city in central Ontario. Pop. 92,884. It lies at the center of Canada's largest mining region, the Sudbury Basin.

**Su·de·ten·land** |sŏŏ'dätn,lænd| area in the NW part of the Czech Republic, on the border with Germany. Allocated to Czechoslovakia after World War I, it became an object of Nazi expansionist policies and was ceded to Germany as a result of the Munich Agreement of September 1938. In 1945 the area was returned to Czechoslovakia. Czech name **Sudety**.

**Su·de·tes** |sŏŏ'dētēz| (also **Sudeten** or **Sudety**) mountain range on the border between Poland and the Czech Republic.

**Su·ez, Isthmus of** |sŏŏ'əz| isthmus between the Mediterranean and the Red seas, connecting Egypt and Africa to the Sinai Peninsula and Asia. The port of Suez lies in the S, at the head of the Gulf of Suez, an arm of the Red Sea. The isthmus is traversed by the Suez Canal.

**Su·ez Canal** |sōō'əz| shipping canal connecting the Mediterranean at Port Said, Egypt with the Red Sea. It was constructed between 1859 and 1869 by Ferdinand de Lesseps. In 1875 it came under British control; it was nationalized by Egypt in 1956. It is 106 mi./171 km. long, providing the shortest route for sea traffic between Europe and Asia.

**Suf·folk**[1] |'səfək| county of E England, on the coast of East Anglia. Pop. 630,000; county seat, Ipswich.

**Suf·folk**[2] |'səfək| commercial and agricultural city in S Virginia, in the Hampton Roads area. Pop. 52,141.

**Suf·folk County** |'səf,ək| suburban, agricultural, and resort county in SE New York, on the E end of Long Island. Pop. 1,321,864.

**Sug·ar Loaf Mountain** |'sHŏŏgər 'lōf| rocky peak to the NE of Copacabana Beach, in Rio de Janeiro, Brazil. It rises to a height of 1,296 ft./390 m.

**Suhl** |sōōl| industrial town in eastern Germany. Pop. 59,000. Until the reunification of Germany, the name was also used for the district surrounding the town.

**Su·i·ta** |sōō'ētä| city in W central Japan, on S Honshu, N of Osaka. Pop. 345,000.

**Su·ka·bu·mi** |sōōkä'bōōmē| resort and commercial town in Indonesia, on W Java, S of Jakarta. Pop. 120,000.

**Su·kho·tai** |',sōōkə'tī| town in NW Thailand. Pop. 23,000. It was formerly the capital of an independent state of the same name, which flourished from the mid-13th to the mid-14th centuries.

**Su·khu·mi** |sōō'kōōmē| port city and capital of the autonomous republic of Abkhazia, in the Republic of Georgia, on the E coast of the Black Sea. It is also a resort known since Roman times for its sulfur baths. Pop. 122,000.

**Suk·kur** |sə'kŏŏr| commercial and industrial city in SE Pakistan, on the Indus River. Pop. 350,000. Nearby is the Sukkur Barrage, a dam across the Indus that directs water through irrigation channels to a large area of the Indus valley.

**Su·la Islands** |sōōlä| (also **Soela Islands**) group of islands in Indonesia, part of the Moluccas group, between Sulawesi (W) and the Ceram Sea (E).

**Su·la·we·si** |,sōōlə'wäsē| mountainous island in the Greater Sunda group in Indonesia, to the E of Borneo; chief town,

Ujung Pandang. It is noted as the habitat of numerous endemic species. Former name **Celebes**.

**Su·lay·ma·ni·yah** |sōōlīmä'nēye| town in NE Iraq, in mountainous S Kurdistan. Pop. 279,000. It is the capital of a Kurdish governorate of the same name. Full name **As Sulaymaniyah**; also spelled **Sulaimaniya**.

**Sul·mo·na** |sōōl'mōnä| commercial and industrial city in central Italy, on the Gizio River. Pop. 25,000.

**Su·lu Sea** |'sōōlōō| sea in the Malay Archipelago. The NE coast of Borneo lies SW, and islands of the Philippines, including the Sulu Archipelago, surround the sea on its other sides.

**Su·ma·tra** |sə'mätrə| large (164,000 sq. mi./424,700 sq. km.) island of Indonesia, to the SW of the Malay Peninsula, from which it is separated by the Strait of Malacca; chief city, Medan. □ **Sumatran** *adj. & n.*

**Sum·ba** |'sōōmbä| island of the Lesser Sunda group in Indonesia, lying to the S of the islands of Flores and Sumbawa; chief town, Waingapu. Also called **Sandalwood Island**.

**Sum·ba·wa** |sōōm'bäwä| island in the Lesser Sunda group in Indonesia, between Lombok and Flores.

**Su·mer** |'sōōmər| ancient region of SW Asia, in present-day Iraq, comprising the S part of Mesopotamia. From the 4th millennium B.C. it was the site of an early civilization, and its city states became part of ancient Babylonia. □ **Sumerian** *adj. & n.*

**Sum·ga·it** |sōōmgä'yēt| Russian name for SUMQAYIT.

**Sum·mer·side** |'səmər,sīd| port town, the second-largest community on Prince Edward Island. Pop. 7,474.

**Sum·mit** |'səmət| city in NE New Jersey, an affluent suburb W of Newark. Pop. 19,757.

**Sum·qay·it** |sōōmkä'yēt| industrial city in E Azerbaijan, on the Caspian Sea. Pop. 235,000. Russian name **Sumgait**.

**Sum·ter** |'səmtər| commercial and industrial city in E central South Carolina. Pop. 41,943.

**Su·my** |'sōōmē| industrial city in NE Ukraine, near the border with Russia. Pop. 296,000.

**Sun·belt, the** |'sən,belt| (also **Sun Belt**) region of the U.S. originally known for its resorts, now more for the move of much business and commerce here from the N and E. It includes Florida, Texas, Arizona, and California.

**Sun·chon** |'sŏon'CHən| **1** industrial city in W North Korea, NE of Pyongyang, in a mining district. Pop. 356,000. **2** commercial city in SW South Korea, in an agricultural district. Pop. 249,000.

**Sun City**[1] |'sən| retirement community in S central Arizona, a suburb NW of Phoenix. Pop. 38,126.

**Sun City**[2] |'sən| resort in the North West province of South Africa, built in the 1980s in the former BOPHUTHATSWANA to attract tourists, especially from other parts of South Africa, with gambling and other entertainments.

**Sun·da Islands** |'sŏondä| chain of islands in the SW part of the Malay Archipelago, consisting of two groups: the *Greater Sunda Islands*, which include Sumatra, Java, Borneo, and Sulawesi, and the *Lesser Sunda Islands*, which lie to the E of Java and include Bali, Sumbawa, Flores, Sumba, and Timor. The Sunda Strait passes between Sumatra and Java, connecting the Java Sea with the Indian Ocean.

**Sun·dar·bans** |'səndər,bənz| region of swampland in the Ganges delta, extending from the mouth of the Hooghly River in West Bengal, E India to that of the Tetulia in Bangladesh.

**Sun·der·land** |'səndərlənd| industrial city in Tyne and Wear, NE England, a North Sea port at the mouth of the Wear River. Pop. 287,000.

**Sund·svall** |'sənds,väl| port and manufacturing center in E Sweden, on the Gulf of Bothnia. Pop. 94,000.

**Sun·flow·er State** |'sən,flowər| nickname for KANSAS.

**Sun·ga·ri River** |'sŏongərē| (also called **Songhua**) river of NE China, flowing 1,150 mi./1,850 km. N from the Changbai Shan range through Jilin and Heilongjiang provinces to the Amur River at the Russian border.

**Sun·ny·vale** |'sənē,väl| city in N central California, one of the technological centers of Silicon Valley. Pop. 117,229.

**Sun·rise** |'sən,rīz| city in SE Florida, a retirement and commercial suburb W of Fort Lauderdale. Pop. 64,407.

**Sun·set Boulevard** |'sən,set| road that links the center of Los Angeles, California, with the Pacific Ocean 30 mi./48 km. to the W. The E section, between Fairfax Avenue and Beverly Hills, is known as the Sunset Strip.

**Sun·shine Coast** |'sən,SHīn| name given to the Pacific coast of Australia between Noosa Heads and Bribie Island, in Queensland, noted for its fine beaches.

**Sun·shine State** nickname for FLORIDA.

**Sun Valley** |'sən| city in S central Idaho, a famed winter sports resort. Pop. 938.

**Suo·mi** |'swawmē| Finnish name for FINLAND.

**Su·pe·ri·or, Lake** |sə'pirēər| the largest of the five Great Lakes of North America, lying between Michigan, Wisconsin, and Minnesota in the U.S. and Ontario, Canada. With an area of 31,800 sq. mi./82,350 sq. km., it is the largest freshwater lake in the world.

**Su·pe·ri·or** |sə'pirēər| port city in NW Wisconsin, on Lake Superior adjacent to Duluth, Minnesota. Pop. 27,134.

**Sur, Point** |'sŏor| see BIG SUR, California.

**Su·ra·ba·ya** |',sŏorə'bīə| industrial port in Indonesia, on the N coast of Java. Pop. 2,473,000. It is Indonesia's principal naval base and its second-largest city.

**Su·ra·kar·ta** |,sŏorə'kärtə| (also called **Solo; Sala**) city in Indonesia, on central Java, SE of Semarang. Pop. 504,000. It is an industrial, commercial, and cultural center.

**Su·rat** |sŏo'ræt; 'sŏorət| city in the state of Gujarat in W India, a port on the Tapti River near its mouth on the Gulf of Cambay. Pop. 1,497,000. It was the site of the first trading post of the East India Company, established in 1612.

**Su·ren·dra·na·gar** |sə'rendrənəgər| commercial and industrial town in W central India, in Gujarat state. Pop. 106,000.

**Su·resnes** |sŏo'rän| residential and industrial W suburb of Paris, France. Pop. 37,000. There is a U.S. military cemetery here.

**Sur·gut** |sŏor'gŏot| oil- and gas-producing town and port in W Siberia, in Russia. Pop. 256,000.

**Su·ri·ba·chi, Mount** |,sŏori'bäCHi| small dormant volcano on IWO JIMA, in the W Pacific, scene of a February 1945 flagraising by U.S. Marines that was the subject of a famous World War II photograph and a monument in the Arlington National Cemetery, Virginia.

**Su·ri·gao** |,sŏorē'gow| port and commercial city in the Philippines, on SE Mindanao. Pop. 100,000. It is one of the oldest Spanish settlements in the Philippines.

**Su·ri·name** |'sŏorə,näm| (also **Surinam**) republic on the NE coast of South America. Area: 63,061 sq. mi./163,265 sq. km. Pop. 457,000. Languages, Dutch (official),

**Surinam**

Creole, Hindi. Capital and largest city: Paramaribo. Former name (until 1948) **Dutch Guiana** or **Netherlands Guiana**. Colonized by the Dutch and the British, Suriname became independent in 1975. The largely African and Asian population relies on sugar, timber, and bauxite exports. □ **Surinamese** *adj. & n.* **Surinamer** *n.*

**Sur•rey**[1] |'sərē| municipality in SW British Columbia, an industrial and commercial suburb SE of Vancouver. Pop. 245,173.

**Sur•rey**[2] |'sərē| county of SE England. Pop. 997,000; county seat, Guildford. Surrey contains many London suburbs.

**Surt•sey**[3] |'sərtsē| small island to the S of Iceland, formed by a volcanic eruption in 1963.

**Su•sa**[1] |'soŏzə| ancient city of SW Asia, one of the chief cities of the kingdom of Elam and later capital of the Persian Achaemenid dynasty.

**Su•sa**[2] |'soŏzə| another name for SOUSSE.

**Sus•que•han•na River** |ˌsəskwə'hænə| river of the NE U.S. It has two headstreams, one rising in New York State and one in Pennsylvania, which meet in central Pennsylvania. The river then flows 150 mi./240 km. S to Chesapeake Bay.

**Sus•sex** |'səsəks| former county of S England. It was divided in 1974 into the counties of East Sussex and West Sussex. Sussex was originally the kingdom of the South Saxons.

**Suth•er•land** |'səTHərlənd| former county of Scotland, since 1975 a district of Highland region.

**Sut•lej** |'sətlij| river of N India and Pakistan that rises in the Himalayas in SW Tibet, and flows for 900 mi./1,450 km. W through India into Punjab province in Pakistan, where it joins the Chenab to form the Panjnad and eventually join the Indus.

**Sut•ton** |'sətn| largely residential borough of S Greater London, England, W of Croydon. Pop. 164,000.

**Sut•ton Cold•field** |'sətn| largely residential town in the West Midlands of England, just N of Birmingham. Pop. 86,000.

**Su•va** |'soŏvə| the capital of Fiji, a port on the SE coast of the island of Viti Levu. Pop. 72,000.

**Su•wan•nee** |'s(ə)wänē| (also **Swanee**) river of the SE U.S. Rising in SE Georgia, it flows for some 250 mi./400 km. SW through N Florida to the Gulf of Mexico.

**Su•won** |'soŏ'wən| historic industrial city in NW South Korea, S of Seoul. Pop. 2,449,000. The capital of Kyonggi province, it is an agricultural research and administrative center.

**Suz•dal** |'soŏzdəl| city in central Russia, now part of NE Moscow. With its ancient buildings, its major industry is tourism.

**Su•zhou** |'soŏ'CHow| (also **Suchou** or **Soochow**) city in E China, in the province of Jiangsu, W of Shanghai on the Grand Canal. Pop. 840,000. Founded in the 6th century B.C., it was the capital of the ancient Wu kingdom.

**Su•zu•ka** |soŏ'zoŏkä| industrial city in central Japan, on S Honshu. Pop. 174,000.

**Sval•bard** |'sväl,bärd| group of islands in the Arctic Ocean about 400 mi./640 km. N of Norway. Pop. 3,700. They came under Norwegian sovereignty in 1925. The chief settlement (on Spitsbergen) is Longyearbyen.

**Svalbard**

**Sverd•lovsk** |ˌsvərd'lawfsk| former name (1924–91) for EKATERINBURG.

**Sver•drup Islands** |'sferdrəp| icebound island group in the Canadian Arctic, W of Ellesmere Island. Explored by the Norwegian Otto Sverdrup in 1898, they did not become Canadian until 1931.

**Sve•ri•ge** |sve'rēyə| Swedish name for SWEDEN.

**Svir River** |'svir| river (140 mi./320 km. long) in NW Russia. It flows from Lake Onega to Lake Ladoga. During World War

II it was the battle line between Russian and Finnish troops.

**Sviz·ze·ra** |'zvĕttserä| Italian name for SWITZERLAND.

**Swa·bia** |'swabēə| former duchy of medieval Germany. The region is now divided among SW Germany, Switzerland, and France. German name **Schwaben**.
□ **Swabian** *adj. & n.*

**Swains Island** |swänz| (also **Quiros**) privately owned island in the S central Pacific, N of and under the jurisdiction of American Samoa. It was formerly part of Tokelau, New Zealand.

**Swa·kop·mund** |'sfäkawpmənt| resort town in W Namibia, on the Atlantic coast. Pop. 18,000. It was formerly the chief port of German Southwest Africa.

**Swan River** |'swän| river of Western Australia. Rising as the Avon to the SE of Perth, it flows N and W through Perth to the Indian Ocean at Fremantle. It was the site of the first-free (nonpenal) European settlement in Western Australia.

**Swan·sea** |'swänzē| industrial port city in S Wales, on the Bristol Channel. Pop. 182,000. Welsh name **Abertawe**.

**Swat** |swät| river in N Pakistan, flowing 400 mi./645 km., from a SE spur of the Hindu Kush into the Kabul River NE of Peshawar.

**Swa·tow** |'swä'tow| former name for SHANTOU.

**Swa·zi·land** |'swäzē,lænd| landlocked kingdom in southern Africa, bounded by South Africa and Mozambique. Area: 6,706 sq. mi./17,363 sq. km. Pop. 825,000. Official languages, Swazi and English. Capital and largest city: Mbabane. Legislative capital: Lobamba. Controlled by South Africa and Britain, Swaziland became independent in 1968. It is largely agricultural.

**Swaziland**

**Swe·den** |'swēdən| kingdom occupying the E part of the Scandinavian Peninsula. Area: 173,798 sq. mi./449,964 sq. km. Pop.

**Sweden**

8,591,000. Language, Swedish. Capital and largest city: Stockholm. Swedish name **Sverige**. A nation from the 12th century, Sweden was an independent kingdom by 1523; in 1814–1905 it was united with Norway. Mining, forest industries, and manufacturing are key to the economy.
□ **Swedish** *adj. & n.* **Swede** *n.*

**Swift Current** |'swift| industrial and commercial city in SW Saskatchewan. Pop. 14,815.

**Swin·don** |'swindən| industrial town in central England. Pop. 100,000. An old market town, it developed rapidly after railroad engineering works were established in 1841 and again in the 1950s as an overspill town for London.

**Swiss Confederation** |'swis| the confederation of cantons forming Switzerland, and the official name of the country.

**Swit·zer·land** |'switsərlənd| mountainous, landlocked republic in W central Europe. Area: 15,949 sq. mi./41,293 sq. km. Pop. 6,673,850. Official languages, French, German, Italian, and Romansch. Capital: Bern. Largest city: Zurich. French name **Suisse**, German name **Schweiz**, Italian name **Svizzera**; also called by its Latin name **Helvetia**. Independent from the 14th–15th centuries, when it threw off Hapsburg and other rulers, Switzerland has a history of neutrality and as a home to international organizations. Tourism, high technology, dairying, and finance are among key industries. □ **Swiss** *adj. & n.*

**Sword Beach** |sawrd| easternmost of the Normandy beaches used during the D-day landing in June 1944, at the village of Lion-sur-Mer. British forces landed here.

**Syb·a·ris** |'sibərəs| ancient city of MAGNA GRAECIA, on the Gulf of Tarentum (Taranto) in S Italy. Its luxury gave rise to the term *sybarite*.

**Syd·ney**[1] |'sidnē| industrial city in E Nova Scotia, on Cape Breton Island. Pop.

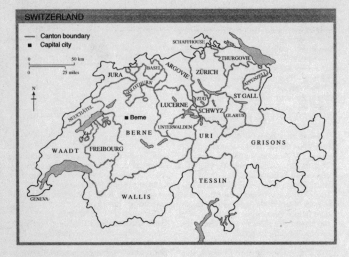

SWITZERLAND

—— Canton boundary
■ Capital city

0        50 km
0     25 miles

26,063. It is a coal-mining and steelmaking center.

**Syd•ney**² |'sidnē| the capital of New South Wales in SE Australia. Pop. 3,098,000. It was the first British settlement in Australia and is the country's largest city and chief port. It has a fine natural harbor, crossed by the Sydney Harbour Bridge (opened 1932), and a striking opera house (opened 1973).

**Syk•tyv•kar** |siktif'kär| city in NW Russia, capital of the autonomous republic of Komi. Pop. 235,000.

**Sylt** |'soolt| island in the North Sea, largest of the Frisian Islands of Germany. Area: 36 sq. mi./96 sq. km. Its largest towns are Westerland, a resort, and Kampen.

**Syr•a•cuse**¹ |'sirə,kyoos| industrial city in central New York, to the SE of Lake Ontario. Pop. 163,860. It was a center of salt production during the 19th century, and is now a manufacturing center.

**Syr•a•cuse**² |'sirə,kyoos| port on the E coast of Sicily. Pop. 125,000. It was a flourishing center of Greek culture, especially in the 5th and 4th centuries B.C. under the rule of Dionysius I and II. It was taken by the Romans at the end of the 3rd century B.C. Italian name **Siracusa**.

**Syr Dar•ya River** |sir'däryə| river (1,370 mi./2,204 km.) in Kyrgyzstan, Uzbekistan, and Kazakhstan, flowing through the Fergana Valley to the Aral Sea.

**Syr•ia** |'sirēə| republic in the Middle East with a coastline on the E Mediterranean Sea. Area: 71,089 sq. mi./184,050 sq. km. Pop. 12,824,000. Language, Arabic. Capital and largest city: Damascus. An ancient country, Syria became an Islamic center in the 7th century, and was dominated by the Turks from the 16th century until World War I. It gained independence in 1941. In 1958–61 it was a member, with Egypt, of the United Arab Republic. Traditionally agricultural, it is now also industrial and an oil producer. □ **Syrian** *adj. & n.*

Syria

**Syr•i•an Desert** |'sirēən| region of SW Asia, a N extension of the Arabian Desert, in SE Syria, E Jordan, SW Iraq, and N Saudi Arabia. Mesopotamia lies to the E.

**Syz•ran** |siz'rən| river port and industrial

city in W Russia, on the Volga River. Pop.
175,000.

**Szcze·cin** |'sHcHet,sHēn| industrial city in
NW Poland, a port on the Oder River near
the border with Germany. Pop. 413,000.
German name **Stettin**.

**Sze·chwan** |'se(t)sH',wän| see Sɪcʜᴜᴀɴ.

**Sze·ged** |'seged| city in S Hungary, a port
on the Tisza River near the border with Ser-
bia. Pop. 178,000. It is noted for food production.

**Szé·kes·fe·hér·vár** |'sekesH,fehärvär| in-
dustrial and transportation center in W
Hungary, the capital of Féjer county. Pop.
110,000. The kings of Hungary were
crowned and buried here from the 11th to
the 16th centuries.

**Szi·get·vár** |'sēget,vär| historic city in SW
Hungary. Pop. 12,000. Its medieval
fortress was defended by Nicholas Zrinyi
against Sulayman I, the Ottoman sultan, in
1566.

**Szol·nok** |'sōl,nōk| agricultural and trans-
portation center in E Hungary, capital of
Solnok county. Pop. 80,000. It was founded as a fortress town in 1076.

**Szom·bat·hely** |'sōmbawt,hā| transporta-
tion center and capital of Vas county in W
Hungary, near the Austrian border. Pop.
86,000.

# Tt

**Ta·bas·co** |təˈbæskō| state of SE Mexico, on the Gulf of Mexico. Area: 9,759 sq. mi./25,267 sq. km. Pop. 1,501,000. Capital: Villahermosa. Agriculture and oil are key to its economy.

**Ta·ble Mountain** |ˌtäbəl| flat-topped mountain near the SW tip of South Africa, overlooking Cape Town and Table Bay, rising to a height of 3,563 ft./1,087 m.

**Ta·bor, Mount** |ˈtābər| (Hebrew name **Har Tavor**) mountain in N Israel, rising to 1,938 ft./588 m. above the Plain of Jezreel.

**Tà·bor** |ˈtäb,awr| historic city in the S central Czech Republic. Pop. 36,000. The economy is based on agriculture and mining.

**Ta·bo·ra** |təˈbawrə| commercial city in W central Tanzania, the capital of the Tabora region. Pop. 120,000.

**Ta·briz** |təˈbrēz| city in NW Iran. Pop. 1,089,000. The capital of East Azerbaijan and a former Armenian and Persian capital, it has been subject to frequent destructive earthquakes. Textile, carpet, and other industries are important.

**Ta·chi·ka·wa** |ˌtäˈCHeˈkäwä| commercial city in E central Japan, on E central Honshu, a suburb W of Tokyo. Pop. 153,000.

**Ta·ching** |ˈtäˈCHiNG| see DAQING.

**Ta·clo·ban** |täˈklōbän| commercial port city in the Philippines, on NE Leyte. Pop. 137,000.

**Tac·na** |ˈtäknə| city in extreme S Peru, the capital of Tacna department, an irrigated agricultural region. Pop. 116,000. The Tacna region was long fought over by Peru, Bolivia, and Chile.

**Ta·co·ma** |təˈkōmə| industrial port city in W central Washington, on Puget Sound S of Seattle. Pop. 176,664.

**Ta·con·ic Mountains** |təˈkänik| (also the **Taconics**) range of the Appalachian system along the E border of New York with Connecticut, Massachusetts, and Vermont.

**Tae·gu** |ˈtægˈoȯ; ˈtīˈgoȯ| industrial city in SE South Korea. Pop. 2,229,000. The third-largest South Korean city, a communications center, it has historic Buddhist sites.

**Tae·jon** |ˈtæjˈawn; ˈtīˈjawn| industrial and technological city in central South Korea. Pop. 1,062,000.

**Ta·gan·rog** |ˈtægənˌrawg| industrial port in SW Russia, on the Gulf of Taganrog, an inlet of the Sea of Azov. Pop. 293,000. It was founded in 1698 by Peter the Great as a fortress and naval base.

**Ta·gus** |ˈtāgəs| river in SW Europe, the longest of the Iberian Peninsula, which rises in the mountains of E Spain and flows over 625 mi./1,000 km. generally W into Portugal, where it turns SW, emptying into the Atlantic near Lisbon. Spanish name **Tajo**, Portuguese name **Tejo**.

**Ta·hi·ti** |təˈhētē| island in the central S Pacific, one of the Society Islands, forming part of French Polynesia. Pop. 116,000. Capital: Papeete. One of the largest islands in the S Pacific, it was claimed for France in 1768. Tourism and fruit production are key to its economy.

**Tah·le·quah** |ˈtæləˌkwaw.| commercial city in E Oklahoma, former capital of the Cherokee nation. Pop. 10,398.

**Ta·hoe, Lake** |ˈtäˌhō| mountain lake on the border of N central California with Nevada, noted for its resorts.

**Tai'an** |ˈtīˈän| industrial and agricultural city in NE China, in Shandong province. Pop. 1,370,000.

**Tai·chung** |ˈtīˈCHȯNG| commercial and cultural city in W central Taiwan. Pop. 774,000.

**Ta'if** |ˈtäif| city in W Saudi Arabia, to the SE of Mecca in the Asir Mts. Pop. 205,000. It is the unofficial seat of government of Saudi Arabia during the summer.

**Tai·myr Peninsula** |tīˈmir| (also **Taymyr**) vast, almost uninhabited peninsula on the N coast of central Russia, extending into the Arctic Ocean and separating the Kara Sea from the Laptev Sea. Its N tip, Cape Chelyuskin, is the northernmost point of Asia.

**Tai·nan** |ˈtīˈnän| industrial city on the SW coast of Taiwan. Pop. 690,000. Settled from mainland China in 1590, it is one of the oldest cities on the island and was its capital from 1684 until 1885, when it was replaced by Taipei. Its original name was Taiwan, the name later given to the whole island.

**Tai·pei** |ˈtīˈpā; ˈtīˌbā| the capital of Taiwan. Pop. 2,718,000, an important center of commerce, finance, and industry. It developed as an industrial city in the 19th century, and became the capital in 1885.

**Tai·ping** |ˈtīˈpiNG| city in central peninsular Malaysia, in the foothills of the Bintang

Mts. Pop. 146,000. The only city in Malaysia with a Chinese name, it was developed by immigrant Chinese in the 1840s.

**Tai·wan** |'tī'wän| island republic off the SE coast of China. Area: 14,000 sq. mi./35,980 sq. km. Pop. 20,400,000. Official language, Mandarin Chinese. Capital: Taipei. Official name **Republic of China.** Former (Portuguese) name **Formosa.** Held at times by the Portuguese and Japanese, the island became in 1949 the refuge of nationalist Chinese fleeing the communist takeover of the mainland. It has since developed a strong industrial economy, despite friction between the exiles and natives and despite loss of UN recognition in 1971 in favor of the mainland, which regards Taiwan as one of its provinces. □ **Taiwanese** *adj. & n.*

Taiwan

**Tai·yuan** |'tīyoŏ'än| industrial city in N China, capital of Shanxi province. Pop. 1,900,000.

**Ta'iz** |tä'ēz| city in SW Yemen. Pop. 290,000. It was the administrative capital of Yemen from 1948 to 1962.

**Ta·jik·i·stan** |tä,jiki'stän| (also **Tadzhikistan**) mountainous republic in central Asia, N of Afghanistan. Area: 55,272 sq. mi./143,100 sq. km. Pop. 5,412,000. Languages, Tajik (official), Russian. Capital and largest city: Dushanbe. A Mongol ter-

Tajikistan

ritory absorbed into the Russian Empire in the 19th century, Tajikistan is inhabited by an Iranian, Sunni Muslim people. Independent from the Soviet Union since 1991, it has an economy based on agriculture and mineral extraction. □ **Tajik** *adj. & n.*

**Taj Ma·hal** |,täzH mə'häl| mausoleum in N central India, near the Jumna River in Agra, completed c. 1648 by Mogul emperor Shah Jahan for his favorite wife.

**Ta·jo** |'tähō| Spanish name for TAGUS.

**Ta·ka·ma·tsu** |,täkä'mätsoō| ferry port and industrial center in W Japan, on NE Shikoku. Pop. 330,000.

**Ta·ka·o·ka** |tä'kowkä| industrial city in central Japan, on central Honshu. Pop. 175,000. It is a center for the Japanese aluminum industry.

**Ta·ka·ra·zu·ka** |tä,kärä'zoōkä| city in W central Japan, on S Honshu, NW of Osaka. Pop. 202,000. It is a suburb and a resort serving the Osaka and Kobe areas.

**Ta·ka·sa·ki** |,täkä'säkē| industrial city in N central Japan, on central Honshu. Pop. 236,000.

**Ta·kat·suki** |tä'kätskē| city in W central Japan, on S Honshu, NNE of Osaka. Pop. 360,000.

**Ta·kli·ma·kan Desert** |,täkləmə'kän| (also **Takla Makan**) desert in the Xinjiang autonomous region of NW China, lying between the Kunlun Shan and Tien Shan mountains and forming the greater part of the Tarim Basin.

**Ta·ko·ra·di** |,täkō'rädē| seaport in W Ghana, on the Gulf of Guinea. Pop. 615,000. It is part of the joint urban area of Sekondi-Takoradi and is one of the major seaports of W Africa.

**Ta·la·ra** |tä'lärä| port town in extreme NW Peru, an oil industry center. Pop. 90,000.

**Ta·la·ve·ra de la Rei·na** |,tälä'värä,dä lä 'ränä| town in central Spain, on the Tagus River. Pop. 69,000. It is known for its fine ceramics.

**Tal·ca** |'tälkä| city in central Chile, capital of the Maule region. Pop. 164,000. It is a wine industry center.

**Tal·ca·hua·no** |,tälkä'wänō| city in S central Chile, a commercial and naval port in the Bío-Bío region. Pop. 247,000.

**Tal·ie·sin** |täl'yesən; tælε'əsən| see SPRING GREEN, Wisconsin and SCOTTSDALE, Arizona.

**Tal·la·de·ga** |,tælə'dägə; ,tælə'dēgə| industrial city in E central Alabama, a mining center also noted for its Talladega Superspeedway. Pop. 18,175.

**Tal·la·has·see** |,tælə'hæsē| university and

industrial city, the capital of Florida, in the NW. Pop. 124,773.

**Tal·la·poo·sa River** |ˌtæləˈpo͞osə| river that flows 268 mi./430 km. from NW Georgia into Alabama, where it joins the Coosa to form the Alabama River.

**Tal·linn** |ˈtælən| the capital of Estonia, an industrial port on the Gulf of Finland. Pop. 505,000. Before 1917 it was called Revel.

**Ta·ma** |ˈtämä| city in E central Japan, on E central Honshu, W of Shinjuku. Pop. 144,000.

**Ta·ma·le** |täˈmälä| commercial and academic city in N Ghana, capital of the Northern region. Pop. 136,000.

**Ta·mal·pa·is, Mount** |ˌtæmalˈpīəs| mountain in Marin County, NW California, N of San Francisco across the Golden Gate, and center of a recreational area.

**Tam·an·ras·set** |ˌtæmənˈræsət| commercial town in S Algeria, at the edge of the Hoggar Mts. and the Sahara. Pop. 38,000. It is a center for the Tuareg people.

**Ta·mar** |ˈtämər| river in SW England that rises in NW Devon and flows 60 mi./98 km. generally southward, forming the boundary between Devon and Cornwall and emptying into the English Channel through Plymouth Sound.

**Tam·a·rac** |ˈtæməˌræk| city in SE Florida, a retirement center NW of Fort Lauderdale. Pop. 44,822.

**Ta·mau·li·pas** |täˌmowˈlēpäs| state of NE Mexico with a coastline on the Gulf of Mexico. Area: 30,662 sq. mi./79,384 sq. km. Pop. 2,244,000. Capital: Ciudad Victoria.

**Tam·bo·ra, Gu·nung** |ˈgo͞oˌnoͦoNG ˈtämbrə| active volcano in Indonesia, on N Sumbawa. Its 1815 eruption was one of the most destructive in the history of the world.

**Tam·bov** |tämˈbawf| industrial city in SW Russia. Pop. 307,000.

**Ta·mil Na·du** |ˌtæməl ˈnädoͦo| state in the extreme SE of the Indian peninsula, on the Coromandel Coast, with a largely Tamil-speaking, Hindu population. Pop. 55,640,000. Capital: Madras. Tamil Nadu was also an ancient kingdom comprising a much larger area, stretching N to Orissa and including the Lakshadweep Islands and part of the Malabar Coast. Former name (until 1968) **Madras**.

**Tam·ma·ny Hall** |ˌtæmənē| name for the traditional Democratic Party in New York City, regarded as occupying a social hall in lower Manhattan. Actual headquarters moved many times.

**Tam·mer·fors** |ˌtämərˈfarsн| Swedish name for TAMPERE.

**Tam·pa** |ˈtæmpə| industrial port and resort on the W coast of Florida. Pop. 280,015.

**Tam·pa Bay** |ˈtæmpə| inlet of the Gulf of Mexico in SW Florida, on which lie Tampa, St. Petersburg, and other cities and resorts.

**Tam·pe·re** |ˈtämpərə| industrial and commercial city in SW Finland. Pop. 173,000. Swedish name **Tammerfors**.

**Tam·pi·co** |tæmˈpē,kō| one of Mexico's principal ports, an oil, fishing, and resort center in Tamaulipas state, on the Gulf of Mexico. Pop. 272,000.

**Tam·worth** |ˈtæm,wərTH| industrial town in central England, in Staffordshire. Pop. 65,000.

**Ta·na, Lake** |ˈtänə| lake in N Ethiopia, the largest in the country and the source of the Blue Nile.

**Ta·na** |ˈtänə| longest river in Kenya. It flows 500 mi./800 km. from near Mount Kenya to the Indian Ocean N of Malindi.

**Tan·a·gra** |ˈtænəgrə| town in ancient Greece, in Boeotia E of Thebes, where the Spartans defeated the Athenians in 457 B.C. during the Peloponnesian War.

**Ta·na·na·rive** |təˈnɒnə,rēv| former name (until 1975) for ANTANANARIVO.

**Tan·a·na River** |ˈtænə,naw| river that flows 600 mi./1,000 km. from the Yukon Territory across Alaska, meeting the Yukon River W of Fairbanks.

**Tan·dil** |tänˈdél| city in E Argentina, S of Buenos Aires. Pop. 90,000. It is a resort and agricultural and university center.

**Tan·ga** |ˈtäNGgä| one of the principal ports of Tanzania, in the NE, on the Indian Ocean, opposite Pemba island. Pop. 188,000.

**Tan·gan·yi·ka, Lake** |ˌtæNGgənˈyēkə| lake in E Africa, in the Great Rift Valley. The deepest lake in Africa and the longest (420 mi./680 km.) freshwater lake in the world, it forms most of the border of the Democratic Republic of Congo (formerly Zaire) with Tanzania and Burundi.

**Tan·gan·yi·ka** |ˌtæNGgənˈēkə| former republic in E Africa, since 1964 part of TANZANIA. Before independence in 1962, it was colonized by the Germans and the British.

**Tan·gier** |tænˈjir| (also **Tangiers, Tanger**) seaport on the N coast of Morocco, on the Strait of Gibraltar commanding the W entrance to the Mediterranean. Pop. 307,000. Portuguese from the end of the 15th century, Tangier was ruled by the sultan of Morocco from 1684 until 1904, when it came under international control; it passed to the newly independent monarchy of Morocco in 1956.

**Tan·gle·wood** see STOCKBRIDGE.

**Tang·shan** |'täNG'shän| industrial city in Hebei province, NE China. Pop. 1,500,000. The city was rebuilt after a devastating earthquake in 1976.

**Ta·nim·bar Islands** |tə'nim,bär| group of islands in Indonesia, between the Aru Islands and Timor in the Banda Sea.

**Tan·jung·ka·rang** |,tänjŏŏNG'käräNG| see BANDAR LAMPUNG.

**Tan·nen·berg** |'tänən,berg| (Polish name **Stebark**) village in NE Poland (formerly in East Prussia), scene of two historic battles In 1410 Poles and allies defeated the invading Teutonic Knights nearby. In 1914 the Germans won a major victory over Russian troops here.

**Tannu-Tuva** |,tänŏŏ'tŏŏvə| former name for TUVA.

**Tan·ta** |'täntə| industrial and commercial city in NE Egypt, N of Cairo in the Nile delta. Pop. 372,000. It is a center of Sufism. The ruins of SAÏS are nearby.

**Tan·za·nia** |,tænzə'nēə| republic in E Africa with a coastline on the Indian Ocean. Area: 362,940 sq. mi./939,652 sq. km. Pop. 27,270,000. Official languages, Swahili and English. Capital: Dodoma. Largest city: Dar es Salaam. A 1964 unification of Tanganyika and Zanzibar, Tanzania stretches from high plateaus including the Serengeti E to the ocean. It is largely agricultural, producing coffee, cotton, sisal, and other export crops. Mount Kilimanjaro and other sites draw tourists. □ **Tanzanian** *adj. & n.*

Tanzania

**Ta·or·mi·na** |,towr'mēnə| resort town on the E coast of Sicily. Pop. 11,000. It was founded by Greek colonists in the 4th century B.C. and was an important city until the 15th century.

**Taos** |tows; 'tä,ōs| town in N New Mexi-

co, in the Sangre de Cristo Mts., a noted resort and arts center. Pop. 4,065.

**Ta·pa·chu·la** |,täpä'CHŏŏlä| city in extreme SE Mexico, in Chiapas state, near the Guatemalan border. Pop. 223,000. It is a commercial and transportation center in a coffee-producing region.

**Ta·pa·jós** |,täpə'zHawsH| (also **Tapajoz**) river that with its headstreams flows 1,256 mi./2,010 km. N from the Mato Grosso in central Brazil, to join the Amazon W of Santarém.

**Tap·pan Zee** |'tæpən 'zē; 'tæ,pæn| broadening of the Hudson River in SE New York, near Tarrytown. Bridged in 1955, it is a well-known fishing and recreational site.

**Tara** |'tærə| hill in County Meath, E central Ireland, site in early times of the residence of the high kings of Ireland and still marked by ancient earthworks.

**Ta·ra·bu·lus Al-Gharb** |tə'räbələs äl 'gärb| Arabic name for TRIPOLI (in sense **1**).

**Ta·ra·bu·lus Ash-Sham** |tə'räbələs esH 'sHæm| Arabic name for TRIPOLI (in sense **2**).

**Ta·ra·na·ki** |,tärä'näkē| Maori name for Mount Egmont (see EGMONT, MOUNT).

**Ta·ran·to** |'tärän,tō| seaport and naval base in Apulia, SE Italy. Pop. 244,000. Founded by the Greeks in the 8th century B.C., it came under Roman rule in 272 B.C.

**Ta·ras·con** |,tärä'skawn| commercial town in SE France, on the Rhone River N of Arles, associated with the writing of Alphonse Daudet. Pop. 12,000.

**Ta·ra·wa** |tə'räwə; 'tärə,wä| atoll in the S Pacific, one of the Gilbert Islands. Pop. 29,000. It is the location of Bairiki, the capital of Kiribati. Tarawa was the scene of intense fighting in World War II.

**Tarbes** |tärb| industrial and market town in SW France, the capital of the Hautes-Pyrénées department. Pop. 50,000.

**Tar Heel State** |'tär,hēl| informal name for NORTH CAROLINA.

**Ta·ri·ja** |tä'rēhä| city in SE Bolivia, capital of Tarija department, on the Guadalquivir River. Pop. 90,000. It is a highland agricultural center.

**Ta·rim** |'tä'rēm; 'dä'rēm| river of NW China, in Xinjiang autonomous region. It rises as the Yarkand in the Kunlun Shan mountains and flows for over 1,250 mi./2,000 km. generally E through the dry Tarim Basin, petering out in the Lop Nor depression. For much of its course the river follows no clearly defined bed and is subject to much evaporation.

**Ta·rim Basin** |'tä'rēm; 'dä'rēm| vast, dry low-lying region in Xinjiang, NW China, lying between the Kunlun Shan and Tian Shan mountains. It includes the Taklimakan Desert and Turfan Depression.

**Tar·lac** |'tär‚läk| commercial town in the Philippines, on central Luzon, N of Manila. Pop. 209,000.

**Tarn** |tärn| river of S France, which rises in the Cévennes and flows 235 mi./380 km/ generally SW through deep gorges before meeting the Garonne NW of Toulouse.

**Tar·nów** |'tär‚nŏŏf| industrial city in S Poland. Pop. 74,000.

**Tar·pe·ian Rock** |tär'pēən| cliff in ancient Rome, at the SW corner of the Capitoline Hill, from which murderers and traitors were thrown.

**Tar·pon Springs** |'tärpən| city in SW Florida, on the Gulf of Mexico, home to a famed sponge-diving industry. Pop. 17,906.

**Tar·qui·nia** |tär'kwēnyə| industrial town in central Italy, NW of Rome. Pop. 14,000. Once capital of the Etruscan League, it came under Roman domination in the 4th century B.C.

**Tar·ra·go·na** |‚tärə'gōnə| port and commercial center in E Spain, on the Mediterranean Sea, capital of Tarragona province. Pop. 113,000.

**Tar·ra·sa** |tə'räsə| (also **Terrassa**) industrial city in Catalonia, NE Spain, N of Barcelona. Pop. 154,000.

**Tar·ry·town** |'tærē‚town| residential and industrial village in SE New York, on the Tappan Zee of the Hudson River. Pop. 10,739.

**Tar·sus** |'tärsəs| ancient city of Asia Minor (present-day S Turkey), the capital of Cilicia and the birthplace of St. Paul. It is now a market town.

**Tar·ta·ry** |'tärtərē| historical region of Asia and E Europe, especially the high plateau of central Asia and its NW slopes, which formed part of the Tartar Empire of Genghis Khan, with its capital at Samarkand, in the Middle Ages.

**Tar·tu** |'tär‚tŏŏ| industrial and port city in E Estonia, on the Ema River. Pop. 115,000.

**Tash·kent** |tæsH'kent| the capital of Uzbekistan, in the far NE of the country in the western foothills of the Tian Shan mountains: pop. 2,094,000. One of the oldest cities in central Asia, Tashkent was an important center on the trade route between Europe and the Orient. It became part of the Mongol Empire in the 13th century, was captured by the Russians in 1865,

and replaced Samarkand as capital of Uzbekistan in 1930.

**Ta·sik·ma·la·ya** |‚täsikmə'lēə| (also **Tasikmalaja**) commercial city in Indonesia, on W Java. Pop. 166,000.

**Tas·man, Mount** |'tæzmən| peak in the Southern Alps range, on South Island, New Zealand; the second-highest in New Zealand: 11,473 ft./3,497 m.

**Tas·ma·nia** |tæz'mānēyə; tæz'mānyə| state of Australia consisting of the mountainous island of Tasmania itself and several smaller islands. Pop. 458,000. Capital and largest city: Hobart. It was known as Van Diemen's Land until 1855. Agriculture and mining are important. □ **Tasmanian** *adj. & n.*

**Tas·man Sea** |'tæzmən| arm of the South Pacific lying between Australia and New Zealand.

**Ta·ta·bán·ya** |'tätä‚bänyä| town in N Hungary, in a coalfield W of Budapest. Pop. 77,000.

**Ta·tar City** |'tä'tär| (also called **Inner City**) walled section of Beijing, China, lying N of the Chinese, or Outer, City. It includes the Forbidden City and most government offices and embassies.

**Ta·tar·stan** |‚tätər'stæn| autonomous republic in European Russia, in the valley of the Volga River. Pop. 3,658,000. Capital: Kazan.

**Tate Gallery** |tāt| noted art gallery in central London, England, on the N bank of the Thames in the Millbank section, opened in 1897.

**Ta·tra Mountains** |'tätrə| (also the **Tatras**) range in E Europe on the Polish–Slovak border, the highest range in the Carpathians, rising to 8,710 ft./2,655 m. at Mount Gerlachovsky.

**Tau·ba·té** |‚towbə'tä| commercial city in SE Brazil, in São Paulo state. Pop. 220,000. It is a processing center in the agricultural Paraiba River valley.

**Taung·gyi** |'town'jē| (also **Tawnggyi**) hill resort town in central Burma, SE of Mandalay. Pop. 108,000.

**Taun·ton**[1] |'tawntn| the county seat of Somerset, in SW England. Pop. 49,000. It is a center of textile and cider production.

**Taun·ton**[2] |'tawntn| industrial city in SE Massachusetts. Pop. 49,832.

**Tau·po, Lake** |'towpō| the largest lake of New Zealand, in the center of North Island. The town of Taupo is on its northern shore. Maori name **Taupomoana**.

**Tau·ran·ga** |tow'räNGə| industrial port on the Bay of Plenty, North Island, New Zealand. Pop. 64,000.

**Tau·rus Mountains** |'tawrəs| (Turkish name **Toros Daglari**) range in S Turkey, parallel to the Mediterranean coast. Rising to 12,250 ft./3,734 m. at Mount Aladaë, it forms the S edge of the Anatolian plateau.

**Ta·voy** |tə'voi| commercial town in Tenasserim division, S Burma, near the mouth of the Tavoy River. Pop. 102,000.

**Tax·co** |'täskō| (official name **Taxco de Alarcón**) historic city in S Mexico, in Guerrero state, famed as a silver-mining and silversmithing center, and for its colonial architecture. Pop. 42,000.

**Tay, Firth of** |'fərTH əv 'tā| the estuary of the Tay River, on the North Sea coast of Scotland. It is spanned by the longest railroad bridge in Britain, a structure opened in 1888 that has 85 spans and a total length of 11,653 ft./3,553 m.

**Tay** |tā| the longest river in Scotland, flowing 120 mi./192 km. E through Loch Tay, and entering the North Sea through the Firth of Tay.

**Tay·lor** |'tālər| city in SE Michigan, a suburb SW of Detroit. Pop. 70,811.

**Tay Ninh** |'tī 'nin| commercial city in southern Vietnam, NW of Ho Chi Minh City. Pop. 37,000. It is the capital of Tay Ninh province, scene of some of the fiercest fighting during the Vietnam War.

**Ta·za** |'täzə| commercial and industrial city in NE Morocco, E of Fez. Pop. 121,000.

**Tbi·li·si** |təbī'lēsē| the capital of the republic of Georgia, on the Kura River in the Caucasus. Pop. 1,267,000. From 1845 until 1936 its name was Tiflis. An ancient city, it is now a commercial and industrial center.

**Tchad** French name for CHAD.

**Tea·neck** |'tē,nek| township in NE New Jersey, a largely residential suburb. Pop. 37,825.

**Tea·pot Dome** |'tē,pät 'dōm| oil field in SE Wyoming, which as a naval reserve was the focus of a 1920s corruption scandal.

**Té·bes·sa** |te'besə| (ancient name **Theveste**) historic commercial and industrial city in NE Algeria, near the Tunisian border. Pop. 112,000.

**Tees** |tēz| river of NE England that rises in Cumbria and flows 80 mi./128 km. generally SE to the North Sea at Middlesbrough.

**Tees·side** |'tē(z),sīd| industrial region in NE England around the lower Tees valley, in Celeveland, including Middlesbrough.

**Te·gal** |tə'gäl| industrial port town in Indonesia, on central Java. Pop. 230,000.

**Te·gern·see** |'tāgərn,zā| lake in Bavaria, in SW Germany, SE of Munich, in the foothills of the Alps, a popular resort area.

**Te·gu·ci·gal·pa** |tə,gōōsə'gälpə| capital and largest city of Honduras. Pop. 670,000. Once a mining center, it now has various industries.

**Te·hach·a·pi Mountains** |ti'hæCHə,pē| range that lies across California, just N of the Transverse Ranges. It is sometimes considered the divider between N and S California.

**Teh·ran** |,tāə'ræn; ,tāə'rän| (also **Teheran**) the capital and largest city of Iran, an industrial center in the foothills of the Elburz Mts. Pop. 6,750,000. It replaced Isfahan as capital of Persia in 1788.

**Te·hua·cán** |,tāwä'kän| city in S central Mexico, in Puebla state. Pop. 139,000. It is a commercial center and a famed spa.

**Te·huan·te·pec, Isthmus of** |tə'wäntə,pek| lowland region in S Mexico, between the Gulf of Campeche (the Gulf of Mexico) on the N and the Gulf of Tehuantepec (the Pacific Ocean) on the S. Highland Chiapas lies to the E, Oaxaca to the W.

**Tei·de, Pi·co de** |'pēkō dā 'ta,dā| volcano on Tenerife, in the Spanish Canary Islands, in the Atlantic. At 3,718 m./12,198 ft., it is the highest peak in Spain.

**Te·jo** |'tā,ZHōō| Portuguese name for TAGUS.

**Te·kir·dağ** |te'kir,däg| port city in European Turkey, W of Istanbul on the Sea of Marmara, the capital of Tekirdağ province. Pop. 80,000.

**Tel Aviv** |,tel ə'vēv| (also **Tel Aviv–Jaffa**) industrial and administrative city on the Mediterranean coast of Israel. Pop. 355,000. It was founded as a suburb of Jaffa by Russian Jewish immigrants in 1909 and named Tel Aviv a year later. The capital of Israel 1948–50, it is still regarded as such by many governments.

**Tel·e·graph Hill** |'telə,græf| hill neighborhood in San Francisco, California, named for the signal stations that surmounted it in the 19th century.

**Tel·e·mark** |'telə,märk| mountain and lake region in S Norway. The highest peak is Gausta (6,178 ft./1,883 m.).

**Tel·ford** |'telfərd| industrial town in Shropshire, W central England. Pop. 115,000.

**Tell el-Amarna** |'tel ,el ə'märnə| see AMARNA, TELL EL-.

**Tel·li·cher·ry** |,teli'CHerē| (also called **Thalassery**) port town in S India, on the Malabar Coast of Kerala state. Pop. 104,000.

**Tel·lu·ride** |'telyə,rīd| resort town in SW Colorado, a former mining center. Pop. 1,309.

**Te·ma** |'tāmä| industrial port city in SE

Ghana, just E of Accra. Pop. 100,000. Developed from the 1950s, it has the largest artificial harbor in Africa.

**Te·mes·vár** |'temesн,vär| Hungarian name for Timişoara.

**Te·mir·tau** |'tämirtow| coal-mining town in Kazakhstan, NW of Qaraghandy. Pop. 213,000.

**Tem·pe, Vale of** |'tempē| valley in E central Greece, between Mount Olympus and Mount Ossa. Its beauty was celebrated by the ancient Greek poets.

**Tem·pe** |,tem'pē; 'tempē| city in S central Arizona, a suburb E of Phoenix and home to Arizona State University. Pop. 141,865.

**Tem·ple** |'tempəl| industrial and commercial city in central Texas. Pop. 46,109.

**Tem·ple, Mount** |'tempəl| name for Mount Moriah, in Jerusalem, as the site of the Temple of Solomon.

**Te·mu·co** |tä'mo͝okō| industrial and commercial city in S central Chile, capital of Araucania region. Pop. 212,000.

**Te·na·li** |tä'näle͝| commercial city in S India, in Andhra Pradesh state, SE of Hyderabad. Pop. 144,000.

**Ten·der·loin, the** |'tendər,loin| generic term for an urban district notorious for vice. It was first used of part of W Manhattan, New York City, in the 19th century.

**Ten·e·dos** |'tenə,däs| see Bozcaada.

**Ten·er·ife** |,tenə'rēfē; ,tenə'rif| volcanic island in the Atlantic, the largest of the Spanish Canary Islands. Pop. 771,000. Capital: Santa Cruz.

**Ten·nes·see** |,tenə'sē| see box. □ **Tennessean** adj. & n.

**Ten·nes·see River** |,tenə'sē| river in the SE U.S., flowing some 875 mi./1,400 km. in a great loop, generally W through Tennessee and Alabama, then N to re-enter Tennessee, joining the Ohio River in W Kentucky. Its flooding was controlled and its flow harnessed for hydroelectric power by the projects of the Tennessee Valley Authority, beginning in 1933.

**Te·noch·ti·tlán** |tä,nawcнtēt'län| the capital of the Aztec empire in ancient Mexico.

**Te·ó·fi·lo Oto·ni** |tä'awfē,lo͞o ō'tōnē| (also **Theophilo Ottoni**) city in E central Brazil, in Minas Gerais state. Pop. 127,000. It is a center for the mining and cutting of semiprecious stones.

**Te·o·ti·hua·cán** |,täaw,tēwä'kän| the largest city of pre-Columbian America, situated about 25 mi./40 km. NE of present-day Mexico City. Built c. 300 B.C., it reached its zenith c. 300–600 A.D., when it was the center of an influential culture that spread

---

| **Tennessee** |
| :--- |
| **Capital:** Nashville |
| **Largest city:** Memphis |
| **Other cities:** Chattanooga, Clarksville, Fayetteville, Jackson, Knoxville, Lexington |
| **Population:** 4,877,185 (1990); 5,430,621 (1998); 5,966,000 (2005 proj.) |
| **Population rank (1990):** 17 |
| **Rank in land area:** 36 |
| **Abbreviation:** TN; Tenn. |
| **Nickname:** Volunteer State; Big Bend State |
| **Motto:** 'Agriculture and Commerce' |
| **Bird:** mockingbird |
| **Flower:** iris (cultivated flower) or maypop (wildflower) |
| **Tree:** tulip poplar |
| **Songs:** "When It's Iris Time in Tennessee"; "The Tennessee Waltz"; "My Tennessee"; "My Homeland, Tennessee"; "Rocky Top" |
| **Noted physical features:** Nashville Basin; Appalachian Mountains; Cumberland Plateau; Clingman's Dome; Tennessee River |
| **Tourist attractions:** Graceland (Memphis); Grand Ole Opry House (Nashville); The Hermitage; Cumberland Gap, Great Smoky Mountains (with North Carolina) and Shiloh national parks |
| **Admission date:** June 1, 1796 |
| **Order of admission:** 16 |
| **Name origin:** For an important Cherokee village, *Tanasi*, on the Little Tennessee River in the eastern part of the state; the meaning of the name is unknown. |

---

throughout Mesoamerica. By 650 it was declining, and it was sacked by invading Toltecs c. 900. Among its monuments are palatial buildings, plazas, and temples, including the Pyramids of the Sun and the Moon and the temple of Quetzalcóatl.

**Te·pic** |tä'pēk| city in W Mexico, capital of the agricultural state of Nayarit. Pop. 238,000.

**Te·pli·ce** |'teplētse| (also **Teplitz**) industrial and transportation center in the NW Czech Republic. Pop. 55,000. In a mining region, it is also a spa.

**Ter·cei·ra** |tər'serə| central and third-largest island in the Portuguese Azores, in the N Atlantic.

**Te·re·si·na** |,tärə'zēnə| river port in NE Brazil, on the Parnaíba river, capital of the state of Piauí. Pop. 591,000.

**Te·re·só·po·lis** |ˌtārä'zawpō͝o͝oˌlĕs| resort city in SE Brazil, in highlands in Rio de Janeiro state. Pop. 123,000.

**Ter·mez** |ter'mez| town in S Uzbekistan, on the N bank of the Amu Darya River, on the Afghan border. Pop. 90,000.

**Ter·na·te** |tər'nätē| volcanic island in Indonesia, in the Moluccas, W of Halmahera. Chief town: Ternate.

**Ter·ni** |'ternē| industrial town in central Italy, on the Nera River, capital of Terni province. Pop. 110,000.

**Ter·no·pol** |ter'nōpəl| (also **Tarnopol**) **1** administrative district in W Ukraine, N of the Dniester River. Pop. 1,175,000. **2** its capital, an industrial city. Pop. 218,000.

**Ter·re·bonne** |'terə,bän| city in S Quebec, a suburb N of Montreal. Pop. 39,768.

**Ter·re Haute** |ˌterə 'hōt; 'hət| commercial and industrial city in W Indiana, on the Wabash River. Pop. 57,483.

**Te·ruel** |täro͞o'wel| market town in E central Spain, on the Turia River, capital of Teruel province. Pop. 31,000.

**Tes·sin** |te'seN| French and German name for TICINO.

**Te·te** |'tātə| commercial town in W central Mozambique, on the Zambezi River. Pop. 112,000. It is the capital of Tete province.

**Te·thys Sea** |'tēTHis| former sea on the E of PANGAEA, thought to have lain along the line between Gondwanaland and Laurasia, roughly from present-day Iberia E to SE Asia.

**Té·touan** |tāt'wän| (also **Tetuán**) industrial and tourist city in N Morocco. Pop. 272,000.

**Te·to·vo** |'tetōvō| city in NW Macedonia, a ski resort and commercial center W of Skopje. Pop. 181,000. It is an Albanian ethnic center.

**Teu·to·bur·ger·wald** |'toitə,bo͝orgər,vält| (also called **Teutoburg Forest**) forested range in NW Germany, between Paderborn and Osnabrück. Its highest peak reaches 1,465 ft./447 m.

**Te·ve·re** |'tāvārā| Italian name for the TIBER River.

**Tewks·bury** |'to͝oksb(ə)rē| town in NE Massachusetts, SE of Lowell. Pop. 27,266. It is an industrial and residential suburb.

**Tex·ar·ka·na** |ˌteksär'kænə| twin cities on the Texas-Arkansas border. The Texas city (pop. 31,656) is home to an army ordnance center. The Arkansas city (pop. 22,631) is also industrial and commercial.

**Tex·as** |'teksəs| see box. □ **Texan** adj. & n.

**Tex·as City** |'teksəs| port city in SE Texas, on Galveston Bay SE of Houston. Pop.

---

| Texas |
|---|
| **Capital:** Austin |
| **Largest city:** Houston |
| **Other cities:** Abilene, Corpus Christi, Dallas, El Paso, Fort Worth, Galveston, Laredo, Lubbock, San Antonio, Waco |
| **Population:** 16,986,510 (1990); 19,759,614 (1998); 21,487,000 (2005 proj.) |
| **Population rank (1990):** 3 |
| **Rank in land area:** 2 |
| **Abbreviation:** TX; Tex. |
| **Nickname:** Lone Star State |
| **Motto:** 'Friendship' |
| **Bird:** mockingbird |
| **Flower:** bluebonnet |
| **Tree:** pecan |
| **Songs:** "Texas, Our Texas"; "The Eyes of Texas" |
| **Noted physical features:** Corpus Christi Bay; Port Corpus Christi, Port Galveston, Port Houston; Guadalupe Peak |
| **Tourist attractions:** The Alamo; Big Bend National Park; Guadalupe Mountains; Lyndon B. Johnson Space Center; Padre Island National Seashore |
| **Admission date:** December 29, 1845 |
| **Order of admission:** 28 |
| **Name origin:** From the Caddo Indian word *teyshas*, 'allies,' used by various native groups to refer to their mutual alliances; in the 1540s, Spanish explorers took this to be a tribal name, recording it as *Teyas* or *Tejas*, and applying it to the land north of the Rio Grande. |

---

40,822. This oil and chemical industry center was the scene of a devastating explosion in April 1947.

**Tex·co·co, Lake** |tās'kōkō| (also **Tezcuco**) dry lake in central Mexico, E of present-day Mexico City. It was the site, on islands, of the Aztec capital Tenochtitlán.

**Tex·el** |'tesəl| island, largest of the West Frisian Islands of the Netherlands, in the North Sea.

**Tha·ba·na Ntlen·ya·na** |tä'bänä ntlen-'yänä| mountain in the Drakensberg Range, in Lesotho. At 11,424 ft./3,482 m., it is the highest peak in Africa S of Mount Kilimanjaro.

**Thai·land, Gulf of** |'tī,lænd; 'tīlənd| inlet of the South China Sea between the Malay Peninsula to the W and Thailand and Cambodia to the E. It was formerly known as the Gulf of Siam.

**Thai·land** |'tī,lænd; 'tīlənd| kingdom in SE Asia, on the Gulf of Thailand. Area:

**Thailand**

198,190 sq. mi./513,115 sq. km. Pop. 56,303,000. Language, Thai. Capital and largest city: Bangkok. Former name (until 1939) **Siam**. A regional power from the 14th to the 19th century, Siam lost territory to British and French colonialism in the 19th century. It was occupied by Japan in World War II and supported the U.S. in the Vietnam War, later experiencing a large influx of refugees from Cambodia, Laos, and Vietnam. The absolute monarchy was abolished in 1931, although the king remained head of state. Thailand produces rice and other crops, tin and other metals, and textiles and consumer goods. □ **Thai** *adj. & n.*

**Thames** |'temz| river of S England, flowing 210 mi./338 km. E from the Cotswolds in Gloucestershire through London to the North Sea. In Oxfordshire it is also called the **Isis**.

**Thames River**[1] |'THāmz; 'tāmz; 'temz| estuarial river in SE Connecticut that flows from Norwich past New London and Groton to Long Island Sound.

**Thames River**[2] |'temz| river that flows 160 mi./260 km. across S Ontario, past London. It was the scene of an 1813 battle in which Tecumseh died.

**Thane** |'tänə| (also **Thana**) industrial and commercial town in W India, in Maharashtra state. Pop. 797,000.

**Than·et, Isle of** |'THænɪt| E peninsula of Kent, in SE England, once separated by channels from the mainland. The resorts of Margate and Ramsgate are here. The Jutes are thought to have landed here in A.D. 449.

**Than·ja·vur** |ˌtənjə'voor| (also **Tanjore**) city in S India, in Tamil Nadu state. Pop. 200,000. It is noted for its temples and is a leading center of dance and music in S India.

**Thap·sus** |'THæpsəs| ancient seaport of NE Tunisia, S of present-day Sousse, the scene of a victory by Julius Caesar over Pompey in 46 B.C., during the Roman civil war.

**Thar Desert** |'tär; 'tər| desert region to the E of the Indus River, in Rajasthan and Gujarat states of NW India and the Punjab and Sind regions of SE Pakistan. Also called **Great Indian Desert**.

**Thá·sos** |'THä,saws| island in Greece, in the N Aegean Sea. Its capital is Límen.

**Thebes**[1] |'THēbz| Greek name for an ancient city of Upper Egypt, whose ruins lie on the Nile about 420 mi./675 km. S of Cairo. It was the capital of Egypt under the 18th dynasty (*c.* 1550–1290 B.C.) and is the site of the temples of Luxor and Karnak.

**Thebes**[2] |'THēbz| city in Greece, in Boeotia, NW of Athens. It became a major power following the defeat of the Spartans at the battle of Leuctra in 371 B.C. It was destroyed by Alexander the Great in 336 B.C. Modern Greek name **Thívai**. □ **Theban** *adj. & n.*

**The·lon River** |'THē,lawn| river that rises in the Northwest Territories and flows 550 mi./900 km. across Nunavut to Hudson Bay.

**The·o·dore Roo·se·velt National Park** |'THēə,dawr 'rōzə,velt| preserve in W North Dakota, incorporating the ranch home of the president as well as extensive badlands areas.

**The·ra** |'THirə| Greek island in the S Cyclades. The island suffered a violent volcanic eruption in about 1500 B.C.; remains of an ancient Minoan civilization have been preserved beneath the pumice and volcanic debris. Also called **Santorini**. Greek name **Thíra**. In legend Metropolis, the capital of Atlantis, was here.

**Ther·mop·y·lae** |THər'mäpəlē| pass between the mountains and the sea in Greece, about 120 mi./200 km. NW of Athens, originally narrow but now much widened by the recession of the sea. In 480 B.C. it was the scene of a heroic defense against the Persian army of Xerxes I by 6,000 Greeks; among them were 300 Spartans, all of whom, including their king Leonidas, were killed.

**Thes·pi·ae** |'THespē,ē| ancient city of Greece, at the foot of Mount Helicon (present Elikón), where, according to Greek mythology, the Muses performed.

**Thes·sa·lo·ní·ki** |ˌTHesələ'nēkē| industrial port in NE Greece, the second-largest city in Greece and capital of the Greek region of Macedonia. Pop. 378,000. Also called **Salonica**; Latin name **Thessalonica**.

**Thes·sa·ly** |ˈTHesəlē| ancient and modern region of NE Greece. Greek name **Thessalía**. □ **Thessalian** adj. & n.

**Thet·ford Mines** |ˈTHetfərd| industrial city in S Quebec, in the Notre Dame Mts. Pop. 17,273. It has been a major asbestos producer.

**Thiès** |ˈtyes| commercial and industrial city in W Senegal, E of Dakar. Pop. 201,000.

**Thim·phu** |ˈTHim'pōō| (also **Thimbu**) the capital since 1952 of Bhutan, in the Himalayas. Pop. 30,000.

**Thing·vel·lir** |ˈTHiNG(g),vet,lēr| lava plain in W Iceland, NE of Reykjavik, seat from A.D. 930 of the Althing, the oldest parliament in the world. It is now a national park.

**Thí·ra** |ˈTHirə| Greek name for THERA.

**Third River** |ˈTHərd| huge drainage canal in Iraq, between the Euphrates and Tigris rivers, completed 1992 as part of a land reclamation project, which is controversial as threatening the way of life of the Marsh Arabs of S Iraq.

**Third World** |ˈTHərd 'wərld| term used during the Cold War to designate countries not aligned with either the capitalist West (the First World) or the communist East (the Second World). It came to connote underdevelopment. See FOURTH WORLD.

**Thí·vai** |ˈTHē,vi| Greek name for THEBES[2].

**Thorn·ton** |ˈTHawrntn| city in N central Colorado, a residential and commercial suburb S of Denver. Pop. 55,031.

**Thou·sand Islands**[1] |ˈTHowzənd| group of about 100 small islands off the N coast of Java, forming part of Indonesia. Indonesian name **Pulau Seribu**.

**Thou·sand Islands**[2] |ˈTHowzənd| noted resort area, a group of about 1,500 islands in a widening of the St. Lawrence River, just below Kingston, Ontario. Some of the islands are in Ontario, some in New York.

**Thou·sand Oaks** |ˈTHowzənd| industrial city in SW California, NW of Los Angeles. Pop. 104,352.

**Thrace** |ˈTHrās| ancient country lying W of the Black Sea and N of the Aegean. It is now divided among Turkey, Bulgaria, and Greece. □ **Thracian** adj. & n.

**Thread·nee·dle Street** |ˈTHred,nēdl| street in central London, containing the premises of the Bank of England ("the Old Lady of Threadneedle Street").

**Three Gor·ges Dam** |THrē 'gawrjəz| dam under construction on the Yangtze River N of Yichang, in Hubei province, E central China. Potentially the largest hydroelectric project in the world, the dam will flood the scenic Yangtze gorges.

**Three Mile Island** |ˈTHrē ,mīl 'īlənd| island in the Susquehanna River near Harrisburg, Pennsylvania, site of a nuclear power station. In 1979 an accident damaged the reactor core, provoking strong reactions against the nuclear industry in the U.S.

**Three Sis·ters** |THrē 'sistərz| glacier-covered volcanic peaks in W central Oregon, in the Cascade Range, in a noted wilderness area.

**Throgs Neck** |ˈTHrägz ,nek| peninsula in the SE Bronx, New York City, that gives its name to a major bridge to Queens (Long Island).

**Thu·le**[1] |ˈtōōlē; 'THōōlē| settlement on the NW coast of Greenland, founded in 1910 by the Danish explorer Knud Rasmussen. Inuit name **Qaanaaq**.

**Thu·le**[2] |ˈtōōlē; 'THōōlē| country described by the ancient Greek explorer Pytheas as being six days' sail N of Britain, most plausibly identified with Norway. It was regarded by the ancients as the northernmost part of the world (in Latin **Ultima Thule**).

**Thun** |tōōn| **1** town in the N foothills of the Bernese Alps, central Switzerland, on the Aare River. Pop. 37,000. **2** a lake in central Switzerland, formed by a widening of the Aare.

**Thun·der Bay** |ˈTHəndər| city on an inlet W of Lake Superior in SW Ontario. Pop. 113,946. One of Canada's major ports, an outlet for grain from the prairies, it was formed by the amalgamation in 1970 of Fort William and Port Arthur.

**Thu·rin·gia** |THōō'rinj(ē)ə| densely forested state of E central Germany, N of the Ore Mountains. Pop. 2,572,000. Capital: Erfurt. German name **Thüringen**.

**Thur·so** |ˈTHərsō| fishing port on the N coast of Scotland, in Highland region, the northernmost town on the mainland of Britain. Pop. 9,000.

**Tia·hua·na·co** |,tēäwä'näkō| archaeological site in W Bolivia, at in the Andes highlands at the SE shore of Lake Titicaca. Its pre-Incan monuments include the Gateway of the Sun.

**Tian·an·men Square** |tē'enə(n),men| large public square in Beijing, China. On the S edge of the Tatar, or Inner, City, it is the site of the Great Hall of People, museums, monuments, and Mao Zedong's tomb. During April–June 1989, massive antigovernment demonstrations were held here until brutally suppressed.

**Tian·jin** |tē'än'jin| (also **Tientsin**) industrial port in NE China, in Hubei province, the third-largest city in the country. Pop. 5,700,000.

**Tian Shan** |tē'än'sHän| (formerly **Tien Shan**) mountain range to the N of the Tarim Basin in Xinjiang, China, extending to the W into Kyrgyzstan.

**Tian·shui** |tē'än'sH(w)ē| city in Gansu province, central China, in the N foothills of the Qin Ling mountains W of Baoji, Shaanxi. Pop. 1,967,000.

**Ti·ber** |'tībər| river of central Italy, upon which Rome stands. It rises in the Tuscan Apennines and flows 252 mi./405 km. generally SW, entering the Tyrrhenian Sea at Ostia. Italian name **Tevere**.

**Ti·be·ri·as, Lake** |tī'birēəs| another name for Sea of Galilee (see GALILEE, SEA OF).

**Ti·be·ri·as** |tī'birēəs| resort town in NE Israel, on the Sea of Galilee. Pop. 36,000. It was a center of Jewish learning from the 2nd century, and the scholar Maimonides is buried here.

**Ti·bes·ti Mountains** |tə'bestē| mountain range in N central Africa, in the Sahara in N Chad and S Libya. It rises to 11,201 ft./3,415 m. at Emi Koussi, the highest point in the Sahara.

**Ti·bet** |tə'bet| mountainous country in Asia on the N side of the Himalayas, since 1965 forming an autonomous region in the W of China. Area: 474,314 sq. mi./1.23 million sq. km. Pop. 2,196,000. Official languages, Tibetan and Chinese. Capital and largest city: Lhasa. Chinese name **Xizang**. On the "roof of the world," Tibet has an average elevation of over 12,500 ft./4,000 m. Ruled by Buddhist lamas since the 7th century, it has been dominated by Mongols, Manchus, and China since the 13th century. After China crushed a revolt in 1959, the Dalai Lama fled into exile, and sporadic unrest continued in this largely pastoral region. □ **Tibetan** adj. & n.

**Ti·ci·no** |tī'cHēnō| predominantly Italian-speaking canton in S Switzerland, on the Italian border. Capital: Bellinzona. It joined the Swiss Confederation in 1803. French and German name **Tessin**.

**Ti·con·der·o·ga** |ˌtī,kändə'rōgə| industrial village in NE New York, in lowlands between Lakes George and Champlain. Pop. 2,770. Nearby Fort Ticonderoga was fought over repeatedly in the 1750s–80s.

**Tide·wa·ter, the** |'tī,wawtər; 'tīd,wätər| coastal regions of E Virginia, in which tidal water flows up the Potomac, Rappahannock, York, James, and smaller rivers. Early

17th-century British settlement focused here.

**Ti·do·re** |tē'dōrä| island in Indonesia, in the Moluccas, W of Halmahera.

**Tien Shan** |tē'en'sHän| see TIAN SHAN.

**Tien·tsin** |tē'ent'sin| see TIANJIN.

**Tier·ra del Fue·go** |tē'erə del 'fwägō| island at the S extremity of South America, separated from the mainland by the Strait of Magellan. Discovered by Ferdinand Magellan in 1520, it is now divided between Argentina and Chile.

**Tie·tê River** |tyä'tä| river that flows 500 mi./800 km. across S Brazil, from near the Atlantic coast, past São Paulo, to the Paraná River.

**Tif·fin** |'tifən| industrial city in NW Ohio, on the Sandusky River. Pop. 18,604.

**Tif·lis** |'tifləs| former official Russian name (1845–1936) for TBILISI.

**Ti·ghi·na** |tī'gēnə| (also known as **Bendery**) manufacturing town in Moldova, near the Dniester River. Pop. 142,000.

**Ti·gray** |tī'grā| (also **Tigré**) province of Ethiopia, in the N of the country, bordering Eritrea. Capital: Mekele. An ancient kingdom, Tigray was annexed as a province of Ethiopia in 1855. It engaged in a bitter guerrilla war against the government of Ethiopia 1975–91, during which time the region suffered badly from drought and famine. □ **Tigrayan** adj. & n.

**Ti·gre** |'tēgrā| city in E Argentina, a port and resort N of Buenos Aires. Pop. 256,000.

**Ti·gris** |'tīgrəs| river in SW Asia, the more easterly of the two rivers of ancient Mesopotamia. It rises in the mountains of E Turkey and flows 1,150 mi./1,850 km. SE through Iraq, passing through Baghdad, to join the Euphrates, forming the Shatt al-Arab, which flows into the Persian Gulf.

**Ti·hwa** |'dē'hwä| former name (until 1954) for URUMQI.

**Ti·jua·na** |ˌtēə'wänə| town in NW Mexico, in Baja California just S of the U.S. border. Pop. 743,000. A tourist center, it has a reputation for rowdiness.

**Ti·kal** |tē'käl| ancient Mayan city in the tropical Petén region of N Guatemala, with great plazas, pyramids, and palaces. It flourished A.D. 300–800.

**Ti·krit** |tī'krēt| (also **Tekrit**) town in N central Iraq, NW of Bagdhad. The Muslim sultan Saladin (c.1138) and Iraqi president Saddam Hussein (1937) were born here.

**Til·burg** |'til,bərg| industrial city, a textile center, in the S Netherlands, in the province of North Brabant. Pop. 159,000.

**Til·bury** |'tilb(ə)rē| the principal port of

**Til·la·mook** |'tiləmək; 'tilə,mʊ͞ok| city in NW Oregon. Pop. 3,001. It is the seat of Tillamook County, a dairying center, and is on Tillamook Bay, a fishing and resort hub.

**Tim·a·ru** |'timə,rʊ͞o| port and resort on the E coast of South Island, New Zealand. Pop. 28,000.

**Tim·buk·tu** |,timbək'tʊ͞o| (also **Timbuctoo**) town in N Mali. Pop. 20,000. It was formerly a trading center for gold and salt on trans-Saharan trade routes, reaching the height of its prosperity in the 16th century but falling into decline after its capture by the Moroccans in 1591. French name **Tombouctou**.

**Times Beach** |'tīmz| abandoned city in E central Missouri, SW of St. Louis, site of a 1980s evacuation due to chemical contamination.

**Times Square** |'tīmz| a focal point of Manhattan, New York City, around the intersection of Broadway and 42nd St. Its long-held reputation for seediness is giving way to redevelopment.

**Tim·gad** |'tim,gæd| (ancient name **Thamugadi**) historic city in NE Algeria, near Batna, founded by the Romans in the 1st century A.D. and abandoned by the 7th century.

**Ti·miş·oa·ra** |,tēmē'sHwärə| industrial and university city in W Romania. Pop. 325,000. Formerly part of Hungary, and the chief city of the Banat region, it has substantial Hungarian and German-speaking populations. Demonstrations here in 1989 led to the collapse of the communist government. Hungarian name **Temesvár**.

**Tim·mins** |'timinz| industrial city in E central Ontario, in a major mining district. Pop. 47,461.

**Ti·mor** |'tē,mawr; tē'mawr| the largest of the Lesser Sunda Islands, in the S Malay Archipelago. Pop.: East Timor 714,000, West Timor 3,383,000. The island was formerly divided into Dutch West Timor and Portuguese East Timor. In 1950 West Timor was absorbed into the newly formed Republic of Indonesia. In 1975 East Timor declared itself independent but was invaded and occupied by Indonesia (see EAST TIMOR). □ **Timorese** adj. & n.

**Ti·mor Sea** |'tē,mawr; tē'mawr| arm of the Indian Ocean between Timor and NW Australia.

**Tin·douf** |tēn'dʊ͞of| oasis town in extreme W Algeria, in the Sahara Desert. Pop. 14,000. It has been involved in tensions between Morocco and Algeria over the WESTERN SAHARA.

**Ti·ni·an** |'tinēən| island in the W Pacific, in the Northern Mariana Islands. Pop. 2,000. Used by U.S. forces during World War II, it is noted as the site from which the planes that dropped atomic bombs on Hiroshima and Nagasaki took off.

**Tin·ker Creek** |'tiNGkər| stream in SW Virginia, near Roanoke, a focus of the nature writing of Annie Dillard.

**Tin Pan Alley** |,tin pæn 'ælē| name for the U.S. popular music business, taken from no particular street, but long associated with lower Manhattan, New York City.

**Tin·ta·gel** |tin'tæjəl| village on the coast of N Cornwall, England. Nearby are the ruins of Tintagel Castle, the legendary birthplace of King Arthur.

**Tin·tern Abbey** |'tintərn| 12th-century ruin in SE Wales, in Gwent, on the Wye River, immortalized in a poem by Wordsworth.

**Tip·pe·ca·noe River** |,tipəkə'nʊ͞o| river that flows 170 mi./275 km. through Indiana. Battle Ground, near its meeting with the Wabash, is the site of the 1811 battle of Tippecanoe.

**Tip·pe·rary** |,tipə'rerē| county in the center of the Republic of Ireland, in the province of Munster. Pop. 134,000; county seats, Nenagh, Clonmel.

**Ti·ra·na** |ti'ränə| (also **Tiranë**) the capital and largest city of Albania, on the Ishm River in the central part. Pop. 210,000. Founded by the Turks in the 17th century, it became capital of Albania in 1920, and is the country's industrial and cultural center.

**Ti·ras·pol** |ti'ræspəl| manufacturing city in E Moldova, on the Dniester River NW of Odessa. Pop. 186,000.

**Tir·go·vi·şte** |tər'gövēsHte| town in S central Romania, in an oil-producing region. Pop. 101,000.

**Tir·gu Jiu** |'tərgʊ͞o 'ZHēʊ͞o| capital of Gorj county in SW Romania. Pop. 93,000.

**Tir·gu Mu·reş** |'tərgʊ͞o 'mʊ͞o,resH| industrial and commercial city in central Romania, on the Mureş River. Pop. 165,000.

**Ti·rich Mir** |'tiriCH'mir| the highest peak in the Hindu Kush, in NW Pakistan, rising to 25,230 ft./7,690 m.

**Tir-nan-Og** |,tirnə'nawg| in Irish folklore, a land of eternal youth, the equivalent of ELYSIUM.

**Ti·rol** |tə'röl| German name for TYROL.

**Tir·u·chi·ra·pal·li** |,tirəCHə'räpəlē| (also **Tiruchchirappalli**) industrial city and rail junction in Tamil Nadu, S India. Pop. 387,000. Also called **Trichinopoly**.

**Ti·ru·nel·ve·li** |,tiro͞o'nelvəlē| commercial and industrial city in S India, in Tamil Nadu state. Pop. 366,000. The Christian saint Francis Xavier began his Indian ministry here in the 1540s.

**Ti·ru·pa·ti** |'tiro͞o,pätē| city in S India, in Andhra Pradesh state, NW of Madras. Pop. 189,000. It is a major Hindu religious site.

**Ti·rup·pur** |'tirə,po͝or| commercial town in S India, in Tamil Nadu state. Pop. 306,000. A temple here to the Hindu god Shiva is a pilgrimage site.

**Ti·ryns** |'tirənz; 'tīrənz| ancient city of Argolis Greece, in the NE Peloponnese. It figures prominently in Greek legend.

**Ti·sa** |'tēsä| Serbian name for TISZA.

**Ti·sza** |'tisäw| river in SE Europe, the longest tributary of the Danube, which rises in the Carpathian Mountains of W Ukraine and flows 600 mi./960 km. W into Hungary, then S, joining the Danube in Serbia NW of Belgrade. Serbian name **Tisa**.

**Ti·ta·no, Monte** |tē'tänō| mountain in the Republic of San Marino, notable for its three peaks. Height: 2,437 ft./743 m.

**Ti·ti·ca·ca, Lake** |,titi'käkə; ,tētē'käkə| lake in the Andes, on the border between Peru and Bolivia. At 12,497 ft./3,809 m., it is the highest large (3,200 sq. mi./8,288 sq. km.) lake in the world.

**Ti·to·grad** |'tētō,gräd| former name (1946–93) for PODGORICA.

**Ti·to·vo Uži·ce** |'tētaw,vaw 'o͞oZHētse| commercial and industrial city in W Serbia. Pop. 83,000.

**Ti·tov Ve·les** |'tētawv 'veles| commercial city in central Macedonia, on the Vardar River SE of Skopje. Pop. 65,000.

**Ti·tus·ville¹** |'titəs,vil| commercial and resort city in E central Florida, near Cape Canaveral. Pop. 39,394.

**Ti·tus·ville²** |'titəs,vil| historic city in NW Pennsylvania, on Oil Creek. Pop. 6,434. The first operative oil well was drilled here in 1859.

**Ti·vo·li** |'tivəlē| commune NE of Rome. Pop. 51,000. A major tourist center, it is known for its waterfalls on the Aniene River and for its many opulent villas, chief among them the Villa d'Este and the remains of the villa of the Emperor Hadrian.

**Ti·vo·li Gardens** |'tivəlē| amusement park in central Copenhagen, Denmark, with theaters, rides, gardens, a lake, and a concert hall.

**Ti·zi Ou·zou** |tē'zi'o͞o'zo͞o| commercial and industrial town in N Algeria, E of Algiers. Pop. 101,000. It is the chief town of **Kabylia**.

**Tlal·ne·pan·tla** |,tlälnə'päntlə| (official name **Tlalnepantla de Baz**) city in central Mexico, just N of Mexico City, of which it is an industrial suburb. Pop. 702,000.

**Tlal·pan** |tläl'pän| (also **Tlalpam**) city in central Mexico, in the Distrito Federal, just S of Mexico City, of which it is a suburb. Pop. 485,000.

**Tla·que·pa·que** |,tläkä'päkä| town in SW Mexico, in Jalisco state, just SE of Guadalajara, of which it is a suburb. Pop. 328,000. Its folk arts are well known.

**Tlax·ca·la** |tlä'skälə| 1 state of E central Mexico, the smallest in the country. Area: 1,551 sq. mi./4,016 sq. km. Pop. 764,000. 2 its capital city. Pop. 25,000.

**Tlem·cen** |tlem'sen| industrial city in NW Algeria. Pop. 146,000. In the 13th–15th centuries it was the capital of a Berber dynasty.

**To·a·ma·si·na** |,to͞oəməsēnə| (formerly **Tamatave**) port city in E Madagascar, on the Indian Ocean. Pop. 127,000. On a rail line from Antananarivo, it is the chief port in Madagascar.

**To·bac·co Road** |tə'bækō| term for economically marginal parts of the U.S. upper South, drawn from a road along which early tobacco growers transported their product to river ports.

**To·ba·go** |tə'bāgō| island in the Lesser Antilles, West Indies, a constituent of TRINIDAD AND TOBAGO. Lying NE of Trinidad, it is 116 sq. mi./300 sq. mi. in area and has a pop. of 50,000. Scarborough is its capital.

**To·bol River** |tə'bawl| river (1,042 mi./1,677 km.) in Kazakhstan and W Russia in Asia, rising in the SE foothills of the Ural Mts. and flowing to the Irtysh River at Tobolsk.

**To·bolsk** |tə'bawlsk| industrial town in W Russia, in Siberia, on the Irtysh River. Pop. 94,000. Its industries center around oil and gas production.

**To·bruk** |'tō,bro͝ok; tō'bro͝ok| port on the Mediterranean coast of NE Libya. Pop. 94,000. It was the scene of fierce fighting during World War II. Arabic name **Tubruq**.

**To·can·tins** |,tōkən'tēNz| 1 river of South America, which rises in central Brazil and flows 1,640 mi./2,640 km. N, joining the Pará to enter the Atlantic through a large estuary at Belém. 2 state of central Brazil, formerly the N part of Goias. Pop. 920,000. Capital: Palmas.

**Todd River** |ˈtäd| river in central Australia that flows only in wet years, 200 mi./320 km. from the MacDonnell Ranges to the Simpson Desert.

**Tog·gen·burg** |ˈtawgən‚bŏŏrg| district in NE Switzerland, on the Thur River. Farming and tourism are the major industries.

**To·gliat·ti** |tawlˈyätē| industrial city and river port in SW Russia, on the Volga River. Pop. 642,000. It was founded in 1738 but relocated in the mid-1950s to make way for the Kuibyshev reservoir. Former name (until 1964) **Stavropol**. Russian name **Tolyatti**.

**To·go** |ˈtōgō| republic in W Africa with a short coastline on the Gulf of Guinea. Area: 21,933 sq. mi./56,785 sq. km. Pop. 3,761,000. Languages, French (official), W African languages. Capital: Lomé. Official name **Togolese Republic**. The former Togoland, lying between Ashanti and Dahomey (Benin), was controlled by Germany and then Britain before independence in 1960. It is agricultural and has mineral resources. □ **Togolese** *adj. & n.*

**Togo**

**To·ho·ku** |tōˈhōkōō| region of Japan, in NE Honshu. Capital: Sendai.

**To·kaj** |ˈtaw‚ki| (also **Tokay**) town in NE Hungary, on the Tisza River. The well-known sweet wine is produced here.

**To·ke·lau** |ˈtōkə‚low| group of three atolls in the W Pacific, between Kiribati and Samoa, forming an overseas territory of New Zealand. Pop. 1,200. Formerly **Union Islands**.

**To·ko·ro·za·wa** |‚tōkō'rōzäwä| city in E central Japan, on E central Honshu, a suburb NE of Tokyo. Pop. 303,000.

**To·ku·shi·ma** |‚tōkōō'sнēmä| port city in W Japan, on SE Shikoku. Pop. 263,000.

**To·ku·ya·ma** |‚tōkōō'yämä| port city in W Japan, on SW Honshu, at W end of Inland Sea. Pop. 111,000.

**Tokelau**

**To·kyo** |ˈtōkē‚ō| the capital and largest city of Japan, capital of Kanto region, on Tokyo Bay, E central Honshu. Pop. 8,163,000. Formerly called Edo (or Yedo), it was the center of the military government under the shoguns (1603–1867). It was renamed Tokyo ("eastern capital") in 1868, when it replaced Kyoto ("western capital") as the imperial capital. An industrial, commercial, financial, and cultural center, it is also, with nearby Yokohama, a major port. The Tokyo metropolitan area, with a pop. of 28 million, is by some calculations the largest in the world.

**Tol·bu·khin** |tawlˈbŏŏкнin| former name (1949–91) for DOBRICH.

**To·le·do**[1] |təˈlēdō| industrial city and port on Lake Erie, in NW Ohio. Pop. 332,943.

**To·le·do**[2] |tōˈlädō| port city in the Philippines, on central Cebu. Pop. 120,000.

**To·le·do**[3] |tōˈlädō| historic city in central Spain, on the Tagus River, capital of Castilla-La Mancha region. Pop. 64,000. It was a preeminent city and cultural center of Castile. Toledan steel and sword blades have been famous since the first century B.C.

**Tol·lund** |ˈtälənd| wetland in central Jutland, Denmark, where the remains of a much-studied Iron Age (c.500 B.C.–A.D. 400) man were found in 1950.

**Tol·pud·dle** |ˈtäl‚pədəl| village in SW England, in Dorset, made famous by the "Tolpuddle Martyrs," farmworkers whose 1830s attempts to form a union led to transportation as criminals to Australia.

**To·lu·ca** |tōˌlōōkä| commercial and industrial city in central Mexico, capital of the state of Mexico. Pop. 488,000. It lies at the foot of the extinct volcano Nevado de Toluca, at an altitude of 8,793 ft./2,680 m. Full name **Toluca de Lerdo**.

**Tol·yat·ti** |tawlˈyätē| Russian name for TOGLIATTI.

**Tom River** |‚tawm| river (450 mi./725 km.

long) in central Russia. It rises in the Altai Mts. and flows NNW into the Ob River near Tomsk.

**To·ma·ko·mai** |tō'mäkō͞,mī| industrial port city in N Japan, on S Hokkaido, SE of Sapporo. Pop. 160,000.

**Tom·big·bee River** |täm'bigbē| river that flows 400 mi. from NE Mississippi through W Alabama, to the Alabama River. In the 1980s the **Tennessee-Tombigbee Waterway** connected it with the Tennessee River.

**Tom·bouc·tou** |,tōnbook'tōō| French name for TIMBUKTU.

**Tomb·stone** |'tōōm,stōn| historic frontier city in SE Arizona. Pop. 1,220. It is the scene of the 1881 gunfight at the O.K. Corral.

**To·mis** |'tōməs| ancient name for CONSTANŢA.

**Tomsk** |tämsk| industrial city in S Siberian Russia, a port on the Tom River. Pop. 506,000.

**Ton·a·wan·da** |,tänə'wändə| industrial city in W New York, on the Niagara River N of Buffalo. Pop. 17,284.

**Ton·ga** |'täNG(g)ə| kingdom in the S Pacific consisting of an island group SE of Fiji. Area: 258 sq. mi./668 sq. km. Pop. 98,000. Official languages, Tongan and English. Capital: Nuku'alofa. Also called the **Friendly Islands**. Comprising some 170 islands and atolls, Tonga was controlled by Britain 1900–70. Fishing and tropical agriculture are important. □ **Tongan** adj. & n.

Tonga

**Tong·a·ri·ro, Mount** |,täNG(g)ə'rirō| mountain in North Island, New Zealand. It rises to a height of 6,457 ft./1,968 m. and is held sacred by the Maoris.

**Ton·gass National Forest** preserve in SE Alaska, the largest U.S. national forest, in the Panhandle and on islands in the Alexander Archipelago, focus of 1990s disputes over logging.

**Tong·a·ta·pu** |,täNG(g)ä'täpōō| largest

(100 sq. mi./260 sq. km.) island of Tonga. Nuku'alofa, the capital, is here.

**Tong·chuan** |'təNG'CHōō(w)än| industrial city in Shaanxi province, central China, N of Xi'an. Pop. 404,000.

**Tong·hua** |'təNG'hwä| city in Jilin province, NE China, E of Shenyang. Pop. 373,000

**Ton·gi** |'tawNGgē| (also **Tungi**) industrial city in central Bangladesh, N of Dhaka. Pop. 165,000.

**Tong·ling** |'tōōNG'liNG| city in Anhui province, E China, in the Yangtze River valley SW of Nanjing. Pop. 228,000.

**Ton·kin, Gulf of** |'tän'kin; 'täNG,kin| arm of the South China Sea, bounded by the coasts of S China and northern Vietnam and the island of Hainan. Its chief port is Haiphong. A disputed naval incident here in 1964 was followed by greatly increased U.S. military involvement in Vietnam.

**Ton·kin** |'tän'kin; 'käNG'kin| (also **Tong·king; Tonking**) former French protectorate in SE Asia, on territory, centered on the Red River delta, constituting most of present-day northern Vietnam.

**Ton·lé Sap** |,tänlä'säp| lake in central Cambodia, linked to the Mekong River by the Tonlé Sap river. It triples in size during the wet season (June–Nov.), and has fisheries. Angkor stands on the NW shore.

**Too·ele** |tōō'welə| city in NW Utah. Pop. 13,887. Once a mining center, it has also been engaged in the building and dismantling of weapons.

**Too·woom·ba** |tə'wōōmbə| town in Queensland, Australia, to the W of Brisbane. Pop. 76,000. It was formerly known as The Swamps.

**To·pe·ka** |tə'pēkə| industrial city, the capital of Kansas, in the E central part. Pop. 119,883.

**Top·ka·pi Palace** former residence of the Ottoman sultans in Istanbul (then Constantinople), Turkey. It is now a museum famed for its jewels and for belongings of the prophet Muhammad.

**Tor·bay** |,tawr'bā| borough in Devon, SW England, on Tor Bay. Pop. 121,000. It was formed in 1968 from the amalgamation of the seaside resorts Torquay, Paignton, and Brixham.

**Tor·de·sil·las** |tawrdə'sē(l)yäs| village in N Spain, on the Duero River. A treaty signed here in 1494 between Spain and Portugal established the boundary between their respective colonial properties worldwide.

**Tor·gau** |'tawr,gow| port city in eastern central Germany, on the Elbe River. Pop.

22,000.The first meeting between U.S. and Soviet troops as they advanced into Germany in 1945 took place here.

**To·ri·no** |tŏ'rēnō| Italian name for TURIN.

**Torn·gat Mountains** |'tawrngæt| section of the E edge of the Canadian Shield, in E Labrador, rising to 5,420 ft./1,652 m. at Mt. Caubvick, on the Quebec border.

**Tor·nio** |'tawrnē,ō| river that rises in NE Sweden and flows 356 mi./566 km. generally S, forming the border between Sweden and Finland before emptying into the Gulf of Bothnia. Swedish name **Torne Älv**.

**To·ron·to** |tə'räntō| the capital of Ontario and center of the largest metropolitan area in Canada, on the north shore of Lake Ontario. Pop. 635,395; metropolitan area pop. 3,893,000. Founded in 1793, it was originally named York but in 1834 was renamed Toronto, from a Huron word mean 'meeting place.' It is the financial, commercial, and industrial hub of Canada.

**Tor·quay** |tawr'kē| resort town in SW England, in Devon, administratively part of Torbay since 1968. Pop. 57,000.

**Tor·rance** |'tawrəns| commercial and industrial city in SW California, S of Los Angeles. Pop. 133,107.

**Tor·re An·nun·zia·ta** |'tawrä ä,nōōnsē-'yätä| port city and seaside resort in S Italy, on the Bay of Naples at the foot of Mount Vesuvius. Pop. 56,000.

**Tor·re del Gre·co** |'tawrä del 'grekō| port and seaside resort in S Italy, on the Bay of Naples, near Mount Vesuvius. Pop. 104,000. It has suffered repeatedly from eruptions from Mount Vesuvius.

**Tor·re·ón** |,tawrā'ōn| industrial and commercial city in N Mexico, in Coahuila state. Pop. 460,000.

**Tor·res Strait** |'tawriz| channel separating the N tip of Queensland, Australia, from the island of New Guinea and linking the Arafura and the Coral seas.

**Tor·res Ve·dras** |'tawrəs 'vādrəsH| commune in W Portugal, N of Lisbon. Pop. 11,000. The town is known for its line of fortifications, erected in 1809 to defend against the French.

**Tor·ring·ton** |'tawriNGtən| historic industrial and commercial city in NW Connecticut, on the Naugatuck River. Pop. 33,687.

**Tórs·havn** |'tawrs,houn| (also **Thorshavn**) the capital of the Faroe Islands, a port on the island of Strømø. Pop. 14,000. It has been a governmental center since the 9th century.

**Tor·to·la** |tawr'tōlə| the principal island of the British Virgin Islands. Its chief town, Road Town, is the capital of the islands.

**Tor·tu·ga Island** |tawr'tōōgə| (French name **Île de la Tortue**) island off the N coast of Haiti, in the Atlantic, a notorious haunt of pirates in the 17th century.

**To·ry Island** |'tō,rē| small island off the coast of NW Ireland, in County Donegal, a noted pirate haven in legend.

**To·sca·na** |tō'skänə| Italian name for TUS-CANY.

**Tot·ten·ham** |'tätnəm| district of N Greater London, England, part of the borough of Haringey.

**Tot·to·ri** |tō'tōrē| port city in W Japan, on S Honshu. Pop. 142,000.

**Toub·kal, Mount** |tōōb'käl| (Arabic name **Djebel Toubkal**) peak in S central Morocco, S of Marrakech. At 13,665 ft./4,165 m., it is the highest point in the Atlas Mts. and in N Africa.

**Toul** |tōōl| fortress town in NE France, on the Moselle River. Pop. 17,000. Primarily agricultural, it also has some light industry.

**Tou·lon** |tōō'lawN| port and naval base on the Mediterranean coast of S France. Pop. 170,000.

**Tou·louse** |tōō'lōōz| city in SW France, on the Garonne River, principal city of the Midi-Pyrénées region. Pop. 366,000. It is a high-tech industrial and educational center.

**Tou·raine** |tōō'rēn| region and former province in W central France, comprising the area around Tours. It is known for its wines and for the medieval and Renaissance chateaus that dot the Loire valley.

**Tou·rane** |tōō'rän| former name for DA NANG.

**Tour·coing** |tōōr'kweN| textile-manufacturing town in N France, near the Belgian border. Pop. 94,000.

**Tour·nai** |tōōr'nā| town in Belgium, a textile center on the Scheldt River near the French border. Pop. 68,000. It was controlled by the counts of Flanders from the 9th century until taken by France in 1188; it returned to the Netherlands in 1814. Flemish name **Doornik**.

**Tours** |'tōōr| industrial and ecclesiastical city in W central France, on the Loire River. Pop. 133,000.

**Tow·er Ham·lets** |'tow,ər 'hæmləts| industrial and residential borough of E London, England, along the N of the Thames River. Pop. 154,000. Bethnal Green, Bow, Limehouse, Millwall, and Wapping are here.

**Tow·er of Lon·don** |'towər əv 'ləndən|

fortress in London, England, just E of the old City walls, on the N side of the River Thames. Begun in the 11th century, it now draws tourists to such attractions as the crown jewels.

**Town 'n' Coun·try** |'town ən 'kəntrē| residential community in W Florida, NW of Tampa. Pop. 60,946.

**Tow·son** |'towsən| suburban community in N Maryland, N of Baltimore. Pop. 49,445.

**Towns·ville** |'townz,vil| industrial port and resort on the coast of Queensland, NE Australia. Pop. 101,000.

**To·ya·ma** |tō'yämä| industrial port city in central Japan, on central Honshu. Pop. 321,000.

**To·yo·ha·shi** |,tōyō'häsHē| city in central Japan, on S central Honshu, S of Nagoya. Pop. 338,000.

**To·yo·na·ka** |tōyō'näkä| city in W central Japan, on S Honshu, a suburb N of Osaka. Pop. 410,000.

**To·yo·ta** |toi'ōtə| (also **Toyoda**) industrial city in central Japan, on S central Honshu. Pop. 332,000. It is dominated by the Toyota Motor Company.

**Trab·zon** |træb'zän| port on the Black Sea in N Turkey. Pop. 144,000. In 1204, after the sack of Constantinople by the Crusaders, an offshoot of the Byzantine Empire was founded with Trabzon as its capital, which was annexed to the Ottoman Empire in 1461. Also called **Trebizond**.

**Tra·cy** |'trāsē| commercial and industrial city in N central California, in the San Joaquin Valley. Pop. 33,558.

**Trades, the** |'trādz| ocean regions in which the trade winds blow steadily from the NE (in the N hemisphere) or SE (in the S hemisphere). They lie within about 25° from the equator in each hemisphere, inside the **horse latitudes** and outside the equatorial **doldrums**.

**Tra·fal·gar, Cape** |trə'fælgər| cape on the coast of S Spain. The British navy won a decisive battle here against the French and Spanish navies in 1805, during the Napoleonic Wars.

**Tra·fal·gar Square** |trə'fælgər| public square in central London, England, in Westminster. Charing Cross is on the S side, the National Gallery on the N side, of this focal point.

**Trail** |trāl| industrial city in SE British Columbia, a mining and metal industry center. Pop. 7,919.

**Trail of Tears** |'trāl əv 'tērz| historic route or routes over which the Cherokee and

other tribes moved W toward Oklahoma after being expelled from Georgia and neighboring states in the 1830s and 1840s.

**Tra·lee** |trə'lē| the county seat of Kerry, a port on the SW coast of the Republic of Ireland. Pop. 17,000.

**Trans Alai Mountains** |'trænz ə'lī| range in Kyrgyzstan, Tajikistan, and China. Lenin Peak, at 23,382 ft./7,127 m., is the highest in the range.

**Trans-Alaska Pipeline** |'trænzə'læskə| oil conduit that extends 800 mi./1,300 km. from Prudhoe Bay, on the North Slope of Alaska, to Valdez, on Prince William Sound.

**Trans·ant·arc·tic Mountains** |,trænz-,ænt'ärk,tik| mountain chain extending across Antarctica, separating Greater Antarctica from Lesser Antarctica and the Ross Ice Shelf. It reaches 14,275 ft./4,351 m. at Mount Markham.

**Trans-Canada Highway** |,trænz'kænədə| route between Victoria, British Columbia, and Saint John's, Newfoundland. At 4,860 mi./7,820 km., it is claimed to be the longest national highway in the world.

**Trans·cau·ca·sia** |,trænzkaw'kāzHə| region lying to the S of the Caucasus Mts., between the Black Sea and the Caspian, and comprising the present-day republics of Georgia, Armenia, and Azerbaijan. It was created the Transcaucasian Soviet Federated Socialist Republic in 1922, but was broken up into its constituent republics in 1936. □ **Transcaucasian** adj.

**Trans·jor·dan** |trænz'jawrdn| former name (until 1949) of the region E of the Jordan River now forming the main part of the kingdom of Jordan. □ **Transjordanian** adj.

**Trans·kei** |træn(t)'skī| former homeland established in South Africa for the Xhosa people, now part of the province of Eastern Cape.

**Trans-Siberian Railway** |trænsī'birēən| rail line that links European Russia with the Pacific coast. Built 1891–1904, it extends from Moscow through Vladivostok to the Sea of Japan, a distance of 5,786 mi./9,311 km. An extension stretches 1,952 mi./3,102 km. from Ust-Kut to the Pacific.

**Trans·vaal** |træns'väl| (also **the Transvaal**) former province in NE South Africa, lying N of the Vaal River. In 1994 it was divided into Northern Transvaal (now Northern), Eastern Transvaal (now Mpumalanga), Pretoria-Witwatersrand-Vereeniging (now Gauteng), and the E part of North-West Province.

**Trans·verse Ranges** |trænz'vərs| term

for various mountain ranges that cross S California, and are often considered the divider between N and S. See also TEHACHAPI Mts.

**Tran·syl·va·nia¹** |ˌtrænsəl'vānēə| large tableland region of NW Romania, separated from the rest of the country by the Carpathian Mts. and the Transylvanian Alps. Part of Hungary until it became a principality of the Ottoman Empire in the 16th century, it was returned to Hungary at the end of the 17th century and was incorporated into Romania in 1918. From Latin *trans* 'across, beyond' + *silva* 'forest'.
□ **Transylvanian** *adj.*

**Tran·syl·va·nia²** |ˌtrænsəl'vānēə| in U.S. history, unrecognized fourteenth colony that was proposed in the 1770s in what is now central Kentucky and neighboring Tennessee.

**Tra·pa·ni** |'träpänē| port and trade center on the NW coast of Sicily, in S Italy, capital of Trapani province. Pop. 73,000.

**Tra·si·me·no, Lake** |ˌträzi'mänō| lake in central Italy, W of Perugia. Hannibal defeated the Romans here in 217 B.C. in the Second Punic War, and there was heavy fighting between German and British troops during World War II.

**Trás-os-Montes** |'træˌzŏŏzH 'mŏn‚tēSH| mountainous region of NE Portugal, N of the Douro River.

**Trav·an·core** |'trævən‚kawr| (also **Tiru-vankur**) region and former state in SW India, between the Malabar Coast and the Western Ghats in present-day Kerala state.

**Trav·erse City** |'trævərs| resort and industrial port in Michigan, in the NW of the Lower Peninsula, on Lake Michigan. Pop. 15,155.

**Trav·nik** |'trävnēk| town in W central Bosnia and Herzegovina. Pop. 64,000. It was the capital of Bosnia 1686–1850.

**Treb·bia River** |'trebyä| river (71 mi./114 km. long) in NW Italy that rises E of Genoa and flows into the Po River NW of Piacenza.

**Treb·i·zond** |'trebə‚zänd| another name for TRABZON.

**Tre·blin·ka** |trə'blinɡkə| site of a World War II Nazi concentration camp outside Warsaw, Poland.

**Trem·blant, Mont** |ˌmō 'trem‚blänt; ‚mō ‚trä'blä| peak of the Laurentians in S Quebec, NW of Montreal, a noted ski resort.

**Treng·ga·nu** |treNG'gänŏŏ| (also **Terengganu**) state of Malaysia, on the E coast of the Malay Peninsula. Capital: Kuala Trengganu.

**Trent** |trent| the chief river of central England, which rises in Staffordshire and flows 170 mi./275 km. generally northeastward, uniting with the River Ouse 15 mi./25 km. W of Hull to form the Humber estuary.

**Trent Canal** |trent| (also **Trent-Severn Waterway**) waterway in S Ontario that connects Lake Huron (at Port Severn on Georgian Bay) with Lake Ontario (at Trenton). It was begun in the 1830s.

**Trentino–Alto Adi·ge** |tren'tēnō ‚ältō 'ädē‚jä| region of NE Italy. Capital: Bolzano. On the border with Austria, it includes the Dolomites.

**Tren·to** |'trentō| historic industrial and commercial city on the Adige River in N Italy. Pop. 102,000.

**Tren·ton¹** |'trentən| industrial city, the capital of New Jersey, in the W central part on the Delaware River. Pop. 88,675.

**Tren·ton²** |'trentən| industrial port city in SE Ontario, on the Bay of Quinte off Lake Ontario. Pop. 16,908. It is the E terminus of the Trent Canal.

**Trèves** |trev| the French name for TRIER.

**Tre·vi·so** |trä'vēzō| agricultural market and industrial city in NE Italy, capital of the province of Treviso, on the Sile and Botteniga rivers. Pop. 84,000.

**Tri·Be·Ca** |trī'bĕkə| residential and commercial section of S Manhattan, New York City, noted for its lofts. Its name derives from *Tri*angle *Be*low *Ca*nal Street.

**Tri·bor·ough Bridge** |'trībə‚rō| bridge complex linking the Bronx, Queens, and Manhattan, in New York City, opened in 1936.

**Trich·i·nop·o·ly** |ˌtriCHə'näpəlē| another name for TIRUCHIRAPALLI.

**Tri·chur** |tri'CHŏŏr| (also **Thrissur**) commercial town in S India, in Kerala state. Pop. 275,000. It is an important Hindu religious center.

**Tri·den·tine Alps** |trī'den‚dīn| another name for the DOLOMITE Mts.

**Trier** |'trir| city on the Mosel River in Rhineland-Palatinate, western Germany. Pop. 99,000. French name **Trèves**. Established by a Germanic tribe, the Treveri, *c.*400 B.C., Trier is one of the oldest cities in Europe. It was a powerful archbishopric from 815 until the 18th century, but fell into decline after the French occupation in 1797. Today it is noted as a wine and industrial center.

**Tri·este** |trē'est| city in NE Italy, the largest port on the Adriatic and capital of Friuli–Venezia Giulia region. Pop. 231,000. Formerly held by Austria (1382–

1918), Trieste was annexed by Italy after World War I. The Free Territory of Trieste was created after World War II but returned to Italy in 1954.

**Tri·glav** |'trē,gläv| mountain in the Julian Alps, NW Slovenia, near the Italian border. Rising to 9,392 ft. (2,863 m), it is the highest peak in the mountains E of the Adriatic.

**Tri·ka·la** |'trəkälä| (also **Trikala**) commercial city in Trikkala department, N central Greece. Pop. 41,000. It is said to be the birthplace of Aesculapius, the father of medicine, and was noted in ancient times for its medical school.

**Tri·mon·ti·um** |trē'mawntēyəm| Roman name for PLOVDIV.

**Trin·co·ma·lee** |,triNGkōmə'lē| the principal port of Sri Lanka, on the E coast. Pop. 44,000. It was the chief British naval base in SE Asia during World War II after the fall of Singapore.

**Trin·i·dad and To·ba·go** |'trinədæd ən tə-'bāgō| republic in the West Indies consisting of two islands of the NE coast of Venezuela. Area: 1,981 sq. mi./5,128 sq. km. Pop. 1,249,000. Languages, English (official), Creole. Capital and largest city: Port-of-Spain (on Trinidad). Trinidad, much larger and inhabited by Arawaks, was a Spanish colony. Tobago, a Carib island, was colonized by France and Britain. Britain controlled both by the early 19th century. Independence came in 1962. Oil refining and trade are central to the economy. □ **Trinidadian** *adj. & n.* **Tobagan** *adj. & n.*

**Trinidad & Tobago**

**Trin·i·ty Mountains** |'triniətē| forested range of the Klamath Mts. in NW California. The Trinity River flows from it.

**Trin·i·ty River** |'trinitē| river that flows 550 mi./900 km. across Texas to the Gulf of Mexico. It rises in four main headstreams, the West, Clear, Elm, and East forks.

**Trip·o·li** |'tripəlē| port in NW Lebanon.

Pop. 160,000. It was founded *c.*700 B.C. and was the capital of the Phoenician triple federation formed by the city-states Sidon, Tyre, and Arvad. Today it is a major port and commercial center of Lebanon. Arabic name **Tarabulus Ash-Sham** ('eastern Tripoli'); also **Trâblous**.

**Trip·o·li²** |'tripələ| the capital and chief port of Libya, on the Mediterranean coast in the NW of the country. Pop. 991,000. Founded by Phoenicians in the 7th century BC, its ancient name was Oea. Arabic name **Tarabulus Al-Gharb** ('western Tripoli').

**Trip·o·lis** |'tripələs| summer resort and commercial center in S Greece, in the Peloponnesus. Pop. 22,000. It is the capital of Arcadia department.

**Trip·o·li·ta·nia** |,tripələ'tānēə| coastal region surrounding Tripoli in North Africa, in what is now NE Libya. □ **Tripolitanian** *adj. & n.*

**Tri·pu·ra** |'tripərə| state in the far NE of India, on the E border of Bangladesh. Pop. 2,745,000. Capital: Agartala. An ancient Hindu kingdom, Tripura acceded to India after independence in 1947, and achieved full status as a state in 1972.

**Tris·tan da Cu·nha** |,tristən də 'kōōn(y)ə| the largest of a small group of volcanic islands in the S Atlantic 1,320 mi./2,112 km. SW of the British colony of St. Helena, of which it is a dependency. Pop. 292. It was discovered in 1506 by the Portuguese admiral Tristão da Cunha and annexed to Britain in 1816.

**Tri·van·drum** |tri'vændrəm| the capital of the state of Kerala, a port on the SW (Malabar) coast of India. Pop. 524,000.

**Tr·na·va** |'tərnəvə| market and ecclesiastical town in W Slovakia, NE of Bratislava. Pop. 72,000.

**Tro·ad** |'trō,æd| (also **Troas**) ancient region of NW Asia Minor, of which ancient Troy was the chief city.

**Tro·bri·and Islands** |'trōbrē,ænd| small group of islands in the SW Pacific, in Papua New Guinea, off the SE tip of the island of New Guinea.

**Tro·ca·de·ro** |tri'träkə'derō| plaza in Paris, France, on the Right Bank of the Seine, opposite the Eiffel Tower. The plaza, built for a 1937 World's Fair, is the site of a major art museum.

**Trois-Rivières** |,trwärēv'yer| (English name **Three Rivers**) historic industrial city in S Quebec, on the St. Lawrence River at the mouth of the St.-Maurice River. Pop. 49,426.

**Trom·sø** |'trōōm,sōō| the principal city of

Arctic Norway, situated on an island in Troms County. Pop. 51,000.

**Trond•heim** |'trɒn,hīm| historic port city in W central Norway, the second-largest city in the country. Pop. 138,000. It was the capital of Norway during the Viking period.

**Troon** |trōōn| town on the W coast of Scotland, In South Ayrshire, noted for its golf course. Pop. 14,000.

**Trop•ics, the** |'träpiks| region that lies between 23° 27′ N (the **Tropic of Cancer**) and 23° 27′ S (the **Tropic of Capricorn**). These are the outer limits of the zone in which the sun is ever directly overhead (June 21 in the N, Dec. 22 in the S). □ **tropical** adj.

**Tros•sachs** |'träsəks| (also **the Trossachs**) picturesque wooded valley in central Scotland, between Loch Achray and the lower end of Loch Katrine.

**Trou•ville** |trōōvēl| (also called **Trouville-sur-Mer**) resort and seaport on the English Channel, in NW France. Pop. 7,000.

**Trow•bridge** |'trō,brij| town in SW England, the county seat of Wiltshire. Pop. 23,000.

**Troy**[1] |troi| (also **Ilium, Ilion,** or **Troia**) ancient city of NW Asia Minor, S of the Dardanelles in present-day Turkey, according to legend besieged and destroyed by Greek forces 3,200 years ago. Its remains have been found at Hissarlik, on the Menderes River. □ **Trojan** adj. & n.

**Troy**[2] |troi| residential and commercial city in SE Michigan. Pop. 72,884.

**Troy**[3] |troi| industrial city in E New York, on the Hudson and Mohawk rivers just NE of Albany. Pop. 54,269.

**Troyes** |trwä| town in N France, on the Seine River. Pop. 61,000. It was capital of the former province of Champagne. It gave its name to a system of weights and measures first used at the medieval fairs held here.

**Tru•cial States** |'trōōshəl| former name (until 1971) for UNITED ARAB EMIRATES, deriving from the 1836 maritime truce they signed with Britain.

**Tru•jil•lo** |trōō'hēyō| industrial city on the coast of NW Peru, capital of La Libertad department. Pop. 509,000.

**Truk Islands** |trōōk; trək| (also **Chuuk**) group of fourteen volcanic islands and numerous atolls in the W Pacific, in the Caroline Islands, forming part of the Federated States of Micronesia. Pop. 54,000. There was a Japanese naval base here during World War II.

**Trum•bull** |'trəmbəl| town in SW Connecticut, an affluent suburb NE of Bridgeport. Pop. 32,016.

**Tru•ro**[1] |'trōōrō| the county seat of Cornwall, in SW England. Pop. 19,000.

**Tru•ro**[2] |'trōōrō| resort town in E Massachusetts, near the end of Cape Cod. Pop. 1,573. It is a well-known arts colony.

**Tru•ro**[3] |'trōōrō| commercial and industrial town in central Nova Scotia, on Minas Basin. Pop. 11,683.

**Truth or Con•se•quen•ces** |,trōōTH 'känsə,kwensəz| commercial city in SW New Mexico, on the Rio Grande. Pop. 6,221. Formerly Hot Springs, it took its current name in 1950 to obtain a live radio broadcast from the city.

**Tsa•ri•tsyn** |tsə'rētsən| former name (until 1925) for VOLGOGRAD.

**Tsar•sko•ye Se•lo** |'tsärskəyə sə'law| earlier name for PUSHKIN.

**Tse•li•no•grad** |tsi'lenə,gräd| former name for ASTANA, Kazakhstan.

**Tsi•nan** |'jē'nän| see JINAN.

**Tsing•hai** |'CHiNG'hī| see QINGHAI.

**Tsing•tao** |'CHiNG'dow| see QINGDAO.

**Tsi•tsi•har** |'CHi'CH'här| see QIQIHAR.

**Tskhin•va•li** |'tskinvəlē| the capital of South Ossetia, in the republic of Georgia. Pop. 43,000.

**Tsu** |(t)sōō| commercial and industrial port city in central Japan, on S Honshu, NW of Nagoya. Pop. 157,000.

**Tsu•chi•u•ra** |(t)sōō'CHēōōra| commercial and cultural center in E central Japan, on central Honshu, a suburb in the Tokyo-Yokohama area. Pop. 127,000.

**Tsu•ga•ru Strait** |(t)sōō'gärōō| strait in N Japan, between Honshu and Hokkaido islands, connecting the Sea of Japan with the Pacific; approximately 100 mi./161 km. long.

**Tsu•ku•ba** |(t)sōō'kōōbä| city in E central Japan, on central Honshu. Pop. 143,000. The government-planned Tsukuba City research and technology center here is home to 46 national research facilities.

**Tsu•shi•ma** |(t)sōō'sHēmä| Japanese island in the Korea Strait, between South Korea and Japan. In 1905 it was the scene of a defeat for the Russian navy during the Russo-Japanese War.

**Tu•a•mo•tu Archipelago** |,tōōə'mōtōō| group of about eighty coral islands forming part of French Polynesia, in the S Pacific. Pop. 12,000. It is the largest group of coral atolls in the world. The islands of Mururoa and Fangataufa have been used by the French since 1966 for nuclear testing.

**Tü·bing·en** |ˈtybɪNGən| city in SW Germany, on the Neckar River. An educational and publishing center, it retains its medieval core. Pop. 75,000.

**Tu·bruq** |too͞oˈbroͦok| Arabic name for TOBRUK.

**Tu·bu·ai Islands** |too͞oˈbwäē| group of volcanic islands in the S Pacific, forming part of French Polynesia; chief town, Mataura (on the island of Tubuai). Pop. 6,500. Also called the **Austral Islands**.

**Tuc·son** |ˈtoo͞o,sän| city in SE Arizona, a center of manufacturing and tourist destination with a desert climate. Pop. 405,390.

**Tu·ge·la River** |too͞oˈgälə| river that flows 300 mi./483 km. from KwaZulu-Natal province, South Africa, to the Indian Ocean. **Tugela Falls**, with a total drop of 3,110 ft./948 m., is the highest in Africa.

**Tui·ler·ies** |ˌtwēlə'rē| public gardens adjacent to the Louvre, in Paris, France, on the Right Bank. The grounds were originally bought by Catherine de Medici in 1563 for a garden next to the Tuileries Palace (demolished 1871).

**Tu·la**[1] |ˈtoo͞olə| the ancient capital city of the Toltecs, generally identified with a site near the town of Tula in Hidalgo State, central Mexico.

**Tu·la**[2] |ˈtoo͞olə| industrial city in European Russia, to the S of Moscow. Pop. 543,000.

**Tu·la·gi** |too͞oˈlägē| (also **Tulaghi**) small island in the central Solomon Islands, just S of Florida Island and N of Guadalcanal, the scene of an Allied attack on Japanese troops in August 1942.

**Tu·lare** |too͞oˈlærē; too͞oˈlær| commercial city in S central California, an agricultural center in the San Joaquin Valley. Pop. 33,249.

**Tul·cea** |ˈtoo͞olCHä| industrial town in SE Romania, in the Danube delta, capital of Tulcea county. Pop. 95,000.

**Tu·le Lake** |ˈtoo͞olē| lake in N California, on the Modoc Plateau, a noted wildfowl refuge and scene of fighting in the 1870s Modoc War.

**Tul·la·more** |ˌtələˈmōr| the county seat of Offaly, in the Republic of Ireland. Pop. 9,000.

**Tulle** |too͞ol| industrial city, capital of Corrège department in S central France. Pop. 21,000. The cloth known as tulle was first made here.

**Tul·sa** |ˈtəlsə| commercial and industrial city, on the Arkansas River in NE Oklahoma. Pop. 367,302.

**Tu·lum** |ˌtoo͞oˈloo͞om| archaeological site in SE Mexico, a 6th-century Mayan city on the Caribbean coast of Quintana Roo state.

**Tum·kur** |too͞omˈkoͦo| commercial city and health resort in S central India, in the Devarayadurga Hills in Karnataka state. Pop. 180,000.

**Tunb Islands** |ˈtoo͞onəb| two small islands (Greater and Lesser Tunb) in the Persian Gulf, administered by the emirate of Ras al Khaimah until occupied by Iran in 1971.

**Tun·bridge Wells** |ˈtənbrij ˈwelz| spa town in Kent, SE England. Pop. 58,000. Founded in the 1630s after the discovery of iron-rich springs, the town was patronized by royalty throughout the 17th and 18th centuries. Official name **Royal Tunbridge Wells**.

**Tung·shan** |ˈtoo͞oNGˈsHän| see XUZHOU.

**Tun·gu·ra·hua** |ˌtoo͞oNGgoo͞oˈräwä| active volcano in the Andes in central Ecuador: 16,457 ft./5,016 m. It gives its name to surrounding Tungurahua province.

**Tun·gu·ska** |too͞oNGˈgoo͞oskə| two rivers in Siberian Russia, the *Lower Tunguska* and *Stony Tunguska*, flowing W into the Yenisei River through the forested, sparsely populated Tunguska Basin. The area was the scene in 1908 of a devastating explosion believed to have been due to the disintegration in the atmosphere of a meteorite or small comet.

**Tu·nis** |ˈt(y)oo͞onəs| the capital of Tunisia, an industrial port on the Mediterranean coast of N Africa, near the site of ancient Carthage. Pop. 597,000.

**Tu·ni·sia** |t(y)oo͞oˈnēzHə| republic in N Africa, on the Mediterranean. Area: 63,403 sq. mi./164,150 sq. km. Pop. 8,223,000. Language, Arabic. Capital and largest city: Tunis. The sucessor to classical Carthage, Tunisia was long controlled by the Turks and (1886–1956) by France. Agriculture, oil and mineral extraction, and tourism are all important to its economy. □ **Tunisian** *adj. & n.*

**Tun·ja** |ˈtoo͞oNG,hä| historic commercial city

**Tunisia**

in central Colombia, the capital of Boyacá department. Pop. 112,000.

**Tuol Sleng** prison in Phnom Penh, Cambodia, a notorious execution site of the 1970s Khmer Rouge regime, now a museum of the history of the period.

**Tu·ol·um·ne River** |tŏŏˈäləmē| river that flows from Yosemite National Park, California. It is impounded in the Hetch Hetchy Reservoir, which supplies San Francisco with water.

**Tu·pe·lo** |ˈt(y)ŏŏpə,lō| industrial city in NE Mississippi. Pop. 30,685. Site of Civil War battles, it is also the birthplace of Elvis Presley.

**Tu·ran** |tŏŏˈrän| region of steppes and deserts in central Asia, S and E of the Aral Sea, extending from Kazakhstan through Uzbekistan and Turkmenistan; home of the Turanian people.

**Tur·fan Depression** |tŏŏrˈfän| see TURPAN DEPRESSION.

**Tu·rin** |ˈt(y)ŏŏrən| industrial and commercial city in NW Italy, on the Po River, capital of Piedmont region. Pop. 992,000. Turin was the capital of the kingdom of Sardinia from 1720 and became the first capital of a unified Italy (1861–64). It is a center of publishing, auto, and other industries. Italian name **Torino**.

**Tur·ka·na, Lake** |tŏŏrˈkänə| salt lake in NW Kenya and extending into S Ethiopia; it has no outlet, and is increasing in salinity. Also called **the Jade Sea.**

**Tur·ke·stan** |ˌtərkəˈstæn| (also **Turkistan**) region of central Asia between the Caspian Sea and the Gobi Desert, inhabited mainly by Turkic peoples. It is divided by the Pamir and Tien Shan mountains into E Turkestan, now the Xinjiang autonomous region of China, and W Turkestan, which comprises present-day Turkmenistan, Kazakhstan, Uzbekistan, Tajikistan, and Kyrgyzstan.

**Tur·key** |ˈtərkē| republic comprising the whole of the Anatolian peninsula in W Asia, as well as a peninsula in SE Europe. Area: 301,063 sq. mi./779,452 sq. km. Pop. 56,473,000. Language, Turkish. Capital: Ankara. Largest city: Istanbul. The center of the Ottoman Empire before World War I, Turkey became a secular republic in the 1920s. It has a sizable Kurdish minority in the E. Agriculture, coal mining, industry, and tourism are all important. □ **Turkish** adj. **Turk** n

**Turk·me·ni·stan** |tərkˈmenə,stæn| republic in central Asia, lying between the Caspian Sea and Afghanistan. Area: 188,528 sq. mi./488,100 sq. km. Pop. 3,861,000. Languages, Turkoman (official), Russian. Capital and largest city: Ashgabat. Also called **Turkmenia**. The Karakum Desert comprises 90% of Turkmenistan, which had been Turkestan and then (1924–91) a constituent republic of the Soviet Union. Traditionally pastoral, the country has substantial mineral resources. □ **Turkmen** adj. & n.

**Turkmenistan**

**Turks and Cai·cos Islands** |ˈtərks ən ˈkäkəs ,| British dependency in the Caribbean, comprising two island groups between Haiti and the Bahamas. Pop. 12,000. Capital: Cockburn Town (on the island of Grand Turk).

**Tur·ku** |ˈtŏŏrkŏŏ| industrial port in SW Finland. Pop. 159,000. It was the capital of Finland until 1812. Swedish name **Åbo**.

**Turkey**

**Turks & Caicos**

**Tur·lock** |'tər,läk| commercial city in N central California, in the San Joaquin Valley. Pop. 42,198. It is an agricultural hub.

**Tur·nu Ro·șu** |'toornoō 'raw,sнoō| historic mountain pass in the Transylvanian Alps of central Romania. It is traversed by the Olt River.

**Tur·nu Se·ve·rin** |'toornoō ,säve'rēn| see DROBETA–TURNU SEVERIN, Romania.

**Tur·pan Depression** |'toor'pän| (also called **Turfan Depression**) deep depression in Xinjiang, W China, in the Tarim Basin, the lowest point in the country: 505 ft./154 m. below sea level. Area: 20,000 sq. mi./50,000 sq. km.

**Tur·qui·no, Pi·co** |'pēkō toor'kēnō| see SIERRA MAESTRA, Cuba.

**Tus·ca·loo·sa** |,təskə'loōsə| industrial city in W central Alabama, on the Black Warrior River. Pop. 77,759. The University of Alabama is here.

**Tus·can Archipelago** |'təskən| group of small islands, belonging to Italy, in the Mediterranean Sea between France, Corsica, and Italy. Among the islands are Elba and Pianosa.

**Tus·ca·ny** |'təskənē| region of W central Italy, on the Ligurian Sea. Pop. 3,563,000. Capital: Florence. Italian name **Toscana**.

**Tus·ca·ro·ra Mountains** |,təskə'rōrə| range in NE Nevada that has been the scene of gold and silver booms.

**Tus·cu·lum** |'təsk(y)ələm| ancient town in Italy, SE of Rome. According to legend, it was a rival to Rome until defeated; later it became a resort for wealthy citizens of the city.

**Tus·cum·bia** |təsk'əmbēə| industrial city in NW Alabama, in the Muscle Shoals area on the Tennessee River. Pop. 8,413. The writer Helen Keller was born here.

**Tus·ke·gee** |təsk'ēgē| city in E central Alabama, home to Tuskegee Uinversity. Pop. 12,257.

**Tus·tin** |'təstən| city in SW California, a suburb SE of Los Angeles. Pop. 50,689.

**Tu·ti·co·rin** |,tootikə'rin| industrial port city in S India, in Tamil Nadu state. Pop. 284,000.

**Tu·va** |'toovə| autonomous republic in S central Russia, on the border with Mongolia. Pop. 314,000. Capital: Kyzyl. Former name **Tannu-Tuva**.

**Tu·va·lu** |too'väloo| country in the SW Pacific consisting of a group of nine main islands, formerly called the Ellice Islands. Area: 10 sq. mi./26 sq. km. Pop. 8,500. Official languages, English and Tuvaluan (an Austronesian language). Capital: Funafu-

**Tuvalu**

ti. The islands formed part of the British colony of the Gilbert and Ellice Islands but separated from the Gilberts after a referendum in 1975. Tuvalu became independent in 1978. The chief product is coconuts. □ **Tuvaluan** *adj. & n.*

**Tux·e·do Park** |tək'sēdō| village in SE New York. Pop. 706. Developed in the 1880s as a refuge for the rich, it gave its name to the evening jacket.

**Tux·tla Gu·ti·ér·rez** |'toostlä gootē'yärās| commercial city in SE Mexico, capital of the state of Chiapas. Pop. 296,000.

**Tuz·la** |'toozlä| town in NE Bosnia. Pop. 132,000. A Muslim enclave, it suffered damage and heavy casualties when besieged by Bosnian Serb forces in 1992–94.

**Tver** |tver| industrial port in European Russia, on the Volga River NW of Moscow. Pop. 454,000. It was known as Kalinin from 1931 until 1991. Tver is also the name of a historic principality in the area.

**Tweed** |twēd| river that rises in the Southern Uplands of Scotland and flows 97 mi./155 km. generally E, crossing into NE England and entering the North Sea at Berwick-upon-Tweed. For part of its lower course it forms the border between Scotland and England.

**Twen·ty·nine Palms** |'twentē,nīn ,pälmz| desert city in S California, E of Los Angeles, just S of the Twentynine Palms Marine Corps air center. Pop. 11,821.

**Twick·en·ham** |'twikənəm| residential district of the borough of Richmond-upon-Thames, W London, England, headquarters to the Rugby Football Union and former home to poet Alexander Pope.

**Twin Cities** |twin| popular name for the adjacent cities of Minneapolis and Saint Paul, Minnesota.

**Twin Falls** |twin| commercial and industrial city in S central Idaho, on the Snake River. Pop. 27,591.

**Ty·burn** |'tībərn| place in London, England, near Marble Arch, where public hangings were held *c.* 1300–1783.

**Ty•chy** |'təhə| industrial town in S Poland, S of Katowice. Pop. 192,000.

**Ty•ler** |'tīlər| industrial city in E Texas. Pop. 75,450. It is a center of horticultural industries, famed for its roses.

**Tyne** |tīn| river in NE England, formed by the confluence of two headstreams, the North Tyne, which rises in the Cheviot Hills, and the South Tyne, which rises in the N Pennines. It flows 31 mi./50 km. generally E, entering the North Sea at Tynemouth.

**Tyne and Wear** |'tīn ən 'wir| metropolitan county of NE England. Pop. 1,087,000. County town: Newcastle upon Tyne.

**Tyne•side** |'tīn,sīd| industrial urban region on the banks of the Tyne River, in NE England, stretching from Newcastle-upon-Tyne to the coast. □ **Tynesider** *n.*

**Tyre** |tīr| historic port on the Mediterranean in S Lebanon. Pop. 14,000. Founded in the 2nd millennium B.C. as a colony of Sidon, it was for centuries a Phoenician port and trading center, before its decline in the 14th century. □ **Tyrian** *adj. & n.*

**Ty•rol** |tə'rōl| Alpine state of W Austria. Capital: Innsbruck. The S part was ceded to Italy after World War I. German name **Tirol.** □ **Tyrolean** *adj. & n.* **Tyrolese** *adj. & n.*

**Ty•rone** |ti'rōn| one of the Six Counties of Northern Ireland, W of Lough Neagh. Pop. 144,000; chief town, Omagh.

**Tyr•rhe•ni•an Sea** |tə'rēnēən| part of the Mediterranean Sea between mainland Italy and the islands of Sicily and Sardinia.

**Tyu•men** |tyōō'men| city in W Siberian Russia, in the E foothills of the Ural Mts. Pop. 487,000. Founded in 1586 on a Tartar site, it is regarded as the oldest city in Siberia.

**Tzu-po** |'dzə'bō| see ZIBO.

# Uu

**Uban·gi River** |(y)ळ'bæNGgē| (French spelling **Oubangui**) river that flows 660 mi./1,060 km. from the border of the Central African Republic and Congo (formerly Zaire), along the border of the latter with the Republic of Congo, to join the Congo River, of which it is the chief N tributary.

**Ubangi-Shari** |(y)ळ'bæNGgē 'sHärē| former name (until 1958) for CENTRAL AFRICAN REPUBLIC.

**Ube** |'ळbē| industrial port city in W Japan, on SW Honshu. Pop. 175,000.

**Ube·ra·ba** |,ळbe'räbə| commercial city in E Brazil, in Minas Gerais state, in an agricultural and cattle-raising region. Pop. 232,000.

**Uber·lân·dia** |'ळbər'ländēə| commercial city in E Brazil, in Minas Gerais state, in an agricultural and cattle-raising area. Pop. 437,000.

**Ubon Rat·cha·tha·ni** |ळ'bən, räCHə'tänē| (also **Ubol Rajadhani**) commercial town in E Thailand, on the Mun River just below its junction with the Chi. Pop. 99,000.

**Uca·ya·li River** |,ळkə'yälē| river that flows 1,000 mi./1,600 km. through central and N Peru. It joins the Marañón River to form the Amazon.

**Uc·cle** |'əklə| (also **Ukkel**) commune in central Belgium. Pop. 76,000. It is a suburb of Brussels.

**Udai·pur** |ळ'dī,poor| historic city in NW India, on Lake Pichola in Rajasthan state. Pop. 308,000.

**Udha·ga·man·da·lam** |,ळdəgəmən'däləm| (also **Udagamandalam**) historic hill resort town in S India, in Tamil Nadu state. Pop. 82,000.

**Udi·ne** |'ळdē,nā| manufacturing city in NE Italy, capital of Udine province. Pop. 99,000.

**Ud·mur·tia** |ळd'moorsHə| autonomous republic in central Russia. Pop. 1,619,000. Capital: Izhevsk. Also called **Udmurt Republic**.

**Ue·da** |ळ'ädä| (also **Uyeda**) industrial and resort city in central Japan, on central Honshu, S of Nagano. Pop. 119,000.

**Ue·le River** |'welē| (also **Welle**) river that flows 700 mi./1,125 km. across N Congo (formerly Zaire), joining the Bomu River to form the Ubangi River.

**Ufa** |ळ'fä| industrial city, the capital of Bashkiria, S central Russia, in the Ural Mts. Pop. 1,094,000.

**Ufa River** |ळ'fä| river (580 mi./933 km) in W Russia. It rises in W Chelyabinsk oblast and flows through the Southern Ural Mts. into the Belaya River at Ufa.

**Uf·fi·zi Gallery** |ळ'fitsē; ळ'fētsē| art museum in Florence, Italy, housed in a Renaissance palace, that is home to some of the best-known Renaissance masterworks.

**Ugan·da** |(y)ळ'gændə| landlocked republic in E Africa. Area: 93,140 sq. mi./241,139 sq. km. Pop. 16,876,000. Languages, English (official), Swahili, and others. Capital and largest city: Kampala. Ethnically diverse Uganda was controlled by Britain before independence in 1962. It exports coffee, tea, tobacco, cotton, and other products. □ **Ugandan** adj. & n.

Uganda

**Uga·rit** |ळgə'rēt| ancient port and Bronze Age trading city in N Syria, founded in Neolithic times and destroyed by the Sea Peoples in about the 12th century B.C. Late Bronze age remains include a palace, temples, and private residences containing legal, religious, and administrative cuneiform texts in Sumerian, Akkadian, Hurrian, Hittite, and Ugaritic languages. Its people spoke Ugaritic, a Semitic language written in a distinctive cuneiform alphabet, whose study has contributed to better understanding of biblical Hebrew. □ **Ugaritic** adj. & n.

**Ui·jong·bu** |'wē,jəNG'bळ| industrial city in NW South Korea, a satellite of Seoul. Pop. 276,000.

**Uin·ta Mountains** |yळ'intə| range of the Rocky Mts. in NE Utah. Kings Peak, at 13,528 ft./4,123 m. is its high point, and the high point in Utah.

**Uist** |'(y)ळist| two islands in the Outer Hebrides, Scotland, *North Uist* and *South Uist*, lying to the S of Lewis and Harris and separated from each other by the island of Benbecula.

**Uji** |'ōōjē| Resort city in W central Japan, on S Honshu, S of Kyoto. Pop. 177,000.

**Uji·ji** |ōō'jējē| commercial town in W Tanzania, on Lake Tanganyika just S of Kigoma, noted as the place where journalist Henry M. Stanley "found" explorer David Livingstone in 1871.

**Uji·ya·ma·da** |ˌōōjēyä'mädä| former name (until 1956) for ISE.

**Uj·jain** |'ōōˌjīn| historic city in W central India, in Madhya Pradesh, a Hindu holy site. Pop. 376,000.

**Ujung Pan·dang** |'ōōˌjōōNG'pän,däNG| the chief seaport of the island of Sulawesi in Indonesia. Pop. 944,300. Former name (until 1973) **Makassar**.

**Uki·ah** |yōō'kīə| city in NW California, on the Russian River. Pop. 14,599.

**Ukraine** |yōō'krān| (also formerly called **the Ukraine**) republic in E Europe, to the N of the Black Sea. Area: 233,179 sq. mi./603,700 sq. km. Pop. 51,999,000. Languages, Ukrainian and Russian. Capital and largest city: Kiev. The home of the Scythians and Sarmatians, Ukraine was united with Russia by the 9th century. It was an original republic of the Soviet Union, becoming independent in 1991. Its vast steppes produce grain, and heavy industry dominates the Donets Basin. Mining is also a key to the economy. □ **Ukrainian** *adj. & n.*

**Ukraine**

**Ula·la** |ōō'lälə| former name (until 1932) for GORNO-ALTAISK.

**Ulan Ba·tor** |ˌōōˌlän 'bä,tawr| (also **Ulaanbaatar**) the capital of Mongolia. Pop. 575,000. It was founded in the 17th century as a Buddhist center. Former name (until 1924) **Urga**.

**Ulan-Ude** |ˌōōˌlänōō'dä| industrial city in S Siberian Russia, capital of the republic of Buryatia. Pop. 359,000. Former name (until 1934) **Verkhneudinsk**.

**Ule·å·borg** |'ōōleō'bawrē| Swedish name for OULU.

**Ul·has·na·gar** |ˌōōlhəs'nägər| city in W India, in the state of Maharashtra. Pop. 369,000.

**Uli·thi** |ōō'lēTHē| atoll in the W Caroline Is., in the Federated States of Micronesia. U.S. forces took its harbor from the Japanese in 1944.

**Ulm** |'ōōlm| industrial city on the Danube River in Baden-Württemberg, S Germany. Pop. 112,000. It is noted for its Gothic cathedral, with a spire 528 ft./161 m. tall.

**Ul·san** |'ōōl'sän| industrial port on the S coast of South Korea. Pop. 683,000.

**Ul·ster** |'əlstər| former province of Ireland, in the N of the island. The nine counties of Ulster are now divided between Northern Ireland (Antrim, Down, Armagh, Londonderry, Tyrone, and Fermanagh) and the Republic of Ireland (Cavan, Donegal, and Monaghan). □ **Ulsterman** *n.* **Ulsterwoman** *n.*

**Ul·ster County** |'əlstər| county in SE New York, W of the Hudson River. Pop. 165,304. Many Catskills resorts are here.

**Ul·ti·ma Thule** |ˌəltimə'tōōlē| see THULE.

**Ulugh Muz·tagh** |'ōōˌlōōg mōōztäg| see MUZTAG.

**Ulun·di** |ōō'lōōndē| town in KwaZulu/Natal, South Africa, formerly the seat of Zulu kings, later capital of Zululand and KwaZulu. Pop. 11,000.

**Ulu·ru** |ōō'lōōrōō| Aboriginal name for AYERS ROCK.

**Ul·ya·novsk** |ōōl'yänəfsk| former name (1924–92) for SIMBIRSK.

**Uman** |ōō'män| historic industrial city in central Ukraine, S of Kiev. Pop. 93,000.

**Um·bria** |'əmbrēə| predominantly agricultural region of central Italy, in the valley of the Tiber. Pop. 823,000. Capital: Perugia.

**Umeå** |'ōōmä,ō| port city in NE Sweden, on an inlet of the Gulf of Bothnia. Pop. 91,000.

**Umm al Qai·wain** |'ōōm äl ki'wīn| **1** one of the seven member states of the United Arab Emirates. Pop. 35,000. **2** its capital city.

**Um·ta·li** |ōōm'tälē| former name (until 1982) for MUTARE.

**Umtaåta** |ōōm'tätä| commercial town in S South Africa, in Eastern Cape province. Pop. 55,000. It was formerly the capital of TRANSKEI.

**Una River** |'ōōnä| river, 159 mi./256 km. long, that forms part of the border between Bosnia and Herzegovina and Croatia, emptying into the Sava River.

**Un·a·las·ka** |ˌənəˈlæskə| island in the E Aleutian Islands of Alaska. The naval base of Dutch Harbor and the city of Unalaska are the chief settlements.

**Un·ga·va** |ənˈgävə| (also **Labrador-Ungava**) peninsular region of E Canada, in N Quebec and Labrador. Thinly populated, it has vast hydroelectric and mineral resources.

**Un·ion** |ˈyōōnyən| industrial and residential township in NE New Jersey. Pop. 50,024.

**Un·ion City**[1] |ˈyōōnyən| city in N central California, a reidential and industrial suburb S of Oakland. Pop. 53,762.

**Un·ion City**[2] |ˈyōōnyən| industrial city in NE New Jersey, across the Hudson River from New York City. Pop. 58,102.

**Un·ion·dale** |ˈyōōnyən,dāl| residential and commercial village in SE New York, on Long Island, site of the Nassau Memorial Coliseum. Pop. 20,328.

**Un·ion Square** |ˈyōōnyən| park in S Manhattan, New York City, noted as a former theater and, later, labor union hub.

**Un·ion Territory** |ˈyōōnyən| any of several territories of India that are administered by the central government.

**Un·ion·town** |ˈyōōnyən,town| historic city in SW Pennsylvania, in the Allegheny foothills and on the former National Road. Pop. 12,034.

**United Arab Emirates** |yōōˈnītəd ˈerəb ˈemərits| abbrev. **UAE**) independent state on the S coast of the Persian Gulf, W of the Gulf of Oman. Area: 30,010 sq. km./77,700 sq. km. Pop. 2,377,000. Language, Arabic. Capital: Abu Dhabi. The United Arab Emirates was formed in 1971 by the federation of the independent sheikhdoms formerly called the Trucial States: Abu Dhabi, Ajman, Dubai, Fujairah, Ras al Khaimah (joined early 1972), Sharjah, and Umm al Qaiwain. Oil and gas, fishing, and manufacturing are important to the economy.

**United Arab Emirates**

**United Arab Republic** |yōōˈnītəd ˈerəb rəˈpəblik| abbrev. **UAR**) former political union established by Egypt and Syria in 1958. It was seen as the first step toward the creation of a pan-Arab union in the Middle East, but only Yemen entered into loose association with it (1958–66) and Syria withdrew in 1961. Egypt retained the name United Arab Republic until 1971.

**United Kingdom** |yōō,nītəd ˈkiNGdəm| abbrev. **U.K.**) country of W Europe consisting of England, Wales, Scotland, and Northern Ireland. Area: 94,295 sq. mi./244,129 sq. km. Pop. 55,700,000. Language, English. Capital and largest city: London. Full name **United Kingdom of Great Britain and Northern Ireland.** England (with Wales) and Scotland have had the same monarch since 1603, and were formally joined in 1707. Ireland was joined to Great Britain in 1801, but all except present-day Northern Ireland broke away in 1921. The U.K. has been a great maritime, colonial, industrial, and financial power; this historic prominence contributes to the reluctance of many Britons to enter fully into the European Union.

**United Kingdom**

**United Nations** |yōō,nītəd ˈnāsHənz| international organization headquartered on the East Side of Manhattan, New York City, but with offices (and subsidiary headquarters) in cities around the world.

**United Provinces**[1] |yōō,nītəd ˈprävinsəz| Indian administrative division formed by the union of Agra and Oudh and called Uttar Pradesh since 1950.

**United Provinces**[2] |yōō,nītəd ˈprävinsəz| *hist.* the seven provinces, united in 1579, that formed the basis of the republic of the Netherlands.

**United Provinces of Cen·tral Amer·i·ca** |yōō,nītəd ˈprävinsəz əv ˈsentrəl əˈmerikə| former federal republic in Central America, formed in 1823 to unite the states of Guatemala, El Salvador, Honduras,

Nicaragua, and Costa Rica, all newly independent from Spain. The federation collapsed in 1838.

**United States of Amer·i·ca** |yōō'nītəd 'stāts əv ə'merikə| (abbrev. **U.S.** or **USA**; see map, next page) federal republic occupying most of the S half of North America and including also Alaska and the Hawaiian Islands. Area: 3.62 million sq. mi./9.37 million sq. km. Pop. 248,710,000. Capital: Washington, D.C. Largest city: New York City. Established under the constitution of 1787, the U.S. now comprises 50 states and the District of Columbia. Since emerging from World War II as the leading power in the non-communist world, it has held a dominant military, industrial, financial, and cultural position.

**Uni·ver·sal City** |'yōōnə,vərsəl| district of NW Los Angeles, California, in the San Fernando Valley, home to Universal Studios and other entertainment facilities.

**Uni·ver·sity City** |,yōōnə'vərsətē| city in E Missouri, on the W boundary of St. Louis, home to Washington University. Pop. 40,087.

**Uni·ver·sity Park** |,yōōnə'vərsətē| city in NE Texas, enclosed by N Dallas, home to Southern Methodist University. Pop. 22,259.

**Un·na** |'ōōnə| industrial city in NW Germany, E of Dortmund. Pop. 64,000.

**Un·ter den Lin·den** |,ōōntər den 'lindən| tree-lined ("under the lindens") avenue in Berlin, Germany, stretching from the Brandenburg Gate to the Spree River.

**Up·land** |'əplənd| city in SW California, a suburb E of Los Angeles and N of Ontario. Pop. 63,374.

**Upo·lu** |ōō'pōlōō| volcanic island in the SW Pacific, the most populous of the republic of Samoa. Pop. 163,000. Apia, the capital, is here. Vailima, the last home of Robert Louis Stevenson, is now a government residence.

**Up·per Aus·tria** |'awstrēə; 'ästrēə| state of NW Austria. Capital: Linz. German name **Oberösterreich**.

**Up·per Can·a·da** |'cænədə| the mainly English-speaking region of Canada N of the Great Lakes and W of the Ottawa River, in what is now S Ontario. A British colony in 1791–1841, it was then united with LOWER CANADA.

**Up·per Dar·by** |'därbē| suburban township in S Pennsylvania, just SW of Philadelphia. Pop. 81,177.

**Up·per Egypt** |'ējipt| term for regions of Egypt S of Cairo and the delta of the Nile

River. They are "up" the Nile from the region around its delta, which is called **Lower Egypt**.

**Up·per Peninsula** |pə'ninsələ| the N section of Michigan, with shores on Lake Superior (N) and Lake Michigan (S) and Lake Huron (SE). Sparsely populated, it has fishing, mining, and resort industries.

**Up·per Vol·ta** |'vätə| former name (until 1984) for BURKINA FASO.

**Upp·sa·la** |'əpsələ| industrial and cultural city in E Sweden. Pop. 167,000. Its university, founded in 1477, is the oldest in N Europe.

**Upstate** |,əp'stät| in New York, parts of the state N of New York City, thought of as distinct culturally and politically.

**Ur** |ər; ōōr| ancient Sumerian city on the Euphrates, in S present-day Iraq. It was one of the oldest cities of Mesopotamia, dating from the 4th millennium B.C., and reached its zenith in the late 3rd millennium B.C. According to the Bible it was Abraham's place of origin. Much of the city was sacked and destroyed by the Alamites, but it recovered and underwent a revival under Nebuchadnezzar. Ur was conquered by Cyrus the Great in the 6th century B.C., after which it fell into decline and was finally abandoned in the 4th century B.C. The site was excavated 1922–34, revealing spectacular royal tombs and vast ziggurats.

**Ura·ga** |ōō'rägä| port in central Japan, on Uraga Strait on SE Honshu. It was here that U.S. emissaries were repulsed when they first tried to establish relations with Japan in 1846.

**Ural Mountains** |'yōōrəl| (also **the Urals**) mountain range in N Russia, extending 1,000 mi./1,600 km.) S from the Arctic Ocean to the Aral Sea, in Kazakhstan, and rising to 6,214 ft./1,894 m. at Mount Narodnaya. It forms part of the conventional boundary between Europe and Asia.

**Ural River** |'yōōrəl| river (1,575 mi./2,534 km.) rising at the S end of the Ural Mts. in W Russia and flowing through W Kazakhstan to the Caspian Sea at Atyraū.

**Ura·wa** |ōō'räwä| commercial city and cultural center in E central Japan, on E central Honshu, a suburb of the Tokyo-Yokohama metropolitan area. Pop. 418,000.

**Ur·bana** |ər'bænə| industrial and commercial city in E central Illinois, with neighboring Champaign home to the University of Illinois. Pop. 36,344.

**Ur·bi·no** |ōōr'bēnō| historic town in the Marches region of central Italy. Pop.

15,000. The palace here is a noted example of Renaissance architecture and contains a collection of Renaissance masterpieces.

**Ur·fa** |'ŏŏrfä| (also **Sanliurfa**; ancient name **Edessa**) commercial city in SE Turkey, the capital of Urfa province. Pop. 279,000. It is at the center of an agricultural district.

**Ur·ga** |'ŏŏrgə| former name (until 1924) for ULAN BATOR.

**Ur·ganch** |ŏŏr'gyenCH| (also **Urgench**) commercial city in W Uzbekistan, on Amu Darya River. Pop. 130,000.

**Urua·pán** |ŏŏ'rwä,pän| commercial city in W Mexico, in Michoacán state. Pop. 217,000. A Tarascan Indian center, it is noted for its folk arts. The surrounding district is agricultural.

**Uru·guay** |'(y)ŏŏrə,gwī| republic on the Atlantic coast of South America, S of Brazil. Area: 68,063 sq. mi./176,215 sq. km. Pop. 3,110,000. Language, Spanish. Capital and largest city: Montevideo. Liberated from Spanish colonial rule in 1825, Uruguay is a land of grassy plains devoted to livestock-raising, with fishing and light industries also important. □ **Uruguayan** *adj. & n.*

**Uraguay**

**Uruk** |'ŏŏrŏŏk| ancient city in S Mesopotamia, to the NW of Ur. One of the greatest cities of Sumer, it was built in the 5th millennium B.C. and is associated with the legendary hero Gilgamesh. Excavations begun in 1928 revealed great ziggurats and temples. Arabic name **Warka**; biblical name **Erech**.

**Ürüm·qi** |ŏŏ'rŏŏmCHē| (formerly **Urumchi; Tihwa**) industrial city and capital of Xinjiang, NW China. Pop. 1,100,000. At the junction of ancient caravan routes, Ürümqi has long been an important trading center.

**Uşak** |'ŏŏSHäk| commercial city in W Turkey, the capital of Uşak province, an agricultural area. Pop. 105,000.

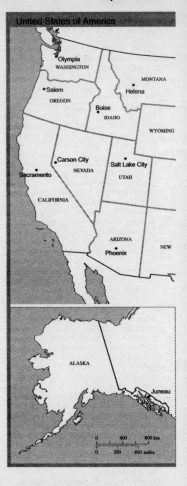

**Us·hua·ia** |ŏŏ'swäyä| port in Argentina, in Tierra del Fuego. Pop. 11,000. It is the southernmost town in the world.

**Üs·kü·dar** |,ŏŏskŏŏ'där| suburb of Istanbul, Turkey, on the E side of the Bosporus where it joins the Sea of Marmara. Pop. 396,000. Former name **Scutari**.

**Us·pal·la·ta Pass** |,ŏŏspä'yätä; ,ŏŏspä-'zHätä| pass over the Andes near Santiago,

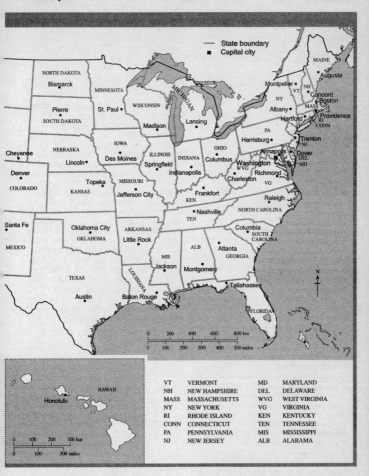

| | | | |
|---|---|---|---|
| VT | VERMONT | MD | MARYLAND |
| NH | NEW HAMPSHIRE | DEL | DELAWARE |
| MASS | MASSACHUSETTS | WVG | WEST VIRGINIA |
| NY | NEW YORK | VG | VIRGINIA |
| RI | RHODE ISLAND | KEN | KENTUCKY |
| CONN | CONNECTICUT | TEN | TENNESSEE |
| PA | PENNSYLVANIA | MIS | MISSISSIPPI |
| NJ | NEW JERSEY | ALB | ALABAMA |

in S South America, linking Argentina with Chile. The statue 'Christ of the Andes' is here.

**Us·su·riysk** |ˌo͞oso͞o'rēsk| coal-mining center and transportation junction in E Russia, N of Vladivostok. Pop. 161,000.

**Ust-Abakanskoe** |o͞ost ˌäbə'känsko͞e| former name (until 1931) for ABAKAN.

**Us·ti nad La·bem** |'o͞ostyē 'näd lä,bem| in-dustrial city in the NW Czech Republic. Pop. 107,000. It is a river port and transportation hub.

**Us·ti·nov** |'o͞ostə,nawf| former name (1984–87) for IZHEVSK.

**Usu·ma·cin·ta River** |ˌo͞oso͞omä'sēntä| river that flows 600 mi./1,000 km. from W Guatemala, where its headstreams include the Chixoy, along the border with Chiapas,

Mexico, then N through Mexico to the Gulf of Campeche.

**Usum·bu·ra** |ˌo͞osəm'bo͝orə| former name (until 1962) for BUJUMBURA.

**Utah** |'yo͞o,taw; 'yo͞o,tä| see box. □ **Utahan** *adj. & n.*

**Utah Beach** |'yo͞o,taw; 'yo͞o,tä| name given to the westernmost of the beaches, N of Carentan in Normandy, where U.S. troops landed on D-day in June 1944.

**Uti·ca**[1] |'yo͞otikə| industrial city in central New York, on the Mohawk River. Pop. 68,637.

**Uti·ca**[2] |'yo͞otikə| ancient Phoenician city in N Africa, in present-day N Tunisia, NW of Tunis. It was for a time a Roman provin-

---

### Utah

**Capital/largest city:** Salt Lake City
**Other cities:** Ogden, Provo
**Population:** 1,722,850 (1990); 2,099,758 (1998); 2,411,000 (2005 proj.)
**Population rank (1990):** 35
**Rank in land area:** 13
**Abbreviation:** UT; Ut.
**Nickname:** Beehive State
**Motto:** 'Industry'
**Bird:** California gull
**Fish:** rainbow trout
**Flower:** sego lily
**Tree:** blue spruce
**Song:** "Utah, We Love Thee"
**Noted physical features:** Great Basin; Great Salt Lake; Sevier Desert; Colorado Plateau, Tavaputs Plateau, Uinta Mountains, Wasatch Plateau and Range
**Tourist attractions:** Bonneville Salt Flats; Rainbow Bridge; Glen Canyon Dam, Flaming Gorge; Golden Spike National Historic Site; Dinosaur and Natural Bridges national monuments; Arches, Bryce Canyon, Canyonlands, Capital Reef and Zion national parks
**Admission date:** January 4, 1896
**Order of admission:** 45
**Name origin:** For the Ute Indians, who lived in the area; *Ute* or *Eutaw* is vaiously translated as 'in the tops of the mountains,' 'high up,' 'the hill dwellers,' 'the land of the sun,' or 'the land of plenty.'

---

cial capital, and declined by the 3rd century A.D.

**Utrecht** |'o͞o,treKHt; 'yo͞o,trekt| commercial and cultural city in the central Netherlands, capital of a province of the same name. Pop. 231,000.

**Utsu·no·mi·ya** |ˌo͞otso͞o'nōmēyä| industrial city in N central Japan, on central Honshu. Pop. 427,000.

**Ut·tar Pra·desh** |ˌo͞otə prə'däsh; prə'desh| state in N India, bordering on Tibet and Nepal. Pop. 139.03 million. Capital: Lucknow. It was formed in 1950 from the United Provinces of Agra and Oudh.

**Uu·si·kau·pun·ki** |'o͞osē'kä,po͞oNGkē| (Swedish name **Nystad**) industrial port in SW Finland, on the Gulf of Bothnia. Pop. 14,000.

**Ux·mal** |o͞osH'mäl| archaeological site in SE Mexico, in Yucatán state S of Mérida, the remains of a Mayan city built from about 600 A.D.

**Uz·bek·i·stan** |o͝oz'bekə,stæn; o͝oz'bekə,stän| republic in central Asia, lying S and SE of the Aral Sea. Area: 172,808 sq. mi./447,400 sq. km. Pop. 20,955,000. Language, Uzbek. Capital and largest city: Tashkent. Home to a Turkic people, Uzbekistan was part of the Soviet Union 1924–91. It has vast irrigated agricultural and pasture land, mineral wealth, and some heavy industry. □ **Uzbek** *adj. & n.*

Uzbekistan

**Uzh·go·rod** |'o͞ozHgərət| (also **Uzhhorod**) industrial city and transportation hub in W Ukraine, in the foothills of the Carpathian Mountains. Pop. 120,000.

# Vv

**Vaal** |väl| river of South Africa, the chief tributary of the Orange River, rising in the Drakensberg Mts. and flowing 750 mi./1,200 km) SW to the Orange River near Douglas, in Northern Cape.

**Vaa·sa** |'väsä| port in W Finland, on the Gulf of Bothnia. Pop. 53,000. Swedish name **Vasa**.

**Vac·a·ville** |'vækə,vil| city in W central California, SW of Sacramento. Pop. 71,479. It is an agricultural trade center.

**Va·do·dara** |və'dōdərə| city in the state of Gujarat, W India. Pop. 1,021,000. The capital of the former state of Baroda, the city was known as Baroda until 1976.

**Va·duz** |fä'dōots| the capital of Liechtenstein. Pop. 5,000.

**Vail** |väl| town in N Colorado, a noted ski resort. Pop. 3,659.

**Val·dai Hills** |väl'dī| glacial highland in NW Russia, in the upper Volga region. The highest point is 1,053 ft./321 m.

**Val-de-Marne** |,väldə'märn| department in N France, in the Île-de-France, SE of Paris. Pop. 1,216,000. The capital is Créteil.

**Val·dez** |væl'dēz| port city in SE Alaska, on Prince William Sound, the S terminus of the Trans-Alaska Pipeline. Pop. 4,068.

**Val·di·via** |väl'dēvēə| industrial city in S central Chile, in the Los Lagos region. Pop. 114,000.

**Val-d'Oise** |väl'dwäz| department in N France, in the Île-de-France, N of Paris. Pop. 1,050,000. The capital is Pontoise.

**Val-d'Or** |väl'dawr| city in SW Quebec, a gold-mining center. Pop. 23,842.

**Val·dos·ta** |væl'dästə| industrial city in S Georgia. Pop. 39,806.

**Va·lence** |vä'läNs| manufacturing city, capital of Drôme department , in SE France, on the Rhône River. Pop. 66,000.

**Va·len·cia** |və'lensēə| **1** autonomous region of E Spain, on the Mediterranean coast. It was formerly a Moorish kingdom (1021–1238). **2** its capital, a port on the Mediterranean coast. Pop. 777,000.

**Va·len·cia** |və'lensēə| industrial city in N Venezuela, on Lake Valencia. Pop. 903,000.

**Va·len·ci·ennes** |,väläN'syen| town in N France. Pop. 39,000. Its name is given to a decorative type of lace produced from the 15th century.

**Va·le·ra** |və'lärə| commercial city in W Venezuela, in Trujillo state. Pop. 111,000.

**Val·hal·la** |væl'hælə| in Scandinavian myth, the hall assigned to heroes who have died in battle. Here they feast with the god Odin.

**Val·la·do·lid**[1] |,väyädō'lēd| former name (until 1828) for **MORELIA**.

**Val·la·do·lid**[2] |,väyädō'lēd| city in N Spain, capital of Castilla-León region. Pop. 345,000. It was the principal residence of the kings of Castile in the 15th century.

**Val·le d'Aos·ta** |,välädä'awstə| largely French-speaking Alpine region in the NW corner of Italy. Capital: Aosta.

**Val·le·du·par** |,väyädōo'pär| commercial city in N Colombia, the capital of César department. Pop. 252,000.

**Val·le·jo** |və'laō; və'lä,hō| industrial port city in N central California, on San Pablo Bay NE of San Francisco. Pop. 109,199.

**Val·let·ta** |və'letə| the capital and chief port of Malta. Pop. 9,000; urban harbor area pop. 102,000.

**Val·ley, the** |'vælē| capital of Anguilla, in the West Indies. Pop. 2,000. It is a tourist center.

**Val·ley Forge** |'vælē 'fawrj| site on the Schuylkill River in Pennsylvania, about 20 mi./32 km. NW of Philadelphia, where George Washington's Continental Army spent the winter of 1777–78 in conditions of extreme hardship during the Revolutionary War.

**Val·ley of the Kings** valley near ancient Thebes in Egypt where the pharaohs of the New Kingdom (c.1550–1070 B.C.) were buried. Most of the tombs were looted in antiquity; the exception was that of Tutankhamen, almost untouched until discovered in 1922.

**Val·ley of the Sun** nickname for the valley in central Arizona in which Phoenix and most of its suburbs lie.

**Val·ley Stream** |,vælē 'strēm| industrial and commercial village in W central Long Island, SE New York. Pop. 33,946.

**Val·my** |väl'mē| village in NE France, in the Argonne region. Pop. 290. The first engagement of the French Revolutionary Wars, between the French and the Prussians, was fought here on September 20, 1792.

**Va·lois** |väl'wä| medieval duchy of N France, home of the Valois royal dynasty (1328–1589).

**Va·lo·na** |və'lōnə| Italian name for **VLORË**.

**Val·pa·rai·so** |,välpärä'ēzō| the principal

port of Chile, in the center of the country, near Santiago. Pop. 277,000.

**Val·pa·rai·so** |ˌvælpəˈrāzō| commercial and industrial city in NW Indiana. Pop. 24,414.

**Van** |væn| commercial town in E Turkey, capital of Van province. Pop. 153,000. A Kurdish center, it is on the SE shore of saline **Lake Van,** the largest (1,450 sq. mi./3,755 sq. km.) in the country.

**Va·nad·zor** |ˈvänädˌzawr| (formerly **Kirovakan**) industrial city in N Armenia. Pop. 169,000. It is a rail and manufacturing center.

**Van·cou·ver**[1] |vænˈkoovər| port city in SW British Columbia, on the mainland opposite Vancouver Island. Pop. 471,844. It is the largest city in W Canada, and its chief Pacific port.

**Van·cou·ver**[2] |vænˈkoovər| industrial port city in SW Washington, on the Columbia River N of Portland, Oregon. Pop. 46,380.

**Van·cou·ver Island** |vænˈkoovər| large island off the Pacific coast of Canada, in SW British Columbia. Its capital, Victoria, is the capital of British Columbia. It became a British Crown Colony in 1849, later uniting with British Columbia.

**Van·da** |ˈvändə| Swedish name for VANTAA.

**Van·den·berg Air Force Base** |ˈvændən-ˌbərg| facility on the Pacific coast of SW California, N of Santa Barbara, an important space program site.

**Van·der·bijl·park** |ˌvändər,bīl,pärk| steel-manufacturing city in South Africa, in the province of Gauteng, S of Johannesburg. Pop. 540,000 (with Vereeniging).

**Van Die·men's Land** |vænˈdēmənz| former name (until 1855) for TASMANIA.

**Vä·nern** |ˈvenərn| (also **Vaner**) lake in SW Sweden, the largest (1,450 sq. mi./3,755 sq. km.) lake in Sweden and the third-largest in Europe.

**Va·ni·ko·lo** |ˌvänēˈkōlō| (also **Vanikoro**) island in the S central Solomon Islands, in the Santa Cruz group, scene of the 1788 loss of the French explorer La Pérouse.

**Vannes** |vän| agricultural and tourist center, capital of the department of Morbihan, in Brittany, NW France. Pop. 48,000.

**Van Nuys** |vænˈīz| industrial and residential section of NW Los Angeles, California, a center of aerospace manufacturing.

**Van·taa** |ˈväntä| city in S Finland, a N suburb of Helsinki. Pop. 155,000.

**Va·nua Le·vu** |vəˌnooə ˈlävoo| (formerly **Sandalwood Island**) island in N Fiji, in the SW Pacific. At 2,146 sq. mi./5,556 sq.

km. it is the second-largest island in the country.

**Va·nu·atu** |ˌvänəˈwä,too| republic consisting of a group of islands in the SW Pacific. Area: 5,716 sq. mi./14,800 sq. km. Pop. 156,000. Official languages, Bislama, English, and French. Capital: Vila (on Efate). The Melanesian islands were administered jointly by Britain and France 1906–80 as the condominium of the New Hebrides. Vanuatu became independent in 1980. Copra and fish are among its local products. □ **Vanuatuan** *adj. & n.*

Vanuatu

**Var** |vär| department in extreme SW France. Pop. 815,000. The capital is Toulon.

**Va·ra·na·si** |vəˈränəsē| historic city on the Ganges, in Uttar Pradesh, N India. Pop. 926,000. It is a holy city and a place of pilgrimage for Hindus, who undergo ritual purification in the Ganges. Former name **Benares.**

**Var·dar River** |ˈvär,där| (Greek name **Axios**) river that flows 240 mi./390 km. from W Macedonia into NE Greece, into the Gulf of Salonika in the Aegean Sea.

**Va·re·se** |vəˈräsā| town in Lombardy, N Italy, in a resort region. Pop. 88,000.

**Varna** |ˈvärnə| industrial port and resort in E Bulgaria, on the W shore of the Black Sea. Pop. 321,000.

**Va·sa** |ˈväsä| Swedish name for VAASA.

**Vas·lui** |väsˈlooē| commercial city in E Romania, capital of Vaslui county. Pop. 74,000.

**Väs·ter·ås** |ˌvestəˈraws| port on Lake Mälaren in E Sweden, the capital of Västmannland county. Pop. 120,000.

**Vat·i·can City** |ˈvætikən| independent papal state in the city of Rome, the seat of government of the Roman Catholic Church. Pop. 1,000. It covers an area of 109 acres/44 hectares around St. Peter's Basilica and the palace of the Vatican. Having been suspended after the incorporation of the former Papal States into Italy in 1870, the temporal power of the pope was restored by the Lateran Treaty of 1929. Castel Gandolfo and several churches in Rome constitute extraterritorial possessions.

**Vät·tern** |ˈvetərn| large lake in S Sweden, connected to the North and Baltic seas by canal. Jönköping lies on its S.

**Vau·cluse** |vōˈklŸz| department in SE France, in Provence. Pop. 467,000. The capital city is Avignon. The scenery of the Vaucluse attracts tourists.

**Vaud** |vō| canton on the shores of Lake Geneva in W Switzerland. Pop. 584,000. Capital: Lausanne. German name **Waadt**.

**Vaude·ville** |ˌvawd(ə)ˈvēl| corruption of the name of the valley **Vau-de-Vire** in NW France, home of Olivier Basselin, a 15th-century musician who supposedly composed the light love and drinking songs that first became known as vaudeville.

**Vaux** |vō| **1** village in NE France, NE of Verdun. The village experienced fierce fighting during World War I and was captured by German forces in June 1916. **2** Vaux-le-Vicomte, 17th-century chateau built for Nicolas Fouquet, finance minister to Louis XIV. Its magnificence so enraged the king that he had Fouquet jailed; it also inspired him to build the chateau at Versailles.

**Väx·jö** |ˈvek,SHŒ| industrial town in S Sweden, a glassmaking center and capital of Kronoborg county. Pop. 47,000.

**Ve·ii** |ˈvēī| ancient city in Etruria, N of Rome. It was an important member of the Etruscan League and fought against Rome for centuries before being captured after a 10-year siege.

**Vel·bert** |ˈfel,bert| manufacturing city in NW Germany, NE of Düsseldorf. Pop. 90,000.

**veld** |velt| (also **veldt**) high, treeless interior grasslands and savanna of South Africa and of Zimbabwe. The Boers settled much of the area in their Great Trek of the 1830s, and used it for grazing.

**Ve·li·ki·ye Lu·ki** |vəˈlēkēə ˈlo͞okē| transportation center and town in W Russia, W of Tver. Pop.116,000.

**Ve·li·ko Tur·no·vo** |ˈveli,kaw ˈtərnəvō| historic town in central Bulgaria, a former (1187–1396) capital, in the N foothills of the Balkan Mts. Pop. 100,000.

**Vel·la La·vel·la** |ˌvelə ləˈvelə| island in the central Solomon Islands, in the SW Pacific, in the New Georgia group, NW of Guadalcanal, site of a 1943 victory by U.S. naval forces over the Japanese.

**Vel·lore** |vəˈlawr| historic commercial town

in S India, in the foothills of the Eastern Ghats in Tamil Nadu state. Pop. 305,000.

**Vel·sen** |ˈvelsən| seaport in N Netherlands, near the mouth of the North Sea Canal. Pop. 61,000.

**Vence** |väNs| resort town in SE France, W of Nice. Pop. 15,000. It is a noted arts center.

**Ven·da** |ˈvendə| former homeland established in South Africa for the Venda people, now part of Northern Province.

**Ven·dée** |väNˈdā| largely agricultural department in W France, on the Bay of Biscay. Pop. 509,000. The capital is La-Roche-sur-Yon. It was the center of 1790s rebellion against the Revolutionary government in Paris.

**Ven·dôme** |väNˈdawm| **1** manufacturing town in N central France. Pop. 17,000. The title of duke of Vendôme was created by Henri IV and given to an out-of-wedlock son in 1598. **2** Place Vendôme square in Paris, France, on the Right Bank built 1687–1720, in classical style. In the center is a column cast from cannons captured by Napoleon I at the Battle of Austerlitz, topped by a statue of the emperor.

**Ve·ne·to** |ˈvänə,tō| (also **Venetia**) largely agricultural autonomous region in NE Italy The capital is Venice. Pop. 4,385,000.

**Ve·ne·zia** |vəˈnetsēə| Italian name for VENICE.

**Ve·ne·zia Giu·lia** |vəˈnetsēə ˈjo͞olyä| former region in NE Italy, on the Adriatic Sea. Much of it was ceded to Yugoslavia after World War II; the rest merged with the province of Udine to form Friuli–Venezia Giulia.

**Ven·e·zu·e·la** |ˌvenəz(ə)ˈwālə| republic on the N coast of South America, with a coastline on the Caribbean Sea. Area: 352,279 sq. mi./912,050 sq. km. Pop. 20,191,000. Language, Spanish. Capital and largest city: Caracas. Venezuela won independence from Spain in 1821, and seceded from Colombia in 1830. A major oil exporter, it

**Venezuela**

also mines metals and grows coffee and other crops. □ **Venezuelan** *adj. & n.*

**Ven·ice**[1] |'venəs| city in NE Italy, capital of the Veneto region. Pop. 318,000. Italian name **Venezia**. Situated on a lagoon of the Adriatic, it is built on numerous islands that are separated by canals and linked by bridges. It was a powerful republic in the Middle Ages and from the 13th to the 16th centuries a leading sea power, controlling trade to and ruling parts of the E Mediterranean. Its commercial importance declined after the Cape route to India was discovered at the end of the 16th century, but it remained an important center of art and music. After the Napoleonic Wars Venice was placed under Austrian rule and was incorporated into a unified Italy in 1866. □ **Venetian** *adj. & n.*

**Ven·ice**[2] |'venəs| beachfront section of Los Angeles, California, W of downtown.

**Vè·nis·sieux** |ˌvānē'syœ| town in E France, a SE suburb of Lyons. Pop. 61,000.

**Ven·lo** |'venlō| industrial and commercial city in Limbourg province, SE Netherlands, near the German border. Pop. 65,000.

**Ven·ti·mi·glia** |ˌventē'mēlyä| beach resort and seaport in NW Italy, on the Ligurian Sea, on the Italian Riviera near the French border. Pop. 26,000. It has a major flower market.

**Ven·tu·ra** |ven'CHoͦorə| (official name **San Buenaventura**) city in S California, on the Pacific, in an oil-producing and agricultural area. Pop. 92,575.

**Ve·ra·cruz** |ˌverə'krōͦoz| **1** state of E central Mexico, with a long coastline on the Gulf of Mexico. Capital: Jalapa Enriquez. **2** city and port in Veracruz state, on the Gulf of Mexico. Pop. 328,000.

**Ver·cel·li** |vər'CHelē| market town and industrial center in NW Italy, capital of Vercelli province. Pop. 50,000. It is in a rice-growing area.

**Ver·dun**[1] |ver'dən| fortified town on the Meuse River in NE France. Pop. 23,000. The site of one of the longest and bloodiest battles in World War I, Verdun has large military cemeteries and several war memorials.

**Ver·dun**[2] |vər'dən| city in S Quebec, a suburb just S of Montreal on the St. Lawrence River. Pop. 61,307.

**Ve·ree·ni·ging** |vəˈrēnikiNG| industrial city in South Africa, in the province of Gauteng. Pop. 774,000 (with Vanderbijlpark).

**Verkh·ne·u·dinsk** |ˌvyerknə'ōͦodinsk| former name (until 1934) for ULAN-UDE.

**Ver·kho·yansk** |ˌverkə'yänsk| river port and fur-trading town in Siberia, W Russia, NE of Yakutsk. Near the Arctic Circle and one of the coldest places on Earth, it was formerly used to house political exiles.

**Ver·mont** |vər'mänt| see box. □ **Vermonter** *n.*

**Verny** |'vərnyē| former name (until 1921) for ALMATY.

**Ve·ro Beach** |'virō| resort and commercial city in E central Florida. Pop. 17,350.

**Ve·ro·na** |vəˈrōnə| commercial and industrial city on the Adige River, in NE Italy. Pop. 259,000.

**Verrazano-Narrows Bridge** |ˌverəˌzänō 'nærōz| suspension bridge linking Staten Island, and Brooklyn, New York, completed in 1964. It crosses the Narrows of New York Bay.

**Ver·sailles** |ver'sī; vər'sī| town, SW of Paris, in N central France, capital of the department of Yvelines. Pop. 91,000. The opulent palace of Versailles, built by King Louis XIV, with its expansive gardens, was the royal residence until 1789. International treaties, including that ending World War I, have been signed here.

**Ver·viers** |ver'vyä| manufacturing town in E Belgium; pop 53,000.

---

### Vermont

**Capital:** Montpelier
**Largest city:** Burlington
**Other cities:** Brattleboro, Rutland, Stowe
**Population:** 562,758 (1990); 590,883 (1998); 638,000 (2005 proj.)
**Population rank (1990):** 48
**Rank in land area:** 45
**Abbreviation:** VT; Vt.
**Nickname:** Green Mountain State
**Motto:** 'Freedom and Unity'
**Bird:** hermit thrush
**Fish:** brook trout (cold water); walleye pike (warm water)
**Flower:** red clover
**Tree:** sugar maple
**Song:** "Hail, Vermont!"
**Noted physical features:** Green Mountains
**Tourist attractions:** ski resorts
**Admission date:** March 4, 1791
**Order of admission:** 14
**Name origin:** From French *vert*, 'green,' and *mont*, 'mountain,' originally applied to the Green Mountains east of Lake Champlain by French explorer Samuel de Champlain on his map of 1612.

**Ves·ter·å·len** |'vestə,raw| group of islands of Norway, N of the Arctic Circle.

**Vest·man·na·ey·jar** |'vest,män'ä,yär| Icelandic name for WESTMANN ISLANDS.

**Ve·su·vi·us** |və'sōōvēəs| active volcano near Naples, in S Italy, 4,190 ft./1,277 m. high. A violent eruption in A.D. 79 buried the nearby towns of Pompeii and Herculaneum.

**Vesz·prém** |'ves,präm| town in W Hungary. Pop. 65,000. A commercial center, it is popular with tourists.

**Vet·lu·ga River** |vit'lōōgä| river (528 mi./850 km. long) in W Russia, flowing into the Volga River in the SW of Mari El Republic.

**Ve·vey** |və'vā| commune and tourist resort in W Switzerland, on the NE shore of Lake Geneva, SE of Lausanne. Pop. 16,000.

**Via Ap·pia** |,vēə 'æpēə; 'vīə| Latin name for APPIAN WAY.

**Via·reg·gio** |,vēä'rejō| beach resort and seaport on the Tyrrhenian Sea in W Italy. Pop. 57,000. The body of the English poet Shelley washed up on shore near here.

**Vi·borg** |'vē,bawr| historic rail junction and commercial town in N Denmark. Pop. 29,000.

**Vi·cen·te Ló·pez** |vē,sentä 'lōpes| city in E central Argentina, a suburb just NW of Buenos Aires. Pop. 289,000.

**Vi·cen·za** |vē'cHensä| industrial city in NE Italy, capital of Vicenza province. Pop. 109,000. It is noted for its Renaissance architecture.

**Vi·chy** |'vēsHē| town in S central France. Pop. 28,000. A noted spa, it is a source of effervescent mineral water. During World War II it was the headquarters of the regime (1940–44) set up under Marshal Pétain after the German occupation of N France, to administer unoccupied France and the colonies, which functioned as a puppet for the Nazis.

**Vicks·burg** |'viks,bərg| city on the Mississippi River, in W Mississippi. Pop. 20,908. In 1863 it was successfully besieged by Union forces under U.S. Grant. It was the last Confederate outpost on the river, and its loss effectively split the Confederacy in half.

**Vic·to·ria**[1] |vik'tawrēə| state of SE Australia. Pop. 4,394,000. Capital: Melbourne. Originally a district of New South Wales, it became a separate colony in 1851 and was federated with the other states of Australia in 1901.

**Vic·to·ria**[2] |vik'tawrēə| port at the S tip of Vancouver Island, capital of British Columbia. Pop. 71,228.

**Vic·to·ria**[3] |vik'tawrēə| business center, port, and capital of Hong Kong, S China. Pop. 591,000. Victoria Harbor is one of the greatest natural harbors in the world and has excellent dockyard facilities.

**Vic·to·ria**[4] |vik'tawrēə| the capital of the Seychelles, a port on the island of Mahé. Pop. 24,000.

**Vic·to·ria**[5] |vik'tawrēə| city in S Texas, a center of the oil and cattle industries. Pop. 55,076.

**Vic·to·ria, Lake** |vik'tawrēə| the largest (26,820 sq. mi./69,464 sq. km.) lake in Africa, with shores in Uganda, Tanzania, and Kenya, and drained by the Nile. Also called **Victoria Nyanza**.

**Vic·to·ria de Du·ran·go** |vik'tawrēä dä dōō,räNGgō| full name for the city of DURANGO, Mexico.

**Vic·to·ria Falls** |vik'tawrēä| waterfall 355 ft./109 m. high on the Zambezi River, on the Zimbabwe–Zambia border.

**Vic·to·ria Island** |vik'tawrēə| third-largest island in the Canadian Arctic, divided between the Northwest Territories and Nunavut. The administrative center of Cambridge Bay is on its SE coast.

**Vic·to·ria Nile** |vik'tawrēə 'nīl| the upper part of the White Nile, between Lake Victoria and Lake Albert.

**Vic·to·ria Ny·an·za** |vik'tawrēə nē'ænzə; nī'ænzə| another name for Lake Victoria (see VICTORIA, LAKE).

**Vic·tor·ville** |'viktər,vil| industrial and residential city in S California, NE of Los Angeles. Pop. 40,674.

**Vi·da·lia** |və'dālyə| city in SE Georgia, in an area noted for onion production. Pop. 11,708.

**Vi·din** |'vēdin| port city in extreme N Bulgaria, on the Danube River. Pop. 91,000. It is known for wine and ceramics.

**Vi·en·na** |vē'enə| the capital of Austria, an historic administrative, financial, and cultural center in the NE on the Danube River. Pop. 1,533,000. From 1278 to 1918 it was the seat of the Habsburg dynasty. It has long been a center of the arts, especially music, associated with famed composers. German name **Wien**. □ **Viennese** adj. & n.

**Vi·en·na Woods** |vē'enə| English name for WIENERWALD.

**Vienne** |vyen| **1** department in W central France, in the Poitou-Charentes region. Pop. 380,000. The capital is Poitiers. **2** river in central France that rises near Limoges and flows N and W for 220 mi./350 km., into the Loire River SE of Saumur. **3** the French form of VIENNA.

**Vien·tiane** |vyen'tyän| the capital and chief port of Laos, on the Mekong River. Pop. 377,000.

**Vie·ques** |vē'äkäs| (English name **Crab Island**) island municipality in E Puerto Rico, a resort and naval firing range. Pop. 8,602.

**Vier·sen** |'firzən| industrial city in western Germany, W of Düsseldorf. Pop. 78,000.

**Vier·wald·stät·ter·see** |fir'vält‚stetər‚zä| German name for Lake Lucerne (see LUCERNE, LAKE).

**Vi·et·nam** |vē'et'näm; ‚vēet'næm| republic in SE Asia, with a coastline on the South China Sea. Area: 127,295 sq. mi./329,566 sq. km. Pop. 67,843,000. Language, Vietnamese. Capital: Hanoi. Largest city: Ho Chi Minh City. Long dominated by China, Vietnam was part of French Indochina 1862–1954.With French withdrawal, it was partitioned into North and South Vietnam, and was reunified in 1975, following the Vietnam War. Its economy is traditionally based on agriculture. □ **Vietnamese** *adj. & n.*

**Vietnam**

**Vi·go** |'vēgō| port city in Galicia, NW Spain, on the Atlantic. Pop. 277,000.

**Vi·ja·ya·na·gar** |‚vijəyə'nəgər| ruined city in S India, near present-day Hampi in Karnataka state; capital of the Hindu Vijayanagar empire of the 14th to 16th centuries.

**Vi·ja·ya·wa·da** |‚vijəyə'wädä| commercial and religious city on the Krishna River in Andhra Pradesh, SE India. Pop. 701,000.

**Vi·jo·së River** |vē'ōsə| river (148 mi./238 km. long) in NW Greece that flows through Albania to the Adriatic Sea N of Vlorë

**Vi·la** |'vēlə| (also **Port Vila**) the capital of Vanuatu, on the SW coast of the island of Efate. Pop. 20,000.

**Vi·la No·va de Ga·ia** |‚vēlə 'nawvə dä 'gīə| city in NW Portugal, an industrial suburb of Oporto. Pop. 68,000.

**Vi·la Re·al** |‚vēlə rē'äl| town on the Corgo River in N Portugal, capital of Vila Real district. Pop. 15,000.

**Vi·la Ve·lha** |‚vēlə 'velyə| port city in E Brazil, in Espírito Santo state, just S of Vitória. Pop. 269,000.

**Vil·lach** |'fil‚äKH| industrial town and transportation center in S Austria. Pop. 55,000.

**Vil·la d'Este** |‚vilä'destä| villa near Tivoli, E of Rome, Italy. Built for a cardinal of the Catholic Church in 1550, it is famous for its gardens.

**Vil·lage, the** |'vilij| see GREENWICH VILLAGE, New York City.

**Vil·la·her·mo·sa** |‚vēyäer'mōsä| city in SE Mexico, capital of the state of Tabasco. Pop. 390,000. Full name **Villahermosa de San Juan Bautista**.

**Vil·la·no·va** |‚vilə'nōvə| academic community in SE Pennsylvania, NW of Philadelphia, home to Villanova University.

**Vil·la·vi·cen·cio** |‚vēyävē'sensē‚ō| commercial city in central Colombia, the capital of Meta department. Pop. 233,000. It is the trading center for agricultural E Colombia.

**Villefranche-sur-Mer** |vēl'fränSHsyr 'mer| seaport and resort, SE France, on the Riviera, E of Nice. Pop. 8,000.

**Ville·juif** |vēlZHə'wēf| commune, a S suburb of Paris, in N central France. Pop. 49,000.

**Vil·leur·banne** |‚vēlYœr'bän| industrial E suburb of Lyons, E France. Pop. 120,000.

**Villingen-Schwenningen** |'viliNGən 'SHfeniNGən| twin manufacturing city in SW Germany, E of Freiburg. Combined pop. 80,000.

**Vil·ni·us** |'vilnēəs| historic industrial and academic city, the capital of Lithuania, on the Neris River. Pop. 593,000.

**Vi·lyui River** |vil'yōōē| (also **Vilyuy**) river (1,520 mi./2,450 km. long) in Asian Russia, flowing into the Lena River, NW of Yakutsk.

**Vim·i·nal** |'vimənl| one of the seven hills upon which Rome, Italy, was built.

**Vi·my Ridge** |vē'mē| ridge near commune of Vimy, in N France, N of Arras. It was captured by Canadian forces in 1917, after bloody fighting.

**Vi·ña del Mar** |‚vēnyə del 'mär| city in central Chile, a seaside resort and suburb just N of Valparaiso. Pop. 281,000.

**Vin·cennes¹** |ven'sen| industrial and residential E suburb of Paris, France. Pop.

45,000. A former royal residence here is now a museum.

**Vin·cennes**² |vin'senz| historic commercial and industrial city in SW Indiana, on the Wabash River. Pop. 19,859.

**Vin·dhya Range** |'vindyə| range in central India extending from Gujarat to the Ganges Valley; historically, the dividing line between N and S India.

**Vine·land** |'vīnlənd| commercial and industrial city in S New Jersey, in an agricultural area. Pop. 54,780.

**Vinh Long** |'vin 'lawNG| (also **Vinhlong**) port city in southern Vietnam, SW of Ho Chi Minh City. Pop. 82,000.

**Vin·land** |'vinlənd| region of the NE coast of North America that was visited in the 11th century by Norsemen led by Leif Ericsson. It was so named from the report that grapevines were found growing there. The exact location is uncertain: sites from the northernmost tip of Newfoundland (see L'ANSE AUX MEADOWS) to Cape Cod and even Virginia have been proposed.

**Vin·ny·tsya** |'vēnitsyə| industrial city in central Ukraine. Pop. 379,000. Russian name **Vinnitsa**.

**Vin·son Mas·sif** |'vinsən 'mæsif| the highest mountain range in Antarctica, in Ellsworth Land, rising to 16,863 ft./ 5,140 m.

**Vire** |vēr| **1** commercial town in NW France, on the Vire River **2** river in NW France, flowing N past Vire and Saint Lô into the Bay of the Seine. Its estuary was the dividing point between Omaha and Utah beaches in the D-day landings, June 1944.

**Vir·gi·lio** |vir'jēlēō| commune in N Italy, S of Mantova. Pop. 7,600. Ancient Andes, on this site, was the birthplace of the poet Virgil.

**Vir·gin·ia** |vər'jinyə| see box. □ **Virginian** *adj. & n.*

**Vir·gin·ia Beach** |vər'jinyə| city and resort on the Atlantic coast of SE Virginia. Pop. 393,069.

**Vir·gin·ia City** |vər'jinyə| historic settlement in W Nevada, S of Reno, site of the 1850s–60s Comstock Lode gold and silver boom.

**Vir·gin Islands** |'vərjən| group of Caribbean islands at the E extremity of the Greater Antilles, divided between British and U.S. administration. The islands were encountered by Columbus in 1493 and settled, mainly in the 17th century, by British and Danish sugar planters, who introduced African slaves. The British Virgin Islands

**US Virgin Islands**

consists of about forty islands in the NE of the group. Pop. 17,000. Capital: Road Town (on Tortola). They have constituted a British Crown Colony since 1956, having

---

## Virginia

**Official name:** Commonwealth of Virginia

**Capital:** Richmond

**Largest city:** Norfolk

**Other cities:** Arlington, Hampton, Lexington, Newport News, Charlottesville, Roanoke, Virginia Beach, Williamsburg

**Population:** 6,187,358 (1990); 6,791,345 (1998); 7,324,000 (2005 proj.)

**Population rank (1990):** 12

**Rank in land area:** 35

**Abbreviation:** VA; Va.

**Nickname:** Old Dominion; Mother of Presidents; Mother of States

**Motto:** *Sic semper tyrannis* (Latin: 'Thus ever to tyrants')

**Bird:** cardinal

**Flower:** American dogwood flower

**Tree:** American dogwood

**Song:** "Carry Me Back to Old Virginia"

**Noted physical features:** Chesapeake Bay; Natural Bridge; Luray Caverns; Newport News, Norfolk, Portsmouth, Richmond (ports)

**Tourist attractions:** Bull Run, Chancellorsville, Fair Oaks, Fredericksburg, Manassas, Petersburg, Richmond, Seven Pines, Spotsylvania, Wilderness and Yorktown battle sites; Monticello, Mount Vernon, Stratford Hall and Williamsburg historical sites; George Washington Birthplace National Monument; Virginia Beach; Shenandoah National Park

**Admission date:** June 25, 1788

**Order of admission:** 10

**Name origin:** For Elizabeth I of England, "the Virgin Queen"; the name originally applied to all the territory claimed by the British in North America.

previously been part of the Leeward Islands. The remaining islands (about fifty) make up the U.S. unincorporated territory of the Virgin Islands. Pop. 101,809. Capital: Charlotte Amalie (on St. Thomas). They were purchased from Denmark in 1917 because of their strategic position.

**Vi•run•ga** |vē'ro͝oNGgə| (also **Mfumbira**) mountain range in E central Africa, in the Rift Valley and N of Lake Kivu on the border of Congo (formerly Zaire) with Rwanda and Uganda. It reaches 14,787 ft./4,507 m. at Karisimbi, and has several active volcanoes.

**Vis** |vēs| island in the Adriatic Sea, part of Croatia. Pop. 4,000. A resort, its main towns are Vis and Komiža.

**Vi•sa•kha•pat•nam** |ˌvēsäkə'pətnəm| port on the coast of Andhra Pradesh, in SE India. Pop. 750,000.

**Vi•sa•lia** |vi'sālyə| city in S central California, an agricultural hub in the San Joaquin Valley. Pop. 75,636.

**Vi•sa•yan** |vē'sīən| (also **Visayas; Bisayas**) island group in the central Philippines, between Luzon and Mindanao.

**Vis•by** |'vizbē| port on the W coast of the Swedish island of Gotland, of which it is the capital. Pop. 57,000.

**Vis•ta** |'vistə| city in SW California, a suburb N of San Diego. Pop. 71,872.

**Vis•tu•la** |'visCHələ| river in Poland that rises in the Carpathian Mts. and flows 592 mi./940 km. generally N, through Cracow and Warsaw, to the Baltic near Gdańsk. Polish name **Wisła**.

**Vi•tebsk** |vē'tepsk| Russian name for VITSEBSK.

**Vi•ter•bo** |vē'terbō| agricultural center in central Italy, capital of Viterbo province. Pop. 60,000.

**Vi•ti Le•vu** |'vētē 'lāvo͞o| the largest (4,028 mi./10,429 sq. km.) of the Fiji islands. Its chief settlement is Suva.

**Vi•tim River** |və'tēm| river (1,133 mi./1,823 km. long) in S Russia. It rises in central Buryatia and flows NE into the Lena River on the SW border of Sakha.

**Vi•to•ria** |vē'tawrēə| industrial city in NE Spain, capital of the Basque Provinces. Pop. 209,000.

**Vi•tó•ria** |vē'tawrēə| port in E Brazil, capital of the state of Espírito Santo. Pop. 276,000.

**Vi•tó•ria da Con•qui•sta** |vē'tawrēyə dä kawn'kēstä| city in E Brazil, in Bahia state. Pop. 264,000. It is a cattle industry center in the Batalha Mts.

**Vitry-sur-Seine** |vēˌtrē sYr 'sen| industrial suburb of Paris, in N central France. Pop. 85,000.

**Vit•sebsk** |'vētsyipsk| industrial city in NE Belarus, on the Western Dvina River. Pop. 356,000. Russian name **Vitebsk**.

**Vit•to•ria** |vi'tawrēə| city in SE Sicily, a center of wine and olive-oil production. Pop. 54,000.

**Vit•to•rio Ve•ne•to** |vi'tawrēō 'venāˌtō| commune in NE Italy. Pop. 29,000. After winning a decisive battle here against Austrian forces, Italians achieved an armistice with Austro-Hungarian forces in World War I.

**Viz•ca•ya** |vis'kī(y)ə| province in N Spain, in the Basque Country, bordering on France. Pop. 1,155,000. The capital is Bilbao.

**Viz•i•a•na•ga•ram** |ˌvizēə'nəgərəm| commercial and industrial city in S India, in Andhra Pradesh state. Pop. 177,000.

**Vlaar•ding•en** |'vlärdiNGgən| industrial city in SW Netherlands, on the Nieuwe Maas River. Pop. 74,000.

**Vla•di•kav•kaz** |ˌvlədiˌkəf'käz| city in SW Russia, capital of the autonomous republic of North Ossetia. Pop. 306,000. Former names **Ordzhonikidze** (1931–44 and 1954–93) and **Dzaudzhikau** (1944–54).

**Vlad•i•mir** |vlə'dēˌmir; 'vlædəˌmi(ə)r| historic industrial city in European Russia, E of Moscow. Pop. 353,000. It is the former (12th–13th century) capital of the principality of Vladimir.

**Vla•di•vos•tok** |ˌvlædəvə'stäk; ˌvlædə'västäk| city in the extreme SE of Russia, on the Sea of Japan, capital of Primorsky Krai. Pop. 643,000. It is the chief port of Russia's Pacific coast and terminus of the Trans-Siberian Railway.

**Vlis•sing•en** |'vlisiNGə| Dutch name for FLUSHING.

**Vlo•rë** |'vlawr| naval and commercial port in SW Albania, on the Adriatic coast. Pop. 56,000. Also called **Vlona**, Italian name **Valona**.

**Vl•ta•va** |'vəltəvə| river of the Czech Republic, which rises in the Bohemian Forest on the German border and flows 270 mi./435 km. generally N, passing through Prague before joining the Elbe N of the city. German name **Moldau**.

**Voj•vo•di•na** |'voivəˌdēnə| mainly Hungarian-speaking province of N Serbia, on the Hungarian border. Pop. 2,035,000. Capital: Novi Sad.

**Vol•ca•no Islands** |väl'kānō; vawl'kānō| island group of Japan, in the W Pacific, S of Bonin Island; the largest is Iwo Jima.

**Vol·ga** |'võlgə| the longest river in Europe, which rises in NW Russia and flows 2,292 mi./3,688 km. generally E to Kazan, where it turns SE to the Caspian Sea. It has been dammed at several points to provide hydroelectric power, and is navigable for most of its length.

**Vol·go·donsk** |,vəlgə'dawnsk| city in W Russia, on the Don River NE of Rostov. Pop. 178,000.

**Vol·go·grad** |,vəlgə'grät| industrial city in SW Russia, at the junction of the Don and Volga rivers. Pop. 1,005,000. Former names **Tsaritsyn** (until 1925) and **Stalingrad** (1925–61).

**Vol·hyn·ia** |väl'hinēə| (also **Volynia**) historic region in NW Ukraine, originally a Russian principality. It is now largely an agricultural and coal-mining area.

**Vo·log·da** |'vawləgdə| industrial city in N Russia, on the Vologda River. Pop. 286,000.

**Vo·los** |'vaw,laws; 'vō,läs| port on an inlet of the Aegean Sea, in Thessaly, E Greece. Pop. 77,000. Greek name **Vólos**.

**Vol·scian Mountains** |'vawlsHən| (also called **Lepini Mountains**) range in central Italy. Its highest peak rises to 5,039 ft./1,536 m.

**Vol·ta** |'vältə; 'vōltə| river of W Africa, which is formed in central Ghana by the junction of its headwaters, the Black Volta, the White Volta, and the Red Volta, which rise in Burkina Faso. At Akosombo in SE Ghana it has been dammed, creating Lake Volta, one of the world's largest manmade lakes.

**Vol·ta Re·don·da** |,vawltə re'dändə| industrial city in SE Brazil, in Rio de Janeiro state, on the Paraíba River. Pop. 229,000. It is a steel industry center.

**Vol·ter·ra** |vawl'terə| town in central Italy. Pop. 13,000. An Etruscan stronghold later controlled Florence, it contains Etruscan and Roman structures.

**Vol·tur·no River** |vawl'tŏŏrnō| river (109 mi./175 km.) in S central Italy that rises in the Apennine range and flows into the Gulf of Gaeta SE of Gaeta. Its valley was the scene of heavy fighting in World War II.

**Vo·lu·bi·lis** |və'lŏŏbiləs| Roman town in ancient Mauretania Tingitana, now an area of ruins near Meknès, NW Morocco.

**Vol·un·teer State** |,välən'tir| nickname for TENNESSEE.

**Volzh·sky** |'vawlsHkē| industrial city in SW Russia, on the Volga near Volgograd. Pop. 275,000.

**Vor·arl·berg** |'fawr,ärl,bərg| Alpine state of W Austria. Pop. 331,000. Capital: Bregenz.

**Vor·ku·ta** |vawr'kŏŏtə| city in Russia, in the N Ural Mts., above the Arctic Circle. Pop. 117,000. It was founded as a prison labor camp during the Stalin era.

**Vo·ro·nezh** |və'rawniZH| industrial city in Russia, S of Moscow on the Voronezh River. Pop. 895,000.

**Vo·ro·shi·lov·grad** |,vərəsHə,low'grät| former (1935–91) name for LUHANSK.

**Vosges** |vōzH| mountain system of E France, in Alsace near the border with Germany, rising to 4,669 ft./1,423 m.

**Vos·tok** |vä'stawk| Russian scientific station in central Antarctica, near the S magnetic pole, cited as the coldest known place on earth.

**Vot·kinsk** |'vawt,kinsk| industrial city in W Russia, on the Kama River. Pop. 104,000.

**Voy·a·geurs National Park** |,voiä'zHər| preserve in N Minnesota, along the Ontario border, whose name recalls the French fur traders of the 18th century.

**Vra·tsa** |'vrätsə| industrial city in NW Bulgaria, in the foothills of the Balkan Mountains. Pop. 102,000.

**Vrin·da·van** |'vrindəvən| (also **Brindaban; Bindraban; Vrindaban**) historic town in N India, in Uttar Pradesh state, S of Delhi. Pop. 48,000. It is a Hindu holy city.

**Vu·ko·var** |'vŏŏkə,vär| town in extreme E Croatia, on the Danube River (the border with Serbia). Pop. 45,000.

**Vung Tau** |'vŏŏNG 'tow| port in southern Vietnam, SE of Ho Chi Minh City, on the South China Sea. Pop. 134,000.

**Vyat·ka** |'vyätkə| industrial town in N central European Russia, on the Vyatka River. Pop. 487,000. Former name (1934–92) Kirov.

**Vy·borg** |'vē,bawrg| (Swedish name **Viborg**; Finnish name **Vipuri**) seaport in NW Russia, on the Gulf of Finland, NE of Saint Petersburg and near the Finnish border. Pop. 80,000.

**Vy·cheg·da River** |'vicHegdə| river (700 mi./1,120 km. long) in W Russia, rising in the N Ural Mts. and flowing W to join the Northern Dvina River at Kotlas.

# Ww

**Waadt** |vät| German name for VAUD.

**Waal** |väl| river of the S central Netherlands. The more southerly of two major tributaries of the Rhine, it flows for 52 mi./84 km. from the point where the Rhine forks, just W of the border with Germany, to the estuary of the Meuse (Maas) on the North Sea.

**Wa·bash River** |'waw,bæsн| river that flows 475 mi./765 km. from W Ohio across Indiana and then along the Indiana-Illinois border, to the Ohio River.

**Wa·co** |'wākō| commercial and industrial city in E central Texas. Pop. 103,590.

**Wa·di Hal·fa** |'wädē 'hälfə| town in N Sudan, on the border with Egypt. Situated on the Nile at the S end of Lake Nasser, it is the terminus of the railroad from Khartoum.

**Wad Me·da·ni** |wäd 'medn-ē| (also **Wad Madani**) city in E Sudan, capital of Gezira state, SE of Khartoum on the Blue Nile. Pop. 141,000. It is the center of a cotton-producing region.

**Wag·ga Wag·ga** |'wägə ,wägə| agricultural town on the Murrumbidgee River, in New South Wales, SE Australia. Pop. 41,000.

**Wa·gram** |'vä,gräm| village in E Austria, site of a battle (July 5–6, 1809) won by Napoleon against troops led by Archduke Charles Louis of Austria.

**Wah** |wä; vä| town in central Pakistan, S of Hasan Abdal. Pop. 122,000. A famous Mogul garden is here.

**Wai·ka·to** |wī'kätō| the longest river of New Zealand, which flows 270 mi./434 km. generally NW from Lake Taupo, at the center of North Island, to the Tasman Sea.

**Wai·ki·ki** |,wīki'kē| Hawaiian beach resort, a suburb of Honolulu, on the island of Oahu.

**Wai·mea Canyon** |wī'māə| (also **the Grand Canyon of the Pacific**) deep canyon in W Kauai Island, Hawaii, a tourist attraction.

**Wai·tan·gi** |'wī,täNGgē| historic village in New Zealand, on North Island, site of the signing of the Treaty of Waitangi, which formed the basis for British annexation of New Zealand (1840).

**Wa·ka·ya·ma** |,wäkə'yämə| commercial and industrial city in W central Japan, on S Honshu. Pop. 397,000.

**Wake·field** |'wāk,fēld| industrial town in E Massachusetts, N of Boston. Pop. 24,825.

**Wake Forest** |wāk| town in N central North Carolina, the original home of Wake Forest University, now in Winston-Salem. Pop. 5,769.

**Wake Island** |wāk| coral atoll in the Pacific, N of the Marshall Islands. Controlled by the U.S. since 1898, it was the scene of World War II fighting after the Japanese occupied it in December 1941.

**Wak·han Salient** |wä'кнän 'salēənt| narrow corridor of land, 188 mi./300. km in length, in the NE corner of Afghanistan, which was formerly a demarcating line between Russian and British spheres of influence.

**Wal·brzych** |'välbzнik| coal-mining and industrial city in SW Poland. Pop. 141,000.

**Wal·deck** |'väl,dek| administrative district, a former principality, in Hesse, central Germany.

**Wal·den Pond** |'wawldən| pond in Concord, Massachusetts, associated with the writer Henry David Thoreau. It is now within a state park.

**Wales** |wālz| principality of Great Britain and a constituent of the United Kingdom, to the W of central England. Area: 8,020 sq. mi./20,766 sq. km. Pop. 2,798,000. Capital and largest city: Cardiff. Welsh name **Cymru**. Wales is mainly mountainous and forms a large peninsula extending into the Irish Sea. The earliest inhabitants appear to have been overrun by Celtic peoples in the Broze and Iron ages. The Romans established outposts linked by a system of roads. After the Roman withdrawal in the 5th century the Celtic Welsh successfully maintained independence against the Anglo-Saxons who settled in England, and in the 8th century Offa, king of Mercia, built an earthwork, Offa's Dyke, marking the border. In the Dark Ages Christianity was spead through Wales by missionaries, but the country remained somewhat isolated. Colonization from Norman England began in the 12th century, and was assured by Edward I's conquest (1277–84). Wales was formally brought into the English legal and parliamentary system in 1536, but has retained a distinct cultural identity; the Welsh language is still widely used. In the 1990s moves toward greater autonomy grew. □ **Welsh** *adj. & n.*

**Wall·a·bout Bay** |'wawlə,bowt| former inlet of the East River in Brooklyn, New York, scene of the imprisonment during the Revolutionary War of thousands of American prisoners, many of whom died here.

**Wal·la·chia** |wə'lākēə| (also **Walachia**) former principality of SE Europe, between the Danube and the Transylvanian Alps. In 1861 it was united with Moldavia to form Romania. □ **Wallachian** *adj. & n.*

**Wal·la·sey** |'wäləsē| residential town in Merseyside, NW England, on the Wirral Peninsula. Pop. 63,000.

**Wal·la Wal·la** |,wälə 'wälə| historic commercial and industrial city in SE Washington. Pop. 26,478.

**Wal·ling·ford** |'wawliNGfərd| industrial town in S central Connecticut. Pop. 40,822.

**Wal·lis and Fu·tu·na Islands** |'wälis ənd fə'tōōnə| overseas territory of France comprising two groups of islands to the W of Samoa in the central Pacific. Pop. 15,000. Capital: Mata-Uta (on Uvea).

**Wallis & Fatuna**

**Wal·loo·nia** |wä'lōōnēə| (also **Wallonia**) French-speaking region in S Belgium, comprising the provinces of Hainaut, Liège, Luxembourg, Namur, and part of Brabant.

**Wal·lops Island** |'wäləps| island in E Virginia, on the Delmarva Peninsula, site of a U.S. rocket and high-altitude balloon facility.

**Wal·lowa Mountains** |wä'lawə| range in NE Oregon, noted for its alpine topography and plants. The Wallowa River valley, on its E, is home to the Nez Perce Indians.

**Wall·send** |'wawl,zend| industrial town in NE England, in Tyne and Wear, on the Tyne River. Pop. 45,000.

**Wall Street** |wawl| street at the S end of Manhattan, New York City, where the New York Stock Exchange and other leading financial institutions are located. □ **Wall Streeter** *n.*

**Wal·nut Creek** |'wäl,nət| residential and industrial city in N central California, a suburb NE of Oakland. Pop. 60,569.

**Wal·sall** |'wawl,sawl| industrial town in the West Midlands of England. Pop. 256,000.

**Wal·sing·ham** |'wawlziNGəm| village in E central England, in Norfolk, formerly site of Walsingham Abbey, a major place of pilgrimage.

**Wal·tham** |'wawl,THæm| historic industrial and academic city in E Massachusetts, on the Charles River W of Boston. Pop. 57,878.

**Wal·tham Forest** |'wawltəm; 'wawlTHəm| residential borough of NE Greater London, England. Pop. 203,400. **Waltham Abbey**, burial place of King Harold, last pre-Norman English king, is just N, in Essex.

**Wal·vis Bay** |'wawlvəs| port in Namibia. Pop. 25,000. It was an exclave of the former Cape Province, South Africa until it was transferred to Namibia in 1994.

**Wands·worth** |'wän(d)z,wərTH| largely residential borough of S London, England, S of the Thames River. Pop. 238,000. Battersea and Putney are here.

**Wan·ga·nui** |,wäNGgə'nōōē| port in New Zealand, on the W coast of North Island. Pop. 41,000.

**Wan·kie** |'wäNGkē| former name (until 1982) for HWANGE.

**Wann·see** |'vän,zä| lakeside resort site, near Berlin, Germany, of a 1942 conference at which the Nazis set forth their doctrine of the "final solution," calling for the extermination of the Jews.

**Wan·xian** |'wänSHē'än| city in Sichuan province, central China, an inland port on the Yangtze River above the Yangtze Gorges. Pop. 157,000.

**Wap·si·pin·i·con River** |,wäpsə'pinikən| river that flows 225 mi./360 km. across E Iowa, to the Mississippi. Its valley is associated with the regional painting of Grant Wood and others.

**Wa·ran·gal** |'wawrəNGgəl| commercial and industrial city in S central India, in Andhra Pradesh state. Pop. 467,000.

**War·dha** |'wawrdə| **1** city in central India, in Maharashtra state, SW of Nagpur. Pop. 103,000. It was the headquarters of Mohandas Gandhi, father of Indian independence. **2** river in central India that flows 290 mi./465 km., from NW of Maharashtra state to its S border, where it meets the Wainganga to form the Pranhita.

**War·ka** |'värkə| Arabic name for URUK.

**Warley** |'wawrlē| industrial town in W central England, in the West Midlands, just W of Birmingham. Pop. 152,000.

**Warm Springs** |wärm| resort city in NW Georgia, associated with Franklin D. Roosevelt and his "Little White House," where he died. Pop. 407.

**War·ner Rob·ins** |ˌwärnər 'räbinz| industrial and military city in central Georgia. Pop. 43,726.

**War·ren**[1] |'wawrən; 'wärən| industrial city, an auto center, in SE Michigan, just N of Detroit. Pop. 144,864.

**War·ren**[2] |'wawrən; 'wärən| industrial city in NE Ohio, on the Mahoning River. Pop. 50,793.

**War·ring·ton** |'wawriNGtən| industrial town on the Mersey River in Cheshire, NW England. Pop. 83,000.

**Warr·nam·bool** |'wärnəm,bool| coastal resort and former whaling port in SE Australia, in Victoria. Pop. 24,000.

**War·saw** |'wawr,saw| historic city, the capital of Poland, on the Vistula River. Pop. 1,656,000. The city suffered severe damage and the loss of 700,000 lives during World War II and since has been almost completely rebuilt. It is a cultural and industrial center. Polish name **Warszawa**.

**War·saw Pact** |'wawr,saw| military alliance, formed by a 1955 treaty and surviving until 1991, of countries allied with the Soviet Union. A response to NATO, it included also Bulgaria, Czechoslovakia, Hungary, Poland, Romania, and (until 1968) Albania.

**War·ta River** |'värtə| river (502 mi./808 km. long) in Poland, rising NW of Kraków and flowing W into the Oder River.

**War·wick**[1] |'wär,wik; 'wawr(w)ik| city in E central Rhode Island, an industrial and residential suburb S of Providence. Pop. 85,427.

**War·wick**[2] |'wärik; 'wawr(w)ik| the county seat of Warwickshire, in central England, on the Avon River. Pop. 22,000.

**War·wick·shire** |'wärik,SHir; 'wärikSHər| county of central England. Pop. 477,000; county seat, Warwick.

**Wa·satch Range** |'wawsæCH| range of the Rocky Mts., extending S from Idaho into central Utah, where Salt Lake City and its suburbs lie on its W, along the **Wasatch Front**.

**Wash, the** inlet of the North Sea in E England, between Lincolnshire and Norfolk. Boston and King's Lynn lie near it.

**Wash·ing·ton**[1] |'wawsHiNGtən; 'wäsH-iNGtən| industrial town in NE England. Pop. 49,000. The original village of Wash-

ington was the ancestral home of George Washington, first President of the United States.

**Wash·ing·ton**[2] |'wawsHiNGtən; 'wäsH-iNGtən| historic city in W Pennsylvania, SW of Pittsburgh. Pop. 15,864.

**Wash·ing·ton**[3] |'wawsHiNGtən; 'wäsH-iNGtən| see box. □ **Washingtonian** adj. & n.

**Wash·ing·ton**[4] |'wawsHiNGtən; 'wäsH-iNGtən| the capital of the U.S. Pop. 606,900. It is coextensive with the District of Columbia, a federal district on the Potomac River between Virginia and Maryland. Founded in 1790, it was planned and built as a capital. In addition to government, it is a business, cultural, and tourist center. Generally known as **Washington, D.C.**. □ **Washingtonian** adj. & n.

**Wash·ing·ton, Mount** |'wäsHiNGtən; 'wäsHiNGtən| peak in N central New Hampshire, highest in the Presidential Range of the White Mts. and in the NE U.S.: 6,288 ft./1,918 m.

**Wash·ing·ton Crossing** |'wawsHiNGtən; 'wäsHiNGtən| historic site on the Delaware River N of Trenton, New Jersey, where George Washington and American forces crossed from Pennsylvania for an attack on

---

## Washington

**Capital:** Olympia
**Largest city:** Seattle
**Other cities:** Everett, Spokane, Tacoma
**Population:** 4,866,692 (1990); 5,689,263 (1998); 6,258,000 (2005 est.)
**Population rank (1990):** 18
**Rank in land area:** 18
**Abbreviation:** WA; Wash.
**Nickname:** The Evergreen State
**Motto:** Alki (Chinook: 'By and By')
**Bird:** willow goldfinch
**Fish:** steelhead trout
**Flower:** coast rhododendron
**Tree:** Western hemlock
**Song:** "Washington, My Home"
**Noted physical features:** Puget Sound, Rosario Sound
**Tourist attractions:** Bonneville Dam, Gran Coulee Dam; Mount Rainier, Olympic, and North Cascades National Parks
**Admission date:** November 11, 1889
**Order of admission:** 42
**Name origin:** For George Washington (1732-99), the first president of the United States.

Hessian troops on Christmas, 1776. There are parks on both sides of the river.

**Wash·ing·ton Square** |'wawSHiNGtən; 'wäSHiNGtən| park in lower Manhattan, New York City, a focal point of Greenwich Village.

**Wash·i·ta River** |'wäSHə,taw; 'wawSHə ,taw| river that flows 500 mi./800 km. from the Texas Panhandle across S Oklahoma to the Red River at Lake Texoma.

**Wa States** |'wä| mountainous region of Burma, in Shan state E of the Salween River, inhabited by the Wa; it constitutes a large part of the GOLDEN TRIANGLE.

**Wa·ter·bury** |'wawtər,berē; 'wätər,berē| industrial city in W Connecticut, on the Naugatuck River. Pop. 108,961. It is an historic brass-manufacturing center.

**Wa·ter·ford**[1] |'wawtərfərd; 'wätərfərd| town in SE Connecticut, a largely residential suburb of New London. Pop. 17,930.

**Wa·ter·ford**[2] |'wawtərfərd; 'wätərfərd| **1** county in the SE of the Republic of Ireland, in the province of Munster. Pop. 92,000; main administrative center, Dungarvan. **2** its county seat, a port on an inlet of St. George's Channel. Pop. 40,000. It is noted for its colorless flint glass, known as Waterford crystal.

**Wa·ter·ford**[3] |'wawtərfərd; 'wätərfərd| residential suburb NW of Pontiac, in SE Michigan. Pop. 66,692.

**Wa·ter·gate, the** |'wätər,gāt; 'wätər,gāt| apartment and office complex in Washington, D.C., site of a 1972 break-in at Democratic headquarters that led eventually to the resignation of President Richard Nixon.

**Wa·ter·loo**[1] |,wawtər'lōō; wätər'lōō| village in central Belgium. Pop. 28,000. The Battle of Waterloo (1815) ended in Napoleon's decisive defeat by the British troops of the Duke of Wellington and Prussian troops.

**Wa·ter·loo**[2] |,wawtər'lōō; wätər'lōō| industrial and commercial city in NE Iowa. Pop. 66,467.

**Wa·ter·loo**[3] |,wawtər'lōō; wätər'lōō| commercial and industrial city in S Ontario, next to Kitchener. Pop. 71,181.

**Wa·ter·town**[1] |'wawtər,town; 'wätər,town| industrial town in E Massachusetts, on the Charles River just W of Boston. Pop. 33,284.

**Wa·ter·town**[2] |'wawtər,town; 'wätər,town | industrial and commercial city in N central New York, near Lake Ontario and the Thousand Islands. Pop. 29,429.

**Wa·ter·town**[3] |'wawtər,town; 'wätər,town |

industrial city in S central Wisconsin. Pop. 19,142.

**Wa·ter·ville** |'wawtərvil; 'wätər,vil| commercial city in S central Maine, on the Kennebec River. Pop. 17,173.

**Wa·ter·vliet** |'wawtər,vlēt; wätər,vlēt| historic industrial town in E New York, just NE of Albany on the Hudson River. Pop. 11,061. The site of the first U.S. Shaker settlement and a large arsenal are here.

**Wat·ford** |'wätfərd| industrial town in Hertfordshire, SE England. Pop. 74,000.

**Wat·kins Glen** |'wätkinz| resort village in W central New York, at the S end of Seneca Lake. Pop. 2,207.

**Wat·ling Street** |'wätliNG| Roman road (now largely underlying modern roads) running NW across England, from Richborough in Kent through London and St. Albans to Wroxeter in Shropshire.

**Wat·son·ville** |'wätsən,vil| city in W central California, in an agricultural area S of San Jose. Pop. 31,099.

**Watts** |wäts| district of S Los Angeles, California, home to much of the black population of the city.

**Watts Bar** |'wäts 'bär| locality on the Tennessee River, NE of Chattanooga, Tennessee, site of major hydroelectric and nuclear facilities.

**Wau·ke·gan** |waw'kēgən| industrial port city in NE Illinois, on Lake Michigan. Pop. 69,392.

**Wau·ke·sha** |'wawki,SHaw| industrial city in SE Wisconsin, W of Milwaukee. Pop. 56,958.

**Wau·sau** |'waw,saw| industrial and commercial city in central Wisconsin. Pop. 37,060.

**Wau·wa·to·sa** |,waw-wə'tōsə| city in SE Wisconsin, a suburb W of Milwaukee. Pop. 51,308.

**Wa·ver·ley** |'wävərlē| **1** town in Australia, a residential suburb E of Sydney, in New South Wales. Pop. 59,000. **2** town in SE Australia, a suburb SE of Melbourne, in Victoria. Pop. 118,000.

**Wax·a·hach·ie** |,wawksə'hæCHē| industrial and commercial city in NE Texas, S of Dallas. Pop. 18,168.

**Wax·haw** |'wæk,shä| town in S North Carolina, near the South Carolina border. Pop 1,294. Andrew Jackson was born in a settlement in the area in 1767, in which state is unclear.

**Wayne**[1] |wān| industrial city in SE Michigan, a suburb SW of Detroit. Pop. 19,899.

**Wayne**[2] |wān| residential and commercial

township in NE New Jersey, just NW of Paterson. Pop. 47,025.

**Wayne County** |wān| county in SE Michigan, site of Detroit and many suburbs. Pop. 2,111.687.

**Wa·zir·i·stan** |wə‚ziri'stän| arid mountainous region of NW Pakistan, on the border with Afghanistan.

**Weald** |wēld| formerly wooded district of SE England including parts of Kent, Surrey, and East Sussex.

**Web·ster Groves** |‚webstər 'grōvz| city in E Missouri, a residential and academic suburb SW of St. Louis. Pop. 22,987.

**Wed·dell Sea** |'wedl| arm of the Atlantic Ocean, off the coast of Antarctica.

**Wee·nen** |'vēnen| town in KwaZulu-Natal province, E South Africa, SE of Ladysmith, scene of an 1838 massacre of Boer settlers (Voortrekkers) by Zulu forces.

**Wei·fang** |'wā'fäNG| industrial city in Shandong province, E China. Pop. 565,000. Former name **Weihsien**.

**Wei·hai** |'wā'hī| city in Shandong province, E China, a port on the Yellow Sea. It was leased from 1898 to 1930 by the British, who called it Port Edward. Pop. 129,000.

**Wei·mar** |'vī‚mär| city in Thuringia, central Germany. Pop. 59,000. It was famous in the late 18th and early 19th century for its intellectual and cultural life. The German National Assembly ratified the Treaty of Versailles here in 1919, and established a government called the **Weimar Republic**, which lasted until 1933.

**Wei·nan** |'wā'nän| city in Shaanxi province, central China, NE of Xi'an, on the Wei River. Pop. 709,000.

**Wei River** |wā| (Chinese name **Wei Shui**) river of N central China, flowing 537 mi./864 km. from SE Gansu province to the Yellow River at Huatin. XIAN lies on the Wei.

**Weir·ton** |'wirtn| industrial city in N West Virginia, on the Ohio River. Pop. 22,124.

**Wel·kom** |'velkəm| mining town in central South Africa, in Free State. Pop. 185,000.

**Wel·land** |'welənd| industrial and commercial city in S Ontario, on the Welland Canal. Pop. 47,914.

**Wel·land Canal** |'welənd| (also **Welland Ship Canal**) canal in S Ontario, 26 mi./42 km. long, linking Lake Erie with Lake Ontario, bypassing Niagara Falls and forming part of the Great Lakes–St. Lawrence Seaway.

**Welles·ley** |'welzlē| town in E Massachusetts, a suburb W of Boston. Pop. 26,615. It is home to Wellesley College.

**Well·fleet** |'wel‚flēt| resort town in SE Massachusetts, near the tip of Cape Cod, noted for its arts colony. Pop. 2,493.

**Wel·ling·ton** |'weliNGtən| the capital of New Zealand, situated at the S tip of North Island. Pop. 150,000. It became the capital in 1865, succeeding Auckland.

**Wells** |welz| city in SW England, in Somerset, site of one of the best-known medieval cathedrals in Britain. Pop. 9,000.

**Wels** |vels| industrial and market town in N Austria, SW of Linz. Pop. 53,000. It was important during the Roman period.

**Welsh Marches** |welsH| name for the countryside on either side of the border between Wales and England. *March* is an old word for 'boundary.'

**Wel·wel** |'wel‚wel| pastoral village in SE Ethiopia, in the Ogaden, scene of a 1934 clash that preceded the Italo-Ethiopian War of 1935–36.

**Wel·wyn Garden City** |'welən| industrial city in SE England, in Hertfordshire. Pop. 41,000. Established in 1920 to ease crowding in London, to the S, it is also a commuter suburb.

**Wem·bley** |'wemblē| residential district of W Greater London, England, in the borough of Brent. It is famous for its sports stadium.

**We·natch·ee** |wə'næCHē| city in central Washington, an agricultural-procesing center on the Columbia River near the Wenatchee Mts. Pop. 21,756.

**Wens·ley·dale** |'wenzlē‚dāl| upper valley of the Ure River in North Yorkshire, N England, which gave its name to types of cheese and sheep.

**Wen·zhou** |'wen'jō| (also **Wen-Chou**) industrial city in Zhejiang province, E China. Pop. 1,650,000.

**Wer·ri·bee** |'werəbē| town in SE Australia, in Victoria, SW of Melbourne. Pop. 72,000.

**We·sel** |'vāzəl| industrial and port city in western Germany, on the Rhine River. The city was nearly destroyed in March 1945, when the Allies crossed the Rhine, and has has been rebuilt.

**We·ser** |'wāzər| river of NW Germany, which is formed at the junction of the Werra and Fulda rivers in Lower Saxony and flows 182 mi./292 km. N to the North Sea near Bremerhaven.

**Wes·sex** |'wesiks| the kingdom of the West Saxons, established in Hampshire in the early 6th century and gradually extended to include much of S England. Under Alfred the Great and his successors it formed the nucleus of the Anglo-Saxon kingdom of England. Athelstan, Alfred's grandson, became king of England. The name was revived in the 19th century by Thomas Hardy to designate the SW counties of England (especially Dorset) in which his novels are set.

**West, the** |west| in 20th-century politics, the largely capitalist nations of W Europe and the Americas.

**West Af·ri·ca** |'æfrikə| the W part of the African continent, especially the countries bounded by and including Mauritania, Mali, and Niger in the N and Gabon in the S. □ **West African** adj. & n.

**West Al·lis** |'æləs| industrial city in SE Wisconsin, a suburb of Milwaukee. Pop. 63,221.

**West Bank** |'west 'bæNGk| region west of the Jordan River and NW of the Dead Sea. Covering some 2,270 sq. mi./5,879 sq. km., it contains Jericho, Hebron, Nablus, Bethlehem, and other settlements. It became part of Jordan in 1948 and was occupied by Israel following the Six Day War of 1967. In 1993 an agreement was signed that granted limited autonomy to the Palestinians, who comprise 97 percent of its inhabitants; withdrawal of Israeli troops began in 1994.

**West Bend** |'west 'bend| industrial city in SE Wisconsin, on the Milwaukee River. Pop. 23,916.

**West Ben·gal** |ben'gäl| state in E India. Pop. 67.98 million. Capital: Calcutta. It was formed in 1947 from the predominantly Hindu area of former Bengal.

**West Ber·lin** |bər'lin| the W half of the city of Berlin (divided in 1945) and, until German reunification in 1990, a state of the Federal Republic of Germany. Surrounded on all sides by East Germany, it was occupied by U.S., French, and British troops and separated from East Berlin in 1961 by the Berlin Wall.

**West Branch** |'west ˌbræncH| agricultural city in E central Iowa, the birthplace of Herbert Hoover. Pop. 1,908.

**West Brom·wich** |'brämwicH| industrial town in the West Midlands, England, NW of Birmingham. Pop. 155,000.

**West·ches·ter County** |'wes,cHestər| suburban county in SE New York, just NE of New York City. Pop. 874,866. White Plains is its seat.

**West Country** |west| the SW counties of England, specifically Cornwall, Devon, Somerset, Avon, Wiltshire, and W Dorset.

**West Co·vi·na** |kō'vēnə| city in SW California, a suburb E of Los Angeles. Pop. 96,086.

**West End** |'west'end| the W part of central London, England, long noted for its theaters, clubs, and shopping.

**Wes·ter·ly** |'westərlē| industrial and resort town in SW Rhode Island, on the Connecticut border. Pop. 21,605.

**West·ern Aus·tra·lia** |aws'trālyə| state comprising the W part of Australia. Area: 975,473 sq. mi./2.53 million sq. km. Pop. 1,643,000. Capital: Perth. It was colonized by the British in 1826, and was federated with the other states of Australia in 1901.

**West·ern Cape** |'western 'kāp| province of SW South Africa, formerly part of Cape Province. Pop. 3,635,000. Capital: Cape Town.

**West·ern Channel** |'western 'cHænl| channel between South Korea and the Japanese island of Tsushima; it connects the Sea of Japan with the Yellow and East China seas.

**West·ern Desert** |'western 'dezərt| Egyptian name for the LIBYAN DESERT.

**West·ern Em·pire** |'western 'em,pīr| the W part of the ROMAN EMPIRE from the 3rd to the 5th centuries A.D. It included Italy, Gaul, Spain, Britain, Illyricum (the E coast of the Adriatic Sea), and N Africa.

**West·ern hem·i·sphere** |'western 'hemə-ˌsfēr| the half of the earth containing the Americas.

**West·ern Isles** |'western 'īlz| **1** another name for the HEBRIDES. **2** an administrative region of Scotland, consisting of the Outer Hebrides. Pop. 29,000; administrative center, Stornoway.

**West·ern Re·serve** |'western ri'zərv| historic region of the U.S., comprising lands formerly owned by Connecticut, in present-day NE Ohio. Cleveland is the largest city.

**West·ern Sa·hara** |'western sə'hærə| region of NW Africa, on the Atlantic coast between Morocco and Mauritania. Area: 97,383 sq. mi./252,126 sq. km. Pop. 187,000. Capital: La'youn. Formerly the

**Western Sahara**

Spanish Sahara, the region has been controlled since 1976 by Morocco (Mauritania briefly controlled a part). The Polisario Front has continued to struggle for independence as the Saharabi Arab Democratic Republic. The area has vast rock phosphate deposits.

**West·ern Sa·moa** |'western se'mōe| see republic of SAMOA.

**Western Samoa**

**West·ern Wall** |'western 'wawl| (also called **Wailing Wall**) wall in Jerusalem, Israel, originally part of the temple structure built by Herod the Great and destroyed by the Romans in A.D. 70. A place of Jewish prayer, it also forms the W wall of the sanctuary enclosing the Muslim holy place, the Dome of the Rock.

**Wes·ter·ville** |'wester,vil| city in central Ohio, a suburb NE of Columbus. Pop. 30,193.

**Wes·ter·wald** |'vester,vält| mountainous region in western Germany, stretching E from Koblenz and the Rhine River for 70 mi./115 km. Its highest peak, Fuchskauten, reaches 2,156 ft./657 m.

**West·fa·len** |'vest,fälen| German name for WESTPHALIA.

**West·field**[1] |'west,fēld| industrial city in W Massachusetts. Pop. 38,372.

**West·field**[2] |'west,fēld| historic town in NE New Jersey, a suburb W of Elizabeth. Pop. 28,870.

**West Flan·ders** |'flændərz| province of NW Belgium. Pop. 1,107,000. Capital: Bruges.

**West Fri·sian Islands** |'frēzHen| see FRISIAN ISLANDS.

**West Ger·ma·ny** |'jermenē| (officially **Federal Republic of Germany**) former republic in Europe, formed in 1949 from the German zones occupied after World War II by the U.S., France, and Great Britain. Bonn was its acting capital. It was reunited with East Germany in 1990. German name **Bundesrepublik Deutschland**.

**West Gla·mor·gan** |glə'mawrgən| former county of S Wales, formed in 1974 and dissolved in 1996.

**West Ham** |west 'hæm| see NEWHAM, London, England.

**West Hart·ford** |west 'härtfərd| town in central Connecticut, a residential and industrial suburb W of Hartford. Pop. 60,110.

**West Ha·ven** |west 'hāvən; 'west ,hāven| city in SW Connecticut, a suburb W of New Haven. Pop. 54,021.

**West Hills** |west 'hilz| section of the town of Huntington, New York, on Long Island, the birthplace of Walt Whitman.

**West Hol·ly·wood** |'hälē,wŏŏd| city in SW California, a largely residential suburb NE of Beverly Hills. Pop. 36,118.

**West In·dies** |west 'indēz| chain of islands extending from the Florida peninsula to the coast of Venezuela, lying between the Caribbean and the Atlantic. They consist of three main island groups, the Greater and Lesser Antilles and the Bahamas, with Bermuda lying farther to the N. Originally inhabited by Arawak and Carib Indians, the islands were visited by Columbus in 1492 and named by him in the belief that he had reached the coast of India. The Spanish settlements of the 16th and 17th centuries were fiercely contested by other European powers, principally the British, the French, and the Dutch; the region became notorious for buccaneering and piracy in the 17th century. Many of the islands became British colonies in the 17th and 18th centuries, and were centers for the cultivation of sugar and large plantations worked by slaves imported from W Africa. The islands now include a number of independent states and British, French, Dutch, and U.S. dependencies. □ **West Indian** adj. & n.

**West Ir·i·an** |'irē,än| see IRIAN JAYA.

**West Jor·dan** |west 'jawrdn| city in N central Utah, a largely residential suburb S of Salt Lake City. Pop. 42,892.

**West La·fay·ette** |läfā'yet| city in W central Indiana, a suburb of Lafayette and home to Purdue University. Pop. 25,907.

**West·mann Islands** |'westmən| group of fifteen volcanic islands off the S coast of Iceland. Icelandic name **Vestmannaeyjar**.

**West·meath** |west'mēTH| county of the central Republic of Ireland, in the province of Leinster. Pop. 62,000; county seat, Mullingar.

**West Mem·phis** |'memfəs| industrial and commercial city in NE Arkansas, across the

Mississippi River from Memphis, Tennessee. Pop. 28,259.

**West Mid·lands** |'midləndz| metropolitan county of central England. Pop. 2,500,000. County town: Birmingham.

**West Mif·flin** |'miflən| industrial borough in SW Pennsylvania, SE of Pittsburgh. Pop. 23,644.

**West·min·ster¹** |'wes(t),minstər| industrial and commercial city in SW California, SE of Los Angeles. Pop. 78,118.

**West·min·ster²** |'wes(t),minstər| city in N central Colorado, a suburb NW of Denver. Pop. 74,625.

**West·min·ster³** |'wes(t),minstər| inner borough of London, England, which contains the Houses of Parliament and many government offices. Pop. 181,000. Full name **City of Westminster**. The name is also used in reference to the British Parliament.

**West·min·ster Ab·bey** |'wes(t),minstər| church of St. Peter in Westminster, London, England, facing the Houses of Parliament. It is the site of royal coronations and burials, and is famous for its Poet's Corner, with the graves of many literary notables.

**West·mor·land** |'westmərlənd; west 'mawrlənd| former county of NW England. In 1974 it was united with Cumberland and N parts of Lancashire to form the county of Cumbria.

**West·mount** |'westmownt| affluent residential city in S Quebec, just SW of Montreal. Pop. 20,329.

**West New York** |n(y)ōō 'yawrk| industrial and residential town in NE New Jersey, on the Hudson River across from New York City. Pop. 38,125.

**Weston-super-Mare** |'westən,sōōpər 'mer| resort in Avon, SW England, on the Bristol Channel. Pop. 62,000.

**West Orange** |'awr(y)nj; 'ärənj| suburban township in NE New Jersey, NW of Newark. Pop. 39,013.

**West Pak·i·stan** |'pæki'stæn; ,päki'stän| see PAKISTAN.

**West Palm Beach** |,west ,pä(l)m 'bēCH| commercial and industrial city in SE Florida. Pop. 67,643.

**West·pha·lia** |,west'fälyə| former province of NW Germany. Previously a duchy of the archbishop of Cologne, it became a province of Prussia in 1815. In 1946 the major part was incorporated in the state of North Rhine–Westphalia, the northern portion becoming part of Lower Saxony. German name **Westfalen**. □ **Westphalian** adj. & n.

**West Point** |west 'point| community in SE New York, on the Hudson River, home to the U.S. Military Academy. Pop. 8,024.

**West·port¹** |'west,pawrt| town in SW Connecticut, an affluent suburb W of Bridgeport. Pop. 24,410.

**West·port²** |'west,pawrt| former town, now part of Kansas City, Missouri, that was a 19th-century gateway to the westbound Santa Fe Trail.

**West Prus·sia** |'prəSHə| former province in Prussia, NE Germany, on the Baltic Sea. After World War I it was divided between Poland and Germany; at the end of World War II the entire region was given to Poland. Its capital was Danzig.

**West Quod·dy Head** |'kwädē| easternmost (66° 57' W) point of the U.S., in Lubec, Maine, S of Passamaquoddy Bay.

**West River** |,west| see XI RIVER.

**West Rox·bury** |'räks,berē| SW district of Boston, Massachusetts. Largely residential, it was a separate town until 1874, and was the site of the experimental Brook Farm.

**West Sen·e·ca** |'senikə| town in W New York, a suburb SE of Buffalo. Pop. 47,830.

**West Side** |'west 'sīd| in Manhattan, New York City, the residential and commercial districts W of Fifth Avenue, regarded in general as less affluent, more diverse, and more intellectual than the East Side.

**West Sus·sex** |'səsiks| county of SE England. Pop. 693,000; county seat, Chichester. It was formed in 1974 from part of the former county of Sussex.

**West Val·ley City** |west 'vælē| city in N central Utah, a residential suburb S of Salt Lake City. Pop. 86,976.

**West Vir·gin·ia** |vər'jinyə| see box, p. 408. □ **West Virginian** adj. & n.

**West·wood** |'west,wŏŏd| section of W Los Angeles, California, home to the University of California at Los Angeles (UCLA).

**West York·shire** |'yawrkSHər| metropolitan county of N England. Pop. 1,985,000. County town: Wakefield.

**Weth·ers·field** |'weTHərz,fēld| historic town in central Connecticut, just S of Hartford on the Connecticut River. Pop. 25,651.

**Wet·ter·stein Mountains** |'vetər,SHtīn| range in S Germany. It includes the ZUGSPITZE, the highest peak in Germany.

**Wetz·lar** |'vet,slär| manufacturing city in central Germany, N of Frankfurt. Pop. 51,000.

**We·wak** |'wä,wäk; 'wē,wæk| town in N New Guinea Island, Papua New Guinea, the capital of Sepik district. Pop. 23,000. It

## West Virginia

**Capital:** Charleston

**Largest city:** Huntington

**Other cities:** Morgantown, Parkersburg, Vienna, Weirton, Wheeling

**Population:** 1,793,477 (1990); 1,811,156 (1998); 1,849,000 (2005 proj.)

**Population rank (1990):** 34

**Rank in land area:** 41

**Abbreviation:** WV; W. Va.

**Nickname:** Mountain State; Panhandle State

**Motto:** *Montani Semper Liberi* (Latin: 'Mountaineers Are Always Free')

**Bird:** cardinal

**Fish:** brook trout

**Flower:** big laurel

**Tree:** sugar maple

**Songs:** "The West Virginia Hills"; "West Virginia, My Home Sweet Home"; "This Is My West Virginia"

**Noted physical features:** Seneca Cavern; Allegheny Plateau; Seneca Rock; Berkeley Springs, White Sulphur Springs; Spruce Knob

**Tourist attractions:** Harper's Ferry; Cumberland National Road

**Admission date:** June 20, 1863

**Order of admission:** 35

**Name origin:** The area was part of Virginia until the time of the Civil War. When Virginia voted to secede, the western counties that comprise West Virginia objected strongly and chose instead to remain loyal to the Union, forming a new state.

was the scene of fighting between U.S. and Japanese forces in World War II.

**Wex•ford** |'weksfərd| **1** county of the Republic of Ireland, in the SE, in the province of Leinster. Pop. 102,000. **2** its county seat, a port on the Irish Sea. Pop. 10,000.

**Wey•mouth**[1] |'wāməTH| resort and port on the coast of Dorset, S England. Pop. 38,000.

**Wey•mouth**[2] |'wāməTH| town in E Massachusetts, an industrial and residential suburb SE of Boston. Pop. 54,063.

**Wham•poa** |'hwäm'pwä| see HUANGPU.

**Whang•a•rei** |,(h)wäNGə'rā| port on the NE coast of North Island, New Zealand. Pop. 44,000.

**Whea•ton** |'wētn| suburban city in NE Illinois, W of Chicago, noted for its many religious institutions. Pop. 51,464.

**Whee•ler Peak** |,(h)wēlər| highest peak in New Mexico, in the Sangre de Cristo Mts. NE of Taos: 13,161 ft./4,011 m.

**Whee•ling** |'(h)wēliNG| historic industrial city in N West Virginia, on the Ohio River. Pop. 34,822.

**Whid•bey Island** |'(h)widbē| island in NW Washington, just N of Puget Sound. It is agricultural, residential, and a tourist attraction.

**Whis•tler** |'(h)wis(ə)lər| municipality in SW British Columbia, N of Vancouver, noted as a ski resort. Pop. 4,459.

**Whit•by**[1] |'(h)witbē| port town on the coast of North Yorkshire, NE England, a former ecclesisastical center. Pop. 13,000.

**Whit•by**[2] |'(h)witbē| town in SE Ontario, a largely residential suburb E of Toronto on Lake Ontario. Pop. 61,281.

**White Bear Lake** |'wit 'ber| city in SE Minnesota, a suburb NE of St. Paul. Pop. 24,704.

**White•chap•el** |'(h)wit,CHӕpəl| district in the East End of London, England, E of the Tower of London, notorious as the scene of murders by Jack the Ripper in 1888. It is today more affluent.

**White•hall** |'(h)wit,hawl| street in Westminster, London, England, in which many government offices are located; the name is used in reference to the British government.

**White Hill** |'(h)wit| (also **White Mountain**) hill near Prague, the Czech Republic, where, in November 1620, Czech Protestants were decisively defeated by Catholic forces, ending the independence of Bohemia and marking the start of the Thirty Years War.

**White Horse, Vale of the** |'(h)wit 'hawrs| district in S central England, around Wantage in Oxfordshire, named for the huge figure of a horse carved out of a hill at Uffington. Its date is uncertain.

**White•horse** |'(h)wit,hawrs| the capital of Yukon Territory. Pop. 17,925. Situated on the Alaska Highway, it is the center of a copper-mining and fur-trapping region.

**White House, the** |'(h)wit ,hows| official home of the U.S. president, on the N side of the Mall, at 1600 Pennsylvania Avenue, in Washington, D.C. Built 1792–1800, it was rebuilt after being burned by the British in 1814. Its Oval Office, East Room, and Rose Garden are especially familiar.

**White Mountains**[1] |'(h)wit| range in E Arizona, rising to 11,420 ft./3,481 m. at Baldy Peak (also, White Mt.), and home to the White Mountain Apache.

**White Mountains**[2] |'(h)wit| range of the Appalachian system in N New Hampshire, rising to 6,288 ft./1,918 m. at Mount Washington, in the Presidential Range. Known for their resorts, the Whites continue NE into Maine as the Longfellow Mts.

**White Nile** |'(h)wīt 'nīl| the name for the main, W branch of the Nile between the Uganda–Sudan border and its confluence with the Blue Nile at Khartoum.

**White Pass** |'(h)wīt| pass from Skagway, Alaska into British Columbia that provided a route for gold seekers in the 1890s Klondike rush. A railroad here, opened in 1900, draws tourists.

**White Plains** |'(h)wīt 'plānz| commercial city in SE New York, the seat of Westchester County. Pop. 48,718.

**White River**[1] |'(h)wīt| river that flows 720 mi./1,160 m. from NW Arkansas across the Ozark Plateau, to the Mississippi River.

**White River**[2] |'(h)wīt| river that flows in two main branches through Indiana, past Indianapolis, to the Wabash River.

**White River**[3] |'(h)wīt| river that flows 500 mi./800 km. from NW Nebraska into South Dakota, to the Missouri River.

**White Rus·sia** |'(h)wīt 'rəSHə| another name for BELARUS. □ **White Russian** adj. & n.

**White Sands** |'wīt 'sændz| area of gypsum flats in central New Mexico, designated a national monument in 1933. It is surrounded by a large missile-testing range, which in 1945 was the site of the detonation of the first nuclear weapon.

**White Sea** |'(h)wīt| inlet of the Barents Sea on the coast of NW Russia.

**White·stone** |'(h)wīt,stōn| largely residential section of N Queens, New York, on the East River across from the Bronx, to which it is joined by the Bronx-Whitestone Bridge.

**White Sul·phur Springs** |,(h)wīt ,səlfər 'spriNGz| historic resort city in SE West Virginia, in the Allegheny Mts. Pop. 2,779.

**Whit·ney, Mount** |'(h)witnē| mountain in the Sierra Nevada in California. Rising to 14,495 ft./4,418 m., it is the highest peak in the continental U.S. outside Alaska.

**Whit·ti·er** |'(h)witēər| industrial city in SW California, a suburb SE of Los Angeles. Pop. 77,671.

**Why·al·la** |(h)wī'ælə| steel-manufacturing town on the coast of South Australia, on the Spencer Gulf. Pop. 26,000.

**Wich·i·ta** |'wiCHə,taw| largest city in Kansas, the S on the Arkansas River. Pop. 304,011. It has aircraft and other industries and is an agricultural and commercial center.

**Wich·i·ta Falls** |'wiCHə,taw| industrial and commercial city in N central Texas. Pop. 96,259.

**Wick·low** |'wiklō| **1** county of the Republic of Ireland, in the E, in the province of Leinster, S of Dublin. Pop. 97,000. **2** its county seat, on the Irish Sea. Pop. 6,000.

**Wick·low Mountains** |'wiklō| low range in SE Ireland, S of Dublin, covering much of County Wicklow. Its famed beauty spots include AVOCA and GLENDALOUGH.

**Wie·licz·ka** |vye'lēCHkə| commune in S Poland, SE of Cracow, a salt-mining center. Pop. 17,000.

**Wien** |'vēn| German name for VIENNA.

**Wie·ner Neu·stadt** |,vēnər 'noi,SHtät| industrial town in NE Austria. Pop. 35,000. It is a manufacturing center and a rail junction.

**Wie·ner·wald** |'vēnər,vält| (also called **Vienna Woods**) a forested range in NE Austria, just W of Vienna. A picturesque region of hills and streams, it is a popular vacation area.

**Wies·ba·den** |'wēsbädn| city in western Germany, the capital of the state of Hesse, on the Rhine opposite Mainz. Pop. 264,000. It has been a spa town since Roman times.

**Wig·an** |'wigən| industrial town in NW England, in Greater Manchester. Pop. 89,000.

**Wight, Isle of** |wīt| island off the S coast of England, a county since 1974. Pop. 127,000. Administrative center: Newport. It lies at the entrance to Southampton Water and is separated from the mainland by the Solent and Spithead channels.

**Wil·ber·force** |'wilbər,fawrs| village in SW Ohio, NE of Xenia, home to Wilberforce University. Pop. 2,702.

**Wil·der·ness, the** |'wildərnəs| wooded region of Spotsylvania County, NE Virginia, site of an inconclusive Civil War battle in 1864.

**Wil·der·ness Road** |'wildərnəs| historic route opened by Daniel Boone in the 1770s and used until the 1840s, allowing W migration through the Allegheny Mts. by way of the Cumberland Gap between Tennessee and Kentucky.

**Wild·spit·ze** |'vilt,SHpitsə| highest peak in the Otztaler Alps, in the Tyrol, W Austria, and second-highest in Austria: 12,382 ft./3,774 m.

**Wild·wood** |'wil'd,wŏŏd| resort city in S New Jersey, on the Atlantic. Pop. 4,484.

**Wil·helm, Mount** |'vil,helm| peak in central New Guinea Island, Papua New

Guinea, the highest in the country: 14,739 ft./4,509 m.

**Wil·helms·ha·ven** |'wil,helmz,häfən| port and resort in NW Germany, on the North Sea. Pop. 91,000. It was a major naval base until 1945.

**Wilkes-Barre** |'wilks,bærə; 'wilks,bærē| industrial city in NE Pennsylvania, on the Susquehanna River in the Wyoming Valley. Pop. 47,523.

**Wilkes Land** |'wilks| region of Antarctica with a coast on the Indian Ocean. It is claimed by Australia.

**Wil·lam·ette River** |wə'læmət| river that flows 300 mi./480 km. through W Oregon, through Portland, to the Columbia River. Its fertile valley was the goal of 19th-century settlers.

**Wil·lem·stad** |'viləm,stät| the capital of the Netherlands Antilles, on the SW coast of the island of Curaçao. Pop. 50,000.

**Wil·liams·burg**[1] |'wilyəmz,bərg| residential and industrial section of N Brooklyn, New York, noted for its Hasidic Jewish community and arts colony.

**Wil·liams·burg**[2] |'wilyəmz,bərg| city in SE Virginia, between the James and York rivers. Pop. 11,530. First settled as Middle Plantation in 1633, it was the capital of Virginia from 1699, when it was renamed in honor of William III, until 1799, when Richmond became the state capital. Much of the town has been reconstructed to appear as it was during the colonial era.

**Wil·liams·port** |'wilyəmz,pawrt| industrial city in N central Pennsylvania, on the Susquehanna River. Pop. 31,933. It is noted as the birthplace of Little League baseball.

**Will·ing·bo·ro** |'wiliNG,bərə| residential township in W central New Jersey, near the Delaware River. Pop. 36,291. It was founded as Levittown in 1959.

**Wil·lis·ton Lake** |'wilistən| largest North American reservoir, on the Peace River in NE British Columbia, created by the W.A.C. Bennett Dam (completed 1968).

**Wil·lough·by** |'wiləbē| city in SE Australia, a residential suburb N of Sydney, in New South Wales. Pop. 52,000.

**Wil·ming·ton**[1] |'wilmiNGtən| largest city in Delaware, an industrial and commercial hub on the Delaware River, in the NE. Pop. 71,529.

**Wil·ming·ton**[2] |'wilmiNGtən| industrial port city in SE North Carolina, on the Cape Fear River and the Atlantic. Pop. 55,530.

**Wil·son, Mount** |'wilsən| peak in the San Gabriel Mts. of SW California, near Pasadena, site of a major astronomical observatory.

**Wil·son** |'wilsən| industrial city in E central North Carolina. Pop. 36,930.

**Wil·ton** |'wiltn| historic town in SW England, in Wiltshire. Pop. 4,000. Once the seat of the kings of Wessex, it is known for its carpet industry.

**Wilt·shire** |'wilt,SHir; 'wiltsHər| county of SW England. Pop. 553,000 ; county seat, Trowbridge.

**Wim·ble·don** |'wimbəldən| residential district of SW London, England, in the borough of Merton, famed as home to the All England Lawn Tennis and Croquet Club and its annual tennis tournament.

**Wim·mera** |'wimərə| **1** river in SE Australia, in Victoria, that flows 155 mi. /249 km. from the Great Dividing Range to Lake Hindmarsh. **2** wheat-growing area through which the river flows.

**Win·ches·ter**[1] |'win,CHestər; 'winCHəstər| historic city in S England, the county seat of Hampshire. Pop. 36,000. Known to the Romans, it became capital of the kingdom of Wessex in 519.

**Win·ches·ter**[2] |'win,CHestər; 'winCHəstər| historic city in NW Virginia, an agricultural center in the Shenandoah Valley. Pop. 21,947.

**Wind Cave National Park** |wind| preserve in the Black Hills of South Dakota, noted for its caves and wildlife.

**Win·der·mere** |'wində(r),mir| lake in Cumbria, in the Lake District. At about 10 mi./17 km. in length, it is the largest lake in England. The town of Windermere lies on its E shore.

**Wind·hoek** |'vint,hŏŏk| the capital of Namibia, in the center of the country. Pop. 59,000. It was the capital of the former German protectorate of South West Africa from 1892 until 1919, emerging as capital of independent Namibia in 1990.

**Win·dow Rock** |'windō| community in NE Arizona, capital of the Navajo Indian reservation. Pop. 3,306. It is named for a limestone formation.

**Wind River Range** |wind| range of the Rocky Mts. in W Wyoming, rising to 13,804 ft./4,207 m. at Gannett Peak, the highest in the state. The Wind River flows from the range.

**Wind·scale** |'win(d),skāl| former name (1947–81) for SELLAFIELD.

**Wind·sor**[1] |'winzər| commercial and residential town in N central Connecticut, N of Hartford. Pop. 27,817. **Windsor Locks,**

just N, is the site of Bradley International Airport.

**Wind·sor**² |'winzər| town in S England, on the Thames River opposite Eton. Pop. 32,000. It is the site of Windsor Castle, the primary residence of the British royal family.

**Wind·sor**³ |'winzər| industrial city and port in S Ontario, on Lake Ontario opposite Detroit, Michigan. Pop. 191,435.

**Wind·ward Islands**¹ |'windwərd| group of islands in the E Caribbean. Constituting the S part of the Lesser Antilles, they include Martinique, Dominica, St. Lucia, Barbados, St. Vincent and the Grenadines, and Grenada. Their name refers to their position farther upwind (in terms of the prevailing SE winds) than the Leeward Islands.

**Wind·ward Islands**² |'windwərd| (French name **Iles du Vent**) island group in the E Society Islands, French Polynesia, including Moorea and Tahiti.

**Wind·ward Passage** |'windwərd| ocean channel between Cuba, on the W, and Haiti, on the E, connecting the Caribbean Sea with the Atlantic.

**Windy City** |'windē 'sitē| nickname for Chicago, Illinois, given for its winds but for the volubility of its 19th-century promoters.

**Win·ne·ba·go, Lake** |,winə'bāgō| largest lake in Wisconsin, in the E central part. The city of Oshkosh and many resorts lie on it.

**Win·ne·muc·ca** |,winə'məkə| commercial and industrial city in N central Nevada, on the Humboldt River. Pop. 6,134.

**Win·net·ka** |wi'netkə| affluent residential village in NE Illinois, a suburb N of Chicago. Pop. 12,174.

**Win·ni·peg, Lake** |'winə,peg| large lake in the province of Manitoba in Canada, to the N of the city of Winnipeg. Fed by the Saskatchewan, Winnipeg, and Red rivers from the E and S, the lake is drained by the Nelson River, which flows NE to Hudson Bay.

**Win·ni·peg** |'winə,peg| the capital of Manitoba, an agricultural processing and administrative city in the S of the province at the confluence of the Assiniboine and Red rivers, to the S of Lake Winnipeg. Pop. 616,790. First settled as a French trading post in 1738, it became a post of the Hudson's Bay Company in 1821.

**Win·ni·peg·o·sis, Lake** |,winəpə'gōsis| lake in S central Manitoba whose waters drain E into Lake Manitoba, and thence into Lake Winnipeg.

**Win·ni·pe·sau·kee, Lake** |,winəpə'säkē|

largest lake in New Hampshire, a resort center in the E central part.

**Wi·no·na** |wə'nōnə| industrial city in SE Minnesota, on the Mississippi River. Pop. 25,399.

**Winston-Salem** |,winstən'sāləm| industrial and commercial city in N central North Carolina, a tobacco-processing center. Pop. 143,485.

**Win·ter Ha·ven** |'wintər ,hāvən| resort and industrial city in central Florida. Pop. 24,725.

**Win·ter Palace** |,wintər 'pæləs| former Russian imperial palace in Saint Petersburg, one of the largest in the world and now an art museum. It was stormed in 1917 by Revolutionary forces.

**Win·ter Park** |,wintər| resort and citrus-growing city in E central Florida, NE of Orlando. Pop. 22,242.

**Win·ter·thur**¹ |'wintər,THoor| former estate of the du Pont family in N Delaware, in Centerville, now noted for its art and craft museums.

**Win·ter·thur**² |'vintər,toor| industrial town in N Switzerland, in Zurich canton. Pop. 86,000.

**Win·throp** |'winTHrəp| resort and residential town in NE Massachusetts, on the N of Boston Harbor. Pop. 18,127.

**Wir·ral, the** |'wirəl| peninsula in NW England, between the Dee River and the Mersey estuary, SW of Liverpool, to which it is connected by tunnels. It contains industrial and residential suburbs, including Birkenhead.

**Wis·con·sin** |wis'känsən| see box, p. 412. □ **Wisconsinite** *n.*

**Wis·con·sin River** |wis'känsən| river that flows 430 mi./690 km. through central Wisconsin to the Mississippi River at Prairie du Chien. The **Dells of the Wisconsin** are a popular scenic area.

**Wis·ła** |'vēswä| Polish name for VISTULA.

**Wis·mar** |'vis,mär| port in NE Germany, on the Baltic Sea, between Rostock and Lübeck. Pop. 54,000.

**Wit·bank** |'wit,bæNGk| industrial town in NE South Africa, a mining center in Mpumalanga province. Pop. 173,000.

**Wit·ten** |'vitn| industrial city on the Ruhr River E of Essen, in western Germany. Pop. 106,000.

**Wit·ten·berg** |'vitn,berk| town in eastern Germany, on the Elbe River NE of Leipzig. Pop. 87,000. It was the scene in 1517 of Martin Luther's campaign against the Roman Catholic Church, a major factor in the rise of the Reformation.

## Wisconsin

**Capital:** Madison
**Largest city:** Milwaukee
**Other cities:** Eau Claire, Green Bay, Kenosha, Oshkosh, Racine, Sheboygan, Wausau, West Allis
**Population:** 4,891,769 (1990); 5,223,500 (1998); 5,479,000 (2005 proj.)
**Population rank (1990):** 16
**Rank in land area:** 23
**Abbreviation:** WI; Wis.
**Nickname:** Badger State; America's Dairyland
**Motto:** 'Forward'
**Bird:** robin
**Fish:** muskellunge
**Flower:** wood violet
**Tree:** sugar maple
**Song:** "On, Wisconsin!"
**Noted physical features:** Kettle Moraine Glacial Hills; The Dells Rock Formations; Timms Hill
**Tourist attractions:** Apostle Islands National Lakeshore
**Admission date:** May 29, 1848
**Order of admission:** 30
**Name origin:** For the Wisconsin River, which flows through the central part of the state; itself named probably from Ojibwa *Wees-kon-san,* meaning 'the gathering of the waters.'

**Wit·wa·ters·rand** |'wit,wawtərz,ränd| (also **the Witwatersrand**) region of South Africa, around the city of Johannesburg. Consisting of a series of parallel rocky ridges, it forms a watershed between the Vaal and Olifant rivers. The region contains rich gold deposits, first discovered in 1886. Also called **the Rand**.

**Wło·cła·wek** |'vlätslävek| agricultural market center and industrial city in central Poland, on the Vistula River. Pop. 122,000.

**Wo·burn**[1] |'w̄,bərn| village in S central England, in Berkshire, noted as the site of Woburn Abbey, 18th-century seat of the dukes of Bedford, now a major tourist attraction.

**Wo·burn**[2] |'wŏŏ,bərn; 'wŏbərn| industrial city in NE Massachusetts, NW of Boston. Pop. 35,943.

**Wo·dis·ław Śląs·ki** |vō'jĕswäf 'slawNskē| industrial city in S Poland, in a coal-mining region. Pop. 112,000.

**Wo·king** |'wōkiNG| residential town in Surrey, SE England. Pop. 82,000.

**Wolds, the** |wŏldz| upland district in NE England, in Lincolnshire, Yorkshire, and Humberside, composed of a range of chalk hills.

**Wol·fen·büt·tel** |'vawlfen,bytl| agricultural market and manufacturing city in N central Germany, on the Oker River. Pop. 52,000.

**Wolf River** |wŏolf| river that flows 210 mi./340 km. through central Wisconsin. With a lumbering history, it is also noted for its fishing.

**Wolfs·berg** |'vawlfs,berk| industrial town and summer resort in S Austria. Pop. 28,000.

**Wolfs·burg** |'vawlfs,bŏork| industrial city on the Mittelland Canal in Lower Saxony, NW Germany, noted as the home of the Volkswagen company. Pop. 129,000.

**Wol·lon·gong** |'wŏolən,gawNG| industrial port city on the coast of New South Wales, SE Australia. Pop. 211,000.

**Wol·ver·hamp·ton** |'wŏolvər,hæm(p)tən| industrial city in the West Midlands, England, NW of Birmingham. Pop. 240,000.

**Wol·ver·ine State** |,wŏolvə'rēn| informal name for MICHIGAN.

**Won·ju** |'wawn'jŏo| industrial and military city in N South Korea, SE of Seoul. Pop. 237,000.

**Won·san** |'wawn'sän| industrial port city in E North Korea, on the Sea of Japan. Pop. 350,000.

**Wood·bridge** |'wŏod,brij| industrial, commercial, and residential township in NE New Jersey. Pop. 93,086.

**Wood Buf·fa·lo National Park** |'wŏod ,bəfəlō| preserve in N Alberta and the S Northwest Territories, the largest Canadian national park.

**Wood·land** |'wŏodlənd| city in N central California, in an agricultural area NW of Sacramento. Pop. 39,802.

**Wood·land Hills** |'wŏodlənd| affluent residential section of NW Los Angeles, California, in the San Fernando Valley.

**Wood·lawn** |'wŏod,lawn| residential section of the N Bronx, New York City, site of the noted Woodlawn Cemetery.

**Woods Hole** |'wŏodz 'hōl| village in Falmouth, SE Massachusetts, at the SW corner of Cape Cod, a resort and noted ocean research center.

**Wood·stock**[1] |'wŏod,stäk| town in central England, in Oxfordshire, NW of Oxford. Pop. 3,000. Nearby is Blenheim Palace, the 18th-century house built for the Duke of Marlborough, and birthplace of statesman Winston Churchill.

**Wood·stock**[2] |'wŏod,stäk| resort town in SE New York, near the Catskills. Pop.

6,290. It gave its name in the summer of 1969 to a huge rock festival actually held in Bethel, 60 mi./96 km. to the SW.

**Wood·stock**³ |'wŏŏd,stäk| industrial city in S Ontario, on the Thames River. Pop. 30,075.

**Wool·lah·ra** |wŏŏ'lärə| city in SE Australia, a suburb SE of Sydney, in New South Wales. Pop. 51,000.

**Woo·me·ra** |'wŏŏmərə| town in central South Australia, the site of a vast military testing ground used in the 1950s for nuclear tests and since the 1960s for tracking space satellites.

**Woon·sock·et** |wŏŏn'säkət; 'wŏŏn'säkət| industrial city in N Rhode Island, on the Blackstone River. Pop. 43,877.

**Woos·ter** |'wŏŏstər| industrial and academic city in N central Ohio. Pop. 22,191.

**Worces·ter**¹ |'wŏŏstər| cathedral city in W England, on the River Severn, the administrative center of Worcestershire. Pop. 81,000. It was the scene in 1651, during the English Civil War, of a battle in which Oliver Cromwell defeated a Scottish army under Charles II. It has been a center of porcelain manufacture since 1751.

**Worces·ter**² |'wŏŏstər| industrial and university city in central Massachusetts, on the Blackstone River.

**Worces·ter·shire** |'wŏŏstər,sHir; 'wŏŏs-tərsHər| county of W central England, part of Hereford and Worcester between 1974 and 1998.

**World's View** |'wərldz 'vyŏŏ| height in S Zimbabwe, in the Matopo Hills SE of Bulawayo, where the British colonialist Cecil Rhodes is buried.

**World Trade Center** twin-towered office complex in S Manhattan, at 1,368 ft./417 m. the tallest building in New York City. It opened in 1973.

**Worms** |vawrms; 'wərmz| industrial town in western Germany, on the Rhine NW of Mannheim. Pop. 77,000. It was the scene in 1521 of the condemnation of Martin Luther's teaching, at the Diet of Worms.

**Wor·thing** |'wərTHiNG| resort town on the S coast of England, in West Sussex. Pop. 92,000.

**Wounded Knee** |,wŏŏndəd 'nē| village in SW South Dakota, in the Pine Ridge Indian reservation, scene of an 1890 massacre and 1973 demonstrations.

**Wran·gel Island** |'ræNGgəl| island in the East Siberian Sea, off the coast of NE Russia.

**Wran·gell Mountains** |'ræNGgəl| range in SE Alaska, within the Wrangell–St. Elias

National Park, along the Pacific coast and the border of the Yukon Territory.

**Wre·kin, the** |'rēkən| volcanic hill in W England, in Shropshire, that figures in the poetry of A. E. Housman.

**Wrex·ham** |'reksəm| mining and industrial town in NE Wales, in Clwyd. Pop. 41,000.

**Wro·cław** |'vrawt,swäf| industrial port city on the Oder River in W Poland. Pop. 643,000. Held by the Habsburgs from the 16th century, it was taken by Prussia in 1741. It passed to Poland in 1945. German name **Breslau**.

**Wu·hai** |'wŏŏ'hī| industrial city in Inner Mongolia, N China, on the Yellow River N of Yinchuan. Pop. 264,000.

**Wu·han** |'wŏŏ'hän| port in E China, the capital of Hubei province. Pop. 3,710,000. Situated at the confluence of the Han and the Yangtze rivers, it consists of three adjacent towns (Hankow, Hanyang, and Wuchang), administered jointly since 1950.

**Wu·hsi** |'wŏŏ'sHē| see WUXI.

**Wu·hsien** |'ŏŏsHē'en| see SUZHOU.

**Wu·hu** |'wŏŏ'hŏŏ| deepwater port on the Yangtze River in Anhui province, E China, SW of Nanjing. Pop. 426,000. It is an important agricultural processing and distribution center.

**Wup·per·tal** |'vŏŏpər,täl| industrial city in western Germany, in North Rhine–Westphalia NE of Düsseldorf. Pop. 385,000.

**Wu River** |wŏŏ| (Chinese name **Wu Jiang**) river of central China, flowing 700 mi./1,130 km. from central Guizhou province to the Yangtze River at Fuling, Sichuan, below Chongqing.

**Würt·tem·berg** |'vŏŏrtəm,berk| former state in SW Germany, now part of Baden-Württemberg.

**Würz·burg** |'vŏŏrts,bŏŏrk| industrial city on the Main River in Bavaria, S Germany. Pop. 128,000.

**Wu·tai Shan** |'wŏŏ'tä'sHän| mountain in Shanxi province, NE China, N of Taiyuan: 10,000 ft./3,060 m. high. It is sacred to Buddhism and a pilgrimage site.

**Wu·xi** |'wŏŏ'sHē| (also **Wu-hsi**) city, a textile center, on the Grand Canal in Jiangsu province, E China. Pop. 930,000.

**Wu·xing** |'wŏŏ'siNG| see HUZHOU.

**Wu·zhou** |'wŏŏ'jō| city in Guangxi, S China, on the Xun River, W of Guangzhou (Canton). Pop. 210,000.

**Wy·an·dotte** |'wīən,dät| industrial city in SE Michigan, S of Detroit. Pop. 30,938.

**Wye** |wī| river that rises in the mountains of W Wales and flows 132 mi./208 km. gen-

## Wyoming

**Capital:** Cheyenne
**Largest city:** Casper
**Other cities:** Green River, Laramie, Rock Springs, Sheridan
**Population:** 453,588 (1990); 480,907 (1998); 568,000 (2005 proj.)
**Population rank (1990):** 50
**Rank in land area:** 10
**Abbreviation:** WY; Wyo.
**Nickname:** Equality State; Cowboy State
**Motto:** 'Equal Rights'
**Bird:** meadowlark
**Flower:** Indian paintbrush
**Tree:** plains cottonwood
**Song:** "Wyoming"
**Noted physical features:** Jackson Hole; Wyoming Basin; Shoshone Cave; Thermopolis Hot Springs; Gannett Peak
**Tourist attractions:** Buffalo Bill Center; Shoshone Dam; Fort Laramie; Fort Bridger Historical Preserve; Thunder Basin National Grassland; Devil's Tower and Fossil Butte National Monuments; Grand Teton and Yellowstone National Parks; Flamingo Gorge Reservoir
**Admission date:** July 10, 1890
**Order of admission:** 44
**Name origin:** From the Delaware Indian words *maugh-wau-wa-ma*, 'large plains' or 'upon the great plain'; originally applied to a valley in northeastern Pennsylvania.

erally SE, entering the Severn estuary at Chepstow. In its lower reaches it forms part of the border between Wales and England.

**Wy‧o‧ming** |wī'ōmiNG| see box.

**Wy‧o‧ming Valley** |wī'ōmiNG| valley in NE Pennsylvania, along the Susquehanna River, in an anthracite-producing industrial region. Wilkes-Barre is the chief city.

**Wy‧ong** |'wī,äNG; 'wīawNG| town in SE Australia, in New South Wales, N of Sydney. Pop. 100,000.

# Xx

**Xai•xai** |'shī'shī| (also **Xai-Xai**; formerly **Vila de João Belo**) town in S Mozambique, a seaport at the mouth of the Limpopo River on the Indian Ocean. Pop. 94,000.

**Xan•a•du** |'zænə,dōō| old name for Shangdu, Inner Mongolia, China. The imperial summer residence here, built during the Yuan dynasty, in the late 13th century, was the inspiration for Samuel Taylor Coleridge's famous poem "Kubla Khan: A Vision in a Dream."

**Xan•kän•di** |zän'kændē| the capital of Nagorno-Karabakh, in S Azerbaijan. Pop. 58,000. Russian name **Stepanakert**.

**Xán•thi** |'ksänThē| **1** department in NE Greece. Pop. 90,000. **2** its capital. Pop. 32,000.

**Xan•thus** |'zænThəs| (also **Xanthos**) ancient city of Lycia, in S Asia Minor (present-day SW Turkey), on the Xanthus (now Koca) River in Muğla province.

**Xe•nia** |'zēnyə| commercial and industrial city in SW Ohio. Pop. 24,664.

**Xia•men** |shē'ä'mən| (also **Hsia-men**) port in Fujian province, SE China. Pop. 639,000. Also called **Amoy**.

**Xi'an** |shē'än| (formerly **Sian; Siking; Chang'an**) industrial city and capital of Shaanxi province, N China. Pop. 2,710,000. Inhabited since the 11th century B.C., the city was the capital of the Qin (Ch'in), Han, and Sui dynasties and was the W capital of the Tang (T'ang) dynasty. The tomb of Qin emperor Shi Huangdi (c. 259–210 B.C.), guarded by 10,000 terracotta soldiers, was discovered nearby in 1974.

**Xiang•fan** |shē'äNG'fän| city in Hubei province, E central China, NW of Wuhan, on the Han River. Pop. 410,000.

**Xiang•gang** Pinyin name for HONG KONG.

**Xiang River** |shē'äNG| (Chinese **Xiang Jiang**; formerly **Siang River**) river, S central China, rising in NE Guangxi province and flowing 715 mi./1,150 km. N through Hunan to Lake Dongting.

**Xiang•tan** |shē'äNG'tän| industrial city in Hunan province, S central China, on the Xiang River SW of Changsha. Pop. 442,000.

**Xian•yang** |shē'ä'yäNG| city in Shaanxi province, central China, to the N of the Wei River, NW of Xi'an. Pop. 352,000.

**Xi•chang** |'shē'chäNG| city in S Sichuan province, central China. Pop. 436,000.

**Xi•ga•zê** |'shē'gäd'zə| (formerly **Shigatse**) city in S Tibet, to the S of the Yarlung Zangbo (Brahmaputra) River, SW of Lhasa; the second-largest city in Tibet. Pop. 84,000. The Tashi Lumpo monastery to the W is the traditional seat of the Panchen Lama.

**Xing•tai** |'shiNG'tī| industrial city in NE China, to the S of Shijiazhuang in the province of Hebei. Pop. 1,167,000.

**Xin•gú** |shiNG'gōō| river that rises in the Mato Grosso of W Brazil and flows 1,230 mi./1,979 km. generally N to join the Amazon delta.

**Xi•ning** |'shē'niNG| (formerly **Sining**) industrial city and capital of Qinghai province, W central China. Pop. 698,000. An old trading town on the Tibetan caravan route, it is now an agricultural processing and distribution center.

**Xin•jiang** |'shiNjē'äNG| (formerly **Sinkiang**) autonomous region in NW China. Area: 636,100 sq. mi./1,646,800 sq. km. Pop. 15.17 million. Capital: Ürümqi. Occupying one sixth of China, Xinjiang includes the Tian Shan mountains and the vast Taklimakan Desert. The region has important mineral resources.

**Xin•xiang** |'shiNshē'äNG| city in Henan province, E central China, NE of Zhengzhou, on the Wei River. Pop. 474,000.

**Xin•yang** |'shin'yäNG| city in S Henan province, E central China, in the foothills of the Tongbai Shan range. Pop. 193,000.

**Xin•yu** |'shin'yōō| industrial city in Jiangxi province, SE central China, an iron and steel center SW of Nanchang, on the Yuan River. Pop. 226,000.

**Xi River** |shē| (English name **West River**; Chinese name **Xi Jiang**; formerly **Si River**) river, SE China. Rising in Yunnan province, where it is known as the Hongshui, the Xi flows 1,250 mi./2,010 km. E through Guangxi and Guangdong provinces to a large delta on the South China Sea, where Guangzhou (Canton), Hong Kong, and Macao are situated.

**Xi•xa•bang•ma Feng** |,shēshə'bäNG,mä 'feNG| see GOSAINTHAN.

**Xi•zang** |'shī'zäNG| see TIBET.

**Xo•chi•cal•co** |,sōchē'kälkō| archaeological site in central Mexico, SW of Cuernavaca in Morelos state. Religious and military, the ruins reflect the influence of several different ancient cultures.

**Xo·chi·mil·co** |ˌsōCHē'mēlkō| town in central Mexico, in the Distrito Federal, S of Mexico City. Pop. 271,000. It is famous for its Floating Gardens, remnants of a 2,000-year-old system of lake shore agriculture.

**Xu·chang** |'SHY'CHäNG| city in Henan province, E central China, S of Zhengzhou. Pop. 254,000.

**Xu·zhou** |'SHOO'jō| (also **Hsu-chou, Suchow**) city in Jiangsu province, E China. Pop. 910,000. Former name (1912–45) **Tongshan**.

# Yy

**Ya·an** |'yä'än| (formerly **Yachow**) city in Sichuan province, central China, SW of Chengdu. Pop. 282,000. It is an important tea processing center.

**Ya·blo·no·vy Range** |'yä,blənəvē| mountain range in SE Siberia, S Russia, extending NE from the Mongolian border to E of Lake Baikal. The highest peak is Sokhondo (7,192 ft./2,192 m.).

**Ya·chi·yo** |'yäCHē,ō; yä'CHēō| city in E central Japan, on E central Honshu, N of Chiba. Pop. 149,000.

**Ya·cui·ba** |yä'kwēbə| commercial town in S Bolivia, in Tarija department, on the Argentine border, in the Gran Chaco region. Pop. 31,000.

**Yad·kin River** |'yädkən| river that flows 200 mi./320 km. through W North Carolina, joining the Uwharrie to form the Pee Dee River.

**Ya·fo** |'yäfō| Hebrew name for JAFFA.

**Yai·zu** |īzōō| port city in E central Japan, on central Honshu. Pop. 112,000.

**Ya·ke·shi** |'yä'kə'sHē| city in Inner Mongolia, NE China, on the Hailar River E of Hailar. Pop. 393,000.

**Yak·i·ma** |'yæki,maw| commercial and industrial city in S central Washington. Pop. 54,827.

**Ya·ku·tia** |yä'kōōsHə| autonomous republic in E Russia. Pop. 1,081,000. Capital: Yakutsk. It is the coldest inhabited region of the world, with 40 percent of its territory lying to the N of the Arctic Circle. Official name **Republic of Sakha**.

**Ya·kutsk** |yə'kōōtsk| city in E Russia, on the Lena River, capital of the republic of Yakutia. Pop. 187,000.

**Ya·la** |'yälə| town in SW Thailand, S of Pattani. Pop. 69,000.

**Ya·long River** |'yä'lōoNG| (Chinese name **Yalong Jiang**) river, S China, flowing 800 mi./1,290 km. S from S Qinghai province through W Sichuan to the Yangtze River at the Sichuan-Yunnan border; one of the longest tributaries of the Yangtze.

**Yal·ta** |'yawltə| port and spa in S Ukraine, on the Black Sea. It was the site of an Allied conference in 1945 that was attended by Roosevelt, Churchill, and Stalin, who laid the initial plans for post–World War II Europe.

**Ya·lu River** |'yä'lōo| river of E Asia, which rises in the mountains of Jilin province in NE China and flows 500 mi./800 km. generally SW to the Yellow Sea, forming most of the border between China and North Korea. In November 1950 the advance of UN troops toward the Yalu precipitated the Chinese advance into Korea.

**Ya·ma·ga·ta** |'yä,mägä,tä| industrial city in NE Japan, on N Honshu, W of Mount Zao. Pop. 250,000.

**Ya·ma·gu·chi** |,yämä'gōōCHē| commercial city in W Japan, on SW Honshu. Pop. 129,000. It has many Buddhist temples.

**Ya·ma·to** |yä'mätō| city in E central Japan, on E central Honshu, SW of Tokyo. Pop. 195,000.

**Yamato-koriyama** |yä'mätō,kawrē'yämä| city in W central Japan, on S Honshu, S of Nara. Pop. 93,000.

**Yam·bol** |'yäm,bōl| (also **Jambol**) port city in SE Bulgaria, on the Tundzha River. Pop. 99,000.

**Ya·mous·sou·kro** |,yämə'sōōkrō| the capital of Côte d'Ivoire. Pop. 120,000. It was designated as capital in 1983, replacing Abidjan.

**Yam·pa River** |'yæmpä| river that flows 250 mi./400 km. across NW Colorado to join the Green River. It is a recreational attraction.

**Ya·mu·na** |'yəmənə| Hindi name for JUMNA.

**Yan·an** |'yän'än| (formerly **Yenan**) market and tourist city in Shaanxi province, central China. Pop. 113,000. The destination of the communists' Long March during the Chinese civil war, it was the site of the communist headquarters for most of 1936–49.

**Yan·cheng** |'yän'&chəNG| (also **Yen-cheng**) industrial city in Jiangsu province, E China. Pop. 380,000.

**Yang·chow** |'yäNG'jō| see YANGZHOU.

**Yan·gon** |yäNG'gōn| Burmese name for RANGOON.

**Yang·quan** |'yäNGCHōō'än| city in Shanxi province, E China, E of Taiyuan, in a coal- and iron-mining region. Pop. 362,000.

**Yang·tze River** |'yäNG(t)'sē| (Chinese name **Chang Jiang**) principal and longest river of China: 3,964 mi./6,380 km. It rises as the Jinsha in the Tibetan highlands and flows S, then E through central China, entering the East China Sea at Shanghai.

**Yang·zhou** |'yäNG'jō| (formerly **Yang-chow**) city in Jiangsu province, E China, on the Grand Canal. Pop. 313,000. It was a capital of the Sui dynasty and important cultural and religious center under the Tang (T'ang) dynasty.

**Yan·ji** |'yän'jē| city in Jilin province, NE China, W of Tumen. Pop. 231,000.

**Yank·ton** |'yæNGktən| commercial and industrial city in SE South Dakota. Pop. 12,703.

**Yan·tai** |'yän'tī| (also **Yen-tai**) port on the Yellow Sea in Shandong province, E China. Pop. 3,204,600. Former name (3rd century B.C.–15th century) **Chefoo.**

**Yan·tra River** |'yäntrə| 178 mi./287 km. long, that rises in Bulgaria in the Balkan Mts. and flows N into the Danube River E of Nikopol.

**Yao** |yow; 'yäō| city in W central Japan, on S Honshu, a residential suburb S of Osaka. Pop. 278,000.

**Ya·oun·dé** |yown'dā| the capital of Cameroon, an agricultural trade center. Pop. 800,000.

**Yap** |yäp; yæp| (also **Uap**) island group in the SW Pacific, one of the four Federated States of Micronesia. Pop. 14,000. Previously held by Germany, then Japan, it was captured by U.S. forces in 1945.

**Ya·qui River** |yä'kē| river in NW Mexico that with headstreams flows 420 mi./680 km. from N Sonora state into the Gulf of California near Guaymas.

**Ya·ren** |'yä,ren| unofficial capital of the Pacific nation of Nauru.

**Yar·kand River** |yär'känd| (also called **Yarkant;** Chinese name **Yarkant He**) river in Xinjiang, W China. Rising near K2 in the Karakorum Mts. it flows 500 mi./800 km. NE to join the Kashgar and form the Tarim River.

**Yar·mouth**[1] |'yärməTH| resort town in SE Massachusetts, on S Cape Cod. Pop. 21,174.

**Yar·mouth**[2] |'yärməTH| port town in SW Nova Scotia. Pop. 7,781.

**Yar·muk River** |yär'mŏŏk| river that flows 50 mi./80 km. W from NW Jordan, to the Jordan River just S of the Sea of Galilee. It forms part of the Jordan-Syria border.

**Ya·ro·slavl** |yärä'slävəl| port in European Russia, on the Volga River NE of Nizhni Novgorod. Pop. 636,000.

**Yar·row Water** |'yærō| river that flows from the Borders region in SE Scotland into Ettrick Water and the Tweed River near Selkirk. It is celebrated by English and Scottish poets.

**Yas·na·ya Po·lya·na** |'yäsnəyə pəl'yänə| village in W Russia, S of Tula. It was the birthplace of Leo Tolstoy, and he is buried at his estate here.

**Ya·tsu·shi·ro** |yät'sŏŏ,sHērō| commercial city in SW Japan, on W Kyushu, on Yatsushiro Bay. Pop. 108,000.

**Ya·vat·mal** |'yävət,mäl| (also **Yeotmal**) commercial town in E central India, in Maharashtra state. Pop. 122,000.

**Ya·wa·ta** |yä'wätə| city in W central Japan, on S Honshu, S of Kyoto. Pop. 76,000.

**Yax·chi·lan** |,yäsHcHē'län| archaeological site in SE Mexico, in Chiapas state near the Guatemalan border, on the Usumacinta River. Mayan ruins here remain largely cloaked in jungle foliage.

**Yazd** |'yäzd| (also **Yezd**) historic city in central Iran, in a desert region. Pop. 275,000. It is known for its silk weaving.

**Yaz·oo River** |yæ'zŏŏ| river that flows 190 mi./305 km. from N Mississippi to join the Mississippi River at Vicksburg. The fertile land between the rivers is the Mississippi **Delta,** or **Yazoo Delta.**

**Ybor City** |'ēbawr| industrial and commercial section of Tampa, Florida, noted for its Cuban culture and cigar industry.

**Ye·do** |'yedō| earlier name for TOKYO, Japan. Also, **Edo.**

**Ye·lets** |yil'yets| (also **Elets**) industrial city in W Russia, S of Moscow. Pop. 121,000.

**Yel·low·head Pass** |'yelō,hed| rail and highway pass through the Rocky Mts. W of Edmonton, Alberta.

**Yel·low·knife** |'yelō,nīf| the capital since 1967 of the Northwest Territories, on the N shore of Great Slave Lake. Pop. 15,179.

**Yel·low River** |'yelō| the second largest river in China, which rises in the mountains of W central China and flows over 3,000 mi./4,830 km. in a huge semicircle before entering the gulf of Bo Hai. Chinese name **Huang Ho.**

**Yel·low Sea** |'yelō| arm of the East China Sea, separating the Korean peninsula from the E coast of China. Chinese name **Huang Hai.**

**Yel·low Springs** |'yelō| academic village in SW Ohio, home to Antioch College. Pop. 3,972.

**Yel·low·stone National Park** |'yelə,stōn| preserve in NW Wyoming and Montana. Its features include Old Faithful, a geyser that erupts every 45 to 80 minutes to a height of about 100 ft./305 m.

**Yem·en** |'yemən| republic in the S and SW of the Arabian Peninsula. Area: 208,960 sq. mi./540,000 sq. km. Pop. 12,533,000. Language, Arabic. Capital and largest city: Sana'a. Economic and commercial capital: Aden. Islamic since the 7th century, Yemen was part of the Ottoman Empire from the

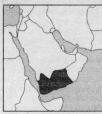

**Yemen**

16th century, then dominated by the British from the 19th century until 1967, when the country split into South Yemen (the People's Democratic Republic) and North Yemen (the Arab Republic). Reunification occurred in 1990. Oil, coffee, cotton, and trade are key to the economy. □ **Yemeni** *adj. & n.*

**Ye·na·ki·ye·ve** |yeˈnäkēyivə| (formerly **Ordzhonikidze**) city in E Ukraine. Pop. 120,000. It is a suburb of Donetsk.

**Yen·an** |ˈyäˈnän| see YANˈAN.

**Ye·nan·gyaung** |ˈyenänˈjowNG| town in W central Burma, on the Irrawaddy River N of Magwe; the main oil-producing center in Burma.

**Ye·ni·sei** |ˌyenəˈsā| river in Siberia, which rises in the mountains on the Mongolian border and flows 2,566 mi./4,106 km. generally N to the Arctic coast, emptying into the Kara Sea.

**Yeo·vil** |ˈyō͝vil| commercial and industrial town in SW England, in Somerset. Pop. 37,000.

**Yer·ba Bue·na** |ˌyərbä ˈbwenä| name of an island in San Francisco Bay, California, and also of the 1820s mainland settlement that became the city of San Francisco.

**Ye·re·van** |ˌyerəˈvän| (also **Erevan**) industrial city, the capital of Armenia, in the S Caucasus. Pop. 1,202,000.

**Yes·sen·tu·ki** |ˌyəsəntŏŏˈkē| resort town in W Russia, a spa on the N slopes of the Caucasus Mts., W of Pyatigorsk.

**Yev·pa·to·ri·ya** |ˌyefpäˈtawrēəä| (also **Eupatoria**) seaport in Ukraine, on the W coast of the Crimean Peninsula. Pop. 111,000.

**Ye·zo** |ˈyezō| see HOKKAIDO.

**Yi·bin** |ˈēˈbin| commercial and industrial city in Sichuan province, central China, on the Min River S of Chengdu. Pop. 806,000.

**Yi·chang** |ˈēˈCHäNG| city in Hubei province, E central China, at the head of navigation on the Yangtze River, W of Wuhan. Pop. 372,000.

**Yi·chun** |ˈēˈCHŏŏn| (also **I-chun**) city in Heilongjiang province, NE China. Pop. 882,000.

**Yin·chuan** |ˈyinˈCHwän| industrial city, the capital of Ningxia province, NE China. It produces textiles, rubber goods, chemicals, and machine tools. Pop. 658,000.

**Ying·kou** |ˈyiNGˈkō| (formerly **Newchwang**) city in Liaoning province, NE China, a port on the Liao River near where it flows into Liaodong Bay. Pop. 422,000.

**Yi·ning** |ˈyēˈniNG| (also called **Gulja**) city in Xinjiang, NW China, a former caravan trading center in the W Tian Shan mountains. Pop.177,000.

**Yi·yang** |ˈyēˈyäNG| city in Hunan province, E central China, an industrial port on the Zi River, NW of Changsha. Pop. 372,000.

**Yog·ya·kar·ta** |ˌyägyˈkərtə| (also **Jogjakarta**) city in S central Java, Indonesia. Pop. 412,000. It was formerly the capital of Indonesia (1945–49).

**Yo·ho National Park** |ˈyōhō| preserve in the Rocky Mts. in SE British Columbia. Kicking Horse Pass, opened for the Canadian Pacific Railway, is here, as is the Burgess Shale, a famed fossil resource.

**Yok·kai·chi** |yōˈkiCHē| industrial port city in central Japan, on S Honshu. Pop. 274,000.

**Yok·na·pa·taw·pha County** |ˌyawknəpəˈtawfə| fictional county in N Mississippi, the setting for most of the work of William Faulkner.

**Yo·ko·ha·ma** |ˌyōkəˈhämə| seaport on the island of Honshu, Japan, S of Tokyo. Pop. 3,220,000. It is the second-largest city in Japan.

**Yo·ko·su·ka** |yōˈkōsəkä| port city and naval base in E central Japan, on E central Honshu. Pop. 433,000.

**Yol·la Bol·ly Mountains** |ˈyälə ˌbälē| range of the Klamath Mts. in NW California, noted for its wilderness and wildlife.

**Yo·na·go** |yōˈnägō| port city in W Japan, on S Honshu. Pop. 131,000.

**Yo·ne·za·wa** |yōˈnäzäˌwä; ˌyōnəˈzäwə| city in NE Japan, on N Honshu, S of Yamagata. Pop. 95,000. It has long been noted for silk weaving.

**Yon·kers** |ˈyäNGkərz| industrial city in SE New York, on the Hudson River just N of the Bronx, New York City. Pop. 188,082.

**Yonne** |yawn| **1** department in NE France. Pop. 323,000. The capital is Auxerre. **2** river, 184 mi./293 km. long, in central France that flows NW into the Seine River near Montereau.

**Yor·ba Lin·da** |ˌyawrbə ˈlində| city in SW

California, a suburb SE of Los Angeles and the birthplace of Richard Nixon. Pop. 52,422.

**York**¹ |yawrk| historic commercial city in N England, on the Ouse River. Pop. 101,000. The Romans occupied the site, known as Eboracum, from A.D. 71 until about A.D. 400; in A.D. 867 it was taken by the Vikings. It is the seat of the Archbishop of York and is noted for its cathedral, York Minster.

**York**² |yawrk| suburban city in S Ontario, just N of Toronto. Pop. 140,525. York is also the early name for Toronto itself.

**York**³ |yawrk| commercial and industrial city in SE Pennsylvania. Pop. 42,192.

**York, Cape**¹ |yawrk| the northernmost point in Australia, on the Torres Strait in N Queensland, at the tip of the Cape York Peninsula.

**York, Cape**² |yawrk| SW tip of Hayes Peninsula, on Baffin Bay, Greenland. It served as a base for U.S. explorer Robert E. Peary's polar expedition. A 100-ton meteorite found here was brought to the U.S. by Peary.

**York·shire** |'yawrkSHər; 'yawrk,SHir| former county of N England, traditionally divided into East, West, and North Ridings. Since 1996 the N part of the area has formed the county of North Yorkshire, while the rest of the Yorkshire area consists of separately administered regions. □ **York·shireman** *n.* **Yorkshirewoman** *n.*

**York·town** |'yawrk,town| historic site in SE Virginia, on the York River N of Newport News, scene of both the last (October 1781) battle of the American Revolution and a Civil War battle (1862).

**York·ville**¹ |'yawrk,vil| district of the Upper East Side of Manhattan, New York City, long German in character.

**York·ville**² |'yawrk,vil| fashionable shopping and arts district of Toronto, Ontario.

**Yo·ru·ba·land** |'yawrəbə,lænd| (also **Yoruba**) region of coastal W Africa, home to the Yoruba people, and centered in SW Nigeria, in and around Lagos, Ibadan, and Oshogbo.

**Yo·sem·i·te National Park** |yō'semətē| preserve in the Sierra Nevada in central California. It includes Yosemite Valley, with sheer granite cliffs and the mile-high rock face of El Capitan and several famed waterfalls, including Yosemite Falls, the highest in the U.S., with a drop of 2,425 ft./739 m.

**Yoshkar-Ola** |yəSH'kärə'lä| industrial city, the capital of the republic of Mari El, in E central Russia. Pop. 246,000.

**Yo·su** |'yə'sōo| port city in S South Korea, on the Korea Strait. Pop. 184,000. It is a fishing, tourist, and oil refining center.

**Youghal** |yawl| historic port town in County Cork, S Ireland, on Youghal Bay, at the mouth of the Blackwater River. Pop. 6,000.

**Yough·io·ghe·ny River** |,yäkə'gānē| river that flows 135 mi./220 km. from West Virginia into Pennsylvania, joining the Monongahela River at McKeesport.

**Youngs·town** |'yəNGz,town| industrial city in NE Ohio, in the Mahoning River valley. Pop. 95,372. It is an historic steel center.

**Yous·sou·fia** |yōō'sōōfēə| (formerly **Louis Gentil**) town in W central Morocco, NE of Safi, in a phosphate-mining area. Pop. 60,000.

**Yoz·gat** |yawz'gät| city in central Turkey, E of Ankara, capital of Yozgat province. Pop. 50,000.

**Ypres** |'ēpr(ə)| town in NW Belgium, near the border with France, in the province of West Flanders. Pop. 35,000. Ypres was the scene of some of the bitterest fighting of World War I. Flemish name **Ieper**.

**Yp·si·lan·ti** |,ipsə'læntē| industrial city in SE Michigan, near Ann Arbor. Pop. 24,846.

**Yre·ka** |wī'rēkə| commercial and resort city in N California, near the Oregon border. Pop. 6,948.

**Yser River** |ē'zer| river that flows through France and Belgium for 48 mi./77 km., emptying into the North Sea near Nieuwpoort, Belgium.

**Yu·ba City** |'yōōbə| commercial city in N central California, in an agricultural area NW of Sacramento. Pop. 27,437.

**Yu·cai·pa** |yōō'kīpə| suburban city in S California, SE of San Bernardino. Pop. 32,824.

**Yu·ca·tán** |,yōōkə'tän| state of SE Mexico, at the N tip of the Yucatán Peninsula. Area: 14,833 sq. mi./38,402 sq. km. Pop. 1,364,000. Capital: Mérida.

**Yu·ca·tán Peninsula** |,yōōkə'tän| peninsula in S Mexico, lying between the Gulf of Mexico and the Caribbean Sea. The region was the seat of the Mayan civilization.

**Yuc·ca Mountain** |'yəkə| mountain in SW Nevada, NW of Las Vegas, that is the proposed storage site for the most hazardous U.S. radioactive wastes.

**Yu·ci** |'yōō'zē| industrial city in Shanxi province, E China, SE of Taiyuan. Pop. 425,000.

**Yue·yang** |yōō'a'yæNG| city in Hubei province, E central China, SW of Wuhan, on the NE shore of Lake Dongting. Pop. 303,000.

**Yu·go·sla·via** |ˌyōōgə'slävēə| federation of states in SE Europe, in the Balkans. Created as the Kingdom of the Serbs, Croats, and Slovenes after World War I, it took the name Yugoslavia in 1929, its capital at Belgrade. In the 1990s, four of its republics (Croatia, Slovenia, Bosnia and Herzegovina, and Macedonia) seceded, amid regional conflicts. Serbia and Montenegro in 1992 declared a new Yugoslavia, but this has not received widespread recognition. □ **Yugoslavian** *adj. & n.*

Yugoslavia

**Yu·kon River** |'yōō,kän| river that rises in the Yukon Territory and flows 1,870 mi./3,020 km. W through central Alaska to the Bering Sea.

**Yu·kon Territory** |'yōō,kän| territory of NW Canada, on the border with Alaska. Area: 186,661 sq. mi./482,515 sq. km. Pop. 27,797. Capital and largest city: White-

horse. Mountainous, isolated, and undeveloped, the Yukon has little economic activity except for mining. The population increased briefly during the Klondike gold rush (1897–99).

**Yu·lin** |'yōō'lin| industrial and commercial city in Guangxi, S China, E of Nanning, on the Nanliu River. Pop. 1,255,000.

**Yu·ma** |'yōōmə| historic commercial city in SW Arizona, on the Colorado and Gila rivers near the California and Mexico borders. Pop. 54,923.

**Yu·men** |'yY'mən| (also called **Laojunmiao**) city in NW Gansu province, N China. Near the Jade Gate of the Great Wall, it is an important petroleum center. Pop. 109,000.

**Yun·dum** |'yōōn,dōōm| village in W Gambia, SW of Banjul and site of its international airport.

**Yun·nan** |'yY'næn| province of SW China, on the border with Vietnam, Laos, and Burma. Pop. 36.97 million. Capital: Kunming.

**Yu·yao** |'yY'yow| city in Zhejiang province, E China, NW of Ningbo. Pop. 778,000.

**Yuzhno-Sakhalinsk** |'yōōzHnə səkHə-'linsk| chief town on Sakhalin Island, in far E Russia. Pop. 165,000.

**Yu·zov·ka** |'yōōzefkə| former name (1872–1924) for DONETSK.

**Yve·lines** |ēv'lēn| department W of Paris in N central France. Pop. 1,307,000. The capital is Versailles.

**Yver·don** |ēver'dōN| (also **Yverdon-les-Bains**) spa town in W Switzerland, N of Lausanne. Pop. 22,000.

# Zz

**Zaan·dam** |zän'däm| manufacturing municipality in W Netherlands, near Amsterdam. Pop. 130,000. Peter the Great of Russia lived here (1697) in order to study shipbuilding.

**Zaan·stad** |'zän,stät| industrial town in W Netherlands. Pop. 131,000.

**Zab·rze** |'zäbzʜe| industrial and mining city in Upper Silesia, S Poland. Pop. 205,000. From 1915 to 1945 it was a German city bearing the name Hindenburg.

**Za·ca·te·cas** |,säkə'täkəs| **1** state of N central Mexico. Area: 28,293 sq. mi./73,252 sq. km. Pop. 1,278,000. **2** its capital, a silver-mining city situated at an altitude of 8,200 ft. (2,500 m). Pop. 165,000.

**Za·dar** |'zä,där| port town and resort in W Croatia, on the Adriatic Sea. Pop. 76,000.

**Za·ga·zig** |zə'gäzig| (also **Zaqaziq**) commercial ity in the Nile delta, N Egypt. Pop. 279,000. Ancient Bubastis is nearby.

**Za·greb** |'zä,greb| the capital of Croatia, an industrial and communications center on the Sava River. Pop. 707,000.

**Zag·ros Mountains** |zäg'rəs| range in W Iran, rising to 14,921 ft./4,548 m. at Zard Kuh. Most of Iran's oil fields lie along the W foothills.

**Za·he·dan** |,zähi'dän| city in SE Iran, near the borders with Afghanistan and Pakistan. Pop. 362,000.

**Zah·le** |zä'la| commercial and resort town in central Lebanon, E of Beirut in the Bekaa Valley. Pop. 200,000.

**Za·ire** |zä'ir| (also **Zaïre**) former name for the Democratic Republic of the CONGO.

**Za·ire River** |zä'ir| another name for the CONGO River.

**Za·kin·thos** |'zäkēn,ᴛʜaws| (also **Zakynthos**) island off the SW coast of mainland Greece, in the Ionian Sea, most southerly of the Ionian Islands. Pop. 33,000. Also called **Zante**.

**Za·ko·pa·ne** |,zäkə'pänə| a winter-sports resort in the Tatra Mts. of S Poland. Pop. 29,000.

**Za·la·e·ger·szeg** |'zawlaw,eger,seg| market town in W Hungary, on the Zala River. Pop. 63,000. It is the capital of Zala county.

**Za·ma**[1] |'zämə; 'zämə.| ancient town in N Africa, probably SW of Carthage (near Tunis, Tunisia), where the Roman Scipio Africanus defeated Carthaginian forces under Hannibal in 202 B.C.

**Za·ma**[2] |'zämä| city in E central Japan, on E central Honshu, W of Yokohama. Pop. 112,000.

**Zam·be·zi River** |zæm'bēzē| river of East Africa, which rises in NW Zambia and flows for 1,600 mi./2,560 km. S through Angola and Congo (formerly Zaire) to the Victoria Falls, turning E along the border between Zambia and Zimbabwe, before crossing Mozambique and entering the Indian Ocean.

**Zam·bia** |'zæmbēə| landlocked republic in central Africa, divided from Zimbabwe by the Zambezi River. Area: 290,696 sq. mi./752,613 sq. km. Pop. 8,373,000. Languages, English (official), various Bantu languages. Capital and largest city: Lusaka. A British colony from 1889, called Northern Rhodesia 1911–64, Zambia exports copper, cobalt, and other minerals. □ **Zambian** adj. & n.

Zambia

**Zam·bo·an·ga** |,zämbō'äɴɡgə| port on the W coast of Mindanao, in the S Philippines. Pop. 442,000.

**Za·mo·ra** |sä'mawrə| communications and marketing center in NW Spain, on the Duero River. Pop. 62,000.

**Za·mość** |'zä,mawsʜcʜ| industrial town in SE Poland, SE of Lublin. Pop. 59,000.

**Zand·voort** |'zänt,vawrt| resort town in the Netherlands, on the North Sea coast. Pop. 16,000.

**Zanes·ville** |'zänz,vil| industrial city in N central Ohio, E of Columbus. Pop. 26,778. On the old National Road, it is a noted ceramics center.

**Zan·jan** |zæn'jän| commercial city in NW Iran, at the W end of the Elburz Mts. Pop. 254,000.

**Zan·te** |'dzäntə| another name for ZA-KINTHOS.

**Zan·zi·bar** |'zænzə,bär| island off the coast of E Africa, part of Tanzania. Pop. 641,000. Under Arab rule from the 17th century, Zanzibar was a prosperous trading port. It became a British protectorate in 1890 and an independent Commonwealth state in 1963, but in the following year the sultan was overthrown and the country became a republic, uniting with Tanganyika to form Tanzania. □ **Zanzibari** *adj. & n.*

**Zao·zhuang** |'zow'zHwäNG| (also **Tsaochuang**) city in Shandong province, E China, a center for coal mining, heavy industry, and agricultural trade. Pop. 3,192,000.

**Za·po·pan** |,säpō'pän| commercial town in SW Mexico, in Jalisco state, a satellite just W of Guadalajara. Pop. 668,000.

**Za·po·rizh·zhya** |,zäpə'rawzHə| industrial city of Ukraine, on the Dnieper River. Pop. 891,000. It developed as a major industrial center after the construction of a hydroelectric dam in 1932. Russian name **Zaporozhye**; former name (until 1921) **Aleksandrovsk**.

**Za·qa·ziq** |,zäkä'zēk| variant spelling of ZAGAZIG.

**Za·ra·go·za** |'zärə'gōsə| Spanish name for SARAGOSSA.

**Zá·ra·te** |'zärä,tä| (formerly **General Uriburu**) commercial town in E Argentina, a port in the delta of the Paraná River, NW of Buenos Aires.

**Za·ria** |'zärēə| city in N Nigeria, an agricultural and light industrial center. Pop. 345,000.

**Zar·qa** |'zärkə| (also **Az Zarqa**) industrial city in NW Jordan, NE of Amman. Pop. 359,000.

**Za·wier·cie** |zä'vyerCHe| industrial city in S Poland, NW of Katowice, on the Warta River. Pop. 60,000.

**Zea·land** |'zēlənd| the principal island of Denmark, situated between the Jutland peninsula and the S tip of Sweden. Its chief city is Copenhagen. Danish name **Sjælland**.

**Zee·brug·ge** |'zā,brykə| industrial and ferry port on the coast of Belgium, linked by canal to Bruges.

**Zee·land** |'zā,länt; 'zēlənd| agricultural province of the SW Netherlands, at the estuary of the Maas and Scheldt rivers. Pop. 357,000. Capital: Middelburg.

**Ze·fat** |'tse,fät| (also **Safed; Safad; Tsefat**) historic city in N Israel, NNW of the Sea of Galilee. Pop. 22,000. It is one of Israel's four holy cities.

**Zeist** |zīst| residential community in cen-

tral Netherlands, near Utrecht. Pop. 62,000.

**Zeitz** |tsīts; sīts| industrial city in eastern central Germany, on the Weisse Elster River, SSW of Leipzig. Pop. 44,000.

**Ze·la·zo·wa Wo·la** |zell,äzawvä'vawlə| village in E central Poland, W of Warsaw, birthplace of the composer Chopin.

**Ze·ni·ca** |'zenētsə| (also **Zenitsa**) industrial town in central Bosnia and Herzegovina. Pop. 133,000.

**Zen·tsu·ji** |zent'sōōjē| city in W Japan, on N Shikoku, SW of Takamatsu. Pop. 38,000. The founder of the Shingon sect of Buddhism was born here.

**Zer·matt** |tsər'mät| Alpine ski resort and mountaineering center near the Matterhorn, in S Switzerland.

**Ze·ya River** |'zāyə| river (800 mi./1,290 km. long) in E Russia, rising in the Stanovoy Range and flowing S into the Amur River at Blagoveshchensk.

**Zgierz** |zəgyesH| town in central Poland, a textile center. Pop. 59,000.

**Zham·byl** |jäm'bil| (formerly **Dzhambul**) industrial city, capital of Zhambyl region, S Kazakhstan. Pop. 312,000.

**Zhang·jia·kou** |'jäNGjē'ä'kō| (also **Changchiakow**) city along the Great Wall in Hebei province, NE China, in an ironmining area. Pop. 720,000. Mongolian name **Kalgan**.

**Zhang·ye** |'jäNG'yə| commercial and industrial city in Gansu province, N China, in the N foothills of the Qilian Shan mountains. Pop. 400,000.

**Zhang·zhou** |'jäNG'jō| city in Fujian province, SE China, W of Xiamen. Pop. 318,000.

**Zhan·jiang** |'jänjē'äNG| (also **Chan-chiang**) port in Guangdong province, S China. Pop. 1,049,000.

**Zhao·dong** |'jow'dōōNG| agricultural and industrial city in Heilongjiang province, NE China, NW of Harbin. Pop. 754,000.

**Zhao·tong** |'jow'tōōNG| city in NE Yunnan province, S China, E of the Jinsha (Yangtze) River. Pop. 560,000.

**Zhda·nov** |'zHdänəf| former name (1948–89) for MARIUPOL.

**Zhe·jiang** |'jəjē'äNG| (formerly **Chekiang**) mountainous province in E China to the S of Yangtze River. Pop. 41.45 million. Capital: Hangzhou. It is the smallest mainland province in land area (39,230 sq. mi./101,800 sq. km.).

**Zhe·lez·no·do·ro·zhnyy** |zHə,liznədə-'rawzHnē| (also **Zheleznodorozhny**) industrial city in W Russia, E of Moscow. Pop. 99,000.

**Zhe·lez·no·gorsk** |ZHə,liznə'gawrsk| city in W Russia, NW of Kursk. Pop. 88,000.

**Zheng·zhou** |jəNG'jō| (also **Chengchow**) the capital of Henan province, in NE central China. Pop. 1,660,000.

**Zhen·jiang** |'jənjē'äNG| (also **Chen-chi-ang, Chinkiang**) port in Jiangsu province, on the Yangtze River, E China. Pop. 1,280,000.

**Zhez·qaz·qhan** |ZHəzkäz'kнän| (also **Zhezkazgan**; formerly **Dzezjazgab**) copper-mining city in central Kazakhstan. Pop. 110,000.

**Zhi·to·mir** |ZHi'taw,mir| Russian name for ZHYTOMYR.

**Zhlo·bin** |ZHlōbyin| industrial city in SE Belarus, on the Dnieper River. Pop. 57,000.

**Zhob river** |zhōb| seasonal river in central Pakistan, flowing 230 mi./370 km., from the Toba-Kakar Range to the Gomal River.

**Zhong·shan** |'jōōNG'sнän| (also **Chung-shan**) agricultural and industrial city in Guangdong province, SE China, the birthplace of political leader Sun Yat-sen. Pop. 1,073,000.

**Zhu·kov·skiy** |ZHōō'kawfskē| (also **Zhukovsky**) industrial city in W Russia, SE of Moscow. Pop. 101,000.

**Zhu River** |jōō| see PEARL RIVER.

**Zhu·zhou** |'jōō'jō| city in Hunan province, S central China, on the Xiang River S of Changsha. Pop. 410,000.

**Zhy·to·myr** |ZHi'taw,mir| industrial city in central Ukraine. Pop. 296,000. Russian name Zhitomir.

**Zi·bo** |'dzə'bō| (also **Tzu-po**) industrial city in Shandong province, E China. Pop. 2,484,000.

**Zie·lo·na Go·ra** |ZHə'lawnə'gōōə| industrial town in W Poland, capital of Zielona Gora county. Pop. 114,000.

**Zi·gong** |'dzə'gōōNG| industrial and agricultural city in Sichuan province, central China, SE of Chengdu, a center of salt production. Pop. 1,673,000.

**Zi·guin·chor** |,zēgēn'sHawr| commercial city in SW Senegal, an inland port on the Casamance River. Pop. 149,000.

**Zi·hua·ta·ne·jo** |,sēwätä'nähō| resort and fishing and cruise ship port in S Mexico, on the Pacific coast in Guerrero state.

**Zi·le** |zi'lä| commercial town in N central Turkey, in Tokat province. Pop. 46,000. As ancient **Zela**, it was the place from which Julius Caesar, after a victory, sent the message "Veni, vidi, vici (I came, I saw, I conquered)."

**Ži·li·na** |'ZHēli,nä| industrial town in NW Slovakia, on the Váh River. Pop. 84,000.

**Zil·ler·ta·ler Alps** |tsili,tälər| range of the E Alps on the border between Austria and Italy. The Brenner Pass divides it from the Otztal Alps to the W.

**Zim·ba·bwe** |zim'bäb,wä| landlocked republic in SE Africa, divided from Zambia by the Zambezi River. Area: 151,058 sq. mi./391,090 sq. km. Pop. 10,080,000. Languages, English (official), Shona, Ndebele, and others. Capital and largest city: Harare. An ancient civilization that gave the country its name was overrun by Bantu peoples 500 years ago. The British dominated what was called Rhodesia from the late 19th century. In 1965–79 a white minority government declared independence. Majority (African) rule came in 1979. Mining and agriculture are the basis of the economy. □ **Zimbabwean** adj. & n.

Zimbabwe

**Zin·der** |zin'der| commercial town in S Niger. Pop. 121,000. A walled town on ancient caravan routes, it was a French colonial capital before 1926.

**Zi·on** |'zīən| (also **Mount Zion** or **Sion**) part of the city of Jerusalem, originally the hill (see MORIAH, MOUNT) on which the Temple of Solomon was built. The name came to mean Jerusalem itself, and the Promised Land in general.

**Zi·on National Park** |'zīən| preserve in SW Utah, noted for its colorful sandstone formations and deep canyons.

**Zi·tá·cua·ro** |,sētä'kwärō| historic city in S Mexico, in Michoacán state. Pop. 108,000. It was important during the Mexican War of Independence.

**Zla·to·ust** |zlətä'ōōst| industrial city in central Russia, in the S Ural Mts. Pop. 208,000.

**Zlin** |zlēn| industrial town in the E central Czech Republic. Pop. 85,000. It is a center of the Czech shoe-manufacturing industry.

**Zó•ca•lo** |sō'kälō| central public square in a Mexican city, especially the Plaza de la Constitución in Mexico City, one of the largest city squares in the world, the site of the National Palace and other important buildings.

**Zoe•ter•meer** |ˌzo͞otər'mer| industrial and administrative town in W Netherlands, N of Rotterdam. Pop. 103,000.

**Zom•ba** |'zŏmbə| commercial city in S Malawi, in the agricultural Shire Highlands. Pop. 63,000. It was the first capital of Malawi.

**Zo•na Ro•sa** |ˌsōnə 'rōsä| entertainment district of Mexico City, Mexico, just E of Chapultepec Park along the Paseo de la Reforma.

**Zon•gul•dak** |ˌzawNGgo͞ol'däk| port city in N Turkey, on the Black Sea, capital of Zonguldak province, a coal mining district. Pop. 120,000.

**Zoue•rate** |zwē'rät| (also **Zouîrâte**) mining town in N central Mauritania, near the Western Sahara border. Pop. 26,000.

**Zoug** |tso͞ok| French name for **Zug**.

**Zren•ja•nin** |'zrenyəinin| (formerly called **Petrovgrad** and, earlier, **Velike Beçk-erek)** port town in Vojvodina, N Serbia, on the Begej River. Pop. 81,000.

**Zug** |tso͞ok| **1** mainly German-speaking canton in central Switzerland. Pop. 85,000. The smallest (265 sq. mi./685 sq. km.) canton, it joined the confederation in 1352. **2** its capital. Pop. 21,000. French name **Zoug**.

**Zug•spit•ze** |'tso͞ok,sHpitsə| peak in the Wetterstein Mts. of the Bavarian Alps, S Germany, near the Tyrol. It is the highest peak in Germany (9,720 ft./2,963 m.).

**Zui•der Zee** |ˌzīdər 'zä| former large shallow inlet of the North Sea, in the Netherlands. In 1932 a dam across the entrance was completed, and large parts have been drained and reclaimed as polders. The remainder forms the IJsselmeer.

**Zu•lu•land** |'zo͞olo͞o,lænd| see **KwaZulu**.

**Zun•yi** |'dzo͞on'e| city in Guizhou province, S China, N of Guiyang. Pop. 354,000.

**Zu•rich** |'tsYriKH; 'zo͞orik| city in N central Switzerland, on Lake Zurich. Pop. 343,000. The largest city in Switzerland, it is an international financial center and a tourist destination.

**Zut•phen** |'zytfə| historic industrial and commercial town in E central Netherlands, on the IJssel River. Pop. 31,000.

**Zvi•sha•va•ne** |ˌzvēsHə'väni| (formerly **Shabani)** mining town in S central Zimbabwe, E of Bulawayo. Pop. 27,000. It is an asbestos producing center.

**Zwei•brück•en** |'sfībrʏkən| historic industrial city in western Germany, in Rhineland-Palatinate near the Saarland border. Pop. 35,000.

**Zwick•au** |'tsfikow| mining and industrial city in SE Germany, in Saxony. Pop. 113,000.

**Zwol•le** |'zwawlə| town in the E Netherlands, capital of Overijssel province. Pop. 96,000.

# Appendixes

# OCEANS AND SEAS OF THE WORLD

| | Area | | Maximum depth | |
|---|---|---|---|---|
| | Sq. miles | Sq. km. | Feet | Meters |
| *Oceans* | | | | |
| Pacific Ocean | 63,800 | 165,250 | 36,200 | 11,034 |
| Atlantic Ocean | 31,830 | 82,440 | 30,246 | 9,219 |
| Indian Ocean | 28,360 | 73,440 | 24,442 | 7,450 |
| Arctic Ocean | 5,400 | 14,090 | 17,881 | 5,450 |
| *Seas* | | | | |
| South China Sea | 1,331 | 3,447 | 18,241 | 5,560 |
| Caribbean Sea | 1,063 | 2,754 | 25,197 | 7,680 |
| Mediterranean Sea | 967 | 2,505 | 16,470 | 5,020 |
| Sea of Okhotsk | 610 | 1,580 | 11,063 | 3,372 |
| Gulf of Mexico | 596 | 1,544 | 14,370 | 4,380 |
| Hudson Bay | 475 | 1,230 | 850 | 259 |
| Sea of Japan | 389 | 1,007 | 12,280 | 3,733 |
| East China Sea | 290 | 752 | 9,126 | 2,782 |
| North Sea | 222 | 575 | 2,170 | 659 |
| Black Sea | 178 | 461 | 7,360 | 2,237 |
| Red Sea | 169 | 438 | 7,370 | 2,240 |
| Baltic Sea | 163 | 422 | 1,440 | 437 |
| Yellow Sea | 161 | 417 | 300 | 91 |

# WORLD LAND AREA BY CONTINENT

|  | Area | | Percent of the |
|  | Sq. miles | Sq. km. | world's land |
|---|---|---|---|
| Asia | 17,100,000 | 44,350,000 | 29.6 |
| Africa | 11,700,000 | 30,300,000 | 20.2 |
| North America | 9,350,000 | 24,250,000 | 16.2 |
| South America | 6,900,000 | 17,800,000 | 11.8 |
| Antarctica | 5,500,000 | 14,250,000 | 9.5 |
| Europe | 4,050,000 | 10,500,000 | 7.0 |
| Oceania (incl. Australia and New Zealand | 3,300,000 | 8,500,000 | 5.7 |
| TOTAL | 57,900,000 | 149,950,000 | 100.0 |

# WORLD POPULATION BY CONTINENT

|  | Pop. (1990) | Pop. density (people/sq. mile) |
|---|---|---|
| Asia | 3,112,700,000 | 293 |
| Africa | 642,111,000 | 54 |
| Europe | 498,371,000 | 249 |
| North America | 427,226,000 | 34 |
| South America | 296,716,000 | 44 |
| Oceania | 26,481,000 | 8 |
| TOTAL | 5,292,200,000 | 101 |

# MAJOR MOUNTAINS OF THE WORLD

| Mountain | Location | Height Feet | Meters |
|---|---|---|---|
| Everest | Nepal-China | 29,028 | 8,848 |
| K2 | Kashmir | 28,250 | 8,611 |
| Kanchenjunga | Nepal-India | 28,209 | 8,598 |
| Annapurna | Nepal | 26,503 | 8,078 |
| Communism Peak | Tajikstan | 24,590 | 7,495 |
| Aconcagua | Argentina-Chile | 22,834 | 6,960 |
| Ojos del Salado | Argentina-Chile | 22,664 | 6,908 |
| Bonete | Argentina | 22,546 | 6,872 |
| McKinley | Alaska, USA | 20,110 | 6,194 |
| Logan | Yukon, Canada | 19,850 | 6,054 |
| Kilimanjaro | Tanzania | 19,340 | 5,895 |
| Elbrus | Caucasus, Russia | 18,481 | 5,642 |
| Citlaltépetl | Mexico | 18,503 | 5,699 |
| Kenya | Kenya | 17,058 | 5,200 |
| Ararat | Turkey | 16,946 | 5,165 |
| Vinson Massif | Antarctica | 16,863 | 5,140 |
| Margherita Peak | Uganda-Zaire | 16,763 | 5,109 |
| Mont Blanc | France-Italy | 15,771 | 4,807 |
| Wilhelm | Papua New Guinea | 14,739 | 4,509 |
| Whitney | California, USA | 14,495 | 4,418 |
| Matterhorn | Italy-Switzerland | 14,688 | 4,477 |
| Elbert | Colorado, USA | 14,431 | 4,399 |
| Pikes Peak | Colorado, USA | 14,110 | 4,300 |
| Jungfrau | Switzerland | 13,642 | 4,158 |
| Cook | New Zealand | 12,349 | 3,764 |
| Hood | Oregon, USA | 11,239 | 3,426 |
| Olympus | Greece | 9,570 | 2,917 |
| Kosciusko | Australia | 7,234 | 2,228 |

# MAJOR VOLCANOES OF THE WORLD

| Volcano | Location | Height (feet) | Last eruption (other notable eruptions) |
|---|---|---|---|
| Cameroon | Cameroon | 13,354 | 1982 |
| El Chichon | Mexico | 7,300 | 1982 |
| Erebus | Ross Is., Antarctica | 12,450 | 1998 |
| Etna | Italy | 10,990 | 1998 |
| Fuji | Honshu, Japan | 12,368 | 1708 |
| Kelud | Java, Indonesia | 5,679 | 1990 |
| Kilauea | Hawaii, USA | 4,090 | 1998 |
| Krakatau (Krakatoa) | Indonesia | 2,667 | 1995 (1883) |
| Mauna Loa | Hawaii, USA | 13,678 | 1984 |
| Nevado del Ruiz | Colombia | 17,457 | 1991 (1985) |
| Pelée | Martinique | 4,583 | 1932 (1902) |
| Pinatubo | Luzon, Philippines | 5,249 | 1995 |
| Rainier | Washington, USA | 14,410 | 1894 |
| St. Helens | Washington, USA | 8,312 | 1991 (1980) |
| Santa Maria | Guatemala | 12,375 | 1998 (1902) |
| Santorini | Greece | 1,850 | 1950 (c. 1500 B.C.) |
| Shasta | California, USA | 14,162 | 1786 |
| Stromboli | Italy | 3,038 | 1998 |
| Taal | Luzon, Philippines | 984 | 1977 (1911) |
| Unzen | Japan | 4,462 | 1996 (1792) |
| Vesuvius | Italy | 4,190 | 1944 (A.D. 79) |
| Wrangell | Alaska, USA | 14,269 | 1907 |

# MAJOR NATURAL LAKES OF THE WORLD

|  | Area | |
|---|---|---|
|  | Sq. miles | Sq. km. |
| Caspian Sea | 143,240 | 370,992 |
| Lake Superior | 32,526 | 84,243 |
| Lake Victoria | 26,820 | 69,464 |
| Aral Sea | 24,904 | 64,501 |
| Lake Huron | 24,361 | 63,096 |
| Lake Michigan | 22,300 | 57,757 |
| Lake Tanganyika | 12,650 | 32,764 |
| Lake Baikal | 12,160 | 31,494 |
| Great Bear Lake | 12,095 | 31,328 |
| Lake Nyasa | 11,150 | 28,879 |
| Great Slave Lake | 11,030 | 28,568 |
| Lake Erie | 9,966 | 25,812 |
| Lake Winnipeg | 9,416 | 24,387 |
| Lake Ontario | 7,336 | 19,001 |
| Lake Balkhash | 7,115 | 18,428 |
| Lake Ladoga | 6,835 | 17,703 |
| Lake Chad* | 6,300 | 16,317 |
| Lake Maracaibo | 5,120 | 13,261 |
| Patos | 3,920 | 10,153 |
| Lake Onega | 3,710 | 9,609 |
| Lake Eyre* | 3,600 | 9,320 |
| Lake Titicaca | 3,200 | 8,288 |
| Lake Nicaragua | 3,100 | 8,029 |
| Lake Mai-Ndombe* | 3,100 | 8,029 |
| Lake Athabasca | 3,064 | 7,935 |

*indicates large seasonal variations

# MAJOR RIVERS OF THE WORLD

|  | Length | |
| --- | --- | --- |
| **River** | **Miles** | **Km.** |
| Nile | 4,160 | 6,695 |
| Amazon | 4,150 | 6,683 |
| Yangtze (Chiang Jiang) | 3,964 | 6,380 |
| Mississippi-Missouri-Red Rock | 3,741 | 6,019 |
| Ob-Irtysh | 3,481 | 5,410 |
| Yenesei-Angara | 3,100 | 4,989 |
| Yellow (Huang He) | 3,000 | 4,830 |
| Congo | 2,800 | 4,630 |
| Lena | 2,750 | 4,400 |
| Amur-Shilka | 2,744 | 4,390 |
| Mackenzie-Peace-Finlay | 2,635 | 4,241 |
| Mekong | 2,600 | 4,180 |
| Missouri-Red Rock | 2,564 | 4,125 |
| Niger | 2,550 | 4,100 |
| Mississippi | 2,470 | 3,975 |
| Plate-Paraná | 2,450 | 3,943 |
| Murray-Darling | 2,331 | 3,751 |
| Missouri | 2,315 | 3,736 |
| Volga | 2,292 | 3,688 |
| Purus | 2,100 | 3,400 |
| São Francisco | 1,990 | 3,200 |
| Rio Grande | 1,880 | 3,030 |
| Yukon | 1,870 | 3,020 |
| Tunguska, Lower | 1,861 | 2,995 |
| Brahmaputra | 1,800 | 2,900 |
| Indus | 1,800 | 2,900 |
| Japurá | 1,750 | 2,815 |
| Danube | 1,700 | 2,736 |
| Euphrates | 1,700 | 2,736 |
| Ganges | 1,678 | 2,700 |
| Para-Tocantins | 1,640 | 2,640 |
| Nelson-S. Saskatchewan-Bow | 1,600 | 2,560 |
| Zambezi | 1,600 | 2,560 |
| Paraguay | 1,584 | 2,549 |
| Ural | 1,575 | 2,534 |
| Amu Darya | 1,500 | 2,400 |
| Kolyma | 1,500 | 2,400 |
| Salween | 1,500 | 2,400 |
| Colorado | 1,468 | 2,333 |
| Arkansas | 1,450 | 2,320 |
| Dnieper | 1,370 | 2,200 |
| Syr Darya | 1,370 | 2,200 |
| Orange | 1,155 | 1,859 |
| St. Lawrence | 750 | 1,200 |

# LARGEST METROPOLITAN AREAS OF THE WORLD

| Metropolitan Area | Country | Pop. (1990) in millions |
|---|---|---|
| Mexico City | Mexico | 20.2 |
| Tokyo | Japan | 18.1 |
| São Paulo | Brazil | 17.4 |
| New York City | USA | 16.2 |
| Shanghai | China | 13.4 |
| Bombay (Mumbai) | India | 12.6 |
| Los Angeles | USA | 11.9 |
| Calcutta | India | 11.8 |
| Buenos Aires | Argentina | 11.5 |
| Seoul | Korea | 11.0 |
| Beijing | China | 10.8 |
| Rio de Janeiro | Brazil | 10.7 |
| Tianjin | China | 9.4 |
| Jakarta | Indonesia | 9.3 |
| Cairo | Egypt | 9.0 |
| Delhi | India | 8.8 |
| Moscow | Russia | 8.8 |
| Manila | Philippines | 8.5 |
| Osaka | Japan | 8.5 |
| Paris | France | 8.5 |